# A Flexible Organization for Instructors

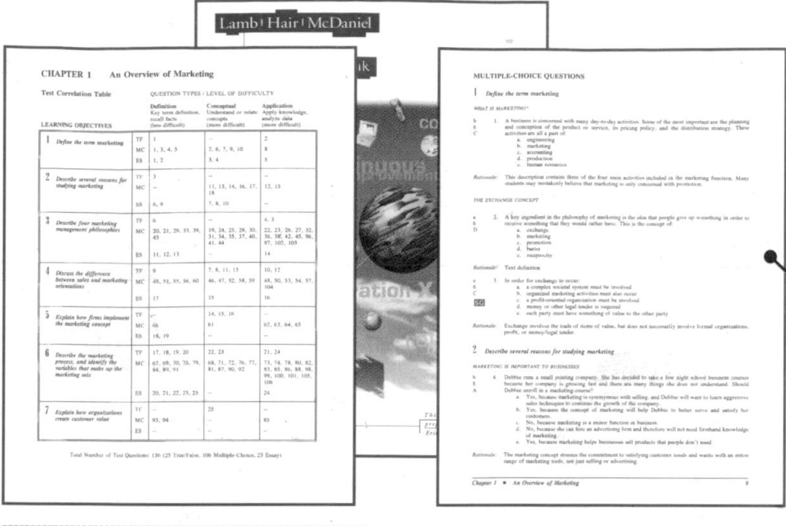


**TEST BANK QUESTIONS**

are grouped by learning objective, so that you can thoroughly test all objectives—or emphasize the ones you feel are most important. Correlation tables at the beginning of each chapter make it easy to prepare tests that cover the objectives at the level of difficulty appropriate for your students.

**MicroExam 4.0**

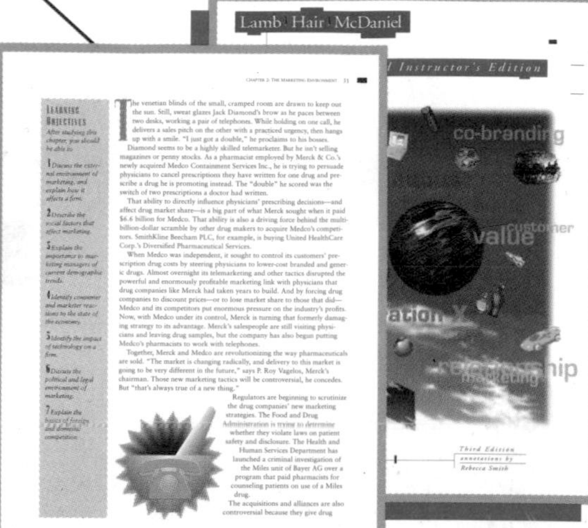


**TEXT LEARNING OBJECTIVES**

form the framework for organizing your lectures, selecting support materials, and customizing tests for your students.

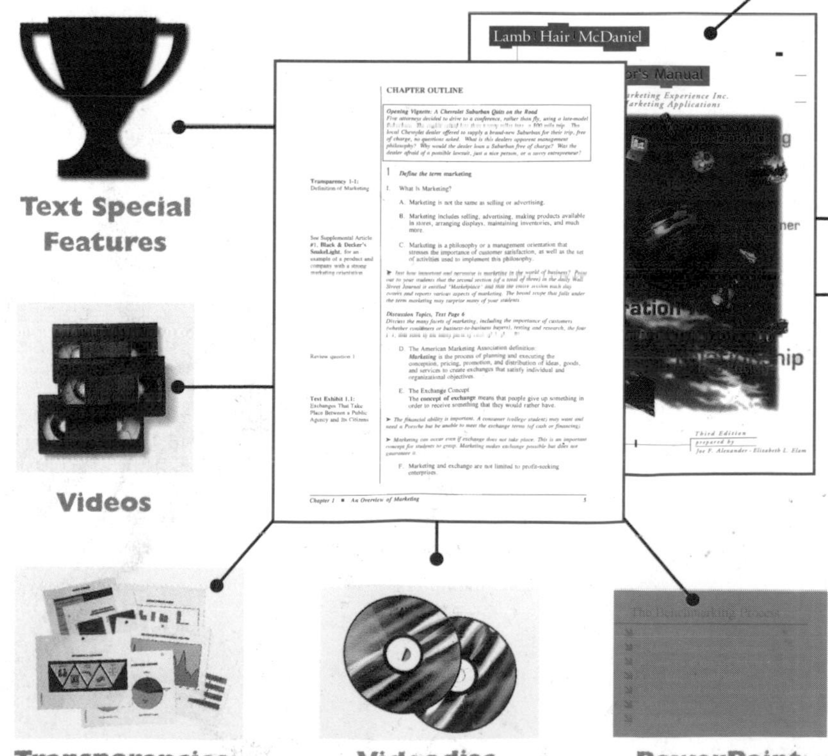


**SUPPLEMENTAL ARTICLES**

**CLASS ACTIVITIES**

**ALL LECTURE SUPPORT MATERIALS**

come together under their appropriate objectives in the *Instructor's Manual Lecture Outlines,* for thorough coverage of all objectives. Annotations tell you the appropriate times to integrate transparencies, text special features, additional examples, supplemental articles and activities, and end-of-chapter pedagogy into your lectures—a smorgasbord of teaching aids from which to choose.

Lamb | Hair | McDaniel

*Charles W. Lamb, Jr.*
*M. J. Neeley Professor of Marketing*
*M. J. Neeley School of Business*
*Texas Christian University*

*Joseph F. Hair, Jr.*
*William A. Copeland III Endowed Professor of Business Administration*
*Chairman, Department of Marketing*
*College of Business Administration*
*Louisiana State University*

*Carl McDaniel*
*Chairman, Department of Marketing*
*College of Business Administration*
*University of Texas at Arlington*

# marketing

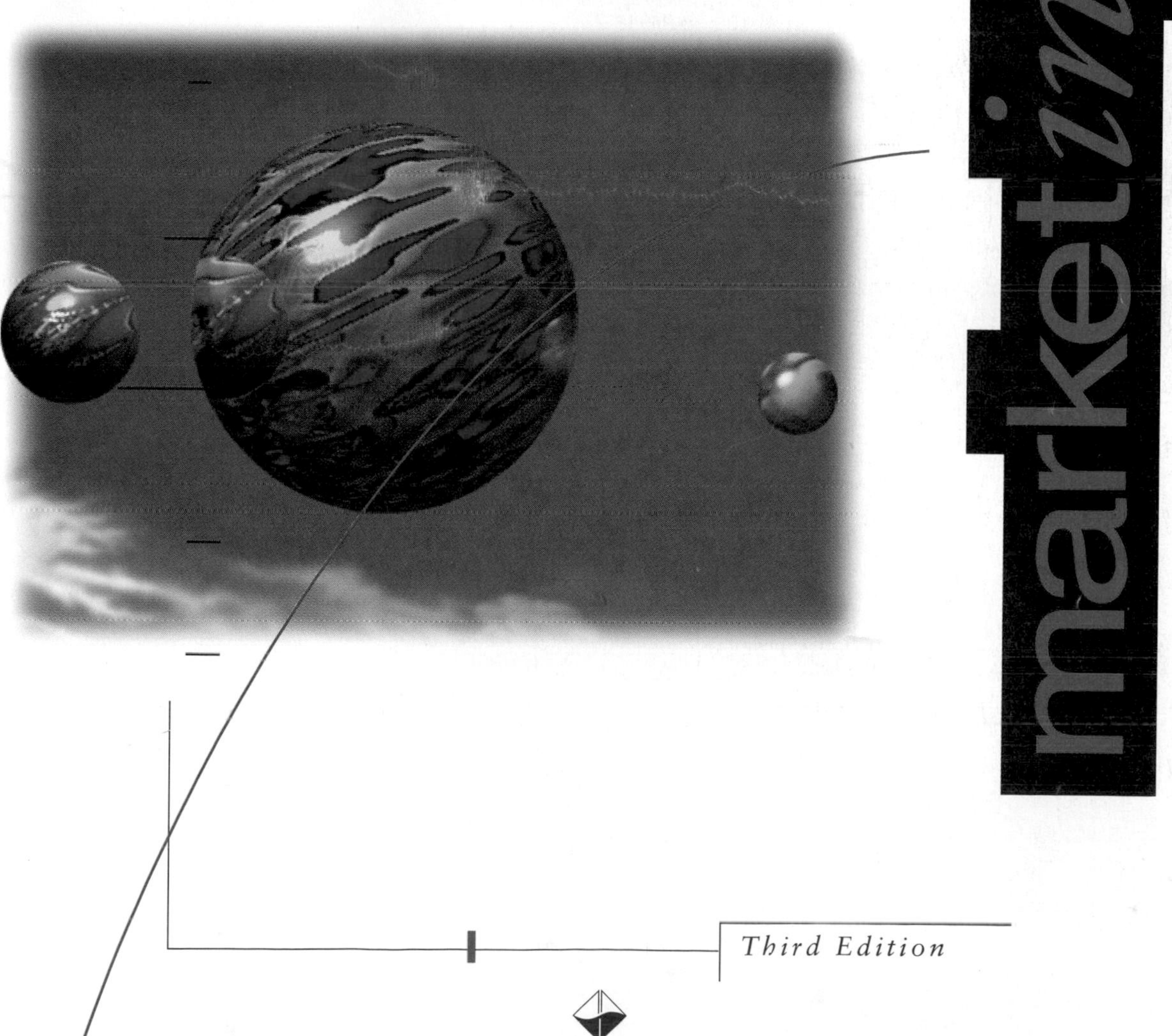

*Third Edition*

SOUTH-WESTERN College Publishing
*An International Thomson Publishing Company*

Developmental Editor: Cinci Stowell
Production Editor: Sharon L. Smith
Production House: PC&F, Inc.
Cover Illustration and Design: Michael Lindsay Design
Internal Design: John Odam Design
Special Page Illustrator: John Odam Design
Photo Research: Alix Roughen
Marketing Manager: Stephen E. Momper



Library of Congress Cataloging-in-Publication Data
Lamb, Charles W.
Marketing/Charles W. Lamb, Jr., Joseph F. Hair, Jr., Carl McDaniel.—3rd ed.
p. cm.
Rev. ed. of: Principles of marketing, 1993.
Includes bibliographical references and index.
ISBN 0-538-84948-7
1. Marketing. 2. Marketing—Management I. Hair, Joseph F. II. McDaniel, Carl D. III. Lamb, Charles W. Principles of marketing. IV. Title.
HF5415.L2624 1995
658.8—dc20 95-2874
CIP

ISBN: 0-538-84948-7

2 3 4 5 6 7 VH 0 9 8 7 6

Printed in the United States of America

I(T)P
International Thomson Publishing

To my daughters
Christine and Jennifer Lamb
—*Charles W. Lamb, Jr.*

To my wife Dale
and son Joey
—*Joseph F. Hair, Jr.*

To my love,
Corinne
—*Carl McDaniel*

## Brief Contents

## Contents

## Part Three Product Decisions 280

### Chapter 9 Product Concepts 282



### Chapter 10 Developing and Managing Products 312

## Part Six Pricing Decisions 612

Chapter 18

# A SPECIAL FEATURES SAMPLER

## For Students

Marketing students who have come before you have taught us a lot about what you want your textbook to be. You want current topics that relate to the real world. You want interesting examples that are relevant to your life. You want an enjoyable writing style. You want videos. You want an easy-to-understand organization with study aids to help you succeed on tests.

This text will meet or exceed your expectations in all of these important areas—and many others. Here is just a sample of the features you will find as you explore with us the exciting world of marketing.

# REAL INSIGHTS FROM REAL PEOPLE...PLUS VIDEOS!



## PART TWO
## ANALYZING MARKETING OPPORTUNITIES



Kristin Knapp is Vice President of External Relations of AIESEC, the largest student organization in the world. She rose to this leadership position while serving as a volunteer with AIESEC during college. Though Kristin majored in public relations, it was her classes in international business and marketing that prepared her for the environment in which she operates every day. Kristin works with five other people from different AIESEC chapters throughout the United States, helping undergraduates become more aware of foreign cultures through business opportunities. She also interfaces with AIESEC's corporate sponsors—such as AT&T, Arthur Andersen, IBM, and GE—to develop outside ties that will benefit AIESEC.

AIESEC has over 820 chapters in 78 countries. The organization seeks to promote cultural understanding while developing tomorrow's global leadership.

This objective is met through two programs. The core program involves an international exchange of members for practical work internships in foreign markets. The other program is the global theme project, in which a of AIESEC's chapters host projects relating to a common theme. These projects are designed to give the students a better perspective on global business and the different cultures of the world. In fact, one recent theme of the project was education toward international and cultural understanding.

Kristin feels that it is vital that companies be aware of differences among cultures, given the global nature of business today. U.S. firms must be open to new ideas

### ◀ CAREERS VIDEO VIGNETTES

Most of you attend college for one main purpose . . . to land the job that is right for you. But what kinds of marketing jobs are out there, and what are they like? Learn from recent graduates speaking to you on video about their jobs. Accompanying printed vignettes appear at the beginning of each text Part. The "Careers in Marketing" appendix extends your careers preview with job descriptions, career paths, and typical salaries for marketing jobs.



the tone for the rest of the 50-plus magazines. The publication features personality profiles and articles like a story on volunteers titled "Everyday Heroes: They're Helping Reshape America." The stories in *Modern Maturity* don't shy away from the age issue, but the subjects are active, optimistic, and energetic.

The final element of its strategy concerns the magazine's advertising policy. The magazine turns away advertisements that have a "downer attitude." For example, *Modern Maturity* does not accept ads for crutches, wheelchairs, or similar products. Although advertising revenues would probably increase 30 percent if it did accept such ads, the editor feels that these types of ads would detract from the upbeat tone of the magazine.



Questions

1. Do you think there is a need for magazines that target readers over 50 years old? Would it be better to reach this market through other types of publications? Give reasons to support your answer.
2. Do you agree with the editor of *Modern Maturity* that advertising influences readers' perceptions of the publication? Why or why not?
3. Does *Modern Maturity* share a frame of reference with its readers? How important is a shared frame of reference to the 50-plus market?

References


David Astor, "Cartoonist Wants to Reach Older Readers," *Editor & Publisher,* 5 June 1993, pp. 35–36.
Glen Cameron and John Haley, "Feature Advertising: Policies and Attitudes in Print Media," *Journal of Advertising,* September 1992, pp. 47–55.
Michael Kavanagh, "Using the Grey Matter," *Marketing,* 31 March 1994, pp. 30–32.
Patrick M. Reilly, "Older Readers Prove Elusive as Magazines Rethink Strategies for the Mature Market," *The Wall Street Journal,* 12 July 1990, pp. B1, B4.


### SIGNATURE SERIES CASES ▶

Have you ever wondered what makes famous athletes such good product spokespeople? Shaquille O'Neal has his own theory about this phenomenon . . . and he explains it to you himself beginning on page 526—with videos of his commercials as examples. Throughout the text you will find similar insights in "Signature Series Cases" written for you and signed by successful business people.

**SIGNATURE SERIES VIDEO CASE**

Dreamful Attraction and the Role of Athletes in Marketing

SIGNATURE SERIES VIDEO

*by Shaquille O'Neal*

What is marketing, and why is it so important? Marketing is the process of planning and executing the concept, pricing, promotion, and distribution of ideas, goods, and services to create exchanges that satisfy individuals and organizational objectives. All companies would like to be successful and make money. Marketing contributes directly to achieving these objectives. Marketing includes assessing the wants and satisfactions of present and potential customers, designing and managing product offerings, determining prices and pricing policies, developing distribution strategies, and communicating with present and potential customers. This case discusses the role athletes can play in the marketing of products and is based on my experiences as an athlete and a marketer.

Marketing Background and Concepts

While on the outside looking in, I did not realize that marketing was so complicated. I never knew that a person, such as an athlete, could have such a powerful effect on peoples' thought processes and purchasing behavior. The use of a well-known athlete in marketing a good or service can have a great impact on the sales of that good or service. Look at Michael Jordan. Before we knew it, almost every kid seemed to be wearing or wanted to wear Air Jordan shoes.

Why does this happen? Is it the appeal of a great athlete, or is it great marketing? The answer is "none of the above." It's both. In my time as a professional basketball player, I have seen firsthand the dramatic appeal that athletes have for the fans and the public in general. Most top-name athletes are like E.F. Hutton: When they talk, people listen. But why do they listen? I believe they listen to us, the athletes, because we have credibility. You will read in this book that "companies sometimes use sports figures and other celebrities to promote products hoping they are appropriate opinion leaders. Research has shown that the effectiveness of celebrity endorsements depends largely on how credible and attractive the spokesperson is and how familiar people are with him or her. The endorsement is most likely to succeed if an association between the spokesperson and the product can be established."

But marketers have to be careful when they select a celebrity to endorse a product. Bill Cosby failed as an

# THE MOST CURRENT TOPICS





## ◄▲ QUALITY AND VALUE

In business today, everyone is talking quality and customer value. Companies have found that to stay competitive, all operations—from marketing to billing—must focus on adding value for customers. To give you a sense for how quality and value permeate marketing practice, we have integrated these topics throughout the text, marked with a trophy icon like the one shown here. Also, special "Creating Customer Value" boxes like the one shown here deal with value issues in more depth.

CHAPTER 4: CONSUMER DECISION MAKING 133

then, through these beliefs, form a *brand image*—a set of beliefs about a particular brand. In turn, the brand image shapes consumers' attitudes toward the product.

**attitude**
Learned tendency to respond consistently toward a given object.

Attitudes tend to be more enduring and complex than beliefs, because they consist of clusters of interrelated beliefs. An **attitude** is a learned tendency to respond consistently toward a given object, such as a brand. Attitudes also encompass an individual's value system, which represents personal standards of good and bad, right and wrong, and so forth.

For an example of the nature of attitudes, consider the differing attitudes of consumers around the world toward the habit of purchasing on credit. Americans have long been enthusiastic about charging goods and services and are willing to pay high interest rates for the privilege of postponing payment. But to many European consumers, doing what amounts to taking out a loan—even a small one—to pay for anything seems absurd. Germans especially are reluctant to buy on credit. Italy has a sophisticated credit and banking system well suited to handling credit cards, but Italians prefer to carry cash, often huge wads of it. Most Japanese consumers have credit cards, but card purchases amount to less than 1 percent of all consumer transactions. The Japanese have long looked down on credit purchases but acquire cards to use while traveling abroad.[29]

If a good or service is meeting its profit goals, positive attitudes toward the product merely need to be reinforced. However, if the brand is not succeeding, the marketing manager must strive to change target consumers' attitudes toward it. This change can be accomplished in three ways: changing beliefs about the brand's attributes, changing the relative importance of these beliefs, and adding new beliefs.

### Changing Beliefs about Attributes

The first technique is to turn neutral or negative beliefs about product attributes into positive ones. For example, pork was losing sales to chicken because consumers thought pork was fatty and unhealthy. To counter this belief, pork producers launched the Pork: The Other White Meat campaign to reposition their product in the minds of consumers. The campaign tells consumers that pork is leaner, lower in calories, and lower in saturated fat than they think.

Likewise, BMW is continuing its efforts to reposition itself as a safe, affordable vehicle for the entire family and to steer away from its image as a yuppie statement. Its new commercials concentrate on safety features, such as traction control; its print ads show children for the first time. BMW also hopes the campaign will convince consumers that the cars are not as expensive as they might think.[30]

Changing beliefs about a service can be more difficult, because service attributes are intangible. Convincing consumers to switch hairstylists or lawyers or to go to a mall dental clinic can be much more difficul
razor blades. Image, which is also largely int
patronage. What is a "better doctor"? How
they will get better dental care in a mall thar
keting is explored in detail in Chapter 11.

### Changing the Importance of Beliefs

The second approach to modifying attitudes
beliefs about an attribute. For years, consu
high in natural fiber. The primary belief asso
tends to act as a mild, natural laxative. Tod

## ◀▼ GLOBAL MARKETPLACE

The world is getting smaller. Former communist countries are opening their markets to the West. Improved communications and distribution systems are creating opportunities in third-world countries. Europe and the Pacific Rim are becoming formidable competitors as well as market opportunities. To be successful, marketers must think globally. The text will help you think globally too, by integrating global issues and examples throughout the book, marked with a globe icon as shown here. "Global Perspectives" boxes and end-of-Part "Global Marketing Cases" delve into marketing issues beyond our borders in more depth.

CHAPTER 4: CONSUMER DECISION MAKING 143

Children were considered an asset because they could help with the farmwork. Today, in an industrial economy, large families are not necessary.

Culture is dynamic. It adapts to changing needs and an evolving environment. The rapid growth of technology in this century has accelerated the rate of cultural change. TV has changed entertainment patterns and family communication and has heightened public awareness of political and other news events. Automation has increased the amount of leisure time we have and, in some ways, has changed the traditional work ethic. Cultural norms will continue to evolve because of our need for social patterns that solve problems.

Without understanding a culture, a firm has little chance of selling products in it. Colors, for example, may have different meanings in global markets than they do at home. In China, white is the color of mourning, and brides wear red; in the United States, black is for mourning, and brides wear white. Pepsi had a dominant market share in Southeast Asia until it changed the color of its coolers and vending equipment from deep regal blue to light ice blue. In that part of the world, light blue is associated with death and mourning.

Language is another important aspect of culture that global marketers must deal with. They must take care in translating product names, slogans, and promotional messages into foreign languages so as not to convey the wrong message. Consider the following examples of blunders made by marketers when delivering their message to Spanish-speaking consumers: General Motors discovered too late that Nova (the name of an economical car) literally means "doesn't go" in Spanish; Coors encouraged its English-speaking customers to "Turn it loose," but the phrase in Spanish means "Suffer from diarrhea"; and when Frank Perdue said, "It takes a tough man to make a tender chicken," Spanish speakers heard "It takes a sexually stimulated man to make a chicken affectionate."[51]

As more companies expand their operations globally, the need to understand the cultures of foreign countries becomes more important. Marketers should become familiar with the culture and adapt to it. Or marketers can attempt to bring their own culture to other countries, as Domino's Pizza originally sought to do in Japan.

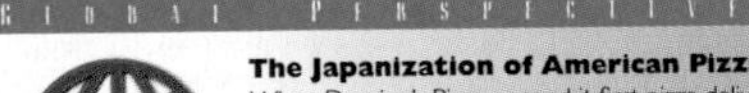

**The Japanization of American Pizza**

When Domino's Pizza opened it first pizza delivery outlet in Japan in 1986, its mission was to educate Japanese consumers about true American pizza. After years of Domino's-inspired education, Japanese today know very well what pepperoni and bell peppers are. But by far their favorite pizza toppings are things like curry topped with bits of squid.

These days, the streets of Tokyo swarm with pizza-delivery scooters. As many as 1,000 local pizza stores offer such Japanized toppings as apple, rice, German sausage, potato, and mayonnaise sauce. Domino's devised some creative alternatives of its own for its 100-plus stores in Japan. It now offers a ten-inch chicken teriyaki gourmet pizza topped with Japanese-style grilled chicken, spinach, onion, and corn—which is the most common pizza topping in Japan. Domino's also offers squid and tuna topping and corn salad, as well as such Oriental toppings as barbecued beef and sauteed burdock root.

Domino's attempts to go Japanese are a big switch from its early days in Japan, when it struggled to convince consumers that a $20 pizza delivered in a cardboard box was truly American—and thus fashionable. Back then, only noodle shops and sushi restaurants delivered. But trend-conscious young Japanese got hooked on the Western dish, and the success of Domino's soon attracted Japanese imitators. The local outlets, more in tune with Japanese tastes, promptly introduced more exotic recipes at cheaper prices. For example, one local outlet says older consumers in the countryside like the taste of shrimp in chili sauce over a sweetened pizza crust. Another local outlet delivers what it calls the ultimate Japanese-style pizza: a chicken, seaweed, and shredded bonito topping with sauce made from fish stock.[52]

What important lessons has Domino's learned from its experiences in Japan? Other than pizza toppings, what other marketing variables might Domino's need to adapt for Japanese culture?

338 PART THREE: PRODUCT DECISIONS

4. Describe some products whose adoption rates are or have been affected by complexity, compatibility, relative advantage, observability, and trialability.

5. What types of communication aid the product diffusion process? Identify some products you use, and tell how you found out about them. Explain what influenced you to buy them.

✍6. Your firm is phasing out a product. Write a memo explaining why the phaseout will be gradual rather than immediate.

### Application for Small Business

In the course Marketing 4123, Marketing Planning, students are required to develop a business plan for a new business. Jennifer Lamb created a fictional marketing research firm that specializes in conducting customer satisfaction surveys for small businesses in the community. The rationales for the firm's offering a single product are that (1) measuring customer satisfaction is a very "hot" topic in business today and (2) most firms offering this type of service target large firms, and their services cost more than most small businesses can afford.

Jennifer's fictitious firm uses college students, especially marketing majors, to conduct personal interviews and telephone surveys. When she wrote her business plan, she had several friends in mind who she thought would be interested in doing this kind of work for the experience and a little extra spending money. She also thought that many small businesses could be convinced to retain her services if the price was significantly lower than that charged by other research firms in the area.

Jennifer got an A on her paper and is now thinking seriously about creating the company she described in her business plan. She wants to know if you would be interested in becoming her partner in this venture.

#### Questions

1. Prepare a list of questions to ask Jennifer about the proposed business.
2. Prepare a list of questions to ask some small-business owners or managers in your community. The answers to these questions should help you decide whether or not to give Jennifer's proposal further consideration.
3. Prepare a list of criteria similar to those in the Marketing and Small Business box in this chapter that might be used to evaluate Jennifer's new product idea.

**CRITICAL THINKING CASE**

### Mane 'N Tail

Straight Arrow is a maker of animal care products based in Lehigh Valley, Pennsylvania. Among its products is Mane 'N Tail, a shampoo for horses. Straight Arrow is planning to reposition its shampoo toward a new target market—humans. The appeal for the product is simple, says Gene Carter, executive vice president of marketing and sales for Straight Arrow. ...oks beautiful. ...ir," he said. ...as first serious- ...arch by Carter ...t revealed that ...out of a case of ... 30 million last ...nd begin mar- ...ores. Dunavant and Carter know that they will be competing against hair care giants like Procter & Gamble and Nexxus.

#### Questions

1. Propose a series of steps that Straight Arrow should follow before introducing Mane 'N Tail for humans.
2. Assuming the idea is viable, propose a positioning strategy for the new product.
3. Propose a market entry strategy.
4. Assess the chances of this product being successful.

#### Reference

Pam Weisz, "HBA Companies Are Making Hay with a Little Horse Sense," *Brandweek*, 16 May 1994, p. 32.

324 PART THREE: PRODUCT DECISIONS

MARKETING AND SMALL BUSINESS

**Checklist for Evaluating New Product Concepts**

If a small business is lucky enough to have stable or increasing sales, new product additions can boost profits and market share. Small-business managers must be careful, however, not to expand beyond the firm's financial capacities. A new product requires shelf space, investment in inventory and perhaps spare parts, and maybe even a new salesperson—all of which require an extra financial commitment.

A new small business usually has only one chance "to do it right." A failure in introducing a new product means bankruptcy and perhaps the loss of a person's life savings. Conversely, for the owner of an established small business who suddenly finds that his or her source of livelihood has evaporated, the right new product can help offset declining demand.

The product development process is generally the same for both large and small firms. However, many entrepreneurs must do most steps in the process themselves rather than rely on specialists or outside consultants.

Here's a simple checklist for evaluating new product concepts for a small business. By adding up the points, a small-business owner can more accurately estimate success.

1. Contribution to before-tax return on investment:
   - More than 35 percent +2
   - 25–35 percent +1
   - 20–25 percent –1
   - Less than 20 percent –2
2. Estimated annual sales:
   - More than $10 million +2
   - $2 million–$10 million +1
   - $1 million–$1.99 million –1
   - Less than $1 million –2
3. Estimated growth phase of product life cycle:
   - More than three years +2
   - Two or three years +1
   - One or two years –1
   - Less than one year –2
4. Capital investment payback:
   - Less than a year +2
   - One to two years +1
   - Two to three years –1
   - More than three years –2
5. Premium-price potential:
   - Weak or no competition, making entry easy +2
   - Mildly competitive entry conditions +1
   - Strongly competitive entry conditions –1
   - Entrenched competition that makes entry difficult –2

This checklist is by no means complete. But a neutral or negative total score should give an entrepreneur reason to consider dropping the product concept.

subjects products to much more severe treatment than is expected by end users. The Consumer Product Safety Act of 1972 requires manufacturers to conduct a "reasonable testing program" to ensure that their products conform to established safety standards.

Many products that test well in the laboratory are also tried out in homes or businesses. Examples of product categories well suited for such use tests include human and pet food products, household cleaning products, and industrial chemicals and supplies. These products are all relatively inexpensive, and their performance characteristics are apparent to users.

Most products require some refinement based on the results of laboratory and use tests. A second stage of development often takes place before test marketing.

**TEST MARKETING**

After products and marketing programs have been developed, they are usually tested in the marketplace. **Test marketing** is the limited introduction of a product and a marketing program to determine the reactions of potential customers in a market situation. Test marketing allows management to evaluate alternative strategies and to assess how well the various aspects of the marketing mix fit together. Quest, Seagram's low-calorie line of sparkling waters, was test marketed for nearly a year before its national introduction.[32]

The cities chosen as test sites should reflect market conditions in the new product's projected market area. Yet no "magic city" exists that can universally represent market conditions, and a product's success in one city doesn't guarantee it will be a nationwide hit. When selecting test market cities, researchers should therefore find locations where the demographics and purchasing habits mirror the overall market. The company should also have

## ◀▲ SMALL BUSINESS ISSUES

Did you know that roughly 35 percent of all U.S. employees work for companies of less than 100 people, and close to half work for companies of under 500 people? Chances are good that you will work for a small business too at some point in your career. With this in mind, we integrated examples from small enterprises throughout the book. In addition, "Marketing and Small Business" boxes look at specific issues from a small-business point of view. An "Application for Small Business" at the end of every chapter gives you a chance to apply what you have learned to a small-business setting.

ETHICS IN MARKETING

**Are "Kiddie" Cocktails for Kids?**

The liquor industry has launched a fresh wave of low-alcohol cocktails that critics say will be tempting for teenagers. Low-alcohol cocktails, bearing such familiar brand names as Jack Daniel's and mixed with fruit juice or soda, are one of the few promising segments in the stagnant spirits industry. New drinks with a sweet taste, brightly colored labels, and names like Tahitian Tangerine and Dixie Jazzberry are flooding into grocery stores and liquor outlets.

These low-alcohol cocktails are a growth opportunity for the stagnant spirits industry. But critics contend they are a kind of kiddie cocktail that will increase alcohol abuse among teenagers.

Brown-Forman, flush with the success of its Jack Daniel's Country Cocktails, introduced a line of Southern Comfort Cocktails. Grand Metropolitan PLC's Heublein followed its twelve-proof José Cuervo Margaritas with Smirnoff Quenchers, a lower-power line of fruity, vodka-laced drinks.

The new concoctions amount to a kind of kiddie cocktail, critics contend. Some are even sold in familiar, twelve-ounce aluminum cans with pop-tops—just like Coke and Pepsi.

"It's an easy leap from Coca-Cola to Jim Beam and Cola. These are transitional products deliberately intended to blur lines between soft drinks and alcoholic drinks," says Jean Kilbourne, a frequent critic of the spirits industry who advises federal officials on alcohol abuse.[11]

Liquor marketers deny that they are targeting underage drinkers or that these new products are intended to be "transitional," as some critics claim. Do you consider it ethical to market these low-alcohol prepared cocktails? Do you think these new products will increase alcohol consumption and abuse among teenagers? Are some populations more vulnerable than others? Should these low-alcohol products be available in grocery stores where beer is sold, or should they be restricted to liquor stores and other outlets licensed to sell high-alcohol products?



The Ethics in Marketing box in this section describes questionable product line extensions by alcoholic beverage marketers.

### Product Line Contraction

Sometimes product lines become overextended. When this happens, some items in the product line need to be eliminated. Symptoms of product line overextension include the following:

- Some products in the line do not contribute to profits because of low sales or cannibalize sales of other items in the line.
- Manufacturing or marketing resources are disproportionately allocated to slow-moving products.
- Some items in the line are obsolete because of new product entries in the line or new products offered by competitors.

Three major benefits are likely when a firm contracts overextended product lines. First, resources become concentrated on the most important products. Second, managers no longer waste resources trying to improve the sales and profits of poorly performing products. Third, new product items have a greater chance of being successful because more financial and human resources are available to manage them.

## ◀▼ ETHICS IN MARKETING

Is it ethical to market low-alcohol cocktails to teenagers? As a buyer for a large department store, would you accept dinner from a supplier? Would you accept a speaking engagement, for which you would be paid $500? Ethical issues are seldom black-and-white. Where do you draw the line? Find out by putting yourself into the situations described in the text's "Ethics in Marketing" boxed features and the "Ethics Cases" at the end of several text Parts.



## PART FOUR ETHICS CASE

**THE GENEROUS SALESPERSON**

Jill McCarthy, a retail buyer for a large department store, was told during her training as a buyer that the company was very sensitive to any type of inducements given buyers beyond "modest tokens of friendship." The company felt that as long as buyers were entertained or received tokens of appreciation of little or no value, their position as buyers would not be compromised.

- Why would a company feel the need for such a policy? What would constitute "a modest token of friendship"? What would be excessive?

The first year of Jill's job involved nothing that could even remotely be linked to the "bribery policy." One salesperson for a large dress manufacturer had become good friends with Jill and offered to take her to dinner so they could quietly discuss some of the emerging fashion trends that would be affecting the next season's lines. Jill was happy to go to dinner because it was a good opportunity to enjoy quiet conversation with her friend Barbara, the sales representative. The dinner went very well and was very productive for both Jill and her store.

- Does anyone feel uncomfortable accepting dinner under this policy?

Later that year Barbara invited Jill to attend an ice show with her, as a recreational activity. Jill remembered the dinner, felt that it would be very pleasant to attend anything with Barbara, and quickly accepted. On the date of the planned entertainment, Jill received four tickets and a note from Barbara saying that she was terribly sorry that she could not come to town but that she wanted Jill to invite other friends and enjoy the ice show.

- Should Jill accept the tickets? Why or why not? What are the issues in this situation?

A month later, with a note of apology, Jill received a smoked turkey and a fruitcake from Barbara in the name of Barbara's company.

- What should Jill do? Why? What harm has been done?

The following spring Barbara asked Jill to speak to the retail apparel manufacturers' trade association on the buyer's view of sales and service in retailing. Jill was very happy to receive the invitation to speak and was happier later to hear that there was an honorarium of $500 associated with the speaking engagement. She worked hard on her speech, and it was very well received. She felt she earned every penny of the $500.

- Did Jill do anything wrong by accepting? Was Barbara's involvement a problem? What danger might exist in this situation?

In late summer Barbara spent almost two days with Jill, acquainting her with some of the changes that would be made in the line and bringing her up-to-date on some new trends that were to be watched in the industry. Two weeks later Jill received a $1,000 check from Barbara's company with a notation that it was in appreciation for the time she spent advising Barbara on the needs of retailers.

- How has Jill compromised her position as a buyer? As long as she intends to be uninfluenced by the money, can she take it?

Jill realized she was in clear violation of the "bribery policy" but was not sure where she crossed the line.

- Where did Jill cross the line? Could she have continued working with Barbara after saying no to a gift or other act of friendship?

## RELATIONSHIP MARKETING ▶

Being truly customer-driven means building relationships with customers. In Chapters 1, 5, and 11, you will learn what "relationship marketing" means, how it extends to strategic alliances, and how it applies to services marketing.

IBM Canada, noticing that business customers weren't always getting the service they wanted, started a new program called "customer obsession." It began with a two-day workshop for senior IBM Canada managers in information and marketing services.[23] The goal was to reassess and redefine the firm's customer-service strategy. After the workshop, participating executives shared their new plans with all 11,000 employees, regardless of whether these employees dealt directly with customers.

*7 Discuss the role of relationship marketing and strategic alliances in business-to-business marketing.*

### RELATIONSHIP MARKETING AND STRATEGIC ALLIANCES

As Chapter 1 explained, relationship marketing is the strategy that entails seeking and establishing ongoing partnerships with customers. Relationship marketing is redefining the fundamental roles of business buyers and sellers. Suppliers are making major adjustments in their thinking, management styles, and methods of responding to purchaser's standards and operational requirements. Relationship marketing is not a faddish trend but rather is driven by strong business forces: the competitive need for quality, speed, and cost-effectiveness, as well as new design techniques.[24]

**strategic alliance (strategic partnership)** Cooperative agreement between business firms, taking the form of a licensing or distribution agreement, joint venture, research and development consortium, or partnership.

A **strategic alliance**, sometimes called a strategic partnership, is a cooperative agreement between business firms. Strategic alliances can take the form of licensing or distribution agreements, joint ventures, research and development consortia, and partnerships. For example, Citibank Visa and Ford have introduced the Ford Citibank Visa and MasterCard. The card offers customers an opportunity to earn substantial rebates on the purchase or lease of new Ford, Lincoln, and Mercury automobiles.[25]

The trend toward forming strategic alliances is accelerating rapidly, particularly among high-tech firms. Xerox management, for example, has decided that in order to maintain its leadership position in the reprographics industry, the company must "include suppliers as part of the Xerox family."[26] This strategy often means reducing the number of suppliers, treating those that remain as allies, sharing strategic information freely, and drawing on supplier expertise in developing new products that can meet the quality, cost, and delivery standards of the marketplace.

Many strategic alliances fail to produce the benefits expected by the partners. Some fail miserably. Three general problems have been identified:

- Partners are often organized quite differently, complicating marketing and design decisions and creating problems in coordinating actions and establishing trust.
- Partners that work together well in one country may be poorly equipped to support each other in other countries, leading to

GLOBAL PERSPECTIVES

**Ford and Mazda**

Strategic alliances between U.S. carmakers and their European and Asian counterparts have typically resulted in more headaches than profits. A noteworthy exception is the relationship between Ford and Mazda.

The two carmakers have collaborated on ten ...rt, Explorer, and Probe and the ...s provided Mazda with assis... and styling. Mazda has shared ...elopment expertise with Ford. ...uarter of the Fords and Mazdas ...in some way from the fifteen-...

...and Mazda should use in ...other guidelines would you ...gic alliance between these



$14.4 billion a year to spend as they wish, and children influence household purchases amounting to more than $132 billion a year.[26] Almost without thinking about it, parents are creating the next generation of spenders.

How does spending behavior begin? When do children start making consumer choices and influencing those of their parents? Exhibit 2.3 shows the five-stage process for becoming a shopper:

- Stage 1, observing, consists of children's initial interactions with the marketplace. The first thing children learn is that the satisfying objects they usually get from their parents have commercial sources. In this stage, children make sensory contact with the marketplace and construct their first mental images of marketplace objects and symbols, such as Ronald McDonald.
- Stage 2, making requests, occurs while babies are still totally dependent on their parents. Through pointing, gesturing, and vocalizing, very young children convey to parents that they see something they want.
- Shopping actually begins at stage 3—making selections. Choosing something is the first physical act taken by an independent consumer, and it occurs as children learn to walk. As children make requests and parents fulfill them, children begin to develop a memory of the store location of certain products. Children also express their desire for independence by locating and retrieving satisfying products themselves. With permission, children leave their parents and move on their own through the store maze.
- Stage 4, making assisted purchases, begins when children give money in exchange for goods while the parent supervises. Instead of obtaining desired objects from their parents, children in this stage are asking and receiving permission to obtain objects from others. Children become primary consumers who spend their own money on their own needs and wants. On average, children reach this stage at the age of 5½.[27]
- The final stage is stage 5, making independent purchases. Some children make purchases without parents as early as 4 years old, but the average age is 8. The interval between stage 4 and stage 5 is the longest period of time between stages. It reflects the difficulty of learning a complex exchange system and the reluctance of many parents to let children go to stores on their own.

Many marketers recognize the importance of reaching the children's market early. Kodak not only donates cameras and film to schools as part of its Using Cameras in the Curriculum program (for kids in kindergarten through grade six) but also lines up photofinishers who will donate development of the film. The company weaves environmental themes into its program. Kodak hopes to draw the 6-to-11-year-old crowd with the school program, as it did with its single-use camera decorated with characters from the hit movie *Aladdin*. For kids "too old" for such things, Kodak launched the Photo fX 35mm camera for $39.95—a "real" camera that "looks like Mom and Dad's."[28]

### Generation X: Savvy and Cynical

**generation X** People who are currently between the ages of 18 and 29.

In 1995, approximately 47 million consumers were between the ages of 18 and 29. This group has been labeled **generation X.** It is the first generation of latchkey children—products of dual-career households or, in roughly half of cases, of divorced or separated parents. Generation X began entering the work force in the era of downsizing and downturn, so they're likelier than the previous generation to be unemployed, underemployed, and living at home with Mom and Dad. They're alienated

## ◀ GENERATION X

Generation X—young adults between the ages of 18 and 29—present some unique challenges for marketers. They grew up in an environment very different from their parents'. Learn the demographics of this new customer group and how they affect buying behavior.

# LEARNING TOOLS FROM THE REAL WORLD



**LEARNING OBJECTIVES**

*After studying this chapter, you should be able to*

1 *Define the term* marketing.

2 *Describe several reasons for studying marketing.*

3 *Describe four marketing management philosophies.*

4 *Discuss the differences between sales and marketing orientations.*

5 *Explain how firms implement the marketing concept.*

6 *Describe the marketing process, and identify the variables that make up the marketing mix.*

7 *Explain how organizations create customer value.*

Five attorneys from Boise, Idaho, decided to drive together to a conference in Portland, Oregon—a distance of 500 miles—leaving the afternoon before the conference. One of the attorneys volunteered to drive his late-model Chevrolet Suburban. Less than 20 miles outside Boise, the Suburban developed engine problems. The engine quit completely, and the lawyers were stranded alongside the freeway.

Now they were in a real dilemma. Even if they could get on a flight to Portland, the airfare would be extremely high due to the same-day purchase of the tickets. So the owner of the Suburban phoned the dealer where he bought the vehicle and explained the problem. The lawyer was hoping to rent another Suburban.

Instead, the dealer offered to supply a brand-new Suburban free of charge. The dealer delivered the new Suburban to the attorneys beside the freeway, the switch was made, and the dealer rode back with the tow truck.

The Suburban had broken down because the engine had seized. The attorney who was driving had been engrossed in conversation and hadn't paid close attention to the gauges. It seems that a technician in a fast-lube-and-oil-change place had forgotten to tighten the oil drain plug. The plug fell out, the oil drained, and within minutes the engine overheated and seized completely. The dealer had the diagnosis in hand when the attorneys returned several days later.[1]

Describe the Chevrolet dealer's apparent management philosophy. Why would the dealer lend the attorney a brand-new Suburban free of charge? Was the dealer afraid of a possibl... sav... exp...

## ◀ OPENING EXAMPLES PREVIEW THE CHAPTER

Each chapter begins with an interesting real-life situation, with questions that anticipate key issues in the chapter.

Creating customer value by delivering quality products is essential for achieving success in today's competitive markets. Many chapters include specially identified boxes describing successful strategies for enhancing customer value. Other examples of efforts to enhance customer value and quality are provided throughout the book and marked with the second icon shown in the margin.

Marketing ethics is another important topic selected for special treatment throughout the book. Many business executives and educators have suggested that business education focus more on ethical issues. Thus many chapters include highlighted stories about firms or industries that have faced ethical dilemmas or have engaged in practices that some consider unethical. Questions are posed to focus your thinking on the key ethical issues raised in each story.

Entrepreneurship and small business applications are also highlighted in special boxes in many chapters. Every chapter also includes an application case related to small business. This material illustrates how entrepreneurs and small businesses can use the principles and concepts discussed in the book.

Chapters conclude with a final comment on the chapter-opening vignette ("Looking Back"), a summary of the major topics examined, a listing of the key terms introduced in the chapter, discussion and writing questions (writing questions marked with an icon), and two or three cases with discussion questions. All these features are intended to help you develop a more thorough understanding of marketing and enjoy the learning process.

The remaining chapters in Part One introduce you to the dynamic environment in which marketing decisions must be made and to global marketing. Part Two covers consumer decision making and buyer behavior; business-to-business marketing; the concepts of positioning, market segmentation, and targeting; the nature and uses of marketing research and decision support systems; and customer value and quality issues. Parts Three through Six examine the elements of the marketing mix—product, distribution, promotion, and pricing. Part Seven focuses on the unique challenges of marketing to multicultural target markets; marketing ethics and social responsibility; and strategic planning, forecasting, and control. Three appendixes—one concerning careers in marketing, the second concerning financial arithmetic for marketing, and the third providing experiential marketing exercises—conclude the book.

**LOOKING BACK**

Look back at the story at the beginning of this chapter about the attorney whose Chevrolet Suburban broke down during a trip from Boise, Idaho, to Portland, Oregon. You should now find the questions that appear at the end of the story to be simple and straightforward. The dealer's actions suggest that he or she is marketing-oriented. The dealer recognized the attorney's misfortune as an opportunity to demonstrate a commitment to customer satisfaction even after the sale and even when the problem was caused by a third party.

The attorneys were so impressed with the service and the new Suburban they used on their trip that three of them bought new Suburbans from the dealer within two weeks. A fourth, the owner of the original Suburban, bought the loaned Suburban because he didn't like the idea of a rebuilt engine. The payoff for the dealer was the sale of four Suburbans and an engine rebuild. The total sales figure for the four Suburbans was well over $100,000.

## "LOOKING BACK" AT THE OPENING EXAMPLES ▶

You have finished reading the chapter . . . so what have you learned? Can you now answer the questions posed in the opening example? Test yourself. Then read the "Looking Back" section at the end of the chapter where we answer the questions for you. If you got the right answers, then you are ready to go on to the chapter cases!

businesses, (c) General Motors, (d) oil companies, and (e) the airline industry? Which environmental factors do you feel have most greatly influenced them?

7. What is environmental management? Cite an example.

### Application for Small Business

After selling his small computer business, James Munch set out on an eighteen-month sailboat trip with his wife and young children. He had founded the business several years earlier, and it had become a million-dollar enterprise. Now he was looking for a new venture.

While giving his five children reading lessons on board the sailboat—they each had slight reading disabilities—Munch had an inspiration for a new company. He wondered why a computer could not be programmed to drill students in special-education classes who needed repetition to recognize and pronounce new words correctly.

Questions

1. Refer back to Exhibit 2.1 and explain to James how the external environment could affect his new company.

2. How could each uncontrollable variable influence the new venture?

**CRITICAL THINKING CASE**

### Calvin Klein, Inc.

Calvin Klein has come down from his ivory tower—and none too soon. "I had become too isolated," says Klein, conceding that he lost touch with consumers by cloistering himself in his showroom. "When I'm out there in the stores, I learn."

The result: After several years of sluggish sales and occasional losses, Calvin Klein, Inc., is transforming itself into a design, marketing, and licensing company. Having finally conceded that outside manufacturers could make some of its lines more efficiently and profitably, the company found buyers for its jeans and underwear businesses, which will now be converted to licensees.

In the future, Calvin Klein will derive virtually all its income from the royalties it collects from licensees. In a sense, this is a return to the past; when the company introduced its jeans in the late 1970s, it used a licensee to make them. Calvin Klein fragrances—Obsession, Eternity, and Escape—have always been sold under license. And now that the company has licensees for its … is actively pur- … menswear and … yers are found, … will remain in- … image. … Klein's revenues … censees assume … nsing also pro- … s are based on … usinesses grow, … s 51 years old, … rry Schwartz, also 51, to focus on what they do best: designing and marketing the apparel that others will now produce. A high priority is improving the CK "bridge" collection of lower-priced women's wear. Klein criticized it as "too young-looking" and lacking styles that women could wear to work.

"We've gone through a difficult period," concedes the designer, who has been dubbed "Calvin Clean" by the fashion press for his spare, minimalist fashions. "We're not all the way there yet, but we've developed a real long-term strategy to grow our businesses." Adds Schwartz: "Manufacturing wasn't our forte."

Calvin Klein initially gained fame with his designer jeans, which generated sales as high as $240 million in 1982, when the label was licensed to Puritan Fashions, the jeans manufacturer. But after Calvin Klein bought Puritan in 1983, the company neglected jeans—which at one time accounted for 80 percent of its overall revenues—and by last year jeans sales had shrunk to about $50 million.

New York–based Rio Sportswear bought the jeans division for $35 million and will pay a royalty ranging from 5 to 10 percent to Calvin Klein. Arnold Simone, Rio's president, expects that sales of Calvin Klein jeans can be lifted quickly. Rio, which already produces 1.5 million pairs of jeans a month under labels such as Bill Blass, says manufacturing efficiencies will enable it to lower prices from about $60 a pair to about $45—matching Gap and Levi's brands. "The beautiful part of Klein is that the company is really the best marketer in the industry, with wonderful, sexy, and sophisticated ads," Simone says. Rio will also launch a line of Calvin Klein children's jeans.

## CRITICAL THINKING CASES ▶

Now apply what you just learned to the real company situation posed in the chapter-end "Critical Thinking Case." Do you agree with what the company did? What concepts from the chapter support your point of view? Once you have mastered these brief cases for all chapters in a text Part, challenge yourself with the "Integrative Cases" that require you to apply your knowledge from several chapters.

Calvin Klein, Inc., is also counting on generating much of its future growth abroad. The company has opened licensed Calvin Klein boutiques in Barcelona, St. Moritz, and Singapore and has formed a partnership with four Japanese companies to create in-store shops and produce more licensed apparel. As for Klein himself, the designer is now preoccupied with what he calls a "breakthrough" concept: a unisex perfume.



Questions

1. Can a fashion designer dictate to the market what is "really in" at the moment? Is marketing necessary?

2. Would you say that Calvin Klein ignored the external environment in the past? What external factors should the firm be concerned with in the future?

3. How would you describe the competitive structure of the fashion industry?

4. Do you believe that Klein is now making the best use of his time for the company? If not, what should he be doing?

Reference

Teri Agins, "Shaken by a Series of Business Setbacks, Calvin Klein Inc. Is Redesigning Itself," *The Wall Street Journal*, 21 March 1994, pp. B1, B6.

**VIDEO CASE**

### Life Fitness Company

In 1977, Augie Neato had an idea for combining an exercise bike and a computer. For nine months, Neato hit the road in his motor home trying to sell his idea. During that time, he sold eleven bikes instead of the thousands that he had imagined. Neato decided that the only way to make sales was to get people to try the product first. So he began putting the bikes in health clubs and letting people rent them by the half hour. Once the health club owners saw that customers liked the bike, sales of Neato's company, Life Fitness, began to escalate rapidly.

In 1984 Neato sold the company to Bally Manufacturing, a producer of gaming devices. Bally didn't just provide capital for a growing business; it already owned a chain of 350 health clubs. Those clubs were a captive market for Life Fitness products and a place to test new ideas. Over the next seven years, Life Fitness products were sold to thousands of health clubs around the nation. Bally then restructured and decided Life Fitness no longer fit its strategic plan. Neato jumped at the opportunity to reacquire, with the help of an investment banking group, his idea and products.

Neato noted two basic changes in consumers' fitness behavior in the early 1990s: Membership in health clubs was slowing down, and people were beginning to exercise at home. Baby boomers, the primary target market for health clubs, were experiencing an ever-increasing poverty of time. Neato knew that if he could provide the same quality exercise experience in the home as in the club, he would have a winner.

In 1993 Neato decided to tackle the consumer market. His decision posed a critical challenge for Life Fitness Company: How could it expand into the consumer market without losing market share in the professional market? Neato knew that he could capitalize on the well-known Life Fitness name. One immediate problem, however, was balancing the quality level of the professional Life Fitness equipment with the price that individual consumers were willing to pay.

Life Fitness's new direction is paying off. Consumer products accounted for 25 percent of company sales in 1994. Life Fitness expects that consumer products will make up 66 percent of total sales by 1999.

Questions

1. Explain how Life Fitness could capitalize on a poverty of time.

2. What other external variables might affect Life Fitness Company?

3. Describe the target market for Life Fitness consumer products.

4. How might the marketing mixes for Life Fitness consumer products and professional products differ?

Reference

CNBC, 1994.

## ◀ VIDEO CASES

Videos add an extra dimension to case studies. Not only will you read about a company, but you will also see and hear about the situation in the videos. Many of the chapter-end video cases come from CNBC Business News, so they are current and professionally produced.

# INTEGRATED LEARNING SYSTEM

The text and supplements have been organized around the learning objectives, to create for you a tightly integrated learning system.



LEARNING OBJECTIVES

*After studying this chapter, you should be able to*

1 *Discuss the importance of global marketing.*

2 *Discuss the impact of multinational firms on the world economy.*

3 *Describe the external environment facing global marketers.*

4 *Identify the various ways of entering the global marketplace.*

5 *List the basic elements involved in developing a global marketing mix.*

Terry S. Prindiville gazed at the women jammed into a bustling shop in Shanghai and saw opportunity. All this tumult, the JCPenney executive thought, to buy lingerie that his company could offer at lower prices and higher quality. JCPenney isn't selling goods in China yet, but Prindiville and his staff are masterminding an ambitious expansion that is transforming the company into a major international retailer.

Already, JCPenney stores are under construction in Mexico. The company added nearly a million square feet of retail space in Japan in 1995 by offering its private-label apparel in 300 department stores owned by Aoyama Trading Co., Japan's largest retailer of men's suits. JCPenney has been scouting sites in Chile after surveys showed that many Chileans are so

## ◀ CHAPTER OBJECTIVES

The learning objectives listed at the beginning of every chapter briefly state the skills you will acquire from reading the chapter.



1 *Discuss the importance of global marketing.*

**global marketing**
Use of a global vision to effectively market goods and services across national boundaries.

**global vision**
Ability to recognize and react to international marketing opportunities, awareness of threats from foreign competitors in all markets, and effective use of international distribution networks.

### THE REWARDS OF GLOBAL MARKETING

Today, global revolutions are underway in many areas of our lives: management, politics, communications, technology. The word *global* has assumed a new meaning, referring to a boundless mobility and competition in social, business, and intellectual arenas. No longer just an option, **global marketing** (marketing to target markets throughout the world) has become an imperative for business.

U.S. managers must develop a global vision not only to recognize and react to international marketing opportunities but also to remain competitive at home. Often a U.S. firm's toughest domestic competition comes from foreign companies. Moreover, a global vision enables a manager to understand that customer and distribution networks operate worldwide, blurring geographic and political barriers and making them increasingly irrelevant to business decisions.[2] In summary, having

## NUMBERED ICONS ▶

Each objective, with its numbered icon, then appears in the chapter margin where the objective is fulfilled, so that you can quickly locate the applicable material.



KEY TERMS

*balance of payments 70*
*balance of trade 69*
*boycott 81*
*buyer for export 89*
*contract manufacturing 92*
*countertrade 98*
*direct foreign investment 92*
*dumping 98*
*exchange control 81*
*export agent 90*
*export broker 90*
*exporting 89*
*fully industrialized society 79*
*General Agreement on Tariffs and Trade (GATT) 81*
*global marketing 67*
*global marketing standardization 73*
*global vision 67*
*industrializing society 78*
*joint venture 92*
*keiretsu 82*
*licensing 91*
*Maastricht Treaty 85*
*market grouping 81*
*multinational corporation (MNC) 71*
*North American Free Trade Agreement (NAFTA) 83*
*preindustrial society 77*
*quota 81*
*takeoff economy 78*
*tariff 81*
*trade agreement 81*
*trade deficit 69*
*traditional society 77*

### SUMMARY

1 **Discuss the importance of global marketing.** Businesspeople who adopt a global vision are better able to identify global marketing opportunities, understand the nature of global networks, and engage foreign competition in domestic markets. In addition, U.S. exports help us reduce the trade deficit and the balance of payments problem.

2 **Discuss the impact of multinationals on the world economy.** Multinational corporations are international traders that regularly operate across national borders. Because of their vast size and financial, technological, and material resources, multinational corporations have a great influence on the world economy. They have the ability to overcome trade problems, save on labor costs, and tap new technology.

3 **Describe the external environment facing global marketers.** Global marketers face the same environmental factors as they do domestically: culture, economic and technological development, political structure, demography, and natural resources. Cultural considerations include societal values, attitudes and beliefs, language, and customary business practices. A country's economic and technological status depends on its stage of industrial development: traditional society, preindustrial society, takeoff economy, industrializing society, or fully industrialized society. Political structure is shaped by political ideology and such policies as tariffs, quotas, boycotts, exchange controls, trade agreements, and market groupings. Demographic variables include population, income distribution, and growth rate.

4 **Identify the various ways of entering the global marketplace.** Firms use the following strategies to enter global markets, in descending order of risk and profit: direct investment, joint venture, contract manufacturing, licensing, and export.

5 **List the basic elements involved in developing a global marketing mix.** A firm's major consideration is how much it will adjust the four P's—product, promotion, place (distribution), and price—within each country. One strategy is to use one product and one promotion message worldwide. A second strategy is to create new products for global markets. A third strategy is to keep the product basically the same but alter the promotional message. A fourth strategy is to slightly alter the product to meet local conditions.

Discussion and Writing Questions

1. Why is it important that U.S. businesses become more involved in global marketing?
2. Discuss the role of multinational corporations in developing nations.
3. How viable is global marketing standardization for multinational corporations?

## SUMMARIES ▶

The summary at the end of the chapter is organized around the learning objectives as well, reinforcing the key points under each objective.

## SUPPLEMENT INTEGRATION ▼▶

The Study Guide summaries, outlines, and questions are all organized around the learning objectives, to tie these study aids to text content. Your instructor's materials are also tied to text content through the learning objectives, assuring that your objectives and the ones your instructor has for you are the same.

____ 4. The government of Bolimia has announced that it will no longer permit U.S. cars to be exported into its country. This is an example of a quota.

____ 5. GATT, NAFTA, and the EC are all examples of market groupings.

____ 6. Some countries in Africa are highly populated. However, the size of the population alone does not tell an exporter enough about the country's potential as a target market.

4 *Identify the various ways of entering the global marketplace*

____ 7. The Crafty Corporation produces arts and crafts materials at its U.S. manufacturing plant. Crafty then sells the products to markets in Germany, Japan, and Mexico. This is an example of exporting.

____ 8. Licensing globally is similar to the concept of franchising locally, except that global licensing agreements do not require control in the same way that franchises do.

____ 9. Active ownership of a foreign company or overseas manufacturing or marketing facilities is direct foreign investment.

5 *List the basic elements involved in the development of a global marketing mix*

____ 10. Wave surfboards are produced in Australia and sold both in Australia and in the United States. The price in the United States for the surfboards is below the price charged for the same product in its country of origin. This is an example of dumping.



4 *Identify the various ways of entering the global marketplace*

9. Selling domestically produced products in another country is ________________. The most common intermediary for international trade is the export merchant, also known as a(n) ________________. This intermediary assumes all risks and sells internationally for its own account. A second type of intermediary brings buyers and sellers together. This intermediary is called a(n) ________________ and deals primarily in agriculture and raw materials. A foreign sales agent-distributor or a hired purchasing agent of foreign customers is a(n) ________________.

10. A legal process whereby one firm agrees to let another firm use its manufacturing process, trademarks, patents, trade secrets, or other proprietary knowledge is called ________________. This is an effective way for a firm to move into the international market with relatively low risk.

11. If a firm does not want to become involved in licensing arrangements it may engage in private-label manufacturing by a foreign company. This strategy is called ________________. Another alternative is for a domestic firm to join with a foreign firm to form a new entity. This strategy is called a(n) ________________. Finally, a domestic firm could have active, majority ownership is a foreign company. This alternative is known as ________________.

### CHAPTER 3 Developing a Global Vision

#### LEARNING OBJECTIVES

1 *Discuss the importance of global marketing*

As world trade barriers are removed and domestic competition increases, international marketing is becoming a viable and important opportunity for U.S. businesses. However, the United States' ability to compete in global markets has significantly declined in the last four decades, and many domestic firms are losing market share to foreign businesses.

2 *Discuss the impact of multinational firms on the world economy*

Because of their vast size and financial, technological, and material resources, multinational corporations (MNCs) have a tremendous influence on the world economy. These firms have the potential to solve complex social, economic, and environmental problems in both developed and undeveloped nations. But if these corporations misuse their power, they can have a devastating effect on economic conditions in the world.

3 *Describe the external environment facing global marketers*

Global marketers face the same environmental factors domestically or internationally: culture, level of economic development, political and legal structure, demographics, and natural resources. Several of these will have a greater impact and be more difficult to understand in the global environment. Cultural considerations will include the language, societal values, attitudes and beliefs, and customary business practices. Level of economic development may vary widely between countries. The political and legal structure will probably include tariffs, quotas, boycotts, exchange controls, trade agreements, and market groupings. In short, all the external environment factors may be different and more complicated.

4 *Identify the various ways of entering the global marketplace*

Representing descending levels of risk and profit, firms use these strategies to enter global markets: direct investment, joint ventures, contract manufacturing, licensing, and exporting.

5 *List the basic elements involved in the development of a global marketing mix*

In developing a global marketing mix, a firm's major consideration is how much it will adjust the four P's--product, place, promotion, and price--within each country. Using a global marketing approach, a firm makes few or no adjustments to product and promotion strategies. However, national differences in distribution channels and economic conditions usually require such firms to adjust place and price.

#### CHAPTER OUTLINE

1 *Discuss the importance of global marketing*

I. The Rewards of Global Marketing

**Global marketing**, marketing to target markets throughout the world, is an imperative for almost every business. Managers must recognize and react to international opportunities as well as to foreign competition via imports, which is found in almost every industry.

In addition, managers need to understand how customer and supplier networks operate worldwide.

A. Many successful global firms find that they derive a majority of their firm's profits from international operations.

B. **Global vision** means recognizing and reacting to international marketing opportunities, being aware of threats from foreign competitors in all markets, and effectively using international distribution networks.

C. The Importance of Global Marketing to the United States

1. The United States exports about a fifth of its industrial production and a third of its farm products.
2. One out of every sixteen jobs in the United States is directly or indirectly supported by exports.
3. Almost one-third of corporate profits is derived from international trade and foreign investment.

40 *Chapter 3 ▪ Developing a Global Vision*

## A STUDY SYSTEM

After reading the text chapter and summary, review the Study Guide outline and summary, and answer the questions. If you find from these review activities that you need further study on a particular objective, you can easily locate all applicable material by simply looking for the numbered icon. Also, your instructor will be testing your knowledge of these key concepts as the final link in the learning system.

# PREFACE

A basic tenet of this text is to understand your customers and then do your very best to deliver outstanding value and service to those customers. We have tried very hard to follow this important principle. The acid test for how well we are doing in meeting the needs of our target market is the market response. We are very gratified and proud of the results of *Marketing,* Second Edition. By more than doubling the sales of the first edition, you have demonstrated your confidence in our product.

## WITH SUCCESS COMES RESPONSIBILITY

We believe that your demonstrated trust in *Marketing,* Second Edition, places an even greater responsibility on us to deliver the finest textbook and supplementary package on the market in this Third Edition. Our goal is not just to meet, but to exceed your expectations. We have accomplished this with value-added innovations within the text and with new supplements.

Instructors and students have told us that our text is lively, interesting, and filled with student-oriented, current examples. We have gone to great lengths to make certain that "lively and interesting" never means "superficial" or "shallow." We have done extensive research to provide a comprehensive introduction to the field of marketing which is enjoyable to read. The latest concepts and theories are covered in a practical and contemporary manner. Our responsibility is to build on the strengths of previous editions to make marketing come alive for the students while delivering an efficient and effective total teaching package for you, the professor.

## VALUE-DRIVEN INNOVATIONS FOR THE THIRD EDITION

### NEW! SIGNATURE CASE SERIES BY SUCCESSFUL BUSINESS PEOPLE

To help bring the text to life for the students, we have asked some of America's most successful business people to prepare a short written case—most with videos—about specific marketing concepts. For example, Shaquille O'Neal talks directly to students from his own experience about the role of athletes in marketing products (Chapter 15). He offers his own ideas about why an athlete's endorsement works—he calls it "Dreamful Attraction."

John Roach, Chairman and CEO of Tandy Corporation, explains Tandy's actual retail growth strategies as management moved to divest parts of the business and build on Tandy's strengths (Chapter 13). In Chapter 8, Raymond Kordupleski, Customer Satisfaction Director at AT&T, describes how AT&T reengineered its billing operation to be customer-focused, to attack MCI's perceived competitive advantage in customer service.

We call this our "Signature Series," because we have asked these authors to sign their cases, signifying that they personally prepared the case for *Marketing,* Third Edition. Most authors supplied videos to accompany their cases. For example, Shaquille O'Neal authorized use of his Pepsi commercials to reinforce his words on the role of the athlete in promoting products. Cases with accompanying videos are identified as "Signature Series Video Cases."

Short biographical sketches of each Signature Series author appear on p. xlvii of the text. Students will no doubt find the Signature Series enjoyable as well as educational.

## NEW! MARKETBUILDER SOFTWARE, BY JIAN

JIAN—producer of the popular BizPlan*Builder* commercial software—now has a comprehensive software tool for marketing. More than a game, Market*Builder* contains everything students need to develop a real marketing plan, communicate it, and measure their performance. This software was carefully designed to be easy to use and produce professional results. It is available for either IBM or MacIntosh.

## NEW! CNBC VIDEO EXAMPLES FOR EACH CHAPTER

Add video examples to spice up your lectures! For each chapter, we have chosen four to six current CNBC news clips on the very latest developments on issues discussed in the chapter. Some segments provide current profiles of companies discussed in the chapter. Others demonstrate text concepts with visual examples from the real world. A video instructor's manual previews each clip and keys it to the chapter content for easy integration. The CNBC examples are also available on videodisc.

## NEW! CUSTOM-PRODUCED CAREER VIDEO VIGNETTES OPEN EACH PART

Many students taking an introductory marketing course have not yet chosen a career field. They often have limited knowledge of the many career opportunities in marketing. These videos accomplish two objectives. First, they describe marketing jobs that are available to recent college graduates. Second, the videos illustrate the relevance of the material the student is preparing to read. We searched America's businesses to find young, successful recent college graduates to discuss their careers. The graduates explain to the students why and how the marketing principles the students are preparing to read are important in the real world. Students quickly learn that *Marketing,* Third Edition, is providing relevant and useful information for their future careers in business.

## NEW! FOCUS ON QUALITY AND VALUE

Delivering superior customer value is becoming the key to success in building and sustaining a long-range advantage in an increasingly competitive marketplace. In this new edition, we have increased our coverage of quality and value with the following new features:

- Integrated examples throughout the text, marked with icons like the one shown here.
- "Creating Customer Value" boxed features that profile customer-value initiatives at real companies.
- Additional examples called "Quality in Marketing" that appear in the margins of the Annotated Instructor's Edition to enhance your lectures.

In addition, Chapter 8, "Customer Value and Quality," has been thoroughly revised and updated for the Third Edition. The chapter describes how the Total Quality Management movement has evolved into a focus on customer value. The three components of customer value are goods quality, service quality, and value-based prices. Goods quality is discussed in terms of TQM principles and practices, such as quality function deployment, benchmarking, and Pareto analysis. The Gap Model of service quality is used as a framework for discussing service quality. The value-based pricing approach starts with the customer, considers the competition, and then determines the appropriate price. Numerous examples of companies successful in implementing customer value are provided.

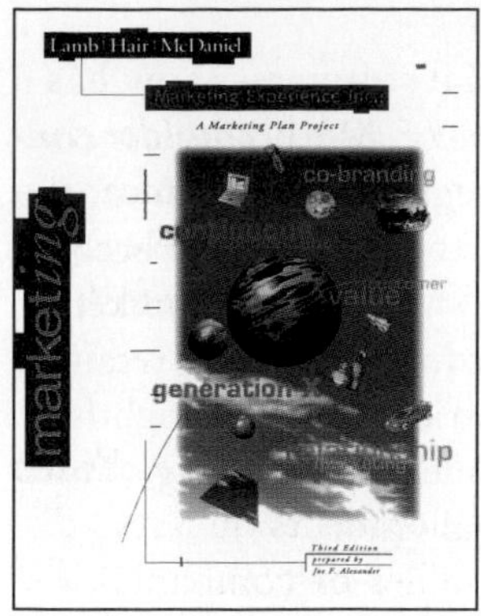


### NEW! MARKETING APPLICATIONS SUPPLEMENT TO THE TEXT

Students must do more than read about marketing principles; they must learn how to apply them in the world of business. With this in mind, we offer a new supplement that challenges students with marketing experiential exercises and applied, short marketing tasks for every chapter. In addition, the supplement contains a comprehensive class exercise for developing interpersonal marketing skills. With this new supplement, students will learn how to put basic marketing concepts into practice.

### WE COVER TODAY'S HOT TOPICS IN MARKETING

A sample of our coverage of today's contemporary hot topics in marketing include:

NAFTA—Chapter 3
World Trade Organization—Chapter 3
Component Life Styles—Chapter 2
Generation X—Chapter 2
Personalized Economy—Chapter 2
Poverty of Time—Chapter 2
Co-branding—Chapter 9
Customer Value—Chapters 1, 5, 10, and all of 8
Re-engineering—Chapter 10
Relationship Marketing—Chapters 1, 5, and 11
Continuous Improvement—Chapter 8
ISO 9000—Chapter 8
Quality Function Deployment (QFD)—Chapter 8
Value-Based Pricing—Chapter 8
Total Quality Management—Chapter 8

## POPULAR TEXT THEMES HAVE BEEN RETAINED AND ENHANCED

### INCREASED SMALL BUSINESS COVERAGE

Many students, at some point in their careers, will either own or work for a small company. In addition to small business examples in each chapter and our feature boxes entitled "Focus on Small Business," we have added "Application for Small Business" at the end of each chapter. These are minicases designed to illustrate how small businesses can create strategies and tactics using the material in the chapter. We have used these applications in our own classes and have found them very useful for integrating marketing principles and small business.

### A CHAPTER ON MULTICULTURAL MARKETING IN THE UNITED STATES

The United States has become a multicultural society. We live in a country that offers a richly interwoven fabric of customs, cultures, traditions, purchasing patterns, values, and attitudes. As the year 2000 nears, the United States is evolving toward a society characterized by three large racial and ethnic minorities. Chapter 20 explores the meaning of cultural diversity, the sociodemographic characteristics of the largest minority markets, and marketing strategies used to successfully target these markets.

## AN EMPHASIS ON GLOBAL MARKETING THROUGHOUT THE BOOK

Professors and accrediting associations stress the importance of global business concepts in today's world and recommend their thorough integration throughout the business curriculum. "Thinking globally" cannot be an afterthought. It must become part of every manager's tactical and strategic planning. Nor should global marketing be an afterthought in a principles of marketing text. Accordingly, we have retained the subject in the front of the book as Chapter 3. Global marketing is now rightfully positioned as a key component of the business environment. *Marketing,* Third Edition, stresses early the importance of developing a "global vision."

Global marketing is fully integrated throughout the book as well. Our "Global Perspectives" boxes, which appear in most chapters, provide expanded global examples and concepts. Each box concludes with thought-provoking questions carefully prepared to stimulate class discussion. For example, the box in Chapter 6 describes how marketing toys in Europe is a different game for U.S toy manufacturers, and asks students to consider the pros and cons of changing toys to fit European tastes versus standardizing.

We have also integrated numerous global examples within the body of the text. An icon like the one shown here marks key global examples for ready reference. For example, on p. 143 we discuss the meanings of colors in different cultures to exemplify how cultural differences affect marketing decisions.

Finally, to give students an opportunity to analyze global issues, we have provided comprehensive global marketing cases after several part divisions. Also, a number of our video cases have a global orientation.

## FOCUS ON ETHICS

In this edition we continue our emphasis on ethics. From the Second Edition we have retained and updated the chapter on ethics and social responsibility (Chapter 21). The Ethical Issues boxes, complete with questions focusing on ethical decision making, have been revised and added to every chapter.

The end-of-part Ethics Cases place students in ethical dilemmas that change and get more perplexing as more information is revealed. Additional ethics cases appear in the Instructor's Resource Guide. With these additional cases, you can give students the initial facts of the situation, and then see how their thinking evolves as you reveal additional facts along the way. Students really enjoy these cases and get a feel for the complexity of ethics issues as the cases lead them to look at the issues from all sides.

## CAREERS IN MARKETING

Appendix A presents information on a variety of marketing careers, with job descriptions and career paths, to familiarize students with employment opportunities in marketing. This appendix also indicates what people in various marketing positions typically earn and how students should go about marketing themselves to prospective employers. This appendix, along with the career video vignettes discussed on p. xxxvi of this preface, provides students with a realistic preview of jobs in marketing.

## FINANCIAL TOOLS IN MARKETING

Marketers need to know the basic components of various financial analyses. We have presented these basics in Appendix B, "Financial Arithmetic for Marketing" and Appendix C, "Tools of Marketing Control."

## PEDAGOGY THAT WORKS

Your feedback told us what pedagogy you and students liked most from our Second Edition and what new features you would welcome. You told us that current examples are important to you, so we have included all new opening vignettes, new examples throughout the text, and CNBC video examples correlated to every chapter. You told us that cases that students find relevant are important to you, so we have added Signature Series Cases and replaced most of the video cases with new, current videos. You told us that, in this time of "lean-and-mean" competition, small business applications are becoming increasingly important, so we expanded our small business focus with applied small business exercises at the end of every chapter. Finally, you told us that the integrated learning system helped you organize your lectures and helped your students study more effectively, so we have retained that important feature.

Below is a brief description of the pedagogical features that we selected to meet and exceed your expectations.

### FULLY INTEGRATED LEARNING SYSTEM

The text and all major supplements are organized around the learning objectives that appear at the beginning of each chapter, to provide you and the students with an easy-to-use, integrated learning system. A numbered icon like the one shown here 2 identifies each objective and appears next to its related material throughout the text, annotated instructor's edition, instructor's manual, test bank, and study guide.

The learning objectives are the key to the fully integrated system. They provide a structure for your lesson plans. Everything you need to assure complete coverage of each objective is identified by the objective icon. A correlation table at the beginning of every chapter in the test bank enables you to create tests that fully cover every learning objective or that emphasize the objectives you feel are most important.

The integrated system also gives structure to students as they prepare for tests. The icons identify all the material in the text and study guide that fulfill each objective. Students can easily check their grasp of each objective by reading the text sections, reviewing the corresponding summary section, answering the study guide questions for that objective, and returning to the appropriate text sections for further review when they have difficulty with any of the questions. Students can quickly identify all material relating to an objective by simply looking for the icon.

### TEXT PEDAGOGY THAT EXCITES AND REINFORCES

Pedagogical features are meant to reinforce learning, but they need not be boring. We have tried to create teaching tools within the text that will excite student interest as well as teach.

- **New Opening Vignettes, Revisited at Chapter Conclusion:** Each chapter begins with a new, current, real-world story about a marketing decision or situation facing a company. These vignettes have been carefully prepared to stimulate student interest in the topics to come in the chapter and can be used to begin class discussion. A special section before the chapter summary called "Looking Back" answers the teaser questions posed in the opening vignette and helps illustrate how the chapter material relates to the real world of marketing.
- **Key Terms:** Key terms appear in boldface in the text, with definitions in the margins, making it easy for students to check their understanding of key definitions. Then if they need a fuller explanation of any term, the discussion is right there—

next to the definition. A complete alphabetical list of key terms appears at the end of each chapter as a study checklist, with page citations for easy reference.

- **Chapter Summaries:** Each chapter ends with a summary that distills the main points of the chapter. Chapter summaries are organized around the learning objectives, so that students can use them as a quick check on their achievement of learning goals.
- **Discussion and Writing Questions:** College placement offices around the country inform us that employers are demanding graduates with better written communication skills. To meet this need, we have included writing exercises along with the discussion questions at the end of each chapter. These exercises are marked with the icon shown here. The writing questions are designed to be brief, so that students can accomplish writing assignments in a short time and grading time is minimized.
- **New! Application for Small Business:** These short scenarios prompt students to apply marketing concepts to small business settings. Each scenario ends with provocative questions to aid student analysis.
- **Critical Thinking Chapter and Part Cases:** Our society has an enormous capacity for generating data, but our ability to use the data to make good decisions has lagged behind. Experts contend that this is because too often we accept the data presented to us at face value instead of evaluating them critically and making the effort to understand and interpret them. In the hope of better preparing the next generation of business leaders, many educators are beginning to place greater emphasis on developing critical thinking skills.

  *Marketing*, Third Edition, contributes to this effort with short end-of-chapter Critical Thinking Cases and a more challenging, comprehensive Integrative Case at the end of each of the seven major parts—four of them new for this edition. Integrative Cases include "Kraft General Foods" and "Software Pricing."

- **Video Cases:** A video case appears at the end of every chapter to add a visual dimension to case analysis. Most of the cases are new for this edition. Many are from CNBC Business News, so that they are as real-world and current as possible. We screened hundreds of videos to find the select few that best demonstrate chapter concepts. Companies featured in the video cases include Euro-Disney, Head Golf, and Southwest Airlines.
- **New! Signature Series Cases:** Several chapters also conclude with cases from our new Signature Series, most of which have accompanying videos. Written and signed by prominent business people, these cases speak directly to students from the real world of marketing. These cases are discussed in more detail on p. xxxv of this preface.
- **Glossary:** A comprehensive glossary of key terms appears at the end of the book.
- **Indexes:** Two indexes—a names/companies/products index and a subject index—are included to help students quickly find text topics and examples.

## INNOVATIVE STUDENT SUPPLEMENTS

*Marketing,* Third Edition, provides an excellent vehicle for students to learn the fundamentals. However, to truly understand the subject, students need to apply the principles to real-life situations. We have provided a variety of supplements that give students the opportunity to apply concepts through hands-on activities.

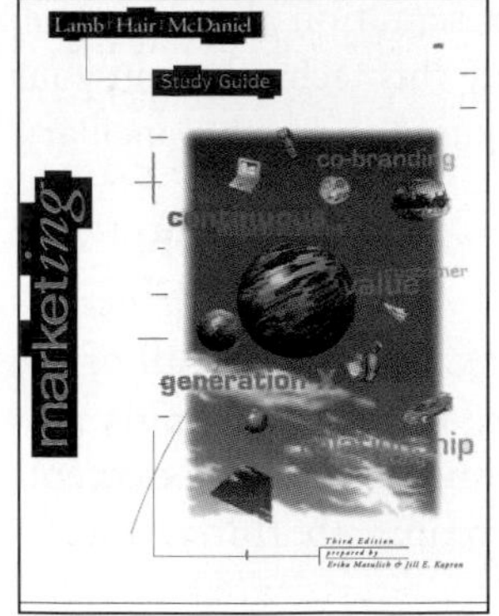

- **A Comprehensive Student Study Guide:** All questions in the study guide are keyed to the learning objectives by numbered icons. As students work through the study guide, they may find they need further review on some topics. They can easily find all related material in the text and study guide by simply looking for the icon.

  In addition to true/false, multiple choice, and essay questions, every chapter includes application questions, many in the form of short scenarios. Study guide questions were designed to be similar in type and difficulty level to the test bank questions, so that review using the study guide will help students improve their test scores. The guide also includes chapter outlines with definitions of key terms, a synopsis of key points under the learning objectives, and vocabulary practice.
- **Market*Builder* Software:** We are pleased to make available to users of *Marketing,* Third Edition, a new software by JIAN, specifically designed for marketing applications. The software—called Market*Builder*—is described in more detail on p. xxxvi of this preface.
- ***Fancy Footwork—The Marketing Program:*** This computer simulation enables students to make real-world product decisions for a new line of athletic footwear through the four stages of the product life cycle. Students develop strategies for the four P's in marketing their products and receive performance feedback and suggestions for improving their marketing mix.
- ***Export to Win!*** This six- to nine-hour computer simulation helps students understand exporting and international marketing while playing an interesting and challenging game. It is based on a successful commercial version developed for the U.S. Department of Commerce which helps business professionals learn to expand markets by exporting.

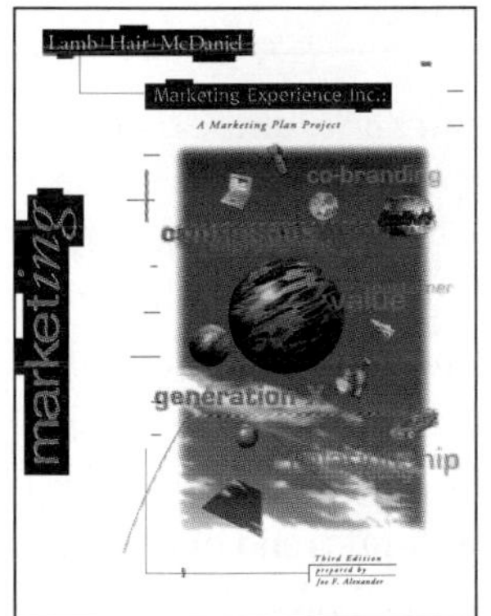

- **Marketing Applications Supplement:** This new supplement, discussed in more detail on p. xxxvii of this preface, offers short applied tasks, to give students hands-on experience with marketing concepts.
- **A Comprehensive Marketing Plan Project:** For those of you who want to challenge your students to create a realistic marketing plan, we offer *The Marketing Experience, Inc.* This marketing plan project enables student teams to actually design a comprehensive marketing plan during the course of the term.

## INNOVATIVE INSTRUCTOR'S SUPPLEMENTS

All components of our comprehensive support package have been developed to help you prepare lectures and tests as quickly and easily as possible. We provide a wealth of information and activities beyond the text to supplement your lectures, as well as teaching aids in a variety of formats to fit your own teaching style. Changing to *Marketing,* Third Edition, will lighten your teaching load while giving your students the tools they need to master the principles of marketing.

### VIDEODISC TECHNOLOGY TO MAKE LECTURES COME ALIVE

For instructors interested in multimedia presentations, our laser videodisc will excite your students with color and variety. The *Marketing,* Third Edition, videodisc contains animated illustrations, transparencies, and videos for classroom projection. In addition to video cases and part opener careers videos, the videodisc includes the CNBC video examples. The videos, transparencies, and illustrations can be viewed in any order you choose, and, with an optional computer and South-Western software, you can prepare a complete video "script" of your classroom presentation ahead of time. An accompanying videodisc guide describes how to integrate this technology in your classroom. A compatible "CAV-type" videodisc player is required to use this ancillary.

## ABUNDANT ANNOTATIONS IN THE INSTRUCTOR'S EDITION

We have gone to great lengths to provide the most useful *Annotated Instructor's Edition* ever prepared for teaching principles of marketing. We provide all of the margin information you want most—the tips, examples, and teaching aids that enrich your course, ease your preparation, and help you connect marketing concepts to "real life" business events. Each chapter contains approximately thirty annotations, which fall into these categories:

- **Teaching Tips:** Suggestions for activities from marketing instructors around the country who have found effective ways to involve students. About half the activities are described fully in the annotations; the other half are described in more detail in *Great Ideas for Teaching Marketing*, Third Edition, edited by the textbook authors.
- **Themes:** Examples that relate text concepts to areas of current interest in marketing:

  New! Quality in Marketing

  Cross-Cultural Marketing

  Global Marketing

  Ethics in Marketing

  Environmental Concerns

  Service Marketing

  Small Business Marketing

  Nonprofit Marketing
- **Company Examples:** Examples about well-known companies that illustrate points mentioned in the text.
- **More on . . . :** Supplements to the text discussion, in the form of alternative views, insights from business experts, interesting examples, and trend analyses.
- **Transparencies:** Cues and discussion prompts linking text concepts to the transparencies that are part of the teaching package.

## THE HOTTEST NEWS IN MARKETING, SENT EVERY WEEK BY FAX

Every two weeks, South-Western's "FACTS Service" sends subscribers by fax summaries of two current and exciting marketing articles chosen from leading publications. Articles are chosen to follow the text sequence throughout the term. This free service also includes chapter and page correlations with the text and questions for class discussion. South-Western's "FACTS Service" will provide you with the very latest examples for your lectures.

## A COMPREHENSIVE INSTRUCTOR'S MANUAL, THE CORE OF OUR INTEGRATED LEARNING SYSTEM

Each chapter of the *Instructor's Manual* begins with the learning objectives and a brief summary of the key points covered by each objective. The integrated system then comes together in the detailed outlines of each chapter. Each outline, integrated with the textbook and with other supplements through the learning objectives,

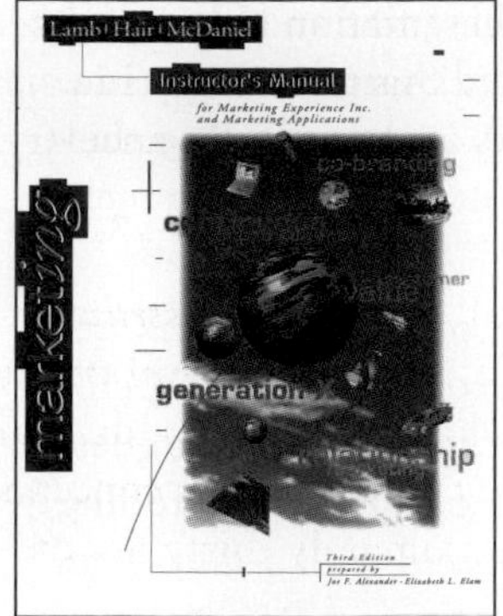


refers you to the support materials at the appropriate points in the lecture: transparencies with discussion suggestions, additional examples not included in the text, exhibits, supplemental articles, additional activities, boxed material, and discussion questions. These outlines assist you in organizing lectures, choosing support materials, bringing in outside examples not mentioned in the book, and taking full advantage of text discussion. Our lecture outlines are something that you can really use—not just a list of headings.

In addition to complete solutions to text questions and cases, the manual supplies additional cases for selected chapters, twelve ethical scenarios, summaries of current articles, and class activities. Our manual is truly "one-stop shopping" for everything you need for your complete teaching system.

## COMPREHENSIVE TEST BANK INTEGRATED INTO THE SYSTEM

To complete the system, our enhanced *Test Bank*, like the other supplements, is organized around the learning objectives. At the beginning of each test bank chapter is a correlation table that classifies each question according to type, complexity, and learning objective covered. Using this table, you can create exams with the appropriate mix of question types and level of difficulty for your class. You can choose to prepare tests that cover all learning objectives or emphasize those you feel are most important.

The *Test Bank* is one of the most comprehensive on the market, with over 3,300 true/false, multiple-choice, and essay questions. We've added numerous application questions, many of which are short scenarios, to test student understanding beyond memorization. All questions have been carefully reviewed for clarity and accuracy. Questions are identified by topic and show the rationales and text pages where the rationales appear.

## OTHER OUTSTANDING SUPPLEMENTS

- **Transparency acetates:** More than 225 full-color transparency acetates are provided with *Marketing*, Third Edition. Most are creatively prepared visuals that do not repeat the text. Only acetates that highlight concepts central to the chapter are from the textbook. All acetates use greatly enlarged type and strong colors, so that they can be read in the back row of a large lecture hall.

  The transparencies are tied to the integrated learning system through the instructor's manual lecture outlines and the margins of the annotated instructor's edition of the text. In both places, transparencies and their discussion prompts appear within the learning objective content where they apply.

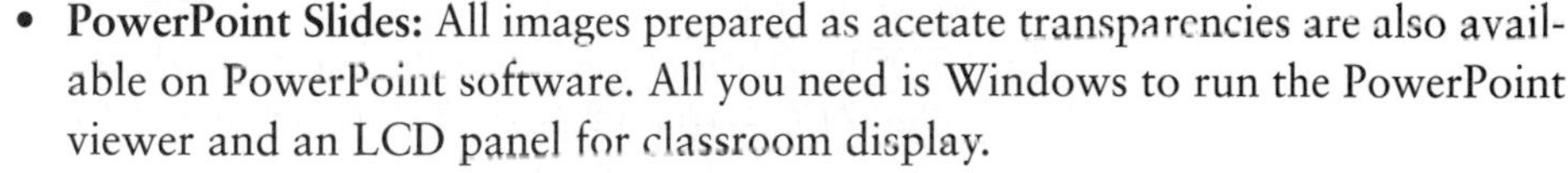

- **PowerPoint Slides:** All images prepared as acetate transparencies are also available on PowerPoint software. All you need is Windows to run the PowerPoint viewer and an LCD panel for classroom display.

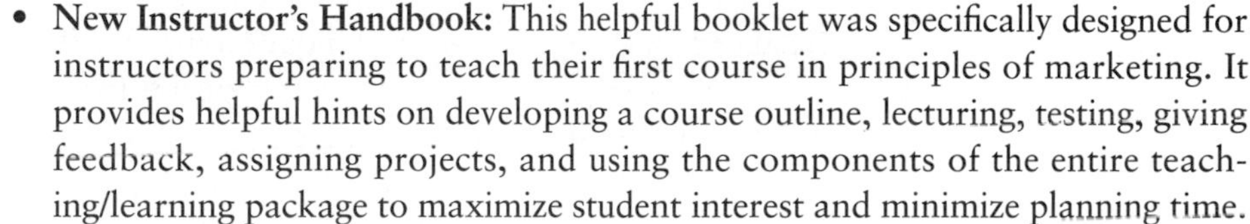

- **New Instructor's Handbook:** This helpful booklet was specifically designed for instructors preparing to teach their first course in principles of marketing. It provides helpful hints on developing a course outline, lecturing, testing, giving feedback, assigning projects, and using the components of the entire teaching/learning package to maximize student interest and minimize planning time.

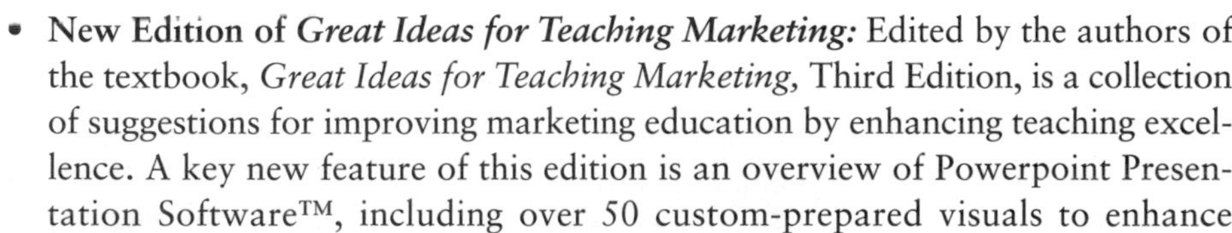

- **New Edition of *Great Ideas for Teaching Marketing:*** Edited by the authors of the textbook, *Great Ideas for Teaching Marketing,* Third Edition, is a collection of suggestions for improving marketing education by enhancing teaching excellence. A key new feature of this edition is an overview of Powerpoint Presentation Software™, including over 50 custom-prepared visuals to enhance

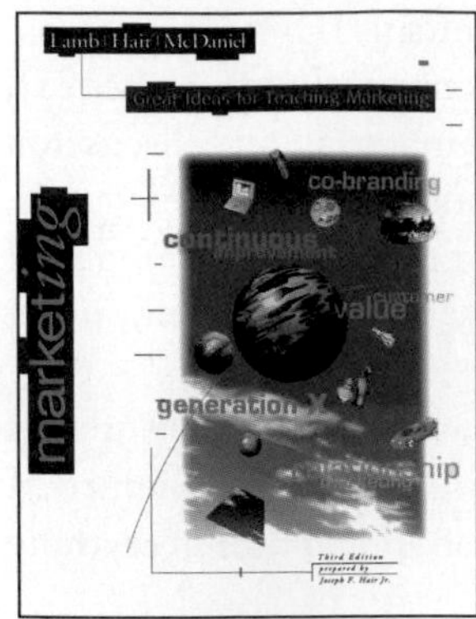

presentation effectiveness. The publication includes teaching tips and ideas submitted by over 200 marketing educators from the United States and Canada. Contributors' names, addresses, and telephone numbers are provided so they can be reached directly for additional information about their teaching techniques.

- **Testing Software (MicroExam 4.0):** All items from the printed test bank are available on disk through South-Western's automated testing program, *MicroExam 4.0*. This program allows instructors to create exams by selecting questions as provided by the program, modifying existing questions, or adding questions. MicroExam 4.0 will run on MS-DOS computers with a minimum 640K memory, a $3\frac{1}{2}$" disk drive, and a hard drive. MicroExam 4.0 is provided free of charge to instructors at educational institutions that adopt *Marketing*, Third Edition, by Lamb, Hair, and McDaniel.
- **Instructor's Manuals for Simulation Games:** The manuals that accompany the two software simulation games—*Fancy Footwork* and *Export to Win!*—provide concise descriptions of these games and suggestions for getting students started using the games. They also provide game variations, sample computer output for both student and instructor, the logic used in building each simulation, and much more.

## ACKNOWLEDGEMENTS

Every textbook owes its content, personality, and features not just to the authors, but to a team of hardworking individuals behind the scenes. The most pleasant task in writing a textbook is the expression of gratitude to people and institutions that have helped the authors. We appreciate the support and encouragement we have received from our colleagues and deans at Texas Christian University, Louisiana State University, and the University of Texas at Arlington. We could not have done without the advice and help of Cinci Stowell who has made the Third Edition a reality. Also, a special thanks goes to Steve Momper, our Marketing Manager, for his suggestions and support.

Our secretaries and administrative assistants, Fran Eller at TCU, RoseAnn Reddick at UTA, and Mary Jennings and Susan Sartwell at LSU, typed and retyped thousands of pages of manuscript, provided important quality control, and helped keep the project (and us) on schedule. Their dedication, hard work, and support were exemplary.

We would also like to acknowledge several other colleagues who played important roles in the development of this book. Julie Baker, University of Texas at Arlington, revised Chapter 11 and contributed the TQM material in Chapter 8. Amelie Storment provided invaluable input and assistance on the revisions of several chapters. Elizabeth Elam, Stan Madden, Linda Catlin, and Tom White contributed interesting cases on a variety of current topics. Special thanks are due Robbie Vitrano and Debbie Currier for their assistance in preparation of the Louisiana Lottery video case, and to Pam Parker for the Woman's Hospital video case. Finally, Alexandra Moustakatou prepared the Jergens Soap case and Danita Baggs prepared the Enviro Care Ethics case.

Thanks, too, to the following people for preparing the high-quality supplements our customers expect: Erika Matulich, Jill Kapron, Elizabeth Elam, Joe Alexander, Diana Haytko, and Rebecca Smith.

Finally, we are particularly indebted to our reviewers:

M. Wayne Alexander
Moorhead State University

Linda Anglin
Mankato State University

James C. Boespflug
Arapahoe Community College

G.L. Carr
University of Alaska Anchorage

William M. Diamond
SUNY—Albany

Kevin M. Elliott
Mankato State University

Karen A. Evans
Herkimer County Community College

Randall S. Hansen
Stetson University

Hari S. Hariharan
University of Wisconsin-Madison

Timothy S. Hatten
Black Hills State University

James E. Hazeltine
Northeastern Illinois University

Patricia M. Hopkins
California State Polytechnic

Kenneth R. Laird
Southern Connecticut State University

J. Gordon Long
Georgia College

Cathy L. Martin
Northeast Louisiana University

Donald R. Self
Auburn University at Montgomery

Mark T. Spence
Southern Connecticut State University

Janice E. Taylor
Miami University of Ohio

Ronald D. Taylor
Mississippi State University

Sandra T. Vernon
Fayetteville Technical Community College

Charles R. Vitaska
Metro State College, Denver

William R. Wynd
Eastern Washington University

# MEET THE SIGNATURE SERIES AUTHORS

## SHAQUILLE O'NEAL

### CENTER, ORLANDO MAGIC

Shaquille O'Neal, the number one pick in the 1992 NBA Draft, was the most anticipated player in the history of basketball, and he delivered what the world was waiting for with his rim-bending, backboard-breaking dunks.

Known worldwide as the Shaq Attaq, he stands at 7-1, 305 pounds, dominating some of the best NBA teams. His first year awards were more than impressive: 1993 NBA Rookie of the Year, the first rookie to ever win Player of the Week in his first week in the NBA, and the first rookie to be voted a starter in the All-Star Game in nine years.

Since the day he was drafted, the media have been comparing Shaquille to NBA's greatest. "He is in the company of the most productive centers in the last quarter of a century: Ewing, Robinson, Olajuwon, Walton, Abdul-Jabbar," Malcom Moran of the *New York Times* wrote. "Shaquille is measured only against the all-time greats . . . and he probably possesses the most impressive physical attributes," wrote *Inside Sports*.

In just his second season, Shaquille led the Orlando Magic to its first ever playoff appearance, was in the top five of the NBA in scoring and field goal percentage, and was voted as a starter above Patrick Ewing for the eastern team in the NBA All-Star game for the second time. Between his second and third season, Shaq participated in the World Games in Toronto with other NBA greats including Alonso Mourning, Dominique Wilkins, and Shawn Kemp. Not only did the Americans win the 1994 World Championship but Shaquille was awarded the Most Valuable Player for the Games. Shaq's basketball talents continue to shine as he is the leading scorer in the league this year and Orlando Magic has the best record in the NBA.

While basketball has certainly made this talented gentleman a household name, it is his off-court demeanor that has attracted even more rave reviews. Ahmad Rashad, host of NBC's "Inside Stuff" stated, "Of all the guys I've interviewed, I had more fun hanging out with Shaquille O'Neal than almost anybody." "If you know him, you like him," said Joel Smith, athletic director at Cole High School in San Antonio where Shaquille spent two years. "I don't think you'll find anyone in this town that doesn't."

While Shaquille's size might intimidate, he marvels fans with his well-mannered, charismatic personality and his contagious smile. Shaquille has a knack for practical joking and a love for music. His extraordinary talents landed him a starring role in Paramount Pictures' "Blue Chips" with veteran actor Nick Nolte, released on February 18, 1994; his own rap career, which includes a platinum debut album "Shaq Diesel" and a second album "Shaq Fu: Da Return"; and an autobiography titled *Shaq Attaq,* which recaps his lifestyle from when he was a teenager to his rookie year in the NBA.

As the most popular celebrity in sports today, Shaq has been featured in global cutting-edge commercials endorsing Reebok products and Pepsi soft drinks, and his name and likeness are featured on Spalding basketballs, SkyBox trading cards, ScoreBoard memorabilia, Electronic Arts video games, and Kenner toys. He is one of the most sought-out figures for product endorsement worldwide. In fact, when marketing executives from 250 of the most successful corporations were asked for their wish list of athlete endorsers for the Steiner Sports Marketing annual survey, Shaquille O'Neal topped the list.

Shaquille says he owes most of his success to his family network, especially his parents. "My parents have always been my role models," Shaquille has said numerous times. "They taught me dedication and respect. If I didn't have them, I wouldn't have the discipline I have now and I probably wouldn't have the basketball skills I have now."

Shaquille's sensitive side extends beyond his family. Through actions, not just monetary donations, Shaq has touched the hearts of the less fortunate and the needy. Each year on Thanksgiving, he personally serves homeless people in the city of Orlando, Florida, a Thanksgiving meal, and on Christmas he transforms into Shaq-A-Clause, bringing gifts to lonesome, needy children in Orlando hospitals.

It is the combination of Shaquille's winning personality, million-dollar smile, and love for others that has made this basketball superstar a role model for both children and adults.

## PAUL C. P. McILHENNY

### VICE PRESIDENT, McILHENNY COMPANY

Paul C. P. McIlhenny began his career with McIlhenny Company in 1967 after receiving his Bachelor of Arts degree in Political Science with a minor in English from the University of the South in Sewanee, Tennessee.

He worked for a year and a half with the largest TABASCO® sauce food broker in the U. S. in southern California. His initial responsibilities were in food service sales after which he became Purchasing Agent. He is the Vice-President and Secretary and a Director of McIlhenny Company, manufacturer of TABASCO® brand products.

He is a founder and Director of Fuelman/Fleetman, Inc., and he also serves as an Associate Director of Avery Island, Inc. He is Iberia Parish Coordinator for the Louisiana Coastal Wetlands Conservation and Restoration Plan, and serves as a Board Member of the Louisiana Old State Capital. He served as a founding Director and Officer of the Episcopal School of Acadiana, as well as the President of The Rotary Club of New Iberia, Louisiana.

He is an active member of several gourmet societies as follows: He is the Grand Sénéchal of La Confrèrerie des Chevaliers du Tastevin Chapître de la Nouvelle Orléans, a Member of L'Ordre des Canardiers, and a member of the La Société des Escargots Orléanais.

He co-authored the 125th Anniversary TABASCO® Cookbook, and his hobbies include wing shooting, red fish and speckled trout fishing, game cooking, and wine tasting.

## VICKI L. ROMERO

### PRESIDENT AND CEO, WOMAN'S HEALTH FOUNDATION

Ms. Romero currently serves as President and Chief Executive Officer of Woman's Health Foundation, one of the largest free-standing women's specialty centers in the country, located in Baton Rouge, Louisiana. As President and CEO, Ms. Romero is among the 10 percent of women at the helm of major healthcare institutions in the country.

Ms. Romero is the Chair of the Board of the Capital Area United Way and the secretary of the Greater Baton Rouge Chamber of Commerce. Additionally, she is a member of the Board of Directors of City National Bank. She is a graduate of the 1992 Chamber of Commerce Leadership Program and the 1994 Louisiana Leadership program sponsored by Council for a Better Louisiana. She was recipient of the YWCA Women of Achievement Award in 1990, and was named by Sales and Marketing International as the 1994 Marketer of the Year. She was also named the 1994 Woman of Achievement by the American Society of Women Accountants.

At the state level, she serves as Chairperson of the Commission of Perinatal Care and Prevention of Infant Mortality, is a member of the advisory council of the Louisiana Healthcare Alliance and is a member of the Board of Directors of the Louisiana Hospital Association Trust Fund.

Nationally, Ms. Romero has been recognized by Modern Healthcare magazine as a 1991 "Up and Comer" in healthcare. She serves on the governing council of the American Hospital Association Maternal-Child Section and is a board member of the National Perinatal Information Center. She has been an invited speaker on leadership in healthcare by the Healthcare Financial Management Association, American Hospital Association, Jacobs Institute of Women's Health, and the Joint Commission on the Accreditation of Healthcare Organizations. The Healthcare Forum recently named Ms. Romero as a 1994 Emerging Leader in Healthcare.

Ms. Romero is a graduate of Nicholls State University with a B.S. in Accounting. She has a daughter who is a sophomore at Loyola University in New Orleans.

## JOHN V. ROACH

### CHAIRMAN AND CEO, TANDY CORPORATION

John V. Roach began his career at Tandy Corporation in 1967 as General Manager of Tandy Computer Services. In 1982, he was named Chairman of the Board and Chief Executive Officer. He also serves as a member of the Board of Directors of Justin Industries, City Club, Van Cliburn Foundation, and Electronic Industries Association. He is Chairman of the Board of his alma mater, Texas Christian University, where he earned a B.A. in Physics and Math and an MBA.

Mr. Roach has received many leadership awards including *Financial World's* Chief Executive Officer of the Year in 1981, *Forbes* Magazine's Business Speaker of the Year in 1988, and Financial World's CEO of the Decade in Specialty Retailing in 1989. He has been recognized by Texas Christian University as a Distinguished Alumnus and by the University of Texas at Arlington College of Business as a Distinguished Business Leader. He was inducted into the Texas Business Hall of Fame in 1994.

## RAY KORDUPLESKI

### AT&T CUSTOMER SATISFACTION DIRECTOR

As AT&T's Customer Satisfaction Director, Ray Kordupleski is responsible for overall development, implementation, and strategic use of customer satisfaction data and information throughout AT&T. Mr. Kordupleski has over twenty-eight years of experience in the telecommunications industry, including positions with Illinois Bell, New Jersey Bell, Bell Atlantic, and AT&T. Highlights of Mr. Kordupleski's assignments include:

- Installation and Repair Service District Manager, Chicago, IL

- AT&T Liaison for the Federal Communications Commission
- Advisor to U.S. Congress during the competitive Interconnect Policy transition period
- V.P. Operations for Bell Atlanticom Systems, Inc.

Mr. Kordupleski's work in quality and customer satisfaction is well recognized. He has served as an advisor on the subject to organizations such as Walt Disney World, Milliken, Farber Castel, Bull Inc., the Environmental Protection Agency, the Department of Defense Communications Agency, Swedish Televerkert, Quality Association of Finland, Telecom New Zealand, and Telecom Australia.

Mr. Kordupleski received his B.S. in electrical engineering from the University of Illinois, an MBA from Loyola University of Chicago, and has completed advanced studies in business at Dartmouth College.

## KEN BRICKMAN

### VICE PRESIDENT, SALES AND MARKETING, LOUISIANA LOTTERY CORPORATION

One of the original officers of the Louisiana Lottery Corporation, Ken Brickman served as Secretary/Treasurer from June of 1991 to July of 1992; as Executive Vice President until January 1995; and most recently as Vice President, Sales and Marketing. Before joining the Louisiana Lottery Start-Up, he served as General Counsel and then as Deputy Director with the Illinois Lottery.

Brickman is a graduate of Culver-Stockton College, Canton, Missouri, and the University of Missouri (Columbia) School of Law.

## GIAN M. FULGONI

### CHAIRMAN AND CHIEF EXECUTIVE OFFICER, INFORMATION RESOURCES, INC.

Mr. Fulgoni is Chairman and Chief Executive Officer of Information Resources, Inc. IRI offers a complete line of scanner-based information services for the consumer packaged goods industry and decision support software for use across a wide variety of industries and governmental agencies worldwide. Since its founding in 1979, IRI has grown rapidly to become the second largest market research company in the world and the fortieth largest independent software vendor. In both 1984 and 1985, the company was listed by Inc. Magazine in the "Inc. 100" list of fastest growing public companies. In the words of the *Wall Street Journal* and the *New York Times,* IRI has become known as "the pioneer/trail blazer in the field of marketing research using UPC scanners."

IRI introduced the BehaviorScan® system in January 1980. BehaviorScan® combines the technologies of UPC scanning and targetable TV (patented by IRI) in a system that precisely measures the sales impact of alternative marketing strategies (i.e., ad weight, ad copy, price, promotions, etc.) for new and established brands. The service was described at a meeting of the Association of National Advertisers as the "most talked about innovation in the history of research services."

IRI's most recent innovative service is InfoScan. Introduced in 1987, InfoScan monitors the consumer purchasing of every UPC coded product sold in supermarkets, drug stores and mass merchandisers, convenience stores, and price clubs. InfoScan combines weekly scanner sales and price data from 2,700 supermarkets,

500 drug stores, and 250 mass merchandisers nationwide with the daily purchases of over 60,000 panel households and complete information on the promotional conditions affecting consumer purchasing. With annual sales of information and software now exceeding $200 million per year, InfoScan has become the fastest growing new service in the history of the market research industry.

In recognition of his efforts in guiding the development of InfoScan, Mr. Fulgoni was honored in 1990 by Peat Marwick as one of four Illinois High Tech Entrepreneurs of the Year. In 1991, Mr. Fulgoni was awarded the "bronze award" by the *Wall Street Transcript,* one of three awards recognizing the extent to which a company's CEO has taken proper steps to enhance the overall value of the company for the benefit of its shareholders.

Active in industry affairs, Mr. Fulgoni is a frequent speaker at management conferences and trade association meetings.

Educated in England, Mr. Fulgoni holds an Honors Degree in Physics from the University of Manchester and a Masters Degree in Marketing from the University of Lancaster.

# Meet the Authors

## CHARLES W. LAMB, Jr.—TEXAS CHRISTIAN UNIVERSITY

Charles Lamb is the M. J. Neeley Professor of Marketing, M. J. Neeley School of Business, Texas Christian University. He served as chair of the TCU marketing department from 1982 to 1988.

Lamb has authored or co-authored more than a dozen books and anthologies on marketing topics and over 100 articles that have appeared in academic journals and conference proceedings.

He is vice president for publications for Academy of Marketing Science, a member of the American Marketing Association Education Council, a member of the board of directors of the American Association for Advances in Health Care Research, and a past president of the Southwestern Marketing Association.

Lamb earned an associate degree in business administration from Sinclair Community College, a bachelor's degree from Miami University, an MBA from Wright State University, and a doctorate in business administration from Kent State University. He previously served as assistant and associate professor of marketing at Texas A&M University.

## JOSEPH E. HAIR, JR.—LOUISIANA STATE UNIVERSITY

Joseph Hair is William A. Copeland III Endowed Professor of Business Administration and Chairman, Department of Marketing, Louisiana State University. Previously, Hair was an associate professor of marketing and held the Phil B. Hardin Chair of Marketing at the University of Mississippi. He has taught graduate and undergraduate marketing and marketing research courses.

Hair has authored twenty-seven books, monographs, and cases and over sixty articles in scholarly journals. He also has participated on many university committees and has chaired numerous departmental task forces. He serves on the editorial review board of several journals.

He is a member of the American Marketing Association, Academy of Marketing Science, Southern Marketing Association, and Southwestern Marketing Association.

Hair holds a bachelor's degree in economics, a master's degree in marketing, and a doctorate in marketing, all from the University of Florida. He also serves as a marketing consultant to businesses in a variety of industries, ranging from food and retailing to financial services, health care, electronics, and the U. S. Departments of Agriculture and Interior.

## CARL McDANIEL—UNIVERSITY OF TEXAS, ARLINGTON

Carl McDaniel is a professor of marketing at the University of Texas—Arlington, where he has been chairman of the marketing department since 1976. He has been an instructor for more than twenty years and is the recipient of several awards for outstanding teaching. McDaniel has also been a district sales manager for Southwestern Bell Telephone Company. Currently he serves as a board member of the North Texas Higher Education Authority.

In addition to *Principles of Marketing,* McDaniel also has co-authored numerous textbooks in marketing and business. McDaniel's research has appeared in such publications as the *Journal of Marketing Research, Journal of Marketing, Journal of the Academy of Marketing Science,* and *California Management Review.*

McDaniel is a member of the American Marketing Association, Academy of Marketing Science, Southern Marketing Association, Southwestern Marketing Association, and Western Marketing Association.

Besides his academic experience, McDaniel has business experience as the co-owner of a marketing research firm. During the winter and spring of 1995 McDaniel served as Senior Consultant to the International Trade Centre (ITC), Geneva, Switzerland. The ITC's mission is to help developing nations increase their exports. He has a bachelor's degree from the University of Arkansas and his master's degree and doctorate from Arizona State University.

# Part One
# The World of Marketing



As a busy college student, Chad Mattix used his computer for everything from composing term papers to balancing his budget. When minor equipment or software problems arose, he was frustrated by the scarcity of companies offering advice and technical aid geared to student computing needs. Recognizing an unfilled niche, he and three others joined forces to develop a small business that provides a wide range of support to other computer users on campus. The partners' complementary backgrounds contributed to the company's success. Some members provided business savvy, others technical expertise.

Pinnacle Computer Corporation is still going strong. Two years out of college, Chad is now president of the company, which recently began offering its services to small and medium-size businesses. Pinnacle designs work-group applications for internal communications through e-mail (electronic mail) and project management programs. The goal is to use computer technology to better manage small companies' work loads and streamline their communication. Pinnacle works closely with clients, identifying their processes and then determining the best means of automating them.

Chad's role as president requires that he focus on several aspects of the business, including marketing, accounting, operations, and legal issues. His degree in finance has been a big help, but he feels that a broader background in other areas of business studies, such as marketing, would have better prepared him for the challenges he now faces.

Chad believes entrepreneurs will find more opportunities as major corporations reduce the size of their workforces and turn to outside companies to perform jobs once done in-house. Pinnacle Computer Corporation plans to continue expanding its customer base—and profits—by keeping abreast of new technology and the changing needs of their clients. Judging by their success thus far, it is a potent recipe for success.

# CHAPTER 1

# AN OVERVIEW OF MARKETING

## LEARNING OBJECTIVES

*After studying this chapter, you should be able to*

1 *Define the term* marketing.

2 *Describe several reasons for studying marketing.*

3 *Describe four marketing management philosophies.*

4 *Discuss the differences between sales and marketing orientations.*

5 *Explain how firms implement the marketing concept.*

6 *Describe the marketing process, and identify the variables that make up the marketing mix.*

7 *Explain how organizations create customer value.*

Five attorneys from Boise, Idaho, decided to drive together to a conference in Portland, Oregon—a distance of 500 miles—leaving the afternoon before the conference. One of the attorneys volunteered to drive his late-model Chevrolet Suburban. Less than 20 miles outside Boise, the Suburban developed engine problems. The engine quit completely, and the lawyers were stranded alongside the freeway.

Now they were in a real dilemma. Even if they could get on a flight to Portland, the airfare would be extremely high due to the same-day purchase of the tickets. So the owner of the Suburban phoned the dealer where he bought the vehicle and explained the problem. The lawyer was hoping to rent another Suburban.

Instead, the dealer offered to supply a brand-new Suburban free of charge. The dealer delivered the new Suburban to the attorneys beside the freeway, the switch was made, and the dealer rode back with the tow truck.

The Suburban had broken down because the engine had seized. The attorney who was driving had been engrossed in conversation and hadn't paid close attention to the gauges. It seems that a technician in a fast-lube-and-oil-change place had forgotten to tighten the oil drain plug. The plug fell out, the oil drained, and within minutes the engine overheated and seized completely. The dealer had the diagnosis in hand when the attorneys returned several days later.[1]

Describe the Chevrolet dealer's apparent management philosophy. Why would the dealer lend the attorney a brand-new Suburban free of charge? Was the dealer afraid of a possible lawsuit, just a nice person, or a savvy entrepreneur? These issues are explored in Chapter 1.

1 *Define the term* marketing.

## WHAT IS MARKETING?

What does the term *marketing* mean to you? Many people think it means the same as *selling*. Others think marketing is the same as personal selling and advertising. Still others believe marketing has something to do with making products available in stores, arranging displays, and maintaining inventories of products for future sales. Actually, marketing includes all these activities and more.

Marketing has two facets. First, it is a philosophy, an attitude, a perspective, or a management orientation that stresses customer satisfaction. Second, marketing is a set of activities used to implement this philosophy. The American Marketing Association's definition encompasses both perspectives: "**Marketing** is the process of planning and executing the conception, pricing, promotion, and distribution of ideas, goods, and services to create exchanges that satisfy individual and organizational objectives."[2]

**marketing**
Process of planning and executing the conception, pricing, promotion, and distribution of ideas, goods, and services to create exchanges that satisfy individual and organizational objectives.

**concept of exchange**
Idea that people give up something to receive something they would rather have.

*Exchange* is the key term in this definition of marketing. The **concept of exchange** is quite simple. It means that people give up something to receive something they would rather have. Normally we think of money as the medium of exchange. We "give up" money to "get" the goods and services we want. Exchange does not require money, however. Two persons may barter or trade such items as baseball cards or oil paintings.

Five conditions must be satisfied for any kind of exchange to take place:

- There must be at least two parties.
- Each party must have something the other party values.
- Each party must be able to communicate with the other party and deliver the goods or services sought by the other trading party.
- Each party must be free to accept or reject the other's offer.
- Each party must believe that it is appropriate or desirable to deal with the other party.[3]

Exchange will not necessarily take place even if all these conditions exist. They are, however, necessary for exchange to be possible. For example, you may place an

Marketing is a set of activities (planning, promotion, etc.) implemented to create a mutually satisfying exchange between the seller and the buyer.

© Steven Chenn/Westlight
© Tony Stone Worldwide/Andy Sack

Exhibit 1.1

Exchanges between a Public Agency and Its Citizens

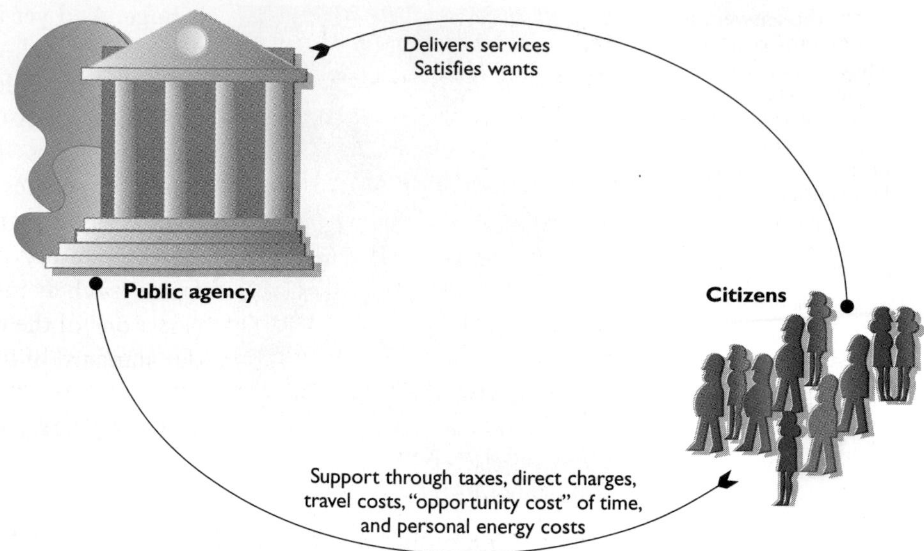


advertisement in your local newspaper stating that your used automobile is for sale at a certain price. Several people may call you to ask about the car, some may test-drive it, and one or more may even offer you your asking price. All five conditions necessary for an exchange exist. But unless you reach an agreement with a buyer and actually sell the car, an exchange will not take place.

Notice that marketing can occur even if an exchange does not occur. In the example just discussed, you would have engaged in marketing even if no one bought your used automobile.

Exchange is not restricted to profit seeking enterprises. Exhibit 1.1 illustrates the exchange relationship between a public agency and its citizens. An agency, such as a public library or a municipal recreation and parks department, delivers want-satisfying services that citizens perceive as valuable. Citizens support the agency through their payments of tax dollars, direct charges for using the services, and travel and transportation costs. Citizen support also includes the opportunity costs of not engaging in other activities while they use a service and the personal energy costs spent to use the service.

2 *Describe several reasons for studying marketing.*

## WHY STUDY MARKETING?

You may be asking, "What's in it for me?" or "Why should I study marketing?" These are important questions whether you are majoring in a business field other than marketing (such as accounting, finance, or management information systems) or a nonbusiness field (such as journalism, economics, or agriculture). There are several important reasons to study marketing: Marketing plays an important role in society, marketing is important to businesses, marketing offers outstanding career opportunities, and marketing affects your life every day.

### MARKETING PLAYS AN IMPORTANT ROLE IN SOCIETY

The U.S. Bureau of the Census predicts that the total population of the United States will reach 268 million by the end of the 1990s. Think about how many transactions are needed each day to feed, clothe, and shelter a population of this size. The number

The person who answers the phone is often the customer's only contact with a firm. In marketing-oriented organizations, a strong interest in satisfying customers or clients is an important characteristic of all employees—but especially of those who interact directly with the public.



is huge. And yet it all works quite well, partly because the well-developed U.S. economic system efficiently distributes the output of farms and factories. A typical U.S. family, for example, consumes 2.5 tons of food a year. Marketing makes food available when we want it, in desired quantities, at accessible locations, and in sanitary and convenient packages and forms (such as instant and frozen foods). Food is just one of the many products that are part of our standard of living.

## MARKETING IS IMPORTANT TO BUSINESSES

The fundamental objectives of most businesses are survival, profits, and growth. Marketing contributes directly to achieving these objectives. Marketing includes these activities, which are vital to business organizations: assessing the wants and satisfactions of present and potential customers, designing and managing product offerings, determining prices and pricing policies, developing distribution strategies, and communicating with present and potential customers.

All businesspeople, regardless of specialization or area of responsibility, need to be familiar with the terminology and fundamentals of accounting, finance, management, and marketing. People in all business areas need to be able to communicate with specialists in other areas. Therefore, a basic understanding of marketing is important to all businesspeople.

## MARKETING OFFERS OUTSTANDING CAREER OPPORTUNITIES

Between a fourth and a third of the entire civilian work force in the United States performs marketing activities. Marketing offers great career opportunities in such areas as professional selling, marketing research, advertising, retail buying, distribution management, product management, product development, and wholesaling. Marketing career opportunities also exist in a variety of nonbusiness organizations, including hospitals, museums, universities, the armed forces, and various government and social service agencies (see Chapter 11).

As the world marketplace becomes more challenging, U.S. companies are going to have to become better marketers. In high-tech and low-tech industries, profit and nonprofit organizations, the demand for marketing-educated personnel is growing.

Korn/Ferry International, an executive search firm, and the Graduate School of Management at the University of California, Los Angeles, conducted a study of 1,362 senior executives from *Fortune* 500 firms. According to their study, marketing is the fastest route to the top in today's corporate world. When asked to predict what the fastest route will be in ten years, senior executives once again said marketing. For more detailed information about careers in marketing, see Appendix A. The American Marketing Association also publishes a book, *Careers in Marketing and the Employment Kit,* that provides extensive information about career opportunities in marketing.

### MARKETING AFFECTS YOUR LIFE EVERY DAY

Marketing plays a major role in your everyday life. You participate in the marketing process as a consumer of goods and services. About half of every dollar you spend pays for marketing costs, such as marketing research, product development, packaging, transportation, storage, advertising, and sales expenses. By developing a better understanding of marketing, you will become a better-informed consumer. You will better understand the buying process and be able to negotiate more effectively with sellers. Moreover, you will be better prepared to demand satisfaction when the goods and services you buy do not meet the standards promised by the manufacturer or the marketer.

3 *Describe four marketing management philosophies.*

## MARKETING MANAGEMENT PHILOSOPHIES

Four competing philosophies strongly influence an organization's marketing activities. These philosophies are commonly referred to as production, sales, marketing, and societal marketing orientations.

### PRODUCTION ORIENTATION

**production orientation**
Philosophy that focuses on the internal capabilities of the firm rather than on the desires and needs of the marketplace.

A **production orientation** is a philosophy that focuses on the internal capabilities of the firm rather than on the desires and needs of the marketplace. A production orientation means that management assesses its resources and asks these questions: "What can we do best?" "What can our engineers design?" "What is easy to produce given our equipment?" In the case of a service organization, managers ask, "What services are most convenient for the firm to offer?" and "Where do our talents lie?"

There is nothing wrong with assessing a firm's capabilities; in fact, such assessments are major considerations in strategic marketing planning (see Chapter 22). A production orientation falls short because it does not consider whether the goods and services that the firm produces most efficiently also meet the needs of the marketplace.

A production orientation does not doom a company to failure, particularly not in the short run. Sometimes what a firm can best produce is exactly what the market wants. In other situations, as when competition is weak or demand exceeds supply, a production-oriented firm can survive and even prosper.

### SALES ORIENTATION

**sales orientation**
Philosophy that assumes buyers resist purchasing items that are not essential.

A **sales orientation** assumes that buyers resist purchasing items that are not essential. It is also based on the ideas that people will buy more goods and services if aggressive sales techniques are used and that high sales result in high profits. Not only are sales to the final buyer emphasized, but intermediaries are also encouraged to push manufacturers' products more aggressively. To sales-oriented firms, marketing means selling things and collecting money.

The fundamental problem with a sales orientation, as with a production orientation, is a lack of understanding of the needs and wants of the marketplace. Sales-oriented companies often find that, despite the quality of their sales force, they cannot convince people to buy goods or services that are neither wanted nor needed.

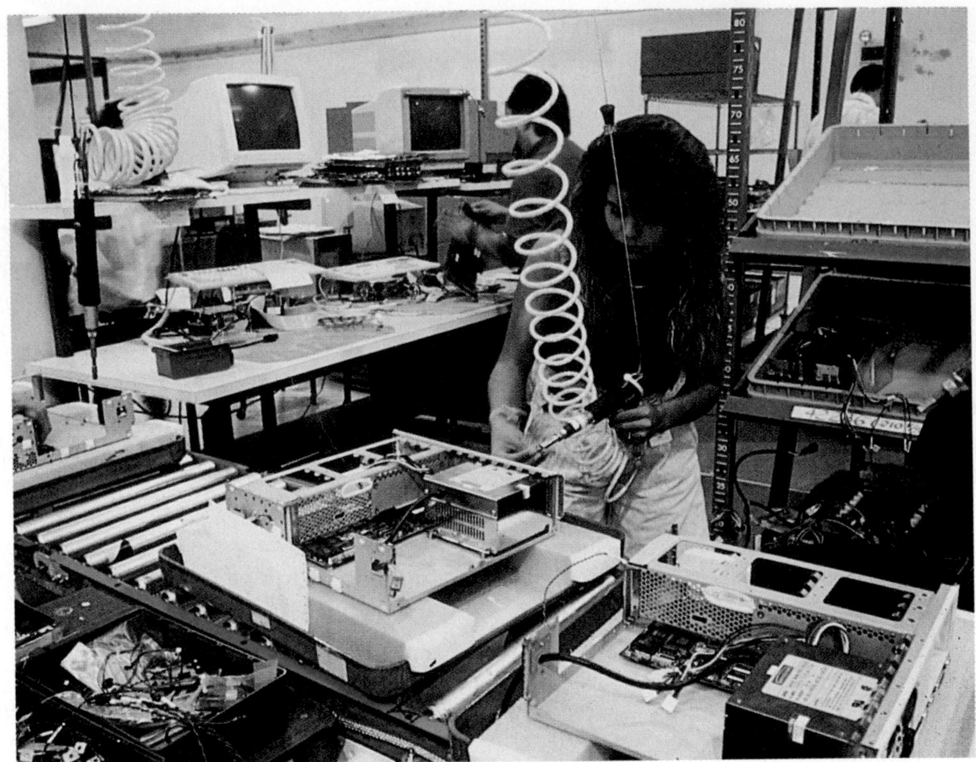

Dell Computer has prospered because every employee, from the executive suite to the assembly line, has adopted the marketing orientation and is committed to customer satisfaction.



**marketing orientation**
Philosophy that assumes responsiveness to customer wants should be the central focus of all marketing activities.

**marketing concept**
Idea that the social and economic justification for an organization's existence is the satisfaction of customer wants and needs while meeting organizational objectives.

ETHICS IN MARKETING

**Should Mass Merchandisers Sell Firearms?**

The National Sporting Goods Association calculates that discount retailers, including Kmart and Wal-Mart, sell $158 million worth of rifles and shotguns per year.[6] Wal-Mart is probably also the largest seller of handguns in the United States. According to industry experts, Kmart and Wal-Mart use firearms to position themselves as one-stop hunting shops, aiming to attract male customers who also buy highly profitable hunting clothing and accessories. A spokesperson for the National Rifle Association notes that firearm salespeople do not need any specialized training. He claims that "selling a firearm is like selling anything else. As long as a person can read, it's fairly straightforward."[7]

Many mass merchandisers—such as Sears Roebuck, JCPenney, Montgomery Ward, Target, and Ames Department Stores—have stopped selling firearms. When asked why Target no longer carries hunting rifles, a spokesperson reported, "We see ourselves as a family store, and we didn't see firearms as a fit."[8]

Is it ethical for mass merchandisers to sell firearms? Would you say that selling firearms is illustrative of a production, sales, marketing, or societal marketing orientation? What about the decision not to sell firearms?

## MARKETING ORIENTATION

A **marketing orientation,** which is the foundation of contemporary marketing philosophy, is based on an understanding that a sale does not depend on an aggressive sales force but rather on a customer's decision to purchase a product. What a business thinks it produces is not of primary importance to its success. Instead, what a customer thinks he or she is buying—the perceived value—defines a business. Perceived value also determines a business's products and its potential to prosper. To marketing-oriented firms, marketing means building relationships with customers.

This philosophy, called the **marketing concept,** is simple and intuitively appealing. It states that the social and economic justification for an organization's existence is the satisfaction of

| | What is the organization's focus? | What business are you in? | To whom is the product directed? | What is your primary goal? | How do you seek to achieve your goal? |
|---|---|---|---|---|---|
| **Sales orientation** | Inward, upon the organization's needs | Selling goods and services | Everybody | Profit through maximum sales volume | Primarily through intensive promotion |
| **Marketing orientation** | Outward, upon the wants and preferences of customers | Satisfying consumer wants and needs | Specific groups of people | Profit through customer satisfaction | Through coordinated marketing activities |

*Exhibit 1.2*

Differences between Sales and Marketing Orientations

customer wants and needs while meeting organizational objectives. The marketing concept includes the following:

- Focusing on customer wants so the organization can distinguish its product(s) from competitors' offerings
- Integrating all the organization's activities, including production, to satisfy these wants
- Achieving long-term goals for the organization by satisfying customer wants and needs legally and responsibly

Today, companies of all types are applying the marketing concept. For example, Wal-Mart Stores has become the leading discount retailer in the United States by focusing on what its customers want: everyday low prices, items always in stock, and cashiers always available. At DuPont, a team of chemists, sales and marketing executives, and regulatory specialists developed a herbicide that corn growers can apply less often.[4] And at Dell Computer, employees from top managers to assembly workers meet weekly to carefully examine customer complaints and employee suggestions, with the goal of ensuring that customers have a "quality experience" and are "pleased, not just satisfied."[5]

### SOCIETAL MARKETING ORIENTATION

One reason a marketing-oriented organization may choose not to deliver the benefits sought by customers is that these benefits may not be good for individuals or society. This important refinement of the marketing concept, called the **societal marketing concept**, states that an organization exists not only to satisfy customer wants and needs and to meet organizational objectives but also to preserve or enhance individuals' and society's long-term best interests. Marketing "environmentally friendly" products and containers, discussed in Chapter 21, is consistent with a societal marketing orientation. The Ethics in Marketing story in this section shows how complex societal marketing issues can be.

**societal marketing concept**
Idea that an organization exists not only to satisfy customer wants and needs and to meet organizational objectives but also to preserve or enhance individuals' and society's long-term best interests.

4 *Discuss the differences between sales and marketing orientations.*

## THE DIFFERENCES BETWEEN SALES AND MARKETING ORIENTATIONS

As noted at the beginning of this chapter, many people confuse the terms *sales* and *marketing*. These orientations are substantially different, however. Exhibit 1.2 compares the two orientations in terms of five characteristics.

### THE ORGANIZATION'S FOCUS

Most sales-oriented firms are highly bureaucratic. Personnel tend to be "inward-looking," preoccupied with employment security and working conditions. They focus on satisfying their own short-term needs rather than their customers' needs.

In contrast, marketing-oriented firms recognize that customers direct the activities of the firm, and their internal organization reflects this awareness. A marketing orientation means that all departments coordinate their activities and focus on satisfying customers. According to Leslie H. Wexner, CEO and founder of The Limited, a chain of women's apparel stores, "The common thread among retailers who really are doing it right is that they realize that the customer is the one calling the shots, not the other way around."[9]

De Mar, a plumbing, heating, air conditioning, and refrigeration company in Clovis, California, grew in six years from just over $200,000 annual revenue to $3.3 million by focusing on customers' most pressing need—timely service in emergencies. De Mar provides service twenty-four hours a day, seven days a week. De Mar also guarantees same-day service for customers requiring it. Customers also want accurate cost estimates, and so De Mar guarantees estimates before work begins.[10] This organization's focus is truly the customer.

## Customer-Oriented Personnel

For an organization to be focused on customers, employees' attitudes and actions must be customer-oriented. An employee may be the only contact a particular customer has with the firm. In that customer's eyes, the employee is the firm. Any person, department, or division that is not customer-oriented weakens the positive image of the entire organization. For example, a potential customer who is greeted discourteously may well assume that the employee's attitude represents the whole firm.

To promote the right attitude, Chrysler Corporation has begun paying dealers for high scores on customer satisfaction surveys.[11] According to J. W. "Bill" Marriott, Jr., CEO of Marriott International, "Our basic philosophy is to make sure our associates (employees) are very happy and that they work to go the extra mile—take care of customers and have fun doing it."[12] Every employee is cross-trained to handle all major guest services. Many other successful companies are making sure their employees focus on customers' needs.

These companies also recognize that, when employees are happy, they provide better customer service. Companies like Metropolitan Life, American Express, and Federal Express are offering employee benefits such as flexible work hours, compressed work weeks, and job sharing because having contented workers leads to better customer service and greater employee retention.[13]

## The Role of Training

Leading marketers recognize the role of employee training in customer service. For example, all new employees at Disneyland and Walt Disney World must attend Disney University, a special training program for Disney employees. They must first pass Traditions 1, a day-long course focusing on the Disney philosophy and operational procedures. Then they go on to specialized training. Similarly, McDonald's has Hamburger University. At American Express's Quality University, line employees and managers learn how to treat customers. Some Japanese department stores provide elevator operators with two months' training. Because elevator operators have so much contact with customers, they must know how to respond to customers' questions.[14]

### Empowerment

In addition to training, some marketing-oriented firms are giving employees more authority to solve customer problems on the spot. The term used to describe this delegation of authority is **empowerment.** Montgomery Ward sales clerks, for example, are now authorized to approve checks and handle merchandise return problems. Before, only store managers performed these functions.[15] Empowerment gives customers the feeling that their concerns are being addressed and gives employees the feeling that their expertise matters. The result, again, is greater satisfaction all the way around.

**empowerment**
Practice of giving employees expanded authority to solve customer problems as they arise.

## THE FIRM'S BUSINESS

As Exhibit 1.2 illustrates, a sales-oriented firm defines its business (or mission) in terms of goods and services. A marketing-oriented firm defines its business in terms of the benefits its customers seek. People who spend their money, time, and energy expect to receive benefits, not just goods and services. This distinction has enormous implications.

Because of the limited way it defines its business, a sales-oriented firm often misses opportunities to serve customers whose wants can be met through only a wide range of product offerings instead of specific products. For example, in 1990 Encyclopedia Britannica earned more than $40 million after taxes. Just four years later, after three consecutive years of losses, the sales force had collapsed. How did this respected company sink so low? Britannica managers saw that competitors were beginning to use CD-ROM to store huge masses of information but chose to ignore the new computer technology.[16] It's not hard to see why parents would rather give their children an encyclopedia on a compact disc instead of a printed one. The CD versions are either given away or sold by other publishers for under $400. A full set of the Encyclopedia Britannica costs a minimum of $1,500, weighs 118 pounds, and takes four and a half feet of shelf space.[17] If Britannica had defined its business as providing information instead of publishing books, it might not have suffered such a precipitous fall.

Cunard offers passengers much more than just transportation by ship. Its real product is a bundle of services that pamper and entertain passengers.



Defining a business in terms of goods and services rather than in terms of the benefits that customers seek is sometimes called **marketing myopia.** In this context, the term *myopia* means narrow, short-term thinking. This orientation can threaten an organization's survival. For example, some of the large luxury passenger ships that were threatened by competition from the airlines survived because

**marketing myopia**
Practice of defining a business in terms of the goods and services it produces rather than in terms of the benefits customers seek.

they redefined themselves as being in the floating hotel business, not the transportation business. Another example is movie theater operators like American Multi-Cinema (AMC), which have learned that good movies alone will not attract customers. The same movie may be showing in five or six theaters in the same area, so AMC has made convenience a top priority. Most AMC box offices accept credit cards and phone-ahead ticket sales. Some AMC theaters offer such tasty treats as iced cappuccino, mineral water, crab cakes, salads, quiche, egg rolls, and croissant sandwiches. Many theater operators also understand that they are not just competing against other movie houses in the neighborhood. The real threat comes from other forms of entertainment—everything from going out for a steak to taking in the ballet.[18] Both these examples show how products emerge to better deliver the benefits consumers seek and what can happen when a company adapts to changing customer needs.

Answering the question "What is this firm's business?" in terms of the benefits customers seek, instead of goods and services, has at least three important advantages:

- It ensures that the firm keeps focusing on customers and avoids becoming preoccupied with goods, services, or the organization's internal needs.
- It encourages innovation and creativity by reminding people that there are many ways to satisfy customer wants.
- It stimulates an awareness of changes in customer desires and preferences so that product offerings are more likely to remain relevant.

The marketing concept and the idea of focusing on customer wants do not mean that customers will always receive everything they want. It is not possible, for example, to profitably manufacture and market for $25 each automobile tires that will last for 100,000 miles. Furthermore, customers' preferences must be mediated by sound professional judgment as to how to deliver the benefits they seek. As one adage suggests, "People don't know what they want—they only want what they know." Consumers have a limited set of experiences. They are unlikely to request anything beyond those experiences because they are not aware of benefits they may gain from other potential offerings. For example, before the automobile, people knew they wanted quicker, more convenient transportation but could not express their need for a car.

### THOSE TO WHOM THE PRODUCT IS DIRECTED

A sales-oriented organization targets its products at "everybody" or "the average customer." A marketing-oriented organization aims at specific groups of people (see Exhibit 1.2). The fallacy of developing products directed at the average user is that relatively few average users actually exist. Typically, populations are characterized by diversity. An average is simply a midpoint in some set of characteristics. Because most potential customers are not "average," they are not likely to be attracted to an average product marketed to the average customer.

Consider the market for shampoo as one simple example. There are shampoos for oily hair, dry hair, and dandruff. Some shampoos remove the gray or color hair. Special shampoos are marketed for infants and elderly people. There is even shampoo for people with average or normal hair (whatever that is), but this is a fairly small portion of the total market for shampoo.

Companies with a marketing orientation tend to develop a selection of specialized products that meet diverse customer needs. Head & Shoulders, for instance, sells not just dandruff shampoo but also shampoo for people with a dry scalp or for those who want a shampoo combined with conditioner.



A marketing-oriented organization recognizes that different customer groups and their wants vary. It may therefore need to develop different goods, services, and promotional appeals. A marketing-oriented organization carefully analyzes the market and divides it into groups of people who are fairly similar in terms of selected characteristics. Then the organization develops marketing programs that will bring about mutually satisfying exchanges with one or more of those groups. Consider this example:

> Paying attention to the customer isn't exactly a new concept. Back in the 1920s, General Motors Corporation helped write the book on customer satisfaction by designing cars for every lifestyle and pocketbook. This was a breakthrough for an industry that had been largely driven by production needs ever since Henry Ford promised any color as long as it was black.[19]

Chapter 6 thoroughly explores the topic of analyzing markets and selecting those that appear to be most promising to the firm.

## THE FIRM'S PRIMARY GOAL

A sales-oriented organization seeks to achieve profitability through sales volume and tries to convince potential customers to buy, even if the seller knows that the customer and product are mismatched. Sales-oriented organizations place a higher premium on making a sale than on developing a long-term relationship with a customer.

**relationship marketing**
Strategy of developing strong customer loyalty and forging long-term partnerships by creating satisfied customers who will buy additional products from the firm.

In contrast, the ultimate goal of most marketing-oriented organizations is to make a profit from satisfying customers. **Relationship marketing** is the name of a strategy that entails forging long-term partnerships with customers.

One way to build relationships with customers is to consistently offer them good value (the topic of Chapter 8). Frequent-user programs and personalized service are just two of the methods frequently used to build relationships with customers. For example, Parisian, a growing and profitable fashion chain, has a "Call Customer Program." Sales associates maintain a call book containing detailed information about their regular customers' sizes and style preferences. The associates act as "purchasing agents" for customers, phoning to tell them about special events or the arrival of appropriate merchandise and to remind them of important personal dates, such as a spouse's birthday.[20]

Business-to-business relationship marketing means, in effect, becoming a part of the customer's organization and contributing to its success, not just closing a sale. It is based on a philosophy that customers are not a target for the firm's marketing efforts but instead are partners with whom the firm must work to enhance the value of goods and services that it supplies. For example, when Boeing considered developing a more fuel-efficient aircraft, it involved representatives from eight major customer airlines in the initial concept discussions. Major suppliers were also brought into the process during the early design stage to provide ideas and suggestions.[21] Baxter International developed ValueLink, a computer-based inventory control system, to help its hospital customers reduce inventory costs while improving the internal distribution of supplies. Baxter takes on the time-consuming task of making sure essential items like needles, bandages, and syringes wind up in the right place in the proper numbers. With ValueLink, Baxter can often become a hospital's sole source of supplies.[22]

## TOOLS THE ORGANIZATION USES TO ACHIEVE ITS GOALS

Sales-oriented organizations seek to generate sales volume through intensive promotional activities, mainly personal selling and advertising. In contrast, marketing-oriented organizations recognize that promotion is only one of four basic marketing tools: product decisions, place (or distribution) decisions, promotion decisions, and pricing decisions. Chapters 9 through 19 focus on these topics. A marketing-oriented organization recognizes each of these four components as equally important. On the other hand, sales-oriented organizations view promotion as the primary means of achieving their goals.

## A WORD OF CAUTION

This comparison of sales and marketing orientations is not meant to belittle the role of promotion, especially personal selling, in the marketing mix. Promotion is the means by which organizations communicate with present and prospective customers about the merits and characteristics of their organization and products. Effective promotion is an essential part of effective marketing. Salespeople who work for marketing-oriented organizations are generally perceived by their customers to be problem solvers and important links to supply sources and new products. Chapter 17 and Appendix A examine the nature of personal selling in more detail.

5 *Explain how firms implement the marketing concept.*

## IMPLEMENTATION OF THE MARKETING CONCEPT

Although the marketing concept is a simple and appealing management philosophy, firms seem to have trouble implementing it. Three difficult hurdles must be overcome: organized resistance, slow learning, and fast forgetting.[23] Organized resistance means that some departments, such as manufacturing and finance, may feel threatened if marketing is identified as the key function of all employees. Slow learning means that diffusion of the marketing concept takes a long time, even with the endorsement of top management. Fast forgetting means that successful firms sometimes forget how and why they became successful and unintentionally abandon the marketing concept.

In an established organization, changing to a customer-driven corporate culture must occur step by step. Furthermore, middle managers alone cannot effect a change in corporate culture; they must have the total support of the CEO and other top executives.[24] According to Thomas J. Pritzker, president of Hyatt Hotels, the notion that a customer orientation can just be turned on is a fallacy: "Management has to set a tone and then constantly push, push, push."[25]

The success of Nordstrom, the Seattle-based retailer, illustrates the results of strong management support for customer-oriented service. Employees can do almost anything to satisfy shoppers. One story, which the company doesn't deny, tells of a customer who got his money back on a tire, even though Nordstrom doesn't sell tires. In 1993 Nordstrom received the highest overall customer satisfaction rating from 2,000 shoppers who participated in a study ranking seventy U.S. retail and department store chains on attributes such as price, convenience, and quality of offerings.[26]

### CHANGES IN AUTHORITY AND RESPONSIBILITY

Changing from a production or sales orientation to a marketing orientation often requires major revisions in relationships within the firm. Nonmarketing people who have been making marketing decisions, such as production managers, may suddenly lose their authority. Personnel in such areas as marketing research may find that they have gained considerable authority.

One way of winning acceptance for the marketing concept is to get everyone who will be affected by the change to participate in the planning process. It is important to remember, however, that during a period of change, some human relations problems are inevitable. Implementing the marketing concept slowly rather than in a revolutionary fashion normally smooths the transition.

Sometimes companies fool themselves into thinking they've implemented the marketing concept when they really have not. Management may concentrate on some of these trappings of marketing:

- *Declarations of support from top management:* speeches, annual reports
- *Creation of a marketing organization:* appointment of a marketing head and product or market managers, transfer of the product development and service functions to marketing, reassignment of salespeople around markets, strengthening of the advertising function

Walt Disney World's white-collar workers all get a chance to interact with guests for one week each year. Mickey Mouse's shoes are among those they fill.



- *Adoption of new administrative mechanisms:* formal marketing planning, more and better sales information, restructuring of the reporting system around markets
- *Increased marketing expenditures:* staffing, training and development, advertising, research

Although these are actions taken by firms that actually implement the marketing concept, by themselves they are not enough to change old production-focused ideas and habits.

When a person or a company has been doing something a certain way for many years, change often comes very hard. For example, the top management of Xerox Corporation spent much of the 1970s building huge layers of bureaucracy and wasting millions of dollars developing products that never reached the marketplace. It took Xerox ten years to realize that its old strategy of throwing people at problems and raising prices as costs went up just wouldn't work. It wasn't until 1980 that Xerox finally realized how capable its Japanese counterparts were and how little Xerox knew about customer wants.[27] At that point, the company started making the changes that eventually pulled it out of the doldrums.

### FRONT-LINE EXPERIENCE FOR MANAGEMENT

Detroit Diesel Corporation requires all managers and distributors to call or visit four customers a day. At Xerox, executives spend one day a month taking complaints from customers about machines, bills, and service. At Hyatt Hotels, senior executives, including the president, put in time as bellhops.[28] Marriott International's CEO logs an average of 200,000 travel miles each year visiting the company's hotels, inspecting them, and talking to employees at all levels in the organization. According to Bill Marriott, "CEOs don't listen enough. The people who work for them know more about their particular areas than the chief executive."[29] Walt Disney World's managers also join the "front line" each year to participate in

*Exhibit 1.3*

The Marketing Process

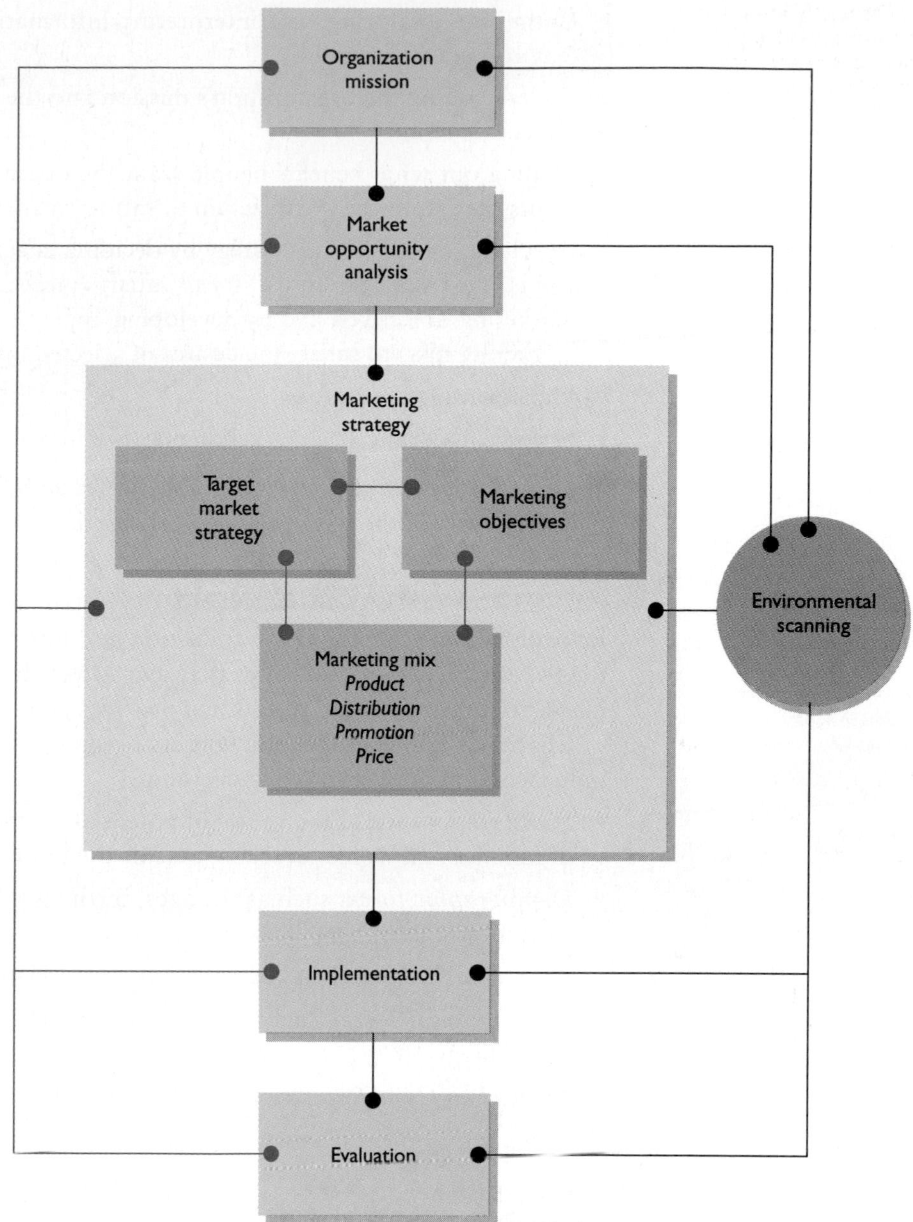


a program called cross utilization. For a week, the bosses sell tickets or popcorn, dish out ice cream or hot dogs, load and unload rides, park cars, drive the monorail or trains, or take on any of the 100 "on-stage" jobs that make the park come alive for guests.

*6 Describe the marketing process, and identify the variables that make up the marketing mix.*

## THE MARKETING PROCESS

Earlier in this chapter, marketing was defined as the process of planning and executing the conception, distribution, promotion, and pricing of ideas, goods, and services to create exchanges that satisfy individual and organizational objectives. Marketing therefore includes the following activities:

- Gathering, analyzing, and interpreting information about the environment (environmental scanning)
- Understanding the organization's mission and the role marketing plays in fulfilling this vision
- Finding out what benefits people want the organization to deliver and what wants they want the organization to satisfy (market opportunity analysis)
- Developing a marketing strategy by deciding exactly which wants, and whose wants, the organization will try to satisfy (target market strategy); by setting marketing objectives; and by developing appropriate marketing activities (the marketing mix) to satisfy the desires of selected target markets
- Implementing the strategy
- Periodically evaluating marketing efforts and making changes if needed

These activities and their relationships, shown in Exhibit 1.3, form the foundation on which most of the rest of the book is based.

## ENVIRONMENTAL SCANNING

**environmental scanning**
Collection and interpretation of information about forces, events, and relationships that may affect the future of an organization.

**Environmental scanning** is the collection and interpretation of information about forces, events, and relationships that may affect the organization. It helps identify market opportunities and threats and provides guidelines for the marketing strategy.

Chapter 2 examines the following six categories of uncontrollable environmental influences that affect marketing decisions:

- *Social forces* such as the values of potential customers and the changing roles of families and women working outside the home
- *Demographic forces* such as the ages, birth and death rates, and locations of various groups of people
- *Economic forces* such as changing incomes, inflation, and recession
- *Technological forces* such as advanced communications and data retrieval capabilities
- *Political and legal forces* such as changes in laws and regulatory agency activities
- *Competitive forces* from domestic and foreign-based firms

## ORGANIZATION MISSION

One of top management's most important responsibilities is to formulate the organization's basic statements of purpose and mission. As noted earlier, an organization's mission statement answers the question "What is this firm's business?" Mission statements are based on a careful analysis of the benefits sought by present and potential customers, as well as existing and anticipated environmental conditions. This long-term vision of what the organization is or is striving to become establishes the boundaries within which objectives, strategies, and actions must be developed. The topic of organization mission is addressed in Chapter 22.

## MARKET OPPORTUNITY ANALYSIS

**market opportunity analysis**
Description and estimation of the size and sales potential of market segments of interest to a firm and assessment of key competitors in these market segments.

A market segment is a group of individuals or organizations that share one or more characteristics. They therefore have relatively similar product needs. A **market opportunity analysis** describes market segments of interest to the firm, estimates their size and sales potential, and assesses key competitors in these market segments.

GLOBAL PERSPECTIVES

**Electrolux**

Think back to 1983, when the dream of a single European market was just starting to take shape. Leif Johansson, then 32 and a manager at Electrolux, the Swedish appliance maker, was captivated by marketing studies showing a convergence of European lifestyles. "More pasta was being eaten in certain neighborhoods of Stockholm than in Italy," he recalls. Johansson figured that Europe would become like the United States, where a few powerful companies compete across an entire continent, and that 325 million European consumers would be eager to buy the same refrigerators, ovens, and dishwashers.

Marshaling his evidence, he persuaded his bosses to buy Italy's Zanussi Group. With that key move, Electrolux became Europe's largest appliance maker.

Over a decade later, after Johansson became Electrolux's president, he and the diplomats in Brussels are still trying to forge a united Europe. Despite increased pasta consumption in some unlikely places, national tastes and national markets remain strong—especially when it comes to appliances. Northern Europeans want large refrigerators because they shop only once a week, in supermarkets; southern Europeans prefer small ones because they pick through open-air markets almost every day. Northerners like their freezers on the bottom, southerners on top. And Britons, who devour frozen foods, insist on units with 60 percent freezer space.[30]

What led Johansson to conclude that European consumers would be eager to buy the same refrigerators, ovens, and dishwashers? Why hasn't his vision become a reality? What does this conclusion suggest for Electrolux and other appliance manufacturers competing in Europe?

From William Echikson, "The Trick to Selling in Europe," *Fortune*, 20 September 1993. 

## MARKETING STRATEGY

As Exhibit 1.3 illustrates, **marketing strategy** involves three activities: selecting one or more target markets, setting marketing objectives, and developing and maintaining a **marketing mix** (product, distribution, promotion, and pricing) that will produce mutually satisfying exchanges with target markets.

### Target Market Strategy

The three general strategies for selecting target markets are to try to appeal to the entire market with a single marketing mix, to concentrate on only one segment of the market, or to attempt to appeal to multiple market segments using multiple marketing mixes. The characteristics, advantages, and disadvantages of each strategic option are examined in Chapter 6.

### Marketing Objectives

A **marketing objective** is a statement of what is to be accomplished through marketing activities—for example, getting 100 people to test-drive a new car during the month of November or getting 2,000 passengers to fly on a new commuter airline during the first week in June. Marketing objectives should be consistent with organization objectives, should be measurable, and should specify the timeframe during which they are to be achieved.

Carefully specifying marketing objectives offers two major benefits. First, when the objectives are attainable and challenging, they motivate those charged with achieving the objectives. They also serve as standards by which everyone in the organization can gauge their performance. Second, the process of writing specific marketing objectives forces executives to sharpen and clarify their thinking. Written objectives also allow marketing efforts to be integrated and pointed in a consistent direction.

### Marketing Mix

As noted earlier, the term marketing mix refers to a unique blend of product, distribution (place), promotion, and pricing strategies (the **four P's**) designed to produce mutually satisfying exchanges with a target market. The marketing manager can control each component of the marketing mix, but the strategies for all four components must be blended to achieve optimal results. Any mix is only as good as its weakest component. For example, an excellent product with a poor distribution system will likely fail.

**marketing strategy**
Plan that involves selecting one or more target markets, setting marketing objectives, and developing and maintaining a marketing mix that will produce mutually satisfying exchanges with target markets.

**marketing mix**
Unique blend of product, distribution, promotion, and pricing strategies designed to produce mutually satisfying exchanges with a target market.

**marketing objective**
Statement of what is to be accomplished through marketing activities.

**four P's**
Product decisions, distribution (or place) decisions, promotion decisions, and pricing decisions, which together make up the marketing mix.

A respected brand name adds perceived value to a product, as it does for Godiva chocolates and Gucci handbags.



MARKETING AND SMALL BUSINESS

**The Importance of Good Marketing Skills**

Most of you will not end up working for a major corporation. Instead, many of you will go to work for a small or medium-size company. Some will start your own enterprise.

People who start their own business are often called entrepreneurs. They are pulled toward entrepreneurship by several powerful incentives. First, the financial return is potentially greater than one could achieve working for someone else. Second, entrepreneurship offers freedom from supervision and the rules of bureaucratic organizations. Third, it offers freedom from routine, boring, and unchallenging work. On the other hand, starting and operating one's own business requires hard work, long hours, and much emotional energy. Sometimes people invest their life savings in a small business only to see it fail.

Two keys to success for the 16 million small U.S. firms are adequate capital and good marketing skills. A good rule of thumb is to have enough start-up capital to establish the operation plus enough working capital to get through the first two years without earning a profit. Many entrepreneurs start with far less and, as a result, fail.

Money alone, however, does not guarantee success. Entrepreneurs still need to understand and implement the marketing concept. Hundreds of thousands of small businesses have failed because they offered a good or a service that no one wanted. Other firms couldn't get adequate distribution, priced their offerings incorrectly, failed to develop a good promotional strategy, or failed to spend enough money promoting their organization and product.

Successful marketing mixes have been carefully tailored to satisfy target markets. At first glance, McDonald's and Wendy's may appear to have roughly identical marketing mixes. After all, they are both in the fast-food business. However, McDonald's targets parents with young children. It has Ronald McDonald, special children's Happy Meals, and playgrounds. Wendy's generally targets the adult crowd. Wendy's doesn't have a playground, but it does have carpeting (for a more adult atmosphere), and it pioneered fast-food salad bars.

Variations in marketing mixes do not occur by chance. They represent fundamental marketing strategies devised by astute marketing managers attempting to gain advantages over competitors and to achieve competitive success.

## Product Strategies

Typically the marketing mix begins with the product offering. It is hard to devise a distribution system or set a price without knowing the product to be marketed. Thus, the heart of the

CREATING CUSTOMER VALUE

### The Lexus Story

The marketplace for luxury automobiles is clogged with such prestigious nameplates as Mercedes, BMW, Porsche, Volvo, Saab, Cadillac, and Lincoln. It's hard to imagine that anyone would need another model of luxury car.

Not only is competition fierce in this market segment, but the consumers are extremely quality conscious and demanding. They are typically 45 to 50 years old, college educated, with a median income of $160,000. Twenty percent are company presidents or CEOs. Consumers in this niche are as knowledgeable and demanding as anyone in any segment anywhere.

To successfully penetrate this market, Toyota's Lexus division adopted a customer-driven approach, with particular emphasis on service. Lexus stressed product quality with a standard of zero defects in manufacturing. The service quality goal was to treat each customer as one would treat a guest in one's home, to pursue the perfect person-to-person relationship, and to strive to improve continually. Maximizing customer value would depend on keeping the price competitive. The integrating theme was "The relentless pursuit of perfection."

In the auto industry, the individual dealer is the face of the company. Therefore, Lexus was highly selective, evaluating dealers' customer satisfaction performance, management experience, capitalization, and willingness to meet the high standards of luxury set by the manufacturer. The average dealer spent between $3 million and $5 million on facilities, with 80 percent of the dealers building new facilities.

Lexus assisted dealers with design of the dealership, just as McDonald's offers design expertise to its franchisees. Layout, decor, landscaping, and furnishings were integrated into a high-quality, luxury image. Diagnostic equipment and computer information systems were customized for Lexus and integrated into a national computer data base. A dealer can access the full service record of any Lexus sold anywhere in the United States and update the information on that individual car. Dealers are empowered to achieve customer satisfaction on any concern without prior approval, regardless of cost.

In 1990, when one customer contacted Lexus twice about a problem, Lexus immediately recalled the LS400 model. Dealers personally got in touch with most owners and made arrangements for the pickup and repair of their cars. If the customer lived more than 100 miles from a dealer, a technician was sent to the customer to perform the work on-site so as to reduce customer inconvenience. In one case, a technician flew from Los Angeles to Anchorage, Alaska, to service a car.

This relentless pursuit of perfection has a direct impact on customer satisfaction. In *Car and Driver*'s annual buyers' survey, the LS400 received a score of 9.7 on a 10-point scale—the highest ever for any car. The J. D. Power Quality Survey, conducted during the LS400 recall, rated the Lexus highest of any car. The result? Lexus has established a clear quality image and captured a significant share of the luxury car market in just a few years by maximizing customer value.[32]

How would you explain the success of the Lexus automobile in terms of customer value? How does the marketing strategy for the Lexus differ from the strategies used by Mercedes-Benz and BMW for comparable automobiles?

marketing mix is a firm's product offerings.

Marketers view products in a much larger context than you might imagine. A product includes not only the physical unit but also many other factors, including the package, warranty, service subsequent to sale, and brand and company image. The names Yves St. Laurent and Gucci, for example, create additional value for everything from cosmetics to bath towels. We buy things not only for what they do but also for what they mean to us.

## Distribution (Place) Strategies

Distribution strategies are concerned with making products available when and where customers want them. Wholesalers and retailers assist manufacturers in distributing products to end users. Physical distribution consists of all business activities concerned with storing and transporting products so that they arrive in usable condition at designated places when needed. Physical distribution is also part of distribution strategy.

## Promotion Strategies

Promotion includes personal selling, advertising, sales promotion, and public relations. Its role is to help bring about mutually satisfying exchanges with target markets by informing, educating, persuading, and reminding them about the benefits of an organization or a product. A good promotion strategy can sometimes dramatically increase a firm's sales. Each element of promotion is coordinated and managed with the others to create a promotional blend or mix.

## Pricing Strategies

Price, what a buyer must give up to obtain a product, is the most flexible of the four components of the marketing mix. Marketers can raise or lower prices more frequently than they can change any other marketing mix variable. Thus price is an important competitive weapon.

### IMPLEMENTATION

**implementation**
Phase of the marketing process in which marketers turn their plans into action assignments and ensure that these assignments are executed in a way that will accomplish the marketing plans' objectives.

**Implementation** is the process that turns marketing plans into action assignments and ensures that these assignments are executed in a way that accomplishes the plans' objectives.[31] Although implementation is essentially "doing what you said you were going to do," many organizations repeatedly experience failures in strategy implementation. Brilliant marketing strategies are doomed to fail if they are not properly implemented.

### EVALUATION

**evaluation**
Phase of the marketing process in which marketers gauge the extent to which objectives have been achieved during a specified time period.

**Evaluation** entails gauging the extent to which marketing objectives have been achieved during a specified time period. Four common reasons for failing to achieve a marketing objective are unrealistic marketing objectives, inappropriate marketing strategy, poor implementation, and changes in the environment after the objective was specified and the strategy was implemented.

*7 Explain how organizations create customer value.*

## THE CREATION OF CUSTOMER VALUE

**customer value**
The ratio of benefits to the sacrifice necessary to obtain those benefits.

**Customer value** is the ratio of benefits to the sacrifice necessary to obtain those benefits. The customer determines the value of both the benefits and the sacrifices. Customer value is created when customer expectations regarding product quality, service quality, and value-based price are met or exceeded. Understanding the relationship among these three components is essential to creating customer value and achieving success in today's highly competitive markets.

Creating customer value is the core business strategy of many successful firms. Toyota's successful introduction of the Lexus, described in the Creating Customer Value box, provides an example of how to maximize value to customers in a highly competitive industry.

## LOOKING AHEAD

This book is divided into twenty-two chapters organized into seven major parts. The chapters are written from the marketing manager's perspective. Each chapter begins with a brief list of learning objectives followed by a short story about a marketing situation faced by a firm or industry. At the end of each of these opening vignettes, several thought-provoking questions link the story to the subject addressed in the chapter. Your instructor may wish to begin chapter discussions by asking members of your class to share their views about the questions.

The examples of global marketing highlighted in most chapters will help you understand that marketing takes place all over the world, between buyers and sellers in different countries. These and other global marketing examples throughout the book, marked with the icon shown in the margin, are intended to help you develop a global perspective on marketing.

Creating customer value by delivering quality products is essential for achieving success in today's competitive markets. Many chapters include specially identified boxes describing successful strategies for enhancing customer value. Other examples of efforts to enhance customer value and quality are provided throughout the book and marked with the second icon shown in the margin.

Marketing ethics is another important topic selected for special treatment throughout the book. Many business executives and educators have suggested that business education focus more on ethical issues. Thus many chapters include highlighted stories about firms or industries that have faced ethical dilemmas or have engaged in practices that some consider unethical. Questions are posed to focus your thinking on the key ethical issues raised in each story.

Entrepreneurship and small business applications are also highlighted in special boxes in many chapters. Every chapter also includes an application case related to small business. This material illustrates how entrepreneurs and small businesses can use the principles and concepts discussed in the book.

Chapters conclude with a final comment on the chapter-opening vignette ("Looking Back"), a summary of the major topics examined, a listing of the key terms introduced in the chapter, discussion and writing questions (writing questions marked with an icon), and two or three cases with discussion questions. All these features are intended to help you develop a more thorough understanding of marketing and enjoy the learning process.

The remaining chapters in Part One introduce you to the dynamic environment in which marketing decisions must be made and to global marketing. Part Two covers consumer decision making and buyer behavior; business-to-business marketing; the concepts of positioning, market segmentation, and targeting; the nature and uses of marketing research and decision support systems; and customer value and quality issues. Parts Three through Six examine the elements of the marketing mix—product, distribution, promotion, and pricing. Part Seven focuses on the unique challenges of marketing to multicultural target markets; marketing ethics and social responsibility; and strategic planning, forecasting, and control. Three appendixes—one concerning careers in marketing, the second concerning financial arithmetic for marketing, and the third providing experiential marketing exercises—conclude the book.

## LOOKING BACK

Look back at the story at the beginning of this chapter about the attorney whose Chevrolet Suburban broke down during a trip from Boise, Idaho, to Portland, Oregon. You should now find the questions that appear at the end of the story to be simple and straightforward. The dealer's actions suggest that he or she is marketing-oriented. The dealer recognized the attorney's misfortune as an opportunity to demonstrate a commitment to customer satisfaction even after the sale and even when the problem was caused by a third party.

The attorneys were so impressed with the service and the new Suburban they used on their trip that three of them bought new Suburbans from the dealer within two weeks. A fourth, the owner of the original Suburban, bought the loaned Suburban because he didn't like the idea of a rebuilt engine. The payoff for the dealer was the sale of four Suburbans and an engine rebuild. The total sales figure for the four Suburbans was well over $100,000.

## SUMMARY

1 **Define the term *marketing*.** The ultimate goal of all marketing activity is to facilitate mutually satisfying exchanges between parties. The activities of marketing include the conception, pricing, promotion, and distribution of ideas, goods, and services.

2 **Describe several reasons for studying marketing.** First, marketing affects the allocation of goods and services that influence a nation's economy and standard of living. Second, an understanding of marketing is crucial to understanding most businesses. Third, career opportunities in marketing are diverse, profitable, and expected to increase significantly during the 1990s. Fourth, understanding marketing makes consumers more informed.

3 **Describe four marketing management philosophies.** The role of marketing and the character of marketing activities within an organization are strongly influenced by its philosophy and orientation. A production-oriented organization focuses on the internal capabilities of the firm rather than on the desires and needs of the marketplace. A sales orientation is based on the beliefs that people will buy more products if aggressive sales techniques are used and that high sales volumes produce high profits. A marketing-oriented organization focuses on satisfying customer wants and needs while meeting organizational objectives. A societal marketing orientation goes beyond a marketing orientation to include the preservation or enhancement of individuals' and society's long-term best interests.

4 **Discuss the differences between sales and marketing orientations.** First, a sales-oriented firm focuses on its own needs; marketing-oriented firms focus on customers' needs and preferences. Second, sales-oriented companies consider themselves to be deliverers of goods and services, whereas marketing-oriented companies view themselves as satisfiers of customers. Third, sales-oriented firms direct their products to everyone; marketing-oriented firms aim at specific segments of the population. Fourth, although the primary goal of both types of firms is profit, sales-oriented businesses pursue maximum sales volume through intensive promotion, whereas marketing-oriented businesses pursue customer satisfaction through coordinated marketing activities.

5 **Explain how firms implement the marketing concept.** To implement the marketing concept successfully, management must enthusiastically embrace and endorse the concept and encourage its spread throughout the organization. Changing from a production or sales orientation to a marketing orientation often requires changes in authority and responsibility and front-line experience for management.

6 **Describe the marketing process, and identify the variables that make up the marketing mix.** The marketing process includes scanning the environment, analyzing market opportunities, setting marketing objectives, selecting a target market strategy, developing and implementing a marketing mix, implementing the strategy, and evaluating marketing efforts and making changes if needed. The marketing mix combines product, distribution (place), promotion, and pricing strategies (the four

### KEY TERMS

*concept of exchange* 6
*customer value* 24
*empowerment* 13
*environmental scanning* 20
*evaluation* 24
*four P's* 21
*implementation* 24
*marketing* 6
*marketing concept* 10
*marketing mix* 21
*marketing myopia* 13
*marketing objective* 21
*marketing orientation* 10
*marketing strategy* 21
*market opportunity analysis* 20
*production orientation* 9
*relationship marketing* 16
*sales orientation* 9
*societal marketing concept* 11

P's) in a way that creates exchanges satisfying to individual and organizational objectives.

7 **Explain how organizations create customer value.** Customer value is created when customer expectations regarding product quality, service quality, and value-based price are met or exceeded.

## Discussion and Writing Questions

✍1. In your new position as marketing manager for the nonprofit National Wildlife Federation, you have made the adoption of a marketing orientation your first goal. Write a memo to your staff explaining why you believe the organization will benefit from this new approach.

2. Donald E. Petersen, chairman of the board of Ford Motor Company, remarked, "If we aren't customer-driven, our cars won't be either." Explain how this statement reflects the marketing concept.

3. How does the concept of marketing myopia reflect the fundamental difference between sales and marketing orientations?

✍4. A friend of yours agrees with the adage "People don't know what they want—they only want what they know." Write your friend a letter expressing the extent to which you think marketers shape consumer wants.

5. How does direct experience in serving customers help managers implement the marketing concept?

6. Can a firm be successful without adopting a marketing orientation? Why or why not?

## Application for Small Business

Christine Louise graduated from college in June 1995 and decided to open a women's footwear store called Sisi's Shoes. Since high school, she had always wanted to run her own business. On the very first day the store was open, a customer asked Christine if she guaranteed the products she sold. Christine proudly replied, "Every shoe that is purchased from Sisi's Shoes has a lifetime guarantee. If at any time you are not satisfied with your shoes, you can return them to the store for a full refund of your purchase price."

### Questions

1. What marketing management philosophy is Christine expressing? Why have you reached this conclusion?

2. Do you think a lifetime guarantee for this kind of product is too generous? Why or why not?

3. Do you think this policy will contribute to success or to bankruptcy?

4. Suggest other customer-service policies that might be appropriate for Sisi's Shoes.

## CRITICAL THINKING CASE

### The Limited

How would you like to turn around a huge, struggling retailer in an economy that has all the zip of linen on a humid day? That's the task confronting Leslie Wexner, chairman of The Limited, and his top merchants.

The Limited was hailed in the 1980s as the most successful innovator in its industry. Now its two biggest divisions, Limited Stores and Lerner New York, both nationwide chains, have been losing traditional customers. Express, a sister store that carries hip sportswear at reasonable prices—just what Limited Stores was once known for—is luring the older shops' younger customers away. And Lerner's once loyal budget customers no longer frequent the malls where most Lerner shops reside. Instead, the customers have been shopping more at Wal-Mart, Kmart, and other discounters that sell the same type of clothes as Lerner does but at lower prices.

The numbers reflect the shift. Comparable-store sales—that is, sales at stores open for more than a year, an important measure of performance—have been slumping at both Limited Stores and Lerner New York for nearly two years. Some of the company's other operations (which besides Express include Structure, a men's store, Henri Bendel, Lane Bryant, and Victoria's Secret) turned in strong results earlier this year, but the Limited and Lerner stores account for about a third of total sales.



### Questions

1. Why do you think Limited Stores is experiencing declining sales while other divisions of The Limited are producing strong sales and profits?
2. Describe the target market for Limited Stores and for Lerner New York.
3. What recommendations would you offer Wexner and his top managers to help reverse the sales and profit trends at Limited Stores and Lerner's?

### Reference

Susan Caminiti, "In Search of the '90s Consumer," *Fortune*, 21 September 1992, p. 100.

**VIDEO CASE**

## Euro Disney

Euro Disney opened April 12, 1992, with hopes of repeating the success of Walt Disney Co.'s U.S. theme parks. However, Euro Disney has been troubled by negative publicity, low attendance, and financial losses. Built on sugar beet and sunflower fields twenty miles east of Paris, the $5 billion theme park and resort complex lost over $300 million in 1993 and roughly $1 million each day in 1994. Walt Disney Co., which owns 49 percent of the park, had hoped that the European Magic Kingdom would contribute at least $75.5 million to its net income each year, but Euro Disney has yet to earn a profit.

Although the Disney theme parks have enjoyed great success in the United States and Japan, Euro Disney has struggled to attract visitors. The economic recession in Europe, as well as competition from the 1992 Summer Olympics and the World's Fair in Spain, contributed to a dismal opening year. The French have not embraced the American concept of family entertainment and disapprove of the alcohol ban in the park. Attendance records indicate there have been very few French visitors. In addition, visitors to Euro Disney are not spending as much money on food and merchandise as visitors to the other Disney parks do (an average of $85 each). The Europeans tend to be more money-conscious than U.S. or Japanese visitors. They are also less likely to make repeat visits. Hotel occupancy rates have remained low, averaging around 55 percent.

Because of the lackluster performance of Euro Disney, the second phase of construction did not start in 1993 as scheduled. Plans for an MGM movie studio, a water theme park, and more hotels have been postponed. In fact, Walt Disney Co. has tried to sell several of its six hotels at Euro Disney to raise capital to relieve some of the park's debt. Hotel rates and entry fees to Euro Disney have been reduced to attract visitors, and prices have also been cut on food and merchandise within the park. Nevertheless, despite disappointing performance, Walt Disney Co. continues to support the theme park and remains optimistic about the future of the European Magic Kingdom.

### Questions

1. What marketing management philosophy does Disney's entry into Europe illustrate? Explain the rationale for your answer.
2. Describe Euro Disney's target market strategy.
3. Describe Euro Disney's marketing mix.
4. Suggest ideas for improving Euro Disney's performance.

References

Scott Kraft, "Ailing Euro Disney Given Sweeping Bailout Package," *Los Angeles Times*, 15 March 1994, p. A1.

Robert Neff, "In Japan, They're Goofy about Disney," *Business Week*, 12 March 1990, p. 64.

Richard Turner and Peter Gumbel, "Major Attraction: As Euro Disney Braces for Its Grand Opening, the French Go Goofy," *Wall Street Journal*, 10 April 1992, pp. A1, A8.

Sharon Waxman, "In Europe, Can Mickey Be the Mouse That Soared?" *Washington Post*, 14 August 1993, p. B1.

# Chapter 2

# The Marketing Environment

## LEARNING OBJECTIVES

*After studying this chapter, you should be able to*

1 *Discuss the external environment of marketing, and explain how it affects a firm.*

2 *Describe the social factors that affect marketing.*

3 *Explain the importance to marketing managers of current demographic trends.*

4 *Identify consumer and marketer reactions to the state of the economy.*

5 *Identify the impact of technology on a firm.*

6 *Discuss the political and legal environment of marketing.*

7 *Explain the basics of foreign and domestic competition.*

The venetian blinds of the small, cramped room are drawn to keep out the sun. Still, sweat glazes Jack Diamond's brow as he paces between two desks, working a pair of telephones. While holding on one call, he delivers a sales pitch on the other with a practiced urgency, then hangs up with a smile. "I just got a double," he proclaims to his bosses.

Diamond seems to be a highly skilled telemarketer. But he isn't selling magazines or penny stocks. As a pharmacist employed by Merck & Co.'s newly acquired Medco Containment Services Inc., he is trying to persuade physicians to cancel prescriptions they have written for one drug and prescribe a drug he is promoting instead. The "double" he scored was the switch of two prescriptions a doctor had written.

That ability to directly influence physicians' prescribing decisions—and affect drug market share—is a big part of what Merck sought when it paid $6.6 billion for Medco. That ability is also a driving force behind the multi-billion-dollar scramble by other drug makers to acquire Medco's competitors. SmithKline Beecham PLC, for example, is buying United HealthCare Corp.'s Diversified Pharmaceutical Services.

When Medco was independent, it sought to control its customers' prescription drug costs by steering physicians to lower-cost branded and generic drugs. Almost overnight its telemarketing and other tactics disrupted the powerful and enormously profitable marketing link with physicians that drug companies like Merck had taken years to build. And by forcing drug companies to discount prices—or to lose market share to those that did—Medco and its competitors put enormous pressure on the industry's profits. Now, with Medco under its control, Merck is turning that formerly damaging strategy to its advantage. Merck's salespeople are still visiting physicians and leaving drug samples, but the company has also begun putting Medco's pharmacists to work with telephones.

Together, Merck and Medco are revolutionizing the way pharmaceuticals are sold. "The market is changing radically, and delivery to this market is going to be very different in the future," says P. Roy Vagelos, Merck's chairman. Those new marketing tactics will be controversial, he concedes. But "that's always true of a new thing."

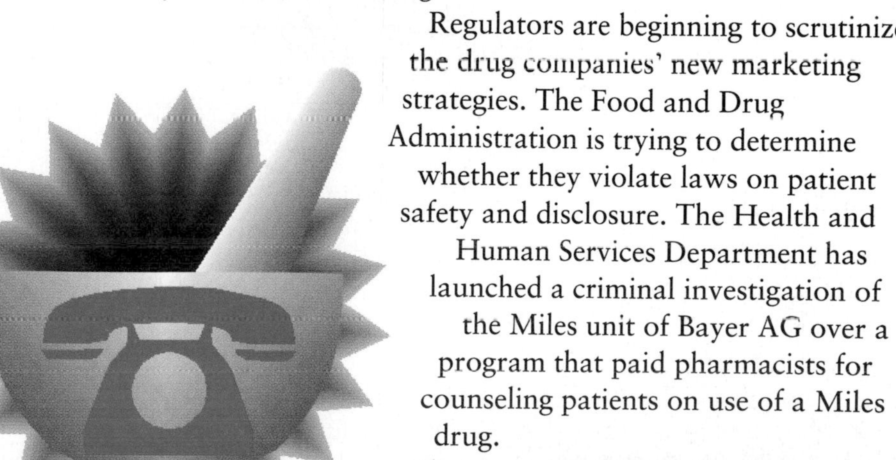

Regulators are beginning to scrutinize the drug companies' new marketing strategies. The Food and Drug Administration is trying to determine whether they violate laws on patient safety and disclosure. The Health and Human Services Department has launched a criminal investigation of the Miles unit of Bayer AG over a program that paid pharmacists for counseling patients on use of a Miles drug.

The acquisitions and alliances are also controversial because they give drug companies direct access to specific information about individuals and their prescriptions. Such data can be used to intervene in relationships among physicians, patients, and pharmacists in order to influence drug selection and use. The patient information also gives drug companies a data base to help them try to prove that their drugs are more cost-effective than competing drugs or other treatments.

Many retail pharmacists, already angry at Medco and its competitors for imposing low reimbursement rates and for excluding some pharmacists from health-plan networks, profoundly resent Merck for joining Medco's side. The National Association of Retail Druggists, an association of independent pharmacists, wrote to Dr. Vagelos complaining that "Merck has increasingly initiated programs that will result in the demise of the independent retail pharmacist if not challenged." NARD added that it won't accept financial support from Merck anymore.

The new marketing tactics may be generating ill will, but they work. Medco's telemarketing pharmacists at its eleven facilities across the country expect to switch some 75,000 prescriptions a month, or nearly a million over a year's time.[1]

Competition, technology (database marketing), and government regulation have all had a profound impact on Merck in the past few years. What other uncontrollable factors in the external environment have also affected the company? Does the external environment affect the marketing mix of most companies? What often occurs when an organization ignores the external environment?

1 *Discuss the external environment of marketing, and explain how it affects a firm.*

**target market**
Group for which an organization designs, implements, and maintains a marketing mix intended to meet the needs of that group, resulting in mutually satisfying exchanges.

## THE EXTERNAL MARKETING ENVIRONMENT

As you learned in Chapter 1, managers create a marketing mix by uniquely combining product, distribution, promotion, and price strategies. The marketing mix is, of course, under the firm's control and is designed to appeal to a specific group of potential buyers. A **target market** is a defined group that managers feel is most likely to buy a firm's product.

Over time, managers must alter the marketing mix because of changes in the environment in which consumers live, work, and make purchasing decisions. Some new consumers become part of the target market; others drop out. Those who remain may have different tastes, needs, incomes, lifestyles, and buying habits than the original target consumers.

Although managers can control the marketing mix, they cannot control elements in the external environment that continually mold and reshape the target market. Exhibit 2.1 shows the controllable and uncontrollable variables that affect the target market, whether it consists of consumers or business purchasers. The uncontrollable elements in the center of the diagram continually evolve and create changes in the target market. In contrast, managers can shape and reshape the marketing mix, depicted on the left side of the exhibit, to influence the target market.

### ENVIRONMENTAL SCANNING

Unless marketing managers understand the external environment, the firm cannot intelligently plan for the future. Thus many organizations assemble a team of specialists to continually collect and evaluate environmental information, a process called environmental scanning. The goal in gathering the environmental data is to identify future market opportunities and threats.

For example, because of the growing number of women in the work force, more men are doing the household chores previously done by women. Today about 20 percent of married men are the primary grocery shopper for the family—up from 14 percent in 1988.[2] But they are not doing the job very well yet. For men, being a

*Exhibit 2.1*

Effect of Uncontrollable Factors in the External Environment on the Marketing Mix

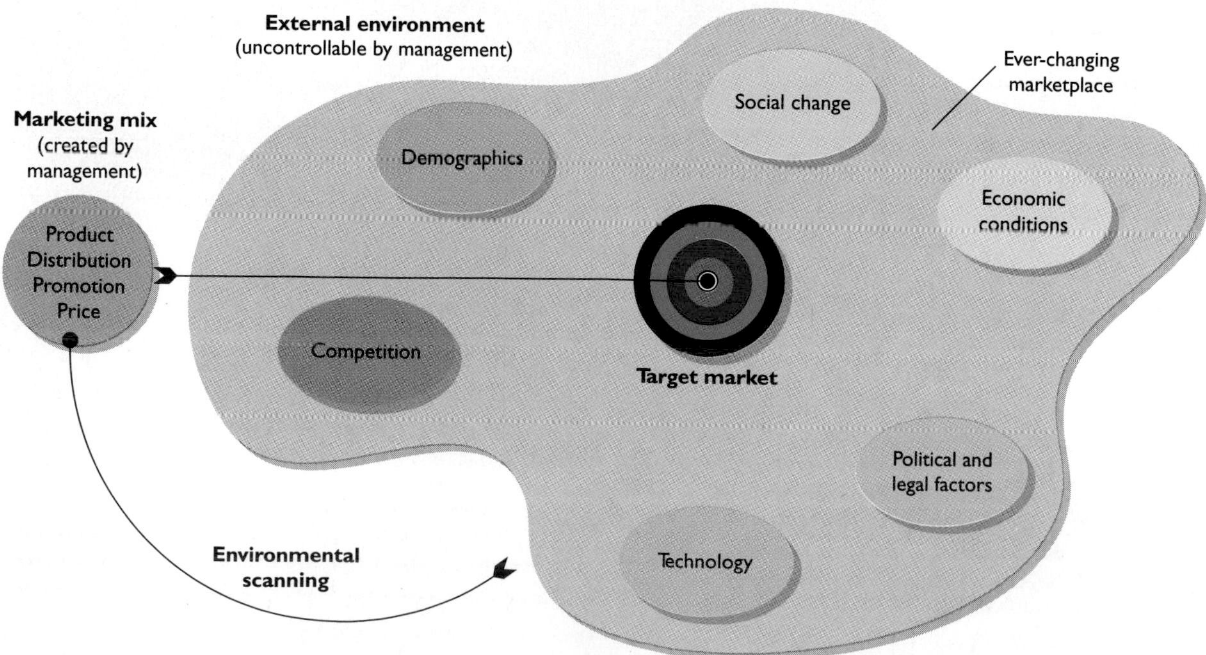

lousy shopper "is part of a kind of macho image," says Steve Barnett, an anthropologist and principal with Global Business Network, who has studied men's shopping behavior. The attitude is " 'I can't shop well; I do it if my wife makes me do it,' " he says. Barnett divides male shoppers into two categories: "lost in space" (they wander around in a disorganized state) and "demons of efficiency" (they rip through the aisles as quickly as possible). Because they are less interested in bargains and tend to buy on the run, men are more likely to grab a big-name brand than women. Yet at the same time, many male shoppers—particularly married ones—pay little attention to which name brands they use at home.[3] The increase in male shoppers means that marketing managers at Procter & Gamble, Kraft General Foods, Kroger, and countless other organizations must analyze their old marketing strategies and make changes that will help them meet both male and female shoppers' needs.

Note how three companies have responded to other environmental trends:

- DuPont, recognizing Americans' increased interest in eating healthy food, has developed a high-fiber flour substitute that can make ordinary white bread the nutritional equivalent of whole-wheat bread.[4]
- The Jackson Hole Ski Corporation, citing government health reports and changing attitudes, has decided to stop hosting races sponsored by tobacco and alcohol companies.
- Sales representatives for Hanes Hosiery use hand-held computers equipped with wands that read bar codes to keep track of retailer inventories. When representatives complete the inventory, they use a lightweight printer to create a full report. After comparing the inventory report against the store's target

Initially, U.S. carmakers sought government protection in response to the threat posed by Japanese rivals. But when U.S. carmakers decided to compete by offering customers more car for their money, they learned that the threat was really an opportunity.

© Cadillac Motor Car Division

> stock level, sales representatives use a laptop computer to generate a new order and electronically transmit it to Hanes's main office. The system drastically cuts the time needed to restock the store.

Evolving lifestyles, changing attitudes, and emerging technology—all outside the direct control of the companies—led DuPont to develop a new product, Jackson Hole to alter its promotional plans, and Hanes to improve its distribution.

Sometimes the changing environment can pose a threat. When it does, the challenge to marketing managers is to convert the threat to an opportunity. Consider the following example:

> What do you do when you're in the suntan business and America decides to end its love affair with the sun? As the sale of sun blocks climbed, Coppertone was frustrated in its attempt to get its share of the emerging market. "Coppertone is for tanning, not for blocking," consumers seemed to be saying.
>
> So the company went back to its origins—a cute little girl with a dog nipping at her bathing suit and the slogan "Tan, Don't Burn." Whom do you want to protect most from the sun? Children. What's the most important quality a children's sun block should have? Waterproofing.

Coppertone called its new sun block Water Babies and featured the name on the package along with the little girl and the dog. The Coppertone logo was visible but smaller. Water Babies has been an enormous success. Not only is it a new profit center, but it's also helping Coppertone keep pace with a trend toward sensible skin care.[5]

## ENVIRONMENTAL MANAGEMENT

No one business is large or powerful enough to create major change in the external environment. Thus marketing managers are basically adapters rather than agents of change. For example, despite the huge size of General Motors, Ford, and Chrysler, they have only recently been able to stem the competitive push by the Japanese for an ever-growing share of the U.S. automobile market. Competition is basically an uncontrollable element in the external environment.

However, a firm is not always completely at the mercy of the external environment. Sometimes a firm can influence external events. For example, extensive lobbying may help persuade Congress to pass legislation limiting Japanese automobile imports. A company may help tame an overly aggressive competitor by filing an antitrust suit. When a company implements strategies that attempt to shape the external environment within which it operates, it is engaging in **environmental management.**

**environmental management**
Implementation of strategies that attempt to shape the external environment within which a firm operates.

The factors within the external environment that are important to marketing managers can be classified as social, demographic, economic, technological, political and legal, and competitive.

2 *Describe the social factors that affect marketing.*

## SOCIAL FACTORS

Social change is perhaps the most difficult external variable for marketing managers to forecast, influence, or integrate into marketing plans. Although there are hundreds, perhaps thousands, of economic forecasters, very few firms venture into analyzing and forecasting social trends. Managers have to depend largely on their knowledge of the past and on their observations.

During the United States' first 150 years, four basic values strongly influenced attitudes and lifestyles:

- *Self-sufficiency:* Every person should stand on his or her own two feet.

- *Upward mobility:* Success would come to anyone who got an education, worked hard, and played by the rules.
- *Work ethic:* Hard work, dedication to family, and frugality were moral and right.
- *Conformity:* No one should expect to be treated differently from everybody else.

For eighteen years DDB Needham Worldwide, one of the world's largest advertising agencies, has been surveying 4,000 heads of household to determine how Americans see themselves, how they live, and what they think. In a nutshell, Americans are hard to figure out. They are skeptical on the one hand but surprisingly optimistic on the other. Here is a snapshot from the latest survey:

- We wear seat belts, subscribe to cable, approve of pollution standards, and own microwaves and VCRs.
- We approve of couples living together before marriage and think women's liberation is a good thing. We approve of abortion and shared child-rearing responsibilities between parents.
- We like the look of a large lamp in a picture window.
- We long for the good old days.
- We are giving up on cleanliness at all costs. Messy homes are becoming more tolerable. We don't mind dirty ashtrays. Unseen dirt is worse than the dirt we can see. Disinfectants are important.
- We have less free time.
- We eat dinner with our families less often. We eat big Sunday brunches less often. Men snack more often than women.
- We don't play cards.
- Although we're a mobile society, we'd rather lay down roots. Small towns are preferred over big cities and suburbs. We prefer traveling in the United States to visiting foreign countries.
- Our greatest achievements are still ahead. If we had the chance to live our lives over, many of us would do things differently. About half of us would try anything once.
- Our days follow routines, but we aren't good at scheduling.
- We like a good bargain.
- A growing number of people, especially men, like sports cars. A growing number of people, especially men, like driving fast. A growing number of people, especially women, are going to museums, movies, libraries, and concerts.
- Communism no longer threatens us.
- We cook outdoors, with gas grills. Regular charcoal is passé.
- We don't like to shop, but when we do, we shop with lists (women more so than men).
- We are watching less TV.
- We try to buy American. We are buying more generics. We are less loyal to brand-name products.
- We approve of police using whatever force is necessary to maintain law and order. We feel smoking should not be allowed in public places. A growing number of people think there should be a gun in every home. A growing number of people think marijuana should be legal.

- We are serious and reserved. We work hard most of the time and feel we are under a great deal of pressure. We never seem to get ahead.[6]



## MYTHS ABOUT TODAY'S VALUES

Every decade has its attitudinal myths, and the 1990s are no exception. Here are a few of the more common ones:

- *The 1990s are a rerun of the 1950s.* Even if you took away personal computers and microwave ovens, the 1990s would not be like the 1950s. Attitudes have evolved dramatically. Back in the 1950s, cigarette smoking was fashionable and abortion was illegal. "Separate but equal" treatment of African-Americans was not considered discriminatory. Women, minorities, older Americans, and homosexuals had no employment rights. These groups are especially unlikely to want to return to the "good old days."
- *Women will quit working and return to their families in the 1990s.* Household finances in the 1990s are forcing many women to stay in their jobs. It now takes more than one earner to maintain the average household's standard of living. The media jumped on the news that women's labor-force participation rates dipped during the 1991 recession, but this drop only mimicked similar declines in men's labor-force participation during those hard times. The Bureau of Labor Statistics predicts that the labor-force participation rate for women 25 to 54 years old will grow to 82 percent by 2005, up from 74 percent in 1990.
- *Men will help more with housecleaning.* Men are spending more time on housework than ever before. Much of this increase is due to the fact that divorced and never-married men are a growing share of all men, and these men are responsible for all their own housework. Husbands and fathers are also spending more time on overall housework. But these increases are primarily in the areas of child care and shopping, according to Cathleen Zick of the University of Utah. Household cleaning has yet to become trendy among married men.[7]
- *If it's not good for you, people won't eat it.* Low-fat and low-cholesterol foods are now a $12 billion a year market. Yet the number of "lite" food introductions has dropped each year during the 1990s. There is definitely a trend toward full-flavored foods. Full flavor often means plenty of salt, sugar, and fat. For example, the new Roasted Honey Nut Skippy peanut butter has more than 4 percent of the market; the chunky version has thirty-two grams of fat per serving, or 72 percent of total calories. The percentage of people who frequently eat salty snacks has risen from 40 to 45 percent in the 1990s. Campbell Soup, too, has learned that consumers don't always live up to their own best intentions. Its low-sodium soups have lagged behind its "traditional categories." Cream of broccoli, launched in 1991, is Campbell's best-selling flavor in thirty-five years—with seven grams of fat per serving.[8]

## MARKETING-ORIENTED VALUES OF THE 1990s

Today's consumers are demanding, inquisitive, and discriminating. No longer willing to tolerate products that break down, they are insisting on high-quality goods that save time, energy, and often calories. U.S. consumers rank the characteristics of product quality as (1) reliability, (2) durability, (3) easy maintenance, (4) ease of use, (5) a trusted brand name, and (6) a low price. Shoppers are also concerned about nutrition and want to know what's in their food. In the late 1980s, barely a third of grocery shoppers read labels on the foods they bought; today half of them do.[9]

Today's shoppers are also environmentalists. Eight in ten U.S. consumers regard themselves as environmentalists, and half of those say they are strong ones.[10] Four out of five shoppers are willing to pay 5 percent more for products packaged with recyclable or biodegradable materials. Many marketers predict that by the year 2000 it will be very hard to sell a product that isn't environmentally friendly.

**poverty of time**
Lack of time to do anything but work, commute to work, handle family situations, do housework, shop, sleep, and eat.

In the 1990s, fewer consumers say expensive cars, designer clothes, pleasure trips, and "gold" credit cards are necessary components of a happy life. Instead, they put value on nonmaterial accomplishments, such as having control of their lives and being able to take a day off when they want.[11] Dual-career families have a **poverty of time,** with few hours to do anything but work and commute to work, handle family situations, do housework, shop, sleep, and eat. In a recent study of 1,010 people, half said they would sacrifice a day's pay for an extra day off each week. Of those surveyed, 21 percent said they had "no time for fun anymore," 33 percent said they don't accomplish what they set out to do each day, and 38 percent reported cutting back on sleep to make up for lost time.[12] Compared to 1989, the number of consumers engaging in time-saving activities has grown sharply: 70 percent save time by eating at fast-food restaurants (up 11 percentage points); 60 percent save time by bringing home takeout meals (up 13 points); 55 percent shop in convenience stores despite higher prices (up 12 points); 42 percent eat frozen prepared meals to save time (up 11 points); and 29 percent save time by ordering merchandise by phone, mail, or computer (up 7 points).[13]

More broadly, consumers are attracted to whatever they perceive as being "fun." Fed up with the world of work, more of them look for leisure activities that give pure pleasure. The most pleasurable activities, in rank order, are being intimate, playing sports, fishing, being involved with art and music, playing with and talking to our children, sleeping, going to church, and attending movies.[14]

## THE GROWTH OF COMPONENT LIFESTYLES

**component lifestyle**
Practice of choosing goods and services that meet one's diverse needs and interests rather than conforming to a single, traditional lifestyle.

People in the United States today are piecing together **component lifestyles.** In other words, they are choosing products and services that meet diverse needs and interests rather than conforming to traditional stereotypes.

In the past, a person's profession—for instance, banker—defined his or her lifestyle. Today a person can be a banker and also a gourmet, fitness enthusiast, dedicated single parent, and conservationist. Each of these lifestyles is associated with different goods and services and represents a target audience. For example, for the gourmet, marketers offer cooking utensils, wines, and exotic foods through magazines like *Bon Appetit* and *Gourmet.* The fitness enthusiast buys Adidas equipment and special jogging outfits and reads *Runner* magazine. Component lifestyles increase the complexity of consumers' buying habits. The banker may own a BMW but change the oil himself or herself. He or she may buy fast food for lunch but French wine for dinner, own sophisticated photographic equipment and a low-priced

The changing role of women has been a major shift in the marketing environment. (*left*) In the 1950s, marketers viewed women mainly as housewives. (*right*) Today women are also viewed as career women with a complex mix of roles.

(*left*) H. Armstrong Roberts; (*right*) © 1991 P. Barry Levy/ProFiles West

home stereo, shop for socks at Kmart or Wal-Mart and suits or dresses at Brooks Brothers.

### THE CHANGING ROLE OF FAMILIES AND WORKING WOMEN

Component lifestyles have evolved because consumers can choose from a growing number of goods and services, and most have the money to exercise more options. Rising purchasing power has resulted from the growth of dual-income families. Approximately 58 percent of all females between 16 and 65 years old are now in the work force, and female participation in the labor force is expected to grow to 63 percent by 2005.[15] This phenomenon has probably had a greater effect on marketing than any other social change.

Although dual-career families typically have greater household incomes, they have less time for family activities (poverty of time). Their purchasing roles (which define the items traditionally bought by the man or the woman) are changing, as well as their purchasing patterns. Consequently, new opportunities are being created. For example, small businesses are opening daily that cater to dual-career households by offering specialized goods and services. Ice cream and yogurt parlors, cafes, and sports footwear shops have proliferated. With more women than ever working full time, there is a special demand for new household services. San Francisco Grocery Express, a warehouse operation, uses computers to take customers' telephone orders. Customers refer to a catalog listing grocery items and prices. Later, vans deliver the food to the purchasers' front doors.

Also, many traditionally male-oriented products are being modified for or promoted to women because of the growth in female purchasing power. For example, many people would say there is no more masculine product than a Smith & Wesson revolver. Yet after Smith & Wesson launched LadySmith, a line of guns specifically for women, the gunmaker's sales to women jumped from 5 percent of the company's total to nearly 18 percent. Toyota sells almost 60 percent of its cars to women. "Women have become extremely knowledgeable about the car business," says corporate marketing manager Ren Rooney. "They have some influence on 80 percent of our purchases."[16] Avis also decided to start targeting women after it noted that the number of female business travelers was growing faster than the business travel market in general. The company gave discounts to members of the National

Association for Female Executives, created an ad campaign showing a woman in a car, and placed the ads in women's magazines such as *Lear's*, *Entrepreneurial Woman*, and *New Woman*. The tag line: "We make the road a little less lonely."

Targeting women for traditionally male-oriented products is not without controversy, however, as the Ethics in Marketing box explains.

## THE GROWING SINGLES MARKET

About 23 million people in the United States live by themselves.[18] Two trends lie behind this singles surge: Unprecedented numbers of adults never marry, and by some estimates, 60 percent of all couples divorce.

It's an attractive market but a tough one. Studies show that singles share such traits as a tendency to spend more than married adults on travel, convenience foods, and restaurants. But this vast, fragmented group includes everyone from carefree 21-year-olds to elderly widows. They are also widely scattered geographically, although the greatest concentration of single households is in the Midwest (see Exhibit 2.2).

There is also the delicate task of getting a message across without offending. According to Jane R. Fitzgibbon, a group director of Ogilvy & Mather Advertising, too often marketers have been "treating singles as if they were just some sort of extramarital aberration."[19] Campbell made that mistake with its Soup for One line. "Our consumers told us Soup for One is a lonely name. They are eating alone, and they don't need to be reminded," says Robert Bernstock, a vice president in the soup division.[20] In 1990, after years of mediocre sales, the Soup for One label was removed. Sales of single-serving sizes have since improved. On the other hand, Procter & Gamble has been very successful with Folgers Singles, coffee in single-serve bags. Advertising uses the song "One" from the Broadway musical *A Chorus Line* to position the product as "One sensational way to wake up." Trans World Airlines, responding to research showing that 35 percent of airline travelers are single, has created a series of commercials targeting the market. One spot followed a 30-something young man traveling alone in Europe, reflecting on his father's advice to take the trip now, while he's still young.[21]

Spending patterns of singles vary widely by gender. For example, single men spend 52 percent more than single women on food away from home. They spend $1,600 a year on restaurant meals, almost as much as the amount spent by the average 2.6-person household. Yet single women spend less than $800 a year on meals out.[22] Some of this difference may be explained by the fact that men are more likely than women to pick up the

ETHICS IN MARKETING

### Should Brewers Target Women?

Given the overall decline in beer consumption over the past ten years, it is no wonder that beer marketers have been seeking new target markets. Women have been a logical option, although men still decide nearly twice as often as women what brand of beer to buy. But according to Steve LeResche, director of public communications at Anheuser-Busch, things are changing. Brewers have an interest in marketing to women because of their increasing buying power.

As beer marketers have tried to gain an edge on this untapped market, they have faced a couple of controversies. One is the patronizing and male-oriented tone of traditional beer commercials. Women will never be major consumers of beer if commercials continue to be designed to appeal only to male drinkers.

Health organizations have also expressed concern about beer marketing aimed at women, just as they expressed concern about the increase in cigarette marketing to women. Because beer drinkers are traditionally a younger market, critics complain that beer makers are targeting women of childbearing age.

Smart beer marketers are discovering a middle ground. They are designing ads for their primary audience—men—that are not offensive to the growing number of women beer drinkers.[17]

Is there anything wrong with brewers targeting women? Are they simply satisfying an existing need? As long as a product is legal, should marketers target whomever they want?

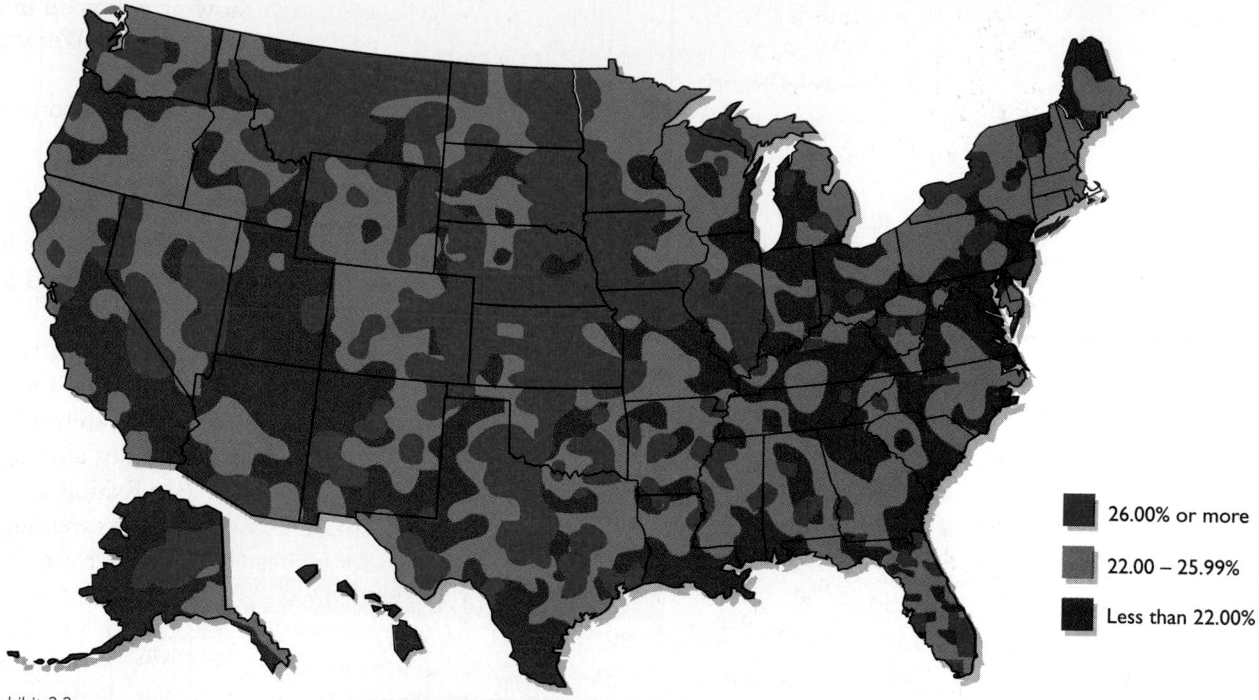


*Exhibit 2.2*

Where the Singles Live

Source: "The Singles Scene," *American Demographics*, July 1992, p. 18. Reprinted with permission © *American Demographics* July 1992. For subscription information please call (800) 828-1133.

check on dates. But the main reason is less romantic. Many single women are elderly, and elderly people are less likely than younger adults to eat out. Another reason for the discrepancy is that few single men enjoy cooking.

Overall, single men spend 39 percent more than single women on new and used cars. But single women ages 35 to 44 spend more on cars than single men their age, and the most affluent single women—those with annual incomes of $40,000 or more—spend an average of $2,200 a year on new cars. That is nearly double the average of $1,200 spent by affluent single men. It's not surprising that single women spend more than single men on clothing, shoes, dry cleaning, and jewelry. But the margin isn't great; women spend about $1,000 a year, and men spend almost $900. Single men spend over twice as much as single women on entertainment and education.[23]

*3 Explain the importance to marketing managers of current demographic trends.*

**demography**
Study of people's vital statistics, such as their age, race, and location.

## DEMOGRAPHIC FACTORS

Demographic factors—another uncontrollable variable in the external environment—are also extremely important to marketing managers. **Demography** is the study of people's vital statistics, such as their age, race and ethnicity, and location. Demographics are significant because the basis for any market is people. This section describes some marketing trends related to age and location; Chapter 20 discusses marketing issues related to race and ethnicity.

### U.S. POPULATION TRENDS

The 1990 census revealed that the U.S. population had risen to 255 million from 227 million in 1980, representing an annual growth rate of less than 1 percent. The population should reach 383 million by 2050.[24] Nevertheless, this is the slowest U.S. growth rate since the Great Depression.

The significance of these figures is that consumer goods marketers can no longer

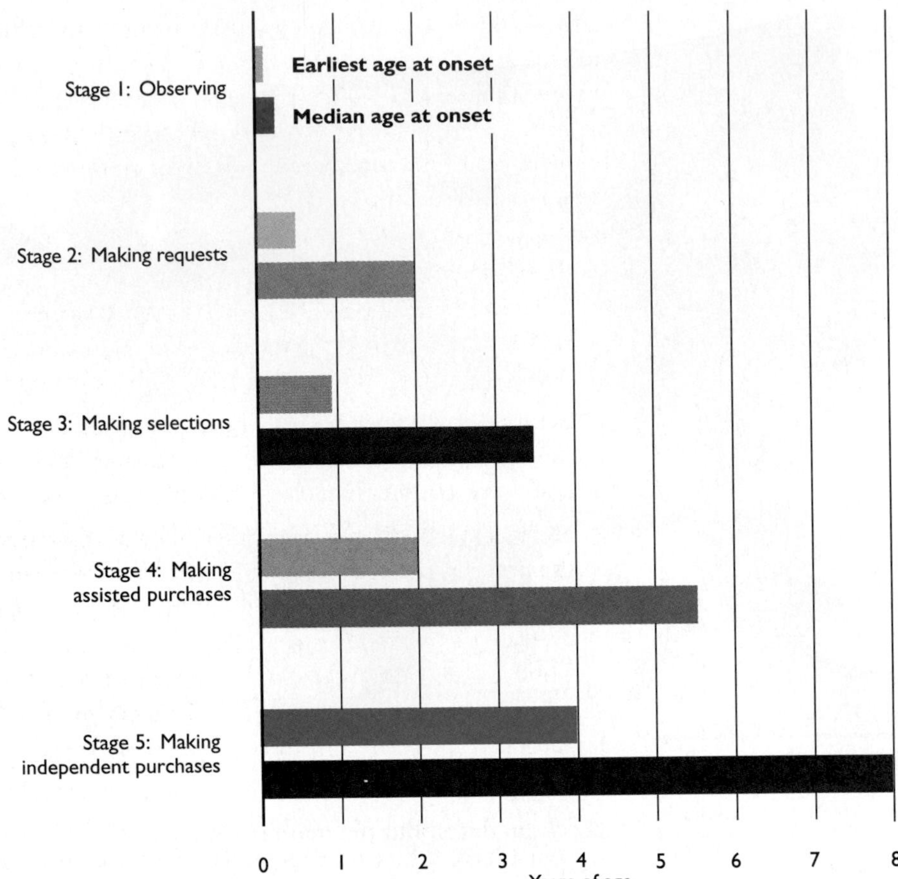


*Exhibit 2.3*

Five Stages of Consumer Development

Source: Adapted from James McNeal and Chyon-Hwa Yeh, "Born to Shop," *American Demographics*, June 1992, p. 36.

count on an expanding U.S. population to fuel sales increases. To prosper in the domestic market, some companies will try to take competitors' customers—sometimes by acquiring the competitors. Already, several of the big consumer goods mergers—for example, R.J. Reynolds with Nabisco and Kraft with General Foods—have been partially driven by demographics. If a marketer can't count on many new customers entering the marketplace, buying existing customers may make sense. Another tactic that makes sense is to try to build brand loyalty in the young. Yet another is to tap into specialized niches, such as the elderly market, before competitors do.

The elderly market may indeed become more important to marketers, because the United States is getting older. The number of 24- to 44-year-olds increased 32 percent between 1980 and 1994, and the number of 10- to 24-year-olds fell by 13 percent. The baby boomlet of the 1980s resulted in a modest 11 percent increase in the number of children under age 10. Meanwhile, the population 65 years or older has grown 24 percent since 1980, more than twice as fast as the population as a whole. The biggest spurt has come among the very old, with the number of people over 85 growing 44 percent. That group remains small, however; only 1 percent of the people in the United States are 85 or older.[25] Let's take a closer look at some of these age groups.

## Today's Preteens: Born to Shop

**discretionary income**
Income after taxes and necessities.

By some measures, preteens have greater **discretionary income** (money beyond necessities and taxes) than college students do. Parents give preteens as much as

$14.4 billion a year to spend as they wish, and children influence household purchases amounting to more than $132 billion a year.[26] Almost without thinking about it, parents are creating the next generation of spenders.

How does spending behavior begin? When do children start making consumer choices and influencing those of their parents? Exhibit 2.3 shows the five-stage process for becoming a shopper:

- Stage 1, observing, consists of children's initial interactions with the marketplace. The first thing children learn is that the satisfying objects they usually get from their parents have commercial sources. In this stage, children make sensory contact with the marketplace and construct their first mental images of marketplace objects and symbols, such as Ronald McDonald.
- Stage 2, making requests, occurs while babies are still totally dependent on their parents. Through pointing, gesturing, and vocalizing, very young children convey to parents that they see something they want.
- Shopping actually begins at stage 3—making selections. Choosing something is the first physical act taken by an independent consumer, and it occurs as children learn to walk. As children make requests and parents fulfill them, children begin to develop a memory of the store location of certain products. Children also express their desire for independence by locating and retrieving satisfying products themselves. With permission, children leave their parents and move on their own through the store maze.
- Stage 4, making assisted purchases, begins when children give money in exchange for goods while the parent supervises. Instead of obtaining desired objects from their parents, children in this stage are asking and receiving permission to obtain objects from others. Children become primary consumers who spend their own money on their own needs and wants. On average, children reach this stage at the age of 5½.[27]
- The final stage is stage 5, making independent purchases. Some children make purchases without parents as early as 4 years old, but the average age is 8. The interval between stage 4 and stage 5 is the longest period of time between stages. It reflects the difficulty of learning a complex exchange system and the reluctance of many parents to let children go to stores on their own.

Many marketers recognize the importance of reaching the children's market early. Kodak not only donates cameras and film to schools as part of its Using Cameras in the Curriculum program (for kids in kindergarten through grade six) but also lines up photofinishers who will donate development of the film. The company weaves environmental themes into its program. Kodak hopes to draw the 6-to-11-year-old crowd with the school program, as it did with its single-use camera decorated with characters from the hit movie *Aladdin*. For kids "too old" for such things, Kodak launched the Photo fX 35mm camera for $39.95—a "real" camera that "looks like Mom and Dad's."[28]

### Generation X: Savvy and Cynical

**generation X**
People who are currently between the ages of 18 and 29.

In 1995, approximately 47 million consumers were between the ages of 18 and 29. This group has been labeled **generation X.** It is the first generation of latchkey children—products of dual-career households or, in roughly half of cases, of divorced or separated parents. Generation X began entering the work force in the era of downsizing and downturn, so they're likelier than the previous generation to be unemployed, underemployed, and living at home with Mom and Dad. They're alienated

Generation X is particularly difficult to target because they are wary of many advertising schemes. This ad for Guess "cuts through the clutter" of traditional ads to appeal to the twenty-something consumer.

by a culture that has been dominated by the previous generation for as long as they can remember. They're angry as they look down a career path that's crowded with 30- and 40-somethings who are in no hurry to clear the way. Furthermore, as a generation that's been bombarded by multiple media since their cradle days, they're savvy and cynical consumers.

The members of generation X don't mind indulging themselves. Among the young women of generation X, 38 percent go to the movies in a given month, compared with 19 percent of the women who are now in their 30s and 40s. The members of generation X devote a larger-than-average share of their spending dollars to restaurant meals, alcoholic beverages, clothing, and electronic items such as televisions and stereos.[29] One survey found that the members of generation X aspire to having a home of their own (87 percent), a lot of money (42 percent), a swimming pool (42 percent), and a vacation home (41 percent).[30] They are more materialistic than past generations but have less hope of achieving their goals.

Perhaps it is this combination of high aspirations and low expectations that makes generation X such a challenge for marketers. "This is a generation that hates to be marketed to," says cScott Kauffman, vice president of broadcast and new media at *Entertainment Weekly.* "You have the youth of America reading novels in which chapters are titled, 'I am not a target market.'"[31]

Marketers have made some embarrassing attempts to woo generation X, including Subaru's now-infamous Impreza ad. Using a dizzying array of camera angles and quick cuts, the spot featured an intense young guy comparing the car to punk rock, which "challenged corporate thinking and reminded us what was cool about music." The ad is now held up as a textbook example of how not to market to generation X.

Perhaps the biggest rule in marketing to generation X is not to take yourself too seriously. One of the print ads in Converse's campaign for its Chuck Taylor All-Star athletic shoes, for example, showed a girl wearing purple Chucks standing on top of a building. The copy, set in very small type, simply read: "Tracy in NYC. She said if she spit her gum out from up here and it hit someone below, the force would totally split them in half." The Converse logo appeared in the lower left corner of the ad. The ad worked because it had a light touch, and although the girl's fashion statement was a bit forward at the time, Converse didn't try to claim its shoes were the hottest new thing.

## Baby Boomers: America's Mass Market

Almost 76 million babies were born in the United States between 1946 and 1964, which created a huge market. The oldest **baby boomers** are pushing 50, but they cling to their youth. One study found that baby boomers see themselves as continuing to be very active after they turn 50. They won't even think of themselves as being senior citizens until after they turn 60 (39 percent) or 70 (42 percent).[32]

**baby boomer**
Person born between 1946 and 1964.

This group cherishes convenience, which has resulted in a growing demand for home delivery of items like large appliances, furniture, and groceries. In addition, the spreading culture of convenience explains the tremendous appeal of prepared takeout foods and the necessity of VCRs and portable telephones.

Baby boomers' parents raised their children to think for and of themselves. Studies of child-rearing practices show that parents of the 1950s and 1960s consistently ranked "to think for themselves" as the number-one trait they wanted to nurture in their children.[33] Postwar affluence also allowed parents to indulge their children as never before. They invested in their children's skills by sending them to college. They encouraged their children to succeed in a job market that rewarded competitive drive more than cooperative spirit and individual skills more than teamwork.

In turn, the sheer size of the generation encouraged businesses to promote to the emerging individuality of baby boomers. Even before the oldest baby boomers started earning their own living more than two decades ago, astute businesspeople saw the profits that come from giving millions of young people what they want. Businesses offered individualistic baby boomers a growing array of customized products and services—houses, cars, furniture, appliances, clothes, vacations, jobs, leisure time, and even beliefs.

**personalized economy**
Economic structure in which goods and services are delivered at a good value on demand.

The importance of individualism among baby boomers led to a personalized economy. A **personalized economy** delivers goods and services at a good value on demand. Successful businesses in a personalized economy give customers what they want when they want it. To do this, they must know their customers extremely well. In fact, the intimacy between producer and consumer is exactly what makes an economy personalized.

In the personalized economy, successful products share three characteristics:

- *Customization:* Products are custom-designed and marketed to ever-smaller target markets. Today, for example, there are hundreds of cable TV channels from which to choose. In 1950 the average grocery store carried about 4,000 items; today, that number is closer to 16,000, as manufacturers target increasingly specific needs.[34]
- *Immediacy:* Successful businesses deliver products and services at the convenience of the consumer rather than the producer. Banc One, with locations in the eastern and southern states, for example, opens some of its branches on Saturdays and Sundays. Its twenty-four-hour hot line, staffed by real people, solves problems at the customer's convenience. The immediacy of the personalized economy explains the booming business in one-hour film processing, walk-in medical clinics, and thirty-minute pizzas.
- *Value.* Businesses must price competitively or create innovative products that can command premium prices. Even the most innovative products quickly become commodities in the fast-paced personalized economy, however. Apple fell prey to this danger. Its once-innovative Macintosh computers must now compete against less expensive machines that offer similar functions.

As the age of today's average consumer moves toward 40, average consumption patterns are also changing. People in their early 40s tend to focus on their families and finances. As this group grows in numbers, they will buy more furniture from manufacturers like Lazy Boy, American Martindale, Baker, and Drexel-Heritage to replace the furniture they bought early in their marriage. The demand for family counselors and wellness programs should also increase. Additionally, discount investment brokers like Charles Schwab and mutual funds like Fidelity and Dreyfus

Consumers over 50 have the time, financial resources, and good health to enjoy many leisure activities. In fact, they are the prime market for the U.S. travel industry.



should profit. Because middle-aged consumers buy more reading materials than any other age group, the market for books and magazines should remain strong throughout the 1990s. People who buy magazines on the newsstand tend to be younger, so newsstand sales may falter while subscription sales take off.

During the remainder of the 1990s, merchants will offer more products and services aimed at middle-aged markets. Styles will have a more conservative look, commercials will feature more middle-aged actors, and the general atmosphere of retail stores will be less youth-oriented. Already, Dayton Hudson department stores have been redecorated to reflect this changing image.

## Older Consumers: Not Just Grandparents

Today's 50-plus consumers are wealthier, healthier, and better educated than earlier generations.[35] Although they make up only 26 percent of the population, 50-plus consumers buy half of all domestic cars, half of all silverware, and nearly half of all home remodeling.[36] Smart marketers are already targeting this growing segment. By 2020, over a third of the population will be 50 years old or older.

Many marketers have yet to tap the full potential of the huge and lucrative senior market because of enduring misconceptions about mature adults, all based on stereotypes. Here are a few:

- *Stereotype:* Older consumers are sick or ailing. *Fact:* A full 85 percent of mature citizens report themselves to be in good or excellent health. Over two-thirds of the elderly have no chronic health problems.[37]
- *Stereotype:* Older consumers are sedentary. *Fact:* Of all travel dollars spent in the United States, 80 percent are spent by people over 50 years old.
- *Stereotype:* Older consumers have a poor retention rate. *Fact:* Senior citizens are readers and much less influenced by TV than younger consumers. They not only retain what they read, but they are willing to read far more copy than younger people are.

- *Stereotype:* Older consumers are interested only in price and are intolerant of change. *Fact:* Although senior citizens are as interested in price as anyone else, they are more interested in value. And a generation that has survived the better part of a century characterized by more technological change than any other in history can hardly be considered resistant to change.[38]

Acceptance of change, however, doesn't mean a lack of brand loyalty. For example, the most critical factor in determining car-owner loyalty is age. The oldest consumers (ages 65 and up) are twice as loyal to the make of car as the youngest customers are.[39] The cars most popular with older Americans are Lincoln, Cadillac, and Buick.

Marketers who want to actively pursue the mature market must understand it. Aging consumers create some obvious opportunities. JCPenney's Easy Dressing clothes feature Velcro-fastened clothing for women with arthritis or other ailments who may have difficulty with zippers or buttons. Sales from the first Easy Dressing catalog, distributed in 1991, were three times higher than expected.[40] Other retailers are adding more rest stops in stores and arranging shelving so customers needn't bend over. Grocers are considering using elastic cords to attach magnifying glasses to grocery carts. General Motors and Toyota are adding "older" features to their cars: Toyota is installing simpler audio systems with fewer gadgets in its Camry sedans, and some GM cars now offer a "head-up display" that flashes vehicle speed and other signals on the front windshield, making them easier to read.[41] On the cruise ship *Crown Odyssey,* owned by Royal Cruise Line, passengers take water aerobics classes, order broiled fish with lemon, and attend seminars on stress reduction. Are the passengers health-conscious yuppies? No, Royal is simply trying to meet the wishes of its 50-plus target market. Sales of Post Natural Bran Flakes rose rapidly when Kraft General Foods began using durable entertainers Lena Horne and Steve Allen in its advertising.

### AMERICANS ON THE MOVE

The average U.S. citizen moves every six years.[42] This trend also has implications for marketers. A large influx of new people into an area creates many new marketing opportunities for all types of businesses. Conversely, significant out-migration from a city or town may force many of its businesses either to move or close down.

The United States experiences both immigration from other countries and migration within U.S. borders. In the past decade, the six states with the highest levels of immigration from abroad were California, New York, New Jersey, Illinois, Texas, and Massachusetts. The six states with the greatest population increases due to interstate migration were Florida, Georgia, North Carolina, Virginia, Washington, and Arizona.[43]

4 *Identify consumer and marketer reactions to the state of the economy.*

## ECONOMIC FACTORS

In addition to social and demographic factors, marketing managers must understand and react to the economic environment. The three economic areas of greatest concern to most marketers are the distribution of consumer income, inflation, and recession.

### RISING INCOMES

As disposable (or after-tax) incomes rise, more families and individuals can afford the "good life." Fortunately, U.S. incomes have continued to rise. After adjustment for inflation, median incomes in the United States rose 4 percent between 1980 and 1994.

Today about two-thirds of all U.S. households earn a "middle-class" income. The rough boundaries for a middle-class income are $18,000, comfortably above poverty, to about $75,000, just short of wealth. In 1995 almost half the households were in the upper end of the $18,000 to $75,000 range, as opposed to only a quarter in 1980. The percentage of households earning above $75,000 rose from 2.6 percent to 7.4 percent of the total households.[44] As a result, Americans are buying more goods and services than ever before. For example, in raising a child to age 17, a middle-class family will spend about $122,000 in 1995 dollars. This new level of affluence is not limited to professionals or even individuals within specific age or education brackets. Rather, it cuts across all household types, well beyond what businesses traditionally consider to be markets for high-priced goods and services. This rising affluence primarily stems from the increasing number of dual-income families.

Unfortunately, the recession of the early 1990s kept poor people from moving into the middle class. The real purchasing power of lower-income households has stagnated since 1980. A college education is the single most important factor in moving up economically.[45]

During the remainder of the 1990s, many marketing managers will focus on families with incomes over $35,000, because this group will have the most discretionary income. The average American household has over $12,000 in discretionary income each year.[46] Some marketers will concentrate their efforts on higher-quality, higher-priced goods and services. The Lexus automobile and American Airlines' "international class" service for business-class seats on transcontinental flights are examples of this trend.

## INFLATION

**inflation**
General rise in prices resulting in decreased purchasing power.

**Inflation** is a general rise in prices resulting in decreased purchasing power. Fortunately, the United States has had a low rate of inflation for over a decade. The 1990s have been marked by an inflation rate under 4 percent. These economic conditions benefit marketers, because real wages and hence purchasing power go up when inflation stays down. A significant increase in inflation almost always depresses real wages and the ability to buy more goods and services.

In times of low inflation, businesses seeking to increase their profit margins can do so only by increasing their efficiency. If they significantly increase prices, no one will purchase their goods or services.[47]

In more inflationary times, marketers use a number of pricing strategies to cope (see Chapter 19 for more on these strategies). But in general, marketers must be aware that inflation causes consumers to either stock up or decrease their brand loyalty. In one research session, a consumer panelist noted, "I used to use just Betty Crocker mixes, but now I think of either Betty Crocker or Duncan Hines, depending on which is on sale." Another participant said, "Pennies count now, and so I look at the whole shelf, and I read the ingredients. I don't really understand, but I can tell if it's exactly the same. So now I use this cheaper brand, and honestly, it works just as well." Inflation pressures consumers to make more economical purchases. However, most consumers try hard to maintain their standard of living.

In creating marketing strategies to cope with inflation, managers must realize that, despite what happens to the seller's cost, the buyer is not going to pay more for a product than the subjective value he or she places on it. No matter how compelling the justification might be for a 10 percent price increase, marketers must always examine its impact on demand. Many marketers try to hold prices level as long as practical.

## RECESSION

**recession**
Period of economic activity when income, production, and employment tend to fall.

A **recession** is a period of economic activity when income, production, and employment tend to fall—all of which reduce demand for goods and services. The problems of inflation and recession go hand in hand, yet recession requires different marketing strategies:

- *Improve existing products and introduce new ones:* The goal is to reduce production hours, waste, and the cost of materials. Recessions increase demand for goods and services that are economical and efficient, offer value, help organizations streamline practices and procedures, and improve customer service.
- *Maintain and expand customer services:* In a recession, many organizations postpone the purchase of new equipment and materials. Sales of replacement parts and other services may become an important source of income.
- *Emphasize top-of-the-line products and promote product value:* Customers with less to spend will seek demonstrated quality, durability, satisfaction, and capacity to save time and money. High-priced, high-value items consistently fare well during recessions.

5 *Identify the impact of technology on a firm.*

## TECHNOLOGICAL AND RESOURCE FACTORS

Sometimes new technology is an effective weapon against inflation and recession. New machines that reduce production costs can be one of a firm's most valuable assets. Unfortunately, the United States isn't developing new technology nearly as well as it should be at a time when innovation has become more important than ever.

Although the United States still generates more patents than any other nation, other countries, especially Japan, are catching up. In 1993, the three companies to register the most U.S. patents were Japanese—Canon, Hitachi, and Toshiba. IBM and General Electric were ranked fourth and fifth.[48] Since 1983, Japan has gained against the United States in thirty-eight of forty-eight product categories, particularly office computers, electronics, transportation equipment, and shipbuilding. U.S. spending on research and development has been averaging about 2 percent of gross domestic product, but the Japanese have dramatically increased their spending to 3 percent.[49] Moreover, growth in R&D spending in the United States slowed during the second half of the 1980s and then began to fall.[50]

Another telling statistic is how R&D money is spent. The U.S. government spends about $76 billion a year on R&D; private industry spends another $85 billion.[51] In the 1990s, the United States has spent 16 percent more on R&D than Japan, Germany, France, and the United Kingdom combined. Yet these four countries together spend 12 percent more than the United States on R&D not related to defense.[52]

**basic research**
Attempt to expand the frontiers of scientific knowledge without concern for commercial viability.

U.S. companies often have difficulty translating the results of R&D into goods and services. The Japanese are masters at making this transformation. For example, VCRs, flat-panel displays, and compact disc players are based on U.S. research that wasn't exploited at home. The United States excels at **basic research** (or pure

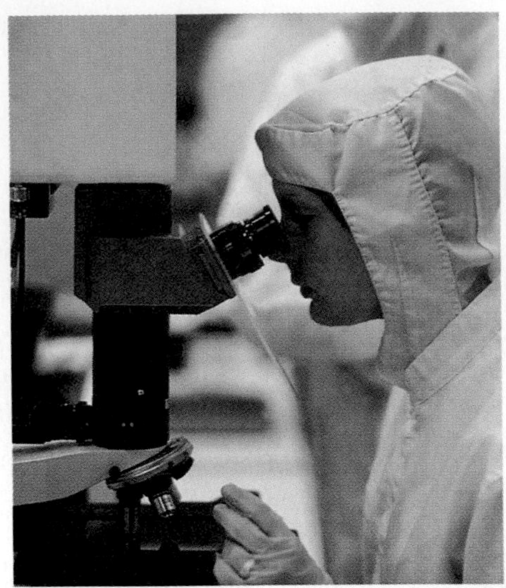

Research and development expenditures often pay off in new products and a bigger share of global markets. The key to innovation and competitiveness, however, is not just the amount spent but the uses to which R&D findings are put.



**applied research**
Attempt to find practical solutions to existing or potential real-world problems.

research), which attempts to expand the frontiers of knowledge but is not aimed at a specific, pragmatic problem. Basic research aims to confirm an existing theory or to learn more about a concept or phenomenon. For example, basic research might focus on high-energy physics. **Applied research,** in contrast, attempts to develop new or improved products. It is where the United States sometimes falls short, although many U.S. companies do conduct applied research. For example, IBM is conducting applied research into the use of holograms to store vast amounts of computer data.

Today, both Congress and industry are demanding more relevance from R&D expenditures. Congress has ordered the National Science Foundation to spend 60 percent of its $2 billion research budget on projects deemed relevant to national needs.[53] Depending on how relevance is defined, the effect could be dramatic. Even weapons laboratories, whose R&D budgets exceed $22 billion a year, are attempting to help U.S. industry become more globally competitive by undertaking cooperative projects. Yet the peculiar culture of the weapons laboratories is making the transition difficult. In 1993 Quadrax Corporation, a high-tech composites maker, asked the Livermore National Laboratory to analyze some of Quadrax's materials. Livermore kept the results secret—even from Quadrax.[54]

R&D expenditures are only a rough measure of where the United States stands in terms of innovation. A look at management of the R&D process can be even more revealing. U.S. managers tend to be obsessed with short-term profits (one to three years) and minimal risk taking. The result is an infatuation with slight variations of existing products, which are often very profitable, instead of true innovations. Developing new products like Honey Nut Cheerios and Diet Cherry Coke is probably not the path to world economic leadership.

To regain its world leadership, the United States must promote innovation. One way is to reduce the tax on capital gains, which slashes the reward for successful innovation. The capital-gains tax is higher in the United States than in any other developed country. In the United States, a start-up company that had doubled in value over the past decade would have provided its investors with a return, after inflation and the capital-gains tax, of just over 1 percent annually.[55] Under those rules, many managers ask, "Why bother?"

Companies must also learn how to innovate, and large R&D budgets aren't the sole answer. One of the biggest R&D spenders in the United States is General Motors, which by most standards is not a leading innovator. On the other hand, Corning has relatively low R&D budgets but is arguably one of the five most innovative companies in the world.[56] The difference is in management and corporate culture.

Again, we might take a clue from the Japanese. In Japan, a team composed of engineers, scientists, marketers, and manufacturers works simultaneously at three levels of innovation. At the lowest level, they seek small improvements in an existing product. At the second, they try for a significant jump, such as Sony's move from the

*Exhibit 2.4*

Top Twenty Technologies for the Remainder of the 1990s

Source: Adapted from Daniel Burrus, "A Glimpse of the Future," *Managing Your Career,* Spring 1991, pp. 6, 10. Copyright by Daniel Burrus.

**1. Genetic engineering.** The mapping, restructuring, and remodeling of the human and animal gene code will allow us to eliminate or enhance a specific trait. Agricultural applications will include crops that are insect-proof, drought-resistant, and nitrogen-fixing. Human applications will range from predicting inherited genetic diseases to applying gene therapy to correct genetic disorders.

**2. Advanced biochemistry.** Using genetic engineering techniques, scientists will create new drugs, such as Interleukin-2, to fight such diseases as cancer in humans and animals.

**3. Bioelectricity.** Damaged or dysfunctioning nerves, muscles, and glands will be stimulated through bioelectricity. For example, bioelectricity is currently being used in humans to stimulate the growth of severed bones, regulate defective hearts and lungs, speed the healing rate of wounds, and act as an alternative to addictive painkillers.

**4. Advanced computers.** The development of faster, more powerful computers will be based on evolving chip technologies. A single Sarnoff chip contains 100 or more tiny lasers, creating the first functional optoelectric integrated circuit. By the late 1990s, these chips will be used in powerful new desktop computers.

**5. Multisensory robotics.** A new generation of robots will be able to handle duties beyond repetitive functions. In a few years, we'll see the first useful service robots, such as smart shopping carts, mobile helpers used in factories, and personal robots.

**6. Artificial intelligence.** The continued expansion of computers will enable them to perform functions normally attributed to human intelligence, such as learning, adaptation, recognition, and self-correction.

**7. Parallel processing.** Multiple computers attack a problem simultaneously, thus speeding the process.

**8. Digital electronics.** The digitizing of audio, video, and film will yield better organization. Soon, companies will begin digitizing all types of information on such a large scale that any tidbit can be retrieved almost instantaneously.

**9. Lasers.** Improvements will include the expanded use of lasers in surgery (microwave scalpels will completely replace metal scalpels) and holography (3-D imagery will become common in advertising).

**10. Fiber optics.** Optical fibers will improve communications in the majority of U.S. households and businesses. By the end of the decade, the majority of U.S. homes will have fiber-optic connections that can carry four signals at once: telephone, TV, radio, and computer data.

**11. Optical data storage.** Optical memory systems will expand to read and store information in digital form. Examples include all optical disks, optical film, floptical disks, and bar code readers.

**12. Microwaves.** Currently microwaves have two major applications: sending wireless digital information (satellite dishes) and heating objects (ovens). New applications in the 1990s will range from microwave clothes dryers to cancer treatments.

**13. Advanced satellites.** As more countries send satellites into orbit, additional and improved uses for satellite technology will emerge.

**14. Photovoltaics (PV).** New uses will be found for PV cells, which convert sunlight into energy. In the next few years, solar hydrogen (an economical, pollution-free energy source) will be used increasingly for rural electrification and as an alternative for automobile and jet fuel.

**15. Micromechanics.** Micromechanics is the design and construction of tiny mechanisms able to link up with microelectronic circuits, allowing the creation of smaller, faster electronic products. The first quantum transistor, recently developed, is 100 times smaller and 1,000 times faster than current transistors. Mass-produced, these transistors will revolutionize the electronics industry.

**16. Molecular design.** A supercomputer creates new materials built molecule by molecule, atom by atom. The first products to move out of the lab are tailor-made enzymes for individual use.

**17. New polymers.** The adaptation of complex chemical structures makes them lighter, stronger, more resistant to heat, and able to conduct electricity. Applications range from garbage bags and army tanks to running shoes, ball bearings, and moldable batteries.

**18. High-tech ceramics.** New versions of ceramic materials are resistant to corrosion, wear, and high temperatures. We'll soon see ceramic auto engine parts, which yield cleaner-running engines, and a ceramic-based automotive gas turbine engine.

**19. Fiber-reinforced composites.** Lightweight, noncorrosive composite materials will continue to develop; they often are stronger than steel. Applications include home building materials, bridges, and aircraft.

**20. Superconductors.** Superconductors are inexpensive materials that carry electricity without any loss of energy. Near-term uses range from less expensive but more advanced magnetic imaging machines for hospitals, superconducting TV antennas, and faster computer circuits. By the 21st century, scientists hope to complete development of superconducting cables that transmit electricity and magnetically levitated trains.

CREATING CUSTOMER VALUE

**The Value of Technology**

You arrive at the hotel, pop your "smart" card in a slot to introduce yourself, then go straight to your room, which was assigned earlier by computer. To enter your room, you merely say your name, and the door magically opens. You hang up your coat, punch in channel 162 on the TV, and hold a videoconference with colleagues. When the meeting ends, you flip to another channel to shop for a gift, then call home on the videophone to see how the family is faring while you are on the road. Scenes like this will be commonplace soon, because companies like the hotel chain Marriott are scurrying to satisfy customer demands with just the right combination of technology.

Companies determined to delight customers in the twenty-first century are preparing for the day when technology will personalize customer service in new ways. Don't always expect consumers to catch on immediately, though. Says Thomas I. Rubel, a partner at Price Waterhouse's Management Horizons division: "You've got the technology in one hand, and Bubba and his wife, who may not accept it, in the other." Better be ready for both, because invariably customers will expect service delivery on their own terms.

The trend, however, is toward "disintermediation," which essentially means removing intermediaries from the provision of services—that is, customer self-service. Rapid advances in hardware and software are making self-service easier and more fun—two requirements for consumer acceptance of any new technology.

With voice-recognition technology, for example, customers simply speak to a computer instead of pushing buttons or typing. Although a staple of science fiction films and TV shows since the 1950s, this technology has frustrated scientists for decades. AT&T, which has been coaxing machines to recognize human speech for forty years, says the technology is finally ready. AT&T's Universal credit card outfit is planning what it calls a twenty-first-century Personal Servant for its 17 million–plus cardholders. A cardholder will communicate with PS via phone or computer. PS will then make hotel reservations, balance the checkbook, or do any number of mundane chores. It will even make recommendations, such as "Jack, the Ralph Lauren outlet is having a sale on men's shirts. Should I order you a few?" Most remarkably, a cardholder will be able to design his or her PS's voice and personality. If the Arthur Treacher or John Gielgud type doesn't please you, create one that is more like Marilyn Monroe or Madonna.[60]

What other technologies do you see companies developing in order to deliver better customer value? Some companies are charging just as much for high-tech services as they are for human ones, even though the high-tech services cost less to provide. For example, about 10 percent of all U.S. banks charge customers for using an ATM. The banks reason that customers value the service enough to pay for it. Is this attitude fair? Is it ethical? When companies achieve lower costs, shouldn't part of the savings be passed on to consumers?

microcassette tape recorder to the Walkman. The third is true innovation, an entirely new product. The idea is to produce three new products to replace each present product, with the same investment of time and money. One of the three may then become the new market leader and produce the innovator's profit.[57]

Companies must also learn to foster and encourage innovation. Rubbermaid teaches its people to let ideas flow from its so-called core competencies, the things it does best. Bud Hellman, who used to run a Rubbermaid subsidiary, was touring one of the company's picnic-cooler plants in the late 1980s when he suddenly realized he could use its plastic blow-molding technique to make a durable, lightweight, inexpensive line of office furniture. The result was the Work Manager System, which accounts for 60 percent of sales at Rubbermaid's furniture division. Toro, a Minnesota maker of mowers and other lawn equipment, fosters innovation by letting all employees know they won't be penalized for taking a risk on new ideas that fail. Bell Atlantic started what it calls its Champion program. Any employee with a good idea gets to leave his or her job for a while, at full pay and benefits, and receive training in such skills as writing a business plan and organizing a development schedule. The innovator also gets money to invest in the idea. The employee becomes the idea's champion, with a strong incentive to develop it successfully. The innovator can invest 10 percent of his or her salary in the project and give up bonuses in return for 5 percent of the revenues if the product gets to market. Since the company started the program in 1989, Champion has generated two patents, with eleven more pending.[58]

Despite some problems, innovation is alive and well. Many scientists believe the world will see more innovations between 1995 and 2005 than we have seen in the previous hundred years.[59] Exhibit 2.4 (on page 51) forecasts the technologies that will shape innovation for the remainder of the 1990s. Technology will also play an important role in the drive toward better customer service, as the Creating Customer Value box explains.

6 *Discuss the political and legal environment of marketing.*

## POLITICAL AND LEGAL FACTORS

Business needs government regulation to protect the interests of society, protect one business from another, and protect consumers. In turn, government needs business, because the marketplace generates taxes that support public efforts to educate our youth, protect our shores, and so on. The private sector also serves as a counterweight to government. The decentralization of power inherent in a private enterprise system supplies the limitation on government essential for the survival of a democracy.

Every aspect of the marketing mix is subject to laws and restrictions. It is the duty of marketing managers or their legal assistants to understand these laws and conform to them, because failure to comply with regulations can have major consequences for a firm. Sometimes just sensing trends and taking corrective action before a government agency acts can help avoid regulation.

However, the challenge is not simply to keep the marketing department out of trouble but to help it implement creative new programs to accomplish marketing objectives. It is all too easy for a marketing manager or sometimes a lawyer to say no to a marketing innovation that actually entails little risk. For example, an overly cautious lawyer could hold up sales of a desirable new product by warning that the package design could prompt a copyright infringement suit. Thus it is important to understand thoroughly the laws established by the federal government, state governments, and regulatory agencies to control marketing-related issues.

### FEDERAL LEGISLATION

Federal laws that affect marketing fall into several categories. First, the Sherman Act, the Clayton Act, the Federal Trade Commission Act, the Celler-Kefauver Antimerger Act, and the Hart-Scott-Rodino Act were passed to regulate the competitive environment. Second, the Robinson-Patman Act was designed to regulate pricing practices. Third, the Wheeler-Lea Act was created to control false advertising. These key pieces of legislation are summarized in Exhibit 2.5 (on page 54).

Many other laws have been passed to protect purchasers, users, and innocent third parties. A sampling of these consumer protection laws is shown in Exhibit 2.6 (on page 55). Note that all aspects of marketing—product, price, promotion, and distribution—are regulated. For instance, tying contracts, which require a customer to buy something he or she does not want in order to get a full line of a firm's products, are illegal. If a manufacturer requires a dealer to carry a full line of its products, it may be in violation of the Clayton and Sherman acts. Also, if a franchise agreement allows the franchise holder to sell only to customers within an assigned sales territory, the agreement is illegal. Nor can a franchise agreement prohibit a franchise holder from carrying a competitor's products.

### STATE LAWS

State legislation that affects marketing varies. Oregon, for example, limits utility advertising to 0.5 percent of the company's net income. California has forced industry to improve consumer products and has also enacted legislation to lower the energy

| Legislation | Impact on marketing |
|---|---|
| **Sherman Act of 1890** | Makes trusts and conspiracies in restraint of trade illegal; makes monopolies and attempts to monopolize a misdemeanor |
| **Clayton Act of 1914** | Outlaws discrimination in prices to different buyers; prohibits tying contracts (which require the buyer of one product to also buy another item in the line); makes illegal the combining of two or more competing corporations by pooling ownership of stock |
| **Federal Trade Commission Act of 1914** | Creates the Federal Trade Commission to deal with antitrust matters; outlaws unfair methods of competition |
| **Robinson-Patman Act of 1936** | Prohibits charging different prices to different buyers of like grade and quantity merchandise; requires sellers to make any supplementary services or allowances available to all purchasers on a proportionately equal basis |
| **Wheeler-Lea Amendment to the FTC Act of 1938** | Broadens the Federal Trade Commission's power to prohibit practices that might injure the public without affecting competition; outlaws false and deceptive advertising |
| **Lanham Act of 1946** | Establishes protection for trademarks |
| **Celler-Kefauver Antimerger Act of 1950** | Strengthens the Clayton Act to prevent corporate acquisitions that reduce competition |
| **Hart-Scott-Rodino Act of 1976** | Requires large companies to notify the government of their intent to merge |

*Exhibit 2.5*

Primary U.S. Laws That Affect Marketing

consumption of refrigerators, freezers, and air conditioners. Several states, including New Mexico and Kansas, are considering levying a tax on all in-state commercial advertising.

## REGULATORY AGENCIES

Although state regulatory bodies more actively pursue violations of their marketing statutes, federal regulators generally have the greatest clout. The Consumer Product Safety Commission, the Federal Trade Commission, and the Food and Drug Administration are the three federal agencies most directly and actively involved in marketing affairs. These agencies, plus others, are discussed throughout the book, but a brief introduction is in order at this point.

**Consumer Product Safety Commission (CPSC)**
Federal agency established to protect the health and safety of consumers in and around their homes.

The sole purpose of the **Consumer Product Safety Commission** (CPSC) is to protect the health and safety of consumers in and around their homes. The CPSC has the power to set mandatory safety standards for almost all products that consumers use (about 15,000 items). The CPSC consists of a five-member committee and about 1,100 staff members, who include technicians, lawyers, and administrative help. The commission can fine offending firms up to $500,000 and sentence their officers to up to a year in prison. It can also ban dangerous products from the marketplace.

**Federal Trade Commission (FTC)**
Federal agency empowered to prevent persons or corporations from using unfair methods of competition in commerce.

The **Federal Trade Commission** (FTC) also consists of five members, each holding office for seven years. The Federal Trade Commission is empowered to prevent persons or corporations from using unfair methods of competition in commerce. It is authorized to investigate the practices of business combinations and to conduct hearings on antitrust matters and deceptive advertising. The FTC has a vast array of

| Legislative action | Impact or change in consumer environment |
|---|---|
| **Mail Fraud Act, 1872** | Makes it a federal crime to defraud consumers through use of the mail |
| **Pure Food & Drug Act, 1906** | Regulates interstate commerce in misbranded and adulterated foods, drinks, and drugs |
| **Federal Food, Drug & Cosmetic Act, 1938** | Strengthens the Food and Drug Act of 1906 by including cosmetics; requires predistribution clearance on any new drugs |
| **Flammable Fabrics Act, 1953** | Prohibits interstate shipments of flammable apparel or material |
| **Automobile Information Disclosure Act, 1958** | Requires auto manufacturers to post suggested retail prices on new cars |
| **Food Additives Amendment, 1958** | Prohibits new feed additives until approved by the Food and Drug Administration |
| **Fair Packaging and Labeling Act, 1965** | Regulates packaging and labeling; establishes uniform sizes |
| **Child Safety Act, 1966** | Prevents the marketing of harmful toys and dangerous products |
| **Cigarette Label Act, 1966** | Requires labels that warn about smoking hazards |
| **Consumer Credit Protection, 1968** | Requires full disclosure of annual interest rates and other financial charges on loans and revolving charges |
| **Fair Credit Report Act, 1970** | Regulates the reporting and use of credit information; limits consumer liability for stolen credit cards to $50 |
| **Consumer Product Safety Act, 1972** | Creates the Consumer Product Safety Commission |
| **Fair Debt Collection Practice Act, 1978** | Makes it illegal to harass or abuse any person, to make false statements, or to use unfair methods when collecting a debt |

*Exhibit 2.6*

Examples of U.S. Legislation Designed to Protect Consumers

regulatory powers (see Exhibit 2.7 on page 56). Nevertheless, it is not invincible. For example, the FTC had proposed to ban all advertising to children under age 8, to ban all advertising of the sugared products that are most likely to cause tooth decay to children under age 12, and to require dental health and nutritional advertisements to be paid for by industry. Business reacted by lobbying to reduce the FTC's power. The two-year lobbying effort resulted in passage of the FTC Improvement Act of 1980. The major provisions of the act are as follows:

- It bans the use of unfairness as a standard for industrywide rules against advertising. All the proposals concerning children's advertising were therefore suspended, because they were based almost entirely on the unfairness standard.
- It requires oversight hearings on the FTC every six months. This congressional review is designed to keep the commission accountable. Moreover, it keeps Congress aware of one of the many regulatory agencies it has created and is responsible for monitoring.

Businesses rarely band together to create change in the legal environment as they did to pass the FTC Improvement Act. Generally, marketing managers only react to legislation, regulation, and edicts. It is usually less costly to stay attuned to the regulatory

| Remedy | Procedure |
|---|---|
| **Cease-and-desist order** | A final order is issued to cease an illegal practice—and is often challenged in the courts. |
| **Consent decree** | A business consents to stop the questionable practice without admitting illegality. |
| **Affirmative disclosure** | An advertiser is required to provide additional information about products in advertisements. |
| **Corrective advertising** | An advertiser is required to correct the past effects of misleading advertising (for example, 25% of media budget for FTC-approved advertisements or FTC-specified advertising). |
| **Restitution** | Refunds are required to be given to consumers misled by deceptive advertising. According to a 1975 court of appeals decision, this remedy cannot be used except for practices carried out after the issuance of a cease-and-desist order (still on appeal). |
| **Counteradvertising** | The FTC proposed that the Federal Communications Commission permit advertisements in broadcast media to counteract advertising claims (also that free time be provided under certain conditions). |

*Exhibit 2.7*

Powers of the Federal Trade Commission

environment than to fight the government. If marketers had toned down their hard-hitting advertisements to children, they might have avoided an FTC inquiry altogether.

**Food and Drug Administration (FDA)**
Federal agency charged with enforcing regulations against selling and distributing adulterated, misbranded, or hazardous food and drug products.

The **Food and Drug Administration** (FDA), another powerful agency, is charged with enforcing regulations against selling and distributing adulterated, misbranded, or hazardous food and drug products. The FDA can be a very difficult hurdle for small entrepreneurial firms, as the accompanying box reveals.

## COMPETITIVE FACTORS

*7 Explain the basics of foreign and domestic competition.*

The competitive environment encompasses the number of competitors a firm must face, the relative size of the competitors, and the degree of interdependence within the industry. Management has little control over the competitive environment confronting a firm. Yet the marketing mix, particularly pricing, depends on the type and amount of competition.

### THE ECONOMICS OF COMPETITION

Economists recognize four basic models of competition. These models are mainly based on the number of competitors and the nature of the products produced. Exhibit 2.8 (on page 58) summarizes the characteristics of the four basic models and the key task of the marketing manager within each competitive situation. The type of competition has a great effect on pricing strategies, which are discussed in further detail in Chapter 19.

**monopoly**
Form of economic competition in which one firm controls the output and price of a product for which there are no close substitutes.

At one extreme of economic competition is the **monopoly.** One firm controls the output and price of a product for which there are no close substitutes. In other words, the firm is the industry; there are no direct competitors. Utility companies are the most common form of monopoly in the United States. In addition, a patent can give a company monopoly power for a time. Xerox, for example, held the patent on the dry-paper copying process. Not until the patent expired and competitors entered the marketplace did dry-paper copiers fall significantly in price.

**purely competitive market**
Form of economic competition characterized by a large number of sellers marketing a standardized product to a group of buyers who are well informed about the marketplace.

At the other extreme of the competitive spectrum is pure competition. A **purely competitive market** is characterized by a large number of sellers marketing a standardized product to a group of buyers who are well informed about the marketplace. New competitors can easily enter the marketplace and sell their entire output at the prevailing market price. In a purely competitive market, it would not make sense for one firm to raise the price. A buyer would simply go elsewhere and get the same merchandise at the prevailing market price. Similarly, there would be no reason to advertise, because the pure competitor can sell its entire output at the prevailing market price without advertising. A purely competitive market doesn't exist in the real world. However, some industries closely mirror the model—most notably such agricultural markets as wheat, cotton, soybeans, and corn.

**oligopoly**
Form of economic competition in which a small number of firms dominate the market for a good or service.

**monopolistic competition**
Form of economic competition in which a relatively large number of suppliers offer similar but not identical products.

When a relatively small number of firms dominate the market for a good or service, the industry is an **oligopoly.** Automobile, aircraft, supercomputer, and tire and rubber producers all compete in oligopolistic markets. Oligopolies can also exist at a lower competitive level. If a town in the Arizona desert had only four or five service stations, they would be competing as an oligopoly. Because they have few competitors, the actions of one firm have a direct impact on the others. This interdependence characterizes an oligopoly. The close relationship among firms often leads to collusion and price fixing, which are illegal under federal and state laws. Rather than fix prices, some industries simply follow a price leader. The leader is typically the dominant firm in terms of assets, market share, or geographic coverage. Marketing managers do not have a lot of pricing flexibility in an oligopoly. They must be alert to price changes and quickly match price decreases or lose a significant amount of market share. To further secure a position in the marketplace, marketing managers should stress service, product quality, and other nonprice forms of competition.

**Monopolistic competition** refers to a situation in which a relatively large number of suppliers offer similar but not identical products. Examples include laundries, hair stylists, aspirin or gasoline producers, lawyers, and airlines in major markets. Each firm has a comparatively small percentage of the total market, so each has limited control over market price. Firms attempt to distinguish their offerings through brand names, trademarks, packaging, advertisements, and services. With monopolistic competition, consumers tend to prefer the products of specific firms and, within limits, will pay a higher price. In other words, they tend to think, "I like Prell shampoo

MARKETING AND SMALL BUSINESS

### Inventive Products, Inc.

The Sensor Pad is about as simple as a medical device can get: two sealed plastic sheets with lubricant in between. But Glenda Richardson thinks it probably spared her death from breast cancer. John Withers, a surgeon at the Maui Clinic in Hawaii, says it is one of the most effective weapons to be deployed against breast cancer in years. And Patricia Redmond, a New York radiologist, says it "can absolutely save lives."

Breast cancer took an estimated 46,000 lives in the United States last year and was second among cancers killing women. Early detection is essential in defeating it, and frequent self-examination is essential to that effort. That is where the pad comes in. Its lower sheet clings to the skin while the top sheet floats on a thin layer of liquid silicon, eliminating friction so a finger can explore the contours of an object as small as a grain of salt.

But don't try buying the Sensor Pad in the United States. Although years ago it sailed through government approval processes in Europe and Asia, the U.S. Food and Drug Administration won't let Inventive Products sell it in this country. Grant Wright, the president of Inventive Products, and his father, Earl, the pad's co-inventor, have been fighting for nine years to get clearance for the product. What began as an FDA

*(continued)*

| Type of competition | Number of firms | Type of product | Ease of market entry | Price control | Importance of promotion | Key marketing task |
|---|---|---|---|---|---|---|
| **Monopoly** | One | Unique (no substitute) | Blocked | Complete | Little or none | Maintain blocked entry through public relations, huge advertising expenditures, or other means |
| **Monopolistic competition** | Numerous | Similar | Few | Some | Very important | Maintain differentiated product |
| **Oligopoly** | Few | Similar | Major barriers | Some, with care | Important | Understand competition and react quickly; strive for non-price advantage |
| **Pure competition** | Numerous | Homogeneous | No barriers | None | None | Attempt to lower product and distribution costs |

*Exhibit 2.8*

Types of Economic Competition

because it's a little different. But if the price goes up too much, I know Prell is not that different, so I'll switch to something else." Thus the seller has some control over price—but only within a limited range. If the marketing manager raises prices too high, the company could lose its entire market.

## MARKETING AND SMALL BUSINESS

request for more information has degenerated into a long, debilitating struggle and allegations that the Wrights violated federal law. So frustrated did the Wrights become about the bureaucratic maze that six years ago they started selling the pad to U.S. hospitals without FDA clearance. That move triggered a court battle that they lost in 1992. Now they are back to trying to win FDA blessing for the pad.

But if the dispute isn't resolved soon, Grant Wright says, he will close his Decatur, Illinois, company. It costs about $4,000 a month to operate and has already burned through $356,000 in legal fees. "I'm 33, with a wife and three kids," he says. "I've got to do something with my life."

Wright's struggle, in the eyes of some, is more than just the tale of a small-town entrepreneur's tangle with far-away bureaucrats; it is a study of how the medical-devices industry in the United States copes with the world's most stringent regulatory system. The FDA has a backlog of about 5,000 applications for new medical devices. In a recent year only twelve new medical devices were given premarket approval. The FDA responds that it is the watchdog that guards against unsafe and unhealthy products reaching the market.

Furthermore, the dispute between companies with innovative products and the FDA is a manifestation of the way litigation-driven aversion to risk can stifle innovation in the medical marketplace. "We as a society refuse to take risks and want 100 percent guarantees that our lives are going to be perfect," says Mary Palmore, a Chicago gynecologist.[61]



## COMPETITION FOR MARKET SHARE

As U.S. population growth slows, costs rise, and available resources tighten, firms find they must work harder to maintain their profits and market share regardless of the form of the competitive market. Take, for example, the seemingly staid breakfast cereal market. An avalanche of cereal promotions threatened to bury consumers as Kellogg and General Mills went head to head for a bigger share of the $7.5 billion breakfast cereal market. The two companies sought an advantage by pricing competitively and by bashing each other's products. Boxes of Total Corn Flakes from General Mills proclaimed the product "more nutritious and better-tasting than Kellogg's Corn Flakes." Kellogg countered with streamers on packages of Just Right saying its "taste beats Total." Kellogg spends several hundred million dollars on promotion each year, for one simple

In monopolistic competition, a large number of firms offer similar products. Thus no firm can raise prices much higher than the prices charged by competitors. (*top*) A service-industry example is the quick-copy printing shop; (*bottom*) the hardware store is an example in the consumer goods market.

(*bottom*) © Gabe Palmer/The Stock Market

reason: A single share point, or 1 percent of total sales, means $75 million in revenue.[62]

Smaller firms can often survive in highly competitive markets by generating products of exceptional quality or by offering goods and services that fulfill unique needs. For example, Steiger Tractor Company has become a viable competitor in an old and stable market. The company produces a big articulated tractor, which bends in the middle to make turning easier. Using all four wheels for traction enables it to pull bigger loads. An articulated tractor can cut a farmer's labor costs by as much as 33 percent per acre.

The Steiger tractor example illustrates that, with a good marketing mix, small firms can still compete effectively against the giants. Regardless of company size, the marketing mix—product, distribution, promotion, and price—represents management's tools of competition. Steiger developed a unique product in order to compete. Lexus, AT&T, and IBM have used product quality to gain and hold market share. Coca-Cola, Frito Lay, and 7-Eleven stores use distribution to gain competitive advantage. Firms like Wal-Mart, Toys R Us, and Thrifty Car Rental use price as a primary means of competition. Some companies, like Kraft General Foods and Procter & Gamble, are superior competitors in every aspect of their marketing mix. They have an excellent research staff that enables them to bring out the right products, an efficient distribution system involving thousands of stores and institutions, aggressive pricing, and a very large promotion budget. For example, Kraft General Foods spends over $100 million a year advertising Maxwell House coffee, and Procter & Gamble does the same for Folgers.

## GLOBAL COMPETITION

Both Kraft General Foods and Procter & Gamble are savvy international competitors as well. They each conduct business in over a hundred different nations. Many foreign competitors also consider the United States to be a ripe target market. Thus a U.S. marketing manager can no longer worry about only domestic competitors. In automobiles, textiles, watches, television, steel, and many other areas, foreign competition has been strong. Global competition is discussed in much more detail in Chapter 3.

In the past, foreign firms penetrated U.S. markets by concentrating on price, but today the emphasis has switched to product quality. Nestlé, Sony, Rolls Royce, and Sandoz Pharmaceuticals are noted for quality, not cheap prices.

With the expansion of global marketing, U.S. companies often battle each other in international markets just as intensively as in the domestic market. Consider Hasbro and Mattel toy companies, which have been competing in the United States for years. Hasbro acquired Sindy, a pudgy bike-riding teenager of a doll, from a British maker in 1986. Now Sindy has been transformed into a flashy, champagne-sipping, long-haired blonde. Although Sindy is not sold in the United States, Mattel claims she is now just a pirated version of its Barbie doll. Mattel has won a number of European court orders preventing Hasbro from selling Sindy in Holland, Belgium, France, and Germany. Lawsuits are pending in five other jurisdictions, and proceedings began in the United Kingdom, Sindy's homeland, in 1993. Sindy has warded off Barbie's challenge in Greece and Spain and has an impressive following in Europe and Australia. A British television special even celebrated her birthday.[63]

## LOOKING BACK

Looking back at the story on Merck and its acquisition of Medco, you should now understand that the external environment affects all firms and their marketing mixes. The opening vignette illustrated how competition, technology, and government regulation affect Merck. Other uncontrollable factors also have a profound effect on the firm. Changing attitudes toward personal health (fewer people smoking and more exercising), an aging population, a declining birthrate, and skyrocketing medical costs (an economic factor) have all altered the way Merck does business. Any industry that ignores the external environment is doomed to failure in the long run.

## SUMMARY

**1 Discuss the external environment of marketing, and explain how it affects a firm.** The external marketing environment consists of social, demographic, economic, technological, political and legal, and competitive variables. Marketers generally cannot control the elements of the external environment. Instead, they must understand how the external environment is changing and the impact of change on the target market. Then marketing managers can create a marketing mix to effectively meet the needs of target customers.

**2 Describe the social factors that affect marketing.** Within the external environment, social factors are perhaps the most difficult for marketers to anticipate. Several major social trends are currently shaping marketing strategies. First, people of all ages have a broader range of interests, defying traditional consumer profiles. Second, changing gender roles are bringing more women into the work force and increasing the number of men who shop. Third, a greater number of dual-career families has led to a poverty of time, creating a demand for time-saving goods and services. Fourth, the rapidly expanding singles market is creating a need for different package sizes and promotional messages.

**3 Explain the importance to marketing managers of current demographic trends.** Today, several basic demographic patterns are influencing marketing mixes. Because the U.S. population is growing at a slower rate, marketers can no longer rely on profits from generally expanding markets. Marketers are also faced with increasingly experienced consumers among the younger generations. And because the population

KEY TERMS

*applied research* 50
*baby boomer* 44
*basic research* 49
*component lifestyle* 38
*Consumer Product Safety Commission (CPSC)* 54
*demography* 41
*discretionary income* 42
*environmental management* 35
*Federal Trade Commission (FTC)* 54
*Food and Drug Administration (FDA)* 56
*generation X* 43
*inflation* 48
*monopolistic competition* 57
*monopoly* 56
*oligopoly* 57
*personalized economy* 45
*poverty of time* 38
*purely competitive market* 57
*recession* 49
*target market* 33

is also growing older, marketers are offering more products that appeal to middle-aged and elderly markets.

4 **Identify consumer and marketer reactions to the state of the economy.** Marketers are currently targeting the increasing number of consumers with higher discretionary income by offering higher-quality, higher-priced goods and services. During a time of inflation, marketers generally attempt to maintain level pricing in order to avoid losing customer brand loyalty. During times of recession, many marketers maintain or reduce prices to counter the effects of decreased demand; they also concentrate on increasing production efficiency and improving customer service.

5 **Identify the impact of technology on a firm.** Monitoring new technology is essential to keeping up with competitors in today's marketing environment. For example, in the technologically advanced United States, many companies are losing business to Japanese competitors, who are prospering by concentrating their efforts on developing marketable applications for the latest technological innovations. In the United States, many R&D expenditures go into developing refinements of existing products. U.S. companies must learn to foster and encourage innovation. Without innovation, U.S. companies can't compete in global markets.

6 **Discuss the political and legal environment of marketing.** All marketing activities are subject to state and federal laws and the rulings of regulatory agencies. Marketers are responsible for remaining aware of and abiding by such regulations. Some key federal laws that affect marketing are the Sherman Act, Clayton Act, Federal Trade Commission Act, Robinson-Patman Act, Wheeler-Lea Amendment to the FTC Act, Lanham Act, Celler-Kefauver Antimerger Act, and Hart-Scott-Rodino Act. The Consumer Product Safety Commission, the Federal Trade Commission, and the Food and Drug Administration are the three federal agencies most involved in regulating marketing activities.

7 **Explain the basics of foreign and domestic competition.** The four economic models of competition are monopoly, pure competition, oligopoly, and monopolistic competition. Declining population growth, rising costs, and resource shortages have heightened domestic competition. Yet with an effective marketing mix, small firms continue to be able to compete with the giants. Meanwhile, dwindling international barriers are bringing in more foreign competitors and offering expanding opportunities for U.S. companies abroad.

## Discussion and Writing Questions

1. What is the purpose of environmental scanning? Give an example.
2. Why is adaptability a crucial aspect of marketing management? Think of an example of marketing adaptability that you have observed in a business or industry.
3. ✍ You have been asked to address a local business group on the subject of component lifestyles and the challenges they represent to marketers. Prepare an outline for your talk.
4. Explain the concept of poverty of time and how it shapes marketing strategies. Name some products not discussed in the chapter that were developed in response to the prevailing poverty of time.
5. ✍ You want your firm to start using new technology to improve its production of computer components. As marketing manager of the firm, prepare a report for your boss specifying the potential economic and ecological benefits of the new technology.
6. Which tools of the marketing mix do you think are the focus of (a) McDonald's, (b) mail-order catalog

businesses, (c) General Motors, (d) oil companies, and (e) the airline industry? Which environmental factors do you feel have most greatly influenced them?

7. What is environmental management? Cite an example.

## Application for Small Business

After selling his small computer business, James Munch set out on an eighteen-month sailboat trip with his wife and young children. He had founded the business several years earlier, and it had become a million-dollar enterprise. Now he was looking for a new venture.

While giving his five children reading lessons on board the sailboat—they each had slight reading disabilities—Munch had an inspiration for a new company. He wondered why a computer could not be programmed to drill students in special-education classes who needed repetition to recognize and pronounce new words correctly.

### Questions

1. Refer back to Exhibit 2.1 and explain to James how the external environment could affect his new company.
2. How could each uncontrollable variable influence the new venture?

## CRITICAL THINKING CASE

### Calvin Klein, Inc.

Calvin Klein has come down from his ivory tower—and none too soon. "I had become too isolated," says Klein, conceding that he lost touch with consumers by cloistering himself in his showroom. "When I'm out there in the stores, I learn."

The result: After several years of sluggish sales and occasional losses, Calvin Klein, Inc., is transforming itself into a design, marketing, and licensing company. Having finally conceded that outside manufacturers could make some of its lines more efficiently and profitably, the company found buyers for its jeans and underwear businesses, which will now be converted to licensees.

In the future, Calvin Klein will derive virtually all its income from the royalties it collects from licensees. In a sense, this is a return to the past; when the company introduced its jeans in the late 1970s, it used a licensee to make them. Calvin Klein fragrances—Obsession, Eternity, and Escape—have always been sold under license. And now that the company has licensees for its underwear and, once again, its jeans, it is actively pursuing a licensing deal for its CK menswear and women's wear divisions. If and when buyers are found, only the women's couture collection will remain in-house, as the engine driving the label's image.

By licensing its brand name, Calvin Klein's revenues will fall—but so will its costs, as its licensees assume much of the business's overhead. Licensing also provides a cushion against risk: Royalties are based on sales, not profits, and as long as the businesses grow, so do the royalties.

The restructuring allows Klein, who is 51 years old, and his longtime business partner, Barry Schwartz, also 51, to focus on what they do best: designing and marketing the apparel that others will now produce. A high priority is improving the CK "bridge" collection of lower-priced women's wear. Klein criticized it as "too young-looking" and lacking styles that women could wear to work.

"We've gone through a difficult period," concedes the designer, who has been dubbed "Calvin Clean" by the fashion press for his spare, minimalist fashions. "We're not all the way there yet, but we've developed a real long-term strategy to grow our businesses." Adds Schwartz: "Manufacturing wasn't our forte."

Calvin Klein initially gained fame with his designer jeans, which generated sales as high as $240 million in 1982, when the label was licensed to Puritan Fashions, the jeans manufacturer. But after Calvin Klein bought Puritan in 1983, the company neglected jeans—which at one time accounted for 80 percent of its overall revenues—and by last year jeans sales had shrunk to about $50 million.

New York–based Rio Sportswear bought the jeans division for $35 million and will pay a royalty ranging from 5 to 10 percent to Calvin Klein. Arnold Simone, Rio's president, expects that sales of Calvin Klein jeans can be lifted quickly. Rio, which already produces 1.5 million pairs of jeans a month under labels such as Bill Blass, says manufacturing efficiencies will enable it to lower prices from about $60 a pair to about $45—matching Gap and Levi's brands. "The beautiful part of Klein is that the company is really the best marketer in the industry, with wonderful, sexy, and sophisticated ads," Simone says. Rio will also launch a line of Calvin Klein children's jeans.

Calvin Klein, Inc., is also counting on generating much of its future growth abroad. The company has opened licensed Calvin Klein boutiques in Barcelona, St. Moritz, and Singapore and has formed a partnership with four Japanese companies to create in-store shops and produce more licensed apparel. As for Klein himself, the designer is now preoccupied with what he calls a "breakthrough" concept: a unisex perfume.



### Questions

1. Can a fashion designer dictate to the market what is "really in" at the moment? Is marketing necessary?
2. Would you say that Calvin Klein ignored the external environment in the past? What external factors should the firm be concerned with in the future?
3. How would you describe the competitive structure of the fashion industry?
4. Do you believe that Klein is now making the best use of his time for the company? If not, what should he be doing?

### Reference

Teri Agins, "Shaken by a Series of Business Setbacks, Calvin Klein Inc. Is Redesigning Itself," *The Wall Street Journal*, 21 March 1994, pp. B1, B6.

**VIDEO CASE**

## Life Fitness Company

In 1977, Augie Neato had an idea for combining an exercise bike and a computer. For nine months, Neato hit the road in his motor home trying to sell his idea. During that time, he sold eleven bikes instead of the thousands that he had imagined. Neato decided that the only way to make sales was to get people to try the product first. So he began putting the bikes in health clubs and letting people rent them by the half hour. Once the health club owners saw that customers liked the bike, sales of Neato's company, Life Fitness, began to escalate rapidly.

In 1984 Neato sold the company to Bally Manufacturing, a producer of gaming devices. Bally didn't just provide capital for a growing business; it already owned a chain of 350 health clubs. Those clubs were a captive market for Life Fitness products and a place to test new ideas. Over the next seven years, Life Fitness products were sold to thousands of health clubs around the nation. Bally then restructured and decided Life Fitness no longer fit its strategic plan. Neato jumped at the opportunity to reacquire, with the help of an investment banking group, his idea and products.

Neato noted two basic changes in consumers' fitness behavior in the early 1990s: Membership in health clubs was slowing down, and people were beginning to exercise at home. Baby boomers, the primary target market for health clubs, were experiencing an ever-increasing poverty of time. Neato knew that if he could provide the same quality exercise experience in the home as in the club, he would have a winner.

In 1993 Neato decided to tackle the consumer market. His decision posed a critical challenge for Life Fitness Company: How could it expand into the consumer market without losing market share in the professional market? Neato knew that he could capitalize on the well-known Life Fitness name. One immediate problem, however, was balancing the quality level of the professional Life Fitness equipment with the price that individual consumers were willing to pay.

Life Fitness's new direction is paying off. Consumer products accounted for 25 percent of company sales in 1994. Life Fitness expects that consumer products will make up 66 percent of total sales by 1999.

### Questions

1. Explain how Life Fitness could capitalize on a poverty of time.
2. What other external variables might affect Life Fitness Company?
3. Describe the target market for Life Fitness consumer products.
4. How might the marketing mixes for Life Fitness consumer products and professional products differ?

### Reference

CNBC, 1994.

# CHAPTER 3

# DEVELOPING A GLOBAL VISION

## LEARNING OBJECTIVES

*After studying this chapter, you should be able to*

1 *Discuss the importance of global marketing.*

2 *Discuss the impact of multinational firms on the world economy.*

3 *Describe the external environment facing global marketers.*

4 *Identify the various ways of entering the global marketplace.*

5 *List the basic elements involved in developing a global marketing mix.*

Terry S. Prindiville gazed at the women jammed into a bustling shop in Shanghai and saw opportunity. All this tumult, the JCPenney executive thought, to buy lingerie that his company could offer at lower prices and higher quality. JCPenney isn't selling goods in China yet, but Prindiville and his staff are masterminding an ambitious expansion that is transforming the company into a major international retailer.

Already, JCPenney stores are under construction in Mexico. The company added nearly a million square feet of retail space in Japan in 1995 by offering its private-label apparel in 300 department stores owned by Aoyama Trading Co., Japan's largest retailer of men's suits. JCPenney has been scouting sites in Chile after surveys showed that many Chileans are so eager to buy American goods that they regularly fly to the United States to shop. Licensed JCPenney shops are racking up impressive sales in the United Arab Emirates and Singapore. The company is talking with potential licensees, including one in Greece and another in Portugal that is already selling JCPenney private-label goods. JCPenney is considering anchoring a new regional mall in Taiwan. It is looking into Thailand and Indonesia. It offers catalogs in Iceland, Brazil, and Russia and is translating a trimmed-down catalog into Spanish to tap the Latin American market.

JCPenney has ventured into the international marketplace before, only to back out later. The collapse of the Soviet Union after the abortive coup against Mikhail Gorbachev scuttled one joint venture. A year of negotiations to buy a retail chain in Hungary failed after the government raised the price repeatedly. Chinese tariffs remain a barrier. To develop malls to its specifications in Mexico, JCPenney had to persuade Mexican developers to work with U.S. developers.

A failed acquisition of retail chains in Italy and Belgium in the late 1970s further undermined the company's confidence. In Belgium, JCPenney's plan to build giant stores was thwarted by the local equivalent of zoning boards—stacked with competing merchants. JCPenney was left with small, outdated stores in congested downtown areas, and competitors built spacious suburban stores. "There was no way we could grow the business," says Narina Vaira, a vice president of JCPenney's international division. JCPenney also had assumed it could turn the chains around by slashing bloated payrolls and raising productivity, but labor laws in both countries made layoffs prohibitively expensive and time-consuming.

Despite the problems it had encountered before, JCPenney decided to reenter the international market in 1990. But this time, the company wouldn't buy existing retail chains; in fact, it would avoid buying property at all. It would link up with local partners who would know, for example, that Chilean men consider short pants suitable only for boys and that Abu Dhabi women, although they wear full-length robes outdoors, like party dresses. And it would tailor its retailing to each country while banking on its strong suits: private labels and merchandise presentation. As a result, JCPenney insisted that Liwa Trading, a licensee in Dubai, send people to Dallas to learn the retailer's merchandising, training, and accounting methods. JCPenney's initial list of thirty promising countries was whittled to twenty after its executives gauged their political and economic stability (which eliminated much of Eastern Europe), their willingness to allow the repatriation of profits, and their economic growth and demographics.

Eventually, the company settled on four fundamental strategies:

- In "understored" countries where real estate was affordable, laws allowed foreign ownership, and labor and construction regulations wouldn't hamstring expansion, JCPenney would open and operate stores itself.
- In more saturated markets or where regulations or other problems make it too tough to run company-owned stores, the company would license local retailers to operate JCPenney Collection stores, which sell its branded apparel and other soft goods.
- In still tougher markets, such as Singapore and Japan, where high property costs and regulations make it almost impossible to build large stores, JCPenney would license other retailers to operate in-store shops selling specific brands, such as the Hunt Club shop in Robinson's Department Store in Singapore.
- In places with strong consumer demand but insurmountable barriers, JCPenney would sell through catalogs, usually distributing goods through a third party that would take orders, buy the goods from JCPenney in the United States, and ship them.[1]

Why are international markets becoming increasingly important to U.S. companies like JCPenney? Is globalization the wave of the future in international marketing? When should domestic and global marketing mixes be significantly different? These are some of the issues addressed in Chapter 3.

1 *Discuss the importance of global marketing.*

**global marketing**
Use of a global vision to effectively market goods and services across national boundaries.

**global vision**
Ability to recognize and react to international marketing opportunities, awareness of threats from foreign competitors in all markets, and effective use of international distribution networks.

## THE REWARDS OF GLOBAL MARKETING

Today, global revolutions are underway in many areas of our lives: management, politics, communications, technology. The word *global* has assumed a new meaning, referring to a boundless mobility and competition in social, business, and intellectual arenas. No longer just an option, **global marketing** (marketing to target markets throughout the world) has become an imperative for business.

U.S. managers must develop a global vision not only to recognize and react to international marketing opportunities but also to remain competitive at home. Often a U.S. firm's toughest domestic competition comes from foreign companies. Moreover, a global vision enables a manager to understand that customer and distribution networks operate worldwide, blurring geographic and political barriers and making them increasingly irrelevant to business decisions.[2] In summary, having **global vision** means recognizing and reacting to international marketing opportunities, being aware of threats from foreign competitors in all markets, and effectively using international distribution networks.

Over the past two decades, world trade has climbed from $200 billion a year to $4 trillion. Countries and companies that were never considered major players in global marketing are now important, some of them showing great skill.

Today, marketers face many challenges to their customary practices. Product development costs are rising, the life of products is getting shorter, and new technology is spreading around the world faster than ever. But marketing winners relish the pace of change instead of fearing it.

An excellent example of a company with global vision is Whirlpool Corporation, headquartered in Benton Harbor, Michigan. Whirlpool recently purchased the remaining interest in a joint venture it had formed with the Major Appliance Division of Philips, which is headquartered in Eindhoven, Holland. The administrative offices of Whirlpool Europe are in Comerio, Italy. On the twelve-person management committee sit managers from Sweden, Holland, Italy, the United States, India, South Africa, and Belgium. Managers from different cultures help companies refine their global vision.

Global vision is equally apparent at the top of other leading companies. For instance, IBM prides itself on having five different nationalities represented among its highest officers and three among its outside directors. Four nationalities are represented on Unilever's board; three on the board of Shell Oil. Sony America named as its president and chief operating officer Ron Sommer, who was born in Israel, raised in Austria, and carries a German passport.

Adopting a global vision can be very lucrative for a company. Gillette, for example, gets about two-thirds of its revenue from its international division. About 70 percent of General Motors' profits come from operations outside the United States.[3] Similarly, Colgate-Palmolive's success in international markets has often helped offset its weakness in its domestic market.[4] The corporate strategies and major brands of R.J. Reynolds are also global. Lester Pullen, the CEO of R.J. Reynolds, notes, "In perhaps ten years it may be virtually impossible to rise to the top in any major American business without international experience."[5]

Global marketing is not a one-way street, whereby only U.S. companies sell their wares and services throughout the world. Foreign competition in the domestic market used to be relatively rare but now is found in almost every industry. In fact, in many industries the United States has lost significant market share to imported products. In the last ten years, the percentage of machine tools imported from other countries grew from 23 percent to 46 percent.[6] In electronics, cameras, automobiles, fine china, tractors, leather goods, and a host of other consumer and industrial products, U.S. companies must struggle at home to maintain their market shares against foreign competitors.

In personal computers, American companies have achieved a hollow victory. Their share of the global computer market increased from 59 percent in 1985 to 71 percent in 1993. Yet computers produced in the United States increasingly come with peripherals—disk drives, printers, monitors, and flat-screen displays—imported from Japan and other parts of Asia. The United States imported $16 billion more computer peripherals from Asia than it exported in 1994.[7]

## THE IMPORTANCE OF GLOBAL MARKETING TO THE UNITED STATES

Many countries depend more on international commerce than the United States does. For example, France, Great Britain, and Germany all derive more than 19 percent of their gross domestic product from world trade, compared to about 11 percent for the United States.[8] Nevertheless, the impact of international business on the U.S. economy is still impressive:

- The United States exports about a fifth of its industrial production and a third of its farm products.[9]
- One of every sixteen jobs in the United States is directly or indirectly supported by exports.
- U.S. businesses export over $300 billion in goods to foreign countries every year, and almost a third of U.S. corporate profits is derived from our international trade and foreign investment.
- The United States is the world's leading exporter of grain, selling more than $12 billion of this product a year to foreign countries, or about one-third of all agricultural exports.[10]

The United States ships more than three times as much grain as the next biggest exporter, according to the World Resources Institute. U.S. grain is shipped around the world to both developed and developing nations.

© Tony Stone Images/Andy Sacks

- Chemicals, office machinery and computers, automobiles, aircraft, and electrical machinery make up almost half of all nonagricultural exports.

These statistics might seem to imply that practically every business in the United States is selling its wares throughout the world, but nothing could be further from the truth. About 85 percent of all U.S. exports of manufactured goods are shipped by 250 companies; less than 10 percent of all manufacturing businesses, or around 25,000 companies, export their goods on a regular basis. Most small and medium-size firms are essentially nonparticipants in global trade and marketing. Only the very large multinational companies have seriously attempted to compete worldwide. Fortunately, more of the smaller companies now are aggressively pursuing international markets.

With the proper manufacturing processes and superior products, U.S. companies can be successful against foreign competition. One tool-making company, Giddings and Lewis, watched as foreign competition intensified in the United States, eventually capturing nearly half the market. To remain competitive, the company switched to a more flexible manufacturing system. It then saw its sales increase by 38 percent.[11] Another company, Fusion Systems, makes industrial equipment used to produce a variety of goods, including optical fibers, automobile parts, and semiconductor chips. The company prospered in the Japanese market, largely because it produces superior products. The Japanese, one of Fusion's managers acknowledges, are the world's most demanding customers. But if provided with the best product, they will buy it. Donald Spero, president of Fusion, adds, "Our business is market-driven. If we are unable to sell to the leading customers, then we're not really in business."[12]

Where U.S. firms have always been very successful compared to foreign companies is in the area of services. More than 70 percent of U.S. output consists of services rather than goods, and services are effectively insulated from international competition because they are hard to transport. Services account for only about 20 percent of U.S. trade.[13] Yet the trade surplus (exports minus imports) in services grew nearly fivefold between 1981 and 1993, to $56 billion.[14] U.S. airlines, fast-food chains, software firms, and financial service organizations all help to build our services trade surplus. For instance, U.S. companies, led by Microsoft, have three-fourths of the world's software business, compared with only 20 percent for all of Europe and a mere 4.3 percent for Japan.[15] Merrill Lynch, the first U.S. securities firm allowed to operate in China, already is doing about $4 billion a year in business there.

## THE BALANCE OF TRADE PROBLEM

**balance of trade**
Difference between the value of a country's exports and the value of its imports during a certain time.

The more U.S. firms export their wares, the better our **balance of trade**—which is the difference between the value of a country's exports and the value of its imports during a certain time. A country that exports more goods or services than it imports is said to have a favorable balance of trade; a country that imports more than it exports is said to have an unfavorable balance of trade.

**trade deficit**
Excess of imports over exports.

Although U.S. exports have been booming, we still import more than we export. We have had an unfavorable balance of trade throughout the past decade. In 1993 the United States had a **trade deficit** (an excess of imports over exports) of over $100 billion. When imports exceed exports, more money flows out of the country than into it. As long as we continue to buy more goods from abroad than we sell abroad, we will have a trade deficit and an unfavorable balance of trade.

**balance of payments**
Difference between a country's total payments to other countries and its total receipts from other countries.

The difference between a country's total payments to other countries and its total receipts from other countries is its **balance of payments**. This figure includes the balance of trade and then some. It includes imports and exports (balance of trade), long-term investments in overseas plants and equipment, government loans to and from other countries, gifts and foreign aid, military expenditures made in other countries, and money deposits in and withdrawals from foreign banks.

From the beginning of this century until 1970, the United States had a favorable balance of trade. But in the other areas that make up the balance of payments, U.S. payments have long exceeded receipts, mainly because of the large U.S. military presence abroad. Hence, in almost every year since 1950, the United States has had an unfavorable balance of payments. And since 1970, both the balance of payments and the balance of trade have been unfavorable.

*2 Discuss the impact of multinational firms on the world economy.*

## MULTINATIONAL FIRMS

**multinational corporation (MNC)**
Company that moves resources, goods, services, and skills across national boundaries without regard to the country in which the headquarters is located.

The United States has a number of large companies that are global marketers. Many of them have been very successful. A company that is heavily engaged in international trade, beyond exporting and importing, is called a **multinational corporation** (MNC). Multinational corporations move resources, goods, services, and skills across national boundaries without regard to the country in which the headquarters is located. The leading multinational firms in the world are listed in Exhibit 3.1.

A multinational corporation is more than a business entity, as the following paragraph explains:

> The multinational corporation is, among other things, a private "government," often richer in assets and more populous in stockholders and employees than are some of the nation-states in which it carries on business. It is simultaneously a "citizen" of several nation-states, owing obedience to their laws and paying them taxes, yet having its own objectives and being responsive to a management located in a foreign nation. Small wonder that some critics see in it an irresponsible instrument of private economic power or of economic "imperialism" by its home country. Others view it as an international carrier of advanced management science and technology, an agent for the global transmission of cultures bringing closer the day when a common set of ideals will unite mankind.[16]

Many multinational corporations are enormous. For example, the sales of both Exxon and General Motors are larger than the gross domestic product of all but twenty-two nations in the world. A multinational company may have several worldwide headquarters, depending on where certain markets or technologies are. Britain's APV, a maker of food-processing equipment, has a different headquarters for each of its worldwide businesses. Hewlett-Packard moved the headquarters of its personal computer business from the United States to Grenoble, France. Siemens A.G., Germany's electronics giant, is relocating its medical electronics division headquarters from Germany to Chicago. Honda is planning to move the worldwide headquarters for its power-products division to Atlanta, Georgia. ABB Asea Brown Boveri, the European electrical engineering giant based in Zurich, Switzerland, groups its thousands of products and services into fifty or so business areas. Each is run by a leadership team that crafts global business strategy, sets product development priorities, and decides where to make its products. None of the teams work out of Zurich headquarters; they are scattered around the world. Leadership for power transformers is based in Germany, electric drives in Finland, process automation in the United States.[17]

*Exhibit 3.1*

The World's Largest Multinational Firms, by Industry

Source: "Biggest Companies in the World by Industry," *Fortune Global 500,* 25 July 1994, p. 142. 

| Industry | Company | Country | Company sales (in millions) |
|---|---|---|---|
| Aerospace | Boeing | U.S. | $25,285 |
| Apparel | Levi Strauss | U.S. | 5,892 |
| Beverages | PepsiCo | U.S. | 25,021 |
| Building materials, glass | Saint-Gobain | France | 12,630 |
| Chemicals | DuPont | U.S. | 32,621 |
| Computers, office equipment | IBM | U.S. | 62,716 |
| Electronics, electrical equipment | Hitachi | Japan | 68,582 |
| Food | Philip Morris | U.S. | 50,621 |
| Forest and paper products | International Paper | U.S. | 13,685 |
| Industrial and farm equipment | Mitsubishi Heavy Industries | Japan | 25,804 |
| Jewelry, silverware | Citizen Watch | Japan | 3,501 |
| Metal products | Pechiney | France | 11,127 |
| Metals | IRI | Italy | 50,488 |
| Mining, crude-oil production | Ruhrkohle | Germany | 14,155 |
| Motor vehicles and parts | General Motors | U.S. | 133,622 |
| Petroleum refining | Exxon | U.S. | 97,825 |
| Pharmaceuticals | Johnson & Johnson | U.S. | 14,138 |
| Publishing, printing | Bertelsmann | Germany | 10,957 |
| Rubber and plastic products | Bridgestone | Japan | 14,377 |
| Scientific, photographic, and control equipment | Eastman Kodak | U.S. | 20,059 |
| Soaps, cosmetics | Procter & Gamble | U.S. | 30,433 |
| Textiles | Toray Industries | Japan | 8,193 |
| Tobacco | RJR Nabisco Holdings | U.S. | 15,104 |
| Toys, sporting goods | Nintendo | Japan | 4,500 |
| Transportation | Hyundai Heavy Industries | South Korea | 6,735 |

### THE MULTINATIONAL ADVANTAGE

Large multinationals have several advantages over other companies. For instance, multinationals can often overcome trade problems. Taiwan and South Korea have long had an embargo against Japanese cars for political reasons and to help domestic carmakers. Yet Honda USA, a Japanese-owned company based in the United States, sends Accords to Taiwan and Korea. Another example is Germany's BASF, a major chemical and drug manufacturer. Its biotechnology research at home is challenged by the environmentally conscious Green movement. So BASF moved its cancer and immune-system research to Cambridge, Massachusetts.

Another advantage for multinationals is their ability to sidestep regulatory problems. U.S. drugmaker SmithKline and Britain's Beecham decided to merge in part so they could avoid licensing and regulatory hassles in their largest markets. The merged company can say it's an insider in both Europe and the United States. "When we go to Brussels, we're a member state [of the European Community]," one executive explains. "And when we go to Washington, we're an American company."[18]

Multinationals can also shift production from one plant to another as market conditions change. When European demand for a certain solvent declined, Dow Chemical instructed its German plant to switch to manufacturing a chemical that had been imported from Louisiana and Texas. Computer models help Dow make decisions like these so it can run its plants more efficiently and keep costs down.

Multinationals can also tap new technology from around the world. Xerox has introduced some eighty different office copiers in the United States that were designed and built by Fuji Xerox, its joint venture with a Japanese company. Versions of the superconcentrated detergent that Procter & Gamble first formulated in Japan in response to a rival's product are now being sold under the Ariel brand name in Europe and being tested under the Cheer and Tide labels in the United States. Also consider Otis Elevator's development of the Elevonic 411, an elevator that is programmed to send more cars to floors where demand is high. It was developed by six research centers in five countries. Otis's group in Farmington, Connecticut, handled the systems integration; a Japanese group designed the special motor drives that make the elevators ride smoothly; a French group perfected the door systems; a German group handled the electronics; and a Spanish group took care of the small-geared components. Otis says the international effort saved more than $10 million in design costs and cut the process from four years to two.

Finally, multinationals can often save a lot in labor costs, even in highly unionized countries. For example, Xerox started moving copier-rebuilding work to Mexico, where wages are much lower. Its union in Rochester, New York, objected because it saw that members' jobs were at risk. Eventually the union agreed to change work styles and to improve productivity to keep the jobs at home. Sometimes, however, the potential to save on labor costs can create major ethical dilemmas for multinationals, as the Ethics in Marketing story explains.

ETHICS IN MARKETING

**A Matter of Human Rights or of Profits?**

Levi Strauss & Company has decided to cut its ties to China because of what it calls "pervasive human rights violations" there. Levi Strauss says it will gradually withdraw about $40 million worth of production contracts with about thirty Chinese companies. The apparel marketer has annually bought about 5 million shirts and pairs of pants from the Chinese, representing about 2 percent of the company's total output.

Although there is a certain symbolism in the retreat of a major marketer whose jeans are so closely linked with Yankee capitalism and the Western lifestyle, the money involved is not substantial, and Levi Strauss has made no direct investments in China. Most experts downplay the significance of the decision, questioning whether Levi Strauss is really making a major sacrifice or just looking for some good public relations.

"This was a pure business decision, related to bottom-line profitability," says Chin-Ning Chu, president of Asian Marketing Consultants, San Francisco. "Levi can give any reason they want to for the decision, and tying it to human rights is good PR image, but I don't think that's what's really going on." The company simply found alternative production markets in places like Thailand and Southeast Asia that provide better profit margins, according to Chu.

Levi Strauss said the decision was based on guidelines that the company adopted in 1992 to govern its dealings in the estimated fifty foreign countries in which it makes or markets clothing. The guidelines include a provision stipulating that the company should not start or renew contracts in countries with pervasive violations of human rights. Burma and China were the only two countries where the company found human rights policies disturbing enough to warrant withdrawal. Levi Strauss pulled out of Burma last year. In China's case the human rights violations include the export of goods made with forced prison

## GLOBAL MARKETING STANDARDIZATION

Traditionally, marketing-oriented multinational corporations have operated somewhat differently in each country. They use a strategy of providing different product features, packaging, advertising, and so on. However, Ted Levitt, a Harvard professor, described a trend toward what he referred to as "global marketing," with a slightly different meaning.[20] He contended that communication and technology have made the world smaller, so that almost everyone everywhere wants all the things they have heard about, seen, or experienced. Thus he saw the emergence of global markets for standardized consumer products on a huge scale, as opposed to segmented foreign markets with different products. In this book, global marketing is defined as individuals and organizations using a global vision to effectively market goods and services across national boundaries. To make the distinction, we can refer to Levitt's notion as **global marketing standardization.**

**global marketing standardization**
Production of uniform products that can be sold the same way all over the world.

Global marketing standardization presumes that the markets throughout the world are becoming more alike. Firms practicing global marketing standardization produce "globally standardized products" to be sold the same way all over the world. Uniform production should enable companies to lower production and marketing costs and increase profits. However, research indicates that superior sales and profits do not necessarily follow from global standardization.[21]

Levitt cited Coca-Cola, Colgate-Palmolive, and McDonald's as successful global marketers. However, Levitt's critics point out that the success of these three companies is really based on variation, not on offering the same product everywhere. McDonald's, for example, changes its salad dressings for French tastes and sells beer and mineral water in its restaurants there. It also offers different products to suit tastes in Germany (where it offers beer) as well as in Japan (where it offers sake). Also, the fact that Coca-Cola and Colgate-Palmolive sell some of their products in more than 160 countries does not signify that they have adopted a high degree of standardization for all their products globally. Only three Coca-Cola brands are standardized, and one of them, Sprite, has a different formulation in Japan. Some Colgate-Palmolive products are marketed in just a few countries. Axion paste dishwashing detergent, for example, was formulated for developing countries, and La Croix Plus detergent was custom-made for the French market. Colgate toothpaste is marketed the same way globally, although its advanced Gum Protection Formula is used in only twenty-seven nations.

Nevertheless, some multinational corporations are moving toward a degree of global marketing standardization. Nike, for example, designed a standardized global marketing plan for its Air 180 shoes. Their advanced air cushioning system is visible through the shoe's clear midsole. For greater adaptability, the television commercials for the shoes are not narrated. Instead, the commercials use title cards, translated into various languages, to identify Nike and promote the worldwide availability of the Air 180 model. Ads use the company's "Just do it" theme. Similarly, Eastman Kodak has launched a world brand of blank tapes

ETHICS IN MARKETING

labor and the imprisonment of union organizers and pro-democracy leaders.

Levi Strauss expects it will need several years to pull out of China, and the company has set no deadline. It is developing a plan "to make this orderly withdrawal and place the production in other locations." Levi Strauss will continue to buy fabric from Chinese manufacturers. Those contracts are also subject to the new guidelines, but Linda Butler, manager of corporate communications, says the company is still "working its way down the supply chain" and has not reviewed the contracts. Butler says the company will continue to monitor the situation and conduct biannual reviews.

Richard Brecher, director of business advisory services for the U.S.-China Business Council, sees Levi Strauss's pullout as an isolated incident. "I don't see broad support of it." Furthermore, says Brecher, by withdrawing from the market, Levi Strauss "is abdicating any role they might play in economic improvement or reform." According to Brecher, well-run companies can serve as good role models for the Chinese: "In their own companies, they operate under very strong requirements that don't discriminate against race, ethnic, or political backgrounds, that pay fairly, and that don't allow them to use prison or forced labor." Brecher says Levi Strauss could be missing a major opportunity: "The Chinese are very fashion-conscious and Levi is a very important brand name."[19]

Do you agree with Levi Strauss's decision to pull out of China? Is the decision simply a public relations ploy, given the fact that the company doesn't own any manufacturing facilities there? If it is a public relations ploy, is it a good one? Would you pay more for Levi's jeans knowing that the manufacturer doesn't deal with countries that violate human rights? Do you agree with the argument that by staying in China, Levi Strauss can help show other Chinese enterprises how to treat workers fairly? In addition, China is a market with 1.2 billion people. Doesn't Levi Strauss have an obligation to its stockholders to maximize its profits?

American Marketing Association

A McDonald's restaurant anywhere in the world has recognizable features. But it may offer some variations to suit the local market, as at this outlet in Beijing.

H. Zeng/Agence-Chine Nouvelle/SIPA-Press

for videocassette recorders. Procter & Gamble calls its new philosophy "global planning." The idea is to determine which product modifications are necessary from country to country while trying to minimize those modifications. P&G has at least four products that are marketed similarly in most parts of the world: Camay soap, Crest toothpaste, Head and Shoulders shampoo, and Pampers diapers. However, the smell of Camay, the flavor of Crest, and the formula of Head and Shoulders, as well as the advertising, vary from country to country.

3 *Describe the external environment facing global marketers.*

## THE EXTERNAL ENVIRONMENT FACING GLOBAL MARKETERS

A global marketer or a firm considering global marketing faces problems, many due to the external environment. Many of the same environmental factors that operate in the domestic market also exist internationally. They include culture, economic and technological development, political structure, demographic makeup, and natural resources.

### CULTURE

Central to any society is the common set of values shared by its citizens that determine what is socially acceptable. Culture underlies the family, the educational system, religion, and the social class system. The network of social organizations generates overlapping roles and status positions. These values and roles have a tremendous effect on people's preferences and thus on marketers' options. Swiss homemakers, for example, consider the performance of household chores central to the homemaking role and find it difficult to accept the idea of labor-saving machines or commercial products. They reject commercial appeals emphasizing the time and effort saved in performing household tasks.

Exhibit 3.2 shows how culture can influence one's view of the world. It is taken from a Japanese Airline route map. To people from the United States, our country

*Exhibit 3.2*

Japanese View of North America

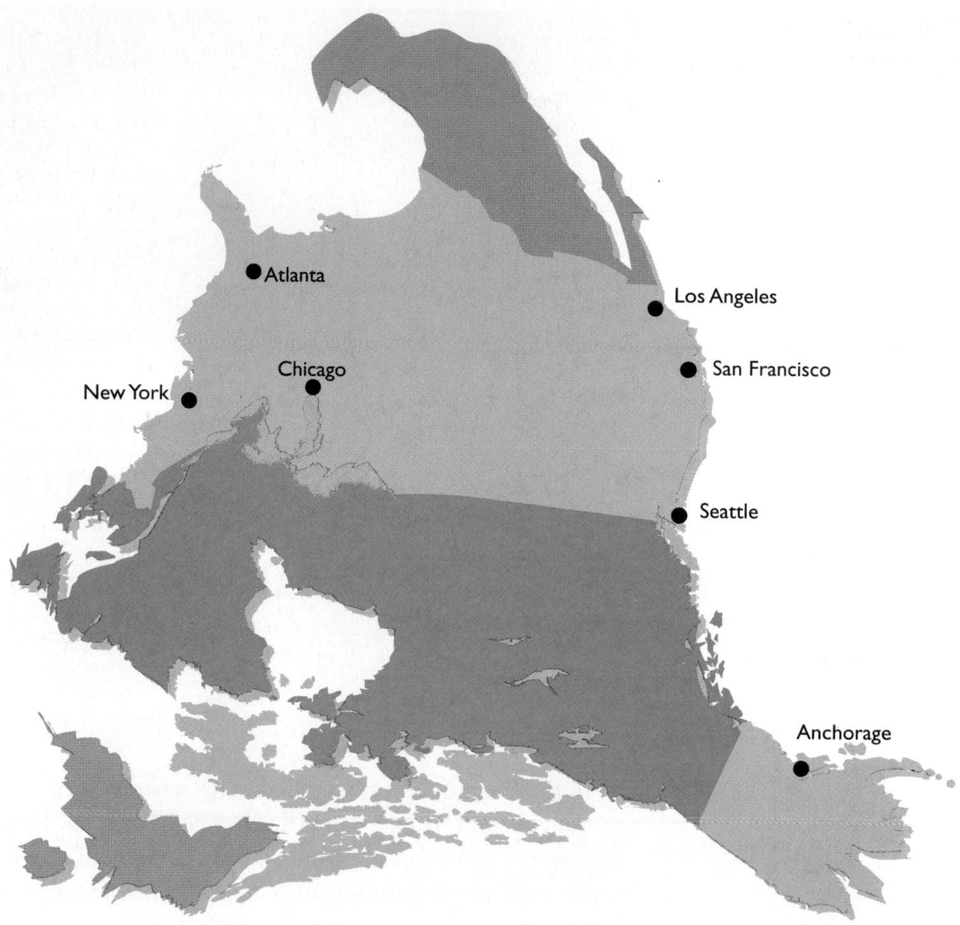


looks upside down and backward on the map. But the map accurately reflects the Japanese view of the world. From a viewpoint on the other side of the globe, Japan would be in the center and right side up.

Language is another important aspect of culture. Marketers must take care in translating product names, slogans, and promotional messages so as not to convey the wrong meaning. For example, when Coca-Cola reentered China in 1979, it discovered that the literal representation of Coca-Cola in Chinese characters means "bite the wax tadpole." With the help of language specialists, the company substituted new characters that sound like Coca-Cola but mean "can happy, mouth happy."[22] Likewise, a Mexican magazine promotion for a U.S.-brand shirt carried a message stating the opposite of what it was intended to communicate. Instead of reading "When I used this shirt, I felt good," the advertisement translated into "Until I used this shirt, I felt good."[23]

Each country has its own customs and traditions that determine business practices and influence negotiations with foreign customers. In many countries, personal relationships are more important than financial considerations. For instance, skipping social engagements in Mexico may lead to lost sales. Negotiations in Japan often include long evenings of dining, drinking, and entertaining, and only after a close personal relationship has been formed do business negotiations begin. The importance of punctuality also varies from culture to culture. Most U.S. businesspeople consider punctuality at meetings to be a sign of respect and are often frustrated by Latin Americans, who consider time relatively less important.

*Exhibit 3.3*

Important Cultural Considerations in International Marketing

| Differences in these cultural factors . . . | . . . Affect values and habits relating to: |
|---|---|
| Assumptions and attitudes | Time<br>One's proper purpose in life<br>The future<br>This life versus the hereafter<br>Duty and responsibility |
| Personal beliefs and aspirations | Right and wrong<br>Sources of pride<br>Sources of fear and concern<br>Extent of one's hopes<br>Individual versus society |
| Interpersonal relationships | Source of authority<br>Care or empathy for others<br>Importance of family obligations<br>Objects of loyalty<br>Tolerance for personal differences |
| Social structure | Interclass mobility<br>Class or caste systems<br>Urban-village-farm origins<br>Determinants of status |

In the United States, we also prefer written contracts. If a party violates the terms of the contract, legal actions are frequently taken. However, in China, where trust is important to business dealings, oral agreements mean more. The written contract represents the beginning of a negotiation process, and many changes are to be expected.

Even if English is spoken during negotiations, communication problems still occur. For instance, the Japanese may say yes or maybe when they really mean no, to avoid making their foreign counterparts lose face and feel embarrassed. When the Taiwanese shake their heads back and forth they mean yes, not no.

Businesspeople from the United States are learning that global success requires patience and cultural understanding. Consider the following:

> Recently, as finishing touches were being added to Motorola Inc.'s $400 million Silicon Harbor complex in Hong Kong, Tam Chung Ding summoned his favorite geomancer, or diviner. Tam, president of Motorola's Asia-Pacific semiconductor division, wanted the 87-year-old soothsayer to double-check the new facility's *feng shui*—literally, its wind and water—for good luck. Yes, the omens were favorable. Built on reclaimed land, the project had water—a symbol of wealth—on three sides and was ringed by mountains—a source of power. . . . "This office has about the best *feng shui* in Hong Kong," Tam boasts.[24]

Exhibit 3.3 summarizes some important cultural considerations; several additional examples are discussed in this chapter's section on marketing mix. Successful multinational marketers understand that employees must learn to appreciate these differences among cultures. Motorola, for example, has opened a special center for cultural training at its headquarters in Schaumburg, Illinois. Many firms are hiring "cultural consultants," such as Bob Waisfisz of The Hague, Netherlands, to speak to their employees. Waisfisz often uses humor in his presentations. He notes, for example, that "in Germany, everything is forbidden unless it's allowed. In Britain, everything is allowed unless it's forbidden. And in France, everything is allowed even if it's forbidden."[25]

Economic development differs in Mexico, an industrializing society (represented *left* by a street market in Oaxaca), and Canada, a fully industrialized society (represented *right* by the skyscrapers of downtown Toronto). The North American Free Trade Agreement was proposed to link both economies with that of the United States.



## ECONOMIC AND TECHNOLOGICAL DEVELOPMENT

A second major factor in the external environment facing the global marketer is the level of economic development in the countries where it operates. In general, complex and sophisticated industries are found in developed countries, and more basic industries are found in less-developed nations. Yet exceptions do exist. For example, a government of a less-developed nation may buy complex facilities to improve its status with the local population, even though it has neither the skills to operate the machinery nor the market to dispose of the goods.

To appreciate marketing opportunities (or lack of them), it is helpful to examine the five stages of economic growth and technological development: traditional society, preindustrial society, takeoff economy, industrializing society, and fully industrialized society.

### The Traditional Society

**traditional society**
Largely agricultural society, with a social structure and value system that provide little opportunity for upward mobility.

Countries in the traditional stage are in the earliest phase of development. **A traditional society** is largely agricultural, with a social structure and value system that provide little opportunity for upward mobility. It is custom-bound, and its economy typically operates at the subsistence level because of backward or primitive technology. The culture may be highly stable, and economic growth may not get started without a powerful disruptive force. Therefore, to introduce single units of technology into such a country is probably wasted effort. In Ghana, for instance, a tollway sixteen miles long and six lanes wide, intended to modernize distribution, does not connect to any city or village or other road. Similarly, a modern fertilizer plant in India was built but not used because the distribution system was inadequate to market the fertilizer. Clearly, these projects were not integrated into the culture.

### The Preindustrial Society

**preindustrial society**
Society characterized by economic and social change and the emergence of a rising middle class with an entrepreneurial spirit.

The second stage of economic development, the **preindustrial society**, involves economic and social change and the emergence of a middle class with an entrepreneurial spirit. Nationalism may begin to rise, along with restrictions on multinational organizations. Countries like North Korea and Uganda are in this stage. Effective marketing in these countries is very difficult because they lack the modern distribution and communication systems that U.S. marketers often take for granted. Peru, for example, did not establish a television network until 1975.

## The Takeoff Economy

**takeoff economy**
Period of transition from a developing to a developed nation, during which new industries arise.

The **takeoff economy** is the period of transition from a developing to a developed nation. New industries arise, and a generally healthy social and political climate emerges. Thailand, Malaysia, and Vietnam have entered the takeoff stage. For example, in recent years Thailand has had one of the fastest rates of economic growth in the world. Investors from Japan, Taiwan, and the United States are bringing capital and new technology to Thailand. Consumer markets are beginning to emerge among the more prosperous Thais, creating opportunities for foreign companies. In an effort to develop its economy, Vietnam now offers large tax breaks to foreign investors who promise jobs. Gold Medal Footware, headquartered in Taiwan, now employs 500 young workers in Danang and hopes to increase the number to 2,500.[26] The firm chose Vietnam because of multiple tax breaks from the Vietnamese government.

## The Industrializing Society

**industrializing society**
Society characterized by the spread of technology to most sectors of the economy.

The fourth phase of economic development is the **industrializing society.** During this era, technology spreads from sectors of the economy that powered the takeoff to the rest of the nation. Mexico, China, and Brazil are among the nations in this phase of development.

Countries in the industrializing stage begin to produce capital goods and consumer durable products. Demands for parts and materials create many secondary industries, such as tires for automobiles, motors for refrigerators, and electronic components. These industries also foster economic growth. As a result, a large middle class begins to emerge, and the demand for luxuries and services grows.

One of the fastest-growing economies in the world today (about 10 percent per year) is China.[27] A population of 1.2 billion is producing a gross domestic product of over $1.2 trillion a year.[28] This new industrial giant will be the world's largest manufacturing zone, the largest market for such key industries as telecommunications and aerospace, and one of the largest users of capital. Although China will be an economic superpower in size, it won't compete as directly with U.S. or European technology-based industries as Japan does. Instead, its strengths will be mostly light manufacturing and low-tech industries.

A loosening of government controls to allow private ownership, along with city and provincial ownership, has been the key to economic growth in China. Old-style nationally owned companies simply can't compete. Consider the case of two refrigerator companies. In the southern city of Rongqi, the Rongsheng Refrigerator Factory is a model of the locally owned factories that are quietly reaching Western standards of quality. As a result, Rongsheng's 3,500 workers are struggling to fill orders for China's most popular brand. The glistening complex, which has a modern steel sculpture in front, a recreation complex nearby, and three Mercedes among the cars in the parking lot, made $32 million profit in 1993. In stark contrast, the nationally owned Shenyang Medical Instrument Factory in Liaoning province has a warehouse full of its Great Wall refrigerators awaiting repairs. Although 300 of its 2,400 workers have no jobs, they stay on the payroll. The factory lost $5.3 million in two years. "We should learn from this lesson," says Lu Zizhun, the plant's Communist Party secretary.[29] The factory has given up trying to compete with Rongsheng, turning instead to new products such as pruning shears and x-ray equipment. The exploding Chinese economy has also given rise to countless entrepreneurial efforts, like the one described in the accompanying box.

## The Fully Industrialized Society

**fully industrialized society**
Society that is an exporter of manufactured products, many of which are based on advanced technology.

The **fully industrialized society,** the fifth stage of economic development, is an exporter of manufactured products, many of which are based on advanced technology. Examples include automobiles, computers, airplanes, oil exploration equipment, and telecommunications gear. Great Britain, Japan, Germany, France, Canada, and the United States fall into this category.

The wealth of the industrialized nations creates tremendous market potential. Therefore, industrialized countries trade extensively. Also, industrialized nations usually ship manufactured goods to developing countries in exchange for raw materials like petroleum, precious metals, and bauxite.

MARKETING AND SMALL BUSINESS

**All China Marketing Research Co.**

In Beijing, a statistician named Gao Yuxian is methodically building the biggest data base in China. Gao, the president of newly formed All China Marketing Research Co., is creating statistics on millions of stores, factories, and farms. He is using data that for many years were kept hidden by one of the world's most secretive societies. The statistics will become the basis for a firm supplying information on China's industrial concerns.

All China's headquarters is little more than a cell with bare pipes, concrete-block walls, and exposed wiring. In the basement, a dozen men and women sit in cubicles, poring over data gleaned from thousands of bureaus scattered throughout China's thirty provinces. All enterprises must supply local bureaucrats with detailed quarterly statements on finances, production, employment, and other data. The information eventually makes its way to the State Bureau, which sells it to All China.

The information arrives on paper documents neatly filled out in Chinese characters. Gao's workers then type the reams of entries into their Taiwanese-made personal computers. The result provides a close look at thousands of individual offices and factories. Anita Yuan, the company's data-service manager, demonstrates the emerging data base. Under the heading "Trades Query," she searches listings for individual industries. "Freeze Egg Production" and "Citric Acid Processing" light up on her screen. She taps a couple of more times to get a breakout of employees, finances, and productivity numbers on the Hong Yu Ferment Factory, Dong Kung District. The information is available to customers on computer disk, in both English and Chinese.

Bell Labs is helping to plan a networking system that will let business customers throughout China tap into All China's data base. Bell Labs, through a research unit called EastGate Services, is also forming a joint venture with All China that will have exclusive worldwide marketing rights to the tightly controlled data. Gao is relying heavily on Bell Labs to guide All China beyond mere data storage and into the information age, which will demand much more sophisticated data manipulation and transmission. "AT&T wants to build its information superhighway," Gao says, adding enthusiastically: "We'll be the biggest shop along its road."[30]



### POLITICAL STRUCTURE

Political structure is a third important variable facing global marketers. Government policies run the gamut from no private ownership and minimal individual freedom to little central government and maximum personal freedom. As rights of private property increase, government-owned industries and centralized planning tend to decrease. But rarely will a political environment be at one extreme or the other. India, for instance, is a republic with elements of socialism, monopoly capitalism, and competitive capitalism in its political ideology.

Many countries are changing from a centrally planned economy to a market-oriented one. Germany has made the fastest transformation because its dominant western half was already there. Eastern European nations like Hungary and Poland have also been moving quickly with market reforms. Many of the reforms have increased foreign trade and investment. For example, in Poland, foreigners are now

Although the economy of the former Soviet Union has been unstable for the past few years, it still offers many marketing opportunities for adventurous Western companies.



allowed to invest in all areas of industry, including agriculture, manufacturing, and trade. Poland even gives companies that invest in certain sectors some tax advantages.

Companies from Western Europe, Japan, and the United States have been taking advantage of the new opportunities. For example, Japan's Suzuki Motors Company has a $138 million joint venture with a consortium of nineteen Hungarian auto suppliers. General Electric has a $150 million agreement for the majority share of Tungsram, a Hungarian lighting equipment manufacturer. Although severe economic problems still must be addressed, companies willing to take a long-term view will find increasing opportunities in Eastern Europe.

Russia is progressing more slowly than many Eastern European countries, but it also is headed in the direction of a market-oriented economy. Over 5,000 Russian managers are studying abroad, and many more are studying market-oriented principles within Russia.[31] By 1994, some 18,000 foreign companies had invested in Russia.[32] However, many changes in the Russian economy are still desperately needed. Shortages of food, daily necessities, and housing are widespread. Economic "shock therapy," to make a rapid transition to a market-oriented economy, has resulted in skyrocketing inflation and many hardships. About 90 percent of all Russians are living below the poverty level.[33] Shortages of wood have limited the supply of caskets; the only people who can acquire a casket are those who can supply their own wood. Moreover, many consumer products are of poor quality. For example, the majority of Moscow's house fires are started by faulty TV sets. Finally, the region has the ability to grow its own food, yet its agricultural distribution system is so inefficient that up to half the food is wasted. Thus the countries of the former Soviet Union must annually buy $3.3 billion in corn, wheat, and soybeans from abroad. Despite this dire situation, plenty of opportunity exists. RJR Nabisco is trying to process and market tomato products, hoping to save some of the 40 percent of the crop lost each year.[34] More opportunities exist in many other inefficient industries, such as mining, oil drilling and explorations, and consumer durable goods.

Changes leading to market-oriented economies are not restricted to Eastern Europe and Russia. Many countries within Latin America are also attempting market reforms. Countries like Brazil, Argentina, and Mexico are reducing government control over many sectors of the economy. They are also selling state-owned companies to foreign and domestic investors and removing trade barriers that have protected their markets against foreign competition.[35] Brazil has now overtaken Italy and Mexico to become the tenth largest automobile manufacturer in the world.[36]

Another trend in the political environment is the growth of nationalist sentiments among citizens who have strong loyalties and devotion to their country. Failure to appreciate emerging nationalist feelings can destroy a company's chances of doing business in that country. Such problems can be avoided by allowing citizens of the host country to have partial ownership of the operation.

Another potential cloud on the horizon for some types of companies doing business abroad is the threat of nationalization. Some countries have nationalized (taken ownership of) certain industries or companies, such as airlines in Italy and Volvo in Sweden, to infuse more capital into their development. Industries are also nationalized to allow domestic corporations to sell vital goods below cost. For example, for many years France has been supplying coal to users at a loss.

## Legal Considerations

Closely related to and often intertwined with the political environment are legal considerations. Legal structures are designed to either encourage or limit trade. Some examples follow:

**tariff**
Tax levied on the goods entering a country.

- ***Tariff:*** tax levied on the goods entering a country. For example, trucks imported into the United States face a 25 percent tariff.[37] Since the 1930s, tariffs have tended to decrease as a barrier to trade. But they have often been replaced by nontariff barriers, such as quotas, boycotts, and other restrictions.

**quota**
Limit on the amount of a specific product that can enter a country.

- ***Quota:*** limit on the amount of a specific product that can enter a country. The United States has strict quotas for imported textiles, sugar, and many dairy products. Several U.S. companies have sought quotas as a means of protection from foreign competition. For example, Harley-Davidson convinced the U.S. government to place quotas on large motorcycles imported into the United States. These quotas gave the company the opportunity to improve its quality and compete with Japancse motorcycles.

**boycott**
Exclusion of all products coming from certain countries or companies.

- ***Boycott:*** exclusion of all products from certain countries or companies. Governments use boycotts to exclude companies from countries with whom they have a political **dispute.** Several Arab nations boycotted Coca-Cola because it maintained distributors in Israel.

**exchange control**
Law compelling a company earning foreign exchange from its exports to sell that foreign exchange to a control agency, usually a central bank.

- ***Exchange control:*** law compelling a company earning foreign exchange from its exports to sell it to a control agency, usually a central bank. A company wishing to buy goods abroad must first obtain foreign exchange from the control agency. Generally, exchange controls limit the importation of luxuries. For instance, Avon Products drastically cut back new production lines and products in the Philippines because exchange controls prevented conversion of pesos to dollars to ship back to the home office. The pesos had to be used in the Philippines. China restricts the amount of foreign currency each Chinese company is allowed to keep from its exports. Therefore, Chinese companies must usually get the government's approval to release funds before they can buy products from foreign companies.

**market grouping**
Trade alliance in which several countries agree to work together to form a common trade area that enhances trade opportunities.

- ***Market grouping:*** also known as a common trade alliance; occurs when several countries agree to work together to form a common trade area that enhances trade opportunities. The best-known market grouping is the European Community (EC), whose members are Belgium, France, Germany, Italy, Luxembourg, the Netherlands, Denmark, Ireland, Spain, the United Kingdom, Portugal, and Greece. The EC has been evolving for nearly four decades, yet until recently, many trade barriers existed among member nations.

**trade agreement**
Agreement to stimulate international trade.

- ***Trade agreement:*** agreement to stimulate international trade. Not all government efforts are meant to stifle imports or investment by foreign corporations. The General Agreement on Tariffs and Trade is a good example of a structure designed to increase international trade.

**General Agreement on Tariffs and Trade (GATT)**
Multinational agreement that reduces tariffs and other barriers to trade, the eighth version of which was signed in 1994 by representatives of 117 countries.

The eighth **General Agreement on Tariffs and Trade** (GATT) since World War II was signed by ministers from 117 nations in 1994. The agreement cuts overall tariffs by about 40 percent, which will lower the prices on thousands of products worldwide.[38] GATT officials estimate that the accord will increase global income by $235 billion a year.[39] The 1994 GATT agreement makes several major changes in world trading practices:

- *Agriculture:* Europe will gradually reduce farm subsidies, opening new opportunities for such U.S. farm exports as wheat and corn. Japan and Korea will begin to import rice. But growers of U.S. sugar, citrus fruit, and peanuts will have their subsidies trimmed.
- *Automotive products:* The United States will be permitted to protect just one industry with a "voluntary" restraint agreement that limits imports. Detroit fears it will not be that one industry and will lose its ability to restrict Japanese exporters' share of U.S. car sales.
- *Entertainment, pharmaceuticals, and software:* New rules will protect patents, copyrights, and trademarks for twenty years. But many developing nations will have a decade to phase in patent protection for drugs, and France refused to liberalize market access for the U.S. entertainment industry. France limits the number of U.S. movies and TV shows that can be shown.
- *Financial, legal, and accounting services:* Services come under international trading rules for the first time, potentially creating a vast opportunity for these competitive U.S. industries. But specific terms of market access remain to be worked out, mainly with developing countries.
- *Textiles and apparel:* Strict quotas limiting imports from developing countries will be phased out over ten years, causing further job loss in the U.S. clothing trade. But retailers and consumers will be the big winners, because quotas now add $15 billion a year to clothing prices.
- *A new trade organization:* GATT will be replaced by the World Trade Organization. The new organization will have far greater authority to resolve trade disputes than GATT has ever had. It will also oversee world trade in services and agriculture.[40]

The trend toward globalization has brought to the fore several specific examples of the influence of political structure and legal considerations: Japanese keiretsu, the North American Free Trade Agreement, and the European Union.

## Japanese Keiretsu

**keiretsu**
Japanese society of business, which takes one of two main forms: a bank-centered keiretsu, or a massive industrial combine centered around a bank; and a supply keiretsu, or a group of companies dominated by the major manufacturer they provide with supplies.

Japanese nationalism produced the **keiretsu,** or societies of business, which take two main forms. Bank-centered keiretsu are massive industrial combines of twenty to forty-five core companies centered on a bank (see Exhibit 3.4). They enable companies to share business risk and provide a way to allocate investment to strategic industries. Supply keiretsu are groups of companies dominated by the major manufacturer they provide with supplies. Keiretsu exist with the blessing of the Japanese government. After World War II, it wanted to help reestablish industry by encouraging cooperation. The Japanese government was also hoping the strong networks would help keep out foreign companies.[41]

Keiretsu have indeed blocked U.S. companies, and others, from the Japanese market. Consider the Matsushita keiretsu. Matsushita, one of the world's top twenty manufacturers, makes Panasonic, National, Technics, and Quasar brands. Matsushita also controls a chain of about 25,000 National retail stores in Japan, which together generate more than half Matsushita's domestic sales. From batteries to refrigerators, these shops agree to sell no other brands or just a few others. And the dealers agree to sell at manufacturers' recommended prices. In return, Matsushita essentially

*Exhibit 3.4*

A Japanese Keiretsu

Source: Adapted by permission of *Harvard Business Review* from A Brief History of Japan's Keiretsu in "Computers and the Coming of the U.S. Keiretsu," by Charles H. Ferguson (July–August 1990). Copyright 1990 by the President and Fellows of Harvard College; all rights reserved.

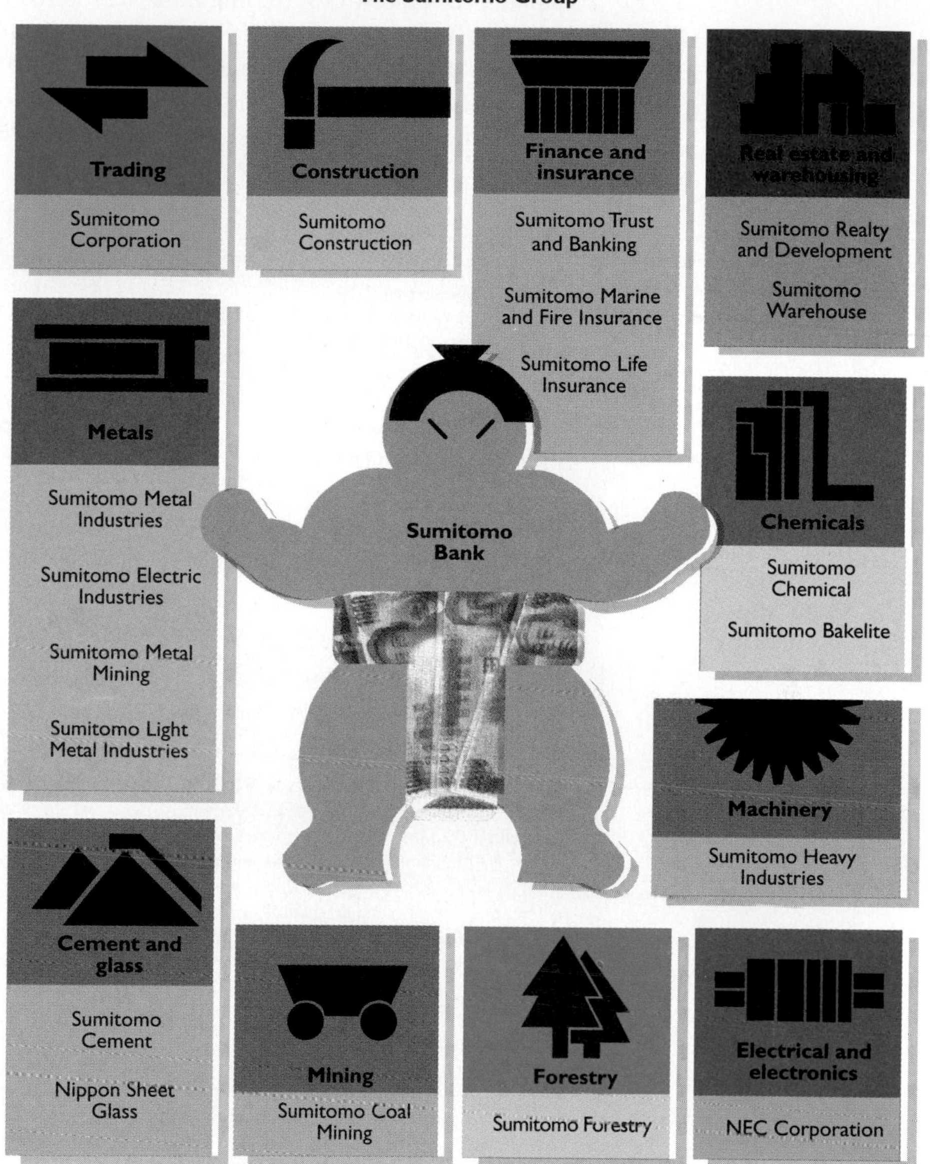


guarantees the livelihoods of the stores' owners. The Japan Fair Trade Commission has estimated that almost 90 percent of all domestic business transactions are "among parties involved in a long-standing relationship of some sort."[42]

Trade talks between Japan and the United States in 1992 centered on keiretsu, with little success. The U.S. government demanded that the keiretsu be opened to U.S. companies. But Japanese officials were reluctant to acknowledge the need to reform the keiretsu, arguing that they make the Japanese economy more efficient.[43]

## The North American Free Trade Agreement

**North American Free Trade Agreement (NAFTA)**
Treaty establishing the world's largest free-trade zone, which includes Canada, the United States, and Mexico.

In 1992, negotiators concluded the **North American Free Trade Agreement** (NAFTA), which created the world's largest free-trade zone. The agreement was ratified by the U.S. Congress in 1993.[44] It includes Canada, the United States, and Mexico, with a combined population of 360 million and economy of $6 trillion.[45] The key benefits to the United States from NAFTA are summarized in Exhibit 3.5.

Canada, the largest U.S. trading partner, entered a free-trade agreement with the United States in 1988. Most of the new opportunities for U.S. business under NAFTA are thus in Mexico, America's third largest trading partner. U.S.-Mexican trade doubled between 1988 and 1993 to $76 billion a year.[46] Tariffs on Mexican exports to the U.S. averaged just 4 percent before the treaty was signed, and most

*Exhibit 3.5*

Benefits to the United States from the North American Free Trade Agreement

Source: "Border Crossings," *Business Week*, 22 November 1993, pp. 40–41; "What's It All About?" *Dallas Morning News*, 21 March 1993, p. 12J; Kenneth Bacon, "Trade Pact Is Likely to Step Up Business Even Before Approval," *Wall Street Journal*, 13 August 1992, p. A10; Louis Richman, "How NAFTA Will Help America," *Fortune*, 19 April 1993, pp. 95–102.

**Elimination of Tariffs and Barriers**

Approximately 65% of U.S. industrial and agricultural exports to Mexico are eligible for duty-free treatment within 5 years. In addition, Mexican export performance requirements, which require U.S. companies to export as a condition of being allowed to invest in Mexico, and Mexican "local content" regulations have been eliminated. Key industries affected include the following:

**Motor vehicles and parts:** Mexican tariffs on vehicles and light trucks were halved immediately. Within 5 years, duties on 75% of U.S. parts exports to Mexico will be eliminated. The Mexican automobile market is the fastest growing in the world. The Big Three U.S. auto manufacturers expect sales to rise from 7,700 units in 1993 to over 60,000 in 1996.

**Auto rule of origin:** Only autos that contain 62.5% North American content benefit from the tariff cuts, to ensure that benefits of trade liberalization flow to North American companies.

**Textiles and apparel:** Barriers to $250 million—approximately 20%—of U.S. exports were eliminated immediately, with barriers to a further $700 million in U.S. exports dropped within 6 years. All North American trade restrictions will be eliminated within 10 years, with rules-of-origin provisions to ensure that benefits of liberalization accrue to North American producers. U.S. apparel exports should increase 30 percent, but imports will increase about 60 percent.

**Land transportation:** U.S. trucking companies are permitted to carry international cargo to Mexican states contiguous to the United States and to all of Mexico by 1999. Railroads are able to provide service to Mexico. U.S. companies are able to invest in and operate land-side port services in Mexico. Currently 90 percent of U.S. trade with Mexico is shipped by land. Before the treaty, U.S. truckers had to "hand off" trailers to Mexican truck drivers at the border.

**Consumer Goods:** Wal-Mart, JCPenney, and Radio Shack are already part of a U.S. movement into Mexico. Soon fast-food franchisers, such as McDonald's and Wendy's, will join the rush to Mexico. Procter & Gamble and other packaged-goods manufacturers will increase their investments in the Mexican and Canadian markets.

**Telecommunications:** U.S. companies will receive nondiscriminatory access to the Mexican public telephone system, and investment restrictions were eliminated. Southwestern Bell purchased part of Telefonos de Mexico. AT&T, MCI, and Sprint are moving into the Mexican long-distance market.

**Financial services:** U.S. banks and securities firms are allowed to establish wholly owned subsidiaries in Mexico. Transitional restrictions will be phased out by January 1, 2000. Credit cards, mortgages, and life and property insurance are all new markets for U.S. firms.

**Energy:** Contracts for oil field services and electric power generation equipment will now be open to U.S. companies. However, U.S. companies still cannot engage in oil exploration or open retail service stations in Mexico.

**Agriculture:** Mexican import licenses, which cover about 25% of U.S. exports, were dropped. The remaining Mexican tariffs will be phased out over 10 to 15 years. Mexico will supply more citrus, vegetables, and fruits. The U.S. will ship more meat and grains, including corn and soybeans. Canadian wood exports will continue to grow.

**Intellectual property rights:** U.S. high-tech, entertainment, and consumer goods producers have realized substantial gains in patent, trademark, and copyright protections. Compulsory licensing is limited, resolving an important issue with Canada.

**Environment/Labor Rights/Adjustment Safeguards**

**Environment:** The U.S. was allowed to maintain its stringent environmental, health, and safety standards.

**Worker rights:** The parties assume that the benefits of the trade pact will provide Mexico with resources to enforce labor initiatives.

**Adjustment safeguards:** For import-sensitive U.S. industries, U.S. tariffs will be phased out over 10 years—15 years for some particularly vulnerable industries. U.S. workers who lose their jobs because of the trade pact will receive timely, comprehensive, and effective services and retraining through an existing or newly created program.

goods entered the U.S. duty-free. Therefore, NAFTA primarily opened the Mexican market to U.S. companies. When the treaty went into effect, tariffs on about half the items traded across the Rio Grande disappeared. The pact removed a web of Mexican licensing requirements, quotas, and tariffs that limited transactions in U.S. goods and services. For instance, the pact allows U.S. and Canadian financial-services companies to own subsidiaries in Mexico for the first time in fifty years.

The first industries that benefited from NAFTA were autos, textiles, capital goods, financial services, construction equipment, electronics, telecommunications, and petrochemicals. Sales of companies in such industries have been rising for some time as a result of Mexico's growing economy, but NAFTA is speeding the process. In 1983 Caterpillar sold only twelve pieces of heavy construction equipment to Mexico; in 1994 it shipped over 1,400. NAFTA removed tariffs on Caterpillar equipment sold in Mexico while maintaining duties against Japanese rival Komatsu. As protections are lifted from the Mexican car industry, Rockwell International will sell more door latches, sunroofs, and window mechanisms. It already plans to build a new plant in Mexico.

Canadian companies are also eager to do business in Mexico. Magna International, Canada's largest auto parts maker, is building its first Mexican production facility near a Volkswagen assembly plant in Puebla. Another Canadian company, Northern Telecom, had only ten employees in Mexico in 1988. It plans to build sales from an estimated $200 million now to over $500 million by the late 1990s. That's not an unreasonable goal, because industry experts foresee the Mexican telecommunications market expanding by 15 percent annually.

In the end, the real test of NAFTA will be whether it delivers rising prosperity on both sides of the Rio Grande. For Mexicans, NAFTA must provide rising wages, better benefits, and an expanding middle class with enough purchasing power to keep buying goods from the United States and Canada. That scenario is plausible but not guaranteed.

As for the United States, its gross domestic product will grow about $30 billion a year once NAFTA is fully implemented.[47] But for Americans, the trade agreement will need to prove that it can produce more well-paying jobs than it destroys. Although estimates of the employment effects of NAFTA vary widely, almost every study agrees that there will be gains. The Commerce Department's rule of thumb is that each extra $1 billion in exports creates over 19,000 U.S. jobs, implying an additional increase under NAFTA of some 60,000 jobs by the end of the decade. Such export-oriented jobs will likely command higher wages than occupations that service or supply only the domestic economy. David Walters, chief economist for the Office of the U.S. Trade Representative, calculates that in 1990 workers who made goods exported to Mexico enjoyed a 12.2 percent hourly pay premium over the average $10 an hour earned by nonagricultural workers in the private sector.[48] At the same time, there will be job losses in specific industries—makers of household glass products and brooms, among others—as some labor-intensive work shifts south. By some estimates, freer trade with Mexico will have eliminated about 145,000 jobs between 1990 and 1996.[49] But these losses, painful as they are for the individuals affected, will be more than offset by the new jobs that expanded trade will create.

## The European Union

**Maastricht Treaty**
Agreement among the twelve members of the European Community to pursue economic, monetary, and political union.

In 1993, all twelve member countries of the European Community ratified the Maastricht Treaty. The **Maastricht Treaty,** named after the Dutch town where it was developed in 1991, proposes to take the EC further toward economic, monetary, and political union. Officially called the Treaty on European Union, the document outlines plans for tightening bonds among the member states and creating a single market. The European Commission, which drafted the treaty, predicts that Maastricht will create 1.8 million new jobs by 1999. Also, retail prices in the European Union are expected to fall by a minimum of 6 percent.[50]

Although the heart of the treaty deals with developing a unified European market, Maastricht is also intended to increase integration among the European Union members in areas much closer to the core of national sovereignty. The treaty calls for economic and monetary coordination, including a common currency and an independent central bank by 1999. Common foreign, security, and defense policies are also goals, as well as European citizenship—whereby any European Union citizen can live, work, vote, and run for office anywhere in the member countries. The treaty standardizes trade rules and taxes and coordinates health and safety standards. Duties, customs procedures, and taxes are also standardized. A driver hauling cargo from Amsterdam to Lisbon can now clear four border crossings by showing a single piece of paper. Before the Maastricht Treaty, the same driver would have carried two pounds of paper to cross the same borders. The overall goal is to end the need for a special product for each country—for example, a different Braun electric razor for Italy, Germany, France, and so forth. Goods marked *GEC* (goods for EC) can be traded freely, without being retested at each border.

Some economists have called the European Union the "United States of Europe." It is an attractive market, with 320 million consumers and purchasing power almost equal to that of the United States. But the European Union will probably never be a United States of Europe. For one thing, even in a united Europe, marketers will not be able to produce a single Europroduct for a generic Euroconsumer. With nine different languages and individual national customs, Europe will always be far more diverse than the United States. Thus product differences will continue. It will be a long time, for instance, before the French begin drinking the instant coffee that Britons enjoy. Preferences for washing machines also differ: British homemakers want front-loaders, and the French want top-loaders; Germans like lots of settings and high spin speeds; Italians like lower speeds. Even European companies that think they understand Euroconsumers often have difficulties producing "the right product":

> Atag Holdings NV, a diversified Dutch company whose main business is kitchen appliances, reckoned it was well-placed to expand abroad. Its plant is a mile from the Dutch/German border and near Europe's geographic and population center. And Lidwien Jacobs, a product manager, says she was confident Atag could cater to both the "potato" and "spaghetti" belts—marketers' terms for consumer preferences in northern and southern Europe. But, as Atag quickly discovered, preferences vary much more than that. "To sell in America, you need one or two types of ceramic stove top," Ms. Jacobs says. "In Europe, you need 11."
>
> Belgians, who cook in huge pots, require extra-large burners. Germans like oval pots, and burners to fit. Italians boil large pots of water quickly, for pasta. The French need small burners and very low temperatures for simmering sauces and broths. Such quirks affect every detail. Germans like oven knobs on the front, the French on top. Even clock placement differs. And Atag has had to test market 28 colors. While Continentals prefer black and white, the British demand a vast range, including peach, pigeon blue and mint green.
>
> "Whatever the product, the British are always different," Ms. Jacobs says with a sigh. Another snag: "Domestic," the name of Atag's basic oven, turns off buyers in Britain, where "domestic" is a synonym for "servant."
>
> Atag's kitchenware unit has lifted foreign sales to 25 percent of its total from 4 percent in the mid-1980s. But it now believes that its range of designs and speed in delivering them, rather than the magic bullet of a Euro-product, will keep it competitive.

"People would fight another war, I think, to keep their own cooking habits," Ms. Jacobs jokes.[51]



An entirely different type of problem facing global marketers is the possibility of a protectionist movement by the European Union against outsiders. For example, European automakers have proposed holding Japanese imports at roughly their current 10 percent market share. The Irish, Danes, and Dutch don't make cars and have unrestricted home markets; they would be unhappy about limited imports of Toyotas and Datsuns. But France has a strict quota on Japanese cars to protect Renault and Peugeot. These local carmakers could be hurt if the quota is raised at all.

U.S. companies realize they have to be perceived as European or risk similar trade barriers. Their adaptation is remarkable. For example, consider H.J. Heinz. Although it is a huge company, it is only a sixth the size of its big European rivals Nestlé and Unilever. Heinz spent almost $1 billion in modernizing its European plant and in marketing. Its primary goal was to push its Weight Watchers' meals ahead of Nestlé's Lean Cuisine meals. Heinz has excellent distribution networks in Britain and Italy, but in the huge and affluent German market, Nestlé has the edge. Still, Heinz is gaining market share in Germany with Weight Watchers' beef stroganoff and apple strudel. This kind of marketing battle is likely to be waged in many European markets.

Interestingly, a number of big U.S. companies are already considered more "European" than many European companies. Coke and Kellogg's are considered classic European brand names. Ford and General Motors compete for the largest share of auto sales on the continent. IBM and Digital Equipment dominate their markets. General Electric, AT&T, and Westinghouse are already strong all over Europe and have invested heavily in new manufacturing facilities throughout the continent.

Although many U.S. firms are well prepared to contend with European competition, the rivalry is perhaps more intense there than anywhere else in the world. In the long run, it is questionable whether Europe has room for eight mass-market automakers, including Ford and GM, when the United States sustains just three. Similarly, an integrated Europe probably doesn't need twelve national airlines.

## DEMOGRAPHIC MAKEUP

The three most densely populated nations in the world are China, India, and Indonesia. But that fact alone is not particularly useful to marketers. They also need to know whether the population is mostly urban or rural, because marketers may not have easy access to rural consumers. In Belgium about 90 percent of the population lives in an urban setting, whereas in Kenya almost 80 percent of the population lives in a rural setting. Belgium is thus the more attractive market.

Just as important as population is personal income within a country. The wealthiest countries in the world include Japan, the United States, Switzerland, Sweden, Canada, Germany, and several of the Arab oil-producing nations. At the other extreme are countries like Mali and Bangladesh, with a fraction of the per capita purchasing power of the United States. However, a low per capita income is not in itself enough reason to avoid a country. In countries with low per capita incomes, wealth is not evenly distributed. There are pockets of upper- and middle-class consumers in just about every country of the world. In some cases the number of consumers is surprisingly large. For example, India, a country with close to a billion people, has a very low per capita income. But between 10 and 20 percent of its population

Many corporations are recognizing that India holds prime marketing potential for reaching 100 million middle-class consumers.

can be considered middle class, creating a potential market of over 100 million consumers.

The most significant global economic news of the past decade is the rise of a global middle class. From Shekou, China, to Mexico City and countless cities in between, there are traffic jams, bustling bulldozers, and people hawking tickets to various events. These are all symptoms of a growing middle class. In China, per capita incomes rose 8.5 percent annually from 1983 to 1993; they grew at a 6.5 percent annual rate in East Asia.[52] Developing countries, excluding Eastern Europe and the former Soviet Union, should grow about 5 percent annually over the next decade.

Growing economies demand professionals. In Asia, accountants, stock analysts, bankers, and even middle managers are in short supply. Rising affluence also creates demand for consumer durables such as refrigerators, VCRs, and automobiles. As Central Europe's middle class grows, Whirlpool expects its sales to grow over 6 percent annually.[53] Companies like Procter & Gamble and Gillette offer an array of products at different price points to attract and keep customers as they move up the income scale.

The percentage of the world's population that lives in industrialized nations has been declining since 1960, because industrialized nations have grown slowly and developing nations have grown rapidly. In this decade more than 90 percent of the world's population growth will occur in developing countries and only 10 percent in the industrialized nations. The United Nations reports that by the year 2000, 79 percent of the world's population will reside in developing countries—for example, Guinea, Bolivia, and Pakistan.

## NATURAL RESOURCES

A final factor in the external environment that has become more evident in the past decade is the shortage of natural resources. For example, petroleum shortages have created huge amounts of wealth for oil-producing countries such as Norway, Saudi Arabia, and the United Arab Emirates. Both consumer and industrial markets have blossomed in these countries. Other countries—such as Indonesia, Mexico, and Venezuela—were able to borrow heavily against oil reserves in order to develop more rapidly. On the other hand, industrial countries like Japan, the United States, and much of Western Europe experienced rampant inflation in the 1970s and an enormous transfer of wealth to the petroleum-rich nations. But during much of the 1980s and 1990s, when the price of oil fell, the petroleum-rich nations suffered. Many were not able to service their foreign debts when their oil revenues were sharply reduced. However, Iraq's invasion of Kuwait in 1990 led to a rapid increase in the price of oil and focused attention on the dependence of industrialized countries on oil imports. The price of oil once again declined following the defeat of Iraq, but the U.S. dependence on foreign oil will likely remain high in the 1990s.

Petroleum is not the only natural resource that affects international marketing. Warm climate and lack of water mean that many of Africa's countries will remain importers of foodstuffs. The United States, on the other hand, must rely on Africa for many precious metals. Japan depends heavily on the United States for timber and logs. A Minnesota company manufactures and sells a million pairs of disposable chopsticks to Japan each year. The list could go on, but the point is clear. Vast differences in natural resources create international dependencies, huge shifts of wealth, inflation and recession, export opportunities for countries with abundant resources, and even a stimulus for military intervention.

4 *Identify the various ways of entering the global marketplace.*

## GLOBAL MARKETING BY THE INDIVIDUAL FIRM

A company should consider entering the global marketplace only after its management has a solid grasp of the global environment. Some relevant questions are "What are our options in selling abroad?" "How difficult is global marketing?" "What are the potential risks and returns?" Concrete answers to these questions would probably encourage the many U.S. firms not selling overseas to venture into the international arena. Foreign sales could be an important source of profits.

Many firms form multinational partnerships—called strategic alliances—to assist them in penetrating global markets; strategic alliances are examined in Chapter 5. Five other methods of entering the global marketplace are, in order of risk, export, licensing, contract manufacturing, joint venture, and direct investment (see Exhibit 3.6 on page 90).

### EXPORT

**exporting**
Practice of selling domestically produced products in another country.

When a company decides to enter the global market, exporting is usually the least complicated and least risky alternative. **Exporting** is selling domestically produced products to buyers in another country. Leading exports from the United States are aircraft, auto parts, and computers and computer-related products; the fifteen largest U.S. exporters are listed in Exhibit 3.7 (on page 90).

**buyer for export**
Intermediary in the international market that assumes all ownership risks and sells internationally for its own account.

A company deciding to export can sell directly to foreign importers or buyers, or it may decide to sell to intermediaries located in its domestic market. The most common intermediary is the export merchant, also known as a **buyer for export,** who is usually treated like a domestic customer by the domestic manufacturer. The buyer for export assumes all risks and sells internationally for its own account. The domestic firm is involved only to the extent that its products are bought in foreign markets.

A second type of intermediary is the export broker, who plays the traditional broker's role by bringing buyer and seller together. The manufacturer still retains title

*Exhibit 3.6*

Risk Levels for Five Methods of Entering the Global Marketplace

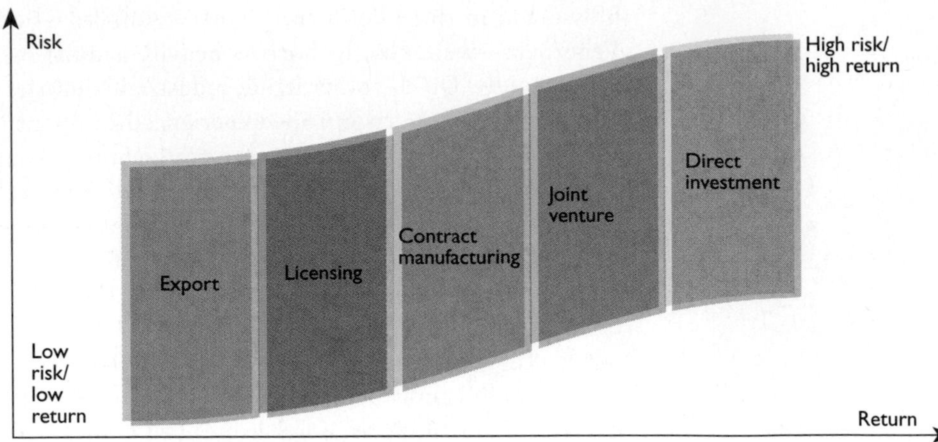


**export broker**
Broker that operates primarily in exporting agricultural products and raw materials.

**export agent**
Intermediary who either lives in a foreign country and performs the same functions as a domestic manufacturer's agent or lives in the manufacturer's country but represents foreign buyers.

and assumes all the risks. **Export brokers** operate primarily in agriculture and raw materials.

**Export agents** are a third type of intermediary. A foreign sales agent-distributor lives in the foreign country and performs the same functions as a domestic manufacturer's agent, helping with international financing, shipping, and so on. The U.S. Department of Commerce has an agent-distributor service that helps about 5,000 U.S. companies a year find an agent or distributor in virtually any country of the world. A second category of agents resides in the manufacturer's country but represents foreign buyers. This type of agent acts as a hired purchasing agent for foreign customers operating in the exporter's home market.

The Department of Commerce maintains offices in sixty-seven U.S. cities to provide aid and information to companies interested in exporting. These offices can

*Exhibit 3.7*

Fifteen Largest U.S. Exporters

Source: "Top 50 U.S. Industrial Exporters," *Fortune*, 22 August 1994, p. 132. © 1994 Time Inc. All rights reserved.

| Company and headquarters | Products | Exports as percentage of total sales |
|---|---|---|
| **Archer-Daniels-Midland,** Decatur, IL | Protein meals, vegetable oils, flour, grain | 29.6% |
| **Boeing,** Seattle | Commercial aircraft | 57.8 |
| **Caterpillar,** Peoria, IL | Heavy machinery, engines, turbines | 32.2 |
| **Chrysler,** Highland Park, MI | Motor vehicles and parts | 19.3 |
| **DuPont,** Wilmington, DE | Specialty chemicals | 10.7 |
| **Ford Motor,** Dearborn, MI | Motor vehicles and parts | 8.7 |
| **General Electric,** Fairfield, CT | Jet engines, turbines, plastics, medical systems, locomotives | 14.0 |
| **General Motors,** Detroit | Motor vehicles and parts | 11.2 |
| **Hewlett-Packard,** Palo Alto, CA | Measurement and computation products and systems | 23.3 |
| **IBM,** Armonk, NY | Computers and related equipment | 11.6 |
| **Intel,** Santa Clara, CA | Microcomputer components, modules, and systems | 38.8 |
| **McDonnell Douglas,** St. Louis, MO | Aerospace products, missiles, electronic systems | 23.5 |
| **Motorola,** Schaumburg, IL | Communications equipment, semiconductors | 29.4 |
| **Philip Morris,** New York | Tobacco, beer, food products | 8.1 |
| **United Technologies,** Hartford, CT | Jet engines, helicopters, cooling equipment | 16.9 |

provide sales leads, alert companies to overseas trade fairs, evaluate competition in specific countries, and even evaluate the market for a firm's product. In 1995, the Commerce Department also opened export centers in Los Angeles, Miami, Chicago, and Baltimore to provide "one-stop shopping" for potential exporters. The export centers offer assistance from up to nineteen different federal agencies.[54]

Creating a solid international marketing strategy, developing a level of international competence, and having managerial commitment are the key factors to success in exporting.[55] Another big hurdle for many companies is export financing. The Export-Import Bank in Washington, D.C., tries to help smaller businesses get loans from commercial banks by providing loan guarantees and insurance. "The impediment companies typically experience is that they can't get enough financing to build the inventory" and begin exporting, claims Robert J. Kaiser, marketing vice president with the Export-Import Bank.[56] The bank has a program to help small businesses that works with city and state agencies in twenty-six offices around the country.

## LICENSING

Another effective way for a firm to move into the global arena with relatively little risk is to sell a license to manufacture its product to someone in a foreign country. **Licensing** is the legal process whereby a licensor agrees to let another firm use its manufacturing process, trademarks, patents, trade secrets, or other proprietary knowledge. The licensee, in turn, agrees to pay the licensor a royalty or fee agreed on by both parties.

**licensing**
Legal process whereby a licensor agrees to let another firm use its manufacturing process, trademarks, patents, trade secrets, or other proprietary knowledge.

Because it has many advantages, U.S. companies have eagerly embraced the licensing concept. For instance, Philip Morris licensed Labatt Brewing Company to produce Miller High Life in Canada. The Spalding Company receives more than $2 million annually from licensing agreements on its sporting goods. Fruit-of-the-Loom manufactures nothing itself abroad but lends its name through licensing to forty-five consumer items in Japan alone, for at least 1 percent of the licensee's gross sales.

A licensor must make sure it can exercise the control over the licensee's activities needed to ensure proper quality, pricing, distribution, and so on. Licensing may also create a new competitor in the long run, if the licensee decides to void the license agreement. International law is often ineffective in stopping such actions. Two common ways of maintaining effective control over licensees are shipping one or more critical components from the United States or locally registering patents and trademarks to the U.S. firm, not to the licensee.

Franchising is one form of licensing that has grown rapidly in recent years. Over 350 U.S. franchisors operate more than 32,000 outlets in foreign countries, bringing in sales of $6 billion. Over half the international franchises are for fast-food restaurants and business services. As with other forms of licensing, maintaining control over the franchisees is important. For instance, McDonald's was forced to take legal action to buy back its Paris outlets, because the franchisee failed to maintain quality standards. McDonald's claimed the Paris franchise was dirty and provided poor service and food. Investigators found dog droppings inside one outlet, and the franchise charged extra for catsup and hid the straws from customers. Because of the damage to McDonald's reputation, the chain was able to develop only 67 outlets in all of France, compared to 270 in Great Britain and 270 in Germany. To reestablish itself, McDonald's decided to project French style and class. The first outlet to appear after McDonald's repurchased its franchise was in a handsome turn-of-the-century building on one of Paris's grand boulevards.

## CONTRACT MANUFACTURING

**contract manufacturing**
Private-label manufacturing by a foreign company.

Firms that do not want to become involved in licensing or to become heavily involved in global marketing may engage in **contract manufacturing,** which is private-label manufacturing by a foreign company. The foreign company produces a certain volume of products to specification, with the domestic firm's brand name on the goods. The domestic company usually handles the marketing. Thus the domestic firm can broaden its global marketing base without investing in overseas plant and equipment. After establishing a solid base, the domestic firm may switch to a joint venture or direct investment.

## JOINT VENTURE

**joint venture**
Arrangement in which a domestic firm buys part of a foreign company or joins with a foreign company to create a new entity.

Joint ventures are quite similar to licensing agreements. In a **joint venture,** the domestic firm buys part of a foreign company or joins with a foreign company to create a new entity. A joint venture is a quick and relatively inexpensive way to "go global."

It also can be very risky. Many joint ventures fail. Others fall victim to a takeover, in which one partner buys out the other. In a survey of 150 companies involved in joint ventures that ended, three-quarters were found to have been taken over by Japanese partners. Gary Hamel, a professor at the London Business School, regards joint ventures as "a race to learn": The partner that learns fastest comes to dominate the relationship and can then rewrite its terms.[57] Thus, a joint venture becomes a new form of competition.

The Japanese excel at learning from others, Hamel says. U.S. and European companies are not as good at it. Toshiba, the oldest and third largest of Japan's electronic giants (after Hitachi and Matsushita), has entered into more joint ventures than any other Japanese company. Some of its U.S. partners include Apple Computer, United Technologies, Time Warner, Sun Microsystems, Motorola, National Semiconductor, and General Electric. The joint ventures aid Toshiba in two ways. They are helping the company weather the economic slowdown in Japan and giving it access to some of the most important technologies of the digital age.[58]

In a successful joint venture, both parties gain valuable skills from the alliance. In the General Motors–Suzuki joint venture in Canada, for example, both parties have contributed and gained. The alliance, CAMI Automotive, was formed to manufacture low-end cars for the U.S. market. The plant, run by Suzuki management, produces the Geo Metro/Suzuki Swift—the smallest, highest-gas-mileage GM car sold in North America—as well as the Geo Tracker/Suzuki Sidekick sport utility vehicle. Through CAMI, Suzuki has gained access to GM's dealer network and an expanded market for parts and components. GM avoided the cost of developing low-end cars and obtained models it needed to revitalize the lower end of its product line and its average fuel-economy rating. The CAMI factory may be one of the most productive plants in North America. There GM has learned how Japanese carmakers use work teams, run flexible assembly lines, and manage quality control.[59]

## DIRECT INVESTMENT

**direct foreign investment**
Active ownership of a foreign company or of overseas manufacturing or marketing facilities.

Active ownership of a foreign company or of overseas manufacturing or marketing facilities is **direct foreign investment.** Direct investors have either a controlling interest or a large minority interest in the firm. Thus they have the greatest potential reward and the greatest potential risk. Federal Express lost $1.2 billion in its attempt to build a hub in Europe.[60] It created a huge infrastructure but couldn't generate the package volume to support it. To control losses, the company fired 6,600 international employees and closed offices in over 100 European cities. On the other hand, direct investment can often lead to rapid success. MTV has only been in the European market since 1988, yet in 1994 it had more viewers in Europe (56.5 million households) than in the United States. It also earned over $100 million on its European investment in 1994.[61]

Sometimes firms make direct investments because they can find no suitable local partners. Also, direct investments avoid the communication problems and conflicts of interest that can arise with joint ventures. IBM, for instance, requires total ownership of foreign investments because it does not want to share control with local partners.

A firm may make a direct foreign investment by acquiring an interest in an existing company or by building new facilities. It might do so because it has trouble transferring some resource to a foreign operation or getting that resource locally. One important resource is personnel, especially managers. If the local labor market is tight, the firm may buy an entire foreign firm and retain all its employees instead of paying higher salaries than competitors.

The United States is a popular place for direct investment by foreign companies. In 1994 the value of foreign-owned businesses in the United States was over $425 billion.

5 *List the basic elements involved in developing a global marketing mix.*

## THE GLOBAL MARKETING MIX

To succeed, firms seeking to enter into foreign trade must still adhere to the principles of the marketing mix. Information gathered on foreign markets through research is the basis for the four P's of global marketing strategy: product, place (distribution), promotion, and price. Marketing managers who understand the advantages and disadvantages of different ways to enter the global market and the effect of the external environment on the firm's marketing mix have a better chance of reaching their goals.

The first step in creating a marketing mix is developing a thorough understanding of the global target market. Often this knowledge can be obtained through the same types of marketing research used in the domestic market (see Chapter 7). However, global marketing research is conducted in vastly different environments. Conducting a survey can be difficult in developing countries where telephone ownership is rare and mail delivery is slow or sporadic. Drawing samples based on known population parameters is often difficult because of the lack of data. In some cities in South America, Mexico, and Asia, street maps are unavailable, streets are unidentified, and houses are unnumbered. Moreover, the questions a marketer can ask may differ in other cultures. In some cultures, people tend to be more private than in the United States and do not like to respond to personal questions on surveys. For instance, in France questions about one's age and income are considered especially rude.

### PRODUCT AND PROMOTION

With the proper information, a good marketing mix can be developed. One important decision is whether to alter the product or the promotion for the global marketplace. One study suggests that a standardized global marketing strategy may be the best approach, at least for marketing efforts in Western nations.[62] Other options are to radically change the product or to adjust either the promotional message or the product to suit local conditions.

## One Product, One Message

The strategy of global marketing standardization, which was discussed earlier, means developing a single product for all markets and promoting it the same way all over the world. For instance, the American Express "Don't leave home without it" campaign for the American Express card now runs in over thirty nations, from Hong Kong to Brazil to France. The only difference is which well-known persons are featured in the ads in each country. The ads star Sir Terence Conran in Britain and hotelier Karl Nuser in Germany, for example.[63]

Global media—especially satellite and cable TV networks like Cable News Network International, MTV Networks, and British Sky Broadcasting—make it possible to beam advertising to audiences unreachable a few years ago. "Eighteen-year-olds in Paris have more in common with eighteen-year-olds in New York than with their own parents," says William Roedy, director of MTV Europe. MTV's advertisers almost all run unified, English-language campaigns in the twenty-eight nations it reaches. The audiences "buy the same products, go to the same movies, listen to the same music, sip the same colas. Global advertising merely works on that premise."[64]

When Ford unveiled its Mondeo global car in Europe, it decided on a direct-mail campaign in fifteen nations. The advertising theme was "Beauty with inner strength," which plays well with the primarily male, young-to-middle-aged target market. Both Ford and non-Ford owners were targeted, using dealer-generated mailing lists and lists purchased from brokers. Each direct-mail packet contained the name and address of the local Ford dealer. The campaign mailed 850,000 packets, which resulted in a stunning 160,000 showroom visits. Perhaps one reason for the success of the campaign is that most Europeans rarely receive direct-mail promotions. The average Belgian gets seventy-eight pieces of direct mail a year, a German sixty-one pieces, a French consumer fifty-five, and an English citizen forty-two pieces a year. In Spain it's twenty-four. In Ireland, the average person gets just eleven—less than one direct-mail letter or catalog every month.[65]

Both Nike and Reebok spend over $100 million a year in promotion outside the United States. Each company practices global marketing standardization to keep its messages clear and its products desirable. Both companies have exploited basketball's surging popularity around the world. Nike sends Charles Barkley of the Phoenix Suns to Europe and Asia touting its products. Reebok counters by sending basketball superstar Shaquille O'Neal overseas as its ambassador. One of the main appeals of sneakers is their American style; therefore the more American an advertising commercial, the better. The tag lines—whether in Italy, Germany, Japan, or France—all read the same way in English: "Just do it" and "Planet Reebok."[66] NBA All Star Patrick Ewing has created his own global marketing standardization program. He owns Ewing Athletic, which manufactures his signature footware. His commercials, now shown in seventy overseas markets, feature the "Ew the Man" tag line.[67]

Many U.S. television programs are distributed worldwide without modification—especially in Europe, where a significant part of the population is familiar with English and has a lifestyle similar to that of Americans.

© Gamma Liaison/Yvonne Hemsey

Even a one-product, one-message strategy may call for some changes to suit local needs, such as variations in the product's measurement units, package

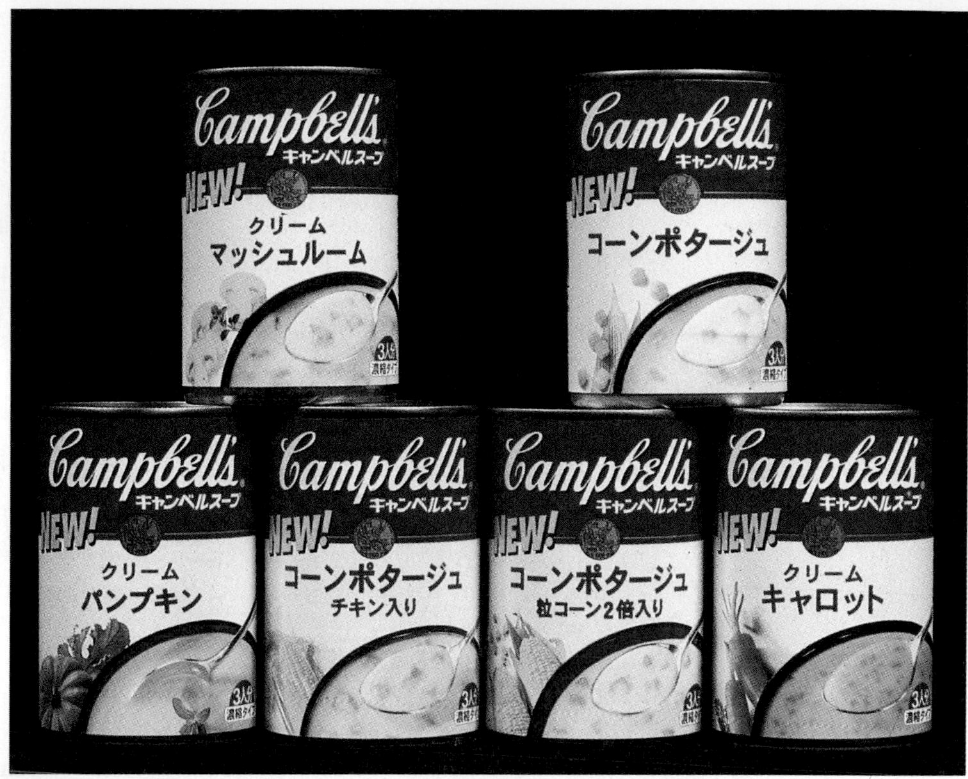


Sometimes companies design new products to meet the needs of a different market. Campbell's Soup has developed a new line of flavors that appeals to Japanese consumers.

sizes, and labeling. Pillsbury, for example, changed the measurement unit for its cake mixes because adding "cups of" has no meaning in many developing countries. Also, in developing countries packages are often smaller so consumers with limited incomes can buy them. For instance, cigarettes, chewing gum, and razor blades may be sold individually instead of in packages.

## Product Invention

In the context of global marketing, product invention can be taken to mean either creating a new product for a market or drastically changing an existing product. For the Japanese market, Nabisco had to remove the cream filling from its Oreo cookies because Japanese children thought they were too sweet. Campbell Soup invented a watercress and duck-gizzard soup that is now selling well in China. It is also considering a cream of snake soup.[68] Apple Computer had difficulty penetrating the Japanese personal computer market for many years. It refused to pay Japanese software developers to convert their programs to run on the Macintosh or to lend developers machines so they could write programs directly for Apple's computers. But after Apple formed close ties with Japanese software companies, it saw sales take off.

Consumers in different countries use products differently. For example, in many countries, clothing is worn much longer between washings than in the United States, so a more durable fabric must be produced and marketed. For Peru, Goodyear developed a tire that contains a higher percentage of natural rubber and has better treads than tires manufactured elsewhere in order to handle the tough Peruvian driving conditions.

## Message Adaptation

Another global marketing strategy is to maintain the same basic product but alter the promotional strategy. Bicycles are mainly pleasure vehicles in the United States. In many parts of the world, however, they are a family's main mode of transportation. Thus promotion in these countries should stress durability and efficiency. In contrast, U.S. advertising may emphasize escaping and having fun.

Harley-Davidson decided that its American promotion theme, "One steady constant in an increasingly screwed-up world," wouldn't appeal to the Japanese market. The Japanese ads combine American images with traditional Japanese ones: American riders passing a geisha in a rickshaw, Japanese ponies nibbling at a Harley motorcycle. Waiting lists for Harleys in Japan are now six months long.[69]

Global marketers find that promotion is a daunting task in some countries. For example, commercial television time is readily available in Canada but severely restricted in Germany. Until recently, marketers in Indonesia had only one subscription TV channel with few viewers (120,000 out of a nation of 180 million people). Because of this limited television audience, several marketers, such as the country's main Toyota dealer, had to develop direct-mail campaigns to reach their target markets.

Some cultures view a product as having less value if it has to be advertised. In other nations, claims that seem exaggerated by U.S. standards are commonplace. On the other hand, Germany does not permit advertisers to state that their products are "best" or "better" than those of competitors, a description commonly used in U.S. advertising. The hard-sell tactics and sexual themes so common in U.S. advertising are taboo in many countries. Procter & Gamble's advertisements for Cheer detergents were voted least popular in Japan because they used hard-sell testimonials. The negative reaction forced P&G to withdraw Cheer from the Japanese market. In the Middle East, pictures of women in print advertisements have been covered with censor's ink.

Language barriers, translation problems, and cultural differences have generated numerous headaches for international marketing managers. Consider these examples:

- A toothpaste claiming to give users white teeth was especially inappropriate in many areas of Southeast Asia, where the well-to-do chew betel nuts and black teeth are a sign of higher social status.
- Procter & Gamble's Japanese advertising for Camay soap nearly devastated the product. In one commercial a man meeting a woman for the first time immediately compared her skin to that of a fine porcelain doll. Although the ad had worked in other Asian countries, the man came across as rude and disrespectful in Japan.
- Pepsi-Cola's slogan "Come alive with Pepsi" translated into German as "Come out of the grave with Pepsi."[70]
- Coca-Cola took out full-page ads in Greek newspapers apologizing for an earlier ad that showed the Parthenon's white marble columns tapered like a Coke bottle. Greeks have great respect for their ancient temples and were highly indignant. The general secretary of the Greek Culture Ministry said, "Whoever insults the Parthenon insults Greece."[71]

### Product Adaptation

Another alternative for global marketers is to slightly alter a basic product to meet local conditions. Additional pizza toppings offered by Domino's in Japan include corn, curry, squid, and spinach.[72] The best-selling doll in the United States is Barbie, but initially she did not sell well in Japan. Parents and children felt that the doll's breasts were too big and the legs too long. After making minor modifications and changing Barbie's eyes from blue to dark brown, Mattel sold 2 million Barbie dolls in Japan in just two years. In spite of this apparent success, Mattel still believed the sales of Barbie were not as high as they should be. Since then, the company's ongoing marketing research has shown that Japanese consumers, particularly younger ones, have become much more receptive to Western products and trends. As a result Mattel decided again to market the more voluptuous, blue-eyed Barbie that it sells in all its other markets.[73]

Regardless of whether a company adapts an existing product, sells a product that is identical to one in the United States, or invents something entirely new, it may need to meet global quality standards like ISO 9000, which is discussed in the accompanying box.

CREATING CUSTOMER VALUE

**An International Standard for Quality**

What is ISO 9000? Dial-a-horoscope? A foreign sports car? A new galaxy? No, ISO 9000 (pronounced "ice-o nine thousand") is a standard of quality management, hugely popular in Europe, that is rapidly taking hold in the United States and around the globe.

The ISO 9000 series was created in the late 1980s by the International Organization for Standardization. The set of five technical standards, known collectively as ISO 9000, was designed to offer a uniform way of determining whether manufacturing plants and service organizations have sound quality procedures. To register, a company must undergo a third-party audit of its manufacturing and customer-service processes, covering everything from how it designs, produces, and installs its goods to how it inspects, packages, and markets them. Worldwide, more than 30,000 certificates have been issued to document compliance with the standards.

Think of ISO 9000 not as another variant of total quality management but as a set of generally accepted accounting principles for documenting quality procedures. It is rapidly becoming an internationally recognized system, comprehensible to buyers and sellers. Says Richard Thompson, vice president and general manager of Caterpillar's engine division, whose Mossville, Illinois, plant was among the first U.S. diesel engine factories to win the certificate: "Today, having ISO 9000 is a competitive advantage. Tomorrow, it will be the ante to the global poker game."

DuPont, General Electric, Eastman Kodak, British Telecom, and Philips Electronics are among the big-name companies that are urging—or even coercing—suppliers to adopt ISO 9000. GE's plastics business, for

*(continued)*

## PRICING

Once marketing managers have determined a global product and promotion strategy, they can select the remainder of the marketing mix. Pricing presents some unique problems in the global sphere. Exporters must not only cover their production costs but also consider transportation costs, insurance, taxes, and tariffs. When deciding on a final price, marketers must also determine what customers are willing to spend on a particular product. Marketers also need to ensure that their foreign buyers will pay them.

Because developing nations lack mass purchasing power, selling to them often poses special pricing problems. Sometimes a product can be simplified in order to lower the price. However, the firm must not assume that low-income countries are willing to accept lower quality. Although the nomads of the Sahara are very poor, they still buy expensive fabrics to make their clothing. Their survival in harsh conditions and extreme temperatures requires this expense. Additionally, certain expensive luxury items can be sold almost anywhere.

## Dumping

**dumping**
Practice of selling products either below cost or below their selling price in their domestic market.

Some companies overproduce certain items and end up dumping them in the international market. **Dumping** occurs when products are sold either below cost or below their selling price in the domestic market.

Dumping of products by foreign producers is illegal in the United States and Europe. During the early 1990s, Japanese producers were charged with dumping computer chips in the U.S. market and VCRs and compact disc players in Europe. In 1993 the U.S. Commerce Department imposed dumping tariffs of up to 109 percent on steel imports from nineteen nations.[75]

## Countertrade

**countertrade**
Form of trade in which all or part of the payment for goods or services is in the form of other goods or services.

Global trade does not always involve cash. Countertrade is a fast-growing way to conduct global business. In **countertrade,** all or part of the payment for goods or services is in the form of other goods or services. Countertrade is thus a form of barter (swapping goods for goods), an age-old practice whose origins have been traced back to cave dwellers. The U.S. Commerce Department says that roughly 30 percent of all global trade is countertrade.[76] In fact, both India and China have made billion-dollar government purchasing lists, with most of the goods to be paid for by countertrade.

One common type of countertrade is straight barter. For example, PepsiCo sends Pepsi syrup to Russian bottling plants and in payment gets Stolichnaya vodka, which is then marketed in the West. Another form of countertrade is the compensation agreement. Typically, a company provides technology and equipment for a plant in a developing nation and agrees to take full or partial payment in goods produced by that plant. For example, General Tire Company supplied equipment and know-how for a Romanian truck tire plant. In turn, General Tire sold the tires it received from the plant in the United States under the Victoria brand name. Pierre Cardin gives technical advice to China in exchange for silk and cashmere. In these cases, both sides benefit even though they don't use cash.

### CREATING CUSTOMER VALUE

instance, commanded 340 vendors to meet the standard by June 1994. Declares John Yates, general manager of global sourcing for the company: "There is absolutely no negotiation. If you want to work with us, you have to get it."

In the United States, the biggest problem surrounding ISO 9000 is ignorance. Nearly two-thirds of the executives at midsize manufacturers have either never heard of ISO 9000 or think it will have no impact on their companies, according to a poll by management consultant Grant Thornton. Other managers cling to the wrong-headed impression that ISO 9000 is a legal requirement for doing business in the European Community. It isn't, although it is steamrolling through Europe. In Britain about 17,500 certificates have been issued, versus just 1,300 in the United States by late 1993.

ISO 9000 is not a solution. It is, at best, a catalyst. Square D, a part of France's Groupe Schneider, which makes circuit breakers and other electrical and electronic equipment, used ISO 9000 as part of a three-year effort to standardize quality management systems in its twenty-nine U.S. plants. But W. F. Fightmaster, vice president for quality, is not one to overplay the importance of ISO 9000. Says he: "There are some people who believe that once you have ISO you have a quality system. That just isn't so. It's less than one-seventh of the system." The other pieces include training and empowering workers, studying competitors' methods ("benchmarking"), and achieving tough goals for continuous improvement.[74]

Do you see ISO 9000 as being important for U.S. multinationals? Why do you think U.S. businesses have been so slow to embrace ISO 9000? Do you think implementing ISO 9000 actually contributes to quality, or is it just another bureaucratic hoop for a company to jump through?

American Marketing Association

## DISTRIBUTION

Solving promotional, price, and product problems does not guarantee global marketing success. The product still has to get adequate distribution. For example, Europeans don't play sports as much as Americans do, so they don't visit sporting-goods stores as often. Realizing this, Reebok started selling its shoes in about 800 traditional shoe stores in France. In one year, the company doubled its French sales. Harley-Davidson had to open two company-owned stores in Japan to get distribution for its Harley clothing and clothing accessories.

The Japanese distribution system is considered the most complicated in the world. Imported goods wind their way through layers of agents, wholesalers, and retailers. For example, a bottle of ninety-six aspirin costs about $20 because the bottle passes through at least six wholesalers, each of whom increases the selling price. The result is that the Japanese consumer pays the world's most exorbitant prices. These distribution channels seem to be based on historical and traditional patterns of socially arranged tradeoffs, which Japanese officials claim are very hard for the government to change. Today, however, the system seems to be changing because of pressure from the Japanese consumer. Japanese shoppers are now placing low prices ahead of quality in their purchase decisions.[77] The retailer who can cut distribution costs and therefore the retail price gets the sale. Some marketers have tried to bypass traditional channels in Japan for a different reason: to ensure that their products get adequate exposure and sales support. For example, Campbell's Soup, owner of Pepperidge Farm cookies, found that the cookies distributed through traditional import channels were out of date and broken by the time they reached consumers. Consequently, Campbell's began selling cookies directly to 7-Eleven stores, which are very popular in Japan. Sales immediately rose to over $16 million annually.

Retail institutions in other countries also may differ from what a company is used to in its domestic market. The terms *department store* and *supermarket* may refer to types of retail outlets that are very different from those found in the United States. Japanese supermarkets, for example, are large multistory buildings that sell not only food but also clothing, furniture, and home appliances. Department stores are even larger outlets, but unlike their U.S. counterparts, they emphasize foodstuffs and operate a restaurant on the premises. For a variety of reasons, U.S.-type retail outlets do not exist or are impractical in developing countries. For instance, consumers may not have the storage space to keep food for several days. Refrigerators, when available, are usually small and do not allow for bulk storage.

Channels of distribution and the physical infrastructure are also inadequate in many developing nations. In China, for example, most goods are carried on poles or human backs, in wheelbarrows and handcarts, or increasingly (and this is an important advance) on bicycles. In recent years much effort has gone into extending the Chinese rail system, but many of the new lines are more strategic than commercial, and most trains are still pulled by steam locomotives.

## LOOKING BACK

Look back at the story about JCPenney at the beginning of the chapter. With world trade running above $4 trillion a year, companies that do not take part in global marketing are missing a great opportunity. However, in order to take part, the managers of companies like JCPenney must possess a global vision and understand target markets, economic groupings, and distribution networks on a worldwide basis.

Where it can be applied, global marketing standardization of product lines offers significant economic benefits. However, different cultures, languages, levels of economic development, and distribution channels in global markets usually require either new products or modified products. Pricing, promotion, and distribution strategies must often be altered as well.

## KEY TERMS

*balance of payments* 70
*balance of trade* 69
*boycott* 81
*buyer for export* 89
*contract manufacturing* 92
*countertrade* 98
*direct foreign investment* 92
*dumping* 98
*exchange control* 81
*export agent* 90
*export broker* 90
*exporting* 89
*fully industrialized society* 79
*General Agreement on Tariffs and Trade (GATT)* 81
*global marketing* 67
*global marketing standardization* 73
*global vision* 67
*industrializing society* 78
*joint venture* 92
*keiretsu* 82
*licensing* 91
*Maastricht Treaty* 85
*market grouping* 81
*multinational corporation (MNC)* 71
*North American Free Trade Agreement (NAFTA)* 83
*preindustrial society* 77
*quota* 81
*takeoff economy* 78
*tariff* 81
*trade agreement* 81
*trade deficit* 69
*traditional society* 77

## SUMMARY

1 **Discuss the importance of global marketing.** Businesspeople who adopt a global vision are better able to identify global marketing opportunities, understand the nature of global networks, and engage foreign competition in domestic markets. In addition, U.S. exports help us reduce the trade deficit and the balance of payments problem.

2 **Discuss the impact of multinationals on the world economy.** Multinational corporations are international traders that regularly operate across national borders. Because of their vast size and financial, technological, and material resources, multinational corporations have a great influence on the world economy. They have the ability to overcome trade problems, save on labor costs, and tap new technology.

3 **Describe the external environment facing global marketers.** Global marketers face the same environmental factors as they do domestically: culture, economic and technological development, political structure, demography, and natural resources. Cultural considerations include societal values, attitudes and beliefs, language, and customary business practices. A country's economic and technological status depends on its stage of industrial development: traditional society, preindustrial society, takeoff economy, industrializing society, or fully industrialized society. Political structure is shaped by political ideology and such policies as tariffs, quotas, boycotts, exchange controls, trade agreements, and market groupings. Demographic variables include population, income distribution, and growth rate.

4 **Identify the various ways of entering the global marketplace.** Firms use the following strategies to enter global markets, in descending order of risk and profit: direct investment, joint venture, contract manufacturing, licensing, and export.

5 **List the basic elements involved in developing a global marketing mix.** A firm's major consideration is how much it will adjust the four P's—product, promotion, place (distribution), and price—within each country. One strategy is to use one product and one promotion message worldwide. A second strategy is to create new products for global markets. A third strategy is to keep the product basically the same but alter the promotional message. A fourth strategy is to slightly alter the product to meet local conditions.

## Discussion and Writing Questions

1. Why is it important that U.S. businesses become more involved in global marketing?
2. Discuss the role of multinational corporations in developing nations.
3. How viable is global marketing standardization for multinational corporations?

✍4. You are marketing manager for a consumer products firm that is about to undertake its first expansion abroad. Write a memo for your staff reminding them of the role culture will play in the new venture. Give examples.

5. Describe how differences in natural resources can affect the global marketing environment.

6. What is meant by "having a global vision"? Why is it important?

✍7. Your state senator has asked you to contribute to her constituents' newsletter a brief article that answers the question "Will there ever be a 'United States of Europe'?" Write a draft of your article, and include reasons why or why not.

8. Why do you think that more companies don't enter the global marketplace through direct investment? After all, it provides the greatest form of control and profit potential.

9. What are some of the unique distribution problems that U.S. marketers face in other countries? How can they be overcome?

## Application for Small Business

Artais Weather Check Incorporated is a small business with a problem most companies would love: It dominates its market in the United States. The problem is that the market is extremely small. Artais makes weather observation systems for small airports. Each year, only a dozen or so small airports can afford a $45,000 system.

Artais quite sensibly turned to exporting for market growth. However, it immediately ran into some new problems. For example, in Egypt the device had to be programmed in English and Arabic.

### Questions

1. What are some other environmental problems Artais might face?
2. Describe how each element of Artais's marketing mix may have to be altered in order to compete globally.

## CRITICAL THINKING CASE

### Mars Incorporated

We are all familiar with its brand-name products—Snickers, M&Ms, Milky Way, maybe even Pedigree pet food. As a global marketer, Mars spends millions to keep these names before us. Yet the privately owned company otherwise stays hidden. It grants no interviews, allows no pictures of executives.

The most glaring current mystery is the change in the company's performance: Between 1991 and 1994, Mars quietly but dramatically gave up market share in both its U.S. and Western European candy businesses. Its pet-food business, the biggest in the world, is losing money in the United States and slowing down in Europe, even in such strongholds as Germany, where Mars has had 80 percent of the market. Nevertheless, with annual sales estimated at $13 billion, the company remains an enormous power worldwide in a collection of food businesses.

Mars Incorporated seems obsessed with its strategy of global expansion: finding converts to its brands in new country after new country, not worrying about those in existing markets. "You've got to understand," says a former Mars executive, "these guys play for the long haul and they aren't afraid of anybody. That is really the way they capitalize on opportunities."

Why is Mars experiencing problems now? The most basic explanation is probably that Mars has ignored some fundamental changes in its competitive environment over the past five years. For one, major competitors like Philip Morris, Nestlé, and Cadbury Schweppes have been gobbling up smaller competitors. And they are bombarding Mars with new offerings, even as the total European market stagnates. They are also outspending Mars for promotion. As a result, Mars has lost market share in Western Europe. In Germany, for instance, its market share in the candy bar category faded from 30 percent in 1991 to 26 percent in 1994.

For all its problems, Mars still displays great abilities as a field organization. Forrest Mars Sr., a meticulous engineer, spent decades in Europe patiently developing the brands. He started a pet-food industry long before most people in those countries would even consider feeding a pet out of a can. His kind of pioneering required an organization that could execute an expansion strategy without much help. Says one global competitor: "One thing Mars does better than any public company is understand the true importance of international markets." Adds a former European executive of Mars: "Mars's real strength, to their credit, is excellent on-the-ground operations. You can go back to a market three years after it opens, and their brands have distribution on a wide scale."

Mars is not just a believer in global expansion, however. It also practices global marketing standardization, the theory that because we live in a homogenizing universe, many products can be sold the same way everywhere. That's why Mars has heavily backed such global sporting events as the World Cup and the Olympics. This simplicity generates savings in advertising, packaging, distribution, and staff. Global marketing standardization works for a product like Snickers, because the brand's promise—Snickers satisfies hunger—has universal application.

However, Mars is just beginning to recover from the idea that the company could run the same marketing program in Spain as in England, say, without maintaining separate marketing staffs in different countries. It failed terribly. Another mistake was the decision to change the color of all the labels in the Whiskas cat-food line to purple. The company, like its competitors, had traditionally used different colors on the cans to denote different varieties: green for rabbit, red for beef, and so on. But to Mars, building a block of color in the manner of Coke seemed to make more sense. The company further compounded its problems by refusing to invest money in new European pet-food products.

The strategy of global marketing standardization also failed at Kal Kan Foods, the U.S. pet-food division. Over the past decade, Kal Kan brands have been changed to Mars's global brands—Pedigree dog food and Whiskas and Sheba cat foods. The Pedigree change was brilliantly executed. But with Whiskas, Mars lost half its market share in the transition.

From Bill Saporito, "The Eclipse of Mars," *Fortune*, 28 November 1994. 

### Questions

1. Why do you think Mars has had so many problems with global marketing standardization?
2. What elements of the global environment need additional attention from Mars executives?
3. If you were made president of Mars Incorporated, what would you do to improve the company's global marketing?

### Reference

Bill Saporito, "The Eclipse of Mars," *Fortune,* 28 November 1994, pp. 82–92.

**VIDEO CASE**

## The Chinese Market

The pace of change in China seems unstoppable. Although the extremely low wages (by U.S. standards) seem to make the market unattractive, China's huge population has incredible total purchasing power. Rapid economic growth (25 percent during a recent six-month period) means more income and a growing middle class. Busy telephone lines and traffic jams are manifestations of China's growth. After years of saving their money, consumers are on a spending spree, which pushed up inflation 20 percent in one year.

The new governor of China's central bank is trying hard to control growth and inflation. He has raised interest rates, called in bank loans, and cut government spending to curb speculation in real estate. Money-hungry local officials have been fired and put in jail. One person who defrauded many stock market customers was executed.

Eugene Martin, the U.S. Consul General in China, notes that doing business in China isn't easy. He tries to guide U.S. businesspeople around the problems of inflation, bureaucratic red tape, payoffs to officials, and patent violations, among others. Yet Martin believes that the huge opportunities outweigh the problems. The Chinese need everything. For example, China's need for electric power plants in the 1990s is equal to the world's total capacity to build such plants.

Questions

1. Do you think China will become one of the top five markets for U.S. companies before the year 2000? Why or why not?

2. Discuss how each of the uncontrollable variables in the external environment might affect a U.S. company doing business in China.

3. Describe how the marketing mix for the following products might have to be altered for Chinese customers: refrigerator, personal computer, pizza, road grader, air compressor.

# PART ONE INTEGRATIVE CASE

## COCA-COLA

*Sue Cisco*

The U.S. soft-drink industry is, like all other industries, dynamic. Many forces can change business conditions. Historically, soft-drink manufacturers in the United States have been able to increase sales by placing their products in as many stores and restaurants as possible. However, fewer and fewer locations are left that don't already carry soft drinks. The result is what marketers call a "mature" market. Another problem the industry is facing is changing consumer preferences. We now prefer lighter, less sweet, and healthier drinks. Finally, the average American consumer already drinks two eight-ounce glasses of carbonated drinks per day.

U.S. soft-drink manufacturers are trying strategies that they feel will enable them to maintain profits in the face of slowing population growth and changing consumer tastes. But Coke and Pepsi, which together account for about 74 percent of the total soft-drink market, are following different strategies. PepsiCo has chosen to diversify through new product development and is also launching aggressive advertising campaigns designed to gain market share for Pepsi. Coca-Cola, on the other hand, has chosen to increase international operations and expand domestically through joint ventures.

The reunification of Germany created a once-in-a-lifetime marketing opportunity for Coke and Pepsi. The East German soft-drink market had been closed to outside manufacturers for nearly forty years.

Even before removal of the Berlin Wall, Coca-Cola had approached the East German government. Although Coca-Cola was not able to begin operations in East Germany at that time, the company did collect some valuable marketing information that enabled it to pursue the market when it eventually opened up.

When the Wall came down, 17 million thirsty East German residents rushed to try the products they had seen advertised on West German television. Consumer surveys conducted at this time indicated that Coca-Cola was a name recognized by 99 percent of East Germans. Other market research indicated that East Germans were dissatisfied with the two government-produced soft drinks and were particularly interested in all Western products. Coca-Cola was also aware of its strong position in West Germany, where 11 percent of the entire company's profits had been generated in the previous year. (Coca-Cola outsells Pepsi 7 to 1 in Europe.)

Despite its advantages, Coca-Cola knew it had to act quickly to ensure success in eastern Germany. Management was aware that restaurants and small outlets would choose to serve just one cola drink—in most cases, the first one to enter the market. Coca-Cola trucks were placed at border crossings so East Berliners, who were seeing western Germany for the first time in forty years, could be presented with cases and six-packs of free Coke. At one location, 70,000 cans were handed out in just a few hours. This goodwill gesture paved the way for Coke representatives trying to convince eastern German merchants and vendors to carry Coke products.

Coke's advertising and promotion strategy was designed to build on its strong position with restaurant owners and to increase demand for Coke products. In East Berlin, sidewalk vendors began carrying signs that said "Drink Coca-Cola," and restaurants and cafes proudly displayed red-and-white umbrellas with the famous Coke logo. To reflect eastern Germans' preference for Western products, Coke used the slogan "You can't beat the feeling"—in English.

Since Coke was introduced in eastern Germany, sales have skyrocketed. Before retail sales actually began, fewer than 200,000 cases of Coke products were sold annually, and they were sold in only a few locations. From the day in mid-February 1990 when retail sales began until the end of the year, Coca-Cola sold an astonishing 126 million cases of product. In the United States, which has almost twenty times more people than eastern Germany has, annual sales are only about ten times as great. Coca-Cola anticipated that by 1995 it would sell over 600 million cases a year, or 35 cases of Coke products for every person. In the United States, in comparison, Coke sells about 11 cases a year for each American.

One of the keys to Coke's success in the eastern German soft-drink market was the proper use of market research. Another significant element was the ability to work with the local government. Unlike its competitors and many other Western companies, Coca-Cola was willing to build production facilities and distribution networks within the former East Germany's borders and thereby create 1,500 jobs for citizens. Additional jobs were provided by giving contracts for packaging, sugar, and pallet manufacturing to local suppliers. Coca-Cola endeared itself as well by becoming a significant corporate taxpayer and a buyer of local goods and services.

Coca-Cola can attribute its international success to many factors. According to experts, the company's strength is reacting quickly to the opportunities that arise. And by hiring local managers who understand the business and the region, Coca-Cola is able to succeed abroad.

### Questions

1. Evaluate Coca-Cola's expansion into the eastern German market by examining the conditions of the U.S. soft-drink market.
2. Compare the American consumer to the consumer in unified Germany. Plan a marketing strategy for the German consumer.
3. Defend Coca-Cola's decision to use the U.S. slogan "You can't beat the feeling" in its lead-off campaign in the German market.
4. Predict Coca-Cola's future success in Germany. Evaluate the impact of Pepsi entering this market.
5. Judging from Coke's success in Germany, what other American products do you think could be marketed there? Evaluate the threats and opportunities they will encounter.

### Suggested Readings

"A World Ahead," *Beverage World,* Fall 1993, pp. 19–26.

Paul Meller, "Eastern Europe: Testing Western Brands' Eastern Impact," *Marketing,* 23 September 1993, pp. 20–25.

Daniel Michaels, "Eastern Europe Is One Hot Market," *Fortune,* 25 January 1993, p. 14.

Patricia Sellers, "Coke Gets Off Its Can in Europe," *Fortune,* 13 August 1992, pp. 68–72.

# PART ONE
# GLOBAL MARKETING CASE

## THE DÜSSELDORF TRADE SHOW

*Linda B. Catlin, Wayne State University*
*Thomas F. White, Regis University*

Brown Automation Company, located in Davenport, Iowa, manufactures transfer presses* for the automotive and appliance industries. The company employs 125 people and has annual sales of $11 million. Currently, company representatives are making plans to participate in a large manufacturing trade show in Düsseldorf, Germany.

During the last three years, Brown's sales department has received numerous telephone and written requests for information about the company's products from European and Japanese firms. Several of these firms have called back after receiving the Brown sales literature and asked that a Brown representative contact the foreign firm when the representative visits Europe or Japan. Until now, Brown has never sent anyone outside North America on sales trips or to attend trade shows, although the company has sold its equipment to several Canadian firms.

Earlier this year, the company president, Jim Nelson, decided that the company should participate in the Düsseldorf trade show. His decision was based on two considerations: first, domestic sales are down 15 percent because of cutbacks in the automotive industry, and second, the increasing number of requests for information from foreign firms convinced him that there was a large potential market in Europe for Brown's products. Jim began preparing for the trade show by calling together Tom Messaic, marketing manager; John Harper, engineering manager; and Alex Carrero, controller.

This group of managers first interviewed two U.S. consultants who had worked with other U.S. companies in setting up marketing operations in Europe, including Germany, and who had contacts throughout Europe in several industries. When the Brown trade show team discussed the pros and cons of hiring one of these consultants to manage the company's participation in the Düsseldorf trade show, Tom and John were in favor, but Jim and Alex argued that the $15,000 fees were too high. As Jim said, "We've participated in many shows here in the United States, and shows can't be that much different in Germany. I know my managers can handle the Düsseldorf show on their own. Tom, I want you to take charge of this one, and John, I want you to work closely with him to cover the technical aspects related to equipment."

Tom began his preparations by calling a meeting of his staff. His marketing coordinator, Janice Beacon, suggested that they contact the local university to find someone who was familiar with German culture.

"When I studied in France during my junior year in college, I found some big differences between the way we do things here and the way the French do those same things," she said. "I think we need to be aware of how Germans conduct business differently than U.S. citizens do."

"I'm sure you're right, Janice," Tom replied, "but right now I think we need to concentrate on some of the technical details of putting together this trade show in Germany. Remember, we have only four months to figure out how to get our equipment there, what the booth will look like, and who we'll send to staff the booth. And Alex has given us a pretty small budget to do all this, so we need to be careful about how we spend the money.

"I've drawn up a list of our usual planning areas for trade shows," Tom continued. "And I've assigned each one of you to take charge of one or two of these areas. I'd like you to put together a plan for covering these at the Düsseldorf show. We'll meet again in two weeks to go over what you've done. Thanks for your input today."

Tom assigned responsibility for the following list of trade show areas to members of his staff:

- Publications, including sales and technical literature for the company's equipment, information about the firm, and business cards
- Staffing requirements for the booth and the hospitality suite at the nearby hotel
- Physical setup of the booth, including size, equipment displays, and backdrop

*A transfer press is a customized, automated piece of industrial equipment used to move a product through two or more steps in the manufacturing process.

- Promotional items and giveaways for businesspeople visiting the booth

To the Student

Assume that you are Tom Messaic, marketing manager for Brown Automation. What issues and questions should your staff members bring up for each of the areas associated with the trade show in Düsseldorf? What are the details that need to be decided on in each area? What special considerations are necessary since this trade show is in Germany and not in the United States? Considering your answers to these questions, what will you recommend to Mr. Nelson, the company president, regarding Brown's participation in the Düsseldorf trade show this year?

INSA
Western Flyer

# PART TWO

# ANALYZING MARKETING OPPORTUNITIES



Kristin Knapp is Vice President of External Relations of AIESEC, the largest student organization in the world. She rose to this leadership position while serving as a volunteer with AIESEC during college. Though Kristin majored in public relations, it was her classes in international business and marketing that prepared her for the environment in which she operates every day. Kristin works with five other people from different AIESEC chapters throughout the United States, helping undergraduates become more aware of foreign cultures through business opportunities. She also interfaces with AIESEC's corporate sponsors—such as AT&T, Arthur Andersen, IBM, and GE—to develop outside ties that will benefit AIESEC.

AIESEC has over 820 chapters in 78 countries. The organization seeks to promote cultural understanding while developing tomorrow's global leadership. This objective is met through two programs. The core program involves an international exchange of members for practical work internships in foreign markets. The other program is the global theme project, in which a of AIESEC's chapters host projects relating to a common theme. These projects are designed to give the students a better perspective on global business and the different cultures of the world. In fact, one recent theme of the project was education toward international and cultural understanding.

Kristin feels that it is vital that companies be aware of differences among cultures, given the global nature of business today. U.S. firms must be open to new ideas from other cultures if they are to target effective marketing and promotional campaigns at people of different backgrounds. Businesses can no longer hope to reach everyone with a single promotional strategy. Many potential customers would be unreceptive to such a unicultural approach. The more specific advertisers are in addressing their customers' needs and wants, the more successful they will be. Kristin believes that an understanding of cultural differences can help businesses achieve the goal of satisfying their customers.

# Chapter 4

# Consumer Decision Making

## LEARNING OBJECTIVES

*After studying this chapter, you should be able to*

1 *Explain why marketing managers should understand consumer behavior.*

2 *Identify the types of consumer buying decisions.*

3 *Analyze the components of the consumer decision-making process.*

4 *Explain the consumer's postpurchase evaluation process.*

5 *Discuss the importance of high and low involvement in buying decisions.*

6 *Identify and understand the individual factors that affect consumer buying decisions.*

7 *Identify and understand the social factors that affect consumer buying decisions.*

Cereal isn't just for breakfast anymore. To help keep sales and profits growing without having to increase prices, some of the nation's most powerful marketers are hoping to convince Americans to curl up in front of the TV set with a new type of snack. A print ad for Ralston Purina's Cookie-Crisp cereal, for example, features a boy popping the sugary nuggets into his mouth while he does his homework. Boxes of Kellogg's Cracklin' Oat Bran boast that the cereal tastes like oatmeal cookies and makes "a great snack . . . anytime." And commercials for Quaker Oats' 100% Natural cereal promote eating it straight from the box.

Many cereal makers are also creating cereals specifically for snacking. For example, General Mills, the nation's number-two cereal maker after Kellogg, has a cereal called Fingos that was made expressly to be consumed without milk and spoon. It is advertised as "the cereal to eat with your fingers," and even the packaging depicts the cereal being eaten with fingers instead of in a bowl of milk.

Convincing consumers to pack a bag of oats in their lunchbox or to give a handful of wheat squares to their kids as an after-school snack may not be easy. Cereal makers are taking on some of the biggest marketers, including PepsiCo's Frito-Lay division and Anheuser-Busch's Eagle Snacks. And changes in consumers' eating habits typically occur very slowly. Although Ralston has been encouraging consumers to make Chex Party Mix since the 1950s and General Mills has been pitching Cheerios as baby's first finger food for two decades, 90 percent of all cereal is still consumed at breakfast. Less than 3 percent is eaten directly from the box.

General Mills is optimistic about the concept of cereal as a finger food. Although cereal accounts for a small percentage of snacks, its consumption has increased over the past ten years. In addition, Americans consume an average of 200 snacks annually (compared to about 300 breakfasts). General Mills originally conceived of Fingos as a portable meal for breakfast skippers, but it found that nearly 80 percent of the product was eaten in the afternoon or evening. The company is counting on cereal's relatively healthful image to give Fingos an edge over more traditional salty snacks.[1]

Although changes in consumption patterns often come slowly, cereal marketers are betting that consumers will eventually warm up to the idea of cereal as a snack. Through their marketing efforts, companies like General Mills are attempting to change consumers' beliefs about cereal to include the idea that it can be consumed at other times of the day besides breakfast. What other ways can marketers change consumers' beliefs about products and brands? What other factors besides beliefs influence consumers' purchasing patterns? Questions like these will be answered as you read about the consumer decision-making process.

1 *Explain why marketing managers should understand consumer behavior.*

## THE IMPORTANCE OF UNDERSTANDING CONSUMER BEHAVIOR

Consumers' lives are in a constant state of flux. As each generation grows and matures, it adopts values and lifestyles somewhat different from those of the previous generation. What is important also changes as consumers progress through the life cycle. Finally, consumers differ according to their demographic and social characteristics.

If a marketing manager's basic task is to create a proper marketing mix for a well-defined market, the manager must have a thorough knowledge of consumer behavior. **Consumer behavior** describes the processes used by consumers to make purchase decisions, as well as to use and dispose of the purchased good or service. The study of consumer behavior also includes the analysis of factors that influence purchase decisions and product use.

**consumer behavior**
Processes a consumer uses to make purchase decisions, as well as to use and dispose of purchased goods or services; also includes factors that influence purchase decisions and the use of products.

The ability to create a product and to persuade people to buy it instead of competitors' offerings requires insight into the consumer purchase process. Knowledge of consumer behavior reduces uncertainty when creating the marketing mix. For example, a manager can better anticipate the impact of a price increase on a product's quality image if he or she understands consumer decision-making processes. Similarly, an appreciation of the role of culture, social class, and family can help advertisers create more effective promotional campaigns.

2 *Identify the types of consumer buying decisions.*

## TYPES OF CONSUMER BUYING DECISIONS

All consumer buying decisions generally fall into three broad categories: routine response behavior, limited decision making, and extensive decision making. When buying frequently purchased, low-cost goods and services, consumers generally use **routine response behavior.** These goods and services can also be called low-involvement products, because consumers spend little time on search and decision before making the purchase. Usually, buyers are familiar with several different brands in the product category but stick with one brand. A parent, for example, will not stand at the cereal shelf in the grocery store for twenty minutes thinking about which brand of cereal to buy for the children. Instead, he or she will walk by the shelf, find the family's usual brand, and put it into the cart.

**routine response behavior**
Type of decision making exhibited by consumers buying frequently purchased, low-cost goods and services; requires little search and decision time.

Suppose the children's usual brand of cereal, Kellogg's Corn Flakes, is unavailable in the grocery store. Completely out of cereal at home, the buyer now must select another brand. Getting information about an unfamiliar brand in a familiar product

Consumer decision making is not all alike. (*left*) The couple buying new golf clubs is using limited decision making, which requires some time for gathering information and analyzing it. (*right*) A big purchase like a car usually requires extensive decision making.

(*left*) © Superstock; (*right*) © 1992 Bill Bachmann/ProFiles West

**limited decision making**
Type of decision making that requires a moderate amount of time for gathering information and deliberating about an unfamiliar brand in a familiar product category.

**extensive decision making**
Most complex type of consumer decision making, used when buying an unfamiliar, expensive product or an infrequently bought item; requires use of several criteria for evaluating options and much time for seeking information.

category is called **limited decision making.** This type of decision making requires a moderate amount of time for gathering information and deliberating. Before making a final selection, our buyer may pull from the shelf several brands similar to Kellogg's Corn Flakes, such as Corn Chex and Cheerios, to compare their nutritional value and calories and to decide whether the children will like the new cereal. Limited decision making is also used for products bought only occasionally, such as tires, cosmetics, and books.

Consumers practice **extensive decision making** when buying an unfamiliar, expensive product or an infrequently bought item. This process is the most complex type of consumer buying decision. Buyers use several criteria for evaluating their options and spend much time seeking information. Buying a home or a car, for example, requires extensive decision making.

The type of decision making that consumers use to purchase a product does not necessarily remain constant. For instance, if a routinely purchased product no longer satisfies, consumers may practice limited or extensive decision making to switch to another brand. And people who first use extensive decision making may then use limited or routine decision making for future purchases. For example, a new mother may first extensively evaluate several brands of disposable diapers before selecting one. Subsequent purchases of diapers will then become routine.

*3 Analyze the components of the consumer decision-making process.*

**consumer decision-making process**
Step-by-step process used by consumers when buying goods or services.

## THE CONSUMER DECISION-MAKING PROCESS

When buying products, consumers follow the **consumer decision-making process** shown in Exhibit 4.1: (1) problem recognition, (2) information search, (3) evaluation of alternatives, (4) purchase, and (5) postpurchase behavior.

Note that the act of buying something is only one step in the process. Not all consumer decision making leads to an actual purchase; the consumer may end the process at any time. Keep in mind, too, that not all purchase decisions proceed in order through all steps of the process. Typically, people engaged in extensive decision making go through all five steps, but those engaged in routine response behavior and limited decision making may skip one or more steps.

Understanding how consumers make purchase decisions can help marketing

*Exhibit 4.1*

Consumer Decision-Making Process

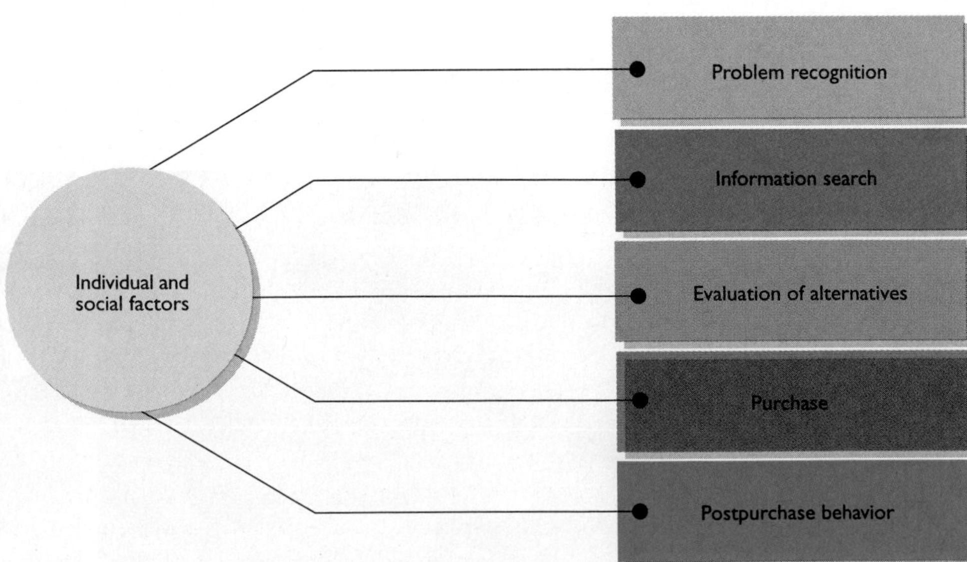

managers in several ways. For example, if a manager knows through research that gas mileage is the most important attribute for a certain target market, the manufacturer can redesign the product to meet that criterion. If the firm cannot change the design in the short run, it can use promotion in an effort to change consumers' decision-making criteria. For example, the manufacturer can advertise the car's maintenance-free features and sporty European style while downplaying gas mileage.

## PROBLEM RECOGNITION

Do you often feel thirsty after strenuous exercise? Has a television commercial for a new sports car ever made you wish you could buy it? Physiological thirst and TV commercials are both stimuli for consumers. A **stimulus** is any unit of input affecting the five senses: sight, smell, taste, touch, hearing. Problem recognition is triggered when a consumer has been exposed to either an internal or an external stimulus. For example, hunger and thirst are *internal stimuli;* the color of an automobile, the design of a package, a brand name mentioned by a friend, an advertisement on television, or cologne worn by a stranger are considered *external stimuli.*

**stimulus**
Any unit of input affecting the five senses: sight, smell, taste, touch, hearing.

An individual experiences **problem recognition** when faced with an imbalance between actual and desired states. The desired state the individual would like to achieve is satisfaction of a need or want. A **need** is anything an individual depends on to function efficiently. Needs are considered the root of all human behavior, for without needs there would be no behavior.

**problem recognition**
Result of an imbalance between actual and desired states.

**need**
Anything an individual depends on to function efficiently; root of all human behavior.

Although marketing managers cannot create needs, they can create wants. A **want** exists when someone has an unfulfilled need and has determined that a particular good or service will satisfy it. Young children might want toys, video games, and baseball equipment. Teenagers may want compact discs, fashionable sneakers, and pizza. A want does not necessarily have to be for a specific product; it can also be for a certain attribute or feature of a product. For instance, older consumers want goods and services that offer convenience, comfort, and security. Remote-control appliances, home deliveries, speaker phones, and motorized carts are all designed for comfort and convenience. Likewise, a transmitter that can signal an ambulance or the police if the person wearing it has an emergency offers security for older consumers.

**want**
Recognition of an unfulfilled need and a product that will satisfy it.

Marketers selling their products in global markets must carefully observe the needs and wants of consumers in various regions. Consumers in Asia, for example, are increasingly looking for products that will simplify their hectic lives and are willing to pay for the right solutions. The desire to save time is already revolutionizing the way Asians shop. Self-service convenience chains and food stores are replacing mom-and-pop shops and street markets. Time-saving products such as Procter & Gamble's Rejoice (known as Pert Plus in the United States), which combines shampoo and conditioner, is a hit with working Asian women. Quick and convenient meals are also a necessity for Asian consumers, who have made both McDonald's and Kentucky Fried Chicken huge successes in the region.[2]

Consumers recognize unfulfilled wants in various ways. The two most common occur when a current product isn't performing properly and when the consumer is about to run out of something that is generally kept on hand. Consumers may also recognize unfulfilled wants if they hear about or see a product whose features make it seem superior to the one currently used. Such wants are usually created by advertising and other promotional activities. For example, a young teenager may develop a strong desire for a new Sega video game set after seeing it on display in a store.

## INFORMATION SEARCH

After recognizing a want, a consumer may or may not search for more information, depending on the perceived benefits of the search versus its perceived costs. The perceived benefits include finding the best price, getting the most desired model, and achieving ultimate satisfaction with the purchase decision. The perceived costs include the time and expense of undertaking the search and the psychological costs of processing information. Consumers will spend time and effort searching as long as the benefits outweigh the costs; that is, the value of more information must be greater than the cost of obtaining it.[3]

**evoked set (consideration set)**
Group of brands, resulting from an information search, from which a buyer can choose.

The information search should yield a group of brands, sometimes called the buyer's **evoked set** (or consideration set), from which the buyer can further evaluate and choose. Consumers do not consider all the brands available in a product category, but they do rather seriously consider a much smaller set. For example, there are more than 30 brands of shampoos and more than 160 types of automobiles available, yet most consumers seriously contemplate only about four shampoos and two to five automobiles when faced with a purchase decision.[4]

### Internal and External Information Searches

**internal information search**
Process of recalling past information stored in the memory.

An information search can occur internally, externally, or both. An **internal information search** is the process of recalling information stored in the memory. This stored information stems largely from previous experience with a product. For instance, perhaps while shopping you encounter a brand of cake mix that you tried some time ago. By searching your memory, you can probably remember whether it tasted good, pleased guests, and was easy to prepare.

**external information search**
Process of seeking information in the outside environment.

**nonmarketing-controlled information source**
Product information source that is not associated with advertising or promotion.

**marketing-controlled information source**
Product information source that originates with marketers promoting the product.

In contrast, an **external information search** seeks information in the outside environment. There are two basic types of external information sources: nonmarketing-controlled and marketing-controlled. A **nonmarketing-controlled information source** is not associated with marketers promoting a product. A friend, for example, might recommend an IBM personal computer because he or she bought one and likes it. Nonmarketing-controlled information sources include personal experience (trying or observing a new product); personal sources (family, friends, acquaintances, and coworkers); and public sources, such as Underwriters Laboratories, *Consumer Reports,* and other rating organizations.

A **marketing-controlled information source,** on the other hand, is biased toward a specific product, because it originates with marketers promoting that product. Marketing-controlled information sources include mass-media advertising (radio, newspaper, television, and magazine advertising), sales promotion (contests, displays, premiums, and so forth), salespeople, and product labels and packaging. Many consumers are wary about the information they receive from marketing-controlled sources, arguing that most marketing campaigns stress the attributes of the product and don't mention the faults. These sentiments tend to be stronger among better-educated and higher-income consumers.

### Factors Influencing the External Search

The extent to which an individual conducts an external search depends on perceived risk, knowledge, prior experience, and level of interest in the good or service.[5] Generally, as the perceived risk of the purchase increases, the consumer enlarges the search and considers more alternative brands in the evoked set. For instance, assume you want to buy a new car. The decision is a relatively risky one, mainly because of cost, so you are motivated to search for information about models, options, gas

Some consumer decision making is influenced by nonmarketing-controlled sources. For example, this woman decided to buy an IBM personal computer because a friend recommended that brand over others.

© IBM

mileage, durability, passenger capacity, and so forth. You may also decide to gather information about more models, because the trouble and time expended in finding the data are less than the cost of buying the wrong car.

The more knowledgeable and better informed consumers are about a potential purchase, the less they need to search. Also, the more that consumers already know, the more efficiently they search; that is, consumers will seek less information about inappropriate alternatives, and their evoked set will be smaller. A second, closely related factor is confidence in one's decision-making ability. A confident consumer not only has plenty of stored information about the product but also feels self-assured about making the right decision. People lacking this confidence will continue an information search even when they know a great deal about the product.

Consumers with prior experience in buying a certain product will have less perceived risk than inexperienced consumers. Therefore, they will spend less time searching and limit the number of products in their evoked set.

Moreover, consumers who have had a positive prior experience with a product are more likely to limit their evoked set to only those items related to the positive experience. For example, many consumers are loyal to Honda automobiles, which enjoy low repair rates and high customer satisfaction, and own more than one.

Finally, the extent of the search undertaken is positively related to the amount of interest a consumer has in a product. That is, a consumer who is more interested in a product will spend more time searching for information and alternatives. For example, suppose you are a dedicated runner who reads jogging and fitness magazines and catalogs. In searching for a new pair of running shoes, you may enjoy reading about the new brands available and spend more time and effort than other buyers in deciding on the right shoe.

## EVALUATION OF ALTERNATIVES AND PURCHASE

After getting information and constructing an evoked set of alternative products, the consumer is ready to make a decision. A consumer will use the information stored in memory and obtained from outside sources to develop a set of criteria. These standards help the consumer evaluate and compare alternatives. One way to begin narrowing the number of choices in the evoked set is to pick a product attribute and then exclude all products in the set that don't have that attribute. For instance, assume that John is thinking about buying a new compact disc player. He is interested in a remote control and the ability to hold several discs at one time (product attributes), so he excludes all compact disc players without these features.

Another way to narrow the number of choices is to use "cutoffs," minimum or maximum levels of an attribute that an alternative must pass to be considered further.[6] Suppose John still must choose from a wide array of remote-control, multidisc players. He then names another product attribute: price. Given the amount of money he has saved, John decides he cannot spend more than $200. Therefore, he can exclude all compact disc players priced above $200. To reach a final decision, John would pick the most important attributes, such as a remote control or ability to hold several discs at a time, weigh the merits of each, and then evaluate alternative players on those criteria.

Adding new brands to an evoked set affects the consumer's evaluation of the existing brands in that set. As a result, certain brands in the original set may become more desirable.[7] For example, suppose John sees two compact disc players priced at $100 and $150. At the time, he may judge the $150 player as too expensive and choose not to purchase it. However, if he then adds to his list of alternatives another compact disc player that is priced at $250, he may come to judge the $150 one as less expensive and decide to purchase it.

A person's tendency to think ahead may also affect his purchase decisions. Consumers who consider how they would feel if they made the wrong choice are likely to make a purchase decision more quickly. Additionally, consumers are likely to prefer a higher-priced, well-known brand over a less expensive, lesser-known brand if they consider how they would feel in the event they made the wrong decision. Say that John is debating whether to buy the $100 or $150 compact disc player. If he fears that he will come to regret choosing the $100 model, research suggests that he will tend to decide to buy the $150 model right

CREATING CUSTOMER VALUE

### Wonder Corporation

Top management of Wonder Corporation decided to initiate a customer satisfaction program, starting with the product that accounts for 30 percent of company sales. A list of twenty-two critically important product attributes was developed from information gathered in a variety of market interviews, and those attributes were grouped into seven categories: Product quality, delivery service, salesperson helpfulness, product design, after-sale service, billing, and value. Wonder executives were shocked to learn the number of variables that influence customer satisfaction.

Furthermore, the executives were chagrined to learn that product quality was only one of seven broad categories of customer concern. Several years earlier, the company had started a quality-improvement program. In retrospect, the executives realized that they had fallen into a common trap, trying to improve in areas chosen by management rather than by customers.

With the list of critically important attributes, Wonder Corporation conducted a telephone survey of about 850 past and current customers as well as competitors' customers. The current Wonder customers seemed pleasantly surprised that the company was concerned about their opinions and were open in their comments about the attributes that were important to them and the company's performance in those areas.

The data were summarized and presented in the form of the grid in Exhibit 4.2. Because survey respondents indicated that salesperson and value attributes were highly important but poorly met by Wonder

*Exhibit 4.2*

Wonder Corporation Priorities for Improvement

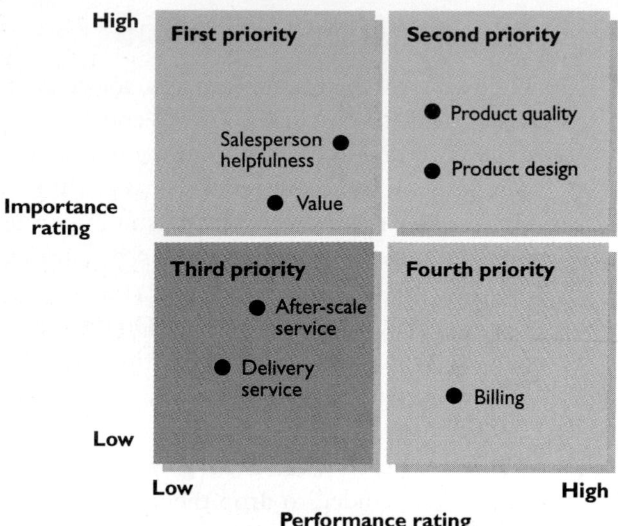


away rather than wait. The lesson for marketers of better-known brands competing with less-expensive and less-well-known alternatives is to try to make consumers think about how they would feel if they made the wrong decision. For example, one Kodak ad showed a consumer who regrets, after the fact, buying a cheaper film.[8]

Even when John has every intention of purchasing a new compact disc player, his purchase decision may be superseded by others' opinions as well as by unexpected situations. What if John's wife strongly opposes his decision to buy a compact disc player because she wants him to save money for their vacation? Then the chances of John's buying one are greatly reduced. Or suppose that John decides to buy a cassette player instead of a compact disc player, because cassettes are cheaper than compact discs. Unexpected situations that may also influence John's actual purchase include a change in family income, an increase in the price of disc players, or a decrease in the perceived value of the product to him.

The accompanying box shows how companies can determine which attributes are most important to consumers. Understanding the criteria used to evaluate competing products can lead directly to increased sales, as Wonder Corporation discovered.

**CREATING CUSTOMER VALUE**

Corporation, they were originally targeted as the first priority for improvement.

These data provided valuable guidance, but the company still needed to know how well it compared with three key competitors. Thus Wonder's executives conducted another survey evaluating similar products from four companies. (Wonder's identity was, of course, disguised.) Respondents were asked to indicate the relative importance of each of the seven categories of attributes and to rate the performance of Wonder Corporation's product as well as the performance of competing products. The results showed which attribute categories were competitive weaknesses and should therefore be a priority. Value came out as the most pressing problem, followed by after-sale service, salesperson helpfulness, delivery service, billing, product design—and, finally, product quality.

The executives used this information to develop an action plan for improving Wonder's primary product. Resources were allocated on the basis of the competitive priorities that had been revealed in the second survey.

After a year of progress on every attribute, Wonder found that customer satisfaction with its product had surpassed customer satisfaction with the market leader's product. That success convinced Wonder's executives to extend the same customer satisfaction program to the company's other five products.

How many attributes should Wonder's marketing action plan emphasize? Which attributes should be the focus? Should the action plan focus on making consumers aware or on persuading them?

4 *Explain the consumer's postpurchase evaluation process.*

## POSTPURCHASE BEHAVIOR

Following the evaluation process, the consumer decides which product to buy (or decides not to buy at all). If the consumer does indeed buy a product, he or she expects certain outcomes from the purchase. How well these expectations are met determines whether the consumer is satisfied or dissatisfied with the purchase.

Consider this example: A person buys a used car with somewhat low expectations for the car's actual performance. Surprisingly, the car turns out to be one of the best cars she has ever owned. Thus the buyer's satisfaction is high, because her fairly low expectations were exceeded. On the other hand, a consumer who buys a brand-new car would expect it to perform especially well. But if the car turns out to be a lemon, she will be very dissatisfied, because her high expectations have not been met.

Price often creates high expectations. One study found that higher monthly cable TV bills were associated with greater expectations for cable service. Over time, cable subscribers tended to drop the premium-priced cable channels because their high expectations were not met.[9]

The degree of satisfaction or dissatisfaction with a product varies from person to person. Obviously, the more a consumer searches for information, the more satisfied he or she may be with a purchase. With increased knowledge, the buyer has more realistic expectations of the product. Also, people who feel competent in their everyday lives, and who therefore tend to feel confident about their decisions, may also be more satisfied with their major purchases than those who feel less competent.

One important element of any postpurchase evaluation is reducing any lingering

The details in these car ads help people who have already bought the advertised model to feel at ease with their purchase. To reduce cognitive dissonance, people often seek confirmation that they made the right decision.

*(left)* © BMW; *(right)* © Mercedes-Benz

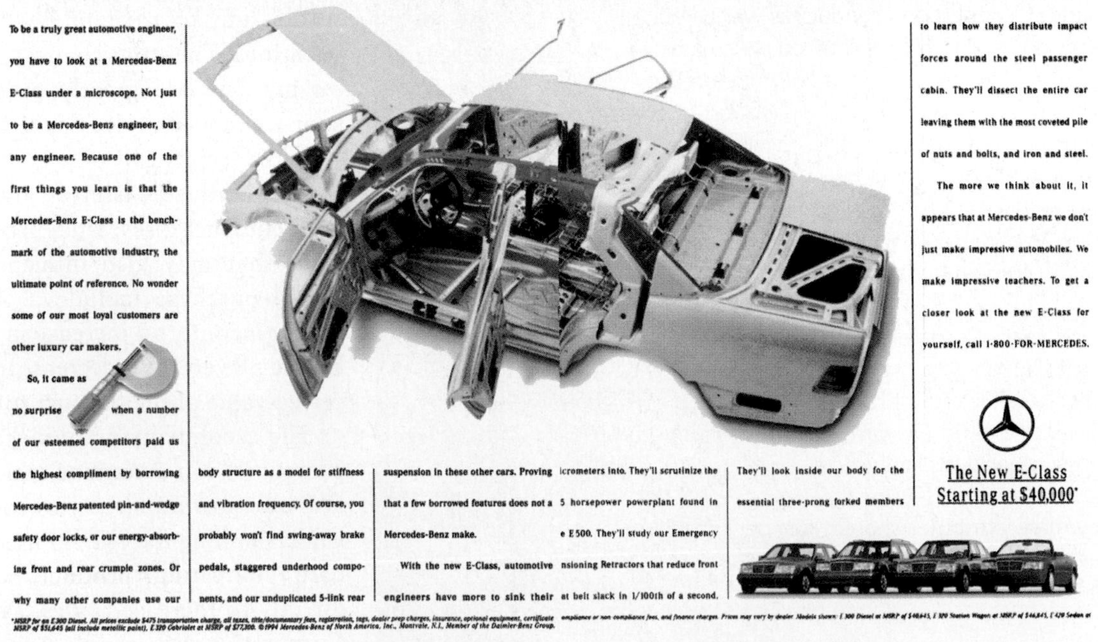

**cognitive dissonance**
Inner tension that a consumer experiences after recognizing an inconsistency between behavior and values or opinions.

doubts that the decision was sound. When people recognize inconsistency between their values or opinions and their behavior, they tend to feel an inner tension called **cognitive dissonance.** For example, suppose a consumer spends half his monthly salary on a new high-tech stereo system. If he stops to think how much he has spent, he will probably feel dissonance. Dissonance occurs because the person knows the purchased product has some disadvantages as well as some advantages. In the case of the stereo, the disadvantage of cost battles the advantage of technological superiority.

Consumers try to reduce dissonance by justifying their decision. They might seek new information that reinforces positive ideas about the purchase, avoid information that contradicts their decision, or revoke the original decision by returning the product. People who have just bought a new car often read more advertisements for the car they have just bought than for other cars in order to reduce dissonance. In some instances, people deliberately seek contrary information in order to refute it and reduce dissonance. Dissatisfied customers sometimes rely on word of mouth to reduce cognitive dissonance, by letting friends and family know they are displeased.

Marketing managers can help reduce dissonance through effective communication with purchasers. For example, a customer-service manager may slip a note inside the package congratulating the buyer on making a wise decision. Postpurchase letters sent by manufacturers and dissonance-reducing statements in instruction booklets may help customers feel at ease with their purchase. Advertising that displays the product's superiority over competing brands can also help relieve the possible dissonance of someone who has already bought the product.

5 *Discuss the importance of high and low involvement in buying decisions.*

## CONSUMER INVOLVEMENT IN BUYING DECISIONS

People usually experience cognitive dissonance only when buying high-involvement products. *Involvement* refers to the amount of time and effort a buyer invests in the search, evaluation, and decision processes of consumer behavior. The level of involvement in the purchase depends on the product's economic and social importance to the consumer. Buying a prestigious car may be more socially important to one consumer than to another. Involvement also varies according to product category and brand.

**high-involvement decision making**
Process of deliberately searching for information about products and brands in order to evaluate them thoroughly.

Consumers who deliberately search for information about products and brands in order to evaluate them thoroughly are most likely engaging in **high-involvement decision making.** This process resembles the model outlined in Exhibit 4.1. These consumers want to make the right decision, so they want to know as much as they can about the product category and the available brands. Goods and services that are usually high-involvement purchases are cars, TV sets, refrigerators, washing machines, home computers, insurance policies, and financial investments. Consumers usually shop around for these products, seeking information from friends, publications, manufacturers, and retailers.

**low-involvement decision making**
Process of deciding to buy a product in which the consumer experiences little perceived risk, low identification with the product, or little personal relevance.

On the other hand, suppose a shopper goes to the grocery store and notices a new brand of chocolate bar. The consumer thinks, "I'd really like some chocolate right now. It looks good. Why not try one?" The consumer perceives little risk if the wrong decision is made. So what if the candy bar doesn't quite meet the consumer's expectations? Such **low-involvement decision making** sharply contrasts with what goes into the purchase of a new car or home. In low-involvement decision making, the consumer experiences little perceived risk, little identification with the product, and little personal relevance.

In low-involvement buying situations, consumers normally don't experience problem recognition until they are exposed to advertising or see an item displayed on a shelf. They tend to learn about low-involvement products in an almost random, spontaneous fashion. They buy first and evaluate later, whereas the reverse is true for high-involvement products. With low-involvement products, buyers seek an acceptable level of satisfaction. They tend to buy familiar brands that they expect will give them the fewest problems. For example, consumers might buy Coke because they are thirsty and want a soft drink. Although they are familiar with other brands of soft drinks, they have learned through experience that Coke tastes good to them. However, few social or financial consequences are associated with buying soft drinks, so consumers risk little in choosing Coke.

Low-involvement decision making is typical in habitual consumer behavior, characterized by brand loyalty. Buyers may plan such a purchase. For example, a shopper may decide to buy Minute Maid orange juice before going to the grocery store. But the purchase decision results from experiences and evaluations that have occurred over a number of purchases. Over time, consumers build brand awareness and develop simple tactics for choosing products, which permit a quick yet satisfactory decision.[10]

### FACTORS AFFECTING INVOLVEMENT LEVEL

Five factors influence a consumer's level of involvement in the purchase process:

- *Previous experience:* When consumers have had previous experience with a good or service, the level of involvement typically decreases. After repeated product trials, consumers learn to make quick choices. Because consumers are familiar with the product and know whether it will satisfy their needs, they become less involved in the purchase. For example, consumers with pollen allergies typically buy the sinus medicine that has relieved their symptoms in the past.

- *Interest:* Involvement is directly related to consumer interests, as in cars, music, movies, bicycling, or electronics. Naturally, these areas of interest vary from one individual to another. Although some people have little interest in nursing homes, a person with elderly parents in poor health may be highly interested.
- *Perceived risk of negative consequences:* As the perceived risk in purchasing a product increases, so does a consumer's level of involvement. Several types of risks concern consumers. First, financial risk is exposure to loss of wealth or purchasing power. Because high risk is associated with high-priced purchases, consumers tend to become extremely involved. Therefore, price and involvement are usually directly related: As price increases, so does the level of involvement. For example, someone who is thinking of buying a home will normally spend much time and effort to find the right one. Second, consumers take social risks when they buy products that can affect people's social opinions of them (for example, driving an old, beat-up car or wearing unstylish clothes). Third, buyers undergo psychological risk if they feel that making the wrong decision might cause some concern or anxiety. For example, should a working parent hire a babysitter or enroll the child in a day-care center?
- *Situation:* The circumstances of a purchase may temporarily transform a low-involvement decision into a high-involvement one. High involvement comes into play when the consumer perceives risk in a specific situation. For example, an individual might routinely buy low-priced brands of liquor and wine. However, when the boss visits, the consumer might make a high-involvement decision and buy more prestigious brands.
- *Social visibility:* Involvement also increases as the social visibility of a product increases. Products often on social display include clothing (especially designer labels), jewelry, cars, and furniture. All these items make a statement about the purchaser and, therefore, carry a social risk.

### INVOLVEMENT IMPLICATIONS FOR THE MARKETING MANAGER

Marketing managers have several responsibilities when dealing with high-involvement product purchases. For one thing, promotion to the target market should be extensive and informative. A good ad gives consumers the information they need for making the purchase decision, as well as specifying the benefits and unique advantages of owning the product. For example, Jaguar runs lengthy ads that detail technical information about its luxury cars.

Want recognition for low-involvement purchases often does not occur until the consumer is in the store. Therefore, in-store promotion is an important tool when promoting low-involvement products. Marketing managers have to focus on package design so the product will be eye-catching and easily recognized on the shelf. Examples of products that take this approach are Campbell's soups, Tide detergent, Velveeta cheese, and Heinz catsup. In-store displays also stimulate sales of low-involvement products. A good display can explain the product's purpose and prompt recognition of a want. Displays of health and beauty-aid items in supermarkets have been known to increase sales many times above normal. Coupons, cents-off deals, and two-for-one offers also effectively promote low-involvement items.

Linking a product to a higher-involvement issue is another tactic that marketing managers can use to increase the sales of a low-involvement product. For example, many food products are no longer just nutritious but also low in fat or cholesterol. Although packaged food may normally be a low-involvement product, reference to health issues raises the involvement level. Special K cereal has been around for several decades. To take advantage of today's interest in health and low-fat foods, it now advertises that its cereal contains no fat. Likewise, Rice Krispies promotes that fact that its formula is low in sugar, and Cheerios advertises that it is also an excellent source of oat bran.

*6 Identify and understand the individual factors that affect consumer buying decisions.*

## INDIVIDUAL FACTORS INFLUENCING CONSUMER BUYING DECISIONS

The consumer decision-making process does not occur in a vacuum. On the contrary, several individual and social factors strongly influence the decision process. Exhibit 4.3 summarizes these influences. They have an effect from the time a consumer perceives a stimulus through postpurchase behavior.

The individual factors that affect consumer behavior are unique to each person. These factors include perception; motivation; learning; values, beliefs, and attitudes; and personality, self-concept, and lifestyle.

### PERCEPTION

**perception**
Process by which people select, organize, and interpret stimuli into a meaningful and coherent picture.

**selective exposure**
Process whereby a consumer notices certain stimuli and ignores other stimuli.

The world is full of stimuli. The process by which we select, organize, and interpret these stimuli into a meaningful and coherent picture is called **perception.** In essence, perception is how we see the world around us and how we recognize that we have a consumption problem.

#### Selective Perception

People cannot perceive every stimulus in their environment. Therefore, they use **selective exposure** to decide which stimuli to notice and which to ignore. A typical

*Exhibit 4.3*

Individual and Social Factors That Affect Consumer Decision-Making Process

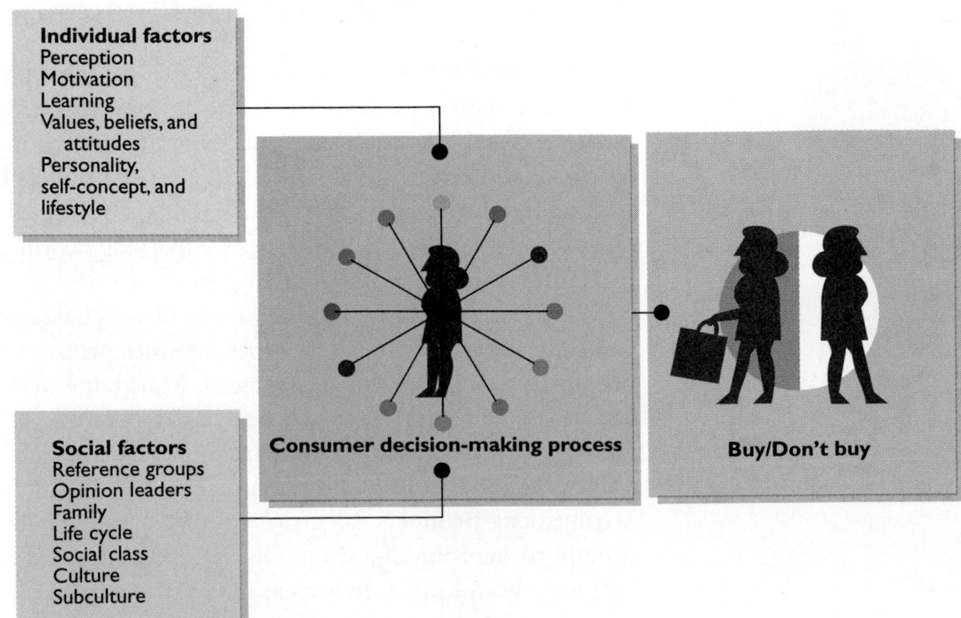

consumer is exposed to over 150 advertising messages a day but notices only between 11 and 20.

The familiarity of an object, contrast, movement, intensity (such as increased volume), and smell are cues that influence perception. Consumers use these cues to identify and define products and brands. Color is another cue, and it plays a key role in consumers' perceptions. One study gave college students three different "flavors" of chocolate pudding that was, in reality, vanilla pudding with food coloring added to varying degrees. Students rated the dark brown pudding as having the best chocolate flavor and the two lighter puddings as being creamier. Not one of the students indicated he or she was tasting a flavor of pudding other than chocolate. Thus, color proved to be a critical cue for judging chocolate pudding. In fact, one might conclude that the color of the pudding was more important than its taste.[11]

What is perceived by consumers may also depend on stimuli's vividness or shock value. Graphic warnings of the hazards associated with a product's use are perceived more readily and remembered more accurately than less vivid warnings.[12] "Sexier" ads excel at attracting the attention of younger consumers. Companies like Calvin Klein and Guess use sensuous ads to "cut through the clutter" of competing ads and other stimuli to capture the attention of the target audience. Similarly, Benetton ads use shock value to cut through the clutter by portraying taboo social issues, from racism to homosexuality.

**selective distortion**
Process whereby a consumer changes or distorts information that conflicts with his or her feelings or beliefs.

Two other concepts closely related to selective exposure are selective distortion and selective retention. **Selective distortion** occurs when consumers change or distort information that conflicts with their feelings or beliefs. For example, suppose a consumer buys a Chrysler. After the purchase, if the consumer receives new information about a close alternative brand, such as a Ford, he or she may distort the information to make it more consistent with the prior view that the Chrysler is better than the Ford. Business travelers who fly often may distort or discount information about airline crashes because they must use air travel constantly in their jobs. People who smoke and have no plans to quit may distort information from medical reports and the Surgeon General about the link between cigarettes and lung cancer.

**selective retention**
Process whereby a consumer remembers only that information that supports his or her personal beliefs.

**Selective retention** is remembering only information that supports personal feelings or beliefs. The consumer forgets all information that may be inconsistent. After reading a pamphlet that contradicts one's political beliefs, for instance, a person may forget many of the points outlined in it.

Which stimuli will be perceived often depends on the individual. People can be exposed to the same stimuli under identical conditions but perceive them very differently. For example, two people viewing a TV commercial may have different interpretations of the advertising message. One person may be thoroughly engrossed by the message and become highly motivated to buy the product. Thirty seconds after the ad ends, the second person may not be able to recall the content of the message or even the product advertised.

## Marketing Implications of Perception

Marketers must recognize the importance of cues, or signals, in consumers' perception of products. Marketing managers first identify the important attributes, such as price or quality, that the targeted consumers want in a product and then design signals to communicate these attributes. For example, consumers will pay more for candy wrapped in expensive-looking foil packages. But shiny labels on wine bottles signify less expensive wines; dull labels indicate more expensive wines. Anheuser-Busch raised the price on many of its less expensive beers to make its

In marketing wine, the label is an important perceptual cue to the value of the product. Consumers perceive wine bottles with dull rather than shiny labels as being worth more.

© Tony Stone Images/Robert D. Smith

premier brand, Budweiser, more attractive to consumers.[13] Marketers also often use product warranties as a signal to consumers that the product is of higher quality than competing products. Consumers who perceive these warranties as highly credible generally perceive the product to be of higher quality.[14]

Of course, brand names send signals to consumers. The brand names of Close-Up toothpaste, DieHard batteries, and Frigidaire appliances, for example, identify important product qualities. Brand names that incorporate numbers or letters, such as Mazda RX-7 or WD-40, invoke images of masculine, high-tech, futuristic products.[15] Consumer also perceive quality and reliability with certain brand names. The ten brand names with the highest perceived value are Disney World, Kodak, Hallmark, UPS, Fisher-Price, Levi's, Mercedes-Benz, Arm & Hammer, AT&T, and IBM.[16]

Naming a product after a place can also add perceived value by association. The names Santa Fe and Dakota convey a sense of openness, freedom, and youth, but products named after New Jersey or Detroit might conjure images of pollution and crime.[17] Brand names that use the word *Texas* evoke feelings of independence, opportunity, and fun because of the state's dramatic history and the fact that many consumers still think of Texas as embodying the American West.[18] Some brand names capitalizing on these associations are shown in Exhibit 4.4.

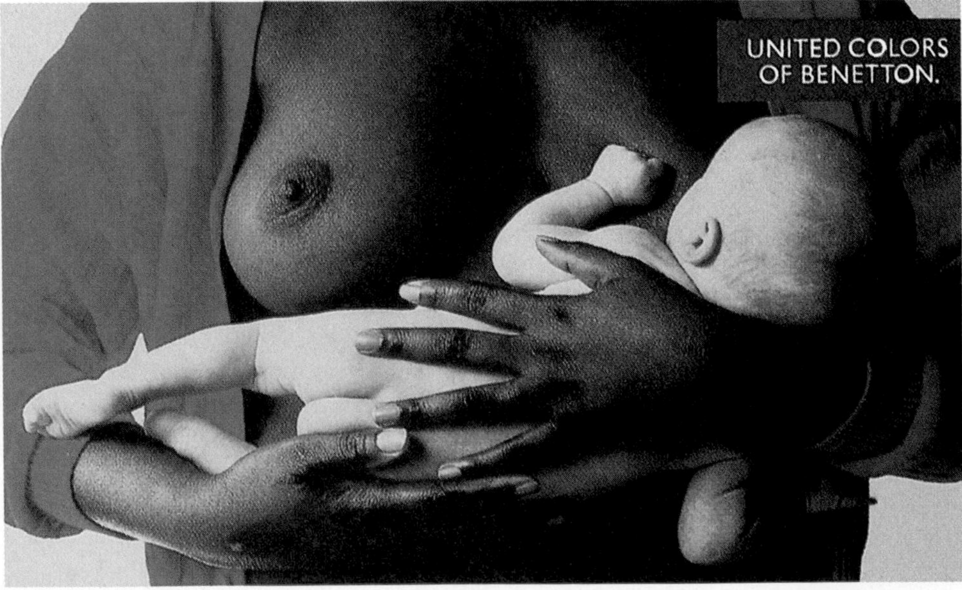

To cut through the clutter of advertising that the average consumer is exposed to, companies like Benetton use startling images on taboo themes to attract attention.

© Benetton

| Brand | Product type | Manufacturer |
| --- | --- | --- |
| Texas Instruments | Calculators, electronic components | Texas Instruments Inc. (Dallas) |
| Big Texas | Hamburger buns | Metz Baking Co. (Dubuque, Iowa) |
| Texas Best | Barbecue and picante sauces | T. Marzetti Co. (Columbus, Ohio) |
| Best of Texas | Sauces, jellies, pickled products | Best of Texas Inc. (Detroit, Tex.) |
| Texas Annies | Sauces | Hecht & Phillips Enterprises (Arlington, Tex.) |
| Lone Star Steakhouse & Saloon | Restaurants | Lone Star Steakhouse & Saloon Inc. (Wichita, Kans.) |
| Lone Star Honey | Honey | Lone Star Honey Co. (Leander, Tex.) |
| Old El Paso | Mexican foods | Pet Inc. (St. Louis, Mo.) |
| Texas Brand | Boots | Texas Boot Co. (Lebanon, Tenn.) |
| Tex Twill | Jeans | Levi Strauss & Co. (San Francisco) |
| Texas Gunpowder | Ground jalapeno seasoning | Texas Gunpowder Inc. (Mesquite, Tex.) |
| Texas Cola | Soft drinks | Texas Beverage Packers Inc. (San Antonio, Tex.) |
| Texas Pride | Baking nuts | Sunshine Nut Co. (San Antonio, Tex.) |
| Texas Pride Barbecue Seasoning | Seasoning | American Spice & Seasonings Inc. (Dallas) |
| Texas Pride | Beer | Pearl Brewing Co. (San Antonio, Tex.) |
| Texas Pete Hot Sauce | Hot sauces | T.W. Garner Food Co. (Winston-Salem, N.C.) |
| TexJoy | Coffee | Texas Coffee Co. (Beaumont, Tex.) |
| Bob's Texas Style Potato Chips | Potato chips | Bob's Texas Style Potato Chips (Brookshire, Tex.) |
| Boone's Texas Shake | Spices | Boones's Texas Shake (Cuero, Tex.) |
| Arlene's Texas Traditions | Jams, peppers, pickled products | Arlene's Texas Traditions (Berclair, Tex.) |
| Tex-O-Gold | Chili | Tex-O-Gold (Fort Worth, Tex.) |
| Texas Star Beef Jerky | Beef jerky | Brenham Sausage Co. (Brenham, Tex.) |
| Texas Chewie Pecan Praline | Candy | Lammes Candies Inc. (Austin, Tex.) |
| Early Texas Tastes | Preserves, relishes, sauces | Early Texas Tastes (Roby, Tex.) |
| Fresh From Texas | Alfalfa sprouts, chop suey mix | Energy Sprouts Inc. (San Antonio, Tex.) |
| Jake's Texas | Peanuts, dandy, spice mixes | Hammered-Down Supply (Hawkins, Tex.) |
| Harley's Texas Style | Seasoning, barbecue | Harley Goerlitz (Giddings, Tex.) |
| Texas Smoke | Wood ships, seasoning | Indian Creek Mesquite Inc. (Brownwood, Tex.) |
| Texas Taste Buds Fire & Brimstone | Jalapeno peanut brittle | Texas Taste Buds (Seabrook, Tex.) |
| Texmati Rice | Rice | RiceTec (Alvin, Tex.) |

*Exhibit 4.4*

Some Brand Names That Capitalize on Favorable Perceptions of the Lone Star State

Source: Kathleen Deveny, "What's in a Name? A Lot if It's 'Texas,'" *The Wall Street Journal*, 24 November 1993, p. T1. Reprinted by permission of *The Wall Street Journal*, © 1993 Dow Jones & Company, Inc. All Rights Reserved Worldwide.

Marketing managers are also interested in the *threshold level of perception:* the minimum difference in a stimulus that the consumer will notice. This concept is sometimes referred to as the "just-noticeable difference." For example, how much would Sony have to drop the price of a VCR before consumers recognized it as a bargain—$25? $50? or more? One study found that the just-noticeable difference in a stimulus is about a 20-percent change. For example, consumers will likely notice a 20-percent price decrease more quickly than a 15-percent decrease. This marketing principle can be applied to other marketing variables as well, such as package size or loudness of a broadcast advertisement.[19] Another study showed that the bargain-price threshold for a name brand is lower than that for a store brand. In other words, consumers perceive a bargain more readily when stores offer a small discount on a name-brand item than when they offer the same discount on a store brand; a larger discount is needed to achieve a similar effect for a store brand.[20]

Besides changing such stimuli as price, package size, and volume, marketers can change the product. For example, how many sporty features will General Motors have to add to a basic two-door sedan before consumers begin to perceive the model as a sports car? How many new services will a discount store like Kmart need to add before consumers perceive it as a full-service department store?

Marketing managers who intend to do business in global markets should be aware of how foreign consumers perceive their products. For instance, in Japan, product labels are often written in English or French, even though they may not translate into anything meaningful. But many Japanese associate foreign words on product labels with the exotic, the expensive, and high quality. Likewise, many Europeans perceive U.S.-made goods as being higher in quality than locally produced goods. Marketers using down-home American imagery in advertising and marketing have experienced huge successes in Europe. For example, Jeep, calling itself "The American Legend" in Europe, saw sales surge to 25,000 in 1993 from 18,000 in 1991. Print advertising in the United Kingdom features a Jeep with English license plates in front of a log cabin flying a U.S. flag.[21]

## MOTIVATION

By studying motivation, marketers can analyze the major forces influencing consumers to buy or not buy products. When you buy a product, you usually do so to fulfill some kind of need. These needs become motives when aroused sufficiently. For instance, suppose this morning you were so hungry before class that you needed to eat something. In response to that need, you stopped at McDonald's for an Egg McMuffin. In other words, you were motivated by hunger to stop at McDonald's. **Motives** are the driving forces that cause a person to take action to satisfy specific needs.

**motive**
Driving force that causes a person to take action to satisfy specific needs.

**Maslow's hierarchy of needs**
Method of classifying human needs and motivations into five categories in ascending order of importance: physiological, safety, social, esteem, and self-actualization.

Why are people driven by particular needs at particular times? One popular theory is **Maslow's hierarchy of needs,** shown in Exhibit 4.5, which arranges needs in ascending order of importance: physiological, safety, social, esteem, and self-actualization. As a person fulfills one need, a higher-level need becomes more important.

The most basic human needs are *physiological*—that is, needs for food, water, and shelter. Because they are essential to survival, these needs must be satisfied first. Ads showing a juicy hamburger or a runner gulping down Gatorade after a marathon exemplify the use of appeals to satisfy physiological needs.

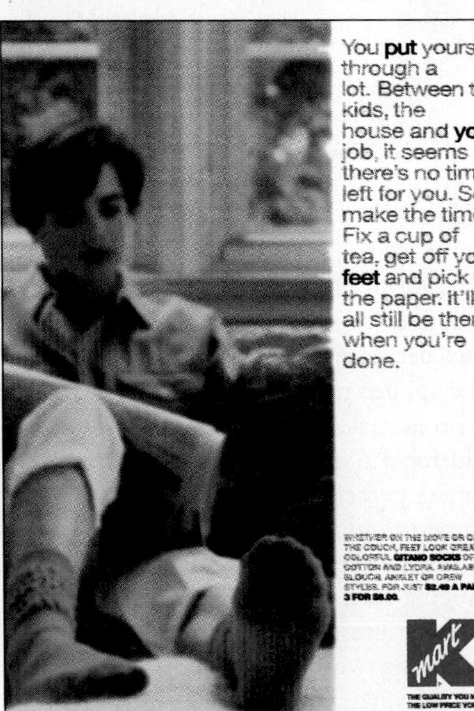


Changing consumer perceptions can be a difficult task. Kmart is using ads like this to enhance its image as a full-service department store that can fulfill the buying needs of the young professional.

*Safety* needs include security and freedom from pain and discomfort. Marketers often exploit consumers' fears and anxieties about safety to sell their products. For example, an ad campaign by Volvo features real people who believe they survived terrible car crashes because they were driving a Volvo.[22] The Ethics in Marketing box on pages 130–131 discusses how marketers often play on consumers' fears to sell their products.

After physiological and safety needs have been fulfilled, *social* needs—especially love and a sense

*Exhibit 4.5*

Maslow's Hierarchy of Needs

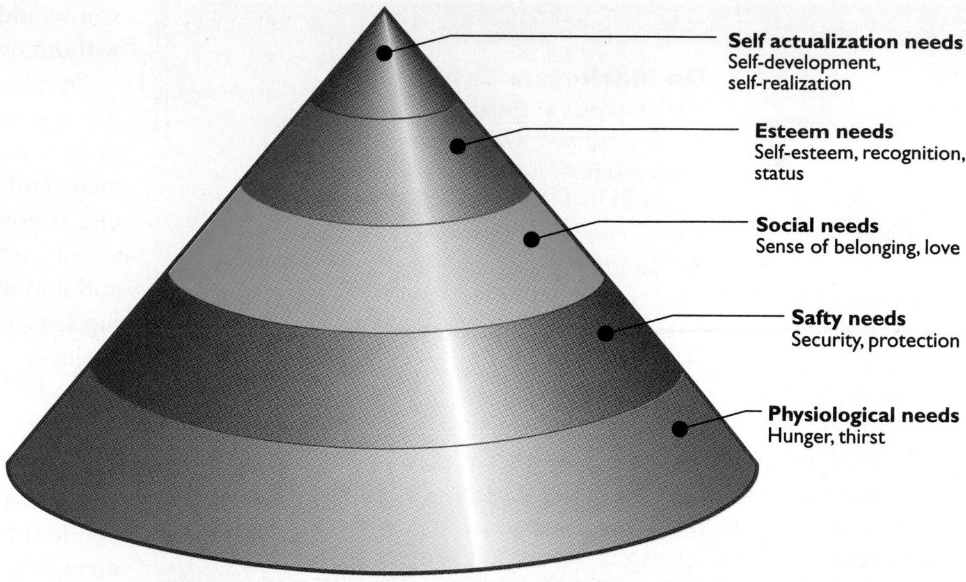


of belonging—become the focus. Love includes acceptance by one's peers, as well as sex and romantic love. Marketing managers probably appeal more to this need than to any other. Ads for clothes, cosmetics, and vacation packages suggest that buying the product can bring love.

Love is acceptance without regard to one's contribution; esteem is acceptance based on one's contribution to the group. *Self-esteem* needs include self-respect and a sense of accomplishment. Esteem needs also include prestige, fame, and recognition of one's accomplishments. Mont Blanc pens, Mercedes-Benz automobiles, and Neiman-Marcus stores all appeal to esteem needs.

The highest human need is *self-actualization*. It refers to finding self-fulfillment and self-expression, reaching the point in life at which "people are what they feel they should be." Maslow felt that very few people ever attain this level. Even so, advertisements may focus on this type of need. For example, American Express ads convey the message that acquiring its card is one of the highest attainments in life. Likewise, the U.S. Armed Forces' slogan urges young people to "Be all that you can be."

## LEARNING

**learning**
Process that creates changes in behavior, immediate or expected, through experience and practice.

Almost all consumer behavior results from **learning,** which is the process that creates changes in behavior through experience and practice. It is not possible to observe learning directly , but we can infer when it has occurred. Suppose you see an advertisement for a new and improved cold medicine. If you go to the store that day and buy that remedy, we infer that you have learned something.

The definition of learning says that experience can change behavior—a process called *experiential learning*. If you try the new cold medicine when you get home and it does not relieve your symptoms, you may not buy that brand again. *Conceptual learning,* which is not learned through direct experience, is also important. Assume, for example, that you are standing at a soft-drink machine and notice a new diet flavor with an artificial sweetener. But someone has told you that diet beverages leave an aftertaste, so you choose a different drink. You have learned that

ETHICS IN MARKETING

**Do Marketers Exploit Consumers' Fears?**

Marketers nowadays seem more willing to play on consumers' fears and anxieties to sell products, and their advertising has become scarier and more graphic than ever. Take, for instance, a TV commercial by Energizer: Flames roar through a lovely home, melting a silent smoke detector into a shapeless glob of plastic. The message: One third of all smoke detectors have dead batteries. The commercial ends with the pink Energizer bunny thumping across the screen.

Similarly, an ad for First Alert carbon monoxide detectors flashes photos of real people who died of carbon monoxide poisoning while a woman tells how her husband carried a picture of their dead daughter in his wallet for twenty-one years. Loving Choice Baby Food Products urges consumers through direct mail to purchase its how-to video on cardiopulmonary resuscitation for children—"now . . . before it's too late."

The scare strategy undoubtedly stems from the sense that many Americans have never been more afraid and desperately want to protect themselves against the world. Never mind that life expectancy is creeping upward and that the incidence of home accidents—including fires, poisonings, and falls—steadily declines. People are bombarded daily with accounts of tragedies involving everything from violent carjackings and gang wars to maladies arising from overexposure to electromagnetic fields from power lines.

Using fear tactics in advertising is not new, although in the past they were used more cautiously. Ads for Kellogg's All-Bran cereal startled people a decade ago by citing links between a high-fiber diet and the prevention of some types of cancer. Even mentioning the word *cancer*

you would not like this new diet drink without ever trying it.

People learn faster and retain the information longer when the material to be learned is important. Reinforcement and repetition also boost learning. If you see a vendor selling frozen yogurt (stimulus), buy it (response), and find the yogurt to be quite refreshing (reward), your behavior has been positively reinforced. On the other hand, if you buy a new flavor of yogurt, such as black cherry, and it does not taste good (negative reinforcement), you will not buy that flavor of yogurt again. Without positive or negative reinforcement, a person will not be motivated to repeat the behavior pattern or to avoid it. Thus if a new brand evokes neutral feelings, some marketing activity, such as a price change or an increase in promotion, may be required to induce further consumption. Learning theory is helpful in reminding marketers that concrete and timely actions are what reinforce desired consumer behavior.

Repetition is a key strategy in promotional campaigns, because it can lead to increased learning. Delta Airlines uses repetitious advertising so consumers will learn that "At Delta, we love to fly, and it shows." Generally, to heighten learning, advertising messages should be spread over time rather than clustered at one time.

**stimulus generalization**
Form of learning that occurs when one response is extended to a second stimulus similar to the first.

A related learning concept useful to marketing managers is **stimulus generalization.** In theory, stimulus generalization occurs when one response is extended to a second stimulus similar to the first. Marketers often use a successful, well-known brand name for a family of products because it gives consumers familiarity with and knowledge about each product in the family. Such brand-name families spur the introduction of new products and facilitate the sale of existing items. Jell-O frozen pudding pops rely on the familiarity of Jell-O gelatin; Clorox laundry detergent relies on familiarity with Clorox bleach; and Ivory shampoo relies on familiarity with Ivory soap.[24] Branding is examined in more detail in Chapter 9.

Another form of stimulus generalization occurs when retailers or wholesalers design their packages to resemble well-known manufacturers' brands. Such imitation often confuses consumers, who buy the imitator thinking it's the original. U.S. manufacturers in foreign markets have sometimes found little, if any, brand protection. For example, in South Korea, Procter & Gamble's Ivory soap competes head-on with the Korean brand Bory, which has an almost identical logo on the package.

ETHICS IN MARKETING

was considered risky back then, because advertisers believed consumers didn't want to be reminded of death.

Marketing experts say it's the use of real people that makes some of the ads seem so ominous. Car ads have long shown images of crash dummies surviving wrecks or of a driver's near-miss of a fatal accident due to the car's safety features. But television ads for Volvo feature images of real people, including a woman and her two children and a man shooting baskets with his sons, while the date of their near-fatal accident appears superimposed over each portrait.

Advertisers today claim their scary ads are more a public service than a sales tactic. BRK Electronics, which manufacturers the First Alert carbon monoxide detector, initially used more straightforward, educational ads, but they didn't catch consumers' attention. When the company decided to use real people in the ads to make viewers realize that carbon monoxide poisoning could also happen to them, demand for its detector skyrocketed.

Many ads and promotions, such as those for Loving Choice Baby Products, play on people's feelings of protectiveness about children and loved ones. Other ads strike a chord by graphically depicting just how much viewers have to lose. A commercial from Allstate Insurance shows the wreckage of a recently burned-out house, as mournful music plays in the background. The camera lingers on melted toys and a smoldering TV remote-control device before focusing on the real problem, a smoke detector with no batteries.[23]

Are marketers taking advantage of consumers' fears to sell their products, or are these ads really a public service to consumers? Would you as a consumer feel offended or well served by such ads?

Source: Reprinted by permission of *The Wall Street Journal*, © 1993 Dow Jones & Company, Inc. All Rights Reserved Worldwide.

Consumers dissatisfied with Bory may attribute their dissatisfaction to Ivory, never realizing that Bory is an imitator.[25] Counterfeit products are also produced to look exactly like the original. For example, counterfeit Levi's jeans made in China are hot items in Europe, where Levi Strauss has had trouble keeping up with demand. The knockoffs look so much like the real thing that unsuspecting consumers don't know the difference—until after a few washes, when the belt loops fall off and the rivets begin to rust.[26] Passage of the General Agreement on Tariffs and Trade, which was discussed in Chapter 3, should help to reduce counterfeiting.

The opposite of stimulus generalization is **stimulus discrimination,** which means learning to differentiate among similar products. Consumers usually prefer one product as more rewarding or stimulating. For example, some consumers prefer Coca-Cola and others prefer Pepsi; many insist they can taste a difference between the two brands.

With some types of products—such as aspirin, gasoline, bleach, paper towels—marketers rely on promotion to point up brand differences that consumers would otherwise not recognize. This process, called product differentiation, is discussed in more detail in Chapter 6. Usually product differentiation is based on superficial differences. For example, Bayer tells consumers that it's the aspirin "doctors recommend most." Exxon has brought back the tiger as an advertising symbol to help differentiate its products from those of other oil companies.

**stimulus discrimination**
Learned ability to differentiate among stimuli.

## VALUES, BELIEFS, AND ATTITUDES

Learning helps people shape their value systems. In turn, values help determine self-concept, personality, and even lifestyle. A **value** is an enduring belief that a specific mode of conduct is personally or socially preferable to another mode of conduct.

**value**
Enduring belief that a specific mode of conduct is personally or socially preferable to another mode of conduct.

People's value systems have a great effect on their consumer behavior. Consumers with similar value systems tend to react alike to prices and other marketing-related inducements. Values also correspond to consumption patterns. People who want to protect the environment try to buy only products that don't harm it. Values can also influence consumers' TV viewing habits or the magazines they read. For instance, people who strongly object to violence avoid crime shows. Likewise, people who oppose pornography do not buy *Playboy.*

Value systems can vary quite a bit across cultures and subcultures. For example,

The values of Japanese workers have traditionally been different from those of American workers. In general, the Japanese have given priority to their work lives, whereas Americans have tried to balance work, family, and leisure. In today's Japan, however, workers are being encouraged to enjoy more free time.



leisure time is valued in the United States. Consumers spend a considerable amount of time and money on sporting events, movies, restaurants, vacations, and amusement parks. U.S. workers traditionally expect eight-hour days, five-day workweeks, and vacation time. Japanese workers, on the other hand, typically work twelve-hour days and often work on Saturdays as well. Only half of Japanese workers use all their vacation time. One reason most Japanese don't take more time off is that they don't want to burden their colleagues by leaving early or taking a holiday. Japanese workers also feel that their work will suffer if they put effort into other things.[27]

The personal values of target consumers may have interesting implications for marketing managers. The personal value systems of baby boomers and generation X are quite different. Baby boomers have a strong sense of individualism. They succeeded in a job market that rewarded competitive drive more than cooperative spirit and that valued individual skills more than teamwork. Baby boomers found pleasure in material possessions and affluence. In contrast, the members of generation X resent baby boomers, who, as they see it, had a party and didn't clean up the mess. Born into an increasingly diverse world, the members of generation X are more likely than their elders to accept differences in race, ethnicity, national origin, family structure, and lifestyle. The members of generation X are more likely to seek work that is personally fulfilling, as opposed to selecting jobs for financial payoff. Growing up in the age of AIDS, divorce, latchkey kids, national economic decline, and rising violence, they are well aware that stability is hard to find and danger is just around the corner.[28]

**belief**
Organized pattern of knowledge that an individual holds as true about his or her world.

Beliefs and attitudes are closely linked to values. A **belief** is an organized pattern of knowledge that an individual holds as true about his or her world. A consumer may believe that Sony's camcorder makes the best home videos, tolerates hard use, and is reasonably priced. These beliefs may be based on knowledge, faith, or hearsay. Consumers tend to develop a set of beliefs about a product's attributes and then, through these beliefs, form a *brand image*—a set of beliefs about a particular brand. In turn, the brand image shapes consumers' attitudes toward the product.

**attitude**
Learned tendency to respond consistently toward a given object.

Attitudes tend to be more enduring and complex than beliefs, because they consist of clusters of interrelated beliefs. An **attitude** is a learned tendency to respond consistently toward a given object, such as a brand. Attitudes also encompass an individual's value system, which represents personal standards of good and bad, right and wrong, and so forth.

For an example of the nature of attitudes, consider the differing attitudes of consumers around the world toward the habit of purchasing on credit. Americans have long been enthusiastic about charging goods and services and are willing to pay high interest rates for the privilege of postponing payment. But to many European consumers, doing what amounts to taking out a loan—even a small one—to pay for anything seems absurd. Germans especially are reluctant to buy on credit. Italy has a sophisticated credit and banking system well suited to handling credit cards, but Italians prefer to carry cash, often huge wads of it. Most Japanese consumers have credit cards, but card purchases amount to less than 1 percent of all consumer transactions. The Japanese have long looked down on credit purchases but acquire cards to use while traveling abroad.[29]

If a good or service is meeting its profit goals, positive attitudes toward the product merely need to be reinforced. However, if the brand is not succeeding, the marketing manager must strive to change target consumers' attitudes toward it. This change can be accomplished in three ways: changing beliefs about the brand's attributes, changing the relative importance of these beliefs, and adding new beliefs.

## Changing Beliefs about Attributes

The first technique is to turn neutral or negative beliefs about product attributes into positive ones. For example, pork was losing sales to chicken because consumers thought pork was fatty and unhealthy. To counter this belief, pork producers launched the Pork: The Other White Meat campaign to reposition their product in the minds of consumers. The campaign tells consumers that pork is leaner, lower in calories, and lower in saturated fat than they think.

Likewise, BMW is continuing its efforts to reposition itself as a safe, affordable vehicle for the entire family and to steer away from its image as a yuppie statement. Its new commercials concentrate on safety features, such as traction control; its print ads show children for the first time. BMW also hopes the campaign will convince consumers that the cars are not as expensive as they might think.[30]

Changing beliefs about a service can be more difficult, because service attributes are intangible. Convincing consumers to switch hairstylists or lawyers or to go to a mall dental clinic can be much more difficult than getting them to change brands of razor blades. Image, which is also largely intangible, significantly determines service patronage. What is a "better doctor"? How do consumers become convinced that they will get better dental care in a mall than through a family dentist? Service marketing is explored in detail in Chapter 11.

## Changing the Importance of Beliefs

The second approach to modifying attitudes is to change the relative importance of beliefs about an attribute. For years, consumers have known that bran cereals are high in natural fiber. The primary belief associated with this attribute is that the fiber tends to act as a mild, natural laxative. Today, however, cereal marketers promote the high fiber content of bran cereals as a possible factor in preventing certain types of cancer, vastly increasing the importance of this attribute in the minds of consumers.

Likewise, with more consumers avoiding products that contain harsh or unnecessary chemicals, many marketers are now promoting the naturalness of their products. For example, Johnson & Johnson advertises its Pure Cotton line of cotton swabs and balls as being made without cheaper rayon fibers and "whitened without harsh chlorine." But the products are really just a repackaged version of the same cotton items the company has always sold.[31]

Whirlpool has tried to change European consumers' beliefs about the attributes that are most important to them in a washing machine. European manufacturers believe that European consumers prefer washing machines that are narrow and load from the top. Whirlpool research, however, indicated that Europeans would gladly trade these characteristics for superior overall performance: a reliable machine that cleans well, is easy to use, and economizes on water, detergent, and energy. Whirlpool contends that if all these criteria are met, other features—such as where the machine opens and how big it is—become less important.[32]

### Adding New Beliefs

The third approach to transforming attitudes is to add new beliefs. Recall the opening vignette about cereal makers attempting to add the belief that cereal can be a healthy snack food as well as a breakfast food. Similarly, chewing gum makers are advertising their product as an alternative to smoking or as a way to remove food residue from one's teeth. For example, Trident sugarless gum advertises that it "actually helps fight cavities when you chew it after meals."[33]

Adding new beliefs is not easy. For example, when Anheuser-Busch first introduced Bud Dry beer, consumers were confused, because the word *dry* is commonly used to describe wines. Nevertheless, many consumers have since added the new belief that beer too can be described as dry. Volvo faced a similar problem in introducing its sporty 850 model. For over a quarter of a century, Volvo has successfully crafted an image as the safest car on the road. However, Volvo did such a good job driving home its safety message that consumers had a hard time imagining a Volvo as anything other than a boxy, steel-reinforced tank. Ads for the Volvo 850 kept the brand's unifying slogan—"Drive safely"— but also attempted to convince drivers that it's fun to drive.[34]

U.S. companies attempting to market their goods in overseas may need to help consumers add new beliefs about a product in general. For example, catsup is a household staple only in the United States, where Americans consume an average of three pounds a year. In its effort to convert the rest of the world to its catsup, Heinz ran advertisements in Greece showing how ketchup can be poured on pasta, eggs, and meat. Heinz also offered cooking lessons in Tokyo on using catsup as an ingredient in Western-style foods, such as omelets, sausages, and pasta.[35]

## PERSONALITY, SELF-CONCEPT, AND LIFESTYLE

**personality**
Way of organizing and grouping the consistencies of an individual's reactions to situations.

Each consumer has a unique personality. **Personality** is a broad concept that can be thought of as a way of organizing and grouping the consistencies of an individual's reactions to situations. Thus personality combines psychological makeup and environmental forces. It includes people's underlying dispositions, especially their most

*Exhibit 4.6*

Some Common Personality Traits

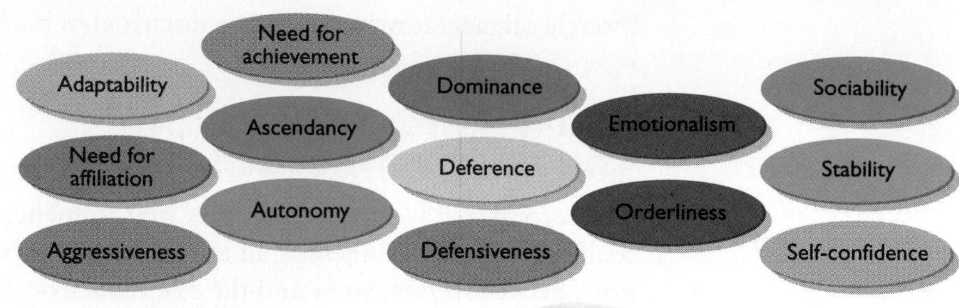


dominant characteristics. Some marketers believe that personality influences the types and brands of products purchased. For instance, the type of car, clothes, or jewelry a consumer buys may reflect one or more personality traits. Personality traits like those listed in Exhibit 4.6 may be used to describe a consumer's personality.

**self-concept**
How a consumer perceives himself or herself in terms of attitudes, perceptions, beliefs, and self-evaluations.

**ideal self-image**
The way an individual would like to be.

**real self-image**
The way an individual actually perceives himself or herself.

**Self-concept,** or self-perception, is how consumers perceive themselves. Self-concept includes attitudes, perceptions, beliefs, and self-evaluations. Although self-concept may change, the change is often gradual. Through self-concept, people define their identity, which in turn provides for consistent and coherent behavior.

Self-concept combines the **ideal self-image** (the way an individual would like to be) and the **real self-image** (how an individual actually perceives himself or herself). Generally, we try to raise our real self-image toward our ideal (or at least narrow the gap). Consumers seldom buy products that jeopardize their self-image. For example, someone who sees herself as a trend setter wouldn't buy clothing that doesn't project a contemporary image.

Human behavior depends largely on self-concept. Because consumers want to protect their identity as individuals, the products they buy, the stores they patronize, and the credit cards they carry support their self-image.

By influencing the degree to which consumers perceive a good or service to be self-relevant, marketers can affect consumers' motivation to learn about, shop for, and buy a certain brand.[36] Marketers also consider self-concept important because it helps explain the relationship between individuals' perceptions of themselves and their consumer behavior.

An important component of self-concept is *body image,* the perception of the attractiveness of one's own physical features. One study showed that patients who had plastic surgery experienced significant improvements in their overall body image and self-concept.[37] Sales of at-home hair color to aging baby boomers have substantially increased as more middle-aged men and women color their hair in order to "age gracefully."[38] Likewise, health clubs, exercise equipment manufacturers, and diet plans target consumers who want to improve their self-concept by exercising and losing weight.

**lifestyle**
Mode of living as identified by a person's activities, interests, and opinions.

Personality and self-concept are reflected in lifestyle. A **lifestyle** is a mode of living, as identified by a person's activities, interests, and opinions. Psychographics is the analytical technique used to examine consumer lifestyles and to categorize consumers. Unlike personality characteristics, which are hard to describe and measure, lifestyle characteristics are useful in segmenting and targeting consumers. Many industries now use psychographics to better understand their market segments. For example, the auto industry has a psychographic segmentation scheme for classifying car buyers into one of six groups according to their attitudes toward cars and the driving experience. At the two extremes are "gearheads," true car enthusiasts who enjoy driving and working on their cars themselves, and "negatives," who view cars as a necessary evil that they would just as soon do without.[39] Psychographics and lifestyle segmentation schemes are discussed in more detail in Chapter 6.

## SOCIAL FACTORS INFLUENCING CONSUMER BUYING DECISIONS

*7 Identify and understand the social factors that affect consumer buying decisions.*

The second major group of factors that influence consumer decision making are social factors, which include all effects on buyer behavior that result from interactions between a consumer and the external environment. Social factors include reference groups, opinion leaders, family, life cycle, social class, culture, and subculture (refer back to Exhibit 4.3).

**reference group**
Group in society that influences an individual's purchasing behavior.

**primary membership group**
Reference group with which people interact regularly in an informal, face-to-face manner, such as family, friends, or fellow employees.

**secondary membership group**
Reference group with which people associate less consistently and more formally than a primary membership group, such as a club, professional group, or religious group.

**aspirational group**
Group that someone would like to join.

**norm**
Value or attitude deemed acceptable by a group.

### REFERENCE GROUPS

All the formal and informal groups that influence the buying behavior of an individual are that person's **reference groups.** Consumers may use products or brands to identify with or become a member of a group. They learn from observing how members of their reference groups consume, and they use the same criteria to make their own consumer decisions.

Reference groups can be categorized very broadly as either direct or indirect (see Exhibit 4.7). Direct reference groups are face-to-face membership groups that touch people's lives directly. They can be either primary or secondary. **Primary membership groups** include all groups with which people interact regularly in an informal, face-to-face manner, such as family, friends, and coworkers. In contrast, people associate with **secondary membership groups** less consistently and more formally. These groups might include clubs, professional groups, and religious groups.

Consumers also are influenced by many indirect, nonmembership reference groups that they do not belong to. **Aspirational groups** are those that a person would like to join. To join an aspirational reference group, a person must at least conform to the norms of that group. (**Norms** are the values and attitudes deemed acceptable by the group.) Thus a person who wants to be elected to public office may begin to dress more conservatively, as other politicians do. He or she may go to

*Exhibit 4.7*

Types of Reference Groups

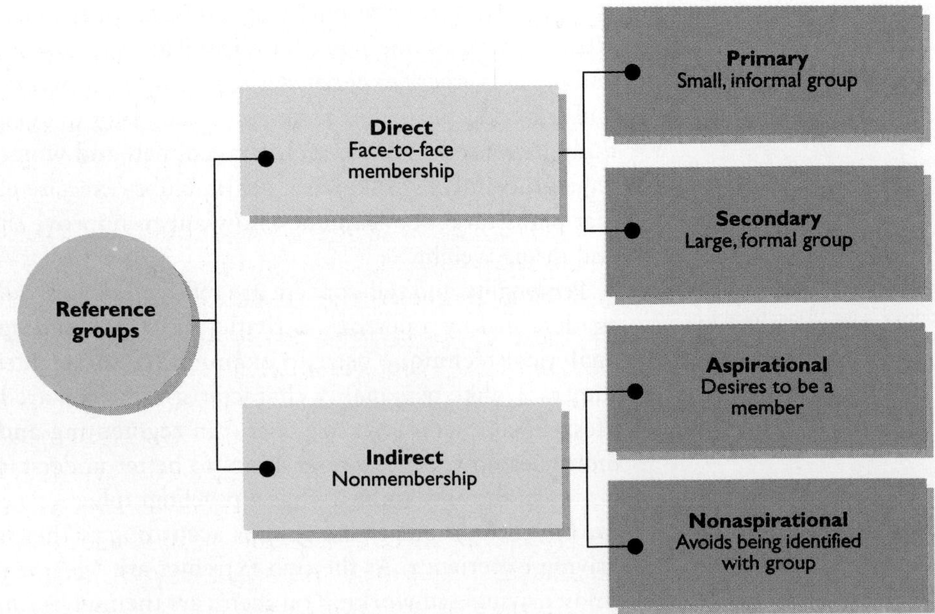

*Exhibit 4.8*

Selling Power of Athletes

Source: Video Storyboard Tests Inc., as reported in Kevin Goldman, "Candice Bergen Leads the List of Top Celebrity Endorsers," *The Wall Street Journal*, 17 September 1993, p. B6. Reprinted by permission of *The Wall Street Journal*, © 1993 Dow Jones & Company, Inc. All Rights Reserved Worldwide.

| Consumer appeal ranking 1993 | 1992 | Name | TV endorsements |
|---|---|---|---|
| 1 | 1 | **Michael Jordan** | Nike, Gatorade, McDonald's |
| 2 | 5 | **Joe Namath** | Flex-All, Nobody Beats the Wiz |
| 3 | 9 | **Larry Bird** | McDonald's |
| 4 | 3 | **Bo Jackson** | Nike, Lipton Tea |
| 5 | 2 | **Earvin "Magic" Johnson** | Pepsi |
| 6 | — | **Joe Montana** | LA Gear, Hanes Menswear |
| 7 | — | **Chris Evert** | Nuprin |
| 8 | 10 | **Charles Barkley** | Nike |
| 9 | — | **Shaquille O'Neal** | Reebok |
| 10 | 7 | **Jimmy Connors** | Nuprin |

many of the restaurants and social engagements that city and business leaders attend and try to play a role that is acceptable to voters and other influential people.

**nonaspirational reference group**
Group with which an individual does not want to associate.

**Nonaspirational reference groups,** or dissociative groups, influence our behavior when we try to maintain distance from them. A consumer may avoid buying some types of clothing or cars, going to certain restaurants or stores, or even buying a home in a certain neighborhood in order to avoid being associated with a particular group.

The activities, values, and goals of reference groups directly influence consumer behavior. For marketers, reference groups have three important implications: They serve as information sources and influence perceptions; they affect an individual's aspiration levels; and their norms either constrain or stimulate consumer behavior. For example, aspiring young executives might check the makes of cars driven by their superiors before buying a car.

## OPINION LEADERS

**opinion leader**
Individual who influences the opinions of others.

Reference groups frequently include individuals known as group leaders or **opinion leaders,** those who influence others. Obviously, it is important for marketing managers to persuade such people to purchase their goods or services.

Opinion leaders on one subject are often not opinion leaders on others. For instance, middle-aged parents who have raised three children may convince younger parents in the neighborhood to buy certain baby-care items. However, they may not be able to sway others to vacation at a particular place.

Opinion leadership is a casual, face-to-face phenomenon and usually very inconspicuous, so locating opinion leaders can be a challenge. Thus marketers often try to create opinion leaders. They may use high school cheerleaders to model new fall fashions or civic leaders to promote insurance, new cars, and other merchandise. On a national level, companies sometimes use sports figures and other celebrities to promote products, hoping they are appropriate opinion leaders (see Exhibit 4.8).

Research has shown that the effectiveness of celebrity endorsements depends largely on how credible and attractive the spokesperson is and how familiar people are with him or her. The endorsement is most likely to succeed if an association between the spokesperson and the product can be established.[40] For example, comedian Bill Cosby failed as an endorser for financial products but succeeded with such products as Kodak cameras and Jell-O gelatin. Consumers could not mentally link Bill Cosby with serious investment decisions but could associate him with leisure activities and everyday consumption. Additionally, in the selection of a celebrity endorser, marketers must consider the broader meanings associated with the endorser. Although the endorser may have certain attributes that are desirable for endorsing the product, he or she may also have other attributes that are inappropriate.[41]

MCI's Friends and Family campaign takes a different approach to the use of endorsers as opinion leaders. Instead of well-known actors, the company's commercials feature actual employees talking about the company's long-distance service. This approach has been very successful. Viewers feel these endorsers have a genuinely close tie to the service they are promoting, unlike actors who only simulate their feelings.[42]

A marketing manager can also try to use opinion leaders through group sanctioning or referrals. For example, some companies sell products endorsed by the American Heart Association or the American Cancer Society. Marketers seek endorsements from schools, churches, cities, the military, and fraternal organizations as a form of group opinion leadership. Salespeople often ask to use opinion leaders' names as a means of achieving greater personal influence in a sales presentation.

## FAMILY

The family is the most important social institution for many consumers, strongly influencing values, attitudes, self-concept—and buying behavior. For example, a family that strongly values good health will have a grocery list distinctly different from that of a family that views every dinner as a gourmet event. Moreover, the family is responsible for the **socialization process,** the passing down of cultural values and norms to children. Children learn by observing their parents' consumption patterns, and so they will tend to shop in a similar pattern.

**socialization process**
How cultural values and norms are passed down to children.

Families comprise two or more distinct personalities, often with wide variations in age. Within a family, therefore, individual wants are unique. But because all families must operate with limited resources, many buying decisions must be based on compromise.

Decision-making roles, particularly the roles of spouses, tend to vary significant-

*Exhibit 4.9*

Who Dominates Purchase Decisions in Different Product Categories

Source: Adapted from Diane Crispwell, "The Brave New World of Men," *American Demographics,* January 1992, p. 40. Source: *American Demographics* magazine © 1992. Reprinted with Permission.

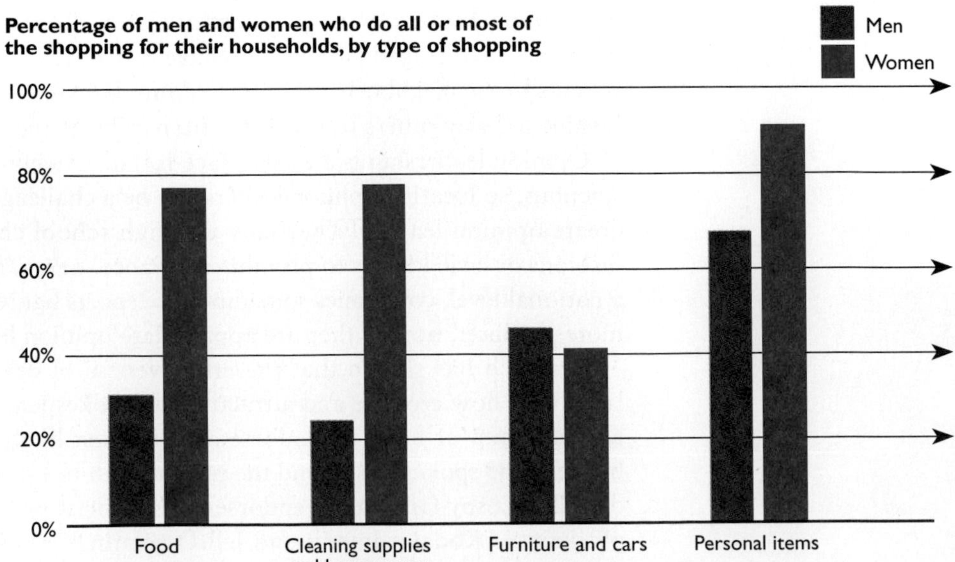

ly, depending on the type of item purchased. *Autonomic* decision making occurs when a husband or wife buys something independently of the other. Usually only personal products are bought independently, such as personal hygiene or hair care items. *Husband-dominant* purchases are decided mostly by the husband; *wife-dominant* purchases are decided mostly by the wife (see Exhibit 4.9). Husbands care more about the larger household purchases, such as furniture or cars or those that ensure the family's financial well-being, and may play a more dominant role than the wife when these purchases are considered. On the other hand, women typically have primary authority over goods and services that are needed to sustain the day-to-day operation of the home or that are associated with care of children.[43] In a *syncratic* purchase situation, decisions are made jointly by husband and wife. Research suggests that husbands and wives tend to compromise in their syncratic purchase decisions in an effort to be fair with each other and to avoid conflict.[44]

Changes in family structure often change the decision-making process. For example, as noted in Chapter 2, more women are now in the work force than ever before, and there are more single heads of households. Therefore, the typical family decision styles may not hold true as often as they did ten years ago. For example, although husbands have historically made decisions about insurance and financial planning, this trend may be changing. Perhaps we should not try to credit one spouse or the other with decisions of a certain type. Indeed, a single head of household has to make all types of decisions.

Family members of both sexes take a variety of roles in the purchase process. *Initiators* are the ones who suggest, initiate, or plant the seed for the purchase process. The initiator can be any member of the family. For example, Sister might initiate the product search by asking for a new bicycle as a birthday present. *Influencers* are those members of the family whose opinions are valued. In our example, Mom might function as a price-range watchdog, an influencer whose main role is to veto or approve price ranges. Brother may give his opinion on certain makes of bicycles. The *decision maker* is the member of the family who actually makes the decision to buy or not to buy. For example, Dad may choose the final brand and model of bicycle to buy after seeking further information from Sister about cosmetic features such as color and imposing additional criteria of his own, such as durability and safety. The *purchaser* (probably Dad or Mom) is the one who actually exchanges money for the product. Finally, the *consumer* is the actual user—Sister, in the case of the bicycle.

Marketers should consider family purchase situations along with the distribution of consumer and decision-maker roles among family members. Ordinary marketing views the individual as both decision maker and consumer. Family marketing adds three other possibilities: Sometimes more than one decision maker is involved; sometimes more than one consumer is involved; and sometimes the decision maker and the consumer are different people. Exhibit 4.10 on page 140 represents the nine patterns of family purchasing relationships that are possible.[45]

Children today can have great influence over the purchase decisions of their parents. In many families, with both parents working and short on time, children may be encouraged to participate.[46] In addition, children in single-parent households become more involved in family decision making at an earlier age than children in two-parent households.[47] Children are especially influential in decisions about food. Over three-fourths of parents say their children help decide where the family goes for fast food, and over half say their kids influence the choice of a full-service restaurant. Most kids also have input into the kinds of food the family eats at home, and many

*Exhibit 4.10*

Relationships among Purchasers and Consumers in the Family

Source: Robert Boutilier, "Pulling the Family's Strings," *American Demographics*, August 1993, p. 46. Source: *American Demographics* magazine © 1993. Reprinted with Permission.

| | | Purchase decision maker | | |
|---|---|---|---|---|
| | | One member | Some members | All members |
| Consumer | One member | 1 | 2 Tennis racquet | 3 |
| | Some members | 4 Sugar pops | 5 | 6 |
| | All members | 7 | 8 | 9 Refrigerator |

even influence the specific brands their parents buy. Children are also influential in purchase decisions for toys, clothes, vacations, recreation, and automobiles, even though they are usually not the actual purchasers of such items.[48]

## FAMILY LIFE CYCLE

The life cycle stage of a family can also have a significant impact on consumer behavior. As Chapter 6 explains in more detail, the family life cycle is an orderly series of stages through which consumers' attitudes and behavioral tendencies evolve, through maturity, experience, and changing income and status.

Family decisions about where to eat and what to eat are strongly influenced by children, especially in single-parent households.

© Tony Stone Images/Howard Grey

Marketers often define their target markets in terms of family life cycle. For instance, young singles spend more than average on alcoholic beverages, education, and entertainment. New parents typically increase their spending on health care, clothing, housing, and food, while they decrease their spending on alcohol, education, and transportation. Households with older children spend more on food, entertainment, personal care products, and education, as well as cars and gasoline. After their children leave home, spending by older couples on vehicles, women's clothing, health care, and long-distance calls typically increases.[49] Marketers should also be aware of the many nontraditional life-cycle paths that are common today, which provide insights into the needs and wants of such consumers as divorced parents, lifelong singles, and childless couples.

## SOCIAL CLASS

**social class**
Group of people in a society who are considered nearly equal in status or community esteem, who regularly socialize among themselves both formally and informally, and who share behavioral norms.

The United States, like other societies, does have a social class system. A **social class** is a group of people who are considered nearly equal in status or community esteem, who regularly socialize among themselves both formally and informally, and who share behavioral norms.

A number of techniques have been used to measure social class, and a number of

| | | |
|---|---|---|
| **Upper classes** | | |
| Capitalist class | 1% | People whose investment decisions shape the national economy; income mostly from assets, earned or inherited; university connections |
| Upper middle class | 14% | Upper-level managers, professionals, owners of medium-sized businesses; college educated; family income nearly twice national average |
| **Middle classes** | | |
| Middle class | 33% | Middle-level white-collar, top-level blue-collar; education past high school typical; income somewhat above national average |
| Working class | 32% | Middle-level blue-collar, lower-level white-collar; income slightly below national average |
| **Lower classes** | | |
| Working poor | 11–12% | Low-paid service workers and operatives; some high school education; below mainstream in living standard but above poverty line |
| Underclass | 8–9% | People who are not regularly employed and who depend primarily on the welfare system for sustenance; little schooling; living standard below poverty line |

*Exhibit 4.11*

U.S. Social Classes

Source: Adapted from Richard P. Coleman, "The Continuing Significance of Social Class to Marketing," *Journal of Consumer Research*, December 1983, p. 267; Dennis Gilbert and Joseph A. Kahl, *The American Class Structure: A Synthesis* (Homewood, IL: Dorsey Press, 1982), ch. 11.

criteria have been used to define it. One view of contemporary U.S. status structure is shown in Exhibit 4.11. Here are some additional observations about members of these classes:

- *Upper classes:* The upper classes consist of the very rich and the well-to-do. Upper-class individuals seem to think of themselves as nice-looking people and are concerned with personal appearance. They are more confident, outgoing, and culturally oriented than people of other social classes. They also seem a bit more permissive and are willing to tolerate alternative views. The upper social classes are more likely than other classes to try to contribute something to society—for example, by government service, volunteer work for charitable organizations, or active participation in civic affairs.
- *Middle classes:* Middle-class consumers have a much different perspective on life. Attaining goals and achieving status and prestige are important. Compared with the lower classes, members of the middle classes have a stronger orientation outward, toward society in general and toward peers in particular. Apparently, the middle-class lifestyle is more dynamic than the relatively static lifestyle of the lower classes. The **working class** is a distinct subclass of the middle class. The working-class person depends heavily on relatives and community for economic and emotional support. Members of this social subclass rely on relatives for tips on job opportunities, get their advice on purchases, and count on them in times of trouble. The emphasis on family ties is one sign of this group's intensely local view of the world. For instance, working-class people like the local news far more than middle-class audiences do, who show more enthusiasm for national and world coverage.

Working-class people also vacation closer to home and are more likely to visit relatives when they go on vacation.

- *Lower classes:* Lower-class members typically fall at or below the poverty level. This social class has the highest unemployment rate, and many individuals or families are subsidized through the welfare system. Many are illiterate, with little formal education. Lower-class members also have poorer physical and mental health and a shorter life span than others do. Compared to more affluent consumers, lower-class consumers have poorer diets and typically purchase much different types of foods when they shop.

Lifestyle distinctions between the social classes are greater than the distinctions within a given class. The most significant separation between the classes is the one between the middle and lower classes. It is here that the major shift in lifestyles appears.

Marketers are interested in social class for two main reasons. First, social class often indicates which medium to use for advertising. Suppose an insurance company seeks to sell its policies to middle-class families. It might advertise during the local evening news, because middle-class families tend to watch more television than other classes do. If the company wants to sell more policies to upscale individuals, it might place a print ad in a business publication like *The Wall Street Journal,* which is read by more educated and affluent people.

Second, social class may also tell marketers where certain types of consumers shop. Wealthy, upper-class shoppers tend to frequent expensive stores, places where members of the other classes might feel uncomfortable. Marketers also know that middle-class consumers regularly visit shopping malls. Therefore, marketers with products to sell to the middle class may decide to distribute their merchandise through malls.

Broad social class categories are becoming less useful to marketers as indicators of purchase behavior. One of the reasons seems to be the fragmentation of U.S. society into scores of distinct subgroups, each with unique tastes and yearnings. Recent economic trends have also added to the disintegration of broad class structures. Many thousands of the jobs that provided for a comfortable middle-class lifestyle have simply vanished, as well as long-term income security. As a result, subgroups have formed within the vast middle class, each defined by different opportunities, expectations, and outlooks.[50]

## CULTURE

**culture**
Set of values, norms, attitudes, and other meaningful symbols that shape human behavior and the artifacts, or products, of that behavior as they are transmitted from one generation to the next.

**Culture** is the set of values, norms, attitudes, and other meaningful symbols that shape human behavior, as well as the artifacts, or products, of that behavior as they are transmitted from one generation to the next. Culture is environmentally oriented. The nomads of Finland have developed a culture for Arctic survival. Similarly, people who live in the Brazilian jungle have created a culture suitable for tropical living.

Human interaction creates values and prescribes acceptable behavior for each culture. By establishing common expectations, culture gives order to society. Sometimes these expectations are coded into laws. For example, drivers in our culture must stop at a red light.

As long as a value or belief meets the society's needs, it remains part of the culture. If it is no longer functional, it fades away. Large families were valued in the nineteenth and early twentieth centuries, when the U.S. economy was more agrarian.

Children were considered an asset because they could help with the farmwork. Today, in an industrial economy, large families are not necessary.

Culture is dynamic. It adapts to changing needs and an evolving environment. The rapid growth of technology in this century has accelerated the rate of cultural change. TV has changed entertainment patterns and family communication and has heightened public awareness of political and other news events. Automation has increased the amount of leisure time we have and, in some ways, has changed the traditional work ethic. Cultural norms will continue to evolve because of our need for social patterns that solve problems.

Without understanding a culture, a firm has little chance of selling products in it. Colors, for example, may have different meanings in global markets than they do at home. In China, white is the color of mourning, and brides wear red; in the United States, black is for mourning, and brides wear white. Pepsi had a dominant market share in Southeast Asia until it changed the color of its coolers and vending equipment from deep regal blue to light ice blue. In that part of the world, light blue is associated with death and mourning.

GLOBAL PERSPECTIVES

### The Japanization of American Pizza

When Domino's Pizza opened it first pizza delivery outlet in Japan in 1986, its mission was to educate Japanese consumers about true American pizza. After years of Domino's-inspired education, Japanese today know very well what pepperoni and bell peppers are. But by far their favorite pizza toppings are things like curry topped with bits of squid.

These days, the streets of Tokyo swarm with pizza-delivery scooters. As many as 1,000 local pizza stores offer such Japanized toppings as apple, rice, German sausage, potato, and mayonnaise sauce. Domino's devised some creative alternatives of its own for its 100-plus stores in Japan. It now offers a ten-inch chicken teriyaki gourmet pizza topped with Japanese-style grilled chicken, spinach, onion, and corn—which is the most common pizza topping in Japan. Domino's also offers squid and tuna topping and corn salad, as well as such Oriental toppings as barbecued beef and sauteed burdock root.

Domino's attempts to go Japanese are a big switch from its early days in Japan, when it struggled to convince consumers that a $20 pizza delivered in a cardboard box was truly American—and thus fashionable. Back then, only noodle shops and sushi restaurants delivered. But trend-conscious young Japanese got hooked on the Western dish, and the success of Domino's soon attracted Japanese imitators. The local outlets, more in tune with Japanese tastes, promptly introduced more exotic recipes at cheaper prices. For example, one local outlet says older consumers in the countryside like the taste of shrimp in chili sauce over a sweetened pizza crust. Another local outlet delivers what it calls the ultimate Japanese-style pizza: a chicken, seaweed, and shredded bonito topping with sauce made from fish stock.[52]

What important lessons has Domino's learned from its experiences in Japan? Other than pizza toppings, what other marketing variables might Domino's need to adapt for Japanese culture?

Source: Reprinted by permission of *The Wall Street Journal*, © 1993 Dow Jones & Company, Inc. All Rights Reserved Worldwide.

Language is another important aspect of culture that global marketers must deal with. They must take care in translating product names, slogans, and promotional messages into foreign languages so as not to convey the wrong message. Consider the following examples of blunders made by marketers when delivering their message to Spanish-speaking consumers: General Motors discovered too late that Nova (the name of an economical car) literally means "doesn't go" in Spanish; Coors encouraged its English-speaking customers to "Turn it loose," but the phrase in Spanish means "Suffer from diarrhea"; and when Frank Perdue said, "It takes a tough man to make a tender chicken," Spanish speakers heard "It takes a sexually stimulated man to make a chicken affectionate."[51]

As more companies expand their operations globally, the need to understand the cultures of foreign countries becomes more important. Marketers should become familiar with the culture and adapt to it. Or marketers can attempt to bring their own culture to other countries, as Domino's Pizza originally sought to do in Japan.

## SUBCULTURE

**subculture**
Homogeneous group of people who share elements of the overall culture as well as unique elements of their own group.

A culture can be divided into subcultures on the basis of demographic characteristics, geographic regions, political beliefs, religious beliefs, national and ethnic background, and the like. A **subculture** is a homogeneous group of people who share elements of the overall culture as well as cultural elements unique to their own group. Within subcultures, people's attitudes, values, and purchase decisions are even more similar than they are within the broader culture. Subcultural differences may result in considerable variation within a culture in what, how, when, and where people buy goods and services.

In the United States alone, countless subcultures can be identified. Many are concentrated geographically. People belonging to the Mormon religion, for example, are clustered mainly in Utah; Cajuns are located in the bayou regions of southern Louisiana. Hispanics are more predominant in those states that border Mexico; the majority of Chinese, Japanese, and Koreans are found in the Pacific region of the United States.

Other subcultures are geographically dispersed. For example, computer hackers, military families, and university professors may be found throughout the country. Yet they have identifiable attitudes and values that distinguish them from the larger culture.

If marketers can identify subcultures, they can then design special marketing programs to serve their needs. Chapter 20 explains how marketers target their efforts for racial and ethnic subcultures in the United States: African-Americans, Hispanics, Asian-Americans, and Native Americans.

## LOOKING BACK

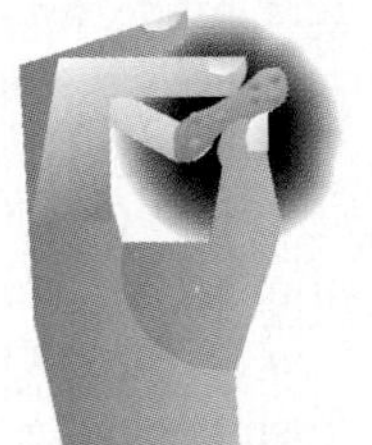

Returning to the discussion that opened the chapter, you should now be able to see how individual and social factors affect the consumer decision-making process. In the vignette, you saw how some of the nation's largest cereal marketers are attempting to change consumers' beliefs and attitudes toward cereal. Specifically, through savvy marketing and advertising they are attempting to add the belief that cereal is not just for breakfast but can also be a delicious and healthy snack at any time of the day. Consumer decision making is a fascinating and often intricate process. An appreciation of consumer behavior and the factors that influence it will help you identify target markets and design effective marketing mixes.

## SUMMARY

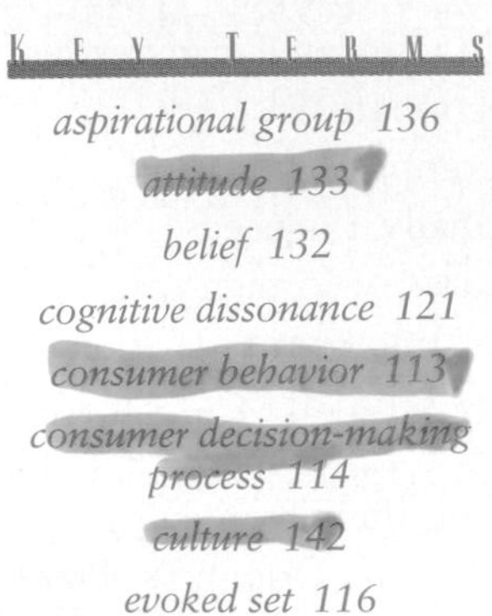

KEY TERMS

*aspirational group* 136
*attitude* 133
*belief* 132
*cognitive dissonance* 121
*consumer behavior* 113
*consumer decision-making process* 114
*culture* 142
*evoked set* 116

**1 Explain why marketing managers should understand consumer behavior.** Consumer behavior describes how consumers make purchase decisions and how they use and dispose of the products they buy. An understanding of consumer behavior reduces marketing managers' uncertainty when they are defining a target market and designing a marketing mix.

**2 Identify the types of consumer buying decisions.** Consumer decision making falls into three broad categories. First, consumers exhibit routine response behavior for frequently purchased, low-cost items that require very little decision effort; routine

*extensive decision making* 114
*external information search* 116
*high-involvement decision making* 122
*ideal self-image* 135
*internal information search* 116
*learning* 129
*lifestyle* 135
*limited decision making* 114
*low-involvement decision making* 122
*marketing-controlled information source* 116
*Maslow's hierarchy of needs* 128
*motive* 128
*need* 115
*nonaspirational reference group* 137
*nonmarketing-controlled information source* 116
*norm* 136
*opinion leader* 137
*perception* 124
*personality* 134
*primary membership group* 136
*problem recognition* 115
*real self-image* 135
*reference group* 136
*routine response behavior* 113
*secondary membership group* 136
*selective distortion* 125
*selective exposure* 124
*selective retention* 125
*self-concept* 135
*social class* 140
*socialization process* 138
*stimulus* 115
*stimulus discrimination* 131
*stimulus generalization* 130
*subculture* 144
*value* 131
*want* 115

response behavior is typically characterized by brand loyalty. Second, consumers engage in limited decision making for occasional purchases or for unfamiliar brands in familiar product categories. Third, consumers practice extensive decision making when making unfamiliar, expensive, or infrequent purchases.

3 **Analyze the components of the consumer decision-making process.** The consumer decision-making process begins with problem recognition, when stimuli trigger awareness of an unfulfilled want. If additional information is required to make a purchase decision, the consumer may engage in an internal or external information search. The consumer then evaluates the additional information and establishes purchase guidelines. Finally, a purchase decision is made.

4 **Explain the consumer's postpurchase evaluation process.** Consumer postpurchase evaluation is influenced by prepurchase expectations, the prepurchase information search, and the consumer's general level of self-confidence. Cognitive dissonance is the inner tension that a consumer experiences after recognizing a purchased product's disadvantages. When a purchase creates cognitive dissonance, consumers tend to react by seeking positive reinforcement for the purchase decision, avoiding negative information about the purchase decision, or revoking the purchase decision by returning the product.

5 **Discuss the importance of high and low involvement in buying decisions.** High-involvement decisions usually include an extensive information search and a thorough evaluation of alternatives. In contrast, low-involvement decisions are characterized by brand loyalty and a lack of personal identification with the product. The main factors affecting the level of consumer involvement are price, interest, perceived risk of negative consequences, situation, and social visibility.

6 **Identify and understand the individual factors that affect consumer buying decisions.** Individual factors include perception; motivation; learning; values, beliefs, and attitudes; and personality, self-concept, and lifestyle. Perception allows consumers to recognize their consumption problems. Motivation is what drives consumers to take action to satisfy specific consumption needs. Almost all consumer behavior results from learning, which is the process that creates changes in behavior through experience. Consumers with similar values, beliefs, and attitudes tend to react alike to marketing-related inducements. Finally, certain products and brands reflect consumers' personality, self-concept, and lifestyle.

7 **Identify and understand the social factors that affect consumer buying decisions.** Social factors include such external influences as reference groups, opinion leaders, family, family life cycle, social class, culture, and subculture. Consumers may use products or brands to identify with or become a member of a reference group. Opinion leaders are members of reference groups who influence others' purchase decisions. Family members also influence purchase decisions; children tend to shop in similar patterns as their parents. Marketers often define their target markets in terms of consumers' life cycle stage, social class, culture, and subculture; consumers with similar characteristics generally have similar consumption patterns. Because all consumer behavior is shaped by individual and social factors, the main goal of marketing strategy is to understand and influence them.

## Discussion and Writing Questions

1. Describe the three categories of consumer decision-making behavior. Name typical products for which each type of consumer behavior is used.
2. The type of decision making a consumer uses for a product does not necessarily remain constant. Why? Support your answer with an example from your own experience.
3. Considering Maslow's hierarchy of needs, give some examples of how marketers appeal to basic human motivations.
4. Recall an occasion when you experienced cognitive dissonance about a purchase. In a letter to a friend, describe the event and explain what you did about it.
5. Discuss a high-involvement purchase decision that you have made. What made it a high-involvement purchase?
6. You are a new marketing manager for a firm that produces a line of athletic shoes to be targeted to the college student subculture. For your boss, write a memo listing some products attributes that might appeal to this subculture, and recommend some marketing strategies.

## Application for Small Business

Deli Depot is a new franchise opportunity offering cold and hot sandwiches, soup and chili, and yogurt, pies, and cookies. It is positioned to compete with Subway and similar sandwich restaurants. Its unique advantages include special sauces on sandwiches, supplementary menu items like soup and pies, and quick delivery within specified zones.

The franchise package offered to franchisees includes information on the factors that typically influence consumers' selection of casual restaurants. These selection factors, in order from most important to least important, include food taste, food variety, value for the money, restaurant reputation, friendliness of employees, and convenience of location.

Robert Powell and a group of investors purchased the right to all franchise locations in the Atlanta metropolitan area. His group estimates that five units can be opened successfully in the first year and that a total of thirty can be opened in the first five years.

Because this is a new franchise, potential customers must first be made aware of Deli Depot and then convinced to try it. Over the long run a loyal customer base must be established to make each Deli Depot a success.

### Questions

1. Are Deli Depot's unique advantages strong enough to attract customers from Subway and other sandwich competitors? Why or why not?
2. Are all the important customer selection factors for sandwich restaurants included in the list? Do you agree with the importance rankings? Explain your answers.
3. How can Robert and his group make potential customers aware of the new Deli Depot locations and menu selections?
4. How can Robert and his group convince individuals who try Deli Depot to become regular customers?

**CRITICAL THINKING CASE**

## The Soap Industry

The U.S. soap industry is mature but far from stagnant. An environmentally conscious public forces continual innovations from the three biggest soap marketers: Procter & Gamble, Colgate-Palmolive, and Unilever. Consumers increasingly want assurances that soap products contain natural ingredients that will not harm or irritate their skin. The soap industry's response has been to formulate new soap products from vegetable oils and starch-derived raw materials, of which there fortunately are a wide variety.

Soap typically is a low-involvement, routine consumer purchase for which little time is spent searching and deciding which brand to buy. Often, consumers are loyal to a certain brand because of previous experience. Marketing managers therefore must somehow persuade people to buy their products instead of the competitors'. They generally have differentiated their products from others in advertising or developed new products in an effort to attract new customers.

Almost half of household members use the same brand, and many of the product choices are made by women. Men purchase only about 20 percent of the small soap bars (face/hand size) but a considerably larger proportion of the large soaps (bath/shower size). Women use more of the smaller soap bars because of their heavier purchases of beauty bars, but men are increasingly buying beauty bars for themselves. The beauty bar category gives soap marketers an opportunity to change soap purchases from low-involvement decisions to high-involvement decisions. Beauty bar purchases can be associated with risk, such as face irritation.

Bar soaps lead the personal soaps category in dollars and sales volume, but liquid soaps, which contain little or no soap, continue to increase their share of the marketplace. Overall, the market share of liquid soaps in the United States is considerably lower than it is in Europe. Nevertheless, liquid soaps have been the fastest-growing category since 1990, with a sales gain of 7.5 percent by 1995. Both women and men use liquid soaps primarily for convenience and deodorant reasons, although men use only a small proportion of liquid soaps.

When women buy soap bars, they use them about equally for complexion or deodorant purposes. Men use soap bars almost exclusively for deodorant reasons. Mildness is the primary feature that consumers expect from soap bars. Overall, deodorant soap bars are the most popular, followed by beauty/cold cream bars. Clear disinfectant soap bars are third in sales but are far less popular than the first two categories.

In response to pressure from consumers, soap marketers are offering multibenefit products that combine functions previously offered separately. For example, Lever Brothers' Lever 2000 is a three-in-one moisturizing, deodorant, and antibacterial cleansing bar. It has proved to be a very successful market entry.

Additionally, many consumers have responded favorably to the addition of natural raw materials to soap formulations, because they like the positive environmental message. Marketing managers have taken the cue. For example, soap bars are being promoted on the basis of their natural and environmentally friendly ingredients—in the process also sending a message of high quality and commitment to customer satisfaction.

In recent years some consumers also have moved toward "value" brands rather than premium labels, asking for better product benefits at little or no extra cost. Soap manufacturers have had to slash prices on name-brand products sold in all outlets in order to compete with products sold at discount stores. Because raw materials are the major cost in soap production, efforts to control costs have focused on ingredients. Soap market analysts note that, although natural ingredients are expected to continue growing in popularity, synthetic ingredients will remain a factor in the intensively competitive soap market.

### Questions

1. Which types and brands of soap do you purchase? Why?
2. Do you believe soap marketers can make soap a high-involvement purchase? Explain your answer.
3. Why do women make the majority of soap purchases?
4. Why do you think liquid soaps have a much lower market share in the United States than in Europe?

### References

S. J. Ainsworth, "Soaps and Detergents," *Chemical and Engineering News,* 24 January 1994, pp. 34–44.

R. Gerry, "The Slippery Soap Business," *Chemical Business,* September 1993, pp. 15–18.

R. Mullin, "Getting Better Performance with Less Surfactant," *Chemical Week,* 26 January 1994, pp. 38–40.

C. Power, "Everyone Is Bellying Up to This Bar," *Business Week,* 27 January 1992, p. 84.

*Soap, Laundry, Paper Products, and Kitchen Wraps,* vol. 20 of *Study of Media and Markets* (Simmons, 1992).

**VIDEO CASE**

## General Tire

For years, General Tire relied on the strength of its own retail operations to market its line of passenger and light-truck tires. During the 1980s, the company abandoned its retail operations to focus its efforts on the production of quality tires.

There are two main markets for tires in the United States: the original equipment manufacturer (OEM) market (automobile manufacturers) and the replacement market (consumers). The OEM market has always been attractive to tire manufacturers because of its high volume and nonexistent promotion cost. However, the profit margin in the OEM market is lower than in the replacement market, because automobile manufacturers are very price-sensitive and often award the contract for tires to the lowest bidder.

During the late 1980s, a weak U.S. dollar enabled foreign manufacturers to buy U.S. tire production facilities and combine operations within their existing plants to generate greater economies of scale. For example, Michelin acquired Uniroyal and B.F. Goodrich. These acquisitions gave Michelin a 20 percent share of the tire market. Goodyear and Bridgestone/Firestone each held a 16 percent share of the market. General Tire, which was purchased by Continental AG of Germany in 1987, was in a distant fourth place, with an 8 percent share of the market.

The tire industry is experiencing slow growth, at 1 to 2 percent per year. The slow growth is attributed mainly to new technology that enables manufacturers to produce longer-lasting tires. The single most important innovation has been the development of the steel-belted radial tire. Today, steel-belted radials account for 95 percent of all passenger car tire sales and 65 percent of all truck tire sales. Every new car comes equipped with radial tires.

Market research conducted by General Tire indicates that consumers have little brand loyalty when it comes to buying tires. The research suggests that consumers are more loyal to the dealer selling the tires than to the brand of tires. Tire purchasers typically compare the original tires with other brands in the market before making a tire purchase. Moreover, purchasers increasingly are shopping for tires at multibrand discount outlets to facilitate comparison shopping.

One of the most attractive segments in the consumer tire market is performance tires. High-performance tires are designed to fit sports cars and performance sedans. These tires give the car better handling characteristics at higher speeds. High-performance tires wear faster and hence need more frequent replacement. Performance tires are premium-priced and offer a higher profit margin to the manufacturer. This segment is also one of the fastest growing in the tire market. When selecting replacement tires for their cars, consumers interested in performance tires look for a variety of product features, such as speed rating, traction, temperature rating, and appearance. General Tire competes head to head with Goodyear and Michelin in this market, but in recent years Firestone has focused on this segment as well.

### Questions

1. Describe the decision-making process for buying performance tires. Use Exhibit 4.1 to explain this process.
2. What sources of information do performance tire consumers seem to use?
3. Are tires a high- or low-involvement product in general? Are performance tires different? Justify your answers.
4. What problems might General Tire have in competing with Goodyear and Michelin in the performance tire market? What does General Tire need to do to solve these problems?

### References

*Million Dollar Directory 1995* (Parsippany, NJ: Dun & Bradstreet Information Services, 1995).

Leah Rickard, "Hoosier Tire's 'Rookie Mistake,'" *Advertising Age,* 7 March 1994, p. 46.

Ramond Serafin and Leah Rickard, "Mercedes, Firestone

Lap Up Indy Cachet," *Advertising Age,* 6 June 1994, p. 12.

*Standard & Poor's Industry Surveys* (New York: Standard & Poor's Corporation, October 1995).

Patricia Strand and Gary Levin, "Tire Makers Take Opposite Routes: Michelin Ads Rely on Brand Loyalty," *Advertising Age,* 6 February 1989, p. 34.

CHAPTER 5

# BUSINESS-TO-BUSINESS MARKETING

## LEARNING OBJECTIVES

*After studying this chapter, you should be able to*

1 *Describe business-to-business marketing.*

2 *Identify the four major categories of business-market customers.*

3 *Explain the standard industrial classification system.*

4 *Explain the major differences between business-to-business and consumer markets.*

5 *Describe the seven types of business-to-business goods and services.*

6 *Discuss the unique aspects of business-to-business buying behavior.*

7 *Discuss the role of relationship marketing and strategic alliances in business-to-business marketing.*

In a pact that could help make electric cars more practical, utility company Boston Edison agreed to market electric-vehicle chargers made by the GM Hughes Electronics unit of General Motors. The utility plans widespread installation of chargers in the Northeast in such places as malls and corporate parking lots, enabling drivers to "refuel" electric cars as readily as they do gasoline-powered vehicles.

The partnership illustrates how two major industries are joining forces to make electric cars a reality. Carmakers, pressured by antipollution laws to put more electric vehicles on the road by 1998, are scrambling to develop better batteries, chargers, and other technologies needed for widespread use of such vehicles. Meanwhile, electric utilities, eager to develop a huge new market for power, are funding electric-vehicle research and developing infrastructure—charging stations, for example—to support wider use of the vehicles.[1]

Why are utilities like Boston Edison eager to promote the use of electric cars? What benefits does General Motors seek from this strategic alliance?

1 *Describe business-to-business marketing.*

**business-to-business marketing**
Marketing of goods and services to individuals and organizations for purposes other than personal consumption.

## WHAT IS BUSINESS-TO-BUSINESS MARKETING?

**Business-to-business marketing** is the marketing of goods and services to individuals and organizations for purposes other than personal consumption. The sale of an overhead projector to your college or university is an example of business-to-business marketing. Business-to-business products include those that are used to manufacture other products, that become part of another product, that aid the normal operations of an organization, or that are acquired for resale without any substantial change in form. The key characteristic distinguishing business-to-business products from consumer products is intended use, not physical characteristics. A product that is purchased for personal or family consumption or as a gift is a consumer good. If that same product, such as a microcomputer or a cellular telephone, is bought for use in a business, it is a business-to-business product.

2 *Identify the four major categories of business-market customers.*

## BUSINESS-TO-BUSINESS CUSTOMERS

The business-to-business market consists of four major categories of customers: producers, resellers, governments, and institutions.

### PRODUCERS

**producer segment**
Portion of the business-to-business market consisting of individuals and organizations that buy goods and services for use in producing other products, for incorporation into other products, or for facilitation of the organization's daily operations.

Exhibit 5.1 shows the types of firms in the **producer segment** of the business-to-business market. It includes profit-oriented individuals and organizations that use purchased goods and services to produce other products, to incorporate into other products, or to facilitate the daily operations of the organization.

Individual producers often buy large quantities of goods and services. Companies like General Motors spend more than $50 billion annually—more than the gross domestic product of Ireland, Portugal, Turkey, or Greece—on such business products as steel, metal components, and tires. Companies like AT&T and IBM spend over $50 million daily for business goods and services, such as computer chips and parts.[2]

*Exhibit 5.1*

Components of the Producer Segment of the Business-to-Business Market

| Kind of organization | Number of firms |
|---|---|
| Agriculture, forestry, fishing | 559,000 |
| Mining | 280,000 |
| Construction | 1,829,000 |
| Manufacturing | 633,000 |
| Transportation, public utilities | 709,000 |
| Finance, insurance, real estate | 2,377,000 |
| Services | 6,813,000 |
| *Total* | 13,200,000 |

Aerospace and military-aircraft manufacturers sell much of their product to the U.S. government, which is the largest single market for goods and services in the world.

© Tony Stone Worldwide/Barry Lewis

## RESELLERS

The **reseller market** includes retail and wholesale businesses that buy finished goods and resell them for a profit. A retailer sells mainly to final consumers; wholesalers sell mostly to retailers and other organizational customers. There are over 1 million retailers and 470,000 wholesalers operating in the United States, with combined annual sales of over $3 trillion.[3] Consumer product firms like Procter & Gamble, Kraft General Foods, and Coca-Cola sell directly to large retailers and retail chains and through wholesalers to smaller retail units. Wholesaling and retailing are explored in detail in Chapters 12 and 13.

**reseller market**
Portion of the business-to-business market consisting of retail and wholesale businesses that buy finished goods and resell them for a profit.

**Business product distributors** are wholesalers that buy business products and resell them to business customers. They often carry thousands of items in stock and employ sales forces to call on business customers. Businesses that wish to buy a gross of pencils or 100 pounds of fertilizer typically purchase these items from local distributors rather than directly from manufacturers such as Empire Pencil or Dow Chemical.

**business product distributor**
Wholesaler that buys business products and resells them to business customers.

## GOVERNMENTS

A third major segment of the business-to-business market is government. Government organizations include thousands of federal, state, and local buying units. They make up what is considered to be the largest single market for goods and services in the world.[4]

Contracts for government purchases are often put out for bid. Interested vendors submit bids (usually sealed) to provide specified products during a particular time. Sometimes the lowest bidder is awarded the contract. When the lowest bidder is not awarded the contract, strong evidence must be presented to justify the decision. Grounds for rejecting the lowest bid include lack of experience, inadequate financing, or poor past performance. Bidding allows all potential suppliers a fair chance at winning government contracts and helps ensure that public funds are spent wisely. For more information about bidding, see Chapter 19.

### Federal Government

Name just about any good or service and chances are that someone in the federal government uses it. The U.S. federal government is the world's largest customer.

Although much of the federal government's buying is centralized, no single federal agency contracts for all the government's requirements, and no single buyer in any agency purchases all that the agency needs. One can view the federal government as a combination of several large companies with overlapping responsibilities and thousands of small independent units.

One of the largest "companies" is the General Services Administration (GSA), which buys general-use items (like cars and desks) for all civilian agencies and military departments. A second large "company" is the Defense Logistics Agency (DLA), which buys billions of dollars worth of food, clothing, and other standard supplies for various branches of the military.

MARKETING AND SMALL BUSINESS

**Finding Gold in the Federal Government**

An excellent target market for small businesses is the federal government. Many small companies have been very successful in this market, and the government offers some distinct advantages over other markets. For one thing, there's no doubt that the government will pay its bills, although it may take its time. Also, as a government contractor, a new small business gains credibility that can help in selling to private customers. In addition, Uncle Sam buys nearly everything—from food to spark plugs to exotic scientific and technical equipment—and doesn't usually subject suppliers to the abrupt cancellations that, in industry, are a feature of recessions. By making progress payments as the steps of a project are completed, the government acts as a financing source for small businesses. Progress payments help small businesses buy the inventory needed to complete the contract. And in the view of some small-business owners, the government is a more objective buyer than many companies are.

However, learning how to bid for government orders can be a major problem. It doesn't take long for the small-business manager to discover that up-and-coming bureaucrats feel more comfortable with big-company suppliers. Government bureaucrats also have a way of moving to a new assignment, leaving the small enterprise to prove itself over again to the replacement.

Small businesses that finally win federal procurement awards may encounter another set of problems. Sometimes the specifications are different from those the company originally understood. The government's time requirements for delivery may be unreasonably short, or the time the government takes to pay may be unreasonably long. Nevertheless, many small businesses conclude that the hassles are more than outweighed by the benefits.

### State, County, and City Government

Selling to states, counties, and cities can be less frustrating for both small and large vendors than selling to the federal government. Paperwork is typically simpler and more manageable than at the federal level. On the other hand, vendors must decide which of the over 82,000 governmental units are likely to buy their wares. State and local buying agencies include school districts, highway departments, government-operated hospitals, and housing agencies.

Purchasing by nonfederal government entities has become more professional and standardized in recent years. Many larger cities and counties and all states use centralized purchasing, with one purchasing agent for each department of a jurisdiction. Standard specifications apply to most items purchased.

States exchange information on buying procedures and specifications through associations like the National Association of State Purchasing Officials. Nonfederal governments also use cooperative purchasing to reduce costs. Under this system, several units of government—for instance, a city and surrounding suburbs—join to buy certain goods and services. The typical result is price breaks for volume purchasing.

### INSTITUTIONS

The fourth major segment of the business-to-business market is institutions that seek to achieve goals different from such ordinary business goals as profit, market share, and return on investment. This segment includes schools, hospitals, colleges and universities, churches, labor unions, fraternal organizations, civic clubs, foundations, and other so-called nonbusiness organizations. The institutional market includes about 6 million organizations and spends about $250 billion annually on goods and services.[5]

Voluntary Hospitals of America, an alliance of nearly 900 not-for-profit hospitals and multihospital systems, buys sutures, staplers, and endoscopic surgical instruments exclusively from Johnson & Johnson Medical. For Johnson & Johnson, this one agreement is worth about $250 million in sales each year.[6]

3 *Explain the standard industrial classification system.*

## CLASSIFICATION OF BUSINESS AND GOVERNMENT MARKETS

**standard industrial classification system (SIC)**
Detailed numbering system developed by the U.S. government in order to classify business and government organizations by their main economic activity.

The **standard industrial classification system** (SIC) is a detailed numbering system developed by the U.S. government to classify business and government organizations by their main economic activity. The SIC system divides the economy into eleven major divisions and assigns two-digit numbers to major industry groups within each division. For each two-digit code, the U.S. Census Bureau publishes data on total industry sales and employment. This information is further broken down by geographic region and is available for each county in the United States.

Two-digit SIC industry categories are then further divided into three-digit and four-digit categories, which represent subindustries within the broader two-digit categories. Exhibit 5.2 on page 156 shows an example of two-, three-, four-, and five-digit codes. The fifth and subsequent digits are product classifications.

Much has been published on uses of the SIC system for marketing.[7] Exhibit 5.3 on page 157 shows several SIC data sources and how they may be used by business-to-business marketers.

Although SIC data are helpful for analyzing, segmenting, and targeting markets, they have important limitations. For example, the federal government assigns only one code to each organization. Therefore, the system does not accurately describe firms that engage in many different activities or that provide various types of products. Another limitation is that four-digit codes are not assigned to industries in geographic areas where two or fewer firms are located. Thus some firms are not represented in the SIC listings. Furthermore, the four-digit system is too general to adequately describe industries that are growing more sophisticated and diversified.[8]

4 *Explain the major differences between business-to-business and consumer markets.*

## BUSINESS-TO-BUSINESS VERSUS CONSUMER MARKETS

The basic philosophy and practice of marketing is the same whether the customer is a business organization or a consumer. Business markets do, however, have characteristics different from consumer markets. Exhibit 5.4 on page 158 summarizes the main differences between business-to-business and consumer markets.

*Exhibit 5.2*

SIC Breakdown for Hand Tools

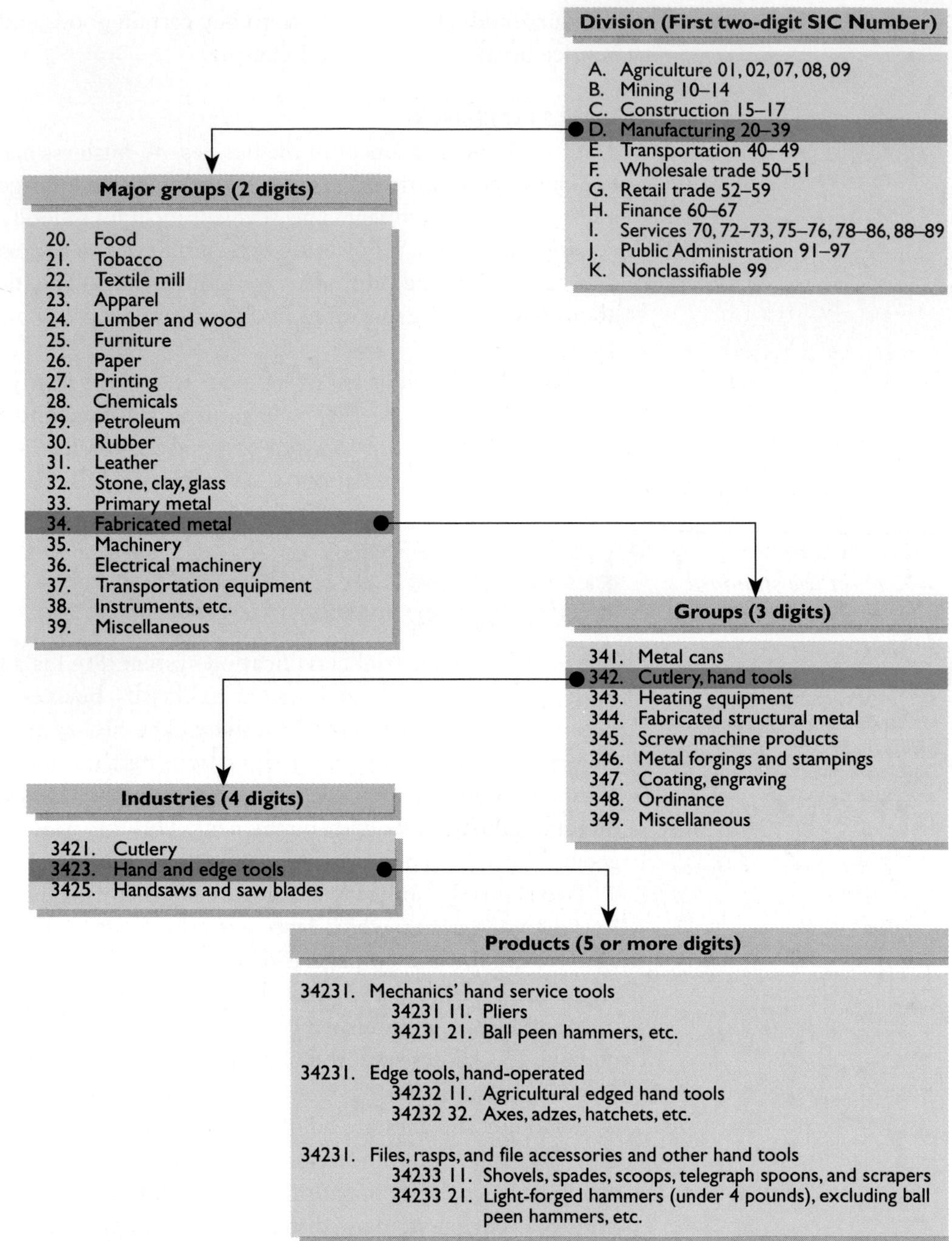


## DEMAND

Consumer demand for products (discussed at length in Chapter 18) is quite different from demand in the business-to-business market. Unlike consumer demand, business-to-business demand is derived, inelastic, joint, and fluctuating.

### Derived Demand

**derived demand** Demand that results from demand for another product.

The demand for business-to-business products is called **derived demand** because organizations buy products to be used in producing consumer products. In other words, the demand for business-to-business products is derived from the demand for

| SIC source | Possible applications to marketing |
|---|---|
| *SIC Manual* | Determining target markets and segments in terms of SIC codes |
| *U.S. Census of Manufacturers* | Determining market size, growth, areas of geographic concentration, number of firms; published every 5 years |
| *Survey of Manufacturers* | Determining market size, growth, areas of geographic concentration, number of firms; published annually |
| *U.S. Industrial Outlook* | Determining number of firms, areas of geographic concentration, past industry trends, projected industry forecasts |
| *Sales & Marketing Management's* "Survey of Industrial & Commercial Buying Power" | Determining number of firms by county, number of large firms, value of shipments for total United States and by state and county |
| *County Business Patterns* | Determining number of firms by county, number of employees |
| Dun's *Census of American Business* | Determining number of firms by employee size, sales volume, and state and county |
| *Predicasts* | Determining market size, annual growth rates; from short- and long-term forecasts by SIC in article abstracts |
| Private industrial directories, such as *Million Dollar Directory, Poor's Register* | Determining company names, addresses, secondary SIC codes, products produced, sales volumes, and names of key executives; on a national basis |
| State and county industrial directories | Similar to private industrial directories, but by individual state or county |
| Data bases, such as Dun & Bradstreet, Trinet, Thomas | Determining company names, addresses, sales volumes, products, number of employees, names of key executives, market share, consumption of products |
| Mailing-list companies | Determining company names and addresses; on labels, printouts, diskettes, tapes |

*Exhibit 5.3*

Selected SIC-Related Sources and Their Marketing Applications

Source: Adapted from Robert W. Haas, "SIC—A Marketing Tool in Transition," *Business*, April–June 1990, pp. 15–22. Reprinted by permission of the author and Georgia State University Press.

consumer products. For example, car and truck manufacturers account for a major share of U.S. steel, rubber, and aluminum consumption. An additional 5 billion pounds of aluminum are used annually in the production of beverage containers.[9]

Because demand is derived, business-to-business marketers must carefully monitor demand patterns and changing preferences in final consumer markets, even though their customers are not in those markets. Moreover, business-to-business marketers must carefully monitor their customers' forecasts, because derived demand is based on expectations of future demand for those customers' products.

Some business-to-business marketers not only monitor final consumer demand and customer forecasts but also try to influence final consumer demand. For example, aluminum producers advertise on television and in magazines the convenience

*Exhibit 5.4*

Major Characteristics of Business-to-Business Markets Compared to Consumer Markets

| Characeristic | Business-to-business market | Consumer market |
|---|---|---|
| Demand | Organizational | Individual |
| Purchase volume | Larger | Smaller |
| Number of customers | Fewer | Many |
| Location of buyers | Geographically concentrated | Dispersed |
| Distribution structure | More direct | More indirect |
| Nature of buying | More professional | More personal |
| Nature of buying influence | Multiple | Single |
| Type of negotiations | More complex | Simpler |
| Use of reciprocity | Yes | No |
| Use of leasing | Greater | Lesser |
| Primary promotional method | Personal selling | Advertising |

and recyclability of aluminum containers. The target of these ads is beverage purchasers and consumers.

## Inelastic Demand

The demand for many business-to-business products is inelastic with regard to price. *Inelastic demand* means that an increase or decrease in the price of the product will not significantly affect demand for the product.

The price of a product used in the production of or as part of a final product is often a minor part of the final product's total price. Therefore, demand for the final consumer product is not affected. If the price of automobile paint or spark plugs rose significantly, say 200 percent in one year, do you think the number of new automobiles sold that year would be affected? Probably not.

## Joint Demand

**joint demand**
Demand for two or more items that are used together in a final product.

**Joint demand** occurs when two or more items are used together in a final product. For example, a decline in the availability of memory chips will slow production of microcomputers, which will in turn reduce the demand for disk drives. Many business products, like hammer heads and hammer handles, also exemplify joint demand.

## Fluctuating Demand

The demand for business-to-business products—particularly new plants and equipment—tends to be more unstable than the demand for consumer products. A small increase or decrease in consumer demand can produce a much larger change in demand

Every car produced at this Saturn plant incorporates products manufactured elsewhere—such as steel, rubber, and aluminum. When the demand for cars increases, so does the demand for the materials used to make them.

© SWC

**multiplier effect (accelerator principle)**
Phenomenon in which a small increase or decrease in consumer demand produces a much larger change in demand for the facilities and equipment needed to make the consumer product.

for the facilities and equipment needed to make the consumer product. Economists refer to this phenomenon as the **multiplier effect** (or accelerator principle).

Boeing Aircraft uses sophisticated surface grinders to make airplane parts. Suppose Boeing is using twenty surface grinders. Each machine lasts about ten years. Purchases have been timed so two machines will wear out and be replaced annually. If the demand for airplane parts does not change, two grinders will be bought this year. If the demand for parts declines slightly, only eighteen grinders may be needed and Boeing won't replace the worn ones. However, suppose in the next year demand returns to previous levels plus a little more. To meet the new level of demand, Boeing will need to replace the two machines that wore out in the first year, the two that wore out in the second year, plus one or more additional machines. The multiplier effect works this way in many industries, producing highly fluctuating demand for business-to-business products.

## PURCHASE VOLUME

Business-to-business customers buy in much larger quantities than consumers. Just think how large an order Kellogg typically places for the wheat bran and raisins used to manufacture Raisin Bran. Imagine the number of tires that Ford buys at one time.

## NUMBER OF CUSTOMERS

Business-to-business marketers usually have far fewer customers than consumer marketers. The advantage is that it is a lot easier to identify prospective buyers, monitor current customers' needs and levels of satisfaction, and personally attend to existing customers. The main disadvantage is that each customer becomes crucial—especially for those business-to-business manufacturers that have only one customer. In many cases, this customer is the U.S. government.

### LOCATION OF BUYERS

Business-to-business customers tend to be much more geographically concentrated than consumers. For instance, more than half the nation's business buyers are located in New York, California, Pennsylvania, Illinois, Ohio, Michigan, and New Jersey. The petroleum, rubber, and steel industries are even more concentrated.

### DISTRIBUTION STRUCTURE

Many consumer products pass through a distribution system that includes the producer, one or more wholesalers, and a retailer. However, because of many of the characteristics already mentioned, channels of distribution are typically shorter in business-to-business marketing. Direct channels, where manufacturers market directly to users, are much more common.

### NATURE OF BUYING

Unlike consumers, business buyers usually approach purchasing rather formally. Businesses use professionally trained purchasing agents or buyers who spend their entire career purchasing a limited number of items. They get to know the items and the sellers quite well. Some professional purchasers earn the designation of Certified Purchasing Manager (CPM) after participating in a rigorous certification program.

**reciprocity**
Practice in which business purchasers choose to buy from their own customers.

### NATURE OF BUYING INFLUENCE

Typically, more people are involved in a single business purchase decision than in a consumer purchase. Experts from fields as varied as quality control, marketing, and finance, as well as professional buyers and users, may be grouped in a buying center (discussed later in this chapter).

### TYPE OF NEGOTIATIONS

Consumers are used to negotiating price on automobiles and real estate. But in most cases, American consumers expect sellers to set the price and other conditions of sale, such as time of delivery and credit terms. On the other hand, negotiating is common in business-to-business marketing. Buyers and sellers negotiate product specifications, delivery dates, payment terms, and other pricing matters. Sometimes these negotiations occur during many meetings over several months. Final contracts are often very long and detailed.

### USE OF RECIPROCITY

Business purchasers often choose to buy from their own customers, a practice known as **reciprocity.** This practice is neither unethical nor illegal unless one party coerces the other and the

ETHICS IN MARKETING

**Symposium or Sales Presentation?**

A young doctor listened intently to a panel of distinguished physicians discussing advances in hypertension treatment at the annual meeting of the American Academy of Family Physicians. By the end of the three-hour presentation, he was thinking about switching some of his hypertension patients to a drug called a calcium channel blocker, which was much discussed at the presentation. The seminar was sponsored by the pharmaceutical company G.D. Searle, as the young physician knew. But he didn't realize that Searle, which was then running a promotional campaign for one of several calcium channel blockers, had carefully picked speakers who were well-known advocates of this class of drugs.

The drug industry's public position is that it supports medical education out of concern for the safe and appropriate use of its products and for the professional advancement of its customers—that is, physicians.[13]

Do you think the drug industry's position is ethical? Do you think it was ethical for Searle to sponsor the seminar on calcium channel blockers? Searle didn't hide its sponsorship of the seminar. Should the company have also announced that the speakers had been carefully selected and were well-known advocates of calcium channel blockers?

Much of the equipment used in business can be leased instead of purchased. Both the lessee and lessor benefit.



result is unfair competition. Reciprocity is generally considered a reasonable business practice. If all possible suppliers sell about the same product for about the same price, doesn't it make sense to buy from those firms that buy from you?

### USE OF LEASING

Consumers normally buy products rather than lease them. But businesses commonly lease expensive equipment like computers, construction equipment and vehicles, and automobiles. Leasing accounts for about a third of all new capital investment in the United States each year.[10] It allows firms to reduce capital outflow, acquire a seller's latest products, receive better services, and gain tax advantages.[11]

The lessor, the firm providing the product, may be either the manufacturer or an independent firm. The benefits to the lessor include greater total revenue from leasing compared to selling and a chance to do business with customers who cannot afford to buy. Leasing, however, is not without risks. When U.S. airlines slashed spending in the early 1990s, hundreds of jets owned by aircraft makers and leasing firms were idled.[12]

### PRIMARY PROMOTIONAL METHOD

Business-to-business marketers tend to emphasize personal selling in their promotion efforts, especially for expensive items, custom-designed products, large-volume purchases, and situations requiring negotiations. The sale of many business-to-business products requires a great deal of personal contact. Personal selling is discussed in more detail in Chapter 17.

With so much riding on a single sale in the business-to-business market, salespeople tend to go to great lengths to sway buyers' opinions. Thus it is perhaps not surprising that ethical questions sometimes arise, as the adjacent Ethics in Marketing story illustrates.

5 *Describe the seven types of business-to-business goods and services.*

## TYPES OF BUSINESS-TO-BUSINESS PRODUCTS

Business-to-business products generally fall into one of the following seven categories, depending on their use: major equipment, accessory equipment, raw materials, component parts, processed materials, supplies, and business services.

**major equipment (installation)**
Capital good, such as a large or expensive machine, mainframe computer, blast furnace, generator, airplane, or building.

### MAJOR EQUIPMENT

**Major equipment** includes such capital goods as large or expensive machines, mainframe computers, blast furnaces, generators, airplanes, and buildings. (These items are also commonly called *installations*.) Major equipment is depreciated over time

Like other producers, farmers must purchase major equipment, such as corn harvesters.

© Tony Stone Worldwide/Curt Mass

rather than charged as an expense in the year it is purchased. In addition, major equipment is often custom-designed for each customer.

Personal selling is an important part of the marketing strategy for major equipment, because distribution channels are almost always direct from the producer to the business user.

**accessory equipment**
Goods, such as portable tools and office equipment, that are less expensive and shorter-lived than major equipment.

## ACCESSORY EQUIPMENT

**Accessory equipment** is generally less expensive and shorter-lived than major equipment. Examples include portable drills, power tools, microcomputers, and fax machines. Accessory equipment is often charged as an expense in the year it is bought rather than depreciated over its useful life. In contrast to major equipment, accessories are more often standardized and are usually bought by more customers. These customers tend to be widely dispersed. For example, all types of businesses buy microcomputers.

Local industrial distributors (wholesalers) play an important role in the marketing of accessory equipment, because business buyers often purchase accessories from them. Regardless of where accessories are bought, advertising is a more vital promotional tool for accessory equipment than for major equipment.

**raw material**
Unprocessed extractive or agricultural product, such as mineral ore, lumber, wheat, corn, fruits, vegetables, or fish.

## RAW MATERIALS

**Raw materials** are unprocessed extractive or agricultural products—for example, mineral ore, lumber, wheat, corn, fruits, vegetables, and fish. Raw materials become part of finished products. Extensive users, such as steel or lumber mills and food canners, generally buy huge quantities of raw materials. Because there is often a large number of relatively small sellers of raw materials, none can greatly influence price or supply. Thus the market tends to set the price of raw materials, and individual producers have little pricing flexibility.

Promotion is almost always personal selling, and distribution channels are usually direct from producer to business user.

To create a consumer preference for its brand, Intel pays computer manufacturers to feature its "Intel inside" logo. Most other component parts are anonymous.

© Toshiba America Information Systems Inc.

**component part**
Finished item ready for assembly or product that needs very little processing before becoming part of some other product.

## COMPONENT PARTS

**Component parts** are either finished items ready for assembly or products that need very little processing before becoming part of some other product. Examples include spark plugs, tires, and electric motors for automobiles. A special feature of component parts is that they often retain their identity after becoming part of the final product. For example, automobile tires are clearly recognizable as part of a car. Moreover, because component parts often wear out, they may need to be replaced several times during the life of the final product. Thus there are two important markets for many component parts: the original equipment manufacturer (OEM) market and the replacement market.

Many of the business-to-business features listed before in Exhibit 5.4 characterize the OEM market. The difference between unit costs and selling prices in the OEM market is often small, but profits can be quite substantial because of volume buying.

Rarely does advertising play a key role in the promotion strategy for OEM markets. Even more rare is advertising to end users. Two exceptions to this generalization are NutraSweet, the artificial sweetener, and Intel, the semiconductor company. NutraSweet encourages the manufacturers of products such as Diet Coke and Extra chewing gum to feature its logo on their containers and packages. Intel pays microcomputer manufacturers to feature its trademark—"Intel inside"—in their ads and on their products. NutraSweet and Intel are trying to create a brand image and customer preference for their brands.[14] Buyers needn't know exactly what NutraSweet is or what Intel makes if those buyers can be convinced that products containing these components are preferable.

The replacement market is composed of organizations and individuals buying component parts to replace worn-out parts. Because components often retain their identity in final products, users may choose to replace a component part with the same brand used by the manufacturer—for example, the same brand of automobile tires or battery. The replacement market operates differently from the OEM market, however. Whether replacement buyers are organizations or individuals, they tend to demonstrate the characteristics of consumer markets that were shown in Exhibit 5.4. Consider, for example, an automobile replacement part. Purchase volume is usually small, and there are many customers, geographically dispersed, who typically buy from car dealers or parts stores. Negotiations do not occur, and neither reciprocity nor leasing is usually an issue.

Manufacturers of component parts often direct their advertising toward replacement buyers. Cooper Tire & Rubber, for example, makes and markets component parts—automobile and truck tires—for the replacement market only. Ford and other carmakers compete with independent firms in the market for replacement automobile parts.

### PROCESSED MATERIALS

**processed material**
Good used directly in manufacturing other products.

**Processed materials** are used directly in manufacturing other products. Unlike raw materials, they have had some processing. Examples include sheet metal, chemicals, specialty steel, lumber, corn syrup, and plastics. Unlike component parts, processed materials do not retain their identity in final products.

Most processed materials are marketed to OEMs or to distributors servicing the OEM market. Processed materials are generally bought according to customer specifications or to some industry standard, as is the case with steel and lumber. Price and service are important factors in choosing a vendor.

### SUPPLIES

**supply**
Consumable item that does not become part of the final product.

**Supplies** are consumable items that do not become part of the final product—for example, lubricants, detergents, paper towels, pencils, and paper. Supplies are normally standardized items that purchasing agents routinely buy. Supplies typically have relatively short lives and are inexpensive compared to other business goods. Because supplies generally fall into one of three categories—maintenance, repair, or operating supplies—this category is often referred to as MRO items.

Competition in the MRO market is intense. Bic and Paper Mate, for example, battle for business purchases of inexpensive ballpoint pens.

### BUSINESS SERVICES

**business service**
Expense item obtained from an outside provider that does not become part of a final product, such as janitorial, advertising, legal, management consulting, marketing research, maintenance, and other services.

**Business services** are expense items that do not become part of a final product. Businesses often retain outside providers to perform janitorial, advertising, legal, management consulting, marketing research, maintenance, and other tasks. Hiring an outside provider makes sense when it costs less than hiring or assigning an employee to perform the task and when an outside provider is needed for particular expertise.

6 *Discuss the unique aspects of business-to-business buying behavior.*

## BUSINESS-TO-BUSINESS BUYING BEHAVIOR

As you probably have already concluded, business buyers behave differently from consumers. Understanding how purchase decisions are made in organizations is a first step in developing a business-to-business selling strategy. Five important aspects of business-to-business buying behavior are buying centers, evaluative criteria, buying situations, the purchase process, and customer service.

### BUYING CENTERS

**buying center**
Group consisting of all those who are involved in a purchase decision for an organization.

A **buying center** includes all those persons in an organization who become involved in the purchase decision. Membership and influence vary from company to company. For instance, in engineering-dominated firms like Bell Helicopter and General Dynamics, the buying center may consist almost entirely of engineers. In marketing-oriented firms like Toyota and IBM, marketing and engineering have almost equal authority. In consumer goods firms like Procter & Gamble, product managers and other marketing decision makers may dominate the buying center. In a small manufacturing company, almost everyone may be a member.

The number of people involved in a buying center varies widely depending on industry, company, and even culture. According to Alan Wolfe, director of marketing services at Primary Contact International and an expert on the phenomenon of "Eurobuyers," an average of nine people influence a typical business buying decision in Europe. The number ranges from an average of three in Italy to twenty in France.[15]

The relationships that truly constitute a firm's buying center do not appear on the formal organization chart. For example, even though a formal committee may have been set up to choose a new plant site, it is only part of the buying center. Other people, like the company president, often play informal yet powerful roles. In a lengthy decision-making process, such as finding a new plant location, some members may drop out of the buying center when they can no longer play a useful role. Others whose talents are needed then become part of the center. No formal announcement of "who is in" and "who is out" is ever made.

## Roles in the Buying Center

As in the purchasing decisions of families, several people may play a role in the business purchase process:

- *Initiator:* the person who first suggests making a purchase.
- *Influencers/evaluators:* people who influence the buying decision. They often help define specifications and provide information for evaluating options. Technical personnel are especially important as influencers.
- *Gatekeepers:* group members who regulate the flow of information. Frequently, the purchasing agent views the gatekeeping role as a source of his or her power. A secretary may also act as a gatekeeper by determining which vendors get an appointment with a buyer.
- *Decider:* the person who has the formal or informal power to choose or approve the selection of the supplier or brand. In complex situations, it is often difficult to determine who makes the final decision.
- *Purchaser:* the person who actually negotiates the purchase. It could be anyone from the president of the company to the purchasing agent, depending on the importance of the decision.
- *Users:* members of the organization who will actually use the product. Users often initiate the buying process and help define product specifications.

An example illustrating these basic roles is shown in Exhibit 5.5 on page 166.

## Implications of Buying Centers for the Marketing Manager

Successful vendors realize the importance of identifying and interacting with the true decision makers. They make sure their sales representatives focus on those who can actually sign a contract or write a check. Alcoa, for instance, claims that every hour its sales engineers contact key design engineers and managers in Detroit and in the aerospace business. As a result, the aluminum industry has made inroads in what was the steel industry's market for car and airplane parts.

In reviewing a customer's buying center, a marketing manager must ask three basic questions:

- *Price:* Business buyers want to buy at low prices—at the lowest prices, under most circumstances. However, a buyer who pressures a supplier to cut prices to a point where the supplier loses money on the sale almost forces shortcuts on quality. The buyer also may, in effect, force the supplier to quit selling to him or her. Then a new source of supply will have to be found.

Many international business buyers use similar evaluative criteria. One study of South African buyers of high-tech laboratory instruments found that they use the following evaluative criteria, in descending order: technical service, perceived product reliability, after-sales support, supplier's reputation, ease of maintenance, ease of operation, price, confidence in the sales representative, and product flexibility.[19]

## BUYING SITUATIONS

Often business firms, especially manufacturers, must decide whether to make something or buy it from an outside supplier. The decision is essentially one of economics. Can an item of similar quality be bought at a lower price elsewhere? If not, is manufacturing it in-house the best use of limited company resources? For example, Briggs & Stratton, a major manufacturer of four-cycle engines, might be able to save $150,000 annually on outside purchases by spending $500,000 on the equipment needed to produce gas throttles internally. Yet Briggs & Stratton could also use that $500,000 to upgrade its carburetor assembly line, which would save $225,000 annually.

If a firm does decide to buy a product instead of making it, the purchase will be a new buy, a modified rebuy, or a straight rebuy.

### New Buy

**new buy**
Buying situation requiring the purchase of a product for the first time.

A **new buy** is a situation requiring the purchase of a product for the first time. For example, suppose a law firm decides to replace word-processing machinery with microcomputers. This situation represents the greatest opportunity for new vendors. No long-term relationship has been established (at least for this product), specifications may be somewhat fluid, and buyers are generally more open to new vendors.

If the new item is a raw material or a critical component part, the buyer cannot afford to run out of supply. The seller must be able to convince the buyer that the seller's firm can consistently deliver a high-quality product on time.

**value engineering (value analysis)**
Systematic search for less expensive substitute goods or services.

New-buy situations often result from value engineering. **Value engineering** (also called value analysis) is the systematic search for less expensive substitutes. The goal is to identify goods and services that perform a given function at a lower total cost than those currently used. There is a growing tendency for buyers and potential suppliers to do value engineering studies. The vendor who can show the results of such studies will benefit during the negotiation process.

### Modified Rebuy

**modified rebuy**
Buying situation in which the purchaser wants some change in the original good or service.

A **modified rebuy** is normally less critical and less time-consuming than a new buy. In a modified-rebuy situation, the purchaser wants some change in the original good or service. It may be a new color, greater tensile strength in a component part, more respondents in a marketing research study, or additional services in a janitorial contract.

Because the two parties are familiar with each other and credibility has been established, buyer and seller can concentrate on the specifics of the modification. But in some cases, modified rebuys are open to outside bidders. The purchaser uses this strategy to ensure that the new terms are competitive. An example would be a law firm deciding to buy more powerful microcomputers. The firm may open the bidding to examine the price/quality offerings of several suppliers.

### Straight Rebuy

**straight rebuy**
Buying situation in which the purchaser reorders the same goods or services without looking for new information or investigating other suppliers.

A **straight rebuy** is a situation vendors relish. The purchaser is not looking for new information or other suppliers. An order is placed, and the product is provided as in previous orders. Usually a straight rebuy is routine, because the terms of the purchase have been hammered out in earlier negotiations. An example would be the law firm previously cited purchasing printer ribbons from the same supplier on a regular basis.

**purchasing contract**
Agreement in which a business buyer promises to purchase a given amount of a product within a specified period.

One common technique used in straight-rebuy situations is the **purchasing contract.** Purchasing contracts are used with products that are bought often and in high volume. In essence, the purchasing contract makes the buyer's decision making routine and promises the salesperson a sure sale. The advantage to the buyer is a quick, confident decision and, to the salesperson, reduced or eliminated competition.

**annual purchasing contract**
Type of purchasing contract that provides a discount schedule for purchases over the period of the contract.

There are two common forms of purchasing contracts. The **annual purchasing contract** provides a discount schedule for purchases over the period of the contract. The more the company buys within a year, the greater the discount it receives. Electronic Data Systems won a landmark annual contract to supply personal computers and training to General Electric worldwide. The four-year contract was estimated to be worth $400 million to $500 million for Electronic Data Systems.[20]

**blanket purchasing contract**
Type of purchasing contract that requires the supplier to provide a certain amount of product at the same price each month during the course of a year.

The **blanket purchasing contract,** on the other hand, obliges the supplier to provide a certain amount of product each month during the year at one set price. Each year the contract and the price are renegotiated. Computer supplies like laser-printer cartridges and paper commonly fall under blanket purchasing contracts.

**forward buying**
Practice of purchasing in advance of need to take advantage of promotional discounts offered by suppliers.

Some firms use forward buying for products that fall into the straight-rebuy category. **Forward buying** is purchasing in advance of need to take advantage of promotional discounts offered by suppliers.

Suppliers must remember not to take straight-rebuy relationships for granted. Retaining existing customers is much easier than attracting new ones.

## THE PURCHASE PROCESS

The business-to-business purchase process is traced in Exhibit 5.6 on page 170. It begins with recognition of a need. For example, a firm may realize that it must replace old machinery or expand its facilities.

The next step in the purchase sequence is a tentative decision on the type of product needed. Sometimes the buying firm then drafts product specifications. More often, though, members of the buying center select several potential sources of supply and begin negotiations. Purchasing agents may even keep lists of approved suppliers for various types of products. Negotiations begin with a discussion of the product needed, the time frame within which it is needed, and the terms of delivery. Negotiations often end when each of the potential suppliers submits a proposal with a bid, or price to be charged for the product. The buyer then analyzes the proposals and either selects the best one or asks suppliers for clarification.

Exhibit 5.6

Business-to-Business Purchase Process

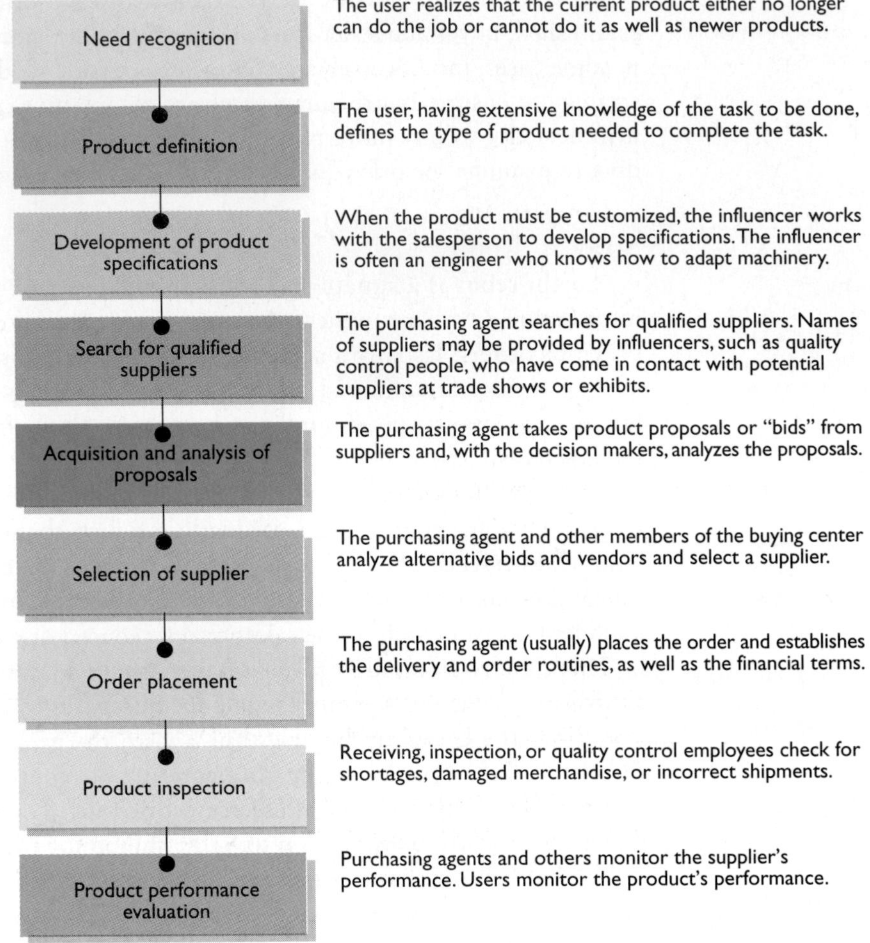


## Vendor Analysis

**vendor analysis**
Practice of comparing alternative suppliers in terms of attributes that the buying center views as important.

Buying centers, particularly in new-buy situations, use vendor rating systems, called **vendor analysis,** to compare suppliers on attributes the buying center views as important. Exhibit 5.7 illustrates the use of vendor analysis to compare microcomputer suppliers. The buying center has identified the six attributes in the left column as most important. Each vendor is then rated on each attribute. A potential vendor's score is determined by adding all the ratings and dividing by the total number of attributes. In the example, the vendor is strong except on the attributes of affordability and product line depth. The purchasing agent has to decide how important these two attributes are.

A more sophisticated approach, which builds in assessments of each attribute's importance, first weights the attributes (for example, 1 for somewhat important, 2 for moderately important, and 3 for very important). These importance ratings are then multiplied by the vendor rating scores, which are totaled to yield an overall vendor score.

## Completion of the Transaction

After analyzing vendors, selecting a source of supply, and negotiating the terms of the purchase, the buying firm issues a purchase order, making the transaction official. Purchase orders often include such details as product identification code or description, quantity and quality to be delivered, method and frequency of delivery, and payment terms.

*Exhibit 5.7*

Example of Vendor Analysis in a Microcomputer Buying Situation

| Attributes | Unacceptable (0) | Poor (1) | Fair (2) | Good (3) | Excellent (4) |
|---|---|---|---|---|---|
| | Rating scale | | | | |
| Compatibility | | | | | X |
| Affordability | | | X | | |
| Reliability | | | | | X |
| Product line depth | | | X | | |
| Service/ support | | | | | X |
| Flexibility | | | | X | |

*Total score:* 4 + 2 + 4 + 2 + 4 + 3 = 19

*Average score:* 19 ÷ 6 = 3.17

When products are received, they are inspected for correctness, quantity, and quality and then checked into inventory. When the seller's invoice has been checked and found in order, payment is authorized. Once payment has been made, the transaction is complete.

Although the transaction is complete at this point, the buyer will take note of the product and the supplier's performance through periodic evaluations. These evaluations will help the buyer determine whether to make future purchases from this supplier.

## The Salesperson's Role

The salesperson plays a very important role throughout the purchase process. Salespeople often are the first to recognize that buyers need their product. Because they are the ones recognizing the need, they are in a position to influence the product's definition and specifications.

Salespeople who emphasize the need to the buyer are usually guaranteed that their company will be one of the suppliers considered. Good salespeople, knowing that at this point they have an "in" with this particular buyer, should ask questions to determine the buyer's potential budget for this purchase. With this type of information, the salesperson can prepare a bid within the buyer's price range. The salesperson's company will have a competitive edge.

If the sale is made, the salesperson should verify that the product is packaged and ready to be delivered on time and is received in good working condition, with all parts included. Finally, throughout their follow-up service, salespeople should ensure that the customer is fully satisfied with the product and that the seller has fulfilled all presale promises.

### CUSTOMER SERVICE

Business-to-business marketers are increasingly recognizing the benefits of developing a formal system to monitor customer opinions and perceptions of the quality of customer service.[21] Companies like Honda, Apple, and Merck build their strategies not only around products but also around a few highly developed service skills.[22] Customer service is explored in more detail in Chapters 8 and 11.

IBM Canada, noticing that business customers weren't always getting the service they wanted, started a new program called "customer obsession." It began with a two-day workshop for senior IBM Canada managers in information and marketing services.[23] The goal was to reassess and redefine the firm's customer-service strategy. After the workshop, participating executives shared their new plans with all 11,000 employees, regardless of whether these employees dealt directly with customers.

7 *Discuss the role of relationship marketing and strategic alliances in business-to-business marketing.*

## RELATIONSHIP MARKETING AND STRATEGIC ALLIANCES

As Chapter 1 explained, relationship marketing is the strategy that entails seeking and establishing ongoing partnerships with customers. Relationship marketing is redefining the fundamental roles of business buyers and sellers. Suppliers are making major adjustments in their thinking, management styles, and methods of responding to purchaser's standards and operational requirements. Relationship marketing is not a faddish trend but rather is driven by strong business forces: the competitive need for quality, speed, and cost-effectiveness, as well as new design techniques.[24]

**strategic alliance (strategic partnership)**
Cooperative agreement between business firms, taking the form of a licensing or distribution agreement, joint venture, research and development consortium, or partnership.

A **strategic alliance,** sometimes called a strategic partnership, is a cooperative agreement between business firms. Strategic alliances can take the form of licensing or distribution agreements, joint ventures, research and development consortia, and partnerships. For example, Citibank Visa and Ford have introduced the Ford Citibank Visa and MasterCard. The card offers customers an opportunity to earn substantial rebates on the purchase or lease of new Ford, Lincoln, and Mercury automobiles.[25]

The trend toward forming strategic alliances is accelerating rapidly, particularly among high-tech firms. Xerox management, for example, has decided that in order to maintain its leadership position in the reprographics industry, the company must "include suppliers as part of the Xerox family."[26] This strategy often means reducing the number of suppliers, treating those that remain as allies, sharing strategic information freely, and drawing on supplier expertise in developing new products that can meet the quality, cost, and delivery standards of the marketplace.

Many strategic alliances fail to produce the benefits expected by the partners. Some fail miserably. Three general problems have been identified:

- Partners are often organized quite differently, complicating marketing and design decisions and creating problems in coordinating actions and establishing trust.
- Partners that work together well in one country may be poorly equipped to support each other in other countries, leading to

GLOBAL PERSPECTIVES

**Ford and Mazda**

Strategic alliances between U.S. carmakers and their European and Asian counterparts have typically resulted in more headaches than profits. A noteworthy exception is the relationship between Ford and Mazda.

The two carmakers have collaborated on ten current models, including the Ford Escort, Explorer, and Probe and the Mazda MX-6, 323, and Protegé. Ford has provided Mazda with assistance in international marketing, finance, and styling. Mazda has shared valuable manufacturing and product development expertise with Ford. According to *Business Week,* at least a quarter of the Fords and Mazdas sold in the United States have benefited in some way from the fifteen-year-old strategic alliance.[28]

What is the main criterion that Ford and Mazda should use in selecting projects for joint efforts? What other guidelines would you suggest for a successful long-term strategic alliance between these companies?

Strategic alliances enable corporations to target new markets. GM and Visa increase the chances of obtaining new customers by enabling customers to earn automobile discounts by using their credit cards.

© SWC

problems in global alliances.

- Because of the quick pace of technological change, the most attractive partner today may not be the most attractive partner tomorrow, leading to problems in maintaining alliances over time.[27]

The two key features of successful strategic alliances are carefully chosen partners and a situation in which both parties benefit from the relationship.

Strategic alliances often involve multinational partnerships. In Japan, IBM has a strategic alliance with Ricoh to distribute low-end computers and with Fuji Bank to market financial systems. IBM has similar links with other Japanese firms. The Global Perspectives story about Ford and Mazda is another example of a multinational strategic alliance.

## LOOKING BACK

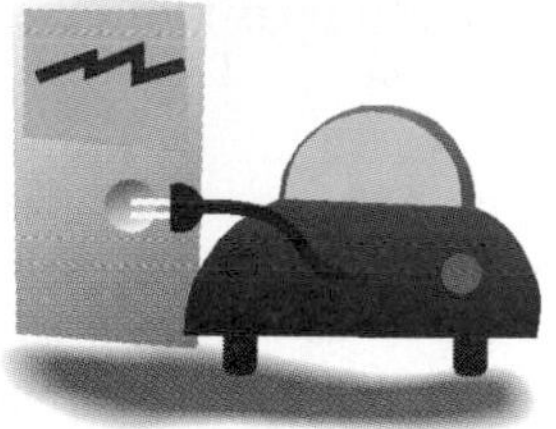

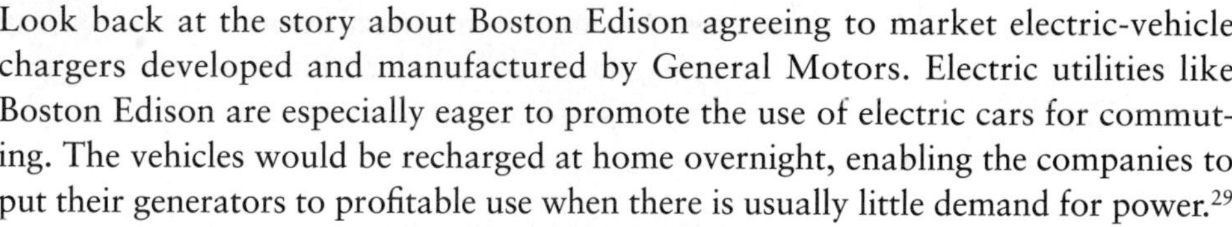

Look back at the story about Boston Edison agreeing to market electric-vehicle chargers developed and manufactured by General Motors. Electric utilities like Boston Edison are especially eager to promote the use of electric cars for commuting. The vehicles would be recharged at home overnight, enabling the companies to put their generators to profitable use when there is usually little demand for power.[29]

By joining with Boston Edison, GM Hughes hopes to establish its recharging technology as an industry standard. Boston Edison will be the sole distributor for GM Hughes rechargers in nine northeastern states.[30] Both firms clearly expect to benefit from this strategic alliance.

## SUMMARY

1 **Describe business-to-business marketing.** Business-to-business marketing provides goods and services that are bought for use in business rather than for personal consumption. Intended use, not physical characteristics, distinguishes a business-to-business product from a consumer product.

2 **Identify the four major categories of business-market customers.** Producer markets consist of for-profit organizations and individuals that buy products to use in producing other products, to use as components of other products, or to use in facilitating business operations. Reseller markets consist of wholesalers and retailers that buy finished products to resell for profit. Government markets include federal, state, county, and city governments that buy goods and services to support their own operations and serve the needs of citizens. Institutional markets consist of very diverse nonbusiness institutions whose main goals do not include profit.

KEY TERMS

*accessory equipment* 162
*annual purchasing contract* 169
*blanket purchasing contract* 169
*business service* 164
*business-to-business marketing* 152
*business product distributor* 153
*buying center* 164
*component part* 163
*derived demand* 156
*forward buying* 169
*joint demand* 158
*major equipment* 161
*modified rebuy* 168
*multiplier effect* 159
*new buy* 168
*processed material* 164
*producer segment* 152
*purchasing contract* 169
*raw material* 162
*reciprocity* 160
*reseller market* 153
*standard industrial classification system (SIC)* 155
*straight rebuy* 169
*strategic alliance* 172
*supply* 164
*value engineering* 168
*vendor analysis* 170

3 **Explain the standard industrial classification system.** The standard industrial classification (SIC) system provides a way to identify, analyze, segment, and target business-to-business and government markets. Organizations can be identified and compared by a numeric code indicating type of economic activity (at the broadest level), industry, geographic region, subindustry, and product classification. Unfortunately, SIC codes are inadequate for identifying organizations that engage in many different activities or that provide a variety of products.

4 **Explain the major differences between business-to-business and consumer markets.** In business-to-business markets, demand is derived, price-inelastic, joint, and fluctuating. Purchase volume is much larger than in consumer markets. Customers are fewer in number and more geographically concentrated. Distribution channels are more direct. Buying is approached more formally, using professional purchasing agents. More people are involved in the buying process, and negotiation is more complex. Reciprocity and leasing are more common. And finally, selling strategy in business-to-business markets normally focuses on personal contact rather than on advertising.

5 **Describe the seven types of business-to-business goods and services.** Major equipment includes capital goods, such as heavy machinery. Accessory equipment is typically less expensive and shorter-lived than major equipment. Raw materials are extractive or agricultural products that have not been processed. Component parts are finished or near-finished items to be used as parts of other products. Processed materials are used to manufacture other products. Supplies are consumable and not used as part of a final product. Business services are intangible products that many companies use in their operations.

6 **Discuss the unique aspects of business-to-business buying behavior.** Business-to-business buying behavior is distinguished by five fundamental characteristics. First, buying is normally undertaken by a buying center consisting of many people who range widely in authority level. Second, business buyers typically evaluate alternative products and suppliers based on quality, service, and price—in that order. Third, business-to-business buying falls into three general categories: new buys, modified rebuys, and straight rebuys. Fourth, business-to-business purchasing is a process that involves several steps, including developing product specifications, choosing a supplier, and evaluating supplier performance. Fifth, customer service before, during, and after the sale plays a big role in business-to-business purchase decisions.

7 **Discuss the role of relationship marketing and strategic alliances in business-to-business marketing.** Relationship marketing entails seeking and establishing long-term alliances or partnerships with customers. Companies form strategic alliances for a variety of reasons. Some fail miserably. The keys to success appear to be choosing a partner carefully and creating conditions where both parties benefit.

## Discussion and Writing Questions

✍1. A friend is interested in a career in business-to-business marketing. Write a letter to your friend explaining each type of business-to-business market. For each type of market, cite examples not mentioned in the chapter.

2. List three examples of joint-demand products.

✍3. Choose a business-to-business service not mentioned in the chapter. Assume that you are the marketing manager for a firm selling that service and that the president has asked for a list of your customers. Prepare a memo responding to this request.

4. Name some component parts not mentioned in the chapter. What are the primary markets for these component parts?

5. Identify each type of business-to-business buying situation. For each, list an example not discussed in the chapter.

## Application for Small Business

Russell Moulé wanted to distinguish his Dallas construction company from a host of competitors. So in early 1995 he and his father, Charles, started talking to architects and designers in the Dallas area. They asked these potential customers to identify the worst features of Russell's competitors. The answer: bad manners, workers who track dirt across carpets, and beat-up construction trucks, which high-class clients object to having parked in their driveways.

### Questions

1. Identify the roles that architects and designers play in the new-home construction process (see the list of buying roles in Exhibit 5.5).

2. Prepare a detailed plan showing how Russell might use this information to increase business.

3. Do you think the benefits of implementing your plan would exceed the costs? Justify your answer.

**CRITICAL THINKING CASE**

## The Truck Tire Market

The trucking industry is a highly competitive business. Not only do trucking transport companies compete with one another, but they also compete with air and rail transport companies for long-haul shipments. To remain competitive with other modes of transportation and to increase profits, trucking companies are always looking for ways to cut the costs of operating their fleets. One major expense that concerns the trucking industry is the cost of tires. Environmentalists are also interested in how long truck tires last. One of the problems facing us today is how to dispose of all the used tires.

Most companies retread truck tires to prolong their life. Typically, the process works like this: Trucking companies buy a new tire and use it on the front axle (steering axle of the truck), because this is the most critical location for a quality tire. When the tread becomes worn, the company retreads the tire and moves it to the rear axle (drive axle) of the truck. When the tread becomes worn again, the tire can be retreaded one more time and used on the truck trailer.

Two things have to happen for the tire to last through two retreads and over 300,000 miles of travel. First, the casing (the rubber components that hold the tire on the rim and hold the tread in place) must be manufactured to stand up to this kind of use. Second, the trucking company must keep the wheels aligned and the tires properly inflated. General Tire has a distinct advantage in the truck tire market because its tires have among the most rigorous specifications in the industry. The company relies on its high-tech manufacturing process and state-of-the-art production equipment to produce a high-integrity tire casing (which means that all the components used to produce the tire casing are designed to work together as an integrated package). By designing the casing to accept multiple retreads, General can offer its customers a money-saving product and keep the tire out of the scrap pile longer, which pleases environmentalists.

General Tire also provides its customers with a visual-inspection alignment system. This system allows General Tire's customers to spot alignment problems early. Thus trucking companies can correct problems before a tire becomes unserviceable. Other services offered by General Tire, like scrap pile analysis (looking through customers' scrap piles to identify common problems with used tires), help the company provide better support for its customers.

Questions

1. Using Exhibit 5.6, discuss how General Tire helps facilitate the purchase of its products.
2. Explain how the decision to buy tires is different for consumers than for truck fleet owners.
3. Discuss the nature of demand for truck tires.

**VIDEO CASE**

## Amtech Corporation

When David Cook's father told him that scientists in Los Alamos, New Mexico, had created an interesting technology to track livestock in the fields, Cook investigated. In 1983 his company, Amtech Corporation, bought the patent rights to develop commercial applications. Today the Dallas firm uses the technology to make electronic identification tags for cargo containers, railroad cars, and tollway vehicles. Amtech has become the leader in developing technology to serve the transportation industry around the world.

The original plans for Amtech included applications in everything from inventory control to ski lifts. The company scrapped applications like warehouse tracking systems, because its system offered no advantage over bar coding. Instead, it focused on transportation, where speedy data reading would be an asset. Amtech's technology identifies objects using radio signals to send and receive information, but its advantage is that it can electronically read tags at a good distance, at great speeds, and regardless of whether dirt, snow, or other debris covers the tag.

The most visible application among typical consumers are such tollways as the Lincoln Tunnel in New York City, the Dallas North Tollway, Oklahoma's PikePass, and fourteen other tollways worldwide. Amtech's system uses a small, credit card–sized device, called a tolltag, that is placed on the inside of a car's windshield. Transceivers, installed at the toll plazas, bounce radio beams off each tolltag to identify the motorist and debit his or her account. The system boasts a 99.9 percent accuracy rate in toll collection and has helped decrease traffic congestion and pollution. It has also reduced the operating costs of 350 toll plazas worldwide. Motorists like the convenience of the tolltags, which save time and fuel.

The railroad industry accounts for 67 percent of Amtech's sales. The company has no competition, thanks to an Association of American Railroads mandate that requires all U.S. railroads to employ Amtech's system to track boxcars. The system has also been endorsed by European railroads, including France's TGV bullet train, which can be tracked at speeds of 240 miles per hour. Amtech has enabled the rail industry to monitor performance, improve safety, and lower its costs.

Amtech's system was also selected as the industry standard for identification tags in the intermodal container industry. It is the only system that can track containers at a distance of forty feet when they are being moved from one type of transportation vehicle to another—for example, from ship to train or from train to truck. The system has thus helped save time and money for the intermodal industry.

In addition, Amtech's technology is used by trucking companies and airlines to track freight and improve service. The company is currently exploring the possibilities of sending data to automobiles for onboard navigation.

Amtech Corporation executes the design, manufacturing, testing, installation, and service of its products. The company's innovation and excellence have allowed Amtech to remain the leader in providing the transportation industry with identification systems.

### Questions

1. Select one target market for Amtech products. Go to the library and look up its SIC number in the *SIC Manual.* Prepare a brief analysis of this target market from information in *U.S. Industrial Outlook* and the *Census of Manufacturers.* You may use other sources as well.
2. Use the example of Amtech identification tags to illustrate how business-to-business markets are different from consumer markets.
3. Write a memo to David Cook proposing a new application for Amtech tags. Justify your recommendation.

### References

Mitchell Schnurman, "Innovator's Firm Is Ready to Forge New Industry with Electronic Tags," *Fort Worth (Texas) Star-Telegram,* 6 August 1989, pp. 4-1, 4-7, 4-8.

R. Lee Sullivan, "Fast Lane," *Forbes,* 4 July 1994, pp. 112, 114.

# Chapter 6

# Segmenting and Targeting Markets

## LEARNING OBJECTIVES

*After studying this chapter, you should be able to*

1 *Describe the characteristics of markets and market segments.*

2 *Explain the importance of market segmentation.*

3 *Discuss criteria for successful market segmentation.*

4 *Describe bases commonly used to segment consumer markets.*

5 *Describe the bases for segmenting business markets.*

6 *List the steps involved in segmenting markets.*

7 *Discuss alternative strategies for selecting target markets.*

8 *Explain how and why firms implement positioning strategies and how product differentiation plays a role.*

9 *Discuss global market segmentation and targeting issues.*

No longer is Limited Inc. a mainstay of women's wardrobes and investors' portfolios. The Limited and Express chains are languishing, and so Limited Inc. aims to expand by market segmentation—targeting men. Menswear played virtually no role in the growth of the Limited Inc. empire through the 1980s, but the company set a goal of making menswear a $1 billion business by 1995, or roughly 13 percent of the company's total sales.

In pursuit of that goal, in 1987 Limited Inc. established Structure, a 426-store men's chain that sells "interpretations" of European-style sportswear and suits. The idea for the new chain was conceived when several Express stores started stocking large-size sweaters at the request of men who came in with female customers. Sales of men's apparel are indeed humming, largely because of strong demand for more relaxed office wear. Limited Inc. thinks the trend toward informality will accelerate, as "casual Fridays" spread throughout the week.

Structure is now Limited Inc.'s fastest-growing apparel chain. A quarter of the 300 new stores Limited Inc. opens this year will be Structure outlets. And in Chicago and Southern California, the company is testing a Structure catalog, the first time it has applied the direct-marketing techniques of its Victoria's Secret unit to another retailing division.[1]

Judging from the way the terms are used in this vignette, how would you define *market segmentation* and *targeting*? How would you describe Structure's likeliest customers? What advertising media do you think would work best?

1 *Describe the characteristics of markets and market segments.*

## MARKET SEGMENTATION

The term *market* means different things to different people. We are all familiar with terms like supermarket, stock market, labor market, fish market, and flea market. All these types of markets share several characteristics. First, they are composed of people (consumer markets) or organizations (business markets). Second, these people or organizations have wants and needs that can be satisfied by particular product categories. Third, they have the ability to buy the products they seek. Fourth, they are willing to exchange their resources, usually money or credit, for desired products. In sum, a **market** is (1) people or organizations, with (2) needs or wants, and with (3) the ability and (4) the willingness to buy. A group of people that lacks any one of these characteristics is not a market.

**market**
People or organizations with needs or wants and with the ability, and the willingness, to buy.

**market segment**
Subgroup of people or organizations sharing one or more characteristics that cause them to have similar product needs.

**market segmentation**
Process of dividing a market into meaningful, relatively similar, and identifiable segments or groups.

Within a market, a **market segment** is a subgroup of people or organizations sharing one or more characteristics that cause them to have similar product needs. At one extreme, we can define every person and every organization in the world as a market segment, **because** each is unique. At the other extreme, we can define the entire consumer market as one large market segment and the business-to-business market as another large segment. All people have some similar characteristics and needs, as do all organizations.

From a marketing perspective, it normally makes sense to describe market segments somewhere between the two extremes. The process of dividing a market into meaningful, relatively similar, and identifiable segments or groups is called **market segmentation.** The purpose of market segmentation is to enable the marketer to tailor marketing mixes to meet the needs of one or more specific segments. Exhibit 6.1 shows the criteria that some food and beverage marketers use to segment markets and to develop marketing mixes that will appeal to a brand's best customers.

Exhibit 6.2 further illustrates the concept of market segmentation. Each box

*Exhibit 6.1*

Target Markets for Three Products

Source: Spectra Marketing Systems, with data from Information Resources Inc., Simmons Market Research Bureau, Claritas Corp., and Progressive Grocer. Reported in Michael J. McCarthy, "Marketers Zero In on Their Customers," *The Wall Street Journal,* 18 March 1991, p. B1. Reprinted by permission of *The Wall Street Journal,* © 1991 Dow Jones & Company, Inc. All Rights Reserved Worldwide.

| Brand | Heavy-user profile | Lifestyle and media profile | Top three target stores |
|---|---|---|---|
| Peter Pan peanut butter | Households with kids, headed by 18-to-35-year-olds, in suburban and rural areas | Heavy video renters<br>Theme park visitors<br>Below-average TV viewers<br>Above-average radio listeners | Goodtown Super Market<br>3350 Hempstead Turnpike, Levittown, NY<br>Pathmark Supermarket<br>3635 Hempstead Turnpike, Levittown NY<br>King Kullen Market<br>598 Stewart Ave., Bethpage, NY |
| Stouffers Red Box frozen entrees | Households headed by people 55 and older and upscale suburban households headed by 35-to-54-year-olds | Gambling casino visitors<br>Party givers<br>People involved in public activities<br>Heavy newspaper readers<br>Above-average TV viewers | Dan's Supreme Super Market<br>69-62 188th St., Flushing, NY<br>Food Emporium<br>Madison Ave. & 74th St., New York, NY<br>Waldbaum Super Market<br>196-35 Horace Harding Blvd., Flushing, NY |
| Coors Light beer | Heads of household, 21 to 34, middle to upper income, suburban and urban | Health club members<br>Rock music buyers<br>Plane travelers<br>People who give parties and cookouts<br>Video renters<br>Heavy TV sports viewers | Food Emporium<br>1498 York Ave., New York, NY<br>Food Emporium<br>First Ave. & 72nd St., New York, NY<br>Gristedes Supermarket<br>350 E. 86th St., New York, NY |

No market segmentation

Fully segmented market

Market segmentation by gender: M,F

Market segmentation age group: 1,2,3

Market segmentation by gender and age group

*Exhibit 6.2*

Concept of Market Segmentation

represents a market consisting of seven persons. This market might vary as follows: one homogeneous market of seven people, a market consisting of seven individual segments, a market composed of two segments based on gender, a market composed of three age segments, or a market composed of five age and gender market segments. Age and gender and many other bases for segmenting markets are examined later in this chapter.

2 *Explain the importance of market segmentation.*

## THE IMPORTANCE OF MARKET SEGMENTATION

Until the 1960s, few firms practiced market segmentation. When they did, it was more likely a haphazard effort than a formal marketing strategy. Before 1960, for example, the Coca-Cola Company produced only one beverage and aimed it at the entire soft-drink market. Today Coca-Cola offers over a dozen different products to market segments based on diverse consumer preferences for flavors and calorie and caffeine content. Coca-Cola offers traditional soft drinks, "energy drinks" (such as Power Ade), flavored teas, and fruit drinks (Fruitopia).[2]

Market segmentation plays a key role in the marketing strategy of almost all successful organizations.[3] Market segmentation is a powerful marketing tool for several reasons. Most important, nearly all markets include groups of people or organizations with different product needs and preferences. Market segmentation helps marketers define customer needs and wants more precisely. Because market segments differ in size and potential, segmentation helps decision makers more accurately define marketing objectives and better allocate resources. In turn, performance can be better evaluated when objectives are more precise.

The Waterbed Council offers an interesting example of how market segmentation can revive flagging sales. To dispel the waterbed's hippie-culture image, the industry is marketing not only to loyal baby boomers but also to older and younger generations. Marketing messages to baby boomers stress product design; marketing messages to those over 60 stress health benefits in treating arthritis and bed sores. To appeal to those under 30, the Waterbed Council notes that "It's not your parents' waterbed."[4] The waterbed market has thus been grouped into three distinct segments, each of which can be targeted very precisely.

The rapidly changing character of many markets, such as the college student market, dictates that firms not only employ market segmentation but also think of segmentation as a continuous process. Marketers should regularly identify new market opportunities, assess the strengths and weaknesses of their segmentation strategies, and update market information. Too often, managers rely on the results of five-year-old market segmentation studies, although they are usually obsolete. Many executives in a wide range of industries—such as transportation, telecommunications, computers, automobiles, clothing, and snack products—believe that market segmentation studies more than a year old have little value and may, in fact, provide misleading information.

*3 Discuss criteria for successful market segmentation.*

## CRITERIA FOR SUCCESSFUL SEGMENTATION

Marketers segment markets for three important reasons. First, segmentation enables marketers to identify groups of customers with similar needs and to analyze the characteristics and buying behavior of these groups. Second, segmentation provides marketers with information to help them design marketing mixes specifically matched with the characteristics and desires of one or more segments. Third, segmentation is consistent with the marketing concept: satisfying customer wants and needs while meeting the organization's objectives.

To be useful, a segmentation scheme must produce segments that meet four basic criteria:

- *Substantiality:* A segment must be large enough to warrant developing and maintaining a special marketing mix. This criterion does not necessarily mean that a segment must have many potential customers. Marketers of custom-designed homes and business buildings, commercial airplanes, and large computer systems typically develop marketing programs tailored to each potential customer's needs. In most cases, however, a market segment needs many potential customers to make commercial sense.
- *Identifiability and measurability:* Segments must be identifiable and their size measurable. Data about the population within geographic boundaries, the number of people in various age categories, and other social and demographic characteristics are often easy to get, and they provide fairly concrete measures of segment size. Say that a social service agency wants to identify segments by their readiness to participate in a drug and alcohol program or in prenatal care. Unless the agency can measure how many people are willing, indifferent, or unwilling to participate, it will have trouble gauging whether there are enough people to justify setting up the service.
- *Accessibility:* The firm must be able to reach members of targeted segments with customized marketing mixes. Some market segments are hard to reach—

for example, senior citizens (especially those with reading or hearing disabilities), those who don't speak English, and the illiterate.

- *Responsiveness:* As Exhibit 6.2 illustrates, markets can be segmented using any criteria that seem logical. However, unless one market segment responds to a marketing mix differently from other segments, that segment need not be treated separately. For instance, if all customers are equally price-conscious about a product, there is no need to offer high-, medium-, and low-priced versions to different segments.

4 *Describe bases commonly used to segment consumer markets.*

**segmentation base (variable)**
Characteristic of individuals, groups, or organizations used as a basis for dividing a market into segments.

## BASES FOR SEGMENTING CONSUMER MARKETS

Marketers use **segmentation bases** or **variables**—characteristics of individuals, groups, or organizations—to divide a total market into segments. The choice of segmentation bases is crucial, because an inappropriate segmentation strategy may lead to lost sales and missed profit opportunities. The key is to identify bases that will produce substantial, measurable, and accessible segments that exhibit different response patterns to marketing mixes.

Markets can be segmented using a single variable, such as age group, or several variables, such as age group, gender, and education. Although it is less precise, single-variable segmentation has the advantage of being simpler and easier to use than multiple-variable segmentation. The disadvantages of multiple-variable segmentation are that it is often harder to use than single-variable segmentation; usable secondary data are less likely to be available; and as the number of segmentation bases increases, the size of individual segments decreases. Nevertheless, the current trend is toward using more rather than fewer variables to segment most markets. Multiple-variable segmentation is clearly more precise than single-variable segmentation.

Consumer goods marketers commonly use one or more of the following characteristics to segment markets: geography, demographics, psychographics, benefits sought, and usage rate. A more detailed description of these characteristics follows. Note that these bases are only examples. Marketers use many other characteristics to segment consumer markets. For example, social class or socioeconomic status (which was examined in Chapter 4) is frequently used to segment consumer markets.

**geographic segmentation**
Method of dividing markets based on region of the country or world, market size, market density, or climate.

### GEOGRAPHIC SEGMENTATION

**Geographic segmentation** refers to segmenting markets by region of the country or world, market size, market density, or climate. *Market density* means the number of people within a unit of land, such as a census tract. Climate is commonly used for geographic segmentation because of its dramatic impact on residents' needs and purchasing behavior. Snow blowers, water and snow skis, clothing, and air-conditioning and heating systems are products with varying appeal, depending on climate.

Consumer goods companies take a regional approach to marketing for four reasons.[5] First, many firms need to find new ways to generate sales because of sluggish and intensely competitive markets. Second, computerized checkout stations with scanners enable retailers to assess accurately which brands sell best in their region. Third, many packaged-goods manufacturers are introducing new regional brands intended to appeal to local preferences. Fourth, a more regional approach allows consumer goods companies to react more quickly to competition. Coca-Cola USA, for example, developed a special marketing campaign for Texas. The campaign included a geographic theme, "Coca-Cola Texas—home of the real thing," and

The spread of checkout scanners has increased interest in geographic segmentation. The data collected by scanner can easily be analyzed to show which goods sell best in a region.
© IBM

**demographic segmentation**
Method of dividing markets based on demographic variables, such as age, gender, income, ethnic background, and family life cycle.

GLOBAL PERSPECTIVES

### Rules of the European Toy Game

Kids are not the same the world over. In Europe, for example, kids tend to be more disciplined and have more structured lives, because European parents are stronger gatekeepers than American parents are. Less freedom, a stronger family orientation, and smaller play areas all affect the type of games and toys popular in Europe.

Some toys sold in the United States cannot even be sold in Europe. According to the European marketing director for Fisher-Price, one of its hottest toys in the United States in the early 1990s was a miniature leaf blower. But the adults in Europe don't use leaf blowers, so their kids wouldn't have known what to do with the toy version. Fisher-Price also had problems selling its toy lawnmowers and vacuum cleaners. The European versions are so different from U.S. versions that kids overseas needed time to figure out what the toys were supposed to be.

On the other hand, Mattel successfully sells All-American Barbie in Europe by calling her Barbie Week-End and removing the American flag from her Levi's jacket. Toys R Us—which has stores in the United Kingdom, Germany, France, Spain, and Austria—does not alter its format from country to country.

Companies wishing to market toys in Europe are required to follow advertising guidelines set up by the Toy Manufacturers of Europe. TME aims to uphold minimum standards of responsibility while allowing companies to implement local marketing strategies.[7]

What are the advantages and disadvantages of changing toys to fit the tastes of markets outside the United States? What are the advantages and disadvantages of offering a standardized product to all markets?

participation in the state's Don't Mess with Texas antilitter effort. Coca-Cola USA and its Texas bottlers contributed 50,000 trash bags to the voluntary cleanup effort, provided recycling bins for aluminum cans, and supplied a million schoolbook covers and half a million auto litterbags bearing antilitter messages.[6] The Global Perspectives story included here provides another example of geographic market segmentation.

## DEMOGRAPHIC SEGMENTATION

As noted in Chapter 2, marketers often segment markets on the basis of demographic information, because it is widely available and often related to consumers' buying and consuming behavior. Some common bases of **demographic segmentation** are age, gender, income, ethnic background, and family life cycle. The discussion here provides some important information about the main demographic segments (except for those based on ethnic background, which are discussed in Chapter 20).

## Age Segmentation

Children 4 to 12 years old influence a great deal of family spending, especially for food and beverages. Preteens spend over $1 billion annually on such play items as toys, bikes, and roller blades; $3.2 billion on food and beverages; about $800 million on movies and spectator sports; over $500 million on consumer electronics; and $620 million at the video arcade. The teen market, which is expected to grow at twice the rate of the overall population in the next decade, spends or influences the spending of nearly $250 billion per year.[8] These age segments are therefore very attractive for a variety of product categories.

Other age segments are also appealing targets for marketers. There are 47 million consumers ages 18 to 29 (generation X), and they have $125 billion in spending power. This segment is a challenge because its members are different from the baby boomers who preceded them, and they dislike being viewed as a "target market."[9]

People between 35 and 44 are likely to have school-age children at home and to outspend all other age groups on food at home, housing, clothing, and alcohol. Those between 45 and 54 spend more than any other group on food away from home, transportation, entertainment, education, personal insurance, and pensions. People from 55 to 64 spend less than those 45 to 54 on almost everything except health care.[10]

## Gender Segmentation

Marketers of products like clothing, cosmetics, personal care items, magazines, jewelry, and footwear commonly segment markets by gender. However, brands that have traditionally been marketed to men—such as Ford Mustang, Cadillac, and Midas Mufflers—are increasing their efforts to attract women. "Women's" products—such as cosmetics, household products, and furniture—are also being marketed to men.[11] Nevertheless, marketers are designing different packaging, advertising, and sales promotion when they market against tradition. The Ethics in Marketing box points out that marketers need to be aware of the special concerns of gender groups.

ETHICS IN MARKETING

### Slim? Or Too Thin?

A growing grassroots campaign would force advertisers to stop using the superthin models who have become so popular. The group called Boycott Anorexic Marketing (BAM) is seeking to end the modeling careers of waiflike models because, it argues, their appearance in ads encourages viewers to undertake starvation diets and promotes eating disorders.

BAM has targeted Coca-Cola for a Diet Sprite ad featuring Kristen McMenamy dressed in a tank top and briefs. "Why should a female who looks like a teenage boy and is nicknamed Skeleton be held up as the model of the '90s?," asks BAM founder Mary Baures.

The Los Angeles chapter of the National Organization for Women has joined the campaign. It has encouraged a nationwide boycott of Calvin Klein products because the company's ads feature superwaif model Kate Moss. Others have defaced some of Calvin Klein's outdoor ads by scrawling the message "I'm so hungry" and "Give me a cheeseburger" by the model's mouth.

Such boycotts are gathering scientific support. Mental health professionals say there is growing evidence that young girls' self-images are greatly influenced by the ads they see. One study found that students in the fifth through the ninth grades were more critical of their body shapes after seeing clothing and perfume ads.

Critics do not claim that advertisers who use superthin models create eating disorders. But the critics do say that advertisers play a role by using a value of extreme thinness in trying to sell products. Jean Kilbourne, who lectures on the images of women in advertising, argues that advertisers often sell things other than the product itself, and whether that additional message is intended or not, it still has an impact.

What women want is to see more real-looking models in ads. The models need not be fat or unattractive, but they should look healthy. Nike ads, for example, feature models who look fit but are not superthin.[12]

Is it ethical for advertisers to use superthin models when starvation diets and eating disorders are of such great concern to women? Do you think the use of superthin models encourages unhealthy eating habits? Is it likely women will change their buying behavior because of the boycotts?

### Income Segmentation

Income is a popular demographic variable for segmenting markets, because income level influences consumers' wants and determines their buying power. Many markets are segmented by income, including the markets for housing, clothing, automobiles, and alcoholic beverages. For example, Budget Gourmet frozen dinners are targeted to lower-income groups, whereas the Le Menu line is aimed at higher-income consumers.

Income segmentation is relevant in the small but growing market for expensive single-malt Scotch and specialty small-batch bourbons, as well as in the market for luxury cars.[13] The lower-income segment also has great potential. U.S. discount retailers, such as Kmart, are planning to open stores in England because of saturated U.S. markets and pent-up demand for discounters in the United Kingdom.[14]

### Family Life Cycle Segmentation

The demographic factors of gender, age, and income often do not sufficiently explain why consumer buying behavior varies. Frequently, differences in consumption patterns among people of the same age and gender result from their being in different stages of the family life cycle. The **family life cycle** (FLC) is a series of stages determined by a combination of age, marital status, and the presence or absence of children. As Chapter 4 explained, it is a valuable basis for segmenting markets.

**family life cycle (FLC)**
Series of life stages determined by a combination of age, marital status, and the presence or absence of children.

Exhibit 6.3 illustrates both traditional and contemporary FLC patterns and shows how families' needs, incomes, resources, and expenditures differ at each stage. The horizontal flow shows the traditional family life cycle. The lower part of the exhibit gives some of the characteristics and purchase patterns of families in each stage of the traditional life cycle. The exhibit also acknowledges that about half of all first marriages end in divorce. When young marrieds move into the young divorced stage, their consumption patterns often revert back to those of the young single stage of the cycle. About four of five divorced persons remarry by middle age and reenter the traditional life cycle, as indicated by the "recycled flow" in the exhibit.

## PSYCHOGRAPHIC SEGMENTATION

Age, gender, income, ethnicity, family life cycle stage, and other demographic variables are usually helpful in developing segmentation strategies, but often they don't paint the entire picture. Demographics provides the skeleton, but psychographics adds meat to the bones. **Psychographic segmentation** is market segmentation on the basis of the following variables:

**psychographic segmentation**
Method of dividing markets based on personality, motives, lifestyle, and geodemographics.

- *Personality:* Personality reflects a person's traits, attitudes, and habits. Many beverages are marketed on the basis of personality segments. For instance, Schlitz beer is targeted toward a personality segment described as "macho men," who feel that because the pleasures in their lives are few and far between, they want something more. Cherry 7-Up is aimed at a personality segment described as "cool" teenagers. Coke South Pacific attracted sports-minded youth with its sponsorship of the Association of Surfing Professionals, which had seventy-one events in twenty-three countries.[15]
- *Motives:* Marketers of baby products and life insurance appeal to consumers'

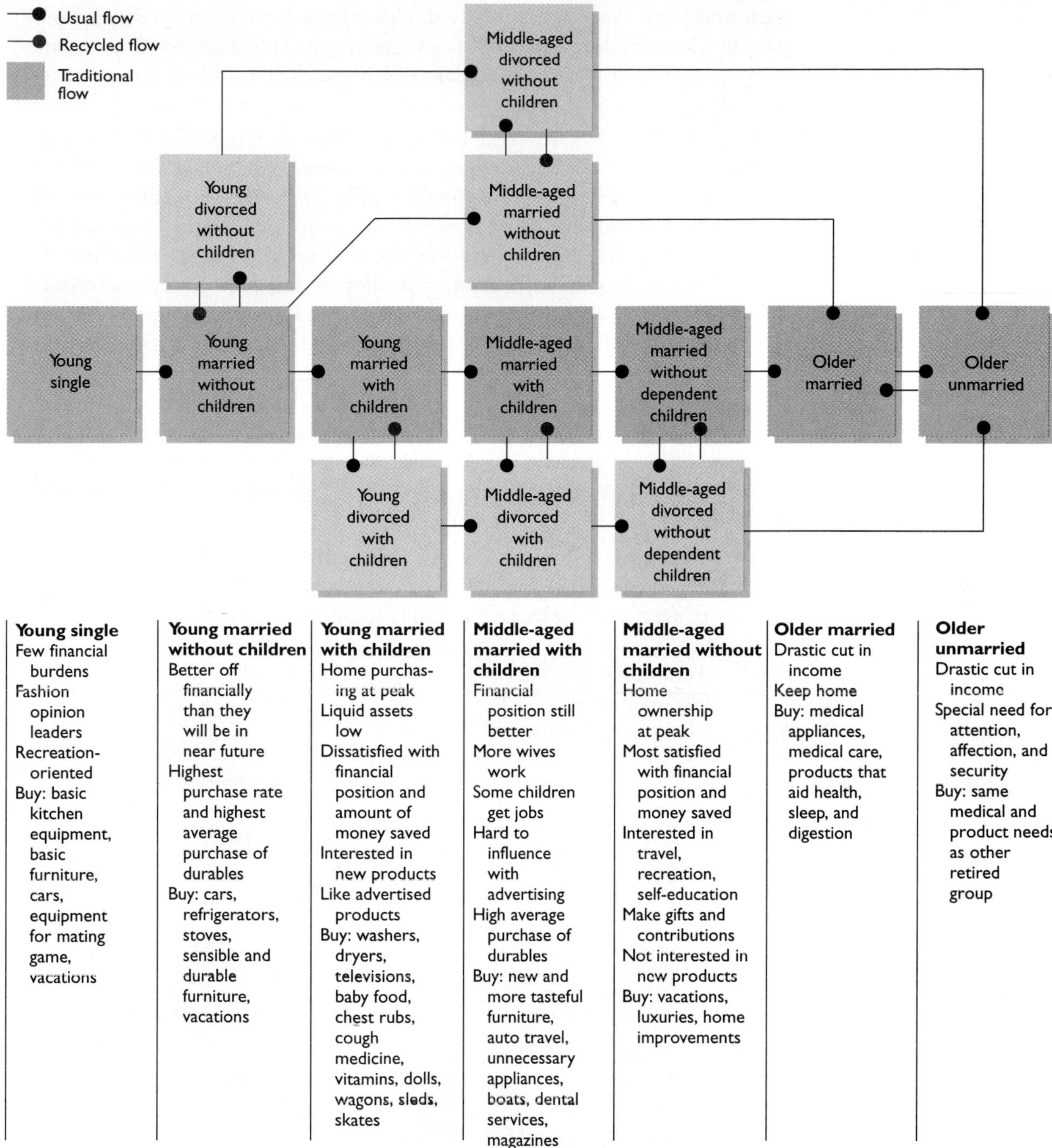


*Exhibit 6.3*

Family Life Cycle

emotional motives—namely, to care for their loved ones. Using appeals like economy, reliability, and dependability, carmakers like Subaru and Suzuki target customers with rational motives. Carmakers like Mercedes-Benz, Jaguar, and Cadillac appeal to status-related motives.

- *Lifestyles:* Lifestyle segmentation divides people into groups according to the way they spend their time, the importance of the things around them, their beliefs, and socioeconomic characteristics like income and education. For example, NPD Market Research identified the following five "eating lifestyles":

meat-and-potato eaters; families with kids whose diets feature soda pop and sweetened cereal; dieters; natural-food eaters; and sophisticates—high-income urban families whose diets feature alcohol, Swiss cheese, and rye and pumpernickel breads.

**geodemographic segmentation**
Method of dividing markets based on neighborhood lifestyle categories.

**micromarketing**
Marketing program tailored to prospective buyers who live in small geographic regions, such as neighborhoods, or who have very specific lifestyle and demographic characteristics.

- *Geodemographics:* **Geodemographic segmentation** clusters potential customers into neighborhood lifestyle categories. It combines geographic, demographic, and lifestyle segmentations. Geodemographic segmentation helps marketers practice **micromarketing,** which is the development of marketing programs tailored to prospective buyers who live in small geographic regions, such as neighborhoods, or who have very specific lifestyle and demographic characteristics. Exhibit 6.1, at the beginning of this chapter, shows how consumer product companies use micromarketing. Working with the idea that people living in the same neighborhood tend to buy the same thing, Claritas developed PRIZM (Potential Rating Index by Zip Market), which classifies Americans by ZIP code. Restaurant chains, banks, and stores use PRIZM to help them choose the best locations for new outlets. PRIZM, along with other research, was used to create MasterCard's Smart Money ads.[16] Micromarketing and PRIZM are explored in more detail in Chapter 7.

These psychographic variables can be used individually to segment markets or can be combined with other variables to provide more detailed descriptions of market segments. One well-known combination approach, offered by SRI International, is called VALS 2 (version 2 of SRI's Values and Lifestyles program).[17] VALS 2 categorizes U.S. consumers by their values, beliefs, and lifestyles rather than by traditional demographic segmentation variables. Many advertising agencies have used VALS segmentation to create effective promotion campaigns.

*Exhibit 6.4*

VALS 2 Dimensions

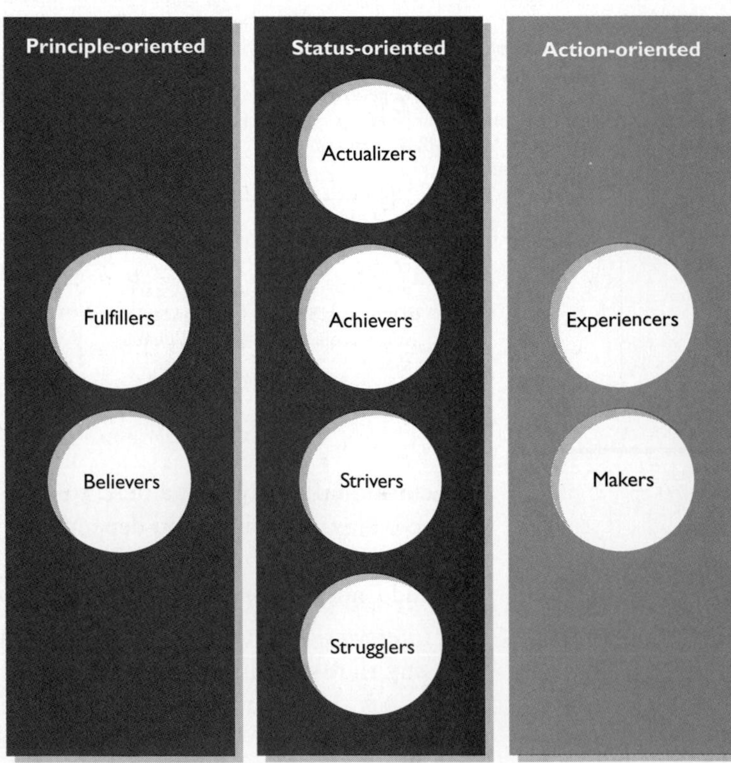

*Exhibit 6.5*

VALS 2 Psychographic Segments

**Actualizers** are successful, sophisticated, active, "take-charge" people with high self-esteem and abundant resources. They are interested in growth and seek to develop, explore, and express themselves in a variety of ways. Their possessions and recreation choices reflect a cultivated taste for the finer things in life.

**Fulfillers** are mature, satisfied, comfortable, reflective people who value order, knowledge, and responsibility. Most are well educated, well informed about world events, and professionally employed. Fulfillers are conservative, practical consumers; they are concerned about value and durability in the products they buy.

**Believers** are conservative, conventional people with concrete beliefs and strong attachments to traditional institutions—family, church, community, and nation. As consumers they are conservative and predictable, favoring U.S. products and established brands.

**Achievers** are successful career- and work-oriented people who like to, and generally do, feel in control of their lives. Achievers live conventional lives, are politically conservative, and respect authority and the status quo. As consumers they favor established goods and services that demonstrate success to peers.

**Strivers** seek motivation, self-definition, and approval from the world around them. They are easily bored and impulsive. Money defines success for strivers, who lack enough of it. They emulate those who own more impressive possessions, but what they wish to obtain is generally beyond their reach.

**Experiencers** are young, vital, enthusiastic, and impulsive. They seek variety and excitement and combine an abstract disdain for conformity and authority with an outsider's awe of others' wealth, prestige, and power. Experiencers are avid consumers and spend much of their income on clothing, fast food, music, movies, and video.

**Makers** are practical people who value self-sufficiency. They live within a traditional context of family, practical work, and physical recreation and have little interest in what lies outside that context. They are unimpressed by material possessions other than those with a practical or functional purpose (for example, tools, pickup trucks, or fishing equipment).

**Strugglers** have lives that are constricted—chronically poor, ill educated, and low skilled. They lack strong social bonds; they are focused on meeting the urgent needs of the present moment. Aging strugglers are concerned about their health. Strugglers are cautious consumers who represent a very modest demand for most goods and services but are loyal to favorite brands.

As Exhibit 6.4 shows, the segments in VALS 2 are classified on two dimensions: vertically by their resources and horizontally by their self-orientation.[18] *Resources* include education, income, self-confidence, health, eagerness to buy, intelligence, and energy level. The resources dimension is a continuum ranging from minimal to abundant. Resources generally increase from adolescence through middle age and decrease with extreme age, depression, financial reverses, and physical or psychological impairment. In contrast, the *self-orientation* dimension classifies three different ways of buying:

- Beliefs or principles—rather than feelings, events, or desire for approval—guide *principle-oriented* consumers in their choices.
- Other people's actions, approval, and opinions strongly influence *status-oriented* consumers.
- *Action-oriented* consumers are prompted by a desire for social or physical activity, variety, and risk.

Exhibit 6.5 describes the eight VALS 2 psychographic segments. Using only the two key dimensions, resources and self-orientation, VALS 2 defines groups of adult

| | Nutritional snackers | Weight watchers | Guilty snackers | Party snackers | Indiscriminate snackers | Economical snackers |
|---|---|---|---|---|---|---|
| **% of snackers** | 22% | 14% | 9% | 15% | 15% | 18% |
| **Lifestyle characteristics** | Self-assured, controlled | Outdoorsy, influential, venturesome | Highly anxious, isolated | Sociable | Hedonistic | Self-assured, price-oriented |
| **Benefits sought** | Nutritious, without artificial ingredients, natural | Low in calories, quick energy | Low in calories, good tasting | Good to serve guests, served with pride, goes well with beverage | Good tasting, satisfies hunger | Low in price, best value |
| **Consumption level of snacks** | Light | Light | Heavy | Average | Heavy | Average |
| **Type of snacks usually eaten** | Fruits, vegetables, cheese | Yogurt, vegetables | Yogurt, cookies, crackers, candy | Nuts, potato chips, crackers, pretzels | Candy, ice cream, cookies, potato chips, pretzels, popcorn | No specific products |
| **Demographics** | Better educated, have younger children | Younger, single | Younger or older, female, lower socio-economic status | Middle-aged, nonurban | Teenager | Have large family, better educated |

*Exhibit 6.6*

Lifestyle Segmentation of the Snack Food Market

consumers who have distinctive attitudes, behavior patterns, and decision-making styles.

## BENEFIT SEGMENTATION

**benefit segmentation**
Method of dividing markets based on the benefits customers seek from the product.

**Benefit segmentation** is the process of grouping customers into market segments according to the benefits they seek from the product. Most types of market segmentation are based on the assumption that the variable and customers' needs are related. Benefit segmentation is different because it groups potential customers on the basis of their needs or wants rather than some other characteristic, such as age or gender. The snack food market, for example, can be divided into six benefit segments, as shown in Exhibit 6.6.

Customer profiles can be developed by examining demographic information associated with people seeking certain benefits. This information can be used to match marketing strategies with selected target markets. For example, American Greetings' Create a Card kiosks located in airports offer benefits to time-pressed businesspeople, who can produce personalized greeting cards during free time spent waiting for a flight.[19]

## USAGE RATE SEGMENTATION

**usage rate segmentation**
Method of dividing markets based on the amount of product bought or consumed.

**Usage rate segmentation** divides a market by the amount of product bought or consumed. Categories vary with the product, but they are likely to include some combination of the following: nonusers, former users, potential users, first-time users, light or irregular users, medium users, and heavy users. Segmenting by usage rate enables marketers to focus their efforts on heavy users or to develop multiple marketing mixes aimed at different segments. Because heavy users often account for a sizable portion of all product sales, some marketers focus on the heavy-user segment. For example, women buy 90 percent of all greeting cards.[20] Therefore, they are an attractive target market.

**80/20 principle**
Idea that 20 percent of all customers generate 80 percent of the demand.

The **80/20 principle** holds that 20 percent of all customers generate 80 percent of the demand. Although the percentages are not usually exact, the general idea often holds true. The alcoholic beverage market illustrates this point clearly. The top 20 percent of bourbon drinkers consume 79 percent of all bourbon, and the top 26 percent of scotch drinkers consume 80 percent of all scotch sold in the United States.[21]

In a variant of usage rate segmentation, some companies try to attract competitors' customers. Subaru developed a marketing campaign to launch its Impreza that was directed to owners of the Honda Civic and the Toyota Corolla. In a 600,000-piece direct mailing, Subaru claimed that the Impreza was a better buy than Honda's Civic. The company offered the incentive of a Columbia Sportswear parka to those who test-drove an Impreza.[22]

5 *Describe the bases for segmenting business markets.*

## BASES FOR SEGMENTING BUSINESS MARKETS

The business market consists of four broad segments: producers, resellers, institutions, and government. (For a detailed discussion of the characteristics of these segments, see Chapter 5.) Whether marketers focus on only one or on all four of these segments, they are likely to find diversity among potential customers. Thus further market segmentation offers just as many benefits to business marketers as it does to consumer product marketers. Business market segmentation variables can be classified into two major categories: macrosegmentation variables and microsegmentation variables.

### MACROSEGMENTATION

**macrosegmentation**
Method of dividing business markets based on such general characteristics as geographic location, type of organization, customer size, and product use.

**Macrosegmentation** variables are used to divide business markets into segments according to the following general characteristics:

- *Geographic location:* The demand for some business products varies considerably from one region to another. For instance, many computer hardware and software companies are located in the Silicon Valley region of California. Similarly, 50,000 people work for 500 companies in the telecommunications industry in Richardson, Texas. In nearby Austin, 450 companies in the computer industry employ 55,000 workers. In Philadelphia, about 166,000 people work for 500 biotechnology and medical firms.[23] Some markets tend to be regional because buyers perceive all producers' offerings to be similar. Buyers prefer to purchase from local suppliers, and distant suppliers often have difficulty competing in terms of price and service. Firms that sell to geographically concentrated industries therefore benefit by locating operations close to the market. Other markets are regional because certain products are used only in a limited area—for example, lobster traps and offshore oil rigs.

- *Customer type:* Segmenting by customer type allows business marketers to tailor their marketing mixes to the unique needs of particular types of organizations or industries. Many companies are finding this form of segmentation to be most responsive to conditions in the marketplace. For example, IBM is reorganizing its global marketing force from a geographic orientation to one

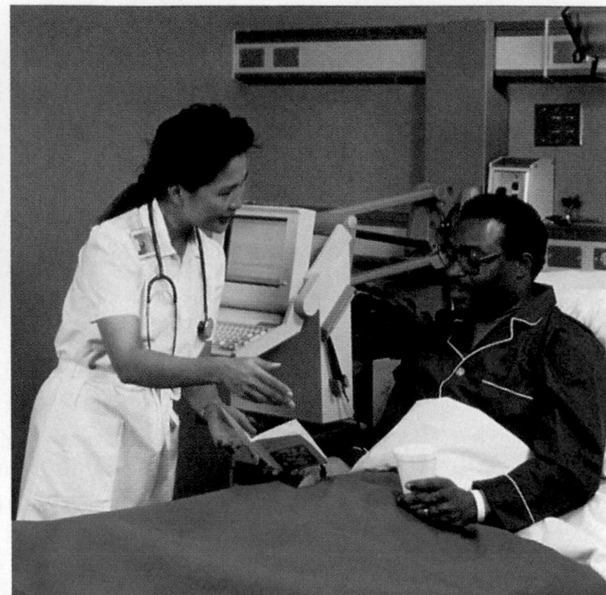

Drug companies use different marketing mixes—(*left*) for pharmacies and (*right*) for hospitals.



based on customer type. The company plans to have fourteen industry segments, including communications, finance, health, and manufacturing.[24] Similarly, some pharmaceutical firms are segmenting by customer type. One sales force may be trained to market to physicians. Others may specialize in pharmacies, health care institutions, or other drug producers. Many companies that do not otherwise distinguish between customer types separate government and nongovernment marketing programs. Marketers targeting government buyers face bureaucratic structures and rules that typically do not exist in nongovernment organizations. Proposals, bids, and contracts have to be prepared according to government specifications.

- *Customer size:* Volume of purchase—heavy, moderate, and light—is a commonly used business-to-business segmentation basis. Another is the buying organization's size, which may affect its purchasing procedures, the types and quantities of products it needs, and its responses to different marketing mixes. Thus banks, for instance, frequently offer different services, lines of credit, and overall attention to commercial customers based on their size. American Express has also segmented the corporate credit card market based on company size, preparing different print ads for small, midsize, and large companies.[25] Often customer size determines a firm's selling strategies. For instance, a firm may make weekly calls to large customers and visit medium-size customers only monthly. A salesperson might never contact small customers, but instead a telemarketing sales force may serve them. Burlington Northern Railroad, for example, markets transportation services using different selling strategies based on customer size.
- *Product use:* Many products—especially raw materials like steel, wood, and petroleum—have diverse applications. How customers use a product may influence the amount they buy, their buying criteria, and their selection of vendors. Many industrial firms use the standard industrial classification (SIC) system, discussed in Chapter 5, to identify end-use segments. For example, a producer of springs may have customers that use the product in making

machine tools, bicycles, surgical devices, office equipment, telephones, and missile systems. Each of these end-use market segments has different needs, motives, and purchase criteria. The springs marketer can choose to target any one end-use segment or to develop unique marketing mixes for multiple segments. However, one marketing mix probably cannot be developed that will appeal to all six end-use market segments.

## MICROSEGMENTATION

Macrosegmentation often produces market segments that are too diverse for targeted marketing strategies. Thus marketers often find it useful to divide macrosegments based on such variables as customer size or product use into smaller microsegments. **Microsegmentation** is the process of dividing business markets into segments based on the characteristics of decision-making units within a macrosegment. Microsegmentation enables the marketer to more clearly define market segments and more precisely define target markets. The marketer can then design marketing mixes that more closely match the desires of target markets. Macrosegmentation can often be done using previously collected data, but microsegmentation usually depends on marketing research to gather the needed information. These are the typical microsegmentation variables:[26]

**microsegmentation**
Method of dividing business markets based on the characteristics of decision-making units within a macrosegment.

- *Key purchasing criteria:* Marketers can segment some business markets by ranking purchasing criteria, such as product quality, prompt and reliable delivery, supplier reputation, technical support, and price. For example, Atlas Corporation developed a commanding position in the industrial door market by providing customized products in just four weeks, much faster than the industry average of twelve to fifteen weeks. Atlas's primary market is companies with an immediate need for customized doors. Sophisticated marketers try to gain access to decision makers early in the purchasing process so they have a chance to influence the selection of key decision criteria and the weighting or ranking of these criteria to favor their own products.
- *Purchasing strategies:* The purchasing strategies of buying organizations can shape microsegments. Two purchasing profiles that have been identified are satisficers and optimizers. **Satisficers** contact familiar suppliers and place the order with the first to satisfy product and delivery requirements. **Optimizers** consider numerous suppliers, (both familiar and unfamiliar), solicit bids, and study all proposals carefully before selecting one. Recognizing satisficers and optimizers is quite easy. A few key questions during a sales call, such as "Why do you buy product X from vendor A," usually produce answers that identify purchaser profiles. These profiles have many implications. For example, a supplier entering the market would be more likely to sell to a decision-making unit composed of optimizers than to a unit consisting of satisficers relying on familiar suppliers.

**satisficer**
Type of business customer that places an order with the first familiar supplier to satisfy product and delivery requirements.

**optimizer**
Type of business customer that considers numerous suppliers, both familiar and unfamiliar, solicits bids, and studies all proposals carefully before selecting one.

- *Importance of purchase:* Classifying business customers according to the significance they attach to the purchase of a product is especially appropriate when customers use the product differently. This approach is also appropriate when the purchase is considered routine by some customers but very important by others. For instance, a small entrepreneur would consider a laser printer a major capital purchase, but a large office would find it a normal expense.
- *Personal characteristics:* The personal characteristics of purchase decision makers (their demographic characteristics, decision style, tolerance for risk,

confidence level, job responsibilities, and so on) influence their buying behavior and thus offer a viable basis for segmenting some business markets. IBM computer buyers, for example, are sometimes characterized as being more risk averse than buyers of less expensive "clones" that perform essentially the same functions. In advertising, therefore, IBM stresses its reputation for high quality and reliability.

6 *List the steps involved in segmenting markets.*

## STEPS IN SEGMENTING A MARKET

The purpose of market segmentation, in both consumer and business markets, is to identify marketing opportunities. The effort spent in devising a segmentation plan is well worthwhile, because it often leads marketers to new groups of potential customers or provides helpful insights into existing customers. Exhibit 6.7 traces the steps in segmenting a market. Note that steps 5 and 6 are actually marketing activities that follow market segmentation (steps 1 through 4).

1. *Select a market or product category for study:* Define the overall market or product category to be studied—one in which the firm already competes, a new but related market or product category, or a totally new one. For instance, Anheuser-Busch closely examined the beer market before introducing Michelob Light and Bud Light. Anheuser-Busch also carefully studied the market for salty snacks before introducing the Eagle brand.
2. *Choose a basis or bases for segmenting the market:* This step requires managerial insight, creativity, and market knowledge. There are no scientific procedures for selecting segmentation variables. The number of possible segmentation bases is limited only by decision makers' imagination. However,

Exhibit 6.7

Steps in Segmenting a Market and Subsequent Activities

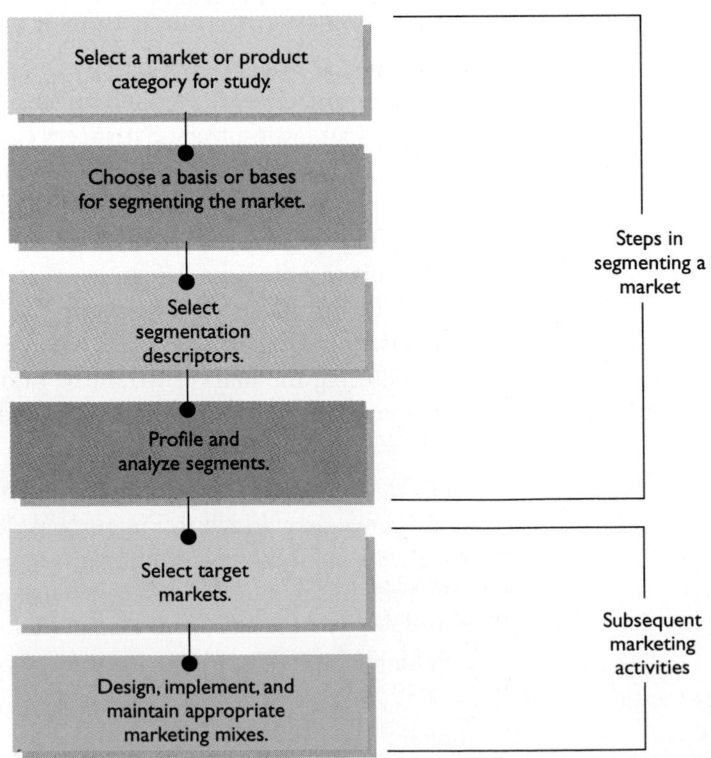

a successful segmentation scheme must produce segments that meet the four basic criteria discussed earlier in this chapter.

3. *Select segmentation descriptors:* After choosing one or more bases, the marketer must select the segmentation descriptors. Descriptors identify the specific segmentation variables to use. For example, if a company selects demographics as a basis of segmentation, it may use age, occupation, and income as descriptors.
4. *Profile and analyze segments:* The profile should include segments' size, expected growth, purchase frequency, current brand usage, brand loyalty, and long-term sales and profit potential. This information can then be used to rank potential market segments by profit opportunity, risk, consistency with organizational mission and objectives, and other factors important to the firm.
5. *Select target markets:* Selecting target markets is not a part of but a natural outcome of the segmentation process. It is a major decision that influences and often directly determines the firm's marketing mix. This topic is examined in greater detail later in this chapter.
6. *Design, implement, and maintain appropriate marketing mixes:* The marketing mix has been described as product, distribution, promotion, and pricing strategies intended to bring about mutually satisfying exchange relationships with target markets. Chapters 9 through 19 explore these topics in detail.

This process of market segmentation was employed by researchers at Texas Christian University, who wanted to better understand what attracted students to TCU. A study was undertaken to help admissions officers, enrollment managers, and institutional marketing representatives identify benefit segments of the college-bound student market. These are the steps that were taken:

1. *Market:* The market was defined as college-bound high school seniors. The study focused on students who had applied to TCU and been admitted to the freshman class.
2. *Segmentation basis:* The segmentation basis selected was benefits sought in a college experience.
3. *Segmentation descriptors:* Forty-three benefit descriptors derived from previous studies and group interviews were selected. The first five were size of school, quality of faculty, attractiveness of campus, distance from home, and student/faculty ratio.
4. *Segment profile and analysis:* A random sample of 1,600 accepted applicants were sent a letter requesting participation in the study, a questionnaire, and a postage-paid return envelope. Subjects were instructed to list their first three college choices and then to rate each school on the forty-three segmentation descriptors.

Analysis of the responses revealed five benefit segments. Members of the first segment were attracted to specific programs, such as business or journalism. The religious affiliation of the university was also important to this group. Members of the second segment were attracted by academic excellence. Members of the third segment sought both specific programs and academic excellence. Members of the fourth segment were attracted by religious affiliation, and members of the fifth segment focused on financial considerations. The decision makers also analyzed such information as the size of each segment and the proportion that ultimately enrolled at TCU.

Recommendations based on the study were to choose one or more target markets from the segments that were identified, to develop survey materials that could be used to identify which segment applicants are in, and to develop marketing mixes tailored to the benefits sought by the target market segments.

7 *Discuss alternative strategies for selecting target markets.*

## STRATEGIES FOR SELECTING TARGET MARKETS

So far this chapter has focused on the market segmentation process, which is only the first step in deciding who to approach about buying a product. The next task is to choose one or more target markets. A target market, as Chapter 2 explained, is a group of people or organizations for which an organization designs, implements, and maintains a marketing mix intended to meet the needs of that group, resulting in mutually satisfying exchanges. The three general strategies for selecting target markets—undifferentiated, concentrated, and multisegment targeting—are illustrated in Exhibit 6.8.

### UNDIFFERENTIATED TARGETING

**undifferentiated targeting strategy**
Marketing approach based on the assumption that the market has no individual segments and thus requires a single marketing mix.

A firm using an **undifferentiated targeting strategy** essentially adopts a mass-market philosophy, viewing the market as one big market with no individual segments. The firm uses one marketing mix for the entire market. A firm that adopts an undifferentiated targeting strategy assumes that individual customers have similar needs that can be met with a common marketing mix.

The first firm in an industry sometimes uses an undifferentiated targeting strategy. With no competition, the firm may not need to tailor marketing mixes to the preferences of market segments. Henry Ford's famous quote about the Model T is a classic example of an undifferentiated targeting strategy: "They can have their car in any color they want, as long as it's black." At one time, Coca-Cola used this strategy with a single product and a single size of its familiar green bottle. Similarly, the

*Exhibit 6.8*

Three Strategies for Selecting Target Markets

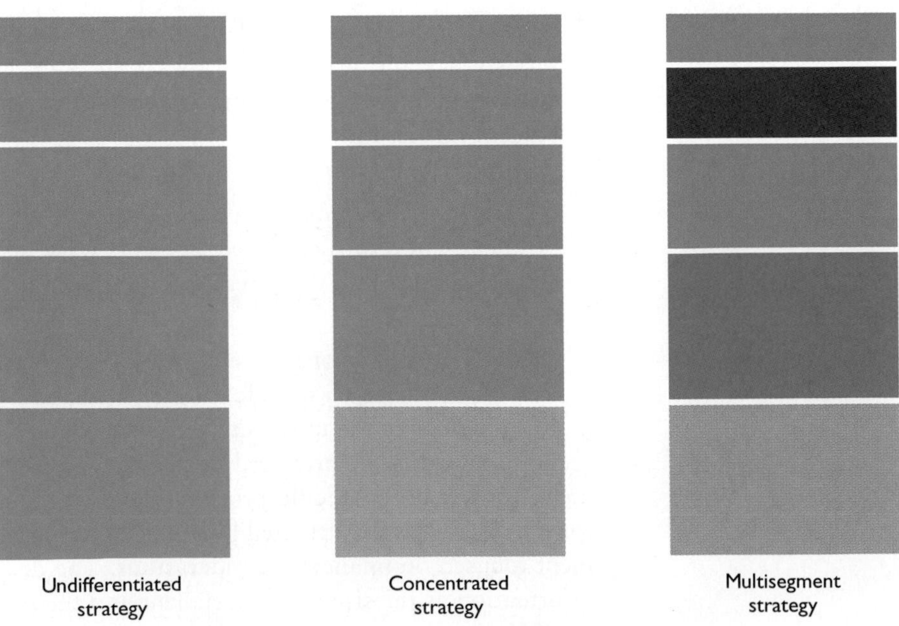

A concentrated targeting strategy, which focuses on a single market niche, helps specialty retailers like this game store compete against the big discount chains and department stores.

© Photonics/Erik VonFischer

Hershey Company marketed one candy bar for everyone, and the Dentyne Company sold only one size package of Dentyne gum. Marketers of commodity products, such as flour and sugar, are also likely to use an undifferentiated targeting strategy.

One advantage of undifferentiated marketing is the potential for saving a lot on production and marketing. Because only one item is produced, the firm should be able to achieve economies of mass production. Also, marketing costs may be lower when there is only one product to promote and a single channel of distribution.

Too often, however, an undifferentiated strategy emerges by default rather than by design, reflecting a failure to consider the advantages of a segmented approach. The result is often sterile, unimaginative product offerings that have little appeal to anyone.

Another problem associated with undifferentiated targeting is that it makes the company very susceptible to competitive inroads. Hershey lost a big share of the candy market to Mars and other candy companies before it changed to a multisegment targeting strategy. Coca-Cola forfeited its position as the leading seller of cola drinks in supermarkets to Pepsi-Cola in the late 1950s, when Pepsi began offering several sizes of containers. Coke lagged in following Pepsi's multisegment targeting strategy.

You might think a firm producing an unexciting product like toilet tissue would adopt an undifferentiated strategy. However, this market has industrial segments and consumer segments. Industrial buyers want an economical, single-ply product sold in boxes of a hundred rolls. The consumer market demands a more versatile product in smaller quantities. Within the consumer market, the product is differentiated as colored or white, designer-print or no-print, cushioned or noncushioned, and economy-priced or luxury-priced. Fort Howard Corporation, the market share leader in industrial toilet paper, does not even sell to the consumer market.

## CONCENTRATED TARGETING

**concentrated targeting strategy** Marketing approach based on appealing to a single segment of a market.

**niche** One segment of a market.

With a **concentrated targeting strategy,** a firm selects a market **niche** (one segment of a market) for targeting its marketing efforts. Because the firm is appealing to a single segment, it can concentrate on understanding the needs, motives, and satisfactions of that segment's members and on developing and maintaining a highly specialized marketing mix. Some firms find that concentrating resources and doing a better job of meeting the needs of a narrowly defined market segment is more profitable than spreading resources over several different segments.

For example, 1st Business Bank targets midsize companies with annual sales between $3 million and $100 million. The bank accepts only ten to fifteen new accounts each month, and these are carefully screened before they are accepted. With this concentrated targeting strategy, the bank has been extremely profitable, and it has had almost no loan losses in ten years.[27] Another example is Nucor Steel, which is small compared to the largest U.S. steel firms. But it concentrates its efforts on the steel joist segment of the steel market, and there it leads the industry.

Small firms often adopt a concentrated targeting strategy to compete effectively with much larger firms. For example, game specialty stores are a growing group of niche retailers. These small, independent operators count on personal service and product selection, rather than price, to differentiate themselves from large discounters like Toys R Us. Many of these game stores target the adult market, carrying classic games like Monopoly as well as exotic chess and backgammon sets and gambling supplies.[28]

Some firms, on the other hand, use a concentrated strategy to establish a strong position in a desirable market segment. Porsche, for instance, targets a very upscale automobile market—"class appeal, not mass appeal."

Concentrated targeting violates the old adage "Don't put all your eggs in one basket." If the chosen segment is too small or if it shrinks because of environmental changes, the firm may suffer negative or even disastrous consequences. Many oil-field supply companies in Texas learned this lesson the hard way in the 1980s, when oil prices dropped and domestic drilling activity declined.

A concentrated strategy can also be disastrous for a firm that is not successful in its narrowly defined target market. Before Procter & Gamble introduced Head and Shoulders shampoo several years ago, several small firms were already selling anti-dandruff shampoos. Head and Shoulders was introduced with a large promotional campaign, and the new brand captured over half the market immediately. Within a year, several of the firms that had been concentrating on this market segment went out of business.

## MULTISEGMENT TARGETING

**multisegment targeting strategy** Marketing approach based on serving two or more well-defined market segments, with a distinct marketing mix for each.

A firm that chooses to serve two or more well-defined market segments and develops a distinct marketing mix for each has a **multisegment targeting strategy.** Stouffer's, for example, offers gourmet entrees for one segment of the frozen dinner market and Lean Cuisine for another. Hershey has dozens of different confections aimed at various segments. For instance, it offers premium candies like Golden Almond chocolate bars, packaged in gold foil and marketed to an adult audience. Another chocolate bar, called RSVP, is targeted toward consumers who crave the taste of Godiva chocolates at the price of a Hershey bar. Cosmetics companies seek to increase sales and market share by targeting multiple age and ethnic groups. Maybelline and Cover Girl, for example, market different lines to teenage women, young adult women, older women, and African-American women. Huge convention hotels like the Chicago Hilton and Towers, which have traditionally targeted the business segment, are now marketing weekend getaways to families. Carnival Cruise Lines recently introduced Fiesta Marina Cruises, the first cruise line specifically designed for Hispanics.[29]

Sometimes organizations use different promotional appeals, rather than completely different marketing mixes, as the basis for a multisegment strategy. For example, different target markets are likely to be attracted to physical fitness programs called Keep Fit, Conditioning, Fitness Training, Slimnastics, Aerobics, Aerobic Dance, Health Club, Figure Control, Jazzercise, or Revitalize. Although the basic program content may be similar, the names are designed to meet different wants.

Public agencies, as well as private organizations, can often benefit from a multisegment strategy. Consider government efforts to persuade citizens to convert to the metric system, which has succeeded in Canada. It is highly desirable that everyone adapt to the metric system at the same time. And yet,

> It is still possible, and more efficient, to work harder with some groups than with others and to work on some segments earlier than others. Age might well be a factor because the young may easily adopt the metric system, while many people over forty will resist the change. Certain manufacturers and industries may be willing to begin using the metric system now. However, others will not change before they have to, and the cooperation of tool makers should be enlisted early. And because reading and viewing habits of citizens differ, it will prove virtually impossible to put together a communications effort that reaches all citizens equally well.[30]

Multisegment targeting offers many potential benefits to firms, including greater sales volume, higher profits, larger market share, and economies of scale in manufacturing and marketing. Yet it also involves costs. Before deciding to use this strategy, firms should compare the benefits and costs of multisegment targeting to those of undifferentiated and concentrated targeting. The following list details the costs:

- *Product design costs:* A multisegment targeting strategy sometimes results in different products for different market segments. It may involve nothing more than a package or labeling change, or it may require a complete redesign of the product itself. An example of a slight modification is packaging Coca-Cola in various sizes and types of containers, such as twelve-ounce cans and two-liter bottles. In contrast, Compaq Computer incurred major costs in developing both desktop and laptop computers. Creating different products with unique features sought by different segments of the market can be very expensive.
- *Production costs:* Total production costs mount as a firm develops and markets different products for different market segments. Each manufacturing run may require a retooling of production equipment, during which time production lines are idle. The result is higher costs for the manufacturer.
- *Promotion costs:* Whether or not a firm produces a different product for each market segment, it normally must develop separate promotional strategies. Significant expenditures of human and financial resources are required. A firm normally must create different advertisements for each segment, and different media may be necessary for the ads.
- *Inventory costs:* The more market segments a firm tries to serve, the higher the inventory costs are likely to be. With inventory costs averaging between 20 and 30 percent of inventory sales value, a multisegment targeting strategy can be very expensive.

In some industries, such as custom-home building, market segments are typically very small; a marketing program may be tailored to a single client. In general, however, each market segment should promise enough sales to warrant a special marketing mix.



- *Marketing research costs:* An effective market segmentation strategy relies on accurate, detailed market information about consumer demographics; consumer reaction to various product designs or promotional appeals; consumer interests, attitudes, opinions; and so on. Gathering this information can be a time-consuming and expensive process. For example, the Kroger supermarket chain conducts more than 250,000 consumer interviews each year to determine changing consumer wants.
- *Management costs:* A multisegment targeting strategy requires extra management time. As the number of segments increases, so does the number of decisions. The firm must coordinate the marketing mix for each targeted market segment.
- *Cannibalization:* **Cannibalization** occurs when sales of a new product cut into sales of a firm's existing products. For example, in 1990 Coors Brewing Company was thinking of introducing a dry beer to compete with Bud Dry, which was already being marketed by Anheuser-Busch. However, Coors discovered that 70 percent of the test market sales of Bud Dry came from other

**cannibalization**
Phenomenon in which sales of a new product cut into sales of a firm's existing products.

Anheuser-Busch brands. This cannibalization effect prompted Coors to place its own dry beer plans on hold. Anheuser-Busch management estimated that, after the first couple of months of test marketing, cannibalization dropped to about 40 percent, with remaining sales coming from Coors Light and Miller Genuine Draft. Industry observers had mixed views about the long-run effect of Bud Dry on sales of other Anheuser-Busch brands.[31]

8 *Explain how and why firms implement positioning strategies and how product differentiation plays a role.*

**positioning**
Developing a specific marketing mix to influence potential customers' overall perception of a brand, product line, or organization in general.

**position**
Place that a product, brand, or group of products occupies in consumers' minds relative to competing offerings.

## POSITIONING

Chapter 1 examined the relationship between an organization's target market strategy and the marketing mix it uses. The term **positioning** refers to developing a specific marketing mix to influence potential customers' overall perception of a brand, product line, or organization in general. (**Position** is the place a product, brand, or group of products occupies in consumers' minds relative to competing offerings.) Consumer goods marketers are particularly concerned with positioning. Procter & Gamble, for example, markets eleven different laundry detergents, each with a unique position, as illustrated in Exhibit 6.9.

Positioning assumes that consumers compare products on the basis of important features. Marketing efforts that emphasize irrelevant features are therefore likely to misfire. For example, Crystal Pepsi and a clear version of Coca-Cola's Tab failed because consumers perceived the "clear" positioning as more of a marketing gimmick than a benefit.[32]

Effective positioning requires assessing the positions occupied by competing products, determining the important dimensions underlying these positions, and choosing a position in the market where the organization's marketing efforts will have the greatest impact. The French have an expression that sums up the positioning concept rather neatly: *Cherchez le creneau,* or "Look for the gap." To find a *creneau* you must think in reverse, go against the grain. If everyone else is going east, see if you can find your *creneau* by going west.[33] If everyone else is making large, five-

*Exhibit 6.9*

Positioning of Procter & Gamble Detergents

Source: Adapted from Jennifer Lawrence, "Don't Look for P&G to Pare Detergents," *Advertising Age*, 3 May 1993, p. 3. Copyright © Crain Communications, Inc.

| Brand | Positioning | Market share |
|---|---|---|
| Tide | Tough, powerful cleaning | 31.1% |
| Cheer | Tough cleaning and color protection | 8.2% |
| Bold | Detergent plus fabric softener | 2.9% |
| Gain | Sunshine scent and odor removing formula | 2.6% |
| Era | Stain treatment and stain removal | 2.2% |
| Dash | Value brand | 1.8% |
| Oxydol | Bleach–boosted formula, whitening | 1.4% |
| Solo | Detergent and fabric softener in liquid form | 1.2% |
| Dreft | Outstanding cleaning for baby clothes, safe for tender skin | 1.0% |
| Ivory Snow | Fabic and skin safety on baby clothes and fine washables | 0.7% |
| Ariel | Tough cleaner, aimed at Hispanics | 0.1% |

This McDonald's restaurant differentiates itself from the many other options available to city dwellers by offering live background music.



passenger automobiles that appeal to luxury, why not build small economy cars? If major competitors are all stressing low price, why not introduce a prestige brand? If your major competitors are colas, perhaps stress that your product is an "uncola."

## PRODUCT DIFFERENTIATION

**product differentiation** Marketing tactic designed to distinguish one firm's products from those of competitors.

**Product differentiation** is a positioning strategy that some firms use to distinguish their products from those of competitors. The distinctions can be either real or perceived. Tandem Computer designed machines with two central processing units and two memories for computer systems that can never afford to be down or lose their database (for example, an airline reservation system). In this case, Tandem used product differentiation to create a product with very real advantages for the target market.

Bleaches, aspirin, unleaded regular gasoline, and some soaps are differentiated by such trivial means as brand names, packaging, color, smell, or "secret" additives. The marketer attempts to convince consumers that a particular brand is distinctive and that they should therefore demand it over competing brands. If a seller can persuade a substantial number of people to demand the brand, the seller can usually raise its price above the general market level.

Product differentiation can be difficult for some products. For instance, consumers do not see much difference in the gambling facilities of riverboat casinos, a growing industry in the United States. The Empress River Casino in the Chicago suburb of Joliet therefore stresses customer service, maintaining that differences do exist in the people behind the tables and the setting in which they are located.[34]

An interesting trend in product differentiation is to market food products, ranging from cookies to mustard to beer, using kosher labeling.[35] Kosher labeling generally requires little more than compliance with certain hygienic processing standards, but it signifies product purity to many consumers regardless of their religious affiliation.

**perceptual mapping**
Means of displaying or graphing, in two or more dimensions, the location of products, brands, or groups of products in customers' minds.

**repositioning**
Changing consumers' perceptions of a brand in relation to competing brands.

## PERCEPTUAL MAPPING

**Perceptual mapping** is a means of displaying or graphing, in two or more dimensions, the location of products, brands, or groups of products in customers' minds. For example, the perceptual map in Exhibit 6.10A is the result of a 1982 study by General Motors of consumers' perceptions of the five GM automobile divisions: Buick, Cadillac, Chevrolet, Oldsmobile, and Pontiac. Consumer perceptions are plotted on two axes. The horizontal axis ranges from conservative and family-oriented at one extreme to expressive and personal at the other. The vertical axis is used to rate price perceptions, and it ranges from high to low. Note that in 1982 the various GM divisions were not perceived as especially distinctive. Consumers didn't clearly distinguish one brand from another, especially on the conservative/family versus expressive/personal dimension.

In 1984 General Motors was reorganized to reduce overlap and duplication among divisions and to produce fewer, more distinctive models. The perceptual map in Exhibit 6.10B shows GM's plans for **repositioning**, or changing consumers' perceptions of the various models in customers' minds, by the late 1980s. As Exhibit 6.10C shows, however, consumer perceptions changed very little between 1982 and 1986.

*Exhibit 6.10*

Perceptual Maps and Positioning Strategies for General Motors Passenger Cars



**(A) Consumer perceptions in 1982**

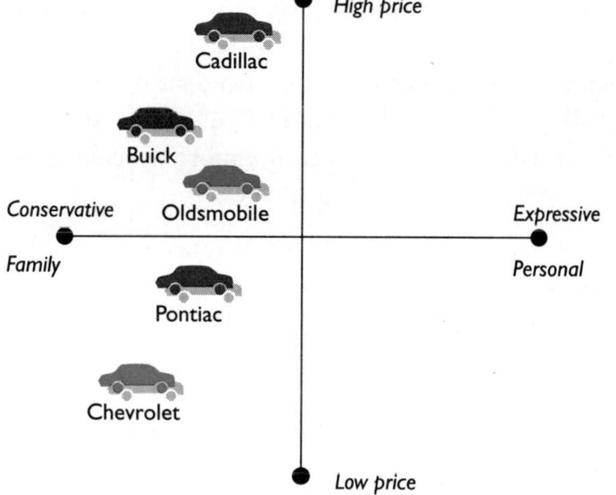


**(B) Repositioning goals for the late 1980s (drafted in 1984)**

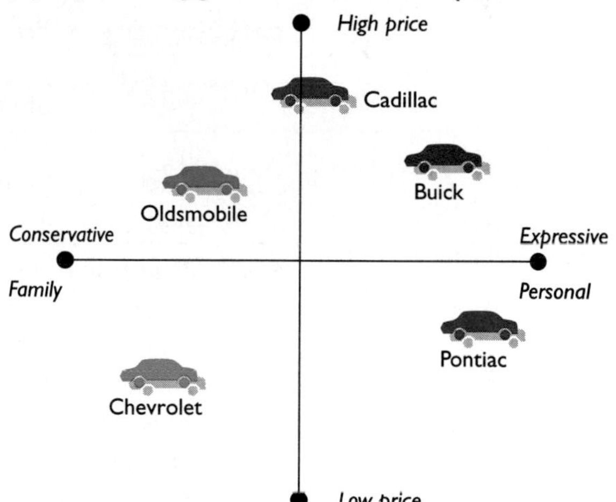


**(C) Consumer perceptions in 1986**

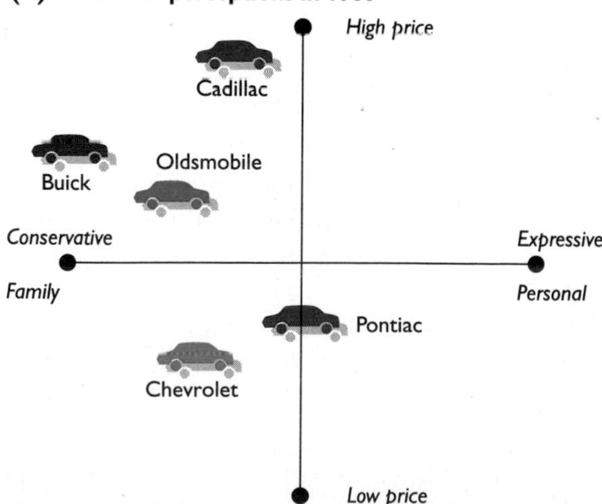


**(D) Repositioning goals for the 1990s (drafted in 1989)**

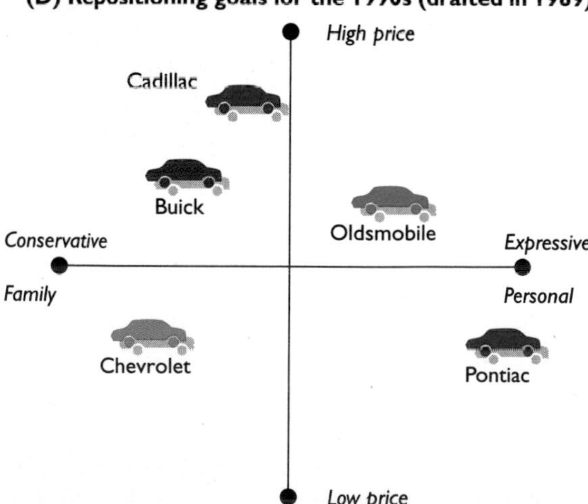

In 1989 General Motors introduced a new overall theme called "Putting quality on the road" that was supported by a $40 million advertising campaign. Exhibit 6.10D illustrates GM's repositioning goals for the 1990s. The following themes were selected to differentiate the divisions from one another:[36]

- *Buick:* "Premium American motorcar"
- *Cadillac:* "Standard luxury worldwide"
- *Chevrolet:* "Customer expectations exceeded"
- *Oldsmobile:* "Innovative technology"
- *Pontiac:* "Performance oriented to young people"

## POSITIONING BASES

Firms use a variety of bases for positioning, including the following:[37]

- *Attribute:* A product is associated with an attribute, product feature, or customer benefit. For example, a promotion for Viva paper towels stressed durability, using product demonstrations. Kirin U.S.A., attempting to position its product as more than a Japanese beer, is advertising Kirin as the purest beer in the world.[38]

- *Price and quality:* This positioning base may stress high price as a signal of quality or emphasize low price as an indication of value. Neiman-Marcus uses the high-priced strategy; Kmart has successfully followed the price and value strategy. However, Kmart has been trying to gain a more upscale image by using national brands and higher-quality Kmart brands.
- *Use or application:* During the past few years, AT&T telephone service advertising has emphasized communicating with loved ones using the Reach Out and Touch Someone campaign. Stressing uses or applications can be an effective means of positioning a product with buyers. The advertising slogan "Orange juice isn't just for breakfast anymore" is an effort to reposition the product, in terms of time and place of use, as an all-occasion beverage.
- *Product user:* This positioning base focuses on a personality or type of user. For instance, Revlon's introductory positioning of the Charlie cosmetic line was designed to fit the lifestyle profile of the liberated woman.
- *Product class:* The objective here is to position the product as being associated with a particular category of products. An exampleis to position a margarine brand with respect to butter.
- *Competitor:* Positioning against competitors is part of any positioning strategy. The Avis rental car positioning as No. 2 exemplifies positioning against specific competitors.

It is not unusual for a marketer to use more than one of these bases. The AT&T Reach Out and Touch Someone campaign that stressed use also emphasized the relatively low cost of long-distance calling. The Milk-Made Company is positioning its Cool Cow, a cholesterol-free milk product, to the youth market as a healthful yet hip alternative to soft drinks.[39]

9 *Discuss global market segmentation and targeting issues.*

## GLOBAL ISSUES IN MARKET SEGMENTATION AND TARGETING

Chapter 3 discussed the trend toward global market standardization, which enables firms like Coca-Cola, Colgate-Palmolive, McDonald's, and Nike to market similar products using similar marketing strategies in many different countries. This chapter has also discussed the trend toward targeting smaller, more precisely defined markets. The Global Perspectives example in this chapter described how some companies adapt their products to fit the tastes of customers in different countries while others offer a standardized product worldwide. Interestingly, both these trends—toward globalization and micromarketing—are occurring at the same time.

The tasks involved in segmenting markets, selecting target markets, and designing, implementing, and maintaining appropriate marketing mixes (described in Exhibit 6.7) are the same whether the marketer has a local perspective or a global vision. The main difference is the segmentation variables commonly used. Countries of the world are commonly grouped using such variables as per capita gross domestic product, geography, religion, culture, or political system.

Some firms have tried to group countries of the world or customer segments around the world using lifestyle or psychographic variables. So-called "Asian yuppies"—in countries like Singapore, Hong Kong, Japan, and South Korea—have substantial spending power and exhibit purchase and consumption behavior similar to that of their better-known counterparts in the United States. In this case, firms may be able to use a global market standardization approach.

## LOOKING BACK

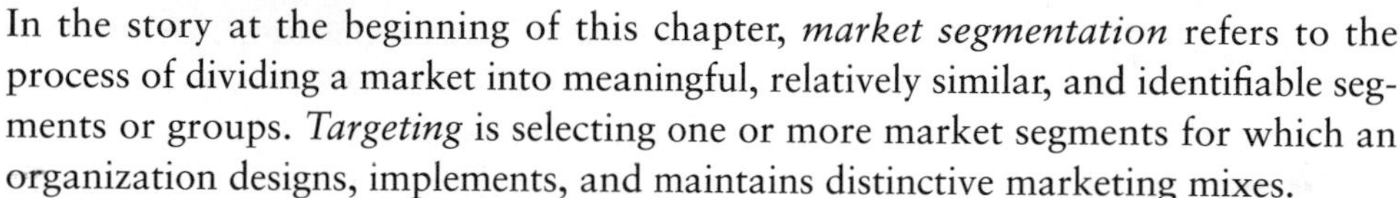

In the story at the beginning of this chapter, *market segmentation* refers to the process of dividing a market into meaningful, relatively similar, and identifiable segments or groups. *Targeting* is selecting one or more market segments for which an organization designs, implements, and maintains distinctive marketing mixes.

Structure's likeliest customers are men 21 to 40 years old who have office jobs and who are concerned with fashion. To determine which advertising media are best to reach this segment, Limited Inc. should research the media habits of its target market. However, some possible media choices are business and sports magazines, the sports section of local newspapers, and radio stations that cater to 21-to-40-year-olds.

## SUMMARY

1 **Describe the characteristics of markets and market segments.** A market is composed of individuals or organizations with the ability and willingness to make purchases to fulfill their needs or wants. A market segment is a group of individuals or organizations with similar product needs as a result of one or more common characteristics.

2 **Explain the importance of market segmentation.** Before the 1960s, few businesses targeted specific market segments. Today, segmentation is a crucial marketing strategy for nearly all successful organizations. Market segmentation enables marketers

to tailor marketing mixes to meet the needs of particular population segments. Segmentation helps marketers identify consumer needs and preferences, areas of declining demand, and new marketing opportunities.

**3 Discuss criteria for successful market segmentation.** Successful market segmentation depends on four basic criteria. First, a market segment must be substantial; it must have enough potential customers to be viable. Second, a market segment must be identifiable and measurable. Third, members of a market segment must be accessible to marketing efforts. Fourth, a market segment must respond to particular marketing efforts in a way that distinguishes it from other segments.

**4 Describe bases commonly used to segment consumer markets.** There are five commonly used bases for segmenting consumer markets: Geographic segmentation is based on region, size, density, and climate characteristics. Demographic segmentation consists of age, gender, income level, ethnicity, and family life cycle characteristics. Psychographic segmentation includes personality, motives, and lifestyle characteristics. Benefits sought is a type of segmentation that identifies customers according to the benefits they seek in a product. Finally, usage segmentation divides a market by the amount of product purchased or consumed.

**5 Describe the bases for segmenting business markets.** Business markets can be segmented on two bases. First, macrosegmentation divides markets according to general characteristics, such as location and customer type. Second, microsegmentation focuses on the decision-making units within macrosegments.

**6 List the steps involved in segmenting markets.** Six steps are involved when segmenting markets: (1) Select a market or product category for study, (2) choose a basis or bases for segmenting the market, (3) select segmentation descriptors, (4) profile and analyze segments, (5) select target markets, and (6) design, implement, and maintain appropriate marketing mixes.

**7 Discuss alternative strategies for selecting target markets.** Marketers select target markets using three different strategies: undifferentiated targeting, concentrated targeting, and multisegment targeting. An undifferentiated targeting strategy assumes that all members of a market have similar needs that can be met with a single marketing mix. A concentrated targeting strategy focuses all marketing efforts on a single market segment. Multisegment targeting is a strategy that uses two or more marketing mixes to target two or more market segments.

**8 Explain how and why firms implement positioning strategies and how product differentiation plays a role.** Positioning is used to influence consumer perceptions of a particular brand, product line, or organization in relation to competitors. The term *position* refers to the place that the offering occupies in consumers' minds. To establish a unique position, firms use product differentiation—emphasizing the real or perceived differences between competing offerings. Products may be differentiated on the basis of attribute, price and quality, use or application, product user, product class, or competitor.

## KEY TERMS

*benefit segmentation* 190
*cannibalization* 200
*concentrated targeting strategy* 198
*demographic segmentation* 184
*80/20 principle* 191
*family life cycle (FLC)* 186
*geodemographic segmentation* 188
*geographic segmentation* 183
*macrosegmentation* 191
*market* 180
*market segment* 180
*market segmentation* 180
*micromarketing* 188
*microsegmentation* 193
*multisegment targeting strategy* 198
*niche* 198
*optimizer* 193
*perceptual mapping* 203
*position* 201
*positioning* 201
*product differentiation* 202
*psychographic segmentation* 186
*repositioning* 203
*satisficer* 193
*segmentation base (variable)* 183
*undifferentiated targeting strategy* 196
*usage rate segmentation* 190

9 **Discuss global market segmentation and targeting issues.** The key tasks in market segmentation, targeting, and positioning are the same regardless of whether the target market is local, regional, national, or multinational. The main differences are the variables used by marketers in analyzing markets and assessing opportunities and the resources needed to implement strategies.

## Discussion and Writing Questions

1. Describe market segmentation in terms of the historical evolution of marketing.
2. List some market segments not discussed in the chapter that are inaccessible to marketing efforts. What makes them hard to reach?
3. Which VALS psychographic segment most accurately reflects your personality and consumer behavior? In several sentences, explain why.
4. ✍ Select a product category and brand that are familiar to you. Using Exhibit 6.8, prepare a market segmentation report and describe a targeting plan.
5. Explain multisegment targeting. Describe an example of a company not mentioned in the chapter that uses a multisegment targeting strategy.
6. ✍ You want your firm to adopt a product differentiation strategy. Write a memo to the president describing how three companies not mentioned in the chapter use product differentiation strategies.
7. Distinguish three positioning strategies, and identify firms that use them.
8. Select a group of people in your community with an unmet consumer need. Do you consider this a viable market segment? Why or why not?
9. Compare and contrast domestic market segmentation and international market segmentation.

## Application for Small Business

Holly Bennett, a recent college graduate, has developed an idea for a theme calendar for college students. The calendar would have small pages that flip—one for every day of the year. At the bottom of each page for the months of September to May would be a study tip or a philosophical statement about education. For the months of June through August, sayings reflecting the way college students spend their summers (for example, traveling, working, sunbathing) would be used.

The calendars will be customized with a specific college's logo on the front cover and throughout the pages, so students will have calendars with their college's name. College colors will also be used to print the calendars.

### Questions

1. Is Holly using a segmentation and targeting strategy? Why or why not?
2. How should she position this product?
3. What are some of the ways she could sell her calendars?

**CRITICAL THINKING CASE**

## The HIV-AIDS Market

A new U.S. niche market is made up of the million people infected with the human immunodeficiency virus (HIV) and the more than 315,000 with AIDS. Ross Products, an Abbott Laboratories unit, targets this market with a drink called Advera, which is fortified with vitamins and minerals. The company claims the drink will boost the immune system, sustain life, and reduce the need for repeated hospitalizations. According to trade promotion materials, the drink is high in calories for weight management and high in protein to maintain lean body mass. Advera is available in two flavors. The drink is sold in six-packs of eight-ounce cans that retail for around $20. The recommended dosage is three cans daily. It is likely that Medicare, Medicaid, and other insurance plans will cover the cost.

Marketing products to individuals with HIV and AIDS involves such issues as product credibility and the approach taken by advertising messages. Sensitivity to confidentiality and customer dignity is important for companies targeting this market.

*Out*magazine, a publication serving the gay community, and *Positive* magazine, geared toward people with HIV and AIDS, are examples of media outlets that carry consumer-directed advertising for products like Advera. Print ads can also be found in health care journals that reach AIDS clinics, physicians in private practice, nurses' associations, hospitals, and home care agencies.

Questions

1. Do consumers with HIV and AIDS make up a valid market segment? Use the four criteria for successful segmentation to answer this question.
2. What can companies do to better market to this segment?
3. What other kinds of goods and services could be successfully marketed to this segment?

**VIDEO CASE**

## Las Vegas

The state of Nevada legalized gambling during the early 1930s. In 1946, Benjamin "Bugsy" Siegel built the first upscale hotel and casino with hopes that Las Vegas would become a gambling paradise. Over the years, the city enticed visitors with elaborate casinos, as well as star-studded shows, wedding chapels, and Elvis impersonators. Today, the neon Strip is lined with hotels and casinos that generate $3 billion and attract over 23 million visitors annually.

The city that was once an adult playground is now targeting a new segment: families. The City of Sin is now the desert Disneyland and the fastest-growing family destination. Investors developing a new wave of resorts and theme parks are wagering that family entertainment will draw crowds, even in a city that was the premier gaming capital for years.

With the opening of three new megaresorts—Luxor, MGM Grand, and Treasure Island—the city boasts 88,000 hotel rooms and occupancy rates of 90 percent or better. Each of the megaresorts emphasizes family entertainment. Treasure Island presents a cannon duel between mock pirate ships every ninety minutes in front of the hotel as well as a forty-foot water slide in its pool. The pyramid-shaped Luxor offers a state-of-the-art Sega arcade and a boat trip on a simulated River Nile through the hotel. The MGM Grand Hotel—the largest in the world, with 5,005 rooms—features Las Vegas's first theme park and the first day-care and children's activities center accompanying a casino. Several other hotels have added attractions, including talking statues at Caesars Palace and an erupting volcano in front of the Mirage. Circus Circus Grand Slam Canyon offers five areas of roller coasters and water rides under a glass dome.

A study conducted by Salomon Brothers found that the new entertainment attractions have prompted visitors to extend their stay in Las Vegas. However, the megaresorts are also threatening the existence of the older hotels. The Dunes and El Rancho have closed, and the Aladdin, Sands, and Sahara are at risk. Even the conservative Desert Inn is expanding and renovating to compete with the megaresorts.

Las Vegas is not worried about competition from the small riverboat casinos that are now operating in twenty-five states. In fact, these operations expose large segments of the public to gambling and lure them to Las Vegas for big-time gaming and entertainment. With all that the city has to offer, Las Vegas hopes to attract both gamblers and families.

Questions

1. Describe the bases that the Las Vegas entertain-

ment community has used in the past to segment the tourist market. What bases are currently being used? Select other appropriate bases and justify your answer.

2. Can the Las Vegas entertainment industry successfully satisfy two target markets?

3. With the influx of families, will Las Vegas's original target market go elsewhere?

4. Develop a perceptual map showing Las Vegas and other tourist destinations, such as Atlantic City; Orlando/Disney World; Branson, Missouri; and Miami Beach.

References

Lee Foster, "Las Vegas: Identity and Illusion," *Dallas Morning News,* 18 September 1994, pp. G1, G6, G7.

Eileen Ogintz, "Resorts Keep Families Amused," *Dallas Morning News,* 18 September 1994, p. G7.

Calvin Sims, "Family Values as a Las Vegas Smash: The Strip's Latest Casino Creations Hope to Take on Disneyland," *The New York Times,* 3 February 1994, p. D1.

# CHAPTER 7

# DECISION SUPPORT SYSTEMS AND MARKETING RESEARCH

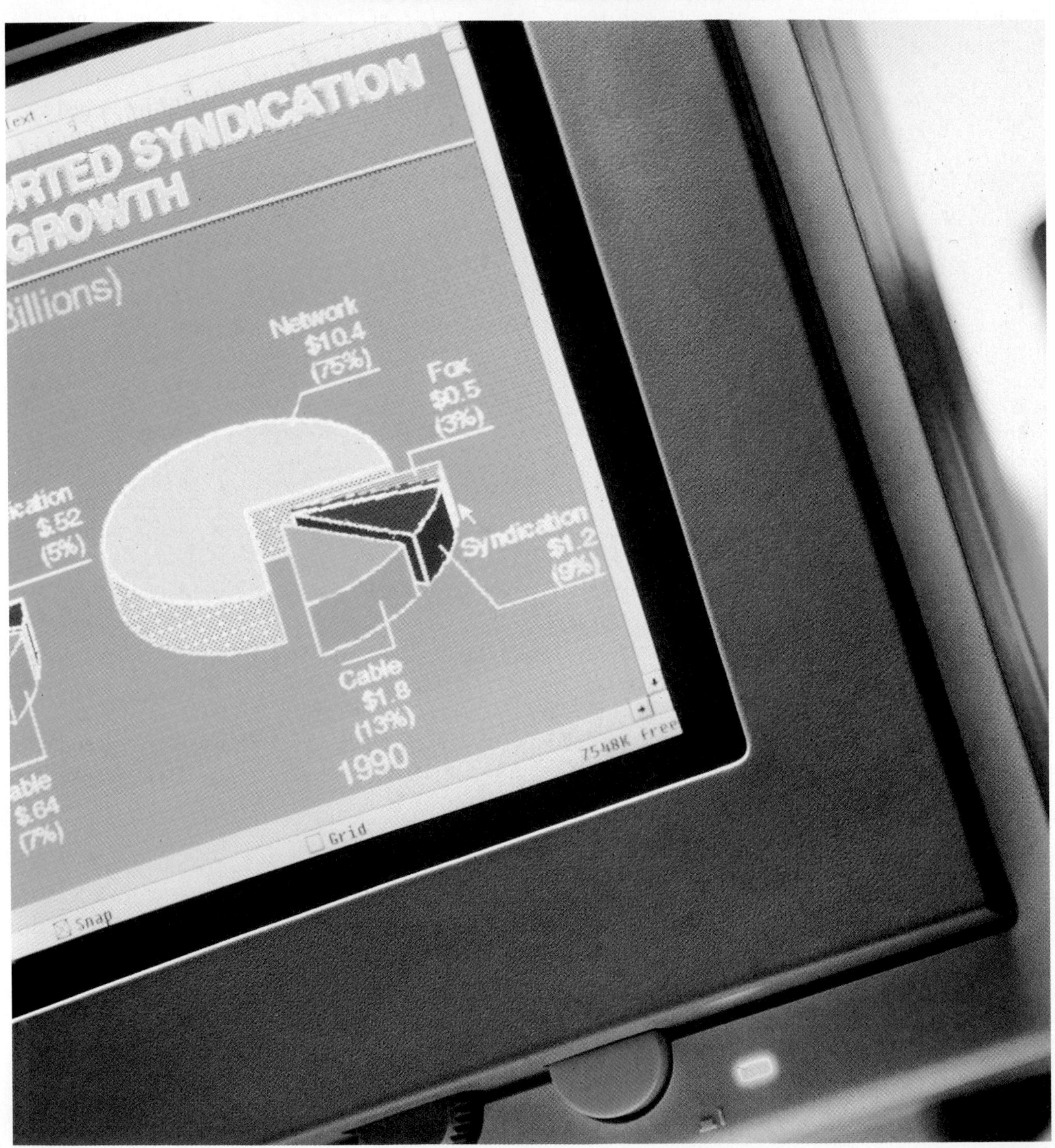

## Learning Objectives

*After studying this chapter, you should be able to*

1 *Explain the concept and purpose of a marketing decision support system.*

2 *Discuss the nature of database marketing and micromarketing.*

3 *Define marketing research, and explain its importance to marketing decision making.*

4 *Describe the steps involved in conducting a marketing research project.*

5 *Discuss the growing importance of single-source research.*

6 *Explain when marketing research should and should not be conducted.*

If a TV commercial Hall of Fame is ever built, a space will surely be reserved for Iron Eyes Cody. Cody was the "star" of the long-running public service announcement for Keep America Beautiful, Inc. (KAB) that ran on TV stations across the country in the 1980s. Few who saw the commercial could forget its image of a single tear crawling down Cody's face as he reacted to the actions of litterbugs.

Effective though the advertisement was, it became outdated as the larger issue of waste management eclipsed littering in the public consciousness. When KAB—a national nonprofit organization dedicated to improving waste-handling practices in U.S. communities—began developing a new public service announcement to address the problem of waste management, it had to figure out how to duplicate the impact of the "crying Indian" ad. With the help of marketing research, KAB and its ad agency developed a new advertisement that just might do that.

The central image of the new KAB ad (see Exhibit 7.1 on page 212) is a baby surrounded by mounds of garbage. The commercial begins with a close-up of the baby and pulls back to a wide shot as actor Michael Douglas narrates over the strains of "America the Beautiful." At the end, viewers are invited to contact KAB for a free booklet. One version asks them to write to the address on the screen; the other flashes a toll-free number.

Using a detailed questionnaire to test the ad concept, KAB found that the image had broad appeal. Jeff Francis, KAB director of communications, says, "We showed them a tape of the idea and then conducted an interview. We found that the baby appealed to everyone. It was an image that, no matter what your age, your sex, if you have children or not, no matter what category you fall into, there was an emotional attachment to that child; which was good because we wanted this ad to be very broad based and hit as many constituency groups as possible. The interviews helped make up our minds about using the baby and the fact that it did appeal to everybody." The interviews lasted about thirty minutes and included discussion of the ad concept and the issue of waste management. Because the ad targeted a broad cross section of people, the respondents came from a variety of backgrounds.[1]

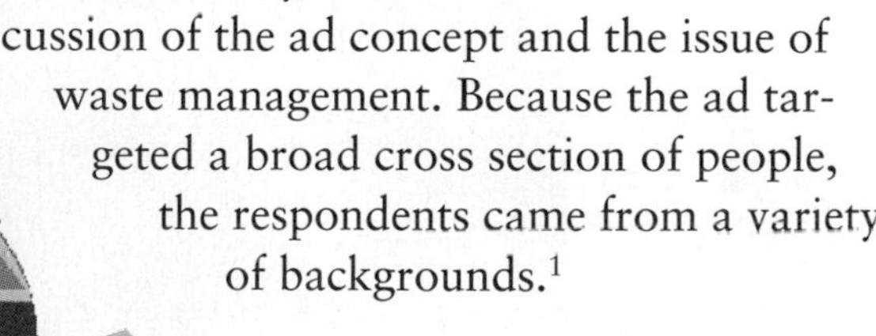

Marketing research was used to create a successful new advertisement for Keep America Beautiful. What are some other uses of marketing research besides creating new advertisements? What are the various techniques for conducting

# KEEP AMERICA BEAUTIFUL, INC.

"For Future Generations" :30 PSA

"Write" Version ZRLI1930; "800"# Version ZRLI2230

*All talents donated: written and conceived by Rotando, Lerch & Iafeliece Advertising; directed and produced by Pytka Productions; postproduction by Susan Grayboff, Big Picture Editorial; music by Russo Grantham Productions; voiceover by Michael Douglas.*

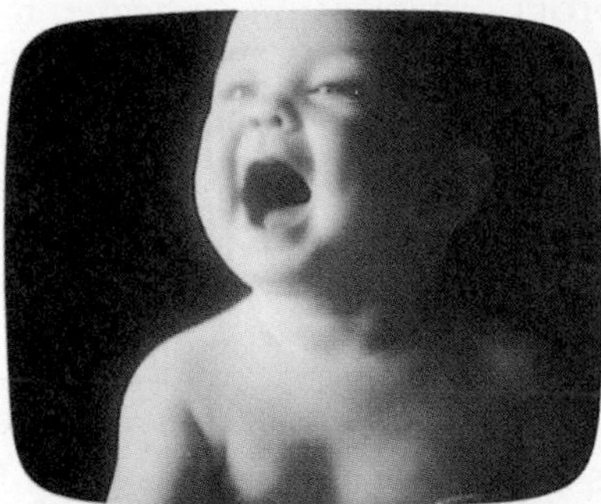

Michael Douglas voiceover with *America the Beautiful* under: For future generations, our country is leaving behind our knowledge, our technologies, our values...

and 190 million tons of garbage every year! Recycling alone just can't do it. Keep America Beautiful is an organization that can do something.

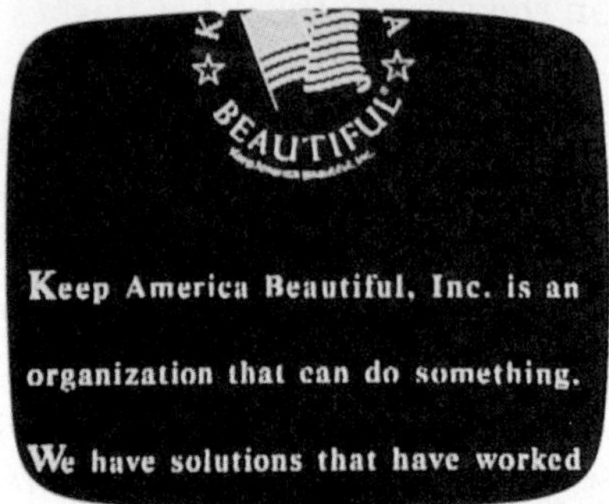


We have solutions that have worked in cities and towns across the country.

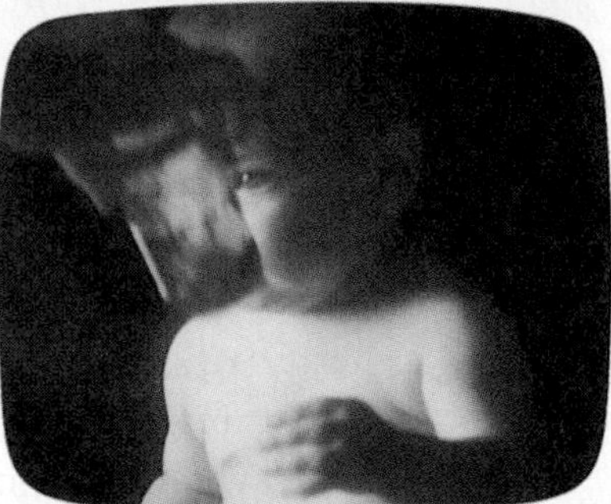

What can you do?

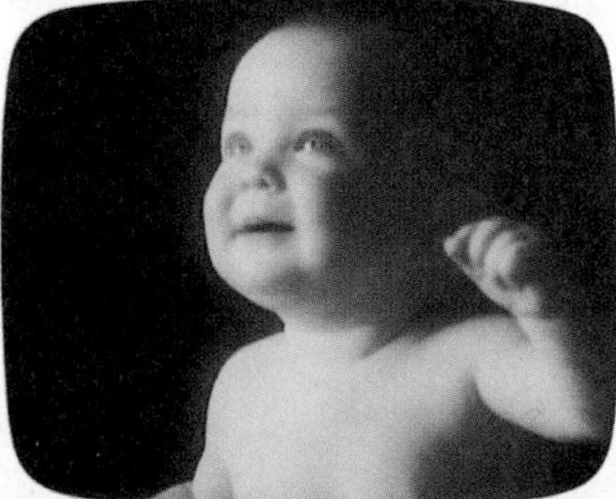

More than you think!

Write to Keep America Beautiful for your free brochure and find out!
("800#" version has "1-800-USA-4-KAB")

*Exhibit 7.1*

New Ad for Keep America Beautiful, Inc.

Keep America Beautiful, Inc.

marketing research? How does marketing research relate to decision support systems?

*1 Explain the concept and purpose of a marketing decision support system.*

## MARKETING DECISION SUPPORT SYSTEMS

Accurate and timely information is the lifeblood of marketing decision making. Good information can help maximize an organization's sales and efficiently use scarce company resources. To prepare and adjust marketing plans, managers need a system for gathering everyday information about developments in the marketing environment—that is, for gathering **marketing intelligence.** The system most commonly used these days for gathering marketing intelligence is called a marketing decision support system.

**marketing intelligence**
Everyday information about developments in the marketing environment that managers use to prepare and adjust marketing plans.

**decision support system (DSS)**
Interactive, flexible information system that enables managers to obtain and manipulate information as they are making decisions.

A marketing **decision support system** (DSS) is an interactive, flexible computerized information system that enables managers to obtain and manipulate information as they are making decisions. A DSS bypasses the information-processing specialist and gives managers access to useful data from their own desks.

These are the characteristics of a true DSS system:

- *Interactive:* Managers give simple instructions and see immediate results. The process is under their direct control; no computer programmer is needed. Managers don't have to wait for scheduled reports.
- *Flexible:* A DSS can sort, regroup, total, average, and manipulate the data in various ways. It will shift gears as the user changes topics, matching information to the problem at hand. For example, the CEO can see highly aggregated figures, and the marketing analyst can view very detailed breakouts.
- *Discovery-oriented:* Managers can probe for trends, isolate problems, and ask "what if" questions.
- *Accessible:* DSS is easy to learn and use by managers who aren't skilled with computers. Novice users should be able to choose a standard, or "default," method of using the system. They can bypass optional features so they can work with the basic system right away while gradually learning to apply its advanced features.

Quaker Oats' DSS, for example, contains about 2 billion facts about products, national trends, and the competition. Management credits the DSS with helping the company achieve a number-one market share in several product categories, covering Quaker Oats cereals, Gatorade, Van de Camp pork and beans, Rice-a-Roni, and Aunt Jemima pancakes. More than 400 marketing professionals at Quaker Oats use the DSS daily. They use it for three major tasks: reporting, tracking, and running the standard reports; marketing planning, which automates the brand planning and budgeting process by adding "what if" analysis and marketing capabilities; and eliciting people's immediate answers to spontaneous marketing questions.

A hypothetical example showing how DSS can be used is provided by Renee Smith, vice president and manager of new products for Central Corporation. To evaluate sales of a recently introduced new product, Renee can "call up" sales by the week, then by the month, breaking them out at her option by, say, customer segments. As she works at her desktop computer, her inquiries can go in several directions, depending on the decision at hand. If her train of thought raises questions about monthly sales last quarter compared to forecasts, she can use her decision support system to analyze problems immediately. Renee might see that her new product's sales were significantly below forecast. Were her forecasts too optimistic? She compares other products' sales to her forecasts and finds that the targets were very accurate. Was something wrong with the product? Is her sales department getting insufficient leads, or is it not putting leads to good use? Thinking a minute

Frito-Lay delivery people use hand-held computers to keep track of the inventory in the stores they serve. The data are transmitted to headquarters to guide production and marketing decisions.



about how to examine that question, she checks ratios of leads converted to sales—product by product. The results disturb her. Only 5 percent of the new product's leads generated orders, compared to the company's 12 percent all-product average. Why? Renee guesses that the sales force is not supporting the new product vigorously enough. Quantitative information from the DSS perhaps could provide more evidence to back that suspicion. But already having enough quantitative knowledge to satisfy herself, the VP acts on her intuition and experience and decides to have a chat with her sales manager.

Companies' successful use of DSS is generating additional popularity.[2] Kmart, Northwestern Mutual Life, and 3M now find that DSS provides an invaluable competitive advantage. Companies such as Federal Express, Avis, Otis Elevator, and Frito-Lay have made it easier to gather marketing intelligence by providing their employees with hand-held computers. Frito-Lay, for instance, has given hand-held computers to all its 10,000 delivery people. The data they collect feed a system that helps the company manage production, monitor sales, and guide promotional strategy. A delivery person can enter orders at each store in a minute or two, running through a programmed product list complete with prices. The machine plugs into a printer in the delivery truck to produce an itemized invoice. At day's end, it generates a sales report and, through a hookup in the local warehouse, transmits the report in seconds to company headquarters in Dallas.[3]

*2 Discuss the nature of database marketing and micromarketing.*

## DATABASE MARKETING AND MICROMARKETING

**database marketing**
Creation of a large computerized file of customers' and potential customers' profiles and purchase patterns as a tool for identifying target markets.

Perhaps the fastest-growing use of DSS is for **database marketing,** which is the creation of a large computerized file of customers' and potential customers' profiles and purchase patterns. It is usually the key tool for successful micromarketing, which relies on very specific information about a market (see Chapter 6). In the 1950s, network television enabled advertisers to get the same message to everyone simultaneously. Today, the use of database marketing and micromarketing enables marketers to get customized, individual messages to everyone simultaneously through direct mail.

Specifically, database marketing can

- Identify the most profitable and least profitable customers
- Identify the most profitable market segments or individuals and target efforts with greater efficiency and effectiveness
- Aim marketing efforts to those goods, services, and market segments that require the most support
- Increase revenue through repackaging and repricing products for various market segments

- Evaluate opportunities for offering new products and services
- Identify products and services that are best-sellers and most profitable

The size of many databases is astounding: Ford Motor Company, 50 million names; Kraft General Foods, 25 million; Citicorp, 30 million; and Kimberly Clark (maker of Huggies diapers), 10 million new parents' names.[4] American Express can retrieve from its database the names of all cardholders who charged purchases at golf pro shops in the past six months, attended symphony concerts, or traveled to Europe more than once in the last year. Its database can even identify the very few people who did all three.

Many companies are having their databases analyzed by marketing database companies to get an even better understanding of their customers. The best known of these special database firms is Claritas, which created PRIZM (Potential Rating Index by Zip Market). PRIZM is founded on the notion that "Birds of a feather flock together." The idea is that people who live in the same neighborhood tend to buy the same types of things. Jonathan Robbin, who designed the original PRIZM database, broke down U.S. Census Bureau data by ZIP code and analyzed each code for social rank, mobility, ethnicity, family life cycle, and housing. The census data are supplemented with market research surveys and other statistics from suppliers such as A.C. Nielsen and with information from 1,600 municipal and regional agencies. The current version of PRIZM further segments the U.S. market by block tracts and ZIP-plus-four codes. ZIP-plus-four codes contain an average of six households.

After examining over 500 million consumer records, PRIZM segmented the U.S. market into sixty-two categories.[5] (A sample of some of the clusters is shown in Exhibit 7.2 on page 215.) Claritas will analyze a company's customer database and then tell the firm into which PRIZM clusters a firm's customers fall. For example, Club Med found that thirteen clusters accounted for over 80 percent of its membership. Also, persons in the Urban Gold Coast cluster were seventeen times more likely to have been to a Club Med than the "average American." Other clusters where Club Med patrons were found in abundance were (in descending order) Blue-Blood Estates, Bohemian Mix, Money and Brains, Furs and Station Wagons, Two More Rungs, and Young Influentials. With this information, Club Med can examine in detail the demographic and lifestyle characteristics of these clusters to better understand its customers and potential customers. For example, because Urban Gold Coast members enjoy sailing, Club Med might seek to lure them with expanded sailing activities. PRIZM can provide Club Med with the names and addresses of persons in the Urban Gold Coast cluster throughout the United States and can identify the media used by this cluster. This information will help Club Med reach its most likely customers. As you can see, database marketing is a very powerful tool.

A broad range of companies use PRIZM. Premier Bank in Baton Rouge, La., merges PRIZM with its internal database to find neighborhoods with lots of households that match the traits of its best customers. Ad agency Ammirati & Puris combined PRIZM with other research to create MasterCard's Smart Money ads. Time, Inc., Ventures used PRIZM to get its new urban-culture magazine, *VIBE,* more advertising revenue. Advertisers were convinced that *VIBE* was just for inner-city kids until PRIZM showed it also appealed to white-collar Young Influentials and middle-aged Money and Brains clusters. The results enabled Time, Inc., to attract consumer electronics and liquor advertising for *VIBE.*[6]

Before they jump into database marketing, however, marketers need to take account of consumer reaction to the growing use of databases. In 1992, under pressure

| Social group | Nickname/description | Cluster numbers | Percent of U.S. households | Predominant adult age range | Key education level | Predominant employment | Key housing type | Lifestyle preferences |
|---|---|---|---|---|---|---|---|---|
| Suburban Elite (S1) | **Blue-Blood Estates**<br>Elite, super rich families<br>*Socioeconomic rank: 1* | 28 | 1.13 | 35–54 | College grads | White collar | Single unit | New convertible car, business/finance magazines, full-service brokerage account |
| | **Money and Brains**<br>Sophisticated townhouse couples<br>*Socioeconomic rank: 2* | 8 | 0.91 | 45–64 | College grads | White collar | Single unit | Tennis 10+ times a year, classical radio, $10,000+ in stock |
| | **Furs and Station Wagons**<br>Executive suburban families<br>*Socioeconomic rank: 3* | 5 | 3.78 | 35–54 | College grads | White collar | Single unit | Own a CD player, all-news radio, 3+ stock transactions per year |
| Affluentials (S2) | **Pools and Patios**<br>Established empty nesters<br>*Socioeconomic rank: 5* | 7 | 3.32 | 45–64 | College grads | White collar | Single unit | Foreign cruise, epicurean magazines, $5,000+ in mutual funds |
| | **Two More Rungs**<br>Mature couples with multi-ethnic roots<br>*Socioeconomic rank: 6* | 25 | 0.66 | 55–65+ | College grads | White collar | Multi 10+ | Broadway cast music, jazz radio, long-term CD |
| | **Young Influentials**<br>Upwardly mobile singles and couples<br>*Socioeconomic rank: 7* | 20 | 3.02 | 18–34 | College grads | White collar | Multi 10+ | New foreign car, science/technology magazines, American Express card |
| Greenbelt Families (S3) | **Young Suburbia**<br>Upscale young suburban families<br>*Socioeconomic rank: 8* | 24 | 6.25 | 25–44 | College grads | White collar | Single unit | 3-door/hatchback, news/talk radio, department store credit card |
| | **Blue-Chip Blues**<br>Upscale blue-collar families<br>*Socioeconomic rank: 10* | 30 | 6.25 | 25–44 | High school grads | Blue/white mix | Single unit | Go fishing, watch headline news, interest checking |
| Urban Gentry (U1) | **Urban Gold Coast**<br>Elite urban singles and couples<br>*Socioeconomic rank: 4* | 21 | 0.44 | 25–65 | College grads | White collar | High-rise | Go sailing, informational TV, $10,000+ in stock |
| | **Bohemian Mix**<br>Bohemian urban singles<br>*Socioeconomic rank: 11* | 37 | 1.02 | 18–34 | College grads | White collar | Multi 10+ | Dance/rap music, watch MTV, educational loan |
| | **Black Enterprise**<br>Upscale African–American families<br>*Socioeconomic rank: 14* | 31 | 0.69 | 35–54 | Some college | White collar | Multi 2–9 | Belong to health clubs, urban/contemporary radio, American Express card |
| | **New Beginnings**<br>Young mobile city singles<br>*Socioeconomic rank: 15* | 23 | 4.14 | 25–34 | Some college | White collar | Multi 10+ | Jog/run, AOR/program radio, have first mortgage |
| Exurban Boom (T1) | **God's Country**<br>Executive exurban families<br>*Socioeconomic rank: 9* | 1 | 3.32 | 25–44 | College grads | White collar | Single unit | Water ski, easy-listening radio, Keogh account |
| | **New Homesteaders**<br>Young middle-class families<br>*Socioeconomic rank: 17* | 17 | 4.78 | 18–34 | Some college | Blue/white mix | Single unit | Ride motorcycles, MOR/nostalgia radio, veterans life insurance |
| | **Towns and Gowns**<br>College-town singles<br>*Socioeconomic rank: 19* | 12 | 1.57 | 18–34 | College grads | White collar | Single unit | New-wave rock, learning channel, educational loan |

*Exhibit 7.2*

Sample PRIZM Clusters

Source: Claritas, Inc., Arlington VA, 1994.

from New York State authorities, American Express disclosed that it was telling merchants more about its cardholders' spending habits than it had previously acknowledged. Information about cardholders' lifestyles and spending habits was being offered for joint marketing efforts with merchants. American Express had told cardholders that it merely provided merchants with a mailing list based on information in the initial application for the card. The New York Attorney General's office made AmEx notify more than 20 million cardholders nationwide that it compiles profiles of spending behavior and that it uses the information for "target marketing" purposes. The cardholders then have the option of excluding personal information from any future marketing efforts.[7]

3 *Define marketing research, and explain its importance to marketing decision making.*

## THE ROLE OF MARKETING RESEARCH

**marketing research**
Process of planning, collecting, and analyzing data relevant to marketing decision making.

**Marketing research** is the process of planning, collecting, and analyzing data relevant to a marketing decision. The results of this analysis are then communicated to management. Marketing research plays a key role in the marketing system. It provides decision makers with data on the effectiveness of the current marketing mix and also insights for necessary changes. Furthermore, marketing research is a main data source for both management information systems and DSS.

Marketing research has three roles: descriptive, diagnostic, and predictive. Its *descriptive* role includes gathering and presenting factual statements. For example, what is the historic sales trend in the industry? What are consumers' attitudes toward a product and its advertising? Its *diagnostic* role includes explaining data. For instance, what was the impact on sales of a change in the design of the package? Its *predictive* function is to address "what if" questions. For example, how can the researcher use the descriptive and diagnostic research to predict the results of a planned marketing decision?

### DIFFERENCES BETWEEN MARKETING RESEARCH AND DSS

Because marketing research is problem-oriented, managers use it when they need guidance to solve a specific problem. Marketing research, for example, has been used to find out what features consumers want in a new personal computer. It has also aided product development managers in deciding how much milk to add in a new cream sauce for frozen peas. The U.S. Army has used marketing research to develop a profile of the young person most likely to be positively influenced by recruiting ads.

In contrast, DSS continually channels information about environmental changes into the organization. This information is gathered from a variety of sources, both inside and outside the firm. One important information source is marketing research. For example, Mastic Corporation, a leading supplier of vinyl siding, asks its nationwide network of distributors and their dealers questions about product quality, Mastic's service to the distributor, the amount of vinyl the distributor sells, and the percentage used for new construction. This information then becomes part of Mastic's DSS. Other data in the system include new housing starts, national unemployment figures, age of housing, and changes in housing styles. Its marketing research is therefore a component or input source for its DSS.

### MANAGEMENT USES OF MARKETING RESEARCH

Marketing research can help managers in several ways. It improves the quality of decision making and helps managers trace problems. Most important, sound marketing research helps managers better understand the marketplace and alerts them to marketplace trends. Finally, marketing research helps managers gauge the perceived value of their goods and services as well as the level of customer satisfaction. A discussion of these benefits follows.

## Improving the Quality of Decision Making

Managers can sharpen their decision making by using marketing research to explore the desirability of various marketing alternatives. For example, some years ago General Mills decided to expand into full-service restaurants. Marketing research indicated that the most popular ethnic food category in the United States was Italian and that interest in pasta and preference for Italian food would continue to increase. The company conducted many taste tests to find appropriate spice levels and to create a menu sure to please target customers. These marketing research studies led to the creation of The Olive Garden Italian restaurants—the fastest-growing and most popular full-service Italian restaurant chain in the nation.

## Tracing Problems

Another way managers use marketing research is to find out why a plan backfires. Was the initial decision incorrect? Did an unforeseen change in the external environment cause the plan to fail? How can the same mistake be avoided in the future?

Reynolds Metals used marketing research to develop a new line of plastic food wrap in transparent shades of red, green, yellow, and blue. Test results among women showed that they loved the product. Yet after the national rollout, sales were sluggish. Again, Reynolds called on marketing research. A telephone survey found that men didn't really see the point of colored plastic wraps. Unfortunately, the purchasing staffs of most supermarkets are men. Armed with this knowledge, Reynolds crafted a simple plan. It sent samples to the supermarket buyers' homes, hoping their wives' reactions would convince them the product would sell. The strategy worked. After ten weeks, colored Reynolds plastic wraps were stocked in three-quarters of the stores nationwide, and sales exceeded expectations.

## Understanding the Marketplace

Managers also use marketing research to understand the dynamics of the marketplace. Assume that you have recently gone to work for a new company that will design, produce, and market a line of casual clothing for college students, called Movin' Up. Perhaps one of your first concerns would be brand loyalty. That is, are college students loyal to the same brands as their parents, or will they consider new brands? You might also ask whether college students are loyal to the same brands they used in high school. The graphs in Exhibit 7.3A show responses to these questions that you might obtain through marketing research. (The data in Exhibit 7.3 are based on an actual marketing research study of 884 undergraduates at fifteen universities across the country.)

Now suppose the company is tentatively planning to promote Movin' Up clothing through direct mail, magazines, and cable television. Management wants to know how much time college students spend each day with various media (see Exhibit 7.3B). The advertising director, Sandra Jarboe, is also interested in the magazines college students read, the cable networks they watch, and the direct-mail pieces to which they respond, as shown in Exhibit 7.3. She is also curious about which print ads college students find most appealing. Sandra believes that this information might help her design the Movin' Up advertising campaign. In addition, the promotion manager, John Gates, is considering doing a fashion show of Movin' Up clothing at various popular spring break locations. Therefore, he needs to find out where college students go for spring break. As you can see, marketing research helps managers develop the marketing mix by providing insights into the lifestyles, preferences, and purchasing habits of target consumers.

**A. Brand loyalty**

Are you loyal to the same brands your parents purchase?

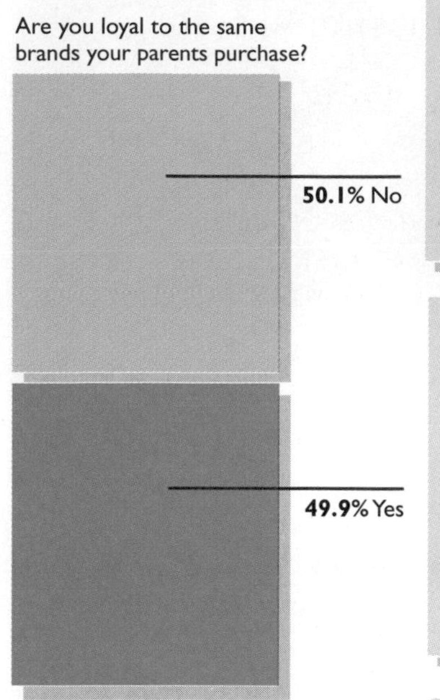


Are you loyal to the same brands that you used in high school?

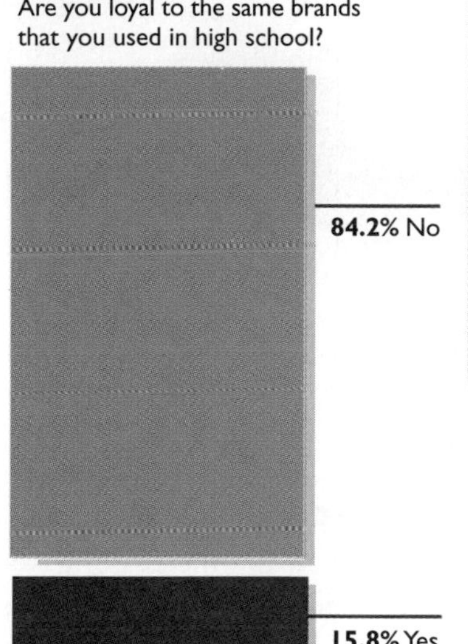


**B. Media use**

| Medium | Average hours per day | *Is that more or less time than spent in high school?* More | Less | Same |
|---|---|---|---|---|
| 1. Radio | 2.21 | 55.0% | 32.5% | 7.9% |
| 2. Network TV | 1.57 | 67.2 | 26.1 | 1.8 |
| 3. Cable TV | 0.98 | 52.7 | 31.4 | 4.4 |
| 4. Newspapers | 0.81 | 36.4 | 48.4 | 6.7 |
| 5. Magazines | 0.67 | 48.5 | 36.2 | 6.2 |

**C. Top 10 favorite magazines (in order)**

| Magazine | Points |
|---|---|
| 1. *Cosmopolitan* | 424 |
| 2. *Sport Illustrated* | 399 |
| 3. *Time* | 325 |
| 4. *Rolling Stone* | 317 |
| 5. *Glamour* | 315 |
| 6. *Vogue* | 261 |
| 7. *Newsweek* | 199 |
| 8. *People Weekly* | 190 |
| 9. *Mademoiselle* | 174 |
| 10. *Elle* | 168 |

**D. Top 10 cable networks (in order)**

| Network | Points |
|---|---|
| 1. MTV | 614 |
| 2. ESPN | 350 |
| 3. HBO | 343 |
| 4. CNN | 240 |
| 5. Showtime | 78 |
| 6. Nick at Nite | 74 |
| 7. Cinemax | 58 |
| 8. Dicovery | 46 |
| 9. VH-1 | 45 |
| 10. TBS | 42 |

**E. Response to direct mail**

| Mailing | Responses |
|---|---|
| 1. J. Crew | 10.4% |
| 2. Citibank Visa | 10.0 |
| 3. American Express | 7.1 |
| 4. L.L. Bean | 6.3 |
| 5. Credit cards (nonspecific) | 5.6 |
| 6. Magazine subscriptions (nonspecific) | 4.8 |
| 7. Lands' End | 3.7 |
| 8. MasterCard | 3.3 |
| 9. Catalogs (nonspecific) | 2.2 |
| 10. Publisher's Clearing House | 2.2 |

**F. Favorite print ads**

| Spot | Responses |
|---|---|
| 1. Absolut Vodka | 12.9% |
| 2. Calvin Klein's Obsession | 10.1 |
| 3. Nike | 5.5 |
| 4. Calvin Klein's Eternity | 2.2 |
| 5. Budweiser | 2.0 |
| 6. Calvin Klein Jeans | 1.8 |
| 7. Guess Jeans | 1.8 |
| 8. Maxell Tapes | 1.7 |
| 9. J&B Scotch | 1.7 |
| 10. Benetton | 1.5 |

**G. Top 5 spring break locations**

| Locations | Responses |
|---|---|
| 1. Home | 33.3% |
| 2. Florida | 10.7 |
| 3. None | 9.4 |
| 4. California | 5.0 |
| 5. Colorado | 4.7 |

*Exhibit 7.3*

A Survey of the College Market

## Fostering Customer Value and Quality

The environment in which business operates is far more competitive and mercurial than it ever has been before. Consumers are less tolerant of poor quality and service, less forgiving, and less loyal to specific brands. Consumer expectations are moving to the highest level. A good product and a fair price are not enough; service must be excellent as well. High product quality, good service, and a fair price mean value—which is, as you will discover in Chapter 8, the cornerstone of customer satisfaction. Satisfied customers are more likely to establish long-term relationships with a company, which are what help create long-term profitability for the firm.

In such an environment, perceived customer satisfaction is the scorecard that tells a company how well it is doing in delivering value. Marketing research is the vehicle for measuring perceived satisfaction. Today virtually all large businesses, ranging

Marketing research plays a key role in proactive management. Con Agra responded to consumers' increasing interest in healthy foods by developing the Healthy Choice line of products.

from IDS Financial Services to Taco Bell, measure customer satisfaction. In addition, countless smaller organizations, both profit and nonprofit, examine how well they are satisfying their customers.

## THE PROACTIVE ROLE OF MARKETING RESEARCH

Understanding—of the nature of the marketing environment and of the customer—is required for successful marketing. By thoroughly knowing the factors that can affect the target market and the marketing mix, management can be proactive rather than reactive. **Proactive management** alters the marketing mix to fit newly emerging economic, social, and competitive trends. In contrast, **reactive management** waits for change to have a major impact on the firm before deciding to take action. The turbulent marketing environment can be viewed as an opportunity (a proactive stance) or a threat (a reactive stance).

**proactive management**
Practice of altering the marketing mix to fit newly emerging economic, social, and competitive trends.

**reactive management**
Practice of waiting for change to have a major impact on the firm before deciding to take action.

Marketing research plays a key role in proactive management. It helps to forecast changes in the market and in consumer desires so that goods and services can be created or modified to meet those needs. ConAgra, for example, used marketing research to examine the growing interest in personal health in the United States. Its research ultimately led to the creation of Healthy Choice frozen dinners, which are low in sodium and cholesterol.

A proactive manager not only makes short-term adjustments in the marketing mix to meet market changes but also seeks to develop a long-run marketing strategy for the firm. A strategic plan, based on the firm's existing and projected internal capabilities and on projected changes in the external environment, guides the long-run use of the firm's resources. For instance, Pitney Bowes has a strategic plan founded on solid marketing research; it helps the firm effectively meet long-run profit and market share goals. Conversely, poor strategic planning can threaten the firm's survival. Montgomery Ward, floundering for almost a decade because of inadequate planning and poor understanding of the marketplace, had to give up its once healthy catalog sales division. Strategic planning is discussed at greater length in Chapter 22.

4 *Describe the steps involved in conducting a marketing research project.*

## STEPS IN A MARKETING RESEARCH PROJECT

Virtually all firms that have adopted the marketing concept engage in some marketing research, because it offers decision makers many benefits. Some companies spend millions on marketing research. But sometimes, particularly at smaller firms, limited-scale research studies are conducted informally. For example, when Eurasia restaurant, serving Eurasian cuisine, first opened along Chicago's ritzy Michigan Avenue, it drew novelty seekers. But it turned off the important business lunch crowd, and sales began to decline. The owner surveyed several hundred businesspeople working within a mile of the restaurant. He found that they were confused by Eurasia's concept and wanted more traditional Asian fare at lower prices. In response, the restaurant altered its concept; it hired a Thai chef, revamped the menu, and cut prices. The dining room was soon full again.

Whether a research project costs $200 or $2 million, the same general process should be followed. The marketing research process is a scientific approach to decision making that maximizes the chance of getting accurate and meaningful results. Exhibit 7.4 traces the steps: (1) defining the marketing problem, (2) planning the research design and gathering primary data, (3) specifying the sampling procedures, (4) collecting the data, (5) analyzing the data, (6) preparing and presenting the report, and (7) following up.

*Exhibit 7.4*

Marketing Research Process

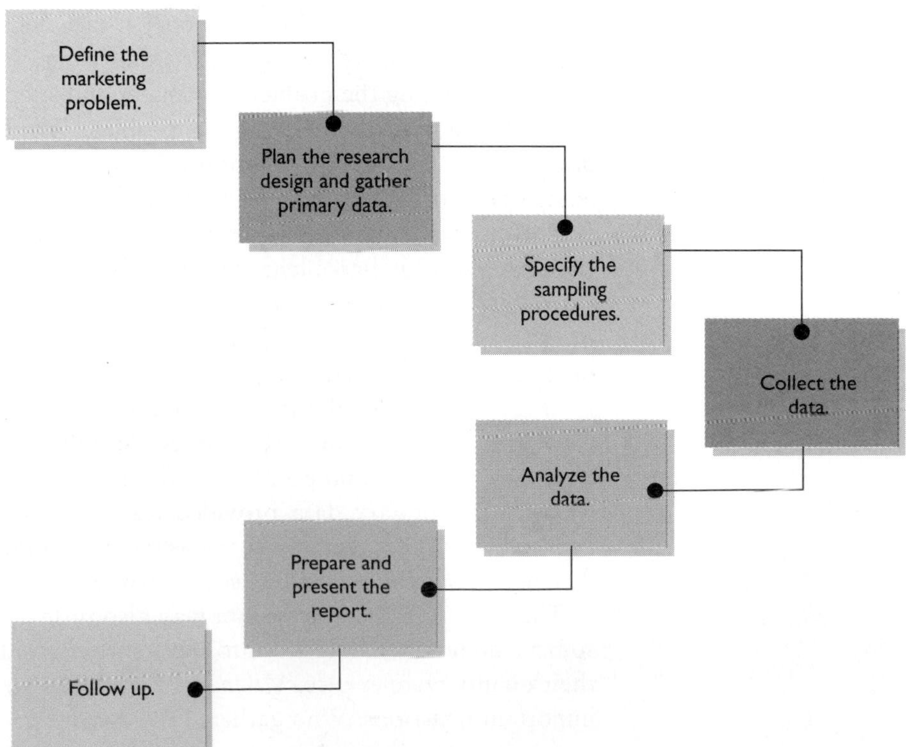

## DEFINING THE MARKETING PROBLEM

The first step in the marketing research process must be to develop either a problem statement or a statement of research objectives on which the decision maker and the researcher can both agree. This step is not as easy as it sounds. But it is important, because this statement directs the rest of the study. Some situations require only a simple problem statement; others lend themselves to a detailed statement of research objectives.

### Situation Analysis

**situation analysis**
Extensive background investigation into a particular marketing problem.

In some cases, identifying and structuring the problem may itself become the objective of a major background investigation called a **situation analysis.** A situation analysis is especially important to the outside consultant or to any researcher dealing with a particular type of problem for the first time. Situation analysis permits the researcher to become immersed in the problem—to learn about the company, its products, its markets, its marketing history, the competition, and so forth. After gathering this background information, the researcher may need to backtrack and revise the problem statement and research objectives.

After completing a situation analysis, the researcher compiles a list of all the data required to meet the research objectives and then determines the types of data required for decision making. Often the researcher will begin with secondary data in order to further refine the problem statement or the statement of research objectives.

### Secondary Data

**secondary data**
Data previously collected for any purpose other than the one at hand.

**Secondary data** are data previously collected for any purpose other than the one at hand. People both inside and outside the organization may have gathered secondary data to meet their needs. Exhibit 7.5 describes major sources of secondary data. Most research efforts rely at least partly on secondary data, which can usually be obtained quickly and inexpensively. The problem is locating relevant secondary data.

Secondary data save time and money if they help solve the researcher's problem. Even if the problem is not solved, secondary data have other advantages. They can aid in formulating the problem statement and suggest research methods and other types of data needed for solving the problem. In addition, secondary data can pinpoint the kinds of people to approach and their locations and serve as a basis of comparison for other data.

The disadvantages of secondary data stem mainly from a mismatch between the researcher's unique problem and the purpose for which the secondary data were originally gathered, which are typically different. For example, a major consumer products manufacturer wanted to determine the market potential for a fireplace log made of coal rather than compressed wood by-products. The researcher found plenty of secondary data about total wood consumed as fuel, quantities consumed in each state, and types of wood burned. Secondary data were also available about consumer attitudes and purchase patterns of wood by-product fireplace logs. The wealth of secondary data provided the researcher with many insights into the artificial log market. Yet nowhere was there any information that would tell the firm whether consumers would buy such a product made of coal.

The quality of secondary data may also pose a problem. Often secondary data sources do not give detailed information that would enable a researcher to assess their quality or relevance. Whenever possible, a researcher needs to address these important questions: Who gathered the data? Why were the data obtained? What

*Exhibit 7.5*

Major Sources of Secondary Data

| Source | Description |
|---|---|
| Internal information | Internal company information may be helpful in solving a particular marketing problem. Examples include sales invoices, other accounting records, data from previous marketing research studies, and historical sales data. |
| Market research firms | Companies such as A. C. Nielsen, Arbitron, and IMS International are major sources of secondary data regarding market share for consumer products and the characteristics of media audiences. |
| Trade associations | Many trade associations, such as the National Industrial Conference Board and the National Retail Merchants Association, collect data of interest to members. |
| University research bureaus, professional associations, foundations | A variety of nonprofit organizations collect and disseminate data of interest to marketing researchers. |
| Commercial publications | *Advertising Age, Sales Management, Product Marketing, Merchandising Week,* and many other commercial publications provide useful research data. |
| Government data | The federal government is a treasure trove of secondary data. Among its reports are *Census of Housing, Census of Retail Trade, Census of Services Industries, Census of Manufacturers, Statistical Abstract of the US., Economic Indicators,* and *U.S. Industrial Outlook.* |

methodology was used? How were classifications (such as heavy users versus light users) developed and defined? When was the information gathered?

*On-Line Databases.* Gathering traditional secondary data is often an arduous task. Researchers write requests for government, trade association, or other reports and then wait several weeks for a reply. Frequently, they make one or more trips to the library only to find that the needed reports are checked out or missing. Today, however, on-line computerized databases have reduced the drudgery associated with gathering secondary data. An **on-line database** is a collection of public information accessible by anyone with the proper computer facilities. With over 7,500 on-line databases available, practically any topic of interest to a marketing researcher is contained in some database.

**on-line database**
Database accessible by anyone with the proper computer facilities.

Hourly fees for consulting databases can range from nominal ($20) to expensive ($200 or more). The network through which users call the databases usually charges by the hour, too, and the charge is roughly equivalent to what you might spend if you had to call the database computer by long-distance telephone. Some databases also charge for the actual information users retrieve. A bibliographic citation might be free, but the full text of an article might cost a few dollars, and a corporate financial report might run $100 or more. Users must be sure to know what costs they're facing before they request a lot of information. Some vendors charge an annual flat fee that allows unlimited searches.

For a look at how an on-line database can affect decision making, consider the experience of Superior, Inc. (not its actual name), a large East Coast consumer goods firm. One morning its president woke up to some unpleasant news. A competitor was rumored to be marshaling its troops for an attack on the market for one of Superior's personal care products, worth $30 million in annual sales. Later that day, concerned executives at Superior were already preparing to take a drastic step: slashing the price to defuse the competitive challenge.

Before taking that step, however, Superior's executives decided to do a little research. Their on-line database told them that the competitor had been bought several years earlier by a conglomerate. Next, a check of local business newspaper databases turned up evidence of an ad agency hiring new personnel to back up the rumored campaign. Further on-line searches revealed that the parent company had once tried to sell the unprofitable subsidiary. Another story indicated that the parent company's bonds were being downgraded and mentioned a lawsuit from a bond holder. And a business news database revealed that a senior executive of the parent company had recently retired, with no successor named. Other stories noted that two other executives had left and hinted at turmoil at the board level.

Superior's executives decided that what at first appeared to be an aggressive threat was actually no more than a gesture by a paralyzed firm unable to take new initiatives. "If there is any gold outside," beamed one Superior executive, "it looks like they just don't have a shovel to pick it up with." Result: Superior's president decided to maintain prices and thereby preserve company profits.

**on-line database vendor**
Intermediary that acquires databases from database creators.

*On-Line Database Vendors.* An **on-line database vendor** is an intermediary that acquires databases from database creators. Such vendors offer electronic mail, news, finance, sports, weather, airline schedules, software, encyclopedias, bibliographies, directories, full-text information, and numeric databases. Thus a user can go to a single on-line vendor and gain access to a variety of databases. Billing is simplified because a single invoice is used for all the databases on the vendor's system. Because all of a vendor's databases have a standardized search procedure, this function is simplified. On-line vendors also provide an index to help researchers determine which databases will most likely meet their needs.

The four most popular on-line databases are CompuServe, a subsidiary of H&R Block; The Source, a subsidiary of Reader's Digest; Dow Jones News/Retrieval Service; and Dialog, a subsidiary of Lockheed Company. Dialog offers over 200 different databases containing more than 100 million items of information. Exhibit 7.6 shows some of the databases offered by the four major on-line vendors.

*Exhibit 7.6*

Selected Offerings of the Four Most Popular On-Line Database Vendors

| **Dow Jones News/Retrieval Service** | **Dialog** |
|---|---|
| Disclosure II (business database)<br>Dow Jones News<br>Current Quotes<br>Wall Street Journal<br>Academic American Encyclopedia<br>Cinemax Movie Reviews<br>AP News | Disclosure II (business database)<br>Management Contents<br>Standard & Poor's Corporate Description<br>Books in Print<br>Electronic Yellow Pages<br>Magazine Index<br>AP News |
| **CompuServe** | **The Source** |
| Standard & Poor's General Information File<br>Washington Post<br>World Book Encyclopedia<br>MicroQuote (stock information)<br>Business Information Wire<br>AP News<br>Comp*U*Store | Management Contents<br>Commodity News Service<br>Cinemax Movie Reviews<br>U.S. News Washington Letter<br>Travel Services<br>Employment Service<br>AP News<br>Comp*U*Store |

On-line database vendors provide several important advantages. First, the researcher can rapidly obtain a much greater variety of information than ever before. Second, by efficiently using on-line search procedures, the researcher can quickly pinpoint relevant data. Third, the large in-house staffs formerly required to research and maintain files can be eliminated, reducing labor costs and increasing productivity. Finally, small firms can study the same secondary data as large organizations and do it just as efficiently.

On-line database vendors have one potential disadvantage. A person unskilled at searching a database may be overwhelmed with data. Researchers must carefully choose the words used to locate the right citations, abstracts, and full-text stories. Thus they must often familiarize themselves with new terminology to narrow the search. Boolean logic, which deals with inclusivity or exclusivity of sets, is a crucial element of successful on-line searches. The basic notions of AND, OR, and NOT are used to broaden or narrow the scope of a request.

Suppose a travel agency is considering setting up packaged tours to Bermuda. The agency owner wants to know more about the competition and about alternatives in Bermuda. An on-line search might begin with the following instruction: travel OR tourism OR cruises OR cruising OR vacations OR vacationing AND Bermuda. With the NOT command, a searcher can eliminate "false drops"—citations that match the search requirements but have nothing to do with the topic of interest. An article about a man who sued a cruise line after suffering an allergic reaction to Bermuda onions can be eliminated by adding the qualifier "NOT Bermuda onion" to the search.[8]

*Computerized Database Packages.* A number of companies are now offering database packages on disk for personal computers. For example, Claritas has created two packages for market segmentation and demographic studies and for perceptual mapping—Compass/Agency for advertising agencies and Compass/Newspapers for newspapers. For Compass/Agency, Claritas recently added Arbitron radio ratings and data on product usage from Simmons Marketing Research Bureau and Mediamark. The Compass/Newspaper system contains more than 200 reports and maps. Users can also obtain data on subscribers, readership, and advertisers and display them as reports and maps or transfer the data to other standard software packages, such as spreadsheet, word-processing, and graphics applications.

The U.S. Department of Commerce has also made census data available for use on personal computers, including 1,300 categories of data on population, education, marital status, number of children in the home, home value or monthly rent, and income. The U.S. Census Bureau offers TIGER files, which map the location of all U.S. streets, highways, railroads, pipelines, power lines, airports, counties, municipalities, census tracts, census block groups, congressional districts, voter precincts, rivers, and lakes.[9]

*On-Line Marketing Research.* Companies are also learning that they can use on-line services to conduct marketing research directly with consumers and potential consumers. Nickelodeon, the cable television network for kids, had many questions that called for marketing research: Is this a good scoring method for a game show? Do kids understand if we show a sequence of program titles and air times? Getting answers to such questions would have required time-consuming and expensive traditional marketing research. Karen Flischel, Nickelodeon's vice president of research, hit upon the idea of using CompuServe for on-line interviewing. Nickelodeon chose viewers who were CompuServe users. The kids, ages 8 to 12, represent households with incomes ranging from $30,000 to $100,000. Half are

In on-line marketing research conducted by Nickelodeon, kids participating in a computer-based meeting clearly communicated their love of pets. Such information is used to determine which programs the cable television network will produce for its young viewers.



minorities. All have personal computers and VCRs in their homes. For those without modems, the network provided them.

Kids post notes on the computer bulletin board whenever they want to. Three times a week, they log on for scheduled meetings, during which Nickelodeon researchers lead discussions on a variety of topics. About a third of the sessions center on specific network programs. Armed with their keyboards, kids provide Nickelodeon with instant feedback. In one instance, they told researchers they were confused by the various locations shown in a segment of "The Tomorrow People," a five-part series with events occurring around the world. Realizing that the sight of a double-decker bus wasn't enough for a kid to identify London, the producers wrote the name of the city on the screen. Other insights come from responses to such survey questions as "How often do you go out to eat?," "Who do you go with?," and "Why do you like it?" One lengthy discussion about pets reminded Nickelodeon executives of the enormous importance of animals to their viewers.[10]

## PLANNING THE RESEARCH DESIGN AND GATHERING PRIMARY DATA

Good secondary data can help researchers conduct a thorough situation analysis. With that information, researchers can list their unanswered questions and rank them. Researchers must then decide the exact information required to answer the questions. The **research design** specifies which research questions must be answered, how and when the data will be gathered, and how the data will be analyzed. Typically, the project budget is finalized after the research design has been approved.

**research design**
Outline of which research questions must be answered, where and when data will be gathered, and how the data will be analyzed.

**primary data**
Information collected for the first time and used to solve a particular problem.

Sometimes research questions can be answered by gathering more secondary data; otherwise, primary data may be needed. **Primary data,** or information collected for the first time, can be used for solving the particular problem under investigation. The main advantage of primary data is that they will answer a specific research question that secondary data cannot answer. For example, suppose Pillsbury has two new recipes for refrigerated dough for sugar cookies. Which one will consumers like better? Secondary data will not help answer this question. Instead, targeted consumers must try each recipe and evaluate the tastes, textures, and appearances of each cookie. Moreover, primary data are current, and researchers know the source. Sometimes researchers gather the data themselves rather than assign projects to outside companies. Researchers also specify the methodology of the research. Secrecy can be maintained because the information is proprietary. In contrast, secondary data are available to all interested parties for relatively small fees.

On the other hand, gathering primary data is expensive. Costs can range from a few thousand dollars for a limited survey to several million for a nationwide study. For instance, a nationwide, fifteen-minute telephone interview with 1,000 adult males can cost $50,000 for everything, including a data analysis and report. Because primary data gathering is so expensive, firms commonly cut back on the number of interviews to save money. Larger companies that conduct many research projects use another cost-saving technique. They piggyback studies, or gather data on two different projects using one questionnaire. The drawback is that answering questions about, say, dog food and gourmet coffee may be confusing to respondents. Piggybacking also requires a longer interview (sometimes a half hour or longer), which tires respondents. The quality of the answers typically declines, with people giving curt replies and thinking, "When will this end!" A lengthy interview also makes people less likely to participate in other research surveys.[11]

However, the disadvantages of primary data gathering are usually offset by the advantages. It is often the only way of solving a research problem. And with a variety of techniques available for research—including surveys, observations, and experiments—primary research can address almost any marketing question.

## Survey Research

**survey research**
Technique for gathering primary data in which a researcher interacts with people to obtain facts, opinions, and attitudes.

The most popular technique for gathering primary data is **survey research,** in which a researcher interacts with people to obtain facts, opinions, and attitudes. Exhibit 7.7 summarizes the characteristics of the most popular forms of survey research.

*In-Home Interviews.* Although in-home, personal interviews often provide high-quality information, they tend to be very expensive because of the interviewers' travel

*Exhibit 7.7*

Characteristics of Several Types of Survey Research

| Characteristic | In-home personal interviews | Mall intercept interviews | Telephone interviews from interviewer's home | Central-location telephone interviews | Focus groups | Self-administered and one-time mail surveys | Mail panel surveys |
|---|---|---|---|---|---|---|---|
| Cost | High | Moderate | Moderate to low | Moderate | Low | Low | Moderate |
| Time span | Moderate | Moderate | Fast | Fast | Fast | Slow | Relatively slow |
| Use of interviewer probes | Yes | Yes | Yes | Yes | Yes | No | Yes |
| Ability to show concepts to respondent | Yes | Yes (also taste tests) | No | No | Yes | Yes | Yes |
| Management control over interviewer | Low | Moderate | Low | High | High | n/a | n/a |
| General data quality | High | Moderate | Moderate to low | High to moderate | Moderate | Moderate to low | Moderate |
| Ability to collect large amounts of data | High | Moderate | Moderate to low | Moderate to low | Moderate | Low to moderate | Moderate |
| Ability to handle complex questionnaires | High | Moderate | Moderate | High if computer-aided | Low | Low | Low |

time and mileage costs. Therefore, market researchers tend to conduct fewer in-home interviews today than in the past.

Nevertheless, this form of survey research has some important advantages. The respondent is interviewed at home, in a natural setting where many consumption decisions are actually made. Also, the interviewer can show the respondent items (for example, package designs) or invite the respondent to taste or use a test product. An interviewer can also probe when necessary—a technique used to clarify a person's response. For example, an interviewer might ask, "What did you like best about the salad dressing you just tried?" The respondent might reply, "Taste." This answer doesn't provide a lot of information, so the interviewer could probe by saying, "Can you tell me a little bit more about taste?" The respondent then elaborates: "Yes, it's not too sweet, it has the right amount of pepper, and I love that hint of garlic."

**mall intercept interview**
Survey research method that involves interviewing people in the common areas of shopping malls.

*Mall Intercept Interviews.* The **mall intercept interview** is conducted in the common areas of shopping malls. It is the economy version of the door-to-door interview—personal contact between interviewer and respondent, minus the interviewer's travel time and mileage costs. To conduct this type of interview, the research firm rents office space in the mall or pays a significant daily fee. One drawback is that it is hard to get a representative sample of the population.

Mall intercept interviews must be brief. Only the shortest ones are conducted while respondents are standing. Usually researchers invite respondents to their office for interviews, which are still rarely over fifteen minutes long. The researchers often show respondents concepts for new products or a test commercial or have them taste a new food product. The overall quality of mall intercept interviews is about the same as telephone interviews.

*Telephone Interviews.* Compared to the personal interview, the telephone interview costs less and may provide the best sample of any survey procedure. Although it is often criticized for providing poorer-quality data than the in-home personal interview, studies have shown that this criticism may not be deserved.[12]

**central-location telephone (CLT) facility**
Specially designed room used for conducting telephone interviews for survey research.

**computer-assisted interviewing**
Interviewing method in which the interviewer reads the questions from a computer screen and enters the respondent's data directly into the computer.

Most telephone interviewing is conducted from a specially designed phone room called a **central-location telephone** (CLT) **facility.** A phone room has many phone lines, individual interviewing stations, sometimes monitoring equipment, and headsets. The use of Wide Area Telephone Service (WATS) lines permits the research firm to interview people nationwide from a single location.

Many CLT facilities offer **computer-assisted interviewing.** The interviewer reads the questions from a computer screen and enters the respondent's data directly into the computer. The researcher can stop the survey at any point and immediately print out the survey results. Thus a researcher can get a sense of the project as it unfolds and fine-tune the research design as necessary. An on-line interviewing system can also save time and money, because data entry occurs as the response is recorded rather than as a separate process after the interview. Hallmark Cards found that an interviewer administered a printed questionnaire for its Shoebox Greeting cards in twenty-eight minutes. The same questionnaire administered with computer assistance took only eighteen minutes.[13]

**focus group**
Group of seven to ten people with desired characteristics who participate in a group discussion about a subject of interest to a marketing organization.

*Focus Groups.* A **focus group** is a type of personal interviewing. Often recruited by random telephone screening, seven to ten people with certain desired characteristics form a focus group. These qualified consumers are usually offered an incentive (typically \$30 to \$50) to participate in a group discussion. The meeting place (sometimes resembling a living room, sometimes featuring a conference table) has audiotaping and perhaps videotaping equipment. It also likely has a viewing room with a one-way mirror, so that clients (manufacturers or retailers) may watch the session. During the session, a moderator, hired by the research company, leads the group discussion.

Focus groups are occasionally used to brainstorm new product ideas or to screen concepts for new products. Ford Motor Company, for example, asked consumers to drive several automobile prototypes. These "test drivers" were then brought together in focus groups. During the discussions, consumers complained that they were scuffing their shoes because the rear seats lacked foot room. In response, Ford sloped the floor underneath the front seats, widened the space between the seat adjustment tracks, and made the tracks in the Taurus and Sable models out of smooth plastic instead of metal.[14]

A new system by Focus Vision Network allows client companies and advertising agencies to view live focus groups in Chicago, Dallas, Boston, and fifteen other major cities. For example, the private satellite network lets a General Motors researcher observing a San Diego focus group control two cameras in the viewing room. The researcher can get a full group view or a close-up, zoom, or pan the participants. The researcher can also communicate directly with the moderator using an ear receiver. Ogilvy and Mather (a large New York advertising agency), StarKist Sea Foods, Seagrams, and others have installed the system.[15]

*Mail Surveys.* Mail surveys have several benefits: relatively low cost, elimination of interviewers and field supervisors, centralized control, and actual or promised anonymity for respondents (which may draw more candid responses). Some researchers feel that mail questionnaires give the respondent a chance to reply more thoughtfully and to check records, talk to family members, and so forth. Yet mail questionnaires usually produce low response rates.

Low response rates pose a problem, because certain elements of the population tend to respond more than others. The resulting sample may therefore not represent the surveyed population. For example, the sample may have too many retired people and too few working people. In this instance, answers to a question about attitudes toward Social Security might indicate a much more favorable overall view of the system than is actually the case. Another serious problem with mail surveys is that no one probes respondents to clarify or elaborate on their answers.

GLOBAL PERSPECTIVES

### Marketing Research in Russia

Opinion and market research in the former Soviet Union dates back to the 1960s, during a brief thaw in the political and economic climate under Nikita Khrushchev. For instance, large-scale youth surveys were conducted under the direction of Dr. Boris Grushin, then head of the Soviet Institute of Public Opinion at the *Komsomolskaya Pravda* newspaper. VNIIKS, All-Union Institute for Market Research, attached to the Ministry of Home Trade, also started doing research on issues of supply and demand around the same time. Much of VNIIKS's early work was "industrial research," which used a network of expert correspondents/informants throughout the Soviet Union.

With a few exceptions, most of the opinion surveys conducted before 1985 were designed to bolster the Communist Party line, not to determine truth. Usually, only positive and favorable findings were published. In addition, little concern was given to proper sampling procedures and interview techniques. Most of this early research was based on self-administered questionnaires distributed at places of work, which provided respondents little promise of anonymity.

The dissolution of the Soviet Union has brought profound changes in the field of marketing research. Research organizations, reformed or newly established, sprang to life to take the public pulse, documenting social change and at the same time serving the needs of a wide variety of clients.

Three types of research organizations operate in Russia today. The first type conducts almost exclusively marketing research projects. It

*(continued)*

GLOBAL PERSPECTIVES

includes groups that at one time or another were affiliated with government industry and trade agencies, and new joint ventures with foreign partners, such as VNIIKS (affiliated with a Finnish research institute) and INFOMARKET (owned by the Russian Ministry of Metallurgy and a Dutch research company).

The second type has a more scholarly orientation, concentrating on public opinion research and social trends. Examples are the Institute of Sociology and the Institute of Applied Social Research. Universities such as Moscow State University and the University of Vilnius have also started centers of public opinion research.

The third type of research organization seeks to combine marketing and opinion research. Their clientele is diverse, ranging from independent news agencies to various government and legislative branches, Western media, research institutes, advertising agencies, and corporations. The All Commonwealth Center for Public Opinion and Market Research and Vox Populi, headed by Boris Grushin, are typical and are two of the best known of this kind.

Taken together, currently available research services include surveys, consumer panels, opinion leader panels, and ad hoc studies covering a wide range of social, economic, political, and marketing or business-related topics. Data-collection techniques include face-to-face interviewing, surveys by mail, and even telephone interviewing among elites or opinion leaders.[16]

Do you think marketing research will ever be as popular in Russia as it is in the United States? What are some unique problems that a researcher would face there?

Mail panels like those operated by Market Facts, National Family Opinion Research, and NPD Research offer an alternative to the one-shot mail survey. A mail panel consists of a sample of households recruited to participate by mail for a given period. Panel members often receive gifts in return for their participation. Essentially, the panel is a sample used several times. In contrast to one-time mail surveys, the response rates from mail panels are high. Rates of 70 percent (of those who agree to participate) are not uncommon.

## Questionnaire Design

All forms of survey research require a questionnaire. Questionnaires ensure that all respondents will be asked the same series of questions.

Questionnaires include three basic types of questions: open-ended, closed-ended, and scaled-response (see Exhibit 7.8). An **open-ended question** encourages an answer phrased in the respondent's own words. Researchers get a rich array of information based on the respondent's frame of reference. In contrast, a **closed-ended question** asks the respondent to make a selection from a limited list of responses. Traditionally, marketing researchers separate the two-choice question (called "dichotomous") from the many-item type (often called "multiple choice"). A **scaled-response question** is a closed-ended question designed to measure the intensity of a respondent's answer.

**open-ended question**
Question worded to encourage unlimited answers phrased in the respondent's own words.

**closed-ended question**
Question that asks the respondent to make a selection from a limited list of responses.

**scaled-response question**
Closed-ended question designed to measure the intensity of a respondent's answer.

Closed-ended and scaled-response questions are easier to tabulate than open-ended questions, because response choices are fixed. On the other hand, if the researcher is not careful in designing the closed-ended question, an important choice might be omitted. For example, suppose this question were asked on a food study: "What do you normally add to a taco, besides meat, that you have prepared at home?"

| | |
|---|---|
| Avocado | 1 |
| Cheese (Monterey Jack/cheddar) | 2 |
| Guacamole | 3 |
| Lettuce | 4 |
| Mexican hot sauce | 5 |
| Olives (black/green) | 6 |
| Onions (red/white) | 7 |
| Peppers (red/green) | 8 |
| Pimento | 9 |
| Sour cream | 0 |

The list seems complete, doesn't it? However, consider the following responses: "I usually add a green, avocado-tasting hot sauce"; "I cut up a mixture of lettuce and

Exhibit 7.8

Types of Questions Found on Questionnaires for National Market Research Surveys

| Open-ended questions | Closed-ended questions | Scaled-response question |
|---|---|---|
| 1. What advantages, if any, do you think ordering from a mail-order catalog company offers compared to shopping at local retail outlet? (*Probe:* What else?)<br><br>2. Why do you have one or more of your rugs or carpets professionally cleaned rather than having you or someone else in the household clean them?<br><br>3. What is there about the color of the eye shadow that makes you like it the best? | ***Dichotomous***<br>1. Did you heat the Danish product before serving it?<br>Yes ..... 1<br>No ..... 2<br><br>2. The federal government doesn't care what people like me think.<br>Agree ..... 1<br>Disagree ..... 2<br><br>***Multiple choice***<br>1. I'd like you to think back to the last footwear of any kind that you bought. I'll read you a list of descriptions and would like for you to tell me which category they fall into. (*Read list and check proper category.*)<br>Dress and/or formal ..... 1<br>Casual ..... 2<br>Canvas/trainer/gym shoes ..... 3<br>Specialized athletic shoes ..... 4<br>Boots ..... 5<br><br>2. In the last three months, have you used Noxzema skin cream . . . (*Check all that apply.*)<br>As a facial wash ..... 1<br>For moisturizing the skin ..... 2<br>For treating blemishes ..... 3<br>For cleansing the skin ..... 4<br>For treating dry skin ..... 5<br>For softening skin ..... 6<br>For sunburn ..... 7<br>For making the facial skin smooth ..... 8 | Now that you have used the rug cleaner, would you say that you . . . (*Check one.*)<br>__ Would definitely buy it<br>__ Would probably buy it<br>__ Might or might not buy it<br>__ Probably would not buy it<br>__ Definitely would not buy it |

spinach"; "I'm a vegetarian; I don't use meat at all. My taco is filled only with guacamole." How would you code these replies? As you can see, the question needs an "other" category.

A good question must also be asked clearly and concisely, and ambiguous language must be avoided. Take, for example, the question "Do you live within ten minutes of here?" The answer depends on the mode of transportation (maybe the person walks), driving speed, perceived time, and other factors. Instead, respondents should see a map with certain areas highlighted and be asked whether they live within one of the areas.

Clarity also implies using reasonable terminology. A questionnaire is not a vocabulary test. Jargon should be avoided, and language should be geared to the target audience. A question like "State the level of efficacy of your preponderant dishwasher powder" would probably be greeted by a lot of blank stares. It would be much simpler to say "Are you (1) very satisfied, (2) somewhat satisfied, or (3) not satisfied with your current brand of dishwasher powder?"

Stating the survey's purpose at the beginning of the interview also improves clarity. The respondents should understand the study's intentions and the interviewer's expectations. Sometimes, of course, to get an unbiased response, the interviewer

While children have fun in the Fisher-Price Play Laboratory, toy designers surreptitiously watch to get ideas for new products and product improvements.



must disguise the true purpose of the study. If an interviewer says "We're conducting an image study for American National Bank" and then proceeds to ask a series of questions about the bank, chances are the responses will be biased. Many times respondents will try to provide answers that they believe are "correct" or that the interviewer wants to hear.

Finally, to ensure clarity, the interviewer should avoid asking two questions in one—for example, "How did you like the taste and texture of the Pepperidge Farm coffee cake?" This should be divided into two questions, one concerning taste and the other texture.

A question should not only be clear but also unbiased. A question like "Have you purchased any quality Black & Decker tools in the past six months?" biases respondents to think of the topic in a certain way (in this case, to link quality and Black & Decker tools). Questions can also be leading: "Weren't you pleased with the good service you received last night at the Holiday Inn?" (The respondent is all but instructed to say yes.) These examples are quite obvious; unfortunately, bias is usually more subtle. Even an interviewer's clothing or gestures can create bias.

**observation research**
Research method that relies on three types of observation: people watching people, people watching physical phenomena, and machines watching people.

## Observation Research

In contrast to survey research, **observation research** does not rely on direct interaction with people. The three types of observation research are people watching people, people watching activity, and machines watching people.

There are two ways of *people watching people:*

- *Mystery shoppers:* Researchers posing as customers observe the quality of service offered by retailers. The largest mystery shopper company is Shop 'N Chek, an Atlanta company that employs over 16,000 anonymous shoppers nationwide. The firm evaluates salespeople's courtesy for General Motors, flight service for United Airlines, and the efficiency of hamburger ordering for Wendy's, among other clients.[17]

- *One-way mirror observations:* At the Fisher-Price Play Laboratory, children are invited to spend twelve sessions playing with toys. Toy designers watch through one-way mirrors to see how children react to Fisher-Price's and other makers' toys. Fisher-Price, for example, had difficulty designing a toy lawn mower that children would play with. A designer, observing behind the mirror, noticed the children's fascination with soap bubbles. He then created a lawn mower that spewed soap bubbles. It sold over a million units in the first year.

**audit**
Examination and verification of the sale of a product.

One form of observation research that features *people watching activity* is known as an **audit,** the examination and verification of the sale of a product. Audits generally fall into two categories: retail audits, which measure sales to final consumers, and wholesale audits, which determine the amount of product moved from warehouses to retailers. Wholesalers and retailers allow auditors into their stores and stockrooms to examine the company's sales and order records in order to verify product flows. In turn, the retailers and wholesalers receive cash compensation and basic reports about their operations from the audit firms.

As for *machines watching people,* four types are used:

- *Traffic counters:* The most common and most popular form of machine-based observation research relies on machines that measure the flow of vehicles over a stretch of roadway. Outdoor advertisers rely on traffic counts to determine the number of exposures per day to a billboard. Retailers use the information to decide where to place a store. Convenience stores, for example, require a moderately high traffic volume to be profitable.
- *VideOCart:* This machine uses infrared sensors in store ceilings to track shopping carts.[18] The new system has spotted a lot of "dippers." These shoppers park their carts at the ends of aisles and then walk down, filling their arms with items from the shelves as they go. Retailers figure such shoppers probably buy less because they are limited by what they can carry. Using VideOcart, Basha's Markets in Chandler, Arizona, found that only 18 percent of the grocery store's customers ever went down the aisle that displays greeting cards, which are high-profit items. So George Fiscus, the store-layout manager, moved the section, sandwiching it between the floral department and an aisle with peanut butter, jelly, and health foods that regularly draws 62 percent of the store's traffic. Sales of greeting cards subsequently jumped 40 percent.[19]
- *Shopper-Trak:* This device uses beams of infrared light to count customers as they pass through the store entrance or past certain locations inside the store. In a test of the Shopper-Trak system, Kmart used it to send salespeople to crowded departments and to open more checkout lanes when lines began to get long. The retailer also wanted to be able to determine for the first time what percentage of shoppers actually make purchases. With such information, the company could perhaps convert browsers into buyers. Departments with little traffic, for instance, could be promoted more heavily with advertised specials, in-store events like the familiar "blue-light specials," and better displays at the ends of the aisles.[20]
- *Passive people meter:* Soon a cameralike device will be available to measure the size of television audiences. The passive system, packaged to resemble a VCR and placed on top of the TV, will be programmed to recognize faces and record electronically when specific members of a family watch TV. It will note when viewers leave the room and even when they avert their eyes from the screen. Strangers would be listed simply as visitors.[21] Passive people meters are eagerly

Observation research helps retailers learn how to get shoppers to buy more on each visit. Envirosell Inc. specializes in surreptitious filming and tracking of consumers as they travel a store's aisles.

Photograph by Chip Simons

anticipated because advertisers are demanding more proof of viewership and the networks are under pressure to show that advertising is reaching its intended targets (ratings are used to help set prices for commercial time). An A.C. Nielsen executive has said that a passive system should yield "even higher quality, more accurate data because the respondents don't have to do anything" other than "be themselves." Already, however, the networks and advertisers are criticizing the passive people meter. One executive noted, "Who would want or allow one of those things in their bedroom?"[22] Others claim that the system requires bright light to operate properly. Also, the box has limited peripheral vision, so it might not sense all the people in a given room. Will the passive people meter work better than the present diary system? Only time will tell.

All observation techniques offer at least two advantages over survey research. First, bias from the interviewing process is eliminated. Second, observation doesn't rely on the respondent's willingness to provide data.

Conversely, the observation technique also has two important disadvantages. First, subjective information is limited, because motivations, attitudes, and feelings are not measured. Second, data collection costs may run high unless the observed behavior patterns occur frequently, briefly, or somewhat predictably.

## Experiments

**experiment**
Method of gathering primary data in which one or more variables are altered to measure their relative influence on another variable.

An **experiment** is another method a researcher can use to gather primary data. The researcher alters one or more variables—price, package design, shelf space, advertising theme, advertising expenditures—while observing the effects of those alterations on another variable (usually sales). The best experiments are those in which all factors are held constant except the ones being manipulated. The researcher can then observe that changes in sales, for example, result from changes in the amount of money spent on advertising.

Holding all other factors constant in the external environment is a monumental and costly, if not impossible, task. Such factors as competitors' actions, weather, and economic conditions are beyond the researcher's control. Yet market researchers have ways to account for the ever-changing external environment. Mars, the candy company, was losing sales to other candy companies. Traditional surveys showed that the shrinking candy bar was not perceived as a good value. Mars wondered whether a bigger bar sold at the same price would increase sales enough to offset the higher ingredient costs. The company designed an experiment in which the marketing mix stayed the same in different markets but the size of the candy bar varied. The substantial increase in sales of the bigger bar quickly proved that the additional costs would be more than covered by the additional revenue. Mars increased the bar size—and its market share and profits.

## SPECIFYING THE SAMPLING PROCEDURES

Once the researchers decide how they will collect primary data, their next step is to select the sampling procedures they will use. A firm can seldom take a census of all possible users of a new product, nor can they all be interviewed. Therefore, a firm must select a sample of the group to be interviewed. A **sample** is a subset from a larger population.

**sample**
Subset for interviewing drawn from a larger population.

**universe**
Population from which a sample is drawn.

Several questions must be answered before a sampling plan is chosen. First, the population or **universe** of interest must be defined. This is the group from which the sample will be drawn. It should include all the people whose opinions, behavior, preferences, attitudes, and so on are of interest to the marketer. For example, in a study whose purpose is to determine the market for a new canned dog food, the universe might be defined to include all current buyers of canned dog food.

After the universe has been defined, the next question is whether the sample must be representative of the population. If the answer is yes, a probability sample is needed. Otherwise, a nonprobability sample might be considered.

### Probability Samples

**probability sample**
Sample drawn from a population in which every element has a known nonzero probability of being selected.

**random sample**
Type of probability sample in which every element of the population has an equal chance of being selected as part of the sample.

A **probability sample** is one in which every element in the population has a known statistical likelihood of being selected. Its most desirable feature is that scientific rules can be used to ensure that the sample represents the population.

One type of probability sample is a random sample. A **random sample** must be arranged in such a way that every element of the population has an equal chance of being selected as part of the sample. For example, suppose a university is interested in getting a cross section of student opinions on a proposed sports complex to be built using student activity fees. If the university can acquire an up-to-date list of all the enrolled students, it can draw a random sample by using random numbers from a table (found in most statistics books) to select students from the list.

### Nonprobability Samples

**nonprobability sample**
Any sample in which little or no attempt is made to get a representative cross section of the population.

**convenience sample**
Nonprobability sample that uses respondents who are convenient or readily accessible to the researcher.

Any sample in which little or no attempt is made to get a representative cross section of the population can be considered a **nonprobability sample.** A common form of a nonprobability sample is the **convenience sample,** based on using respondents who are convenient or readily accessible to the researcher—for instance, employees, friends, or relatives.

Nonprobability samples are acceptable as long as the researcher understands their nonrepresentative nature. Because of their lower cost, nonprobability samples are the basis of much marketing research.

## Types of Errors

Whenever a sample is used in marketing research, two major types of error occur: measurement error and sampling error. **Measurement error** occurs when there is a difference between the information desired by the researcher and the information provided by the measurement process. For example, people may tell an interviewer that they purchase Coors beer when they do not. Measurement error generally tends to be larger than sampling error.

**measurement error**
Error that occurs when there is a difference between the information desired by the researcher and the information provided by the measurement process.

**sampling error**
Error that occurs when a sample is not representative of the target population in some way.

**Sampling error** occurs when a sample somehow does not represent the target population. Sampling error can be one of several types. Nonresponse error occurs when the sample actually interviewed differs from the sample drawn. This error happens because the original people selected to be interviewed either refused to cooperate or were inaccessible. For example, people who feel embarrassed about their drinking habits may refuse to talk about them.

**frame error**
Error that occurs when the sample drawn from a population differs from the target population.

**Frame error,** another type of sampling error, arises if the sample drawn from a population differs from the target population. For instance, suppose a telephone survey is conducted to find out Chicago beer drinkers' attitudes toward Coors. If a Chicago telephone directory is used as the *frame* (the device or list from which the respondents are selected), the survey will contain a frame error. Not all Chicago beer drinkers have a phone, and many phone numbers are unlisted. An ideal sample (for example, a sample with no frame error) matches all important characteristics of the target population to be surveyed. Could you find a perfect frame for Chicago beer drinkers?

**random error**
Error that occurs because the selected sample is an imperfect representation of the overall population.

**Random error** occurs because the selected sample is an imperfect representation of the overall population. Random error represents how accurately the chosen sample's true average (mean) value reflects the population's true average (mean) value. For example, we might take a random sample of beer drinkers in Chicago and find that 16 percent regularly drink Coors beer. The next day we might repeat the same sampling procedure and discover that 14 percent regularly drink Coors beer. The difference is due to random error.

## COLLECTING THE DATA

**field service firm**
Firm that specializes in interviewing respondents on a subcontract basis.

Marketing research field service firms collect most primary data. A **field service firm** specializes in interviewing respondents on a subcontracted basis. Many have offices throughout the country. A typical marketing research study involves data collection in several cities, requiring the marketer to work with a comparable number of field service firms. To ensure uniformity among all subcontractors, detailed field instructions should be developed for every job. Nothing should be open to chance; no interpretations of procedures should be left to subcontractors.

Besides conducting interviews, field service firms provide focus group facilities, mall intercept locations, test product storage, and kitchen facilities to prepare test food products. They also conduct retail audits (counting the amount of a product sold off retail shelves). After an in-home interview is completed, field service supervisors validate the survey by recontacting about 15 percent of the respondents. The supervisors verify that certain responses were recorded properly and that the people were actually interviewed.

## ANALYZING THE DATA

After collecting the data, the marketing researcher proceeds to the next step in the research process: data analysis. The purpose of this analysis is to interpret and draw conclusions from the mass of collected data. The marketing researcher tries to organize

*Exhibit 7.9*

Hypothetical Cross-Tabulation between Gender and Brand of Microwave Popcorn Purchased Most Frequently

| Brand | Purchase by gender | |
|---|---|---|
| | Male | Female |
| Orville Reddenbacher | 31% | 49% |
| T.V. Time | 12 | 6 |
| Pop Rite | 38 | 4 |
| Act Two | 7 | 23 |
| Weight Watchers | 4 | 18 |
| Other | 8 | 0 |

and analyze those data by using one or more techniques common to marketing research: one-way frequency counts, cross-tabulations, and more sophisticated statistical analysis.

Of these three techniques, one-way frequency counts are the simplest. One-way frequency tables record the responses to a question. For example, the answers to the question "What brand of microwave popcorn do you buy most often?" would provide a one-way frequency distribution. One-way frequency tables are always done in data analysis, at least as a first step, because they provide the researcher with a general picture of the study's results.

**cross-tabulation**
Type of data analysis that relates the responses to one question to the responses to one or more other questions.

A **cross-tabulation,** or "cross-tab," lets the analyst look at the responses to one question in relation to the responses to one or more other questions. For example, what is the association between gender and the brand of microwave popcorn bought most frequently? Hypothetical answers to this question are shown in Exhibit 7.9. Although the Orville Reddenbacher brand was popular with both males and females, it was more popular with females. Compared with women, men strongly preferred Pop Rite, whereas women were more likely than men to buy Weight Watchers popcorn.

Researchers can use many other more powerful and sophisticated statistical techniques, such as hypothesis testing, measures of association, and regression analysis. A description of these techniques goes beyond the scope of this book but can be found in any good marketing research textbook. The use of sophisticated statistical techniques depends on the researchers' objectives and the nature of the data gathered.

## PREPARING AND PRESENTING THE REPORT

After data analysis has been completed, the researcher must prepare the report and communicate the conclusions and recommendations to management. This is a key step in the process. If the marketing researcher wants managers to carry out the recommendations, he or she must convince them that the results are credible and justified by the data collected.

Researchers are usually required to present both written and oral reports on the project. These reports should be tailored to the audience. They should begin with a clear, concise statement of the research objectives, followed by a complete, but brief and simple, explanation of the research design or methodology employed. A summary of major findings should come next. The conclusion of the report should also present recommendations for management.

Most people who enter marketing will become research users rather than research suppliers. Thus, they must know what to notice in a report. As with many other items we purchase, quality is not always readily apparent. Nor does a high price guarantee superior quality. The basis for measuring the quality of a marketing research report is the research proposal. Did the report meet the objectives established in the proposal? Was the methodology outlined in the proposal followed? Are the conclusions based on logical deductions from the data analysis? Do the recommendations seem prudent, given the conclusions?

Another criterion is the quality of the writing. Is the style crisp and lucid? It has been said that if readers are offered the slightest opportunity to misunderstand, they probably will. The report should also be as concise as possible.

### FOLLOWING UP

The final step in the marketing research process is to follow up. The researcher should determine why management did or did not carry out the recommendations in the report. Was sufficient decision-making information included? What could have been done to make the report more useful to management? A good rapport between the product manager, or whoever authorized the project, and the market researcher is essential. Often they must work together on many studies throughout the year.

5 *Discuss the growing importance of single-source research.*

## SINGLE-SOURCE RESEARCH

**single-source research**
System for gathering information from a single group of respondents by continuously monitoring the advertising, promotion, and pricing they are exposed to and the things they buy.

**Single-source research** is a system for gathering information from a single group of respondents by continuously monitoring the advertising, promotion, and pricing they are exposed to and the things they buy. The variables measured are advertising campaigns, coupons, displays, and product prices. The result is a huge database of marketing efforts and consumer behavior. Single-source research is bringing ever closer the holy grail of marketing research: an accurate, objective picture of the direct causal relationship between different kinds of marketing efforts and actual sales.

Two electronic monitoring tools are used in single-source systems: television meters and laser scanners, which "read" the bar codes on products and produce instantaneous information on sales. Separately, each monitoring device provides marketers with current information about either the advertising audience or sales and inventories of products. Together, television meters and scanners measure the impact of marketing.

The two major single-source suppliers are Information Resources Incorporated (IRI) and the A.C. Nielsen Company. Each has about half the market for single-source research.[23] However, IRI is the founder of scanner-based research.

**BehaviorScan**
Single-source research program that tracks the purchases of 3,000 households through store scanners.

IRI's first product is called **BehaviorScan.** A household panel (a group of 3,000 long-term participants in the research project) has been recruited and maintained in each BehaviorScan town. Panel members shop with an ID card, which is presented at the checkout in scanner-equipped grocery stores and drugstores, allowing IRI to track electronically each household's purchases, item by item, over time. With such a measure of household purchasing, it is possible to manipulate marketing variables, such as TV advertising or consumer promotions, or to introduce a new product and

In addition to its popular scanner-based research system, Information Resources Incorporated sells Apollo Space Management, which draws these computer-generated schematics of retail shelves.

Courtesy of Information Resources, Inc.

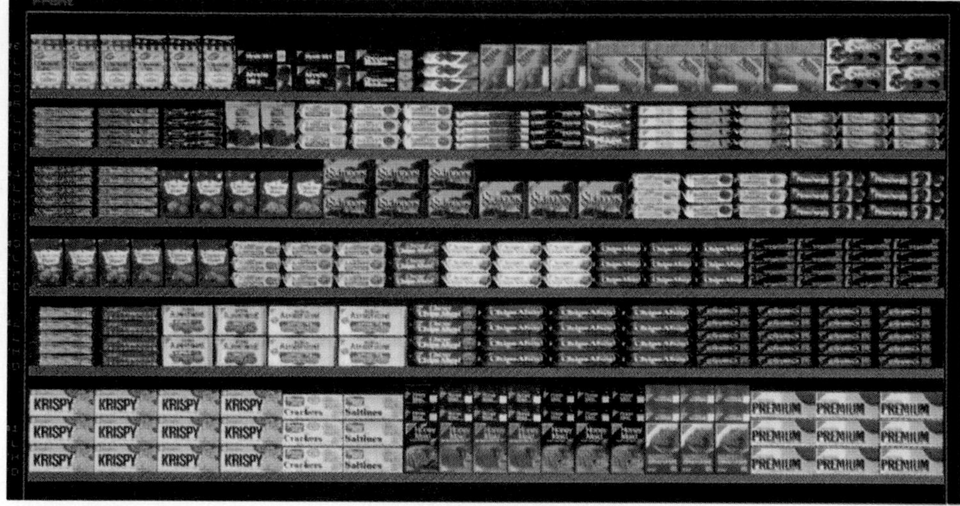


analyze real changes in consumer buying behavior. The BehaviorScan markets are geographically dispersed cities: Pittsfield, Massachusetts; Marion, Indiana; Eau Claire, Wisconsin; Midland, Texas; Grand Junction, Colorado; and Cedar Rapids, Iowa.

**InfoScan**
Scanner-based, national sales-tracking service for the consumer packaged-goods industry, using data from purchases at retail stores.

IRI's most successful product, with sales of over $130 million per year and 740 U.S. clients, is **InfoScan.**[24] InfoScan is a scanner-based sales-tracking service for the consumer packaged-goods industry. Retail sales, detailed consumer purchasing information (including measurement of store loyalty and total grocery basket expenditures), and promotional activity by manufacturers and retailers are monitored and evaluated for all bar-coded products.

InfoScan collects daily purchase data from over 3,000 supermarkets, 600 drugstores, and 300 mass merchandisers. Over time, IRI has also created a huge secondary database. With this database, IRI has examined 780 brands in 116 different packaged-goods product categories. The company has, in essence, what it refers to as thousands and thousands of "naturally occurring experiments"—that is, hundreds of thousands of data points relating weekly sales to price reductions and merchandising activity.

Using this database, IRI researchers were able to look at various marketing mixes and competitive situations and determine the results of managerial decision making. For example, they looked at the weekly sales of an average brand in response to trade promotions. They found that a 10 percent price reduction, on average, led to a 20 percent sales increase during the week of the price reduction. A feature ad and a price reduction generated a 78 percent sales increase during the week of the promotion. An in-store display and a 10 percent price reduction doubled sales. An in-store display, a feature ad, and a 10 percent price reduction tripled sales.

Because of the availability of scanner-based data, physical audits at the retail level may someday all but disappear. Already the largest nonscanner-based wholesale audit company, SAMI, has gone out of business and sold its client list to IRI. Nor does Nielsen use auditors in grocery stores any longer. Nielsen still uses both auditors and scanner data for other types of retail outlets but will probably shift to scanner data alone when most retailers within a store category (such as hardware stores or drugstores) install scanners.

## SCANNER WARS: IRI VERSUS NIELSEN

The scanner data market is the most rapidly growing area of the marketing research industry, with revenues over $500 million in 1993. Kraft General Foods alone spends over $25 million a year for scanner data.[25] Like two heavyweight boxers, IRI and Nielsen are continually punching and counterpunching each other, seeking a competitive advantage that will sway buyers in this attractive market.

A major difference between IRI and Nielsen is the way the data are gathered. IRI scanner panel members present to the retailer an ID card, which has a bar code identifying the household making the purchase. Thus the data are captured at retail sites. Nielsen used a similar system consisting of 15,000 households until 1991 but then replaced its in-store panel with an in-home panel of 40,000 consumers, who use a special scanner at home and transmit the data by a modem. About 4,500 panel members will be connected to Nielsen's Monitor Plus TV program for tracking viewing using a people meter. Nielsen claims its panel will measure all geographic locations. Also, by using home scanners, the system does not depend on retailers' cooperation. Nielsen's panel covers some 1,147 counties, whereas IRI covers only 30 counties. Andy Tarshis, former president of Nielsen, says, "Can households in 30 counties be representative of the total United States?"[26] The new system has other benefits as well, according to Tarshis:

> "By increasing our panel nearly threefold, our ability to do additional analysis increases maybe tenfold," he said. "For example, warehouse clubs are becoming popular, but not everyone is a member. But by expanding our panel to 40,000, the number of households buying at the clubs may be 5,000, which is a much more usable number than we get from 15,000 households."
>
> The same is true for marketers interested in data from minorities. For example, 6 percent of the panel is Hispanic households; as the panel expands, that percentage becomes "a base large enough for us to do dramatically more analysis. We can compare Hispanic household trends on the East Coast vs. the West Coast or even look at a single market," Mr. Tarshis said. Nielsen intends to maintain at least 12 percent of the panel as black households, also enabling expanded analysis of that group.[27]

IRI's InfoScan has historically relied on cooperating supermarkets to supply scanner data. To counter Nielsen, IRI added 600 drugstores, such as Walgreens, Eckerd, and Drug Emporium. The company also added mass merchandisers, including Wal-Mart, Kmart, and Target. This move

MARKETING AND SMALL BUSINESS

### Marketing Research for Small Companies

Because most small businesses have limited financial resources and expertise, they often conclude that doing marketing research and creating an information system isn't worth the cost. Instead, managers of small businesses may rely on hunches or intuition when designing their marketing mix. In the absence of feedback from their customers, they sometimes institute practices that customers object to. Over time, the customer base begins to erode.

Many small-business owners who feel they are doing an outstanding job are unaware of the serious problems confronting them in the area of customer relations. For example, the owner-manager of a car dealership in a small community had this policy: "to present a high-volume, low-price dealership that has a reputation for good service." However, a random survey of customers who had used his service department showed they were dissatisfied and would no longer do business with him.

Marketing research could help small businesses avoid similar misapprehensions. However, "turn-key" marketing research projects, in which a research firm conducts the entire study and makes recommendations, tend to be expensive. A much less expensive alternative is for the small business to do everything but the interviewing, which can be assigned to a market research field service. Perhaps the owner and employees can do the interviewing. Or perhaps an inexpensive mail survey would be better than personal interviews. Another money-saving idea is to create a simple database from customer information cards gathered by offering a drawing for a free lunch or prize. A Polk's Crisscross Directory could be used to get the names and phone numbers of persons living nearby. Also, on-line databases are well within the budget of most small businesses.

was made because only 40 percent of health and beauty aids are sold in supermarkets. Another 40 percent are sold through drugstores, with the remaining 20 percent sold in mass-merchandise outlets.[28] The new IRI sample, therefore, fills out the consumer packaged-goods universe. Recently IRI provided its InfoScan panel members with a "keychain scanner," a portable, pocket-size wand to register product purchases made at nonscanner stores.

And so the battle continues. Some scanner data users give Nielsen the edge in data capture and IRI the software advantage.

### THE FUTURE OF SCANNING

Scanning has become a strategic tool of the highest order. Many marketing research departments have split off scanning, along with its delivery systems and applications, and renamed the function "information management." In fact, in many of these companies information management is no longer part of the marketing research department; it now has its own director or vice president who reports directly to top management.

In these companies the information management function oversees more than just scanning. Other databases may include the company's consumers and trade customers, factory shipments, financial and cost data, and competitive intelligence. A top division executive of one manufacturer estimates that one-third to one-half of its gains in the past several years can be attributed directly to these advanced information technologies.[29]

Scanners themselves are also changing. The next generation of scanners, to be known as Scanner Plus, will have abilities far beyond those of today's machines. These scanners will be able to communicate with personal computers in homes. One function could be to analyze an individual household's consumption based on its prior purchase patterns and to offer menu projections or product use suggestions with an associated shopping list. To encourage the use of that shopping list, special offers may be made on certain listed items. These special offers could be designed for each household, rather than offered to everyone at the same time.

Scanner Plus may also keep track of each household's coupons and the other special offers received directly from advertisers. These offers will simply be entered into the household's electronic account in its personal computer as well as in its "promotion" bank in Scanner Plus. An example of a similar system already in use is the Vision Value card offered by Big Bear Supermarkets in Ohio. It combines scanning with the computerized equivalent of "green stamps" to provide consumers with coupons for products they actually use.[30]

*6 Explain when marketing research should and should not be conducted.*

## WHEN SHOULD MARKETING RESEARCH BE CONDUCTED?

When managers have several possible solutions to a problem, they should not instinctively call for marketing research. In fact, the first decision to make is whether to conduct marketing research at all.

Some companies have been conducting research in certain markets for many years. Such firms understand the characteristics of target customers and their likes and dislikes about existing products. Under these circumstances, further research would be repetitive and waste money. Procter & Gamble, for example, has extensive knowledge of the coffee market. After it conducted initial taste tests with Folger's Instant Coffee, P&G went into national distribution without further research. Consolidated Foods Kitchen of Sara Lee followed the same strategy with its frozen croissants, as did Quaker Oats with Chewy Granola Bars. This tactic, however, does not always work. P&G marketers thought they understood the pain reliever market thoroughly, so they bypassed market research for Encaprin aspirin in capsules. Because it lacked a distinct competitive advantage over existing products, however, the product failed and was withdrawn from the market.

Managers rarely have such great trust in their judgment that they would refuse more information if it were available and free. But they might have enough confidence that they would be unwilling to pay very much for the information or to wait a long time to receive it. The willingness to acquire additional decision-making information depends on managers' perceptions of its quality, price, and timing. Of course, if perfect information were available—that is, the data conclusively showed which alternative to choose—decision makers would be willing to pay more for it than for information that still left uncertainty. In summary, research should only be undertaken when the expected value of the information is greater than the cost of obtaining it.

## LOOKING BACK

Look back at the story about Keep America Beautiful (KAB) that appeared at the beginning of this chapter. You have seen that marketing research provides data to help managers make better decisions. KAB used marketing research to create a very successful new advertisement. Marketing research can also provide clues when a marketing mix fails, as in the example of Reynolds's colored plastic wrap.

Key marketing data often come from a company's own decision support system, which continually gathers data from a variety of sources and funnels it to decision makers. They then manipulate the data to make better decisions. DSS data are often supplemented by marketing research information. This chapter described a variety of survey research techniques, from focus groups to telephone surveys. Other important tools of marketing research are observation research and experiments.

## SUMMARY

**KEY TERMS**

*audit 233*

*BehaviorScan 238*

*central-location telephone (CLT) facility 228*

*closed-ended question 230*

*computer-assisted interviewing 228*

*convenience sample 235*

*cross-tabulation 237*

*database marketing 214*

*decision support system (DSS) 213*

*experiment 234*

1 **Explain the the concept and purpose of a marketing decision support system.** Decision support systems make data instantly available to marketing managers and allow them to manipulate the data themselves to make marketing decisions. Four characteristics of decision support systems make them especially useful to marketing managers: They are interactive, flexible, discovery-oriented, and accessible. Decision support systems give managers access to information immediately and without outside assistance. They allow users to manipulate data in a variety of ways and to answer "what if" questions. And finally, they are accessible to novice computer users.

2 **Discuss the nature of database marketing and micromarketing.** A marketing database is part of a decision support system composed of present and potential customers' profiles and purchasing patterns. Micromarketing is the creation of a large database of customers' and potential customers' profiles and purchasing patterns in order to target households or even individuals. Micromarketing has several important functions. It identifies the potential profitability of specific customers and market

segments. It helps determine effective packaging and pricing strategies for specific market segments. Furthermore, it provides insights into market opportunities for new products and services.

3 **Define marketing research, and explain its importance to marketing decision making.** Marketing research is a process of collecting and analyzing data for the purpose of solving specific marketing problems. Marketers use marketing research to explore the profitability of marketing strategies. They can examine why particular strategies failed and analyze characteristics of specific market segments. Moreover, marketing research allows management to behave proactively rather than reactively, by identifying newly emerging patterns in society and the economy.

4 **Describe the steps involved in conducting a marketing research project.** The marketing research process involves several basic steps. First, the researcher and the decision maker must agree on a problem statement or set of research objectives. Sometimes this step requires a background investigation referred to as a situation analysis, usually drawn partly from secondary sources. The researcher then creates an overall research design to specify how primary data will be gathered and analyzed. Before collecting data, the researcher decides whether the group to be interviewed will be a probability or nonprobability sample. Field service firms are often hired to carry out data collection. Once data have been collected, the researcher analyzes them using statistical analysis. The researcher than prepares and presents oral and written reports, with conclusions and recommendations, to management. As a final step, the researcher determines whether the recommendations were implemented and what could have been done to make the project more successful.

5 **Discuss the growing importance of single-source research.** A single-source research system enables marketers to monitor a market panel's exposure and reaction to such variables as advertising, coupons, store displays, packaging, and price. By analyzing these variables in relation to the panel's subsequent buying behavior, marketers gain useful insight into sales and marketing strategies.

6 **Explain when marketing research should and should not be conducted.** Marketing research helps managers by providing data to make better marketing decisions. However, firms must consider whether the expected benefits of marketing research outweigh its costs. Before approving a research budget, management also should make sure adequate decision-making information doesn't already exist.

## Discussion and Writing Questions

1. One of your employees says, "Marketing research is too expensive, so the company will just have to get by without it." As the manager of a small business, write a memo in reply.
2. How can marketing research help the manager of a service organization? List specific examples for a car rental agency, airline, hotel, and hospital.
3. In analyzing research findings, why is it important to know the methodology used? Provide an example.
4. What could cause a new-product failure despite sound marketing research?
5. Your firm is about to conduct a mail survey. In a memo to the marketing manager, suggest some strategies to encourage response.
6. Discuss the advantages of observation research. Cite an example of a problem that could be solved using observation research.

7. Have you ever participated in a marketing research survey? Describe the experience. Would you say that the researcher was gathering high-quality information?

8. If you were a product manager, would you prefer using IRI or Nielsen for single-source data? Why?

### Application for Small Business

Pizza Heaven is a small, West Coast, independent pizza restaurant that caters primarily to college students. Accordingly, it is located near a campus and promotes its offerings extensively in the college newspaper. In the last year, Pizza Heaven sales have slipped, and management feels that the national chains such as Pizza Hut, Pizza Inn, and Domino's, along with several independent pizza restaurants, are making inroads into its market. Pizza Heaven has decided to conduct marketing research to determine its image among its customers and to see if the company needs to reposition itself or make any other changes.

#### Questions

1. Do you think a small business like Pizza Heaven really needs to conduct formal marketing research? Explain your answer.
2. If Pizza Heaven decides to do marketing research, what are some topics that should be covered in a questionnaire?
3. Who should be interviewed?
4. What survey methods should be considered?

## CRITICAL THINKING CASE

### National Research Group Inc.

In the wildly insecure world of movie executives, Joseph Farrell soothes anxieties. National Research Group Inc., the company he founded and runs, dominates the field of motion-picture research. Such research plays an ever-increasing role in the industry. NRG generates streams of data on everything from which films moviegoers plan to see to which movie ads are most effective. Almost every major film is screened several times in front of test audiences recruited by NRG, which then gathers, quantifies, and analyzes viewer reaction.

NRG research helps determine whether a movie gets promoted a lot or hardly at all. Film endings may be changed and scenes eliminated based on NRG findings. *The Bodyguard,* for instance, was reworked to include more action footage with Kevin Costner after preview screening data from NRG showed that young males were less enthusiastic about the film than their female counterparts. The movie went on to gross more than $400 million for Warner Bros.

NRG's numbers seem to give Hollywood a rare solid scale of measurement, a touchstone of objectivity in a business where big financial decisions are often made on the basis of hype, sizzle, and politics. "You nurture a project for a year or 18 months, and then you go to the first screening, and the lights come up and nobody looks at you. Everybody's looking at Joe Farrell," says Brandon Tartikoff, former chairman of Paramount Pictures.

Nevertheless, the relationship between NRG and the studios is delicate and ambiguous. Ask studio executives or movie producers if they are dependent on NRG, and they frequently avoid the question. Many directors and writers quietly resent the sway that NRG has gained over their creations. Even Hollywood tycoons want people to believe that they treat a movie like art rather than like a new brand of toothpaste.

NRG is the exclusive research firm for the film units of Viacom, Metro-Goldwyn-Mayer, Twentieth Century–Fox, Columbia Pictures, TriStar, and Walt Disney Company. It controls most of the business at Warner Bros. Of the major studios, only Universal doesn't use NRG for screenings, although it subscribes to some of NRG's other survey work.

Some have tried and failed to reduce NRG's influence. While chairman of Fox, Barry Diller—who has always been scornful of market research—became increasingly disenchanted with NRG. Finally, after NRG wrongly predicted that the 1989 hit *War of the Roses* would perform poorly, Diller angrily decreed that Fox would sever ties with NRG. Diller associates say that Joseph Farrell went to work behind the scenes and that, soon after, Fox executives began using NRG again.

In the often upside-down world of Hollywood, pinpoint accuracy isn't always the main thing studio executives seek from NRG. In a business where corporate fortunes and individual careers can ride on the outcome of a single film, executives look to NRG almost desperately for guidance, reassurance—and cover, if things go badly.



## Questions

1. "Producing a movie is an art—marketing research has no place in the world of art." Comment.
2. NRG used focus groups and self-administered questionnaires after a screening. What other techniques might have been used?
3. Can you see any role for decision support systems in Hollywood?

## Reference

Richard Turner and John Emshwiller, "Movie-Research Czar Is Said to Sell Manipulated Findings," *The Wall Street Journal*, 17 December 1993, pp. A1, A6.

**SIGNATURE SERIES CASE**

## Category Management Using Information Resources, Inc. Scanner-Based Information

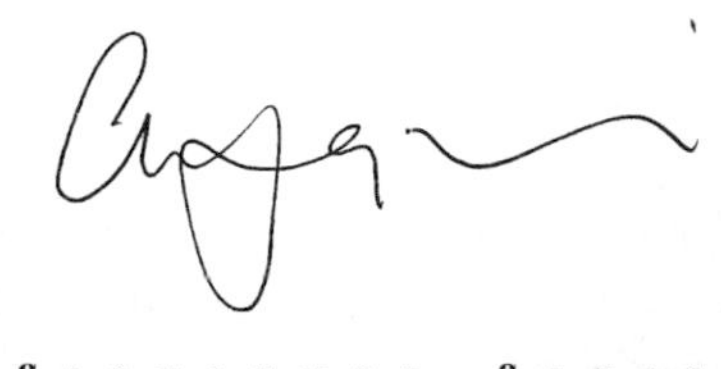

SIGNATURE SERIES

*by Gian M. Fulgoni*
*Chairman and Chief Executive Officer*
*Information Resources, Inc.*

Historically, marketing research had been viewed as a report card: How did the firm do last month? What was our market share? Which brands sold best in the Chicago territory? However, that began to change with the advent of weekly scanner-based data in the late 1980s.

Today, research information is being used by leading edge companies to guide their marketing efforts and increase their sales and profits in many different ways. One of the best examples of how information is being used is the emergence of fact-based selling strategies, in general, category management tactics, in particular. Category management is the sales and inventory management of a group of related products.

Fact-based selling, though simple in concept, requires a significant commitment to information and technology, because management must first have the facts and understand them thoroughly before managers can use them effectively.

Category management, in turn, uses scanner-generated facts and also demands a willingness to move away from a narrow focus on one's own dealer brands (Brand "A" Iced Tea, for example) toward a broader view of the entire product category (ready-to-drink tea). The appeal of the category management approach, which is being adopted by an increasing number of firms today, is that it will create true win/win scenarios for both the retailer and the manufacturer.

Category management techniques can impact sales in a number of ways: (1) by uncovering distribution opportunities; (2) by better utilization of shelf space; (3) by optimal pricing strategies; and (4) by more efficient promotional spending.

Some work Information Resources did with a ready-to-drink tea client illustrates the impact that one of these techniques, in this case a distribution analysis, can have. Following an examination of IRI sales data, the packaged goods manufacturer learned that one retail supermarket chain in a midwestern market was not carrying a number of its items, products that were selling quite well in the other stores in the market. The data also showed that if the retailer added these items to his product mix, and dropped some of the slower-selling items, overall sales of the ready-to-drink category in the grocery chain would increase. And, of course, the manufacturer's sales would increase as well, resulting in a win/win situation.

By analyzing sales results in those stores that carry the items, the manufacturer was able to bring the grocery chain a list of all ready-to-drink tea items that were not being stocked in its stores and the projected sales if the chain were to carry them. Shown below are the five largest sellers from that list and the projected sales of each of those items.

| Item | Projected Annual Sales |
|---|---|
| Brand A tropical iced tea 15.5 oz. | $ 65,600 |
| Brand A regular iced tea 15.5 oz. | 59,400 |
| Brand B raspberry iced tea 16 oz. | 53,500 |
| Brand A peach iced tea 64 oz. | 44,500 |
| Private label lemon iced 16 oz. | 43,400 |
| TOTAL PROJECTED SALES | $266,400 |

(Note the presence of a competitive item, Brand B's raspberry product, on the recommended list.)

A similar list of the items actually carried produced the five slowest selling items, whose total sales were only $31,300, and these were targeted for removal. (Although none of Brand A's products was among these slow moving products, fact-based selling would dictate that the manufacturer present the information to the retailer and, without any mitigating factors, recommend dropping even its own items.)

In this example, the retailer accepted the suggestions and looked forward to a sales increase in the ready-to-drink tea category of $235,100:

| | |
|---|---|
| New sales from new items | $266,400 |
| Lost sales from discontinued items | – 31,300 |
| Net impact on retailer's sales | $235,100 |

Of course IRI's client, Manufacturer A, also anticipated additional sales from his three items that were being added of $169,500 ($65,600 + $59,400 + $44,500).

The tremendous value of a scanner data fact-based approach to selling becomes clear when it is realized that this is the potential impact of **one** type of category management analysis on **one** category in **one** retail account. IRI's manufacturer clients can use this type of analysis for virtually any category with retailers across the country. And if a particular distribution opportunity doesn't exist at another retailer, the manufacturer could examine its shelf space allocation, consider pricing adjustments or review promotional programs. Each one a category management oriented approach based on scanner-data facts.

Those companies who can gather, analyze, and apply information most efficiently will be the market leaders of tomorrow. Marketing research, no longer a simple report on the past, provides the facts to guide the way into that future.

Questions

1. How does scanner-based data provide insights into the future?

2. Why would a manufacturer recommend a competitor's product using category management?

3. What other ways can scanner-based data be used by managers?

**VIDEO CASE**

## Bon-Ton Department Stores

Bon-Ton Department Stores, a Pennsylvania-based chain, decided that it needed a better understanding of the marketplace. A nationally known marketing research firm was hired to determine what customers think of Bon-Ton, how well they like shopping at Bon-Ton, how high the general level of customer satisfaction is, and what attitudes are toward competing department stores. Bon-Ton shoppers were perceived as 25 to 40 years old, female, and professional.

Focus groups were convened in four Bon-Ton markets in Pennsylvania: Greensburg, Harrisburg, York, and Wilkes-Barre. To "loosen up" respondents and begin the conversation, they were asked, "Why do you go shopping?" Among the reasons offered by respondents were these: They saw advertisements announcing a sale, they were seeking a bargain, they were bored, they get a feeling of control from buying something, they shop to keep up with the latest styles, and they shop to reward themselves after going through a bad experience (such as going to the dentist). One woman said she lives alone and doesn't always want to go home after work, so she goes shopping instead.

Another said, "If I'm uptight after work, I'll go shopping to relax." Asking respondents why they go shopping helped to get them thinking about the shopping experience.

Bon-Ton itself was viewed as friendly, well decorated, and stocked with quality, name-brand merchandise for all age groups. The chain was also characterized as computerized, a little homey, but also classy. On the negative side, one person said a gift box from Bon-Ton was "nothing special." Another said that the merchandising wasn't consistent; what was available one week might not be there the next. Yet another said goods were often too crowded together and seemed shopworn. In general, however, the image was positive.

The focus group sessions were followed by a telephone survey of a representative sample of Bon-Ton shoppers.

### Questions

1. Poll fellow students on why they like to shop. What additional reasons for shopping can you uncover?
2. The focus groups revealed a generally positive image for Bon-Ton. Why would the company want to follow up with a telephone survey?
3. What courses of action are suggested by the data from the telephone survey?
4. Was the sample for the telephone survey drawn from the right population? Why or why not?

# CHAPTER 8

# CUSTOMER VALUE AND QUALITY

## LEARNING OBJECTIVES

*After studying this chapter, you should be able to*

1 *Define customer value.*

2 *Describe the customer value triad.*

3 *Describe the techniques of total quality management.*

4 *Describe the roles of management, employees, and suppliers in total quality management.*

5 *Describe the Malcolm Baldrige National Quality Award.*

6 *Discuss the three categories of services.*

7 *Describe the components of service quality.*

8 *Explain the gap model of service quality.*

9 *Discuss the components of value-based pricing.*

10 *Explain the two-factor model of customer satisfaction.*

New car buyers at a New Jersey Chevrolet dealership are invited to an evening seminar for a detailed explanation of their car and its warranty. They are offered coffee and pastries, their questions are answered, and they go home with a certificate for a free oil change.

This is just one example of the simple formula now being tried by many Chevrolet dealers: Make customers happy. That goal, although it may seem obvious, hasn't always been taken seriously by automobile dealers, who consistently rank at or near the bottom in consumer polls on trustworthiness. Looking at the success of General Motors' Saturn division and Toyota's Lexus, Chevy is now making customer satisfaction the focus of a full-scale makeover.

Chevrolet has always been an important General Motors division. But a number of poorly built products and marketing mistakes in the 1980s caused Chevy's market share to plummet. Now, however, Chevy's sales are starting to rise. Chevy officials attribute this increase to the new focus on customers and to a "value pricing" strategy. Chevy is also rolling out several new cars and trucks. It introduced a redesigned Camaro, a new S-10 series of compact pickup trucks, and new Cavalier and Geo Metro subcompacts in 1994. Chevrolet unveiled the Impala SS sedan and redesigned Lumina and Monte Carlo models in 1995.

The key, however, is the customer satisfaction program, which takes inspiration from about 160 companies Chevrolet has studied, including Walt Disney and Federal Express. Chevrolet has designated its workers "customer enthusiasm officers," which means they are responsible for helping the company better serve the needs of its buyers. The division also offers free transportation to buyers who bring their vehicles to Chevy dealerships for warranty service. Analysts and dealers say Chevrolet isn't breaking any new ground with such services. However, they add, Chevy's efforts show that it is serious about customer service.[1]

What is Chevrolet doing to offer customers better value? Why do you think it is studying customer satisfaction programs in other industries? What are some other things you think Chevrolet could do to offer more value to customers?

1 *Define customer value.*

## WHAT IS CUSTOMER VALUE?

Companies today are facing accelerating change in many areas, including better-educated and more-demanding consumers, new technology, and globalization of markets. As a result, competition is the toughest it has ever been. More and more, the key to building and sustaining a long-range competitive advantage is the commitment to delivering superior customer value, as the Chevrolet example in the opening story illustrates.

In Chapter 1 customer value was defined as the customer's perception of the ratio of benefits to the sacrifice necessary to obtain those benefits. Customers receive benefits from quality goods and services. To receive those benefits, they give up money, time, and effort.

For customer value to be a competitive advantage, it must be the focus of all the employees in a company, not just the marketing department. Take the example of Southwest Airlines. People fly Southwest because the airline offers superior value. Although passengers do not get assigned seats or meals (just peanuts or crackers) when they use the airline, its service is reliable and friendly and costs less than most major airlines. All Southwest employees are involved in the effort to satisfy customers. Pilots man the boarding gate when their help is needed, and ticket agents help move luggage. One reservation agent flew from Dallas to Tulsa with a frail, elderly woman whose son was afraid she couldn't handle the plane change by herself on her way to St. Louis.[2]

Customer value is not simply a matter of high quality or a low price. A high-quality product that is available only at a high price will not be perceived as a value. Nor will bare-bones service or low-quality goods selling for a low price. Instead, customers value goods and services of the quality they expect that are sold at prices they are willing to pay. Value marketing can be used to sell a $44,000 Nissan Infiniti Q45 as well as a $3 Tyson frozen chicken dinner.

Marketers interested in customer value

- *Offer products that perform:* This is the bare minimum. Consumers have lost patience with shoddy merchandise.
- *Give consumers more than they expect:* Soon after Toyota launched Lexus, the company had to order a recall. The weekend before the recall, dealers phoned all the Lexus owners in the United States, personally making arrangements to pick up their cars and offering replacement vehicles.
- *Give meaningful guarantees:* Chrysler offers a 70,000-mile power train warranty. Michelin introduced a tire warranted to last 80,000 miles. Both warranties exceed the norm and thus seem more meaningful.
- *Avoid unrealistic pricing:* Consumers couldn't understand why Kellogg's cereals commanded a premium over other brands, and so Kellogg's market share fell 5 percent in the late 1980s.
- *Give the buyer facts:* Today's sophisticated consumer wants informative advertising and knowledgeable salespeople.
- *Build long-term relationships:* American Airlines' AAdvantage frequent-flyer program, Hyatt's Passport Club for repeat guests, and Whirlpool's 800-number hot line for owners of its appliances all maintain links with customers.[3]

The current emphasis on customer value evolved from the "total quality" programs (discussed in more detail later in the chapter) that were popular in the 1980s.

Despite Southwest Airlines' "no-frills" service, its flights are considered a good value because of what customers get for their money. All employees, not just cabin attendants, are committed to satisfying customers' expectations.

Courtesy of Southwest Airlines

These programs mainly tried to improve product quality by improving production processes. Other customer requirements usually got much less attention. For example, Varian Associates, a maker of scientific equipment, adopted quality principles in a number of areas. Its unit that makes vacuum systems for computer clean rooms increased on-time delivery of its products from 42 to 92 percent. But while Varian was obsessed with meeting production schedules, the staff in the vacuum-equipment unit did not return customers' phone calls, and the operation ended up losing market share. Similarly, Varian's radiation equipment service department ranked first in its industry for prompt customer visits. However, the radiation-repair people were so rushed to meet deadlines that they left before explaining their work to customers. The imbalance in approach had a direct effect on the company's bottom line. After a $32 million profit in 1989, Varian's sales grew by only 3 percent in 1990, and the company posted a $4.1 million loss.[4]

Today the most competitive companies are the ones that look beyond the quality of the goods they produce. Better product designs and faster manufacturing are always desirable, but the new perspective goes beyond the narrow quality standards of the past. Instead, managers are trying to ensure that the quality they offer is the quality their customers want to pay for. Relationship marketing, which was discussed in Chapter 1, is often the tool they use to establish customer wants. Smart managers are also starting to use financial tools to make sure quality programs have a payoff—a "return on quality" approach.

After its disappointing experiences with total quality programs, Varian now looks for less expensive ways to please customers and boost quality. When customers complained about the long time needed to set up Varian's radiology equipment at hospitals, the company painstakingly investigated several hundred possible solutions. In the end, Varian decided to change some of its procedures—for example, shipping cables in plastic bags rather than using "popcorn" filler as it had been. This one change saved customers thirty minutes of cleanup time. The company also redesigned key parts to make them fit together more easily. Varian's delighted customers saved an average of ninety-five hours in setup time, worth $50,000 per order to hospitals. Varian also saved $1.8 million a year for itself.

2 *Describe the customer value triad.*

## THE CUSTOMER VALUE TRIAD

**customer value triad**
Goods quality, service quality, and value-based prices—the components of customer value.

To maximize customer value, a firm must know if it is meeting customers' expectations. Real customer value is defined by the customer, not the organization, and can therefore be ambiguous. A useful framework for understanding what customers want is the **customer value triad.**[5] As Exhibit 8.1 shows, the three legs of the triad are perceived goods quality, perceived service quality, and value-based prices. Goods quality and service quality are at the base of the triangle, indicating that they support value-based prices.

Customer value is created when customer expectations in each of the three areas are met or exceeded. A company that fails to meet customer expectations in any one of the three areas is not delivering good customer value. Consider the recent problems at Compaq Computer, which had initially created a niche in portable personal computers. Compaq's goods quality and service quality were good, justifying premium prices 30 to 35 percent higher than the competition's. Compaq's customers believed that they were getting good value. But then Compaq became less responsive to change than competitors were. IBM personal computers, and IBM clones at even lower prices, closed the technological gap. Customers could no longer justify the price premium charged by Compaq, because competitive products conveyed better value. Compaq's goods quality did not deteriorate; the firm still made good computers. Compaq's service did not deteriorate; it still was viewed as very reliable. But the third leg of the value triad—price—was out of line with the other two. As a result, Compaq's sales and profits plummeted.

Although goods quality and service quality are presented as separate parts of the customer value triad, the differences between goods and services are not always clear from a customer's viewpoint. Almost every tangible good has some service associated with it. U.S. auto companies, for example, have typically produced stylish cars. However, customers perceive quality also in terms of the level of service they get from dealerships, and the lackadaisical service that once plagued U.S. nameplates made them vulnerable to Japanese carmakers.[6]

It is also hard to think of a service that doesn't include tangible goods. A restaurant is a service firm, but does anyone doubt that the quality of associated goods (the food) is important? The same can be said for health care, hospitality and

*Exhibit 8.1*

Customer Value Triad

Source: Adapted from Earl Naumann, *Creating Customer Value* (Cincinnati, OH: Thomson Executive Press, 1994), p. 17.

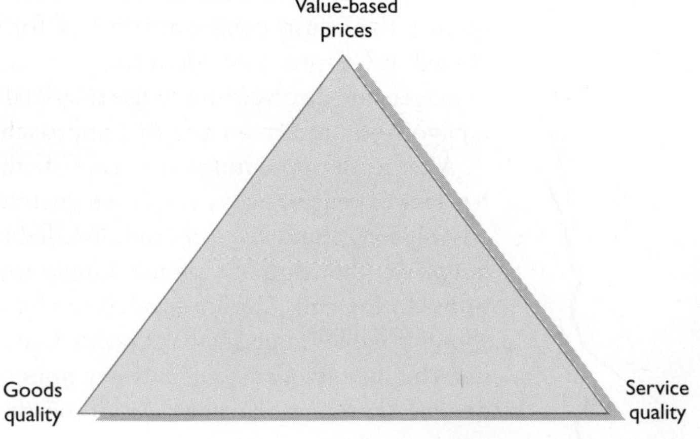

tourism, insurance, and other services. Anyone who has ever had a "bad" haircut, hairstyling, or permanent can readily discuss the goods quality of a service.

Customers tend to bundle price, goods attributes, perceived goods quality, service attributes, and perceived service quality throughout the product's life and attach some value to the bundle. The bundle is then compared to competitive alternatives, and the "best value" is selected. Firms that focus on only one or two dimensions of the customer value triad and neglect the third may thus experience the same difficulties as Compaq.

3 *Describe the techniques of total quality management.*

## GOODS QUALITY: TOTAL QUALITY MANAGEMENT

Of the three elements of the customer value triad, goods quality has received the most attention over the past decade. The quality movement was easily the most important strategic issue of the 1980s and has probably been the most important business concept of the past twenty or thirty years. The organizational philosophy underlying the quality movement is **total quality management** (TQM). TQM is the coordination, throughout the entire organization, of efforts to provide high-quality goods and processes in order to ensure customer satisfaction.

**total quality management (TQM)**
Coordination, throughout the entire organization, of efforts to provide high-quality goods, processes, and services in order to ensure customer satisfaction.

Like the marketing concept, TQM programs are based on the need to understand customer requirements. Thus marketing plays an important role in TQM, and traditional marketing techniques are often used to support the quality focus. For example, marketers know how to create an ongoing dialogue with customers using such techniques as focus groups and customer surveys.

The key idea in TQM is that quality is important at every step of the production process. In contrast, earlier efforts at quality control relied on inspection of the finished goods. TQM strives to eliminate defects from the beginning. A good is inspected at the design stage, and the manufacturing process is engineered to be stable and reliable. Good design and good process result in a high-quality product.

Until recently, many managers were convinced that higher quality costs more. However, companies have come to realize that it costs more to do things poorly and then pay to fix problems than it does to do things right the first time. In addition, greater productivity can result from doing things better. In a firm that relies on inspection for quality control, more than half of all workers may be involved in finding and reworking defective goods. The total investment in this process may account for 20 to 50 percent of production costs.[7] Companies that use a TQM approach, however, have an advantage over competitors of up to 10¢ on every sales dollar. Cabot Corporation, for example, saved $1 million a year and freed up new production capacity by reducing defects at one of its carbon-black plants by 90 percent over a two-year period.[8] Electrolux, a Swedish appliance maker, was able to reduce field-service repairs by 40 percent as a result of changes in design methods and other work processes.[9]

Attention to quality standards has become a significant factor in the global marketplace. For example, the European Union has established **ISO 9000** standards for quality management. These standards,which are being met by many non-European companies, are discussed in the accompanying Global Perspectives box (see the Creating Customer Value box in Chapter 3 as well).

**ISO 9000**
European Union's standards for quality assurance procedures, controls, and documentation.

### ESSENTIAL TQM TECHNIQUES

Several techniques used in the TQM approach distinguish it from traditional ways of doing business. These techniques include quality function deployment, continuous

GLOBAL PERSPECTIVES

### Rice Aircraft

Faced with shrinking sales, Rice Aircraft, an aircraft maintenance company, discovered an unusual survival strategy: compliance with international quality control standards. The ISO 9000 rules, drawn up by the International Standards Organization in Geneva, Switzerland, have been endorsed in about sixty countries. The rules, which spell out how companies should set up their quality assurance systems, focus on procedures, controls, and documentation. The standards are partly designed to assure customers that a company can consistently perform its functions well. Increasingly, U.S. companies realize that they must meet these voluntary standards to compete for business abroad and even to win domestic contracts from U.S.-based multinational companies.

Rice Aircraft doesn't make any of the 60,000 items, mostly fasteners, that it stocks. It adopted the ISO 9000 standards to ensure that orders are filled precisely and promptly. To meet the rules, Rice had to write up detailed procedures for every job and then make sure that employees followed them. The exercise can be excruciating. In writing for the new office manuals, for example, a Rice sales executive in Florida first submitted a two-page summary of her role. By the time the company was satisfied with her document, it had ballooned to forty-five pages. The compliance process "leaves nothing to chance," a Rice executive says.

Rice's new obsession with quality has improved profit margins and helped to win significant new aircraft maintenance business from previously elusive customers. For instance, Rice won a $3 million contract with American Airlines, which was impressed that such a small company was meeting international quality standards.[10]

What is the purpose of the ISO 9000 series of rules? Why did Rice Aircraft implement a strategy to comply with them? Do you think compliance with the rules is going to be necessary in the future for any business wishing to compete globally?

improvement, reduced cycle time, and analysis of process problems.

## Quality Function Deployment

**Quality function deployment** (QFD) is a technique that helps companies translate customer design requirements into product specifications. It is a way for companies to stay close to customers and build their expectations into products.

The QFD quality chart, or matrix, relates what customers want with how goods will be designed and produced to satisfy those wants. An example of a QFD matrix for Writesharp, a pencil maker, is shown in Exhibit 8.2. All the customer expectations that have been identified through research are listed in order of importance on the upper portion of the left side of the chart. Across the top of the chart are listed functional characteristics of the good (pencils), as well as customer satisfaction ratings of Writesharp and two competitors. At each place on the chart where expectation items and functional characteristics intersect, product designers have assigned a value that represents how closely the good meets customer expectations. The QFD chart thus provides customer-based guidelines for developing the best design.

**quality function deployment (QFD)**
Technique that helps companies translate customer requirements into goods specifications by using a quality matrix to relate what customers want with how goods will be designed.

**benchmarking**
Rating a product against the world's best products of all types.

Along with the QFD dimensions, the matrix also incorporates **benchmarking,** which is the process of rating a company's products against the best products in the world, including those in other industries. "The best" includes both functional characteristics of products and customer satisfaction ratings. Benchmarking allows a firm to set performance targets and continuously reach toward those targets. In the example, the functional characteristics of Writesharp pencils (pencil length, time between sharpenings, lead dust, and hexagonality) are benchmarked (on the bottom left-hand side of the matrix) against those characteristics in competitor X's and competitor Y's pencils. Similarly, customer satisfaction benchmarks (is easy to hold, does not smear, keeps a point, does not roll) are ranked at the top right-hand side of the matrix. Looking at both sets of benchmarks and the inner grid that compares functional characteristics with customer expectations, decision makers can see that the improvement with the biggest potential is a better-quality lead that lasts longer and generates less dust.[11]

| | | Functional characteristics | | | | | Customer satisfaction | | | |
|---|---|---|---|---|---|---|---|---|---|---|
| | | Pencil length (inches) | Time between sharpenings (written lines) | Lead dust (particles per line) | Hexagonality | Importance rating (5 = highest) | Writesharp (now) | Competitor X (now) | Competitor Y (now) | Writesharp (target) |
| Customer expectations | Is easy to hold | ● | | | ● | 3 | 4 | 3 | 3 | 4 |
| | Does not smear | | ● | ○ | | 4 | 5 | 4 | 5 | 5 |
| | Keeps a point | ● | ○ | ● | | 5 | 4 | 5 | 3 | 5 |
| | Does not roll | ● | | | ○ | 2 | 3 | 3 | 3 | 4 |
| Benchmarks | Writesharp (now) | 5% | 56% | 10% | 70% | | | | | |
| | Competitor X (now) | 5 | 84 | 12 | 80 | | | | | |
| | Competitor Y (now) | 4 | 41 | 10 | 60 | | | | | |
| | Writesharp (target) | 5.5 | 100 | 6 | 80 | | | | | |

○ Strong correlation

● Some correlation

● Possible correlation

Customer satisfaction scale: 1 to 5 (5 = best)

*Exhibit 8.2*

Quality Function Deployment Matrix

Source: Adapted from Robert Neff, "No. 1—and Trying Harder," *Business Week*, 25 October 1991, p. 23. Reprinted from October 25, 1991 issue of *Business Week* by special permission. Copyright 1991 by McGraw-Hill, Inc.

## Continuous Improvement

**continuous improvement**
Commitment to constantly seek ways to do things better.

**Continuous improvement** is a commitment to constantly seek ways of doing things better in order to maintain quality. Management tries to prevent problems and systematically improve key processes instead of troubleshooting problems as they occur. Continuous improvement also includes finding ways to reduce the time between when a product is first conceived and when it is available for purchase, looking for innovation, and continually measuring performance. TQM thus becomes a never-ending journey rather than a destination.

One of the first steps in implementing continuous improvement is identifying the organization's key processes. Xerox, for example, defined the ten key processes shown in Exhibit 8.3 on page 256. Then each process is carefully analyzed for problems that might affect the quality of products or customers' perceptions of value.

**poka-yoke**
Japanese concept that means finding ways to minimize human error by changing the design.

Designing processes to reduce the potential for mistakes is another form of continuous improvement. ***Poka-yoke,*** a Japanese concept, means finding ways to minimize human error by changing the design. United Electric Controls, a producer of industrial sensors and controls, added beveled edges to its parts so they can only be assembled the correct way. This change allowed the company to reduce delivery times from twelve weeks to three weeks.[12]

## Reduced Cycle Time

**cycle time**
Time from when production begins until the good is received by the customer.

One of the most effective ways to improve the quality of both goods and services is to reduce **cycle time,** which is the time from when production begins until the good

*Exhibit 8.3*

Xerox's Ten Key Business Process Areas

Source: Adapted from Arthur R. Tenner and Irving J. DeToro, *Total Quality Management* (Reading, MA: Addison-Wesley, 1992), p. 102. © 1992 by Addison-Wesley Publishing Company, Inc. Reprinted with permission of the publisher.

| Line functions | Supporting functions |
|---|---|
| Customer marketing | Financial management |
| Customer engagement | Physical asset management |
| Order fulfillment | Business management |
| Product maintenance | Information technology application |
| Billing and collection | Human resource management |

**lead time**
Time between when a customer places and receives an order.

is received by the customer. Companies with faster cycle times than their competitors can earn profits faster and can dramatically increase growth. For example, some manufacturing companies claim to need twenty to forty weeks of **lead time** (the time between when a customer places and receives an order) for delivery of parts that are manufactured in only eight to ten hours. Reducing these lead times improves customer service, increases quality (because parts are handled less), and results in higher profits.[13]

DuPont's Kalrez, a rubbery plastic, had a 90 percent market share in 1988, but Japanese competitors gained market share by offering better customer service. DuPont retaliated by shortening the time that it took to make Kalrez from seventy days to sixteen, cutting its order-filling lead times from forty days to sixteen, and increasing on-time deliveries from 70 percent to 100 percent. Within three years DuPont's Kalrez sales had gone up 22 percent.[14] Motorola Lighting (a subsidiary of Motorola that produces electronic lighting ballasts) cut redesign work that used to take three weeks down to two days, because production and design staff now work together to solve any problem that comes up.[15]

## Analysis of Process Problems

Firms that want to engage in continuous improvement need methods for identifying the causes of problems. Three tools that can be used for this are the following:

**statistical quality control (SQC)**
Method of analyzing deviations in manufactured materials, parts, and goods.

- ***Statistical quality control:*** Statistical quality control (SQC) is a method of analyzing deviations in manufactured materials, parts, and goods. It was pioneered by Dr. W. Edwards Deming, a leader in the TQM movement in Japan, who believed that a statistical understanding of systems allows accurate diagnosis and solution of problems. Data such as output per hour, percentages of defects, and the time each function takes are gathered and analyzed so improvements can be made.[16] SQC enables engineers to determine which errors are avoidable and which are not and to find the causes of the controllable problems.

**Pareto analysis**
Method for identifying a company's biggest problems that uses a bar chart to rank causes of variation in production or service processes by the degree of their impact on quality.

- ***Pareto analysis:*** This is a method for identifying a company's biggest problems. The chief tool of Pareto analysis is a bar chart that ranks the causes of variation in production or service processes by their impact on quality. Most companies find that the worst problems occur again and again. Thus, the most frequent problems can have the most negative impact on quality. The Pareto principle, espoused by Joseph M. Juran, a leader in the quality movement, is that 80 percent of the problems are due to 20 percent of the causes.[17] Pareto

*Exhibit 8.4*

Pareto Chart Showing Elements That Affect Customer Satisfaction for a Package Delivery Company

Source: Data from Donald L. Weintraub, "Implementing Total Quality Management," *Prism* (Cambridge, MA. Arthur D. Little, Inc.), First Quarter 1991, p. 32.

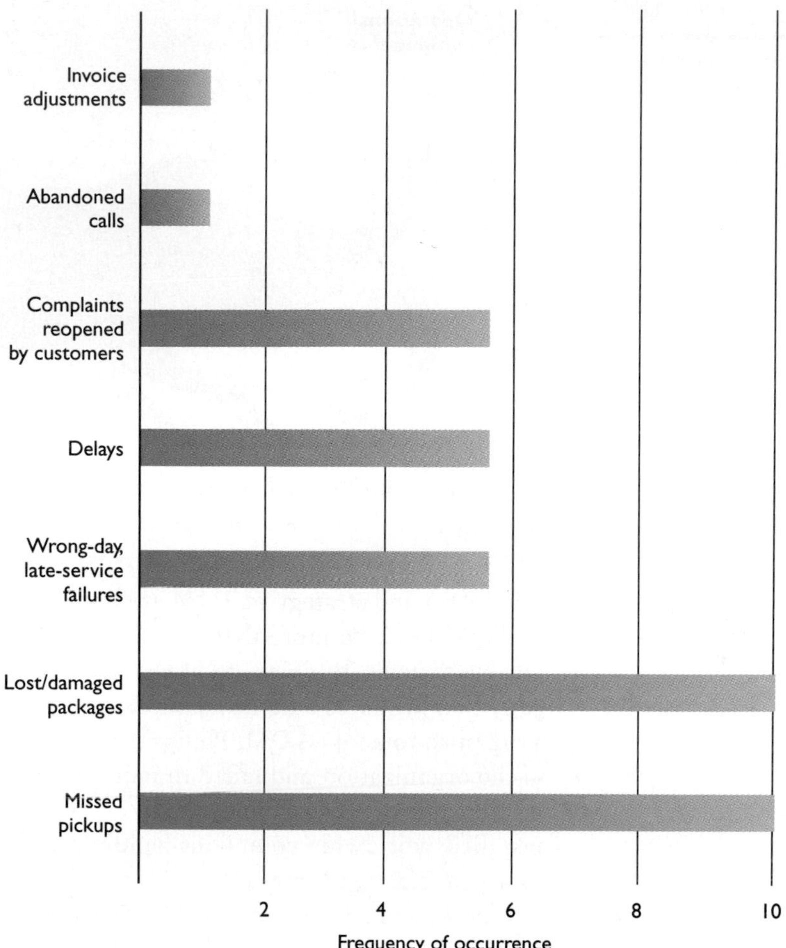


analysis directs management to concentrate on the biggest problems first. Then the next-most-frequent problems can be addressed, and so on, in a continuous attempt to improve quality. Exhibit 8.4 is an example of a Pareto chart for a package delivery company.

**fishbone diagram**
Graph resembling the skeleton of a fish that helps managers visualize cause-and-effect relationships for problems.

- ***Fishbone diagram:*** Once critical problems have been identified, management can determine their root causes. A fishbone diagram—so named because it resembles the skeleton of a fish—helps managers visualize cause-and-effect relationships for each problem. Exhibit 8.5 on page 258 is a simplified version of a fishbone diagram. The problem, or effect, identified by this diagram is order lead time. Its potential causes are operations such as labeling, order entry, pricing, and packaging. Information provided by the fishbone diagram can be used by management to identify areas where quality improvements need to be made.

All three of these tools help pinpoint problems and their causes. When the problems have been identified, they can systematically be attacked.

*4 Describe the roles of management, employees, and suppliers in total quality management.*

## TQM PARTICIPANTS

If TQM is to be successful, all divisions in a company and all employees must support the effort and participate. Top and middle management, employees, and suppliers all play an important role in making TQM work.

Exhibit 8.5

Fishbone Diagram Identifying Factors That Affect Order Lead Time

Source: Data from Tamara J. Erickson, "Beyond the Quality Revolution: Linking Quality to Corporate Strategy," *Prism* (Cambridge, MA. Arthur D. Little, Inc.), First Quarter 1991, p. 18.

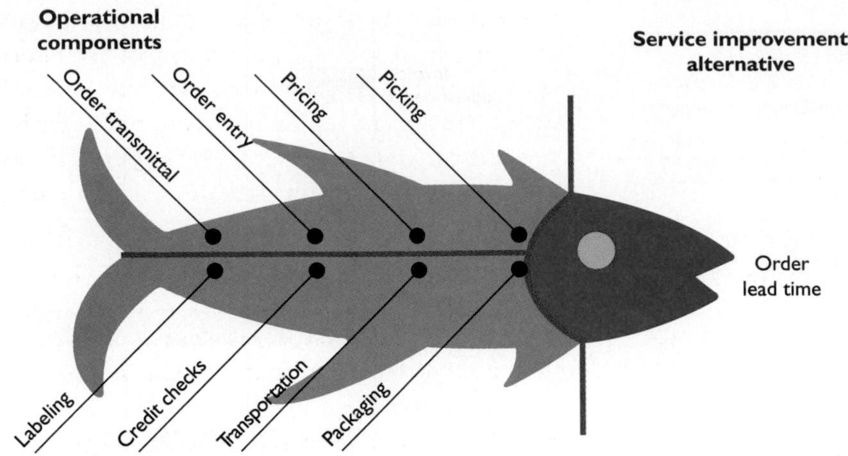


## Management

The vision and strategy of TQM are built by top management, whose commitment to TQM must be more than just lip service. Top management is responsible for putting systems into place to implement quality efforts. Philips Electronics, a company that produces auto headlamps, learned this lesson the hard way. After starting a big push to adopt TQM, Philips management left implementation to lower levels in the organization and failed to monitor the results of the program. Results were unsatisfactory until Philips finally brought top management into the picture, installed worldwide complaint-handling procedures, and began conducting customer satisfaction surveys.[18]

One way to gain top management's support for TQM is to provide compensation or benefits tied to TQM goals. U.S. Healthcare, a health-maintenance organization, surveys its members every year to see how they like their physicians. Incentive pay for physicians is then tied in part to their scores on these patient questionnaires.[19]

Top management's commitment to TQM should filter down to supervisory levels of management. Middle managers become the conduit between top management and the employees who have the most contact with customers. Middle managers also become involved in designing and implementing TQM programs for employees.

## Employees

Employee participation in TQM programs has three key ingredients:

- *Empowerment:* Empowering the work force—delegating decision-making authority to employees, as described in Chapter 1—encourages more positive attitudes toward the job, helps to reduce cycle time, and frees management to spend more time formulating strategy. Examples abound of the positive effects of empowerment. Ten years ago, at a Hewlett-Packard factory, 4 of every 1,000 soldered connections were defective. Engineers cut that rate in half by modifying the production process. But after the company turned the problem over to its workers, defects were reduced to under 2 of every 1 million—a thousandfold improvement.[20] At a Deere & Co. combine plant in Illinois, a worker, not a manager, arranges to fix defective parts delivered by suppliers.[21]
- *Teamwork:* Teamwork is achieved when people work together to reach a common goal. In TQM companies, teamwork means sharing both responsibility and decision making. Instead of competing with one another, as is common in many companies, employees work together. Eastman Kodak has established a

"patent process improvement team" that consists of inventors, laboratory managers, and attorneys. Lawyers meet with scientists during the experimental stage to discuss ways of increasing the chances of yielding a patentable product or process, rather than serving as "patent gatekeepers" at the end of the process. The result has been a 60 percent increase in patent submissions and a doubling of patents issued to the company each year.[22]

- *Training:* Training employees in quality techniques is a central part of TQM. Training helps employees understand the corporate mission, their jobs, and TQM principles and measurement tools. Marlow Industries, a Dallas firm that makes custom thermoelectric coolers, was the 1991 small-business winner of the Baldrige Award for quality. The average Marlow employee spent almost fifty hours in training in 1991. Thomas Interior Systems, a small Chicago-area firm that designs and resells office furnishings, spends an amount equal to 2.5 percent of its total annual payroll costs on education and training. Each Thomas employee is required to spend forty hours per year in training. This training takes place during employees' normal work schedules, and employees are paid their normal wage or salary for participating.[23]

## Suppliers

Companies that adopt TQM tend to encourage suppliers to start quality programs of their own. When one company is trying to produce defect-free output, it cannot tolerate defects in the materials and parts it buys from suppliers. Many firms are moving toward long-term contracts with fewer suppliers but are requiring better quality.[24]

The examples of suppliers' involvement in TQM are plentiful. Philips Electronics, the auto headlamp company mentioned earlier, began to focus on quality after it started supplying Toyota in the early 1980s. Pressure from Toyota forced Philips to change to a more exacting method for measuring quality than it had been using. This pressure led to packaging, manufacturing, and transportation improvements and vast savings in otherwise wasted material. In addition, defect levels dropped dramatically. By 1990, Philips had captured 60 percent of the Japanese market.[25] At the General Motors plant that makes the Buick LeSabre, managers and workers conduct weekly reviews of problem suppliers. About eighty suppliers have been dropped, many for not meeting LeSabre's quality goals.[26] Wilson Oxygen, a regional company in Austin, Texas, sells industrial products like welding supplies, beverage-dispensing systems, and industrial gases. Wilson has a quality evaluation team that works with suppliers to reduce costs by eliminating errors and improving service.[27]

*Prevention* magazine chose LeSabre for its "Safe Car Achievement Award." America chose it as their favorite full-size family car.

BUICK

Without the participation of its management, employees, and suppliers, Buick could not achieve the quality standards it touts in its advertising.

© GM Corporation

The concept of just-in-time (JIT) inventory management, which will be discussed in detail in Chapter 14, is also an example of how TQM has motivated closer cooperation between manufacturers and their suppliers. Quality is critical for suppliers of companies that use JIT, because poor-quality parts and supplies may not be detected if they are delivered at the last minute.

5 *Describe the Malcolm Baldrige National Quality Award.*

## THE MALCOLM BALDRIGE NATIONAL QUALITY AWARD

The Malcolm Baldrige National Quality Award, named for a former Secretary of Commerce, was established by the U.S. Congress in 1987.[28] The award program was inspired by Japan's Deming Prize for quality (named after U.S. quality expert W. Edwards Deming). The Baldrige Award recognizes U.S. companies that offer world-class quality in their goods and services. The award also promotes awareness of quality and transfers information about quality to others in the business community.

The Baldrige Award is administered by the U.S. Department of Commerce's National Institute of Standards and Technology. The Baldrige Award examination board is made up of professionals from business and industry, universities, health care organizations, and government agencies. The most important criterion of the Baldrige Award is whether the firm meets customer expectations. The customer must be No. 1. Examiners evaluate organizations in seven categories, which are described in Exhibit 8.6. To qualify for the award, a company must also show continuous improvement. Company leaders and employees must participate actively, and they must respond quickly to data and analysis.

Companies that have received the Baldrige Award include IBM, Federal Express, the Nuclear Fuel Division of Westinghouse, and—as discussed in the Creating Customer Value box—Xerox Business Products and Systems.

*Exhibit 8.6*

Criteria for the Malcolm Baldrige National Quality Award

Source: Adapted from application guidelines for the Malcolm Baldrige National Quality Award, U.S. Department of Commerce, National Institute for Standards and Technology, Gaithersburg, MD, 1987.

| Criterion | Maximum points | Indicators |
|---|---|---|
| Customer satisfaction | 300 | Commitment to customers, customer relationships, methods of resolving complaints, customer satisfaction results, etc. |
| Quality results | 150 | Supplier relationships, objective measures of quality, quality improvement, total quality picture |
| Human resource utilization | 150 | Training, employee involvement, performance evaluation, staff well-being (at all levels of work force, including upper and middle management) |
| Quality assurance of products and services | 140 | Process quality, continuous improvement, systematic approaches to assuring quality product |
| Leadership | 100 | Senior management's method of setting and maintaining goals and communicating them throughout the organization; social responsibility; values-driven management |
| Information and analysis | 70 | Data collection and analysis, quality of data collected, way company uses data to prevent problems |
| Strategic quality planning | 60 | Methods for setting quality-related goals, plans for meeting company goals in both short term (1–2 years) and longer term (3 years or more) |

6 *Discuss the three categories of services.*

## SERVICE QUALITY

Service quality is an important component of customer value. Indeed, business executives rank the improvement of service quality as one of the most critical challenges facing them today.[30] Thus organizations are looking for creative ways to increase service quality:

- Marriott is empowering many of its hotel employees to solve guests' problems.[31]
- Alaska Airlines, voted the best U.S. airline for three years running by *Condé Nast Traveler,* spends twice the U.S. per-passenger average on meals, provides more leg room, reduces delays due to heavy fog by using special guidance equipment, and encourages a team spirit among employees.[32]
- Humana has created quality action teams that help its hospital employees in their continuous effort to improve quality.[33]
- ServiceMaster trains its janitorial workers in every detail of their jobs, including how to stand straight, pull a mop toward them, and trace an S-shaped pattern on the floor.[34]

### CREATING CUSTOMER VALUE

**The Xerox Story**

Without question, Xerox created the photocopier industry, owned the market, and set the standards against which all photocopiers were compared. For about fifteen years, Xerox was simply unbeatable. But its overwhelming success sowed the insidious seeds of complacency. Xerox paid only superficial attention to customers; the quality of its goods remained unchanged; and the rate of innovation slowed. The company was reluctant to put much effort into bringing out new products while the old ones were still producing handsome profits.

During the mid-1970s, Japanese competitors entered the market. Xerox shrugged off the competition, seeing no need to worry about those distant, low-quality, low-price competitors. The prevailing view at the time was that "made in Japan" was synonymous with low quality. Certainly mighty Xerox didn't have to worry about competitors at the bottom end of the market. Xerox management rationalized that losing market share in low-price, low-margin products wouldn't have much effect on profits anyway. But for more than five years, the competition gained market share, introducing progressively higher-priced, higher-margin goods.

The wake-up call for Xerox came in 1981. Xerox had lost over half its market share in the previous five years, but profits in 1980 remained strong because of the number of copiers in place and the sales of top-end machines. But profits in 1981 fell almost 50 percent, a decline of $500 million to $600 million. CEO David Kearns finally acknowledged that business as usual was completely unacceptable.

In 1983, Xerox formally launched its Leadership Through Quality program. The program had six major elements:

- An executive-level transition team was created to oversee implementation of the program.
- All of Xerox's 100,000 employees went through quality improvement training.
- Management behavior became proactive and customer-oriented and encouraged innovations that improved customer satisfaction.
- Employee empowerment and involvement were instituted to achieve real cultural change.
- An open environment encouraged the free flow of communication in all directions, including communication with customers.
- A performance appraisal, reward, and recognition system was created to reinforce customer-oriented quality improvement.

Only six years after starting the program, Xerox won the 1989 Baldrige Award and regained the number-one position in all six major segments of the copier industry.[29]

What caused Xerox to lose market share? How did Xerox involve the entire company in its quality-improvement efforts? What could Xerox do in the future to maintain its market position?

### CATEGORIES OF SERVICE

Service can be subdivided into three categories.[35] Managers who are concerned about improving service quality need to pay attention to all three of the following categories:

- ***Presale service:*** furnishes the customer with information and assistance in the decision-making process. For example, Stone Container sells a variety of packaging materials—not stone containers—but essentially has a free consulting service that evaluates a customer's packaging needs and comes up with creative solutions. The solutions may include custom-designed cartons, equipment

At Texas Instruments, presale service is a priority. Over 95 percent of those who request information about the company's products get an answer within two hours.



modifications, changes in material flow, or a new plant layout. Stone is so confident of its consulting service that it guarantees customers a cost savings of $300,000 to $500,000 annually. Stone sees its bundle of product attributes as including both presale consulting services and the more tangible packaging materials. However, presale service may be as simple as responding to a potential customer's questions in a timely fashion. Texas Instruments gets about 200,000 inquiries from potential customers each year. Over 95 percent of those inquiries get an answer within two hours, and virtually all inquiries get an answer within twenty-four hours. TI has developed an internal tracking system to ensure that no customer inquiries fall through the cracks. Such a swift response creates a positive image for all TI's products. Presale service is not limited to manufacturing companies: Some insurance companies, for example, do a thorough needs analysis for potential customers to help them choose the best types of insurance.

**presale service**
Service that furnishes the customer with information and assistance in the decision-making process.

- *Transaction service:* directly associated with the exchange transaction between a firm and its customers. One common type of transaction service is providing a fax number so customers can order by fax; some companies go a step further and give customers a computer and modem loaded with ordering software to speed order cycle times. Transaction service could also include prompt dissemination of information about inventory surpluses or shortages, changes in lot sizes, or order fill rates. It could include commitment to firm delivery dates, as well as financing and credit terms. At a hotel or an airline, transaction service might include efficient check-in procedures.

**transaction service**
Service that is directly associated with the exchange transaction between a firm and its customers.

- *Postsale service:* occurs after the transaction. This is the support service that firms have traditionally stressed. For example, if an order is delayed, then the postsale service of providing information about order status, back orders, or shipping delays becomes important. Customer service and complaint resolution processes also become important in such situations.

**postsale service**
Service that occurs after the transaction.

7 *Describe the components of service quality.*

## COMPONENTS OF SERVICE QUALITY

Customers evaluate service quality by the following five components:[36]

- *Reliability:* the ability to perform the service dependably, accurately, and consistently. Reliability is performing the service right the first time. This component has been found to be the one most important to consumers.

**reliability**
Ability to perform a service dependably, accurately, and consistently.

- *Responsiveness:* the ability to provide prompt service. Examples of responsiveness include calling the customer back quickly, serving lunch fast to a someone who is in a hurry, or mailing a transaction slip immediately.

**responsiveness**
Ability to provide prompt service.

- *Assurance:* the knowledge and courtesy of employees and their ability to convey trust. Skilled employees who treat customers with respect, and make

**assurance**
Knowledge and courtesy of service employees and their ability to inspire trust.

The tangible signs of a service, such as automated teller machines, give consumers important clues about the service's quality.

customers feel they can trust the firm, exemplify assurance.

- ***Empathy:*** caring, individualized attention to customers. Firms whose employees recognize customers, call them by name, and learn their customers' specific requirements are providing empathy. When a customer calls Pizza Hut, employees ask for the customer's phone number and enter it into a computer; the computer then shows the type of pizza the customer has ordered in the past, allowing employees to demonstrate empathy.

**empathy**
Caring, individualized attention to customers.

**tangibles**
Physical evidence of a service.

- ***Tangibles:*** the physical evidence of the service. The tangible parts of a service include the physical facilities, tools, and equipment used to provide a service, such as a doctor's office or an ATM, and the appearance of personnel.

Overall service quality is measured by combining customers' evaluations for all five components.

8 *Explain the gap model of service quality.*

## THE GAP MODEL OF SERVICE QUALITY

**gap model**
Model of service quality that identifies five key discrepancies that can cause problems in service delivery and influence evaluations of service quality.

A model of service quality called the **gap model** identifies five discrepancies or gaps that can cause problems in service delivery and influence customer evaluations of service quality. These are the gaps illustrated in Exhibit 8.7 on page 264:

- *Gap 1:* the gap between customer expectations and management's perception of those expectations. This gap results from a lack of understanding or a misinterpretation of the customers' needs, wants, or desires. A firm that does little or no marketing or customer satisfaction research is likely to experience this gap. Managers who assume they know what customers want but who don't have any way of substantiating their views also contribute to this gap. An important step in closing gap 1 is to keep in touch with customer expectations by doing research on customer needs and customer satisfaction.
- *Gap 2:* the gap between management's perception of what customers want and the specifications that management develops to provide the service. Essentially, this gap is the result of management's inability to translate customers' needs into delivery systems within the firm. In order to close this gap, management must be committed to service quality and set service quality goals that can be implemented and measured. Quality function deployment, discussed earlier, can also be used to close this gap. Although QFD was developed for improving the quality of tangible goods, the same concept can easily be applied to services. QFD is simply a way of ensuring that the voice of the customer is heard when designing products.
- *Gap 3:* the gap between the service quality specifications and the service that is actually provided. Assuming for a moment that both gaps 1 and 2 have been closed, gap 3 then is due to the inability of management and employees to do what should be done. Poorly trained, poorly motivated, or alienated workers cause this gap. To close it, management needs to ensure a good match between employees' skills and their jobs and to provide employees with the appropriate

*Exhibit 8.7*

Gap Model of Service Quality

Source: Reprinted with the permission of The Free Press, a Division of Simon & Schuster, from *Delivering Quality Service*, by V. A. Zeithaml, A. Parasuraman, and L. L. Berry. Copyright © 1990 by The Press.

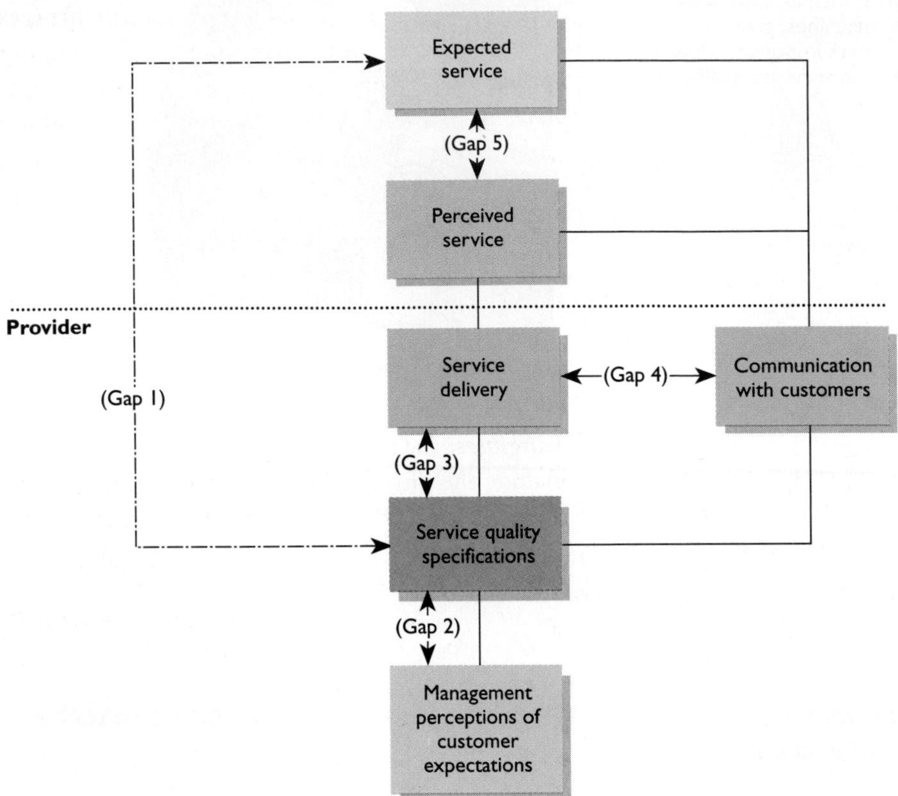


technology to perform their jobs. Other techniques that help to close gap 3 are training employees so they know what management expects and encouraging teamwork. Empowerment—giving employees the authority to make decisions to satisfy customer needs—is also important.

- *Gap 4:* the gap between what the service system provides and what the customer is told it provides. This is clearly a communication gap. It may include misleading or deceptive promotional campaigns promising more than the firm can deliver or doing "whatever it takes" to get the business. To close this gap, companies need to create realistic customer expectations through honest, accurate communication about a firm's service capability. Note in Exhibit 8.7 that a firm's communication with customers is also partly responsible for customer expectations and perceptions of the service.
- *Gap 5:* the gap between customers' perceptions of service performance and their expectations. A gap between expectations and performance can be positive or negative. For example, if a patient expects to wait twenty minutes in the physician's office before seeing the physician but waits only ten minutes, the positive gap increases the patient's evaluation of service quality. However, a forty-minute wait would result in a negative gap and a lower evaluation.

When any of these gaps are large, service quality is perceived as low. As the gaps shrink, service quality improves. Taco Bell, for example, had problems with gap 3, the gap between management's specifications for service quality and actual service delivery. Management's mistake was using the traditional methods to keep workers "under control." The result was high turnover and low morale—and, consequently, poor service to customers. Once management recognized the source of the problem, it instituted a program of employee empowerment and transferred more control to the workers. By narrowing gap 3 and actually delivering the level of service that management knew was necessary in a competitive market, the company started to become more successful.[37]

9 *Discuss the components of value-based pricing.*

## VALUE-BASED PRICING

**value-based pricing**
Pricing strategy that starts with the customer, considers the competition, and then determines the appropriate price.

**Value-based pricing** is a pricing strategy that has grown out of the quality movement. Instead of figuring prices based on costs or competitors' prices, it starts with the customer, considers the competition, and then determines the appropriate price.[38] The basic assumption is that the firm is customer-driven, seeking to understand the attributes customers want in the goods and services they buy and the value of that bundle of attributes to customers. Because very few firms operate in a pure monopoly, however, a marketer using value-based pricing must also determine the value to customers of competitive offerings. Customers evaluate the value of a product (not just its price) relative to the value of other alternatives. In value-based pricing, therefore, the price of the product is set at a level that seems to the customer to be a good price when compared with the prices of other options.

Procter & Gamble developed a new value-based pricing program after recognizing that pricing problems were behind lagging sales of such products as Tide detergent, Crest toothpaste, Vicks cough syrup, and Pampers diapers. Consumer demand for these products had fallen because their prices were higher than prices for competing brands. To restore sales, P&G shifted from a strategy of maintaining high list prices but offering frequent and irregular discounts to a value-pricing strategy based on everyday low prices (a strategy discussed in Chapter 19).[39]

In the automobile industry, value-based pricing is taking the form of one-price selling—that is, selling cars with a fixed set of popular options (such as air conditioning, power windows and door locks, and rear-window defroster) at a low, usually nonnegotiable package price. The base-level automobile plus these options would normally cost more. General Motors pioneered this pricing strategy in 1990 with the introduction of its Saturn line of cars.[40]

Saturn automobiles were among the first products to feature value-based pricing, which calculates prices on the basis of customers' expectations instead of on the basis of the producer's costs or competitors' prices.

An important point about value-based pricing is that it does not simply reduce prices; it takes into account customers' perceptions of value. Earlier in the chapter, customer value was defined as the ratio of benefits to the sacrifice necessary to obtain those benefits. Customer sacrifice usually consists of transaction costs, life cycle costs, and some amount of risk. The **transaction cost** is the immediate financial outlay or commitment that a customer must make—in other words, the purchase price. The **life cycle cost** is the expected additional cost that a customer will incur over the life of the product. Because the life cycle cost is inherently based on expectations, there also is some

**transaction cost**
Immediate financial outlay or commitment a customer makes.

**life cycle cost**
Expected additional outlay a customer incurs over the life of a product.

Many consumers consider Hewlett-Packard laser printers a good value because they cost less than competitors' printers over their life cycle, although they may cost more to buy in the first place.

Courtesy Hewlett-Packard

degree of **risk** involved, which is the uncertainty about long-term costs.

**risk**
Uncertainty about long-term, life cycle costs of buying a good or service.

### TRANSACTION COSTS

For a simple product with a short period of expected use, the transaction cost dominates the customer's decision process. There are very few life cycle costs associated with a can of vegetables, a soft drink, or a bottle of wine. Some small element of risk may be involved, such as choosing a wine that tastes bad, but perceived risk is minor for many products.

Transaction costs represent a major decision criterion for undifferentiated products, those that differ very little from competing offerings. Because the customer can't make a choice on the basis of the product's attributes, the transaction cost, or price, becomes more important. For example, most consumers view gasoline as a generic, undifferentiated product and are sensitive to a price change of only a few cents per gallon. Texaco is attempting to overcome that perception by presenting a high-quality image for its System 3 gasoline. If Texaco succeeds in differentiating its gasoline somewhat, it will be able to charge a slightly higher price and still convey good value to customers.

### LIFE CYCLE COSTS

The longer the expected life of the product, the more important life cycle cost becomes. One of the reasons that Caterpillar has been so successful is that, although transaction costs for its heavy equipment are higher than the competition's, life cycle costs are much lower. Thus the total financial sacrifice is lower. Similarly, Hewlett-Packard has a dominant position in the laser printer market because its high transaction costs are offset by lower life cycle costs.

Life cycle costs are a factor in one of the problems facing the auto industry. The high transaction costs of new cars lead customers to keep their older cars longer. Car buyers see better value in keeping the old car, even with its higher life cycle costs of maintenance and repair.

Marketers of durable goods—such as automobiles, clothes washers and dryers, and televisions—must be aware that customers always form perceptions of expected life cycle costs. In the absence of information on which to base judgments, customer perceptions become subjective and often depend on image. The implication is that managers must understand the relative importance of life cycle costs in customers' decision processes. When life cycle costs are important, marketers should convey specific information that helps customers accurately formulate their expectations.

### RISK

The longer the expected life of the product, the more important a factor risk is. With a long-lived product, the customer has trouble accurately evaluating how long it will last, and so financial sacrifice is harder to determine.

Let's assume that you need a new set of tires for your car. Your expected benefits might consist of 40,000 miles of tire life, certain performance and handling characteristics, and a road hazard warranty. Your sacrifice would be the transaction cost—say $80 per tire—and the life cycle costs of rotating the tires each year and repairing flat tires. But if the tires last for only 25,000 or 30,000 or 35,000 miles instead of the 40,000 you expect, what happens to your perception of value? Unfortunately, you can never know for sure exactly how long tires will last, so some element of risk enters the equation.

To overcome consumers' concerns about risk, marketers often offer warranties. In the auto industry, late-model used cars are often sold with an additional "maintenance policy." These policies, which typically cost $500 to $1,000, are an opportunity for the car buyer to reduce the higher risk of buying a used car. As transaction costs of used cars and their expected life have increased, the perceived risk of buying them also has increased, creating an opportunity to sell a new service.

10 *Explain the two-factor model of customer satisfaction.*

## CUSTOMER SATISFACTION

**customer satisfaction**
Feeling that a product has met or exceeded the customer's expectations.

When maximizing customer value is the organization's goal, it needs to know how well it is meeting customers' expectations. **Customer satisfaction** is the feeling that a product has met or exceeded the customer's expectations. An organization cannot always rely on customers to make their feelings known, however, and so it may deliberately set out to measure customer satisfaction levels.

### MEASUREMENT OF CUSTOMER SATISFACTION

A program to measure customer satisfaction should be a permanent, ongoing process that translates what customers want into usable data. It should define in customers' own words what they want in goods and services in terms of quality. Customer satisfaction measurement should also provide insight into the price perspectives of customers. Current customers, lost customers, and potential customers should be included.

A good example of a comprehensive customer satisfaction measurement program is the one put in place by Fort Sanders Health System, a six-facility health care organization in Knoxville, Tennessee. Fort Sanders believes it is most likely to achieve the goal behind its mission statement—to become the preeminent health care provider in East Tennessee—by responding to the voice of the customer. Fort Sanders began with qualitative research. Patients, physicians, managers, and employees all helped design the questionnaires that were used to elicit the opinions of customers (patients and physicians) about the quality of Fort Sanders's product. Following a baseline measurement of customer satisfaction, Fort Sanders developed a training program to help employees learn more about customer satisfaction and focus on the areas that patients and physicians said required attention. Fort Sanders then formed teams to direct employee efforts in these areas. And it continues to survey customers about their expectations and their perceptions of product quality. This program gives Fort Sanders an advantage over the many organizations that still try to improve product quality by relying on the intuition of management and employees.[41]

### THE TWO-FACTOR MODEL

**hygiene factor**
Factor that contributes to customer dissatisfaction.

**satisfier**
Factor that contributes to customer satisfaction.

When designing customer satisfaction measurement programs, it helps to understand the two-factor model of satisfaction, an adaptation of Frederick Herzberg's two-factor theory of job satisfaction.[42] One category of factors, called **hygiene factors,** has been found to contribute to customer dissatisfaction. The second category, called **satisfiers,** has been found to contribute to customer satisfaction.

Customers can consistently identify why they are satisfied or dissatisfied. In most cases, however, the factors contributing to dissatisfaction are quite different from the factors that contribute to satisfaction. The absence of, or low performance on, some product attributes will quickly cause customer dissatisfaction. High performance on those same attributes contributes very little to high levels of customer satisfaction. However, low performance on these attributes will prevent a firm from ever reaching high levels of customer satisfaction. Conversely, the factors that cause customer satisfaction are usually not identified as factors that cause customer dissatisfaction. Thus, low performance on those attributes causing high satisfaction does not usually cause customer dissatisfaction.

If a firm performs at a very high level in delivering the hygiene factors, customers will perceive the product as being acceptable but not spectacular. Performing at a very high level on hygiene factors might yield the customer response "So what? You're expected to do that." Hygiene factors collectively constitute some threshold level, and failure to meet that threshold level will cause customers to become dissatisfied. For example, let's assume that a customer expects a 40,000-mile life from a set of tires. If the tires last only 25,000 or 30,000 miles, the customer will be dissatisfied. It won't matter how good the traction of the tires is, how quiet the tires are, or how smoothly they ride. Failure to deliver on the hygiene factor of 40,000 expected miles will lead to customer dissatisfaction.

The hygiene factors must be delivered at an acceptable level of performance before the satisfiers become important. Once the customer's expectations on hygiene factors have been met, then the satisfiers have the potential to create high levels of customer satisfaction. In the tire example, if the tire lasts 40,000 miles, then good traction, ride, handling, and low noise may each contribute to high satisfaction levels.

The implications of the two-factor model in measuring customer satisfaction is that both the hygiene factors and the satisfiers important to customers need to be identified and evaluated. The experience of United Parcel Service is a good example of the importance of asking customers directly to identify what they want. UPS had always assumed that on-time delivery was the most important concern of customers and that everything else came second. UPS's definition of quality centered almost exclusively on the results of time-and-motion studies. Knowing the average time it took elevator doors to open on a certain city block and figuring how long it took people to answer their doorbells were critical parts of the quality equation. The corners of delivery vans were shaved off so drivers could climb out of their trucks more easily. Customer satisfaction surveys asked clients whether they were pleased with UPS's delivery time and whether they thought the company could be faster. When UPS began asking broader questions about how it could improve service, it discovered that clients were not as obsessed with on-time delivery as previously thought. UPS management was surprised to learn that customers wanted more interaction with the drivers—the only face-to-face contact any of them had with the company. If drivers were less harried and more willing to talk, customers could get some practical advice on shipping.[43] Thus, for UPS customers, on-time delivery is a hygiene factor; drivers taking the time to interact is a satisfier.

## LOOKING BACK

The story at the beginning of this chapter illustrated that Chevrolet is doing several things to offer customers better value: providing more extensive presale and postsale service, improving its automobile product line, and using a value-based pricing strategy. The company is also studying customer satisfaction programs at other types of businesses renowned for their excellent service. With the product and price components of the customer value triad in place, Chevrolet could look at the service component, perhaps adding or improving other presale, transaction, and postsale services to improve value.

## SUMMARY

**1 Define customer value.** Customer value is the ratio of benefits to the sacrifice necessary to obtain those benefits.

**2 Describe the customer value triad.** The customer value triad is based on three things: goods quality, service quality, and value-based prices. Customer value is created when customer expectations in each of the three areas are met or exceeded. If you fail to meet customer expectations in any one of the three areas, you have not delivered good customer value.

**3 Describe the techniques of total quality management.** There are four important techniques of total quality management (TQM). *Quality function deployment* (QFD) is a technique using a quality chart to relate the goods characteristics that customers want to the way goods will be designed and produced. QFD also includes benchmarking, which is rating a company's product against the best in the world. A second element is *continuous improvement,* a commitment to constantly do things better. Management adopts the perspective of problem prevention and systematic improvement of key processes instead of troubleshooting problems as they occur. A third element of TQM is *reduced cycle time,* reducing the time from when production begins until the good is received by the customer. Companies with faster cycle times than their competitors can earn profits faster and can also dramatically increase growth. The final TQM element is *analysis of process problems,* which can be accomplished with one or more of the following tools: statistical quality control, a method of analyzing deviations in manufactured materials, parts, and products; Pareto analysis, which uses a bar chart to rank causes of variation in production and service in order to identify a company's biggest problems; and fishbone diagrams, visual tools that help managers organize what they know about cause-and-effect relationships for each problem.

**4 Describe the roles of management, employees, and suppliers in total quality management.** TQM involves everyone in the organization. Top management must strongly and visibly commit to TQM, both with words and with actions. Employee empowerment (giving employees the authority to make decisions), teamwork, and training are critical to the success of TQM. Suppliers to TQM companies must also adopt quality practices, because when a company is trying to produce defect-free output, it cannot tolerate defects in the materials and parts it buys from suppliers.

**5 Describe the Malcolm Baldrige National Quality Award.** The Baldrige Award was established by Congress in 1987 to recognize U.S. companies that offer world-class goods and services. The award also promotes awareness of quality and transfers information about quality to others in the business community.

### KEY TERMS

*assurance* 263
*benchmarking* 254
*continuous improvement* 255
*customer satisfaction* 267
*customer value triad* 252
*cycle time* 255
*empathy* 263
*fishbone diagram* 257
*gap model* 263
*hygiene factor* 267
*ISO 9000* 253
*lead time* 256
*life cycle cost* 265
*Pareto analysis* 256
poka-yoke 255
*postsale service* 262
*presale service* 262
*quality function deployment (QFD)* 254
*reliability* 262
*responsiveness* 262
*risk* 266
*satisfier* 267
*statistical quality control (SQC)* 256
*tangibles* 263
*total quality management (TQM)* 253
*transaction cost* 265
*transaction service* 262
*value-based pricing* 265

6 **Discuss the three categories of services.** The first category is presale services. Presale services usually furnish the customer with information and assistance in the decision-making process. The second category of services is transaction services. These are services that are directly associated with the exchange transaction between a firm and its customers. The third category of services consists of those that occur after the transaction, such as automobile maintenance and repair.

7 **Describe the components of service quality.** Customers evaluate service quality on five components. The first is reliability, which is the ability to perform the service dependably, accurately, and consistently. The second component is responsiveness, or the ability to provide prompt service to customers. The third component is assurance, which means the knowledge and courtesy of the employees and their ability to convey trust. Empathy is the fourth component, which involves caring, individualized attention to customers. The fifth component is the tangibles, which are the physical evidence of the service (for example, facilities, equipment, and appearance of personnel).

8 **Explain the gap model of service quality.** The gap model of service quality identifies five key discrepancies that can cause problems in service delivery and influence customer evaluations of service quality. When the gaps are large, service quality is low. As the gaps shrink, service quality improves. Gap 1 is the gap between customer expectations and management's perceptions of those expectations. Gap 2 is the gap between management's perception of what the customer wants and specifications for service quality. Gap 3 is the gap between service quality specifications and delivery of the service. Gap 4 is the gap between what service the company delivers and what the company promises to the customer through external communication. Gap 5 is the gap between customers' expectations of the service and their perceptions of how the service was performed.

9 **Describe the components of value-based pricing.** There are three components of value-based pricing. Transaction costs involve the immediate financial outlay or commitment a customer must make. The life cycle costs are the expected additional costs that a customer will incur over the life of the product. Risk involves uncertainty about life cycle costs.

10 **Explain the two-factor model of customer satisfaction.** The two-factor model of customer satisfaction recognizes that the factors contributing to satisfaction are not necessarily the ones contributing to dissatisfaction. One category of factors, called hygiene factors, has been found to contribute to dissatisfaction. Hygiene factors collectively constitute a threshold level, and failure to meet that level will cause customers to become dissatisfied; however, performing at a high level will not contribute to satisfaction. The second category of factors, called satisfiers, has been found to contribute to satisfaction. Once the hygiene factors are delivered at an acceptable level, the satisfiers become important.

## Discussion and Writing Questions

1. Using the definition and framework of value presented in the chapter, identify several firms in your town that you think are providing good customer value, and explain why. Identify firms that are not providing good value, and explain why.

2. Choose a goods category (for example, soft drinks, computers, or frozen foods) with several competing brands that you are familiar with. For one of the brands, construct a quality function deployment matrix using your expectations and your perceptions of how that brand meets your expectations. If you can, also include benchmarking evaluations based on your knowledge of competing brands.

3. Go to the library and find information on a company that has recently won the Malcolm Baldrige National Quality Award. Write a short report on how this company won its award.

4. Pick a good or service that you have recently purchased, and identify the presale, transaction, and postsale services that are associated with it. In your opinion, which category of service could the firm most improve on?

5. Analyze a recent experience that you have had with a service business (for example, a hairdresser, movie theater, or restaurant) in terms of your expectations and perceptions about each of the five components of service quality.

6. For the good or service you chose in question 4, identify the transaction costs, life cycle costs, and risks that were involved.

7. For the service experience you chose in question 5, identify what you would consider to be the hygiene factors and the satisfiers. How did the company perform on each of these factors?

## Application for Small Business

Paul Brown is the manager of Body Beautiful, a health club for women. The club offers aerobics classes and has a large selection of the latest body-building and weight-loss machines. A lap pool, hot tub, and sauna are also available. Members can purchase exercise clothing and accessories at a small shop on the premises. Prices for Body Beautiful's services are competitive.

Competition is tough for Body Beautiful, from both established clubs and new clubs opening in the area. Membership numbers have been decreasing for the past three months as a result of the competition. Paul is wondering what he can do to attract more new members and keep the members he currently has.

### Questions

1. Explain how Paul could apply the customer value triad to develop a marketing strategy for Body Beautiful.

2. What are some of the tools of total quality management that Paul could use to better understand his customers?

3. What things should Paul keep in mind when developing a customer satisfaction measurement program?

## CRITICAL THINKING CASE

### Xerox

In the late 1970s, Xerox found itself losing ground to the low-volume Japanese copier manufacturers. The industry leader was losing market share so fast that it was shocked into making dramatic changes. Xerox began a Leadership Through Quality program in the early 1980s that involved considerable effort on the part of every employee in the company. Every level of the organization became involved.

Xerox defined quality as total customer satisfaction. This new focus won the company quality awards in Great Britain, France, Holland, Germany, and Japan, but the most prestigious award came in 1989, when Xerox won the Malcolm Baldrige National Quality Award. Only a handful of U.S. companies have won it. The award spurred Xerox to redouble its efforts to achieve excellence.

Part of Xerox's winning strategy was to improve the quality of its service as well as the quality of its machines. Good postsale service—keeping the machines running properly—helps improve customer relations, increases the likelihood of repeat purchases, and increases the sales of consumable products like paper and ink. Much of the profitability in the high-end copier business comes from the sale of consumables.

A group of Xerox employees who call themselves the Hi-Rockers service high-volume copy machines in the Little Rock, Arkansas, area. In 1988, 83 percent of customers rated the Hi-Rockers high on satisfaction. Wanting to increase this percentage, the Hi-Rockers embarked on a program to improve quality. First they asked what their customers wanted. The answer: better response time. The Hi-Rockers then developed a three-level response system based on the seriousness of the equipment breakdown. A priority 1 (emergency) call required a repair person to respond in two hours or less, a priority 2 call required a response in four hours or less, and a priority 3 call required a response in eight hours or less. This program addressed customer requirements, not Xerox requirements.

To implement the new quality programs, Xerox management had to make some changes. Most managers went from a directive, top-down style to a collaborative style. Managers now serve more or less as consultants to those they supervise. Service employees are empowered to do what they think is best for the customer. Everyone works together as a team.

The team approach allowed the Hi-Rockers to successfully follow through on the response-time commitments they made to their customers. Their customer satisfaction ratings rose to 100 percent by 1990. Among the customer comments they received were these: "I never made a priority call that Xerox didn't make" and "You can't beat the service that we now get from Xerox."

### Questions

1. How successful were the Xerox Hi-Rockers in achieving total quality management? To what do you attribute their success?
2. What changes in the management style of the Hi-Rockers' supervisors were required to achieve 100 percent customer satisfaction ratings?
3. What could other companies learn about implementing a quality program from the Hi-Rockers' story?

### References

*Million Dollar Directory 1993* (Parsippany, NJ: Dun & Bradstreet Information Services, 1993).

*Standard & Poor's Industry Surveys* (New York: Standard & Poor's Corporation, October 1993).

*Ward's Business Directory of U.S. Private and Public Companies* (Detroit: Gale Research, 1992).

## SIGNATURE SERIES CASE

### When Is an Improvement Not an Improvement?

Raymond E Kordupleski

SIGNATURE SERIES

*by Raymond Kordupleski*
*Customer Satisfaction Director, AT&T*

An improvement in the efficiency of a company's internal processes, such as accounting, usually makes no difference in the customer's perceived value of the company's products and services. Internal functions are often reengineered from the viewpoint of in-house corporate requirements. For processes that truly have no effect on the customer, this is fine. But, when managers choose to redesign a customer-related process only for internal reasons, they often lose a tremendous opportunity to accomplish much more.

Let's take AT&T's billing process as an example. Before market research was available, the billing operations people knew that the purpose of the billing process was to get the money owed to AT&T by business and residential customers. They were also responsible for handling billing inquiries and collections. The typical quality measurements on the billing process were an accounts receivable score and productivity figures, such as talk time per representative and number of calls handled per day. When reengineering efforts were planned for the billing function, those plans focused on collections and productivity. The results of process improvement did lower costs and increase revenue by reducing receivables, but an important opportunity was missed by focusing only on in-house needs. This oversight would soon cost the company a great deal more than it saved, when a competitor took advantage of customer input.

When customer satisfaction surveys began including questions about the billing process, the analysis showed that 15 percent of a customer's overall satisfaction with AT&T's products and services came from their satisfaction with the bills and billing inquiry services. Now AT&T knew how important the billing service was to a customer when choosing a long-distance carrier. Additional research also showed that MCI had a competitive advantage over AT&T in the perceived quality of the billing statements of MCI, specifically in the amount of detail included for its business customers. AT&T was unable, at that time, to provide the same level of detail in its bills because it did not have access to the information. (Explanatory note: Before deregulation, billing was done by the Regional Bell Operating Companies. For a period of years after divestiture, AT&T had to rely on the operating companies to provide the billing and, therefore, did not have access to detailed information on each business account.)

Unfortunately for AT&T, MCI, through its own customer satisfaction surveys, had the same market information AT&T did. MCI used the customer satisfaction data to attack AT&T and lure its customers away. Television advertisements asked, "What can you do with an AT&T bill?" The implied answer was, pay it and file it. The ad then went on to explain that the detailed account information given by MCI provided strategic data on customer call patterns. Both MCI and AT&T now realized that a bill was more than just a means for collecting money. The bills themselves provided valuable information to business customers. Knowledge of the customer's needs made the bill a competitive weapon. Eventually, AT&T was able to change its billing format to include more detail for business users. We were able to neutralize MCI's competitive advantage in the business market, but not until our market share took a direct hit.

Consumer market research found that the billing process could address residential customers' needs as well. MCI took advantage of billing information to offer the Friends and Family program, which allowed special rates for calls to designated friends and family members. Knowing that customers would respond with their dollars to this new offer, AT&T then countered with its True Value and True Rewards programs, which offered an across-the-board usage discount to all customers. These programs were designed to counter MCI's attack while minimizing the difficulties caused by the transition from regional operating company billing systems to AT&T's in-house billing system. AT&T used what information it did have to best advantage.

Billing service continues to be a strong competitive weapon. An internal operating function that historically had the very simple task of requesting payment on accounts became a new product with its own set of attributes. Customer satisfaction surveys showed that the customer wants three things: no surprises, statements that are easy to understand, and responsive billing inquiry service. The surveys also showed what percentage of the time these three concerns were met and satisfaction levels relative to competitors.

When the marketing function plays an expanded role in the reengineering of internal business functions, every part of the organization can participate in improving customer satisfaction and increasing market share.

### Questions

1. How was MCI able to make a billing statement for business accounts a value-added service to customers? And what was AT&T's response?
2. How did customer satisfaction data indicate that the billing process might provide a competitive edge?
3. Name other examples of businesses where billing, which was not normally considered a strategic product or service, was made into a competitive advantage.

**VIDEO CASE**

## General Motors

During the 1980s, U.S. carmakers suffered from declining sales and image problems due to the increased competition from foreign car producers, namely the Japanese. General Motors was faced with the challenge of restoring its market share and winning back customers. This task involved restoring consumers' confidence in the quality of GM cars as well as offering a product that customers perceived as a good value. In 1993 General Motors launched a value-pricing program to increase sales and lure car buyers back to U.S. products.

GM's value-pricing program offers option-loaded cars at a lower fixed price, greatly reducing or eliminating the need for car buyers and dealers to negotiate on price. In essence, the program aims to convince car buyers that they are receiving the best value for their money. After all, the vehicles in the program are priced below the competition, and everyone pays the same price for the same model with identical options.

This value-pricing program is similar to Saturn's single-price strategy, which sets the price for a specific model loaded with specific options. Saturn, a subsidiary of General Motors, has in fact had a "no dickering" policy since its inception. The "no dicker sticker" concept implies that the sticker price is the best price available to buyers. Saturn has enjoyed overwhelming success with this strategy and has been praised for its customer service.

GM contends that the program is not just a new pricing strategy but is instead a complete strategy shift for the company. Centered around the concept of value, the program incorporates the elements of price, vehicle options, leasing alternatives, promotions, and customer satisfaction. Merely telling consumers that the price is a value will not work by itself.

General Motors introduced its value-pricing program in California, the nation's number-one market for vehicle sales. Today six GM divisions offer forty-six value-priced models in California and thirty-two models nationwide.

GM sales immediately increased 31 percent following the 1993 introduction of the program, but dealers argued that lowering the sticker price would decrease their profit margins. GM maintains that the increase in sales volume will offset the lower prices.

Competitors have followed GM's lead. Ford, for instance, instituted a value-pricing program to try to increase market share and lowered its monthly leasing payments to entice customers.

Meanwhile, the Japanese yen's rise against the U.S. dollar has substantially increased the cost of Japanese automobiles, which makes GM's value pricing even more attractive to potential car buyers. General Motors believes that its cars are now the best buys in the marketplace.

### Questions

1. Does GM's value-pricing program follow the definition of value pricing in the chapter? Why or why not?

2. What are the transaction costs, life cycle costs, and risks associated with purchasing an automobile?

3. In terms of the customer value triad, what has GM put in place so far? What other elements of customer value need to be in place for GM's value-pricing program to be most effective?

# PART TWO
# CRITICAL THINKING CASE

## PETCO PRODUCTS

There are 35.4 million dog owners (38 percent of all households) and 31 million cat owners (33 percent of all households) in the United States. The pet care business exceeds $12 billion annually—almost $4 billion more than we spend on baby food. Add $4.6 billion for medical care for dogs and cats and an additional $1.7 billion for pet gear, and the total appears to be a marketer's dream. Even more astounding is the fact that these figures are most likely understated. Additional expenses for extra housecleaning and home repairs due to damage caused by pets are harder to track and are not included in the totals.

The American Pet Products Manufacturers Association identifies these characteristics of pet owners:

- 23 percent of households owning pets are headed by an adult between 30 and 39 years old. Heads of households between 40 and 49 years old represent 19 percent of the market.
- 14 percent of pet owners are single and over 35 years old. Another 7 percent of pet owners are single and under 35.
- Single pet owners under 35 are more likely to consider their pets part of the family than are older pet owners.
- Single parents are more likely than married parents to agree that a pet can be a best friend.
- 78 percent of pet owners live in houses.
- 53 percent of all pet owners make more than $30,000 annually.

The pet food industry is characterized as a mature and highly competitive business. Yet the dog food market continues to grow at a steady pace. There are more than 20,000 dog food vendors in the United States. Grocery stores, mass merchandisers, and discount and warehouse stores sell the majority of dog food in the United States.

The four major types of dog food sold are dry, canned (wet), soft, and moist. Like dry dog food, soft dog food is sold in bags. Moist dog food, such as Gaines Burgers, is packaged in individually wrapped servings. Dry dog food accounts for the largest percentage of sales (see Exhibit 1). Five large manufacturers dominate the market. These five Companies account for 79 percent of the $3.3 billion annual dog food sales. Ralston Purina is the leader, selling 47 percent of the dry dog food in the United States (see Exhibit 2).

Manufacturers are continually working on new dog food products. Major manufacturers traditionally spend about 3 percent of gross sales on research and development. In answer to specialty companies like Iams, many companies have added high-protein products to their lines. Premium dog foods, foods with higher protein and mineral content, are more expensive, but pet owners can feed their dogs smaller servings.

The premium dog food segment is the fastest-growing segment. Grocers seem to be missing a lot of this business unless the product is tied to a heavy coupon and advertising campaign. The bulk of this segment is being sold through specialty pet stores and veterinarians.

Grocery stores like to stock fast-moving products with large advertising budgets. For the most part, the market is deal-prone; that is, consumers are price-sensitive. Furthermore, dog food takes up a great deal of

*Exhibit 1*

Dog Food Sales (by Product Type)

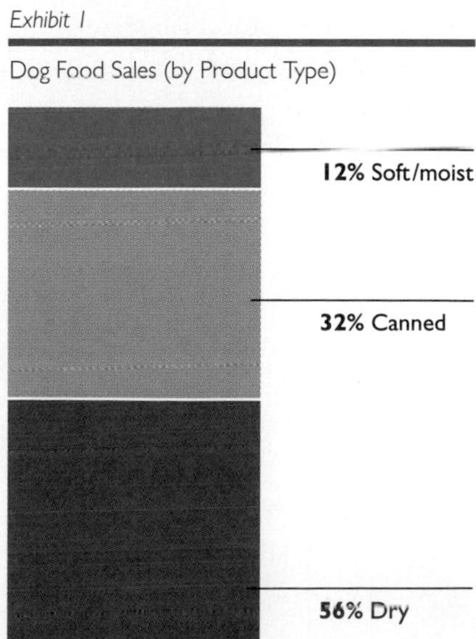

shelf space in the store. Thus grocers are always looking for something new.

Petco's First in Show 27 (FIS-27) is a nutritionally complete and balanced dog food designed to be sold through grocery stores in the traditional five-, twenty-five-, and fifty-pound bags. It is priced well below the competition but has extra vitamin and mineral content. Thus FIS-27 compares favorably with popular pet store dog foods. FIS-27 contains 27 percent highly digestible protein and 12 percent first-grade fats. The formula is designed to meet the high nutritional requirements of growing and active dogs. The product uses only high-grade poultry, lamb, beef, and pork, not the corn and soybean typically found in other dog food products.

Two key ingredients that set FIS-27 apart from other competitors are Odor Bloc and a garlic extract. Odor Bloc, based on an all-natural extract from the yucca plant, reduces odors associated with pet waste by up to 60 percent. It inhibits the production of ammonia, one of the main odor-causing agents in pet waste. The garlic extract is used to reduce the infestation of fleas and ticks. All-natural flavor enhancers are added to FIS-27 to make the product very flavorful.

## Questions

1. Develop profiles of consumers who buy pet food from grocery stores, specialty pet stores, and veterinarians. Differentiate the motives of each group.
2. Propose a multicultural approach for Petco. What type of market research will be necessary?
3. Considering the profile of a grocery store shopper and the existing competition in the dry dog food market, estimate the success of FIS-27.
4. Create a plan to sell FIS-27 to a business market, consisting of kennels.
5. What changes do you think may occur in the pet food market in the next ten years? What adjustments would you recommend to Petco Products?

## Suggested Readings

Julie Liesse, "Superstores Add Bite to Pet Market's Bark," *Advertising Age,* 25 April 1994, p. 42.

"Petco in an Expansionist Mode," *Chain Store Age Executive,* June 1993, p. 26.

*Exhibit 2*

Dry Dog Food (Market Share)

Note: These amounts do not include dog food sold through specialty stores and veterinarians.

| | Dog food sales (in millions of dollars) | | | |
|---|---|---|---|---|
| | Type of product | | | |
| **Company** | **Dry** | **Canned** | **Dry soft/moist** | **Total** |
| Ralston Purina | 889 | 0 | 50 | 939 |
| Grand Met | 157 | 326 | 3 | 486 |
| Quaker Oats | 184 | 83 | 289 | 556 |
| Mars | 66 | 309 | 0 | 375 |
| Carnation | 102 | 158 | 0 | 260 |
| All others | 478 | 184 | 43 | 705 |
| Totals | 1,876 | 1,060 | 385 | 3,321 |

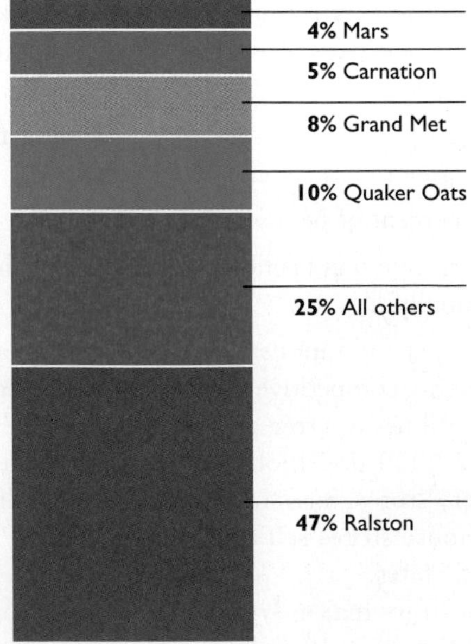

# PART TWO
# GLOBAL MARKETING CASE

## BLANCHWORTH CHINA

*Thomas F. White, Regis University, and Linda L. Catlin, Wayne State University*

The Blanchworth China Company was founded in the British Isles in the eighteenth century and has established a worldwide reputation for premium-quality china designed and handcrafted in the United Kingdom. The china always has sold very well in the United States, and in the early 1980s, fueled by a strong dollar, it experienced an explosive growth in sales. However, as the dollar went into a long decline through the mid- and late 1980s, sales of Blanchworth china dropped by 25 percent in the United States. This decline is particularly important to Blanchworth since the U.S. market accounts for approximately 90 percent of the company's output.

The premium-quality china market is roughly divided into two segments based on price: the high segment is priced from $75 to $300 per plate, while the lower segment ranges from $25 to $75 per plate. Blanchworth has always dominated the high segment with approximately 85 percent of market share, but the company had no presence in the lower segment. Unfortunately, it was the high segment of the market that decreased 25 percent in sales dollars in the late 1980s, while the lower segment grew by 50 percent during the same period. This was clearly a worldwide trend, not only in Blanchworth's market, but also for most other discretionary income items.

In addition to the falling value of the U.S. dollar and the shrinking market for higher-priced china, several other factors helped to create a severe financial crisis for Blanchworth by the end of the 1980s. During the "good times" of the 1980s, when demand and profits were high, Blanchworth's skilled workers' union made heavy wage and work rule demands. The company's managers acceded to these demands in order to avoid any work stoppages. As a result, Blanchworth's craftsmen became some of the highest-paid skilled workers in the British Isles. Workers' salaries increased from 60 percent of the cost of product to nearly 80 percent by the late 1980s. These high labor costs, coupled with company debt incurred by the acquisition of a premium crystal manufacturer, prevented Blanchworth from lowering its prices when U.S. demand decreased.

In 1988, management was forced to propose immediate cost-reducing measures in order to save the company. Among other things, they determined to reduce their labor force by 25 percent and to purchase new equipment that would make the remaining workers more productive. After heated encounters between management and union leaders, the union finally became convinced that the labor force cuts were necessary in order to save the company. The union also agreed to rescind work rules that had worked to preclude higher worker productivity. The union made these concessions to prevent the company from declaring bankruptcy and to save most union jobs.

After a year of operation with the new equipment, Blanchworth management found that increases in productivity were offset by the larger than expected number of senior craftsmen taking advantage of the early retirement package. This package was offered as one means of reducing the labor force by the targeted 25 percent. Profits continued to slide after the work force reduction, and Blanchworth management finally decided the company would have to enter the lower segment of the premium-quality china market. While Blanchworth managers realized that there are many more competitors in this lower segment of the market than in the high-price segment, they believed the company's well-respected name and other marketing strengths would allow it to make a quick entry into this segment.

In late 1990, Blanchworth introduced a new line of products that is lighter in weight and less ornate than its original china place settings. This entire product line is produced in Eastern Europe at a fraction of the labor cost associated with the Blanchworth United Kingdom plant. preliminary market research shows that this line has stronger appeal for the younger, first time china buyer, who sees herself as more contemporary and value-conscious than the traditional Blanchworth customer; moreover, this younger buyer is generally less brand-loyal. Blanchworth calls its new line *Krohn China,* a name that it believes has more of a Continental sound than Blanchworth.

Krohn is carried by the same distribution channel as Blanchworth, but it has its own logo, package design, advertising agency, and display case. Management felt that the name *Blanchworth* associated with the name *Krohn* would help to establish an image of high quality, but at the same time, the name Krohn would differentiate the new line from traditional Blanchworth china. This name association has helped to gain the reseller support necessary in making the new line readily accessible to a large market.

As a result of Blanchworth management's decision to locate its new operations in Eastern Europe, members of the union and residents of the community in which the Blanchworth factory is located feel betrayed. Union leaders were never informed about the new product line, which could have meant the rehiring of many Blanchworth skilled workers. In addition, the move to Eastern Europe has caused ill will among many consumers throughout the United Kingdom and has resulted in some critical editorials in the local and national press.

The union contends that most U.S. customers are brand-loyal to Blanchworth because it is made by skilled workers in the United Kingdom. They argue that this loyalty stems from the fact that many U.S. citizens trace their ancestry to one or more countries in the United Kingdom. Management counters that Blanchworth has never been sold specifically as a U.K. product and that most U.S. buyers neither know nor care where their china products are made. Although there were many bitter feelings between management and the union, there were no work stoppages during 1991.

In early 1992, management announced that after the first year of sales, Krohn generated twice as much profit per plate as Blanchworth. Also, they asserted that Blanchworth employees in the United Kingdom were still not productive enough to offset the high wages these workers earned. As a result, management representatives opened discussions with union leaders about how to solve the continuing low-profit problem. Management suggested that the only solution was a further reduction in wages and benefits, as well as another major change in work rules. The union disagreed with this perspective and countered that the low level of profitability actually resulted from poor management, rather than "overpaid, unproductive workers" as suggested by management.

While they never openly stated so, union leaders suspect that management may he considering moving all Blanchworth operations to Eastern Europe. The union continues to argue that U.S. customers will. not accept Blanchworth china that is not made by U.K. craftsmen. They cite the fact that 100,000 tourists tour the U.K. plant each year and that at least half of these tourists are from the United States. Many of these U.S. tourists purchase over $2,000 in china products during their visit to the plant. The union argues that the tourists who come to the plant feel a strong affinity for Blanchworth china because it is a product of the United Kingdom and that most of these on-site sales would be lost if the plant were moved to Eastern Europe. To further strengthen this argument, the union cites the U.S. Census Bureau's 1990 statistics giving the following breakdown of U.S. citizens by U.K. ancestry: England, 32.6 million; Scotland, 5.4 million; Ireland, 38.7 million; and Wales, 2.0 million.

### To the Student

You are a business consultant who has been brought in to assist Blanchworth's top management with strategic decision making in several areas. During the briefing you are given additional information:

- Management is seriously considering moving all Blanchworth factory operations to Eastern Europe while keeping its other functions in the United Kingdom. They make it clear that the design and quality assurance operations would remain in the United Kingdom. There is concern about how quickly the new European plant and workers could achieve full quality production, especially if the U.K. workers shutdown the British plant before the new plant is on line.
- Management is concerned about political instability in Eastern Europe. If they move both Krohn and

Blanchworth, their. entire production could be compromised, and there would be little chance of reopening a plant in the United Kingdom.

- Sales of Krohn in the United Kingdom are extremely sluggish but are doing well on the continent. Krohn does seem to be gaining acceptance slowly in the United States, mostly among young couples buying it for themselves rather than receiving it as gifts from parents or other friends and relatives.
- The union and the community have threatened to discredit the firm if it moves to Eastern Europe by taking their case directly to the U.K. and U.S. customers.

Answer the following questions about this case:

1. Since management believes its foreign sales will be unaffected by moving all operations to Eastern Europe, it seems to be making the assumption that most people consider fine china to be a functional piece of household ware. Do you agree with this assumption, or would you argue that it is more a work of art with an artist and a history that are "value added" to the physical product? What research should be done before making this decision? Which research methodology do you recommend?

2. Try to anticipate the ways in which the union and the community could discredit the company name if it leaves the United Kingdom. Will U.S. consumers boycott the company *after* the move? Will U.S. consumers voice their disapproval in large numbers *before* the move? How will you get these answers?

3. What specific measures can management take to "inoculate" the firm against the union actions that you anticipated in question 2? Should the firm be proactive rather than dealing with the problem after it is a reality?

4. Should management ask for concessions in order to keep the firm in the United Kingdom? Make a list of possible concessions, and tell who should provide them (for example, union, community, national government, and so on). Concentrate on the long-term solutions when considering how a plan for a win-win solution can be reached in this case.

MORGAN
4

# Part Three
# Product Decisions



Kirk Perry has had a clear vision of his career since his sophomore year in college, when he told his counselor that he wanted to work for Procter & Gamble. He and the counselor developed a plan to help Kirk achieve his goal. They mapped out the courses Kirk would enroll in, the extracurricular activities he would pursue, and the work load he would be expected to shoulder for the next two years as a double major in marketing and finance. Kirk's commitment paid off: He was hired by P&G following his graduation from college and is now a brand manager in the company's health-care advertising division, a position with a tremendous amount of responsibility.

Procter & Gamble is an international company. Most of their products are for the consumer market, and at least one of these products—such as Crest, Scope, Cover Girl, Tide, and Bounty—can be found in approximately 98 percent of the homes in the U.S. and more than 50 percent of households worldwide. Kirk works closely with P&G's advertising agency to develop advertising strategies for the health-care product line.

Companies take their business global in hopes of greater sales and profits. By entering new territories, they increase their market potential. Kirk is well aware that the future of Procter & Gamble lies in countries with developing economies and consumer bases, such as China. While there is certainly some risk involved in investing in these countries, they are home to billions of potential customers. Kirk believes that P&G products will be as popular there as they are in the rest of the world.

# Chapter 9

# Product Concepts

## LEARNING OBJECTIVES

*After studying this chapter, you should be able to*

1 *Define the term* product.

2 *Classify consumer products.*

3 *Define the terms* product item, product line, *and* product mix.

4 *Explain the concept of product life cycles.*

5 *Describe marketing uses of branding.*

6 *Describe marketing uses of packaging and labeling.*

7 *Discuss global issues in branding and packaging.*

8 *Describe how and why product warranties are important marketing tools.*

Eastman Kodak is introducing a new line of 35mm color film called Fun Time. Kodak officials acknowledge that the new line, priced 20 percent below Kodak's GoldPlus line, is intended to compete with lower-priced brands, such as Fuji, that have appeared on the market in recent years.

Promotion of Fun Time will downplay the Kodak name. Fun Time film will not be packaged in Kodak's familiar yellow box, will not be available year-round, and will receive little if any promotional support.[1]

Describe and evaluate Kodak's marketing strategy for Fun Time film.

1 *Define the term* product.

## WHAT IS A PRODUCT?

The product offering, the heart of an organization's marketing program, is usually the starting point in creating a marketing mix. A marketing manager cannot determine a price, design a promotion strategy, or create a distribution channel until the firm has a product to sell. Moreover, an excellent distribution channel, a persuasive promotion campaign, and a fair price have no value with a poor or inadequate product offering.

**product**
Everything, both favorable and unfavorable, that a person receives in an exchange—for example, a good, a service, or an idea.

A **product** may be defined as everything, both favorable and unfavorable, that a person receives in an exchange. A product may be a tangible good like a pair of shoes, a service like a haircut, an idea like obeying driving laws, or any combination of these three. Packaging, style, color, options, and size are some typical product features. Just as important are intangibles such as service, the retailer's image, the manufacturer's reputation, and the way consumers believe others will view the product.

To most people, the term *product* means a tangible good. However, note that services and ideas are also products. (Chapter 11 focuses specifically on the unique aspects of marketing services.) The marketing process identified in Chapter 1 is the same whether the product marketed is a good, a service, an idea, or some combination.

Many products are symbolic; they help us play our roles in society. A man's tie may identify him as a white-collar worker; a pin-striped suit often denotes conservatism. The brand and model of automobile that a person drives may reflect her self-concept. Many other product choices symbolize values, self-concept, and lifestyle—for example, choice of vacations, universities, and memberships in organizations.

People spend their money, time, and energy with the expectation of receiving benefits. A good or service is just a way to deliver user benefits. Charles Revson, the founder of Revlon cosmetics, stated this point succinctly: "In the factory we manufacture cosmetics, but in the store we sell hope." Benefits, not products, are the objective of buying decisions. This distinction has great implications for marketing management. Marketing-oriented firms define their business in terms of the benefits customers seek. Production- and selling-oriented firms often fail because they focus on manufacturing and selling products rather than on satisfying customer wants.

Like other product choices, a person's choice of vacation symbolizes his or her values, self-concept, and lifestyle.

2 *Classify consumer products.*

## TYPES OF CONSUMER PRODUCTS

Products can be classified as either business (industrial) or consumer products, depending on the buyer's intentions. The key distinction between the two types of products is intended use. If the intended use is a business purpose, the product is classified as a business or industrial product. As explained in Chapter 5, a **business product** is used to manufacture other goods or services, to facilitate an organization's operations, or to resell to other customers. A **consumer product** is bought to satisfy an individual's personal wants. Sometimes the same item can be classified as either a business or a consumer product, depending on its intended use. Examples include light bulbs, pencils and paper, and microcomputers.

**business product (industrial product)**
Product used to manufacture other goods or services, to facilitate an organization's operations, or to resell to other customers.

**consumer product**
Product bought to satisfy an individual's personal wants.

We need to know about product classifications because business and consumer products are marketed differently. They are marketed to different target markets and tend to use different distribution, promotion, and pricing strategies.

Chapter 5 examined seven categories of business products: major equipment, accessory equipment, component parts, processed materials, raw materials, supplies, and services. This chapter examines an effective way of categorizing consumer products. Although there are several ways to classify them, the most popular approach includes these four types: convenience products, shopping products, specialty products, and unsought products (see Exhibit 9.1). This approach classifies products according to how much effort is normally used in the shopping process.

### CONVENIENCE PRODUCTS

A **convenience product** is a relatively inexpensive item that merits little shopping effort. That is, a consumer is unwilling to shop extensively for such an item. Candy, soft drinks, combs, aspirin, small hardware items, dry cleaning, and car washes fall into the convenience product category. For some people, a haircut is also a convenience product.

**convenience product**
Relatively inexpensive item that merits little shopping effort.

Consumers buy convenience products regularly, usually without much planning. Nevertheless, consumers do know the brand names of popular convenience products,

*Exhibit 9.1*

Classification of Consumer Products

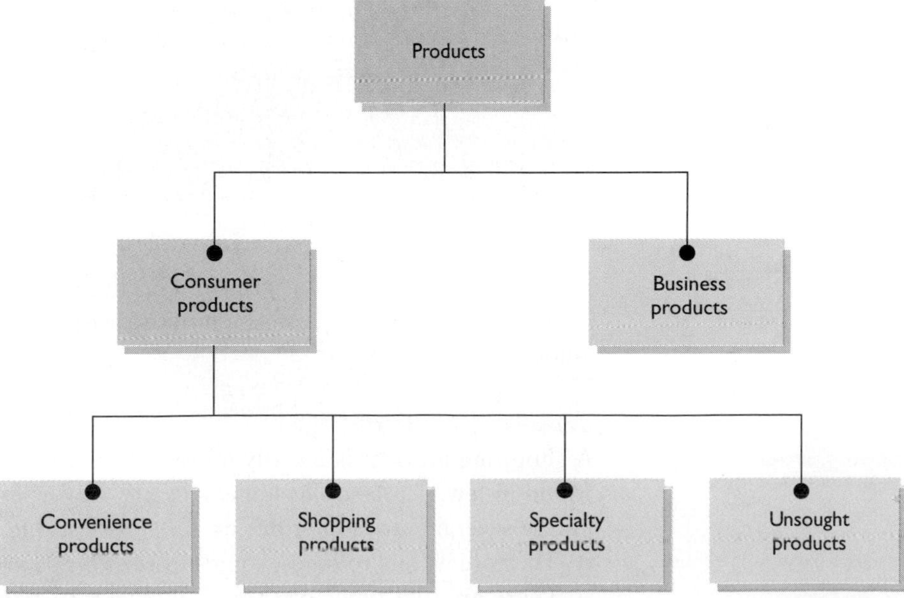

A home *(top)* is a shopping product; people are usually willing to buy a home only after looking at several alternatives and finding the one that best meets their needs. Antiques *(bottom)* may be a shopping product for some people. For people seeking a particular piece, however, antiques are specialty products.

*(top)* © 1992 David Brooks/The Stock Market; *(bottom)* © Jef Apoian/Nawrocki Stock Photo, Inc.

such as Coca-Cola, Bayer aspirin, and Right Guard deodorant. Convenience products normally require wide distribution in order to sell sufficient quantities to meet profit goals.

### SHOPPING PRODUCTS

**shopping product**
Product that requires comparison shopping, because it is usually more expensive than a convenience product and found in fewer stores.

A **shopping product** is usually more expensive than a convenience product and is found in fewer stores. Consumers usually buy a shopping product only after comparing several brands or stores on style, practicality, price, and lifestyle compatibility. They are willing to invest some effort into this process to get the desired benefits.

There are two types of shopping products: homogeneous and heterogeneous.

Insurance is often an unsought product.

Consumers perceive *homogeneous* shopping products as basically similar—for example, washers, dryers, refrigerators, and televisions. With homogeneous shopping products, consumers typically look for the lowest-priced brand that has the desired features.

In contrast, consumers perceive *heterogeneous* shopping products as essentially different—for example, furniture, clothing, housing, and universities. Consumers often have trouble comparing heterogeneous shopping products because the prices, quality, and features vary so much. The benefit of comparing heterogeneous shopping products is "finding the best product or brand for me"; this decision is often highly individual.

## SPECIALTY PRODUCTS

When consumers search extensively for a particular item and are very reluctant to accept substitutes, that item is a **specialty product.** Fine watches, Rolls Royce automobiles, expensive stereo equipment, gourmet restaurants, and highly specialized forms of medical care are generally considered specialty products. A haircut is a specialty product for people who attach great importance to their appearance. These consumers willingly spend much time and effort to have a certain stylist cut their hair. Although many specialty items are very costly, some, like haircuts, are not.

**specialty product**
Product for which consumers search extensively and are very reluctant to accept substitutes.

Specialty products represent a near-perfect fit between the consumer's physical or psychological needs and the product's benefits. Brand names and quality of service are often very important. Marketers of specialty products often use selective, status-conscious advertising to maintain their product's exclusive image. Distribution is often limited to one or a very few outlets in a geographic area.

## UNSOUGHT PRODUCTS

A product unknown to the potential buyer or a known product that the buyer does not actively seek is referred to as an **unsought product.** New products fall into this category until advertising and distribution increase consumer awareness of them.

**unsought product**
Product unknown to the potential buyer or known product that the buyer does not actively seek.

Some goods are always marketed as unsought items, especially needed products we do not like to think about or care to spend money on. Insurance, burial plots, encyclopedias, and similar items require aggressive personal selling and highly persuasive advertising. Salespeople actively seek leads to potential buyers. Because consumers usually do not seek out this type of product, the company must go directly to them through a salesperson, direct mail, or direct-response advertising.

**product item**
Specific version of a product that can be designated as a distinct offering among an organization's products.

3 *Define the terms* product item, product line, *and* product mix.

# PRODUCT ITEMS, LINES, AND MIXES

Rarely does a company sell a single product. More often, it sells a variety of things. A **product item** is a specific version of a product that can be designated as a distinct offering among an organization's products. Gillette's Trac II razor is an example of a product item (see Exhibit 9.2 on page 288).

Exhibit 9.2

Gillette's Product Lines and Product Mix

| | Width of the product mix | | | |
|---|---|---|---|---|
| | **Blades and razors** | **Toiletries** | **Writing instruments** | **Lighters** |
| **Depth of the product lines** | Sensor | Series | Paper Mate | Cricket |
| | Trac II | Adorn | Flair | S. T. Dupont |
| | Atra | Toni | | |
| | Swivel | Right Guard | | |
| | Double-Edge Super Adjustment | Silkience | | |
| | Lady Gillette | Soft and Dri | | |
| | Super Speed | Foamy | | |
| | Twin Injector | Dry Look | | |
| | Techmatic | Dry Idea | | |
| | Three-Piece | Brush Plus | | |
| | Knack | | | |
| | Blades | | | |

**product line**
Group of closely related products offered by the organization.

A group of closely related product items is a **product line.** For example, the column in Exhibit 9.2 titled "Blades and razors" represents one of Gillette's product lines. Different container sizes and shapes also distinguish items in a product line. Diet Coke, for example, is available in cans and various plastic containers. Each size and each container is a separate product item.

**product mix**
All the products that an organization sells.

An organization's **product mix** includes all the products it sells. All Gillette's products—blades and razors, toiletries, writing instruments, lighters—constitute its product mix. Each product item in the product mix may require a separate marketing strategy. In some cases, however, product lines and even entire product mixes share some marketing strategy components. The Pontiac division of General Motors, for example, promotes all Pontiac items and lines with its theme "We build excitement—Pontiac."

Organizations derive several benefits from organizing related items into product lines, including the following:

- *Advertising economies:* Product lines provide economies of scale in advertising. Several products can be advertised under the umbrella of the line. Rising media costs increase the advantages of product line advertising. Campbell Soup, for example, can talk about its soup being "m-m-good" and promote the entire line. Advertising a product line can also enhance the corporate name. For example, *Heinz's 57 Varieties* names both the product line and the corporation.
- *Package uniformity:* A product line can benefit from package uniformity. All packages in the line may have a common look and still keep their individual identities. Yet one item in the line can advertise another. Some examples

include Lean Cuisine frozen dinners, Green Giant frozen vegetables, and Hermes men's toiletries.

- *Standardized components:* Product lines allow firms to standardize components, thus reducing manufacturing and inventory costs. For example, many of the components Samsonite uses in its folding tables and chairs are also used in its patio furniture. General Motors uses the same parts on many automobile makes and models.
- *Efficient sales and distribution:* A product line enables sales personnel for companies like Procter & Gamble to provide a full range of choices to customers. Distributors and retailers are often more inclined to stock the company's products if it offers a full line. Transportation and warehousing costs are likely to be lower for a product line than for a collection of individual items.
- *Equivalent quality:* Purchasers usually expect and believe that all products in a line are about equal in quality. Consumers expect, for example, that all Campbell soups and all Mary Kay cosmetics will be of similar quality.

## DIMENSIONS OF THE PRODUCT OFFERING

**product mix width**
Number of product lines that an organization offers.

**product line depth**
Number of product items in a product line.

**product mix consistency**
Extent to which product lines are similar in terms of end use, distribution outlets used, target markets, and price range.

Marketers often characterize a company's product offering with reference to three dimensions. **Product mix width** refers to the number of product lines an organization offers. In Exhibit 9.2, for example, the width of Gillette's product mix is four product lines. **Product line depth** is the number of product items in a product line. As shown in Exhibit 9.2, the blades and razors product line consists of twelve product items; the toiletries product line includes ten product items. **Product mix consistency** refers to the extent that product lines are similar in terms of end use, distribution outlets, target markets, and price range. According to these characteristics, Gillette's product mix is generally consistent. Product line depth and product mix width and consistency are all related to marketing strategy.

Firms increase the *depth* of product lines to attract buyers with different preferences, to increase sales and profits by further segmenting the market, to capitalize on economies of scale in production and marketing, and to even out seasonal sales patterns. Between 1970 and 1993, for example, Timex increased the depth of its wristwatch line from 300 items to 1,500 items.[7] Exhibit 9.3 on page 290 illustrates Procter & Gamble's product line of eleven laundry detergents, the positioning strategy for each brand, and each brand's market share.

Firms increase the *width* of their product mix to diversify risk. To generate sales and boost profits, firms spread risk across many product lines rather than depending on only one or two. Firms also widen their product mix to capitalize on established reputations. For example, by introducing new product lines, Kodak capitalized on its image as a leader in photographic products. Kodak's product lines now include film, processing, still cameras, movie cameras, paper, and chemicals. Firms may narrow their product mix, too. Avon Products reduced the width of its product mix by selling its health care division. The company could then focus more on its main business—beauty care products.

By maintaining *consistency* in their product mix, firms like Campbell Soup can secure a powerful market position in a general area of specialization. They also can capitalize on economies of scale in development, manufacturing, and marketing. The McIlhenny Company has profited from the reputation of its Tabasco brand pepper sauce by introducing a Bloody Mary mix and a picanté sauce.[3] In contrast, some firms choose to develop inconsistent product mixes, to diversify risk and capitalize on new opportunities in unrelated areas. Neither strategy is necessarily better.

*Exhibit 9.3*

Procter & Gamble's Laundry Detergent Product Line

Source: Jennifer Lawrence, "Don't Look for P&G to Pare Detergents," *Advertising Age*, 31 May 1993, p. 3. Reprinted with permission from the May 3, 1993 issue of *Advertising Age*. Copyright, Crain Communications, Inc., 1993.

| Brand | Positioning | Market share |
|---|---|---|
| Tide | Tough, powerful cleaning | 31.1% |
| Cheer | Tough cleaning and color protection | 8.2 |
| Bold | Detergent plus fabric softener | 2.9 |
| Gain | Sunshine scent and odor-removing formula | 2.6 |
| Era | Stain pretreatment and stain removal | 2.2 |
| Dash | Value brand | 1.8 |
| Oxydol | Bleach-boosted formula, with whitening | 1.4 |
| Solo | Detergent and fabric softener in liquid form | 1.2 |
| Dreft | Outstanding cleaning for baby clothes, safe for tender skin | 1.0 |
| Ivory Snow | Fabric and skin safety on baby clothes and fine washables | 0.7 |
| Ariel | Tough cleaner, aimed at Hispanics | 0.1 |

What works for one firm does not necessarily work for another, although the risks of developing an inconsistent product mix tend to exceed the risks of developing a consistent product mix. For example, Avis, the car rental firm, entered the quick-lube business in the late 1980s. The company opened only 67 franchised quick-lube stations, far fewer than its goal of 200. So bitter were franchisees that many demanded refunds, and some filed lawsuits alleging fraud and misrepresentation.[4] Allegheny Ludlum Steel, on the other hand, successfully markets Allegheny Steel, Jacobsen lawn mowers, True Temper tools and sporting goods, Carmet and IPM audio products, and Arnold magnetic tapes. Allegheny Ludlum's product mix is inconsistent, but its strategy does not pose a handicap.

## ADJUSTMENTS TO PRODUCT ITEMS, LINES, AND MIXES

Over time, firms change product items, lines, and mixes to take advantage of new technical or product developments or to respond to changes in the environment. They may adjust by modifying products, respositioning products, or extending or contracting product lines.

### Product Modifications

**product modification**
Change in one or more of a product's characteristics—for example, its quality, functional characteristics, or style.

Marketing managers must decide if and when to modify existing products. **Product modification** changes one or more of a product's characteristics:

- *Quality modification:* change in a product's dependability or durability. Reducing a product's quality may let the manufacturer lower the price and appeal to target markets unable to afford the original product. The story about Eastman Kodak at the beginning of this chapter illustrates this type of quality modification. On the other hand, increasing quality can help the firm compete with rival firms. Increasing quality can also result in increased brand loyalty, greater ability to raise prices, or new opportunities for market segmentation. Automobile safety features such as antilock brakes and air bags are examples of this type of quality modification.

- *Functional modification:* change in a product's versatility, effectiveness, convenience, or safety. In response to widespread consumer perceptions that aerosol propellants are harmful to the environment, Dow Chemical began offering its bathroom cleaner in a trigger-spray version. The Procter & Gamble deodorant brands Right Guard, Old Spice, and Sure Pro have also been introduced in non-aerosol trigger-spray or pump versions.[5]
- *Style modification:* aesthetic product change, rather than a quality or functional change. Clothing manufacturers commonly use style modifications to motivate customers to replace products before they are worn out. **Planned obsolescence** is a term commonly used to describe the practice of modifying products so those that have already been sold become obsolete before they actually need replacement. Some argue that planned obsolescence is wasteful; some claim it is unethical. Marketers respond that consumers favor style modifications because they like changes in the appearance of goods like clothing and cars. Marketers also contend that consumers, not manufacturers and marketers, decide when styles are obsolete.

**planned obsolescence**
Practice of changing a product's style so that it becomes outdated before it actually needs replacement.

## Repositioning

Repositioning, as Chapter 6 explained, is changing consumers' perceptions of a product. For example, Kentucky Fried Chicken is trying to reposition itself to attract more health-conscious customers. The strategy includes gradually changing the restaurant's name to KFC, reducing dependence on the word *fried,* and adding grilled, broiled, and baked poultry items to the menu. The Colonel's Rotisserie Gold, a marinated, slow-roasted chicken product, is what the company calls "its repositioning linchpin."[6]

Changing demographics, declining sales, or competitors' actions often motivate firms to reposition established products. For example, the changing demographics of snackers and eroding market share led Frito-Lay to reposition its top-selling brand, Fritos, after fifty-eight years of successfully targeting all ages. The repositioning effort includes making major changes in the Fritos logo and packaging, focusing on those between the ages of 9 and 18, and launching a major new radio and TV advertising campaign.[7] Gillette repositioned Dry Idea deodorant from a unisex brand to a women's brand in an effort to increase its sales volume.[8]

## Product Line Extensions

Each product line that an organization offers covers a part of the total range of products offered by the entire industry. For example, Lawn Boy mowers compete in the medium-high price range of the lawn mower market. When a company's management decides to add additional products to an existing product line in order to compete more broadly in the industry, **line extension** occurs. For instance, Procter & Gamble and SmithKline Beecham extended their dental hygiene product lines by introducing items with baking soda.[9] Dockers Authentics, targeted toward a more upscale consumer than the original Docker clothing line, is another recent example of product line extension.[10]

**line extension**
Practice of adding products to a product line.

ETHICS IN MARKETING

## Are "Kiddie" Cocktails for Kids?

The liquor industry has launched a fresh wave of low-alcohol cocktails that critics say will be tempting for teenagers. Low-alcohol cocktails, bearing such familiar brand names as Jack Daniel's and mixed with fruit juice or soda, are one of the few promising segments in the stagnant spirits industry. New drinks with a sweet taste, brightly colored labels, and names like Tahitian Tangerine and Dixie Jazzberry are flooding into grocery stores and liquor outlets.

Brown-Forman, flush with the success of its Jack Daniel's Country Cocktails, introduced a line of Southern Comfort Cocktails. Grand Metropolitan PLC's Heublein followed its twelve-proof José Cuervo Margaritas with Smirnoff Quenchers, a lower-power line of fruity, vodka-laced drinks.

The new concoctions amount to a kind of kiddie cocktail, critics contend. Some are even sold in familiar, twelve-ounce aluminum cans with pop-tops—just like Coke and Pepsi.

"It's an easy leap from Coca-Cola to Jim Beam and Cola. These are transitional products deliberately intended to blur lines between soft drinks and alcoholic drinks," says Jean Kilbourne, a frequent critic of the spirits industry who advises federal officials on alcohol abuse.[11]

Liquor marketers deny that they are targeting underage drinkers or that these new products are intended to be "transitional," as some critics claim. Do you consider it ethical to market these low-alcohol prepared cocktails? Do you think these new products will increase alcohol consumption and abuse among teenagers? Are some populations more vulnerable than others? Should these low-alcohol products be available in grocery stores where beer is sold, or should they be restricted to liquor stores and other outlets licensed to sell high-alcohol products?



The Ethics in Marketing box in this section describes questionable product line extensions by alcoholic beverage marketers.

### Product Line Contraction

Sometimes product lines become overextended. When this happens, some items in the product line need to be eliminated. Symptoms of product line overextension include the following:

- Some products in the line do not contribute to profits because of low sales or cannibalize sales of other items in the line.
- Manufacturing or marketing resources are disproportionately allocated to slow-moving products.
- Some items in the line are obsolete because of new product entries in the line or new products offered by competitors.

Three major benefits are likely when a firm contracts overextended product lines. First, resources become concentrated on the most important products. Second, managers no longer waste resources trying to improve the sales and profits of poorly performing products. Third, new product items have a greater chance of being successful because more financial and human resources are available to manage them.

*Exhibit 9.4*

Four Stages of the Product Life Cycle

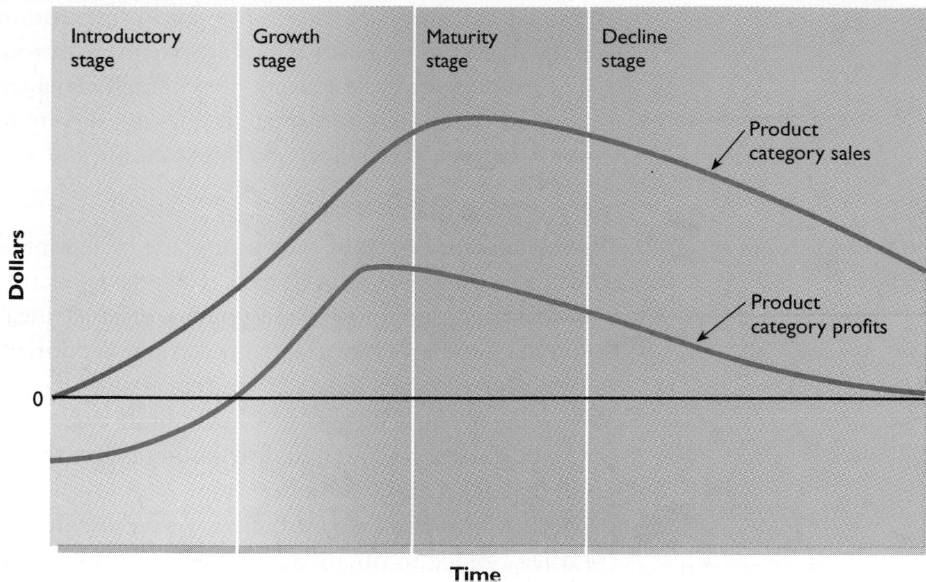


4 *Explain the concept of product life cycles.*

**product life cycle**
Concept describing a product's acceptance in the marketplace over four stages: introduction, growth, maturity, and decline.

**product category**
All brands that satisfy a particular type of need.

## PRODUCT LIFE CYCLES

The **product life cycle** is one of the most familiar concepts in marketing. Few other general concepts have been so widely discussed. Although some researchers have challenged the theoretical basis and managerial value of the product life cycle, most believe it has great potential as a marketing management tool.

The product life cycle concept provides a way to trace the stages of a product's acceptance, from its introduction (birth) to its decline (death). As Exhibit 9.4 shows, a product progresses through four major stages: introduction, growth, maturity, and decline. Note that the product life cycle illustrated in Exhibit 9.4 does not refer to any one brand. Rather it refers to the life cycle for a product category or product class. A **product category** includes all brands that satisfy a particular type of need. Product categories include, for example, passenger cars, cigarettes, soft drinks, and coffee.

The time a product spends in any one stage of the life cycle may vary dramatically. Some products, such as fad items, move through the entire cycle in weeks. Others, such as electric clothes washers and dryers, stay in the maturity stage for decades. Exhibit 9.4 illustrates the typical life cycle for a consumer durable good, such as a washer or dryer. In contrast, Exhibit 9.5 illustrates typical life cycles for styles (such as formal, business, or casual clothing), fashions (such as miniskirts or

*Exhibit 9.5*

Product Life Cycles for Styles, Fashions, and Fads

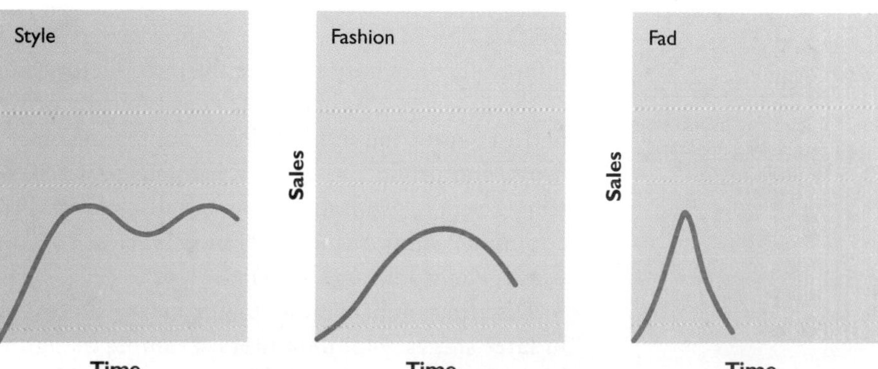

stirrup pants), and fads (such as leopard-print clothing). Changes in a product, its uses, its image, or its positioning can extend that product's life cycle.

The product life cycle concept does not tell managers the length of a product's life cycle or its duration in any stage. It does not dictate marketing strategy. It is simply a tool to help marketers forecast future events and suggest appropriate strategies.

## INTRODUCTORY STAGE

**introductory stage**
First stage of the product life cycle, which represents the full-scale launch of a new product into the marketplace.

The **introductory stage** of the product life cycle represents the full-scale launch of a new product into the marketplace. (Chapter 10 examines the process of developing a new product, or transforming a new-product idea into a marketable product.) Computer databases for personal use, room-deodorizing air conditioning filters, and wind-powered home-electric generators are all product categories that have recently entered the product life cycle. A high failure rate, little competition, frequent product modification, and limited distribution typify the introduction stage of the product life cycle.

Marketing costs in the introductory stage are normally high. High dealer margins are often needed to obtain adequate distribution, and incentives are needed to get consumers to try the new product. Advertising expenses are high because of the need to educate consumers about the new product's benefits. Production costs are also often high in this stage, as product and manufacturing flaws are identified and corrected and efforts are undertaken to develop mass-production economies.

As Exhibit 9.4 illustrates, sales normally increase slowly during the introductory stage. Moreover, profits are usually negative because of research and development costs, factory tooling, and high introduction costs.

The length of the introductory phase is largely determined by product characteristics, such as the product's advantages over substitute products, the educational effort required, and management's commitment of resources to the new item. A short introductory period is usually preferred, to help reduce the impact of negative earnings and cash flow. As soon as the product gets off the ground, the financial burden should begin to diminish. Also, a short introduction helps dispel some of the uncertainty surrounding the new product.

Promotion strategy in the introductory stage focuses on developing product awareness and informing consumers about the product category's potential benefits. At this stage the communication challenge is to stimulate primary demand—demand for the product in general rather than a specific brand. Intensive personal selling is often required to gain acceptance for the product among wholesalers and retailers. Promotion of convenience products often requires heavy consumer sampling and couponing. Shopping and specialty products demand educational advertising and personal selling to the final consumer.

## GROWTH STAGE

**growth stage**
Second stage of the product life cycle, characterized by increasing sales, heightened competition, and healthy profits.

If a product category survives the introductory stage, it advances to the **growth stage** of the life cycle. In this stage, sales typically grow at an increasing rate, many competitors enter the market, large companies may start to acquire small pioneering firms, and profits are healthy. Emphasis switches from primary demand promotion (for example, promoting compact disc players) to aggressive brand advertising and communication of the differences between brands (for example, promoting Sony versus Panasonic and RCA).

Distribution becomes a major key to success during the growth stage, as well as in later stages. Manufacturers scramble to sign up dealers and distributors and to build long-term relationships. Without adequate distribution, it is impossible to establish a strong market position.

Toward the end of the growth phase, prices normally begin falling and profits peak. Price reductions result from increasing economies of scale and increased competition. Also, most firms have recovered their development costs by now, and their priority is in increasing or retaining market share and enhancing profits.

## MATURITY STAGE

**maturity stage**
Third stage of the product life cycle, in which sales begin to level off and the market approaches saturation.

A period during which sales increase at a decreasing rate signals the beginning of the **maturity stage** of the life cycle. New users cannot be added indefinitely, and sooner or later the market approaches saturation. Normally, this is the longest stage of the product life cycle. Many major household appliances are in the maturity stage of their life cycles. For example, over half of all washer, dryer, and refrigerator purchases are replacements for worn-out products rather than purchases by new users.

For shopping products and many specialty products, annual models begin to appear during the maturity stage. Product lines are lengthened to appeal to additional market segments. Service and repair assume more important roles as manufacturers strive to distinguish their products from others. Product design changes tend to become stylistic (how can the product be made different?) rather than functional (how can the product be made better?). Pepsi-Cola North America, for example, is marketing its mature soda line by developing such line extensions as Crystal.[12] R.J. Reynolds is making some changes in the packaging, ingredients, and marketing program for its Winston Select cigarettes so it can compete more effectively against Marlboro.[13] Powdered drink mixes, electric drip coffee pots, and high-meat-content dog foods are examples of other products in the maturity stage.

As prices and profits continue to fall, marginal competitors start dropping out of the market. Dealer margins also shrink, resulting in less shelf space for mature items, lower dealer inventories, and a general reluctance to promote the product. Thus promotion to dealers often intensifies during this stage, in order to retain loyalty.

Heavy consumer promotion by the manufacturer is also required to maintain market share. Consider these well-known examples of competition in the maturity stage: the so-called "cola war" featuring Coke and Pepsi, the "beer war" featuring Anheuser-Busch's Budweiser brands and Philip Morris's Miller brands, and the "burger wars" pitting leader McDonald's against challengers Burger King and Wendy's. In the coffee product category, Kraft General Foods' Maxwell House and Procter & Gamble's Folgers brand each accounted for about 30 percent of the market. After several years of sluggish sales, Maxwell House launched new, hard-hitting comparative ads claiming that consumers prefer its taste to Folgers. Folgers protested to Kraft General Foods and the major television networks, asserting that the results were wrong and the advertising was unfair.[14]

Another characteristic of the maturity stage is the emergence of so-called "niche marketers" that target narrow, well-defined, underserved segments of a market. Starbucks Coffee, for example, targets its gourmet line at the only segment of the coffee market that is growing: new, younger, more affluent coffee drinkers.[15] David Stone, president of Black & Decker's household products group, which markets mature products like irons, has noted that "you can get fanatically loyal customers even if you serve a niche that's only five percent of the marketplace, so now we're serving niches."[16]

## DECLINE STAGE

**decline stage**
Fourth and final stage of the product life cycle, in which sales drop and falling demand forces many competitors out of the market.

A long-run drop in sales signals the beginning of the **decline stage.** The rate of decline is governed by how rapidly consumer tastes change or substitute products are adopted. Many convenience products and fad items lose their market overnight, leaving large inventories of unsold items, such as designer jeans. Others die more slowly, like citizen band (CB) radios, black-and-white console television sets, and nonelectronic wristwatches.

Some firms have developed successful strategies for marketing products in the decline stage of the product life cycle. They eliminate all nonessential marketing expenses and let the brand decline at a normal rate. Cutting advertising does not hurt sales in the decline stage.

## IMPLICATIONS FOR MARKETING MANAGEMENT

The product life cycle concept encourages marketing managers to plan so they can take the initiative instead of reacting to past events. The product life cycle is especially useful as a predicting or forecasting tool. Because products pass through distinctive stages, it is often possible to estimate a product's location on the curve using historical data. Profits, like sales, tend to follow a predictable path over a product's life cycle.

It is important to realize, however, that products and brands in the maturity stage of the product life cycle do not necessarily slip directly into decline and then elimination. Several strategies are available to marketing managers to sustain, and even expand, sales of product categories or brands in the maturity stage:

- *Promoting more frequent use of the product by current customers:* The Florida Orange Growers Association successfully used this strategy in its Orange Juice Is Not Just for Breakfast campaign. Overall juice consumption rose following TV ads reminding people that orange juice is a healthy, refreshing beverage suitable for any time of the day.
- *Finding new target markets for the product:* Johnson's baby shampoo was remarkably successful in adding mothers, sisters, and later fathers and brothers to the original target market of infants. The new theme, "It's mild enough to use every day," was the only change in the product's marketing strategy, yet it was enough to expand the target market's size several hundred percent.
- *Finding new uses for the product:* After decades of level sales, Arm & Hammer baking soda was promoted as a refrigerator freshener, plumbing system cleaner, litter box freshener, and even a toothpaste. Sales surged when each new suggested use appeared in print and television advertisements.
- *Pricing the brand below the market:* Bic pens and Timex watches revolutionized their industries. Their competitors had not successfully introduced brands of acceptable quality at low prices. The introduction of these two brands substantially changed the shape of the product life cycle for ballpoint pens and wristwatches.
- *Developing new distribution channels:* For years Woolite fabric cleaner was sold only in department stores. Then American Home Products introduced the brand in supermarkets and grocery stores without changing the product, the price, or the promotional appeal. Sales tripled in the first year.[17]
- *Adding new ingredients or deleting old ingredients:* The laundry detergent industry has relied on this strategy to extend the life cycles of brands, adding whiteners, brighteners, bleaches, scents, and various other ingredients and attributes. Unscented Bounce, Charmin-Free, decaffeinated beverages, and sugar-free soft drinks all are products with deleted ingredients.
- *Making a dramatic new guarantee:* Spray'n Wash shifted from declining sales to rapidly growing sales almost immediately after offering this guarantee: "If Spray'n Wash doesn't remove a stain from a shirt—any shirt—we'll buy you a new shirt."[18]

Exhibit 9.6 briefly summarizes some typical marketing strategies during each stage of the product life cycle.

5 *Describe marketing uses of branding.*

## BRANDING

The success of any business or consumer product depends in part on the target market's ability to distinguish one product from another. Branding is the main tool marketers use to distinguish their products from the competition's.

**brand**
Name, term, symbol, design, or combination thereof that identifies a seller's products and differentiates them from competitors' products.

**brand name**
Part of a brand that can be spoken, including letters, words, and numbers.

**brand mark**
Elements of a brand that cannot be spoken, such as symbols.

A **brand** is a name, term, symbol, design, or combination thereof that identifies a seller's products and differentiates them from competitors' products. A **brand name** is that part of a brand that can be spoken, including letters (GM, YMCA); words (Chevrolet); and numbers (WD-40, 7-Eleven). The elements of a brand that cannot be spoken are called the **brand mark**—for example, the well-known Mercedes-Benz and Delta Airlines symbols.

### BENEFITS OF BRANDING

Branding has three main purposes: product identification, repeat sales, and new product sales. The most important purpose is *product identification*. Branding allows marketers to distinguish their products from all others. Many brand names are familiar to consumers and indicate quality. Exhibit 9.7 on page 298 lists, in order, the ten brand names that U.S. consumers believe signify the highest-quality products.[19]

**brand equity**
Value of successful company and brand names.

The term **brand equity** refers to the value of company and brand names. Brand equity, not the value of the company's facilities, was the reason RJR Nabisco was bought out for a record price in 1988. RJR Nabisco brands with hefty brand equity include Del Monte fruits and vegetables, Ritz crackers, and Camel cigarettes.[20] *Financial World* magazine has reported that the world's top brands in terms of dollar

*Exhibit 9.6*

Typical Marketing Strategies during the Product Life Cycle

| Marketing mix strategy | Product life cycle stage | | | |
|---|---|---|---|---|
| | **Introduction** | **Growth** | **Maturity** | **Decline** |
| Product strategy | Limited number of models; frequent product modifications | Expanded number of models; frequent product modifications | Large number of models | Elimination of unprofitable models and brands |
| Distribution strategy | Distribution usually limited, depending on product; intensive efforts and high margins often needed to attract wholesalers and retailers | Expanded number of dealers; intensive efforts to establish long-term relationships with wholesalers and retailers | Extensive number of dealers; margins declining; intensive efforts to retain distributors and shelf space | Unprofitable outlets phased out |
| Promotion strategy | Develop product awareness; stimulate primary demand; use intensive personal selling to distributors; use sampling and couponing for consumers | Stimulate selective demand; advertise brand aggressively | Stimulate selective demand; advertise brand aggressively; promote heavily to retain dealers and customers | Phase out all promotion |
| Pricing strategy | Prices are usually high to recover development costs (see Chapter 19) | Prices begin to fall toward end of growth stage as result of competitive pressure | Prices continue to fall | Prices stabilize at relatively low level; small price rises are possible if competition is negligible |

*Exhibit 9.7*

Most Respected Brand Names in the United States

Source: "Measuring Quality Perceptions of America's Top Brands," *Brandweek*, 4 April 1994, pp. 24–26.

| | |
|---|---|
| 1. Disney World | 2. Fisher-Price toys |
| 2. Disneyland | 7. Reynolds Wrap aluminum foil |
| 3. Kodak photographic film | 8. AT&T long-distance telephone service |
| 4. Hallmark greeting cards | 9. Levi's jeans |
| 5. Mercedes-Benz automobiles | 10. Ziploc bags |

value are Marlboro and Coca-Cola—each valued at over $33 billion.[21] Companies like Procter & Gamble spend over $5 million per day to reinforce the brand equity of their products.

**master brand**
Brand so dominant in consumers' minds that they think of it immediately when a product category, use situation, product attribute, or customer benefit is mentioned.

The term **master brand** has been used to refer to a brand so dominant in consumers' minds that they think of it immediately when a product category, use situation, product attribute, or customer benefit is mentioned.[22] Exhibit 9.8 lists the master brands in several product categories. How many other brands can you name in these eleven product categories? Can you name any other product categories in which the master brands listed in Exhibit 9.8 compete? Probably not many. *Campbell's* means soup to consumers; it doesn't mean high-quality food products.

U.S. brands command substantial premiums in many places around the world. Procter & Gamble's Whisper sanitary napkins sell for ten times the price of local brands in China. Johnson & Johnson brands like Johnson's baby shampoo and Band-Aids command a 500 percent premium in China.[23] Gillette disposable razors sell for twice the price of local brands in India.

*Exhibit 9.8*

Master Brands in Selected Product Categories

Source: Peter H. Farquhar et al., "Strategies for Leveraging Master Brands," *Marketing Research*, September 1992, pp. 32–43. Courtesy American Marketing Association.

| Product category | Master brand |
|---|---|
| Baking soda | Arm & Hammer |
| Adhesive bandages | Band-Aid |
| Rum | Bacardi |
| Antacids | Alka-Seltzer |
| Gelatin | Jell-O |
| Soup | Campbell's |
| Salt | Morton |
| Toy trains | Lionel |
| Cream cheese | Philadelphia |
| Crayons | Crayola |
| Petroleum jelly | Vaseline |

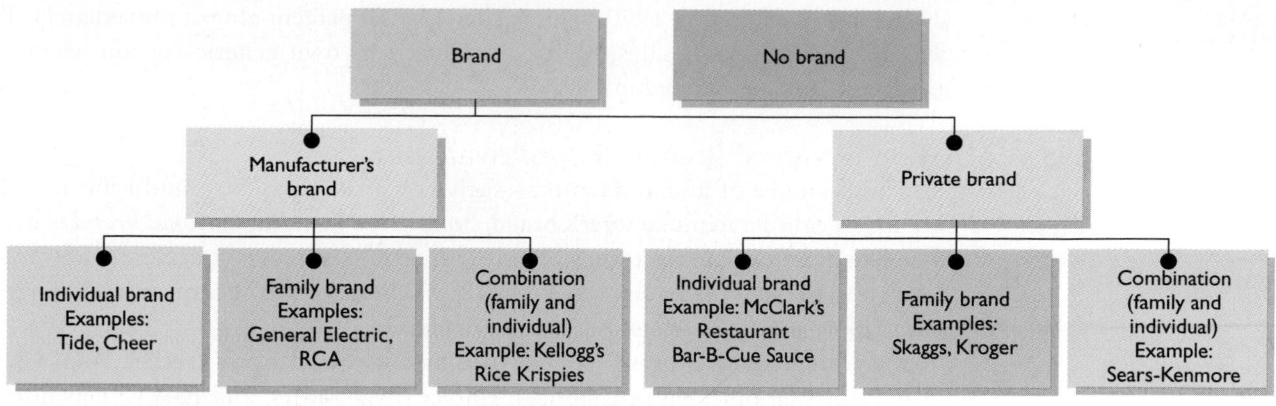


*Exhibit 9.9*

Major Branding Decisions

**brand loyalty**
Consumer's consistent preference for one brand over all others in its product category.

The best generator of *repeat sales* is satisfied customers.[24] Branding helps consumers identify products they wish to buy again and avoid those they do not. **Brand loyalty,** a consistent preference for one brand over all others, is quite high in some product categories. Over half the users in product categories such as cigarettes, mayonnaise, toothpaste, coffee, headache remedies, photographic film, bath soap, and catsup are loyal to one brand. The annual Monitor poll conducted by Yankelovich Partners reports that 74 percent of respondents "find a brand they like, then resist efforts to get them to change." Once consumers are convinced of the quality and value of a particular brand, it takes a lot of money and effort to change their minds.[25] Brand identity is essential to developing brand loyalty.

The third main purpose of branding is to facilitate *new product sales.* Company and brand names like those listed in Exhibit 9.7 and Exhibit 9.8 are extremely useful when introducing new products.

## BRANDING STRATEGIES

Firms face complex branding decisions. As Exhibit 9.9 illustrates, the first decision is whether to brand at all. Some firms actually use the lack of a brand name as a selling point. These unbranded products are called generic products. Firms that decide to brand their products may choose to follow a policy of using manufacturers' brands, private (distributor) brands, or both. In either case, they must then decide among a policy of individual branding (different brands for different products), family branding (common names for different products), or a combination of individual branding and family branding.

### Generic Products versus Branded Products

**generic product**
No-frills, no–brand name, low-cost product.

A **generic product** is typically a no-frills, no–brand name, low-cost product that is simply identified by its product category. The concept of generic products became popular in the late 1970s. (Note that a generic product and a brand name that becomes generic, such as cellophane, are not the same thing.) Generic products have captured significant market shares in some product categories, such as canned fruits, canned vegetables, and paper products.

The main appeal of generics is their low price. Generic grocery products are usually 30 to 40 percent less expensive than manufacturers' brands in the same product category and 20 to 25 percent less expensive than retailer-owned brands.

Pharmaceuticals is another product category where generics have made inroads. When patents on successful pharmaceutical products expire, low-cost generics rapidly appear on the market. When the patent on Merck's popular antiarthritis drug Clinoril expired in 1990, sales declined by 50 percent almost immediately. To avoid a similar loss of sales, Merck introduced its own generic version when its patent on Dolobid expired in 1992.[26]

## Manufacturers' Brands versus Private Brands

**manufacturer's brand**
Manufacturer's name used as a brand name.

**private brand**
Brand name that a wholesaler or a retailer uses for products it sells.

The brand name of a manufacturer—such as Kodak, Lazy Boy, and Fruit-of-the-Loom—is called a **manufacturer's brand.** Sometimes the term *national brand* is used as a synonym for manufacturer's brand. This term is not always accurate, however, because many manufacturers serve only regional markets. The term *manufacturer's brand* more precisely defines the brand's owner.

A **private brand** is a brand name owned by a wholesaler or a retailer. Hunt Club (a JCPenney brand), Sam's American Choice (Wal-Mart), and IGA (Independent Grocers' Association) are all private brands. Private brands account for about 15 percent of total dollar sales in U.S. supermarkets and about 36 percent of total dollar sales in British supermarkets; some experts predict private label products will represent a quarter of U.S. supermarket volume by 1998 and eventually as much as half.[27] About 11 percent of U.S. department stores' apparel sales are private label brands, and further growth is expected.[28] U.S. retailers and wholesalers generally expect the quality of private brand merchandise to improve in the future, providing customers with better value and retailers with opportunities to differentiate themselves from competitors.[29] Consumer experts agree. *Consumer Reports,* for example, rated twenty-five brands of chocolate chip cookies; two of the three most highly rated were private brands.[30]

Despite the growing appeal of private brands, most wholesalers are too small to develop their own brands and rely instead on manufacturers' brands. But as retailers and wholesalers grow, they often must decide whether to establish their own private brands or to continue selling only manufacturers' brands. The advantages of staying with manufacturers' brands include the following:

- Heavy advertising to the consumer by manufacturers like Procter & Gamble helps develop strong consumer loyalties.
- Well-known manufacturers' brands, such as Kodak and Fisher-Price, can attract new customers and enhance the dealer's (wholesaler's or retailer's) prestige.
- Many manufacturers offer rapid delivery, enabling the dealer to carry less inventory.
- If a dealer happens to sell a manufacturer's brand of poor quality, the customer may simply switch brands but remain loyal to the dealer.

The advantages of developing private brands include these:

- A dealer can usually earn higher profits on its own brand. In addition, because the private brand is exclusive, there is less pressure to mark the price down to meet competition.
- A manufacturer can decide to drop a brand or a dealer at any time or even to become a direct competitor to its dealers.
- A private brand ties the customer to the dealer. A person who wants a Die-Hard battery must go to Sears.
- Dealers have no control over the intensity of distribution of manufacturers' brands. Wal-Mart store managers don't have to worry about competing with other sellers of Sam's American Choice products or Ol' Roy dog food. They know that these brands are sold only in Wal-Mart and Sam's Wholesale Club stores.

However, these advantages can be offset by some important disadvantages associated with private brands:

- Dealers must market the brand, thus cutting into profits.
- To obtain a favorable price on products carrying their private brand, dealers must often buy in large quantities. Thus dealers incur all the costs and risks, such as deterioration and obsolescence, of carrying large inventories.
- If the product is of poor quality, customers have only the dealers to blame. Therefore, dealers may lose the customers.
- Some dealers, particularly discounters, have trouble promoting their own brands because consumers perceive them as lower in quality. Kmart, for example, has added more manufacturers' brands in recent years in order to upgrade its image.

## Individual Brands versus Family Brands

**individual branding**
Practice of using a different brand name for each product.

Many companies use different brand names for different products; this practice is referred to as **individual branding.** Companies use individual brands when their products vary greatly in use or performance. For instance, it would not make sense to use the same brand name for a pair of dress socks and a baseball bat. Individual brands are also used when products vary greatly in quality. Holiday Inn distinguishes its upscale hotels with the name Holiday Inn Crowne Plaza. This name enables management to maintain the prestigious image of this high-quality product while fiercely competing in a less prestigious market with Holiday Inn, a lesser-quality, lower-priced brand that offers fewer amenities. Likewise, Procter & Gamble targets different segments of the laundry detergent market with Bold, Cheer, Dash, Dreft, Era, Gain, Ivory Snow, Oxydol, Solo, and Tide. The Dial Corp. markets Dial and Tone soaps, Brillo soap pads, Purex bleach and detergent, Parson's ammonia, Treet luncheon meats, and a host of other brands.[31]

**family brand**
Practice of using the same brand name to market several different products.

On the other hand, a company that markets several different products under the same brand name is using a **family brand.** For example, Sony's family brand includes radios, television sets, stereos, and other electronic products. A brand name can only be stretched so far, however. Such products as Bic pantyhose, Life Savers gum, and Sara Lee dinner entrees soon failed, and Dial deodorant hasn't nearly matched the success of Dial bar soap. Johnson & Johnson was surprised when consumers didn't flock to buy its baby aspirin, but research revealed that the Johnson & Johnson name was synonymous with gentle baby products. Further research showed that parents who use baby aspirin are more concerned with quickly reducing the child's fever than with providing gentleness.

## Co-Branding

**co-branding**
Placing two or more brand names on a product or its package.

**Co-branding** entails placing two or more brand names on a product or its package. Co-branding is a useful strategy when a combination of brand names enhances the prestige or perceived value of a product or when it benefits brand owners and users.

Co-branding may be used to identify product ingredients or components. The brand name NutraSweet and its familiar brand mark appear on more than 3,000 food and beverage products.[32] Intel, the microprocessor company, pays microcomputer manufacturers like IBM, Dell, and Compaq to include "Intel inside" in their advertising, on the computers, and on the boxes they are packed in.

Co-branding may also be used when two or more organizations wish to collaborate to offer a product. For example, food giants ConAgra and Kellogg have joined together to market Healthy Choice multigrain adult cereals. Neither Kellogg nor

Jeep spends a lot on advertising designed to protect its trademarked name. The front grill is also an element of its trademark, an important symbol of its brand identity.

Courtesy of the Chrysler Corporation

ConAgra has been successful in previous attempts to penetrate the adult segment of the breakfast food market.[33]

Sometimes, firms co-brand to add value to products that are generally perceived to be homogeneous shopping goods or services. Citibank co-brands Visa and MasterCards with Ford and with American Airlines. American Airlines also co-brands long-distance telephone service with MCI. Users of these co-brands receive the benefits received by other credit card holders and long-distance subscribers plus additional benefits, such as automobile purchase discounts or frequent-flier miles.

## TRADEMARKS

**trademark**
Legal, exclusive right to use a brand name or other identifying mark.

**service mark**
Trademark for a service.

A **trademark** is the exclusive right to use a brand or part of a brand. Others are prohibited from using the brand without permission. A **service mark** performs the same function for services, such as H&R Block and Weight Watchers. Parts of a brand or other product identification may qualify for trademark protection—for example:

- Shapes, such as the Jeep front grill and the Coca-Cola bottle, or even buildings, like Pizza Hut
- Ornamental color or design, such as the decoration on Nike tennis shoes, the black-and-copper color combination of a Duracell battery, Levi's small tag on the left side of the rear pocket of its jeans, or the cut-off black cone on the top of Cross pens
- Catchy phrases, such as Prudential's "Own a piece of the rock," Merrill Lynch's "We're bullish on America," and Budweiser's "This Bud's for you"
- Abbreviations, such as *Bud, Coke,* or *The Met*

Rights to a trademark last as long as the mark is used. Normally, if the firm does not use it for two years, the trademark is considered abandoned. If a new user picks up the trademark after the owner abandons it, the new user can claim exclusive ownership of the mark.

The Lanham Act of 1946 specifies the types of marks that can be protected and the remedies available for trademark violations. When an organization is convicted of trademark infringement, it faces severe penalties. For example, the injured party can sue for triple the damages actually suffered and for any profits the offending firm made from the mark. Federal law also allows for the destruction of all materials bearing the infringing mark. A company whose warehouse is filled with items bearing the illegal mark could end up losing a lot.

An old law required that a trademark be used in interstate commerce before it could be registered. The Trademark Revision Act of 1988 allows organizations to register trademarks based on a bona fide intention to use the mark (normally within six months following the issuance of the trademark). Furthermore, this act allows a company to register its trademark for ten years, compared with twenty years under the old law. To renew the trademark, the company must prove it is using it.

**generic product name**
Name that identifies a product by class or type and cannot be trademarked.

Companies that fail to protect their trademarks face the problem of their product names becoming generic. A **generic product name** identifies a product by class or type and cannot be trademarked. Former brand names that were not sufficiently protected by their owners and were subsequently declared to be generic product names in U.S. courts include aspirin, cellophane, linoleum, thermos, kerosene, monopoly, cola, and shredded wheat.

Companies like Rolls Royce, Cross, Xerox, Levi's, Frigidaire, and McDonald's aggressively enforce their trademarks. Rolls Royce, Coca-Cola, and Xerox even run newspaper and magazine ads stating that their names are trademarks and should not be used as descriptive or generic terms. Some ads threaten lawsuits against competitors that violate trademarks. In 1992, Xerox began a year-long ad campaign throughout the Commonwealth of Independent States to combat the growing problem of trademark infringement in the former Soviet Union.[34]

Despite severe penalties for trademark violations, trademark infringement lawsuits are not uncommon. One of the major battles is over brand names that closely resemble another brand name. Coors Brewing, for example, sued Robert Corr, who produces a line of soft drinks under the name Corr's Beverages. Hyatt Hotels has blocked Hyatt Legal Services from featuring the term *Hyatt* in its advertising.

Companies must also contend with fake or unauthorized brands, such as fake Levi's jeans, Microsoft software, Rolex watches, Reebok and Nike footwear, and Louis Vuitton handbags. Levi Strauss has spent over $2 million on more than 600 investigations of counterfeit Levi's jeans. Other companies, including IBM and Coca-Cola, are very aggressive in trying to identify and eliminate counterfeiters.[35] The Global Perspectives box on page 304 describes the problem of counterfeit products in China.

*6 Describe marketing uses of packaging and labeling.*

## PACKAGING

**packaging**
Container for protecting and promoting a product and making it safer and more convenient.

Packages have always served a practical function. That is, they hold contents together and protect goods as they move through the distribution channel. Today, however, packaging is also a container for promoting the product and making it easier and safer to use.

### PACKAGING FUNCTIONS

The three most important functions of packaging are to contain and protect products, promote products, and facilitate product storage, use, and convenience. A fourth function of packaging that is becoming increasingly important is to facilitate recycling and reduce environmental damage.

#### Containing and Protecting Products

The most obvious function of packaging is to contain products that are liquid, granular, or otherwise divisible. Packaging also enables manufacturers, wholesalers, and retailers to market products in specific quantities, such as ounces.

Physical protection is another obvious function of packaging. Most products are handled several times between the time they are manufactured, harvested, or otherwise produced and the time they are consumed or used. Many products are shipped,

GLOBAL PERSPECTIVES

**Counterfeit Trademarks in China**

The practice of copying U.S. trademarks is widespread in China, the world's largest and fastest-growing consumer market. In grocery stores, you're likely to see a familiar red and white toothpaste box that looks very much like Colgate, canned foods with "Del Monte green" labels, and cereal boxes featuring a rooster that looks identical to Kellogg's.

Closer inspection, however, reveals that the toothpaste is Cologate, the vegetable canner is Jia Long, and the cereal is Kongalu Corn Strips.

*Chinese cereal (left) copies Kellogg's packaging, and Chinese facial tissues use well-known American name.*

According to the cereal box, "Kongalu is the trustworthy sign of quality which is famous around the world." Kongalu is well known at Kellogg headquarters, where company lawyers are considering possible actions to halt what Kellogg considers to be a flagrant violation of its trademark.[36]

Most people would agree that it is unethical to intentionally deceive customers about the brands of products they are buying. But where should you draw the line between similarity in package design and violation of trademarks and copyrights? Should Colgate have a monopoly on toothpaste boxes in red and white? Does Del Monte's use of green labels mean other vegetable canners must pick another color? And is the barnyard rooster exclusively Kellogg's? What actions might be available to U.S. companies like Kellogg that believe their copyrights and trademarks have been violated? What actions, if any, do you think the U.S. government should take to enforce prohibitions against trademark infringements when they occur in other countries?



stored, and inspected several times between production and consumption. Some, like milk, need to be refrigerated. Others, like beer, are sensitive to light. Still others, like medicines and bandages, need to be kept sterile. Packages protect products from breakage, evaporation, spillage, spoilage, light, heat, cold, infestation, and many other conditions.

## Promoting Products

Over 15,000 new products are introduced annually in U.S. supermarkets alone. To get attention on such crowded shelves, marketers rely on packaging. Thus a key role of packaging is product promotion. Packages are the last opportunity marketers have to influence buyers before they make purchase decisions.

Packaging does more than identify the brand, list the ingredients, specify features, and give directions. A package differentiates a product from competing products and may associate a new product with a family of other products from the same manufacturer. A new Campbell soup, with the familiar red label, benefits from its obvious association with other Campbell soups.

Packages use designs, colors, shapes, and materials to try to influence consumers' perceptions and buying behavior. For example, Warner-Lambert repackaged its Tracer razor so consumers can test the razor's flexible head without opening the package.[37]

Consumers associate certain colors with certain types of products. Green is typically identified with vegetables. Green Giant uses a "sea of green" package design to create a strong brand identity in the freezer case. Yellow, the color of Dole's labels, is associated with canned fruit. Red and pink have long been associated with processed meats, and white and blue are associated with bread and butter products.

Packages are also very important in establishing a brand's image. Coca-Cola USA introduced a twenty-ounce plastic bottle designed to look like an oversized version

For consumers who are concerned about overflowing landfills, Downy fabric softener is sold in cartons instead of in bulky plastic bottles.

of its classic glass Coke bottle. During the 1990s, the company wants to make all Coca-Cola packaging distinctive—and give the new containers patent protection.[38] Procter & Gamble has updated the graphics on its Old Spice packages to appeal more to younger male consumers.[39]

Packaging has a measurable effect on sales. Quaker Oats revised the package for Rice-A-Roni without making any other changes in marketing strategy and experienced a 44 percent increase in sales in one year.[40]

## Facilitating Storage, Use, and Convenience

Wholesalers and retailers prefer packages that are easy to ship, store, and stock on shelves. They also like packages that protect products, prevent spoilage or breakage, and extend the product's shelf life.

Consumers' requirements for convenience cover many dimensions. Consumers are constantly seeking items that are easy to handle, open, and reclose, although some consumers want packages that are tamper-proof or child-proof. Consumers also want reusable and disposable packages. Surveys conducted by *Sales & Marketing Management* magazine revealed that consumers dislike—and avoid buying—leaky ice cream boxes, overly heavy or fat vinegar bottles, immovable pry-up lids on glass bottles, key-opener sardine cans, and hard-to-pour cereal boxes. Such packaging innovations as zipper tear strips, hinged lids, tab slots, screw-on tops, and pour spouts were introduced to solve these and other problems. Spreckels, for example, introduced a resealable four-pound package for its sugar. The package, which looks like a milk or juice carton, overcomes consumer complaints about the traditional sugar packages breaking and not resealing well.[41] Johnson & Johnson has introduced Tylenol FastCap, a new patented package that will open with the flick of the wrist.[42]

Some firms use packaging to segment markets. For example, the Tylenol FastCap is targeted to adults over 50 who suffer from arthritis and to households without young children.[43] Different-size packages appeal to heavy, moderate, and light users. Salt is sold in package sizes ranging from single serving to picnic size to giant economy size. Campbell soup is packaged in single-serving cans aimed at the elderly and singles market segments. Beer and soft drinks are similarly marketed in various package sizes and types. Packaging convenience can increase a product's utility and, therefore, its market share and profits.

## Facilitating Recycling and Reducing Environmental Damage

One of the most important packaging issues in the 1990s is compatibility with the environment. A growing number of consumers are annoyed by wasteful packaging and prefer, if not demand, recyclable, biodegradable, and reusable packages.[44]

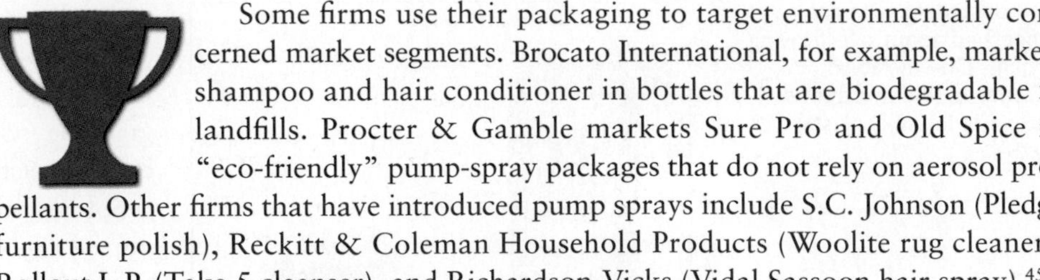

Some firms use their packaging to target environmentally concerned market segments. Brocato International, for example, markets shampoo and hair conditioner in bottles that are biodegradable in landfills. Procter & Gamble markets Sure Pro and Old Spice in "eco-friendly" pump-spray packages that do not rely on aerosol propellants. Other firms that have introduced pump sprays include S.C. Johnson (Pledge furniture polish), Reckitt & Coleman Household Products (Woolite rug cleaner), Rollout L.P. (Take 5 cleanser), and Richardson-Vicks (Vidal Sassoon hair spray).[45]

### LABELING

**persuasive labeling**
Labeling that focuses on a promotional theme or logo rather than on consumer information.

An integral part of any package is its label. Labeling generally takes one of two forms: persuasive or informational. **Persuasive labeling** focuses on a promotional theme or logo, and consumer information is secondary. Price Pfister developed a new persuasive label—featuring a picture of a faucet, the brand name, and the logo—with the goal of strengthening brand identity and becoming known as a brand instead of as a manufacturer.[46] Note that the standard promotional claims—such as "new," "improved," and "super"—are no longer very persuasive. Consumers have been saturated with "newness" and thus discount these claims.

**informational labeling**
Labeling designed to help consumers make a proper product selection and lower their cognitive dissonance after the purchase.

**Informational labeling,** in contrast, is designed to help consumers make proper product selections and lower their cognitive dissonance after the purchase. Sears attaches a "label of confidence" to all its floor coverings. This label gives such product information as durability, color, features, cleanability, care instructions, and construction standards. Most major furniture manufacturers affix labels to their wares that explain construction features, such as type of frame, number of coils, and fabric characteristics. The Nutritional Labeling and Education Act of 1990 mandated detailed nutritional information on most food packages and standards for health claims on food packaging. An important outcome of this legislation is guidelines from the Food and Drug Administration for using terms like *low fat, light, reduced cholesterol, low sodium, low calorie,* and *fresh.*[47] Celentano, a New Jersey maker of Italian frozen foods, has capitalized on the new rules. Its label notes that, "as always," Celentano products don't contain additives, chemicals, preservatives, or artificial ingredients.[48]

### UNIVERSAL PRODUCT CODES

**universal product code (UPC) (bar code)**
Series of thick and thin vertical lines, readable by computerized optical scanners, that represent numbers used to track products.

The **universal product codes** (UPC) that appear on many items in supermarkets and other high-volume outlets were first introduced in 1974. Because the numerical codes appear as a series of thick and thin vertical lines, they are often called *bar codes.* The lines are read by computerized optical scanners that match codes with brand names, package sizes, and prices. They also print information on cash register tapes and help retailers rapidly and accurately prepare records of customer purchases, control inventories, and track sales. The UPC system and scanners are also used in single-source research (see Chapter 7).

*7 Discuss global issues in branding and packaging.*

## GLOBAL ISSUES IN BRANDING AND PACKAGING

As the Global Perspectives box in this chapter indicates, brand imitations are widely available in some countries. Counterfeiting is also a major problem for some international marketers of prestigious brands, including the makers of Levi's jeans, Rolex and Seiko watches, and Gucci and Louis Vuitton handbags. International marketers must also address some other concerns regarding branding and packaging.

## BRANDING

When planning to enter a foreign market with an existing product, a firm has three options for handling the brand name:

- *One brand name everywhere:* This strategy is useful when the company markets mainly one product and the brand name does not have negative connotations in any local market. The Coca-Cola Company uses a one-brand-name strategy in 195 countries around the world. The advantages of a one-brand-name strategy are greater identification of the product from market to market and ease of coordinating promotion from market to market.
- *Adaptations and modifications:* A one-brand-name strategy is not possible when the name cannot be pronounced in the local language, when the brand name is owned by someone else, or when the brand name has a negative or vulgar connotation in the local language. In French, for instance, the brand name Pet is vulgar and the brand name Flic has a negative connotation (it refers to the police). Minor modifications made each of these brand names more suitable for the French market.
- *Different brand names in different markets:* Local brand names are often used when translation or pronunciation problems occur, when the marketer wants the brand to appear to be a local brand, or when regulations require localization. Gillette's Silkience hair conditioner is called Soyance in France and Sientel in Italy. The adaptations were deemed to be more appealing in the local markets. Coca-Cola's Sprite brand had to be renamed Kin in Korea to satisfy a government prohibition on the unnecessary use of foreign words. Snuggle fabric softener is called FaFa in Japan, Cajoline in France, and other cuddly names elsewhere in the world.[49]

## PACKAGING

Three aspects of packaging that are especially important in international marketing are labeling, aesthetics, and climate considerations. The major *labeling* concern is properly translating ingredient, promotional, and instructional information on labels. Care must also be employed in meeting all local labeling requirements. Several years ago, an Italian judge ordered that all bottles of Coca-Cola be removed from retail shelves because the ingredients were not properly labeled. Labeling is also harder in countries like Belgium and Finland, which require bilingual labeling.

Package *aesthetics* may also require some attention. The key is to stay attuned to cultural traits in host countries. For example, colors may have different connotations. Red is associated with witchcraft in some countries, green may be a sign of danger, and white may be symbolic of death. Aesthetics also influence package size. Soft drinks are not sold in six-packs in countries that lack refrigeration. In some countries, products like detergent may be bought only in small quantities because of a lack of storage space. Other products, like cigarettes, may be bought in small quantities, even single units, because of the low purchasing power of buyers.

Extreme *climates* and long-distance shipping necessitate sturdier and more durable packages for goods sold overseas. Spillage, spoilage, and breakage are all more important concerns when products are shipped long distances or frequently handled during shipping and storage. Packages may also have to ensure a longer product life if the time between production and consumption lengthens significantly.

8 *Describe how and why product warranties are important marketing tools.*

## PRODUCT WARRANTIES

Just as a package is designed to protect the product, a warranty protects the buyer and gives essential information about the product. A **warranty** confirms the quality or performance of a good or service. An **express warranty** is a written guarantee. Express warranties range from simple statements—such as "100 percent cotton" (a guarantee of quality) and "complete satisfaction guaranteed" (a statement of performance)—to extensive documents written in technical language. In contrast, an **implied warranty** is an unwritten guarantee that the good or service is fit for the purpose for which it was sold. All sales have an implied warranty under the Uniform Commercial Code.

**warranty**
Guarantee of the quality or performance of a good or service.

**express warranty**
Written guarantee that a good or service is fit for the purpose for which it was sold.

**implied warranty**
Unwritten guarantee that the good or service is fit for the purpose for which it was sold.

Congress passed the Magnuson-Moss Warranty–Federal Trade Commission Improvement Act in 1975 to help consumers understand warranties and get action from manufacturers and dealers. A manufacturer that promises a full warranty must meet certain minimum standards, including repair "within a reasonable time and without charge" of any defects and replacement of the merchandise or a full refund if the product does not work "after a reasonable number of attempts" at repair. Any warranty that does not live up to this tough prescription must be "conspicuously" promoted as a limited warranty.

## LOOKING BACK

Look back at the story about Eastman Kodak's new product line, Fun Time 35mm film. Kodak's objective is to compete in the price-sensitive segment of the amateur photography market without cannibalizing sales of its premium brand, GoldPlus. This is a difficult challenge.

By downplaying the Kodak name and not using the familiar Kodak package, the company is trying to minimize the association of the new product line with the manufacturer. The message seems to be, "If you want low-priced film, buy Fun Time. But it's not the same as Kodak GoldPlus." The reason for not making Fun Time available year-round is to try to keep people from becoming accustomed to paying less for Kodak film.

The strategy for Fun Time appears to be incomplete at best. The positioning strategy for the new film line is very weak. The company needs to provide consumers with answers to the following questions: Is Fun Time a high-quality 35mm film? If so, why should I pay a premium for GoldPlus? If not, why should I buy Fun Time? Why won't Fun Time be available year-round? It does not appear that Kodak is fully committed to making Fun Time a successful product line.

## SUMMARY

1 **Define the term *product*.** A product is anything, desired or not, that a person or organization receives in an exchange. The basic goal of purchase decisions is to receive the tangible and intangible benefits associated with a product. Tangible aspects include packaging, style, color, size, and features. Intangible qualities include service, retailer's image, manufacturer's reputation, and the social status associated with a product. An organization's product offering is the crucial element in any marketing mix.

**2 Classify consumer products.** Consumer products are classified into four categories: convenience products, shopping products, specialty products, and unsought products. Convenience products are relatively inexpensive and require limited shopping effort. Shopping products are of two types: homogeneous and heterogeneous. Because of the similarity of homogeneous products, they are differentiated mainly by price and features. In contrast, heterogeneous products appeal to consumers because of their distinct characteristics. Specialty products possess unique benefits that are highly desirable to certain customers. Finally, unsought products are either new products or products that require aggressive selling because they are generally avoided or overlooked by consumers.

**3 Define the terms *product item, product line,* and *product mix.*** A product item is a specific version of a product that can be designated as a distinct offering among an organization's products. A product line is a group of closely related products offered by an organization. An organization's product mix includes all the products it sells. Product mix width refers to the number of product lines an organization offers. Product line depth is the number of product items in a product line. Product mix consistency is the extent to which product lines are similar. Firms modify existing products by changing their quality, functional characteristics, or style. Product line extension occurs when firms add new products to existing product lines.

**4 Explain the concept of product life cycles.** All product categories undergo a life cycle with four stages: introduction, growth, maturity, and decline. The rate at which products move through these stages varies dramatically. Marketing managers use the product life cycle concept as an analytical tool to forecast a product's future and devise effective marketing strategies.

**5 Describe marketing uses of branding.** A brand is a name, term, or symbol that identifies and differentiates a firm's products. Established brands encourage customer loyalty and help new products succeed. Branding strategies require decisions about individual, family, manufacturer's, and private brands.

**6 Describe marketing uses of packaging and labeling.** Packaging has four functions: containing and protecting products; promoting products; facilitating product storage, use, and convenience; and facilitating recycling and reducing environmental damage. As a tool for promotion, packaging identifies the brand and its features. It also serves the critical function of differentiating a product from competing products and linking it with related products from the same manufacturer. The label is an integral part of the package, with persuasive and informational functions. In essence, the package is the marketer's last chance to influence buyers before they make a purchase decision.

**7 Discuss global issues in branding and packaging.** In addition to brand piracy, international marketers must address a variety of concerns regarding branding and packaging. These include choosing a brand name policy, translating labels and meeting host-country labeling requirements, making packages aesthetically compatible with host-country cultures, and offering the sizes of packages preferred in host countries.

**8 Describe how and why product warranties are important marketing tools.** Product warranties are important tools because they offer consumers protection and help them gauge product quality.

KEY TERMS

## Discussion and Writing Questions

1. Discuss the function of the product in the marketing mix.
2. Identify and describe some examples of product life cycle extension strategies not described in the chapter.
3. Consider Charles Revson's remark: "In the factory we manufacture cosmetics, but in the store we sell hope." What does this statement imply about product benefits?
4. Imagine that you work for a firm that produces several specific products. For new sales employees, write a list of the products and their tangible and intangible benefits.
5. List some specific examples of products that have experienced quality, function, and style modifications.
6. A local business association has asked you, a manufacturer, to give a talk on what the future holds for manufacturers' brands and how they will be able to maintain their share of the market. Write an outline for your speech.

## Application for Small Business

Julie Ann Bradstrum recently joined her father Brad's advertising and public relations firm. Both father and daughter hope that Julie will take over the business when Brad retires in a few years.

Julie's first client is a former sorority sister who is planning to start a word-processing service near campus. Her client wants to call the new business WordPerfect for You. She reasons that most prospective customers are familiar with WordPerfect Corporation's popular word-processing software, and the name Wordperfect for You would describe her service and give it a "touch of class."

### Questions

1. What advice should Julie give her new client?
2. Identify some features of a good company or brand name for this client.
3. Suggest some alternative names for Julie's client's new word-processing service.

## CRITICAL THINKING CASE

### Pepsi Max

In the early days of colas, it was hard to get a Coke to taste the same as every other Coke or a Pepsi to taste the same as every other Pepsi, no matter what fountain or bottle was the source. But today, even though it's much easier to make the product consistent, Pepsi-Cola is doing its best to market under a single name sodas that taste different depending where on the planet you make your purchase. Pepsi Max is a midcalorie soft drink rolling out in Canada. It is also a sugar-free soda pushing through European markets and into Latin America and Asia.

Same name, same package—different products. Pizza Hut and McDonald's adapt pizzas or Big Macs to local market tastes, but Pepsi Max's split personality may prove problematic.

The sugar-free Pepsi Max developed for global markets is aimed at consumers who have otherwise shunned diet drinks. It is not likely to hit the United States, where it would compete directly with well-established Diet Pepsi.



### Questions

1. What are the advantages of using the Pepsi Max name and package design on these distinctly different cola products?
2. What are the disadvantages?
3. Overall, do you think the Pepsi strategy is a good idea?

### Reference

Karen Benezra, "Double Entendre: The Life and the Life of Pepsi Max," *Brandweek*, 18 April 1994, p. 40.

**VIDEO CASE**

## Head Golf

Based in Boulder, Colorado, Head Golf was started in 1991 as a subsidiary of Head Sports. Building on its established brand name in the sporting equipment industry, Head wanted to expand its product portfolio, which primarily included ski and tennis equipment. The subsidiary complements Head Sports' portfolio by reducing the seasonality of ski equipment sales. The company also hoped to generate revenue that had been lost in the declining tennis industry. By providing high-quality golf clubs, shoes, and accessories, Head's vision is to compete as a full-service company against competitors such as Callaway, Cobra, Ping, and Lynx.

In the game of golf, new product developments are aimed at helping all levels of players improve their scores. Golfers, in general, are receptive to new products or concepts that can potentially enhance their golfing performance. Thus Head Golf offers a wide variety of products, including Premise clubs, Big Head woods and irons, putters, shoes, and accessories.

The Premise metal woods and irons were the first line of clubs offered by Head. Premise clubs are built around a patented technology and are available in steel or graphite for both men and women.

The Big Head woods were introduced to compete against the oversized woods like Callaway's Big Bertha and Wilson's Killer Whale, which offer more power and precision to players. With an 11 percent bigger club face than the other oversized woods, the Big Head woods claim to be the most forgiving clubs in golf.

Encouraged by the success of its oversized metal woods, Head opted to extend its product line and develop oversized irons. The Big Head irons have a 33 percent larger effective hitting area, which makes them far more forgiving than conventional irons. In essence, with a two-inch hitting area, Big Head irons enable golfers to "double their sweet spot." A shot that finds the club face will easily find the fairway.

One method that Head Golf uses to promote the Big Head irons is a demonstration known as the "two-ball test." Golfers try hitting two balls at the same time with the Big Head iron. Head advertises a toll-free telephone number that interested persons can call to learn about locations where they can try the two-ball test.

### Questions

1. According to Exhibit 9.1, what type of product is the Big Head iron?
2. When your boss returned from a marketing seminar titled "Managing Marketing over the Product Life Cycle," she asked you to prepare a one-page report explaining the life cycle stage of golf clubs and the implications for Big Head clubs and making specific suggestions for marketing the Big Head line.
3. Evaluate the brand name Big Head. What are its advantages and disadvantages for marketing the new line of golf clubs?

# CHAPTER 10

# DEVELOPING AND MANAGING PRODUCTS

## Learning Objectives

*After studying this chapter, you should be able to*

1 *Describe the six categories of new products, and explain the importance of developing new products.*

2 *Describe the organizational groups or structures used to facilitate new product development.*

3 *Explain the steps in the new product development process.*

4 *Analyze the reasons for the failure or success of a new product.*

5 *Discuss global issues in new product development.*

6 *Explain the diffusion process through which new products are adopted.*

7 *Explain the product management form of organization.*

8 *Identify the cost of sustaining weak products, and explain procedures for deciding to abandon a product.*

Focus groups raved about Oven Lovin' refrigerated cookie dough, which was loaded with Hershey's chocolate chips, Reece's Pieces, and Brach's candies. Pillsbury management was so confident that its new product would be a winner that it skipped test marketing and launched the product nationally. Within months of its launch, the product was available in 90 percent of supermarkets; sales had reached nearly $1.5 million per week and were increasing.

Eighteen months later, sales had declined to less that $60,000 per week. Shoppers apparently didn't think Oven Lovin' was worth 20¢ more than Pillsbury's traditional tube dough product, Pillsbury Best, especially since the Oven Lovin' package was 20 percent smaller.[1]

Why do you think Pillsbury introduced Oven Lovin' refrigerated cookie dough without first test marketing the brand? Was Oven Lovin' a new product? What does this example teach us about focus group research? Why did Oven Lovin' fail?

1 *Describe the six categories of new products, and explain the importance of developing new products.*

**new product**
Product new to the world, the market, the producer, the seller, or some combination of these.

## THE IMPORTANCE OF NEW PRODUCTS

The term **new product** is somewhat confusing, because its meaning varies widely. Actually, there are several "correct" definitions of the term. A product can be new to the world, to the market, to the producer or seller, or to some combination of these.

There are six categories of new products:[2]

- *New-to-the-world products (also called discontinuous innovations):* These products create an entirely new market. The telephone, television, computer, and facsimile machine are commonly cited examples of new-to-the-world products.
- *New product lines:* These products, which the firm has not previously offered, allow it to enter an established market. Williamson-Dickie Manufacturing, after specializing in the "heavy soil" segment of the work clothes market for nearly seven decades, introduced a line of fashion clothing.[3] The rationale for this strategy was to capitalize on the strong image the Dickie brand has among "working people."
- *Additions to existing product lines:* This category includes new products that supplement a firm's established line. Bristol-Myers extended its Ban deodorant line when it introduced Ban Sensitive Tough A.P./deodorant, a hypoallergenic antiperspirant/deodorant for women with sensitive skin.[4]
- *Improvements or revisions of existing products:* The "new and improved" product may be significantly or slightly changed. Haggar's slacks were improved by making them of wrinkle-free cotton; the company shipped over 2 million pairs during the first year they were on the market. Kingsford Products introduced a cleaner-burning charcoal lighter fluid.[5]
- *Repositioned products:* These are existing products targeted at new markets or market segments. Gillette repositioned Dry Idea deodorant from a unisex to a women's brand.[6]
- *Lower-priced products:* This category refers to products that

ETHICS IN MARKETING

### Are Nutrient-Loaded Foods Healthy?

Marketers of snacks and sweets are adding vitamins and minerals to their products and calling the result healthful. But some nutritionists call the claims junk.

In recent years, many foodmakers tried to remove cholesterol and sugar from their fattening fare, often sacrificing taste and losing customers in the process. So some makers of doughnuts, candy, cookies, fruit punch, and other indulgences decided to go the other way: Add nutrients but keep the fat. Franco Harris, for example, keeps all the fat and sugar in his Super Donut but adds fourteen vitamins, minerals, and protein. "We don't just sell a donut, we sell nutrition," says Harris, president of Super Bakery, which sells the product to schools and nursing homes. A single Super Donut, the former Pittsburgh Steeler boasts, contains more than a third of the daily requirement of such nutrients as iron and vitamin C.

Nutritionists are skeptical about the "enriched" products. "They're not any healthier if you think about all the other ingredients contained in the foods," says Keith Levick, director of Childhood Weight Management in Farmington Hills, Michigan. Levick says such products only encourage a disturbing trend: Obesity in children 6 to 11 has increased about 60 percent in the past thirty years.

Nutritionists also caution that the advertised vitamins and minerals aren't necessarily absorbed entirely by the body. The Food and Drug Administration says companies aren't required to prove the absorbability of the nutrients contained in a product. Companies can advertise nutritional contents as long as they don't make any specific health claims.[10]

Does promoting a product as containing specified quantities of vitamins, minerals, and protein suggest that it is healthful? Do you agree with the Food and Drug Administration that companies should be allowed to advertise nutritional contents even if these contents don't really enhance the product's healthfulness? Is it ethical to promote nutritional contents of foods even if these nutrients aren't absorbed entirely by the body?

provide performance similar to competing brands at a lower price. Kimberly-Clark's Kleenex Premium toilet tissue is priced well below the premium lines of other tissue makers.[7]

The product life cycle concept reminds us that developing and introducing new products is vital to business growth and profitability. A continuing stream of new products is needed for most firms to sustain long-term growth in sales and profits. Major consumer and industrial goods manufacturers expect new products to account for a big portion of their total sales and profits. Each year Sony introduces 1,000 new products. About 800 of these products are improvements of existing products, but 200 are aimed at creating whole new markets. Rubbermaid expects to generate 30 percent of its yearly revenue from products launched in the previous five years.[8]

New product development is both expensive and risky. The process of developing and testing a new product can take several years and millions of dollars. For example, Gillette spent $200 million over ten years developing the Sensor razor. However, only a small proportion of all seemingly good ideas result in new product introductions. Furthermore, many products that are introduced fail to meet management's (or consumers') expectations. Johnson & Johnson stopped selling Medipren, an ibuprofen pain reliever, after investing millions of dollars over six years. Like several other J&J products—such as heart valves, kidney dialysis equipment, and magnetic resonance machines—Medipren simply flopped.[9]

*2 Describe the organizational groups or structures used to facilitate new product development.*

## ORGANIZATION FOR NEW PRODUCT DEVELOPMENT

To purposefully cultivate a steady stream of new products, an organized structure is essential. Yet in many firms, top managers tend to receive new product ideas passively rather than actively soliciting them. Moreover, managers often poorly process the ideas they do receive, and chance determines whether or not these ideas are fully considered.

One of the main requirements for generating new product ideas and successfully introducing new products is support from top management. In addition, several kinds of groups or structures within an organization can facilitate the development of new products. These include new product committees and departments, venture teams, and parallel engineering.

### NEW PRODUCT COMMITTEES AND DEPARTMENTS

**new product committee**
Ad hoc group whose members represent various functional interests and who manage the new product development process.

**new product department**
Separate department that manages the new product development process on a full-time basis.

A **new product committee** is an ad hoc group whose members manage the new product development process. The members usually represent functional interests, such as manufacturing, research and development, finance, and marketing. Many organizations use new product committees to screen ideas.

One alternative to a new product committee is a **new product department,** which performs the same functions as a new product committee but on a full-time basis. New product departments typically recommend new product objectives and programs, plan exploratory studies, evaluate concepts and ideas for new products, coordinate testing, and direct interdepartmental teams. Ideally, people in the product development department communicate regularly with their peers in the operating departments.

Setting up a formal department helps ensure that authority and responsibilities are well defined and delegated to specific individuals. As a separate department with authority to develop new products, it can be free from the undue influence of production,

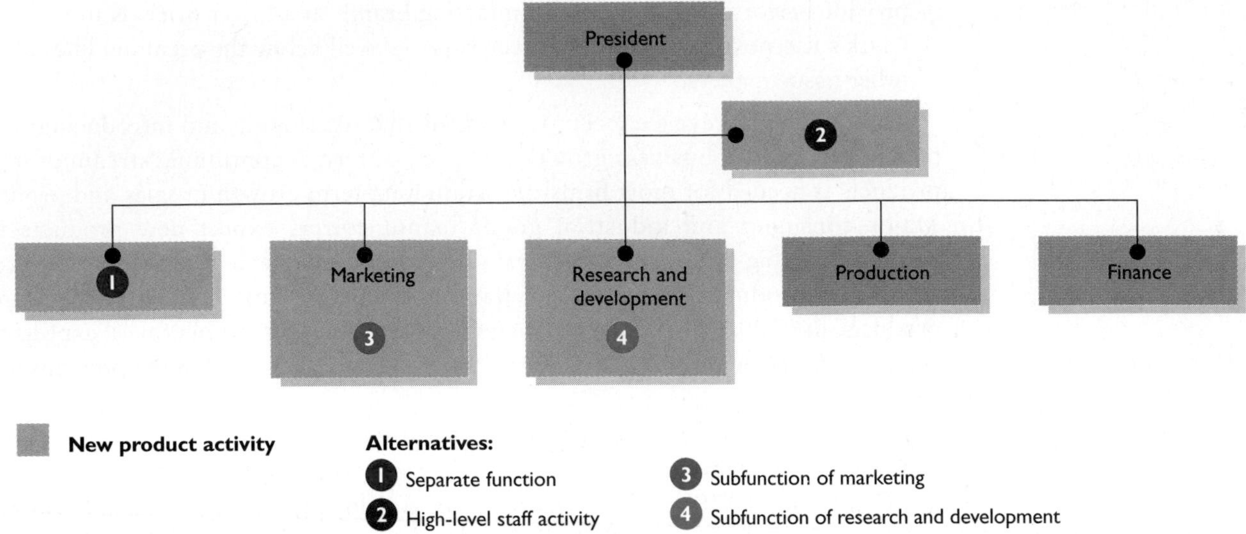


*Exhibit 10.1*

Location of New Product Departments within Organizations

marketing, and other groups. A separate department also has the authority to accomplish its tasks. Thus the new product development manager can rely less on people outside his or her sphere of influence.

As Exhibit 10.1 illustrates, the new product department can be situated in one of several places within the organization. As a high-level staff activity, new product development usually has the strong support of top management. As a staff function, however, it must depend on other functional areas to carry out various activities. For example, the department must rely on marketing to conduct marketing research, production to build prototypes or working models, and finance to develop projections of the product's profitability.

If a company is consumer-oriented, it may choose to place new product development within the marketing function. The result may be new products sharply attuned to customers' needs. On the other hand, production and financial considerations may be skimped. If production management, for example, feels excluded from the planning process, they may show little enthusiasm for estimating production runs, developing prototypes, and so forth.

The last option is to integrate the product development department into research and development. This arrangement is common in chemical, pharmaceutical, and electronics industries, where basic research is a well-funded and essential part of the organization. Grouping new product development and basic research together can offer great advantages. When the two groups work and communicate closely, product development can suggest areas in which basic research might lead to major commercial successes.

## VENTURE TEAMS

**venture team**
Entrepreneurial, market-oriented group staffed by a small number of representatives from different disciplines.

A **venture team** is an entrepreneurial, market-oriented group staffed by a small number of representatives from different disciplines. Team members from marketing, research and development, finance, and other areas focus on a single objective: planning their company's profitable entry into a new business. Venture groups are most often used to handle important business and product tasks that do not fit neatly into the existing organization, that demand more financial resources and longer times to mature than other organizational units can provide, and that require imaginative entrepreneurship neither sheltered nor inhibited by the larger organization.

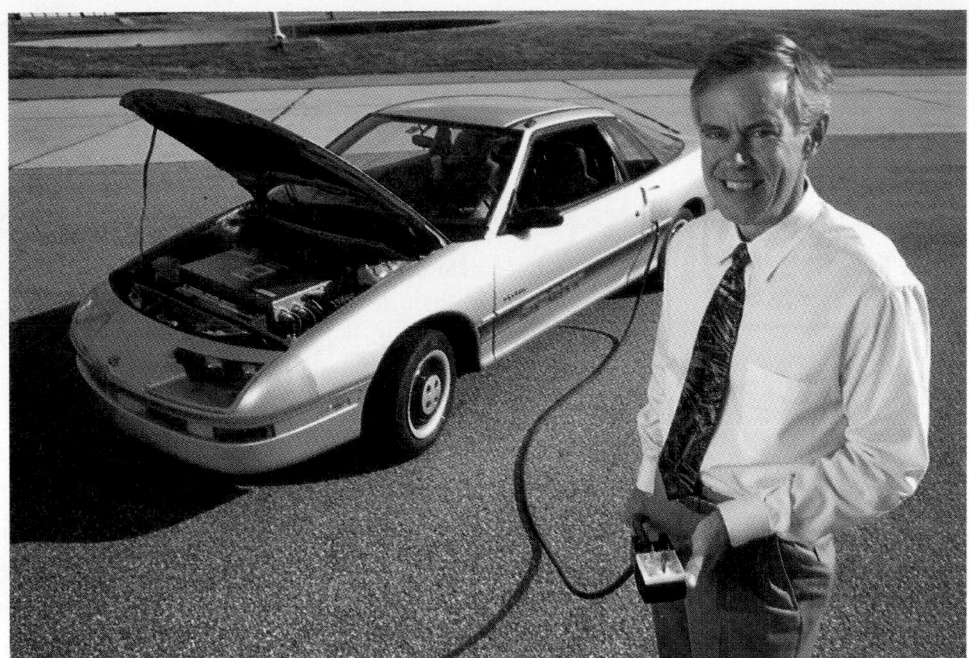

To develop its new electric car, the Impact, General Motors is using parallel engineering. Kenneth R. Baker, who heads the effort, has assembled a small team of engineers, production workers, and marketing experts to bring the product concept to reality.



Unlike new product committees, venture teams require a full-time commitment. In contrast to new product departments, venture teams form and disband as needed instead of being stable departments within the overall organizational structure.

The term *intrapreneur*—an entrepreneur working inside a large organization—is often used to describe members of venture teams. Colgate-Palmolive created Colgate Venture for intrapreneurs to develop specialized, small-market products, such as a deodorizing pad for cat litter boxes and a cleaning solution for teenagers' orthodontal retainers. Colgate Venture has five operating divisions and employs about seventy people.

## PARALLEL ENGINEERING

The earlier a product is brought to market, the greater the chance that profits will be strong. Delays lead to lost sales.[11] Xerox learned that lesson the hard way. Its executives were stunned to discover that Japanese competitors were developing new copier models twice as fast as Xerox and at half the cost. They recognized that Xerox had to greatly reduce its normal four- to five-year product development cycle or continue to lose market share—and possibly its reputation as the world's leading copier manufacturer. After a major reorganization and multimillion-dollar investment, Xerox was able to cut its development time to two years.[12]

Now U.S. manufacturers of all kinds are trying to find new ways to shorten their development cycles and be the first to market new products. Many are completely revising their procedures for developing new products. For example, the Big Three carmakers (General Motors, Ford, and Chrysler) all formed task forces to cut bureaucratic procedures and streamline the new product development process.[13]

**parallel (simultaneous/concurrent) engineering**
Product development process in which all relevant functional areas and outside suppliers participate at all stages, thereby streamlining the development process and reducing its cost.

A new organizational form called **parallel engineering, simultaneous engineering,** or **concurrent engineering** has also emerged to shorten the development process and reduce its cost. With parallel engineering, all relevant functional areas and outside suppliers participate in all stages of the development process. Group members perform development tasks together—thereby avoiding, for example, the need for designers to make changes when engineers or manufacturing are unable to meet design specifications. Involving key suppliers early in the process enables them to design and develop critical component parts. The story about Zytec illustrates this approach.

*3 Explain the steps in the new product development process.*

## THE NEW PRODUCT DEVELOPMENT PROCESS

The management and technology consulting firm Booz, Allen & Hamilton has studied the new product development process for over thirty years. Analyzing five major studies undertaken during this period, the firm has concluded that the companies most likely to succeed in developing and introducing new products are those that take the following actions:

- Make the long-term commitment needed to support innovation and new product development
- Use a company-specific approach, driven by corporate objectives and strategies, with a well-defined new product strategy at its core
- Capitalize on experience to achieve and maintain competitive advantage
- Establish an environment—a management style, organizational structure, and degree of top-management support—conducive to achieving company-specific new product and corporate objectives[15]

**new product strategy**
Plan that links the new product development process with the objectives of the marketing department, the business unit, and the corporation.

CREATING CUSTOMER VALUE

### The Zytec Story

Zytec Corporation, based in Eden Prairie, Minnesota, won a Baldrige Award in 1991. Prior to its creation in 1984, Zytec had been a unit of Magnetic Peripherals, a joint venture of four electronics firms. In 1984, Zytec was almost totally dependent on sales to its former owners.

Today, sales to its former owners account for only a fraction of total revenues. Customized power supplies for original equipment manufacturers of computers, office electronics, and medical and testing equipment account for 90 percent of Zytec's sales. The remaining 10 percent of sales come from repairs to cathode-ray-tube monitors and power supplies, making Zytec the largest repair business of this type in the United Sates.

Immediately following the leveraged buyout that created Zytec, Ronald Schmidt (chairman, president, and CEO) sought to establish a quality culture rather than a quality program. One aspect of this cultural orientation is Zytec's approach to new product development. The design and development of new products are assigned to interdepartmental work teams. These cross-functional teams "own" the new product development process from start to finish. The teams work with both suppliers and customers and are empowered to make decisions regarding the manufacturing process, specifications, and quality standards. This team approach characterizes the entire development process. Once the new product is fully ready for production, the team relinquishes control.[14]

Which form of organization for new product development best describes the Zytec approach? Explain your answer. How does Zytec's approach to new product development contribute to a quality culture?

Most companies follow a formal new product development process, usually starting with a new product strategy. Exhibit 10.2 traces the seven-step process, which is discussed in detail below. The exhibit is funnel-shaped to highlight the fact that each stage acts as a screen. The purpose is to filter out unworkable ideas.

### NEW PRODUCT STRATEGY

A **new product strategy** links the new product development process with the objectives of the marketing department, the business unit, and the corporation. A new product strategy must be compatible with these objectives, and in turn, all three objectives must be consistent with one another.

New product strategy is part of the organization's overall marketing strategy. It sharpens the focus and provides general guidelines for generating, screening, and evaluating new product ideas. The new product strategy specifies the roles that new products must play in the organization's overall

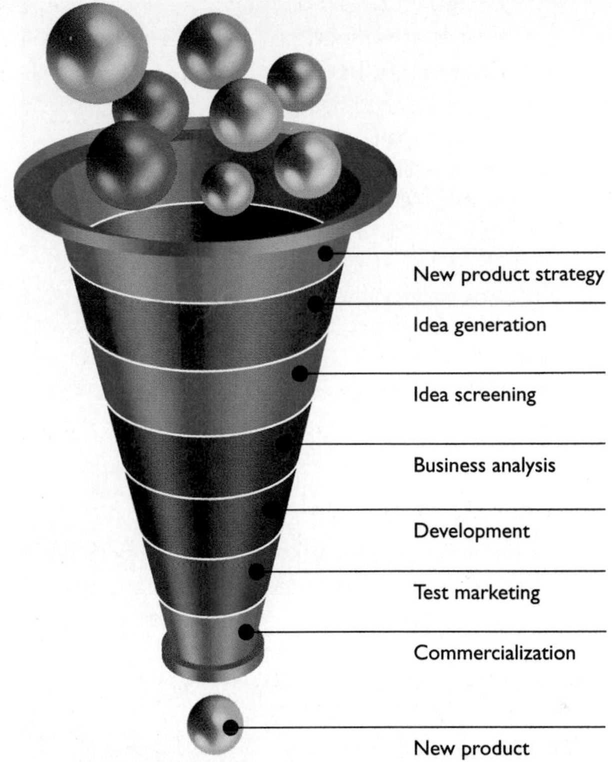


Exhibit 10.2

New Product Development Process

plan and describes the characteristics of products the organization wants to offer and the markets it wants to serve.[16]

As the accompanying story about Motorola shows, quality can be a key component of an organization's new product strategy.

## IDEA GENERATION

New product ideas come from many sources. Exhibit 10.3 on page 321 shows the sources of new product ideas identified in a study of 179 companies. The "Responses" column identifies how often each source was mentioned. The "Most important" column shows how often each source was identified as most important.

Here's some additional detail about important sources of new product ideas:

- *Customers:* The marketing concept suggests that customers' wants and needs should be the springboard for developing new products. Thermos, the vacuum bottle manufacturer, provides an interesting example of how companies tap customers for ideas.[18] The company's first step in developing an innovative home barbecue grill was to send ten members of its interdisciplinary new product team into the field for about a month. Their assignment was to learn all about people's cookout needs and to invent a product to meet them. In cities including Boston, Los Angeles, and Columbus, Ohio, the team conducted focus groups, visited people's homes, and even videotaped barbecues.
- *Employees:* Marketing personnel—advertising and marketing research employees as well as salespeople—often create new product ideas, because they analyze and are involved in the marketplace. Firms should encourage their employees to submit new product ideas and reward them if their ideas are adopted. The very successful introduction of Post-it Notes started with an

## CREATING CUSTOMER VALUE

### The Motorola Story

Although quality had been important to Motorola and many other U.S. firms for years, Motorola was one of the first to establish quality as a dominant strategic issue. In 1981 the company committed itself to improving the quality of its products and processes.

There were a couple of reasons for Motorola's early quality commitment. First, all seven of Motorola's business units were linked somehow to high-tech electronic products. These industries were subject to early, intense international competitive pressure, particularly from Japan. Thus Motorola, unlike some other U.S. firms, was sensitive to the early competitive changes in its market. Fortunately, it understood the need to develop and implement a strategic response without too much delay.

The second reason for Motorola's early quality commitment was rapidly changing customer expectations. Motorola found that customers expected significant and continual increases in quality. To maintain a leadership position in its various businesses, Motorola had to respond. It set a goal of achieving a tenfold increase in quality by 1986.

The response from lower levels of management was about what you would expect. Most managers agreed that quality improvement was important but were skeptical about a tenfold increase. Many viewed the goal as unrealistic. Despite that skepticism, however, Motorola was on its way to quality improvement, and it didn't stop when it achieved its original goal. In 1987, Motorola set the goal of improving quality tenfold by 1989 and a hundredfold by 1991. The "unrealistic, impossible" goal of 1981 had given way to far more ambitious goals. Ironically, largely because of the company's earlier success in meeting such a goal and improved quality awareness, the work force met the new goals established in 1987 with much less skepticism.

The benefits accruing to Motorola from its quality-improvement programs are pervasive. Paul Noakes, vice president and director of external quality programs, estimated that for the first four years of the effort, the company realized cumulative savings in manufacturing operations of $1.5 billion due solely to defect reduction. In 1990 alone, defect reduction saved the company $550 million. Motorola estimates that it has not yet realized potential savings of $1 billion in nonmanufacturing operations.[17]

Discuss the roles that new product strategy plays in Motorola's quality-improvement effort. Why has Motorola been successful in this effort?

employee's idea. In 1974 the research and development department of 3M's commercial tape division developed and patented the adhesive component of Post-it Notes. However, it was a year before an employee of the commercial tape division, who sang in a church choir, identified a use for the adhesive. He had been using paper clips and slips of paper to mark places in hymn books. But the paper clips damaged his books, and the slips of paper fell out. The solution, as we now all know, was to apply the adhesive to small pieces of paper and sell them in packages.

- *Distributors:* A well-trained sales force routinely asks distributors about needs that are not being met. Because they are closer to end users, distributors are often more aware of customer needs than manufacturers are. The inspiration for Rubbermaid's litter-free lunch box, named Sidekick, came from a distributor. The distributor suggested that Rubbermaid place some of its plastic containers inside a lunch box and sell the box as an alternative to plastic wrap and paper bags.[19]
- *Competitors:* No firms rely solely on internally generated ideas for new products. A big part of any organization's marketing intelligence system should be monitoring the performance of competitors' products. One purpose of competitive monitoring is to determine which, if any, of the competitors' products should be copied. Competitive monitoring may include tracking products sold by a company's own customers.
- *Research and development:* R&D is carried out in four distinct ways. *Basic research* is scientific research aimed at discovering new technologies. *Applied research* takes these new technologies and tries to find useful applications for them. **Product development** goes one step further by converting applications into marketable products. *Product modification* makes cosmetic or functional

**product development**
Marketing strategy that entails the creation of new products for present markets; process of converting applications for new technologies into marketable products.

*Exhibit 10.3*

Sources of New Product Ideas

Source: Adapted from Michael Q. Duerr, *The Commercial Development of New Products.* New York: Conference Board, Inc., 1986, p. 263. Reprinted by permission of the Conference Board.

| Sources | Responses | | Most Important | |
|---|---|---|---|---|
| | Number | Percentage | Number | Percentage |
| **Internal sources** | | | | |
| **Marketing** | 157 | 41 (Marketing and Research and development combined) | 33 | 59 (Marketing and Research and development combined) |
| Research and development | 154 | | 41 | |
| Employees | 66 | 9 | 3 | 2 |
| New product committee | 50 | 7 | 4 | 3 |
| Corporate planning | 42 | 5 | 2 | 2 |
| Total | 469 | 62 | 83 | 66 |
| External sources | 130 | 17 | 36 | 28 |
| Acquisitions | 59 | 8 | 4 | 3 |
| Consultants | 48 | 6 | 1 | 1 |
| Inventors | 43 | 6 | 2 | 2 |
| Advertising agency | 8 | 1 | | |
| Total | 288 | 38 | 43 | 34 |
| *Total for all sources* | 757 | 100 | 126 | 100 |

changes in existing products. Many new product breakthroughs come from R&D activities. Pert Plus, Procter & Gamble's combination shampoo and conditioner, was invented in the laboratory.

- *Consultants:* Outside consultants are always available to examine a business and recommend product ideas. Examples include the Weston Group; Booz, Allen & Hamilton; and Management Decisions. Traditionally, consultants determine whether a company has a balanced portfolio of products and, if not, what new product ideas are needed to offset the imbalance. For instance, an outside consultant conceived Airwick's highly successful Carpet Fresh carpet cleaner.

Creativity is the wellspring of new product ideas, regardless of who comes up with them. A variety of approaches and techniques have been developed to stimulate creative thinking. The two considered most useful for generating new product ideas are brainstorming and focus group exercises. The goal of **brainstorming** is to get a group to think of unlimited ways to vary a product or solve a problem. Group members avoid criticism of an idea, no matter how ridiculous it may seem. Objective evaluation is postponed. The sheer quantity of ideas is what matters. As noted in Chapter 7, an objective of focus group

**Some ideas for new products come from distributors, who may have better insights into consumer's needs than do manufacturers. Rubbermaid's litter-free lunch box set is one such idea.**

Photograph by John S. Abbot

**brainstorming**
Technique for generating new product ideas in which group members propose, without criticism or limitation, ways to vary a product or solve a problem.

GLOBAL PERSPECTIVES

**Heinz Catsup**

From Stockholm, Sweden, to Sydney, Australia, catsup isn't the household item it is in the United States. Each American consumes an average of three pounds of catsup each year, more than anywhere else on earth. Still, H.J. Heinz is trying to convert the rest of the world to its thick red sauce. The company doesn't foresee additional growth potential in the United States, where its catsup has a commanding 53 percent market share.

Barry Tilley, London-based general manager of Heinz's Western Hemisphere trading division, says Heinz uses focus groups to determine what foreign consumers want in the way of taste and image. In some regions, the company alters the spices it pours into its vats of catsup. Americans like a relatively sweet catsup, but Europeans prefer a spicier, more piquant variety. "In central Europe and Sweden, we're selling hot catsup and Mexican catsup, and a curry ketchup, in addition to the classic sweet catsup," Tilley says.[20]

Heinz's foreign marketing efforts are most successful when the company quickly adapts to local cultural preferences. Discuss the oft- cited advice "Think globally but act locally" in terms of this example. What new product development and global marketing lessons can we learn from this example? Is Heinz product-, sales-, or marketing-oriented? Why?



interviews is to stimulate insightful comments through group interaction. Focus groups usually comprise seven to ten people. Sometimes consumer focus groups generate excellent new product ideas—for example, Cycle dog food, Stick-Up room deodorizers, Dustbuster vacuum cleaners, and Wendy's salad bar. In the industrial market, machine tools, keyboard designs, aircraft interiors, and backhoe accessories have evolved from focus groups. The Global Perspectives story about Heinz catsup provides another illustration of how focus groups have helped generate ideas for new products.

## IDEA SCREENING

After new ideas have been generated, they pass through the first filter in the product development process. This stage, called **screening,** eliminates ideas that are inconsistent with the organization's new product strategy or are obviously inappropriate for some other reason. The new product committee, the new product department, or some other formally appointed group performs the screening review. Most new product ideas are rejected at the screening stage.

**screening**
Stage in the product development process that eliminates ideas inconsistent with the organization's new product strategy or obviously inappropriate for some other reason.

**concept test**
Evaluation of a new product idea, usually before a prototype has been created.

Concept tests are often used at the screening stage to rate concept (or product) alternatives. A **concept test** evaluates a new product idea, usually before any prototype has been created. Typically, researchers get consumer reactions to descriptions and visual representations of a proposed product.

Concept tests are considered fairly good predictors of success for line extensions. They have also been relatively precise predictors of success for new products that are not copycat items, are not easily classified into existing product categories, and do not require major changes in consumer behavior—such as Betty Crocker Tuna Helper, Cycle dog food, and Libby Fruit Float. However, concept tests are usually inaccurate in predicting the success of new products that create new consumption patterns and require major changes in consumer behavior—such as microwave ovens, videocassette recorders, computers, and word processors.

## BUSINESS ANALYSIS

**business analysis**
Stage in the product development process in which demand, cost, sales, and profitability estimates are made.

New product ideas that survive the initial screening process move to the **business analysis** stage, where preliminary figures for demand, cost, sales, and profitability are calculated. For the first time, costs and revenues are estimated and compared. Depending on the nature of the product and the company, this process may be simple or complex.

The newness of the product, the size of the market, and the nature of competition all affect the accuracy of revenue projections.[21] In an established market like soft drinks, industry estimates of total market size are available. Forecasting market share for a new entry is a bigger challenge.

Analyzing overall economic trends and their impact on estimated sales is especially important in product categories that are sensitive to fluctuations in the business cycle. If consumers view the economy as uncertain and risky, they will put off buying durable goods like major home appliances, automobiles, and homes. Likewise, business buyers postpone major equipment purchases if they expect a recession.

These questions are commonly asked during the business analysis stage:

- What is the likely demand for the product?
- What impact would the new product probably have on total sales, profits, market share, and return on investment?
- How would the introduction of this product affect existing products? Would it cannibalize existing products?
- Would current customers benefit from the product?
- Would this product enhance the image of our overall product mix?
- Would the new product affect current employees in any way? Would it lead to hiring more people or reducing the size of the work force?
- What new facilities, if any, would be needed?
- How might competitors respond?
- What is the risk of failure? Are we willing to take the risk?

Answering these and related questions may require studies of markets, competition, costs, and technical capabilities. But at the end of this stage, management should have a good understanding of the product's market potential. This full understanding is important, because costs increase dramatically once a product idea enters the development stage.

The Marketing and Small Business box provides a checklist that small businesses might use for evaluating new product ideas.

## DEVELOPMENT

**development**
Stage in the product development process in which a prototype is developed and a marketing strategy is outlined.

In the early stage of **development,** the research and development department or engineering department may develop a prototype of the product. During this stage, the firm should start sketching a marketing strategy. The marketing department should decide on the packaging, branding, labeling, and so forth. In addition, it should map out preliminary promotion, price, and distribution strategies. The technical feasibility of manufacturing the product at an acceptable cost should also be thoroughly examined.

The development stage can last a long time and thus be very expensive. Crest toothpaste was in the development stage for ten years. It took eighteen years to develop Minute Rice, fifteen years to develop the Polaroid Colorpack camera, fifteen years to develop the Xerox copy machine, and fifty-five years to develop television.

The development process works best when all the involved areas (R&D, marketing, engineering, production, and even suppliers) work together rather than sequentially. You may recall from earlier in this chapter that this process is called parallel engineering.

Laboratory tests are often conducted on prototype models during the development stage. User safety is an important aspect of laboratory testing, which actually

MARKETING AND SMALL BUSINESS

**Checklist for Evaluating New Product Concepts**

If a small business is lucky enough to have stable or increasing sales, new product additions can boost profits and market share. Small-business managers must be careful, however, not to expand beyond the firm's financial capacities. A new product requires shelf space, investment in inventory and perhaps spare parts, and maybe even a new salesperson—all of which require an extra financial commitment.

A new small business usually has only one chance "to do it right." A failure in introducing a new product means bankruptcy and perhaps the loss of a person's life savings. Conversely, for the owner of an established small business who suddenly finds that his or her source of livelihood has evaporated, the right new product can help offset declining demand.

The product development process is generally the same for both large and small firms. However, many entrepreneurs must do most steps in the process themselves rather than rely on specialists or outside consultants.

Here's a simple checklist for evaluating new product concepts for a small business. By adding up the points, a small-business owner can more accurately estimate success.

1. Contribution to before-tax return on investment:
   - More than 35 percent +2
   - 25–35 percent +1
   - 20–25 percent −1
   - Less than 20 percent −2
2. Estimated annual sales:
   - More than $10 million +2
   - $2 million–$10 million +1
   - $1 million–$1.99 million −1
   - Less than $1 million −2
3. Estimated growth phase of product life cycle:
   - More than three years +2
   - Two or three years +1
   - One or two years −1
   - Less than one year −2
4. Capital investment payback:
   - Less than a year +2
   - One to two years +1
   - Two to three years −1
   - More than three years −2
5. Premium-price potential:
   - Weak or no competition, making entry easy +2
   - Mildly competitive entry conditions +1
   - Strongly competitive entry conditions −1
   - Entrenched competition that makes entry difficult −2

This checklist is by no means complete. But a neutral or negative total score should give an entepreneur reason to consider dropping the product concept.

subjects products to much more severe treatment than is expected by end users. The Consumer Product Safety Act of 1972 requires manufacturers to conduct a "reasonable testing program" to ensure that their products conform to established safety standards.

Many products that test well in the laboratory are also tried out in homes or businesses. Examples of product categories well suited for such use tests include human and pet food products, household cleaning products, and industrial chemicals and supplies. These products are all relatively inexpensive, and their performance characteristics are apparent to users.

Most products require some refinement based on the results of laboratory and use tests. A second stage of development often takes place before test marketing.

### TEST MARKETING

After products and marketing programs have been developed, they are usually tested in the marketplace. **Test marketing** is the limited introduction of a product and a marketing program to determine the reactions of potential customers in a market situation. Test marketing allows management to evaluate alternative strategies and to assess how well the various aspects of the marketing mix fit together. Quest, Seagram's low-calorie line of sparkling waters, was test marketed for nearly a year before its national introduction.[22]

The cities chosen as test sites should reflect market conditions in the new product's projected market area. Yet no "magic city" exists that can universally represent market conditions, and a product's success in one city doesn't guarantee it will be a nationwide hit. When selecting test market cities, researchers should therefore find locations where the demographics and purchasing habits mirror the overall market. The company should also have

*Exhibit 10.4*

Checklist for Selecting Test Markets

| In choosing a test market, many criteria need to be considered, especially the following: |
|---|
| Similarity to planned distribution outlets |
| Relative isolation from other cities |
| Availability of advertising media that will cooperate |
| Diversified cross section of ages, religions, cultural-societal preferences, etc. |
| No atypical purchasing habits |
| Representative population size |
| Typical per capita income |
| Good record as a test city, but not overly used |
| Not easily "jammed" by competitors |
| Stability of year-round sales |
| No dominant television station; multiple newspapers, magazines, and radio stations |
| Availability of retailers that will cooperate |
| Availability of research and audit services |
| Freedom from unusual influences, such as one industry's dominance or heavy tourism |

**test marketing**
Stage in the product development process during which a product is introduced in a limited way to determine the reactions of potential customers in a market situation.

good distribution in test cities. Moreover, test locations should be media-isolated. If the TV stations in a particular market reach a very large area outside that market, the advertising used for the test product may pull in many consumers from outside the market. The product may then appear more successful than it really is. Exhibit 10.4 provides a useful checklist of criteria for selecting test markets. Exhibit 10.5 on page 326 lists the U.S. cities that are the most popular test markets.

## The High Costs of Test Marketing

Test marketing normally covers 1 to 3 percent of the United States, takes about twelve to eighteen months, and costs between $1 million and $3 million.[23] Some products remain in test markets even longer. McDonald's spent twelve years developing and testing salads before introducing them. Despite the cost, many firms believe it is a lot better to fail in a test market than in a national introduction.

Because test marketing is so expensive, some companies do not test line extensions of well-known brands. For example, because the Folger's brand is well known, Procter & Gamble faced little risk in distributing its instant decaffeinated version nationally. Consolidated Foods Kitchen of Sara Lee followed the same approach with its frozen croissants. Other products introduced without being test marketed include General Foods' International Coffees, Quaker Oats' Chewy Granola Bars and Granola Dipps, and Pillsbury's Milk Break Bars.

*Exhibit 10.5*

Best U.S. Test Markets

Source: Judith Waldrop, "All-American Markets," *American Demographics*, January 1992, p. 26. *American Demographics* magazine © 1992. Reprinted with Permission.

| Rank | Metropolitan area | 1990 population |
|---|---|---|
| 1 | Detroit, Mich. | 4,382,000 |
| 2 | St. Louis, Mo.-Ill. | 2,444,000 |
| 3 | Charlotte-Gastonia-Rock Hill, N.C.-S.C. | 1,162,000 |
| 4 | Fort Worth–Arlington, Tex. | 1,332,000 |
| 5 | Kansas City, Mo.-Kans. | 1,566,000 |
| 6 | Indianapolis, Ind. | 1,250,000 |
| 7 | Philadelphia, Pa.-N.J. | 4,857,000 |
| 8 | Wilmington, N.C. | 120,000 |
| 9 | Cincinnati, Ohio-Ky.-Ind. | 1,453,000 |
| 10 | Nashville, Tenn. | 985,000 |
| 11 | Dayton-Springfield, Ohio | 951,000 |
| 12 | Jacksonville, Fla. | 907,000 |
| 13 | Toledo, Ohio | 614,000 |
| 14 | Greensboro–Winston-Salem–High Point, N.C. | 942,000 |
| 15 | Columbus, Ohio | 1,377,000 |
| 16 | Charlottesville, Va. | 131,000 |
| 17 | Panama City, Fla. | 127,000 |
| 18 | Pensacola, Fla. | 344,000 |
| 19 | Milwaukee, Wis. | 1,432,000 |
| 20 | Cleveland, Ohio | 1,831,000 |

The high cost of test marketing is not purely financial. One unavoidable problem is that test marketing exposes the new product and its marketing mix to competitors before its introduction. Thus the element of surprise is lost. Several years ago, for example, Procter & Gamble began testing a ready-to-spread Duncan Hines frosting. General Mills took note and rushed to market with its own Betty Crocker brand, which now is the best-selling brand of ready-to-spread frosting.[24]

Competitors can also sabotage or "jam" a testing program by introducing their own sales promotion, pricing, or advertising campaign. The purpose is to hide or distort the normal conditions that the testing firm might expect in the market. When PepsiCo tested its Mountain Dew sports drink in Minneapolis in 1990, Quaker Oats counterattacked furiously with coupons and ads for Gatorade.[25]

## Alternatives to Test Marketing

Many firms are looking for cheaper, faster, safer alternatives to traditional test marketing. In the early 1980s, Information Resources Incorporated pioneered one alternative: single-source research using supermarket scanner data (discussed in Chapter 7). A typical supermarket scanner test costs about $300,000.

**simulated (laboratory) market test**
Presentation of advertising and other promotion materials for several products, including a test product, to members of the product's target market.

Another alternative to traditional test marketing is **simulated (laboratory) market testing.** Advertising and other promotional materials for several products, including the test product, are shown to members of the product's target market. These people are then taken to shop at a mock or real store where their purchases are recorded. Shopper behavior, including repeat purchasing, is monitored to assess the product's likely performance under true market conditions. Research firms offer simulated market tests for $25,000 to $100,000, compared to $1 million or more for full-scale test marketing.

Despite these alternatives, most firms still consider test marketing essential for most new products. The high price of failure simply prohibits the widespread introduction of most new products without testing. Sometimes, however, when risks of failure are estimated to be low, it is better to skip test marketing and move directly from development to commercialization.

### COMMERCIALIZATION

**commercialization**
Final stage in the product development process, consisting of tasks necessary to begin marketing the product.

The final stage in the new product development process is **commercialization,** the decision to market a product. The decision to commercialize sets several tasks in motion: ordering production materials and equipment, starting production, building inventories, shipping the product to field distribution points, training the sales force, announcing the new product to the trade, and advertising to potential customers.

The time from the initial commercialization decision to the product's actual introduction varies. It can range from a few weeks for simple products that use existing equipment to several years for technical products that require custom manufacturing equipment.

The total cost of development and initial introduction can be staggering. U.S. companies spend over $125 billion each year on research and development, manufacturing, and marketing to introduce around 4,250 new brands.[26] Gillette alone spent over $200 million to develop and start manufacturing the Sensor razor and another $110 million for first-year advertising.[27]

4 *Analyze the reasons for the failure or success of a new product.*

## WHY SOME NEW PRODUCTS SUCCEED AND OTHERS FAIL

Despite the high cost and other risks of developing and testing new products, many companies—such as Rubbermaid, Campbell Soup, and Procter & Gamble—continue to develop and introduce new products. Some new products succeed and some fail. With so much at stake, it is no wonder that marketers have analyzed the factors involved in both success and failure.

The most important factor in successful new product introduction is a good match between the product and market needs—as the marketing concept would predict. Here are other factors that increase the chances of *success* for both consumer and business product introductions:

Unique but superior product

Coordinated, proficient technical and production efforts

Large, high-need, growth market

Reasonably priced product with an economic advantage

Avoidance of a competitive market with satisfied customers

Strong marketing communication and launch effort

Market-derived idea with considerable supporting investment

Associations, trade publications, consultants, and statistical bureaus estimate that the new product failure rate is in the range of 80 to 90 percent and costs over $100 billion each year.[28] Many products fail simply because their manufacturers lack a well-developed marketing strategy. Moreover, they do not realize the importance of creating a product to meet the consumer's need rather than producing "what we know best."

Failure can be a matter of degree. Absolute failure occurs when a company cannot recoup its development, marketing, and production costs. The product actually loses money for the company. A relative product failure results when the product returns a profit but does not meet its profit or market share objectives. Relative failures can sometimes be repositioned or improved to become a viable part of a product line. For instance, Tony's Pizza failed until a home economist developed a crust that didn't taste like cardboard. Similarly, Pepperidge Farm's Deli's floundered until the quality of ingredients was improved.

In the long run, products fail because product characteristics poorly match consumer needs. Other important factors that tend to cause new product *failure* are

Inadequate promotion
Poor packaging
Lack of differential advantage
Poor timing
Overpricing or underpricing
Lack of or inadequate accessories
Poor after-sale service
Inadequate performance
Failure to fulfill promotional claims

5 *Discuss global issues in new product development.*

## GLOBAL ISSUES IN NEW PRODUCT DEVELOPMENT

Increasing globalization of markets and of competition provides a reason for multinational firms to consider new product development from a worldwide perspective. A firm that starts with a global strategy is better able to develop products that are marketable worldwide. In many multinational corporations, every product is developed for potential worldwide distribution, and unique market requirements are built in whenever possible.[29]

Some global marketers design their products to meet regulations and other key requirements in their major markets and then, if necessary, meet smaller markets' requirements country by country. For example, Nissan develops lead-country car models that can, with minor changes, be sold in most markets. For the remaining markets, Nissan provides other models that can readily be adapted. With this approach, Nissan has been able to reduce the number of its basic models from forty-eight to eighteen. This approach also allows a company to introduce new products in all its markets at roughly the same time.

The main goal of the global product development process, therefore, is not to develop a standard product or product line. Rather, it is to build adaptable products that are expected to achieve worldwide appeal.

6 *Explain the diffusion process through which new products are adopted.*

## THE SPREAD OF NEW PRODUCTS

Marketing and product managers have a better chance of successfully guiding a product through its life cycle if they understand how consumers learn about and adopt products. The product life cycle and the adoption process go hand in hand. A person who buys a new product never before tried may ultimately become an

**adopter**
Consumer who was happy enough with a trial experience with a product to use it again.

**adopter,** a consumer who was happy enough with his or her trial experience with a product to use it again.

### STAGES IN THE ADOPTION PROCESS

People progress through distinct stages when deciding whether to adopt or reject a product. One model that describes this process is called *AIDA;* the letters stand for attention, interest, desire, and action. Another model that depicts the adoption process is called the hierarchy of effects model. This model is examined in Chapter 15.

The consumer adoption process has two main marketing implications. First, because adoption is a process, people must progress through awareness, interest, and evaluation stages before proceeding to trial and adoption. Second, different people will be in different stages of the adoption process. Thus marketers face a major challenge in directing their marketing messages. They must attract the interest of some, create interest on the part of others, stimulate trial on the part of still others, and convince other consumers to adopt and continue using the product.

**innovation**
Product perceived as new by a potential adopter.

**diffusion**
Process by which the adoption of an innovation spreads.

**innovator**
Consumer among the small group who first adopt a new idea or product and are eager to try.

### DIFFUSION OF INNOVATION

An **innovation** is a product perceived as new by a potential adopter. It really doesn't matter whether the product is "new to the world" or simply new to the individual. **Diffusion** is the process by which the adoption of an innovation spreads.

Five categories of adopters participate in the diffusion process:

- ***Innovators:*** the first 2½ percent of all those who adopt. Innovators are eager to try new ideas and products, almost as an obsession. In addition to having higher incomes, they are more worldly and more active outside their community

Innovators are those consumers who rush out to buy the newest product, such as the latest computer technology.

Jeffrey MacMillan/*U.S. News & World Report*

than noninnovators. They rely less on group norms and are more self-confident. Because they are well educated, they are more likely to get their information from scientific sources and experts. Innovators are characterized as being venturesome.

**early adopter**
Consumer among the second group to adopt a new idea or product, frequently an opinion leader.

- *Early adopters:* the next 13½ percent to adopt the product. Although early adopters are not the very first, they do adopt early in the product's life cycle. Compared to innovators, they rely much more on group norms and values. They are also more oriented to the local community, in contrast to the innovator's worldly outlook. Early adopters are more likely than innovators to be opinion leaders because of their closer affiliation to groups. The respect of others is a dominant characteristic of early adopters.

**early majority**
Third group of consumers to adopt a new idea or product, characterized by their deliberation.

- *Early majority:* the next 34 percent to adopt. The early majority weigh the pros and cons before adopting a new product. They are likely to collect more information and evaluate more brands than early adopters, therefore extending the adoption process. They rely on the group for information but are unlikely to be opinion leaders themselves. Instead, they tend to be opinion leaders' friends and neighbors. The early majority are an important link in the process of diffusing new ideas, because they are positioned between earlier and later adopters. A dominant characteristic of the early majority is deliberateness.

**late majority**
Fourth group of consumers to adopt a new idea or product, characterized by their reliance on group norms.

- *Late majority:* the next 34 percent to adopt. The late majority adopt a new product because most of their friends have already adopted it. Because they also rely on group norms, their adoption stems from pressure to conform. This group tends to be older and below average in income and education. They depend mainly on word-of-mouth communication rather than the mass media. The dominant characteristic of the late majority is skepticism.

**laggard**
Consumer among the final group to adopt a new idea or product, characterized by ties to tradition.

- *Laggards:* the final 16 percent to adopt. Like innovators, laggards do not rely on group norms. Their independence is rooted in their ties to tradition. Thus the past heavily influences their decisions. By the time laggards adopt an innovation, it has probably been outmoded and replaced by something else. For example, they may have bought their first black-and-white TV set after color television was already widely diffused. Laggards have the longest adoption time and the lowest socioeconomic status. They tend to be suspicious of new products and alienated from a rapidly advancing society. The dominant value of laggards is tradition. Marketers typically ignore laggards, who do not seem to be motivated by advertising or personal selling.

Exhibit 10.6 shows the relationship between the adopter categories and stages of the product life cycle. Note that the various categories of adopters first buy products in different stages of the product life cycle. Sales in the maturity and decline stages almost all represent repeat purchasing.

## PRODUCT CHARACTERISTICS AND THE RATE OF ADOPTION

Five product characteristics can be used to predict and explain the rate of acceptance and diffusion of a new product:

- *Complexity:* the degree of difficulty involved in understanding and using a new product. The more complex the product, the slower its diffusion. For instance, before many of their functions were automated, 35mm cameras were used primarily by hobbyists and professionals. They were just too complex for most people to learn to operate.

Exhibit 10.6

Relationship between the Diffusion Process and the Product Life Cycle

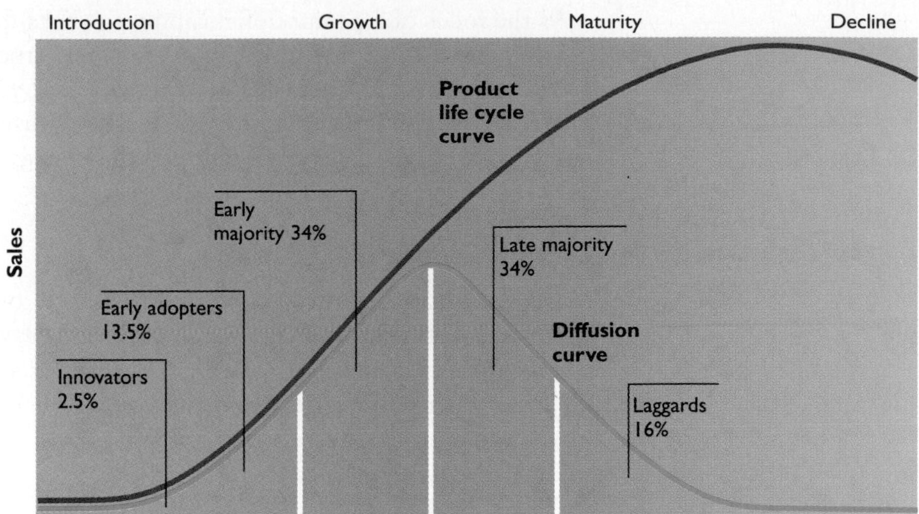


- *Compatibility:* the degree to which the new product is consistent with existing values and product knowledge, past experiences, and current needs. Incompatible products diffuse more slowly than compatible products. For example, the introduction of contraceptives is incompatible in countries where religious beliefs discourage the use of birth control techniques.
- *Relative advantage:* the degree to which a product is perceived as superior to existing substitutes. For example, because it reduces cooking time, the microwave oven has a clear relative advantage over a conventional oven.
- *Observability:* the degree to which the benefits or other results of using the product can be observed by others and communicated to target customers. For instance, fashion items and automobiles are highly visible and more observable than personal care items.
- *Trialability:* the degree to which a product can be tried on a limited basis. It is much easier to try a new toothpaste or breakfast cereal than a new automobile or microcomputer. Demonstrations in showrooms and test drives are different from in-home trial use. To stimulate trial, marketers use free sampling programs, tasting displays, and small package sizes.

## MARKETING IMPLICATIONS OF THE ADOPTION PROCESS

Two types of communication aid the diffusion process: word-of-mouth communication among consumers and communication from marketers to consumers. *Word-of-mouth communication* within and across groups speeds diffusion. Opinion leaders discuss new products with their followers and with other opinion leaders. Marketers must therefore ensure that opinion leaders have the types of information desired in the media that they use. Suppliers of some products, such as professional and health care services, rely almost solely on word-of-mouth communication for new business.

The second type of communication aiding the diffusion process is *communication directly from the marketer to potential adopters.* Messages directed toward early adopters should normally use different appeals than messages directed toward the early majority, the late majority, or the laggards. Early adopters are more important than innovators because they make up a larger group, are more socially active, and are usually opinion leaders.

As the focus of a promotional campaign shifts from early adopters to the early majority and the late majority, marketers should study the dominant characteristics, buying behavior, and media characteristics of these target markets. Then they should revise messages and media strategy to fit. The diffusion model helps guide marketers in developing and implementing promotion strategy.

7 *Explain the product management form of organization.*

**brand manager**
Person who is responsible for a single brand.

**product manager**
Person who is responsible for several brands within a product line or product group.

**category manager**
Person responsible for multiple product lines within a product category.

## PRODUCT MANAGEMENT

Large organizations often use brand, product, or category managers to direct specific marketing efforts. Technically, a **brand manager** is responsible for a single brand. A **product manager** has responsibility for several brands within a product line or product group. A **category manager** has responsibility for multiple product lines within a product category.[30] Exhibit 10.7 shows the responsibilities of brand, product, and category managers.

### THE ORIGINAL PRODUCT MANAGER CONCEPT

During the 1950s and 1960s, major consumer products companies grew in sales, number of product lines, and organizational complexity. Managers developed new organizational arrangements for marketing to cope better with the dynamic nature of the marketing environment. These were the responsibilities of the product manager's job in its original form:

- Creating strategies for improving and marketing assigned product lines or brands
- Making financial and operating plans for those products
- Monitoring the results of those plans and adapting tactics to evolving conditions

*Exhibit 10.7*

Product Management Hierarchy

| Product level | Management level | Responsibilities |
|---|---|---|
| Brand | Brand manager (or product manager) | Develops marketing strategies for a new brand<br>Recommends changes in strategy for an existing brand<br>Positions the brand<br>Identifies target segments for the brand<br>Evaluates the effect of alternative marketing strategies on brand performance |
| Product line | Product manager | Evaluates products in a given line<br>Considers extensions of the line within the product category<br>Assesses an expansion of the line to other product categories<br>Considers candidates for deletion from the line<br>Considers the effects of additions to and deletions from the line on the profitability of other products in the line |
| Product category | Category manager (or top management) | Evaluates existing product lines in the product category<br>Evaluates the mix of new and existing products within the category<br>Considers the relative emphasis on new versus existing products<br>Considers the effects of line additions and deletions on the profitability of other lines in the category<br>Considers the introduction of new product lines |

Apple Computer is one of those firms that uses market managers instead of product managers. Market managers focus on a single segment of the target market—such as the educational market for computers—instead of on a product or product line.

Apple Computer Inc.

Procter & Gamble, originator of the product management form of organization, has fine-tuned the concept. Now individual brand managers report to a category manager, who has profit-and-loss responsibility for an entire product line. For example, a category manager for laundry detergents would have the brand managers of Tide, Cheer, Liquid Tide, and Ivory Flakes reporting to him or her.

Before P&G's reorganization, brand managers fought not only external competitors but also internal brands. Thus the brand managers of Tide and Cheer might both launch massive couponing campaigns during the same month. Both campaigns would suffer. A category manager thinks in terms of product groups and makes sure the brand managers aren't sabotaging one another. Now the brand managers can go directly to the category manager, who has the authority to make quick decisions and coordinate campaigns and other efforts. The category manager can also back up the brand managers with as much as $1 million per project.

## MARKET MANAGEMENT

**market manager**
Person who is responsible for coordinating the marketing efforts designed to reach a particular group of customers.

Some firms, dissatisfied with the product manager concept, have instead created the position of market manager. A **market manager** is like a product manager except that he or she is responsible for coordinating marketing efforts designed to reach a particular group of customers rather than guiding a particular group of products. For example, personal computers are used by households, educational institutions, small businesses, government institutions, and large businesses. Apple Computer has a market manager to serve each market segment. Previously, Apple used a product manager approach, developing and marketing each product in isolation.

A market manager is responsible for annual budgets, long-range plans, sales forecasts, and profit analysis in his or her market. The market manager knows the product need in the market and thus is better able to suggest product modifications, new product ideas, and service enhancements.

8 *Identify the cost of sustaining weak products, and explain procedures for deciding to abandon a product.*

## PRODUCT ABANDONMENT

The product life cycle concept reminds us that all products eventually decline in popularity and profitability. To maintain an effective marketing mix, firms must delete obsolete products as well as develop and introduce new ones.

Abandoning a product is not cost-free. A grocery industry task force found that the costs to manufacturers of deleting products—including disposal of inventory—ranged from $7,100 to $660,770.[31] Wholesalers spend only about $300 on average to drop products from their lines.

However, sometimes the cost of keeping a weak product outweighs the cost of abandoning it. Perhaps the greatest cost of a weak product is its effect on new product ideas. While the firm struggles to maintain a weak product, it can't give new products the attention they deserve. The price for sustaining old products may be the sacrifice of new ones and future profits.

**product-review committee**
Group of high-level executives—representing the marketing, production, and finance departments—appointed to review products for elimination from a company's product line.

Decisions to abandon a product are too important for one person to handle alone. Firms often have a **product-review committee** of high-level executives representing the marketing, production, and finance departments. Typically, the marketing executive discusses marketing strategy, customer relations, sales potential, and competitive offerings. The production executive discusses scheduling, production, and inventory problems. Finally, the finance executive discusses the company's potential profit position if the weak product were eliminated.

### PRODUCT ABANDONMENT CHECKLIST

One of the first tasks of the product-review committee is to set a procedure for periodically evaluating the firm's products. Firms that market a large number of products find some sort of screening procedure for identifying weak products to be a necessity. Most screening procedures list product abandonment, or "early warning," criteria. Exhibit 10.8 is a sample.

After members of the product-review team agree on the screening criteria, they combine the criteria into a checklist like the one shown in Exhibit 10.9. If the product-review committee's time is limited, it can rank products just by their mean scores, from weakest to strongest. In the exhibit, the average score of 2.33 indicates that the product is in trouble. Normally the firm would want to look closely at any product with an average score of 2 or greater.

The product abandonment checklist could be more sophisticated, however. Some criteria could be weighted more heavily than others. The purpose of this type of analysis is to pinpoint weak products and then evaluate them more intensively.

Note that a product with a bad average score should not necessarily be removed from the market, especially if it completes a product line. But another product with the same score may be a good candidate for abandonment.

### TIMING OF PRODUCT ABANDONMENT

After deciding to abandon a product, the product-review team should decide how quickly to withdraw it. The alternatives range from dropping the product immediately to phasing it out over a period of months. This decision should be made only

*Exhibit 10.8*

Sample Product Abandonment Criteria

| | |
|---|---|
| **Product sales trend** | A persistent downward trend in the sales of a product may indicate that it has reached the maturity or decline stage of its life cycle. |
| **Price trend** | A downward trend in the price of a new product may not be a big surprise, but if the trend continues when the product is better established, then it may be in trouble. |
| **Profit trend** | Declining profit, expressed as a percentage of either sales or invested capital, should raise questions about the wisdom of keeping the product on the market. |
| **Substitute products** | Many new products are improved versions of more established products. In such cases, it's a good idea to withdraw the earlier versions from the market. |
| **Product effectiveness** | If a product no longer performs its intended function, then it probably should be withdrawn from the market. For example, household bug sprays lose their effectiveness when insects develop resistance to them. |
| **Executive time** | The more time managers spend on a product, the stronger the argument for abandoning it. Sick products require constant attention; this time can be better spent elsewhere. |

*Exhibit 10.9*

Sample Product Abandonment Checklist

| | **Rating** | | |
|---|---|---|---|
| **Early warning criteria** | **Negative (3)** | **Neutral (2)** | **Positive (1)** |
| Product sales trend | | X | |
| Price trend | X | | |
| Profit trend | X | | |
| Substitute products | | X | |
| Product effectiveness | | | X |
| Executive time | X | | |
| *Average score:* 14 ÷ 6 = 2.33 | | | |

after reviewing current inventory levels and obligations to dealers and customers. Manufacturers of industrial products seldom drop weak products overnight. Products are normally phased out gradually to give customers time to find adequate substitutes.

## LOOKING BACK

Look back at the story at the beginning of this chapter about Pillsbury's Oven Lovin' refrigerated cookie dough. Pillsbury skipped the test marketing stage of the new product development process because management thought the focus group results were sufficient evidence that this revision of existing products would succeed. Furthermore, test marketing takes time, is expensive, and lets competitors see your new products before they are officially introduced.

Focus groups have a serious limitation, however: Consumers often find it difficult to evaluate products based on limited experience. Just because a new product "tastes great" doesn't mean consumers will purchase and repurchase it. Although focus group members liked the Oven Lovin' product and consumers were eager to try it—perhaps motivated by discount coupons—the product was ultimately judged to be too expensive. After an initial trial, most consumers returned to brands they had purchased previously or continued trying other new brands.

Why did Oven Lovin' fail? Two apparent reasons are value and targeting. The price per ounce of dough was higher than other Pillsbury brands, partly because of Oven Lovin's more expensive resealable package. Furthermore, the package provided a benefit most consumers didn't need, because few had any leftover dough to save. Although Oven Lovin' and its resealable package may fill a need for small families and single consumers, these shoppers don't bake cookies very often. Most cookie dough buyers are families with young children, who are often on a tight budget.

Pillsbury hasn't completely dropped Oven Lovin' cookie dough from its product mix. The remaining chocolate-chip variety is available in about a third of U.S. supermarkets. But promotion has been dramatically scaled back.

## SUMMARY

1 **Describe the six categories of new products, and explain the importance of developing new products.** New products can be classified as new-to-the-world products (discontinuous innovations), new product lines, additions to existing product lines, improvements or revisions of existing products, repositioned products, or lower-cost products. To sustain or increase profits, a firm must introduce at least one new successful product before a previous product advances to the maturity stage and profit levels begin to drop. Several factors make it more important than ever for firms to consistently introduce new products: shortened product life cycles, rapidly changing technology and consumer priorities, the high rate of new product failures, and the length of time needed to implement new product ideas.

2 **Describe the organizational groups or structures used to facilitate new product development.** Firms facilitate the development of new products with new product committees and departments, venture teams, and parallel engineering. New product committees are composed of representatives of various branches of an organization and mainly play an advisory role. A new product department may be a separate department, a high-level staff function, a part of marketing, or a part of research and development. Venture team members are recruited from within an organization to work full-time on specific projects and are encouraged to take an "intrapreneurial" approach to new product development. Some U.S. firms use an organizational structure popular in Japan, called parallel engineering, in which all departments work together to develop new products.

3 **Explain the steps in the new product development process.** First a firm forms a new product strategy by outlining the characteristics and roles of future products. Then new product ideas are generated by customers, employees, distributors, competitors, and internal research and development personnel. Once a product idea has survived initial screening by an appointed screening group, it undergoes business analysis to determine its potential profitability. If a product concept seems viable, it progresses into the development phase, in which the technical and economic feasibility

KEY TERMS

adopter 329
brainstorming 321
brand manager 332
business analysis 322
category manager 332
commercialization 327
concept test 322
development 323
diffusion 329
early adopter 330
early majority 330
innovation 329
innovator 329
laggard 330
late majority 330
market manager 333
new product 314
new product committee 315
new product department 315
new product strategy 318
parallel (simultaneous/concurrent) engineering 317
product development 320
product manager 332
product-review committee 334
screening 322
simulated (laboratory) market test 326
test marketing 324
venture team 316

of the manufacturing process is evaluated. The development phase also includes laboratory and use testing of a product for performance and safety. Following initial testing and refinement, most products are introduced in a test market to evaluate consumer response and marketing strategies. Finally, test market successes are propelled into full commercialization. The commercialization process means starting up production, building inventories, shipping to distributors, training a sales force, announcing the product to the trade, and advertising to consumers.

4 **Analyze the reasons for the failure or success of a new product.** The most important factor in new product success is a good match between the product and market needs. Most new product failures can be linked to inappropriate marketing strategy or poor implementation of the marketing strategy.

5 **Discuss global issues in new product development.** A marketer with global vision seeks to develop products that can easily be adapted to suit local needs. The goal is not simply to develop a standard product that can be sold worldwide.

6 **Explain the diffusion process through which new products are adopted.** The diffusion process is the spread of a new product from its producer to ultimate adopters. Adopters in the diffusion process belong to five categories: innovators, early adopters, early majority, late majority, and laggards. Product characteristics that affect the rate of adoption include product complexity, compatibility with existing social values, relative advantage over existing substitutes, visibility, and trialability. The diffusion process is facilitated by word-of-mouth communication and communication from marketers to consumers.

7 **Explain the product management form of organization.** Some firms use the product management form of organization. The product manager plans product objectives and strategy, monitors progress, coordinates budget development and control, and cooperates with other departments on product cost and quality.

8 **Identify the cost of sustaining weak products, and explain procedures for deciding to abandon a product.** In addition to introducing financial losses, weak products drain a firm in other ways. They demand more time from management, advertising, and sales personnel than they deserve. And they take company resources away from potentially profitable new products. Product-review committees periodically evaluate a firm's products and set criteria for product abandonment decisions. If a product meets the abandonment criteria, it is phased out immediately or gradually, depending on obligations to dealers and customers.

## Discussion and Writing Questions

1. An executive at Purex commented, "I turn down new products at least twice as often as I did a year ago. But in every case, I tell my people to go back and bring me some new product ideas." Interpret this statement in terms of today's domestic market conditions.

✍2. Imagine that you have just become the director of new product development. Describe in a memo your department's role in the organization.

3. John Luther, management consultant at Marketing Corporation of America, remarked, "People just can't shake the corporate culture's baggage. They still want to do all that market research and testing." Why is new product development often too time-consuming and complicated?

4. Describe some products whose adoption rates are or have been affected by complexity, compatibility, relative advantage, observability, and trialability.

5. What types of communication aid the product diffusion process? Identify some products you use, and tell how you found out about them. Explain what influenced you to buy them.

✍6. Your firm is phasing out a product. Write a memo explaining why the phaseout will be gradual rather than immediate.

## Application for Small Business

In the course Marketing 4123, Marketing Planning, students are required to develop a business plan for a new business. Jennifer Lamb created a fictional marketing research firm that specializes in conducting customer satisfaction surveys for small businesses in the community. The rationales for the firm's offering a single product are that (1) measuring customer satisfaction is a very "hot" topic in business today and (2) most firms offering this type of service target large firms, and their services cost more than most small businesses can afford.

Jennifer's fictitious firm uses college students, especially marketing majors, to conduct personal interviews and telephone surveys. When she wrote her business plan, she had several friends in mind who she thought would be interested in doing this kind of work for the experience and a little extra spending money. She also thought that many small businesses could be convinced to retain her services if the price was significantly lower than that charged by other research firms in the area.

Jennifer got an A on her paper and is now thinking seriously about creating the company she described in her business plan. She wants to know if you would be interested in becoming her partner in this venture.

### Questions

1. Prepare a list of questions to ask Jennifer about the proposed business.

2. Prepare a list of questions to ask some small-business owners or managers in your community. The answers to these questions should help you decide whether or not to give Jennifer's proposal further consideration.

3. Prepare a list of criteria similar to those in the Marketing and Small Business box in this chapter that might be used to evaluate Jennifer's new product idea.

## CRITICAL THINKING CASE

## Mane 'N Tail

Straight Arrow is a maker of animal care products based in Lehigh Valley, Pennsylvania. Among its products is Mane 'N Tail, a shampoo for horses. Straight Arrow is planning to reposition its shampoo toward a new target market—humans. The appeal for the product is simple, says Gene Carter, executive vice president of marketing and sales for Straight Arrow. "Here's a $100,000 animal that looks beautiful. People want the same thing for their hair," he said.

The idea for marketing to humans was first seriously considered three years ago, when research by Carter and company president Roger Dunavant revealed that as many as ten bottles of Mane 'N Tail out of a case of twelve were being used on human hair.

The company, which had sales of $30 million last year, plans to repackage Mane 'N Tail and begin marketing it through hair salons and drugstores. Dunavant and Carter know that they will be competing against hair care giants like Procter & Gamble and Nexxus.

### Questions

1. Propose a series of steps that Straight Arrow should follow before introducing Mane 'N Tail for humans.

2. Assuming the idea is viable, propose a positioning strategy for the new product.

3. Propose a market entry strategy.

4. Assess the chances of this product being successful.

### Reference

Pam Weisz, "HBA Companies Are Making Hay with a Little Horse Sense," *Brandweek,* 16 May 1994, p. 32.

**VIDEO CASE**

## Mary Kay Cosmetics

Mary Kay Cosmetics began in 1963. Some thirty years later, the company's beauty consultants have over 20 million customers and sell more than $1 billion in Mary Kay products. The company strives to be a pre-eminent force in the distribution and marketing of beauty and health-related products.

Mary Kay Cosmetics relies on direct marketing for its sales. The company uses recruited beauty consultants to sell its product line directly to consumers. Each beauty consultant is treated as a small-business owner.

To support its beauty consultants, the company offers training programs in finance, marketing, distribution, and human resources. These programs cover such topics as inventory control, business record keeping, screening and planning of sales calls, and recruitment of other interested beauty consultants. The company prides itself on the support it offers consultants.

One of the biggest problems facing the cosmetics industry is the testing of new products before introducing them to the market. Historically, cosmetics companies have relied on animal testing to see if new products might be safe for human consumption. However, animal rights activists have lobbied long and hard to keep companies from using animals to test new products. It has become such an important issue that many companies now use "Never tested on animals" as part of their advertising or promotional message.

Mary Kay Cosmetics has always been one of the industry leaders in the development and testing of new cosmetics. To test new products, the company now relies on employee volunteers instead of animals. Each product is thoroughly tested before it is ever shipped out to the beauty consultants for sale.

In addition to this type of product testing, Mary Kay beauty consultants make follow-up calls to all new clients to see how well the cosmetics are performing for them. The company wants to make sure that consumers have no adverse reactions to its products. Follow-up calls also give beauty consultants the chance to make sure that Mary Kay products are being used properly. This sort of attention helps improve customer satisfaction.

In addition to introducing new products, Mary Kay Cosmetics strives to improve its product packaging. The company now uses recycled paper in its packaging and uses recycling codes to support local recycling efforts. Because of its new product testing and recyclable packaging, Mary Kay Cosmetics continues to be an industry leader in the area of social responsibility.

### Questions

1. How important are new products to a company like Mary Kay Cosmetics?
2. Do you think product-safety testing is more important for companies like Mary Kay than for cosmetic companies that rely on more traditional sales outlets? Explain your answer.
3. Do you think Mary Kay customers care about the packaging? Explain your answer.

# CHAPTER 11

# SERVICES AND NONBUSINESS MARKETING

## LEARNING OBJECTIVES

*After studying this chapter, you should be able to*

1 *Discuss the importance of services to the economy.*

2 *Discuss the differences between services and goods.*

3 *Explain why services marketing is important to manufacturers.*

4 *Develop marketing mixes for services.*

5 *Explain internal marketing in services.*

6 *Discuss relationship marketing in services.*

7 *Discuss global issues in services marketing.*

8 *Describe nonbusiness marketing, and develop marketing strategies for nonbusiness organizations.*

Two cars at a crash scene are battered, and their drivers, although not hurt, are shaken and scared. Moments after the collision, a neatly dressed young man arrives on the scene with a clipboard, a camera, and a cassette recorder. He is a senior claims representative for Progressive Corp., an insurance company that specializes in high-risk drivers. In the comfort of an air-conditioned van equipped with an office, Progressive's policyholder is offered a settlement for the market value of his totaled car—before the wreckage has been towed away.

Introduced four years ago, Progressive's Immediate Response program provides a level of service that is exceptional in the auto insurance industry. Representatives now make contact with 80 percent of accident victims less than nine hours after learning of the crash, and adjusters complete most collision damage claims within a week. Progressive's automated claims management system reduces costs, builds customers' goodwill, and helps keep the liability lawyers away.

Progressive has created six-person teams of adjusters to deal with claims. The company invests heavily in training, not only in insurance regulation but also in the art of negotiation and in grief counseling, because part of the job is dealing with the relatives of dead crash victims.

Progressive believes that because auto insurance is a commodity, the company's differential advantage lies in its people. The company looks for the best people and pays them top salaries. A gain-sharing program that is based on a formula including revenues, profits, and costs gives adjusters opportunities to make more than their base salary. Progressive's net income has increased at an average annual compound rate of 20 percent since 1989.[1]

What makes Progressive's service different from competing auto insurance companies' service? Why do you think Progressive's management is so concerned with treating employees well? What is the importance of training in providing good service?

1 *Discuss the importance of services to the economy.*

**service**
Product in the form of an activity or a benefit provided to consumers, with four unique characteristics that distinguish it from a good: intangibility, inseparability, heterogeneity, and perishability.

## THE IMPORTANCE OF SERVICES

A **service** is the result of applying human or mechanical efforts to people or objects. Services involve a deed, a performance, or an effort that cannot be physically possessed. Today, the service sector substantially influences the U.S. economy. Roughly 79 percent of the U.S. work force is employed in services, and the service sector accounts for 74 percent of the U.S. gross domestic product. In addition, services produced a balance-of-trade surplus that reached $55.7 billion in 1993 (compared to a $132.4 billion deficit for goods), which significantly reduces this country's overall trade deficit.[2]

The demand for services is expected to continue. According to the Bureau of Labor Statistics, service occupations will be responsible for all net job growth through the year 2005. Much of this demand results from demographics. An aging population will need nurses, home health care, physical therapists, and social workers; two-earner families need child care, housecleaning, and lawn care services. Also increasing will be the demand for information managers, such as computer engineers, systems analysts, and paralegals.[3]

Services are also important to the world economy. In Great Britain, 73 percent of jobs are in services; 57 percent of German workers and 62 percent of Japanese workers are in services.[4]

The marketing process described in Chapter 1 is the same for all types of products, whether they be goods or services. Many ideas and strategies discussed throughout this book have been illustrated with service examples. In many ways, marketing is marketing, regardless of the product's characteristics. However, services have some unique characteristics that distinguish them from goods, and marketing strategies need to be adjusted for these characteristics.

2 *Discuss the differences between services and goods.*

## HOW SERVICES DIFFER FROM GOODS

Services have four unique characteristics that distinguish them from goods: intangibility, inseparability, heterogeneity, and perishability.

### INTANGIBILITY

**intangibility**
Characteristic of services that prevents them from being touched, seen, tasted, heard, or felt in the same manner in which goods can be sensed.

**search quality**
Characteristic of a product that can be easily assessed before purchase.

**experience quality**
Characteristic of a product that can be assessed only after purchase or use.

**credence quality**
Characteristic of a product that consumers have difficulty assessing even after purchase because they do not have the necessary knowledge or experience.

The basic difference between services and goods is that services are intangible. Because of their **intangibility,** they cannot be touched, seen, tasted, heard, or felt in the same manner in which goods can be sensed. Services cannot be stored and are often easy to duplicate. Moreover, services are seldom based on any hidden technology, and no patent protection exists for services.

Evaluating the quality of services before or even after making a purchase is harder than evaluating the quality of goods because, compared to goods, services tend to exhibit fewer search qualities. A **search quality** is a characteristic that can be easily assessed before purchase—for instance, the color of an appliance or automobile. At the same time, services tend to exhibit more experience and credence qualities.[5] An **experience quality** is a characteristic that can be assessed only after use, such as the quality of a meal in a restaurant or the actual experience of a vacation. A **credence quality** is a characteristic that consumers may have difficulty assessing even after purchase because they do not have the necessary knowledge or experience. Medical and consulting services are examples of services that exhibit credence qualities.

These characteristics also make it harder for marketers to communicate the benefits of an intangible service than to communicate the benefits of tangible goods.

Although a vacation experience like white-water rafting is a service, and thus intangible, buyers judge the experience at least in part on the basis of such tangible factors as the condition of the rafts.

Thus, marketers often rely on tangible cues to communicate a service's nature and quality. For example, the Clinton Administration's proposed health program was to include "health security cards" issued to all U.S. citizens, certifying their right to health care. The card would be a tangible symbol of a person's enrollment in the health program.[6] Allstate Insurance Company's use of the "good hands" symbol helps tangibilize the benefit of protection that insurance provides.

The facilities that customers visit, or from which services are delivered, is a critical part of the total service offering. For example, Barnes & Noble, the nation's top bookseller, was founded on the knowledge that for many consumers shopping is a form of entertainment. The stores were designed to provide a unique shopping experience, using a woody, traditional, soft-colored library atmosphere to please book lovers. Additionally, sophisticated modern architecture and graphics and stylish displays were used to satisfy customers. The company's superstores have cafes and big, heavy chairs and tables where people can browse through piles of books. Management makes sure the stores' restrooms are clean.[7]

Messages about the organization are communicated to customers through such elements as the decor, the clutter or neatness of service areas, and the staff's manners and dress. The Walt Disney organization is one of the best at managing tangible cues. Disneyland and Walt Disney World focus on the set (facility), the cast (personnel), and the audience. Hosts and hostesses (not employees) serve guests (not customers) at attractions and shops (not rides and stores). When cast members are hired, they are given written information about what training they will receive, when and where to report, and what to wear. They spend the first day on the job at "Disney University" learning about the Disney philosophy, management style, and history. The cast members also discover how all parts of the organization work together to provide the highest possible level of guest satisfaction. In the Magic Kingdom, the cast is just as important as the set.

### INSEPARABILITY

**inseparability**
Characteristic of services that allows them to be produced and consumed simultaneously.

Goods are produced, sold, and then consumed. In contrast, services are often sold and produced and consumed at the same time. In other words, their production and consumption are inseparable activities. **Inseparability** means that, because consumers must be present during the production of services like haircuts or surgery, they are actually involved in the production of the services they buy. That type of consumer involvement is rare in goods manufacturing. Inseparability also means that services cannot normally be produced in a centralized location and consumed in decentralized locations, as goods typically are. Services are also inseparable from the perspective of the service provider. Thus, the quality of service that firms are able to deliver depends on the quality of their employees.

### HETEROGENEITY

**heterogeneity**
Characteristic of services that makes them less standardized and uniform than goods.

One great strength of McDonald's is consistency. Whether customers order a Big Mac and french fries in Fort Worth, Tokyo, or Moscow, they know exactly what they are going to get. This is not the case with many service providers. **Heterogeneity** means that services tend to be less standardized and uniform than goods. For example, physicians in a group practice or barbers in a barber shop differ within each group in their technical and interpersonal skills. A given physician's or barber's performance may even vary depending on time of day, physical health, or some other factor. Because services tend to be labor-intensive and production and consumption are inseparable, consistency and quality control can be hard to achieve.

Standardization and training help increase consistency and reliability. Limited-menu restaurants like Pizza Hut and KFC offer customers high consistency from one visit to the next because of standardized preparation procedures. Another way to increase consistency is to mechanize the process. For example, banks have reduced the inconsistency of teller services by providing automated teller machines. Airport x-ray surveillance equipment has replaced manual searching of baggage. Automatic coin receptacles on toll roads have replaced human collectors. Automatic car washes have replaced the uneven quality of hand washing, waxing, and drying.

### PERISHABILITY

**perishability**
Characteristic of services that prevents them from being stored, warehoused, or inventoried.

**Perishability** means that services cannot be stored, warehoused, or inventoried. An empty hotel room or airplane seat produces no revenue that day. The revenue is lost. Yet service organizations are often forced to turn away full-price customers during peak periods.

One of the most important challenges in many service industries is thus finding ways to synchronize supply and demand. The philosophy that some revenue is better than none has prompted many hotels to offer deep discounts on weekends and during the off-season and has prompted airlines to adopt similar pricing strategies during off-peak hours. Car rental agencies, movie theaters, and restaurants also use discounts to encourage demand during nonpeak periods.

*3 Explain why services marketing is important to manufacturers.*

## SERVICES MARKETING IN MANUFACTURING

A comparison of goods and services marketing is beneficial, but in reality it is hard to distinguish clearly between manufacturing and service firms. Indeed, many manufacturing firms can point to service as a major factor in their success. For example, maintenance and repair services are important to buyers of copy machines.

One reason that goods manufacturers stress service is that it might give them a strong competitive advantage, especially in industries in which products are perceived as similar. In the automobile industry, for example, few quality differences between car brands are perceived by consumers. Knowing that, General Motors has developed new guidelines for sales techniques and quality customer service and will link dealer incentive payments to how well the guidelines are followed. Radio Shack is expanding its product offerings from just consumer electronics (goods) to include delivery of merchandise and repair of consumer electronics (services).[8]

4 *Develop marketing mixes for services.*

## MARKETING MIXES FOR SERVICES

Services' unique characteristics—intangibility, inseparability, heterogeneity, and perishability—make marketing more challenging. Elements of the marketing mix (product, distribution, promotion, and pricing) need to be adjusted to meet the special needs created by these characteristics.

### PRODUCT (SERVICE) STRATEGY

The development of "product" strategy in services marketing requires planning focused on the service process.[9] Three types of processing occur:

**people processing**
Type of service directed at the customer.

**possession processing**
Type of service directed at something the customer owns.

**information processing**
Type of service that involves the use of technology or brainpower.

- **People processing** takes place when the service is directed at a customer. Examples: transportation services, hairstyling, health clubs, dental and health care.
- **Possession processing** occurs when the service is directed at something a customer owns. Examples: lawn care, car repair, dry cleaning, veterinary services.
- **Information processing** involves the use of technology (for example, computers) or brainpower. Examples: accounting, education, legal and financial services.

Because customers' experiences and involvement differ for each of these types of services, marketing strategies may also differ. For example, people-processing services require more customer participation than do possession-processing services, which means marketing strategies for the former will need to focus more on inseparability and heterogeneity issues.

Services are generally heterogeneous, meaning that they may vary considerably from one instance to another. But automation increases standardization. Thus this car wash produces a more standardized service than does an individual washing a car by hand.

© Mitch Kezar/Tony Stone Images

#### Core and Supplementary Services

**core service**
Most basic benefit a customer is buying.

**supplementary service**
Service that supports or enhances the core service offered by an organization.

The service offering can be viewed as a bundle of activities that include the **core service,** which is the most basic benefit the customer is buying, and a group of **supplementary services** that support or enhance the core service. Exhibit 11.1 on page 346 illustrates these concepts for Federal Express. The core service is overnight transportation and delivery of packages, which involves possession processing.

Exhibit 11.1

Core and Supplementary Services for Federal Express

Source: Adapted from Christopher H. Lovelock, *Services Marketing*, 2nd ed. (Englewood Cliffs, NJ: Prentice-Hall, 1991), p. 18.

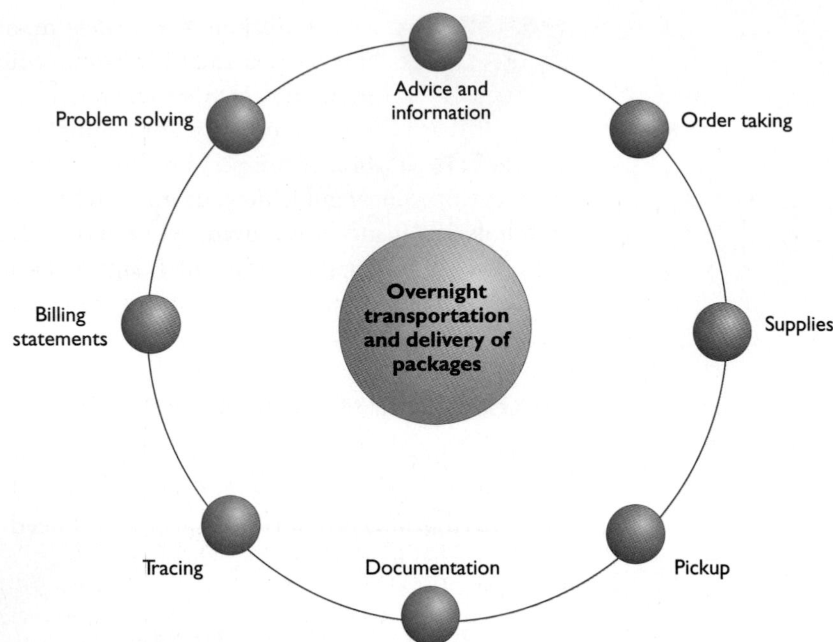


The supplementary services, some of which involve information processing, include problem solving, advice and information, billing statements, and order taking.

In most service industries, the core service becomes a commodity as competition increases. Thus, firms usually emphasize supplementary services to create a competitive advantage. Hospitals like Richardson Medical Center in Texas are marketing AT&T's video telephones as a part of their maternity services. This supplementary service allows the family to see and hear the new baby. New parents pay the cost of a long-distance call; distant relatives rent a videophone at an AT&T Phone Center or take a videophone home for twenty-four hours.[10]

## Customization versus Standardization

Another important issue in developing the service offering is whether to customize or standardize it. Customized services are more flexible and respond to individual customers' needs. They also usually command a higher price. The traditional law firm, which treats each case differently according to the client's situation, offers customized services.

Standardized services are more efficient and cost less. Unlike the traditional law firm, for example, Hyatt Legal Services offers low-cost, standardized service "packages" for those with uncomplicated legal needs, such as drawing up a will or mediating an uncontested divorce.

## The Service Mix

Most service organizations market more than one service. For example, ChemLawn offers lawn care, shrub care, carpet cleaning, and industrial lawn services. Each organization's service mix represents a set of opportunities, risks, and challenges. Each part of the service mix should make a different contribution in achieving the firm's goals. To succeed, each service may also need a different level of financial support.

Designing a service strategy therefore means deciding what new services to introduce to which target market, what existing services to maintain, and what services to eliminate. For example, Walt Disney Company considered adding a cruise line targeting families to its product mix. Disney was responding to market trends that indicate the family market has doubled since 1989, with 28 percent of all first-time adult cruisers taking children with them.[11]

## DISTRIBUTION STRATEGY

Distribution strategies for service organizations must focus on such issues as convenience, number of outlets, direct versus indirect distribution, location, and scheduling. A key factor influencing the selection of a service provider is *convenience*. Therefore, service firms must offer convenience. American Airlines, for example, invested millions of dollars developing the SABRE reservation system to make the reservation process more convenient for independent travel agents. Some competitors complained to the Civil Aeronautics Board, however, because the computer system gave priority listing to American flights. The system has since been modified but remains the most widely used reservation system in the industry.

An important distribution objective for many service firms is the *number of outlets* to use or the number of outlets to open during a certain time. Generally, the intensity of distribution should meet, but not exceed, the target market's needs and preferences. Having too few outlets may inconvenience customers; having too many outlets may boost costs unnecessarily. Intensity of distribution may also depend on the image desired. Having only a few outlets may make the service seem more exclusive or selective.

The next service distribution decision is whether to distribute services to end users *directly or indirectly* through other firms. Because of the intangible nature of services, many service firms have to use direct distribution or franchising. Examples include legal, medical, accounting, and personal care services. Union Marketing and Communications, a Denver-based ad agency that specializes in health care advertising, plans to franchise its services across the United States in order to broaden its distribution. The franchisees will offer sales and services for Union's ready-made health care advertising and marketing campaigns.[12] Other firms with standardized service packages—such as stock funds, airlines, and insurance companies—have developed indirect channels using independent intermediaries. For instance, American Airlines has developed very effective distribution networks through car rental firms, travel agencies, hotels, and tour managers.

The *location* of a service most clearly reveals the relationship between its target market strategy and distribution strategy. Reportedly, Conrad Hilton claimed that the three most important factors in determining a hotel's success are "location, location, and location." Taco Bell, a subsidiary of PepsiCo, has changed from a regional quick-service restaurant chain with 1,500 outlets into a multinational food delivery company with more than 15,000 "points of access" (POAs). A POA is any place where people eat—airports, supermarkets, school cafeterias, or street corners.[13]

For time-dependent service providers like airlines, physicians, and dentists, *scheduling* is often a more important factor. For example, passengers want to know which of the carriers serving a route offer flights at the desired time of day. Sometimes scheduling is the most important factor in a customer's choice of airline.

## PROMOTION STRATEGY

Before they make a purchase decision, consumers and business users have more trouble evaluating services than goods, because services are less tangible. In turn, marketers have more trouble promoting intangible services than tangible goods. Here are four promotion strategies they can try:

For customized services (for example, legal services and construction services), customers may also have the ability to negotiate price.

5 *Explain internal marketing in services.*

## INTERNAL MARKETING IN SERVICE FIRMS

Services are performances, so the quality of a firm's employees is an important part of offering superior service. Employees who like their jobs and are happy with the firm they work for are more likely to deliver high-quality service to customers. In other words, a firm that makes its employees happy has a better chance of making its customers happy. Thus it is critical that service firms practice **internal marketing,** which means treating employees as customers and developing systems and benefits that satisfy their needs. These are the activities involved in internal marketing: competing for talent, offering a vision, training employees, stressing teamwork, giving employees more freedom to make decisions, measuring and rewarding good service performance, and knowing employees' needs.[18]

**internal marketing**
Policy of treating employees as customers and developing systems and benefits that satisfy their needs.

Companies have instituted a wide variety of programs designed to satisfy employees. Federal Express practices internal marketing by offering skills and knowledge training, promotion from within, extensive communication with employees, and an employee grievance process. ServiceMaster's housecleaning branch, Merry Maids, rejects nine out of ten applicants for the entry-level position of "teammate" in an attempt to ensure a good match between the job and the worker. At Metropolitan Life, 90 percent of the company's 28,000 administrative employees have flexible hours, starting work between 7:30 and 10:00 a.m.[19] These examples illustrate how service firms can invest in their most important resource—their employees.

6 *Discuss relationship marketing in services.*

## RELATIONSHIP MARKETING IN SERVICES

Many services involve ongoing interaction between the service organization and the customer. Thus they can benefit from relationship marketing, the strategy described in Chapter 1 as a means of attracting, developing, and retaining customer relationships. The idea is to develop strong loyalty by creating satisfied customers who will buy additional services from the firm and are unlikely to switch to a competitor. Satisfied customers are also likely to engage in positive word-of-mouth communication, thereby helping to bring in new customers.

Many businesses have found that it is more cost-effective to hang on to the customers they have than only to try to attract new ones. A bank executive, for example, found that increasing customer retention by 2 percent can have the same effect on profits as reducing costs by 10 percent.[20]

It has been suggested that relationship marketing can be practiced at three levels (see Exhibit 11.2):[21]

- *Level 1:* The firm uses pricing incentives to encourage customers to continue doing business with it. Examples include the frequent-flyer programs offered by many airlines and the free or discounted travel services given to frequent hotel guests. This level of relationship marketing is the least effective in the long term because its price-based advantage is easily imitated by other firms.
- *Level 2:* This level of relationship marketing also uses pricing incentives but seeks to build social bonds with customers. The firm stays in touch with customers, learns about their needs, and designs services to meet those needs.

*Exhibit 11.2*

Three Levels of Relationship Marketing

Source: Adapted from Leonard L. Berry and A. Parasuraman, *Marketing Services: Competence through Quality* (New York: The Free Press, 1991), p. 137. Reprinted with the permission of The Free Press, a Division of Simon & Schuster. Copyright © 1991 The Free Press.

| Level | Type of bond | Degree of service customization | Main element of marketing mix | Potential for long-term advantage over competitors |
|---|---|---|---|---|
| 1 | Financial | Low | Price | Low |
| 2 | Financial, social | Medium | Personal communication | Medium |
| 3 | Financial, social, structural | Medium to high | Service delivery | High |

Manhattan East Suite Hotels, for example, has compiled a database on the guests who have stayed at its nine luxurious New York City properties. Doormen greet arriving guests by name, and reservation agents know whether a guest prefers a room facing a certain direction or a nonsmoking room.[22] Level 2 relationship marketing has a higher potential for keeping the firm ahead of the competition than does level 1 relationship marketing.

- *Level 3:* At this level, the firm again uses financial and social bonds but adds structural bonds to the formula. Structural bonds are developed by offering value-added services that are not readily available from other firms. Hertz's #1 Club Gold program allows members to call and reserve a car, board a courtesy bus at the airport, tell the driver their name, and get dropped off in front of their car. Hertz also starts up the car and turns on the air conditioning or heat, depending on the temperature.[23] Marketing programs like this one have the strongest potential for sustaining long-term relationships with customers.

7 *Discuss global issues in services marketing.*

## GLOBAL ISSUES IN SERVICES MARKETING

The international marketing of services is a major part of global business, and the United States has become the world's largest exporter of services. Competition in international services is increasing rapidly, however.

To be successful in the global marketplace, service firms must first determine the nature of their core product. Then the marketing mix elements (additional services, pricing, promotion, distribution) should be designed to take into account each country's cultural, technological, and political environment.

Because of their competitive advantages, many U.S. service industries have been able to enter the global marketplace. U.S. banks, for example, have advantages in customer service and collections management. The field of construction and engineering services offers great global potential; U.S. companies have vast experience in this industry, so economies of scale are possible for machinery and materials, human resource management, and project management. The U.S. insurance industry has substantial knowledge about underwriting, risk evaluation, and insurance operations that it can export to other countries. The credit card industry also has great potential for globalization, as the Global Perspectives box illustrates.

*8 Describe nonbusiness marketing, and develop marketing strategies for nonbusiness organizations*

## NONBUSINESS MARKETING

A **nonbusiness organization** is an organization that exists to achieve some goal other than the usual business goals of profit, market share, or return on investment. Few people realize that nonbusiness organizations account for over 20 percent of the economic activity in the United States. The cost of government, the predominant form of nonbusiness organization, has become the biggest single item in the American family budget—more than housing, food, or health care. Together, federal, state, and local governments collect revenues that amount to more than a third of the U.S. gross domestic product. Moreover, they employ nearly one of every five nonagricultural civilian workers. In addition to government entities, nonbusiness organizations include hundreds of thousands of private museums, theaters, schools, churches, and other nonprofit organizations.

**nonbusiness organization**
Organization that exists to achieve some goal other than the usual business goals of profit, market share, and return on investment.

GLOBAL PERSPECTIVES

### Overseas Strategies of U.S. Credit Card Companies

American consumers are long used to credit cards, so Visa, MasterCard, and American Express are trying to court consumers in other countries. Last year, more than $1 trillion was spent globally via credit cards, and this market is expected to double by the year 2000.

But the big credit card companies face significant problems in their efforts to go global. Some of these problems involve variations in government regulations, and some involve deficiencies in electronics and telecommunications networks. Credit card marketers must also learn to understand consumers in different cultures.

Although Americans are willing to pay high interest rates for the ability to postpone payment, many European customers cannot accept the notion of, in essence, taking out a loan to pay for something. Germans are particularly averse to buying on credit. Europeans prefer debit cards.

Italy has a sophisticated credit and banking system that could easily be set up to handle credit and debit cards. However, Italians prefer to carry cash and often pay large bills in person with huge amounts of cash.

Many Japanese consumers have credit cards, but card purchases amount to less than 1 percent of all consumer transactions. The Japanese have long looked down on credit purchases but get cards to use when they travel abroad. The challenge is to find ways to persuade the Japanese to use their cards at home.

In China, credit cards are almost entirely for business use. Companies like to use cards because China lacks an efficient means of transferring money or paying bills. Few consumers have credit cards, however, and the large credit card companies are proceeding cautiously in China because of ambiguous laws governing payment collection.[24]

Why are U.S. credit card companies finding it difficult to market their services in other countries? Can you suggest some marketing strategies these companies could use to break into foreign markets?

### WHAT IS NONBUSINESS MARKETING?

**Nonbusiness marketing** includes marketing activities conducted by nonbusiness organizations. It can be divided into two categories: social marketing and nonprofit organization marketing. **Social marketing** is the use of marketing methods to spread socially beneficial ideas or behaviors. Examples include efforts to get people to seek help for problems like alcohol or drug dependency, child or spouse abuse, and depression. Social marketing is also used to urge people to vote, stop smoking, get health checkups, refrain from polluting, prevent forest fires, support the American Cancer Society, and do a variety of other socially beneficial things. Social marketing can be used by private, for-profit organizations as well as nonprofit organizations, as when the liquor companies urge people not to drink and drive.

**Nonprofit organization marketing,** on the other hand, is the effort by nonprofit organizations to bring about mutually satisfying exchanges with target markets. Although these organizations vary substantially in size and purpose and operate in different environments, most perform the following marketing activities:

- Identify the customers they wish to serve or attract (although they usually use another term, such as *clients, patients, members,* or *sponsors*)

ETHICS IN MARKETING

**Is It Fair to Seek Big Donors in Databases?**

More and more nonprofit groups, eager to tap big givers, are using computers to find wealthy people. These groups are hiring prospect researchers, who are skilled in the use of computer databases, to provide detailed biographical and sometimes financial records to fund-raisers who then go after potential donors. Most prospect researchers feel that, as long as they legally find details about prospects in public sources, they're doing worthy work for a worthy cause.

Others are doubtful. Mary Culnan, a Georgetown University business professor and expert on privacy, told a meeting of the American Prospect Research Association, "I'm somewhat appalled at what's going on. This group represents the worst fears of the privacy advocates."

Nonprofits say they have a special need to learn about the people who are already contributing. Knowing that a donor has $10 million in stock options from taking his company public, fund-raisers can suggest a new level of giving.

Many nonprofits are better than corporations at using computers to spot the most lucrative targets. "I was amazed how much research these people do. They're way ahead of stockbrokers," says Mark C. Desmery, president of Prospex, a New York company that sells information about rich people.

The results can be impressive. During an Iowa State University fund-raising campaign, a wealthy alumnus in California who came to light through prospect research said, "Why is it you never came to me before?" The graduate contributed a seven-figure gift.[26]

Do you think prospect research for the purpose of nonprofit fund-raising is ethical? Should the government regulate access to public information about individuals? In what other ways could nonprofit marketers gather information about prospective donors?



- Explicitly or implicitly specify objectives
- Develop, manage, and eliminate programs and services
- Decide on prices to charge (although they use other terms, such as *fees, donations, tuition, fares, fines,* or *rates*)
- Schedule events or programs and determine where they will be held or where services will be offered
- Communicate their availability through brochures, signs, public service announcements, or advertisements

Often the nonprofit organizations that carry out these functions do not realize they are engaged in marketing.

The biggest obstacle to introducing marketing into a nonbusiness organization may be the word *marketing* itself. Many people think marketing is appropriate only in commercial, profit-seeking organizations. Some even consider marketing activities unprofessional, unethical, or otherwise inappropriate for nonbusiness organizations. These views clearly reflect inaccurate perceptions of marketing. "Some nonprofit people used to think that if you're doing good, somehow God will provide," says John R. Garrison, president of the National Easter Seal Society. "But almost everyone now realizes that commitment isn't enough anymore. You also have to have professionalism, or you're going to go out of business."[25]

**nonbusiness marketing**
Marketing activities conducted by nonbusiness organizations.

**social marketing**
Application of marketing methods to spread socially beneficial ideas or behaviors.

**nonprofit organization marketing**
Effort by public and private nonprofit organizations to bring about mutually satisfying exchanges with target markets.

Some nonprofit organizations have perhaps gone too far in adopting marketing techniques, as the accompanying box explains.

## BENEFITS OF NONBUSINESS MARKETING

A commitment to understanding and enhancing marketing skills offers nonbusiness managers three major benefits. First, because marketing is a systematic process and offers a framework for decision making, relationships between actions once regarded as independent are likely to become more apparent. For example, what if a marketing problem or opportunity is seen only as a communication, price, program, or distribution need? It is unlikely to be resolved in the best way. Coordinated marketing requires that all marketing activities be resolved at the same time and that integrated action be taken.

Second, familiarity with marketing tools is likely to improve decision making.

The American Heart Association is just one of the many nonprofit and for-profit organizations that engage in social marketing. The AMA uses advertising to persuade people to engage in heart-healthy behavior.

Courtesy of the American Heart Association

Unfortunately, some of the concepts and techniques used by marketers are unfamiliar to many nonbusiness managers. They have not been exposed to these tools in their formal training or experience.

Finally, a commitment to marketing is likely to result in more support from customers, prospective donors, foundations, regulators, legislators, and other interest groups. To the extent that marketing improves the satisfaction levels of client groups, the organization is likely to receive improved support. The municipal government of Portland, Oregon, is an example of a nonprofit organization that uses some unusual marketing techniques. The water bureau, for instance, conducts customer surveys. In the sewer department, engineers, planners, and policymakers work on projects as a team rather than independently. Performance audits evaluate whether services are effective and efficient. Police force employees go through cultural-diversity training. The goal of these programs is to make government more accountable to the public and, ultimately, to increase the city's quality of life.[27]

## UNIQUE ASPECTS OF NONBUSINESS MARKETING STRATEGIES

Like their counterparts in business organizations, nonbusiness managers develop marketing strategies to bring about mutually satisfying exchanges with target markets. However, marketing in nonbusiness organizations is unique in many ways—including the setting of marketing objectives, the selection of target markets, and the development of appropriate marketing mixes.

### Objectives

In the private sector, the profit motive is both an objective for guiding decisions and a criterion for evaluating results. Nonbusiness organizations do not seek to make a profit for redistribution to owners or shareholders. Rather, their focus is often generating enough funds to cover expenses. For example, the Methodist Church does not gauge its success by the amount of money left in offering plates. The Museum of Science and Industry does not base its performance evaluations on the dollar value of tokens put into the turnstile.

Most nonbusiness organizations are expected to provide equitable, effective, and efficient services that respond to the wants and preferences of multiple constituencies. These include users, payers, donors, politicians, appointed officials, the media, and the general public. Nonbusiness organizations cannot measure their success or failure in strictly financial terms.

The lack of a financial "bottom line" and the existence of multiple, diverse, intangible, and sometimes vague or conflicting objectives makes prioritizing objectives, making decisions, and evaluating performance hard for nonbusiness managers.

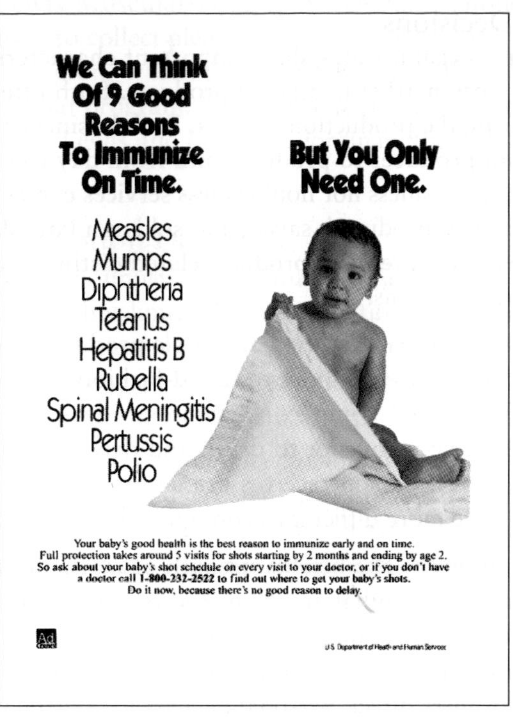


A special challenge facing many nonbusiness marketers is the need to convince the most resistant "customers" to accept a message. With this ad, the U.S. Department of Health and Human Services is trying to reach parents who are disinclined to immunize their babies against common childhood diseases.

Courtesy of U.S. Department of Health and Human Services

They must often use approaches different from the ones commonly used in the private sector. For example, Planned Parenthood has devised a system for basing salary increases on performance:

> Without clear profit and loss responsibility, how does a nonprofit pay people for performance? At Planned Parenthood, all employees must set personal objectives every year. Each goal is assigned a percentage weight to determine its importance. Managers evaluate progress against each goal, grading them from 1 for unsatisfactory to 5 for superior performance. Pay hikes are dished out based on the overall grade.[28]

## Target Markets

Three issues relating to target markets are unique to nonbusiness organizations:

- *Apathetic or strongly opposed targets:* Private-sector organizations usually give priority to developing those market segments that are most likely to respond to particular offerings. In contrast, nonbusiness organizations must often target those who are apathetic about or strongly opposed to receiving their services, such as vaccinations, family-planning guidance, help for problems of drug or alcohol abuse, and psychological counseling. Given the desire or need to reach unresponsive markets, should the organization focus on the least-resistant segment, the most-resistant segment, or both? Valid arguments can be made for any of these options, depending on availability of financial resources, public health or welfare considerations, and the like.
- *Pressure to adopt undifferentiated segmentation strategies:* Nonbusiness organizations often adopt undifferentiated strategies (see Chapter 6) by default. Sometimes they fail to recognize the advantages of targeting, or an undifferentiated approach may appear to offer economies of scale and low per-capita costs. In other instances, nonbusiness organizations are pressured or required to serve the maximum number of people by targeting the average user. The problem with developing services targeted at the average user is that there are few "average" users. Therefore, such strategies typically fail to fully satisfy any market segment. Most profit-seeking firms are well aware of the need for segmenting markets and developing targeted marketing programs.
- *Complementary positioning:* The main role of many nonbusiness organizations is to provide services, with available resources, to those who are not adequately served by private-sector organizations. As a result, the nonbusiness organization must often complement rather than compete with the efforts of others. The positioning task is to identify underserved market segments and to develop marketing programs that match their needs rather than to target the niches that may be most profitable.

If universities were to set prices high enough to fully cover their costs, tuition and fees would rise significantly. Many nonbusiness organizations set their prices below cost.



importance of those costs is illustrated by the large number of eligible citizens who do not take advantage of so-called "free services" for the poverty-stricken. In many public assistance programs, about half the people who are eligible don't participate.[30] Nonmonetary costs consist of the opportunity cost of time, embarrassment costs, and effort costs.

- *Indirect payment:* Indirect payment through taxes is common to marketers of "free" services, such as libraries, fire protection, and police protection. Indirect payment is not a common practice in the profit sector.
- *Separation between payers and users:* By design, the services of many charitable organizations are provided for those who are relatively poor and largely paid for by those who have better finances. Although examples of separation between payers and users can be found in the profit sector (such as insurance claims), the practice is much less prevalent.
- *Below-cost pricing:* An example of below-cost pricing is university tuition. Virtually all private and public colleges and universities price their services below full cost. This practice also exists in the profit sector, although it is generally an undesirable, temporary situation.

## LOOKING BACK

Look back at the story about Progressive Corp. that appeared at the beginning of this chapter. After reading this chapter, you should know the answers to the questions posed at the end of the story. Progressive's service differs from competing auto insurance companies' service because of the quick response to customer needs. In part, this quick response is due to Progressive's distribution strategy—immediately going to where the customer is instead of waiting for the customer to come to it.

Progressive's management treats employees well because it believes in internal marketing, which includes teamwork and suitable reward systems. Keeping employees happy is key to keeping the company's customers happy. Training is also an important part of internal marketing and critical to employees' ability to deal with customers' needs.

## SUMMARY

1 **Discuss the importance of services to the economy.** The service sector plays a crucial role in the U.S. economy, employing about three-quarters of the work force and accounting for more than 60 percent of the gross domestic product.

2 **Discuss the differences between services and goods.** Services are distinguished by four characteristics: intangibility, inseparability, heterogeneity, and perishability. Services are intangible in that they lack clearly identifiable physical characteristics, making it difficult for marketers to communicate their specific benefits to potential customers. The production and consumption of services are typically inseparable. Services are heterogeneous because their quality depends on such variables as the service provider, individual consumer, location, and so on. Finally, services are perishable in the sense that they cannot be stored or saved. As a result, synchronizing supply with demand is particularly challenging in the service industry.

3 **Explain why services marketing is important to manufacturers.** Although manufacturers are mainly marketing goods, the related services they provide often give them a competitive advantage—especially when competing goods are quite similar.

4 **Develop marketing mixes for services.** "Product" (service) strategy issues include what is being processed (people, possessions, information), core and supplementary services, customization versus standardization, and the service mix or portfolio. Distribution decisions involve convenience, number of outlets, direct versus indirect distribution, and scheduling. Stressing tangible cues, using personal sources of information, creating strong organizational images, and engaging in postpurchase communication are effective promotion strategies. Pricing objectives for services can be revenue-oriented, operations-oriented, patronage-oriented, or any combination of the three.

5 **Explain internal marketing in services.** Internal marketing means treating employees as customers and developing systems and benefits that satisfy their needs. Employees who like their jobs and are happy with the firm they work for are more likely to deliver good service. Internal marketing activities include competing for talent, offering a vision, training employees, stressing teamwork, giving employees freedom to make decisions, measuring and rewarding good service performance, and knowing employees' needs.

6 **Discuss relationship marketing in services.** Relationship marketing in services involves attracting, developing, and retaining customer relationships. There are three levels of relationship marketing: Level 1 focuses on pricing incentives; level 2 uses pricing incentives and social bonds with customers; and level 3 uses pricing, social bonds, and structural bonds to build long-term relationships.

7 **Discuss global issues in services marketing.** The United States has become the world's largest exporter of services. Although competition is keen, the United States has a competitive advantage because of its vast experience in many service industries. To be successful globally, service firms must adjust their marketing mix for the environment of each target country.

8 **Describe nonbusiness marketing, and develop marketing strategies for nonbusiness organizations.** Nonbusiness organizations pursue goals other than profit, market share, and return on investment. Nonbusiness marketing includes social marketing, which fosters socially beneficial ideas or behaviors, and nonprofit organization marketing, which facilitates mutually satisfying exchanges between nonprofit organizations and their target markets. Several unique characteristics distinguish

### KEY TERMS

*core service* 345
*credence quality* 342
*experience quality* 342
*heterogeneity* 344
*information processing* 345
*inseparability* 344
*intangibility* 342
*internal marketing* 350
*nonbusiness marketing* 352
*nonbusiness organization* 352
*nonprofit organization marketing* 353
*operations-oriented pricing* 349
*patronage-oriented pricing* 349
*people processing* 345
*perishability* 344
*possession processing* 345
*public service advertisement (PSA)* 357
*revenue-oriented pricing* 349
*search quality* 342
*service* 342
*social marketing* 353
*supplementary service* 345

nonbusiness marketing strategy, including a concern with services and social behaviors rather than manufactured goods and profit; a difficult, undifferentiated, in some ways marginal target market; a complex product that may have only indirect benefits and elicit very low involvement; a short, direct, immediate distribution channel; a relative lack of resources for promotion; and prices only indirectly related to the exchange between the producer and the consumer of services.

## Discussion and Writing Questions

1. Explain what search, experience, and credence qualities are. Cite examples of each that are not discussed in the chapter.

✍2. Assume that you are a service provider. Write a list of implications for your firm of service intangibility.

✍3. You are applying for a job as a marketing manager for a service firm and have been asked how you would handle a mismatch between supply and demand. Write your answer as a memo to the vice president of marketing.

4. Come up with an idea for a new service. Develop a marketing mix strategy for your new service.

5. Describe the three levels of relationship marketing, and give an example of each that is not discussed in the chapter.

✍6. Write a list of some of the issues you would have to consider in taking your new service (from question 4) global. How would you change your marketing mix to address those issues?

7. Search your local community for examples of the two types of nonbusiness marketing described in the chapter.

## Application for Small Business

Susan Brown is a former auto salesperson who wants to start her own consulting business. Knowing that many people hate to buy cars, Susan thinks there is a market for a service offering advice about car purchases. As part of the service, Susan plans to supply clients with information about vehicles, dealers' fees, and manufacturers' incentives. She will also handle the client's negotiations with a dealer.

### Questions

1. How can Susan turn the intangible benefits of her advice into something more tangible for prospective clients?
2. How should Susan determine how much to charge for her service?
3. What consumer or business segments should Susan target with her service?

**CRITICAL THINKING CASE**

## The Rolling Stones

Despite all the talk about the Rolling Stones being past their prime, the rock band's *Voodoo Lounge* compact disc and tour have received great reviews and plenty of publicity. At the outset, the tour was expected to gross 25 percent more than the Stones' 1989 tour, which earned a then-record $98 million. The band's fan base is large and one of the few that spans teens to 20-somethings to baby boomers.

"The Rolling Stones have two things: nostalgic value and current interest. *Voodoo Lounge* is popular, and at the same time you have guys like me in their late 30s, early 40s, who have listened to the Stones since they were kids," said Mark Abramoff, president of Ralph Marlin and Co., which is selling a line of Rolling Stones ties. Featuring reproductions of Stones album covers and tour artwork, the ties come with hangtags in the shape of a tongue, the group's trademark. The line is being sold through a Rolling Stones catalog and at department and specialty stores, but they were most popular on the Stones tour.

Another company that jumped on the Stones bandwagon is the Chevy Chase Bank of Maryland. The bank issued a credit card emblazoned with the group's trademark tongue logo. Chevy Chase Bank was "deluged with applications" for it, said Dan Page, CEO of Affinity Cards, Colorado, which developed the concept. "To a Stones fan, this is what an American Express gold card is to a businessman," he said. "It's an identification of something they believe in. They like being able to slap that tongue down."

Using the card earns a cardholder points for discounts on licensed goods. In addition, Camelot Music offers discounts and special offers to customers who use the card at participating stores. Page said he's negotiating similar deals with other retailers. The card is being promoted in the catalog, and about 20,000 promotional fliers were distributed at each concert site.

Questions

1. Why would the Rolling Stones' *Voodoo Lounge* tour be considered a service?

2. What strategies are being used to promote the tour and the band? Do you think these strategies will be effective? Why or why not?

3. Evaluate the marketing strategies described here in terms of relationship marketing. Suggest other relationship marketing strategies that might be effective.

References

Cyndee Miller, "Stones Strut Their Marketing Stuff," *Marketing News,* 7 November 1994, p. 1, 18.

**VIDEO CASE**

## 1-800-FLOWERS

Venture capitalists were losing $400,000 each month on their Dallas-based 1-800-FLOWERS business when Jim McCann made an offer to buy the ailing company. McCann, owner of New York–based floral retail chain Flora Plenty, took over the telephone rights and moved 1-800-FLOWERS to Westbury, New York. In an attempt to revive the business, McCann used his established network of 2,500 florists and his experience in the industry to provide excellent customer service. Today, the company enjoys annual sales of over $100 million, and McCann attributes this success to its impossible-to-forget name and its repeat customers.

In a time when consumers want convenience and expect good service, 1-800-FLOWERS has prospered. With its toll-free phone number and twenty-four-hour service, the company has made ordering flowers as simple as making a phone call from home. The company receives orders from all over the globe in its three telemarketing centers and then transmits the customer requests via computer to a florist near the intended recipient. Customers like the guarantee, which promises a refund if customers are not satisfied for any reason.

In trying to build this business, 1-800-FLOWERS' advertisements have targeted the largest flower-buying group: white-collar men between 25 and 45 years old. The company also uses interactive computer media to market its products. Currently, 5 percent of 1-800-FLOWERS' sales come from the interactive market, but the company hopes to increase this number by joining the American Classified Network, an interactive classified-advertising service.

New entrants in the flower-delivery business—such as 1-800-FLOWERS, Calyx & Corolla flower catalog, and other on-line computer services—have threatened Florists' Transworld Delivery Association (FTD), a company that dominated the floral business for years. After customers place their orders at a local florist, FTD uses wire transfer to send the orders to florists across the globe. But consumers now prefer the convenience of ordering directly from their homes and the timely delivery that the new companies provide.

In response to the success of its flower service, 1-800-FLOWERS has launched other 800 numbers specifically for gift baskets, candy, and other goodies. As toll-free services have gained popularity among consumers, many other industries have initiated toll-free numbers to offer services, such as 1-800-DOCTORS and 1-800-DENTIST.



## Questions

1. Earlier in this chapter, four unique characteristics of services were discussed. How are the new flower-ordering services effectively dealing with these characteristics in their marketing efforts?
2. If you were a marketer for FTD, how would you respond to the challenge of the new floral services in order to remain competitive?
3. How might floral services like the ones described here foster long-term relationships with customers?

## References

James F. McCann, "Be Perfect or Die" [interview], *Success,* June 1993, p. 14.

Patrick M. Reilly, "Competitive Floral Delivery Networks Claim a Rose Isn't a Rose Isn't a Rose," *The Wall Street Journal,* 14 February 1994, pp. B1, B3.

PART THREE

# INTEGRATIVE CASE

## GILLETTE

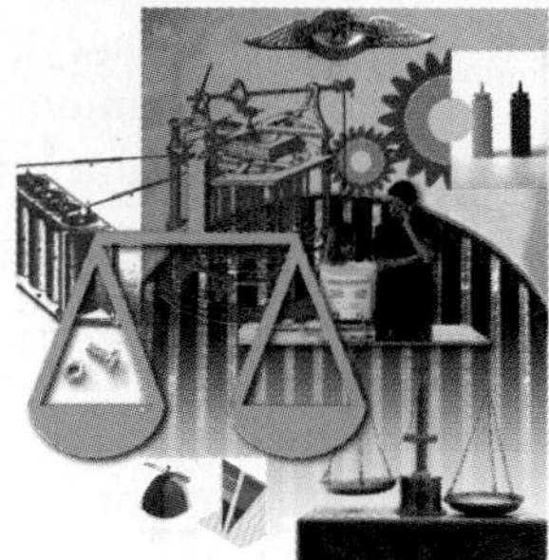

When King Camp Gillette founded the Gillette Company in 1903, he laid the foundation for a company that not only would be renowned the world over but also would be guided by two principles—quality and market dominance—that would continue to make it a world-class force into the twenty-first century. Although Boston-based Gillette is best known for its shaving systems, it is in fact a diversified conglomerate with a commanding edge in the markets for writing instruments, household appliances, and toothbrushes and with a respectable share of the toiletries market.

Since the 1950s, Gillette has acquired several new businesses, nurturing some of them into industry leaders. Gillette's writing-instruments division, for example, was launched with the acquisition of Papermate Pens in 1955. In 1987, Gillette acquired the Waterman Pen Company of France, thereby covering both the low end of the writing-instruments market with disposable Papermates and the high end with high-quality, high-priced Watermans. By 1990 Gillette was the largest writing-instruments company in the world. As if this was not enough, Gillette further consolidated its share of the refillable-pens market with the acquisition of Parker Pen in 1993.

For another example of Gillette's ability to nurture an acquisition into an industry leader, consider its success with Oral-B toothbrushes. The company bought the Oral-B line of dental products from Cooper Labs in 1984, and by 1990 Oral-B toothbrushes were the best-selling toothbrushes in the United States.

Perhaps the best example of Gillette's strategic ability comes from its appliance division. In 1967 the company acquired Braun AG of Germany for $64 million. By 1990 Braun's sales were around $1 billion, and operating earnings for the year were about $125 million. Braun's phenomenal growth was due to the addition of coffee makers, coffee grinders, hair dryers, curlers, and dental hygiene products to complement Braun's existing line of electric shavers.

Most analysts agree that it was during the reign of CEO Colman M. Mockler, Jr., from 1975 to 1990, that Gillette achieved world-class leadership. In an effort to cut costs and streamline the company, Mockler sold or closed twenty-one businesses. Moreover, productivity increased by 6 percent a year during Mockler's stewardship. According to one estimate, the company's 1990 sales were triple those of 1975, but it had fewer employees than it had in 1974.

Today, despite diversification and multiple-market leadership, Gillette's shaving-implements business still produces over 60 percent of the company's operating income. Gillette is now headed by company veteran Alfred Zeien. This is Zeien's vision for the company: "We are in personal-use, personal-care consumer products where we are the *clear* world leader or have a plan to achieve that leadership."

### Close Shaves Before Sensor

One particular product exemplifies Gillette's skill in introducing new products. The name Gillette has always graced the most trusted blades to graze a man's chin. The first Gillette safety razor was introduced in 1903 and the one-piece razor in 1934. The Trac II razor appeared in 1971 and the Atra system in 1977. All were notable successes. Then in 1990, the company launched its revolutionary Sensor system. Within the first year of its introduction, the Sensor had captured 9 percent of the shaving-implements market.

Sensor was introduced during a crucial period in the company's history. Throughout the 1980s, the market for disposable razors steadily rose at the expense of the more durable cartridge shaving systems. One study of the European shaving market revealed that most shavers under 45 years of age were regular users of disposable razors and were not particularly loyal to the Gillette brand name. In fact, Gillette was engaged in a head-on battle with the French company Bic in the market for bulk-packaged, low-cost disposable shavers. Shaving implements were fast becoming a commodity, with most consumers shopping on the basis of price rather than quality or brand name.

Although many believed that the trend toward disposable razors was unavoidable, John Symons, the head of European operations for Gillette, disagreed. He concentrated his attention on Contour Plus (the European name for Atra Plus) shaving cartridge systems, proving that there was a significant market for high-quality shaving systems. He also believed that the low-margin disposable razors could be displaced by the higher-quality, higher-margin replaceable-blade systems. Symons's confidence and success in the European market won him the job of running the American shaving business as well. The combined market was renamed the North Atlantic group. Symons's immediate task was to set the stage for the launch of the Sensor.

## Development of the Sensor

By the time the Sensor was introduced in 1990, $200 million had been spent on research and development—and it was money well spent. The Sensor—a twin-blade cartridge shaving system—was so flexible that it adjusted to the contours of the shaver's face. This flexibility was achieved by mounting the blades on a backing bar, enabling them to move up and down (but not laterally) on springs. If conventional welding had been used to mount the blades, they would have lost their edge more readily.

Laser welding was preferable, but existing laser technology did not work at the speeds necessary for Gillette's manufacturing process. The company spent an estimated $10 million to test a manufacturing system and finally developed something that worked round the clock and provided a very low rejection rate even at very high speeds. This laser welding system is the heart of the Sensor assembly line. The new system completes the fifteen necessary welds on each blade in less than one-fifth of a second, thus producing five twin blades every two seconds. All ten parts of the razor fit together with a margin of error of 0.00004 inch. During assembly, each Sensor passes through almost a hundred electronic and mechanical inspections. The innovative technology, precision manufacturing, and extensive quality control have their dividends: The reject rate, even in the Sensor's first year of production, was only ten twin blades per million.

While the manufacturing process was being perfected, the market was being prepared. John Symons and his team had one clear goal: Enhance the image of Gillette as a manufacturer and marketer of premium-quality branded products in the shaving-instruments market. The team worked closely with the company's advertising agency, BBDO, to create a corporate campaign that would not only convey a high-tech image for the company but would also foster consumer acceptance of the Gillette brand name when the Sensor was launched. The campaign, with its slogan "Gillette—the best a man can get," was ranked first in most consumer surveys in 1989. The television commercials actually had to be pulled off the air after Sensor's introduction in 1990, because consumer demand for the new product was far in excess of manufacturing capability.

## The Sensor's Introduction and Success

The Sensor was introduced in January 1990 in the United States, Europe, and Japan. Instead of using the conventional process for introducing new products in the market—a series of test markets, product refinements, and marketing strategy refinements—Gillette launched the Sensor with an intense publicity campaign.

The Sensor had a high price when compared with disposables. A Sensor razor and cartridge had a suggested list price of $3.75 and actually retailed for anywhere from $1.99 to $3.00. Nevertheless, sales of the product in its initial months were brisk. The most steady stream of profits came from the almost endless sales of replacement blades. At 75¢ each, these had a gross margin of almost 90 percent. The key question, however, was, how many customers would adopt the Gillette Sensor shaving system.

The company predicted that it would be able to sell 18 million razors and 200 million blades in the first year, for a market share of 6 percent in the United States. However, by year's end, it was clear that the Sensor was a resounding success, with actual sales of 27 million razors and 350 million blades. It commandeered a 7 percent market for replacement blades in the United States and in Europe and 42 percent of the combined U.S. and European markets for nondisposable razors.

For customers, the Sensor provided tremendous functionality. Moreover, the high-tech image of the Sensor made it something more than a simple personal hygiene tool, and at its affordable price it provided excellent value.

For the company, however, the Sensor had far-reaching implications. The product asserted Gillette's position as a market leader in shaving systems, leaving the company's close competitor, Warner-Lambert's Schick, far behind. But more important, the product heralded the decline of the disposable, low-margin razors that had been so popular a decade earlier. The unsurpassed quality and the manufacturing edge made it difficult for competitors to manufacture a Sensor imitation at a comparable price.

## After the Sensor

Many companies may have relaxed for a bit after such a phenomenal new product success. But Gillette was busy developing new markets for the Sensor as well as newer versions of the Sensor. If the Sensor was "the best a man can get," what about women? Women represent just under 20 percent of the total shaving market. They shave their legs less frequently than men shave beards, so an average woman needs only about ten blades a year compared to the thirty that an average man might use. Nevertheless, the women's market held promise for the future. Using essentially the same cartridge technology, but modifying the design, Gillette introduced the Sensor for Women. The new shaving system had improved styling for a better grip and better access to areas behind the knees and around ankles. The product was introduced in the summer of 1992. Since the technology was already in place, Gillette spent under $10 million for research and development. The ad budget was $14 million—small compared to the $110 million spent to launch the Sensor. But within a few months of the product's introduction, Sensor for Women was a hit, cornering almost 41 percent of the women's market for nondisposable razors.

In late 1992, the company introduced a new line of men's toiletries in an effort to boost the sagging toiletries division and to complement the Sensor razor. The new line—Gillette Series—included about a dozen items, ranging from shaving creams and shaving gels to deodorants and antiperspirants. Here, as with the Sensor and Gillette's other products, superior technology gave the company a distinct competitive advantage.

When Gillette introduced its Atra razor systems in 1977, they cannibalized Gillette's own Trac II system. Similarly, the Sensor virtually eliminated the other brands in Gillette's line of nondisposable shaving systems. With each new product, the company aims not only to retain the loyalists but also to garner additional market share from competitors and new users. New product development is therefore a continuous process of innovation.

Within three years of the Sensor's introduction, the company launched the Sensor Excel in Europe and Japan. This new razor has tiny "fins" that stretch the skin and allow the whiskers to stand up to meet the blades' sharp edges. In late 1994 the new Sensor was set to be launched in North America.

### Questions

1. Explain in detail the key elements behind the success of the Sensor.
2. How did the Sensor's launch differ from a conventional launch of a new product? What was at stake for the company if the new product had failed?
3. Compared to other divisions at Gillette, the toiletries division (with products such as Right Guard antiperspirant, Soft & Dri antiperspirant, and White Rain shampoo) was, before the introduction of the Gillette Series, seen by some observers as not faring too well. Judging from the company's strategies in other divisions, can you figure out why the toiletries division is less successful?
4. Continuous innovations in companies such as Gillette have their associated risks. Each new product cannibalizes the company's existing products in the same line. What are some essential criteria that such companies might use to judge each new product?

### References

"The Best a Plan Can Get," *The Economist,* 15 August 1992, pp. 59–60.

Subrata N. Chakravarty, "We Had to Change the Playing Field," *Forbes,* 4 February 1991, pp. 82–86.

"Hot Products," *Business Week,* 7 June 1993, pp. 54–57.

"How Gillette Is Honing Its Edge," *Business Week,* 28 September 1992, pp. 60, 65.

William H. Miller, "Gillette's Secret to Sharpness," *Industry Week,* 3 January 1994, pp. 24–30.

*The Wall Street Journal,* 21 February 1990, p. C1; 23 April 1990, p. A14; 8 October 1990, p. B-1; 6 April 1992, p. R6; 17 December 1992, p. B1; 28 June 1993; 27 July 1993, p. A5; 22 April 1994, p. A8.

# PART THREE ETHICS CASE

## THE FAIL-PROOF PRODUCT

Beth Harmon, an employee for a large and respected marketing research firm, had been working for over four years in the area of new market analysis. It had been the custom at her firm for teams of researchers to work on projects. Beth was offered her first assignment as a team leader on a project for a large consumer packaged-goods client.

As the first step in planning the project, Beth met with her boss, Bob Luck, and a representative of the client firm, Roger Howell. They discussed how Beth and her team would design and implement research for a new type of tooth polish. It seemed strange to Beth that Bob and Roger kept stressing the importance of a strong research design that the client's top management would support. She reassured both Bob and Roger that she had studied the problem and would use a very appropriate research design. They seemed to mean something different from what she meant when they discussed research design.

- Were Bob and Roger trying to send Beth a signal, or were they just concerned that she do a good job? What might they have been trying to tell her?

Shortly after that first meeting, Beth met with her team to assign them tasks and deadlines. The research process continued, with the team collecting data and interpreting the results. They soon realized that the new product being proposed would not be accepted by the target market at all. Beth seemed disappointed that her first research project would reach such negative conclusions. But she was glad that she could save her client a lot of money in the long run by stopping the launch of a product that was destined to fail.

- Is this an appropriate outcome for a research project? How can such findings be a good investment for a firm?

The following week, while meeting with her boss, Beth alerted him to the problem with the findings for the new tooth polish. She was startled by his reaction. Bob asked her to "put a spin on the data to make it sound supportive to launching the new product." His reasoning was that Roger had already invested a great deal of time in developing the product and that Roger's career was on the line. Even if the product failed, Roger would probably not be held accountable. But if the product was shown to be a poor idea before the launch, Roger would probably lose his job. Bob explained that Roger had an excellent track record for making products successful, that the research was mostly "window dressing," and that the client was already committed to launching the product. Finally, Bob pointed out that Beth would probably have a brief career in marketing research if she discouraged the client from launching the product.

- What should Beth do and why? What are the likely consequences if she (1) discourages the product launch or (2) encourages the product launch?

After thinking long and hard about the advice her boss had given her, Beth decided to "shave the data" to make it appear at least ambivalent. In her report, she noted that although the market was not distinctly supportive of the new product, the product launch would probably be successful. Bob read her report, praised it, and asked her to reduce it to a single page and sign it.

- How is the letter different from the initial report? Should Beth sign such a letter?

While preparing the letter, Beth recalled a recent court case that had made the news: A packaged-goods manufacturer sued a major marketing research organization for advising it to launch a new product that then failed.

- What kind of risk is Beth taking? What could happen? Would you do what she did to keep your job? How might this experience affect the way Beth does her job in the future?

CAV

# Part Four
# Distribution Decisions



Subway is one of the fastest-growing franchise businesses in the world, and managing one of the sandwich stores is a fast-paced, demanding job. Just ask Dean Dameron. In the five years he's been with the Subway organization, he's worked as a sandwich/salad prep person, an assistant manager, and a night manager. This "through the ranks" experience has given Dean a thorough knowledge of scheduling, product ordering, customer and employee relations, and the evaluation of food and labor costs. It is knowledge he now puts to good use in his current position, store manager.

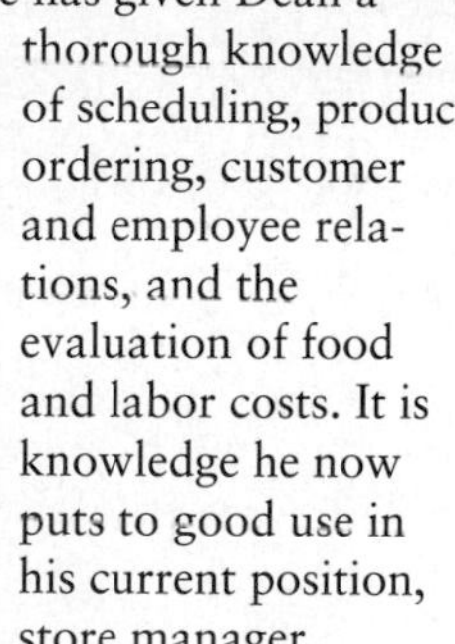

Subway prides itself on promoting from within, and Dean Dameron is proof of the wisdom of this policy. This means of advancement gives employees confidence in themselves and trains them in all aspects of running a store. When other employees see people like Dean advance to higher positions, it encourages them to continue to do a good job.

An electronic media and communications major in college, Dean also took a variety of introductory level business courses. He utilizes the skills he learned at school to help him interact with customers, employees, and suppliers. His business background and communications skills have made him a better manager. This, combined with his on-the-job training and determination, will allow him to continue his rise in this fast-growing company. His aspiration is to own his own Subway franchise one day.

# CHAPTER 12

# MARKETING CHANNELS AND WHOLESALING

## LEARNING OBJECTIVES

*After studying this chapter, you should be able to*

1 *Explain what a marketing channel is and why intermediaries are needed.*

2 *Describe the functions and activities of marketing channel members.*

3 *Discuss the differences among marketing channels for consumer and industrial products.*

4 *Describe alternative channel arrangements.*

5 *Discuss what vertical marketing systems are and how they differ from conventional marketing channels.*

6 *Explain the concepts of power and conflict within marketing channels.*

7 *Discuss the issues that influence channel strategy.*

8 *List the steps in designing marketing channels.*

9 *Discuss channel structure and decisions in global markets.*

10 *List the types of firms that perform wholesaling activities, and explain their functions.*

In Pleasantville, New Jersey, the merchandising manager for Kramer Beverage Company, a Coors beer distributor, is making five stops today. He chats with customers and store employees as he replaces banners, straightens pallets of beer cases on the floors of small retail stores, and puts up table tents and posters at bars. Across the county, a Kramer sales representative cheerfully fulfills a request for a Coors Extra Gold keg sign at a liquor store. And one of Kramer's draft technicians stops at a rural pub to clean draft beer lines and shine levers on the Coors tap.

New brands and glitzy advertising campaigns may grab attention, but it's the wholesale distributors like Kramer that mobilize to place tap handles, secure inches of prime shelf space, instigate local promotions, and provide special services to customers. Simultaneously, these front-line field workers gather crucial market information to send back to the breweries' marketing experts.

The three-tier system of beer making and marketing—brewer, distributor, and retailer—was created by Congress in 1933 to keep brewers from gaining control over the sale of beer to the public, which brewers had done before Prohibition. The current 3,000 or so beer distributors, mostly small businesses with fewer than thirty employees, manage the $24 billion business of delivering beer. The brewers each have hundreds of distributors, granted exclusive territories as small as a single town or as big as several counties (except in Indiana, the only state where exclusive beer distribution territories are illegal).

Today, however, distributors like Kramer are pitted against their own brewers and against retailers. Huge warehouse clubs, discounters, and grocery chains are pressuring brewers to cut prices and to deliver beer directly to their stores rather than go through middlemen. As a result, the antiquated distribution laws are now being challenged in many states.

The current three-tier distribution system does have obvious failings. The practice of loading beer onto brewery trucks, unloading it at distributor warehouses, putting it back on distributor trucks, and then sending it out to retailers may be too costly in today's retail environment. For retailers that can buy entire truckloads, direct deliveries from the brewery make more sense, logistically and economically. Computers, able to transmit inventory data from the big retailers to brewers, make the sales and inventory-tracking functions of the distributor unnecessary. Additionally, more and more retailers are ordering private-label beers and therefore don't need any marketing or inventory help from wholesalers.

Although brewers can't legally distribute beer directly

to retailers, many have set up special distributors that provide beer exclusively to big retailers, often cutting out their longtime distributors. Many distributors wonder if they can survive without the major retail accounts. Big retailers can live without wholesalers, they argue, but small retailers can't. Bars, taverns, liquor stores, small convenience stores, and restaurants would be most hurt if wholesalers went out of business. Furthermore, if direct deliveries become legal, big retailers have the economic power to command heavily discounted prices from brewers. Many smaller retailers that must pay the additional costs of going through a wholesaler will suffer considerably, possibly even being forced out of business.[1]

The beer industry's marketing channel structure is currently mandated by law. What other channel structures could brewers choose if not for the law? What type of channel power are the big retailers exerting over brewers? How is this pressure creating conflict in the channel of distribution? These and other questions will be answered as you read the chapter.

1 *Explain what a marketing channel is and why intermediaries are needed.*

**marketing channel (channel of distribution)**
Set of interdependent organizations that ease the transfer of ownership as products move from producer to business user or consumer.

## MARKETING CHANNELS AND CHANNEL MEMBERS

The term *channel* is derived from the Latin word *canalis,* which means canal. A marketing channel can be viewed as a large canal or pipeline with products (chiefly goods), their ownership, communication, financing and payment, and accompanying risk flowing through it. Formally, a **marketing channel** (also called a **channel of distribution**) is a business structure of interdependent organizations, reaching from the point of product origin to the consumer, through which channel members motivate and communicate with customers and sell, ship, store, deliver, and service products.[2]

Many different types of organizations participate in marketing channels. Channel members (also called intermediaries, resellers, and middlemen) negotiate with one another, buy and sell products, and facilitate the change of ownership between buyers and sellers. Today, there are over 300,000 wholesalers and distributors in the United States.[3] Nonmember channel participants, such as advertising agencies and transportation firms, do not negotiate and only support the activities of the channel members.

Some intermediaries take title to products and resell them. Taking title means they own the merchandise and control the terms of sale—for example, price and delivery date. Wholesalers and retailers often are examples of this type of intermediary. **Wholesalers** are firms that sell mainly to producers, resellers, governments, institutions, and retailers. In contrast, **retailers** are firms that sell mainly to consumers. Other intermediaries do not take title to the goods and services they market but do facilitate the exchange of ownership between sellers and buyers. Brokers, manufacturer's representatives, and agents are examples of this type of intermediary.

**wholesaler**
Firm that sells mainly to producers, resellers, governments, institutions, and retailers.

**retailer**
Firm that sells mainly to consumers.

Intermediaries fulfill three important functions: providing specialization and division of labor, overcoming discrepancies, and providing contact efficiency.

### PROVIDING SPECIALIZATION AND DIVISION OF LABOR

Manufacturers achieve economies of scale through the use of efficient equipment capable of producing large quantities of a single product. According to the concept of specialization and division of labor, breaking down a complex task into smaller, simpler ones and allocating them to specialists will also create much greater efficiency. Economies of scale, specialization and division of labor, and professional management normally lower the average production costs.

Marketing channels can also attain economies of scale through specialization and division of labor. Some producers lack the motivation, financing, or expertise to market directly to end users or consumers. In some cases, as with most consumer convenience goods, the cost of marketing directly to millions of consumers—taking and shipping individual orders—is prohibitive. Producers essentially hire channel members to do what the producers are not equipped to do or what these intermediaries are better prepared to do. Channel members can do some things more efficiently than producers can because they have built good relationships with their customers. Their specialized expertise enhances the overall performance of the channel.

### OVERCOMING DISCREPANCIES

Economies of scale in production require the development of distribution channels capable of overcoming barriers to exchange. For example, assume that Pillsbury can efficiently produce its Hungry Jack instant pancake mix only at a rate of 5,000 units in a typical day. Not even the most ardent pancake fan could consume that amount in a year, much less in a day. The quantity produced to achieve low unit costs has

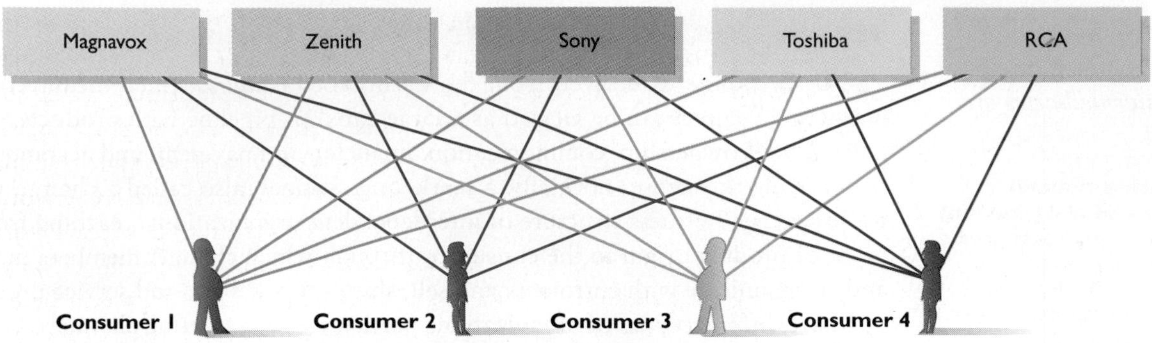


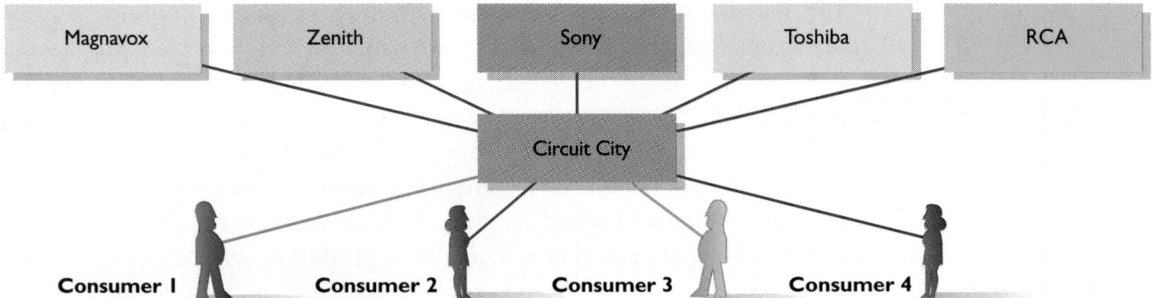


*Exhibit 12.1*

How Intermediaries Reduce the Number of Required Transactions

created a **discrepancy of quantity,** which is the difference between the amount of product produced and the amount an end user wants to buy. Marketing channels overcome quantity discrepancies by making products available in the quantities that consumers and business buyers desire.

**discrepancy of quantity**
Difference between the amount of product produced and the amount a customer wants to buy.

Mass production creates not only discrepancies of quantity but also discrepancies of assortment. A **discrepancy of assortment** is the lack of all the items needed to receive full satisfaction from a product or products. For pancakes to have maximum utility, several other products are required to complete the assortment. At the very least, most people want a knife, fork, plate, butter, and syrup. Others might add orange juice, coffee, cream, sugar, eggs, and bacon or sausage. Even though Pillsbury is a large consumer products company, it does not come close to providing the optimal assortment to go with its Hungry Jack pancakes. To overcome discrepancies of assortment, marketing channels assemble in one place the products that buyers want.

**discrepancy of assortment**
Lack of all the items a customer needs to receive full satisfaction from a product or products.

A **temporal discrepancy** is created when a product is produced but a consumer is not ready to buy it. Marketing channels overcome temporal discrepancies by maintaining inventories in anticipation of demand.

**temporal discrepancy**
Difference between when a product is produced and when a customer is ready to buy it.

Furthermore, because mass production requires many potential buyers, markets are usually scattered over large geographic regions, creating a **spatial discrepancy.** Often global, or at least nationwide, markets are needed to absorb the outputs of mass producers. Marketing channels overcome spatial discrepancies by making products available in locations convenient to consumers and business buyers.

**spatial discrepancy**
Difference between the location of the producer and the location of widely scattered markets.

## PROVIDING CONTACT EFFICIENCY

Consider your extra costs if supermarkets, department stores, and shopping centers or malls did not exist. Suppose you had to buy your milk at a dairy and your meat at a stockyard. Imagine buying your eggs and chicken at a hatchery and your fruits and vegetables at various farms. You would spend a great deal of time, money, and energy just shopping for a few groceries. Channels simplify distribution by cutting the number of transactions required to get products from manufacturers to consumers.

Consider another example, which is illustrated in Exhibit 12.1. Four students in your class each want to buy a television set. Without a retail intermediary like Circuit City, television manufacturers Magnavox, Zenith, Sony, Toshiba, and RCA would each have to make four contacts to reach the four buyers who are in the target market, totaling twenty transactions. However, each producer only has to make one contact when Circuit City acts as an intermediary between the producer and consumers, reducing the number of transactions to nine. Each producer sells to one retailer rather than to four consumers. In turn, your classmates buy from one retailer instead of from five producers.

This simple example illustrates the concept of contact efficiency. U.S. manufacturers sell to millions of individuals and families. Using channel intermediaries greatly reduces the number of required contacts. As a result, producers are able to offer their products cost-effectively and efficiently to consumers all over the world.

2 *Describe the functions and activities of marketing channel members.*

## CHANNEL FUNCTIONS

Intermediaries in marketing channels perform several essential functions that make the flow of goods between producer and buyer possible. These are the three basic functions that intermediaries perform (see Exhibit 12.2):

- *Transactional functions:* At the most basic level, intermediaries perform the transactional functions of contacting buyers, promoting the product to be sold, negotiating the sale, and taking on the risks associated with owning and keeping a product in inventory. Producing high-quality items and offering them at fair prices do not guarantee success. The contacting and promoting

*Exhibit 12.2*

Marketing Channel Functions Performed by Intermediaries

| Type of function | Description |
|---|---|
| Transactional functions | ***Contacting and promoting:*** Contacting potential customers, promoting products, and soliciting orders |
| | ***Negotiating:*** Determining how many goods or services to buy and sell, type of transportation to use, when to deliver, and method and timing of payment |
| | ***Risk taking:*** Assuming the risk of owning inventory |
| Logistical functions | ***Physically distributing:*** Transporting and storing goods to overcome temporal and spatial discrepancies |
| | ***Sorting:*** overcoming discrepancies of quantity and assortment by |
| | • *Sorting out:* Breaking down a heterogeneous supply into separate homogeneous stocks |
| | • *Accumulation:* Combining similar stocks into a larger homogeneous supply |
| | • *Allocation:* Breaking a homogeneous supply into smaller and smaller lots ("breaking bulk") |
| | • *Assortment:* Combining products into collections or assortments that buyers want available at one place |
| Facilitating functions | ***Researching:*** Gathering information about other channel members and consumers |
| | ***Financing:*** Extending credit and other financial services to facilitate the flow of goods through the channel to the final consumer |

This barge hauling goods in Alaska is performing a logistical function for the goods' producers: physical distribution or, more specifically, transportation.



functions make prospective buyers aware of existing products and explain their features, advantages, and benefits. Sellers and buyers must also agree on the terms of the sale, such as how much to buy and sell, which type of transportation to use to get the product to the customer, and when to deliver. They also must agree on the method and timing of payment. Sometimes buyers and sellers agree to terms covering exchanges over a specified period, such as one year. A long-term agreement eliminates the need to negotiate each transaction and may result in straight rebuy arrangements (see Chapter 5).

- *Logistical functions:* Intermediaries also provide the logistical functions of physical distribution and sorting. *Logistics* describes several activities related to the movement of goods from producer to consumer or end user. Transportation and storage of goods overcome temporal and spatial discrepancies. Sorting functions overcome discrepancies of quantity and assortment. These functions might include sorting out, accumulating, allocating, and assorting products into either homogeneous or heterogeneous collections. For example, grading agricultural products typifies the sorting-out process. The consolidation of many lots of grade A eggs from different sources into one lot illustrates the accumulation process. Allocating at the wholesale level—for example, breaking down a tank-car load of milk into gallon jugs—is called "breaking bulk." A buyer of case lots, in turn, sells individual units. Last, supermarkets or other retailers perform the assorting function by assembling thousands of different items that match their customers' desires.
- *Facilitating functions:* Intermediaries also perform the *facilitating* functions of research and financing. Research provides information about channel members and consumers and asks appropriate questions: Who are the buyers? Where are they located? What are their characteristics? Why do they buy? Where do they buy? How will they respond to changes in package style, price, size, promotional appeal, or product features? Who are the major competitors, and what are their strengths and weaknesses? Financing helps producers make goods more attractive to buyers. Inventories are often financed as products flow through or are held in a channel. Manufacturers often provide credit to wholesalers and retailers that buy directly from them. Some wholesalers also

furnish credit for retailers, and many retailers provide credit for final purchasers. Financial institutions may supply credit to any or all members of a channel to finance raw material purchases, operations, accounts receivable, or even purchases of major equipment. For example, a department store chain may secure credit from an insurance company to finance the construction of a new outlet.

Now think back to the opening story about Kramer Beverage Company. As a beer distributor, it provides transactional, logistical, and facilitating channel functions. Kramer sales representatives contact local bars and restaurants to negotiate the terms of the sale, possibly giving the customer a discount for large purchases, and make arrangements for when the beer will be delivered. At the same time, Kramer also provides a facilitating function by extending credit to the customer. Kramer merchandising representatives, meanwhile, assist in promoting the beer on a local level by hanging Coors beer signs and posters. Kramer also provides logistical functions by accumulating the many types of Coors beer from the Coors manufacturing plant in Golden, Colorado, and storing them in its refrigerated warehouse. When an order needs to be filled, Kramer then sorts the beer into heterogenous collections for each particular customer. For example, the local Chili's Grill & Bar may need two kegs of Coors, three kegs of Coors Light, and two cases of Killian's Red in bottles. The beer will then be loaded onto a refrigerated truck and transported to the restaurant. Upon arrival, the Kramer delivery person will transport the kegs and cases of beer into the restaurant's refrigerator and may also restock the coolers behind the bar.

Although individual members can be added to or deleted from a channel, someone must still perform these essential functions. They can be performed by producers, end users or consumers, channel intermediaries such as wholesalers and retailers, and sometimes nonmember channel participants. For example, if a manufacturer decides to eliminate its private fleet of trucks, it must still have a way to move the goods to the wholesaler. This task may be accomplished by the wholesaler, which may have its own fleet of trucks, or by a nonmember channel participant, such as an independent trucking firm. Nonmembers also provide many other essential functions that may have at one time been provided by a channel member. For example, research firms may perform the research function; advertising agencies, the promotion function; transportation and storage firms, the physical distribution function; and banks, the financing function.

3 *Discuss the differences among marketing channels for consumer and industrial products.*

## CHANNEL STRUCTURES

There are many routes a product can take to reach its final consumer. Marketers search for the most efficient channel from the many alternatives available. Marketing a consumer convenience good like gum or candy differs from marketing a specialty good like a Mercedes-Benz. The two products require much different distribution channels. Likewise, the appropriate channel for a major equipment supplier like Boeing Aircraft would be unsuitable for an accessory equipment producer like Black & Decker.[4]

**direct channel**
Distribution channel in which producers sell directly to consumers.

### CHANNELS FOR CONSUMER PRODUCTS

Exhibit 12.3 on page 378 illustrates the four ways manufacturers can route products to consumers. Producers use the **direct channel** to sell directly to consumers. Direct

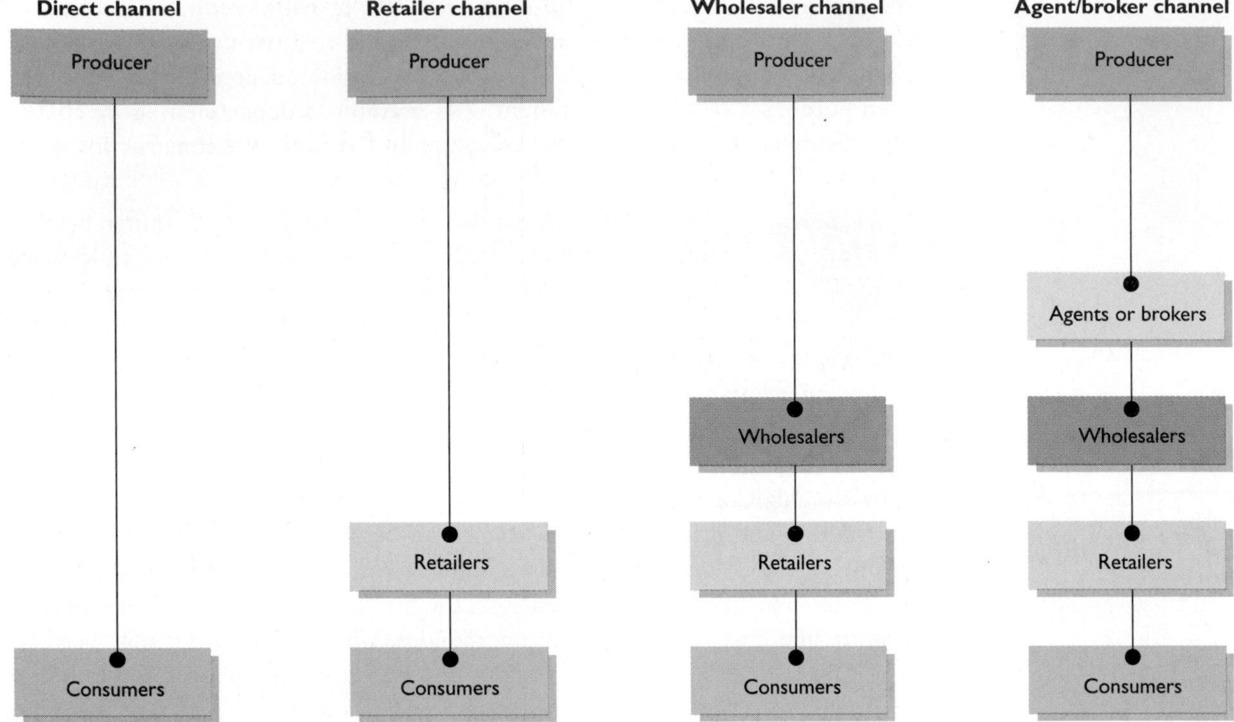


*Exhibit 12.3*

Marketing Channels for Consumer Products

marketing activities—including telemarketing, mail-order and catalog shopping, and forms of electronic retailing like on-line shopping and shop-at-home television networks—are a good example of this type of channel structure. For example, consumers can order Dell, Compaq, and Apple computers directly from a catalog. There are no intermediaries. Producer-owned stores and factory outlet stores—like Sherwin-Williams, Ralph Lauren, Oneida, and West Point Pepperel—are other examples of direct channels. Farmers' markets are also direct channels. Direct marketing and factory outlets are discussed in more detail in Chapter 13.

One direct channel for consumer products is the farmers' market, like this example in Boston, which puts producers in direct contact with end users.

At the other end of the spectrum, an *agent/broker channel* involves a fairly complicated process. Agent/broker channels are typically used in markets with many small manufacturers and many retailers that lack the resources to find each other. Agents or brokers bring manufacturers and wholesalers together for negotiations. Ownership passes to one or more wholesalers and then to retailers. Finally, retailers sell to the ultimate consumer of the product. For example, a food broker represents buyers and sellers of grocery products. The broker acts on behalf of many different producers and negotiates the sale of their products to wholesalers that specialize in foodstuffs. These wholesalers in turn sell to grocers and convenience stores.

Most consumer products are sold through distribution channels similar to the *retailer channel* and the *wholesaler channel,* although more direct channels are becoming popular. A retailer channel is most common when the retailer is large and can buy in large quantities from the manufacturer. Wal-Mart, Sears, and car dealers are examples of retailers that often bypass a wholesaler. A wholesaler is frequently used for low-cost items that are frequently purchased, such as candy, cigarettes, and magazines. For example, Mars sells candies and chocolates to wholesalers in large quantities. The wholesalers then break these quantities into smaller quantities to satisfy individual retailer orders.

### CHANNELS FOR INDUSTRIAL PRODUCTS

As Exhibit 12.4 illustrates, five channel structures are common in industrial, or business-to-business, markets. In contrast to consumer markets, *direct channels* are more typical in industrial markets. For example, manufacturers buy large quantities of raw materials, major equipment, processed materials, and supplies directly from other manufacturers. Manufacturers that require suppliers to meet detailed technical specifications often prefer direct channels. The direct communication required between Chrysler and its suppliers, for example, along with the tremendous size of the orders, makes anything but a direct channel impractical. The channel from producer to government buyers is also a direct channel. As indicated in Chapter 5, much government buying is done through bidding. Thus a direct channel is attractive.

*Exhibit 12.4*

Major Channels for Industrial Products

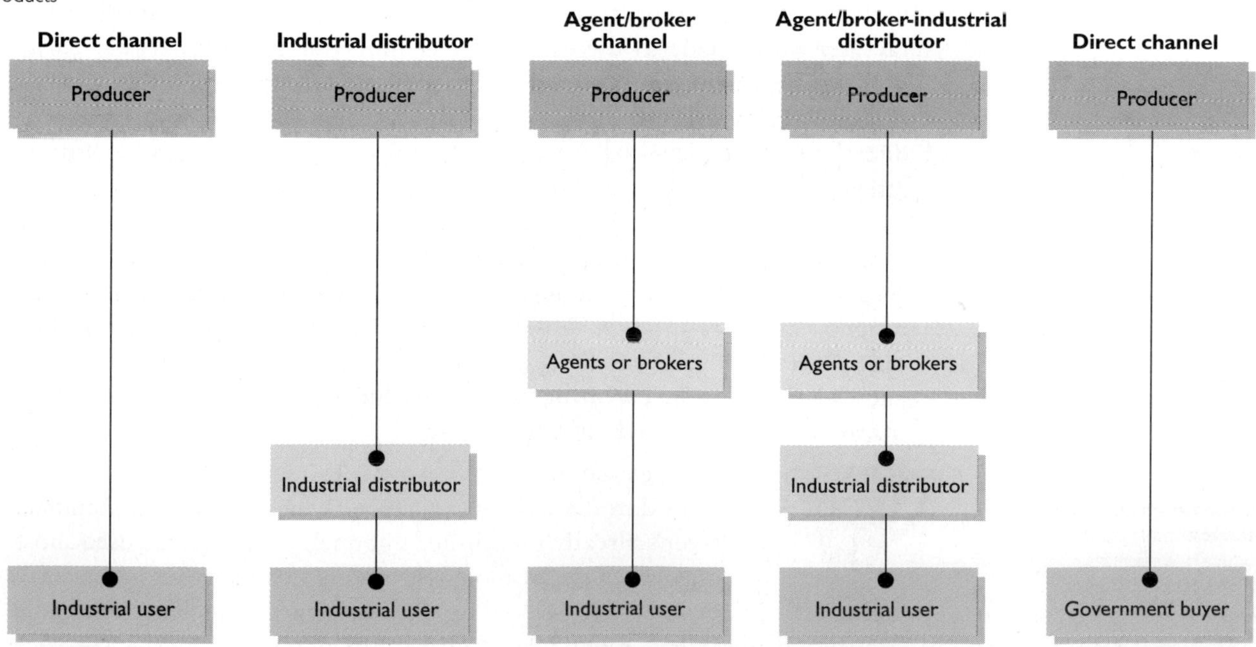

Companies selling standardized items of moderate or low value often rely on *industrial distributors.* In many ways, an industrial distributor is like a supermarket for organizations. Industrial distributors are wholesalers and channel members that buy and take title to products. Moreover, they usually keep inventories of their products and sell and service them.

Often small manufacturers cannot afford to employ their own sales force. Instead, they rely on manufacturers' representatives or selling agents to sell to either industrial distributors or users. For example, Alflex Corporation in Long Beach, California, relies on thirty-four independent manufacturers' representatives around the nation to sell its flexible conduit, a product used to protect copper wire and other products. The reps provide warehousing in their territories and ship the product to the distributor, which in turn sells to industrial users.[5] However, manufacturers' reps and selling agents are not used solely by small manufacturers. Many large firms also use manufacturers' reps rather than funding an internal sales effort.

4 *Describe alternative channel arrangements.*

## ALTERNATIVE CHANNEL ARRANGEMENTS

Rarely does a producer use just one type of channel to move its product. It usually employs several different or alternative channels, which include the following:

**dual distribution (multiple distribution)**
Use of two or more channels to distribute the same product to target markets.

- *Multiple channels:* When a producer selects two or more channels to distribute the same product to target markets, this arrangement is called **dual distribution** (or **multiple distribution**). For example, Whirlpool sells its washers, dryers, and refrigerators directly to home and apartment builders and contractors, but it also sells these same appliances to retail stores that sell to consumers. Spiegel, which has traditionally used direct-mail channels, has now opened several retail stores. Producers also use alternative channels for unique second brands. For example, Timex introduced its more expensive Nautica line of wristwatches to a new niche with a new level of distribution. To gain a foothold in the upscale market, Nautica watches are sold only in specialty stores, as opposed to the mass-merchandiser channels that Timex typically uses for its less expensive lines of watches.[6]
- *Nontraditional channels:* Often nontraditional channel arrangements help differentiate a firm's product from the competition. For example, a small manufacturer may decide to use mail-order channels or infomercials to sell its products instead of going through traditional retailer channels. Although nontraditional channels may limit a brand's coverage, they can give a small producer serving a niche market a way to gain market access and customer attention without having to establish channel intermediaries. Nontraditional channels may also provide another avenue of sales for a large producer. For example, Taco Bell is testing sales of prepackaged Mexican-style food in grocery stores, airports, and schools. McDonald's is experimenting with selling burgers and fries through kiosks inside convenience stores, free-standing restaurants at Texaco stations, catering services, and home delivery. Kellogg and General Mills are exploring vending machines as an option to expand the distribution of their snack-oriented brands.[7]

**strategic channel alliance**
Producers' agreement to jointly use one producer's already-established channel.

- *Strategic channel alliances:* More recently, producers have formed **strategic channel alliances,** which use another manufacturer's already-established channel. Alliances are used most often when the creation of marketing channel relationships may be too expensive and time-consuming. Ocean Spray formed a strategic channel alliance with Pepsi-Cola to help increase the market presence of Ocean Spray's brands. By sharing Pepsi's distribution channels, Ocean Spray can make cans and bottles of Ocean Spray cranberry juice cocktail, cranapple juice, and other juice drinks available in convenience stores, mini-marts, and Pepsi-Cola vending machines. Similarly, Rubbermaid formed a close merchandising alliance with discounter Phar-Mor to supply most of the retailer's plastic housewares. Specially designed Everything Rubbermaid departments were created in Phar-Mor stores, which showcase as many as 560 Rubbermaid items.[8] Strategic channel alliances are also common for selling in global markets where cultural differences, distance, or other barriers can inhibit channel establishment. Anheuser-Busch struck an alliance with Kirin Brewing Company, which controls about half the Japanese beer market. Under the agreement, Budweiser Japan Company, as the alliance is called, will market and distribute Bud through Kirin's channels.[9]

**reverse channel**
Distribution channel in which products move from consumer back to producer.

- *Reverse channels:* **Reverse channels** occur when products move in the opposite direction of traditional channels—from consumer back to producer. This type of channel is important for products that require repair or recycling. For example, automobile dealers generally have a service department to which consumers can bring their cars when they need repairs. A number of producers of high-tech products, like Sony, have established a national network of service centers that will repair the manufacturers' brands of electronic entertainment equipment. Soft-drink and beer manufacturers use reverse channels to collect and recycle glass bottles. They have also been big promoters of aluminum can recycling, mostly because it makes economic sense. Reverse channels for recycling have become more prevalent as producers realize the importance of limiting the solid waste that is normally dumped in landfills. Procter & Gamble is one producer that has redesigned its plastic bottles and containers to use recycled plastics instead of new plastics. To do so, P&G had to devise a reverse channel to get discarded plastic containers back for recycling. Now P&G works with channel intermediaries that collect, sort, shred, clean, and "pelletize" discarded plastic containers. The plastic pellets are then shipped back to P&G to become an ingredient in new plastic bottles and containers.[10]

5 *Discuss what vertical marketing systems are and how they differ from conventional marketing channels.*

## VERTICAL MARKETING SYSTEMS

Goods and services in the U.S. economy have historically been distributed through highly fragmented conventional channels (similar to those in Exhibits 12.3 and 12.4). A **conventional marketing channel** is a network of loosely aligned manufacturers, wholesaling institutions, and retailers that bargain with each other at arm's length, negotiate aggressively over the terms of sale, and otherwise behave independently. Conventional channels typically lack coordination, overall goals, interdependence, and routine procedures. Examples include the channels often used by small manufacturers and small retail outlets, such as independent supermarkets and shoe stores.

In contrast, a **vertical marketing system** (VMS) consists of producers and intermediaries acting together. (Exhibit 12.5 on page 382 illustrates the basic differences between a conventional channel and a VMS.) A VMS is designed to achieve operating economics and maximum market impact. Wholesalers that are part of a vertical marketing system view themselves as marketing partners with the manufacturer or supplier, not just distributors. Both parties recognize that their primary purpose is to develop effective and efficient marketing programs for the entire channel. For example,

*Exhibit 12.5*

Comparison of a Conventional Channel and a Vertical Marketing Channel

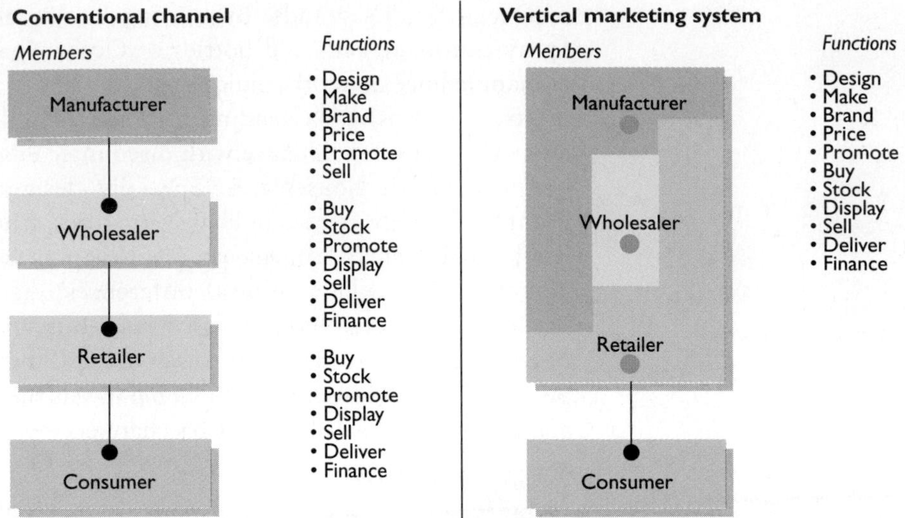


grocery wholesaler SuperValu has developed comprehensive merchandising programs for affiliated retailers that range from private labels, store planning and development, electronic information services, and advertising.[11] The benefits of vertical marketing systems include increased market information to all channel members, financial protection, profitability, future stability and growth, technology sharing, greater bargaining power, discouragement of competitors, and improved distribution services.[12] The three major types of vertical marketing systems are corporate, contractual, and administered.

## Corporate Systems

**corporate system**
Vertical marketing system in which one firm owns successive stages in a channel of distribution.

A **corporate system,** in which one firm owns successive stages in a channel of distribution, is the ultimate vertical marketing system. A single firm that owns the entire channel has no need to worry about intermediaries. The firm can be sure of supplies of raw materials, long-term contact with customers, adequate distribution, and adequate product exposure in the marketplace. Channel members' decision making is not independent or subject to major change without the firm's agreement. Moreover, policies about price levels and product mixes for separate markets or heavier promotion in certain geographic regions can easily be implemented. An example of a corporate system is Tandy, which produces electronics and sells them in its own Radio Shack retail stores. By doing so, the company controls all aspects of production, distribution, and marketing of its products.

**forward integration**
Manufacturer's or wholesaler's acquisition of an intermediary closer to the target market or performance of the functions of an intermediary closer to the target market.

Corporate systems are integrated either forward or backward. **Forward integration** occurs when a manufacturer or wholesaler acquires an intermediary closer to the target market or begins performing the functions of an intermediary closer to the target market. A wholesaler could integrate forward by purchasing a retailer; examples include Sherwin-Williams, which operates over 2,000 paint stores, and Hart Schaffner and Marx, which owns over a hundred menswear outlets. Or a manufacturer like Pepsi-Cola might integrate forward by buying a wholesaler.

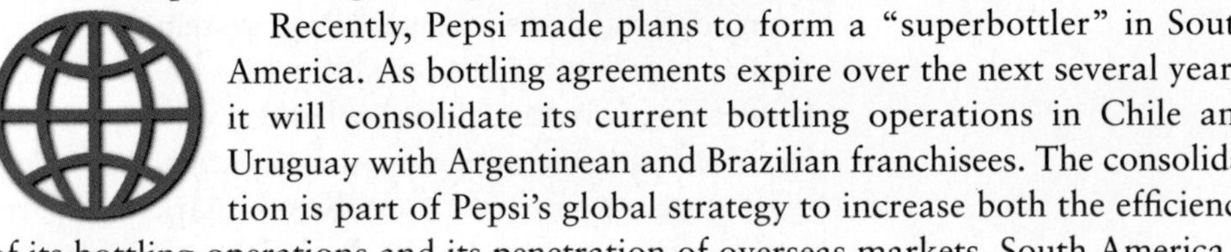

Recently, Pepsi made plans to form a "superbottler" in South America. As bottling agreements expire over the next several years, it will consolidate its current bottling operations in Chile and Uruguay with Argentinean and Brazilian franchisees. The consolidation is part of Pepsi's global strategy to increase both the efficiency of its bottling operations and its penetration of overseas markets. South America is an especially attractive market because per capita soft-drink consumption is low in comparison to Pepsi's better markets. With this new arrangement, Pepsi will gain broader distribution of its product and keep prices affordable because of improved efficiency.[13]

**backward integration**
Retailer's or wholesaler's acquisition of an intermediary closer to the manufacturing stage or performance of the functions formerly performed by an intermediary closer to the manufacturing stage.

**Backward integration** is just the opposite of forward integration. Many large retail organizations integrate backward by developing or acquiring wholesaling and, in some cases, manufacturing operations. Large supermarkets get almost 10 percent of their stock from "captive" manufacturing facilities (those owned by the supermarket chains), many of which were acquired in the 1950s. Similarly, the Ponderosa steakhouse chain was interested in both producing and selling steak, an unusual strategy within the restaurant industry. The steakhouse integrated backward to acquire a meat distributor and a separate beef-supply company. Ponderosa also sponsors research aimed at developing beefier and more disease-resistant cattle.[14]

## Contractual Systems

**contractual system**
Vertical marketing system composed of independent firms at different channel levels (manufacturer, wholesaler, retailer) coordinating their distribution activities by contractual agreement.

A **contractual system** can be defined as a system of independent firms at different channel levels (manufacturer, wholesaler, retailer) coordinating their distribution activities by contractual agreement. Three variations of contractual relationships exist:

- The *franchise*—such as McDonald's, Arby's, Burger King, Holiday Inn, and automobile dealerships—is the most visible form of contractual system. A franchise system is the licensing of an entire business format. One firm (the franchisor) licenses a number of outlets (franchisees) to market a good or service and engage in a business developed by the franchisor. In turn, this licensed business uses the franchisor's trade names, trademarks, service marks, know-how, and business methods. Franchise systems are discussed in detail in Chapter 13.
- A *wholesaler-sponsored voluntary chain* is created when a wholesaler develops a contractual relationship with small independent retailers. This organization allows the wholesaler to standardize and coordinate buying practices, merchandising programs, and inventory management efforts. There is strength in numbers; wholesaler-sponsored voluntary chains can achieve economies of scale and volume discounts. Some examples of wholesaler-sponsored voluntary chains include Western Auto, IGA, and Ben Franklin stores.
- A *retailer-sponsored cooperative,* such as True Value hardware stores, exists when many small independent retailers cooperatively own a wholesaling organization. Like their wholesaler counterpart, a retailer-sponsored cooperative is able to concentrate its buying power and achieve economies of scale.

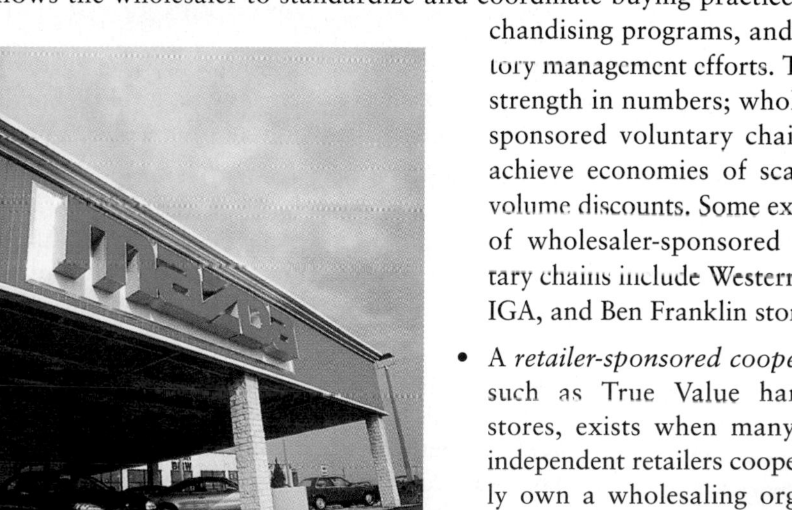

The relationship between a car manufacturer and a franchised dealer is a vertical marketing system, specifically a contractual system. A legal agreement formalizes the partnership between producer and intermediary.

### Administered Systems

**administered system**
Vertical marketing system in which a strong organization assumes a leadership position.

An **administered system** is a marketing channel in which a strong organization assumes a leadership position. The leader's power may consist of sheer economic domination of other channel members. Its authority can also stem from a well-known brand name. Companies like Gillette, Hanes, Campbell Soup, and Westinghouse are leaders of administered systems. The leader of an administered system is not always a manufacturer, however. Increasingly, large retailers are evolving administered systems. For example, Wal-Mart, with over $67 billion in annual sales and over 2,000 retail stores, gains numerous price concessions from manufacturers.

The leader of an administered system can often influence or control the policies of other channel members without the costs and expertise required in a corporate system—perhaps by threatening to withdraw well-known brand names or by offering advertising rebates. Yet the vertically aligned companies can still work as an integrated unit to achieve information, transportation, warehousing, promotion, and other economies. Compared to a conventional system, the net result is usually a lower overall cost, a better assortment of merchandise, faster inventory turnover, and flexibility in adjusting to changing consumer preferences.

In Japan, vertically administered systems called *keiretsu* are led by some of the country's largest companies, such as Toyota and Nissan. These alliances coordinate government, industry, capital, and the best information on advanced technology from around the world (see Chapter 3). Each *keiretsu* typically contains a bank, a trading company, and over twenty groups of industrial enterprises. Nearly all of Japan's leading corporations belong to a *keiretsu*. Each *keiretsu* typically has only one member company representing each industrial sector in order to minimize intergroup competition and to maximize harmony.[15] These *keiretsu* typically lead an administered system of primary and secondary suppliers and may have distribution alliances with thousands of retailers throughout Japan.

*6 Explain the concepts of power and conflict within marketing channels.*

## MARKETING CHANNEL RELATIONSHIPS

A marketing channel is more than a set of institutions linked by economic ties. Social relationships play an important role in building unity among channel members. The basic social dimensions of channels are power, control, leadership, conflict, and legal considerations.

### CHANNEL POWER, CONTROL, AND LEADERSHIP

**channel power**
Capacity of a particular marketing channel member to control or influence the behavior of other channel members.

**channel control**
Situation that occurs when one marketing channel member intentionally affects another member's behavior.

**channel leader (channel captain)**
Member of a marketing channel that exercises authority and power over the activities of other channel members.

**Channel power** is a channel member's capacity to control or influence the behavior of other channel members.[16] **Channel control** occurs when one channel member affects another member's behavior. To achieve control, a channel member assumes channel leadership and exercises authority and power. This member is termed the **channel leader** (or **channel captain**). In one marketing channel, a manufacturer may be the leader because it controls new product designs and product availability. In another, a retailer may be the channel leader because it wields power and control over the retail price, inventory levels, and postsale service.

Regardless of the locus of power, channel members rely heavily on one another. Even the most powerful manufacturers depend on dealers to sell their products; even the most powerful retailers require the products provided by suppliers.

Channel power can take five forms:

- *Reward power:* when a channel member believes that an intermediary can help the firm achieve its goals. For example, a manufacturer may give a wholesaler a full line to sell, thereby raising the wholesaler's profit potential. That manufacturer has reward power.
- *Coercive power:* when a channel member feels threatened. For example, a manufacturer like Compaq Computer is exercising its coercive power if it threatens to discontinue sales to a distributor like MicroAge or a retailer like Computer City. Slow vehicle delivery to car dealers has been used as a means of coercion in the auto industry.
- *Legitimate power:* when the channel leader has a right to make decisions. This type of power stems from values internalized by a company that give it a feeling that another company "should" or "has a right" to exert influence and that it has an obligation to accept the other company's influence. IBM, General Electric, and Xerox are widely perceived as legitimate channel leaders.
- *Referent power:* when one channel member identifies with another. Referent power usually stems from the company's reputation. For instance, some independent motels like to be affiliated with a particular motel chain, which can then be said to have referent power. Manufacturers often enjoy seeing their brands carried at high-prestige stores, such as Neiman Marcus or Saks Fifth Avenue.
- *Expert power:* when channel members believe that another channel member's knowledge and expertise can make the system more efficient. For example, small retailers often rely on manufacturers like Procter & Gamble and Frito-Lay for advice.[17]

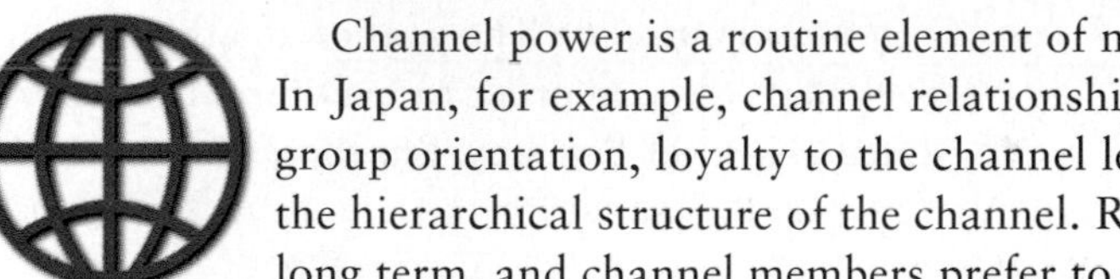

Channel power is a routine element of many business activities. In Japan, for example, channel relationships are characterized by group orientation, loyalty to the channel leader, and adherence to the hierarchical structure of the channel. Relationships are for the long term, and channel members prefer to deal with partners they know well. The relationships are nurtured by personal contacts, visits, gifts, and support in hard times.[18] Many U.S. manufacturers find Japanese retailers and end-user customers unwilling to disrupt their longstanding, personal relationships with Japanese suppliers—even when the U.S. company can offer a product of superior or equal quality at a cheaper price. U.S. firms trying to break into the Japanese market have found that developing and maintaining the customary relationships entails frequent business trips and socializing after hours.[19]

The exercise of channel power is not unique to Japan, however. A small but growing number of manufacturers are deliberately spurning large discounters and mass merchandisers like Wal-Mart and instead selling only to independent stores. These manufacturers resent their lack of control over the huge discounts at which some retailers sell products. For example, Sashco Sealants, a manufacturer of caulks, won't sell its product to Home Depot, Wal-Mart, Homebase, or Kmart and its Builders Square subsidiary. Still others, such as lawn-products maker Scotts Company, sell only certain product lines to the mass merchants and keep other product lines for exclusive sale to independent lawn and garden stores.[20]

Retailers that want to balance their power relationship with manufacturers or even to gain control over suppliers can employ several strategies:

- Developing expert power by obtaining information about consumers' needs and providing this information to suppliers

- Maintaining multiple sources of supply to avoid the coercive power of any single supplier
- Establishing referent power by encouraging consumers to become more loyal to the store than to a supplier's brand
- Developing a strong private-brand program to avoid the coercive power of national producers
- Banding together with other retailers to buy in larger quantities and thereby enhancing their ability to exercise reward power with suppliers[21]

Large retailers do indeed exert considerable power over their suppliers and manufacturers. Traditionally, retailers pay for goods as soon as they receive them. Kmart, however, has asked many of its toy vendors to ship goods on consignment. Under this agreement, Kmart would not pay for the goods until they appeared in stores. The toy vendors, meanwhile, would have to keep the inventory on their own books, even while it sat in Kmart's distribution centers, and risk writing off goods that don't sell. Although many toy vendors have dismissed the idea as ridiculous, some have accepted the proposal for fear of losing an important customer.[22]

## CHANNEL CONFLICT

**channel conflict**
Clash of goals and methods between distribution channel members.

Inequitable channel relationships often lead to **channel conflict,** which is a clash of goals and methods among the members of a distribution channel. In a broad context, conflict may not be bad. Often it arises because staid, traditional channel members refuse to keep pace with the times. Removing an outdated intermediary may result in reduced costs for the entire system.

The sources of conflict within marketing channels can be grouped as follows:

- *Goal incompatibility:* The goal of an athletic footwear store is to sell as many shoes as possible in order to maximize profits, whether the shoes be made by Adidas, Nike, or Saucony. But the Adidas manufacturer wants a certain sales

One source of conflict in a distribution channel is goal incompatibility. This shoe store aims to sell as many pairs of shoes as possible, regardless of the manufacturer. Each manufacturer, however, wants the store to sell the maximum quantity of its own brand.

© Alan Brown/Photonics Graphics

volume and market share in each market. Therefore, the athletic footwear store and Adidas may have conflicting goals.

- *Role incongruence:* A channel member is expected to fulfill certain roles. For instance, imagine that the owner of a McDonald's franchise insists on serving hot dogs instead of hamburgers, french fries, and shakes. The owner doesn't enforce McDonald's cleanliness standards or require employees to wear the traditional McDonald's uniform. The owner is clearly not fulfilling the expectations of the franchisor. Thus role incongruence exists.
- *Communication breakdowns:* When a manufacturer changes the marketing mix and fails to notify other channel members, conflict can result. For example, the failure to notify dealers of reduced warranty coverage from six months to three months could cause a major problem. Unaware of expired warranties, dealers could make repairs with the expectation that they would be reimbursed by the manufacturer.
- *Different perceptions of reality:* A manufacturer may feel that the profit margins offered to the intermediaries are ample for the demands it places on them. Yet if margins seem too low to the intermediaries, they may reduce the space, service, and sales effort they provide to the manufacturer.
- *Ideological differences:* Sometimes channel members' values or viewpoints differ. Retailers may believe "the customer is always right" and offer a very liberal return policy. Wholesalers or manufacturers may feel that people "try to get something for nothing" or don't follow product instructions carefully. Their views of allowable returns might conflict with the retailers'.

**horizontal conflict**
Channel conflict that occurs among channel members on the same level that handle the same manufacturer's brands, such as between two different wholesalers or two different retailers.

Conflict within a channel can either be horizontal or vertical. **Horizontal conflict** occurs among channel members on the same level, such as two or more different wholesalers or two or more different retailers, that handle the same manufacturer's brands. This type of channel conflict is found most often when manufacturers practice dual or multiple distribution strategies. For example, microcomputers initially were sold only in computer specialty stores. Today, however, microcomputer manufacturers also sell their computers in discount stores, department stores, warehouse clubs, and giant electronics superstores, such as CompUSA and Circuit City. Apple, Compaq, and Dell also sell computers to consumers through direct channels, such as direct mail and catalogs. Horizontal conflict may occur among these diverse types of retailers.

**vertical conflict**
Channel conflict that occurs between different levels in a marketing channel, most typically between the manufacturer and wholesaler or between the manufacturer and retailer.

Many regard horizontal conflict as healthy competition. Vertical conflict is much more serious. **Vertical conflict** occurs between different levels in a marketing channel, most typically between the manufacturer and wholesaler and the manufacturer and retailer. Producer-versus-wholesaler conflict often occurs when the producer chooses to bypass the wholesaler and deal directly with the consumer or retailer. For example, conflict arose when several producers agreed to Wal-Mart's request to deal with it directly, bypassing middlemen altogether. Manufacturers' representatives and brokers immediately formed a coalition and began a national campaign, contending that the policy could put thousands out of work. Critics argued that small and medium-size suppliers and retailers would not have the expertise or financial resources to bring products to market and would eventually go out of business.[23]

Dual distribution strategies can also cause vertical conflict in the channel. For example, when Goodyear announced plans to sell Goodyear-brand tires through Sears, hundreds of Goodyear's 2,500 independent dealers, which had been selling

**exclusive dealing**
Channel control practice in which a manufacturer prohibits its dealers from carrying competing products.

**tying contract**
Channel control practice in which a manufacturer sells a product to an intermediary only under the condition that it purchase another (possibly unwanted) product.

**refusal to deal**
Channel control practice in which a producer refuses to allow certain intermediaries to carry its products.

only the Goodyear brand, adopted other brands. Many went so far as to change their signs or consider joining with other chains.[24] Producers and retailers may also disagree over the terms of the sale or other aspects of the business relationship. When Procter & Gamble introduced "everyday low pricing" to its retail channel members, a strategy designed to standardize wholesale prices, many retailers retaliated by trimming the variety of P&G sizes they carried or eliminating marginal brands. Others moved P&G brands from prime, eye-level space to less visible shelves.[25]

## LEGAL CONSIDERATIONS IN CHANNEL RELATIONSHIPS

Channel conflict is typically resolved through negotiation or the exercise of power by a channel member. However, sometimes channel conflict produces legal action. For example, several Mail Boxes Etc. franchisees sued the national franchisor over its response to accusations that it made deceptive claims to sell franchises. The disgruntled franchisees say the company exaggerated the franchise success rate and understated start-up costs.[26] Channel members might also create a coalition to alter the power structure and lobby for a new law that will protect them. For example, auto dealers banded together to form the National Association of Automobile Dealers to fight what they saw as the unfair practices of auto manufacturers.

Seven major federal laws affect the relationships between marketing channel members:

Sherman Antitrust Act (1890)

Clayton Act (1914)

Federal Trade Commission Act (1914)

Robinson-Patman Act (1936)

Wheeler-Lea Amendment to the FTC Act (1938)

Celler-Kefauver Antimerger Act (1950)

Hart-Scott-Rodino Act (1976)

These acts focus on protecting and encouraging competition in the marketplace. They ban a wide range of anticompetitive behavior and address relationships between manufacturers and channel intermediaries. Exhibit 2.5 in Chapter 2 summarizes these key pieces of federal legislation. These laws affect a number of practices that may be legal unless (1) competition is substantially restricted, (2) a monopoly is created, or (3) trade is restrained.

The Clayton Act specifically prohibits exclusive dealing and tying contracts when they restrict competition or create monopolies. **Exclusive dealing**

---

ETHICS IN MARKETING

### How Can Gray Marketing Be Combated?

Many well-known products have been sold through gray-market channels, including IBM personal computers, Seiko watches, Olympus cameras, Duracell batteries, Mercedes-Benz cars, and even Caterpillar tractors and excavators. It is almost impossible to determine the scale of gray marketing, although some estimates indicate that anywhere from $10 billion to $15 billion worth of goods flow annually through gray-market channels in the United States alone.[29]

The driving force behind gray marketing is price differentials. In consumer packaged-goods markets, regional or local marketing programs that offer products at a special price increase the opportunities for gray marketing. Intermediaries purchase these goods in one region and then ship them to another part of the country where they can be sold at a higher price. In industrial goods markets, where significant quantity discounts are common, large industrial customers can buy in large quantities and then sell some of the merchandise to gray marketers, which in turn sell to smaller customers that would otherwise have to buy at the higher price. Internationally, gray markets are driven largely by differences in exchange rates. Global marketing programs that produce standardized products, often with multilingual labels and instructions, make gray marketing easier.[30]

Gray marketing appears to be increasing by over 20 percent each year, and it has a noticeable impact on the sales of major U.S. manufacturers. Thus holders of many well-known U.S. trademarks and a number of trade associations have been seeking control of gray markets through intense lobbying and legal efforts.[31] The manufacturers, charging that

**resale restriction**
Channel control practice in which the producer stipulates to whom distributors may resell its products and in what geographic territories they may be sold.

**exclusive-territory policy**
Channel control practice in which a manufacturer requires an intermediary to sell only to customers located within an assigned territory.

**gray marketing**
Selling trademarked products through unauthorized channels.

occurs when a manufacturer prohibits its dealers from carrying competing products. Although this practice is the basis of most franchise agreements, such an arrangement is illegal when a manufacturer's sales volume is so large that competitors are excluded from the market. For example, if Coca-Cola held a 90 percent market share of all soft drinks sold in the United States and prohibited its bottlers from carrying other brands, this exclusive arrangement would be considered illegal. When a manufacturer sells a product to an intermediary only on the condition that the intermediary purchase another (possibly unwanted) product, the two companies have entered into a **tying contract.** Some manufacturers require a channel member to carry their full line of products to obtain the right to carry the desired product. Tying contracts are illegal, generally under antitrust laws, if the tied products could have been purchased at fair market value from another supplier. Tying contracts are common in franchise arrangements, where the producer sees the franchisee as a captive buyer for all the equipment and supplies needed to operate the franchise.

Even though a producer has the right to decide which intermediaries will carry its products through the distribution channel, the **refusal to deal** with certain channel members may be illegal. For example, Eastman Kodak was accused of refusing to deal with independent service contractors for Kodak photocopier replacement parts. The company was subsequently charged with attempting to monopolize the business of repairing its brand of photocopiers.[27]

Other practices that may create legal problems are resale restrictions and exclusive territories. When a producer stipulates to whom distributors may resell its products and in what territories they may be sold, it is engaging in **resale restriction.** Under an **exclusive-territory policy,** a manufacturer requires an intermediary to sell only to customers located within an assigned territory. Because they lessen competition and restrain trade, many exclusive-territory policies have been deemed illegal.

Another channel practice with legal implications is **gray marketing,** in which trademarked products are sold through unauthorized channels of distribution. Gray marketing can occur within a market or across markets. Gray marketing *within* a market is when a manufacturer's authorized distributors sell the trademarked goods to unauthorized intermediaries. These intermediaries then distribute the goods to customers within the same market area. For consumer products,

## ETHICS IN MARKETING

gray marketers unfairly damage the value of their brands, seek government protection under trademark laws and the Lanham Act. For instance, perfume maker Parfums Givenchy got the courts to order Drug Emporium to stop selling the diverted fragrance Amarige at any of its 228 drugstores.[32]

Gray marketing has several ethical implications as well. Gray marketing upsets pricing policies in the distribution channel, impedes after-sale service, and can create customer dissatisfaction. In some cases, the gray-market goods differ substantially from products distributed through authorized channels. Often they are of inferior quality or conform to government standards. Some gray-market products do not come with the warranties or services offered by the authorized dealer. All of these situations can potentially harm the manufacturer's reputation.[33] Under some circumstances, manufacturers could even be held liable for defective gray-market products.[34]

Purchasers of gray-market goods face a number of risks. For example, microcomputers sold through gray-market dealers typically do not have any warranty protection. Some manufacturers will not honor the warranty unless the machine was purchased from an authorized dealer. A microcomputer from the gray market may either be missing its warranty card or not have a dealer stamp on the card. Some gray marketers alter or remove the machine's serial numbers to make it more difficult to track the source. The best way a consumer can tell whether a dealer is authorized is to call the manufacturer and check the dealer's authorization.[35]

How might customer satisfaction suffer if gray marketing is left unchecked? How might a manufacturer combat gray marketing? Would eliminating special price promotions be a likely cure for gray marketing?

this practice is often called "diverting." Gray marketing *across* markets, or distributing goods to customers in different market areas, especially across international markets, is called "parallel importing."[28] Gray marketing is posing a problem for many manufacturers these days, as the Ethics in Marketing box explains.

*7 Discuss the issues that influence channel strategy.*

## CHANNEL STRATEGY DECISIONS

Devising a marketing channel strategy requires several critical decisions. Marketing managers must decide what role distribution will play in the overall marketing strategy. In addition, they must be sure that the channel strategy they choose is consistent with product, promotion, and pricing strategies. In making these decisions, marketing managers must analyze what factors will influence the choice of channel and what level of distribution intensity will be appropriate.

### FACTORS AFFECTING CHANNEL CHOICE

Marketers must answer many questions before choosing a marketing channel. The final choice depends on analysis of several factors, which often interact. These factors can be grouped as market factors, product factors, and producer factors.

#### Market Factors

Among the most important market factors affecting the choice of distribution channels are *target customer* considerations. Specifically, marketing managers should answer the following questions: Who are the potential customers? What do they buy? Where do they buy? When do they buy? How do they buy? These questions imply that customers have preferences regarding products, sellers, time, and credit that marketing managers should be aware of. Additionally, the choice of channel depends on whether the producer is selling to consumers or to industrial customers. Industrial customers' buying habits are very different from those of consumers. Industrial customers tend to buy in larger quantities and require more customer service. Consumers usually buy in very small quantities and sometimes do not mind if they get no service at all, as in a discount store.

*Geographic location* and *size of the market* are also important to channel selection. As a rule, if the target market is concentrated in one or more specific areas, then direct selling through a sales force is appropriate. When markets are more widely dispersed, intermediaries would be less expensive. The size of the market also influences channel choice. Generally, a very large market requires more intermediaries. For instance, Procter & Gamble has to reach millions of consumers with its many brands of household goods. It needs many intermediaries, including wholesalers and retailers.

*Competition* in the marketplace is also a criterion for choosing a channel. Entering a channel where competition is fierce is difficult. Each year thousands of new products are introduced into the marketplace, making distribution channels crowded and difficult to enter. However, a producer may find a marketing channel that has been overlooked or avoided by its competitors. Many manufacturers have also found direct channels, such as direct mail, to be very profitable. OshKosh B'Gosh, a manufacturer of children's clothing, is testing its own children's apparel catalog to help reverse a sales decline.[36]

#### Product Factors

Products that are more *complex and customized and expensive* tend to benefit from

When a product is complex, customized, and expensive—as an airplane is—the marketing channel is likely to be rather direct. That is, the producer and the customer will usually strike a deal with few, if any, intermediaries involved.

© John Madere

shorter and more direct marketing channels. These types of products sell better through a direct sales force. Examples include pharmaceuticals, scientific instruments, airplanes, and mainframe computer systems. On the other hand, the more standardized a product is, the longer its distribution channel can be and the greater the number of intermediaries that can be involved. For example, the formula for chewing gum is about the same from producer to producer, with the exception of flavor and shape. Chewing gum is also very inexpensive. As a result, the distribution channel for gum tends to involve many wholesalers and retailers.

The product's *life cycle* is also an important factor in choosing a marketing channel. In fact, the choice of channel may change over the life of the product. For example, when photocopiers were first available, they were typically sold by a direct sales force. Now, however, photocopiers can be found in several places, including warehouse clubs, electronics superstores, and mail-order catalogs. As products become more common and less intimidating to potential users, producers tend to look for alternative channels. Gatorade was originally sold to sports teams, gyms, and fitness clubs. As the drink became more popular, mainstream supermarket channels were added, followed by convenience stores and drugstores. Now Gatorade can be found in vending machines and even in some fast-food restaurants.[37]

Another factor is the *delicacy* of the product. Perishable products like vegetables and milk have a relatively short life span. Fragile products like china and crystal require a minimum amount of handling. Therefore, both require fairly short marketing channels.

## Producer Factors

Several factors pertaining to the producer itself are important to the selection of a marketing channel. In general, producers with large financial, managerial, and marketing *resources* are better able to use channels that require fewer intermediaries. These producers have the ability to hire and train their own sales force, warehouse their own goods, and extend credit to their customers. Smaller or weaker firms, on the other hand, must rely on intermediaries to provide these services for them.

Compared to producers with only one or two *product lines,* producers that sell several products in a related area are able to choose channels that are more direct. Sales expenses can be spread over more products.

A producer's desire to *control* pricing, positioning, brand image, and customer support also tends to influence channel selection. For instance, firms that sell products with exclusive brand images, such as designer perfumes and clothing, usually avoid channels in which discount retailers are present. Manufacturers of upscale products, such as Dooney & Bourke or Gucci (handbags) and Godiva (chocolates), may sell their wares only in expensive stores in order to maintain an image of exclusivity. Many producers have opted to risk their image, however, and test sales in discount channels. Levi Strauss expanded its distribution in the early 1980s to include JCPenney and Sears. JCPenney is now Levi Strauss's biggest customer.

## LEVELS OF DISTRIBUTION INTENSITY

Organizations have three options for intensity of distribution, or how available a product is: intensive distribution, selective distribution, or exclusive distribution.

### Intensive Distribution

**intensive distribution**
Form of distribution aimed at having a product available in every outlet where target customers might want to buy it.

**Intensive distribution** is distribution aimed at maximum market coverage. The manufacturer tries to have the product available in every outlet where potential customers might want to buy it. If buyers are unwilling to search for a product (as is true of convenience goods and operating supplies), the product must be very accessible to buyers. A low-value product that is purchased frequently may require a lengthy channel. For example, candy is found in almost every type of retail store imaginable. It is typically sold to retailers in small quantities by a food or candy wholesaler. The Wrigley Company could not afford to sell its gum directly to every service station, drugstore, supermarket, and discount store. The cost would be too high.

Most manufacturers pursuing an intensive distribution strategy sell to a large percentage of the wholesalers willing to stock their products. Retailers' willingness (or unwillingness) to handle items tends to control the manufacturer's ability to achieve intensive distribution. For example, a retailer already carrying ten brands of gum may show little enthusiasm for one more brand.

### Selective Distribution

**selective distribution**
Form of distribution achieved by screening dealers to eliminate all but a few in any single area.

**Selective distribution** is achieved by screening dealers to eliminate all but a few in any single area. For example, Maytag uses a selective distribution system by choosing a select handful of appliance dealers in a geographic area to sell its line of washers and dryers and other appliances. Likewise, DKNY clothing is sold only in select retail outlets. Because only a few retailers are chosen, the consumer must seek out the product. Shopping goods and some specialty products are distributed selectively. Accessory equipment manufacturers in the business-to-business market also tend to follow a selective distribution strategy.

Many image-conscious clothing manufacturers, such as Ralph Lauren, choose a selective distribution strategy. A few carefully chosen retailers offer these goods, so consumers must make an effort to find them.

Several screening criteria are used to find the right dealers. An accessory equipment manufacturer like NEC may seek firms that are able to service its products properly. A television manufacturer like Zenith may look for service ability and a quality dealer image. If the manufacturer expects to move a large volume of merchandise through each dealer, it will choose only those dealers that seem able to handle such volume. As a result, many smaller retailers may not be considered.

### Exclusive Distribution

**exclusive distribution**
Form of distribution that establishes one or a few dealers within a given area.

The most restrictive form of market coverage is **exclusive distribution,** which entails only one or a few dealers within a given area. Because buyers may have to search or travel extensively to buy the product, exclusive distribution is usually confined to consumer specialty goods, a few shopping goods, and major industrial equipment. Products such as Rolls Royce automobiles, Chris-Craft power boats, Pettibone tower cranes, and Coors beer are distributed under exclusive arrangements. Sometimes exclusive territories are granted by new companies (such as franchisors) to obtain market coverage in a particular area. Limited distribution may also serve to project an exclusive image for the product.

Retailers and wholesalers may be unwilling to commit the time and money necessary to promote and service a product unless the manufacturer guarantees them an exclusive territory. This arrangement shields the dealer from direct competition and enables it to be the main beneficiary of the manufacturer's promotion efforts in that geographic area. With exclusive distribution, channels of communication are usually well established, because the manufacturer works with a limited number of dealers rather than many accounts.

Although exclusivity has its advantages, it also can have its pitfalls. An exclusive network may not be large enough, for instance, if demand is brisk. In addition, the producer's insistence on exclusivity might put the channel in financial jeopardy during times of weak demand. Honda's Acura division, for example, uses an exclusive distribution strategy to create a distinctive image for its high-priced cars. But Acura dealers did not experience much initial success because of the car's small niche market, low resale demand, and ironically, infrequent need for follow-up service and repair.[38]

8 *List the steps in designing marketing channels.*

## MARKETING CHANNEL DESIGN

Once a marketing manager has determined which factors influence the choice of marketing channel, then he or she is ready to design the marketing channel. Exhibit 12.6 on page 394 shows the major stages in marketing channel design, along with the criteria that producers use in choosing channels and channel participants. Frequently, wholesalers and retailers can also design channels.

Before marketing channel design can begin, marketers must determine where and how target customers want to buy the product. Market research will tell the manufacturer what type of retailing or wholesaling establishments target customers prefer, as well as how they would like to buy the product. For example, market studies might reveal that customers prefer to buy bath towels at discount stores rather than department stores. They may want to buy towels in sets that include a bath towel, a hand towel, and a face cloth. These customer preferences will provide the foundation for the manufacturer's channel strategy.

### IDENTIFYING CHANNEL ALTERNATIVES

Once customer preferences have been determined, the next step is to identify the channel alternatives that match the organization's channel objectives and channel strategy. Three questions guide the identification of channel alternatives: Which one has the best access to end users? What are the prevailing distribution practices in the industry? What activities and functions must be performed by channel members?

#### Access to End Users

The intermediaries that might be used to reach the target market can best be identified by working backward from the end user. For example, a seller of air network

*Exhibit 12.6*

Channel Design Decisions and Decision Criteria

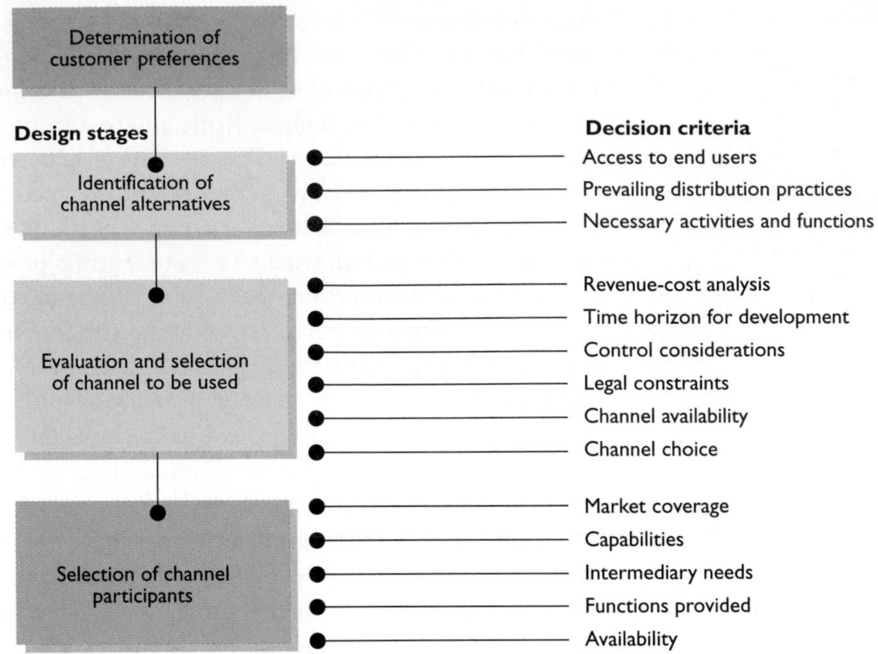


time for cellular mobile telephones might first look at who are the prime users of cellular phones. Management might then consider the following channel alternatives:

- *Established outlets:* One option is to create a distribution channel using established dealers or retailers from a broad segment of cellular-related businesses, such as Sears or Radio Shack.
- *Direct sales force:* Another possibility is to sell directly to end users via an internal sales force. This alternative would increase the intensity of the selling effort but would be quite expensive.
- *Company-owned stores:* The cellular phone manufacturer could also establish a network of company-owned stores to market the hardware, subscriptions, installation, and maintenance.
- *Franchising:* Another alternative might be a franchise network of established companies with diverse backgrounds. Franchisees could perform both wholesaling and retailing activities.
- *Piggybacking:* A final distribution option to consider is using manufacturers of cellular equipment to market the air network.

## Prevailing Distribution Practices

Considering the channel practices of firms selling similar products can help identify the main options. Management can gain insight by studying competitors' distribution strategies and weighing their strengths and weaknesses. Management should be careful, however, not to restrict its marketing channel options to those being used by competitors.

A cellular phone service company might examine the distribution strategies of its major competitors, such as GTE Mobilnet and Bell Cellular. Others' experiences will enable the company to draw conclusions about the strengths and weaknesses of some distribution options.

## Necessary Activities and Functions

Earlier, this chapter described several essential marketing channel functions (refer back to Exhibit 12.2). Producers, intermediaries, and end users must perform these functions. An important step in pinpointing feasible channel alternatives is assessing the functions and activities that need to be performed. Then management must identify which are best performed by producers and which are best performed by intermediaries. Moreover, it must determine the capabilities of the different types of intermediaries under consideration.

Returning to our cellular service example, the company might have recognized that a direct sales force would be very costly per customer contacted compared to other channel options. It may also have realized that channel intermediaries with well-known names and favorable images could help overcome its unfamiliarity to end users. Physical distribution could be discounted as an important factor in selecting a channel, because the product (use of the airwaves) does not require storage or delivery.

## EVALUATING AND SELECTING CHANNELS

The evaluation of channel alternatives should include revenue and cost analyses, the time required for channel development, control considerations, channel availability, and channel choice.

### Revenue and Cost Analyses

A key factor in evaluating channel alternatives is the expected economic performance of each option. Intensive distribution through a variety of retail outlets may be more costly than other choices. Yet compared to selective distribution, it should generate a larger sales volume.

Marketers often describe the ideal channel as one that performs the needed distribution tasks at the lowest possible cost. Distribution cost analysis is a useful tool for comparing the performance of existing marketing channels and estimating the revenues and costs associated with potential channels.

Channel length, channel control, and the amount of financial resources that must be invested in channel activities often are related. In general, short or direct channels allow the manufacturer more control over channel functions and activities. As a result, the manufacturer typically must commit more financial resources to the shorter channel. Conversely, manufacturers give up some of this control with longer channels that incorporate more intermediaries, but less of an investment is required. An important aspect of marketing channel selection is examining the trade-offs between desired control and desired investment in channel activities.

### Time for Development

Time is another significant factor in designing a marketing channel. For example, Ethan Allen spent many years developing its extensive retail network. The Limited grew from one women's specialty store to a $1 billion corporate chain over a twenty-year period. Controlled growth was perceived to be an asset rather than a liability.

Sometimes time is a critical factor. For instance, assume the cellular service marketer rejected the channel option of building a direct sales force. Management might have been convinced that it would not be able to hire and train sales representatives fast enough to beat competitors into the market. The first firm to establish a position in the market would gain a big competitive advantage.

### Control Considerations

The extent to which an organization wishes to control the marketing activities within a channel directly affects the channel selection process. The longer the marketing channel, the less control the manufacturer has. Furthermore, the more intensive the pattern of distribution, the less control the manufacturer has to decide how the product will be marketed. Direct channels and vertical marketing systems offer the most control to the channel leader.

## Channel Availability

An issue often overlooked in channel design is the availability of the intermediary. Sometimes the preferred channels either have exclusive arrangements with other suppliers or for some other reason are uninterested in the supplier. Snap-on Tools had this experience nearly seventy-five years ago. The socket wrench that Snap-on developed enabled users to reduce by two-thirds the number of tools they needed. Wholesalers and retailers neither welcomed this large cutback in sales opportunity nor wanted to stock the new tools. Frustrated by lack of channel availability, Snap-on targeted professional mechanics and developed its own sales force. Essentially, the firm was forced to seek an alternative channel of distribution. Now it has over 5,000 franchised dealers worldwide who call on professional mechanics in familiar "traveling store" vans.

Some Texas wineries haven't been so lucky in finding channels through which to distribute their product. The winemakers once saw their state as the next Napa Valley. But because many of the wineries are located in "dry" areas, where alcohol cannot be sold, they must find distributors in "wet" areas to sell their wine. Many state distributors are reluctant to carry another brand of wine, however, much less a low-profile Texas vintage. Thus Texas wineries are often required to discount their wine by as much as 50 percent to get a distributor to handle it.[39]

## Channel Choice

Channel selection is a vital task because it locks in much longer commitments than do other marketing decisions. Setting up channel networks and building channel relationships often takes a great deal of time and money. Channel selection also affects decisions about other elements of the marketing mix.

Short distribution channels are commonly used for expensive consumer or business products with high profit margins. Promotion strategy typically emphasizes personal

Because wholesalers and retailers did not want to stock its innovative product, Snap-on Tools designed a unique marketing channel. Driving clearly identified "traveling store" vans full of tools, franchised Snap-on dealers call directly on professional mechanics.

Courtesy of Snap-on Tools Corporation

*Exhibit 12.7*

Criteria for Selecting Channel Members

1. Size of prospective channel member
   - Sales
   - Financial strength
2. Sales strength
   - Number of sales personnel
   - Sales and technical competence
3. Product lines
   - Competitive products
   - Compatible products
   - Complementary products
   - Quality of lines carried
4. Reputation
   - Leadership
   - Longevity
5. Market coverage
   - Geographic coverage (outlets per market area)
   - Industry coverage
   - Call frequency or intensity of coverage
6. Sales performance
   - Performance with related lines
   - General sales performance
   - Growth prospects
7. Management
8. Advertising and sales promotion
9. Sales compensation
10. Acceptance of training assistance
11. Transportation savings
12. Inventory
    - Kind and size
    - Inventory minimums (safety stocks)
    - Reductions in manufacturer inventories
    - Extent of postponement (speculation)
13. Warehousing
    - Field locations
    - Ability to handle shipments efficiently
14. Lot quantity costs
    - Willingness to accept ordering policies

selling. In contrast, long channels are commonly used for rather inexpensive consumer or business goods. Stock turnover is often high, unit margins are low, and promotion strategy emphasizes advertising.

## SELECTING CHANNEL PARTICIPANTS

After management selects a channel structure, the next step is to evaluate prospective channel members. A useful approach is to first develop a short list of *mandatory* requirements for each type of channel member, the functions and activities that wholesalers and retailers absolutely must perform. Next, the marketing manager develops a list of *desirable* qualities for the intermediary to possess. After compiling these two lists, prospective channel members can be ranked and evaluated according to how well they meet the criteria.

Exhibit 12.7 shows some key criteria for assessing channel candidates. Management can weight the items according to company needs and objectives, sales strength, product lines, and reputation. The firms with the highest overall scores can then be approached for membership.

After choosing the channel members, management must often recruit them. Chosen channel members are often reluctant to join the channel team. In particular, retailers may be indifferent to adding, say, a tenth brand of gum or a fifth brand of presweetened cereal. In this case, aggressive personal selling may be needed to convince the firm to join the channel.

9 *Discuss channel structure and decisions in global markets.*

## GLOBAL MARKETING CHANNELS

Global marketing channels are important to U.S. corporations that export their products or manufacture abroad. Executives should recognize the unique cultural, economic, institutional, and legal aspects of each market before trying to design marketing channels in foreign countries. They should spend a great deal of time designing the best channel strategy for each country.

GLOBAL PERSPECTIVES

**China, the Pearl of the Orient**

Today there's a fervor among Westerners to break into Chinese markets. Current Chinese leadership readily acknowledges that the country needs foreign technology and expertise—and is giving foreign firms increasing freedom to pursue Chinese markets. With an economy that continues to grow at more than 10 percent a year, China's demand for foreign commodities, especially industrial and agricultural goods, will only continue to grow.

Distribution in China has improved vastly since the 1970s, when all goods were allocated according to a central plan and each ministry in China had complete control over its distribution channel. The result was endless red tape and barely surmountable transportation problems. Since the official "open door policy" of 1979, however, China's distribution channels have changed incrementally. Today only a few items, such as some key agricultural products, are still distributed by the central government. All other items are now distributed more or less according to market demand and price. That diffusion of channel power has created thousands of new, independent dealers.

Unfortunately, access to the Chinese market is not an instant formula for success. Many foreign firms have found that profits in China remain elusive, for many reasons. For one, China is not one market but several, and regional blockades effectively discriminate against certain goods. In addition, distribution channels are undeveloped, and infrastructure bottlenecks stifle the flow of goods. Not least among the problems is an economy that is still run far too much by administrative fiat, with the Chinese bureaucratic apparatus a major hindrance to trade. Finally, the legal system in China is still far from easy to work with. If a dealer simply disappears with a company's product, the company has little or no recourse to recover the goods.

Despite these challenges, U.S. firms can navigate through the channels to find success in China. By learning the Chinese system, a number of firms have discovered how to ride the wave of China's continued growth. One such company is Xerox of Shanghai. The company first entered China in 1987 using a direct channel through its own sales organization. After realizing the vastness of the market for its product, however, Xerox decided to establish a network of dealers. Xerox's dealer network relies on the Chinese system of *guanxi*, or relationships. Xerox credits much of its 43 percent market share in China to the friendships that have been developed over time by its dealers.

Xerox readily admits, however, that all is not perfect. For every one of its roughly one hundred main dealers in the country, there are probably three subdealers. Sometimes there is crossover. For instance, a volume discount may be given to a huge dealer in Shanghai or Beijing. If it

Manufacturers introducing products in global markets face a tough decision: what type of channel structure to use. Specifically, should the product be marketed directly, mostly by company salespeople, or through independent foreign intermediaries, such as agents and distributors?[40] Using company salespeople generally provides more control and less risk than using foreign intermediaries. However, setting up a sales force in a foreign country also entails a greater commitment, both financially and organizationally.

Companies wanting to sell in global markets are more likely to succeed with a company-controlled sales force when

- The product category is relatively new and the products within it are not standardized.
- The product is closely related to the company's core business.
- Product trade secrets are at risk pending patents to protect the technology.
- The product requires high service levels.
- Few legal restrictions constrain direct foreign investment.
- The company already has experienced salespeople who would be hard to replace with foreign agents.
- The company already has an established channel of distribution in the foreign country.
- Close competitors have set up their own direct distribution channels.
- The foreign country's culture is very similar to U.S. culture.[41]

For example, suppose a major software manufacturer wants to introduce a new software package in Europe. The software provides innovative solutions for finance-related customers, such as banks and stockbrokers, and requires specialized training and technical support after the sale. Being a veteran in the European financial

GLOBAL PERSPECTIVES

cannot sell all the product in its territory, it might invade another dealer's area.

Xerox has to deal with such a large tangle of dealers because of China's two-tiered distribution system. One tier is composed of a network of companies that have a base in a major city, such as Shanghai or Beijing. Although these large companies have so-called national distribution, the reality is that very few Chinese companies have access to all major Chinese territories, either for political or logistical reasons. The second tier of China's distribution system is a loose network of local dealers scattered throughout the country that handle distribution channels down to the village level. Given the regional blockades, transportation bottlenecks, and other hassles of moving goods through China, Xerox—along with any other company that desires to do business there—must deal with local distributors in each major city or region in which it wants to sell products.[45]

What are the advantages to Xerox of using foreign intermediaries in China? What would be the advantages of creating its own internal sales force in China? What would be the disadvantages of both types of channel structure in a global market?

software market, the company already has distribution channels and a direct sales force. Given these conditions, the manufacturer would likely use a direct channel to market its new product.

The benefits of using independent foreign intermediaries are in many cases the opposite of the conditions stated previously. For instance, if the product is fairly standardized, does not require a high level of service, is not at risk of losing patent protection, and is within a product category that does not use leading-edge technology, then independent foreign intermediaries are probably the better choice. In countries where the culture and customs are fairly different from those of the United States, inexperienced marketers may have trouble without the help of foreign middlemen. Other benefits of using foreign intermediaries include the economies of scale and scope they obtain by providing distribution services for several manufacturers. Furthermore, the manufacturers avoid having to deal with government regulations and politics in foreign countries.[42]

Marketers should be aware that the channel structure abroad may not be very similar to channels in the United States. For instance, U.S. firms wishing to sell goods in Japan must frequently go through three layers of wholesalers and subwholesalers: the national or primary wholesalers, the secondary or regional wholesalers, and the local wholesalers.[43] The channel types available in foreign countries usually differ as well. The more highly developed a nation is economically, the more specialized its channel types. Therefore, a marketer wishing to sell in Germany or Japan will have several channel types to choose from. Conversely, developing countries like India, Ethiopia, and Venezuela have limited channel types available; there are typically few mail-order channels, vending machines, or specialized retailers and wholesalers.[44]

**10** *List the types of firms that perform wholesaling activities, and explain their functions*

## WHOLESALING INTERMEDIARIES

Variations in channel structures are due in large part to variations in the numbers and types of wholesaling intermediaries. Some of these intermediaries take title to the product (ownership rights); others simply facilitate the sale of a product from producer to end user. Typically, merchant wholesalers take ownership of the products; agents and brokers do not. Exhibit 12.8 on page 400 shows these two main types of wholesaling intermediaries.

Generally, product characteristics and market conditions determine which type of wholesaling intermediary the manufacturer should use. Exhibit 12.9 shows these determining factors. For example, a manufacturer that produces a few engines a

*Exhibit 12.8*

Major Types of Channel Intermediaries

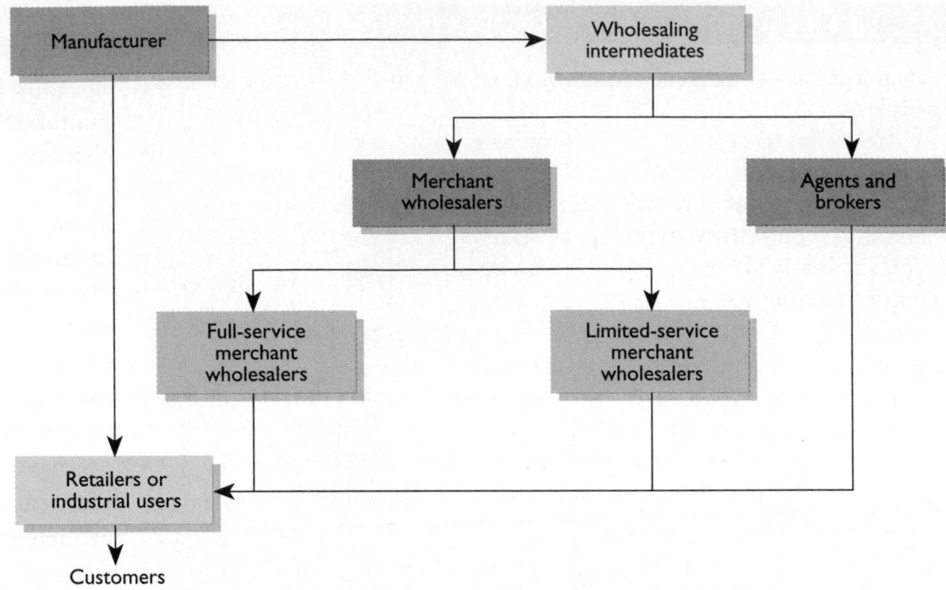


year for space rockets will probably use an agent or broker to sell its product. In addition, the handful of customers that need the product are most likely concentrated near rocket launching sites, again making an agent or broker more practical. On the other hand, a book publisher has many widely dispersed customers with year-round demand for its product. Thus a merchant wholesaler makes sense.

**merchant wholesaler**
Institution that buys goods from manufacturers and resells them to businesses, government agencies, and other wholesalers or retailers and that receives and takes title to goods, stores them in its own warehouses, and later reships them.

## MERCHANT WHOLESALERS

Slightly under 60 percent of all wholesale sales are conducted by merchant wholesalers, which make up 80 percent of all wholesaling establishments.[46] A **merchant wholesaler** is an institution that buys goods from manufacturers and resells them to businesses, government agencies, other wholesalers, or retailers. All merchant wholesalers take title to the goods they sell. Most merchant wholesalers operate one or more warehouses in which they receive goods, store them, and later reship them.

*Exhibit 12.9*

Factors Suggesting Type of Wholesaler to Use

Source: Reprinted by permission of the publisher from Donald M. Jackson and Michael F. d'Amico, "Products and Markets Served by Distributors and Agents," *Industrial Marketing Management*, February 1989, pp. 27–33. Copyright 1989 by Elsevier Science Inc.

| Factor | Merchant wholesalers | Agents or brokers |
|---|---|---|
| Nature of product | Standard | Nonstandard, custom |
| Technicality of product | Complex | Simple |
| Product's gross margin | High | Low |
| Frequency of ordering | Frequent | Infrequent |
| Time between order and receipt of shipment | Buyer desires shorter lead time | Buyer satisfied with long lead time |
| Number of customers | Many | Few |
| Concentration of customers | Dispersed | Concentrated |

Customers are mostly small- or moderate-size retailers, but merchant wholesalers also market to manufacturers and institutional clients. Merchant wholesalers can be categorized as either full-service or limited-service wholesalers, depending on the number of channel functions they perform (refer back to Exhibit 12.2).

## Full-Service Merchant Wholesalers

**full-service merchant wholesaler**
Wholesaler that assembles an assortment of products, provides credit for clients, offers promotional help and technical advice, maintains a sales force to contact customers, and delivers merchandise and that may offer research, planning, installation, and repair.

**Full-service merchant wholesalers** perform all channel functions. They assemble an assortment of products for their clients, provide credit, and offer promotional help and technical advice. In addition, they maintain a sales force to contact customers, store and deliver merchandise, and perhaps offer research and planning support. Depending on the product line, full-service merchant wholesalers sometimes provide installation and repair as well. *Full service* also means "going the extra mile" to meet special customer needs, such as offering fast delivery in emergencies.

**general merchandise wholesaler (full-line wholesaler)**
Wholesaler that stocks a full assortment of products within a product line.

Although they typically carry only one or two lines of merchandise, **general merchandise wholesalers** (or **full-line wholesalers**) stock a full assortment of products within the line. For instance, a hardware wholesaler will stock a full array of tools, paints, fasteners, ropes, chains, and so on. General merchandise wholesalers are common in the drug, grocery, and clothing markets in addition to the hardware market. SYSCO Corporation is one of the nation's largest full-line, full-service merchant wholesalers in the food-service distribution industry. The company supplies restaurants, nursing homes, hospitals, hotels, schools, colleges, and other customers with thousands of types of foods, cooking supplies, tableware, cleaning chemicals, and disposable products, ranging from caviar to chef's hats. SYSCO assembles these products from various manufacturers, stores and delivers them, and offers promotional assistance and technical advice through its sales force.

**specialty merchandise wholesaler**
Wholesaler that offers part of a product line to target customers but in greater depth than general merchandise wholesalers offer.

**Specialty merchandise wholesalers** offer part of a product line to target customers—for instance, a meat or seafood wholesaler as opposed to a grocery wholesaler. Specialty merchandise wholesalers usually offer much greater depth within the

SYSCO Corporation is the nation's largest full-service merchant wholesaler in the food-service distribution industry, with vast warehouses for storing goods and a large fleet of trucks for distributing them to customers.

Sysco Corporation

scope of the product line. For example, seafood wholesalers might carry unusual or exotic seafood. Specialty wholesalers usually have excellent product knowledge in their specialized line of merchandise, which can be very important. Suppose a sausage packing house needs to buy spices for a new brand of sausage and has to choose from hundreds of spices and combinations. A specialty wholesaler of spices can help make the correct choice.

**industrial distributor**
Full-service merchant wholesaler that sells to manufacturers rather than to retailers.

**Industrial distributors** can be described as full-service merchant wholesalers that sell to manufacturers rather than to retailers. Industrial wholesalers typically stock the following products:

- Maintenance, repair, and operating (MRO) supplies (such as hammers, paint, and replacement belts)
- Original equipment manufacturer (OEM) supplies (such as fasteners, power transmission components, hydraulic equipment, and small rubber parts that become part of a finished product)
- Equipment used in the operation of the business (such as hand tools, power tools, and conveyors)
- Machinery used in making raw materials and semifinished goods into finished products (such as grinders, stamping machines, and dryers)

Distributors that carry a general line or a wide assortment of industrial products are called "mill supply houses." Conversely, single-line industrial distributors offer expertise in one area, such as cutting tools or abrasives. Mill supply houses hold a larger piece of the market than single-line industrial distributors because of the economies of scale achieved by large mill supply houses. Buyers also prefer to have as few contracts for MRO supplies as possible, so they tend to choose vendors with broad product lines. Additionally, large mill supply houses can provide expertise rivaling that of single-line specialists.

**rack jobber**
Full-service wholesaler that performs the merchant wholesaler's functions and some usually carried out by the retailer, such as stocking shelves.

**Rack jobbers** perform the merchant wholesaler's functions along with some usually carried out by the retailer—namely, stocking nonfood merchandise on racks or shelves. Rack jobbers serve drug, grocery, and general merchandise retailers like Kmart and Target with such familiar products as hosiery, toys, housewares, and health and beauty aids. Rack jobbers typically sell on consignment, which means that they keep title to the goods and don't collect payment for the merchandise until it is sold. Rack jobbers hire delivery people to maintain inventory records, price the goods, and keep the merchandise fresh. In addition, they restock the racks or shelves and assemble promotional display materials.

**limited-service merchant wholesaler**
Wholesaler that performs only a few of the full-service merchant wholesaler's activities.

**cash-and-carry wholesaler**
Limited-service merchant wholesaler that sells for cash and usually carries a limited line of fast-moving merchandise.

**warehouse club**
Limited-service merchant wholesaler that sells a limited selection of brand-name appliances, household items, and groceries on a cash-and-carry basis to members, usually small businesses and groups.

## Limited-Service Merchant Wholesalers

As the name implies, **limited-service merchant wholesalers** perform only a few of the full-service merchant wholesaler's activities. Limited-service wholesalers represent just a small part of the merchant wholesaling industry.

The **cash-and-carry wholesaler** sells for cash and usually carries a limited line of fast-moving merchandise. Customers must go to the cash-and-carry wholesaler's warehouse and then transport the goods to their retail outlets. Cash-and-carry wholesalers do not make deliveries, extend credit, or supply market information. Compared to the prices charged by full-service wholesalers, the prices of cash-and-carry wholesalers are usually lower. However, retailers' total costs may be higher, because the retailers have to perform some wholesaling functions themselves.

Warehouse clubs are a special form of cash-and-carry wholesaler. A **warehouse club**

You might think that Sam's Club is a retailer, because it is patronized by a great many consumers. However, warehouse clubs can also be considered wholesalers, because they offer merchandise selected (and packaged) for utility to small businesses, which in turn may sell the merchandise to their customers.

sells a limited selection of brand-name appliances, household items, and groceries on a cash-and-carry basis to members, usually small businesses and groups. Members pay an annual membership fee. Merchandise is typically sold in bulk-size cartons or in smaller containers banded or wrapped together. For example, members can buy five-pound boxes of Velveeta cheese, cartons of 1,000 ketchup "tear-packs," or shrink-wrapped packages of a dozen boxes of pencils. Warehouse clubs carry a limited assortment of merchandise—for instance, high-volume office supplies like legal pads and copier paper. Small-business members must still shop at the traditional office supply store for some of their needs. The major warehouse club chains now operating in the United States are Price-Costco and Sam's Club (a division of Wal-Mart). Because warehouse clubs act as a wholesaler to small businesses and a retailer to group customers, this question arises: How should a warehouse club be classified? The answer: It is both a wholesaling and a retailing intermediary. Retail customers generally make up the largest number of patrons, but wholesale buyers account for most of the sales.

**truck jobber**
Limited-service merchant wholesaler that performs the functions of salesperson and delivery person.

The **truck jobber** combines the functions of salesperson and delivery person. Normally, truck jobbers carry a very limited line of semiperishable merchandise, such as milk, bread, snack foods, beer, and candy. Truck jobbers usually sell for cash. Their main customers are supermarkets, but they also serve hospitals, restaurants, factory refreshment shops, and hotels.

**drop shipper**
Limited-service merchant wholesaler that places orders for its customers with the manufacturer but does not physically handle the products it sells.

The **drop shipper** does not store or handle the products it sells. Instead, drop shippers place orders for their customers with the manufacturer, which then ships directly to the customers. Drop shippers are usually found in the bulk industries—for example, coal, lumber, bauxite, heavy equipment, and some agricultural products. Because of their weight, these items have high freight costs relative to their unit value. Direct shipment to customers thus makes sense. Like cash-and-carry wholesalers, drop shippers can offer lower prices, because they perform relatively few wholesale functions. In their case, warehousing and storage are eliminated. Drop shippers are still merchant wholesalers, however, even though they may never see the goods. They take title to the merchandise and therefore set the terms of the sale. Moreover, drop shippers arrange shipping and take the risks of ownership during shipment.

**mail-order wholesaler**
Limited-service merchant wholesaler that sells goods by catalog to businesses, institutions, government, and other organizations.

The **mail-order wholesaler** is the counterpart to the mail-order retailer. The only difference is that the mail-order wholesaler sells goods to businesses, institutions, government, and other organizations, whereas the mail-order retailer concentrates on consumers.

## AGENTS AND BROKERS

Agents and brokers represent retailers, wholesalers, or manufacturers and do not take title to the merchandise. Title reflects ownership, and ownership usually implies control. Unlike wholesalers, agents or brokers only facilitate sales and generally have little input into the terms of the sale. They do, however, get a fee or commission based on sales volume. Many perform fewer functions than limited-service merchant wholesalers.

*Exhibit 12.10*

Functions and Services Provided by Wholesaling Intermediaries

| Wholesaler type | **Contacting and promoting** ■ Sales force ■ Advertising | **Negotiating** ■ Establishing terms of sale | **Risk taking** ■ Ownership of inventory | **Physical distribution** ■ Storage and transportation | **Sorting** ■ Sorting out ■ Accumulation ■ Allocation ■ Assorting | **Research** ■ Market information | **Financing** ■ Credit |
|---|---|---|---|---|---|---|---|
| General merchandise wholesaler | ■ | ■ | ■ | ■ | ■ | ■ | ■ |
| Specialty merchandise wholesaler | ■ | ■ | ■ | ■ | ■ | ■ | ■ |
| Industrial distributor | ■ | ■ | ■ | ■ | ■ | ■ | ■ |
| Rack jobber | ■ | ■ | ■ | ■ | ■ | ■ | ■ |
| Cash-and-carry wholesaler | | ■ | ■ | Storage only | ■ | | |
| Warehouse club | ■ | | ■ | Storage only | ■ | | |
| Truck jobber | ■ | ■ | ■ | ■ | ■ | | |
| Drop shipper | ■ | ■ | ■ | * | | | ■ |
| Mail-order wholesaler | ■ | ■ | ■ | ■ | ■ | | |
| Broker | ■ | ■ | | * | | ■ | |
| Manufacturer's agent or representative | ■ | ■ | | * | | ■ | |
| Selling agent | ■ | ■ | | * | | ■ | |
| Manufacturer's sales branch | ■ | ■ | ■ | ■ | ■ | ■ | ■ |
| Manufacturer's sales office | ■ | ■ | ■ | | ■ | ■ | ■ |

*Coordination of transportation only

**broker**
Wholesaling intermediary that brings buyers and sellers together.

The function of a **broker** is to bring buyers and sellers together. Brokers exist in markets where these two parties would otherwise have trouble finding each other. Brokers do not usually handle the goods involved in the sale or finance either the buyer or seller. Their basic function is to represent the buyer or seller in finding another party to complete the transaction. Typically, a broker locates a potential buyer or seller (called a *principal*) and then lets the two parties resolve matters of price, quantity, delivery date, and specifications. Brokers receive a fee from the principal engaging their services.

**manufacturers' agent**
Wholesaling intermediary that represents one manufacturer or several manufacturers of complementary lines and follows the terms set by the manufacturer.

Like brokers, manufacturers' agents, sometimes called manufacturers' representatives, rarely have much voice in the terms of a sales contract. A **manufacturers' agent** represents one manufacturer, or several manufacturers of complementary lines, and follows the terms set by the manufacturer. Agents are paid on commission and therefore must be good salespeople. They generally have excellent product knowledge and understand customer preferences within their territory.

**selling agent**
Wholesaling intermediary used mostly by small firms on a commission basis and contracted to sell the manufacturer's entire output.

A final type of agent is a selling agent, which is used mostly by small firms. Actually, the term **selling agent** is somewhat misleading, because the agent usually assumes responsibility for the whole marketing operation of a company. In some industries, such as textiles, selling agents may even offer financial help to clients. Selling agents work on commission, usually contracting to sell the manufacturer's entire output.

Exhibit 12.10 summarizes the functions of all the types of wholesaling intermediaries just discussed. These functions correspond to those originally described in Exhibit 12.2.

## TRENDS IN WHOLESALING

Some large retailers find wholesaling intermediaries unnecessary. Although wholesalers were once vital links in the distribution pipeline, their value is now being questioned in such business segments as groceries, mass merchandising, pharmaceuticals, and industrial supplies. Manufacturers worry that wholesalers' markups will hinder their competitiveness. Retailers and end users feel their bargaining power is diminished when they can't deal directly with vendors.[47] Thus pressure is coming from both ends of the marketing channel. Even in Japan, many retailing entrepreneurs are slashing prices by avoiding wholesalers altogether. By purchasing goods directly from the manufacturer, efficient new retailers are able to sell their goods for two-thirds the department store price.[48]

Realizing that few of them will survive today on inventory alone, many savvy wholesalers are repositioning themselves as "value-added distributors" and playing more of a coordinating role between manufacturers and retailers. Wholesalers that can help identify and weigh distribution options, serve as the channel's information center, and at the same time reduce the delivered cost of product will be the winners in the future world of wholesaling.[49]

## LOOKING BACK

As you complete this chapter, you should be able to see how marketing channels operate and how channel members interact to move goods from the manufacturer to the final consumer. The structure of marketing channels often changes over time as marketers respond to changing consumer preferences. For example, as the opening story discussed, many beer manufacturers are pressuring regulatory bodies to let them use direct channels, where it is more profitable to do so, in an attempt to answer the consumer's need for low prices. You may also remember from the opening of the chapter that beer wholesalers originally enjoyed great power over retailers. However, the balance of power has now shifted from wholesaler to retailer. As you've discovered in this chapter, marketing channels and wholesalers play an important role in the marketing process.

## SUMMARY

**1 Explain what a marketing channel is and why intermediaries are needed.** Marketing channels are composed of members that perform negotiating functions. Some intermediaries buy and resell products; other intermediaries aid the exchange of ownership between buyers and sellers without taking title. Nonmember channel participants do not engage in negotiating activities and function as an auxiliary part of the marketing channel structure.

Wholesaler and retailer intermediaries are often included in marketing channels for three important reasons. First, the specialized expertise of intermediaries may improve the overall efficiency of marketing channels. Second, intermediaries may help overcome discrepancies by making products available in quantities and assortments desired by consumers and business buyers and at locations convenient to them. Third, intermediaries reduce the number of transactions required to distribute goods from producers to consumers and end users.

**2 Describe the functions and activities of marketing channel members.** Marketing channel members perform three basic types of functions. Transactional functions include contacting and promoting, negotiating, and risk taking. Logistical functions performed by channel members include physical distribution and sorting functions. Finally, channel members may perform facilitating functions, such as researching and financing.

**3 Discuss the differences between marketing channels for consumer and industrial products.** Marketing channels for consumer and business products vary in degree of complexity. The simplest consumer product channel involves direct selling from producers to consumers. Businesses may sell directly to business or government buyers. Marketing channels grow more complex as intermediaries become involved. Consumer product channel intermediaries include agents, brokers, wholesalers, and retailers. Business product channel intermediaries include agents, brokers, and industrial distributors.

**4 Describe alternative channel arrangements.** Marketers often use alternative channel arrangements to move their products to the consumer. With dual distribution or multiple distribution, they choose two or more different channels to distribute the same product. Nontraditional channels help differentiate a firm's product

### KEY TERMS

from the competitor's or provide a manufacturer with another avenue for sales. Strategic channel alliances are arrangements that use another manufacturer's already-established channel. Finally, reverse channels exist when products move in the opposite direction of traditional channels—from consumer back to the producer. Reverse channels are often used for products that require repair or recycling.

5 **Discuss what vertical marketing systems are and how they differ from conventional marketing channels.** Conventional marketing channels are typically loosely aligned and lack coordination among independent manufacturers, wholesalers, and retailers. In contrast, vertical marketing systems consist of producers and intermediaries acting as a unified system. There are three types of vertical marketing system: corporate, contractual, and administered.

6 **Explain the concepts of power and conflict within marketing channels.** Power, control, leadership, and conflict are the main social dimensions of marketing channel relationships. Channel *power* refers to the capacity of one channel member to control or influence other channel members. Channel power can be based on reward or categorized as coercive, legitimate, referent, or expert power. Channel *control* occurs when one channel member intentionally affects another member's behavior. Channel *leadership* is the exercise of authority and power. Sources of channel *conflict* include goal incompatibility, role incongruence, communication breakdowns, and differing perspectives and ideologies. Channel conflict can be either horizontal, among channel members at the same level, or vertical, among channel members at different levels of the channel. Channel control practices that may be affected by law include exclusive dealing, tying contracts, refusal to deal, resale restrictions, and exclusive territories.

7 **Discuss the issues that influence channel strategy.** When determining marketing channel strategy, the marketing manager must determine what market, product, and producer factors will influence the choice of channel. The manager must also determine the appropriate level of distribution intensity.

8 **List the steps in designing marketing channels.** The marketing channel design process consists of three major steps: (1) identifying channel alternatives, (2) evaluating and selecting channels, and (3) selecting channel participants. Criteria for identifying channel alternatives include access to end users, prevailing distribution practices, and necessary activities and functions. Channel evaluation and selection are based on revenue and cost analyses, development time, control considerations, and channel availability. Finally, considerations for selecting channel participants are market coverage, compatibilities, intermediaries' needs, functions provided, and availability factors.

9 **Discuss channel structure and decisions in global markets.** Global marketing channels are becoming more important to U.S. companies seeking growth abroad. Manufacturers introducing products in foreign countries must decide what type of channel structure to use—in particular, whether the product should be marketed through direct channels or through foreign intermediaries. Marketers should be

*forward integration* 382
*full-service merchant wholesaler* 401
*general merchandise wholesaler (full-line wholesaler)* 401
*gray marketing* 389
*horizontal conflict* 387
*industrial distributor* 402
*intensive distribution* 392
*limited-service merchant wholesaler* 402
*mail-order wholesaler* 404
*manufacturers' agent* 405
*marketing channel (channel of distribution)* 373
*merchant wholesaler* 400
*rack jobber* 402
*refusal to deal* 389
*resale restriction* 389
*retailer* 373
*reverse channel* 381
*selective distribution* 392
*selling agent* 405
*spatial discrepancy* 374
*specialty merchandise wholesaler* 401
*strategic channel alliance* 380
*temporal discrepancy* 374
*truck jobber* 403
*tying contract* 389
*vertical conflict* 387
*vertical marketing system (VMS)* 381
*warehouse club* 402
*wholesaler* 373

aware that channel structures in foreign markets may be very different from those they are accustomed to in the United States.

10 **List the types of firms that perform wholesaling activities, and explain their functions.** Wholesalers are classified into two basic categories: merchant wholesalers, and agents and brokers. *Merchant wholesalers* are independent businesses that take title to goods and assume ownership risk. Full-service merchant wholesalers perform all channel functions and include general merchandise wholesalers, specialty merchandise wholesalers, industrial distributors, and rack jobbers. As their name suggests, limited-service merchant wholesalers perform only a few of the channel functions; this classification includes cash-and-carry wholesalers, warehouse clubs, truck jobbers, drop shippers, and mail-order wholesalers. *Agents and brokers* facilitate sales but do not take title to goods or set sales conditions. Brokers bring buyers and sellers together, whereas agents function as salespeople for one particular manufacturer or several manufacturers of complementary product lines.

## Discussion and Writing Questions

1. Describe the most likely distribution channel for each of these consumer products: candy bars, Tupperware products, nonfiction books, new automobiles, farmer's market produce, and stereo equipment.
2. List three reasons for redesigning marketing channels. Illustrate your answer with specific examples.
3. When Procter & Gamble instituted everyday low pricing in place of various discounts to wholesalers and retailers, what kind of channel power was it exercising? Discuss the implications of P&G's action.
4. If you were a retailer, how might you respond to coercive behavior on the part of large manufacturing companies? Describe your reaction in the form of a letter to the president of one of the offending firms.
5. Identify the types of wholesalers that would be most likely to carry the following goods: fresh produce, industrial machinery, expensive wines, lumber, and agricultural fertilizer. Justify your choices.
6. Describe the distribution channel for some product you are familiar with. Explain why you think the channel is structured as you describe it.
7. Describe a current example of channel conflict that is not discussed in the chapter. Imagine that you are one of the participants in the conflict, and write a letter to the other channel members proposing a resolution.
8. You have been hired to design a distribution channel for a new firm specializing in the manufacturing and marketing of novelties for college student organizations. In a memo to the president of the firm, describe how the channel operates.

## Application for Small Business

Boudreaux has owned and operated a small spice-manufacturing business in south Louisiana for about ten years. Boudreaux has also experimented with preparing and selling several sauces, mostly for meats and salads. For the most part, his firm has sold its products locally. But on occasion, distributors have signed contracts to sell Boudreaux's products regionally.

Boudreaux's most recent product—a spicy Cajun mayonnaise—has been a huge success locally, and several inquiries have come from large distributors about the possibilities of selling the mayonnaise regionally and perhaps nationally. No research has been conducted to determine the level or scope of demand for the mayonnaise. Also, it has been packaged and sold in only a twelve-ounce bottle. The red-and-white label just says "Boudreaux's Cajun Mayonnaise" and lists the major ingredients.

Questions

1. What should Boudreaux do to help the firm decide how best to market the new Cajun mayonnaise?

2. Should Boudreaux sign a contract with one of the distributors to sell the Cajun mayonnaise, or should his firm try to sell the product directly to one or more of the major supermarket chains?

## CRITICAL THINKING CASE

### Perrier

Perrier sparkling water had a 57 percent share of the U.S. designer water market in 1988. In February 1990 a problem in the company's filtration system caused the product to become contaminated with benzene, a minor carcinogen. The company chose to fully disclose the facts, accept full responsibility, and recall $70 million worth of sparkling water.

In April 1990 Perrier was about to resume shipping its product to the United States. Kim Jeffrey, senior vice president of marketing, expected Perrier to be in 90 percent of the U.S. market within six weeks. For each new market entered, Perrier had scheduled a two-week media blitz to announce the reintroduction of the product. The campaign was called We're Back. Perrier also scheduled sales promotion activities to tie in with the ad campaign. In the fifteen largest markets, workers in Perrier Cafes wore We're Back apparel to pass out samples. Perrier saw advertising and promotions as a major way to reestablish its market position, and so it increased its advertising budget fourfold to $25 million.

According to Jeffrey, the key to the success of the reintroduction was going to be distribution. Lost shelf space was going to have to be recaptured in the supermarkets. Perrier had never paid a retailer for shelf space, a common industry practice, and did not intend to do so now. Space for the product was expected to come from space that retailers had saved for the Perrier brand by stocking it with other Perrier products. Some retailers felt Perrier's high profit margin (18 to 20 percent) would more than compensate for using the shelf space. Others insisted that Perrier not only would have to pay to get the shelf space back but also would have to spend a lot of money on advertising and sales promotion.

Restaurateurs were another major stumbling block for Perrier. After Perrier's "perfect and pure" product image had been tarnished, it became just one of several bottled waters vying for restaurants' and diners' attention. Perrier sparkling water had had about a third of the total bar and restaurant market in 1989. Some restaurants took the Perrier brand back and offered two brands of designer water to diners; others would not take the Perrier brand back at all. In the end, restaurateurs were influenced by consumer demand. If they got enough requests for Perrier, restaurants were willing to stock it.

Consumer research at the time indicated that 85 percent of Perrier customers would buy the product again. Ninety percent of consumers felt that by admitting its mistake, Perrier had acted responsibly. These figures led Perrier management to believe that the company could recapture 85 percent of its sales by the end of 1991. Although by the end of 1991 most of Perrier's heavy users had come back, random users had dropped off. In 1992 bottled water sales grew by 3.2 percent. Perrier was still the top brand, but market share had fallen from a high of 70 percent to 40 percent. Perrier was having image problems, and new drinkers were turning to newer products.

By late 1993 Perrier had managed to regain most of its distribution in supermarkets but was still struggling in restaurants, bars, and clubs. Although Perrier's comeback was slower than anticipated, prospects for the future still appeared bright, with a renewed focus on image, packaging, advertising, and distribution. The company has a strong market position, bolstered by its acquisition in 1992 by Nestlé, a Swiss food conglomerate.

Questions

1. What type of advertising strategy should Perrier use to regain its market share? Why?

2. Many feel that the distribution channel contributes to the success or failure of a product. Is it important for Perrier?

3. Should Perrier pay channel members to carry the Perrier brand? What potential problems would arise from this decision?

Suggested Readings

Daniel Butler, "Perrier's Painful Period," *Management Today,* August 1990, pp. 72–73.

Bruce Crumley, "Perrier: Heavy Users Came Back," *Advertising Age,* 21 October 1991, p. 36.

Mike Johnson, "Pumping Perrier into the 90s," *Marketing,* 11 June 1992, pp. 22–23.

Gary Kurzbard and George Siomkos, "Crafting a Damage Control Plan," *Journal of Business Strategy,* March–April 1992, pp. 39–43.

Mark Landler and Lisa Driscoll, "You Can Lead a Restaurateur to Perrier, But . . .," *Business Week,* 25 June 1990, pp. 25–26.

Barbara Lippert, "Perrier Is Reformulated for a New Era," *Adweek's Marketing Week,* 7 May 1990, p. 69.

"Perrier Aims to Recapture Lost Young Drinkers," *Marketing,* 4 March 1994, p. 1.

Greg Prince, "Back, Back, Back, Back . . .," *Beverage World,* March 1994, pp. 72–80.

Patricia Sellers, "Perrier Plots Its Comeback," *Fortune,* 23 April 1990, pp. 277–278.

Patricia Winters, "Perrier's Back," *Advertising Age,* 23 April 1990, p. 22.

**VIDEO CASE**

## Lillian Vernon

Lillian Vernon is a thriving catalog business on the rise with big plans for expansion in its future. The business, which generates over $160 million in annual revenues, successfully competes in an industry that has grown into a $230 billion annual business, with names like L.L. Bean, Lands' End, Sharper Image, and others. Lillian Vernon, named after its founder, was started at her kitchen table when she was only 22 years old, with a $2,000 wedding gift. She placed a $495 ad in *Seventeen* magazine, which offered free personalization of a purse or belt and generated over $32,000 in orders.

The Lillian Vernon catalog is designed to appeal to the thrifty-minded, and in a typical year the company will ship more than 4.5 million orders. Indeed, during the Christmas season it processes over 50,000 items a day through its national distribution center in Virginia Beach, Virginia. Compared to other catalogs that offer much-higher-cost merchandise (average order size for Lands' End is $90; for Sharper Image, $140; for Crate & Barrel, $65), Lillian Vernon's average item cost is less than $20, and the average order size is only about $40. The Lillian Vernon secret is to offer customers high-quality merchandise, such as household, gardening, decorative, and children's products, at exceptionally good values.

Much of the success of Lillian Vernon and other specialty catalog operators is due to capable management and astute marketing. But a lot has to do with responding to demographic and social trends. More women are working or returning to the work force than ever before, and catalogs provide a valuable service by offering them more time to spend with their families and the convenience of shopping at home by mail, phone, or fax—twenty-four hours a day, 365 days a year. There is a growing senior market, many with mobility problems due to poor health. And the recent increase in carjackings and crime in mall parking lots has made it more appealing to shop from the safety of the home. Indeed, the Direct Marketing

Association estimates that almost 60 percent of the adult population orders merchandise by phone, fax, or mail on an annual basis. This is a 70 percent increase over the last decade.

Lillian Vernon has been a true catalog success story. According to founder Lillian Vernon, the company is successful because of its targeted marketing strategy (90 percent of its customers are women), the larger selection of exclusive, inexpensively priced merchandise, the focus on customer satisfaction, and the ability to learn what its customers want. Merchandising decisions are based on a formal market research process, including focus groups and customer surveys, and marketers also go to stores to see what is in the marketplace.

Questions

1. How have catalog companies like Lillian Vernon competed successfully with tradional retailers?
2. What other developments have helped its success?
3. Is the growth of catalog retailers likely to continue?

# CHAPTER 13

# RETAILING

## LEARNING OBJECTIVES

*After studying this chapter, you should be able to*

1 *Discuss the importance of retailing in the U.S. economy.*

2 *Explain the dimensions by which retailers can be classified.*

3 *Describe the major types of retail operations.*

4 *Discuss nonstore retailing techniques.*

5 *Describe the nature of franchising.*

6 *List the major tasks involved in developing a retail marketing strategy.*

7 *Explain the wheel of retailing and the retail life cycle.*

8 *Describe future trends in retailing.*

9 *Discuss present problems in retailing.*

Music lovers are finding it more fun to visit music stores these days. No longer are store interiors just rows and rows of compact discs and tapes, filed in alphabetical order. Instead, music stores are organizing their products better and, in the process , have become quite entertaining.

Music retailers have compelling reasons to revise their retailing strategies. Although total sales of recorded music have been growing by about 15 percent annually, music stores' share of music purchases has been steadily dropping since 1990. Many music buyers find purchasing music selections out of a catalog easier than visiting a store. And music retailing's prime market, the 24-year-old-and-under crowd, has decreased 12 percent since 1988. After finding that over half of the people who enter music stores leave without buying—48 percent of them because they couldn't find the music they wanted—music stores decided they were due for a major change.

One big change is an expansion in what a store carries. Some music retailers are opening "megastores" that carry close to 100,000 music titles—compared with the 30,000 to 50,000 normally carried in stand-alone stores—along with videos, books, and even video-game software. Minneapolis-based Musicland Stores is the largest U.S. music store chain, with over 870 stores. Its megastore, called Media Play, has lots of interaction and such attractions as cafes, popcorn machines, and couches for those who might want to sit and read. Other megastores are experimenting with unconventional alliances, combining with youth-oriented merchants like apparel stores and pizza restaurants. Some have amphitheaters for live performances and in-store radio stations.

To lure more shoppers into the stores, many music retailers are turning to listening posts, evolved from the 1950s listening booth, and multimedia music-previewing systems. The aim is both to entertain shoppers and to get them to buy not only the music they came for but also the tunes they hear in the store. Musicland is testing a hand-held system that uses a computerized listening device resembling a cellular phone. A shopper runs the device's sensor over an album's bar code and then holds the device to the ear to listen to three songs. The music is fed to the device from a central computer carrying as many as 20,000 different albums.

Tower Records, a music store chain based in

California, allows shoppers to preview new music selections through Tower CD listening stations. Each station is a multidisc CD player that can hold twelve albums. A remote-control panel allows shoppers to listen to any track for as long as they want.

The most technologically advanced of the computerized listening and previewing devices is the "i-station," which resembles an automatic teller machine. I-stations can hold 75,000 CD-quality albums. An i-station is activated with a card or the bar code on a CD or cassette. The shopper uses headphones to listen to up to five thirty-second cuts per album and can view full-color music videos. An i-station can call up the latest release or scan through a group's entire repertoire.[1]

In today's fiercely competitive industry, music retailers are struggling to find fresh ways to woo shoppers. Consumers increasingly think of shopping as a chore. To counteract this perception, music stores are seeking to entertain customers as well as to make shopping easier. What other factors would be important to a music store's retailing mix? What special skills should its sales personnel possess?

*1 Discuss the importance of retailing in the U.S. economy.*

**retailing**
All activities directly related to the sale of goods and services to the ultimate consumer for personal, nonbusiness use or for consumption.

## THE ROLE OF RETAILING

**Retailing**—all the activities directly related to the sale of goods and services to the ultimate consumer for personal, nonbusiness use—has enhanced the quality of our daily lives. When we shop for groceries, hair styling, clothes, legal advice, books, and many other products and services, we are involved in retailing. The millions of goods and services provided by retailers mirror the needs and styles of U.S. society.

Retailing affects all of us directly or indirectly. The retailing industry is one of the largest employers; over 2 million U.S. retailers employ about 19 million people. Retailers ring up over $1.9 trillion in sales annually.[2]

Although most retailers are quite small, a few giant organizations dominate the industry. Fewer than 10 percent of all retail establishments account for over half of total retail sales and employ about 40 percent of all retail workers. Who are these giants? Exhibit 13.1 lists the ten largest U.S. retailers.

*2 Explain the dimensions by which retailers can be classified.*

## CLASSIFICATION OF RETAIL OPERATIONS

A retail establishment can be classified according to its ownership, level of service, product assortment, and price. Specifically, retailers use the latter three variables to position themselves in the competitive marketplace. (As noted in Chapter 6, positioning is the strategy used to influence how consumers perceive one product in relation to all competing products.) These three variables can be combined in several ways to create distinctly different retail operations. Exhibit 13.2 on page 416 lists the major types of retail stores discussed in this chapter and classifies them by level of service, product assortment, and price.

### OWNERSHIP

Retailers can be broadly classified by form of ownership: independent, part of a chain, or a franchise outlet. Retailers owned by a single person or partnership and

*Exhibit 13.1*

Ten Largest U.S. Retailers

Source "Fortune's Service 500: The 50 Largest Retailers," *Fortune*, 30 May 1994, pp. 214–215. © 1994 Time Inc. All rights reserved Sears' retail-only sales from company 10-K report (31 December 1993).

| 1993 Rank | Company | Sales (in billions) | Employees (in thousands) |
|---|---|---|---|
| 1 | Wal-Mart Stores (Bentonville, Ark.) | $67 | 520 |
| 2 | Kmart (Troy, Mich.) | 34 | 344 |
| 3 | Sears Roebuck (Chicago) | 30 | 309 |
| 4 | Kroger (Cincinnati) | 22 | 190 |
| 5 | JCPenney (Plano, Tex.) | 20 | 192 |
| 6 | Dayton Hudson (Minneapolis) | 19 | 174 |
| 7 | American Stores (Salt Lake City) | 19 | 127 |
| 8 | Safeway (Oakland) | 15 | 106 |
| 9 | Albertson's (Boise) | 11 | 75 |
| 10 | May Department Stores (St. Louis) | 11 | 113 |

| Type of retailer | Level of service | Product assortment | Price | Gross margin |
|---|---|---|---|---|
| Department store | High | Broad | Moderate to high | Moderately high |
| Mass merchandiser | Moderately high | Broad | Moderate | Moderate |
| Specialty store | Moderately high to high | Narrow | Moderate to high | High |
| Supermarket | Low | Broad | Moderate | Low |
| Convenience store | Moderately low | Medium to narrow | Moderately high | Moderately high |
| Discount store | Moderate to low | Medium to broad | Moderately low | Moderately low |
| Off-price retailer | Low | Medium to narrow | Low | Low |
| Factory outlet | Low | Very narrow | Very low | Low |
| Warehouse club | Low | Broad | Low to very low | Low |

*Exhibit 13.2*

Types of Stores and Their Characteristics

not operated as part of a larger retail institution are **independent retailers.** Around the world, most retailers are independent, operating one or a few stores in their community. Local florists, shoe stores, and ethnic food markets typically fit this classification.

**independent retailer**
Individual or partnership that owns one or several retail establishments that are not part of a larger retail organization.

**chain store**
Retail store that is one of a group owned and operated by a single corporation with central authority.

**franchise outlet**
Retail store owned and operated by an individual who is a licensee of a larger supporting organization.

**Chain stores** are owned and operated as a group by a single organization. Under this form of ownership, many administrative tasks are handled by the home office for the entire chain. The home office also buys most of the merchandise sold in the stores.

**Franchise outlets** are owned and operated by individuals but are licensed by a larger supporting organization. Franchising combines the advantages of independent ownership with those of the chain store organization. Franchising is discussed in detail later in this chapter.

## LEVEL OF SERVICE

The level of service that retailers provide can be classified along a continuum, from full service to self-service. Some retailers, such as exclusive clothing stores, offer high levels of service. They provide alterations, credit, delivery, consulting, liberal return policies, layaway, gift wrapping, and personal shopping. Discount stores usually offer fewer services, and even these are often limited. Retailers like factory outlets and warehouse clubs offer virtually no services.

## PRODUCT ASSORTMENT

The third basis for positioning or classifying stores is by the breadth and depth of their product line (discussed more fully in Chapter 9). Specialty stores—for example, Hallmark card stores, Lady Foot Locker, and TCBY yogurt shops—are the most concentrated in their product assortment, usually carrying single or narrow product lines but in considerable depth. Mass merchandisers (Sears and Montgomery Ward) and department stores (Bloomingdale's, Macy's, and Marshall Field's) may have a product assortment of considerable breadth but with depth in only some product lines.

Discounters like Kmart, Wal-Mart, and Target carry broad assortments of merchandise with limited depth. For example, Target carries automotive supplies, household cleaning products, and pet food. However, Target may carry only four or five brands of canned dog food; a supermarket may carry as many as twenty. Other retailers, such as factory outlet stores, may carry only part of a single line. Liz Claiborne, a major manufacturer of women's clothing, sells only its own brand in its many outlet stores.

### PRICE

Price is a fourth way to position retail stores. Traditional department stores and specialty stores typically charge the full "suggested retail price." Discounters, factory outlets, and off-price retailers use low prices as a major lure for shoppers.

**gross margin**
Amount of money the retailer makes, stated as a percentage of sales, after the cost of goods sold is subtracted.

The last column in Exhibit 13.2 shows the typical gross margin for each type of store. **Gross margin** is how much the retailer makes as a percentage of sales after the cost of goods sold is subtracted. The level of gross margin and the price level generally match. For example, a traditional jewelry store has high prices and high gross margins. A factory outlet has low prices and low gross margins. Supermarkets are the exception to this general rule, especially when competition is intense. Price wars among competing supermarkets, in which stores lower prices on certain items in an effort to win customers, cause gross margins to decline. When Wal-Mart entered the grocery business in a small Arkansas community, for example, a fierce price war ensued. By the time the price war was in full swing, the price of a quart of milk had plummeted to 58¢ (below the price of a pint) and a loaf of bread sold for only 9¢.[3]

3 *Describe the major types of retail operations.*

## MAJOR TYPES OF RETAIL OPERATIONS

There are several types of retail stores. Each offers a different product assortment and service and price level, according to its customers' shopping preferences.

### DEPARTMENT STORES

**department store**
Retailer that carries a wide variety of shopping and specialty goods, including apparel, cosmetics, housewares, electronics, and sometimes furniture.

**buyer**
Person who selects the merchandise for retail stores and may also be responsible for promotion and for personnel.

Housing several departments under one roof, a **department store** carries a wide variety of shopping and specialty goods, including apparel, cosmetics, housewares, electronics, and sometimes furniture. Each department is treated as a separate buying center to achieve economies in promotion, buying, service, and control. Each department is usually headed by a **buyer**, who not only selects the merchandise for his or her department but may also be responsible for promotion and for personnel. For a consistent, uniform store image, central management sets broad policies about the types of merchandise carried and price ranges. Central management is also responsible for the overall advertising program, credit policies, store expansion, customer service, and so on. The buyer within each department is relatively free to operate within top management's guidelines and policies.

Because of their size and buying power, most department stores buy directly from manufacturers. Sometimes the manufacturer produces merchandise under the store's brand name (see Chapter 9). Some department stores have so much buying strength that they dominate small manufacturers, dictating manufacturers' profit margins, delivery dates, merchandise specifications, and transportation methods. This arrangement is a major shift in channel power from the manufacturer to the retailer (see Chapter 12).

Large independent department stores are rare today. Most are owned by national chains. The four largest U.S. department store chains are Dayton-Hudson, May

Department Stores, Federated Department Stores, and R.H. Macy. All operate more than one chain of retail stores, from discount chains to upscale clothiers.[4] Two up-and-coming department store chains are Dillard's, based in Little Rock, Arkansas, and Nordstrom, with corporate headquarters in Seattle. Until recently, both chains were family owned, but they are now listed on the New York Stock Exchange. Dillard's is known for its distribution expertise; Nordstrom offers innovative customer service. In the past few years, much attention has been centered on these two growing chains, and both have a very promising future.

Each year brings a dramatic new event to the department store sector of retailing. Consumers of the late 1980s witnessed the chaos of corporate takeovers, mergers, and acquisitions among the nation's largest and most widely recognized department store chains. Retail giants such as Bloomingdale's, Saks Fifth Avenue, and Marshall Field's were among the many put up for sale because of oversized debt and sluggish consumer demand. Many others were forced to cut expenses drastically to pay off debt. In the process, they became less innovative and in some cases were forced out of business.

In the 1990s, consumers became more cost-conscious and value-oriented. Specialty retailers like The Gap, discounters, and even catalog outlets capitalized on the department stores' plight by offering superior merchandise selection and presentation, sharper pricing, and greater convenience. They have also been quicker to adopt new technology and invest in labor-saving strategies. In addition, their leaner cost structure translates into lower prices for the customer. Meanwhile, manufacturers like Liz Claiborne, Calvin Klein, and Ralph Lauren have opened outlet stores of their own, taking more sales away from department stores.

Department store managers are using several strategies to preserve their market share. One is to reposition department stores as specialty outlets. They are dividing departments into miniboutiques, each featuring a distinct fashion taste, as specialty stores do. Department stores are also enhancing customer service to shift the focus from price. Services include complimentary alterations, longer store hours, personalized attention, after-sale follow-up, and personal wardrobe planning. Finally, department stores are expanding, remodeling, and revitalizing to show off new merchandising directions and to reflect the growth in their marketing areas.

## MASS MERCHANDISERS

Like department stores, mass merchandisers like Sears, JCPenney, and Montgomery Ward have wide product assortments. What distinguishes them from regular department store chains is their sheer size in terms of sales volume and number of stores. **Mass merchandising** is the retailing strategy of using moderate to low prices on large quantities of merchandise, coupled with big promotion budgets, to stimulate high turnover of products. The larger mass merchandisers are also vertically integrated; they own either all or part of many of the manufacturers that supply their merchandise, enabling them to control costs and distribution more effectively.

**mass merchandising**
Retailing strategy of using moderate to low prices on most merchandise, coupled with big promotion budgets, to stimulate high turnover of products.

Because Sears and JCPenney cover most of the U.S. market geographically, network TV advertising is both feasible and economical for them. One ad broadcast on national TV reaches many of their customers. Heavy national TV exposure also gives them name identification and a strong company image. Network promotion usually centers on high-margin, dealer-brand items—for example, Sears Diehard batteries or Road Handler steel-belted radial tires.

During the past several years, both Sears and JCPenney have gained only slightly in sales, while their overall earnings have declined. Sears was the leading U.S. retailer until it was overtaken by Wal-Mart and Kmart in the late 1980s. JCPenney also enjoyed a strong retail position in years past but has since given way to niche merchandisers with strong target-marketing strategies. Many believe the era of the general mass merchandiser has passed.

Responding to this bleak outlook, Sears and JCPenney have searched for new strategies and market niches. In an ambitious program to reposition itself into a competitive, moderate-priced department store, Sears has increased the amount of store space dedicated to clothes and home fashions and deemphasized tools and appliances.[5] In a similar effort, JCPenney's management redefined its target market to include more upscale consumers. The chain stopped selling hard goods like furniture, sporting goods, major appliances, and hardware and instead concentrated on the major profit makers of department stores: clothing, jewelry, and cosmetics. Stores were also remodeled to appeal to upscale consumers.

Sears and JCPenney are also looking for growth in foreign markets to make up for stagnant growth at home. Sears has been quite successful in Mexico. Although the retailer has been present in Mexico since the late 1940s, it has boosted sales in the last several years by upgrading its stores to appeal to Mexico's affluent consumers. Sears de Mexico stores feature marble floors and subdued lighting and upscale fragrances, shoes, and fashions.[6] JCPenney, meanwhile, is constructing stores in Mexico and adding nearly a million square feet of retail space in Japan by offering its private-label apparel in 300 department stores owned by Aoyama Trading Company, Japan's largest retailer of men's suits. JCPenney is also studying its prospects for retail locations in Chile, Greece, Taiwan, and Thailand.[7]

## SPECIALTY STORES

**specialty store**
Retail store specializing in a given type of merchandise.

Specialty stores are becoming more common as retailers refine their segmentation strategies and tailor their merchandise to specific target markets. A **specialty store** is not only a type of store but also a method of retail operations—namely, specializing in a given type of merchandise. Examples include children's clothing, men's clothing, candy, baked goods, sporting goods, and pet supplies. A typical specialty store carries a deeper but narrower assortment of merchandise in its specialty than a department store does. Generally, specialty stores' knowledgeable sales clerks offer more attentive customer service. The format has become very powerful in the apparel market and other areas. Benetton, Waldenbooks, Victoria's Secret, The Body Shop, Foot Locker, and Crate & Barrel are several successful specialty retailers.

Consumers in specialty outlets usually consider price to be secondary. Instead, the distinctive merchandise, the store's physical appearance, and the caliber of the staff determine its popularity. Manufacturers often favor selling their goods in small specialty stores rather than in the larger retailers and department stores. The manufacturer of the popular Thomas the Tank Engine toys, for example, withdrew its line of toys from big retailers like Toys R Us and offered it instead to mom-and-pop stores and other small specialty retailers. Selling through specialty toy stores creates an image of exclusivity for Thomas the Tank. Small specialty shops also provide a low-risk testing ground for new toy concepts.[8]

## SUPERMARKETS

**supermarket**
Large, departmentalized, self-service retailer that specializes in foodstuffs and a few nonfood items.

U.S. consumers spend about 8 percent of their disposable income in supermarkets.[9] A **supermarket** is a large, departmentalized, self-service retailer that specializes in food and some nonfood items.

A decade ago, industry experts predicted the decline of the supermarket industry,

Today's supermarkets often compete with other types of retailers, such as superstores and discounters, by adding specialty departments.

© 1989 Michael Melford/The Image Bank

whose slim profit margins of just 1 to 2 percent of sales left it vulnerable. Supermarkets would need an ever-growing customer base to sustain volume and compensate for low margins, they said. But annual population growth is averaging less than 1 percent a year.

Population trends and a glut of supermarkets have prompted supermarket experts to look more closely at demographic and lifestyle changes. They have discovered several trends affecting their industry. For example, consumers are eating out more. Of the $500 billion or so that consumers spend on food products annually, only half is spent on food prepared at home, a decline from 70 percent in 1965. If this trend continues, spending on restaurants and takeout food will overtake the nation's grocery bill by 1996. This growth in the away-from-home food market has been driven by the entry of more women into the work force and their need for convenience and time-saving products.[10] Working couples need one-stop shopping, and the increasing number of affluent customers are willing to pay for specialty and prepared foods.

As stores seek to meet consumer demand for one-stop shopping, conventional supermarkets are being replaced by bigger *superstores,* which are usually twice the size of supermarkets. Superstores meet the needs of today's customers for convenience, variety, and service. Superstores offer one-stop shopping for many food and nonfood needs, as well as many services—including pharmacies, flower shops, salad bars, in-store bakeries, takeout food sections, sit-down restaurants, health food sections, video rentals, dry-cleaning services, shoe repair, photo processing, and banking. Some even offer family dentistry or optical shops. Offering a wide variety of nontraditional goods and services under one roof is called **scrambled merchandising.**

**scrambled merchandising**
Practice of offering a wide variety of nontraditional goods and services in one store.

Another trend affecting supermarkets is consumers' focus on value. They have increasingly turned to warehouse clubs and discounters, which stock food staples at rock-bottom prices. Discounters like Wal-Mart and Kmart have added produce, meats, and bakeries; at the same time, supermarkets are now stocking more club-pack products, such as twelve-roll bundles of toilet paper, twenty-four-can cases of soft drinks, and cereal multipacks. As the distinction between these different types of retailers blurs, price usually becomes the focal point. Double and triple coupons, everyday low pricing, and price promotions have intensified the price wars.

Many supermarket chains are tailoring marketing strategies to appeal to specific consumer segments for an advantage over competitors that attempt to attract customers solely on the basis of low prices. By offering greater convenience and a broad variety of products, particularly in perishables and service departments, supermarkets are finding a way to stand out in an increasingly crowded marketplace. Supermarkets are also giving more shelf space to private-label products (see Chapter 9), which are priced far less than comparable brand-name goods.[11]

## CONVENIENCE STORES

**convenience store**
Miniature supermarket, carrying only a limited line of high-turnover convenience goods.

A **convenience store** can be defined as a miniature supermarket, carrying only a limited line of high-turnover convenience goods. These self-service stores are typically located near residential areas and are open twenty-four hours, seven days a week. Convenience stores offer exactly what their name implies: convenient location, long hours, fast service. However, prices are usually higher at a convenience store than at a supermarket. Thus the customer pays for the convenience.

From the mid-1970s to the mid-1980s, hundreds of new convenience stores opened, many with self-service gas pumps. Full-service gas stations fought back by closing service bays and opening miniature stores of their own, selling convenience items like cigarettes, sodas, and snacks. Supermarkets and discount stores also wooed customers with one-stop shopping and quick checkout. To combat the gas stations' and supermarkets' competition, convenience store operators have changed their strategy. They have expanded their offerings of nonfood items with video rentals, health and beauty aids, upscale sandwich and salad lines, and more fresh produce. Some convenience stores are even selling Pizza Hut and Taco Bell products prepared in the store.

## DISCOUNT STORES

**discount store**
Retail store that is one of a group competing on the basis of low prices, high turnover, and high volume.

A **discount store** is a retailer that competes on the basis of low prices, high turnover, and high volume. The discount industry has mushroomed into a major force in retailing, in part because of cautious spending by consumers brought about by the recession of the 1990s and changing demographics and priorities. The discounter of the 1960s focused solely on a full line of merchandise, but today discounters can be classified into four major categories: full-line discount retailers, discount specialty retailers, warehouse clubs, and off-price retailers.

### Full-Line Discounters

Compared to traditional department stores, full-line discount stores offer consumers very limited service and carry a much broader assortment of well-known, nationally branded "hard goods," including housewares, toys, automotive parts, hardware, sporting goods, and garden items, as well as clothing, bedding, and linens. Some even carry limited nonperishable food items, such as soft drinks, canned goods, and potato chips. As with department stores, national chains dominate the discounters.

Wal-Mart is the largest discount organization, with over 2,100 stores. Wal-Mart has expanded rapidly by locating stores on the outskirts of small towns and absorbing business for miles around. Much of Wal-Mart's success has been attributed to its merchandising foresight, cost-consciousness, efficient communication and distribution systems, and involved, motivated employees. The company expects to add over 100 new stores annually, increasing its revenues by 20 percent. Wal-Mart is now bigger than Kmart and Sears combined and nearly as big as the entire U.S. department store industry.[12]

Besides expanding throughout the United States, Wal-Mart has global expansion plans for Mexico, Canada, Puerto Rico, Brazil, Argentina, and China. Retailing abroad has proved to be quite a challenge for the giant discounter. In Mexico, for example, it has discovered differences in the ways that Mexicans and Americans shop. Its supercenters in Mexico operate on the notion that customers coming for general merchandise will also purchase groceries there. But Mexicans still shop at neighborhood butcher shops, bakeries, *tortillerias,* fruit stands, and egg shops, partly because items such as tortillas and *pan dulce* don't keep well overnight. Many Mexicans also favor neighborhood stores because they believe the meats and vegetables will be fresher.[13]

Kmart, the number-two discounter, has more than 4,700 stores but has annual sales that are roughly half of Wal-Mart's. Kmart is now modernizing over 2,000 stores and boosting its merchandising and advertising to improve its image.[14] Like Wal-Mart, Kmart has also been expanding into Mexico, as well as into Eastern European countries.

**hypermarket**
Retail establishment that combines a supermarket and discount department store in one large building.

A hybrid full-line discounter is the hypermarket, adapted from the Europeans. The flashy **hypermarket** format combines a supermarket and general merchandise discount store in a space ranging from 200,000 to 300,000 square feet. Although they are widely successful in Europe, where consumers have fewer retailing choices, hypermarkets have enjoyed less success in the United States. Most Europeans, for example, still need to visit several small stores just for their food needs, which makes hypermarkets a good alternative. Americans, on the other hand, can easily pick among a host of stores that offer large selections of merchandise. According to retailing executives and analysts, American customers have found hypermarkets to be too big. Both Wal-Mart's Hypermart U.S.A. and Kmart's American Fare hypermarket formats never got beyond the experimental stage.[15]

Similar to a hypermarket, but only half the size, are *supercenters.* Wal-Mart now operates over seventy SuperCenters and plans to replace many older Wal-Marts with this format. Along with Kmart, which is opening similar Super Kmart supercenters of its own, the two retailers pose a significant threat to traditional supermarkets.[16] Target is also planning to open its first supercenter, which will include a more upscale general merchandise and apparel store combined with a grocery, bank branch, pharmacy, photo studio, and restaurant.[17]

Supercenters are also threatening to push Europe's traditional small and medium-size food stores into extinction. Old-fashioned corner stores and family businesses are giving way to larger chains that offer food, drugs, services, and general merchandise all in one place. Many European countries are passing legislation to make it more difficult for supercenters to open. In France, for example, laws were passed that banned authorizations for new supercenters over 1,000 square meters (10,800 square feet). Belgium and Portugal have passed similar bans. In Britain and the Netherlands, areas outside towns and cities are off limits to superstores. By imposing planning and building restrictions for large stores, these countries are trying to accommodate environmental concerns, movements to revive city centers, and the worries of small shopkeepers.[18]

## Discount Specialty Stores

Another discount niche includes the single-line specialty discount stores—for example, sporting goods stores, electronics stores, auto parts stores, office supply stores, and toy stores. These stores offer a nearly complete selection of single-line merchandise and use self-service, discount prices, high volume, and high turnover to their advantage. Discount specialty stores are often termed **category killers** because they so heavily dominate their narrow merchandise segment. Examples include Toys R Us in toys, Circuit City in electronics, Office Depot in office supplies, Home Depot in home repair supplies, and Ikea in furniture.

**category killer**
Discount specialty store that carries a narrow merchandise selection and that dominates its segment.

Toys R Us is the world's largest toy seller and one of the most successful discount specialty store chains. It gained a loyal following by offering a wide selection of toys, usually over 15,000 different items per store, at prices usually 10 to 15 percent less than competitors'. Today Toys R Us operates about 700 stores worldwide. It first went international in 1984—initially in Canada, then in Europe, Hong Kong, and Singapore. Since then, the company has opened over 200 stores in eleven foreign countries. Breaking into the Japanese market was a challenge, however, because of the country's notorious Large-Store Law, aimed at protecting the country's politically powerful small shopkeepers. Additionally, few Japanese toy companies were initially willing to risk offending wholesalers by supplying merchandise directly to Toys R Us. But international sales now account for 21 percent of the chain's total revenues, and Toys R Us plans to add seventy to eighty more stores around the world by the year 2000.[19]

A relatively new discount specialty store concept is the pet superstore that sells pet foods and supplies at discount prices. Capitalizing on Americans' love for their pets, superstores such as Petco, PetsMart, and Petstuff are muscling into the $15 billion pet-products business and stealing customers from supermarkets and small pet shops. Not surprisingly, small pet shops are being hit very hard by pet superstores. On average, small retailer's revenues plummet 25 percent when a pet superstore opens in the area. Along with lower prices, pet superstores also offer an array of services. Each PetsMart, for example, has on-site pet grooming. Other superstores host obedience classes or provide basic veterinary services.[20]

## Warehouse Clubs

As mentioned in Chapter 12, warehouse membership clubs sell a limited selection of brand-name appliances, household items, and groceries. These are usually sold in bulk from warehouse outlets on a cash-and-carry basis to members only. Individual members of warehouse clubs are charged low or no membership fees.

Warehouse clubs have a major impact on supermarkets. Roughly 60 percent of warehouse club sales come from grocery-related items. Warehouse club members tend to be more educated, be more affluent, and have a larger household than regular supermarket shoppers. These core customers are using warehouse clubs for stocking up on staples; then they go to specialty outlets or food stores for perishables.[21]

Fierce competition is commonplace in the warehouse club industry. Common practices include price slashing, selling below cost, locating outlets to compete directly with each other, and sometimes hiring away rivals' employees to get an edge in local markets. Currently, only three warehouse chains hold 80 percent of the market: Wal-Mart's Sam's Club, Price-Costco, and BJ's.[22]

Both Sam's Club and Price-Costco have been busy introducing Mexican consumers to the warehouse club concept. Club Aurrera, a joint venture between Wal-Mart and Cifra, Mexico's largest retailer, and Price Club Mexico have opened stores in Mexico City. Both have plans to blitz the country with warehouse stores.[23]

## Off-Price Discount Retailers

**off-price retailer**
Retailer that sells at prices 25 percent or more below traditional department store prices because it pays cash for its stock and usually doesn't ask for return privileges.

An **off-price retailer** sells at prices 25 percent or more below traditional department store prices because it pays cash for its stock and usually doesn't ask for return privileges. Off-price retailers buy manufacturers' overruns at cost or even less. They also absorb goods from bankrupt stores, irregular merchandise, and unsold end-of-season output. Nevertheless, much off-price retailer merchandise is first-quality, current goods. Because buyers for off-price retailers purchase only what is available or what they can get a good deal on, merchandise styles and brands often change monthly. Today there are hundreds of off-price retailers, the best known being T.J. Maxx, Ross Stores, Marshall's, and Tuesday Morning.

A couple of interesting variations on the off-price concept have emerged:

- *Single-price stores:* One new type of off-price retailer that has proliferated in the past few years is the single-price store. For a lump sum, usually $1 per item, consumers can buy anything in the store, from shoes to shampoo. Single-price stores generally offer no frills, and customers must search through piles of merchandise. Typically, single-price chains buy their merchandise in large quantities from many sources, including wholesalers and independent vendors. Most products they buy are close-out items and discontinued products.

**factory outlet**
Off-price retailer that is owned and operated by a manufacturer and that carries the manufacturer's own line of merchandise.

- *Factory outlets:* A **factory outlet** is an off-price retailer that is owned and operated by a manufacturer. Thus it carries one line of merchandise—its own. Each season, from 5 percent to 10 percent of a manufacturer's output does not sell through regular distribution channels because it consists of close-outs (merchandise being discontinued), factory seconds, and canceled orders. With factory outlets, manufacturers can regulate where their surplus is sold, and they can realize higher profit margins than they would by disposing of the goods through independent wholesalers and retailers. Factory outlet malls typically locate in out-of-the-way rural areas or near vacation destinations. Most are situated at least thirty miles from urban or suburban shopping areas so manufacturers don't alienate their department store accounts by selling the same goods virtually next door at a discount. Several manufacturers reaping the benefits of outlet mall popularity include Liz Claiborne, J. Crew, and Calvin Klein clothiers; West Point Pepperel textiles; Oneida silversmiths; and Dansk kitchenwares. Top-drawer department stores—including Saks Fifth Avenue, Nordstrom, and Neiman Marcus—have also opened outlet stores to sell hard-to-move merchandise.[24]

4 *Discuss nonstore retailing techniques.*

# NONSTORE RETAILING

**nonstore retailing**
Practice of selling goods and services to the ultimate consumer without setting up a store.

The retailing methods discussed so far have been in-store methods, in which customers must physically shop at stores. In contrast, **nonstore retailing** is shopping without visiting a store. Because consumers demand convenience, nonstore retailing is currently growing faster than in-store retailing. The major forms of nonstore retailing are automatic vending, direct retailing, and direct marketing.

## AUTOMATIC VENDING

**automatic vending**
Form of nonstore retailing that uses vending machines to offer products for sale.

A low-profile yet important form of retailing is **automatic vending.** Automatic vending is the use of machines to offer goods for sale—for example, the cola, candy, or snack vending machines found in college cafeterias and office buildings.

Because many vending items, like soft drinks and snacks, have traditional or relatively fixed prices, raising vending machine prices is often difficult. The key to successful management in the vending business is thus reducing costs and streamlining operations. Often old equipment must be replaced with new machines that have greater capacity or more selections. For example, in an attempt to expand its distribution beyond supermarkets, convenience stores, and delicatessens, Snapple has developed a glass-front vending machine capable of offering fifty-four different flavors simultaneously.[25]

One trend in vending is offering nontraditional kinds of merchandise, such as personal-size pizzas, french fries, cappuccino, quick dinners, and videos. Toy marketers are also using vending machines to sell toys in fast-food restaurants; about twenty Burger Kings in the South have installed machines to vend trading cards, and Pizza Hut units across the country are vending stickers and sports cards. Vending machines selling Kodak cameras and film can now be found in sports stadiums, on beaches, and on mountains.[26] Another trend is a debit-card system for vending machines that have repeat customers.

### DIRECT RETAILING

**direct retailing**
Form of nonstore retailing that occurs in a home setting, such as door-to-door sales and party plan selling.

In **direct retailing,** the sales transaction occurs in a home setting. This approach includes door-to-door sales and party plan selling. Companies like Avon, Mary Kay Cosmetics, Fuller Brush, Amway, and World Book Encyclopedia depend on these techniques. Most direct retailers seem to favor party plans these days in lieu of door-to-door canvassing. Party plans call for one person, the host, to gather as many prospective buyers as possible. Most parties are a combination social affair and sales demonstration.

The sales of direct retailers have suffered as women have entered the work force. Working women are not at home during the day and have little time to attend selling parties. Tupperware, which still advocates the party plan method, is betting that working women have more money to spend but are just a little harder to reach. Its sales representatives now hold parties in offices, parks, and even parking lots. They hold "stop and shops" so women can just drop in, "classes" on self-improvement, and "custom-kitchen" parties on cabinet organizing. Although most Avon sales are still made door-to-door, the company is now trying to pick up sales through a program called Avon Select, which offers products to customers via direct mail. The company has a toll-free number for telephone orders and will even take orders by fax.[27]

Direct retailing is catching on in southern China, an area that has long been under communist rule. Avon began manufacturing and selling cosmetics in China in 1990. In the first year, sales were double the projections. Today, the company has more than 15,000 independent representatives selling Avon beauty products, many of whom earn more than $500 in monthly commissions, an amount most Chinese make in a year. More than 60 million people live within a 100-mile radius of Avon's Guangzhou factory, so the company has plenty of potential customers. In addition, Avon advertises on Hong Kong television, which broadcasts into China, so women in the area already recognize the Avon brand.[28]

### DIRECT MARKETING

**direct marketing (direct-response marketing)**
Techniques used to get consumers to buy from their homes, including direct mail, catalogs and mail order, telemarketing, and electronic retailing.

**Direct marketing,** sometimes called **direct-response marketing,** refers to the techniques used to get consumers to buy from their homes. Those techniques include direct mail, catalogs and mail order, telemarketing, and electronic retailing. Shoppers using these methods are less bound by traditional shopping situations and perceive less risk in buying by mail or telephone. Time-strapped consumers and those who live in rural or suburban areas are most likely to be in-home shoppers, because they value the convenience and flexibility that direct marketing provides.

Direct marketing strives for an immediate response from the consumer. For instance, 800 numbers advertised on cable TV stations invite shoppers to "call in now"; Ed McMahon shouts from an envelope, "You may have just won $10 million!"

Direct marketing typically uses a database of customer names. Because marketers can record the number of customers responding to a direct marketing effort, results are more accurately measured. Direct-response advertising techniques are discussed in Chapter 16.

Privacy issues have become a major concern for many consumers and politicians in light of the advances in direct marketing techniques and the use of highly specialized database marketing. Many consumers today feel that direct marketing techniques invade their privacy. Consumers routinely receive mail from complete strangers with such highly personal information in it that they feel uncomfortable. Many consumers are raising questions about how much of the data collected and stored in databases is really necessary to making the sale.[29] Privacy will be a major issue in the 1990s, and addressing these consumer concerns will be paramount for direct marketers.

## Direct Mail

Direct mail can be the most efficient or the least efficient retailing method, depending on the quality of the mailing list and the effectiveness of the mailing piece. With direct mail, marketers can precisely target their customers according to demographics, geographics, and even psychographics. Good mailing lists come from an internal database or are available from list brokers for about $35 to $150 per 1,000 names. For example, a Los Angeles computer software manufacturer selling programs for managing medical records may buy a list of all the physicians in the area. The software manufacturer may then design a direct-mail piece explaining the benefits of its system and send the piece to each physician. Today, direct mailers are even using videocassettes in place of letters and brochures to deliver their sales message to consumers.

Direct mailers are becoming more sophisticated in their targeting of the "right" customers. With a technique called *predictive modeling,* direct mailers can pick out those most likely to buy their products, using census statistics, lifestyle and financial information, and past-purchase and credit history. For example, a direct marketer like Dell Computers might use this technique to target 500,000 people with the right spending patterns, demographics, and preferences. Without it, Dell could easily mail millions of solicitations annually. Some solicitations could be targeted to only 10,000 of the best prospects, however, saving the company millions in postage while still preserving sales.

New computer technology has enabled direct-mail marketers to personalize their appeals. For example, a marketer of consumer credit cards could personalize the sales approach with these lines: "Being a May graduate of the University of Arizona, Ms. Jones, automatically qualifies you for ABC Bank's consumer credit card." The university, recipient, and graduation date would change from letter to letter, giving each a personal appeal.

Rising postage and paper costs, increased competition, and possible government regulation threaten to cut into the profits of direct mailers. Direct-mail companies are now seeking alternative delivery methods—for instance, private delivery services.

Direct mailers have also suffered from the negative image of "junk mail." Consumers' mailboxes are filled daily with direct-mail solicitations, most of which are never read. An average consumer receives about 12.5 pieces of direct mail each

In frustration with the sheer volume and the excesses of unsolicited direct mail, some people call it "junk mail." However, direct mail often works well as a way to bring buyers and sellers together.

week. According to one study, the consumer opens and reads only about 60 percent of these mailings. The industry is also plagued by direct-mail scams. One common ploy is to notify consumers that they have won a fabulous prize or are a winner in a sweepstakes. When they try to collect their prize, they are informed that they must first make a purchase.[30]

## Catalogs and Mail Order

Consumers can now buy just about anything through the mail—from a Connemara pony to a golf cart equipped with stereo and sunroof to a one-person hot-air balloon in any design wanted. Over 13.5 billion catalogs are mailed annually, with the average U.S. household receiving a new mail-order catalog about every four or five days.[31]

Successful catalogs are usually created and designed for highly segmented markets. Sears, whose catalog sales had dropped off, replaced its "big book" with a collection of more successful specialty catalogs targeted to specific market segments. Certain types of retailers are also using mail order to good effect. For example, computer manufacturers have discovered that mail order is a lucrative way to sell computers to home and small-business users. Currently, 17 percent of all personal computers sold in the U.S. market are sold through the mail.[32] Consumers can save up to 20 percent off traditional dealer prices by buying their computers from a mail-order house. Some mail-order computer firms also offer free in-home repairs for a year, thirty-day money-back guarantees, and toll-free phone lines for answers to questions.

Improved customer service and quick delivery policies have boosted consumer confidence in mail order. L.L. Bean and Lands' End are two catalog companies known for their excellent customer service. Shoppers may order twenty-four hours a day and can return any merchandise for any reason for a full refund. Other successful mail-order catalogs—including Spiegel, J. Crew, Victoria's Secret, and

Tweeds—target hard-working, home-oriented baby boomers who don't have time to visit or would rather not visit a retail store.

Like their direct-mail counterparts, catalog retailers are suffering from rising postage rates and increased paper costs. To help cut down the costs of mailing, catalog producers are trying new delivery methods with rates as much as 5 to 15 percent below U.S. Postal Service rates. Alternate delivery, which typically involves hiring people to hang sales materials from doorknobs in plastic bags, provides several advantages over the mail: Arrival dates can be guaranteed, no laws restrict what can be delivered, and clutter is reduced.[33]

U.S. catalog companies are also finding alternatives overseas, especially in Japan and Europe. Spiegel's Eddie Bauer division recently introduced its youthful leisurewear to Germany and has plans for a mailing in Japan. L.L. Bean already mails catalogs to 146 countries. Nearly 70 percent of its foreign sales are from Japan, 20 percent from Canada, and 6 percent from Great Britain. Opportunities for selling by mail have increased overseas with the growth in two-worker families, quicker delivery service, and increased acceptance of shopping by mail. The fate of U.S. catalog companies in overseas markets will depend on how well they can reproduce their domestic marketing and distribution success. They must also adapt their operations to meet local competition. For instance, giant French cataloger La Redoute, wary of J. Crew's impending arrival, launched a book that offered clothing similar to J. Crew's and guaranteed free forty-eight-hour delivery to some 800 points in France.[34]

## Telemarketing

**telemarketing**
Type of personal selling conducted over the telephone.

**Telemarketing** is the use of the telephone in the selling process. It consists of outbound sales calls, usually unsolicited, and inbound calls—that is, orders through toll-free 800 numbers or fee-based 900 numbers. Telemarketing is different from using the phone to support field sales activities. Salespeople use the phone periodically when they need to contact clients; telemarketing is systematic and continuous.[35]

*Outbound* telemarketing is an attractive direct-marketing technique because of rising postage rates and decreasing long-distance phone rates. Skyrocketing field sales costs also have put pressure on marketing managers to use outbound telemarketing. Searching for ways to keep costs under control, marketing managers are discovering how to pinpoint prospects quickly, zero in on serious buyers, and keep in close touch with regular customers. Meanwhile, they are reserving expensive, time-consuming, in-person calls for closing sales.

Many consumers believe outbound telemarketing methods are intrusive. They resent persistent, obnoxious phone calls at inappropriate times by people selling everything from magazines to aluminum siding. When such calls are computerized, consumers' annoyance increases. Although the tarnished image lingers, outbound telemarketing has become a sophisticated, complex business. In particular, technological advances have enabled telemarketing firms to become more sophisticated in finding prospects and checking sales leads.

*Inbound* telemarketing programs, which use 800 and 900 numbers, are mainly used to take orders, generate leads, and provide customer service. Inbound 800 telemarketing has successfully supplemented direct-response TV, radio, and print advertising for more than twenty-five years. The more recently introduced 900 numbers, which customers pay to call, are gaining popularity as a cost-effective way for companies to target customers. One of the major benefits of 900 numbers is that they allow marketers to generate qualified responses. Although the charge may reduce the total volume of calls, the calls that do come through are from customers who have a true interest in the product.[36]

## Electronic Retailing

Electronic retailing includes the twenty-four-hour shop-at-home television networks and on-line retailing.

*Shop-at-Home Networks.* The shop-at-home television networks are specialized forms of direct-response marketing. These shows display merchandise, with the retail price, to home viewers. Viewers can phone in their orders directly on a toll-free line and shop with a credit card. The shop-at-home industry has quickly grown into a billion-dollar business with a loyal customer following. Shop-at-home networks have the capability of reaching nearly every home that has a television set.

The best-known shop-at-home networks are the Home Shopping Network and the QVC (Quality, Value, Convenience) Network. Home shopping networks are now launching new services to appeal to more affluent audiences, and many traditional retailers, like Macy's and Nordstrom, are introducing their own networks. Spiegel plans to introduce a catalog-based home shopping channel, Catalog 1, that will sell merchandise from Sharper Image, Neiman Marcus, Crate & Barrel, Nature Company, and Williams-Sonoma.[37]

Those in the industry foresee that home shopping networks will play a major role in interactive and multimedia services. Future home shopping services would essentially turn the consumer's television into a smart computer and cash register for buying pay-per-view movies, sports, shopping services, and the like. Already, test subscribers in Florida can browse through a menu of 20,000 products from a supermarket and 7,500 items from a drugstore. Using hand-held remote controls, they will also be able to rotate displayed products to read directions or identify ingredients.[38]

*On-Line Retailing.* On-line retailing is a two-way, interactive service offered to people with microcomputers. It provides customers with a variety of information, including news, weather, stock information, sports news, and shopping opportunities. Users "subscribe" to information and shopping services, usually by getting the required hardware and software and paying a monthly fee. They "log on" to on-line services through a modem.

Prodigy, CompuServe, GEnie, and America Online are the most popular electronic shopping and information services. Subscribers to Prodigy, a joint venture of IBM and Sears, receive advertisements from such carmakers as BMW and Mazda. The advertisers provide brochures, catalogs, and other information packets via the on-line service. Shoppers can then ask for more information or order the product directly from their computer screen. For example, a family in the market for a child's bicycle can view a picture of the model they want on the screen and find the retailer offering the best price. Once they decide, they use their computer to send a message to the retailer and electronically transfer the proper amount of money from their bank account to the retailer's. Then a delivery service can transport the bicycle to the home.

Despite its potential convenience, on-line shopping has had a slow start. The biggest problem is that relatively few people subscribe to on-line services, and those who do aren't typically shoppers. Users are overwhelmingly male, but most shopping dollars nationally are spent by women. Additionally, for most American consumers, shopping is fun; computing isn't. However, some on-line merchants are thriving. PC Flowers has become one of the nation's biggest florists via Prodigy. Floral wire service is a perfect match to on-line demographics, because men are the ones who buy the most flowers.[39]

5 *Describe the nature of franchising.*

**franchise**
Right to operate a business or to sell a product.

**franchisor**
Individual or business that grants operating rights to another party to sell its product.

**franchisee**
Individual or business that is granted the right to sell another party's product.

## FRANCHISING

A **franchise** is a continuing relationship in which a franchisor grants to a franchisee the business rights to operate or to sell a product. The **franchisor** originates the trade name, product, methods of operation, and so on. The **franchisee,** in return, pays the franchisor for the right to use its name, product, or business methods. A franchise agreement between the two parties usually lasts for ten to twenty years, at which time the franchisee can renew the agreement with the franchisor if both parties are agreeable.

To be granted the rights to a franchise, a franchisee usually pays an initial, one-time franchise fee. The amount of this fee depends solely on the individual franchisor, but it generally ranges from $5,000 to $150,000. Besides paying this initial franchise fee, the franchisee is expected to pay weekly, biweekly, or monthly royalty fees, usually in the range of 3 to 7 percent of gross revenues. The franchisee may also be expected to pay advertising fees, which usually cover the cost of promotional materials and, if the franchise organization is large enough, regional or national advertising. A Burger King franchise, for example, costs an initial $40,000 per store, with a 3.5 percent royalty fee and an annual advertising contribution of 4 percent of gross sales. Franchisee start-up costs are an additional $73,000 to $511,000.[40]

Franchising offers the following advantages to a person who wants to own and manage a business:

- A chance to become an independent businessperson with relatively little capital
- A product that has already been established in the marketplace
- Technical training and managerial assistance
- Quality-control standards enforced by the franchisor that help the franchisee succeed by ensuring product uniformity throughout the franchise system

In turn, the franchisor gets company expansion with a limited capital investment, motivated store owners, and bulk purchasing of inventory.[41]

Franchising is not new. General Motors has used this approach since 1898, and Rexall drugstores, since 1901. Today there are over half a million franchised establishments in the United States, with combined sales over $800 billion. Most franchises are retail operations. Of the $1.8 trillion in total retail sales, franchising accounts for about 35 percent.[42] Exhibit 13.3 provides some more facts about franchising.

There are two basic forms of franchises today: product and trade name franchising, and business format franchising. In *product and trade name franchising,* a dealer agrees to sell certain products provided by a manufacturer or a wholesaler. This approach has been used most widely in the auto and truck, soft-drink bottling, tire, and gasoline service industries. For example, a local tire retailer may hold a franchise to sell Michelin tires. Likewise, the Coca-Cola bottler in a particular area is a product and trade name franchisee licensed to bottle and sell Coca-Cola's soft drinks.

*Business format franchising* is an ongoing business relationship between a franchisor and a franchisee. Typically, a franchisor "sells" a franchisee the rights to use the franchisor's format or approach to doing business. This form of franchising has

*Exhibit 13.3*

Franchising Facts

Source: International Franchise Association, 1993.

| | |
|---|---|
| **Sales** | • Franchises had $803.2 billion in sales in 1992.<br>• Franchises accounted for 35% of all retail sales.<br>• Total franchise sales could reach $1 trillion by the year 2000. |
| **Jobs** | • More than 8 million people are employed by franchise establishments.<br>• In the past year, franchise establishments created more than 170,000 new jobs. |
| **Growth** | • A new franchise opens every 8 minutes of each business day.<br>• The total number of franchises grew from 542,496 in 1991 to 558,125 in 1992.<br>• According to studies conducted by the U.S. Commerce Department from 1971 to 1987, less than 5% of franchises have failed or discontinued annually. |
| **Franchisees** | • According to a recent Gallup poll, 94% of franchise owners are successful.<br>• The poll indicated that 75% of franchise owners would repeat their franchise again; only 39% of U.S. citizens would repeat their job or business.<br>• Average gross income of franchisees before taxes was $124,290.<br>• Average total investment cost of a franchise was $147,570. |

rapidly expanded since the 1950s through retailing, restaurant, food-service, hotel and motel, printing, and real estate franchises.[43] Fast-food restaurants like McDonald's, Wendy's, and Burger King use this kind of franchising.

Like other retailers, franchisors are seeking new growth abroad, especially in emerging nations like Mexico, Turkey, and Venezuela. In fact, the U.S. government is making it easier to open franchises in developing countries by guaranteeing 50 percent of loans obtained to open foreign franchise locations.[44] Franchising is popular in Eastern European countries, too. Pizza Hut opened its first foreign franchise in Hungary and regularly has as many as 150 customers lined up outside. Fifteen more Pizza Huts will open in Hungary, as well as twenty-two KFC and forty Dunkin' Donuts outlets.[45]

Franchisors sometimes allow franchisees to alter their business format slightly in foreign markets. For example, McDonald's, with over 800 franchise locations in Japan, is testing food items with a Japanese touch, such as steamed dumplings, curry with rice, and roast pork-cutlet burgers with melted cheese. KFC's Japanese franchisees are experimenting with grilled versions of rice balls and a fried salmon sandwich.[46]

6 *List the major tasks involved in developing a retail marketing strategy.*

## RETAIL MARKETING STRATEGY

Retailers must develop marketing strategies based on overall goals and strategic plans. Retailing goals might include more traffic, higher sales of a specific item, a more upscale image, or heightened public awareness of the retail operation. The strategies that retailers use to obtain their goals might include a sale, an updated decor, or a new advertisement. The key tasks in strategic retailing are defining and selecting a target market and developing the "six P's" of the retailing mix to successfully meet the needs of the chosen target market.

### DEFINING A TARGET MARKET

The first and foremost task in developing a retail strategy is to define the target market. This process begins with market segmentation, the topic of Chapter 6. Successful retailing has always been based on knowing the customer. Sometimes retailing chains have floundered because the market the firm should be serving is different from the one chosen. In other cases, management loses sight of the customers the stores should be serving. For example, The Limited experienced phenomenal growth in the 1980s selling trendy apparel to young women. Today, however, many of the customers who made The Limited so successful have matured, and they now shop at stores that better reflect the sensibilities of an older consumer. Furthermore, The Limited moved into careerwear, an unsuccessful strategy that only confused its remaining customers. As a result, the company was forced to close some units.[47]

Target markets in retailing are often defined by demographics, geographics, and psychographics. A convenience store may define its main target as married men under 35 years old, in the lower income ranges, with two young children. A small local grocer might limit its target market to those living in the surrounding neighborhood. A department store may target fashion-conscious juniors, contemporaries who spend more money than other segments on quality clothing, and conservatives who want comfort and value.

Determining a target market is a prerequisite to creating the retailing mix. For example, Target's merchandising approach for sporting goods is to match its product assortment to the demographics of the local store and region. The amount of space devoted to sporting goods, as well as in-store promotions, also varies according to each store's target market.[48]

Retailers must monitor and evaluate trends affecting their target market so the retailing mix can be adjusted if necessary. For instance, many retailers are responding to the expanding home-office market. In 1993, an estimated 7.6 million company employees worked from home, up 15 percent from the previous year. There were also 24.3 million self-employed home-based workers and 9.2 million after-hours home workers. These home-based workers account for roughly $5 billion in annual spending for microcomputers, fax machines, and telephone products and services. Sears, one retailer tapping into the trend, has developed home-office centers specializing in equipment for home-based workers in 250 of its stores.[49]

## CHOOSING THE RETAILING MIX

**retailing mix**
Combination of the six P's—price, place, product, promotion, personnel, and presentation—to sell goods and services to the ultimate customer.

Retailers combine the elements of the retailing mix to come up with a single retailing method to attract the target market. The **retailing mix** consists of six P's: the four P's of the marketing mix (product, place, promotion, and price) plus personnel and presentation (see Exhibit 13.4).

The combination of the six P's projects a store's image, which influences consumers' perceptions. Using these impressions of stores, shoppers position one store against another. A retail marketing manager must make sure that the store's positioning is compatible with the target customers' expectations. As discussed at the beginning of the chapter, retail stores can be positioned on three broad dimensions: service provided by store personnel, product assortment, and price. Management should use everything else—place, presentation, and promotion—to fine-tune the basic positioning of the store.

### The Product Offering

**product offering (product assortment)**
The mix of products offered to customers by the retailer.

The first element in the retailing mix is the product offering, also called the **product assortment** or merchandise mix. Retailers decide what to sell on the basis of what their target market wants to buy. They can base their decision on market research, past sales, fashion trends, customer requests, and other sources. Developing a product

Exhibit 13.4

Retailing Mix

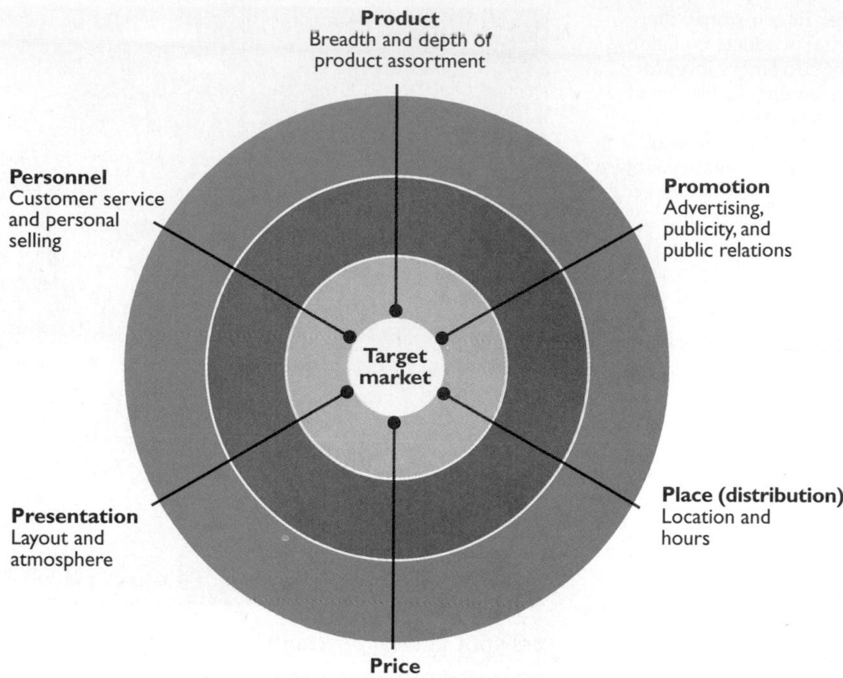


offering is essentially a question of width and depth of the product assortment. Price, store design, displays, and service are important to consumers in determining where to shop, but the most critical factor is merchandise selection.[50]

After determining what products will satisfy target customers' desires, retailers must find sources of supply and evaluate the products. When the right products are found, the retail buyer negotiates a purchase contract. The buying function can either be performed in-house or be delegated to an outside firm. The goods must then be moved from the seller to the retailer, which means shipping, storing, and stocking the inventory. The trick is to manage the inventory by cutting prices to move slow goods and keeping adequate supplies of hot-selling items in stock. As in all good systems, the final step is to evaluate the entire process to seek more efficient methods and eliminate problems and bottlenecks.

One of the more efficient new methods of managing inventory and streamlining the way products are moved from supplier to distributor to retailer is called *efficient consumer response,* or ECR. At the heart of ECR is *electronic data interchange,* or EDI, the computer-to-computer exchange of information, including automatic shipping notifications, invoices, inventory data, and forecasts. In a full implementation of ECR, products are scanned at the retail store when purchased, which updates the store's inventory lists. Headquarters then polls the stores to retrieve the data needed to produce an order. The vendor confirms the order, shipping date, and delivery time, then ships the order and transmits the invoice electronically. The item is received at the warehouse, scanned into inventory, and then sent to the store. The invoice and receiving data are reconciled, and payment via an electronic transfer of funds completes the process.[51]

Many retailers are experimenting with or have successfully implemented ECR and EDI. Dillard's, one of the fastest-growing regional department store chains, has one of the most technologically advanced ECR systems in the industry. Every item

Baxter International, the hospital products company, offers customers inventory management. At Hermann Hospital in Houston, a Baxter employee checks inventory and electronically transmits ordering data to the warehouse.



Dillard's sells has a bar code, so on any given day management knows how many pairs of 9 West slingback ladies' shoes, for instance, have been sold. If the shoes are selling fast, Dillard's ECR system automatically orders more from the company warehouse. The warehouse, in turn, reorders automatically from the vendor. Thus, Dillard's stores are less likely than competitors' to be out of popular items or loaded up with unfashionable ones that eventually have to be marked down.

Advances in computer technology have also helped retailers spot new opportunities, such as the latest fashions. These styles can be re-created on a computer, and the designs can be transmitted electronically to manufacturers for production. New merchandise can be produced and put on store shelves in weeks rather than months. This speed gives retailers like Dillard's a competitive advantage over other fashion retailers.

## Promotion Strategy

Retail promotion strategy includes advertising, public relations and publicity, and sales promotion. The goal is to help position the store in consumers' minds. Retailers design intriguing ads, stage special events, and develop promotions aimed at their target markets. For example, today's grand openings are a carefully orchestrated blend of advertising, merchandising, goodwill, and glitter. All the elements of an opening—press coverage, special events, media advertising, and store displays—are carefully planned.

Retailers' advertising is carried out mostly at the local level, although retail giants like Sears and JCPenney can advertise nationally. In their ads, retailers communicate information about their stores, such as location, merchandise, hours, prices, and special sales. The Softer Side of Sears national advertising campaign was used to help reposition Sears as a low-priced but fashion-conscious apparel retailer. An accompanying campaign, Come See the Many Sides of Sears, was used to promote the retailer's nonapparel merchandise, such as tools, paint, and car parts.[52]

Often large retailers and well-known clothing designers or manufacturers of exclusive specialty products share the spotlight in an advertisement. For example, ads linking Ralph Lauren and Foley's, a department store chain, let everyone know that Foley's sells the latest fashions. In turn, they enhance Ralph Lauren's prestige by associating it with a successful, distinguished fashion retailer. This is called cooperative advertising; it will be discussed in more detail in Chapter 16.

Many retailers are forgoing media advertising these days in favor of direct mail or sales promotion. For example, Macy's and Bloomingdale's are both testing frequent shopper programs that shower top shoppers with perks ranging from advance warning on sales and free gift wrapping to store discounts based on spending. Other retailers are flocking to direct-mail and catalog programs in the hopes they will

Cooperative advertising, like this ad for both Donna Karan fashions and Bloomingdale's department store, is a way to promote a retailer and a manufacturer simultaneously.

prove a cost-effective means of increasing brand loyalty and spending by core customers. Nordstrom mails catalogs featuring brand-name and private-brand clothing, shoes, and accessories to target the shop-at-home crowd.[53]

Sponsoring community events or supporting a good cause can also generate a lot of local publicity and goodwill for a retail establishment. Many large department stores still sponsor holiday parades; other retailers support community programs. Target, for example, donates 5 percent of its pretax profits to community service programs. The company is a large sponsor of Habitat for Humanity, an organization that builds homes for the poor. Target employees build fifty new homes each year, and Target contributes cash, supplies, and furnishings. Target also participates in the Good Neighbor Volunteer program, through which employees donate thousands of volunteer hours annually to various agencies; Child Care Aware, which helps parents identify and select quality child care; and Earth Day.[54]

## The Proper Location

Another element in the retailing mix is place, or site location. Selecting a proper site is a critical decision. First, it is a large, long-term commitment of resources that can reduce a retailer's future flexibility. Whether the retailer leases or purchases, the location decision implies some degree of permanence. Second, the location will affect future growth. The chosen area should be growing economically so it can sustain the original store and any future stores. Last, the local environment may change over time. If the location's value deteriorates, the store may have to be relocated or closed.

Site location begins by choosing a community. This decision depends largely on economic growth potential and stability, the competition, political climate, and so on. Some of the savviest location experts in recent years have been T.J. Maxx and Toys R Us. Both retailers put the majority of their new locations in rapidly growing areas where the population closely matches their customer base.

Sometimes it is not the economic profile or political climate that makes a community a good location but its geographic location. One of Wal-Mart's most successful stores is located in Laredo, Texas, a city bordering Mexico. The store draws not only customers from Laredo but also Mexicans who cross the border to shop for U.S. goods.[55]

After settling on a geographic region or community, retailers must choose a specific site. In addition to growth potential, the important factors are neighborhood socioeconomic characteristics, traffic flows, land costs, zoning regulations, existing competition, and public transportation.

The undisputed winner in the locations race is Wal-Mart, whose strategy of being the first discounter to locate in small and rural markets made it the number-one retailer in the nation.[56] Retailers like McDonald's, Target, and Kmart now follow

Wal-Mart's strategy, locating in small towns instead of large metropolitan areas, where the competition has grown fierce. However, many large retailers have not received the warm welcomes they expected, especially from small towns in the Northeast. Many merchants and citizens in small towns worry that a large national retailer will undermine local retailers, create traffic problems, and destroy the historic character of the town. Offering such services as hair salons, mail centers, optometrists, travel agencies, pharmacies, and food outlets, a discounter like Wal-Mart has every retail destination that the average small town has, translated to a single site.[57] Read about how some small town residents are going head-to-head with Wal-Mart in the accompanying Ethics in Marketing article.

*Freestanding Stores.* One final decision about location faces retailers: whether to have a freestanding unit or to become a shopping mall tenant. An isolated, freestanding location can be used by large retailers like Wal-Mart, Kmart, or Target and sellers of shopping goods like furniture and cars, because they are "destination" stores. In other words, customers will seek them out. An isolated store location may have the advantages of low site cost or rent and no nearby competitors. On the other hand, it may be hard to attract customers to a freestanding location, and no other retailers are around to share costs.

One store that thrives on its isolation is the Domino's outlet near Twenty-Nine Palms, California. The only pizza joint on a military base that is home to 11,000 Marines and their families, it sells close to 4,000 pizzas a week. Marines returning from Operation Desert Storm who wanted to satisfy their pizza cravings pushed annual sales for the store well over $1 million.[59]

*Shopping Centers.* The tremendous boom in shopping centers began after World War II, as the U.S. population started migrating to the suburbs. The first shopping centers were strip centers, typically located along a busy street. They included a supermarket, a variety store, and perhaps a few specialty stores. Essentially unplanned business districts, these strip centers remain popular.

Next, the small community shopping centers emerged, with one or two small department store branches, more specialty shops, one or two restaurants, and several apparel stores. These centers offer a broader variety of shopping, specialty, and convenience goods, provide large off-street parking lots, and usually span 75,000 to 300,000 square feet of retail space.

Finally, along came the huge regional malls. Regional malls are either

---

ETHICS IN MARKETING

### Is Wal-Mart a Threat to Small Towns?

When Wal-Mart unveiled plans to build a store in Westford, Massachusetts, residents stuck "Stop Wal-Mart" bumper stickers on their cars and matching signs in their front yards. Irate townspeople organized phone drives and personally called 500 Westfordians to protest the giant discounter. They also distributed buttons that read, "If they build it, we won't come."

Residents of Sturbridge, Massachusetts, were treated to a last-minute advertising blitz by Wal-Mart that touted the benefits of letting it build a supercenter in a new shopping center on the edge of town: more jobs and a bigger local tax base. Nevertheless, Sturbridge voted against the proposal. Townspeople weren't opposed to the construction of the mall, just to Wal-Mart. The retailer, they said, was just too big and would cause traffic problems and hurt local merchants.

Many small-town New Englanders are rebelling against Wal-Mart's plans to expand into the region—one of its last U.S. frontiers. The discounter has seen plenty of resistance before, but its opponents in New England are more plentiful and possibly more effective than those elsewhere. Indeed, it seems that some stubborn Yankees are slowing, at least temporarily, the chain's expansion plans.

Wal-Mart denies that its expansion into the New England states has been slowed, although it is now reconsidering its plans to build stores in four Massachusetts towns. In Vermont, the sole state where there is no Wal-Mart, its plans for one site are being held up by legal action, and another site is being reviewed by the state government. It takes Wal-Mart an average of thirty months to put a store in New England—allowing for land acquisition, local approval, and construction—compared with six to nine months in other regions.

As much a regional entertainment center as a shopping center, Minnesota's Mall of America can lure customers even in a difficult retail environment.



entirely enclosed or roofed to allow shopping in any weather. Many are landscaped with trees, fountains, sculptures, and the like to enhance the shopping environment. They have acres of free parking. The "anchor stores" or "generator stores" (JCPenney, Sears, or major department stores) are usually located at opposite ends of the mall to create heavy foot traffic.

The largest mall in the United States opened in 1992 near St. Paul and Minneapolis, Minnesota. Covering seventy-eight acres and 4.2 million square feet under one roof, The Mall of America boasts 400-plus stores, an eighteen-hole miniature golf course, fourteen movie theaters, thirteen restaurants, two food courts, and a seven-acre Camp Snoopy amusement park operated by Knott's Berry Farm. The mall promotes itself as a tourist attraction, and some 30 percent of its traffic comes from 150 miles away or more.[60]

Locating in a community shopping center or regional mall offers several advantages. First, the facilities are designed to attract shoppers. Second, the shopping environment, anchor stores, and "village square" activities draw customers. Third, ample parking is available. Fourth, the center or mall projects a unified image. Fifth, tenants share the expenses of the mall's common area and promotions for the whole mall. Finally, malls can target different demographic groups. For example, some malls are considered upscale; others are aimed at people shopping for bargains.

Locating in a shopping center or mall does have disadvantages. These include expensive leases, the chance that common promotion efforts will not attract customers to a particular store, lease restrictions on merchandise carried and hours of operation, the anchor stores' domination of the tenants' association, and the possibility of having direct competitors within the same facility.

Strip centers and small community shopping centers account for 87 percent

### ETHICS IN MARKETING

Many New Englanders are concerned about the additional traffic a Wal-Mart store will create, but most are choosing to center their complaints on more legally compelling arguments: zoning requirements and environmental impact. In Westford, for example, 5,000 people, about 30 percent of the town's residents, signed a petition protesting the proposed site. A thousand residents heckled Wal-Mart officials at a town meeting. Westford residents claimed that a local water well system could be contaminated by spillage from a Wal-Mart garden center. Moreover, local vernal pools, the puddles that frogs and other amphibians use for breeding during a few months a year, might be destroyed by Wal-Mart construction.

In Vermont, tough state land-use and environmental laws have slowed approval of Wal-Mart sites in many towns. Other critics argue that big commercial development on the edge of town often sucks the vitality out of downtown shopping areas.

Some small New England towns have lost the battle against Wal-Mart. In Bath, Maine, for example, residents campaigned against a local Wal-Mart, but one eventually opened in nearby Brunswick. Bath launched a new campaign to protect its local merchants. Whereas shopping in downtown Bath's 100 stores used to be uneventful, now the area boasts weekly outdoor concerts, street dances, a Thanksgiving parade, and extended store hours.[58]

Realistically, in the long run can New Englanders prevent Wal-Mart and similar stores from opening there? What good things have emerged from this resistance to Wal-Mart?

The price range of the goods that a retailer sells helps categorize the store in shoppers' minds. For instance, a store selling expensive Cartier watches is likely to be perceived as quality-oriented and prestigious.

of all retail centers and 51 percent of total shopping center retail sales. Retail analysts expect that by the year 2000, U.S. consumers will do most of their shopping at neighborhood strip shopping centers. With increasing demands on their time, they will choose speed and convenience instead of the elegance and variety offered by large regional malls.[61]

## Retail Prices

Another important element in the retailing mix is price. The strategy of pricing is explained in Chapters 18 and 19. For now it is important to understand that retailing's ultimate goal is to sell products to final consumers and that the right price is critical in ensuring sales. Because retail prices are usually based on the cost of the merchandise, an essential part of pricing is efficient and timely buying.

Price is a key element in a retail store's positioning strategy and classification. Higher prices often indicate a level of quality and help reinforce the prestigious image of retailers, as they do for Lord & Taylor, Saks Fifth Avenue, Gucci, Cartier, and Neiman Marcus. On the other hand, discounters and off-price retailers offer a good value for the money.

A pricing trend among retailers that seems to be here to stay is "everyday low pricing," or EDLP. Introduced to the retail industry by Wal-Mart, EDLP offers consumers a low price all the time rather than holding periodic sales on merchandise. For example, The Gap cut prices on its popular denim jeans, denim shirts, socks, and other items to protect and broaden the company's share of the casual clothes market.[62]

## Presentation of the Retail Store

The presentation of a retail store helps determine the store's image and positions the retail store in consumers' minds. For instance, a retailer that wants to position itself as an upscale store would use a lavish or sophisticated presentation.

**atmosphere**
Overall impression conveyed by a store's physical layout, decor, and surroundings.

The main element of a store's presentation is its **atmosphere,** the overall impression conveyed by a store's physical layout, decor, and surroundings. The atmosphere might create a relaxed or busy feeling, a sense of luxury or of efficiency, a friendly or cold attitude, a sense of organization or of clutter, or a fun or serious mood. For example, the look at Express stores is designed to make suburban shoppers feel as though they have just strolled into a Parisian boutique. Signage is often in French, and the background music has a European flair. The Nike Town store in Chicago looks more like a museum than like a traditional retail store. The three-story space displays products amid life-size Michael Jordan and Bo Jackson statues and glassed-in relics like baseball legend Nolan Ryan's shoes. A History of Air exhibit explains the pockets of air on the bottom of some Nike shoes. A video theater plays Nike commercials and short films featuring Nike gear.[63]

These are the most influential factors in creating a store's atmosphere:[64]

- *Employee type and density:* Employee type refers to an employee's general characteristics—for instance, neat, friendly, knowledgeable, or service-oriented. Density is the number of employees per 1,000 square feet of selling space. A discounter like Kmart has a low employee density that creates a "do-it-yourself," casual atmosphere. In contrast, Neiman Marcus's density is much higher, denoting readiness to serve the customer's every whim. Too many employees and not enough customers, however, can convey an air of desperation and intimidate customers.
- *Merchandise type and density:* A prestigious retailer like Saks or Marshall Field's carries the best brand names and displays them in a neat, uncluttered arrangement. Discounters and off-price retailers may sell some well-known brands, but many carry seconds or out-of-season goods. Their merchandise may be stacked so high that it falls into the aisles, helping create the impression that "We've got so much stuff, we're practically giving it away."
- *Fixture type and density:* Fixtures can be elegant (rich woods), trendy (chrome and smoked glass), or old, beat-up tables. The fixtures should be consistent with the general atmosphere the store is trying to create. Retailers should beware of using too many fixtures, because they may confuse the customers about what the store is selling. By displaying its merchandise on tables and shelves rather than on traditional pipe racks, The Gap creates a relaxed and uncluttered atmosphere. The display tables also allow customers to see and touch the merchandise more easily.
- *Sound:* Sound can be pleasant or unpleasant for a customer. Classical music at a nice Italian restaurant helps create ambience, just as country-and-western music does at a truck stop. Music can also entice customers to stay in the store longer and buy more or eat quickly and leave a table for others. Music is likely to have its greatest effect when shoppers are involved in a highly emotional buying decision. For most consumers, that means buying jewelry, sportswear, cosmetics, and beer. Retailers can tailor their musical atmosphere to their shoppers' demographics and the merchandise they're selling. Music can control the pace of the store traffic, create an image, and attract or direct the shopper's attention. For example, Harrods in London features music by live harpists, pianists, and marching bagpipers to create different atmospheres in different departments.[65]
- *Odors:* Smell can either stimulate or detract from sales. The wonderful smell of pastries and breads entices bakery customers. Conversely, customers can be repulsed by bad odors, such as cigarette smoke, musty smells, antiseptic odors, and overly powerful room deodorizers. If a grocery store pumps in the smell of baked goods, sales in that department increase threefold. Several department stores have tested the effects of pumping in fragrances that are pleasing to their target market.[66]
- *Visual factors:* Colors can create a mood or focus attention and therefore are an important factor in atmosphere. Red, yellow, and orange are considered warm colors and are used when a feeling of warmth and closeness is desired. Cool colors like blue, green, and violet are used to open up closed-in places and create an air of elegance and cleanliness. Some colors are better for display. For instance, diamonds appear most striking against black or dark blue velvet. The lighting can also have an important effect on store atmosphere.

Jewelry is best displayed under high-intensity spotlights and cosmetics under more natural lighting.

## Personnel and Customer Service

People are a unique aspect of retailing. Most retail sales involve a customer-salesperson relationship, if only briefly. When customers shop at a grocery store, the cashiers check and bag their groceries. When customers shop at a prestigious clothier, the sales clerks may help select the styles, sizes, and colors. They may also assist in the fitting process, offer alteration services, wrap purchases, and even offer a glass of champagne. Sales personnel provide their customers with the amount of service prescribed in the retail strategy of the store.

Good service is even more important in a slow-growth economy, when companies survive by keeping the customers they have. Studies show that customer retention results in above-average profits and superior growth. Home Depot is one company that has embraced that philosophy and provides its customers with excellent service. Home Depot salespeople—often recruited from the ranks of carpenters and electricians—are encouraged to spend all the time needed with customers, even if it's hours.[67]

Retail salespeople serve another important selling function: They persuade shoppers to buy. They must therefore be able to persuade customers that what they are selling is what the customer needs. Salespeople are trained in two common selling techniques: trading up and suggestion selling. *Trading up* means persuading customers to buy a higher-priced item than they originally intended to buy. However, to avoid selling customers something they do not need or want, salespeople should take care when practicing trading-up techniques. *Suggestion selling,* a common practice among most retailers, seeks to broaden customers' original purchases with related items. For example, McDonald's cashiers may ask customers whether they would

Good customer service, offered by knowledgeable and helpful sales personnel, is a critical factor in a customer's decision to buy.

like hot apple pie with their hamburger and fries. Suggestion selling should always be founded on helping shoppers recognize true needs rather than selling them unwanted merchandise, just as in trading up.

As noted at the beginning of the chapter, the level of service helps in classifying and positioning retail establishments. The level of service refers to the types of services offered (credit, delivery) and the quality of service. Examples of quality service include fast checkout versus slow checkout and knowledgeable, helpful salespeople versus uninformed, sloppy, and inaccessible clerks. These are some of the factors managers should consider when setting the service level:

- Services offered by the competition
- Type of merchandise handled (furniture and major appliances usually require delivery)
- Socioeconomic characteristics of the target market
- Cost of providing the service
- Price image of the store (a high price usually demands a high level of service)

*7 Explain the wheel of retailing and the retail life cycle.*

## THE CHANGING FACE OF RETAILING

Retailing is the most dynamic component of the distribution channel. New retailers are always entering the market, searching for a new position that will attract customers. For example, the warehouse club format was developed for consumers wanting no-frills, low-cost goods. The evolution of competition in retailing can be explained by two related theories: the wheel of retailing and the retail life cycle.

### THE WHEEL OF RETAILING

**wheel of retailing**
Model describing the constant changes in retailing in which new retail institutions enter a market as low-cost, low-price operations and gradually increase services and prices.

The **wheel of retailing** depicts the constant state of change in retailing (see Exhibit 13.5). According to this model, new retail institutions enter a market as low-cost, low-price operations by reducing or eliminating services. As a retailer becomes established, however, it adds services, and prices gradually increase. The retailer may then move to better locations, offer higher-quality merchandise, install better

*Exhibit 13.5*

Wheel of Retailing

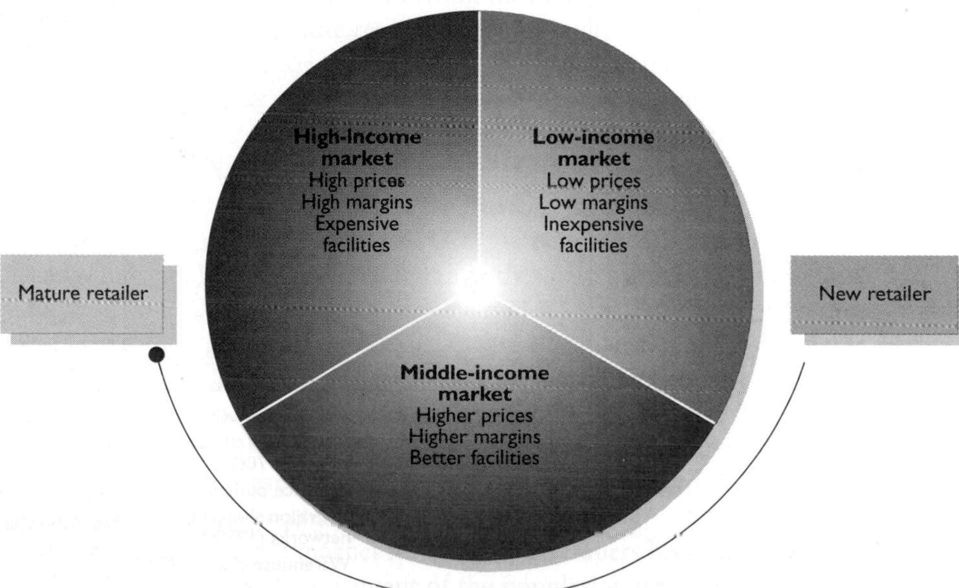

efficient or gain a thorough understanding of the competitive market, leading to their stores' demise. Second, because of the overexpansion of chain retailers, the growth of retail space has consistently outstripped both population growth and consumer spending for the past several years. There are now too many stores for the number of shoppers. Third, by offering an enormous selection in a single product category at lower prices, category killers threaten traditional department stores and mass merchandisers and severely squeeze the smaller chains and the few remaining independent retailers. Additionally, alternative retail formats, such as home shopping and electronic retailing, also pose a significant threat to traditional retail stores. Last, slow job growth and recession have caused consumer spending to slacken in the United States. As a result, today's consumers are less interested in shopping than they were in the 1980s.

## Discussion and Writing Questions

1. Discuss the possible marketing implications of the recent trend toward supercenters, which combine a supermarket and a full-line discount store.
2. Explain the function of warehouse clubs. Why are they classified as both wholesalers and retailers?
3. Identify a successful retail business in your community. What marketing strategies have led to its success?
4. You want to convince your boss, the owner of a retail store, of the importance of store atmosphere. Write a memo citing specific examples of how store atmosphere affects your own shopping behavior.
5. Discuss the potential challenges of global retailing.
6. You have been asked to write a brief article about the way consumer demand for convenience and efficiency is influencing the future of retailing. Write the outline for your article.
7. Why is retailing said to be "an industry that eats its young"?

## Application for Small Business

Earl Schabb and Joe Schabb own three Home Appliance Outlets that sell to a metropolitan market of approximately 500,000 people in the Northeast. The product

Exhibit 13.7

Store Selection Factors When Buying Home Audio Equipment

| Importance | Store selection factors | Home appliance outlets | Score: Competitor #1 | Score: Competitor #2 |
|---|---|---|---|---|
| 1 | Reputation of store | 5 | 4 | 3 |
| 2 | Customer service | 3 | 5 | 2 |
| 3 | Brands of audio equipment | 4 | 3 | 4 |
| 4 | Value and pricing | 4 | 3 | 5 |
| 5 | Knowledge of salespeople | 3 | 4 | 2 |
| 6 | Repair services | 3 | 4 | 2 |
| 7 | Friendliness of personnel | 4 | 2 | 3 |
| 8 | Convenience of location | 4 | 3 | 1 |

line includes audio equipment, TV sets, VCRs, phones, copiers, fax machines, and related items. Audio equipment is the most important product line, accounting for 44 percent of sales. The owners have decided to initiate a customer satisfaction program for that product line and then extend the program to all product lines.

Earl and Joe brainstormed with employees and identified eight "critically important" factors that influence the decision to purchase home audio equipment. A questionnaire was then developed and administered by a telephone survey of fifty current customers and fifty past customers. Results of the survey are shown in Exhibit 13.7. The result was a ranking of store selection factors, with 1 being most important. Home Appliance Outlets and two other competitors were then compared for their perceived performance on the eight selection factors, with a score of 5 meaning excellent performance and a score of 1 meaning poor performance. Earl and Joe developed a customer satisfaction action plan for audio equipment using this information.

### Questions

1. What changes, if any, need to be made in store operations before implementing the customer satisfaction program?
2. What do you believe the customer satisfaction program should emphasize?

## CRITICAL THINKING CASE

### Ann Taylor Stores

Once considered the mecca for sophisticated, urban career women, Ann Taylor Stores has stumbled on some bad times. The Ann Taylor chain became a fixture in upscale malls around the country in the 1980s, thanks to its shrewd targeting of urban working women. The specialty clothier experienced astonishing growth during the eighties. In 1989, same-store sales (sales at stores open at least one year) grew over 14 percent. Then the company unraveled. In 1990, same-store sales inched ahead only 2 percent, and the following year same-store sales dropped almost 6 percent. For its fiscal year ending in February 1992, the company reported a net loss of $15.8 million on sales of $437.7 million.

In part, Ann Taylor's troubles reflect the demise of the dress-for-success uniform insisted on by businesswomen in the 1980s. Back then, a boxy suit, silk blouse, and pearls were standard workday dress for businesswomen. But in the 1990s, working women wear just about anything from walking shorts to print dresses. Ann Taylor's management failed to recognize this trend soon enough and continued manufacturing merchandise that doesn't fit the working woman's new relaxed style.

Ann Taylor compounded its problems with a series of financial and marketing missteps. To pay down its heavy debt load, the company resorted to a maneuver that would prove disastrous: Suppliers were told to produce goods more cheaply, and stores were told to sell them at a higher markup. The standard markup on the company's apparel increased from 45 percent to as high as 65 percent. An astounding number of loyal Ann Taylor customers noticed the higher prices and the second-rate merchandise and complained to the company. Many abandoned the specialty retailer altogether, finding plenty of other options available. Ann Taylor also embarked on a costly and overly ambitious expansion strategy. Between 1989 and 1991, the company grew from 139 stores to 200 stores. The drastic growth in such a short time added greatly to Ann Taylor's already burdensome debt.

In the mid-1990s Ann Taylor launched a major new strategy to mend the chain's image and improve brand status. Through a joint manufacturing venture, Ann Taylor started producing higher-quality goods at a lower cost. The store's inventory of mostly private-label merchandise was repositioned to include finer wools, silks, and cottons—replacing the rayons and polyester blends that had become the standard. To entice today's more casually attired working women, Ann Taylor now devotes a third of its merchandise to weekend wear. Prices have also been cut across the board, in some instances up to 20 percent. The chain has also curbed its empire building. Instead, it will focus on improving existing stores, with many outlets being enlarged to accommodate the retailer's expanded array of merchandise.

With these changes the chain has committed itself to getting back to the basics of selling quality merchandise. The main challenge for Ann Taylor now is to woo back the thousands of customers who have written off the chain.

### Questions

1. Reversing sales declines will be less painful for Ann Taylor stores in newer locations, where customers are less likely to have had bad experiences. Courting former customers will take time. If you were Ann Taylor's new CEO, what would be your message to once-loyal Ann Taylor customers to get them to reconsider the chain?

2. To regain consumer confidence, analysts believe Ann Taylor will be forced to announce its changes with heavy advertising. The company has traditionally done little advertising, however, relying more on catalogs and direct mail to the million or so Ann Taylor charge-account customers. As CEO, how would you promote the changes at Ann Taylor? Defend your answer.

✍3. Ann Taylor made a serious fashion blunder by failing to recognize the needs and wants of its target market. Write a detailed description of who you think Ann Taylor's target market is. Include demographic, geographic, and psychographic descriptors, if possible.

4. Given the target market description you developed for question 3, draft a marketing plan describing a new retail strategy in terms of product, price, promotion, place, presentation, and personnel.

### References

Teri Agins, "Ann Taylor Aims to Resew Torn Image," *The Wall Street Journal,* 14 September 1992, pp. B1, B5.

Sunita Bhargava, "Ann Retaylored," *Business Week,* 17 May 1993, pp. 70–72.

Susan Caminiti, "How to Win Back Customers," *Fortune,* 14 June 1993, p. 118.

Mary Colacecchi, "Ann Taylor at a Crossroads," *Catalog Age,* February 1992, p. 12.

Maggie Mahar, "Mission Impossible?" *Working Woman,* December 1993, pp. 60–63.

## SIGNATURE SERIES VIDEO CASE

## Tandy Corporation

John V. Roach

SIGNATURE SERIES VIDEO

*by John V. Roach*
*Chairman of the Board and Chief Executive Officer, Tandy Corporation*

1993 was an "incredible" year. At the beginning of the year, we were ready to state unequivocally that Tandy Corporation could add more value to the consumer electronics and personal computer retailing world than we could to the consumer electronics and personal computer manufacturing world. Therefore, we announced on January 10, 1993, that we would spin off our manufacturing assets.

As our management energetically pursued the spin-off, the opportunity came to divest most of our manufacturing assets. Bill Bousquette, Bob McClure, and their team divested five multiplant entities essentially in parallel—an "incredible" task—and the result is about $615 million in cash and $100 million in notes receivable. As a result, Tandy strengthened its balance sheet for its planned retail growth in the 1990s.

Our retail growth strategy was simple: modest growth from the Radio Shack division; strong growth from Computer City, which opened twenty stores during the year; and the expansion of our newest concept, Incredible Universe. The strategy was vigorously executed by our divisions.

In 1994, our retail growth strategy—basically the same simple strategy—had more ambitious goals:

- Radio Shack set its sights higher, with a commitment to increase its productivity, position itself even stronger in the marketplace, and introduce new programs to increase its top-of-mind awareness in the marketplace.

- Computer City planned to open even more stores—twenty-four or more—and to continue testing its new smaller-market format, Computer City Express, a half-size store for markets of 100,000 to 400,000 population.
- Our Tandy Name Brand Retail Group planned to continue strengthening its formats for secondary markets and malls.
- The Incredible Universe opened its fourth store in February 1994 in Miami, Florida—our biggest opening yet—and planned up to five more openings.

Executing these ambitious plans would bring in excess of $5 billion in revenue in 1994.

The heart of our strategy is to grow from strength. Radio Shack is unique as a consumer electronics service concept. Our geographic convenience; the availability of products in neighborhoods and remote areas not covered by competitors; our unique selection of products, parts, and accessories; our strong after-the-sale service; and our highly respected people in the store make it possible for us to say that Radio Shack has very little direct competition. Radio Shack's plan is to increase its services this year with its new repair shop and "gift express" programs, further differentiating Radio Shack from others who sell electronic products.

Computer City's strategy is focused on providing the best brands, super selection, and great prices. The real focus is winning the battle for customer shopping experience. With only one national competitor, the competitive environment is better in the computer warehouse superstore business than in many other highly competitive retail industries.

Incredible Universe is a unique shopping experience, one we think is perfect for the future. Its real strength is that it caters to customers' intelligence. The customers—we call them "guests"—are offered incredible information about a great selection of products, a selection two to five times greater than competitors'. There is no pressure to buy specific products, service contracts, or other add-ons. Guests are encouraged to touch, use, understand, and have fun with the products and to enjoy a fun environment with everything from karaoke to food. As an Incredible Universe guest, you will receive incredible service, from speedy transactions and entertainment for your child while you shop, to help with loading your purchase in your car. Most important, with single locations per market and limited advertising, we offer "everyday low prices" so that our guests don't have to worry about the deal-driven mania of most competitors. Our strength is clearly our differentiation from other retailers.

Another of our strengths is a comprehensive infrastructure that is highly focused on customers' shopping experience. Our excellent financial position is also a major asset; when combined with our enviable market position, it permits us to deal from strength in this industry.

We will continue to develop ways of increasing the strengths of all of our formats. We currently have about half a dozen tests underway to enhance our retailing activities. We simply want to be the market leader—the trusted market leader—in consumer electronics and personal computer retailing.

The Tandy team is made up of 42,000 people with a lot of pride in their achievements. Our management team is strong, with a deep sense of fairness for our customers and our employees. We thrive every day in a highly competitive arena, and I believe we've earned a high degree of trust from all those with whom we do business.

I know that our team can vigorously execute our retail growth strategy. My dream is that we will make Tandy one of the most exciting retail growth stories for the 1990s.

Questions

1. Assess Tandy's decision to spin off its manufacturing assets and to focus on retailing in consumer electronics and personal computers.
2. Compare and contrast the retailing mixes (the six P's) used to position Radio Shack, Computer City, and Incredible Universe.
3. Propose appropriate growth strategies for 1997 for Radio Shack, Computer City, and Incredible Universe .
4. Identify important environmental changes that you think will affect retailers of consumer electronics and personal computers in the next decade. What actions should Tandy take to benefit from these advancements, shifts, trends, and events?

**VIDEO CASE**

## Subway

Subway was founded in 1965 and began franchising operations in 1974. Subway is one of the fastest-growing franchise operations in the United States and currently has over 7,500 units. The secret to this rapid growth is the low franchise fee ($10,000), low required investment ($45,000), and ease of store operations. The only equipment needed to open a Subway franchise is bread-baking equipment, two freezers, and a soda-dispensing machine. This equipment can all fit in a relatively small space, and so store overhead is very low. In addition, Subway offers its franchisees one of the most attractive franchise packages around. Each new franchise owner receives a two-week training program in store operations, personnel management, and marketing.

Restaurant spending is increasing at the rate of about 5 percent per year. Some of this growth can be attributed to the value focus of many restaurants. Most of the big fast-food restaurants now feature lower-priced value items. Supermarkets are also trying to tap into the prepared-food takeout market by offering salad bars and expanded deli services.

Demographic trends in the United States are likely to have a major impact on the restaurant business. Two significant factors are the aging population and the rising birth rate. As consumers age, they move away from fast-food restaurants toward midscale restaurants. These aging consumers also have an interest in eating healthful foods. Larger family size means that families are more likely to eat at home.

The sandwich category continues to gain a larger share of overall restaurant sales. Current trends in this category include broader menus designed to appeal to the nonsandwich customer, and nontraditional sites. Since 1992, Subway has established itself as the category leader.

Sandwich shops have the unique advantage of being able to vary their product line without changing their identity or making extensive capital investments. Also, in today's health-conscious world, sandwiches offer a light and healthy alternative to the more traditional offerings of other fast-food outlets.

The key problem facing sandwich shops like Subway is attracting the nonlunch customer. Typically, people see Subway as a good place for lunch, not dinner. By promoting hot sandwiches, like the meatball sub, these stores hope to bring in dinner business. The company has also begun exploring some breakfast items; early results show a 7 percent sales increase. Another good marketing opportunity for submarine sandwich outlets has always been catering. What could possibly be better for a large informal party than a gigantic submarine sandwich?

Adapting the menu to local markets is another strength at Subway. Subway allows its franchisees the opportunity to add up to two sandwiches to the corporate list. These sandwiches are tailored to local tastes. For example, Subway outlets in Alaska have added caribou sandwiches to the menu. Stores in Bahrain offer lamb to their customers. By allowing franchisees to meet the local market demand, Subway continues to be one of the fastest-growing franchises in the world.

Subway has also begun targeting the kid's market with "kid's meals" that are specially priced and packaged and that include prizes. Adopting the kid's marketing ploys practiced by other chains will enable Subway to compete directly for this market. The strategy is that parents will follow their kids' lead in choosing brands. Also, in an effort to capture their share of the summer fast-food sales, Subway developed its Subway Dream Game to compete directly with the promotional efforts of McDonald's (Dream Team 2) and Burger King (The Lion King).

### Questions

1. Discuss the advantages that Subway offers its franchisees. What advantages does Subway gain through having these franchisees?
2. What can Subway do to more effectively compete with the larger fast-food companies, such as McDonald's and Burger King?

References

Sam Bradley and Betsy Spethmann, "Subway Kid's Pack: The Ties That Sell," *Brandweek,* 10 October 1994, p. 22.

John Cortez, "Subway Builds Its Way to No. 2," *Advertising Age,* 5 July 1993, pp. 144–150.

Theresa Howard, "Subway Boosts Morning Daypart with New Menu," *Nation's Restaurant News,* 16 May 1994, p. 7.

Terry Lefton, "Subway Aims for Kids Biz," *Brandweek,* 21 June 1993, p. 6.

Susan Boyles Martin (ed.), *Worldwide Franchise Directory* (Detroit: Gale Research, 1995).

*Standard & Poor's Industry Surveys* (New York: Standard & Poor's Corporation, October 1995).

Jeanne Whalen, "A Sizzling Season of Fast-Food Promos," *Advertising Age,* 30 May 1994, pp. 1–2.

# CHAPTER 14

# PHYSICAL DISTRIBUTION MANAGEMENT

## LEARNING OBJECTIVES

*After studying this chapter, you should be able to*

1 *Explain the importance of physical distribution.*

2 *Discuss the concept of balancing physical distribution service and cost.*

3 *Describe the subsystems of the physical distribution system.*

4 *Identify the special problems and opportunities associated with physical distribution in service organizations.*

5 *Discuss new technology and emerging trends in physical distribution.*

While most of the large retailers and apparel makers in the United States have just been talking about using modern distribution techniques, Italy's Benetton Group, located in the tiny village of Ponzano Veneto, has been setting the world standard for apparel distribution for a decade. Benetton ships 80 million items each year to over 7,000 United Colors of Benetton, Sisley, and other stores in over 100 countries.

An order from a Benetton retailer can be received, filled, and shipped in as little as seven days. Most of the items are shipped from one automated warehouse near the company's headquarters. Each Benetton store communicates electronically with headquarters, either directly or through one of eighty company agents. The entire distribution and transportation process is paperless. Benetton's 200 suppliers and 850 subcontractors are tied to the company's distribution and manufacturing information system, as are its major transportation carriers and its in-house freight forwarders.

The payoff of this distribution system is near-perfect customer satisfaction levels and the best order turnaround times in the apparel industry. Benetton carries no excess stock in the distribution pipeline. As a result, there is no end stock that has to be liquidated.

Because the apparel market changes so quickly, Benetton's distribution system must be highly responsive. The company must be capable of having entirely new fashion collections in its stores every few months. A traditional logistics and distribution system would exact too high a price in lost sales and obsolescence.

Almost every one of the 15,000 Benetton cartons shipped each day comes from the company's highly automated warehouse in Italy. Each carton, which has already been bar coded, enters the warehouse through either one of fifty receiving bays or an underground conveyor system from an adjoining factory. After the items for an order are pulled from the shelves, they are packed in a carton and sent to a preloading area, where transportation personnel complete invoicing and transportation documents. The in-house customs broker prepares customs documents and consolidates ocean and air containers. These documents are then transmitted electronically to points of entry in the destination country, so the apparel is not delayed in customs.

The distribution center sends three types of shipments to Benetton stores. For the two seasonal collections, which are scheduled ten months in advance and consist of thousands of pieces for each store, ocean transport is used. Benetton has plenty of time for these shipments to reach their destination, so the long transit time of about twenty-two days is not a concern. Ocean shipment is also much less expensive than other modes. The second type of shipment, regular store replenishment, may occur every week or two depending on demand. Most stores receive shipments about every twelve days. These shipments are sent by air, and they typically take no more than seven to eight days from order to receipt to almost any point in the world. Emergency shipments, the third type, all go by air.

Benetton expects to double its sales by the end of the decade, primarily through expansion into developing countries—which will bring different logistics and distribution challenges to the company. To further challenge its logistics system, Benetton also plans to begin manufacturing more of its clothing and accessories through joint ventures in China, Turkey, Egypt, India, and Mexico.[1]

What benefits does a highly automated distribution center contribute to Benetton's logistics and distribution system? How does its order-processing system benefit the entire system? For what specific reasons did Benetton choose air and ocean modes of transportation?

*Distribution Magazine*, October 1993, Chilton Way, Radnor, PA 19089

1 *Explain the importance of physical distribution.*

**physical distribution**
Ingredient in the marketing mix that describes how products are moved and stored.

**logistics**
Procurement and management of raw materials for production.

## THE IMPORTANCE OF PHYSICAL DISTRIBUTION

**Physical distribution** is the ingredient in the marketing mix that describes how products are moved and stored. Physical distribution consists of all business activities concerned with stocking and transporting materials and parts or finished inventory so they arrive at the right place when needed and in usable condition.

A broader term that encompasses physical distribution is **logistics,** which also includes the procurement and management of raw materials and component parts for production. Logistics management includes these activities:

- Managing the movement and storage of raw materials and parts from their sources to the production site
- Managing the movement of raw materials, semimanufactured products, and finished products within and among plants, warehouses, and distribution centers
- Planning and coordinating the physical distribution of finished goods to intermediaries and final buyers

In summary, logistics managers are responsible for directing raw materials and parts to the production department and the finished or semifinished product through warehouses and eventually to the intermediary or end user. Exhibit 14.1 depicts the logistics process. Most of this chapter is about the distribution of goods within warehouses and to final users.

Exhibit 14.1

Logistics Process

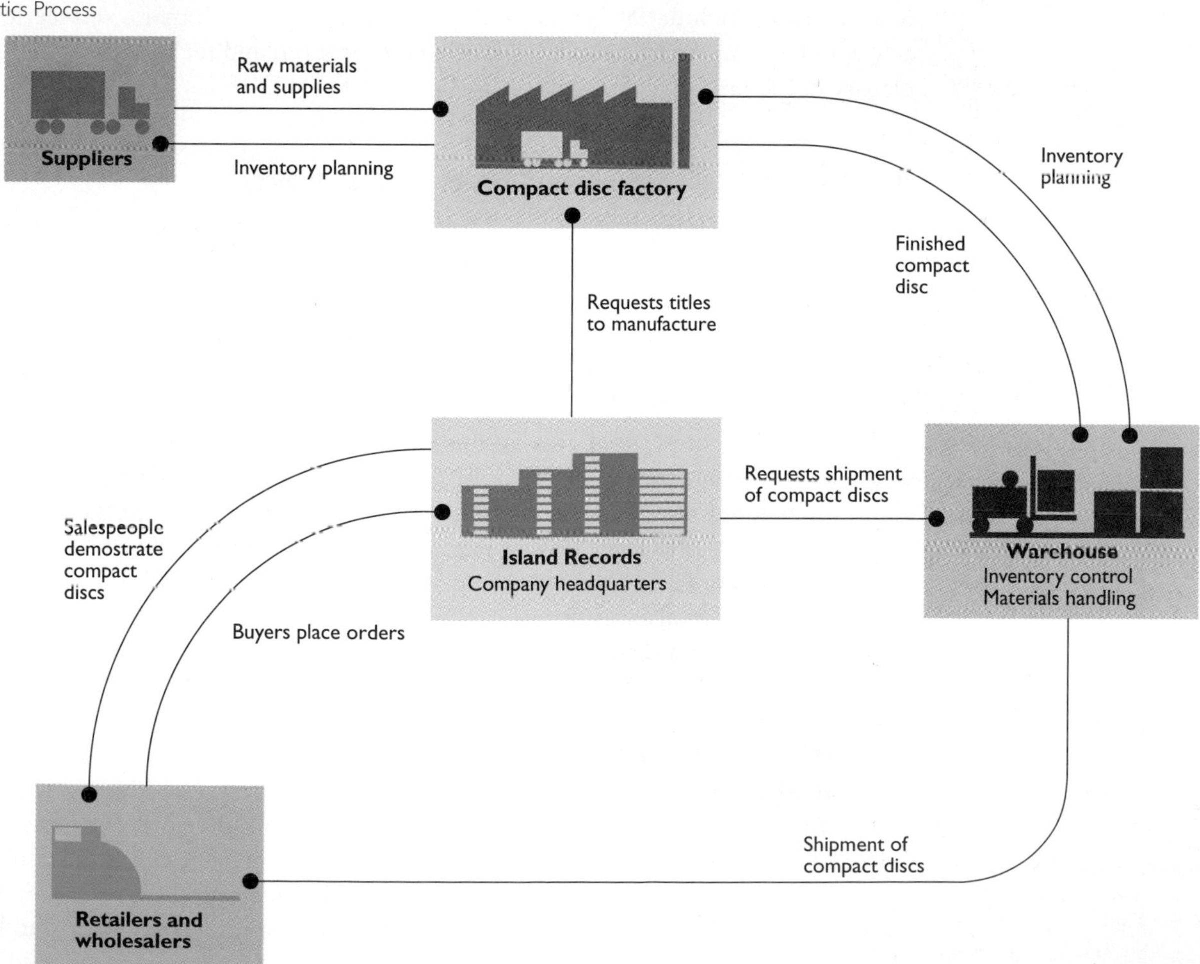

### PHYSICAL DISTRIBUTION AND THE MARKETING CONCEPT

Because it can decrease costs and increase customer satisfaction, physical distribution is a central part of the marketing concept. It creates the time and place utility so important to consumers; they value receiving the products they want, when they want them, and where they want them. Physical distribution also broadens the variety of goods available to consumers. Few people would own a Toyota or Honda if they had to go to Japan to buy one. Similarly, consumers can buy a Lands' End sweater for the same price anywhere in the United States, even though the sweaters are shipped from Wisconsin. Physical distribution not only provides a greater variety of goods but also broadens the area of competition.

Logistics and physical distribution are becoming more important in marketing strategies for both changing markets and existing markets. Instead of differentiating themselves from rivals on price or product superiority, organizations are achieving an advantage through more effective physical distribution, especially in markets with standardized products. They can enhance physical distribution by shortening the time needed for storage, handling, and transportation of products.

### THE ROLE OF THE PHYSICAL DISTRIBUTION MANAGER

The need for better service and cost control in a competitive environment underscores the importance of distribution. Physical distribution managers' scope of authority and responsibility has broadened to meet the challenge. Distribution managers do periodic strategy audits to strengthen their departments. The issues that concern them include the levels of service expected by customers, service levels achieved by competitors, warehouse and plant location, and technological and regulatory developments.

2 *Discuss the concept of balancing physical distribution service and cost.*

## THE BALANCE BETWEEN SERVICE AND COST

Physical distribution encompasses many activities, but only recently have all these activities been combined in a single department. As distribution departments have evolved, their emphasis has changed from getting the lowest transportation rates to the broader issue of minimizing total distribution cost. Distribution costs are both explicit (for example, actual costs associated with distribution) and implicit (for example, missed opportunities, such as lost sales due to slow delivery systems).

The main goal of physical distribution is getting the right goods to the right place at the right time for the least cost. Unfortunately, few physical distribution systems can both maximize customer service and minimize distribution costs. The best customer service requires large inventories and rapid transportation, which drive up costs. Although reduced inventories and slower transportation may lower distribution costs, they can also result in customer dissatisfaction. Distribution managers, therefore, strive for a reasonable balance between customer service and total distribution cost.

### PHYSICAL DISTRIBUTION SERVICE

**physical distribution service**
Interrelated activities performed by a supplier to ensure that the right product is in the right place at the right time.

**Physical distribution service** is the package of activities performed by a supplier to ensure that the right product is in the right place at the right time. Customers are rarely interested in the activities themselves; instead, they are interested in the results or the benefits they receive from those activities—namely, efficient distribution. Specifically, customers are concerned with how long it takes to receive an order and how consistent delivery is, how much effort it takes to place an order, and what condition

*Exhibit 14.2*

How to Set the Service Level at the Least Cost

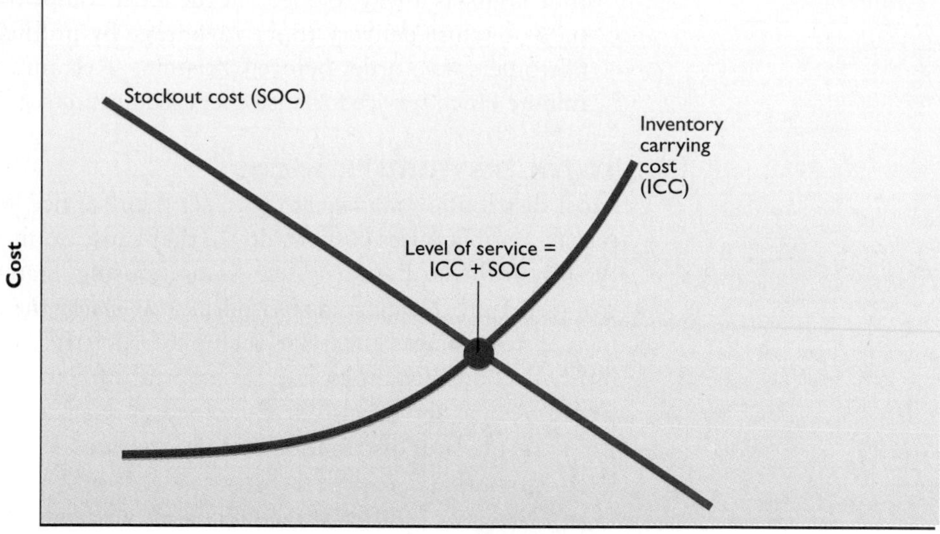


the product is in when it is finally received. Order processing, order assembly, and delivery are of no consequence to the buyer. What matters most are the quality and timeliness of the supplier's performance.[2]

When setting service levels, physical distribution managers must be sensitive to their customers' needs. At the most basic level, customers demand availability, timeliness, and quality. *Availability* is the proportion or percentage of orders that can be completely filled right away. Unavailable goods must be back ordered, causing time delays and extra costs, or the customer can simply cancel the order. *Timeliness* in physical distribution service is, for the buyer, minimal time elapsed between placing the order and receiving it. *Quality* is a low incidence of in-transit damage, shipment of incorrect items, and incorrect shipment quantity.[3]

How does a distribution manager actually set the level of service? There are four possible strategies:

- The first strategy is to cut costs to the minimum and eliminate service entirely. In this case, the distribution manager's main concern is storing, handling, and transporting the product at the least cost possible.
- The second strategy is to offer maximum service at any cost. Because this strategy is so expensive, it is very seldom followed.
- The third strategy sets the level of service where the sum of the costs of being out of stock and carrying inventory is at its lowest point. This approach assumes that service is synonymous with inventory levels and that customers become dissatisfied when a product is not in stock. The cost of being out of stock (**stockout cost**) includes direct costs due to lost sales and indirect costs due to the loss of dissatisfied customers. The graph in Exhibit 14.2 illustrates this concept. As you can see, stockout costs are highest when inventory levels are kept at a minimum. Conversely, when excess inventory is maintained, then inventory carrying costs are high.

**stockout cost**
Cost of being out of stock, which includes direct costs due to lost sales and indirect costs due to the loss of dissatisfied customers.

- The fourth strategy is to seek a competitive advantage. The firm sets physical distribution service at a level just slightly higher than the competition's. For instance, a furniture company may offer customers free delivery within twenty-four hours as a way to edge out the local competition. A mail-order gift company may use delivery to its advantage by promising three-day shipment to customers who order before Christmas. Restaurants often guarantee fifteen-minute lunch service for customers who need to get back to work.

## TOTAL DISTRIBUTION COST

Most distribution managers try to set their service level at a point that maximizes service yet minimizes cost. To do so, they must examine the total cost of all parts of the physical distribution system—warehousing, materials handling, inventory control, order processing, and transportation—using the total cost approach. The basic idea is to examine the relationship of such factors as number of warehouses, finished-goods inventory, and transportation expenses. Of course, the cost of any single element should also be examined in relation to the level of customer service. Thus the physical distribution system is viewed as a whole, not as a series of unrelated activities.

Often the high cost of air transportation can be justified under the total cost approach. Rapid delivery may drastically reduce the number of warehouses required at distant locations. Therefore, the higher cost of using air freight may be more than justified by the savings in inventory and warehouse expenses, as shown in Exhibit 14.3. For example, by using air transport, Swedish carmaker Volvo is able to quickly get automobile parts to its North American Volvo dealers, thereby keeping customers happy and inventories down. Everything from nuts and bolts to parts as large as fenders are flown or trucked from Gothenburg to Oslo or Copenhagen in order to meet one of the shipper's daily U.S.-bound flights. The shipments are cleared through customs ahead of time so they can move quickly. Once in the United

*Exhibit 14.3*

How Using Air Freight Lowers Distribution Costs under the Total Cost Approach

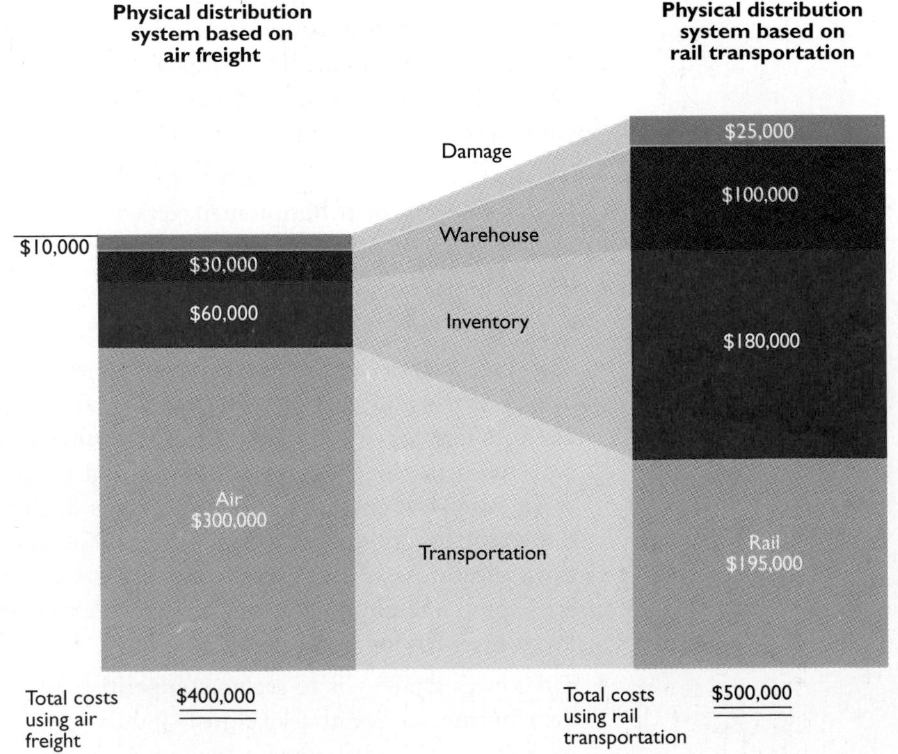

Although air freight is the costliest transportation mode, it is fast and offers special handling for high-value goods.

© John Madere

States, the shipment is transferred to a nearby Federal Express facility in time to make that evening's departure. With this system, Volvo can typically get parts to its U.S. dealers in as little as two days. This form of transportation is expensive, but Volvo's distribution system has become an integral part of its customer satisfaction program.[4]

Implementing the total cost approach requires trade-offs. For example, a supplier that wants to provide next-day delivery to its customers and also minimize transportation costs must make a trade-off between the desired level of service (expensive next-day delivery) and the transportation goal (minimal costs). The options are setting a new service standard, perhaps two-day delivery instead of next-day delivery, or accepting the high cost. Intel, for example, wanted to decrease variability in delivery times and reduce customers' inventory levels. It turned to FedEx for distribution of its new Pentium microprocessor from a Manila plant to customers' receiving docks. Although the transportation method itself is more expensive, Intel increased on-time deliveryies, cut the time it takes to process and deliver an order from fourteen days to four days, and reduced the costs of in-transit inventory.[5]

Ideally, the distribution manager would like to optimize overall distribution performance—that is, to balance distribution activities so that overall distribution costs are minimized while the desired level of physical distribution service is maintained. If attempts to minimize costs and maximize service don't work, the result is *suboptimization.* The problem may be a conflict between physical distribution components. For instance, the transportation people may want to provide customers with same-day delivery, but the order-processing people may take two to three days to process an order.

Suboptimization often occurs in physical distribution because different managers oversee the distribution functions. For example, inventory handling may be a responsibility of the production department, and order processing may be assigned to accounting. More than likely, these managers have different goals for customer service and costs. The only cure is for top management to recognize the role of logistics and physical distribution in helping the firm reach its overall objectives and to build better coordination into the organizational structure.

3 *Describe the subsystems of the physical distribution system.*

## PHYSICAL DISTRIBUTION SUBSYSTEMS

The physical distribution system consists of five distinct subsystems, which serve several key functions of physical distribution managers: deciding on warehouse location, number, size, and type; setting up a materials-handling and packaging system; maintaining an inventory control system; setting procedures for processing orders; and selecting modes of transportation. These subsystems are shown in Exhibit 14.4.

*Exhibit 14.4*

Subsystems of Physical Distribution

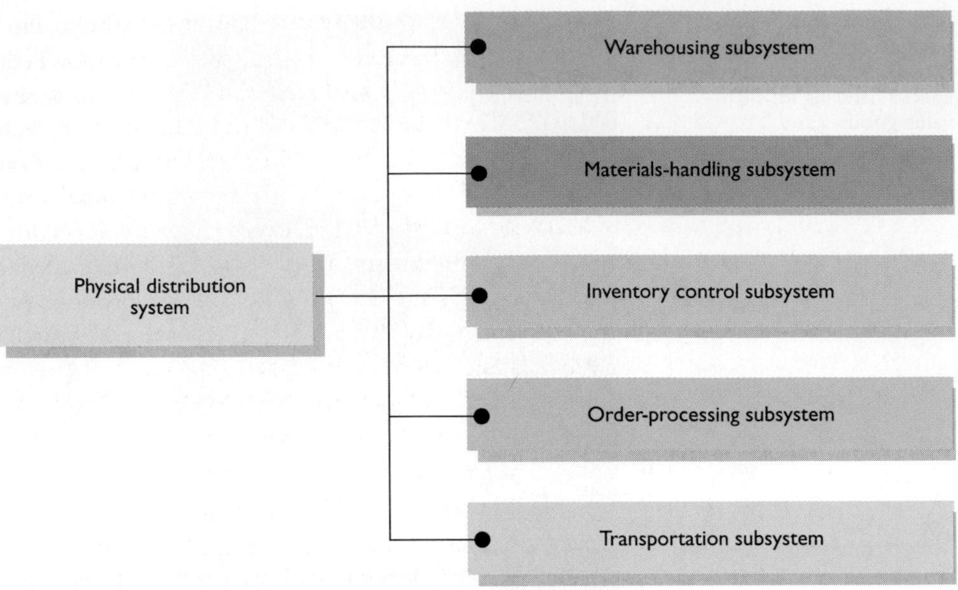


Although these subsystems are discussed here separately, they are, of course, highly interdependent.

## WAREHOUSING

Distribution managers oversee the constant flow of goods from the manufacturer to the ultimate consumer. However, the final user may not need or want the goods at the same time the manufacturer produces and wants to sell them. Products like grain and corn are produced seasonally, but consumers demand them year-round. Other products, such as Christmas ornaments and turkeys, are produced year-round, but consumers do not want them until autumn or winter. Therefore, management must have a storage system to hold these products until they are shipped.

Storage is what helps manufacturers manage supply and demand, or production and consumption. It provides time utility to buyers and sellers, which means that the seller stores the product until the buyer wants or needs it. Even when products are used regularly, not seasonally, many manufacturers store excess products in case the demand surpasses the amount produced at a given time. Storing additional product does have disadvantages, however, including the costs of insurance on the stored product, taxes, obsolescence or spoilage, theft, and warehouse operating costs. Another drawback is opportunity costs—that is, the lost opportunities of using for something else the money that is tied up in stored product.

If a product does require storage, the manufacturer needs somewhere to house it. Warehouses are places for holding a product until it is demanded by consumers. Distribution managers must make several key decisions about warehousing: Where are the best locations? How many warehouses are needed? How big should they be? What type of warehouse should be used?

## WAREHOUSE LOCATION, NUMBER, AND SIZE

Warehouse locations are typically chosen to be near the markets to be served and near the production facilities. In general, if markets are near the plant, then storage facilities are usually nearby, too. Sometimes markets are widely dispersed, however.

For instance, when the manufacturer distributes nationally or globally, then warehouses may be located in each regional or national market served.

Other important considerations affecting warehouse location are the quality and versatility of transportation, the quantity and quality of labor, the cost and quality of industrial land, taxes, local government regulations, and local utility costs. For example, when selecting a site for its centralized warehouse, Becton Dickinson, a leading provider of health care products in Europe, was primarily concerned with labor and transportation costs, tax factors, geography (to achieve the right balance among customers, ports, and manufacturing locations), the quality of the roads and harbors, and the compatibility of the local culture with Becton Dickinson's objectives. Its final choice was Belgium, mostly because of Antwerp's large, modern, and convenient port, Belgian government tax grants and financial incentives, and the area's strong base of information technology.[6]

The number of warehouses needed and their size depend mainly on the level of customer service required. A supplier that wishes to provide next-day delivery anywhere in the country may need many warehouses, located in each major region of the country. A supplier that promises never to be out of stock may need a larger warehouse to store surplus product.

More, larger, and more widely dispersed warehouses are needed when supply sources and markets are widely separated and when customer service is important. Fewer, smaller, or closer warehouses may be warranted when suppliers and markets are located near each other and service is kept at a minimum.

## TYPES OF WAREHOUSES

There are also several types of warehouses: private warehouses, public warehouses, and distribution centers.

### Private Warehouses

**private warehouse**
Storage facility either leased or owned by a company that needs to store a large amount of its own merchandise.

A **private warehouse** is either leased or owned by a company that needs to store large amounts of its own merchandise. Whether to lease or own a private warehouse or to use a public warehouse is mainly a financial issue. Ownership entails expenses for land, building, insurance, and taxes. Although private warehouses can represent a significant investment, the firm can design them to its exact specifications and have complete control over their operation.

### Public Warehouses

**public warehouse**
Independently owned storage facility that stores merchandise for others and that may specialize in certain types of products, such as furniture, refrigerated foods, or household goods.

A **public warehouse** is independently owned (not owned by the firms storing goods there). It often specializes in certain types of products, such as furniture, refrigerated foods, or household goods. Using public warehouses, a producer can place inventories close to key customers for quick delivery without the cost of building private facilities. Public warehouses also offer specialized services, such as inventory-level maintenance, local delivery, materials handling and packaging, price marking, marketing information systems, and office and display space.

A warehouse may be partly or entirely vacant in lean economic times. If it is a private warehouse, the company still must maintain it and pay insurance and real estate taxes, among many other costs. But a company using public warehouses can expand its storage and distribution network during an economic upswing or reduce inventory space during slow periods without causing a cash-flow problem. When

The most successful companies invest in quality distribution systems, to make sure the product gets to the right places in a timely manner. Shown here is The Gap's new high-tech distribution center outside Baltimore, which channels the chain's clothing to East Coast stores.



the company enters new markets, using public warehouses may reduce distribution risks and increase flexibility. It can also more effectively meet seasonal demand.

Manufacturers often use public warehouses for short-term needs, usually for thirty days. For longer-term storage space, manufacturers typically use private warehouses or may enter into a contractual arrangement with a public warehouse. Under **contract warehousing,** both the manufacturer and the warehouse are legally committed in a business relationship for a specified period. Contract warehousing is most appropriate when the manufacturer asks the warehouse to make a major investment in facilities, equipment, or people. For example, a stored product may require extra care in handling or may be so large that additional storage space must be constructed or allocated. A long-term warehousing contract may also allow the manufacturer to lock in favorable rates.[7]

**contract warehousing**
Agreement between a manufacturer and a public warehouse facility to provide storage space for a specified period.

## Distribution Centers

Many corporations use distribution centers to efficiently move products to market. A **distribution center** is a special form of warehouse that specializes in making bulk (consolidating shipments) or breaking bulk (breaking up shipments that will leave the distribution center in smaller quantities). For example, Benetton's distribution center in Italy receives merchandise from its many warehouses and consolidates orders to be shipped to its stores around the globe.

**distribution center**
Type of warehouse that specializes in making bulk or breaking bulk and that strives for rapid inventory turnover.

A distribution center differs from a warehouse in many ways. Specifically, a distribution center is a centralized warehousing operation, usually serving a regional market, that processes and regroups products. Most distribution centers are highly computerized, with automated materials-handling equipment, rather than physical labor, to place and pick items. Distribution centers also improve customer service by cutting delivery time and ensuring product availability. Exhibit 14.5 illustrates the concept of a distribution center.

A distribution center strives for rapid inventory turnover, as opposed to long-term

*Exhibit 14.5*

Distribution Center Concept

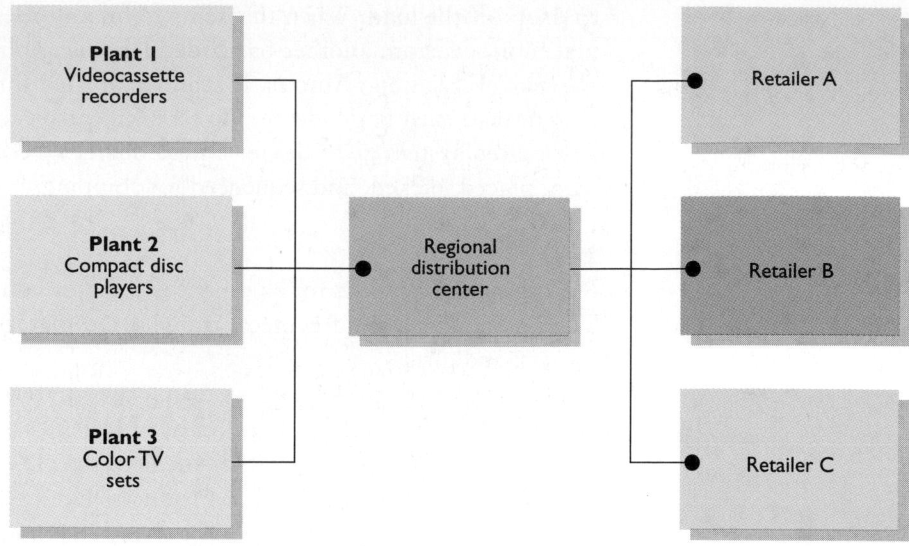


**cross docking**
Method used by many distribution centers to increase efficiency, in which goods are moved directly from the receiving dock to the shipping dock or are held in a temporary area before moving them to the outbound dock, without putting the goods into storage.

storage. Thus many distribution centers use the method called **cross docking,** which eliminates the need to put products into storage before sending them to retail stores or other customers. Instead, the goods move from the receiving dock directly to the shipping dock or are held in a temporary storage area before moving to the outbound dock.[8] Wal-Mart uses cross docking at its distribution centers to avoid excessive warehousing and inventory-handling costs. Wal-Mart places full truckload orders with its vendors, receives these goods at one of its nineteen distribution centers, and then, within a forty-eight-hour window, unpacks and repacks the goods in the configuration needed by each individual store and dispatches the shipments on some of its 2,000 company-owned trucks. In essence, the goods move straight from the receiving dock to the shipping dock.[9]

## MATERIALS HANDLING

**materials-handling system**
Method of moving inventory into, within, and out of the warehouse.

A **materials-handling system** moves inventory into, within, and out of the warehouse. Materials handling includes these functions:

- Receiving goods into the warehouse or distribution center
- Identifying, sorting, and labeling the goods
- Dispatching the goods to a temporary storage area
- Recalling, selecting, or picking the goods for shipment (may include packaging the product in a protective container for shipping)

The goal of the materials-handling system is to move items quickly with minimal handling. With a manual, nonautomated materials-handling system, a product may be handled more than a dozen times. Each time it is handled, the cost and risk of damaging it increase; each lifting of a product stresses its package.

Baxter Health Care, a leading manufacturer and marketer of health care products, uses a sophisticated materials-handling system to reduce product handling and keep costs to a minimum. As goods are received into the warehouse, bar-coded labels are affixed to the pallets of incoming product, which are then placed on a fully automated conveyor to be sent to the storage area. There, truck operators scan the labels while an on-board, radio-controlled computer tells the operator exactly where to drop off the load. When the items to fill an order are picked off the shelves and placed in a carton, another bar-coded label is applied, and the carton is placed on the conveyer system. Automatic scanners posted throughout the intricate conveyor system read each bar code and divert each carton to the proper shipping lane. This automated system gives Baxter a high degree of control over how orders are handled, placed, picked, and sequenced for shipping.[10]

## Packaging

Packaging the product for shipment is a major concern of materials management. The packaging is what protects transported materials against breakage, spoilage, insects, and dirt.

Well-designed packaging restricts the material's movement. For instance, Waterford/Wedgwood, the distributor of Ireland's famed Waterford crystal, uses an adhesive-coated bubble wrap that sticks to the glass to cut down handling time and reduce product damage. Larger products, like furniture or computer equipment, may be shipped in vehicles that are themselves padded for protection.

## Automatic Identification and Bar Coding

**automatic identification (auto ID)**
Use of identification technology to mark and read products as they enter and leave the supplier's warehouse or as they are received by a manufacturer or retailer.

Materials handling, like many other subsystems in physical distribution, is being driven by the need for fast, accurate information. **Automatic identification,** or **auto ID,** is the use of identification technology to mark and read products as they enter and leave the warehouse or as they are received by a manufacturer or retailer. Auto ID may employ voice identification, radio frequencies, or magnetic strips, although bar coding is the most common method.

As Chapter 9 explains, bar coding is the marking of the good or its package with a computer-readable bar pattern. Bar codes store information in a pattern of parallel black and white lines. The traditional bar codes can hold up to twenty or thirty characters per inch, or enough to spell out the universal product code, which is fed into a computer that tells the cash register how much to ring up. New technology, however, has increased the amount of information that can be held in bar codes, and they are no longer limited to just identifying the product. The new high-density bar codes can also tell where the product came from, where it's supposed to go, and what special handling it requires.[11]

## Automatic Storage and Retrieval

**automatic storage and retrieval systems (AS/RS)**
Technology that enables material handlers to automatically store and pick goods from a warehouse or distribution center, in order to decrease product handling, increase order fulfillment accuracy, and increase on-time shipments.

Working side-by-side with auto ID are **automatic storage and retrieval systems** (AS/RS) that automatically store and pick goods in the warehouse or distribution center. These systems decrease product handling and ensure accurate placement of product. AS/RS systems also improve the accuracy of order picking and the rates of on-time shipment.

When a new shipment arrives at the warehouse, the product is generally bar coded and entered into the AS/RS. From there the product may be placed on an automated conveyor system. An automated guided vehicle can then pick it up and place it exactly where it belongs on the warehouse shelves. When an order is placed into the AS/RS, the automated guided vehicle scans the bar-coded products on the warehouse shelves, pulls the right ones, and places them on the automated conveyor system, which sends them to be packaged and shipped.

## Unitization and Containerization

Two important elements of modern materials handling are unitization and con-

Containerization has revolutionized the shipping industry.



tainerization. **Unitization,** or unitizing, is a technique for handling small packages more efficiently. It means grouping boxes on a pallet or skid, which is then moved mechanically, by a forklift, truck, or conveyor system.

**unitization**
Increasing the efficiency of handling small packages by grouping boxes on a pallet or skid for movement from one place to another.

**Containerization** is the process of putting large quantities of goods in sturdy containers that can be moved from ship to truck to airplane to train without repacking. The containers are sealed until delivery, thereby reducing damage and theft. They are essentially miniature mobile warehouses that travel from manufacturing plant to receiving dock. A container, often a special form of truck trailer body, can be reused repeatedly. The average container lasts ten years and can be repaired if damaged.

**containerization**
Putting large quantities of goods in sturdy containers that can be moved from ship to truck to airplane to train without repacking.

## INVENTORY CONTROL

Another important function of physical distribution is establishing an inventory control system. An **inventory control system** develops and maintains an adequate assortment of products to meet customers' demands.

**inventory control system**
Method of developing and maintaining an adequate assortment of products to meet customers' demands.

Inventory decisions have a big impact on physical distribution costs and the level of physical distribution service provided. If too many products are kept in inventory, costs increase—as do risks of obsolescence, theft, and damage. If too few products are kept on hand, then the company risks product shortages and angry customers. The goal of inventory management, therefore, is to keep inventory levels as low as possible while maintaining an adequate supply of goods to meet customer demand.

Two major decisions managers must make regarding inventory are when to buy (order timing) and how much to buy (order quantity). Their task is complicated by the popularity of just-in-time inventory management, which essentially requires smaller but more frequent shipments.

### Order Timing

The **reorder point** is the inventory level that signals when more inventory should be ordered. Three factors determine the reorder point. First, the *order lead time* is the expected time between the date an order is placed and the date the goods are received and made ready for resale to customers. Second, the *usage rate* specifies the rate at which a product is sold or consumed. Third, the *quantity of **safety stock*** needed is the amount of extra merchandise kept on hand to protect against running out of stock. If the safety stock is inadequate, unpredictable usage or unreliable deliveries may cause lost sales.

**reorder point**
Inventory level that signals when more inventory should be ordered.

**safety stock**
Extra merchandise kept on hand to protect against running out of stock.

The reorder point is calculated by first multiplying the order lead time by the usage rate. This figure tells an inventory manager the level of basic stock to have. To avoid stockouts, the manager would then add the quantity of safety stock to this figure to arrive at a final reorder point quantity. The computation is

$$\text{Reorder point quantity} = (\text{Order lead time} \times \text{Usage rate}) + \text{Safety stock quantity}$$

Suppose that Target stocks and sells a limited line of sheets and bedding. Suppose the company sells 100 sheet sets per week (20 per day), and the sheets normally arrive two weeks after ordering. The company also needs at least two days' worth of safety stock. The computation would look like this:

$$\text{Reorder point quantity} = (2 \times 100) + 40 = 240$$

Target would need to reorder sheet sets when its inventory dropped to 240 sets.

This procedure for calculating the reorder point is typically used by companies with computerized inventory control systems, which automatically place an order when the inventory reaches the reorder point. However, most small companies do not have computerized inventory control systems, and some other companies have a computerized system for only part of their inventory management process. These companies need to consider a couple of other variables when they calculate reorder points: how often inventory levels are assessed and how often orders are placed.

**economic order quantity (EOQ)**
Order volume that minimizes order processing costs and inventory carrying costs.

**order processing cost**
Total of operating expenses for the ordering or purchasing department, costs of required follow-up, operating expenses for the receiving department, expenses incurred in paying invoices, and the portion of data-processing costs related to purchasing and acquiring inventory.

**ordering cost**
Average cost per order, calculated by dividing the order processing cost by the number of orders placed per year.

**inventory carrying cost**
Total of all expenses involved in maintaining inventory, including the cost of capital tied up in idle merchandise, the cost of obsolescence, space charges, handling charges, insurance costs, property taxes, losses due to depreciation and deterioration, and opportunity costs.

## Order Quantity

The amount to order or the level of inventory that should be ordered at any one time is guided by the **economic order quantity** (EOQ), which is a measure of the order volume that minimizes these two costs:

- ***Order processing cost:*** total of operating expenses for the ordering or purchasing department, costs of required follow-up, operating expenses for the receiving department, expenses incurred in paying invoices, and the portion of data-processing costs related to purchasing and acquiring inventory. This sum is then divided by the number of orders placed per year, to arrive at an **ordering cost.**
- ***Inventory carrying cost:*** total of all expenses involved in maintaining inventory. These expenses include the cost of capital tied up in idle merchandise, the

*Exhibit 14.6*

Economic Order Quantity (EOQ)

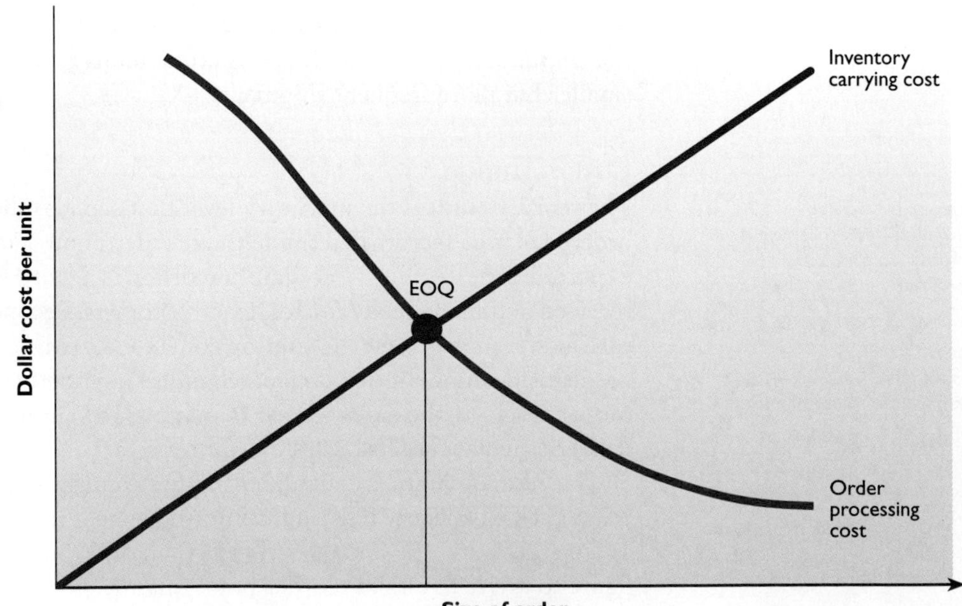

cost of obsolescence, space charges, handling charges, insurance costs, property taxes, losses due to depreciation, losses due to deterioration, and opportunity costs.

Exhibit 14.6 shows the relationship between these costs.

The EOQ can be computed by using this formula:

$$\text{EOQ} = \sqrt{\frac{2 \times \text{Units sold (or average usage)} \times \text{Order cost}}{\text{Unit cost} \times \text{Inventory carrying cost (\%)}}}$$

A simple example will help explain the EOQ. Assume that a software distributor sells an average of 600 word-processing programs a year, at a unit cost of $24. The ordering cost of such software is $48 per order. The cost of carrying it in the warehouse is 24 percent per year (24 percent of the unit cost per year, or 2 percent per month, is a typical figure for most businesses). For calculating the EOQ, it is important that units sold and inventory carrying costs be in the same time unit, such as years. We can now compute the EOQ for this software distributor:

$$\text{EOQ} = \sqrt{\frac{2 \times 600 \times 48}{24 \times 0.24}} = 100 \text{ units (or two months' sales)}$$

The result shows that it is most economical for the software distributor to order 100 copies of word-processing programs at a time.

The application of EOQ presents many practical problems. For instance, small businesses need simple, easy-to-use, inexpensive inventory management systems keyed to current data sources and operations. Using EOQ requires continuous monitoring of inventory, and keeping EOQ values current requires frequent updating of the order processing cost and the inventory carrying cost. Furthermore, computation of the EOQ demands accurate knowledge of order processing cost per order and inventory carrying cost per dollar of inventory.[12] However, with today's wide availability of low-cost computers and cost-estimating software, large and small firms alike have the opportunity to use EOQ to improve their inventory management.

Scanner technology also simplifies calculation of the EOQ. Nintendo of America ships video games directly to more than 8,000 retail customers from its one distribution center in Washington. All video games entering the Nintendo distribution center are entered into the inventory management system by means of bar codes and scanners. A sophisticated computer system automatically determines when the distribution center needs to replenish certain games and automatically shifts slower-moving games to less trafficked areas of the distribution center.[13]

## Just-in-Time Inventory Management

**just-in-time (JIT) inventory management**
Redesigning and simplifying manufacturing by reducing inventory levels and delivering parts just when they are needed on the production line.

Borrowed from the Japanese, **just-in-time** (JIT) **inventory management** is a way to redesign and simplify manufacturing. For the manufacturer, JIT means that raw materials arrive at the assembly line in guaranteed working order "just in time" to be installed, and finished products are generally shipped to the customer immediately after completion. For the supplier, JIT means supplying its customers with products in just a few days, or even a few hours, rather than weeks. More and more U.S. manufacturing firms are using just-in-time inventory management systems. As a result, the percentage of products shipped in a just-in-time environment increased by 19 percent from 1991 to 1992. By 1995, nearly 40 percent of all shipments were expected to be sent just in time.[14]

The basic assumption of JIT is that carrying excessive inventory is bad because it ties up capital. Thus the purchasing firm reduces the amount of raw materials and parts it keeps on hand by ordering more often and in smaller amounts. General Motors and other carmakers, for example, generally maintain just an eight-hour supply of parts. Packard Electric supplies several of them, consolidating and distributing automobile wiring harnesses. Because the wiring harnesses are scheduled to arrive on the assembly line as they are needed, shipment accuracy is crucial for Packard Electric.[15]

Production facilities that adopt JIT techniques are usually redesigned to position all the machines involved in a process closer together, thus reducing work time. The JIT system transports parts to the point where they are needed, just when they are needed, on the production line. Hence, there are no piles of inventory waiting by each machine.

JIT benefits manufacturers foremost by reducing their inventories. For example, at Saturn's powertrain manufacturing and assembly plant in Spring Hill, Tennessee, the inventory of powertrains at any given time is barely two hours, in sharp contrast to the two weeks of inventory generally carried by other auto manufacturers.[16] Additionally, JIT creates shorter lead times, or the time it takes to get parts from a supplier after an order has been placed. Manufacturers also enjoy better relationships with suppliers and can decrease their production and storeroom costs. Because there is little safety stock, and therefore no margin for error, the manufacturer cannot afford to make a mistake. As a result, a manufacturer using JIT must be sure it receives high-quality parts from all vendors and must be confident that the supplier will meet all delivery commitments. Finally, JIT tends to reduce the amount of paperwork.

Just-in-time inventory management is not without its risks, however.[17] (Exhibit 14.7 summarizes the benefits and risks of JIT.) Implementation of JIT is a process of continuous improvement, characterized by many small gains in efficiency over a long period. Many managers have tried to institute JIT too rapidly, only to be disappointed in the results. Shigeo Shingo, one of the initiators of the JIT movement, acknowledges that it took Toyota Motors twenty years to develop JIT fully. He estimates that companies wanting to implement JIT now should expect that it will take at least ten years to realize satisfactory results. In addition, many companies have incorrectly assumed that JIT means slashing inventory levels only, without paying attention to the other aspects of JIT, such as quality control, efficient plant layout, regularly scheduled maintenance, and simpler product design. Managers who ignore these related issues risk delivery delays, shortages of goods, and customer dissatisfaction.

Because of the lower inventory levels, JIT also demands smaller, more frequent,

*Exhibit 14.7*

Benefits and Risks of Just-in-Time Inventory Management

| Benefits of JIT: | Risks of JIT: |
|---|---|
| Reduced inventory levels | Implementing JIT principles too rapidly |
| Shorter lead times | Cutting inventory without implementing other JIT principles |
| Improved supplier relations | Increased delivery costs |
| Lower production and storeroom costs | "Supplier shock" |
| Better-quality supplies | Employee stress |
| Less paperwork | Potential bottlenecks caused by supplier delays |

precisely timed deliveries from suppliers. At Saturn's plant, as many as 850 deliveries may be made by suppliers in a twenty-four-hour period. Deliveries must be made within a five-minute window to be counted as "on time." Tardy suppliers that cause a production delay face being fined $500 a minute.[18]

JIT also has been known to create "supplier shock." Many suppliers have been strong-armed into cutting delivery times by manufacturers practicing JIT. In other instances, manufacturers' inventories have simply shifted from their warehouses to suppliers' warehouses. JIT can also create stress among workers. Experiences with a number of Japanese and U.S. companies show that sharp reductions in inventory may lead to a regimented work flow and increased levels of stress among production-line employees. Finally, JIT has the potential for causing disastrous bottlenecks in production due to even the slightest delays by suppliers. Consider the impact on General Motors' production if a labor strike should occur at its sole supplier of seat belts.

## ORDER PROCESSING

Another important activity of physical distribution is order processing. The role of proper order processing in providing good service cannot be overemphasized.

### The Flow of Goods and Information

As an order enters the system, management must monitor two flows: the flow of goods and the flow of information. Often the best-laid plans of marketers can get entangled in the order-processing system. Obviously, good communication among sales representatives, office personnel, and warehouse and shipping personnel is essential to correct order processing. Shipping incorrect merchandise or partially filled orders can create just as much dissatisfaction as stockouts or slow deliveries. The flow of goods and information must be continually monitored so mistakes can be corrected before an invoice is prepared and the merchandise shipped.

**order entry**
First step in order processing, in which a customer order is taken.

**order handling**
Second step in order processing, in which the order is transmitted to the office, usually on a standardized order form, and then to the warehouse floor.

Order processing begins with the customer's placement of an order, or **order entry.** The customer can be a final user or an intermediary, and the order can be placed directly by the customer or indirectly through a sales representative. The next step, **order handling,** transmits the order to the office, usually on a standardized order form, and then to the warehouse floor. At this point, credit approval and invoice preparation occur. When the order reaches the warehouse, inventory is checked to make sure the product is in stock. If the item is available and credit has been approved, the order can be filled. The goods are located, picked from the shelves, packaged for shipping, and scheduled for delivery. If the item requested is not in stock, the result is a back order, or an order sent to the production facility so an item can be produced to fill the order.

### Benefits of Automation

**electronic data interchange (EDI)**
Computer technique that electronically transmits data about retail inventories to warehouses so orders can be filled more quickly and accurately.

Like inventory management, order processing is becoming more automated through the use of computer technology known as EDI—**electronic data interchange.** The basic idea behind EDI is to replace the paper documents that usually accompany business transactions, such as purchase orders and invoices, with electronic transmission of the needed information. Companies that use EDI can reduce inventory levels, improve cash flow, streamline operations, and increase the speed and accuracy of information transmission. EDI is also believed to create a closer relationship between buyers and sellers.[19] Approximately a third of all Fortune 1,000 firms—as well as their customers and suppliers—have adopted EDI. Purchase orders are the most common document electronically sent and received.[20]

It should not be surprising that retailers have become major users of EDI. For Wal-Mart, Target, Kmart, and the like, logistics speed and accuracy are crucial competitive tools in an overcrowded retail environment. Many big retailers are mandating that their suppliers acquire EDI technology.[21] EDI works hand in hand with retailers' "efficient consumer response" programs, which are designed to have the right products on the shelf, in the right styles and colors, through improved inventory, ordering, and distribution techniques. (See Chapter 13 for more discussion of retailers' use of EDI techniques.)

## TRANSPORTATION

Physical distribution managers must also decide which mode of transportation to use to move products from producer to buyer. This decision is, of course, related to all other physical distribution decisions. The five major modes of transportation are railroads, motor carriers, pipelines, water transportation, and airways. Exhibit 14.8 presents some statistics on these major transportation modes.

Distribution managers generally choose a mode of transportation on the basis of several criteria:

- *Cost:* total amount a specific carrier charges to move the product from the point of origin to the destination. Cost is usually figured in ton-miles (a ton-mile is the movement of one ton, or 2,000 pounds, of freight a distance of one mile).
- *Transit time:* total time a carrier has possession of goods, including the time required for pickup and delivery, handling, and movement between the point of origin and the destination.
- *Reliability:* consistency with which the carrier delivers goods on time and in acceptable condition.
- *Capability:* ability of the carrier to provide the appropriate equipment and conditions for moving specific kinds of goods, such as those that must be transported in a controlled environment (for example, under refrigeration).
- *Accessibility:* carrier's ability to move goods over a specific route or network.

*Exhibit 14.8*

Modes of Transportation in the United States

Source: U.S. Department of Commerce, Bureau of the Census, *Statistical Abstracts of the United States* (Washington, DC: Government Printing Office, 1993), p. 610.

| Mode | Annual ton-miles (in billions) | Percentage of total annual ton-miles | Typical cargo |
|---|---|---|---|
| Railroads | 1,078 | 37% | Coal, farm products, minerals, sand, chemicals |
| Motor carriers | 758 | 26 | Clothing, food, computers, paper goods |
| Pipelines | 578 | 20 | Oil, coal, chemicals |
| Water transportation (inland waterways only) | 462 | 16 | Oil, grain, sand, metallic ores, coal |
| Airways | 10 | Less than 1 | Technical instruments, perishable products, documents |

*Exhibit 14.9*

Criteria for Ranking Modes of Transportation

| | Highest | | | | Lowest |
|---|---|---|---|---|---|
| Relative cost | Air | Truck | Rail | Pipe | Water |
| Transit time | Water | Rail | Pipe | Truck | Air |
| Reliability | Pipe | Truck | Rail | Air | Water |
| Capability | Water | Rail | Truck | Air | Pipe |
| Accessibility | Truck | Rail | Air | Water | Pipe |
| Traceability | Air | Truck | Rail | Water | Pipe |

- *Traceability:* relative ease with which a shipment can be located and transferred.

The mode of transportation used depends on the needs of the shipper. All shippers are concerned with cost, transit time, reliability, capability, accessibility, and traceability. Exhibit 14.9 ranks the basic modes of transportation on these six criteria.

Now let's examine the unique advantages and problems that these modes of transportation present to a physical distribution manager today.

## Railroads

Railroads have long been the backbone of U.S. freight transportation, and today they transport 37 percent of the total ton-miles of freight traffic. Coal is the most commonly carried rail product; over 560 million tons of coal are carried per year, over a third of all material transported by the rail system.[22] Railroads also are the main carriers of grain and other farm products, chemicals, and raw metals and minerals.

Rail is ideal for transporting over long distances bulky items that are low in value relative to their weight. Compared to other carriers, rail is inexpensive for carload lots. Raw materials that can withstand rough handling are more suitable for rail transportation than are finished goods.

A main advantage of rail over other modes is reliability, because weather rarely interrupts rail freight schedules. Most rail service, however, is relatively slow and limited.

The rail industry reached its heyday in the 1920s, when it transported three-quarters of the nation's intercity freight. Since that peak, railroads have witnessed a steady erosion in demand for their services. The construction of the nation's interstate highway system and the arrival of affordable air transport cut the industry's share of freight. However, the Staggers Rail Act of 1980 revived the industry by deregulating the rail system, allowing the railroads more operating freedom. Among other changes, the act brought flexible rates and the ability to contract with individual customers.[23]

A turn in the industry's fortunes is evident. As commerce has broadened from local and regional trade to national and global markets, railroads have combined to offer longer single-line routes. Mergers among railroads have provided cost savings, lower capital spending requirements, and lower labor expenses, as well as a reduction in competing routes. Not only are railroads getting a larger slice of bulk shipments, but they are handling more high-value freight, such as automobiles, and more consumer goods.[24] Additionally, railroads have begun to make major inroads in the long-haul market for general freight through their success with double-stack

Within the transportation subsystem, railways and trucking companies compete to carry many of the same types of products.



container service, which is simply the stacking of two containers on a modified flatcar. Double-stack transport offers about a 25 to 30 percent savings over conventional flatcar service and now accounts for almost all rail container movements.[25]

## Motor Carriers

Motor carriers are the most flexible freight-hauling mode. Almost every product used by industry or consumers moves, at some time, by truck. Over 80 percent of motor carrier freight is short haul—that is, carried locally or under 200 miles.[26] Rates are usually economical over the short haul, and speed is better than with most other modes. Many carriers provide door-to-door service, thus reducing packing costs (because the goods are not handled as often, there is less need for protective packaging). Unfortunately, weather can affect motor carrier service. However, minimal handling and generally smooth rides make trucking desirable for finished goods and fragile items.

Before 1980, motor carriers were bound to limited markets and rates. But with passage of the Motor Carrier Act of 1980, which deregulated the industry, price became for a time the most important selection factor. Many changes and problems for the trucking industry followed. These included rate slashing, increased competition, growing demands from shippers for service and price discounts, and rising costs for insurance and equipment. As a result, many marginal trucking companies were eliminated or absorbed by larger, stronger firms. Many also went bankrupt because of competitors' aggressive pricing tactics, many of which were later found to be illegal.

Over the past few years, motor carriers have embraced a wide array of new technology to boost productivity and enhance service to shippers. Among these advances are hand-held computers, scanners, and satellite tracking systems. For example, industry leader J.B. Hunt Transport installed IBM computers on all 7,000 of its trucks. The hand-held computers allow drivers to send and receive messages, enter shipment statistics, estimate the time of arrival, and monitor engine conditions and vehicle speed. The computers are linked by satellite to Hunt's mainframe computer and can give the precise location of each vehicle. Large motor carriers are expected to continue to invest in satellite communication as a way to differentiate their services. Companies that ship time-sensitive freight find the continuous flow of information valuable, because it can provide early warning of any potential disruption of the delivery schedule.[27]

Motor carriers play an important role in JIT programs. Manufacturers that use JIT rely on the timely delivery of raw materials directly to the assembly line, a feat achieved most successfully through the use of motor carriers. For example, an automobile manufacturing plant that has a special partnership agreement with a trucking firm will notify the trucker which models are scheduled for production during the next few days. The trucking company then takes over, picking up the needed materials from various suppliers, keeping track of where everything is in the system, and delivering the materials to the assembly line just in time for the operator to install them. JIT production methods have essentially redefined the motor carrier, from a simple delivery service to the manufacturer's warehouse on wheels.

## Pipelines

Pipelines are quite slow as a transportation mode but offer continuous, low-cost product flow. There is no route flexibility with a pipeline, and route capacity is limited by the diameter of the pipe. Pipeline routes carry products in one direction, and storage terminals are required at the receiving end. Gases, liquids (oil or chemicals), and some solids (coal or watery mixtures movable in slurries) constitute the market for pipelines. Because pipelines are designed to carry only one or two products, most of them are owned by the companies that use them, such as oil and gas producers.

Despite their limited flexibility, pipelines account for almost a fifth of all intercity ton-miles.[28] Perhaps the greatest advantage of pipelines, other than low cost, is dependability. Weather and labor strikes rarely affect them. Moreover, pipelines are the lowest consumers of energy.

## Water Transportation

Like rail, water transportation is ideal for shipping heavy, low-value, nonperishable goods. Examples include ore, coal, grain, sand, and petroleum products. However, water transportation has a number of drawbacks. Routes, of course, are limited, because a large cargo ship or barge can transport its goods only in oceans or deep inland channels. Because of high fixed costs, water transport requires heavy traffic from point to point in order to achieve economies of scale. Locks, channels, and ports in major industrial areas are often overused, creating costly delays. Even without the bottlenecks, service is usually slow, and in some northern areas icing problems in the winter cause further delays. Weather can also be a problem during droughts, which cut water depth and force lightening of loads. Conversely, floods and high water can also create problems.

Even though service is slow and weather may be a nuisance, water is still one of the cheapest means of moving raw materials and some semifinished goods regularly over long distances. Sometimes it is also economical to ship finished goods by ocean carrier, as when Benetton ships the thousands of pieces of clothing for its two semiannual fashion collections. Because these merchandise shipments are scheduled ten months in advance, the relatively long transit time over the ocean is not a problem. By choosing water transport, Benetton is able to keep transportation costs relatively low.

Inland waterways have made a dramatic comeback since the mid-1950s, when they hauled roughly 3 percent of the nation's freight. Today they haul about 16 percent.[29] New towboats have greatly increased the capacity of many carriers. Special barges now handle refrigerated commodities. Others contain specialized equipment for carrying asphalt, and traditional tank barges now have special linings for hauling chemicals. The growth of containerization and improved port facilities will mean continued expansion for transportation via inland waterways.

Not surprisingly, U.S. ocean carriers are a major player in global trade. They originate from ports along the East and West coasts and the Gulf of Mexico. Some of the largest ports, in import and export volume, are Houston, New Orleans, New York/New Jersey, Baton Rouge, Corpus Christi, and Los Angeles. Resurgent Latin American economies—led by Mexico, Argentina, Brazil, Panama, and Guatemala—are a particular target of many of these U.S. ports. The Port of Los Angeles, for example, is actively promoting partnerships between the big U.S. steamship lines and smaller Latin American lines. One such partnership, between Latin American carrier NYK and U.S. carrier Sea-Land, has created an Asian–Latin American route dubbed the Margarita Service. NYK's vessels call at ports in Guatemala, El Salvador, Costa Rica, and Panama and three ports on the Mexican west coast. Cargo is then transferred to Sea-Land's larger Pacific Ocean vessels at Los Angeles, generally for transport to Hong Kong.[30]

### Airways

Airways are the fastest way to move freight, and speed and limited handling of freight enable shippers to use lighter packaging. But airways are the most expensive mode. Therefore, the market is confined to high-value merchandise and certain perishable items. Examples include electronic parts, fresh-cut flowers, emergency materials, and live seafood. Participants in the air freight market include the passenger airlines (which haul cargo in the holds of their passenger aircraft), all-cargo air freight carriers, and specialists in the express air delivery of small packages and shipments, such as FedEx, United Parcel Service, and Airborne Express.

Specialized cargo planes, roll-on containerization, and efficient ground operations have helped reduce the cost of air freight. However, aircraft have a lower overall weight capacity than other modes, such as barge or rail, and so air freight will always have limitations. Weather and a lack of adequate runways in smaller communities also affect service quality and availability.

By using air transport, a manager can often eliminate costly warehouses and the inventory tied up in those warehouses. Fast service enables the shipper to provide timely and sometimes emergency service. For example, a broken $25 part has been known to shut down an entire General Motors assembly line. Shipping crucial parts by air eliminates costly production delays. Speed also tends to reduce theft, damage, and spoilage. Because air carriers offer a relatively smooth ride compared to other modes of transportation, costly packing and unpacking can be eliminated.

Although air freight rates are the most expensive, in many instances air shipment is necessary. For example, HBO Studio Productions creates video products for cable giant Home Box Office, as well as for HBO affiliates, external advertising agencies, and other businesses. In the case of an HBO cablecast, local transportation is used to get the final edited version of the tape from the studio in Manhattan to the cable TV facilities where the program is actually linked up to the HBO network. However, projects for affiliates and outside clients—whether basketball shoe commercials for TV stations, promotional videos for the more than 200 HBO affiliates, or videos of upcoming HBO specials for television critics to review—are almost always time-sensitive. As a result, HBO uses overnight air service to deliver between 1,500 and 2,000 videos a month. If next-day delivery will be too late for a customer, HBO uses a same-day service, which will deliver the video in just a few hours by whatever means possible.[31]

Air freight is also important in global trade. Air freight operators, especially those offering express shipments, have looked to the global arena for growth opportunities. As these markets grow, shippers need distribution systems that offer fast, guaranteed deliveries throughout the world. Currently, DHL International, the oldest operator in international markets, is estimated to control more than 40 percent of international air freight. Other U.S. air freight operators have made a determined effort to build their global routes as well, but they have had some problems. For example, FedEx was unsuccessful in its attempt to build a full-service air express network in Europe. The company tried to establish a system in the United Kingdom and in continental Europe based on its domestic operations but eventually sold most of its European operations after huge losses. However, FedEx still provides express service to major European cities and overnight service from Europe to the United States. Along with UPS and other carriers, FedEx is now expanding its efforts into Asia, a promising global market.[32]

## Intermodal Transportation

**intermodal transportation** Combination of two or more modes of moving freight.

**Intermodal transportation** is the combination of two or more modes of moving freight. It allows a transportation buyer to exploit the advantages of each for seamless coast-to-coast or long-haul service. At a growth rate of more than 6 percent a year, intermodal is the fastest-growing mode of surface transportation in the United States today.[33]

**piggyback (trailer on flatcar) (TOFC)** Form of intermodal transportation combining the use of truck and rail to ship containerized goods.

**container on flatcar (COFC)** Form of intermodal transportation involving containers that can be transferred from rail or truck onto ship or barge.

**fishyback** Form of intermodal transportation combining the use of truck, rail, and ship or barge to move containerized goods.

**birdyback** Form of intermodal transportation combining the use of truck and air freight to move containerized goods.

**Piggyback,** or **trailer on flatcar** (TOFC), a truck-rail combination, is the most popular form of intermodal transportation. It allows a shipper to achieve the door-to-door capabilities of a motor carrier service along with the long-haul advantages of rail. Containers can also move in a piggyback service called **container on flatcar** (COFC); the containers can easily be transferred from train to ship or barge. Other popular types of intermodal transportation include **fishyback,** combining the use of truck, rail, and ship or barge to move goods, and **birdyback,** combining the use of truck and air freight to move goods.

One of the major reasons for the fast growth of intermodal transportation is the increased use of rail by motor carriers trying to cut costs and overcome a shortage of truck drivers. Railroads, once considered a laggard in freight shipping, have benefited from the popularity of intermodal transportation, which has offset disappointing bulk shipments of coal and grain. The surge in intermodal shipments also reflects improvements in rail productivity and service coupled with reductions in cost.[34]

Many manufacturers and motor carriers that once lacked confidence in rail's reliability and service quality have now become partners with rail companies. For example, by using intermodal transportation services, Nabisco was able to reduce transportation costs and transit times. Today, about a quarter of Nabisco's transportation budget is spent on intermodal service. Nabisco was once worried that shipping by rail would damage its cookies and crackers. But improved containers and equipment have made intermodal carriers competitive with motor carriers.[35]

## Supplementary Carriers

Shippers can also use several supplementary carriers, including the U.S. Postal Service, United Parcel Service, bus services, courier express carriers, and freight forwarders.

The U.S. Postal Service and United Parcel Service specialize in handling packages under seventy pounds. UPS provides door-to-door delivery and, in many cases, next-day delivery to over 175 countries. Bus lines can also transport a large volume of

UPS package delivery is produced and consumed simultaneously. Like all service providers, therefore, UPS faces the challenge of carefully planning distribution in order to meet demand.

packages economically. Like many passenger airlines, bus companies use excess baggage space for carrying freight from one city to another.

Usually promising overnight delivery, courier express carriers specialize in moving packages and documents quickly. Couriers typically use small trucks or vans to pick up and deliver. FedEx, perhaps the best-known courier express carrier, handles over a million express shipments daily.

**freight forwarder**
Carrier that collects less-than-carload shipments from a number of shippers and consolidates them into carload lots.

A **freight forwarder** collects less-than-carload shipments from a number of shippers and consolidates them into carload lots. Forwarders charge rates equivalent to less-than-carload rates, but then they pay the lower carload rates for the consolidated shipments. Their profit comes from the difference between the two rates. Unlike express services like FedEx, freight forwarders do not own their own long-haul equipment. Instead, they use available modes of transportation. Most offer pick-up and delivery service, along with the speed and efficiency of handling carload merchandise. Historically, ground freight forwarders have handled consumer durable goods—for example, clothing, sporting equipment, and appliances.

Most small companies rely on freight forwarders to handle the details of global shipping to an array of foreign countries rather than tackle tracking and controlling product distribution themselves. International freight forwarders handle consolidations, shipping, and customs. Competition in the global marketplace has prompted forwarders to offer a broad spectrum of additional services, making them "total logistics companies."[36] Connecticut-based Air Express International, one of the country's oldest air freight forwarders, is one of these companies. AEI has a 75,000 square foot distribution facility in Europe and a 200,000 square foot facility in Singapore, which serves most of Asia. The company often assigns AEI personnel to work temporarily in the traffic departments of major shippers to ensure speedy customs clearance and smooth operation of the entire distribution process. AEI also has automated information capabilities and EDI systems to assist customers in tracking shipments and to streamline ordering and payment.[37]

4 *Identify the special problems and opportunities associated with physical distribution in service organizations.*

## PHYSICAL DISTRIBUTION FOR SERVICES

The fastest-growing part of our economy is the service sector. Although distribution in the service sector is difficult to visualize, the same skills, techniques, and strategies used to manage inventory can be used to manage service inventory—for instance, hospital beds, bank accounts, or airline seats. The quality of the planning and execution of distribution can have a major impact on costs and customer satisfaction.[38]

Traditional distribution means getting the right product to the right place at the right time. In the service industry, however, this narrow focus is replaced with a much broader mission: getting the right service and the right people and the right information to the right place at the right time.

One thing that sets service distribution apart from traditional manufacturing distribution is that, in a service environment, production and consumption are simultaneous. In manufacturing, a production setback can often be remedied by using safety stock or a faster mode of transportation. Such substitution is not possible with a service. The benefits of a service are also relatively intangible—that is, you can't normally see the benefits of a service, such as a doctor's physical exam. But a consumer can normally see the benefits provided by a product—for example, a vacuum cleaner removing dirt from the carpet.

ETHICS IN MARKETING

**Is Faster Delivery Always Better?**

After years of capitalizing on its commitment to deliver pizzas in thirty minutes or less, Domino's is giving up the marketing concept around which it built the largest pizza operation in the United States. The decision was made after a jury awarded $78 million to a St. Louis woman who had been hit and injured by a Domino's delivery driver. The jury found that Domino's thirty-minute guarantee showed disregard for the safety of other drivers. Two other people hit by Domino's drivers have won smaller jury awards.

Some of Domino's franchisees ended the thirty-minute pledge months before the St. Louis verdict because owners were worried that the negative publicity about possibly unsafe drivers would hurt business. Still, the news came as a shock to many Domino's store operators, who viewed the guarantee as one of the foundations of the company's marketing philosophy.

Dropping its thirty-minute delivery guarantee could not have come at a worse time for Domino's. The company has been trying to halt sliding sales by adding thin-crust and deep-dish pizzas, salads, and breadsticks to its menu. Some stores also sell submarine sandwiches.

Domino's archrival, Pizza Hut, has never offered a delivery guarantee, instead promoting the quality of its product. To ensure safe delivery, Pizza Hut says it checks driving records of potential drivers, then puts new hires through a driver safety-training program. Pizza Hut drivers who maintain excellent driving records may be eligible for prizes ranging from free car maintenance to Caribbean cruises.

Domino's also screens the driving records of its applicants and requires that they attend defensive-driver training programs. However, the company maintains that no matter what they do to ensure safety and training for its drivers, some of the public will still have a negative perception about the company because of the thirty-minute guarantee. For that reason they are eliminating the very element that creates the negative perception.[39]

The decision to drop the delivery guarantee raises a couple of crucial marketing issues for Domino's. How should it reposition itself against the competition? What should it stress that will bring back former customers, who liked the thirty-minute guarantee?

Because service industries are so customer-oriented, customer service is a priority. Service distribution focuses on three main areas:

- *Minimizing wait times:* Wait times are similar to order cycle times in manufacturing distribution. Minimizing the amount of time customers wait in line to deposit a check, wait for their food at a restaurant, or wait in a doctor's office for an appointment is a key factor in maintaining the quality of service.
- *Managing service capacity:* This area is analogous to managing inventory in a goods-producing organization. For a product manufacturer, inventory acts as a buffer, enabling it to provide the product during periods of peak demand without extraordinary efforts. Service firms don't have this luxury. If they don't have the capacity to meet demand, they must either turn down some prospective customers, let service levels slip, or expand capacity. For instance, at tax time a tax preparation firm may have so many customers desiring its services that it has to either turn business away or add temporary offices or preparers.
- *Improving delivery through new distribution channels:* Like manufacturers, service firms are now experimenting with different distribution channels for their

services. These new channels can increase the time that services are available (like round-the-clock automated teller machines) or add to customer convenience (like pizza delivery or walk-in medical clinics).

Although service organizations provide mostly intangible benefits, they still must have supplies, raw materials, and inventory systems. For example, a bank must have deposit forms, loan information packages, and computers to hold customer account information and produce monthly statements. Likewise, a restaurant keeps an inventory of plates, silverware, and glassware, along with a variety of food and drink, to be able to provide a dining experience for its customers.

FedEx and Domino's Pizza are two firms whose innovative distribution of services has influenced their industries. Both built significant market share by focusing on the time and location of the services delivered to the customer. FedEx satisfied an unmet need by offering guaranteed overnight delivery of packages and documents to commercial and residential customers. Domino's innovation was to concentrate on home delivery of pizza in thirty minutes or less. Now, however, the pizza giant is giving up its delivery guarantee for reasons discussed in the Ethics in Marketing box.

5 *Discuss new technology and emerging trends in physical distribution.*

## TRENDS IN PHYSICAL DISTRIBUTION

Several technological advances and business trends affect the physical distribution industry today. These include automation, environmental issues, third-party contract logistics and partnerships, quality issues in transportation, and global distribution.

### AUTOMATION

Manual handling of distribution is now outdated. Computer technology has boosted the efficiency of physical distribution dramatically—for instance, in warehousing and materials management, inventory control, and transportation. This chapter has presented many examples of the use of computer technology and automation, ranging from satellite tracking for motor carriers to electronic data interchange, computerized inventory systems, and automatic identification techniques using bar codes.

One of the major goals of automation is to bring up-to-date information to the decision maker's desk. Shippers have long referred to the transportation system as the "black hole," where products and materials fall out of sight until they reappear some time later in a plant, store, or warehouse. Now carriers have systems that track freight, monitor the speed and location of carriers, and make routing decisions on the spur of the moment. The rapid exchange of information that automation brings to the distribution process helps each party plan more effectively. The links among suppliers, buyers, and carriers open up opportunities for joint decision making. And as more companies compete in global markets, timely information becomes even more important.

### ENVIRONMENTAL ISSUES

Environmental laws and consumer concerns have a profound effect on how U.S. businesses operate, and logistics and distribution managers are becoming much more involved in the environmental matters that affect their firms. For example, the Department of Transportation now requires that all employees dealing with hazardous materials be trained and tested at least once every two years. This rule applies to all hazardous materials transportation, regardless of shipment size, frequency of shipment, degree of hazard of the products shipped, company size, or number of employees.[40]

Concern over the environment has also made waste reduction a factor in the packaging process. Distribution managers are improving packaging design, eliminating overpackaging, reusing packages that were once discarded after a single use, and switching to less expensive packaging, materials with recycled content, or alternatives that take up less warehouse space.[41] Ethan Allen, one of the largest U.S. furniture makers and retailers, has established an innovative recycling program for its packaging materials. The company contracted with United Parcel Service to retrieve Ethan Allen's foam-sheet shipping materials and return them to Ametek, the manufacturer of the foam sheeting. The program has reduced Ethan Allen's disposal costs and also earned the company additional dollars, because Ametek pays the furniture maker for the returned material.[42]

As distribution becomes more global, U.S. companies will also have to deal with the environmental laws of other countries. In the area of logistics and distribution, environmental standards in Europe alone vary enormously from country to country—for everything from packaging standards and truck sizes and weights to vehicle emissions and noise pollution control.[43] Some European standards are far more stringent than those in the United States. In Germany, for instance, it is against the law to incinerate packaging or to dump it in a landfill. Manufacturers are responsible for taking back packaging after products have been purchased. To show compliance with the law, vendors must purchase "green dots" from government-approved third parties and apply them to all packaging. The money collected is used to subsidize package collection and recycling systems. Manufacturers incur penalties for green-dot packages that have been improperly disposed of. To meet the demands of the German market, Hewlett-Packard now ships its DeskJet printers without the usual cardboard packaging. Instead, the company devised a special tray that holds the printers securely wrapped in clear plastic. This method cuts down not only on packaging waste but also on damage. Handlers can now see they are handling a printer, not just a cardboard box.[44]

## CONTRACT LOGISTICS AND PARTNERSHIPS

**contract logistics**
Manufacturer's or supplier's use of an independent third party to buy and manage an entire subsystem of physical distribution, such as transportation or warehousing.

Contract logistics is a rapidly growing segment of the distribution industry. In **contract logistics,** a manufacturer or supplier turns over the entire function of buying and managing transportation or another subsystem of physical distribution, such as warehousing, to an independent third party. Contract logistics allows companies to cut inventories, locate stock at fewer plants and distribution centers, and still provide the same service level or even better. The companies then can refocus investment on their core business.[45]

There are essentially four types of contract logistics vendors. The first are *asset-based,* offering services related to assets, such as trucking, warehousing, or air freight. *Management-based* vendors offer logistics management through computer systems, databases, and consulting services. These firms do not own transportation or warehouses but instead contract with other companies that do. The third type, *integrated* contract logistics vendors, do own assets, typically trucks, warehouses, or both. However, they are not limited to using just their own assets and will contract with other vendors as needed. The last type of contract logistics vendors are *administration-*

GLOBAL PERSPECTIVES

**Shipping Goods in China**

Today, China is the world's largest emerging economic powerhouse, with over 1.17 billion consumers. Estimates indicate economic growth in China of 13 percent annually. But antiquated port facilities, poor rail and road networks, overcrowded conditions, and the pure vastness of China make getting goods in and out a major dilemma.

Take, for instance, a customer who orders a Volkswagen from VW's joint-venture plant in Shanghai. Delivery can be expected within six to eight weeks, but the customer shouldn't count on a shiny new car with no scratches or dents and hardly any mileage on the odometer. The only way to get the VW to some customers is to drive it—in many cases, some 2,000 miles over mountains, across deserts, and down many dirt roads.

Throughout China, urban roadways are usually clogged. As in other emerging countries, its ports and rail depots generally lack the basic equipment, such as forklifts, to move cargo. Bandits are common along highways and roadways, and in some areas village chiefs erect roadblocks and demand a toll in exchange for passage. Tariffs, as high as 200 percent on some products, stop many goods from even getting into China in the first place.

Traffic laws in many Chinese cities are a particular problem for companies like Coca-Cola. In Shanghai, the city bans delivery trucks from its center during the daytime. So Coke turned some of its distribution over to tricycles. But Shanghai considers tricycles a traffic nuisance as well and severely restricts the number of permits for the vehicles. To get around this law, Coke agreed to hire some of Shanghai's unemployed as peddlers if the city's bureaucrats loosened up on permits. Coke now has rights to a 500-tricycle fleet. In other parts of China,

*based*. These firms mainly provide management services, such as freight payment.[46]

Not surprisingly, contract logistics often leads a supplier, retailer, or manufacturer to form an exclusive partnership with a carrier, warehousing expert, or logistics management supplier. Many of the companies seeking partners are practicing just-in-time inventory management. Often sophisticated distribution systems are required to deliver component parts to assembly lines or fashions to the retail shelf within tight, predefined time windows. Contract logistics partnerships help companies meet delivery dates, speedily fill emergency orders, and achieve high accuracy in filling orders.

Coors Brewing uses asset-based contract logistics vendors to assist with the distribution of beer. After years of shipping its own product directly to more than 650 distributors, the brewer realized that this system could not keep up with demand. Coors set up alliances with twenty-four refrigerated public warehouses, all linked to Coors through a partnership with Burlington Northern Railroad. By using satellite warehouses and Burlington Northern, Coors was able to reduce costs and increase profitability.[47]

## QUALITY IN TRANSPORTATION

Companies that buy transportation know that quality transport is a critical part of their success. Many have developed formal quality measurement programs for the modes of transportation they use. The most important quality characteristics are on-time pickup and delivery, competitive rates and transit times, and dependable schedules.[48] Most carriers have responded by developing systems for tracing and tracking shipments and cutting paperwork.

Buyers of transportation are also using fewer carriers and demanding more from them. It is not unusual to find as few as six or eight carriers handling as much as 90 percent of a shipper's transportation. Sears cut the number of motor carriers it deals with from 350 to fewer than 15. Schneider National, the largest U.S. truckload carrier, transports the bulk of Sears's merchandise through a partnership with the retailer. Sears promised enough freight so that Schneider National could dedicate certain equipment to Sears shipments alone. In return, Sears realizes substantial savings.[49] The advantages of forming partnerships with fewer carriers are many. Communication improves, and the carriers know they can rely on a certain level of business. Meanwhile, transportation buyers gain greater control over a central function in the distribution system.

## GLOBAL PERSPECTIVES

Coke has been just as creative with its distribution decisions. In Beijing Coke is delivered by pushcart, and in the hills near Tianjin it is delivered by mule.

China's freight system also leaves a lot to be desired. Rail traffic is so unpredictable that 30 percent of all coal dug out of the country's mines each year still sits where it was found, waiting for the trains to arrive. China is only meeting a fraction of its aviation freight demand. One Hong Kong garment maker recalls watching his freight get loaded on a flight out of Shanghai and immediately unloaded to make way for some government goods.

A growing number of private trucking companies are taking to the roads, but the highways pose their own hazards. Along one stretch of highway in southern China, villagers have occasionally tossed a dead body into the path of an oncoming truck at night. When the shocked driver stops to investigate, he is accused of running over a pedestrian and made to pay compensation.

For those companies lucky enough to get their products to the warehouse, the next test is getting them out of the warehouse and to the customer. Cadbury distributes its chocolates in China only during the winter because there is no guarantee that the warehouse or the retailer will keep the air conditioner turned on in the summer to prevent its chocolate inventory from melting.[51]

Can you think of other areas of the world in which the transportation infrastructure is underdeveloped? What strategies can shippers and carriers devise to help overcome poor roads, railroads, and port facilities?

Reprinted by permission of *The Wall Street Journal*, © 1993 Dow Jones & Company, Inc. All Rights Reserved Worldwide. And from Karen E. Thuermer, "To Maintain a Stronghold, Improve Service, Carriers Invest in China's Decayed Infrastructure," *Traffic World*, 4 April 1994, 18–19.

## GLOBAL DISTRIBUTION

The world is indeed becoming a friendlier place for marketers. The surging popularity of free-market economics over the past decade or so has swept away many barriers. As a result, businesses are finding that the world market is more appealing than ever.

As global trade becomes a more decisive factor in success or failure for firms of all sizes, a well-thought-out global logistics strategy becomes more important. Uncertainty regarding shipping usually tops the list of reasons why companies, especially smaller ones, resist international markets. Even companies that have scored overseas successes often are vulnerable to logistical problems. Large companies have the capital to create global logistics systems, but smaller companies often must rely on the services of carriers and freight forwarders to get their products to overseas markets.

One of the most critical global logistical issues for importers of any size is coping with the legalities of trade in other countries. Shippers and distributors must be aware of the permits, licenses, and registrations they may need to acquire and, depending on the type of product they are importing, the tariffs, quotas, and other regulations that apply in each country. Another important factor to consider is the transportation infrastructure in a country. For example, the Commonwealth of Independent States (the former Soviet Union) has little transportation infrastructure outside the major cities, such as roads that can withstand heavy freight trucks, and few reliable transportation companies of any type. Pilferage and hijackings of freight are also common.[50] Distributors have had similar experiences in China, as the Global Perspectives box relates.

## LOOKING BACK

Now that you have studied this chapter, turn back to the opening story discussing Benetton's logistics and distribution system. Important to Benetton's operations is its highly automated distribution center, which makes on-time shipments possible. You

should now also understand more clearly the trade-offs among the modes of distribution. For instance, Benetton uses air freight for store replenishments and emergency shipments, when it needs to get product to its stores quickly. Ocean freight is used for its semiannual fashion shipments, where time is not as critical. As Benetton ventures into developing countries, physical distribution will become a critical component of its overall marketing plan. Benetton's physical distribution managers must understand the legalities of trade in each new country. Additionally, they must be prepared to deal with underdeveloped transportation infrastructures, which may make shipments to stores in these countries difficult.

## SUMMARY

**1 Explain the importance of physical distribution.** In today's fiercely competitive environment, marketing managers are becoming aware of the importance of effective physical distribution. Rather than concentrating on product or price differentiation, many companies are developing more efficient methods of distributing goods and services to achieve a competitive advantage.

**2 Discuss the concept of balancing physical distribution service and cost.** Today, physical distribution service is recognized as an area in which a firm can distinguish itself from competitors. Therefore, many physical distribution managers strive to achieve an optimal balance of customer service and total distribution cost. Important aspects of service are availability of merchandise, timeliness of deliveries, and quality (condition and accuracy) of shipments. In evaluating costs, physical distribution managers examine all parts of the distribution system.

**3 Describe the subsystems of the physical distribution system.** The physical distribution system has five basic parts, or subsystems: warehousing, materials handling, inventory control, order processing, and transportation. When evaluating warehousing options, physical distribution managers must determine the number, size, and location of warehouses needed as well as the most appropriate type of warehouse—private warehouse, public warehouse, or distribution center. Important elements of materials handling are packaging, bar coding, automatic storage and retrieval, and unitization and containerization. Inventory control systems regulate when and how much to buy (order timing and order quantity). Order processing monitors the flow of goods and information (order entry and order handling). Finally, the major modes of transportation include railroads, motor carriers, pipelines, waterways, and airways. Alternative methods of transporting goods are intermodal transportation and such supplementary carriers as freight forwarders.

**4 Identify the special problems and opportunities associated with physical distribution in service organizations.** Managers in service industries use the same skills, techniques, and strategies to manage physical distribution functions as managers in goods-producing industries. The physical distribution of services focuses on three main areas: minimizing wait times, managing service capacity, and improving delivery through new distribution channels.

**5 Discuss new technology and emerging trends in physical distribution.** Several trends are emerging in today's physical distribution industry. Technology and

### KEY TERMS

*automatic identification (auto ID) 466*
*automatic storage and retrieval systems (AS/RS) 466*
*birdyback 477*
*containerization 467*
*container on flatcar (COFC) 477*
*contract logistics 481*
*contract warehousing 464*
*cross docking 465*
*distribution center 464*
*economic order quantity (EOQ) 468*
*electronic data interchange (EDI) 471*
*fishyback 477*
*freight forwarder 478*
*intermodal transportation 477*
*inventory carrying cost 468*
*inventory control system 467*
*just-in-time (JIT) inventory management 469*
*logistics 457*
*materials-handling system 465*
*order entry 471*
*order handling 471*
*ordering cost 468*
*order processing cost 468*
*physical distribution 457*

automation are bringing up-to-date distribution information to the decision maker's desk. Technology is also linking suppliers, buyers, and carriers for joint decision making. As in many other industries today, concern for the environment is also making an impact on physical distribution. Companies are responding to government concern over the risks of hazardous shipments and developing programs to reduce packaging. Many companies are saving money and time by hiring third-party carriers to handle some or all aspects of the distribution process. Still another trend in distribution is the quest for quality in transportation. Carriers have improved on-time delivery and pickup, developed systems for tracking shipments, and implemented electronic communication with shippers. Finally, as the world becomes a friendlier place in which to buy and sell goods and services, the need to understand global physical distribution has assumed greater importance for many companies.

## Discussion and Writing Questions

1. Is the goal of a physical distribution system to operate at the lowest possible cost? Why or why not?
2. Which physical distribution strategy do you think is optimal? Why?
3. As the manager of a retail bookstore, you have been given the task of designing an inventory control system for textbooks. The *Principles of Marketing* textbook has average sales of $1,000 each semester at a unit cost of $20 each. The cost of carrying it in the store is 12 percent a semester, and it costs an average of $16 to reorder the textbooks. What is the economic order quantity?
4. You are the distribution manager of a company that sells turkeys to grocery stores. Decide whether you will use a private warehouse, public warehouse, distribution center, or a combination of the three to store your product. Explain your decision.
5. Identify the most suitable method(s) of transporting these goods: lumber, fresh seafood, natural gas, fine china, and automobiles. Justify your choices.
6. Suppose that your firm intends to use intermodal transportation to ship your product. Identify the product, and write a memo explaining why this distribution method makes good business sense.
7. Assume that you are the marketing manager of a hospital. Write a report indicating the physical distribution functions that concern you. Discuss the similarities and dissimilarities of physical distribution for services and for goods.

## Application for Small Business

Rafael Navarre owns three fishing boats in Southern California. Several generations of Navarres have been fishermen. Until Rafael's grandfather emigrated to California in 1951, the Navarres fished out of Mexico. Two of Rafael's three boats were purchased in the past ten years, as Rafael saw the need to expand for the business to survive. The company currently sells the fish and other seafood it catches to distributors at the dock. The boats may remain out several days, and anything caught is kept fresh on ice.

In a recent visit with his banker, Rafael became aware of a new Small Business Administration loan program. The program specifically targets minority small businesses that want to modernize and expand. His banker suggested that he consider a loan to install refrigeration and quick-freeze equipment on his boats and to build a refrigerated warehouse and seafood-processing plant. This investment would enable him to be more competitive with larger operators, which are increasingly taking away Rafael's business. The larger companies can guarantee fresher seafood and more consistent delivery of orders placed.

### Questions

1. What factors should Rafael consider in making his decision?
2. What other strategies should Rafael evaluate to remain competitive?

## CRITICAL THINKING CASE

### Itel Distribution Systems

Itel Distribution Systems is part of the Itel Corporation family of third-party logistics services. Logistics is the whole process of moving the product from the point of production to the ultimate consumer. *Third-party* means that companies like Itel do not take ownership of any of the products they move through the channel.

Third-party warehousing is becoming increasingly popular. As the cost of owning and operating warehouse facilities increases, businesses turn to companies like Itel. No matter what the product is, Itel can offer total distribution and warehousing solutions.

Itel offers four key distribution services:

- *Freight consolidation:* Itel serves many companies. Thus shipments can be combined, reducing total shipping costs.
- *Multimodal transportation:* Itel uses many different modes of transportation, alleviating the need to sign contracts with separate companies for different modes of transportation.
- *Bulk transport and storage:* The company can move and store raw materials and deliver them as needed.
- *Comprehensive inventory system:* Itel offers barcoding services, order processing, and packaging of shipments. In addition, its extensive computer system allows comprehensive information access, including the location of specific shipments.

The advantages for manufacturers using third-party warehousing and distribution companies are twofold. First, the manufacturer can expand or contract its operations, as changes in the market or in sales levels occur, without making major capital investments. Second, the manufacturer does not have to invest in warehouse or distribution vehicles. The capital can instead be used to expand production capacity or improve products.

Using contract logistics is not without disadvantages. The main one is the loss of control. If a company turns over its warehousing and distribution functions, it loses control of the distribution process. The second disadvantage is that the company may have to sign a long-term contract with the third-party distribution company, which cancels many of the advantages.

Current industry findings indicate that flexibility is the most important factor for companies considering third-party distribution. Flexibility has moved ahead of cost reductions and service improvements as the main deciding factor. Areas recommended for improvement within the industry include more proactive relationships, improved communication, better information, and improved systems. On the other side, a long-term partnership is one of the key deciding factors for third-party distributors that are considering new clients.

Itel is well prepared to serve this market with its partnership focus. Itel is not just a supplier of distribution services but a partner in its customers' businesses. By taking total control of the customers' distribution needs, Itel lets them focus on the specific needs of their business (concentrate on what they do best) and not worry about operating and managing distribution facilities. For example, Itel leased railway track next to one of its customer's factories to provide rail shipping directly from the plant to one of Itel's warehouses.

Itel now has a total of 9 million square feet of space in thirty-nine distribution facilities. Through expansions and acquisitions, Itel continues to grow. To better serve its customers' needs, Itel is organized regionally (West, Central, Northeast, and Southeast). Itel's strength lies in building personal relationships within each region, not in applying the same formula in each one. Itel finds specific solutions to best meet each customer's needs. Itel wants its customers to have not only the support of a national company but also the individual attention of a local company.

#### Questions

1. What advantages and disadvantages come from Itel's decision to organize on a regional basis? What are the advantages and disadvantages of a national orientation?
2. Do you think Itel has done a good job of alleviating the disadvantages of using a third-party distribution company? Why or why not?
3. What advantages would Itel's customers have in using Itel? Would you recommend using a third-party distribution company?

#### References

Jan Szymankiewicz, "Contracting-Out or Selling-Out?," *Logistics Focus,* December 1993, pp. 2–5.

Clyde Witt, "Third-Party Warehousing: Customized Approach to Distribution," *Material Handling Eng.,* June 1993, pp. 55–58.

**VIDEO CASE**

## United Parcel Service

United Parcel Service radically changed its corporate culture in order to survive and thrive in the 1990s. Its marketing and customer satisfaction efforts were once handled by only seven employees—too few to handle questions from both existing and potential customers. Once plodding and inflexible, Atlanta-based UPS has been introducing a new service every other month since 1990, and almost 200 employees are part of the marketing team.

After losing business to such aggressive competitors as FedEx, Roadway Package System, and Airborne Express, UPS has been changing the way the world's largest package carrier does business. UPS used to think, and even tell customers, "We know what's best for you!" Today, UPS stresses customer satisfaction. This satisfaction is delivered using over $2 billion of the latest technology to keep up-to-the-minute tabs on shipments. Its system includes an integrated international shipping, tracking, and tracing system that interfaces with customs as well as customers' computers, and a portable electronic clipboard for signatures of package recipients. The system provides information to shippers on where their merchandise is prior to arrival, when it arrived, who signed for it, and how long it took to arrive. It also can show them how to save money on shipping by planning ahead.

Along with this technology, UPS is also offering upgraded services. Flexible pickup and delivery times, as well as customized shipment plans and discount prices to volume shippers, are all available to corporate clients. It is tough to fault the long-time success story of pioneer FedEx, but UPS is delivering what today's customers really want—choice and value, along with speed and reliability.

Attention to detail is another reason UPS has been able to deliver on customer satisfaction. The company has one of the largest fleets of aircraft in the world, has a massive computer network, processes over 11 million packages every day, and spends about $1.5 billion on capital improvements every year. But down-home managers boast that they measure costs in tenths of a cent and can predict within five or six minutes how long a driver will take on his or her 100-mile delivery and pickup round every day. Through such attention to detail as calibrating the depth of delivery drivers' pockets so that they don't have to dig too deeply for loose change, designating the right fingers to hold a key, or making truck seats easier to slide in and out of, UPS has acquired an enviable reputation for reliability. After eighty years, it delivers to more U.S. addresses than the U.S. Postal Service does, reaches over 80 percent of the people in the world, and picks up merchandise from all of the companies on the *Fortune 500* list.

### Questions

1. Why are air freight operators so important to businesses, both in the United States and abroad?
2. How have these carriers changed the distribution function?
3. Why is the information they provide as important as the actual shipment of merchandise?

# PART FOUR INTEGRATIVE CASE

## HOME DEPOT

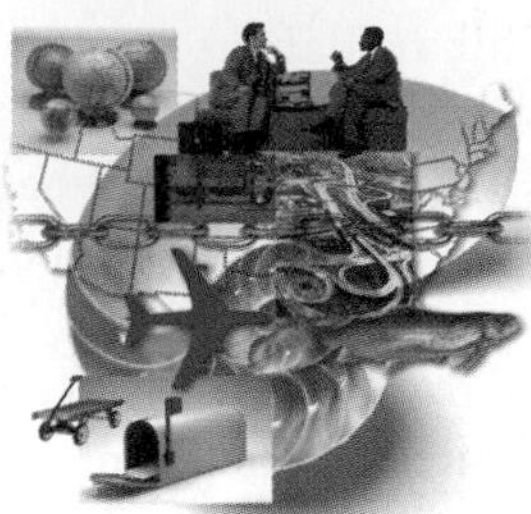

In 1979, two former executives of Handy Dan, a Southern California home center, set up a low-price home improvement store called Home Depot. At the time, many would have dismissed the possibility that Home Depot could upset industry giants within just ten years. A fragmented industry, coupled with low projected gross margins for the company, would have deterred most investors. It deterred Ross Perot, for example, when he was approached in 1979 to provide the financing for the Home Depot idea. He balked at investing $2 million in this project for a 70 percent ownership stake. However, by 1993 that stake would have been worth $12 billion. Today Home Depot is the largest retailer in the home improvement business and the sixteenth largest (by sales) retail chain in the country.

### Home Depot's Phenomenal Growth

Bernard Marcus and Arthur Blank got their $2 million to start Home Depot from a New York investment firm. They set up their first store in an empty storefront on Memorial Drive in Atlanta, Georgia, with an initial inventory of 18,000 items for sale at low prices.

For the opening of their store, Marcus and Blank gave their children 700 crisp one-dollar bills for distribution as thank-you gifts for shoppers. However, by late evening, the kids were in the parking lot handing out the money to entreat people to come into the store. The initial period was disappointing, but eventually people started coming in.

The following year, two more stores were opened. In 1981 Home Depot went public. By 1989, Home Depot had surpassed Lowe's Cos. to become the largest home repair chain in the nation, and sales almost tripled from 1990 to 1993 (see Exhibit 1). In 1994 the company gained entry into the Canadian market through a strategic acquisition and made plans to enter Mexico as well.

Clearly, Home Depot had become a star of retailing. What made it so successful? An emphasis on three factors is credited: customer service, employee motivation, and operational efficiency.

### Customer Service

Almost all home improvement stores carry very similar product lines and attempt to be competitive in prices. What separates Home Depot from others in the industry is its singular commitment to the customer. Most discount retailers focus on low prices, but Home Depot stresses the service provided to customers while incorporating everyday low prices as a company policy.

Most customers at home repair stores are do-it-yourselfers who need crucial product information as well as home repair tips. Thus every Home Depot employee is trained to answer the questions that customers may have about the 30,000 items in the store and to assist customers without pressuring a sale. Moreover, customers buying low-priced items get the same kind of attention as those interested in higher-priced items.

Commitment to customer service is an ingrained value at the company. As Arthur Blank, president of Home Depot notes, "When a customer leaves the store, he or she feels a bond with the store. Something happened in the store beyond buying a product. They found somebody in that store who really cared about their problem, or their project, or their dream list. It

*Exhibit 1*

Home Depot's Growth, 1990–1993

Source: Adapted from "State of the Industry: Executive 100," *Chain Store Age Executive*, August 1992, p. 6A; "State of the Industry," *Chain Store Age Executive*, August 1994, p. 4A.

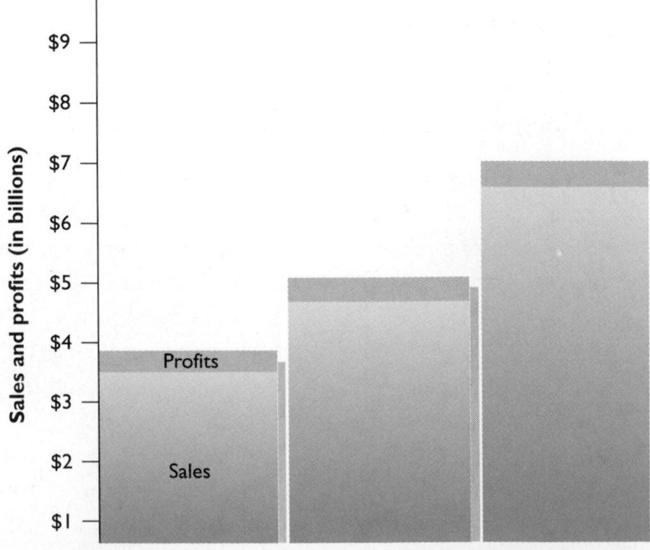

wasn't just someone sticking a product in their hand and sending them on their way. That's what really creates the bond with the customer."

## Employee Motivation

What motivates a Home Depot employee to serve customers with commitment and dedication? Whereas other retailers offer high commissions and regular discounts on employee in-store purchases, Home Depot pays its employees (over 30,000 of them) as if they were partners in the enterprise. Rather than promote the hard-sell, high-pressure sales ethic that sales commissions encourage, Home Depot provides its employees with salaries and shares in the company. After their first year, employees can join a retirement plan that includes Home Depot stock. Employees at the level of assistant manager and above also qualify for lucrative stock options. Many store managers own $1 million or more in Home Depot stock.

Such incentives apart, store managers are given a lot of autonomy in running their stores, and employees are encouraged to suggest and implement new ideas. Employees often act with entrepreneurial zest, implementing new ways to help customers and reacting to new needs. One employee in a store in Louisiana learned sign language on his own so as to be able to assist deaf customers. It is estimated that more than 70 percent of the operational and merchandising changes at Home Depot since its inception were initiated by employees.

The key to such commitment to service is rigorous training. New employees, who are experienced in the building trades, first go through five days of classroom training, where they learn about the company's history, operations, and techniques of customer interaction. Next, each employee spends three weeks under the close tutelage of a department manager, learning everything about ordering, stocking, and selling. After in-depth training in one department, employees spend time learning more about other departments and the items stocked in each. Moreover, every salesperson regularly attends seminars on merchandise-related topics that will help in answering customer questions knowledgeably.

The result of such training is evident. Each salesperson, clad in a bright orange apron, not only is informative and courteous but also acts in the best interests of the customer. Salespeople routinely ask customers detailed questions, lead them personally to the proper aisles, and keep them from overspending.

Employee loyalty and devotion is further instilled when Home Depot's chairman and CEO, Bernard Marcus, and president, Arthur Blank, stop by a store. The two chiefs spend almost 40 percent of their time visiting Home Depot stores—not unlike the legendary Sam Walton, who regularly visited his Wal-Mart stores to talk to employees and customers. Moreover, each of the Home Depot's seven outside directors are required to visit twelve stores every quarter.

Employee morale is boosted by a quarterly broadcast over Home Depot's own closed-circuit TV network connecting all stores. This program, hosted by Marcus and Blank, tells about the operational performance of the company, as well as innovations and ideas suggested by employees. Akin to a staff meeting, the program is yet another tool to create strong employee devotion and a culture of loyalty to the company and commitment to its customers.

## Operational Efficiency

With new stores opening in many different locations each year, how does Home Depot maintain the operational efficiency that ensures competitive prices and avoids stockouts? In this respect as well, Home Depot has been at the forefront, tapping into new technology and devising new systems that best serve its interests.

Fast growth implies rapidly changing needs for information. Such needs can be satisfied efficiently only if the company's information system is flexible. Thus Home Depot relies on an "open" information system as opposed to a customized, closed system. As a result, the company's software can be used on many different types of computer hardware, present and future systems can more easily be integrated, and software can be run on all the company's microcomputers, minicomputers, and mainframe computers. Such open systems enable faster and cheaper changes as well as faster and better access to information. A modern satellite networking system connects terminals in each Home Depot store to a central mainframe computer, enabling multiple transfers to and from stores at any time or all at the same time.

Home Depot's computerized information system ensures closer contact with each store and also closer contact with suppliers. The system speeds order placement, delivery, and payments to suppliers, ensuring that stores are stocked with the items needed by customers.

A system like this one improves Home Depot's ability to manage change and to react to emergencies, as when Hurricane Andrew devastated parts of South Florida in 1992. Home Depot stores that were damaged by the hurricane reopened in tents, often staying open twenty-four hours a day. Powered by generators and linked to headquarters via satellite dishes, they provided home repair and building essentials at cost or, as in the case of much-needed plywood, at a loss.

## The Future

Home Depot's plans are by no means modest. The company plans to expand nationwide from its current base in the East and parts of the West. The numbers of stores and employees are expected to double by 1996.

Store sizes are changing as well. New stores are larger than the older ones, averaging about 98,700 square feet. And some new store formats are being tested. For example, in three towns of the Midwest, the company plans to experiment with larger stores for farming and ranching communities. Called Home Depot CrossRoads, these stores would measure 117,000 square feet, with an additional 100,000 square feet of open space for selling farm and ranch products. Plans are also afoot for providing recycling centers in the store parking lots for consumer recycling of household waste and scrap materials from home repair activities.

Finally, Home Depot is preparing for the day when U.S. population trends, such as the aging of the baby boomers and an increasing tendency for people to switch residences, may reduce interest in home improvement activity. The company is adding home decor and related items to its merchandise mix and providing certified interior designers to cater to customers' needs for design assistance. Simultaneously, Home Depot is testing the global marketplace, in Canada and Mexico. The engine of growth seems set to chug on at Home Depot.

### Questions

1. What general principle for retail success can be drawn from the success of Home Depot?
2. Comment on the competitive position of Home Depot. Can competitors easily emulate Home Depot, to emerge as significant challengers?
3. Identify some major demographic changes that could have an impact on the home repair industry. How is Home Depot responding to these changes?
4. What potential problems do you foresee from Home Depot's recent strategy of enhancing its merchandise mix and increasing store sizes?

### Suggested Readings

"Big 3 Discounters to Big Builders List," *Chain Store Age Executive,* December 1993, pp. 116–124.

Graham Button, "The Man Who Almost Walked Out on Ross Perot," *Forbes,* 22 November 1993.

"Fast Growth Demands Flexibility," *Chain Store Age Executive,* February 1993, pp. 53–56.

*The Fort Wayne Journal-Gazette,* 23 October 1994, p. 2G.

"Home Depot Urges Recycling," *Chain Store Age Executive,* October 1992, pp. 33–36.

Walecia Konrad, "Cheerleading, and Clerks Who Know Awls from Augers," *Business Week,* 3 August 1992, p. 57.

Patricia Sellers, "Companies That Serve You Best," *Fortune,* 31 May 1993.

"State of the Industry" *Chain Store Age Executive,* August 1994, p. 4A.

"State of the Industry: Executive 100," *Chain Store Age Executive,* August 1992, p. 6A.

Roger Thompson, "There's No Place Like Home Depot," *Nation's Business,* February 1992.

"Transporting Data, Openly," *Chain Store Age Executive,* July 1993, pp. 45–48.

Michael Treacy and Fred Wiersema, "Customer Intimacy and Other Value Disciplines," *Harvard Business Review,* January-February 1993.

"Why Open Systems Are Desirable," *Chain Store Age Executive,* November 1992, p. 8A.

# PART FOUR
# ETHICS CASE

## THE GENEROUS SALESPERSON

Jill McCarthy, a retail buyer for a large department store, was told during her training as a buyer that the company was very sensitive to any type of inducements given buyers beyond "modest tokens of friendship." The company felt that as long as buyers were entertained or received tokens of appreciation of little or no value, their position as buyers would not be compromised.

- Why would a company feel the need for such a policy? What would constitute "a modest token of friendship"? What would he excessive?

The first year of Jill's job involved nothing that could even remotely be linked to the "bribery policy." One salesperson for a large dress manufacturer had become good friends with Jill and offered to take her to dinner so they could quietly discuss some of the emerging fashion trends that would be affecting the next season's lines. Jill was happy to go to dinner because it was a good opportunity to enjoy quiet conversation with her friend Barbara, the sales representative. The dinner went very well and was very productive for both Jill and her store.

- Does anyone feel uncomfortable accepting dinner under this policy?

Later that year Barbara invited Jill to attend an ice show with her, as a recreational activity. Jill remembered the dinner, felt that it would be very pleasant to attend anything with Barbara, and quickly accepted. On the date of the planned entertainment, Jill received four tickets and a note from Barbara saying that she was terribly sorry that she could not come to town but that she wanted Jill to invite other friends and enjoy the ice show.

- Should Jill accept the tickets? Why or why not? What are the issues in this situation?

A month later, with a note of apology, Jill received a smoked turkey and a fruitcake from Barbara in the name of Barbara's company.

- What should Jill do? Why? What harm has been done?

The following spring Barbara asked Jill to speak to the retail apparel manufacturers' trade association on the buyer's view of sales and service in retailing. Jill was very happy to receive the invitation to speak and was happier later to hear that there was an honorarium of $500 associated with the speaking engagement. She worked hard on her speech, and it was very well received. She felt she earned every penny of the $500.

- Did Jill do anything wrong by accepting? Was Barbara's involvement a problem? What danger might exist in this situation?

In late summer Barbara spent almost two days with Jill, acquainting her with some of the changes that would be made in the line and bringing her up-to-date on some new trends that were to be watched in the industry. Two weeks later Jill received a $1,000 check from Barbara's company with a notation that it was in appreciation for the time she spent advising Barbara on the needs of retailers.

- How has Jill compromised her position as a buyer? As long as she intends to be uninfluenced by the money, can she take it?

Jill realized she was in clear violation of the "bribery policy" but was not sure where she crossed the line.

- Where did Jill cross the line? Could she have continued working with Barbara after saying no to a gift or other act of friendship?

# PART FIVE
# PROMOTION DECISIONS



When Joe Berninger graduated from college, he went to work for IBM as a marketing representative trainee. He spent his first nine months at the company attending classes and seminars that gave him a thorough understanding of the development, manufacture, delivery, and implementation of computer and information technology.

This initial training helps Joe immensely when he meets with clients. His knowledge of IBM's products and services, both from marketing and technical standpoints, is so extensive that he is able to address his clients' concerns with several solutions. He is currently employed as a marketing specialist for the multi-billion-dollar corporation, and his customer relations range from one-on-one meetings to conducting seminars that promote new technologies.

Joe majored in European history in college and minored in business. This broad background in liberal arts and business has proven to be quite beneficial to him. Perhaps the most important skill Joe gained from his major was the ability to write effectively. Writing is something he does often at IBM—mostly in proposals and internal communications.

IBM will be well served by employees like Joe. His commitment to continuous improvement and customer service, his knowledge of the company's products, and his communication skills will help bolster the company's image as a "total solution provider" in the booming and competitive computer industry.

# Chapter 15

# Promotion Strategy and Marketing Communication

## LEARNING OBJECTIVES

*After studying this chapter, you should be able to*

1 *Discuss the role of promotion in the marketing mix.*

2 *Discuss the elements of the promotional mix.*

3 *Describe the communication process.*

4 *Explain the goals and tasks of promotion.*

5 *Discuss the hierarchy of effects concept and its relationship to the promotional mix.*

6 *Describe the factors that affect the promotional mix.*

7 *Explain how to create a promotion plan.*

8 *Discuss the challenges marketers face when creating global promotion plans for goods and services.*

9 *Describe the ethical and legal aspects of promotion.*

Crested Butte Mountain Resort, a small, family-owned skiing resort in Colorado, sports just 1,100 acres of ski trails—many of them skiable only by experts. It has antiquated ski lifts and very little capital. And as the crow flies, it's just sixteen miles south of Aspen, with its four mountains, trendy international reputation, and 3,700 acres of skiable terrain. Ten years ago, Crested Butte had an annual deficit of $2 million and was little known outside the Rocky Mountain area. It seemed an ideal candidate for extinction.

But thanks to a pioneering spirit and an aggressive promotion plan, today Crested Butte is doing fine. Its survival shows that even a small resort on a shoestring budget can capture national attention with innovative promotions.

Georgians Howard "Bo" Calloway and Ralph O. Walton bought Crested Butte in 1970 after both got into arguments—in separate incidents—with Aspen lift-ticket salespeople. Walton quit his job to run Crested Butte, with advice from Calloway, who already owned a garden resort in Georgia. For the next fourteen years, Crested Butte lost money on skiing but survived through land sales. Then, in 1984, land sales plummeted.

After studying a report about similar problems at Sun Valley Ski Resort in Idaho, Walton zeroed in on Crested Butte's biggest shortcoming: access. Located in a rugged and remote ranching and mining area, the resort is a five-hour drive from Denver. With no direct flights into the area, vacationers found the long and treacherous drive from Denver a major drawback. So in 1985, Walton persuaded American Airlines to fly directly into the area from several major cities. To fill flights, Crested Butte sent letters to past customers that started "HELP." The letter offered one-week packages with airfare, lodging, and lift tickets for only $199. Most of the money went to the airline for the seats, but the offer brought in enough responses —a 10 percent acceptance rate—to keep American Airlines interested in scheduling flights for the next season. Although Crested Butte was still in the red, it plunged forward, offering the same promotion and signing up American Airlines for another year.

Meanwhile, Calloway developed a system to track reservations for twelve different periods of the year in sixty-four separate cities. The system allowed Crested Butte to monitor reservations in these cities and adjust promotions accordingly. For instance, if reservations from Tulsa for the week before Christmas fell below expectations, a promotion was targeted to Tulsa skiers through direct mail and radio ads. If reservations were up, the resort could raise package prices in that city.

Because many travel agents had either never heard of Crested Butte or knew very little about it, the resort sent salespeople to talk to travel agencies about its benefits. The sales pitch focused on Crested Butte's "funky" character and real western setting. Advertising, meanwhile, reinforced Crested Butte's differences from other ski resorts, such as its ruggedness and remote setting. "Heaven forbid we should ever become like Aspen or Vail," the ads said, and "Crested Butte—what Aspen used to be and Vail never was." Ads also compared the resorts' prices.

Lack of capital still strained Crested Butte's ability to attract new skiers, however. Other ski resorts opened their seasons bragging of new lifts, restaurants, and terrain, but Crested Butte had nothing new to brag about. The only land that Crested Butte could develop into ski runs had severe, rocky slopes classified as "extreme," navigable by only the most experienced skiers. Crested Butte developed 400 acres of this terrain anyway and turned it into a plus. Huge signs were put up, warning of the slope's toughness in five languages. New ads compared Crested Butte's huge "extreme" territory with much smaller areas at other resorts, such as Aspen, Snowmass, and Vail.

By the 1988–89 season, Crested Butte was making a profit, but it was still losing money between Thanksgiving and Christmas. So the resort made an unusual offer: free skiing between the holidays. If lodging and restaurant owners in Crested Butte would voluntarily give the resort some revenue from customers who came to ski, the resort might come out ahead. Skiers responded in droves. Lodging from Thanksgiving to Christmas is now booked solid, with about 9,000 skiers jamming the slopes. The resort makes a profit during this season, and the promotion has increased awareness of Crested Butte among skiers to 90 percent from 10 percent.[1]

Crested Butte uses several forms of promotion to communicate with skiers. Advertisements promote the resort's tough terrain and true western ambience; salespeople visit travel agents to boost reservations; and sales promotion activities offer free skiing during the holidays or vacation packages at reduced prices. Crested Butte's success proves that innovative promotion can work for even the smallest company. Focusing on the differences that make Crested Butte better than the competition also contributes to the resort's success. What should be the role of promotion in the marketing mix of a company? What factors influence the choice of a promotional tool? How is a promotion plan created? The rest of the chapter answers these questions.

1 *Discuss the role of promotion in the marketing mix.*

## THE ROLE OF PROMOTION IN THE MARKETING MIX

Few goods or services, no matter how well developed, priced, or distributed, can survive in the marketplace without effective promotion. **Promotion** is communication by marketers that informs, persuades, and reminds potential buyers of a product in order to influence their opinion or elicit a response.

**promotion**
Communication by marketers that informs, persuades, and reminds potential buyers of a product in order to influence an opinion or elicit a response.

**promotional strategy**
Plan for the optimal use of the elements of promotion: advertising, public relations, personal selling, and sales promotion.

**Promotional strategy** is a plan for the optimal use of the elements of promotion: advertising, public relations, personal selling, and sales promotion. As Exhibit 15.1 shows, the marketing manager determines the goals of the company's promotional strategy in light of the firm's overall goals for the marketing mix—product, place (distribution), promotion, and price. Using these overall goals, marketers then combine the elements of the promotional strategy (the promotional mix) into a coordinated plan. The promotion plan then becomes an integral part of the marketing strategy for reaching the target market.

The main function of a marketer's promotional strategy is to convince target customers that the goods and services offered provide a differential advantage over the competition. A **differential advantage** is the set of unique features of a company and its products that are perceived by the target market as significant and superior to the competition. Such features can include high product quality, rapid delivery, low prices, and excellent service. For example, the Sensor Excel razor's differential advantage is a rubber strip that stretches the skin for a closer shave. By effectively

**differential advantage**
Set of unique features of a company and its products that are perceived by the target market as significant and superior to the competition.

*Exhibit 15.1*

Role of Promotion in the Marketing Mix

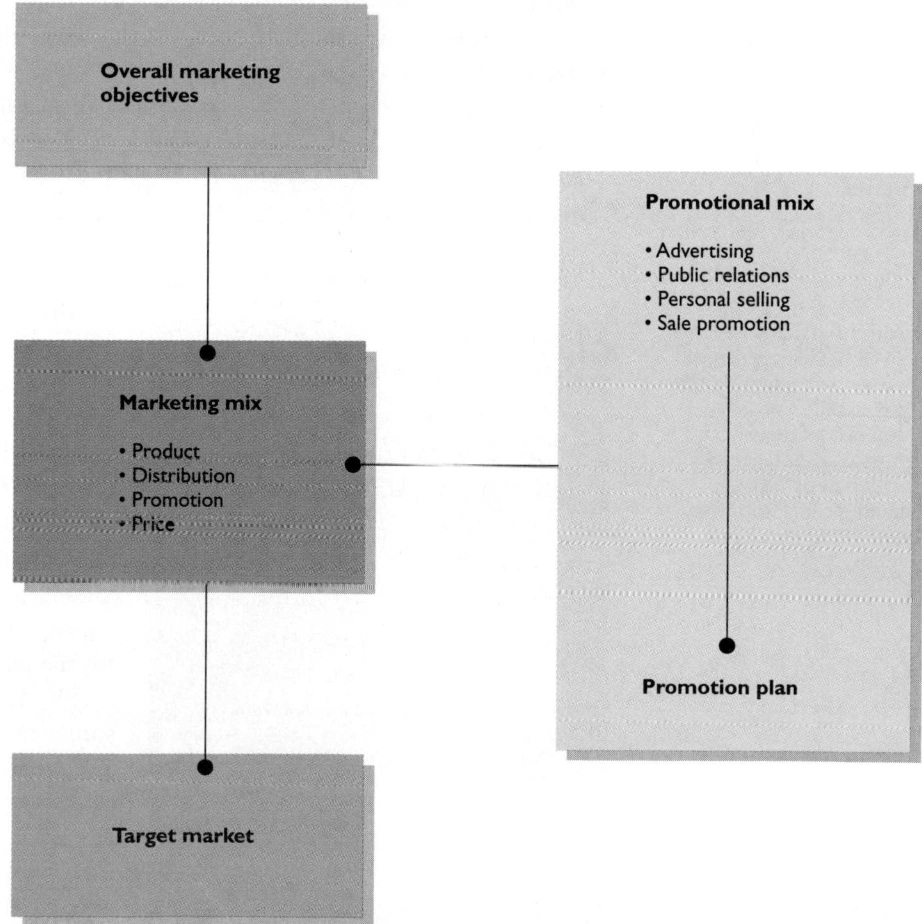

communicating this differential advantage, Gillette can stimulate demand for the Sensor Excel razor. Promotion is therefore a vital part of the marketing mix, informing consumers of a product's benefits and thus positioning the product in the marketplace.

2 *Discuss the elements of the promotional mix.*

## THE PROMOTIONAL MIX

**promotional mix**
Combination of promotion tools—including advertising, public relations, personal selling, and sales promotion—used to reach the target market and fulfill the organization's overall goals.

Most promotional strategies use several ingredients—which may include advertising, public relations, personal selling, and sales promotion—to reach the target market. That combination is called the **promotional mix.** The proper promotional mix is the one that management believes will meet the needs of the target market and fulfill the organization's overall goals. The more funds allocated to each promotional ingredient and the more managerial emphasis placed on each technique, the more important that element is thought to be in the overall mix.

### ADVERTISING

**advertising**
Impersonal, one-way mass communication about a product or organization that is paid for by a marketer.

Almost all companies selling a good or a service use some form of advertising, whether it be in the form of a multimillion-dollar campaign or a simple classified ad in a newspaper. **Advertising** is any form of paid communication in which the sponsor or company is identified. Traditional media—such as television, radio, newspapers, magazines, books, direct mail, billboards, and transit cards (advertisements on buses and taxis and at bus stops)—are most commonly used to transmit advertisements to consumers. Marketers, however, are finding many new ways to send their advertisements, most notably through such electronic means as computer modems and fax machines.

One of the primary benefits of advertising is its ability to communicate to a large number of people at one time. Cost per contact, therefore, is typically very low. Advertising has the advantage of being able to reach the masses (for instance, through national television networks), but it can also be microtargeted to small groups of potential customers, as through direct mail to a select group of customers or through print advertising in a trade magazine.

To promote its new Sensor Excel razor, Gillette devised a strategy that relied heavily on advertising. The ads pointed up the new razor's differential advantage: an innovative design that produces closer, smoother shaves.

Courtesy Gillette Corp.

Although the cost per contact in advertising is very low, the total cost to advertise is typically very high. This hurdle tends to restrict advertising on a national basis to only those companies that are financially able to do so. To introduce its new Sensor Excel razor in the United States, Gillette spent approximately $10 million over twelve months—just on advertisements. Commercials for the new razor were placed on national TV, and print ads appeared in consumer magazines like *Sports Illustrated.* Similarly, Coca-Cola spends $60 million to $80 million each year on Diet Coke's advertising.[2] Few small companies can match this level of spending for a national campaign.

Chapter 16 examines advertising in greater detail.

Cincinnati's annual Tall Stacks event, a celebration of the steamboating era, is sponsored by small companies that want to build awareness and big companies that want to build good will. Last year's official sponsors included Procter & Gamble, Chiquita Brands International, Lenscrafters, Hillshire Farm & Kahn's Company, and Cincinnati Gas & Electric Company.

*The Cincinnati Enquirer*/Jim Callaway

## PUBLIC RELATIONS

Concerned about how they are perceived by their target markets, organizations often spend large sums to build a positive public image. **Public relations** is the marketing function that evaluates public attitudes, identifies areas within the organization that the public may be interested in, and executes a program of action to earn public understanding and acceptance. Public relations helps an organization communicate with its customers, suppliers, stockholders, government officials, employees, and the community in which it operates. Marketers use public relations not only to maintain a positive image but also to educate the public about the company's goals and objectives, introduce new products, and help support the sales effort.

**public relations**
Marketing function that evaluates public attitudes, identifies areas within the organization that the public may be interested in, and executes a program of action to earn public understanding and acceptance.

**publicity**
Public information about a company, good, or service appearing in the mass media as a news item.

A solid public relations program can generate favorable publicity. **Publicity** is public information about a company, good, or service appearing in the mass media as a news item. The organization is not generally identified as the source of the information. For example, the wine industry received favorable publicity after several medical studies found a link between good health and the consumption of red wine. Sales of red wine jumped dramatically after the report.[3] This incident underscores a peculiar reality of marketing: No matter how many millions are spent on advertising, nothing sells a product better than free publicity.

Although an organization does not pay for this kind of mass media exposure, publicity should not be viewed as free. Preparing news releases and persuading media personnel to print or broadcast them costs money. Therefore, originating good publicity can be expensive. For example, winemakers wishing to capitalize on the results of the scientific studies (which they are not allowed to tout in advertising) are sponsoring workshops and conferences that discuss the findings and their benefits to wine drinkers in the hopes that this information will be picked up by the media.[4]

When an oil tanker, the Exxon *Valdez,* spilled its cargo into Alaskan seas, images of the environmental damage were distributed widely. More than five years later, those images were still affecting the company's reputation, despite expensive efforts to overcome the effects of both the oil spill and the bad publicity.

Unfortunately, bad publicity can also cost a company millions. Through the mass media, the world learns when a firm pollutes a stream, produces a defective product, employs executives engaged in payoffs or bribes, or is accused of other undesirable acts. Negative consumer reactions may cost the firm plenty in lost sales. For instance, many motorists avoided using Exxon products after the *Valdez* oil spill in Alaska in 1989.

Public relations is looked at further in Chapter 16.

## PERSONAL SELLING

**personal selling**
Planned presentation to one or more prospective buyers for the purpose of making a sale.

**Personal selling** is a planned presentation to one or more prospective buyers for the purpose of making a sale. Whether it takes place face to face or over the phone, personal selling attempts to persuade the buyer to accept a point of view or convince the buyer to take some action. For example, a car salesperson may try to persuade a car buyer that a particular model is superior to a competing model in certain features, such as gas mileage, roominess, and interior styling. Once the buyer is somewhat convinced, then the salesperson may attempt to elicit some action from the buyer, such as a test drive or a purchase.

Advertising is the prevalent form of promotion for consumer goods, but personal selling is more prevalent for industrial goods. Because industrial products are less standardized, they often are not well suited to mass promotion. Instead, customizing is often required to fit buyers' needs and financial status. To design and sell a custom-made product, firms must secure immediate buyer feedback. Thus personal selling must be used rather than advertising. Advertising still serves a purpose in promoting industrial goods, however. Advertisements in the trade media may be used to create general buyer awareness and interest. Moreover, advertising can help locate potential customers for the sales force. For example, print media advertising often includes coupons soliciting the potential customer to "fill this out for more detailed information."

Personal selling is also discussed in Chapter 17.

## SALES PROMOTION

**sales promotion**
Marketing activities—other than personal selling, advertising, and public relations—that stimulate consumer buying and dealer effectiveness.

**Sales promotion** consists of all marketing activities—other than personal selling, advertising, and public relations—that stimulate consumer purchasing and dealer effectiveness. Sales promotion is generally a short-run tool used to stimulate immediate increases in demand. Sales promotion can be aimed at end consumers, trade customers, or a company's employees. Sales promotions include free samples, contests, bonuses, trade shows, vacation giveaways, and coupons. A major promotional campaign might use several of these sales promotion tools. For example, Fuji Photo Film USA's Kids in Gear promotion allowed an individual child or a team to redeem proofs of purchase from Fuji products for a variety of soccer-related items.

Money-saving coupons also stimulated sales. The promotion was tied into Fuji's cosponsorship of the 1994 World Cup soccer tournament.[5]

Often marketers use sales promotion to improve the effectiveness of other ingredients in the promotional mix, especially advertising and personal selling. Research shows that sales promotion complements advertising by yielding faster sales responses. Gillette, for example, offered cents-off coupons during its promotional campaign to introduce the Sensor Excel razor. Consumers who had seen the advertisements for the Sensor Excel were prompted to try it at a lower introductory price through the coupon. Without the coupon, these consumers may have waited longer to purchase.

Sales promotion is discussed in more detail in Chapter 17.

3 *Describe the communication process.*

## MARKETING COMMUNICATION

**communication**
Process by which we exchange or share meanings through a common set of symbols.

Promotional strategy is closely related to the process of communication. As humans, we assign meaning to feelings, ideas, facts, attitudes, and emotions. **Communication** is the process by which we exchange or share meanings through a common set of symbols. When a company develops a new product, changes an old one, or simply tries to increase sales of an existing good or service, it must communicate its selling message to potential customers. Marketers communicate information about the firm and its products to the target market and various publics through its promotion programs.

**interpersonal communication**
Direct, face-to-face communication between two or more people.

Communication can be divided into two major categories: interpersonal communication and mass communication. **Interpersonal communication** is direct, face-to-face communication between two or more people. When communicating face to face, people see the other person's reaction and can respond almost immediately. A salesperson speaking directly with a client is an example of marketing communication that is interpersonal.

**mass communication**
Communication to large audiences.

**Mass communication** refers to communicating to large audiences. A great deal of marketing communication is directed to consumers as a whole, usually through a mass medium, such as television or newspapers. For example, when a company advertises, it generally does not personally know the people with whom it is trying to communicate. Furthermore, the company is unable to respond immediately to consumers' reactions to its message. Instead, the marketing manager must wait to see whether people are reacting positively or negatively to the mass-communicated promotion. And clutter from competitors' messages or other distractions in the environment can reduce the effectiveness of the mass communication effort.

### THE COMMUNICATION PROCESS

Marketers are both senders and receivers of messages. As *senders,* marketers attempt to inform, persuade, and remind the target market to adopt courses of action compatible with the need to promote the purchase of goods and services. As *receivers,* marketers attune themselves to the target market in order to develop the appropriate messages, adapt existing messages, and spot new communication opportunities. In this way, marketing communication is a two-way, rather than one-way, process.[6] The two-way nature of the communication process is shown in Exhibit 15.2 on page 502.

#### The Sender and Encoding

**sender**
Originator of the message in the communication process.

The **sender** is the originator of the message in the communication process. In an interpersonal conversation, the sender may be a parent, a friend, or a salesperson.

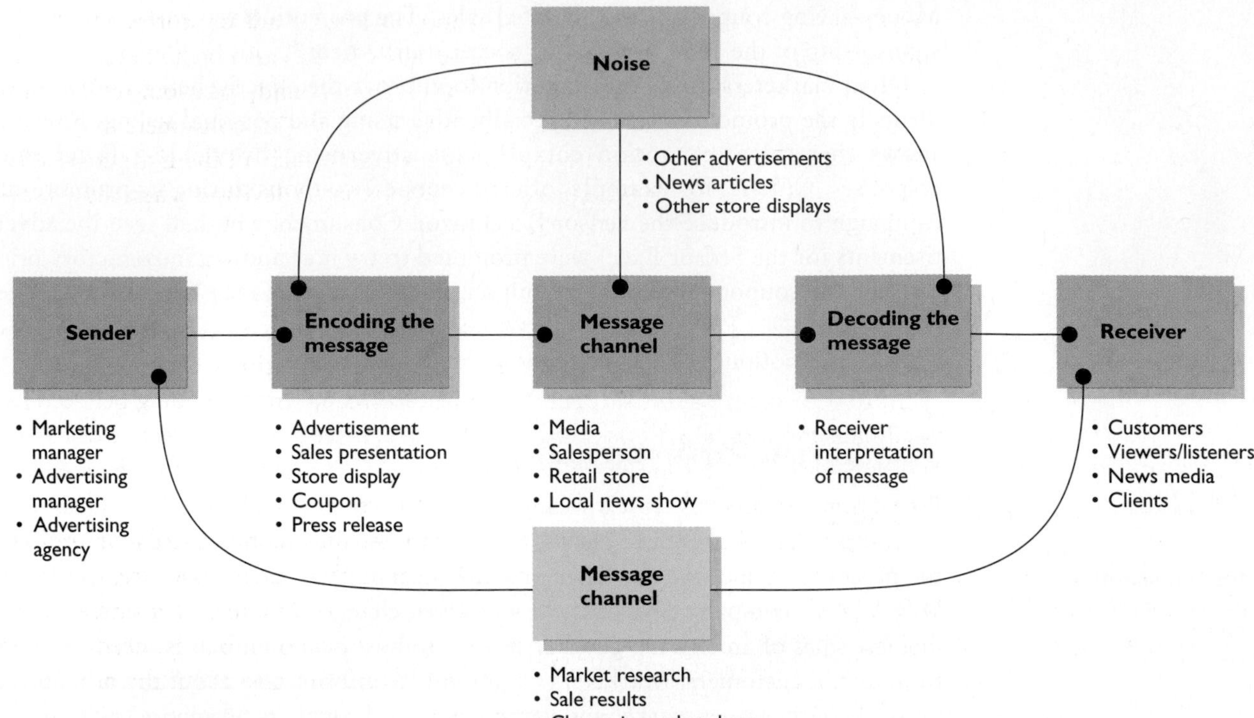


*Exhibit 15.2*

Communication Process

For an advertisement or press release, the sender is the company itself. Compaq Computer, for example, would be the sender of a message introducing the Presario line of low-priced personal computers.[7]

**encoding**
Conversion of the sender's ideas and thoughts into a message, usually in the form of words or signs.

**Encoding** is the conversion of the sender's ideas and thoughts into a message, usually in the form of words or signs. Compaq might encode its message into an advertisement, or a Compaq salesperson might encode the promotional message as a sales presentation.

A basic principle of encoding is that what matters is not what the source says but what the receiver hears. One way of conveying a message that the receiver will hear properly is to use concrete words and pictures. For example, copy for the Presario reads "Congratulations. You've just set up a computer that can edit your novel, balance your checkbook, and beat you at solitaire." The advertisement shows a detailed photograph of the model and points out that one single button turns on the entire machine.

## Message Transmission

**channel**
Medium of communication—such as a voice, radio, or newspaper—for transmitting a message.

Transmission of a message requires a **channel**—for example, a voice, radio, newspaper, or other communication medium. A facial expression or gesture can also serve as a channel.

Reception occurs when the message is detected by the receiver and enters his or her frame of reference. In a two-way conversation, such as a sales presentation given by a Compaq sales representative, reception is normally high.

**noise**
Anything that interferes with, distorts, or slows down the transmission of information.

In contrast, the desired receivers may or may not detect Compaq's message when it is mass-communicated, because most media are cluttered by "noise." **Noise** is anything that interferes with, distorts, or slows down the transmission of information. In some media overcrowded with advertisers, such as newspapers and television, the noise level is high and the reception level is low. For example, reception of

Presario's ads may be hampered by competing computer ads or stories about other computers in a magazine or newspaper. Transmission can also be hindered by situational factors, such as physical surroundings—light, sound, location, weather, and so on; the presence of other people; or the temporary moods consumers might bring to the situation. Mass communication may not even reach all the right consumers. Some members of the target audience may be watching television when the Presario computer is advertised, but others may not be.

## The Receiver and Decoding

**receiver**
Person who decodes a message.

**decoding**
Interpretation of the language and symbols sent by the source through a channel.

Compaq communicates its message through a channel to customers or **receivers,** who will decode the message. **Decoding** is the interpretation of the language and symbols sent by the source through a channel. Common understanding between two communicators, or a common frame of reference, is required for effective communication. Therefore, marketing managers must ensure a proper match between the message to be conveyed and the target market's attitudes and ideas.

Even though a message has been received, it will not necessarily be properly decoded—or even seen, viewed, or heard—because of selective exposure, distortion, and retention (refer back to Chapter 4).[8] Even when people receive a message, they tend to manipulate, alter, and modify it to reflect their own biases, needs, knowledge, and culture. Factors that can lead to miscommunication are differences in age, social class, education, culture, and ethnicity.

A study that examined interpretations of Benetton advertising distributed throughout Europe found significant differences among consumers in Great Britain, France, Norway, and Germany. The differences in interpretation were attributed to differences in culture.[9] A study of U.S. Army recruitment ads confirmed that the target audience, young men between the ages of 18 and 24, received both intended and unintended messages. One television commercial showed the firing of a cannon in order to symbolize teamwork. But the target market interpreted the image as representing a skill that would have little value in civilian life. In this particular study, message interpretation was largely influenced by differences in education, age, race, and prior army experience.[10]

Because people don't always listen or read carefully, they can easily misinterpret what is said or written. Researchers have found that almost a fourth of print communication and about two-thirds of televised communication is misunderstood.[11] Bright colors and bold graphics have been shown to increase consumers' comprehension of marketing communication. However, even these techniques aren't foolproof. A classic example of miscommunication occurred when Lever Brothers mailed out samples of its new dishwashing liquid, Sunlight, which contains real lemon juice. The package clearly stated that Sunlight was a household cleaning product. However, many people saw the word *sunlight,* the large picture of lemons, and the phrase "with real lemon juice" and thought the product was lemon juice.

## Feedback

**feedback**
Receiver's response to a message.

In interpersonal communication, the receiver's response to a message is direct **feedback** to the source. Feedback may be verbal, as in saying "I agree," or nonverbal, as in nodding, smiling, frowning, or gesturing.

Because mass communicators like Compaq are cut off from direct feedback, they must rely on market research or analysis of sales trends for indirect feedback. Compaq might use such measurements as the percentage of radio listeners or magazine readers who recognize, recall, or state that they have been exposed to the Presario message. Indirect feedback enables mass communicators to decide whether to continue, modify, or drop a message.

### THE COMMUNICATION PROCESS AND THE PROMOTIONAL MIX

The four elements of the promotional mix differ in their ability to affect the target audience. Exhibit 15.3 outlines their differences with respect to mode of communication, marketer's control over the communication process, amount and speed of feedback, direction of message flow, marketer's control over the message, identification of the sender, speed in reaching large audiences, and message flexibility.

Most elements of the promotional mix are indirect and impersonal when used to communicate with a target market, providing only one direction of message flow. For example, advertising, public relations, and sales promotion are generally impersonal, one-way means of mass communication. Because they provide no opportunity for direct feedback, they cannot adapt easily to consumers' changing preferences, individual differences, and personal goals.

Personal selling, on the other hand, is personal, two-way communication. The salesperson is able to receive immediate feedback from the consumer and adjust the

*Exhibit 15.3*

Characteristics of the Elements in the Promotional Mix

| | **Advertising** | **Public relations** | **Personal selling** | **Sales promotion** |
|---|---|---|---|---|
| **Mode of communication** | Indirect and impersonal | Usually indirect and nonpersonal | Direct and face-to-face | Usually indirect and nonpersonal |
| **Communicator control over situation** | Low | Moderate to low | High | Moderate to low |
| **Amount of feedback** | Little | Little | Much | Little to moderate |
| **Speed of feedback** | Delayed | Delayed | Immediate | Varies |
| **Direction of message flow** | One-way | One-way | Two-way | Mostly one-way |
| **Control over message content** | Yes | No | Yes | Yes |
| **Identification of sponsor** | Yes | No | Yes | Yes |
| **Speed in reaching large audience** | Fast | Usually fast | Slow | Fast |
| **Message flexibility** | Same message to all audiences | No direct control over message | Tailored to prospective buyer | Same message to varied target audiences |

message in response. Personal selling, however, is very slow in dispersing the marketer's message to large audiences. Because a salesperson can only communicate to one person or a small group of persons at one time, it is a poor choice if the marketer wants to send a message to many potential buyers.

4 *Explain the goals and tasks of promotion.*

## THE GOALS AND TASKS OF PROMOTION

People communicate with one another for many reasons. They seek amusement, ask for help, give assistance or instructions, provide information, and express ideas and thoughts. Promotion, on the other hand, seeks to modify behavior and thoughts in some way. For example, promoters may try to persuade consumers to eat at Burger King rather than at McDonald's. Promotion also strives to reinforce existing behavior—for instance, getting consumers to continue to dine at Burger King once they have switched. The source (the seller) hopes to project a favorable image or to motivate purchase of the company's goods and services.

Promotion can perform one or more of three tasks: *inform* the target audience, *persuade* the target audience, or *remind* the target audience. Often a marketer will try to accomplish two or more of these tasks at the same time. Exhibit 15.4 lists the three tasks of promotion and some examples of each.

### INFORMING

Informative promotion may seek to convert an existing need into a want or to stimulate interest in a new product. It is generally more prevalent during the early stages of the product life cycle. People typically will not buy a product or support a nonprofit organization until they know its purpose and its benefits to them. Consumer

*Exhibit 15.4*

Promotion Tasks and Examples

| **Informative promotion:** |
|---|
| Increasing the awareness of a new brand or product class<br>Informing the market of new product attributes<br>Suggesting new uses for a product<br>Reducing consumers' anxieties<br>Telling the market of a price change<br>Describing available services<br>Correcting false impressions<br>Explaining how the product works<br>Building a company image |
| **Persuasive promotion:** |
| Building brand preference<br>Encouraging brand switching<br>Changing customers' perceptions of product attributes<br>Influencing customers to buy now<br>Persuading customers to receive a call |
| **Reminder promotion:** |
| Reminding consumers that the product may be needed in the near future<br>Reminding consumers where to buy the product<br>Keeping the product in consumers, minds during off times<br>Maintaining consumer awareness |

advocates and social critics generally praise the informative function of promotion, because it helps consumers make more intelligent purchase decisions.

Informative messages are important for promoting complex products, such as automobiles, computers, and investment services. Promotions for these products must detail their technical benefits. Informative promotion is also important for a "new" brand being introduced into an "old" product class. The new product cannot establish itself against more mature products unless potential buyers are aware of it, understand its benefits, and understand its positioning in the marketplace.

### PERSUADING

Persuasion, the second promotional task, may have a negative meaning for many consumers. However, persuasion is simply trying to motivate a consumer to buy a product. Persuasive promotion is designed to stimulate a purchase or an action—for example, to drink more Coca-Cola or to use H&R Block tax services. Often a firm is not trying to get an immediate response but rather trying to create a positive image to influence long-term buyer behavior.

Persuasion normally becomes the main promotion goal when the product enters the growth stage of its life cycle. By this time, the target market should have general product awareness and some knowledge of how the product can fulfill their wants. Therefore, the promotional task switches from informing consumers about the product category to persuading them to buy the company's brand rather than the competitor's. At this time, the marketing manager emphasizes the product's real and perceived differential advantages. Promotional messages used to highlight perceived differential advantages often appeal to emotional needs, such as love, belonging, self-esteem, and ego satisfaction.

Persuasion can also be an important goal for very competitive mature product categories, such as many household items, soft drinks, beer, and banking services. In a marketplace characterized by many competitors, the marketing manager must often encourage brand switching. Informative promotions are only moderately useful in this situation, because most of the target market is familiar with the brand's characteristics. The manager hopes that a persuasive campaign will convert some buyers into loyal users. For example, to persuade new customers to switch their checking accounts, a bank's marketing manager may offer a year's worth of free checks with no fees.

**AIDA concept**
Model that outlines the process for achieving promotional goals in terms of stages of consumer involvement with the message; the acronym stands for Attention, Interest, Desire, and Action.

### REMINDING

Reminder promotion is used to keep the product and brand name in the public's mind. This type of promotion prevails during the maturity stage of the life cycle. It assumes that the target market has already been persuaded of the good's or service's merits. Its purpose is simply to trigger a memory. Crest toothpaste, Tide laundry detergent, Miller beer, and many other consumer products often use reminder promotion.

*5 Discuss the hierarchy of effects concept and its relationship to the promotional mix.*

## AIDA AND THE HIERARCHY OF EFFECTS

The ultimate goal of any promotion is to get someone to buy a good or service or, in the case of nonprofit organizations, to take some action (for instance, donate blood). A classic model for reaching promotional goals is called the **AIDA concept.**[12] The acronym stands for Attention, Interest, Desire, and Action—the stages of consumer involvement with a promotional message.

This model proposes that consumers respond to marketing messages in a cognitive (thinking), affective (feeling), and conative (doing) sequence. First, the promotion manager attracts a person's *attention* by (in personal selling) a greeting and approach or (in advertising and sales promotion) loud volume, unusual contrasts, bold headlines, movement, bright colors, and so on. Next, a good sales presentation, demonstration, or advertisement creates *interest* in the product and then, by illustrating how the product's features will satisfy the consumer's needs, *desire*. Finally, a special offer or a strong closing sales pitch may be used to obtain purchase *action*.

An expanded version of the AIDA concept is the **hierarchy of effects model** (see Exhibit 15.5).[13] This model also proposes that consumers follow a cognitive-affective-conative sequence in responding to promotional messages. It assumes that promotion propels consumers along the following six steps in the purchase-decision process:

1. *Awareness:* The advertiser must first achieve awareness with the target market. A firm cannot sell something if the market does not know that the good or service exists. Imagine that Acme Company, a pet food manufacturer, is introducing a new brand of cat food called Stripes, specially formulated for finicky cats. To increase the general awareness of its new brand, Acme heavily publicizes the introduction and places several ads on TV and in consumer magazines.
2. *Knowledge:* Simple awareness of a brand seldom leads to a sale. The next step is to inform the target market about the product's characteristics. Print ads for Stripes cat food detail the ingredients that cats love—real tuna, chicken, or turkey—as well as the product's nutritional benefits.
3. *Liking:* After the target market learns about the product, the advertiser must generate a favorable attitude. A print ad or TV commercial can't actually tell

*Exhibit 15.5*

AIDA and the Hierarchy of Effects

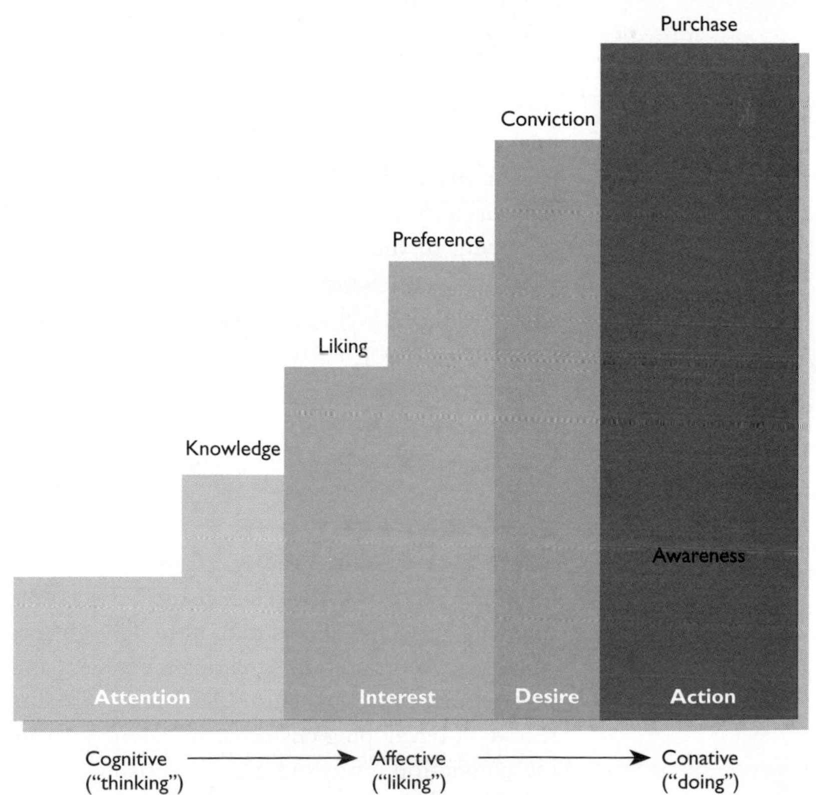


**hierarchy of effects model**
Model that outlines the six-stage process by which consumers make purchase decisions: awareness, knowledge, liking, preference, conviction, and purchase.

pet owners whether their cats will like Stripes. Thus, Acme will compile a list of cat owners in several major metropolitan cities and send each a sample of the new cat food. Acme hopes to establish liking (by the cats as well as the owners) for the new brand.

4. *Preference:* Even though owners (and their cats) may like Stripes, they may not see any advantage over competing brands, especially if owners are brand loyal. Therefore, Acme must create brand preference by explaining the product's differential advantage over the competition. Acme has to convince owners that Stripes is distinctly better than other cat foods in some respect. Specifically, Acme has to show that cats love it and want to eat nothing else. Advertising at this stage claims that Stripes will satisfy "even the pickiest of the litter."
5. *Conviction:* Although pet owners may come to prefer Stripes to other brands, they still may not have developed the conviction (or an intention) to buy the new brand. At this stage Acme might offer the consumer additional reasons to buy Stripes, such as easy-to-open, zip-lock packaging that keeps the product fresh; additional vitamins and minerals that healthy cats need; or feline taste-test results.
6. *Purchase:* Some members of the target market may now be convinced to buy Stripes but have yet to make the purchase. Displays in grocery stores, coupons, premiums, and trial-size packages can often push the complacent shopper into purchase.

### THE HIERARCHY OF EFFECTS AND PROMOTIONAL STRATEGY

Most buyers pass through the six stages of the hierarchy of effects on the way to making a purchase. The promoter's task is to determine where on the purchase ladder most of the target consumers are located and design a promotion plan to meet their needs. For instance, if Acme has determined that about half its buyers are in the preference or conviction stage but have not bought Stripes cat food for some reason, the company may mail cents-off coupons to cat owners to prompt them to buy.

The hierarchy of effects model suggests that promotional effectiveness can be measured in terms of consumers progressing from one stage to the next. However, the order of the stages in the hierarchy of effects model has been much debated. Certainly, conviction does not occur without knowledge or knowledge without awareness. But perhaps purchase can occur without liking or preference—for example, when a low-involvement product is bought on impulse. Or perhaps a consumer can move up several steps simultaneously. Regardless of the order of the stages or consumers' progression through these stages, the hierarchy of effects helps marketers by suggesting which promotional strategy will be most effective.[14]

### THE HIERARCHY OF EFFECTS AND THE PROMOTIONAL MIX

Exhibit 15.6 depicts the relationship between the promotional mix and the hierarchy of effects model. It shows that, although advertising does have an impact in the later stages, it is most useful in creating awareness and knowledge about goods or services. In contrast, personal selling reaches fewer people at first. Salespeople are more effective at developing customer preferences for merchandise or a service and at gaining conviction. For example, advertising may help a potential computer purchaser gain knowledge and information about competing brands, but the salesperson in an

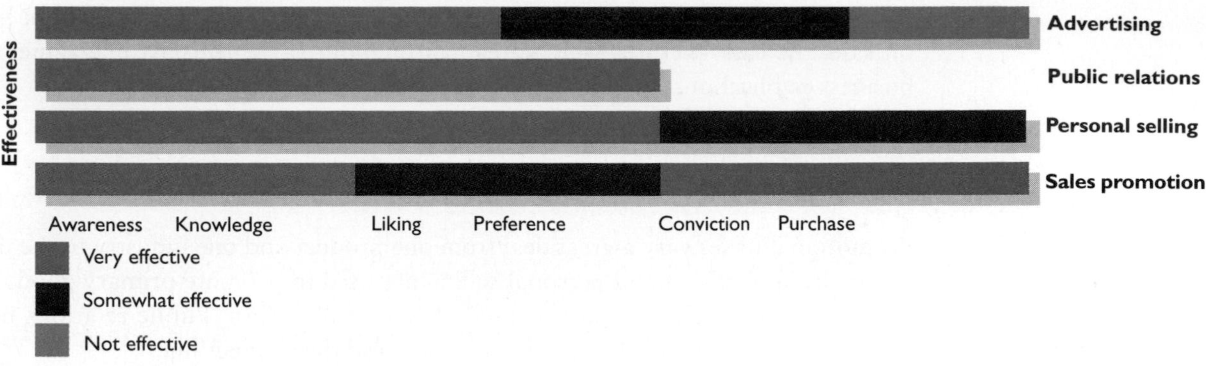


*Exhibit 15.6*

When the Elements of Promotion Are Most Useful

electronics store may be the one who actually encourages the buyer to decide a particular brand is the best choice. The salesperson also has the advantage of having the computer physically there to demonstrate its capabilities to the buyer.

Like advertising, a good sales promotion can build awareness of a new product. Sales promotion also can stir strong purchase intent. For example, coupons and other price-off promotions are techniques used to persuade customers to buy new products. Frequent-buyer sales promotion programs, which allow consumers to accumulate points or dollars that can later be redeemed for goods, tend to increase purchase intent as well as encourage repeat purchases. Consumers who hold a Household Bank MasterCard, for example, receive one entry into the company's sweepstakes for each dollar they charge on their credit card. Cardholders can win free airfare on United Airlines to destinations throughout the world. Because consumers increase their odds of winning each time they use their credit card, they are motivated to use the card more often.

Public relations has its greatest impact in building awareness about a company, good, or service. Many companies can attract attention and build goodwill by sponsoring community events that benefit a worthy cause, such as antidrug and antigang programs. Such sponsorships project a positive image of the firm and its products into the minds of consumers and potential consumers. Good publicity can also help develop consumer preference for a product. For example, when Chrysler rolled out its trio of new 1993 sedans, the market was already waiting. Auto dealers knew them inside and out. Consumers knew them by their factory code name, the LH line, long before they knew the commercial names—Concorde, Vision, and Intrepid. Best of all for Chrysler, the anticipation and desire didn't come from expensive advertising. Instead, the awareness came from aggressive public relations. Working months ahead of the car's public introduction, Chrysler exposed journalists to the LH project. Reporters were given tours of the factory where the cars would be built, as well as engineering

When Chrysler's new LH-series cars finally went on sale, they were snapped up by consumers who had already seen many stories on them in car magazines and business publications. Ads like this one reinforced the awareness that had been developed through the effective public relations campaign.

Courtesy Chrysler Corp.

labs, supplier operations, and worker training centers. By the time the LH line went on sale, the cars' pictures were spread throughout car enthusiast magazines and business publications, accompanied by upbeat feature stories.[15]

6 *Describe the factors that affect the promotional mix.*

## FACTORS AFFECTING THE PROMOTIONAL MIX

Promotional mixes vary a great deal from one product and one industry to the next. Normally, advertising and personal selling are used to promote primary goods and services, supported and supplemented by sales promotion. Public relations helps develop a positive image for the organization and the product line.

The particular promotional mix used for a product depends on several factors: nature of the product, stage in the product life cycle, target market characteristics, type of buying decision, available funds for promotion, and use of either a push or a pull strategy.

### NATURE OF THE PRODUCT

Characteristics of the product itself can influence the promotional mix. For instance, a product can be classified as either a business product or a consumer product (refer back to Chapter 9). Business products are often custom-tailored to the buyer's exact specifications. Therefore, producers of most business goods (except supply items) rely more heavily on personal selling than on advertising. However, advertising is still frequently used for creating awareness. If advertised, business products are promoted chiefly through special trade magazines. Informative personal selling is common for industrial installations, accessories, and component parts and materials.

On the other hand, because consumer products generally are not custom-made, they do not require the selling efforts of a company representative who can tailor them to the user's needs. Thus consumer goods are promoted mainly through advertising to

Shopping goods and business products, like this office furniture, are frequently promoted through personal selling. The salesperson is an important source of information about the features and benefits of the product.

create brand familiarity. Broadcast advertising, newspapers, and consumer-oriented magazines are used extensively to promote consumer goods, especially nondurables. Sales promotion, the brand name, and the product's packaging are about twice as important for consumer goods as for business products. Persuasive personal selling is important at the retail level for shopping goods, such as automobiles and appliances.

The costs and risks associated with a product also influence the promotional mix. As a general rule, when the costs or risks of using a product increase, personal selling becomes more important. Items that are a small part of a firm's budget (supply items) or of a consumer's budget (convenience products) do not require a salesperson to close the sale. In fact, inexpensive items cannot support the cost of a salesperson's time and effort unless the potential volume is high. On the other hand, expensive and complex machinery, new buildings, cars, and new homes represent a considerable investment. A salesperson must assure buyers that they are spending their money wisely and not taking an undue financial risk.

Social risk is an issue as well. Many consumer goods are not products of great social importance because they do not reflect social position. People do not experience much social risk in buying a loaf of bread or a candy bar. However, buying some shopping products and many specialty products, such as jewelry and clothing, does involve a social risk. Many consumers depend on sales personnel for guidance and advice in making the "proper" choice.

### STAGE IN THE PRODUCT LIFE CYCLE

The product's stage in its life cycle is a big factor in designing a promotional mix (see Exhibit 15.7). During the *introduction stage,* the basic goal of promotion is to inform the target audience that the product is available. Initially, the emphasis is on the general product class—for example, personal computer systems. This emphasis gradually changes to awareness of specific brands, such as IBM, Apple, and Compaq. Typically, both extensive advertising and public relations inform the target audience of the product class or brand and heighten awareness levels. Sales promotion

*Exhibit 15.7*

Product Life Cycle and the Promotional Mix

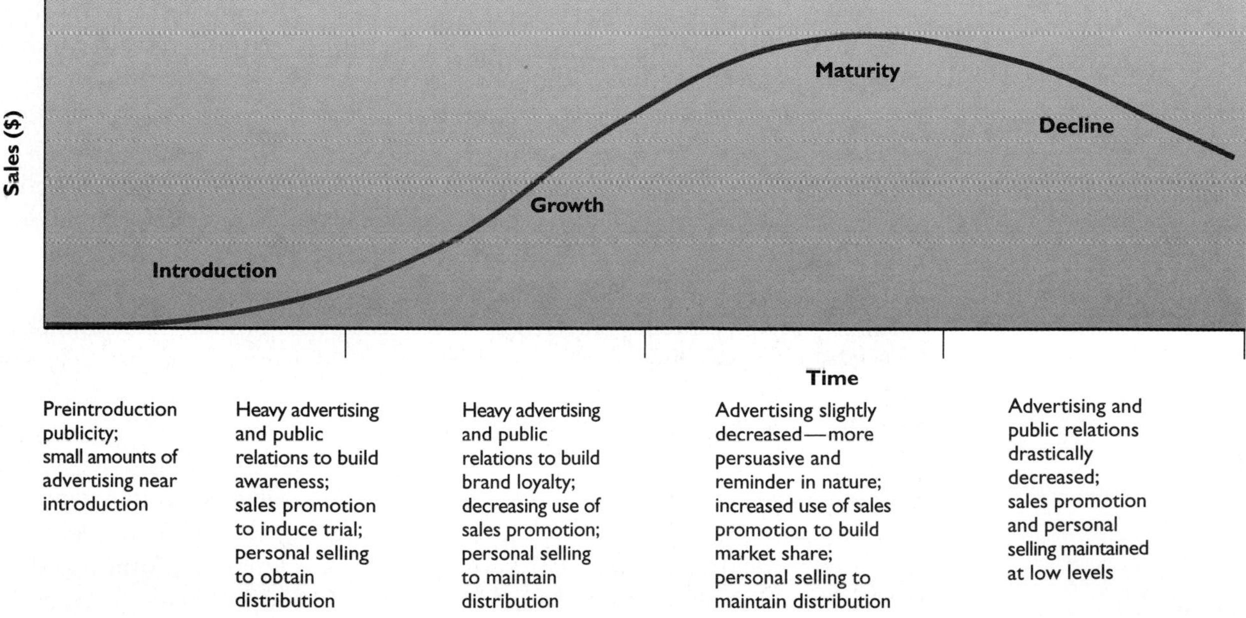

Billboard advertising requires a clear, simple, direct message.



encourages early trial of the product, and personal selling gets retailers to carry the product.

When the product reaches the *growth stage* of the life cycle, the promotion blend may shift. Often a change is necessary because different types of potential buyers are targeted. Although advertising and public relations continue to be major elements of the promotional mix, sales promotion can be reduced, because consumers need fewer incentives to purchase. The promotional strategy is to emphasize the product's differential advantage over the competition. Persuasive promotion is used to build and maintain brand loyalty to support the product during the growth stage. By this stage, personal selling has usually succeeded in getting adequate distribution for the product.

As the product reaches the *maturity stage* of its life cycle, competition becomes fiercer, and thus persuasive and reminder advertising are more strongly emphasized. Sales promotion comes back into focus as product sellers try to increase their market share.

All promotion, especially advertising, is reduced as the product enters the *decline stage*. Nevertheless, personal selling and sales promotion efforts may be maintained.

### TARGET MARKET CHARACTERISTICS

A target market characterized by widely scattered potential customers, highly informed buyers, and brand-loyal repeat purchasers generally requires a promotional mix with more advertising and sales promotion and less personal selling. Sometimes, however, personal selling is required even when buyers are well informed and geographically dispersed. Although industrial installations and component parts may be sold to extremely competent people with extensive education and work experience,

When potential customers are hard to reach with other types of promotion, many marketers use direct-response advertising media, such as print ads and TV commercials that give an 800 number. People with an interest in the good or service can call the number and request additional information.

Courtesy Kaplan

salespeople must still be present to explain the product and work out the details of the purchase agreement.

Often firms sell goods and services in markets where potential customers are hard to locate. Print advertising can be used to find them. The reader is invited to call for more information or to mail in a reply card for a detailed brochure. As the calls or cards are received, salespeople are sent to visit the potential customers.

### TYPE OF BUYING DECISION

The promotional mix also depends on the type of buying decision—for example, a routine decision or a complex decision. For routine consumer decisions, like buying toothpaste or soft drinks, the most effective promotion calls attention to the brand or reminds the consumer about the brand. Advertising and, especially, sales promotion are the most productive promotion tools to use for routine decisions.

If the decision is neither routine nor complex, advertising and public relations help establish awareness for the good or service. For example, suppose a man is looking for a bottle of wine to serve to his dinner guests. Being a beer drinker, he is not familiar with wines. Yet he has seen advertising for Sutter Home wine and has also read an article in a popular magazine about the Sutter Home winery. He may be more likely to buy this brand because he is already aware of it.

In contrast, consumers making complex buying decisions are more extensively involved. They rely on large amounts of information to help them reach a purchase decision. Personal selling is most effective in helping these consumers decide. For example, consumers thinking about buying a car usually depend on a salesperson to provide the information they need to reach a decision.

### AVAILABLE FUNDS

Money, or the lack of it, may easily be the most important factor in determining the promotional mix. A small, undercapitalized manufacturer may rely heavily on free publicity if its product is unique. If the situation warrants a sales force, a financially strained firm may turn to manufacturers' agents, who work on a commission basis with no advances or expense accounts. Even well-capitalized organizations may not be able to afford the advertising rates of publications like *Better Homes and Gardens, Reader's Digest,* and *The Wall Street Journal.* The price of a high-profile advertisement in these media could support a salesperson for a year.

When funds are available to permit a mix of promotional elements, a firm will generally try to optimize its return on promotion dollars while minimizing the *cost per contact,* or the cost of reaching one member of the target market. In general, the cost per contact is very high for personal selling, public relations, and sales promotions like sampling and demonstrations. On the other hand, for the number of people national advertising reaches, it has a very low cost per contact.

Usually there is a trade-off among the funds available, the number of people in the target market, the quality of communication needed, and the relative costs of the promotional elements. For instance, a company may have to forgo a full-page, color

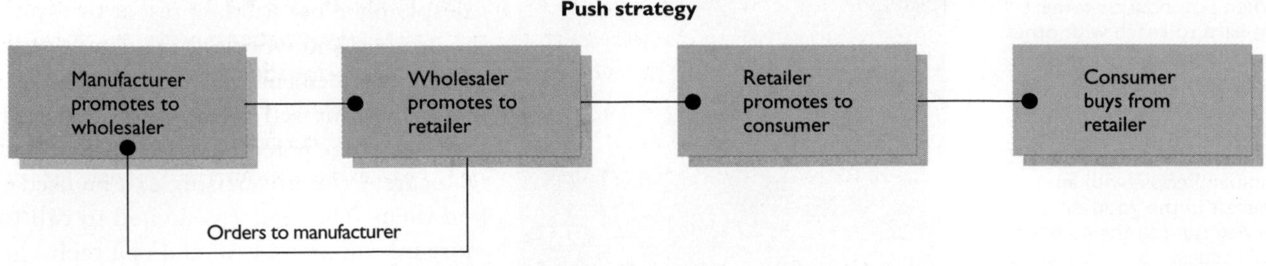


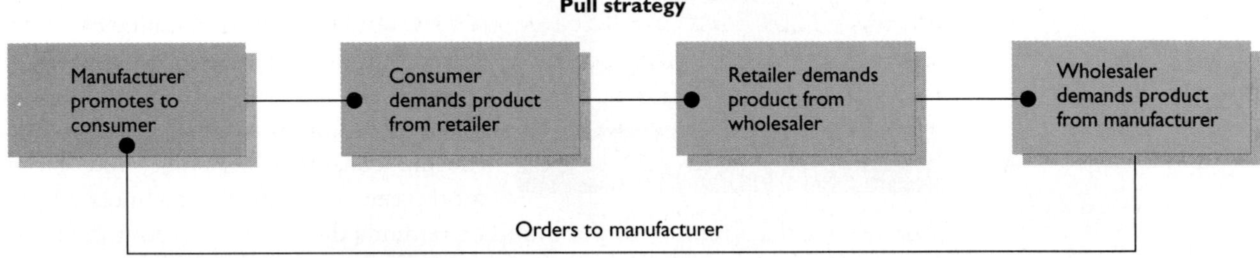


*Exhibit 15.8*

Push Strategy versus Pull Strategy

advertisement in *People* magazine in order to pay for a personal selling effort. Although the magazine ad will reach more people than personal selling, the high cost of the magazine space is a problem.

## PUSH AND PULL STRATEGIES

**push strategy**
Marketing strategy that uses aggressive personal selling and trade advertising to convince a wholesaler or a retailer to carry and sell particular merchandise.

**pull strategy**
Marketing strategy that stimulates consumer demand to obtain product distribution.

Manufacturers may use aggressive personal selling and trade advertising to convince a wholesaler or a retailer to carry and sell their merchandise. This approach is known as a **push strategy** (see Exhibit 15.8). The wholesaler, in turn, must often push the merchandise forward by persuading the retailer to handle the goods. The retailer then uses advertising, displays, and other forms of promotion to convince the consumer to buy the "pushed" products. This concept also applies to services. For example, the Jamaican Tourism Board targets promotions to travel agencies, which in turn tell their customers about the benefits of vacationing in Jamaica.

At the other extreme is a **pull strategy,** which stimulates consumer demand to obtain product distribution. Rather than trying to sell to the wholesaler, the manufacturer using a pull strategy focuses its promotional efforts on end consumers. As they begin demanding the product, the retailer orders the merchandise from the wholesaler. The wholesaler, confronted with rising demand, then places an order for the "pulled" merchandise from the manufacturer. Consumer demand pulls the product through the channel of distribution (see Exhibit 15.8). Heavy sampling, introductory consumer advertising, cents-off campaigns, and couponing are part of a pull strategy. Using a pull strategy, the Jamaican Tourism Board may entice travelers to visit by offering discounts on hotels or airfare. In contrast, a push strategy relies more on extensive personal selling to channel members, on price incentives to wholesalers and retailers, and on trade advertising.

Rarely does a company use a pull or a push strategy exclusively. Instead, the mix will emphasize one of these strategies. For example, the pharmaceutical company Marion Merrell Dow uses a push strategy, through personal selling and trade advertising, to promote its Nicoderm patch nicotine-withdrawal therapy to physicians. Sales presentations and advertisements in medical journals give physicians the detailed information they need to prescribe the therapy to their patients who want to quit smoking. Marion Merrell Dow supplements its push promotional strategy with a pull strategy targeted directly to potential patients through advertisements in consumer magazines and on television. The advertisements illustrate the pull strategy in action: Marion Merrell Dow directs consumers to ask their doctors about the Nicoderm patch.

7 *Explain how to create a promotion plan.*

## STEPS IN DEVELOPING THE PROMOTION PLAN

**promotion plan**
Carefully arranged sequence of promotional efforts designed around a common theme and geared to specific objectives.

A **promotion plan** is a carefully arranged sequence of promotions designed around a common theme and geared to specific objectives. Because promotion is something of an art, developing a promotion plan can be a challenging task. Despite many specific policies and guidelines, creativity still plays a key role. Effective planning can greatly stimulate sales; ineffective planning can waste millions of dollars and actually damage the image of the firm or its products.

The promotion plan consists of several distinct steps:

1. Analyze the marketplace.
2. Identify the target market.
3. Set promotional objectives.
4. Develop a promotion budget.
5. Choose the promotional mix.

### ANALYZE THE MARKETPLACE

If firms truly accept the marketing concept of fulfilling consumer needs and wants, they must conduct research simply to find out what these needs and wants are. With the increasing complexity of the marketplace, proper research is necessary to ensure an effective promotion plan.

Research identifies the product's target market. Research also determines the plan's promotional objectives. As noted in Chapter 8, information can be obtained through either secondary research or primary research. Internal secondary research—using sales data, data about the effectiveness of previous advertising efforts, and the like—provides the marketing manager with valuable information for promoting a current brand. External secondary data are available through research firms that continually conduct research and sell the results to any company willing to pay. For example, national firms offer data on consumer goods, such as total sales volume and market share and the flow of products into homes, as measured by purchase diaries kept by consumer panels or the volume of goods shipped from warehouses.

In this ad for Nicoderm, a skin patch used to help smokers quit, the main goal is to persuade the target audience to ask their doctors for additional information.

Marion Merrell Dow Inc.

In other cases, primary research, or

information collected exclusively for an immediate promotion problem, is necessary for proper planning. Yet market information is usually not available for a new product or a new product category. In that case, primary research might consist of an in-home use test, test marketing, or a focus group. These methods provide valuable insights into potential buyers' characteristics and help the marketer shape the promotion plan.

## IDENTIFY THE TARGET MARKET

Through market research, the market segment the firm wants to reach with a given promotion plan should be explicitly defined geographically, demographically, psychographically, or behaviorally. Naturally, the target market should be those most likely to buy the product within a defined period. For example, Honda has defined its target market for the Honda Civic as young married couples with young children.

Sometimes targeting specific groups with certain products is determined to be unethical by consumer groups, as the Ethics in Marketing box reveals.

## SET PROMOTIONAL OBJECTIVES

Objectives have been discussed in previous chapters, but the need to be specific and realistic requires further explanation. Objectives are the starting point for any promotion plan. Indeed, marketing managers cannot possibly plan a promotion program unless they know what goals they are trying to reach. Of course, promotional objectives should always coincide with overall marketing and corporate objectives.

Promotional objectives should center on the consumer's stage in the hierarchy of effects, or the potential buyer's current stage in the purchasing process. The role of promotion is to change the receiver's attitudes and intentions toward the good or service, moving him or her through the hierarchy

ETHICS IN MARKETING

### Message of Hope or Sly Targeting?

A young black man in shirt and tie sits on a front porch, beckoning to an even younger friend to join him. "I was the first one in my family to go to college," he says. "It was a night-school thing, which is cool, because now I can do some good things. Give back what I learned. And the brothers, they see me and maybe they'll want to do something better for themselves, y'know?"

Is this an ad for Big Brothers or the United Negro College Fund? Not even close. The college grad and his front-porch pal are promoting Colt 45 malt liquor. The new spot is part of a controversial effort by G. Heileman Brewing Company to create a hipper image for Colt 45 and appeal more directly to the malt liquor market's most important customers: young inner-city African-Americans. The campaign has stimulated much debate over ethics.

The creators of the Colt 45 commercials say they meant to portray the values and concerns of inner-city consumers. But critics call them cynical, just a more subtle version of Colt 45's earlier spots featuring Billy Dee Williams, beautiful women, and the tag line "Colt 45. It works every time." The new ads, critics say, are just the same old success tie-in, portraying drinkers as those who are successful. Yet drinking high-alcohol products frequently leads to the opposite result.

Many brewing industry executives see nothing wrong with targeting low-income African-Americans for malt liquor. They say it is no different from targeting a Mercedes-Benz to white, affluent suburbanites. Marketers should be able to target affluent businesspeople as well as urban downscale white women or urban black men or children, they argue.

But critics of the targeting technique say malt liquor makers are unfairly going after a market that suffers disproportionately from alcohol-related disease and inadequate access to health care. For instance, black men are nearly twice as likely as white men to die from liver-related ailments and almost three times as likely to die from other alcohol-related circumstances, according to the Centers for Disease Control and Prevention. Therefore, targeting such people is fundamentally wrong, critics contend.

Health activists also charge that the Colt 45 ads use various visual cues to portray underage drinking as acceptable. The younger guy in the porch scene looks barely out of his teens, especially given the way he defers to the other character. Many contend that Heileman is breaching the beer industry's self-imposed restrictions against advertising alcohol to customers under the legal drinking age of 21.[16]

Do you feel marketers should have the right to target whichever group they determine to be their target market? If so, would you place any limitations on this right?

toward an action. At the same time, the consumer's response to the promotional message helps the marketer move to the next step in promoting the product.[17]

To be effective, objectives should meet these four criteria:

- Objectives should be measurable and written in concrete terms.
- Objectives should be based on sound research and should identify a well-defined target audience.
- Objectives should be realistic.
- Objectives should reinforce the overall marketing plan and relate to specific marketing objectives.

For a good or service, marketing managers may pursue any combination of the five basic promotional objectives: to increase awareness, to improve or change the

The objective of this ad from the Beef Council is attitudinal. Consumers already know about the product, but many have turned from red meat to poultry and fish for diet reasons. The ad seeks to change their opinions about beef.

Exhibit 15.9

Examples of Promotional Objectives for Peter Pan Peanut Butter

| | |
|---|---|
| **Awareness objectives** | To increase the percentage of consumers who are aware of Peter Pan peanut butter from 16% to 24% |
| **Attitudinal objective** | To increase the percentage of parents who feel that Peter Pan peanut butter is the best peanut butter for their children from 22% to 35% |
| **Behavioral objective** | To increase the average number of jars of Peter Pan peanut butter sold each week near large residential areas from 120 to 135 |
| **Reminder objective** | To remind consumers that Peter Pan peanut butter is the creamiest peanut butter and available at their nearest grocery and convenience stores |
| **Recall objective** | To have 25% of the market recall Peter Pan peanut butter is the creamiest |

consumer's attitude, to change a buyer's behavior, to remind the consumer of the product, and to increase the buyer's recall of the product. The **awareness objective** seeks to increase consumers' knowledge of a product or brand. Recall that this is the first stage in the hierarchy of effects model discussed earlier in this chapter. It is an especially important objective for new products or improved brands in the introduction stage of the product life cycle. An **attitudinal objective** can also be thought of as an image objective. The goal is to improve or change the product's image by changing a consumer's attitude toward it. A **behavioral objective** aims to change a buyer's behavior or prompt the buyer to take some action, the last stage in the hierarchy of effects model. The **reminder objective** is simply to cue the consumer that the product is available. Finally, the **recall objective** can be established only after the final execution of the promotion plan. It aims to increase the percentage of the target market that can recall the campaign's message and the product. Examples of some promotional objectives for Peter Pan peanut butter are shown in Exhibit 15.9.

**awareness objective**
Promotional objective that seeks to increase consumers' knowledge of a product or brand.

**attitudinal objective**
Promotional objective that seeks to improve or change a product's image by changing consumers' attitudes toward it.

**behavioral objective**
Promotional objective that aims to change a buyer's behavior or prompt the buyer to take some action.

**reminder objective**
Promotional objective used to cue the consumer that the product is available.

**recall objective**
Promotional objective aimed at increasing the percentage of the target market that can recall the campaign's message and the product.

## DEVELOP A PROMOTION BUDGET

After identifying the target market and specifying the promotion goals, the marketing manager can develop a concrete budget. This is no simple task, nor is there a cookbook approach that will create an ideal promotion budget. Top marketing management usually defines the role of promotion in the marketing mix and allocates funds for it.

Theoretically, the promotion budget should be set at a level that maximizes profitability and return on investment. This theory is not easy to apply, however, because it requires knowledge of the actual monetary benefits resulting from the promotion effort.[18] Easier techniques for setting budgets rely on the following approaches:

**arbitrary allocation**
Method of setting a promotion budget that picks a dollar amount without reference to other factors.

**all-you-can-afford approach**
Method of setting a promotion budget that relies on determining how much the marketer can spend.

- *Arbitrary allocation and all-you-can-afford:* The easiest way to set a promotion budget is simply to pick a dollar amount; this method is called **arbitrary allocation.** Many companies use the arbitrary method for setting their promotion budgets, even though the budget allocated may or may not be enough to promote the product effectively. A variation is for management to figure out how much it can afford to put into promotion. The **all-you-can-afford approach** is a form of arbitrary allocation, because determining what is affordable can be based on many arbitrary criteria. Perhaps the reason for the popularity of these illogical approaches to budget setting is the difficulty of measuring the effectiveness of promotion.
- *Competitive parity:* A second approach for setting a promotion budget is

**competitive parity**
Method of setting a promotion budget that matches a competitor's spending.

called **competitive parity.** The firm allocates enough money to meet the promotional challenge of the competition. If competitor A spends $1 million, then management of firm B allocates $1 million for promotion. Perhaps the biggest problem with this technique is that it ignores creativity and media effectiveness. In assuming the competitor's spending level is correct, the firm disregards its own unique situation, opportunities, strengths, and weaknesses.[19] But if the money is spent in the wrong media or if the campaign is ineffective, spending even $10 million to $50 million won't be enough. One advantage of the competitive parity method is that it does force the firm to examine competitors' actions.

**percent of sales approach**
Method of setting a promotion budget that allocates an amount equal to a certain percentage of total sales.

- *Percent of sales:* Another method of setting a promotion budget is to use a certain percentage of total sales. The formula for a **percent of sales approach** is

$$\text{Promotion dollars} = x\% \times \text{Previous year's total sales}$$

The percent of sales approach is not limited to total sales; it can also be based on sales by product, territory, customer group, and so on. Some firms base their promotion budget on a percentage of the sales forecast for the coming year. The inherent weakness of this approach is that the budget becomes a consequence of sales rather than a determinant of sales. As sales decline, the promotion budget also falls. Research has shown that advertisers maintaining their promotion budgets during slow sales periods achieve better sales than those that do not. For example, airlines that increase their advertising and promotion spending during a recession have been shown to increase sales and market share; airlines that cut promotion spending lose sales and market share. The percent of sales approach also bears little relationship, if any, to a firm's promotional objectives. However, the appeal of the percent of sales approach is its simplicity. It is easy for managers to use and understand, because they often view costs in percentage terms. Although many companies follow this practice, studies have shown that use of the percent of sales method has declined quite a bit among organizations of all sizes.[20]

**market share approach**
Method of setting a promotion budget that allocates the amount needed to maintain or win a certain market share.

- *Market share:* Another approach to budgeting is to calculate how much promotion is needed to maintain or win a certain market share. This is the **market share approach.** If a firm is satisfied with its market share, it may decide to continue spending the dollar amount or percentage it spent in the past. If the organization plans to increase its market share, it can increase its budget to meet its goals. Like the percent of sales approach, however, this method ignores quality and creativity. Who is to say that spending $5 million this year will be more or less effective than spending $5 million last year? Moreover, the firm is letting its competition indirectly set its promotion budget. The market share approach also ignores potential new product offerings. Generally, a new product requires a heavier promotion budget to educate the target market and build product awareness. Aside from recognizing the importance of competition for market share, this approach does not greatly improve on the other methods.

**objective and task approach**
Method of setting a promotion budget that begins with promotional objectives, defines the communication tools required to achieve those objectives, and then adds up the costs of the planned activities.

- *Objective and task:* The most popular and most scientific approach to setting a promotion budget is the **objective and task approach.** First, management sets objectives. Second, it defines the communication tools required to achieve those objectives. Then a budget is built by adding up the costs of the planned promotion activities. This approach requires that management understand the effectiveness of various promotion tools. It also assumes that achieving the

## SELF-REGULATION OF PROMOTION

**National Advertising Division (NAD)**
Complaint bureau for consumers and advertisers, part of the Council of Better Business Bureaus.

**National Advertising Review Board (NARB)**
Appeals board for cases in which the National Advertising Division rules in favor of the complaining party.

Although many laws regulating promotion activities have been enacted, marketers also practice self-regulation. The system they've established for policing promotion practices is the **National Advertising Division** (NAD) of the Council of Better Business Bureaus, which is a complaint bureau for consumers and advertisers. After receiving a complaint about a promotion, NAD starts investigating. It evaluates the information it collects and then decides whether the promotion's claims are substantiated. If the promotion is deemed unsatisfactory, NAD negotiates with the company for either changes or discontinuation of the promotion. If the issue reaches a deadlock or the losing party wishes to appeal, the case is referred to the **National Advertising Review Board** (NARB).

Marketers want to avoid having to drop or modify promotional campaigns because of the potential costs: remaking an ad, overcoming bad publicity and ill will, destroying the timing of a campaign. Yet controversies arise regularly. For instance, Procter & Gamble advertisements for disposable diapers implied that cloth diapers were less healthy for babies—until the National Association of Diaper Services challenged the claims, prompted a NAD investigation, and forced P&G to modify the ads. Similarly, Miller Brewing Company canceled television and print advertising after a government investigation questioned whether Miller was illegally marketing its Ice beer on the basis of higher alcohol content. It is against federal law to disclose a beer's alcoholic content in advertising.[30] And a Volvo commercial in which one of its station wagons withstood the crushing weight of Big Foot, a souped-up pickup truck with oversized tires, was found to be deceptive. In truth, the car had been reinforced with lumber and steel. Volvo was forced to make a public apology, but this confession did not appease the United States Hot Rod Association, which squashed an unreinforced Volvo in a public demonstration broadcast over national media.

## FEDERAL REGULATION OF PROMOTION

When self-regulation doesn't work, the Federal Trade Commission (FTC) steps in. The FTC's main concern is with deception and misrepresentation in promotion. The FTC defines deception as "a representation, omission, or practice that is likely to mislead the consumer acting reasonably in the circumstances, to the consumer's detriment." The courts have ruled that deception can also cover what the consumer infers from the promotion, not only what is literally said. Critics of FTC regulation point out that any message, commercial or not, has the potential for deception. Moreover, even the most honest speaker cannot control the inferences the audience will make.

Often, the FTC will require the promoter to *substantiate* the claims made in its promotional messages. If the claims cannot be substantiated, the FTC's traditional remedy is the *cease-and-desist order,* otherwise known as the "Go and sin no more" approach. This order bans use of claims found to be false or deceptive. *Fines* may also be levied against firms making false claims. In the largest false advertising settlement in FTC history, General Nutrition, a retailer of nutritional supplements, was required to pay $2.4 million in penalties for making unsubstantiated claims for more than forty products. Among the products affected were Sleeper's Diet, which the company claimed can help users lose weight while asleep, and Muscle Fire Power and Liquid Power Energy Lift, which it claimed can enhance muscle development and strength.[31]

**corrective advertising**
Advertisement that is run to amend the false impressions left by previous promotion.

In some cases, the FTC requires a corrective message. **Corrective advertising** is an advertisement run to amend the false impressions left by previous promotion. For example, after investigating several diet-program companies for false and deceptive advertising, the FTC required them to revise their weight-loss claims to reflect accurately the programs' success in helping customers keep off the weight they lose.[32]

What are the effects of corrective advertising? Does it work? In most cases, corrective ads provide useful information to consumers that may change their beliefs and modify their purchasing behavior. However, the variation on the message must be substantial to correct consumers' false impressions. Thus Warner-Lambert had to use the following statement in its ads for sixteen months: "Listerine will not help prevent colds or sore throats or lessen their severity." Nevertheless, after the sixteen months, 57 percent of regular Listerine users still believed it would prevent and reduce the likelihood of colds and sore throats.[33] The overall consensus is that corrective advertising seems to work, at best, moderately well—but not nearly well enough to correct the misrepresentations of deceptive advertising. Furthermore, most corrective ads have little or no impact on company image or on the image of the general product category.

## LOOKING BACK

Crested Butte does not use just one element of the promotional mix to promote its resort to skiers. Rather, it uses a mix of promotional elements: advertising, public relations, public relations, personal selling, and sales promotion. Promotion is crucial to communicating the resort's differential advantage over competing resorts—tough terrain and a real Western setting—and hence crucial to its success. As you read the next two chapters, keep in mind that marketers try to choose the mix of promotional elements that will best promote their good or service. Rarely will a marketer rely on just one method of promotion.

## SUMMARY

1 **Discuss the role of promotion in the marketing mix.** Promotion is communication by marketers that informs, persuades, and reminds potential buyers of a product in order to influence an opinion or elicit a response. Promotional strategy is the plan for using the elements of promotion—advertising, public relations, personal selling, and sales promotion—to meet the firm's overall objectives and marketing goals. Based on these objectives, the elements of the promotional strategy become a coordinated promotion plan. The promotion plan then becomes an integral part of the total marketing strategy for reaching the target market, along with product, distribution, and price.

2 **Discuss the elements of the promotional mix.** The elements of the promotional mix include advertising, public relations, personal selling, and sales promotion. *Advertising* is a form of impersonal, one-way mass communication paid for by the source. *Public relations* is the function of promotion concerned with a firm's public image. Firms can't buy good publicity, but they can take steps to create a positive company image. *Personal selling* involves direct communication, in person or by telephone; the seller tries to initiate a purchase by informing and persuading one or more potential buyers. Finally, *sales promotion* is typically used to back up other components of the promotional mix by motivating employees and stimulating consumer and business-customer purchasing.

3 **Describe the communication process.** The communication process has several steps. When an individual or organization has a message it wishes to convey to a target audience, it encodes that message using language and symbols familiar to the intended receiver and sends the message through a channel of communication. Noise in the transmission channel distorts the source's intended message. Reception

### KEY TERMS

*advertising* 498
*AIDA concept* 506
*all-you-can-afford approach* 518
*arbitrary allocation* 518
*attitudinal objective* 518
*awareness objective* 518
*behavioral objective* 518
*channel* 502
*communication* 501
*competitive parity* 519
*corrective advertising* 522
*decoding* 503

*differential advantage* 497
*encoding* 502
*feedback* 503
*hierarchy of effects model* 507
*interpersonal communication* 501
*market share approach* 519
*mass communication* 501
*National Advertising Division (NAD)* 522
*National Advertising Review Board (NARB)* 522
*noise* 502
*objective and task approach* 519
*percent of sales approach* 519
*personal selling* 500
*promotion* 497
*promotional mix* 498
*promotional strategy* 497
*promotion plan* 515
*publicity* 499
*public relations* 499
*pull strategy* 514
*push strategy* 514
*recall objective* 518
*receiver* 503
*reminder objective* 518
*sales promotion* 500
*sender* 501

occurs if the message falls within the receiver's frame of reference. The receiver decodes the message and usually provides feedback to the source. Normally, feedback is direct for interpersonal communication and indirect for mass communication.

4 **Explain the goals and tasks of promotion.** The fundamental goals of promotion are to induce, modify, or reinforce behavior by informing, persuading, and reminding. *Informative promotion* explains a good's or service's purpose and benefits. Promotion that informs the consumer is typically used to increase demand for a general product category or to introduce a new good or service. *Persuasive promotion* is designed to stimulate a purchase or an action. Promotion that persuades the consumer to buy is essential during the growth stage of the product life cycle, when competition becomes fierce. *Reminder promotion* is used to keep the product and brand name in the public's mind. Promotions that remind are generally used during the maturity stage of the product life cycle.

5 **Discuss the hierarchy of effects concept and its relationship to the promotional mix.** The hierarchy of effects model outlines the six basic stages in the purchase decision-making process, which are initiated and propelled by promotional activities: (1) awareness, (2) knowledge, (3) liking, (4) preference, (5) conviction, and (6) purchase. The components of the promotional mix have varying levels of influence at each stage of the hierarchy. Advertising is a good tool for increasing awareness and knowledge of a good or service. Sales promotion is effective when consumers are at the purchase stage of the decision-making process. Personal selling is most effective in developing customer preferences and gaining conviction.

6 **Describe the factors that affect the promotional mix.** Promotion managers consider many factors when creating promotional mixes. These factors include the nature of the product, product life cycle stage, target market characteristics, the type of buying decision involved, availability of funds, and feasibility of push or pull strategies.

7 **Explain how to create a promotion plan.** Effective promotion planning is crucial to a product's success. Promotion planning involves several distinct steps. First, promotion managers analyze the marketplace, usually by conducting research. Second, they define the target market in terms of demographic, geographic, psychographic, or behavioral variables. The third stage of promotion planning is to set specific promotional objectives. Promotion managers then determine the promotion budget and, finally, select the elements of the promotional mix.

8 **Discuss the challenges marketers face when creating global promotion plans for goods and services.** Global marketers typically face the decision of whether to localize or standardize their promotional message. Localization is advocated by many, who point out that culture plays a large role in the way a promotional message is decoded by the intended receiver. Others recommend standardization, on the grounds that consumers everywhere have the same basic needs and desires and that standardized messages support unified brand images.

9 **Describe the ethical and legal aspects of promotion.** Although many laws are in place to regulate promotional activities, much of the industry practices self-regulation. Promotional practices are monitored by industry and government. Industry regulation is overseen by the National Advertising Division of the Council of Better Business Bureaus and by the National Advertising Review Board. The Federal Trade Commission becomes involved in advertising regulation when industry regulation is inadequate.

## Discussion and Writing Questions

1. Explain the role of promotion in the marketing mix. Describe environments in which it is less important and more important.
2. Why is understanding the target market a crucial aspect of the communication process?
3. With regard to promotion, why is it important for marketers to understand their target market's awareness of and predisposition toward a product?
4. What types of products are promoted using persuasion? Give some examples of persuasive promotion.
5. Discuss the role of personal selling and advertising in promoting industrial products. How does their role differ in promoting consumer products?
6. Assume that your firm's promotion efforts for a new product have failed to meet promotional objectives. Write a report suggesting the reasons.
7. Your company has just developed a complex electronic device that can automatically control all the appliances in a consumer's home. Write a brief promotion plan describing your market analysis efforts, target market, promotional objectives, and promotional mix.
8. Discuss why using the objective and task method to determine a product's promotion budget is superior to other budget-setting methods.
9. Your company would like to develop a promotional campaign for a brand of laundry detergent that will be sold in several different countries. Would you choose to use a localized promotional message or one that is more standardized? Explain your choice. What would your decision be if the product were cosmetics?

## Application for Small Business

The Varsity Shoppes comprise two retail stores selling men's and women's clothing. It is a family operation, and the third-generation son and daughter are currently co-owners. The store has two locations, one near the local college campus and another in a strip center near a major shopping mall developed about twenty years ago east of the downtown area.

Population trends indicate a southerly move by the stores' traditional target market, and so the owners have decided to open a third store in a relatively new strip center south of town. This new location will open in about three months. A promotion campaign is now being planned.

### Questions

1. Which types of promotion should the campaign emphasize—informative, persuasive, or reminder?
2. Suggest a promotion plan that will make the target market aware of the new location. To what extent should the plan emphasize the new location versus the two existing locations?

## CRITICAL THINKING CASE

### *Modern Maturity*

*Modern Maturity*, published by the American Association of Retired Persons (AARP), is the big seller in the magazine market for those over 50. *Advertising Age* picked the 50-plus market as one of the top ten magazine categories to watch. Circulation and revenue are growing quickly in this market, sparking increased interest among publishers—and even among cartoonists, who now create pieces specifically for older readers.

The demographic profile of the mature reader is what attracts magazine editors to this market. People over 50 years old account for 26 percent of the population but control 50 percent of the discretionary income.

The problem is figuring out how to address this market segment. These consumers don't think of themselves as old. "When they look in the mirror they tend to see someone fifteen years younger," says Richard Fontana, publisher of *New Choices* magazine. Magazines like *Second Wind* (targeted to older couples) and *Moxie* (targeted to older working women) were abandoned in the first year. Other magazines never even progressed beyond the testing phase. Consumers may be getting older, but that doesn't mean they are going to read magazines that remind them of that fact. One key is never to refer to age in the title of the publication.

Editors are starting to rethink their strategies for reaching this market. Some are simply hoping to reach older readers through existing magazines. Research indicates that readers from 50 to 59 years old prefer computer magazines. Readers aged 60 to 64 choose boating, women's fashion, and airline magazines.

*Modern Maturity* has achieved success with a three-pronged strategy. The largest single factor contributing to its success is its unique subscription base. The annual subscription cost is only $2.40 and is part of membership in AARP. Thus the magazine has the most paid subscriptions (21.4 million) in the United States. The low subscription cost almost guarantees the magazine a large circulation.

The second element of its strategy is to be relentlessly upbeat. In this respect, *Modern Maturity* has set the tone for the rest of the 50-plus magazines. The publication features personality profiles and articles like a story on volunteers titled "Everyday Heroes: They're Helping Reshape America." The stories in *Modern Maturity* don't shy away from the age issue, but the subjects are active, optimistic, and energetic.

The final element of its strategy concerns the magazine's advertising policy. The magazine turns away advertisements that have a "downer attitude." For example, *Modern Maturity* does not accept ads for crutches, wheelchairs, or similar products. Although advertising revenues would probably increase 30 percent if it did accept such ads, the editor feels that these types of ads would detract from the upbeat tone of the magazine.



### Questions

1. Do you think there is a need for magazines that target readers over 50 years old? Would it be better to reach this market through other types of publications? Give reasons to support your answer.
2. Do you agree with the editor of *Modern Maturity* that advertising influences readers' perceptions of the publication? Why or why not?
3. Does *Modern Maturity* share a frame of reference with its readers? How important is a shared frame of reference to the 50-plus market?

### References

David Astor, "Cartoonist Wants to Reach Older Readers," *Editor & Publisher,* 5 June 1993, pp. 35–36.

Glen Cameron and John Haley, "Feature Advertising: Policies and Attitudes in Print Media," *Journal of Advertising,* September 1992, pp. 47–55.

Michael Kavanagh, "Using the Grey Matter," *Marketing,* 31 March 1994, pp. 30–32.

Patrick M. Reilly, "Older Readers Prove Elusive as Magazines Rethink Strategies for the Mature Market," *The Wall Street Journal,* 12 July 1990, pp. B1, B4.

**SIGNATURE SERIES VIDEO CASE**

## Dreamful Attraction and the Role of Athletes in Marketing

SIGNATURE SERIES VIDEO

*by Shaquille O'Neal*

What is marketing, and why is it so important? Marketing is the process of planning and executing the concept, pricing, promotion, and distribution of ideas, goods, and services to create exchanges that satisfy individuals and organizational objectives. All companies would like to be successful and make money. Marketing contributes directly to achieving these objectives. Marketing includes assessing the wants and satisfactions of present and potential customers, designing and managing product offerings, determining prices and pricing policies, developing distribution strategies, and communicating with present and potential customers. This case discusses the role athletes can play in the marketing of products and is based on my experiences as an athlete and a marketer.

### Marketing Background and Concepts

While on the outside looking in, I did not realize that marketing was so complicated. I never knew that a person, such as an athlete, could have such a powerful effect on peoples' thought processes and purchasing behavior. The use of a well-known athlete in marketing a good or service can have a great impact on the sales of that good or service. Look at Michael Jordan. Before we knew it, almost every kid seemed to be wearing or wanted to wear Air Jordan shoes.

Why does this happen? Is it the appeal of a great athlete, or is it great marketing? The answer is "none of the above." It's both. In my time as a professional basketball player, I have seen firsthand the dramatic appeal that athletes have for the fans and the public in general. Most top-name athletes are like E.F. Hutton: When they talk, people listen. But why do they listen? I believe they listen to us, the athletes, because we have credibility. You will read in this book that "companies sometimes use sports figures and other celebrities to promote products hoping they are appropriate opinion leaders. Research has shown that the effectiveness of celebrity endorsements depends largely on how credible and attractive the spokesperson is and how familiar people are with him or her. The endorsement is most likely to succeed if an association between the spokesperson and the product can be established."

But marketers have to be careful when they select a celebrity to endorse a product. Bill Cosby failed as an endorser for E.F. Hutton but succeeded with such products as Kodak cameras and Coca-Cola. Consumers could not mentally link Bill Cosby with serious investment decisions but could associate him with leisure activities and everyday consumption. Bill Cosby. Investments? I don't think so. That may be why it is important to decide which product an athlete can endorse. If the right product is chosen, then the athlete should have a very good chance at being successful in marketing the product. Because of an athlete's fame and fortune, or attraction, the athlete can often have the right credibility to be a successful spokesperson. The best definition of credibility that I could find was by James Gordon in his book *Rhetoric of Western Thought*. He said that attraction "can come from a person's observable talents, achievements, occupational position or status, personality and appearance, and style." That may be why a famous athlete's personality and position can help him or her communicate more effectively than a not-so-famous athlete.

According to the authors of this book, "persuasion is simply trying to motivate a consumer to buy a product. Persuasive promotion is designed to stimulate a purchase or an action—for example, to drink Coke (or even Pepsi). Often a firm is not trying to get an immediate response but rather to create a positive image to influence long-term buyer behavior." In the cola war, I can see that persuasion is very important for victory. The target audience has to be persuaded to buy a certain drink or to switch to a certain drink. That is a very clear goal that I see all the time when I am around the people at Pepsi. "Persuasion can also be an important goal for very competitive mature product categories, such as many household items, soft drinks, beer, and banking services. The marketplace is now characterized by many competitors, and often the marketing manager must encourage brand switching. The manager hopes that a persuasive campaign will convert some buyers into loyal users."

Credibility is also a positive force because of what I like to call "dreamful attraction." For example, when I was young, I dreamed that I was like Dr. J, the famous basketball player for the Philadelphia 76ers. I would take his head off a poster and put my head on it. I wanted to be Dr. J. That is dreamful attraction. The youth of today are no different. Just the other day a kid stopped me and told me that he wanted to be like me. He had a dreamful attraction.

This dreamful attraction can help sell products. In my case, Pepsi, Spalding, Kenner, and Reebok are hoping that they are able to package properly and market whatever dreamful attraction I might have for their target audience—kids. But it is important that these companies do a good job researching market segmentation and the target market.

Today market segmentation plays a key role in the marketing strategy of almost all organizations. Market segmentation is a powerful marketing tool for several reasons. Most important, nearly all markets include groups of people or organizations with different needs and preferences. Market segmentation helps marketers define customer needs and wants more precisely. Along with market segmentation, the target market is also important. A target market is a group of individuals or organizations for which an organization designs, implements, and maintains a marketing mix intended to meet the needs of that group or groups, resulting in mutually satisfying exchanges.

## Role of Marketing Research

Marketing research entails planning, collecting, and analyzing data relevant to marketing decision making. The results of this analysis are then communicated to management. Marketing research plays a key role in the marketing system. It provides decision makers with data on the effectiveness of the current marketing mix and also insights for necessary changes. It is also important to know that marketing research can be helpful to managers. It improves the quality of decision making and helps managers beter understand the marketplace. Most important, sound marketing research alerts managers to marketplace trends. Thus they can respond to trends early rather than react to situations that have already occurred.

Marketing research can be used to learn what people think about marketing ideas. In my case it could be used to get accurate information on the image of Shaq. It could help get accurate information on a new product. This information could be gathered through focus groups and surveys.

Survey research is a popular way of collecting data. In survey research, the researcher interacts with people to obtain facts, opinions, and attitudes. This can be done by in-home interviews, mall-intercept interviews, telephone interviews, mail surveys, or focus groups.

Focus groups are a type of personal interviewing. Often recruited by random telephone screening, seven to ten people with certain desired characteristics form a focus group. During the session, a moderator hired by the research company leads the group discussion. These groups are also sometimes used to brainstorm new product ideas and to screen concepts for new products.

The information gathered from focus groups or surveys can be used to communicate positive impressions to the public. For example, look at the way in which Michael Jordan is able to communicate a positive impression for all the products that he endorses. The research that was conducted gave the company the information it needed, and Michael was able to successfully communicate the idea to the public. This information also can be used to overcome negative perceptions. For example, look at the negative image that the professional basketball player Dennis Rodman has. With the proper research and information, Dennis's negative image could be corrected, and he could try to communicate this new impression to the public. It seems that good marketing research would also be helpful in using my strategy of dreamful attraction, because it would tell us the best way to appeal to the target audiences of the goods and services I am endorsing.

### Practical Marketing Experiences

Because of my high involvement with Pepsi, I would like to elaborate on how Pepsi uses me to help sell its product. There are many ways to communicate. I find that the most effective way for me is through television commercials. This avenue gives me a chance to express myself and show my real feelings about a message we are trying to communicate—either visually or vocally. I feel that I have what Clint Eastwood has—"Sudden Impaq." My impact is revealed through my sense of humor and my nonverbal communication.

Let us journey into the deep spaces of filming a commercial. My first Pepsi commercial was called "Playground." Only five words were spoken for the entire commercial: "Don't even think about it." There is an old quote that Louisiana State University basketball coach Dale Brown liked to repeat, by a philosopher named Emerson, that says, "What you are speaks so loudly that I cannot hear what you are saying." But the impact was good enough to have an effect on the sales of Pepsi and to earn the producer of the commercial an advertising award. What made the commercial work? Pepsi had a great idea and knew very well the target audience it was aiming to reach. The "Sudden Impaq" of this commercial was toward the end, when the little kid gave his famous line: "Don't even think about it." This impact was similar to the famous "Hey, Kid" commercial that Mean Joe Green made for Coca-Cola in the 1970s. It seems that once again a well-known athlete teaming up with a young kid can truly appeal to audiences of all types.

What pleased me most about the "Playground" commercial was the freedom that the director gave me to have creative control over how I would act. At first, the script called for me to walk through the gate to the playground. I chose to rip off the gate, and they approved the idea and liked it. The script called for me to shoot baskets. I chose to pull the basket to me and slam the ball through, and they approved the idea and liked it. The script called for me to quietly and with no expression look through the cooler for something to drink. I chose to let the world see my real feelings through the use of my facial expressions, and they approved the idea and liked it.

I'm not saying that I'm the only one responsible for the success of the commercial, but I appreciated the Pepsi people allowing me to contribute my creativity to the commercial. I think it helped in the overall image and sudden impact that I was trying to create. In five quick hours, we were able to complete the project, and I was able to learn a great deal from this experience.

From the playground I went to Beverly Hills for the filming of my second Pepsi commercial, titled "A Day in the Life of Shaq." This commercial focused on the theme of being oversized, as in the new oversized Pepsi that was being introduced. The commercial starts with everything around me being a normal size. But everything around me is too small for me. The bed is too small. My breakfast is too small. The hallways are too small. My jacket is too small. Even my Ferrarri is too small. But Pepsi had it figured out. Their introduction of the Big Slam was just right.

Unlike in "Playground," in "A Day in the Life of Shaq" I had a few simple, memorable lines to deliver. The first line I delivered was after they brought me my breakfast. I reacted to my meal by saying in a cute, disgusted manner, "I ordered the big breakfast." Then at the end of the commercial, my last line was "Ain't life grand." Once again, I depended on my use of effective facial expressions and nonverbal communication to really reinforce my Clint Eastwood theory: "Sudden Impaq."

The most recent campaign that Pepsi is using me in is called "Be Young, Have Fun, Drink Pepsi." They are aiming this campaign at their primary audience: young people. According to Ric Rock, vice president for media relations at Pepsi, "Shaquille is a perfect association with Pepsi because he is young, fun, and the most exciting player in basketball—and basketball is the most popular sport among young people."

I spoke to Leonard Armato, my attorney and president of Management Plus, and he gave me his opinion of what he feels is Pepsi's strategy for the new campaign. He said, "In addition to fitting the Pepsi image perfectly, Shaquille's size fits nicely with the trend in packaging—bigger sizes. In 1992–93, Pepsi was developing a new larger-size bottle for soft drinks as part of the 1993 summer promotion. The packaging was called Big Slam.

Pepsi utilized Shaquille's physical presence to enhance its Big Slam product and packaging, which resulted in Pepsi's most successful summer promotion ever."

### Conclusions

Does all of this work? Does Shaq sell? According to Jeff Campbell, senior vice president for international marketing for Pepsi, the 1993 summer sales for Pepsi were up 12 percent. Because of this success, the campaign was extended into 1994.

Why did Shaq sell? Communication.

Although the verbal communication in these commercials was slim, the impact was still there. This makes me believe even more in the quote that who you are can almost be as important as what you say. But if you can blend the two together, who you are and what you have to say, then imagine how much more successful the message can be in the marketing process. Tennis star Andre Agassi's favorite quote from his Canon commercial is "Image is everything." If it is not everything, it is almost everything. If you have the right image, match it with the right product, and market it properly, then success should follow.

I have been involved in commercials and the marketing of products for only two years. But I have learned a great deal in this short time. If there is one formula for success in selling products, it would be this: Marketing + Image + Effective communication = Increase in sales.

Now you can call me Dr. Shaq, M.E. (Marketing Expert).

### Questions

1. Why has Shaquille O'Neal been such a success as an athlete-endorser?

2. What suggestions do you have for improving Shaquille O'Neal's image?

**VIDEO CASE**

## PepsiCo

Coca-Cola's original diet beverage was marketed under the name Tab. It was followed by Diet Pepsi. The original diet drinks used saccharine as the sweetener. Consumers found these drinks to have a bitter aftertaste but bought them for the low-calorie benefits. Then Diet Coke was introduced, with NutraSweet as the sweetener. Consumers preferred the taste of beverages sweetened with NutraSweet, and Diet Coke was a success. In fact, Diet Coke became the number-three soft drink. PepsiCo subsequently changed its formula for Diet Pepsi in order to use the better-tasting sweetener, but it still faced the challenge of convincing diet beverage drinkers (especially Diet Coke drinkers) to switch to Diet Pepsi.

The Diet Pepsi Uh-Huh! campaign was the largest promotional campaign ever developed by PepsiCo. It was begun fifteen years after Pepsi took on Coca-Cola in the Pepsi Challenge. PepsiCo kicked off its Uh-Huh! campaign by sending a million cases of Diet Pepsi to loyal Diet Coke drinkers and followed up with a heavy advertising and sales promotion campaign. The campaign featured Ray Charles and the Uh-Huh! girls (three models who became instant stars).

The Uh-Huh! campaign was a unique blend of promotional efforts. To increase the effectiveness of the ads, PepsiCo ran an Uh-Huh! update column in *USA Today*. Readers of *USA Today* were given an 800 number to call and vote on the best Uh-Huh! headlines of the week.

### Questions

1. How effective do you think advertising and sales promotion are in getting people to switch soft drinks?

2. What stage or stages of the hierarchy of effects model were most likely affected by this promotional campaign?

3. Referring to Exhibit 15.3, how would you categorize the Uh-Huh! campaign? Why?

### References

*Million Dollar Directory 1995* (Parsippany, NJ: Dun & Bradstreet Information Services, 1995).

*Standard & Poor's Industry Surveys* (New York: Standard & Poor's Corporation, October 1995).

# CHAPTER 16

# ADVERTISING AND PUBLIC RELATIONS

## LEARNING OBJECTIVES

*After studying this chapter, you should be able to*

1 *Discuss the effect advertising has on market share, consumers, brand loyalty, and product attributes.*

2 *Identify the major types of advertising.*

3 *Describe the advertising campaign process.*

4 *Describe media evaluation and selection techniques.*

5 *Define the role of advertising agencies.*

6 *Discuss the role of public relations in the promotional mix.*

The Mustang exploded onto the American cultural scene in 1964, capturing the imagination of the era's young people and inspiring musical tributes like "Mustang Sally." The car's low price and sporty styling made it an immediate hit with the leading edge of baby boomers, who were just entering the car market.

Thirty years later, Ford Motor Company capitalized on the romantic lure of the legendary "pony car" as part of a public relations and advertising blitz for its first new version of the Mustang since 1979. The car borrowed styling cues from the 1960s classic: long hood, deep side scoops, stubby back deck with triple taillights, and a galloping pony on the grille.

Ford's $40 million introductory campaign included a unique public relations twist. The company tapped the members of 400 Mustang clubs around the country "to spread the gospel" on the new model. If anyone has a love affair with the car, it is those club members, most of whom own vintage Mustangs. Introductory parties for the redesigned Mustang were held at local Mustang club chapters, with radio tie-ins and Mustang T-shirt giveaways. During development of the new model, Ford even included club members in focus groups previewing designs.

Heritage is the cornerstone of the redesigned Mustang's marketing efforts. The heritage angle is carried throughout an advertising campaign developed by J. Walter Thompson USA, Detroit, with the theme "It is what it was and more." The campaign showed how styling cues on the original 1964 Mustang have been brought back and updated, while also emphasizing today's performance and safety features.

In its advertising effort, images of the original Mustang and the new model are interspersed, separated by billboards that alternately say "It was" and "It is." The same "was/is" dichotomy is used in print advertising in news magazines and auto magazines. A fifteen-second teaser commercial introduced the car during football games telecast on Thanksgiving Day 1994. For the Southern California market, Ford flew over 200 disc jockeys to the Mojave desert, briefed them on the new Mustang, gave them test rides, and then had them create the radio advertisements for the new model.

Ford is hoping this ad campaign can bridge the generation gap. Former Mustang owners are the prime target for the new Mustang GT, the upscale, V-8 model. A younger generation of buyers is the target for the V-6–powered base model. A convertible version is expected to attract buyers with higher incomes and more education.

Research conducted by Ford indicates that under-30 individuals do relate to the Mustang heritage. Even to young people who hadn't been born when the first Mustang was introduced, the Mustang is still an American icon.[1]

Exhibit 16.2

Advertising Response Function

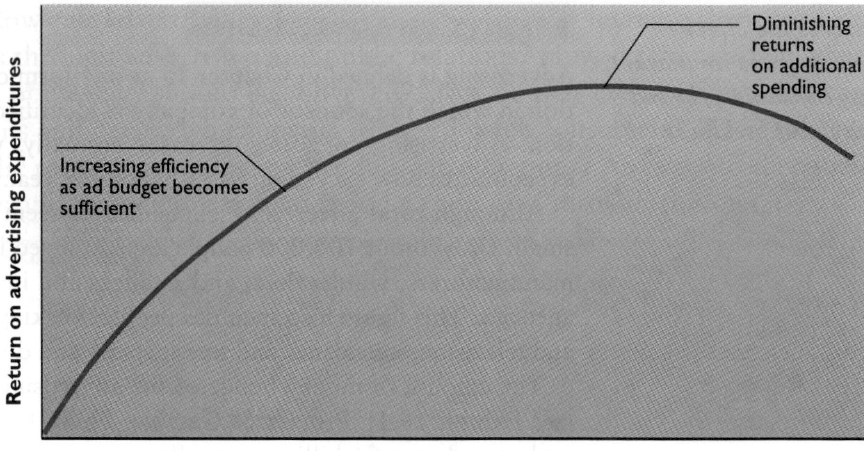


For example, a market leader like Ivory soap spends proportionately less on advertising than a newcomer like Lever 2000 does. Lever 2000 spends more in an attempt to increase awareness and market share. Ivory, on the other hand, spends only as much as needed to maintain market share; anything more would reap diminishing benefits. Because Ivory has already captured the attention of the majority of the target market, it needs only to remind customers of its product.

The second reason that new brands tend to require higher spending for advertising and sales promotion is that a certain minimum level of exposure is needed to measurably affect purchase habits. For example, if Lever 2000 advertised in only one or two publications and bought only one or two television spots, it certainly would not achieve the exposure needed to obtain awareness and ultimately affect consumers' purchase intentions. Instead, Lever 2000 was introduced through advertising in many different media for a sustained period.

## ADVERTISING AND THE CONSUMER

Advertising affects everyone's daily life and influences many purchases. The average U.S. citizen is exposed to about 300 advertisements a day from all types of advertising media. That is about 9,900 a month, or 109,500 per year.[5] Network television airs an average of eighteen minutes of commercials and promotions during each hour of daytime programming.[6] Around 10,000 weekly and daily newspapers, 11,000 magazines, 8,500 AM-FM radio stations, 600 television stations, billions of pieces of direct mail, and thousands of billboards are sure to have an impact on consumers. Advertising affects the TV programs people watch, the content of the newspapers they read, the politicians they elect, the medicines they take, and the toys their children play with. Consequently, the influence of advertising on the U.S. socioeconomic system has been the subject of extensive debate among economists, marketers, sociologists, psychologists, politicians, professors, consumerists, and many others.

Advertising cannot manipulate society as much as some might fear because it cannot change strongly held values. Attitudes and values are deeply rooted within an individual's psychological makeup. Advertising seldom succeeds in changing an attitude that stems from a person's basic value system, or moral code, and that is strongly supported by his or her culture. All the advertising in the world is not going to convince a teenage girl to want Barbie dolls rather than clothes or makeup.

However, advertising may succeed in transforming a person's negative attitude toward a product into a positive one. When prior evaluation of the brand is negative, serious or dramatic advertisements are more effective at changing consumers' attitudes. Humorous ads, on the other hand, have been shown to be more effective at changing attitudes when consumers already have a positive image of the advertised brand.[7]

Credibility is also a factor. Consumers' positive or negative attitudes toward an advertiser can also influence their attitudes toward the advertised product. Research has shown that when consumers believe an advertiser is trustworthy and credible, they are more likely to accept the advertised product's claim and more likely to change their attitudes and buying behavior.[8]

### ADVERTISING AND BRAND LOYALTY

Consumers with a high degree of brand loyalty are least susceptible to the influences of advertising for competing goods or services. For instance, new competitors found it hard to dislodge AT&T after deregulation of the long-distance telephone industry. After relying on "Ma Bell" for a lifetime of service, many loyal customers have shown little response to advertising by competing companies.

Advertising also reinforces positive attitudes toward brands. When consumers have a neutral or favorable frame of reference toward a product or brand, they are often positively influenced by advertising for it. When consumers are already highly loyal to a brand, they may buy more of it when advertising and promotion for that brand increase.[9]

### ADVERTISING AND PRODUCT ATTRIBUTES

Advertising can affect the way consumers rank a brand's attributes, such as color, taste, smell, and texture. For example, in the past a shopper may have selected a brand of luncheon meat based on taste and variety of cuts available. But advertising may influence that consumer to choose luncheon meat on the basis of other attributes, such as calories and fat content. Luncheon meat marketers like Louis Rich, Oscar Mayer, and Healthy Choice now stress the amount of calories and fat when advertising their products.

Automobile advertisers also understand the influence of advertising on consumers' rankings of brand attributes. Car ads have traditionally emphasized brand attributes—in years past, such attributes as roominess, speed, and low maintenance. Today, however, car marketers have added safety to the list. Safety features like antilock brakes, power door locks, and air bags are now a standard part of the message in many carmakers' ads.

*2 Identify the major types of advertising.*

## MAJOR TYPES OF ADVERTISING

The firm's promotional objectives (refer back to Chapter 15) determine the type of advertising it uses. If the goal of the promotion plan is to build up the image of the company, or the industry, **institutional advertising** may be used. In contrast, if the advertiser wants to enhance the sales of a specific good or service, **product advertising** is used.

**institutional advertising**
Form of advertising designed to enhance a company's image rather than promote a particular product.

**product advertising**
Form of advertising that touts the benefits of a specific good or service.

### INSTITUTIONAL ADVERTISING

Advertising in the United States has historically been product-oriented. However, modern corporations market multiple products and need a different type of advertising. This type of advertising promotes the corporation as a whole. Institutional advertising, or corporate advertising, is designed to establish, change, or maintain

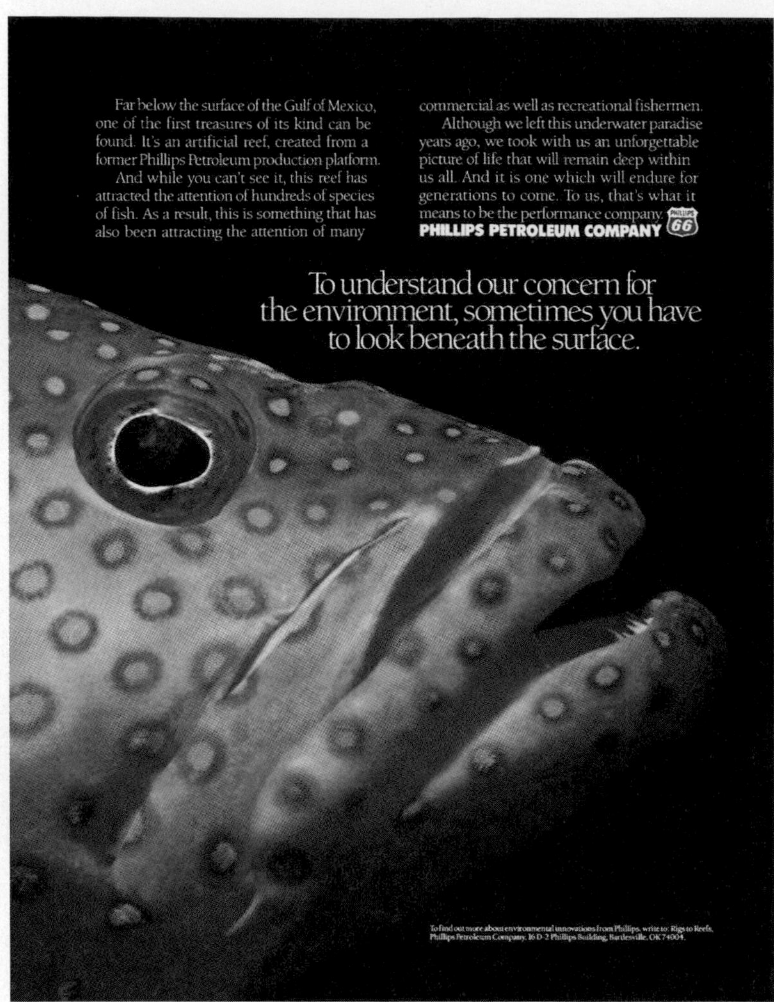


Many big companies use institutional advertising to build a favorable public image, quite apart from the advertising they do for specific products. Environmental themes, like the one in this ad for Phillips Petroleum, are popular in institutional advertising.

© Courtesy Phillips Petroleum Company

the corporation's identity.[10] It usually does not ask the audience to do anything but maintain a favorable attitude toward the advertiser and its goods and services. When using institutional advertising, a corporation has four important audiences to keep in mind: the public, which includes legislators, businesspeople, and opinion leaders; the investment community, mainly stockholders; customers; and the employees of the company.

Competitive pressures and growing consumerism make institutional advertising more critical than ever. Procter & Gamble, Exxon, Toyota, and many other large corporations often use institutional advertising to promote their corporate images. For instance, P&G advertises its environmental efforts—such as recycling plastic detergent bottles and composting disposable diapers—when selling brands.

A form of institutional advertising called **advocacy advertising** is a way for corporations to express their views on controversial issues. Most firms' advocacy campaigns react to criticism or blame, some in direct response to criticism by the media. Other advocacy campaigns may try to ward off increased regulation or damaging legislation. For example, R.J. Reynolds responded to proposed antismoking legislation by using advocacy advertising. In one ad, a nonsmoker declares: "The smell of cigarette smoke annoys me. But not nearly as much as the government telling me what to do."[11]

**advocacy advertising**
Form of advertising in which an organization expresses its views on controversial issues or responds to media attacks.

**pioneering advertising**
Form of advertising designed to stimulate primary demand for a new product or product category.

## PRODUCT ADVERTISING

Unlike institutional advertising, product advertising promotes the benefits of a specific good or service. The product's stage in its life cycle often determines which type of product advertising is used: pioneering advertising, competitive advertising, or comparative advertising.

### Pioneering Advertising

**Pioneering advertising** is intended to stimulate primary demand for a new product or product category. Heavily used during the introductory stage of the product life cycle, pioneering advertising offers consumers in-depth information about the benefits of the product class. Pioneering advertising also seeks to create interest.

Food companies, which introduce many new products, often use pioneering advertising. For example, Mars used pioneering advertising to introduce M&M candies and Snickers bars to Russians. The company embarked on a glitzy ad campaign even before its chocolate appeared in stores. Full-color billboards on Moscow's main

When Mars introduced M&M candies to Russians, it used pioneering advertising. Consumers who are unfamiliar with a product need some extra information about what it is and how it benefits them.

© Bill Swersey/The Gamma Liaison Network

street, Tverskaya, made Russians curious about the chocolate that "Melts in your mouth, not in your hand."[12]

## Competitive Advertising

**competitive advertising**
Form of advertising designed to influence demand for a specific brand.

Firms use competitive advertising when a product enters the growth phase of the product life cycle and other companies begin to enter the marketplace. Instead of building demand for the product category, the goal of **competitive advertising** is to influence demand for a specific brand.

Often promotion becomes less informative and appeals more to emotions during this phase. As products begin to resemble one another, price often becomes a key promotional weapon. Advertisements may begin to stress subtle differences between brands, with heavy emphasis on building recall of a brand name and creating a favorable attitude toward the brand. Automobile advertising has long used very competitive messages, drawing distinctions based on such factors as quality, performance, and image. For example, Ford stresses the theme "Quality is job one" in its advertising. Buick's "The new symbol for quality in America" and Mercury's "All this and the quality of a Mercury" slogans also emphasize superior workmanship. The beer, soft-drink, fast-food, and long-distance telephone service industries also wage advertising "wars."

## Comparative Advertising

**comparative advertising**
Form of advertising that compares two or more specifically named or shown competing brands on one or more specific attributes.

A controversial trend in product advertising is the use of comparative advertising. **Comparative advertising** directly or indirectly compares two or more competing brands on one or more specific attributes. For instance, in a deliberate comparison to Disney theme parks, an advertisement for a Six Flags park readily admits that it is No. 2 and therefore must work harder: "When you're No. 2, you have to have things that No. 1 doesn't have." The spots also imply that visiting Six Flags is easier and quicker than going to a Disney park, with the line "No matter where you live, there is a Six Flags near you."[13]

Before the 1970s, comparative advertising was allowed only if the competing brand was veiled and unidentified. In 1971, however, the Federal Trade Commission (FTC) fostered the growth of comparative advertising by saying that it provided information to the customer and that advertisers were more skillful than the government in communicating this information. Comparative ads soon flooded the media. Today, few marketers would disagree that there seems to be much more direct comparative advertising than ever before. Some advertisers even use comparative advertising against their own brands. Industries experiencing sluggish growth are more likely to employ comparative claims in their advertising.[14]

New federal rulings prohibit advertisers from falsely describing competitors' products and allow competitors to sue if ads show their products or mention their brand names in an incorrect or false manner. These rules also apply to advertisers making false claims about their own products. For example, a federal court ordered Ralston Purina to pay several million dollars in damages to Alpo Pet Foods for making false claims about Ralston's own dog food in comparative advertising.

Is comparative advertising worth the trouble? Much research suggests that comparative advertising is no more effective at increasing purchase intentions than noncomparative advertising is. Marketers also risk brand misidentification and confusion when comparing different brands in advertising. But on the positive side, research has produced these findings:[15]

- Direct comparisons in advertisements attract attention and may thereby enhance purchase intentions.
- Consumers perceive comparative messages as being more relevant than similar noncomparative ads and are able to recall more message points from the comparative ads.
- Comparative ads for relatively unknown brands can increase the association of those unknown brands with well-known brands to which they are compared.
- Comparative ads comparing "objective" brand attributes can generate more positive attitudes than comparative ads focusing on "subjective" brand attributes. For example, the claim that car A has eight more cubic inches of trunk space than car B (objective) is potentially more effective than the claim that soup X is tastier than soup Y (subjective).
- When comparative ads for a new brand are personally relevant and use a brand with high credibility for comparison, they have a more positive effect on purchase intentions than noncomparative ads have.

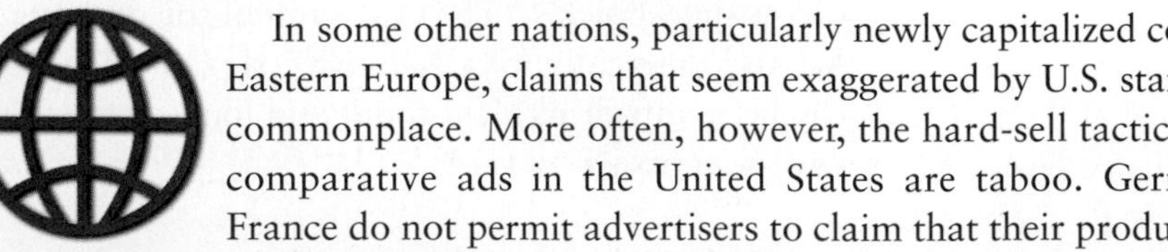

In some other nations, particularly newly capitalized countries in Eastern Europe, claims that seem exaggerated by U.S. standards are commonplace. More often, however, the hard-sell tactics found in comparative ads in the United States are taboo. Germany and France do not permit advertisers to claim that their products are the best or are better than competitors' products, which are common claims in U.S. advertising. Until the 1980s, Japanese regulations all but prohibited comparative ads; ads that failed to compare objectively were considered slanderous. Nevertheless, although the Japanese have traditionally favored a soft-sell advertising approach, consumers are witnessing a trend toward comparative ads. For example, General Motors newspaper ads asked Japanese consumers to "compare our Seville's fuel efficiency with Infiniti's."[16]

3 *Describe the advertising campaign process.*

## STEPS IN CREATING AN ADVERTISING CAMPAIGN

**advertising campaign**
Series of related advertisements focusing on a common theme, slogan, and set of advertising appeals.

An **advertising campaign** is a series of related advertisements focusing on a common theme, slogan, and set of advertising appeals. It is a specific advertising effort for a particular product that extends for a defined period of time. Management of advertising begins with understanding the steps in developing an advertising campaign and then making the important decisions relating to each step. Exhibit 16.3 traces the steps in this process.

The advertising campaign process is set in motion by the promotion plan (discussed in Chapter 15). As you will remember, the promotion planning process identifies the target market, determines the overall promotional objectives, sets the promotion budget, and selects the promotional mix. Advertising, which is usually part of the promotional mix, is used to encode a selling message to the target market. The advertisement is then conveyed to the target market, or receivers of the message, through such advertising vehicles as broadcast or print media.

### DETERMINE CAMPAIGN OBJECTIVES

**advertising objective**
Specific communication task a campaign should accomplish for a specified target audience during a specified period.

The first step in the development of an advertising campaign is to determine the advertising objectives. An **advertising objective** identifies the specific communication task a campaign should accomplish for a specified target audience during a specified period of time. The objectives of a specific advertising campaign depend on the overall corporate objectives and the product being advertised.

The DAGMAR approach (Defining Advertising Goals for Measured Advertising Results) is one method of setting objectives. According to this method, all advertising objectives should precisely define the target audience, the desired percentage change in some specified measure of effectiveness, and the time frame in which that change is to occur. For example, an advertising campaign for the Toyota Camry might set this objective: to increase by 12 percent over the next two years the number of potential 25-to-30-year-old Camry buyers exposed to Camry ads. For BMW's introduction of new, lower-priced models, the objective might be achieving a total of

*Exhibit 16.3*

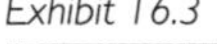

Advertising Campaign Decision Process

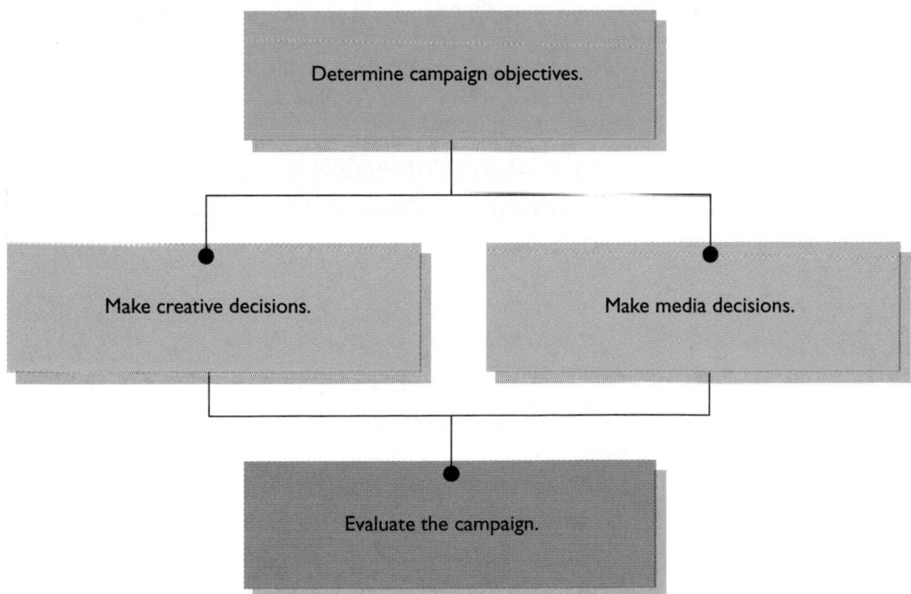

50,000 consumer test drives within the first six months of introduction as a result of mailing video advertisements to a sample of the target audience.

## MAKE CREATIVE DECISIONS

The next step in developing an advertising campaign is to make the necessary creative and media decisions. Note in Exhibit 16.3 that both creative and media decisions are made at the same time. Creative work cannot be completed without knowing which **medium,** or message channel, will be used to convey the message to the target market. However, in this chapter media decisions are addressed after creative decisions.

**medium**
Channel used to convey a message to a target market.

In many cases, the advertising objectives dictate the medium and the creative approach to be used. For example, if the objective is to demonstrate how fast a product operates, then a TV commercial that shows this action may be the best choice.

Creative decisions include identifying the product's benefits, developing possible advertising appeals, evaluating the advertising appeals and selecting one with a unique selling proposition, and executing the advertising message. An effective advertising campaign follows the AIDA and hierarchy of effects models, which were discussed in Chapter 15.

### Identifying Product Benefits

A well-known rule of thumb in the advertising industry is "Sell the sizzle, not the steak." That is, in advertising the goal is to sell the benefits of the product, not its attributes. An attribute is simply a feature of the product, such as its easy-open package or special formulation. A benefit is what consumers will receive or achieve by using the product. A benefit should answer the consumer's question "What's in it for me?" Benefits might be such things as convenience, pleasure, savings, or relief. A quick test to determine whether you are offering attributes or benefits in your advertising is to ask "So?" Consider this example:

> *Attribute:* "The Gillette Sensor razor has twin blades individually mounted on remarkably responsive springs to automatically adjust to the curves and contours of a man's face."
>
> "So . . . ?"
>
> *Benefit:* "So, you'll get a closer, smoother, and safer shave than ever before."

Marketing research and intuition are usually used to list the perceived benefits of a product and to rank consumers' preferences for these benefits.

### Developing Advertising Appeals

An **advertising appeal** identifies a reason for a person to buy a product. Developing advertising appeals, a challenging task, is typically the responsibility of the creative people in the advertising agency.

**advertising appeal**
Reason for a person to buy a product.

Advertising campaigns can focus on one or more advertising appeals. Often the appeals are quite general, thus allowing the firm to develop a number of subthemes or minicampaigns using both advertising and sales promotion. Several possible advertising appeals are listed in Exhibit 16.4.

### Evaluating Advertising Appeals

Choosing the best appeal from those developed normally requires market research. Criteria for evaluation include desirability, exclusiveness, and believability. The appeal first must make a positive impression on and be desirable to the target mar-

*Exhibit 16.4*

Common Advertising Appeals

| | |
|---|---|
| **Profit** | Lets consumers know whether the product will save them money, keep them from losing money, or make them money |
| **Health** | Appeals to those who are body-conscious or who want to be healthy |
| **Love or romance** | Is used often in selling cosmetics and perfumes |
| **Fear** | Can center around social embarrassment, growing old, or losing one's health; because of its power, requires advertiser to exercise care in execution |
| **Admiration** | Is the reason that celebrity spokespeople are used so often in advertising |
| **Convenience** | Is often used for fast-food restaurants and microwave foods |
| **Fun and pleasure** | Are the key to advertising vacations, beer, amusement parks, and more |
| **Vanity and egotism** | Are used most often for expensive or conspicuous items, such as cars and clothing |

ket. It must also be exclusive or unique; consumers must be able to distinguish the advertiser's message from competitors' messages. Most important, the appeal should be believable. An appeal that makes extravagant claims not only wastes promotional dollars but also creates ill will for the advertiser.

**unique selling proposition**
Desirable, exclusive, and believable advertising appeal selected as the theme for a campaign.

The advertising appeal selected for the campaign becomes what advertisers call its **unique selling proposition.** The unique selling proposition usually becomes the campaign's slogan. Lever Brothers' Lever 2000 soap carries the slogan "The deodorant soap that's better for your skin." This is also the soap's unique selling proposition. Effective slogans often become so ingrained that consumers can immediately conjure up images of the product just by hearing the slogan. For example, most consumers can easily name the companies and products behind these memorable slogans or even hum the jingle that goes along with some of them: "Have it your way," "Tastes great, less filling," "Ring around the collar," and "Tum te Tum Tum."[17]

## Executing the Message

Message execution is the way the advertisement portrays its information. In general, the AIDA plan is a good blueprint for executing an advertising message. Any ad should immediately draw the reader's, viewer's, or listener's attention. The advertiser must then use the message to hold consumers' interest, create desire for the good or service, and ultimately motivate action: a purchase.

The style in which the message is executed is one of the most creative elements of an advertisement. Exhibit 16.5 on page 542 lists some examples of executional styles used by advertisers.

Executional styles for foreign advertising are often quite different from those we are accustomed to in the United States. Sometimes they are sex-oriented or aesthetically imaginative. For example, European advertising avoids the direct-sell approaches common in U.S. ads and instead is more indirect, more symbolic, and above all more visual. Italian-based retailer Benetton is widely known for using symbolic images, often described as more art than advertising. Its ads have featured such startling

*Exhibit 16.5*

Ten Common Executional Styles for Advertising

| | |
|---|---|
| **Slice-of-life** | Is popular when advertising household and personal products; depicts people in normal settings, such as at the dinner table. Taster's Choice ads with Tony and Sharon offer a soap opera twist to a slice-of-life. |
| **Lifestyle** | Shows how well the product will fit in with the consumer's lifestyle. Levi's has made this concept popular with Dockers menswear commercials. |
| **Spokesperson/ testimonial** | Can feature a celebrity, company official, or typical consumer making a testimonial or endorsing a product. Basketball superstar Shaquille O'Neal endorses Pepsi. |
| **Fantasy** | Creates a fantasy for the viewer built around use of the product. Diet Coke's spot shows office women fantasizing about the shirtless hardhat from the window above. |
| **Humorous** | Beermakers often use humor in their ads, such as Bud Light's popular "Yes I am" commercials and Miller Light's "Can your beer do this?" spots. |
| **Real/animated product symbols** | Creates a character that represents the product in advertisements, such as the Energizer bunny, 7-Up's red spots, and Coke's polar bears. |
| **Mood or image** | Builds a mood or image around the product, such as peace, love, or beauty. Initial ads for the new-age drink Fruitopia feature kaleidoscope graphics with world peace messages. |
| **Demonstration** | Shows consumers the expected benefit. Many consumer products use this technique. Laundry detergent spots are famous for demonstrating how their product will clean clothes whiter and brighter. |
| **Musical** | Conveys the message of the advertisement through song. Timex ads for its Indiglo watch play off Frank Sinatra singing "Strangers in the Night." |
| **Scientific** | Uses research or scientific evidence to give a brand superiority over competitors. Pain relievers like Advil, Bayer, and Excedrin use scientific evidence in their ads. |

images as close-up photos of male and female genitalia, a black man's hand handcuffed to a white man's, and an AIDS patient and his family moments before his death.[18]

Japanese advertising is known for relying on fantasy and mood to sell products. Ads in Japan notoriously lack the emphatic selling demonstrations found in U.S. advertising, limit the exposure of unique product features, and avoid direct comparisons to competitors' products. Japanese ads often feature cartoon characters or place the actors in irrelevant situations. For example, one advertisement promotes an insect spray while showing the actor having teeth extracted at the dentist's office. One explanation of Japan's preference for soft-sell advertising is cultural: Japanese consumers are naturally suspicious of someone who needs to extol the virtues of a product. Additionally, unlike advertising agencies in the United States, which consider working for competing companies to be unethical, Japan's larger ad agencies customarily maintain business relationships with competing advertisers. Ads are less hard-hitting so as not to offend other clients.[19]

Given the creativity involved in selecting an executional style and the shifting, amorphous nature of cultural preferences, it is understandable that some ads might create controversy. As the Ethics in Marketing box explains, an executional style chosen for Walt Disney Studios had just such an effect.

4 *Describe media evaluation and selection techniques.*

## MAKE MEDIA DECISIONS

As mentioned at the beginning of the chapter, U.S. advertisers spend over $131 billion on media advertising annually. Where does all this money go? About 33 percent, or $43 billion, is spent in media monitored by national reporting services. The remaining 67 percent, or $85 billion, is spent in unmonitored media, such as direct mail, sales promotion, cooperative advertising, couponing, catalogs, and special events. Exhibit 16.6 on page 544 breaks down the dollar amount spent for monitored advertising by media type. As you can see, more than half of every dollar spent on monitored advertising is spent on TV advertising—including *spot TV,* which is TV advertising time bought at the last minute at significantly reduced rates.

**audience selectivity**
Ability of an advertising medium to reach a precisely defined market.

ETHICS IN MARKETING

### Could Mock Newscast Ads Dupe Viewers?

A Walt Disney Studios ad campaign promoting its summer movies created quite a stir—because it didn't look much like an ad campaign. In the advertising, Disney used a relatively new executional style that mimics a newscast.

In the commercials, an "anchorman" sits behind a news desk and hosts "Movie News," an entertainment "news show" that looks very similar to the syndicated show "Entertainment Tonight." The ads, which report all kinds of news about such Disney films as *The Lion King* and *I Love Trouble,* often run during the commercial breaks of real news shows. Many industry critics argued that the ads are clearly designed to dupe viewers into thinking they are watching some kind of editorial programming, not a commercial. It's not until almost the end of the sixty-second ads that the words "Paid for by Buena Vista" are superimposed on the screen in tiny letters. Most viewers probably don't realize that Buena Vista is Disney's in-house film distribution company.

The ads drew fire from many in the TV industry who remember the wave of "fake newscast" ads that surfaced a couple of years ago. The networks had granted approval for such ads but had imposed tough restrictions on when they could be aired. For instance, ABC wouldn't allow a news-style spot for Vaseline Intensive Care lotion featuring Joan Lunden to be run during "Good Morning America," the show she co-hosts.

Critics said the Disney ads are even more confusing, because each one promotes several movies. The spots were also crafted with production values and graphics so smooth that consumers really have to look twice to realize they are not real newscasts. The ads frequently appear in the last commercial segment of news shows—about the time when an entertainment feature is usually reported. Besides appearing during local newscasts, the ads also appear during local station breaks on such shows as "Today," "Good Morning America," "The David Letterman Show," and "Hard Copy."[20]

Do you believe Walt Disney Studios intends to confuse viewers? What sort of regulations would you recommend be imposed on newscast-style ads?



### MEDIA SELECTION CONSIDERATIONS

Promotional objectives and the type of advertising a company plans to use strongly affect the selection of media. Seven major criteria are typically used in selecting media:

- *Target market:* Media selection is a matter of matching the advertising medium with the product's target market. If marketers are trying to reach teenage females, they might select *Seventeen* magazine. If they are trying to reach consumers over 50 years old, they may choose *Modern Maturity.* Even when market profiles match media profiles, marketing managers must also consider other factors, such as circulation and image. *Seventeen* magazine might reach part of the right market, but this might be only a small fraction of the firm's total market. Also, how do teenagers perceive *Seventeen* magazine? If teens consider it a how-to magazine and use it as a reference guide, it should enhance advertisers' credibility.
- *Audience selectivity:* **Audience selectivity** is a medium's ability to reach a precisely defined market. Some media vehicles, like general newspapers and network television, appeal to a wide cross section of the population. Others

*Exhibit 16.6*

National Ad Spending on Monitored Media

Source: "National Ad Spending by Media." Reprinted with permission from the 2 January 1995 issue of *Advertising Age*. Copyright, Crain Communications, Inc., 1995.

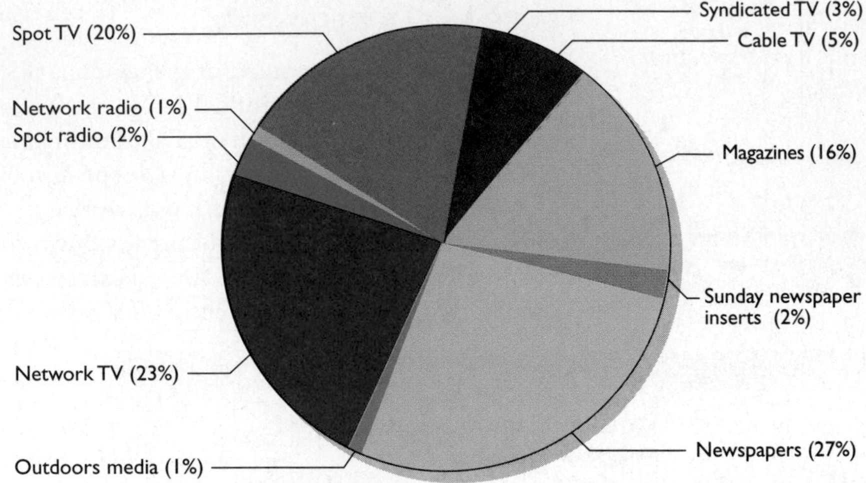


—such as *Bride's, Popular Mechanics, Architectural Digest,* the Disney Channel, ESPN, and Christian radio stations—appeal to very specific groups.

**geographic selectivity**
Ability of an advertising medium to cover a specific area.

- *Geographic selectivity:* **Geographic selectivity** is coverage of a specific area. For example, local radio, newspapers, and television all cover limited geographic areas. Network television and many magazines and newspapers, such as *USA Today* and *The Wall Street Journal,* offer nationwide coverage. Media like *Southern Living, Texas Monthly,* and the local evening newscast offer good coverage in limited areas.

**cost per contact**
Cost of reaching one member of the target market.

- *Cost per contact:* **Cost per contact** is the cost of reaching one member of the target market. Naturally, as the size of the audience increases, so does the total cost. Cost evaluation of media is more thoroughly discussed later in this chapter.
- *Flexibility:* A medium's flexibility can be extremely important to an advertiser. Because of printing timetables, paste-up requirements, and so on, some magazines require final ad copy several months before publication. Thus the advertiser may not be able to adapt to changing market conditions. Radio, on the other hand, provides maximum flexibility. Usually the advertiser can change the ad on the day it is aired, if necessary.
- *Noise level:* The noise level of a medium is the level of distraction it allows for the target audience. For example, to understand a televised promotional message, viewers must watch and listen carefully. But they often watch television with others, who may well provide distractions. Noise can also be created by competing ads, as when a street is lined with billboards. During the three-and-a-half-hour Super Bowl XXVII game, viewers were barraged with sixty-eight commercials and promotions. Postgame research revealed there was so much ad clutter that it was almost impossible for any advertiser to break through. Over 90 percent of the viewers interviewed after the game could not even identify Frito-Lay as the official Super Bowl sponsor.[21] In contrast, direct mail is a private medium with a low noise level. No other advertising media or news stories compete for direct-mail readers' attention.
- *Life span:* Media have either a short or long life span. For example, a radio commercial may last less than a minute. Listeners can't replay the commercial unless they have recorded the program. One way advertisers overcome this problem is by repeating radio ads often. In contrast, a trade magazine has a

One attractive feature of magazines as an advertising medium is that they have a long life span. One person may pick up the same magazine several times and then pass it along for others to read.



relatively long life span. A person may read several articles, put the magazine down, and pick it up a week later to continue reading. In addition, magazines and catalogs often have a high pass-along rate. That is, one person will read the publication and then give it to someone else.

**media mix**
Combination of media to be used for a promotional campaign.

### CRITERIA FOR CHOOSING THE MEDIA MIX

An important element in any advertising campaign is the **media mix,** the combination of media to be used. Media mix decisions are typically based on cost per thousand, reach, and frequency.

**cost per thousand (CPM)**
Standard criterion for comparing media, computed by dividing the price of a single ad by the audience size in thousands.

#### Cost per Thousand

The standard criterion for comparing media is **cost per thousand** (CPM, *M* being the Roman numeral for 1,000). The formula for calculating cost per thousand is

$$\text{CPM} = \text{Price of a single ad} \div \text{Audience size (in thousands)}$$

For example, if the cost of an ad is $50,000 and the audience is 24 million people, the CPM is $2.08:

$$\text{CPM} = \frac{\$50{,}000}{\text{24 million people}} = \$2.08$$

CPM enables an advertiser to compare, for example, *Newsweek* with *Time.* CPM can also be used to compare the cost of different vehicles, such as television versus radio or magazine versus newspaper. An advertiser debating whether to spend local advertising dollars for TV spots or radio spots could consider the CPM of each. The advertiser might then pick the vehicle with the lowest CPM to maximize advertising punch for the money spent.

**audience duplication**
Situation in which the same audience is reached by two different media vehicles.

A factor that complicates media selection is **audience duplication**—that is, the same audience being reached by two different media vehicles. For instance, assume that *Newsweek* has a circulation of 3.1 million and *Time* has a circulation of 4.6 million. If 800,000 people subscribe to both publications, the nonduplicated circulations are 2.3 million for *Newsweek* and 3.8 million for *Time.* In other words, putting an ad in both *Newsweek* and *Time* does not reach 7.7 million different consumers; it reaches 6.9 million (7.7 million - 0.8 million) different consumers. The widespread popularity of *Time* and *Newsweek* often creates a duplication problem with other media types as well. An advertisement aired during the local evening news will most likely have a considerable amount of audience duplication with *Newsweek* and *Time.*

**reach**
Number of target consumers exposed to a commercial at least once during a specific period, usually four weeks.

#### Reach

The number of different target consumers who are exposed to a commercial at least once during a specific period, usually four weeks, measures its **reach.** If 60,000 out of 100,000 radio listeners hear a commercial for the Ford Taurus in San Antonio, Texas, at least once during a four-week period, the commercial's reach would be 60,000, or 60 percent of the total 100,000 listeners.

The media mixes for product introductions and attempts at increasing brand awareness usually emphasize reach. Yet high reach levels do not necessarily mean high degrees of brand awareness or advertising recall. It is not unusual to find that a campaign has achieved 90 percent reach but that only 25 percent of the target audience remembers the ad. Reach is a measurement of potential. That is, a 90 percent reach means that 90 percent of an audience has an opportunity to see or hear a message. It does not measure retention.

### Frequency

**frequency**
Number of times an individual is exposed to a given message during a specific period.

The number of times an individual is exposed to a message is the **frequency.** Average frequency is used by advertisers to measure the intensity of a specific medium's coverage. Suppose that 30,000 people heard the Ford Taurus radio ad three times during the four-week period and that 30,000 heard it five times. The computation of the average frequency is

$$\text{Average frequency} = \frac{\text{Total exposures}}{\text{Audience reach}} = \frac{(30{,}000 \times 3) + (30{,}000 \times 5)}{60{,}000}$$

$$= \frac{\$240{,}000}{60{,}000} = 4$$

Therefore, among the 60,000 listeners reached, the average number of exposures was four.

Because the typical ad is short-lived and because often only a small portion of an ad may be perceived at one time, advertisers repeat their ads. They want consumers to remember the message. Retention tends to peak somewhere between the third and the fifth message perceived by the receiver. Additional exposures tend to be screened out and may create a negative reaction. The ad then loses its effectiveness.

Advertisers must specify the media they wish to use for a campaign, as well as the specific programs (such as "Home Improvement") or other vehicles and the insertion dates for the ads.

© Wayne Williams/Shooting Star

## MEDIA SCHEDULING

**media schedule**
Designation of the media, the specific publications or programs, and the insertion dates of advertising.

After choosing the media for the advertising campaign, advertisers must schedule the ads. A **media schedule** designates the medium or media to be used (such as magazines, television, or radio), the specific vehicles (such as *People* magazine, the "Home Improvement" TV program, or the "Top 40 Countdown" radio show), and the insertion dates of the advertising.

There are three basic types of media schedules:

**continuous media schedule**
Media scheduling strategy, used for products in the latter stages of the product life cycle, in which advertising is run steadily throughout the advertising period.

- Products in the latter stages of the product life cycle, which are advertised on a reminder basis, use a **continuous media schedule.** A continuous schedule allows the advertising to run steadily throughout the advertising period. Examples include Ivory soap, Coca-Cola, and Marlboro cigarettes.

**flighted media schedule** Media scheduling strategy in which ads are run heavily every other month or every two weeks, to achieve a greater impact with an increased frequency and reach at those times.

**pulsing media schedule** Media scheduling strategy that uses continuous scheduling during the best sales periods and a flighted schedule at other times.

**seasonal media schedule** Media scheduling strategy that runs advertising only during times of the year when the product is most likely to be used.

- With a **flighted media schedule,** the advertiser may schedule the ads heavily every other month or every two weeks, to achieve a greater impact with an increased frequency and reach at those times. For example, movie studios schedule television advertising on Wednesday and Thursday nights, when moviegoers are deciding which films to see that weekend.[22] A variation is the **pulsing media schedule,** which combines continuous scheduling with flighting. Continuous advertising is simply heavier during the best sale periods. For instance, a retail department store may advertise on a year-round basis but place more advertising during holiday sale periods, such as Thanksgiving and Christmas.
- Certain times of the year call for a **seasonal media schedule.** Products like Contac cold tablets and Coppertone suntan lotion, which are used more during certain times of the year, tend to follow a seasonal strategy.

## MEDIA TYPES

Advertising media are channels that advertisers use in mass communication. The major advertising media are newspapers, magazines, radio, television, and outdoor media. Exhibit 16.7 summarizes the advantages and disadvantages of these traditional channels. In recent years, however, innovative vehicles have emerged that give

*Exhibit 16.7*

Advantages and Disadvantages of Traditional Advertising Media

| Medium | Advantages | Disadvantages |
|---|---|---|
| Television | Ability to reach a wide, diverse audience; creative opportunities for demonstration; immediacy of messages; entertainment carryover | Little demographic selectivity; short life of message; some consumer skepticism about claims; high cost |
| National | Association of prestige with programming | Long-term advertiser commitments |
| Local | Geographic selectivity; association with programs of local origin and appeal; can be scheduled on short notice | Lack of wide audience on independent stations; high cost for broad geographic coverage; commercial clutter |
| Radio | Low cost; high frequency; immediacy of message; can be scheduled on short notice; relatively no seasonal change in audience; highly portable; negotiable costs; short-term advertiser commitments; entertainment carryover | No visual treatment; short advertising life of message; distractions from background sound; commercial clutter |
| Magazines | Good reproduction, especially for color; permanence of message; demographic selectivity; regional selectivity; local market selectivity; relatively long advertising life; high pass-along rate | Long-term advertiser commitments; slow audience buildup; limited demonstration capabilities; lack of urgency; long lead time |
| Newspapers | Geographic selectivity and flexibility; short-term advertiser commitments; news value and immediacy; advertising permanence; year-round readership; high individual market coverage; co-op and local tie-in availability; short lead time | Little demographic selectivity; limited color capabilities; different local and national rates; low pass-along rate; may be expensive |
| Outdoor media | Repetition; moderate cost; flexibility | Short message; lack of demographic selectivity; high "noise" level distracting audience |

advertisers ways to avoid advertising clutter: direct-response advertising and alternative media.

## Newspapers

The advantages of newspaper advertising include geographic flexibility and timeliness. Because copywriters can usually prepare newspaper ads quickly and at a reasonable cost, local merchants can reach their target market almost daily. The largest source of newspaper ad revenue is local retailers, cooperative advertising, and classified ads.

**cooperative advertising** Arrangement in which the manufacturer and the retailer split the costs of advertising the manufacturer's brand.

In **cooperative advertising,** the manufacturer and the retailer split the costs of advertising the manufacturer's brand. About three-fourths of all cooperative advertising is newspaper advertising. The usual objective of cooperative, or co-op, advertising is to trigger short-term sales. One reason manufacturers use cooperative advertising is the impracticality of listing all their dealers in national advertising. Also, co-op advertising encourages retailers to devote more effort to the manufacturer's lines. Sometimes co-op advertising ties retailers closer to manufacturers and aids in developing goodwill. Most important, manufacturers obtain more total promotion, because retailers share part of the expense.

Because newspapers are generally a mass-market medium, they may not be the best vehicle for marketers trying to reach a very narrow market. For example, local newspapers are not the best media vehicles for reaching purchasers of specialty steel products or even tropical fish. These target consumers make up very small, specialized markets. Newspaper advertising also encounters a lot of distractions from competing ads and news stories; thus one company's ad may not be particularly visible.

## Magazines

Compared to the cost of other media, the cost per contact in magazine advertising is usually high. However, the cost per potential customer may be much lower, because magazines are often targeted to specialized audiences and thus reach more potential customers. The most frequent magazine advertisers include auto manufacturers, toiletries and cosmetics marketers, and direct-response companies.[23]

One of the main advantages of magazine advertising is its market selectivity. Magazines are published for virtually every market segment. For instance, *PC Week* is a leading computer magazine; *Working Mother* targets one of the fastest-growing consumer segments; *Sports Illustrated* is a successful all-around sporting publication; *Marketing News* is a trade magazine for the marketing professional.

## Radio

Radio has several strengths as an advertising medium: selectivity and audience segmentation, a large out-of-home audience, low unit and production costs, timeliness, and geographic flexibility. Local advertising accounts for 78 percent of radio advertising volume.[24] Like newspapers, radio also lends itself well to cooperative advertising.

Radio stations and programs now are segmented on an ever-increasing variety of factors: age, race, income, lifestyle, and others. The *Spot Radio Standard Rates & Data Service* lists more than 160 radio formats, from "adult contemporary" to "young and beautiful."

## Television

Television broadcasters can be divided into three basic types: network television, independent stations, and cable television. The three giants—ABC, CBS, and NBC—

GLOBAL PERSPECTIVES

### Commercial Radio in the Former East Bloc

In the former Czechoslovakia, Prague radio station KISS 98FM offers classic Western hype. Between the Beatles and the latest from Roxette, the rock station promotes itself with outrageous contests for everything from lottery tickets to a new BMW. One man crawled across the Charles Bridge in Prague blowing a ping-pong ball through a straw in order to win a watch.

KISS draws a weekly listening audience of a quarter million, making it one of Prague's top two music stations. Flick across the city's FM dial, and there's something for everyone: Hank Williams, call-in shows, traffic reports. Yet advertisers are scarce and slow to be convinced. Only a few of the most popular stations—rock and country—come close to filling their targets for advertising slots. Most are struggling, airing only a sprinkle of ads even during peak hours.

Part of the problem is that few local advertisers can afford the rates, which average about $65 for a thirty-second spot during prime time. The other reason is that those who can afford the spots, mainly foreign companies, aren't convinced that the results are worth the effort. Currently, about 80 percent of the typical Prague advertiser's media budget goes to television, magazines, and newspapers, with only about 10 to 15 percent going to radio spots—basically the same breakdown as in any major Western city.

Advertisers say Prague radio might be more appealing if they knew better whom they were reaching. Unfortunately, most Prague radio stations aren't sure, because few have done any audience surveys. This lack of data has left many radio stations almost adless.

Most of Prague's small stations are aimed at particular listeners, whether opera buffs or metal heads. But however loyal their audiences, many stations' audiences are too narrow for big advertisers, such as Procter & Gamble and Fiat, which are still trying to introduce products on a large scale.[25]

What could KISS and other Prague radio stations do to convince advertisers that buying advertising air time is worth the money? What types of studies or reports should be conducted? Would making format changes to appeal to different target audiences help gain advertisers?



and a relative newcomer, the Fox Network, dominate network television. The networks rely on advertising income to support programming. In contrast, independent stations often rely on viewer contributions, as well as local advertising, for funds. Consumers pay to have cable television in their homes. Cable systems must carry network and independent stations, as well as certain other types of programs. But they also have the option of offering many other program alternatives that cable operators either buy from someone else or produce themselves.

Before the introduction of cable television, the three major networks attracted over 90 percent of the audience. During the 1980s, their share of the audience dropped to around 65 percent.[26] Although they are still the dominant force in television, the networks have had to become more aggressive to compete with cable TV and the independents.

Television's largest growth market is cable television, with about six of every ten homes subscribing. Today's cable subscribers can receive channels devoted exclusively to particular audiences—for example, women, children, African-Americans, nature lovers, senior citizens, Christians, Hispanics, sports fans, fitness enthusiasts. Other types of special programming feature news, rock and country music, cultural events, and health issues. Because of its targeted channels, cable television is often characterized as "narrowcasting" by media buyers.

Because television is an audiovisual medium, it provides advertisers with many creative opportunities. It also reaches a wide and diverse market. However, television has its disadvantages. Advertising time on television can be very expensive, especially for network stations, and even more so during prime time. Advertisers pay, on average, $110,000 for a thirty-second spot during a network's prime-time programs. The cost to advertise during the Winter Olympics ranges from $250,000 to $350,000, and a thirty-second spot during the Super Bowl is a whopping $900,000. Television advertising can also involve huge production costs. The budget for a professionally produced national commercial averages $222,000.[27]

TV advertising is probably the least globally standardized of all advertising media. Commercial television time is readily available in Canada, is severely restricted in Germany, and before 1992 was totally unavailable in Sweden. In Switzerland, Finland, Ireland, and Austria, television is controlled by state-run monopolies; as a result, it carries few advertisements. Until recently, marketers in Indonesia had access to only a subscription channel with few viewers (120,000 in a nation of 180 million people). Consequently, many advertisers resorted to direct mail to reach their customers.

## Outdoor Media

Outdoor or out-of-home advertising is a flexible, low-cost medium that may take a variety of forms. Examples include billboards, skywriting, giant inflatables, minibillboards in malls and on bus stop shelters, signs in sports arenas, lighted moving signs in bus terminals and airports, and ads painted on the sides of cars and trucks. Outdoor advertising reaches a broad and diverse market. Therefore, it is normally limited to promoting convenience products and selected shopping products, such as cigarettes, business services, and automobiles.

The main advantage of outdoor advertising over other media is that its exposure frequency is very high, yet the amount of clutter from competing ads is very low. Outdoor advertising also has the ability to be customized to local marketing needs. For this reason, retail stores are the largest outdoor advertisers, spending over $150 billion annually.[28]

Advertisers usually base their billboard use on census tract data for the area. They assume that the people who are most likely to see a certain billboard will have demographic characteristics similar to those of the tract where the billboard is located. Billboards can also be targeted to the mobile or business traveler market. For instance, McDonald's bought about 20,000 outdoor boards across the country, in all available sizes and all available markets, to display the message "Great food, great value at McDonald's." The campaign allows McDonald's to use the same message nationally with a variety of products, prices, and promotions. Outdoor advertising provides McDonald's with a way to reach its customers when they're on the road.[29]

**direct-response advertising**
Advertising that calls for consumers' immediate action, or a direct response.

## Direct-Response Advertising

Most **direct-response advertising** uses traditional media targeted to the masses rather than to specific markets. However, the advertising in some way calls for consumers'

In addition to billboards, outdoor advertising includes display boards on bus stop shelters, like these for The Gap.

Outdoor Advertising Association of America

immediate action, or a direct response—perhaps calling a toll-free number or filling out a coupon.

Often direct-response advertising includes an incentive for responding right away. For example, an advertisement for a consumer magazine like *People* may include an order form. If subscribers send in the form immediately, they can receive up to 50 percent off the newsstand price and may also receive a free gift for subscribing.

The traditional direct-response media are television, radio, newspapers, and magazines. Direct-response advertising is also increasingly being seen on billboards, a result of congested traffic and the proliferation of car phones. Cable TV is also becoming popular for many types of direct-response advertising. Many people subscribe to cable, and advertising costs are lower than they are for network stations.

The twenty-four-hour shop-at-home television channels, such as the QVC Network, are specialized direct-response vehicles. These shows display merchandise, with the retail price, to home shopping viewers. Viewers can then phone in their orders. Cable television has benefited from the success of the shop-at-home networks, but smaller direct-response marketers, generally on the air only in brief spot ads, have felt the impact of the home shopping networks on their total sales.

**infomercial**
Thirty-minute or longer advertisement that looks more like a TV talk show than a sales pitch.

A relatively new form of direct-response advertising is the **infomercial,** a thirty-minute or longer advertisement. Infomercials bloomed in the mid-1980s, when deregulation freed television stations and cable networks to sell half-hour blocks of air time for advertising. The otherwise unprofitable late-night time slots have become the special domain of infomercials. Infomercials are an attractive advertising vehicle for many marketers because of the cheap air time and the relatively small production cost. But they are also getting the attention of larger marketers, such as Procter & Gamble, Volvo, Bell Atlantic, General Motors' Saturn division, and Club Med. These advertisers say the infomercial is an ideal way to present complicated information to potential customers, which other advertising vehicles typically don't allow time to do. For example, Philips Electronics aired an infomercial about its new Compact Disc Interactive, a multimedia CD player that attaches to television sets and stereo systems. Philips found that its print advertising was not effective at demystifying the product, even for sophisticated, technologically oriented consumers.[30]

## ALTERNATIVE MEDIA

To cut through the clutter of traditional advertising media, advertisers are now looking for new ways to promote their products. The alternative vehicles include fax machines, video shopping carts in grocery stores, computer screen savers, CD-ROMs, and advertisements run before movies at the cinema and on rented video cassettes. Two of the most exciting alternative media to emerge are electronic "place-based" vehicles and interactive media.

Place-based vehicles have been cropping up in such unlikely places as retail stores, classrooms, doctors' waiting rooms, and health clubs. Channel One, for example, brings a twelve-minute daily newscast of current events, sprinkled with two minutes of commercials, into some high school classrooms. Other contenders include the College Television Network, which programs music videos on monitors in university cafeterias; Channel M, seen in video arcades; and the CNN Airport Network, which provides news at several domestic airports.[31]

Among the *interactive media* currently available to advertisers are on-line computer services like Prodigy and America Online, which can transmit immediate, personalized advertisements through modems to consumers' desktops. Viewers see

- Make a team effort. Rely on senior management, public relations professionals, attorneys, quality control experts, and manufacturing and marketing personnel.

No single approach will work for every crisis, but sketching out some type of crisis management plan before problems arise will help minimize the damage.

A good public relations and crisis management plan helped steer Pepsi-Cola relatively unscathed through a 1993 product tampering hoax. After the first reports surfaced that syringes and hypodermic needles had been found in cans of Pepsi and Diet Pepsi, company officials quickly assembled a crisis team. Pepsi-Cola's president and CEO appeared on network newscasts, along with video footage showing how Pepsi-Cola products are bottled. The process, in which cans are turned upside down and filled within seconds, leaving no room for foreign objects to be inserted, was thoroughly explained. Then the company found surveillance-camera footage of a woman in a supermarket inserting an object into an open Diet Pepsi can. It aired this footage, along with a statement from the director of the Food and Drug Administration, that the tampering was a hoax. Throughout the crisis, Pepsi refused to recall its products, a stance applauded by the industry. The company then ran a national newspaper ad declaring the crisis over, followed up by a massive coupon promotion celebrating its "freedom."[46]

## LOOKING BACK

As you finish reading this chapter, think back to the opening story about the advertising and public relations campaign for Ford's redesigned Mustang. Ford spends millions of dollars on advertising each year in an attempt to increase sales and market share of existing models and to introduce new and redesigned models. Ford goes through the same creative steps as other large marketers, from determining what appeal to use to choosing the appropriate executional style. Ford also expends great effort in deciding which medium will be best to reach each model's target market. The company takes into account such things as audience and geographic selectivity of the medium, cost per contact, audience duplication, and reach. Public relations is also a major element in Ford's promotional mix, especially for new-model introductions.

## SUMMARY

**1 Discuss the effect advertising has on market share, consumers, brand loyalty, and product attributes.** First, advertising helps marketers increase or maintain brand awareness and, subsequently, *market share*. Typically, more is spent to advertise new brands with a small market share than to advertise older brands. Brands with a large market share use advertising mainly to maintain their share of the market. Second, advertising affects *consumers'* daily lives as well as their purchases. Although advertising can seldom change strongly held consumer values, it may transform a consumer's negative attitude toward a product into a positive one. Third, when consumers are highly *loyal* to a brand, they may buy more of that brand when advertising is increased. Last, advertising can also change the importance of a brand's *attributes* to consumers. By emphasizing different brand attributes, advertisers can change their appeal in response to consumers' changing needs or try to achieve an advantage over competing brands.

KEY TERMS

*competitive advertising* 537
*continuous media schedule* 546
*cooperative advertising* 548
*cost per contact* 544
*cost per thousand (CPM)* 545
*crisis management* 559
*direct-response advertising* 550
*flighted media schedule* 547
*frequency* 546
*geographic selectivity* 544
*infomercial* 551
*institutional advertising* 535
*media mix* 545
*media schedule* 546
*medium* 540
*pioneering advertising* 536
*product advertising* 535
*pulsing media schedule* 547
*reach* 545
*seasonal media schedule* 547
*unique selling proposition* 541

2 **Identify the major types of advertising.** Advertising is any form of nonpersonal, paid communication in which the sponsor or company is identified. The two major types of advertising are institutional advertising and product advertising. *Institutional advertising* is not product-oriented; rather, its purpose is to foster a positive company image among the general public, investment community, customers, and employees. *Product advertising* is designed mainly to promote goods and services, and it is classified into three main categories: pioneering, competitive, and comparative. A product's place in the product life cycle is a major determinant of the type of advertising used to promote it.

3 **Describe the advertising campaign process.** An advertising campaign is a series of related advertisements focusing on a common theme and common goals. The advertising campaign process consists of several important steps. Promotion managers first set specific campaign objectives. They then make creative decisions, often with the aid of an advertising agency, centered on developing advertising appeals. Once creative decisions have been made, media are evaluated and selected. Finally, the overall campaign is assessed through various forms of testing.

4 **Describe media evaluation and selection techniques.** Media evaluation and selection make up a crucial step in the advertising campaign process. Promotion managers choose advertising media on the basis of three main variables: characteristics of the target market, audience selectivity, and geographic selectivity. Firms typically use a combination of media, called a media mix. In general, media mix decisions depend on cost per thousand (CPM), reach, and frequency factors. Major types of advertising media include newspapers, magazines, radio, television, and outdoor advertising such as billboards and bus panels. Recent trends in advertising media include fax, video shopping carts, electronic "place-based" media, interactive advertising through microcomputers, minibillboards, and cinema and video advertising.

5 **Define the role of advertising agencies.** Advertising agencies are often hired to develop promotional campaigns. Full-service advertising agencies perform four major functions: creative services, media services, research, and advertising planning.

6 **Discuss the role of public relations in the promotional mix.** Public relations is a vital part of a firm's promotional mix. A company fosters good publicity to enhance its image and promote its products. Public relations is especially useful in boosting new product introductions and positioning brands. An equally important aspect of public relations is managing unfavorable publicity in a way that is least damaging to a firm's image.

## Discussion and Writing Questions

1. How can advertising, sales promotion, and publicity work together? Give an example.
2. Discuss the reasons why new brands with a smaller market share spend proportionately more on advertising and sales promotion than brands with a larger market share.
3. At what stage in a product's life cycle are pioneering, competitive, and comparative advertising

most likely to occur? Give a current example of each type of advertising.

4. What is an advertising appeal? Give some examples of advertising appeals you have observed recently in the media.

5. What are the advantages of magazine advertising? Why are magazines likely to expand as an advertising medium?

✍6. You are the advertising manager of a sailing magazine, and one of your biggest potential advertisers has questioned your rates. Write the firm a letter explaining why you believe your audience selectivity is worth the extra expense for advertisers.

✍7. As the new public relations director for a sportswear company, you have been asked to set public relations objectives for a new line of athletic shoes to be introduced to the teen market. Draft a memo outlining the objectives you propose for the shoe's introduction and your reasons for them.

8. Reports have just surfaced that your company, a fast-food chain, sold contaminated food products that have made several people seriously ill. As your company's public relations manager, devise a plan to handle the crisis.

## Application for Small Business

Quality of service is increasingly the basis for deciding where to do business—particularly in banking. Consumers are five times more likely to have their checking and savings accounts with the bank they perceive as providing the highest quality of service than with any other bank.

Premier Bank is a local bank competing with several much larger regional banks. Biff Motley, director of marketing for Premier, has just completed a workshop for his customer service representatives. He told the participants that when people say they expect good customer service from their bank, they most often mean they want attentive, friendly, courteous, and accurate service from bank employees. He also said that all market segments, not just one or two, expect good customer service.

A marketing research consultant also made a presentation at the training session. She noted that Premier Bank is considered more friendly and courteous than the major competitors but is rated lower than the competitors on quick, accurate service. The research findings also indicate that Premier Bank has more reasonable fees and service charges but is not as competitive on interest rates charged for loans.

### Questions

1. Should Premier Bank's advertising campaign use institutional or product advertising?

2. If product advertising is used, should comparative ads be used?

3. What advertising appeal would be most effective for Premier Bank?

## CRITICAL THINKING CASE

### Borden

After twenty years in retirement, Elsie the Cow is being revived as the centerpiece of an ambitious advertising campaign for Borden dairy products. According to some experts, however, Elsie's return may be too little, too late.

Created in 1936, Elsie was everywhere as Borden's wholesome symbol until she was put out to pasture in the early 1970s. Now the company plans to put an updated version of Elsie on all its dairy products in a major television and print ad campaign. Elsie is scheduled to star in a series of TV commercials featuring an animal farm family, with a talking Elsie as its mother. Borden hopes Elsie's comforting image will stimulate sluggish sales of its dairy brands.

Marketing experts doubt that Elsie will be an effective marketing symbol, however, and caution that her comeback is not a guaranteed success. Several years ago, Timex, Rice-a-Roni, Campbell Soup, and other advertisers tried to revive old slogans and icons. For instance, Timex brought back the slogan "It takes a licking and keeps on ticking" with some success. Likewise, Campbell's "Mmm, mmm, good" slogan rekindled memories for baby boomers. But experts contend that selling Borden's products now is a quite different challenge from selling its products when Elsie was popular. Elsie may remind only an older segment of the population of the brand but not reach the younger consumers that Borden needs to attract.

Other marketing experts say that Elsie's reappearance is an act of desperation and that Borden's troubles cannot be corrected by the return of an animated cow. Borden's reported losses in 1992 indicate that its brands—from Elmer's glue to Cracker Jack caramel-coated popcorn—are in serious trouble. For instance, sales for Borden's processed cheese slid 11 percent while sales for the category rose 1 percent.

Borden's brands lost their consumer appeal in part because of the company's decentralized approach to advertising. In the 1980s, Borden acquired dozens of other food companies and kept practically all their ad agencies. By the end of the decade, the number of agencies had swelled to nineteen. Borden has now decided to take a one-company approach to its advertising.

Despite some analysts' doubts about Elsie's return, others believe bringing her back makes sense. Even when powerful icons like Elsie aren't used for a while, they claim, they remain powerful image builders. On the strength of this theory, Borden plans to use Elsie as a representative for other Borden products after she makes her dairy comeback. The chairman and CEO insists that Elsie recalls a simpler era of wholesomeness and quality that even the MTV generation will relate to.

His view is supported by survey results that found Elsie to be the top logo, one that actually enhances brand image. Findings like these are encouraging Borden to rely on an aggressive one-brand strategy to turn things around for the whole company.

### Questions

1. Describe your perception of Borden's target market, using specific demographic and psychographic descriptors.
2. Assume that you are the advertising manager for Borden's new advertising campaign featuring Elsie's return. What would be the specific objectives of your campaign in light of the target market you described in question 1?
3. ✍ Draft a statement of your creative decisions for the campaign. What will be the chief message or appeal? What will be your style of execution?
4. Do you feel that younger consumers will be able to identify with Elsie's wholesome image? What suggestions would you give Borden's chairman and CEO on his decision to bring Elsie out of retirement?

### References

Kevin Goldman, "Experts Say Borden Has Milked Elsie the Cow for All She's Worth," *The Wall Street Journal,* 12 November 1992, p. B9.

Suein L. Hwang and Kathleen Deveny, "With Elsie as Mascot, Borden Inc. Hopes to Revitalize Its Whole Stable of Brands," *The Wall Street Journal,* 3 September 1992, pp. B1, B8.

Elizabeth Lesly, "The Carving of Elsie, Slice by Slice," *Business Week,* 17 January 1994, p. 29.

Elizabeth Lesly, "Why Things Are So Sour at Borden," *Business Week,* 22 November 1993, pp.78–85.

Gary Levin, "Some Logos Hurt Image," *Advertising Age,* 13 September 1993, p. 40.

Seth Lubove, "Pulling It All Together: Borden, Inc.," *Forbes,* 2 March 1992, pp. 94–96.

Christine Unruh, Bristol Voss, and Jason Wells, "Some Logos a No-Go," *Journal of Business Strategy,* March-April 1994, p. 6.

## SIGNATURE SERIES VIDEO CASE

### Woman's Health Foundation

Vicki Lawson Romero

SIGNATURE SERIES VIDEO

*by Vicki Romero, Chief Executive Officer*

Woman's Health Foundation is the parent company of Woman's Hospital, Woman's Physician Health Organization, Woman's Health Services, Woman's Development Foundation, and Woman's Health Research Institute. For twenty-five years the core business of the foundation has been Woman's Hospital. The hospital is one of the largest women's and infants' specialty hospitals in the United States, delivering almost 7,000 infants annually. The hospital provides care for women of all ages and in all stages of life. Services include obstetrics, gynecology, physical therapy, maternal-fetal medicine, gynecologic oncology, mammography, general surgery, urodynamics, pediatric cardiology, fertility, genetics, day surgery, radiology, and much more.

To respond to changes in the delivery of health care services, the hospital recently completed an ambitious $40 million expansion. Keeping the hospital's products in front of our selected target audiences helps to persuade patients to use its facilities when the need arises, and the marketing staff works at an amazing pace to develop marketing and promotional campaigns to do this. Over the years they have developed many excellent promotional campaigns. Two of the most successful recent campaigns each focused on a different target audience and communicated a unique message.

### Family Album Campaign

The first campaign, Family Album, included general image advertising in addition to several education-based, product-specific ads. Along with mass-media advertising, the campaign used public relations, direct marketing, and educational programming. Individual components of the campaign focused on several different target audiences. The objectives were (1) to create an umbrella campaign to position recent expansion as a recommitment to the community, emphasizing the trust and confidence of patients and families in the area; (2) to begin to position the hospital for its upcoming twenty-fifth anniversary; and (3) to create a campaign format that could encompass labor and delivery services, general surgery, and the neonatal intensive care unit for infants.

The overall theme of the campaign—Family Album—was created from the hospital's management philosophy, which addresses the family of employees and physicians all working together to achieve excellence in the delivery of health care to women and infants. Both broadcast and print advertisements were developed to support the Family Album theme. Four television spots were produced, focusing on different service aspects.

The "family" spot was created in three versions—thirty-second and sixty-second general versions and a thirty-second version with a holiday message tag. The commercial parallels the hospital's growth with the growth of a family. Original music was created for the spot, which weaves the family theme more tightly into the message.

Additional spots were created to showcase other services. The thirty-second "labor and delivery" spot expands on the family concept by invoking the look and feel of a family reunion. The spot's tag line is "Family reunions—held daily at Woman's Hospital." In south Louisiana, these "family reunions" are essential family traditions. The thirty-second "general surgery" spot explained not only the important role women play in the community but also the important role Woman's Hospital plays in their lives. Finally, the "neonatal intensive care unit" spot features the trust and confidence parents have in Woman's Hospital and shows that its nurses are more than just nurses—they're caring friends.

A print campaign was also developed to support each of the television spots. The Family Album theme provides a versatile format to tell stories about our "family." We used real stories about real people who have been touched by the care received at Woman's Hospital. The centerpiece of the campaign was a four-color, eight-page insert placed in the local newspaper, which explained the reasons for expansion to more than 100,000 readers.

To showcase the newest addition to the hospital, two grand-opening events were held. The first, called a Wing Ding, was for the hospital family: physicians, employees, and community VIPs. More than 700 people attended the Friday night event and toured the new wing. The second event was for the general public. In keeping with the construction theme, the Pink n' Blueprints invitations were mailed in print tubes, creating excitement and interest in the event. As a result, more than 2,500 moms, dads, and grandmas attended, participated in education sessions, and toured the new facility. Each participant received a miniature "family album" to take home.

This theme was carried throughout the year, both internally through the Family Album display board, which featured pictures of employee events and hospital departments, and externally through special-purpose ads, such as the ad celebrating quintuplets born at the hospital that same year.

### Breast Cancer Awareness Campaign

The second campaign was a single-product campaign related to breast care. Through various approaches, Woman's Health Foundation hoped to educate women about the importance of the three-step method of early detection for the prevention of breast cancer.

Less than 30 percent of eligible women receive mammography based on guidelines established by the

American College of Radiology. A study supported by the National Cancer Institute found that more than one out of ten older high-risk women have never received a mammogram.

The primary challenge of this campaign was to reach the underserved with a message that the three-step approach for early detection is the key to fighting breast cancer. If women would observe the three-step approach—which includes participating regularly in a screening mammography program, completing monthly breast self-examinations, and having a yearly physician's examination—the breast cancer mortality rate would decrease by more than 30 percent. Education is a vital factor in making women aware of the three-step approach and its benefits.

To determine the current level of understanding about mammography and to discover motivating and deterrent factors for women who comply with the guidelines and those who don't, the foundation conducted a set of consumer focus groups. Separate groups were completed with women ages 35 to 44 who had had mammograms and women ages 35 to 44 who had not, as well as with women ages 55-plus who had had mammograms and women ages 55-plus who had not. Results of this marketing research were then used to develop the campaign strategy, copy, and creative direction.

The results of the survey were also presented to key physician referral sources. The sources included obstetricians/gynecologists, family practitioners, and cardiologists. They were provided with educational posters for display in their patient exam rooms. These posters were reminders for both patients and physicians about the importance of the three-step approach for early detection of breast cancer.

Five marketing objectives were established for this campaign: (1) to increase physician referrals; (2) to motivate women (especially those 55-plus) to have a mammogram and to participate in an ongoing breast care program; (3) to provide more understandable, positive information about the importance of early detection, including mammography and its benefits; (4) to introduce the hospital's first satellite breast center to key constituents within a certain radius and area of town; and (5) to develop a more informational/educational advertising campaign that would address mammography, total breast care, and the new satellite breast center.

The Breast Cancer Awareness Campaign was planned and implemented as a comprehensive marketing effort that included mass-media advertising, specialized education programming, public service announcements, media co-promotions, the grand opening of a new satellite breast center, physician relations, patient communications, and intense public relations activities, including more than fifty broadcast news stories. All materials were created with a timeless message that could be used in years to come, thereby adding to the overall cost-effectiveness of the campaign.

Print ads focused on different aspects unique to Woman's Hospital's breast care program and conveyed important educational information about the three-step approach, with a public service message tone. Positive messages, such as "92 percent of all breast cancer is curable," were derived from the key findings of our consumer research. Models included a variety of ages and races, to reach out to all women in our targeted audiences.

Outdoor boards were used also, as directionals to raise awareness of the new satellite location. A double message—"The mammogram you've been putting off is right around the corner"—created interest in the new satellite clinic location and served as an important reminder about mammography.

Two thirty-second television spots were produced for this campaign. These spots targeted both younger and older women. We also created ten-second spots for cost-effectiveness and frequency.

A direct-mail strategy was used to soften the market prior to the launch of the campaign. Brochures were mailed to women in targeted ZIP codes to inform them of the new satellite location, the hospital's total breast care program, and the importance of mammography.

Direct mail was also used to invite women in the area surrounding the new satellite location to a grand-opening celebration. A presealed postcard that included the invitation and a magnet made a long-lasting impression on the recipients.

The campaign was supported by a tie-in with the national Breast Cancer Awareness month promotion initiated by the American College of Radiology. A pink-ribbon promotion was designed to reach all women with an educational message during Breast Cancer Awareness month. We produced 50,000 pink-ribbon packets, each of which contained a pink-ribbon pin, information about Breast Cancer Awareness month, a page of twelve monthly breast self-examination reminder stickers, and a brochure providing instructions for performing breast self-examination and information about the hospital's breast care program.

These packets were promoted by the media sponsor and distributed through a local pharmacy, the hospital, physicians' offices, and the television station.

In addition to the pink-ribbon packet promotion, the media sponsor provided optimal reach and frequency for messages about breast health and breast cancer. More than fifty news stories were produced and aired during the promotion, which equates to reaching 24 million viewers.

The entire campaign produced extremely positive results. Physician referrals increased during the promotional period, and the Woman's Hospital Breast Center performed a record number of mammograms. In addition, the satellite breast center exceeded expectations by more than 100 percent. More than 2,000 calls were generated during the primary promotional week, with more than half of those calls (1,202) resulting in baseline mammography procedures. The promotion had to be extended because so many women were unable to get their calls through the crowded phone lines to schedule an appointment.

Although the numbers of mammograms performed and awareness levels are important in marketing, the real results and success of this campaign are priceless. Thousands of women are now practicing the three-step approach for early detection of breast cancer. A number of cancers have been successfully detected, and several successful surgeries have been performed. If even one life has been saved as a result of our efforts, this can truly be deemed a successful marketing program.

### Concluding Comments

As with all marketing efforts, results are essential. As Woman's Health Foundation develops any communication campaign, however, it also always has another guiding purpose, which is to provide an educational message to benefit its audience. This philosophical difference is what makes its marketing programs so successful. Education is the key to its success, and marketing is an essential component of education. Providing health education is a vital part of its mission, which positions Woman's Hospital as a national leader in women's health care today.

### Questions

1. Were the two campaigns primarily institutional advertising, product advertising, or a combination? Why was this particular emphasis appropriate?
2. What advertising appeals were used and why?
3. What executional styles were used? Were they effective? Why or why not?

## SIGNATURE SERIES VIDEO CASE

## TABASCO® Sauce: A Louisiana Tradition of Worldwide Renown

SIGNATURE SERIES VIDEO

*by Paul McIlhenny*
*Vice-President, McIlhenny Company*

During George Bush's 1988 presidential campaign, TABASCO® sauce was predicted to replace jelly beans as the White House favorite. It was shown in a photograph of the mess table during the excavation of King Tint's tomb. TABASCO® sauce has made its presence known in the far corners of the world, and even above it. Britain's Queen Mother prefers it in her lobster cocktail and NASA sent TABASCO® sauce up to the Skylab space station.

The little bottle with the distinctive red cap and green neck band has become a household and restaurant fixture in more than 100 countries around the globe. U.S. troops in the Desert Storm conflict received miniatures bottles of the flavorful condiment in their field rations. The military now packs TABASCO® sauce in every individual MRE meal.

After a century and a quarter, TABASCO® sauce is still meticulously produced on Avery Island, Louisiana,

by descendants of Daniel Dudley Avery and his wife, Sarah Craig Marsh. Avery Island, is one of five "islands" arising in atypical fashion above the bayou country of the flat Louisiana Gulf coast. The 2,300-acre tract literally sits atop a mountainous plug of solid salt, perhaps formed by pressures exerted on sediment deposited over eons by the predecessors of the Mississippi River.

In 1859, Edmund McIlhenny, a fifth generation American of Scottish-Irish descent, married Mary Avery, Daniel Avery's daughter. The couple moved to Avery Island to oversee the salt quarrying operation which began shortly after the massive rock salt deposit was discovered. At the same time, McIlhenny began to nurture a special variety of red Capsicum peppers, the seeds of which were given to him by a friend returning from Mexico.

In early 1863, invading Union troops required the entire family to flee Avery Island. On their return in 1865, they found the sugar cane fields destroyed and the salt works inoperable. Mr. McIlhenny's bright red peppers, however, survived the devastation. In fact, he found the pepper plants flourishing in the fertile soil and humid climate of south Louisiana.

He began to experiment with making pepper sauce, and eventually hit upon a formula which involved crushing the ripest, reddest peppers, mixing a half coffee cup of Avery Island salt with each gallon, and aging the concoction in crockery jars for 30 days. The best "French wine vinegar" was added and the mixture was allowed to age for another 30 days, hand-stirring it at regular intervals. After straining the seeds and pepper skins, the sauce was transferred to small cologne-type bottles with narrow necks, then corked and dipped in green sealing wax. When pressed for a name, McIlhenny called his creation "TABASCO," a word indigenous to the Indians of Mexico's central highlands.

"That famous sauce Mr. McIlhenny makes" was so popular with family and friends he was encouraged to market it commercially. In 1868, McIlhenny sent 350 bottles of his pepper sauce to a New York wholesaler at the price of one dollar each. In 1869, orders poured in for thousands of bottles. Today, sales of the familiar two-ounce size alone exceed 75 million bottles annually. Labels are printed in 19 languages for world-wide distribution.

Until the late 60's, all peppers were grown on Avery Island. When a shortage of local pickers developed, McIlhenny Company established contracts with pepper farms in Honduras, Columbia, Venezuela and the Dominican Republic. Today, about 90% of the pepper crop is grown in these countries.

During the annual harvest on Avery Is land, hand-picking is completed at 3 p.m. each day. The boxes of

# CHAPTER 17

# SALES PROMOTION AND PERSONAL SELLING

## LEARNING OBJECTIVES

*After studying this chapter, you should be able to*

1 *State the objectives of sales promotion.*

2 *List the most common forms of consumer sales promotion.*

3 *List the most common forms of trade sales promotion.*

4 *Describe personal selling.*

5 *Identify the different types of selling tasks.*

6 *List the steps in the selling process.*

7 *Describe the functions of sales management.*

Free rooms are nice, but hotels increasingly are offering their best guests something more valuable: frequent-flier miles. Holiday Inn and Sheraton are two hotel chains that offer airline miles on several major carriers as an alternative to earning points toward hotel stays. Marriott has also modified its frequent-stay program by allowing guests to accumulate miles on one of six carriers.

The hotels aren't abolishing their frequent-stay programs; guests can still stockpile points for free rooms, upgrades, and, depending on the hotel, weekend vacation packages, sportswear, or appliances. Many guests do take advantage of the hotel giveaways. But hotel executives have learned what credit card issuers, telephone companies, and other businesses with airline tie-ins already know: In frequency programs, air miles are the currency of choice.

Adding miles to the mix is an important change for hotels. They followed the airlines into the frequency marketing business, and for over ten years they tried in vain to duplicate the airlines' successes. However, the hotels' frequent-stay programs have never generated the intense brand loyalty that the airlines' programs created, partly because travelers decide where to stay based on location or service rather than freebies.

Up until now, many hotels have had airline tie-ins that permitted guests to fatten their frequent-flier accounts, but customers usually were required to fly the same carrier they flew that day to get the miles. What is different now is that hotels are allowing guests to choose among airlines, regardless of which one they flew on. They can even accumulate miles if they drove to the hotel. Holiday Inn, Sheraton, and Marriott have waived membership fees for customers who join their mileage programs.

Holiday Inn's program, for example, offers mileage awards that guests can use with United, Delta, or Northwest Airlines. Guests receive 2.5 miles for each dollar spent on a room. Sheraton's program offers guests 2 points for every dollar spent at its properties, including money spent in restaurants and bars, even if the customer isn't spending the night. Sheraton guests can cash in their air miles with American, United, Continental, or Thai Airlines. Marriott's program benefits travelers who stay in hotels only a short time. Guests receive 500 frequent-flier miles per stay, regardless of dollars spent. After five stays, customers receive a bonus of 2,500 miles. Participating airlines are American, Northwest, Trans World Airlines, USAir, Continental, and British Airways. Because "a mile is a mile is a

mile," consumers can compare which airline has the best program and stick with that airline. But with hotel frequent-stay programs, each hotel is different, making it difficult for consumers to pick a favorite. Brand loyalty, the reason for offering the programs, may therefore remain elusive. Many experts believe that all hotels ultimately will offer mileage programs but that the programs will benefit consumers more than the hotels. If they're all offering the same product—miles—consumers will not need to be brand loyal to any one hotel chain.[1]

What other promotions could hotels offer to increase brand loyalty—that is, loyalty among their current customers? What types of promotions could hotels offer to entice people to switch?

1 *State the objectives of sales promotion.*

## SALES PROMOTION

**sales promotion**
Offer of a short-term incentive in order to induce the purchase of a particular good or service.

In addition to using advertising, public relations, and personal selling, marketing managers can use sales promotion to increase the effectiveness of their promotional efforts. **Sales promotion** is a marketing communication activity in which a short-term incentive motivates consumers to purchase a good or service immediately, either by lowering the price or by adding value.

Advertising offers the consumer a reason to buy; sales promotion offers an incentive to buy. Both are important, but sales promotion is usually cheaper than advertising and easier to measure. A major national TV advertising campaign may cost over $2 million to create, produce, and place. In contrast, a newspaper coupon campaign or promotional contest may cost only about half as much. It is hard to figure exactly how many people buy a product as a result of seeing a TV ad. However, with sales promotion, marketers know the precise number of coupons redeemed or the number of contest entries.

**consumer sales promotion**
Sales promotion activities targeted to the ultimate consumer.

**trade sales promotion**
Sales promotion activities targeted to a channel member, such as a wholesaler or retailer.

Sales promotion is usually targeted toward either of two distinctly different markets. **Consumer sales promotion** is targeted to the ultimate consumer market. **Trade sales promotion** is directed to members of the marketing channel, such as wholesalers and retailers. Consumer products manufacturers spend about a quarter of their promotion budget on consumer sales promotion, half on trade sales promotion, and the remaining quarter on media advertising.[2]

### THE OBJECTIVES OF SALES PROMOTION

Sales promotion usually works best in affecting behavior, not attitudes. Immediate purchase is usually the goal of sales promotion, regardless of the form it takes. Therefore, it seems to make more sense when planning a sales promotion campaign to target customers according to their general behavior. For instance, is the consumer loyal to your product or to your competitor's? Does the consumer switch brands readily in favor of the best deal? Does the consumer buy only the least expensive product, no matter what? Does the consumer buy any products in your category at all?

The objectives of a promotion depend on the general behavior of target consumers (see Exhibit 17.1 on page 574). For example, marketers who are targeting loyal users of their product actually don't want to change behavior. Instead, they need to reinforce existing behavior or increase product usage. An effective tool for strengthening brand loyalty is the frequent-buyer program that rewards consumers for repeat purchases. Other types of promotions are more effective with customers prone to brand switching or with those who are loyal to a competitor's product. The cents-off coupon, free sample, or eye-catching display in a store will often entice shoppers to try a different brand. Consumers who do not use the product may be enticed to try it through the distribution of free samples.

Once marketers understand the dynamics occurring within their product category and have determined the particular consumers and consumer behaviors they want to influence, they can then go about selecting promotional tools to achieve these goals.

2 *List the most common forms of consumer sales promotion.*

## TOOLS FOR CONSUMER SALES PROMOTION

Marketing managers must decide which consumer sales promotion devices to use in a specific campaign. The methods chosen must suit the objectives to ensure success of the overall promotion plan. Popular tools for consumer sales promotion are coupons, premiums, frequent-buyer programs, contests and sweepstakes, samples, and point-of-purchase displays.

*Exhibit 17.1*

Types of Consumers and Sales Promotion Goals

Source: Adapted from Don E. Schultz, William A. Robinson, and Lisa A. Petrison, *Sales Promotion Essentials*, 2nd ed. (Lincolnwood, IL: NTC Business Books, 1993), p. 217.

| Type | Description | Desired results | Sales promotion examples |
|---|---|---|---|
| Current loyals | People who buy your product most or all of the time | Reinforce behavior, increase consumption, change purchase timing | Frequent-flier programs, such as those offered by airlines<br>Bonus packs that give loyal consumers an incentive to stock up |
| Competitive loyals | People who buy a competitor's product most or all of the time | Break loyalty, persuade to switch to your brand | Sampling to introduce your product's superior qualities compared to their brand<br>Sweepstakes or premiums that create interest in the product |
| Switchers | People who buy a variety of products in the category | Persuade to buy your brand more often | Any promotion that lowers the price of the product, such as coupons, price-off packages, and bonus packs<br>Trade deals that help make the product more readily available than competing products |
| Price buyers | People who consistently buy the least expensive brand | Appeal with low prices or supply added value that makes price less important | Coupons, price-off packages, refunds, or trade deals that reduce the price of brand to match that of the brand that would have been purchased |

## Coupons

**coupon**
Certificate that entitles consumers to an immediate price reduction when they buy the product.

A **coupon** is a certificate that entitles consumers to an immediate price reduction when they buy the product. Consumers receive coupons by direct mail; through the media, as in a freestanding insert in Sunday newspapers; on the product's package; through cooperative advertising, which presents a manufacturer's coupon that can be redeemed only at the retailer's store; and through coupon-dispensing machines at retail stores. Coupons are a particularly good way to encourage product trial and repurchase. They are also likely to increase the amount of a product bought.

Coupon distribution has steadily increased over the years. Packaged-goods marketers distribute over 300 billion coupons a year through print media, which equals about 3,000 per household. But shoppers redeem only about one of these coupons in fifty, or about 2 percent. Part of the problem is that coupons are often wasted on consumers who have no interest in the product—for example, dog food coupons that reach the petless. Additionally, coupons are more likely to encourage repeat purchases by regular users of a product than to encourage nonusers to try the brand.[3] Thus some marketers are reevaluating their use of coupons. Procter & Gamble, for

The coupons inserted into the Sunday newspaper are usually combined with a full-page, glossy ad—like this coupon for Zest.

example, has cut the number of coupons it gives to consumers in favor of a lower-price strategy.

In an effort to get a higher yield from promotions, many marketers are directing coupons to the place where they're most likely to affect customer buying decisions: in the aisles where consumers decide which product to buy. Coupon-dispensing machines, attached to the shelf below the featured product, have an 18 percent redemption rate (about one person uses the coupon out of every five who take one), nine times higher than for newspaper inserts. Marketers are also investigating the use of coupons dispensed at the checkout counter in response to a purchase the consumer has just made. Such machines dispense coupons for either the product purchased or a competing brand. Redemption rates for electronic checkout coupons are around 9 percent.[4]

Although the United States remains the world's leading coupon market, several other markets around the world are beginning to experience the same growth in couponing that occurred in the United States during the 1980s. In the European Community, political and economic changes have given marketers more opportunity to use creative promotional techniques. The United Kingdom and Belgium are the EC's most active coupon users; marketers distribute over 5 billion coupons annually in the United Kingdom alone. Couponing continues to grow in Italy, and couponing has just become legal in Denmark. Other European countries still have limited access to coupons, however. For example, in Holland and Switzerland, some major retailers refuse to accept coupons. Other regions are also slow to embrace couponing. In Russia, limited advertising media and the unavailability of many products make couponing difficult. In Japan, coupon redemption is still in its infancy. Although the print media are now allowed to carry coupons, Japanese retailers and consumers are still reluctant to use them. Many consumers feel that using coupons may make them look as though they do not have much money or are being "cheap."[5]

## Premiums

**premium**
Extra item offered to the consumer, usually in exchange for some proof of purchase of the promoted product.

A **premium** is an extra item offered to the consumer, usually in exchange for some proof that the promoted product has been purchased. Premiums reinforce the consumer's purchase decision, increase consumption, and persuade nonusers to switch brands. Premiums like telephones, tote bags, and umbrellas are available when consumers buy cosmetics, magazines, bank services, rental cars, and so on.

The appropriateness of the premium is crucial to its success. For example, Clinique

One effective sales promotion, used frequently by cosmetics makers, is to provide a premium, an extra item, with a purchase. The premium often persuades people to try a product or to buy something right away or in greater quantity than they might otherwise have done.

Courtesy McAlpins

often gives away cosmetics with a customer purchase. *The Wall Street Journal* gives a guide to understanding money and investments to new subscribers. Children's toys are a popular premium in boxes of cereal. Hershey's Bar None candy bar tempts teens with "The Coolest Stuff"—everything from basketballs to boxer shorts—which it gives away in return for ten or more wrappers. For $9.95 plus proof of purchase, M&M/Mars offers a multicolored quartz watch sporting a skateboarding M&M peanut character on the second hand. Fast-food companies often tie into movies or special events to give away souvenir toys and cups. For example, in one summer, McDonald's tied into promotions for the World Cup Soccer championship, Universal Pictures' *The Flintstones,* and the Dream Team 2's participation in the World Championship of Basketball. For the Dream Team 2 promotion, McDonald's issued a dozen collector cups featuring team players, including Shaquille O'Neal and Dominique Wilkins.[6] Similar premium offers by cigarette manufacturers, however, have received quite a bit of criticism, as the Ethics in Marketing article relates.

## Frequent-Buyer Programs

**frequent-buyer program** Promotional program in which loyal consumers are rewarded for making multiple purchases of a particular good or service.

Frequent-buyer programs are one of the fastest-growing forms of consumer sales promotion. In a **frequent-buyer program,** loyal consumers are rewarded for making multiple purchases of a particular good or service. These programs are basically designed to create and reward brand loyalty among consumers who might otherwise switch from brand to brand within a category. One study concluded that improving customer loyalty by 2 percent can boost profits as much as cutting costs by 10 percent can.[8]

The frequent-flier plans offered by airlines are good examples of this promotion tool. The free trips are a relatively easy way for the airlines to build brand loyalty, because they have a high retail value but a relatively low cost to the airline. Retailers' frequent-buyer programs work in much the same way. For example, the Hosiery Club at Dillards department stores rewards hosiery customers with a free pair of hose after the purchase of twelve. Dozens of marketers, from Waldenbooks to Holiday Inn, are also trying variations of frequent-buyer programs to secure customer loyalty.

## Contests and Sweepstakes

Contests and sweepstakes are generally designed to create interest in the good or service, often to encourage brand switching. Contests are promotions in which participants use some skill or ability to compete for prizes. A consumer contest usually requires entrants to answer questions, complete sentences, or write a paragraph

ETHICS IN MARKETING

**Are Premiums a Loophole for Cigarette Makers?**

Cigarette makers have found a new avenue to reach customers in a heavily regulated environment: outfitting smokers with caps, T-shirts, and other merchandise sporting smoking icons like Joe Camel and the Marlboro Man. Antismoking activists and legislators charge that such premiums exploit a loophole in the federal law that requires health-warning labels on cigarette ads.

"The cigarette companies are creating millions of walking billboards," complains a Lutheran minister in Philadelphia who has been arrested for painting over Kool billboards in his inner-city neighborhood. Taking a more law-abiding stance, the minister now gives away free T-shirts with an antidrug message to anyone turning over Salem or Newport cigarette T-shirts or hats.

Other antismoking critics denounce the premiums as encouraging accelerated smoking—the more you puff, the better the prize. More important, they condemn the promotional campaigns as enticements for youngsters to smoke. The premiums typically include merchandise like leather backpacks, biker jackets, sleeping bags, fanny packs, and coolers, all particularly appealing to young people.

Legislation has been introduced that may sharply restrict cigarette companies' promotional campaigns. After the 1991 passage of federal legislation that required warning labels on snuff promotions, the maker of Copenhagen and Skoal brands of chewing tobacco gave up offering customers logo-branded jean jackets, windbreakers, and other gear rather than tarnish its macho image with dire health warnings.

Cigarette makers deny they are skirting federal regulations requiring health warnings. After all, cigarettes are entirely legal, and the federal government has sanctioned their sale and allows their advertising in print media. Tobacco executives also adamantly deny that their promotions are designed to appeal to underage smokers. They say that the premiums are an effective way to reward adult smokers for buying their cigarettes. The promotions are also meant to attract adult smokers to a particular brand by providing them with an incentive to switch.[7]

Do you feel tobacco makers should be required to print health warnings on premiums they give as rewards to smokers? Why or why not? Do you feel these premiums are specifically targeted to young people, as activists claim?



about the product and submit proof of purchase. Winning a sweepstakes, on the other hand, depends on chance or luck, and participation is free. Sweepstakes usually draw about ten times more entries than contests do.

When setting up contests and sweepstakes, managers must make certain that the award will appeal to the target market. For instance, a sweepstakes for an exotic honeymoon destination will definitely capture the attention of the many brides-to-be who read a bridal magazine. A contest sponsored by Guinness Import Company had contestants write a fifty-word essay explaining what Guinness beer means to them. The writer of the best essay won a pub in Ireland. Response to the contest far exceeded any previous Guinness promotion and resulted in worldwide publicity.[9]

In some cases, a contest may succeed without even giving away prizes. For example, 7-Eleven's Sound Off promotion asked customers to vote weekly on whimsical questions, such as "Do men drive better than women?" Customers voted by buying coffee or soft drinks in cups marked yes or no. In-store signs and local radio ads announced the weekly question and the resulting tallies. The promotion yielded a 16 percent increase in soft-drink sales and a 5 percent increase in coffee sales.[10]

## Samples

Consumers generally perceive a certain amount of risk in trying new products. Many are afraid of trying something they will not like (such as a new food item) or spending too much money and getting little reward. Sampling allows the customer to try a product risk-free. However, sampling can be very expensive. As a general rule, then, free samples of a product should be offered only when two conditions exist. First, the benefits of the new product must be clearly superior to those of existing products. Second, the item must have a unique new attribute that the consumer must experience to believe in.

Sampling can be accomplished by directly mailing the sample to the customer, delivering the sample door to door, demonstrating or sampling the product at a retail store, or packaging the sample with another product by the same manufacturer.

Sampling at special events is also becoming popular. Frito-Lay handed out free samples of Frito Scoops! to people attending the concerts of country singer Reba McEntire. Frito-Lay displayed signs bearing the Scoops! logo around the concert hall, and the crowd was shown a one-minute Frito-Lay commercial before the band hit the stage. Similarly, to promote its new raspberry-flavored Nutri-Grain cereal bars, Kellogg handed out free samples to concert goers as they left an outdoor theater in Houston.

Co-op sampling, in which several different products are delivered in the same container, is another method marketers can use to induce trial of their product. This method is less expensive than traditional sampling because the distribution costs are shared by many manufacturers. Manufacturers can also reduce sampling costs by using trial-size containers. Minibottles or cartons of a product, such as shampoo or salad dressing, are offered in stores at low prices. Retailers like this form of promotion, because they share the profit. Consumers also appreciate being able to buy trial-size containers, because they reduce the cost of trying new products.

Sampling is an effective consumer promotion tool in developing countries. However, companies that have successfully sent trial-size samples of new products to U.S. consumers have experienced problems when using this same tactic in Eastern European countries. When Procter & Gamble introduced its Wash & Go shampoo in Poland, it mailed samples directly to people's homes—Poland's first direct-mail sampling campaign. But many of the samples never got to the intended customers. Thieves broke into mailboxes to get them, and P&G ended up paying to fix some broken mailboxes.[11]

## Point-of-Purchase Displays

**point-of-purchase display**
Promotional display set up at the retailer's location to build traffic, advertise the product, or induce impulse buying.

A **point-of-purchase display** is a promotional display set up at the retailer's location to build traffic, advertise the product, or induce impulse buying. One big advantage of point-of-purchase displays is that they offer manufacturers a captive audience in retail stores. Point-of-purchase displays include shelf "talkers" (signs attached to store shelves), shelf extenders (attachments that extend shelves so products stand out), ads on grocery carts and bags, end-aisle and floor-stand displays, television monitors at supermarket checkout counters, in-store audio messages, and audiovisual displays. An in-store display can be simple—for example, a shipping crate that converts to a floor stand—but to be effective, it should provide product information and be creative and entertaining.

Point-of-purchase displays work better for impulse products, those products bought without prior decision by the consumer, than for planned purchases. Consider Borden's launch of a new cheese snack called Doodle O's. Borden decided against expensive advertising and instead created 25,000 cardboard cutouts of an orange fox wearing sunglasses. Dubbed Fox Z. Doodle, the cartoon mascot was part of a point-of-purchase display that held 200 sample-size packages of the cheese snack. The display was so effective in luring the lunchbox set that the displays often had to be refilled daily, instead of on a weekly basis as planned. Success stories like this one support the theory that shoppers may come into a store with a shopping list but are more likely to grab a product from an eye-catching display than to look for the brand on shelves.[12]

Research shows the effectiveness of point-of-purchase displays. One study tested brands in six different product categories and in all instances found that point-of-purchase displays increased sales over stores where displays were not used. Sales of

Computerized greeting-card machines, which let customers inscribe a personalized message, build store traffic and induce impulse purchases.



coffee in point-of-purchase displays, for instance, were over six times higher than sales of coffee displayed in its normal shelf position. Research conducted by Information Resources Inc., which uses scanner technology at cash registers to record the bar codes stamped on purchased items (discussed in Chapter 7), found that point-of-purchase displays could increase the sales of products like frozen dinners, laundry detergent, soft drinks, snack foods, soup, and juice by more than 100 to 200 percent.[13]

Computers and interactive electronic devices are beginning to play an important role in point-of-purchase displays. High-tech displays, whether stand-alone kiosks or on-shelf units, grab attention. Warner-Lambert's Canadian division, for example, installed on-shelf computers in the cough-cold-allergy sections of more than 600 Canadian drugstores. The displays, which help shoppers choose a Warner-Lambert over-the-counter remedy that is appropriate for their symptoms, have increased sales significantly. Hallmark's computerized Personalize It! point-of-purchase displays allow consumers to personalize their greeting cards. Personalize It! can incorporate a nickname, a shared joke, or a special message into the customer's choice of more than 200 preprogrammed cards.[14]

3 *List the most common forms of trade sales promotion.*

## TOOLS FOR TRADE SALES PROMOTION

When selling to members of the distribution channel, manufacturers use many of the same sales promotion tools used in consumer promotions—such as sales contests, premiums, and point-of-purchase displays. Several tools, however, are unique to manufacturers and intermediaries:

**trade allowance**
Price reduction offered by manufacturers to intermediaries, such as wholesalers and retailers.

- *Trade allowances:* A **trade allowance** is a price reduction offered by manufacturers to intermediaries such as wholesalers and retailers. The price reduction or rebate is given in exchange for doing something specific, such as allocating space for a new product, or buying something during special periods. For example, a local dealer could receive a special discount for running its own promotion on GE telephones.

**push money**
Money offered to channel intermediaries to encourage them to "push" products—that is, to encourage other members of the channel to sell the products.

- *Push money:* Intermediaries receive **push money** as a bonus for pushing the manufacturer's brand through the distribution channel. Often the push money is directed toward a retailer's salespeople. For example, the manufacturer may offer $50 to an electronics store's sales force for every television set of its brand sold. This practice, however, may foster more loyalty to the manufacturer than to the retailer.
- *Training:* Sometimes a manufacturer will train an intermediary's personnel if the product is rather complex—as frequently occurs in the computer and telecommunication industries. For example, if a large department store purchases an NCR computerized cash register system, NCR may provide free training so the salespeople can learn how to use the new system.
- *Free merchandise:* Often a manufacturer offers retailers free merchandise in lieu of quantity discounts. For example, a breakfast cereal manufacturer may

throw in one case of free cereal for every twenty cases ordered by the retailer. Occasionally, free merchandise is used as payment for trade allowances normally provided through other sales promotions. For example, instead of giving a retailer a price reduction for buying a certain quantity of merchandise, the manufacturer may throw in extra merchandise "free" (that is, at a cost that would equal the price reduction).

- *Store demonstrations:* Manufacturers can also arrange with retailers to perform an in-store demonstration. For example, food manufacturers often send representatives to grocery stores and supermarkets to let customers sample a product while shopping. Cosmetic companies also send their representatives to department stores to promote their beauty aids by performing facials and makeovers for customers.
- *Business meetings, conventions, and trade shows:* Trade association meetings, conferences, and conventions are an important aspect of sales promotion and a growing, multibillion-dollar market. At these shows, manufacturers, distributors, and other vendors have the chance to display their goods or describe their services to customers and potential customers. The cost per potential customer contacted at a show is estimated to be only 25 to 35 percent that of a personal sales call. Trade shows have been uniquely effective in introducing new products; trade shows can establish products in the marketplace more quickly than can advertising, direct marketing, or sales calls. Companies participate in trade shows to attract and identify new prospects, serve current customers, introduce new products, enhance corporate image, test the market response to new products, enhance corporate morale, and gather competitive product information.

These sales promotion tools help manufacturers gain new distributors for their products, obtain wholesaler and retailer support for consumer sales promotions, build or reduce dealer inventories, and improve trade relations. They are used extensively by many manufacturers. Chevrolet, for example, annually sponsors sixty to eighty-five auto shows for consumers. Many of the displays feature interactive computer stations where consumers enter vehicle specifications and get a printout of prices and local dealer names. In return, the local Chevrolet dealers get the names of good prospects. The shows attract millions of consumers, providing dealers with increased store traffic as well as good leads.[15]

Trade promotions push a product through the distribution channel, whereas consumer promotions pull a product through the channel by creating demand (see Chapter 15). Although consumer promotions are often more effective at increasing sales, trade promotions have become more popular over the past several years. Advertising, a consumer-oriented form of promotion, dropped from 43 percent of marketers' promotion budgets in 1981 to just over 25 percent in 1992. Trade promotion, on the other hand, has soared to about 45 percent of marketers' budgets, mostly at the expense of advertising.[16]

If trade promotion is less effective than consumer promotion, why is it so popular? Sometimes trade deals are offered for competitive reasons—"because everyone else does it." Another source of pressure is retailers. Some big retailers have considerable channel power, and that power allows them to demand product discounts and payments for limited shelf space (called "slotting allowances"), especially for new-product introductions. Too often, however, retailers don't pass on the discounts to the ultimate consumers in the form of lower prices. Retailers have even been known to resell to other retailers, with a markup, the merchandise bought at a discount.

4 *Describe personal selling.*

## PERSONAL SELLING

**personal selling**
Direct communication between a sales representative and one or more prospective buyers, for the purpose of making a sale.

**Personal selling** is direct communication between a sales representative and one or more prospective buyers, for the purpose of making a sale. Salespeople can accomplish this purpose by communicating face to face during a personal sales call or by selling over the telephone (telemarketing).

### PROMOTIONAL ADVANTAGES OF PERSONAL SELLING

Personal selling offers several advantages over other forms of promotion:

- Personal selling provides a detailed explanation or demonstration of the product. This capability is especially needed for complex or new goods and services.
- The sales message can be varied according to the motivations and interests of each prospect. Moreover, when the prospect raises objections, the salesperson is there to provide counterarguments and explanations. In contrast, advertising and sales promotion can only respond to the objections the copywriter thinks are important to customers.
- Personal selling can be directed only to qualified prospects. Other forms of promotion include some unavoidable waste because many people in the audience are not prospective customers.
- Personal selling costs can be controlled by adjusting the size of the sales force (and resulting expenses) in one-person increments. If it is paying salespeople a percentage of sales, the firm does not incur sales expenses until a sale is made. On the other hand, advertising and sales promotion must often be purchased in fairly large amounts.
- Perhaps the most important advantage is that personal selling is considerably more effective than other forms of promotion in closing the sale and getting the customer's signature on the order form.

Personal selling might work better than other forms of promotion given certain customer and product characteristics. Generally speaking, personal selling becomes more important as the number of potential customers decreases, as the complexity of the product increases, and as the value of the product grows (see Exhibit 17.2). When there are relatively few potential customers, the time and travel costs of personally visiting each prospect are justifiable. Of course, the good or service must be of sufficient value to absorb the expense of a sales call—a mainframe computer, a management consulting project, or the construction of a new building, for instance. For highly complex goods, such as business jets or private communication systems,

*Exhibit 17.2*

Comparison of Advertising/Sales Promotion and Personal Selling

| Personal selling is more important if . . . | Advertising/sales promotion is more important if . . . |
|---|---|
| The product has a high value. | The product has a low value. |
| It is a custom-made product. | It is a standardized product. |
| There are few customers. | There are many customers. |
| The product is technically complex. | The product is simple to understand. |
| Customers are concentrated. | Customers are geographically dispersed. |
| Examples: insurance policies, custom windows, airplane engines | Examples: soap, magazine subscriptions, cotton T-shirts |

a salesperson is needed to explain the product's basic advantages and propose the exact features and accessories that will meet the prospective client's needs. Conversely, advertising and sales promotion more effectively and economically promote a product when the number of potential buyers is large, the product is less complex, the buyers are dispersed, and the product is low in value and high in standardization (for instance, toothpaste or cereal).

## CAREERS IN PERSONAL SELLING

In a sense, all businesspeople are salespeople. An individual may become a plant manager, a chemist, an engineer, or a member of any profession and yet still have to sell. During a job search, applicants must "sell" themselves to prospective employers in an interview. To reach the top in most organizations, individuals need to sell ideas to peers, superiors, and subordinates. Most important, people must sell themselves and their ideas to just about everyone with whom they have a continuing relationship and to many other people they see only once or twice. Even our country's Presidents use personal selling skills to sell themselves and their programs to many different constituencies. They must motivate Congressional leaders to provide legislative action, convince the business community and labor to help advance their initiatives, and mobilize public support for their programs. Like successful salespeople, successful Presidents know how to listen, how to solve problems, how to present benefits, how to overcome resistance, and how to motivate action.[17]

Many young people get their first sales experience as retail clerks or fast-food clerks.

*(top)* © 1989 Bill Varie/The Image Bank; *(bottom)* Jan Irish/Leo de Wys, Inc.

About 14 million people are employed in personal selling in the United States.[18] This figure reflects all sorts of sales occupations, including retail sales clerks assisting in department stores, people taking orders at fast-food restaurants, and manufacturers' representatives selling to wholesalers and retailers. In addition, some engineers with MBA degrees design and sell large, complex products. Compared to advertising, which employs only half a million workers, personal selling employs a tremendous number of people. Not surprisingly, the fastest-growing sales jobs are computer related. The number of jobs selling electronic information and computer software is expected to grow over 100 percent by the year 2000.[19]

Chances are that students majoring in business or marketing will start their professional careers in sales. Even students in nonbusiness majors may pursue a sales career. The rewards of choosing a sales career are many. Today the average starting salary for a sales trainee is about $30,500, and a top-level industrial salesperson earns an average salary of nearly $65,600 per year.[20] Besides earning attractive salaries, skilled salespeople can rely on job security. Salespeople who reap profits for their companies are rarely laid off. In addition, salespeople enjoy perhaps more freedom and independence than any other type of employee. Typically, salespeople are neither overly supervised nor chained to their desks. They also receive the satisfaction of seeing a direct correlation between their efforts and their achievements. The enthusiasm and positive attitude that characterize most successful salespeople tend to carry over into their personal lives.

5 *Identify the different types of selling tasks.*

## SELLING TASKS

The sales field affords many job opportunities, such as selling at the wholesale or retail level, telemarketing, selling a manufactured good, selling a service, or just strengthening sales of the good or service by performing a specific support function. In general, all sales positions can be classified into the three basic types of selling tasks: getting orders, taking orders, and supporting sales. However, one salesperson can, and very often does, perform all three tasks in the course of the selling job.

### Getting Orders

**order getter**
Someone who actively seeks buyers for a product.

An **order getter** is someone who actively seeks buyers for a product. An order getter's main task is to convert both prospective and present customers into buyers of the firm's products. To obtain sales, an order getter must aggressively seek prospects, inform them about the product, and then persuade them to buy it. For example, a salesperson for Hewlett-Packard would have to locate people who are interested in buying a computer system, justify buying a Hewlett-Packard system rather than perhaps an IBM or an Apple system, and then close the sale. To do these things, the order getter must thoroughly know the product, the competitive environment, the customer's potential use of the product, and the customer's specific needs.

An order getter can be either a member of a company's own sales force or an independent seller. Manufacturing firms often use manufacturers' representatives to sell to wholesalers, distributors, retailers, and sometimes consumers, as with Amway products and Avon cosmetics.

Telemarketers also serve as order getters. Many companies set up telemarketing operations as a full-fledged selling arm for dealing with designated customer or product segments. In several industries, telemarketers are even replacing field sales representatives.

### Taking Orders

Order takers do not have to go out and seek new buyers for their goods or services because, in most cases, buyers come to them or accounts are assigned to them. Order takers can be either inside order takers or field order takers.

**inside order taker**
Someone who takes orders from customers over the counter, on the sales floor, over the telephone, or by mail.

**Inside order takers** may take orders from customers over the counter, on the sales floor, over the telephone, or by mail. Examples include a cashier in a McDonald's restaurant, a sales clerk in a Macy's department store, and a salesperson for a retail mail-order catalog, such as Dell Computers or J. Crew.

**field order taker**
Someone who visits existing customers regularly, checks inventory, writes up new orders, and then delivers and stocks the product for the customers.

In contrast, **field order takers** focus on building repeat sales and accepting orders. These order takers visit their customers regularly, check inventory, write up new orders, and then deliver and stock the product for customers. They are normally found in the beer, food, and soft-drink industries. For example, Coca-Cola, Frito-Lay, and Miller Brewing Company all employ field order takers to service their retail customers.

### Supporting Sales

Sales support personnel don't actually sell goods or services. Instead, they promote products through goodwill and after-the-sale customer service. Two important types of support personnel are missionary sales representatives and technical specialists.

**missionary sales representative**
Someone who works for a manufacturer to stimulate goodwill within the channel of distribution and to support the company's sales efforts.

**Missionary sales representatives** work for manufacturers to stimulate goodwill within the channel of distribution and to support their company's sales efforts. A missionary sales rep may travel with a wholesaler's representative for a while to reinforce the promotional effort for the product. Sometimes a missionary sales rep works with the manufacturer's new sales personnel to help them learn the territory and the accounts. Missionary sales reps are common in consumer packaged-goods industries such as food and drug products. At the retail level, missionary sales reps may set up displays, check the stock and shelf space, and explain new product offerings to retailers. For industrial goods they usually are a communication link between the manufacturer and key accounts. They relay any problems that arise to the manufacturer. Then new products or product applications are passed forward to the customer.

**technical specialist**
Sales support person with a technical background who works out the details of custom-made products and communicates directly with the potential buyer's technical staff.

**Technical specialists** are salespeople with backgrounds in chemistry, engineering, physics, or a similar field. They work out the details of custom-made products and communicate directly with the potential buyer's technical staff. A sales representative may make an initial presentation to a purchasing committee and then let the technical specialist take over during the question-and-answer phase. If the buyer develops an interest in the seller's product, the specialist plays a larger role, planning the product specifications and installation procedures and overseeing the installation. After making the sale, the sales rep usually relies on feedback from the technical specialist about installation dates, debugging time, and similar information.

6 *List the steps in the selling process.*

## STEPS IN THE SELLING PROCESS

Although personal selling may sound like a relatively simple task, completing a sale actually requires several steps. Some sales take only a few minutes, but others may take months or years to complete. Whether a salesperson spends a few minutes or a few years on a sale, these are the seven basic steps:

1. Generating sales leads
2. Qualifying sales leads
3. Making the sales approach
4. Making the sales presentation
5. Handling objections
6. Closing the sale
7. Following up

Like other forms of promotion, these seven steps of selling follow the AIDA concept (see Chapter 15). Once a salesperson has located a prospect with the authority to buy, he or she tries to get *attention*. An effective presentation and demonstration should generate *interest*. After developing the customer's initial *desire* (preferably during the presentation or demonstration), the salesperson properly handles objections. This step should lower cognitive dissonance and increase desire (refer back to Chapter 4). The salesperson seeks *action* in the close by trying to get an agreement to buy. Follow-up after the sale, the final step in the selling process, not only lowers cognitive dissonance but also may open up opportunities to discuss future sales. Let's look at each step of the selling process individually.

## GENERATING SALES LEADS

**lead generation (prospecting)**
Identification of those firms and people most likely to buy the seller's offerings.

Initial groundwork must precede communication between the potential buyer and the seller. **Lead generation,** or **prospecting,** is the identification of those firms and people most likely to buy the seller's offerings. These firms or people become "sales leads" or "prospects." Naturally, not everyone is a prospect for a firm's good or service, nor are all prospects equally likely to buy. For example, a salesperson may have to make 125 phone calls to schedule 25 interviews. In turn, 5 presentations might result from these interviews, from which a single prospect becomes a buying customer.

Sales leads are secured in several different ways:

- *Advertising and other media* are the foremost ways of securing leads. For business-to-business markets, 30 to 35 percent of all leads are generated through advertising.[21] Advertisements are usually placed in trade publications or in some other highly targeted media vehicle, such as cable television. A coupon or a toll-free number is usually provided for the prospect who would like to request more information.
- Favorable *publicity* also helps to create leads.
- *Direct-mail and telemarketing programs* have become quite popular ways of generating sales leads. This type of lead generation usually starts with a list of potential clients with desirable characteristics, such as a particular occupation. For instance, if a medical equipment company is trying to sell a new piece of equipment used in heart surgery, it may start with a list of all cardiologists in the United States. With these sorts of programs, companies might send direct-mail letters or brochures, usually with a detachable coupon to be returned or an 800 number to be called for more information. Some companies employ telemarketing representatives, who use client lists to contact potential customers by telephone.

**cold calling**
Form of lead generation in which the salesperson approaches potential buyers without any prior knowledge of the prospects' needs or financial status.

**referral**
Recommendation to a salesperson from a customer or business associate.

**networking**
Process of finding out about potential clients from friends, business contacts, coworkers, acquaintances, and fellow members in professional and civic organizations.

- **Cold calling** is a form of lead generation in which the salesperson approaches potential buyers without any prior knowledge of the prospects' needs or financial status. Cold calling requires a lot of footwork. For example, the 700 salespeople who work for the long-distance telephone company Allnet average about forty cold calls a day.[22]
- Another way to gather a lead is through a **referral**—a recommendation from a customer or business associate. **Networking** is the related method of using friends, business contacts, coworkers, acquaintances, and fellow members in professional and civic organizations to find out about potential clients. For example, an insurance agent may rely heavily on networking with neighbors, members of her or his church, or members of community organizations to locate new prospects. Sales representatives selling noncompeting lines and company employees who are not in sales positions are also good sources of

leads. For example, a company might encourage employees to look for sales leads when they're not at work. Employees who secure the most leads in a given time frame may then be eligible for a prize.

- *Trade shows and conventions* are yet another good source of leads. Because these events are designed around the interests of a specific product or industry, most of the leads that are generated are very likely prospects.
- *Company records* of past client purchases are another excellent source of leads.

Sales managers especially value lead generation because it is the main source of new business. Often, however, sales reps don't spend enough of their time prospecting. And many leads requiring a face-to-face sales interview never receive a follow-up visit. Studies have revealed that over half of the prospects who respond to direct mail or advertisements are still in the market six months later for the product they first asked about.[23] Therefore, salespeople who follow up on all leads have a competitive advantage, which should result in increased sales.

### QUALIFYING SALES LEADS

**lead qualification**
Determination of a sales prospect's authority to buy and ability to pay for the good or service.

When a prospect shows interest in learning more about a product, the salesperson has the opportunity to follow up, or qualify, the lead. **Lead qualification** consists of determining whether the prospect has three things:[24]

- *A recognized need:* The most basic criterion for determining whether or not someone is a prospect for a product is a need that is not being satisfied. The salesperson should first consider prospects who are aware of a need but should not discount prospects who have not yet recognized that they have one. With a little more information about the product, they may decide they do have a need for it. Determining whether or not a prospect has a need for a product is not always an easy task. Preliminary interviews and questioning can often provide the salesperson with enough information to determine if there is a need. Some goods and services, however, are designed to meet intangible needs, such as prestige or status, which are hard to detect.
- *Buying power:* Buying power involves both authority to make the purchase decision and access to funds to pay for it. To avoid wasting time and money, the salesperson needs to identify the purchasing authority before making a presentation. An organization chart can provide valuable clues. Asking a switchboard operator or a secretary can also lead the salesperson in the right direction. If the salesperson is still uncertain, he or she can ask a simple, direct question to qualify a prospect—for example, "Can you sign the purchase order for this product?" In some cases, purchasing authority rests with a committee. The salesperson must then identify the most influential committee members. In other situations buying authority may rest with a regional or headquarters officer located in a distant city. Determining ability to pay is often easier. Information about a firm's credit standing can be obtained from Dun & Bradstreet credit ratings or other financial reporting services. For smaller concerns, a local credit bureau can provide the needed information. A salesperson should heed this advice: It is better to qualify ability to pay now than to be left with an unpaid invoice months later.
- *Receptivity and accessibility:* The prospect must be willing to see the salesperson and be accessible to the salesperson. Some prospects simply refuse to see salespeople. Others, because of their stature in their organization, will only see a salesperson or sales manager with similar stature.

Providing sales reps with prequalified leads has proved to be an effective tactic. Robot Research, a manufacturer of closed-circuit video surveillance equipment, sends leads acquired through trade shows and advertising to a telemarketing firm. Telemarketers then call the prospects, asking, "Are you the decision maker? Do you plan to purchase closed-circuit television equipment? Do you want a sales rep to call you?" A yes answer to all three questions classifies the lead as "hot and qualified." Over a third of the prequalified prospects end up buying a Robot product. The result has been increased sales and a more motivated sales force.[25]

## MAKING THE SALES APPROACH

The main goal of the sales approach is either to talk to the prospect or to secure an appointment for a future time. The sales approach should always include an interest-capturing statement so the prospect has a reason for continuing the conversation. For example, the salesperson might say, "Our new robot welding arm has cut production line labor costs up to 40 percent in some installations. More important, the incidence of defective welds drops virtually to zero." An effective approach results in a face-to-face meeting with a qualified prospect. Personally visiting unqualified prospects wastes valuable salesperson time and company resources.

One way to optimize salesperson time and resources is to create a customer profile during the approach. This profile is then used to help develop an intelligent analysis of the prospect's needs in preparation for the sales presentation. For example, one of the jobs of field representatives for SmithKline Beecham, a pharmaceuticals company, is to gather information about their prospects, such as who is the decision maker, who influences him or her, and who are the front-desk contact people. The reps also record important information about the laboratories they call on, such as the size and the type of equipment available. Even though profiling customers requires some extra effort, most of SmithKline Beecham's reps like having the information when the time comes to plan the next sales call or presentation.[26]

The three main ways to get an initial interview are a letter, an unsolicited personal visit, and a telephone call. A letter is usually the least effective technique for gaining an appointment, because it is easy to ignore or turn down. An unsolicited personal visit typically means being screened by a receptionist or secretary who acts as a gatekeeper. Unsolicited visits are also often mistimed. For example, a prospect may be out of the office or otherwise unavailable. Some prospects also resent salespeople who just "drop in." The unexpected salesperson may also have to make an impromptu presentation to a subordinate, who will then decide whether the salesperson should see the decision maker. A telephone call may therefore be the best option. The purpose of a telephone call is to arouse the prospect's interest and introduce the sales proposition without forcing a premature decision.

## MAKING THE SALES PRESENTATION

**sales presentation**
Face-to-face explanation of a product's benefits to a prospective buyer.

Once the salesperson has secured an appointment with a prospect, the next step is a **sales presentation**, a meeting to present the product's benefits to the prospect in person or perhaps through a videotape or videoconferencing. The sales presentation is the heart of the selling process, but it can be expensive. The cost of face-to-face selling for consumer goods was about $210 per sales call in 1992; for industrial goods it was about $227.[27] These figures include the salesperson's compensation, car and transportation costs, and entertainment costs.

Because the salesperson often has only one opportunity to make a case for the product, the quality of the sales presentation can make or break the sale. If the salesperson doesn't have a convincing and confident manner, then the prospect will very often forget the information. Prospects take in body language, voice patterns, dress, and

Videoconferencing is becoming more popular as a means for making sales presentations as the equipment becomes less expensive and more readily available. Videoconferencing is appropriate when a key decision maker cannot be present for the sales presentation.

© Tony Stone Images/Jon Riley

body type. In fact, they are more likely to remember how salespeople present themselves than what salespeople say.[28]

Several presentation techniques can enhance the salesperson's effectiveness. Allowing the prospect to touch or hold the product, using visual aids, and using words that relate important selling points of the product, such as *new, simple,* and *innovative,* can increase message retention and persuasiveness. Presentation experts also agree that beginning the presentation with an overview, being enthusiastic, repeating key ideas, and making eye contact are essential to presentation success.[29]

There are two basic approaches to making a presentation: stimulus-response and need-satisfaction. The second of these approaches has evolved into a third method called consultative selling.

## The Stimulus–Response Approach

**stimulus-response approach**
Sales pitch applying the concept that a given stimulus will produce a given response.

**prepared sales presentation**
Structured, or canned, sales pitch.

The **stimulus-response approach** recognizes that a given stimulus will produce a given response (see Chapter 4). When applied to a selling situation, this term means that the salesperson makes certain points (stimulus) about the good or service that ultimately lead to a sale (response).

A memorized or **prepared sales presentation** lends itself to the stimulus-response approach. Many telephone sales pitches follow this structured or "canned" format. Advantages of the canned approach are that it ensures that the salesperson will tell a complete, accurate story about the product; ensures that sales points will be arranged in a logical, systematic order; and addresses most or all potential objections.

However, the canned approach also has its drawbacks. Perhaps the biggest disadvantage is that it does not allow the salesperson to adapt the presentation to the prospect. Therefore, the salesperson and presentation may seem artificial and mechanical. The canned approach is rather inflexible and discourages the prospect's participation. A salesperson may even have trouble "resuming the pitch" if interrupted by the prospect.

## The Need-Satisfaction Approach

**need-satisfaction approach**
Sales pitch that focuses on satisfying a prospective buyer's particular needs.

In contrast, the **need-satisfaction approach** recognizes that people buy products to satisfy needs and solve problems. A salesperson employing this approach uses the

The salespeople at this Hewlett-Packard outlet have shifted from a product orientation to a need-satisfaction approach, which is more customer-oriented.

Courtesy Hewlett-Packard Company

prospect's particular needs as a springboard for the sales presentation. The salesperson begins by securing the prospect's agreement that a need exists and then offers a solution to satisfy the need. Altering the presentation to suit each prospect in response to the specific sales situation is called **adaptive selling.**[30] This approach is most often used when the salesperson has a complex product line and is selling to a sophisticated audience.

**adaptive selling**
Sales technique using a pitch adapted for each prospect in response to the specific sales situation.

The advantage of the need-satisfaction approach is its strong marketing orientation. It is designed to meet the needs of the marketplace. Because of its marketing orientation, the need-satisfaction approach stresses product benefits, not the physical aspects of the product. For example, people do not buy cars because the cars have nice features and look good. People buy cars to get to work safely, to travel in comfort, to impress others, or to express their good taste. Customers won't buy unless they realize they are receiving value from owning the product.[31]

The need-satisfaction approach has two disadvantages. First, need development can be a long, drawn-out process. Second, the need-satisfaction approach requires a more sophisticated salesperson than someone making a canned presentation. The individual must be able to ask penetrating questions and to integrate the answers into an effective sales presentation that explains how the product satisfies the customer's needs.

## Consultative Selling

**consultative selling**
Sales practice of developing long-term relationships with customers and providing them with information that will help them solve their problems and achieve their short-term and long-term goals.

Many companies are expanding the boundaries of the need-satisfaction approach to emphasize long-term relationships between salespeople and clients. This practice is an outgrowth of relationship marketing, which was discussed in Chapter 5. Relationship selling, or **consultative selling,** is the practice of providing information in the sales situation that will help customers achieve their short- and long-term goals. Consultative salespeople, therefore, become consultants, partners, and problem solvers for their customers. They strive to build long-term relationships with key accounts by developing trust over time.

Consultative selling requires salespeople to learn new skills, particularly in the area of understanding the product, customer needs, the competition, and the industry.[32] The salesperson must be able to determine a client's needs or problems, present all possible solutions, and then recommend the solution that is in the best interests of the customer. Consultative selling therefore requires much more time and considerably more skill than other approaches do. By building a personal and professional relationship with the client, the salesperson becomes more of a partner or a consultant than just another salesperson peddling some good or service.

Consultative selling is very important in Japan, where long-term relationships between seller and customer are the norm. The Japanese traditionally do business only with those they know and trust. Toyota, for example, has more than 100,000 salespeople selling cars, primarily door to door. These salespeople maintain constant contact with customers. A sale typically requires a series of face-to-face meetings. Toyota salespeople call after a purchase to inquire how the car is running and send handwritten greeting cards and special invitations for low-cost oil changes and dealer events. Clients usually purchase cars from the same salesperson many times over many years.[33]

### HANDLING OBJECTIONS

Rarely does a prospect say "I'll buy it" right after a presentation. Often there are objections or perhaps questions about the presentation and the product. For instance, the potential buyer may complain that the price is too high, that he or she does not have enough information for making a decision, or that the good or service will not satisfy present needs. The buyer may also lack confidence in the seller's organization or product. Anticipating specific objections, such as concerns about price, is the best way to prepare for them.

One of the first lessons that every salesperson learns is that objections to the product should not be taken personally, as confrontations or insults. Rather, a salesperson should view objections as requests for information. A good salesperson handles objections calmly and considers them a legitimate part of the purchase decision. Suppose a prospect interrupts early in a presentation and says, "I doubt if your equipment is compatible with our existing equipment." The salesperson might reply, "That's certainly a valid concern, Ms. Jones. I think you'll see as we go along that we've anticipated that possibility and provided compatibility." The salesperson first agrees with the prospect and then goes on to refute the objection. A more direct technique is to meet the prospect's statement head-on and deny it. Some prospects appreciate this straightforward approach.

### CLOSING THE SALE

At the end of the presentation, if the prospect's objections have been met, the salesperson can try to close the sale. Closing requires courage and skill. Naturally, the salesperson wants to avoid rejection, and asking for a sale carries with it the risk of a negative answer. A salesperson should keep an open mind when asking for the sale and be prepared for either a yes or a no. Rarely is a sale closed on the first call. In fact, a salesperson averages about four sales contacts before a sale can be made.[34] Some salespeople may negotiate with large accounts for several years before closing a sale. As you can see, building a good relationship with the customer is very important.

Customers often give signals during the presentation that they are ready to buy or are not interested. Examples include changes in facial expressions, gestures, and questions asked. The salesperson should look for these signals and respond appropriately.

Whenever the customer makes a commitment to buy, order processing should begin. However, if the commitment to buy is not forthcoming, a number of techniques can be used to try to close the sale. Ideally, the salesperson should be able to ask directly for the order. However, other types of closes may be more appropriate:

- One popular approach is the **assumptive close.** The salesperson assumes that the prospect is going to buy and says something like "Which do you want delivered, product A or product B?" or "When do you want the merchandise shipped?"
- The **summative close** summarizes the product's benefits and asks for the sale.
- Sometimes a salesperson will withhold a special concession until the end of the selling process and use it in closing the sale; this strategy is usually called **negotiation,** or the **extra inducement close.** Examples include a price cut, free installation, free service, and a trial order.
- In today's economy, salespeople can use the **urgency close** in many industries. They may say, "Prices will be going up in six weeks" or "We don't anticipate being able to deliver new models for six months because of parts shortages, but we have three of this year's model left."
- A related closing technique, called the **standing-room-only close,** urges customers to buy right away because the product is selling so well that it may not be available later.
- In the **silent close,** the salesperson says nothing at the end of the presentation and waits for the prospect to make a response.

Although some of these closing methods may sound like marketing tricks, successful salespeople avoid using deception and pressure in closing a sale. Instead, they recognize the importance of building trust and a long-term relationship with the customer.

More and more U.S. companies are expanding their marketing and selling efforts into global markets. Salespeople selling in foreign markets should tailor their closing style to each market. For instance, in German-speaking countries—such as Germany, Austria, and parts of Switzerland—salespeople should expect a sober, rigid business climate and negotiations that lack flexibility and compromise. Negotiations with Central and South American customers typically include a great deal of bargaining. Personal relationships are also important in Central and South America, so salespeople should make face-to-face contact with their clients. In China as well, great importance is attached to the personal relationship. Friendship means a lot, and small courtesies and follow-up presents are essential.[35]

**assumptive close**
Technique of ending a sales presentation by assuming the prospect is going to buy.

**summative close**
Technique of ending a sales presentation by summarizing the product's benefits and asking for the sale.

**negotiation (extra inducement) close**
Technique of withholding a special concession until the end of the selling process and using it to close a sale.

**urgency close**
Technique of ending a sales presentation by suggesting a reason for ordering soon, such as an impending price increase.

**standing-room-only close**
Technique of ending a sales presentation by urging customers to buy right away because the product is selling so well that it may not be available later.

**silent close**
Technique of ending a sales presentation by saying nothing and waiting for the prospect to make a response.

## FOLLOWING UP

Unfortunately, many salespeople hold the attitude that making the sale is all that's important. Once the sale is made, they can forget about their customers. They are wrong. Salespeople's responsibilities do not end with making the sales and placing the orders. One of the most important aspects of their jobs is **follow-up.** They must ensure that delivery schedules are met, that the goods or services perform as promised, and that the buyers' employees are properly trained to use the products.

**follow-up**
Final step of the selling process, in which the salesperson ensures that delivery schedules are met, that the goods or services perform as promised, and that the buyers' employees are properly trained to use the products.

A basic goal of any company or professional sales department is to motivate customers to come back, again and again. Most businesses depend on repeat sales, and repeat sales depend on thorough follow-up. Finding a new customer is far more expensive than retaining an existing customer. When customers feel abandoned, cognitive dissonance arises and repeat sales decline. Today this issue is more pertinent than ever, because customers are far less loyal to brands and vendors. Buyers are more inclined to look for the best deal, especially in the case of poor after-the-sale follow-up. More and more companies favor building a relationship with vendors.

*7 Describe the functions of sales management.*

## SALES MANAGEMENT

There is an old adage in business that nothing happens until a sale is made. Without sales there is no need for accountants, production workers, or even a company president. Sales provide the fuel that keeps the corporate engines humming. Companies like West Point Pepperel, Dow Corning, Alcoa, and several thousand other industrial manufacturers would cease to exist without successful salespeople or manufacturers' representatives. Even companies like Procter & Gamble and Kraft General Foods that mainly sell consumer goods and use extensive advertising campaigns still rely on salespeople to move products through the channel of distribution. Thus sales management is one of marketing's most critical specialties. Effective sales management stems from a highly success-oriented sales force that accomplishes its mission economically and efficiently. Poor sales management can lead to unmet profit objectives or even to the downfall of the corporation.

Just as selling is a personal relationship, so is sales management. Although the sales manager's basic job is to maximize sales at a reasonable cost while also maximizing profits, he or she also has many other important responsibilities and decisions. The tasks of sales management are to

1. Set sales objectives
2. Structure the sales force
3. Determine the size of the sales force
4. Develop the compensation plan
5. Recruit the sales force
6. Train the sales force
7. Motivate the sales force
8. Manage sales force turnover
9. Evaluate the sales force

Let's look at each of these tasks.

### SETTING SALES OBJECTIVES

Effective sales management begins with communication of sales goals. Like any marketing objective, sales objectives should be stated in clear, precise, and measurable terms and should always specify a time frame for their fulfillment. Overall sales force objectives are usually stated in terms of desired dollar sales volume, market share, or profit level. For example, a life insurance company may have an objective to sell $50 million in life insurance policies annually (or 1,000 policies), to attain a 12 percent market share, or to achieve $1 million in profits.

**quota**
Statement of the individual salesperson's sales objectives, usually based on sales volume alone but sometimes including key accounts (those with greatest potential), new accounts, and specific products.

Individual salespeople are also assigned objectives in the form of quotas. A **quota** is simply a statement of the salesperson's sales objectives, usually based on sales volume alone but sometimes including key accounts (those with greatest potential), new accounts, and specific products. In addition, quotas can be based on activity or on financial objectives. For example, a sales representative for a cellular phone company may have the sales quota of selling $1,000 worth of equipment or five new cellular systems per week. He or she may also have the objective of completing a certain number of sales calls per week. Many firms are placing more emphasis on financial objectives that require the salespeople to take into account the profit contribution of the products they sell. Those products yielding higher profits for the company will thus receive more attention.

## STRUCTURING THE SALES FORCE

Because personal selling is so costly, no sales department can afford to be disorganized. Therefore, structuring the sales department or sales force is essential. Structure helps the sales manager organize and delegate sales duties and provide direction for salespeople.

Sales departments have traditionally been organized into the four types described and diagramed below. Often firms combine these types.[36]

**sales territory** Particular geographic area assigned to a salesperson.

- *Geographic organization:* A common method for organizing the sales force is assigning a salesperson to a particular geographic area called a **sales territory**—for instance, a region, state, city, or other trading area. A firm like a consumer product organization with a small number of closely related, nontechnical products might use this method. Geographically structured sales departments are most appropriate when customers are widely dispersed or when there are large regional differences in customer buying behavior. For example, sales of snow tires in southern states would not warrant the creation of separate sales territories, but they would in northern states.

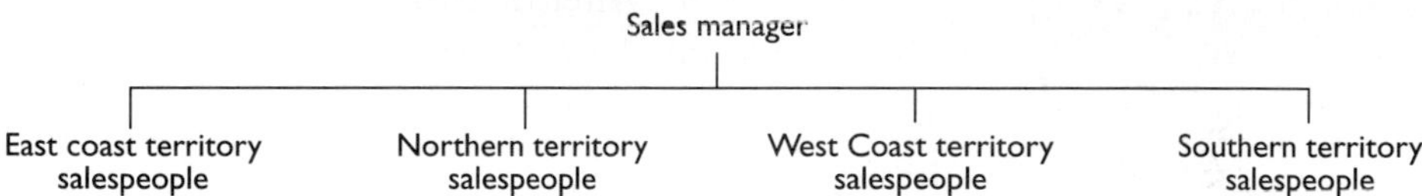


- *Product organization:* Another common method is structuring the sales organization by the product that the salesperson sells. For example, large consumer product companies may structure a sales force around brands. Structuring the sales force in this manner is most appropriate when products are complex, the differences between them are great, and the products or product groups are important enough to justify special attention. A sales force organized by product has greater knowledge of and expertise in specific product categories. Office equipment specialists are a good example of this structuring method.

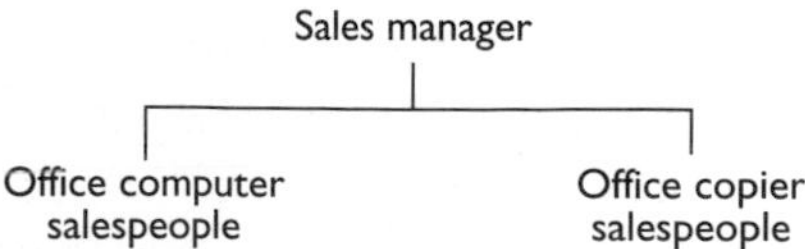


- *Functional organization:* The sales department organized by function focuses on needed sales activities, such as account development or account maintenance. This structure offers specialization and efficiency in performing selling activities and is best for companies selling only a few or very similar products to relatively few target markets. Because it requires more labor, this form of

One popular way to deploy a sales force is by geography, giving each sales representative a specific territory to cover. This structure works best when customers are widely dispersed or when their buying behavior varies from one place to another.

© 1993 Jose Pelaez/The Stock Market

organization is hard for very small firms to maintain. However, it can work well in medium-size to large firms. These firms can afford the luxury of having their salespeople perform only one task or a small number of tasks. For example, many paper makers employ representatives who work solely on selling to major clients. After the negotiations have been completed, service salespeople step in to take care of clients' postsale needs.

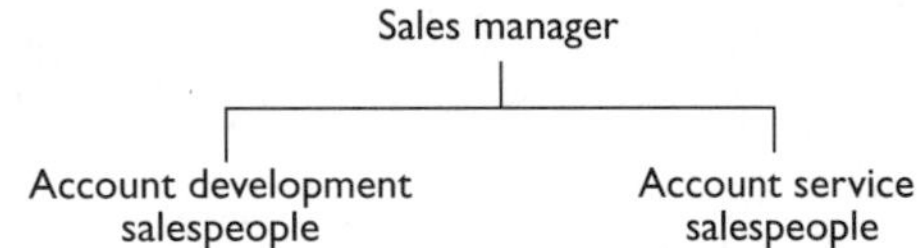


- *Market organization:* In this approach, the sales force is divided by customer groups, or target markets, and each salesperson calls on only one group. A market orientation is most appropriate when customer needs and product purchases vary considerably from one target group to another. This method is also used when there is a great need to identify and solve different customer problems. For example, Boeing, the aircraft manufacturer, uses a market organization for its commercial and government markets. Boeing realizes that the two markets have different needs and problems.

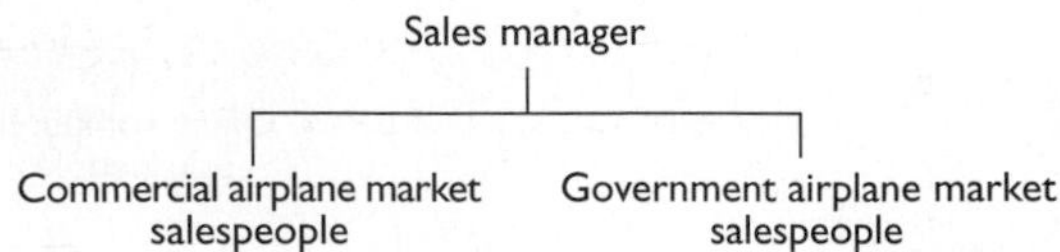

Many companies have been taking the market-oriented structure one step further, to an individual client or account level. This trend has occurred in conjunction with the increased emphasis on consultative selling. The organization typically assigns one salesperson or a team of salespeople to a client to provide better customer service.

For example, IBM restructured so its account reps were assigned to industry-specific groups that work in conjunction with the company's geographically aligned product marketing specialists. Previously, IBM's entire sales force was arranged geographically. IBM's 30,000 salespeople worldwide are now divided into fourteen industry segments: communications, cross industry, distribution, education, finance, government, health, insurance, manufacturing, process, petroleum, travel, transportation, and utilities.[37] By reorganizing the sales force around customers, many companies hope to improve customer service, encourage collaboration with other arms of the company, and unite salespeople into customer-focused teams.

**selling team**
Combination of sales and nonsales people, under the direction of a leader, whose primary objective is to establish and maintain a strong relationship with a particular customer or customers.

As goods and services become more technologically complex, and as buyers come to expect increased levels of service, many sales managers are using the concept of team selling to structure their sales force. A **selling team** can be described as a combination of sales and nonsales people, under the direction of a leader, whose primary objective is to establish and maintain strong customer relationships. A team approach is most profitable when a prospect represents 10 percent or more of a company's total sales and when a prospect that represents a small part of a company's total sales is actually large enough to buy more. Thus most large customers are candidates for a selling team. Xerox, for example, uses a team approach for dealing with AT&T, one of its biggest customers. The sales team consists of over 200 salespeople, most at the district level. In addition, experts from other divisions—such as finance, administration, and service specialists—are also members of the team.[38]

## DETERMINING SALES FORCE SIZE

The ideal size of the sales force can be arrived at using several methods. Two of the most common are the workload approach and the incremental productivity approach. Sales managers rarely rely on one method to determine sales force size. Instead, they combine their own opinions on other issues—such as economic factors, industry trends, growth of the market, and the needs of customers—with these formula methods to come up with the optimal size.

### The Workload Approach

**workload approach**
Method of determining the optimal sales force size, in which the total time required to cover the territory is divided by the selling time available to one salesperson

The **workload approach** divides the total time required to cover the territory by the selling time provided by each salesperson. Here is the formula for using the workload approach:

$$\text{Number of salespeople} = \frac{\text{Ideal number of customers} \times \text{Frequency of calls} \times \text{Length of calls}}{\text{Selling time available from one salesperson}}$$

For example, assume that the ideal number of customers for a firm is 4,000 (3,000 current customers and an estimated 1,000 potential customers). Sales analysis has revealed that each customer should be seen seven times a year and that sales calls average 1.5 hours. Further examination of records has revealed that each salesperson has 2,000 hours of selling time available per year. The computation for this problem is

$$\text{Number of salespeople} = \frac{(3{,}000 + 1{,}000) \times 7 \times 1.5}{2{,}000} = \frac{42{,}000}{2{,}000} = 21$$

If the company now has eighteen people in its sales force, three new people should be hired.

The major advantage of the workload approach is its simplicity. Successful application of the technique depends on the sales manager's ability to estimate the ideal frequency of calls and the number of potential customers. However, the workload approach fails to consider either the cost of increasing the work force or the costs and profits associated with each sales call.

### The Incremental Productivity Approach

**incremental productivity approach**
Method of determining the optimal sales force size, in which salespeople are added as long as the total sales increase is greater than the increase in selling cost.

A second method of determining the optimal size of the sales force is by determining incremental productivity.[39] According to the **incremental productivity approach,** a manager should increase the number of salespeople as long as the additional sales increase is greater than the additional increase in selling cost. Companies with good records know the cost of training a salesperson. This cost, plus field expenses and the salary of a new person, can be compared with the revenue generated by sales activities. Unfortunately, many companies do not have these cost data available.

## DEVELOPING THE COMPENSATION PLAN

Compensation planning is one of the sales manager's toughest jobs. Only good planning will ensure that compensation attracts, motivates, and retains good salespeople. Generally, companies and industries with lower levels of compensation suffer higher turnover rates, which increases costs and decreases effectiveness. Therefore, compensation needs to be competitive enough to attract and motivate the best salespeople. Many firms also take profit into account when developing their compensation plans. Instead of paying salespeople on overall volume, they pay according to the profitability achieved from selling each product. Other firms tie compensation to their quarterly, yearly, or long-range sales and marketing plan. With this method, the firm can easily encourage its salespeople to carry out the company's overall objectives, because it has created a compensation program that balances the interests of the company and those of the sales force.[40]

The three basic compensation methods for salespeople are commission, salary, and combination plans.

### Straight Commission System

**straight commission**
Method of compensation in which the salesperson is paid some percentage of sales.

A typical commission plan gives salespeople a specified percentage of their sales revenue. Firms with limited resources and firms selling high-priced items typically use commission plans for at least part of the compensation package. However, if the plan is a **straight commission** system, the salesperson receives no compensation at all until a sale is made.

A straight commission plan has several disadvantages. Salespeople usually must also pay their expenses from the commission. Moreover, management lacks control over the sales representatives, because they are not paid a salary. In addition, salespeople under this compensation plan normally have little loyalty to the company, and turnover is fairly high if business conditions are slow. Also, commissioned salespeople are reluctant to perform nonselling activities that do not generate commissions.

Nevertheless, to boost sales and upgrade service, many major retail chains have converted the compensation plan in some of their sales departments from hourly wage to straight commission. Commission plans have always existed in department stores but have generally been reserved for high-ticket items, where the extra selling efforts that commissions encourage will pay off. Examples include furniture, electronics, and men's suits. Now some department stores are applying the plan to all departments, from linens to lingerie.

One way to ensure that the sales force is working to forge long-term partnerships with clients is to offer bonuses tied to customer satisfaction rankings as well as to sales and profits. IBM, for example, expects each salesperson to keep up to date on developments at clients' sites.



### Straight Salary System

As its name suggests, a **straight salary** system compensates salespeople with a stated salary regardless of their productivity. Filling out information reports, servicing accounts, calling on smaller customers, and performing other nonselling tasks are very undesirable to the commission salesperson. Yet the salaried salesperson can tolerate these tasks. The straight salary plan works effectively when a territory requires an extensive amount of prospecting. In addition, in firms that use a team approach or that rely on missionary sales representatives, it may be hard to tell who really closed a sale. A salary system tends to work better than a commission system in these cases.

Straight salary plans do have disadvantages. Although they offer maximum control, they may give salespeople little incentive to produce new sales.

### Combination Systems

To achieve the best of both worlds, many companies have turned to a combination system, which offers a salesperson a base salary plus an incentive—usually a commission or a bonus. (Bonuses are often paid as a percentage of salary.) Combination systems have benefits for both the sales manager and the salesperson. The salary portion of the plan helps the manager control the sales force; the incentive provides motivation. For the salesperson, a combination plan offers an incentive to excel while minimizing the extremely wide swings in earnings that may occur when the economy surges or contracts too much.[41]

**straight salary**
Method of compensation in which the salesperson receives a salary regardless of sales productivity.

Some companies are developing creative combination plans. IBM, for example, ties sales bonuses to customer satisfaction (40 percent of the bonus) and the profitability of each sales transaction (60 percent). Local IBM managers survey customers frequently to measure satisfaction. They ask customers not just how happy they are with what they bought but also if the IBM salesperson is keeping up to date on what's going on at each customer's site. To help salespeople determine profit when negotiating a deal, IBM developed special computer software that takes into account such indirect costs as client development. It gives each salesperson a complete profit picture at the point of sale. IBM's bonus plan makes up about half of the average salesperson's compensation and up to 80 percent of total compensation for the top salespeople.[42]

## RECRUITING THE SALES FORCE

Sales management also has the task of recruiting and hiring the best salespeople to sell the firm's products. Sales force recruitment should be based on an accurate, detailed description of the sales task as defined by the company. Sales management should then develop the job description to match the sales force objectives. From the job description, sales management should build a profile of the ideal candidate for the job. Some of the things managers should consider in their sales candidate profile include level of education, employment background and level of experience, stability of employment history, ability to work unsupervised and to travel, knowledge of sales techniques and previous sales training, level of oral and written communication skills and organization skills, and previous compensation.[43]

After sales force recruiters get applications from candidates, they screen them to find the best applicants, using the profile provided by sales management. The chosen applicants are invited to a personal interview in which they may undergo some sort of testing. After initial interviews, the pool of applicants is further pared down for second and even third interviews. Finally, an applicant is chosen for the open position.

## Qualities of a Good Salesperson

What traits should sales recruiters look for in applicants? What traits help ensure that a recruit will become an effective salesperson? The most important quality of top performers is that they are driven by their own goals. That is, they usually set personal goals higher than those management sets for them. Moreover, they are achievement-oriented, talk about their sales accomplishments, and are self-confident. Effective salespeople are also self-competitive; they keep close tabs on their own performance and compare it with their previous performance. They are optimistic, highly knowledgeable about the product, and assertive. They know how to listen to customers and are team players who support their coworkers. They are self-trainers who are continually engaged in upgrading their selling skills.

The way sales candidates close the employment interview suggests how they will close a sale. Do they ask the recruiter how and when they are to follow up for the position or what the next step will be? Effective salespeople always plan the next step before they leave the client's office.

Read the Global Perspectives article to see what qualities U.S. companies are looking for in sales representatives in the Czech Republic.

GLOBAL PERSPECTIVES

### From Socialist to Sales Rep

Caliper Corporation, a U.S. psychological testing and human resources consulting firm, has a seemingly routine assignment: Assess the potential of job candidates who want to sell for U.S. companies. What is different about this assignment, however, is that these U.S. companies are located in the Czech Republic, and the candidates are Czech citizens who grew up in a socialist economy.

The Czech economy is booming, and many U.S. companies with facilities in the country—including Warner Lambert, Kmart, and Amway—are hiring for sales positions. The problem is that the local work force, indeed most of the country's 10 million people, are steeped in the traditions of socialism. Candidates have no track record of selling, servicing, and supervising in a free-market economy.

Caliper tries to find the right people to fill sales jobs for its clients in much the same way it does in the United States: with a sales aptitude test. Translated almost verbatim from the exam given to American candidates, the test looks for such qualities as ego drive, empathy, growth, and leadership. Caliper seeks those who are motivated enough to get a yes out of a sales prospect. Caliper also wants to know what will happen when the person gets rejected by a prospect. Does he or she take a three-day holiday, go on a drinking binge, or bounce right back?

Caliper launched its Eastern European recruiting business in part because of the similarities between Czech and Western culture and the country's pro-American attitude. Despite these positive factors, U.S. companies intent on hiring local talent must be prepared to dispel recruits' long-held socialist beliefs. These companies must also be seriously committed to training a sales force in a country that graduated its first MBA in 1991. Most Czechs are well educated, especially in technical fields, but few candidates know how to sell.[44]

What specific personality traits do you feel Caliper should look for in a candidate? What special training do you think would benefit newly hired Czech salespeople?

## Sources of Candidates

Recruits may come to the company's attention through a number of sources: colleges and universities, other salespeople, trade journal and newspaper ads, employment agencies, and even competitors. Other sources include professional associations, women's groups, customers, employees and former employees, and executive recruiters. Sometimes companies find that their nonselling employees are attracted to sales. To determine the best source of candidates, a company can have its interviewers determine how each candidate learned about the job opening.

Many companies offer selling internships for college students interested in their industry. Northwestern Mutual Life recruits many of its agents from college campuses, where students can participate in the company's unique intern program. At cooperating colleges, 450 selected students undergo regular agent training and then represent Northwestern on their campus. The program introduces students to the industry and gives them a way to learn whether they would enjoy selling life insurance. Ultimately, Northwestern hires an average of one out of three of its interns to full-time sales positions. The college intern program has been a great success for Northwestern. Among its leading agents nationwide, a high percentage began as college agents.[45]

## Candidate Screening

Several tools are used to screen sales candidates. Initial screening takes place when sales recruiters review the candidates' resumes. Recruiters evaluate the job applicants' qualifications, particularly their educational background and previous sales experience. The best candidates are those with some background in the company's field. For example, a pharmaceutical giant like Eli Lilly might prefer candidates with science or health care backgrounds. Likewise, a computer software manufacturer like Lotus may choose candidates with business degrees or with computer experience.

After sifting through the resumes, recruiters choose the best candidates to interview. The personal interview is the most costly screening tool for selecting new salespeople, but it is also by far the most helpful. The sales manager may use role-playing in the interviewing process to see how well the recruit would react in a variety of selling situations. Role-playing tests the candidates' knowledge of real sales situations and demonstrates their communication skills under pressure. Candidates are then compared on the answers to questions like these: How did the candidate handle interview pressures? Were the questions asked by the applicant well conceived and well stated? Does the candidate have a planned career pattern? Does the candidate have realistic goals and expectations? Can the candidate interact at multiple levels with business associates? Does the candidate show signs of being a good self-manager? Is this a major move forward for the candidate in job scope and responsibility?[46]

## Sales Force Diversity

In pursuit of diversity in the work force, many companies are affirming their commitment to minority recruitment and training—and sales staffs are frequently the first area targeted for action. Prudential Insurance is one company with a corporate diversity initiative in place. An assessment conducted several years earlier had suggested to Prudential that minorities and women felt their opportunities within the company were limited. At the same time, market research led the company to believe that its lack of diversity meant that it was not well positioned to penetrate important cultural markets nor to attract the best and brightest new sales agents. As a result, Prudential developed programs to attract and cultivate minority and female employees.[47]

Minorities, however, continue to be underrepresented in sales (see Exhibit 17.3 on page 600). Although the percentages of minorities employed in all sales-related jobs have increased over the past decade, minorities are concentrated in the low-pay sector, among retail and personal services sales workers. Women, however, continue

*Exhibit 17.3*

U.S. Sales Force Statistics

Source: Adapted from U.S. Department of Commerce, Bureau of the Census, *1990 Census of Population Supplementary Reports: Detailed Occupation and Other Characteristics from the EEO File for the U.S.,* 1990 CP-S-1-1 (Washington, DC: Government Printing Office, 1990).

| | Number of salespeople (in millions) | Percent of total | Growth in number since 1980 |
|---|---|---|---|
| Male | 7.3 | 50.8% | 39.4% |
| Female | 7.1 | 49.2 | 42.1 |
| White | 12.1 | 83.5% | 28.1% |
| Black | 1.1 | 7.0 | 89.1 |
| Hispanic | 0.9 | 6.1 | 110.5 |
| Asian | 0.4 | 2.8 | 190.5 |
| All sales occupations | 14.4 | 100.0% | 40.7% |

to move out of low-paying sales jobs into higher-scale ones. For example, the number of women in the low-paying retail and personal services category rose only about 20 percent, but the number in the top-paying category of sales reps soared over 80 percent.[48]

The opportunities in sales for relatively high salaries and independence, combined with the increase in single-parent families, are prompting more women than ever to pursue professional sales careers. Women now make up about half the nation's sales force, with the highest percentages working in amusement and recreation services, apparel and textiles, printing and publishing, and communications. Women are making special strides selling high-tech industrial equipment, a traditionally male-dominated field. On the whole, women perform very well in industrial sales. Successful saleswomen have a high energy level and are perceptive and effective communicators. They also seem to be more solution-oriented than many salesmen, avoiding an aggressive attitude. Another study found few differences between male and female salespeople in job-related attitudes and performance levels.[49]

## TRAINING THE SALES FORCE

After the sales recruit has been hired and given a brief orientation, training begins. A new salesperson generally receives instruction in five major areas: company policies and practices, selling techniques, product knowledge, industry and customer characteristics, and nonselling duties, such as filling out market information reports. A good training program boosts confidence, improves morale, increases sales, and builds better customer relations. Classroom instruction may last several days for company policies and several weeks or months for actual sales techniques. Trainees are taught everything from how to prospect to how to service the account after the sale.

**time management**
Efficient allocation of time to tasks, based on their priority and urgency.

A key lesson for many sales trainees is how to manage their time wisely. **Time management** is the task of efficiently allocating blocks of time to certain tasks in the selling process. The salespeople who know how to manage their time are most effective at covering their territories, tending to customer needs, seeing new prospects, generating leads, and steadily increasing both sales and profits. Exhibit 17.4 breaks down salespeople's time by function. Unfortunately, salespeople cannot distribute their time evenly among all accounts, although exceptional salespeople will make each customer feel like a preferred customer by giving sincere, personalized treatment.

Firms that sell complex products generally offer the most extensive training programs. New salespeople in Kodak's Health Science Division, which sells medical imaging equipment, receive a minimum six-month-long formal education. Trainees

Exhibit 17.4

How Salespeople Spend Their Time

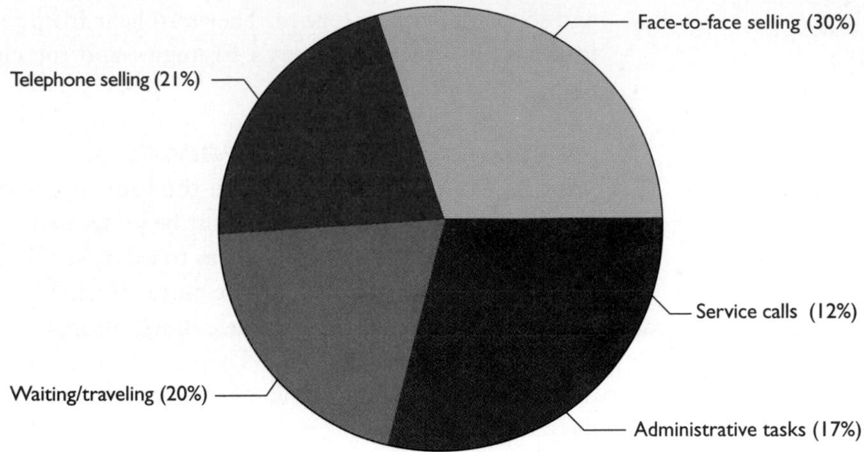


first come to Kodak's Marketing Education Center for six weeks of academics, where they learn Kodak's philosophy and basic selling skills. Then they are sent into the field with a mentor for a week. Because many of the new salespeople have no background in health care, exposure to the hospital environment is absolutely vital. Trainees then come back to the center for four weeks of intensive technical training and lessons in business and selling skills. After this, trainees are sent back into the field for eight weeks to put their new knowledge and skills to use. Once trainees graduate, they spend an additional six months in the field selling with their mentors. At the end of that six months, almost a full year after beginning the training program, the salesperson receives a territory.[50]

Sales training is more customer-, service-, and quality-oriented than ever before. In pursuit of solid company-client partnerships, training programs now seek to improve salespeople's listening skills and to broaden their product and customer knowledge. In addition, training programs stress the interpersonal skills needed to become the contact person for customers. Because negotiation is increasingly important in closing a sale, salespeople are also trained to negotiate effectively without risking profits. Finally, many companies are teaching basic selling techniques to employees who do not sell but who are part of the selling process—for example, engineers and customer-service personnel. Exposing these employees to the selling basics gives them a better understanding of how they can support the sales staff.[51]

Many successful companies have learned that training is not just for newly hired salespeople. Norton, a manufacturer of industrial abrasives, annually brings in roughly a third of its more than 200 salespeople for follow-up training sessions on negotiating skills, product knowledge, and other relevant sales topics. Hershey Chocolate USA provides continuing education for its sales force in the form of a library containing a number of videotapes and books on personal selling. Hershey salespeople are encouraged to use these resources any time.[52]

Training is becoming increasingly important to companies that manage sales forces in foreign countries. FedEx's sheer size and international reach, for example, dictate that it make training a top priority at strategic locations around the globe. All of the company's approximately 2,000 salespeople must be prepared to provide international transportation expertise to a variety of customers. Recruits in Asia and Europe, where the FedEx name is not so well known as it is here, are brought to Memphis headquarters to give them a better understanding of the company. New salespeople are able to see how the superhub works and to get a sense of the size and scope of FedEx's service. They also hear from the company's founder, who talks to them about the company's strategies and the challenges of the global marketplace.[53]

### MOTIVATING THE SALES FORCE

Training equips salespeople with the tools they need for selling. Once they have acquired these sales skills, they must be motivated to use them. Sales managers often use motivational tools or incentives to increase the sales of new products or of high-margin products that may require more effort. Motivational tools also help increase overall sales volume, add new accounts, improve morale and goodwill, move slow items, and bolster slow sales. They can be used to achieve long-term or short-term objectives, such as unloading overstocked inventory and meeting a monthly or quarterly sales goal. Pay increases, promotions, improved working conditions, greater security, recognition, and opportunities for personal growth all help motivate salespeople.

Salespeople's performance often depends on their expectations of the results of their sales efforts. Salespeople who believe that they are realizing their own potential and doing something worthwhile are not only high performers in the present. They are also more likely to perform well in the future.

Two of the most important factors for building salesperson satisfaction and increasing selling motivation are sales quotas and sales incentives. Sales quotas provide a basis for sales planning and can be used as motivators. But setting quotas at the right level is crucial. Motivation may decline if a quota is too easy to reach. In fact, an easy quota is less likely to be attained than a more difficult one. On the other hand, motivation can also decline if a quota is set so high that the salespeople see little hope of ever meeting it. Sales managers should set product or sales quotas at challenging levels and attach significance to the quotas. If the sales force doesn't perceive attaining quotas as important, motivation will suffer.

Sales incentives include various types of rewards, such as recognition at ceremonies, plaques, vacations, merchandise, and pay raises or bonuses. In one survey, salespeople ranked monetary rewards, such as raises, as the incentives that are most important to them. Fittingly, over half of all companies give cash as an employee award.[54] For example, a company might reward its salespeople with a $5 bonus for each order they write, with $1,000 going to the salesperson who generates the most volume.

Sales management should carefully plan the sales incentive program to make sure it will be profitable for the company as well as motivational for the sales force. There is nothing worse than realizing, after the incentive program is in full force, that it is either too generous or not generous enough. The incentive program should also be simple. Poorly planned incentive programs can end up not motivating the sales force at all.

### MANAGING SALES FORCE TURNOVER

Sales force turnover costs the average company nearly a quarter of a million dollars each year. Not only does the company directly lose sales because of the salesperson's leaving, but it also will have to invest time and money in recruiting and training a new employee. Unfortunately, turnover is becoming one of the sales manager's biggest problems.

Salespeople often leave their jobs because of a lack of management support. Many salespeople are also lured to other jobs that promise to pay them more money.

The highest sales force turnover rates occur in companies selling services. Over

30 percent of service companies report turnover rates of over 10 percent annually. Companies selling industrial goods, on the other hand, experience the lowest turnover rates.[55]

## EVALUATING THE SALES FORCE

The final task for sales managers is evaluating the sales force. There are four major methods of evaluation:

- *Call-record reports:* To evaluate the sales force's performance, the sales manager needs feedback—that is, regular information from salespeople. Through call-record reports, sales managers can keep track of salespeople's daily activities. Although call-record reports vary from one firm to another, they generally contain information about the number of calls made and the quality of those calls. Quality is measured by such yardsticks as calls per order, sales or profits per call, or percentage of calls achieving specific goals, such as sales of products that the firm is heavily promoting. Improvement in call quality can increase total volume, change the product mix, or decrease sales cost. The sales manager can use call-record data to increase the number of profitable calls and their quality.
- *Sales force performance ranking:* A second way salespeople can be evaluated is by comparing their sales volume to that of other salespeople and then ranking them according to their performance level. This method traditionally uses data on overall sales volume. However, it may be misleading because of differences from one salesperson to another in competition, customers, and territory. A fairer evaluation method is to rank performance by the salesperson's contribution to profit rather than overall sales volume. The highest-ranked salesperson is the one who not only sells the most (volume) but also concentrates on the most profitable products.
- *Past performance:* Salespeople can also be evaluated by their past performance. Such a comparison is especially important with new salespeople, because it tells the sales manager how well the salesperson is progressing. Progress can be measured in sales and profit trends, as well as by trends in number of calls made and new accounts obtained.
- *Subjective evaluation:* Qualitative, or subjective, methods may also be used to evaluate the sales force. Examples of subjective criteria include the salesperson's knowledge of the company; knowledge of its products, customers, and competitors; and knowledge of sales tasks. The sales manager can also evaluate personal traits. These might include presentation skills, appearance, mannerisms, telemarketing skills, and temperament. This method of evaluation is open to personal biases, however, because it relies on the sales manager's observations and experiences.

## LOOKING BACK

Think back now to the opening article on hotel frequent-stay programs. Many industry analysts fear that by modifying their frequent-stay programs to offer air miles, most hotel programs will become a commodity to consumers. That is, guests will not be loyal to a particular hotel chain, because all hotel chains will be offering the same incentive—miles. To boost loyalty to their particular chain, hotel marketers might consider offering frequent-stay programs whereby guests accumulate points that could be converted into dollars they can spend at a popular restaurant or retailer.

## SUMMARY

**1 State the objectives of sales promotion.** The main objectives of sales promotion are to increase trial purchases, consumer inventories, and repeat purchases. Sales promotion is also used to encourage brand switching and to build brand loyalty. Promotion supports advertising activities.

**2 List the most common forms of consumer sales promotion.** Consumer forms of sales promotion include coupons, premiums, frequent-buyer programs, contests and sweepstakes, samples, and point-of-purchase displays.

**3 List the most common forms of trade sales promotion.** Manufacturers use many of the same sales promotion tools used in consumer promotions, such as sales contests, premiums, and point-of-purchase displays. In addition, manufacturers and channel intermediaries use several unique promotional strategies: trade allowances, push money, training programs, free merchandise, store demonstrations, and meetings, conventions, and trade shows.

**4 Describe personal selling.** Personal selling is direct communication between a sales representative and one or more prospective buyers for the purpose of making a sale. Broadly speaking, all businesspeople use personal selling to promote themselves and their ideas. Personal selling offers several advantages over other forms of promotion. Personal selling allows salespeople to thoroughly explain and demonstrate a product. Salespeople have the flexibility to tailor a sales pitch to the needs and preferences of individual customers. Personal selling is more efficient than other forms of promotion because salespeople target qualified prospects and avoid wasting efforts on unlikely buyers. Personal selling affords greater managerial control over promotion costs. Finally, personal selling is the most effective method of closing a sale.

**5 Identify the different types of selling tasks.** Sales tasks are generally classified into three basic categories: order getting, order taking, and sales support. Order getters, who actively seek prospective buyers and try to persuade them to buy, may be members of a firm's sales force or independent sellers. Order takers handle either inside ordering or field ordering. Inside order takers take orders over the counter, on the sales floor, over the telephone, or by mail. In contrast, field order takers visit clients to service accounts, check inventory, take new orders, and deliver and stock merchandise for customers. Sales support positions include the missionary sales representative and the technical specialist. Missionary sales representatives provide a variety of promotional services to support company sales efforts. Technical specialists help the sales force by describing, designing, and installing products.

**6 List the steps in the selling process.** The selling process is composed of seven basic steps: (1) sales lead generation, (2) sales lead qualification, (3) the sales approach, (4) the sales presentation, (5) the handling of objections, (6) the closing of the sale, and (7) follow-up.

**7 Describe the functions of sales management.** Sales management is a critical area of marketing that performs several important functions. Sales managers set overall company sales objectives and salespeople's individual quotas. They establish a sales force structure based on geographic, product, functional, or customer variables. Managers determine the size of the sales force, typically using either a workload approach or an incremental productivity approach. Sales management develops a compensation plan based on straight commission, straight salary, or a combination of the two. Managers recruit and train the sales force. They motivate the sales force and control turnover by providing sales quotas and sales incentives. Finally, sales

### KEY TERMS

*adaptive selling 589*
*assumptive close 591*
*cold calling 585*
*consultative selling 589*
*consumer sales promotion 573*
*coupon 574*
*field order taker 584*
*follow-up 591*
*frequent-buyer program 576*
*incremental productivity approach 596*
*inside order taker 583*
*lead generation (prospecting) 585*
*lead qualification 586*
*missionary sales representative 584*
*need-satisfaction approach 588*
*negotiation (extra inducement close) 591*
*networking 585*
*order getter 583*
*personal selling 581*
*point-of-purchase display 578*
*premium 575*
*prepared sales presentation 588*
*push money 579*
*quota 592*
*referral 585*
*sales presentation 587*
*sales promotion 573*
*sales territory 593*
*selling team 595*
*silent close 591*
*standing-room-only close 591*
*stimulus-response approach 588*
*straight commission 596*
*straight salary 597*
*summative close 591*
*technical specialist 584*
*time management 600*
*trade allowance 579*
*trade sales promotion 573*
*urgency close 591*
*workload approach 595*

managers evaluate the sales force through call-record reports, performance ranking, past performance, and personal observation.

## Discussion and Writing Questions

1. Why are some firms reducing their use of coupons as a promotional tool?
2. Discuss how different forms of sales promotion can erode or build brand loyalty. If a company's objective is to enhance customer loyalty to its products, what sales promotion techniques would be most appropriate?
3. ✍ You are a new salesperson for a well-known business computer system, and one of your customers is a small business. In a memo to your sales manager, describe the approach you will use to try to make the sale, and explain the reasons for your choice.
4. What does sales follow-up entail? Why is it an essential step in the selling process, particularly in today's marketplace? How does it relate to cognitive dissonance?
5. Explain what is meant by the familiar business adage "Nothing happens until a sale is made."
6. ✍ As the new sales manager for a firm, you have decided to adopt a compensation policy for the sales force that combines salary and commission. Write a memo to the president of the company explaining why you feel your plan will be successful.
7. Suggest some reasons why women are often more effective salespeople than men. What qualities are likely to make them successful salespeople in the market environment of the 1990s?

## Application for Small Business

East Coast Paper is a distributor of paper and plastic products in a three-state area. It enjoys a strong market share and presence, with a sales force of eleven representatives. Robert McClaren, the general manager and part owner, recently committed the company to selling 500,000 pounds of a new product in the upcoming year. The new product is a dense-bodied paper container, microwaveable and capable of withstanding temperatures of 400°F for forty-five minutes.

Almost any size of container can be made, so the new containers would be ideal for restaurant takeouts. Like most innovations, the new paper container would cost somewhat more than currently available containers but would retain the heat in takeout foods much better.

Robert shared this plan with his sales manager, Mary Jennings, and asked for an all-out blitz of the marketplace to ensure movement of the revolutionary product. First thing Monday morning, Mary began the usual sales meeting by explaining the details of the new product to the sales force. To help push it, the company decided to offer an incentive bonus to the salesperson with the highest sales volume for the product over the next three months.

Jane Licata, East Coast Paper's top salesperson, immediately thought of her number-one customer, Copeland's, when she heard about the new product. Copeland's is a family-style restaurant chain operating twenty units in the same three-state market as East Coast Paper. The average daily number of sit-down meals is 756 per unit, with an additional 176 takeout meals per day.

Jane's mission was clear. She needed to demonstrate a need for this new container at Copeland's so she could win the incentive bonus. Jane had already sold Copeland's all its other paper products, including napkins, paper cups, and containers, as well as its plastic takeout bags, styrofoam containers, and some cleaning products.

### Questions

1. Is Jane's personal mission customer-oriented?
2. What kind of sales approach should Jane take to serve the Copeland's account best?

## CRITICAL THINKING CASE

### Coca-Cola MagiCans

On a United Airlines flight in 1990, a flight attendant opened an ordinary-looking can of Coca-Cola Classic. When she tried to pour it, nothing came out, but the can had something in it. After the plane landed, the bomb squad quickly defused the can and found a ten-dollar bill inside, which was supposed to pop out when the can was opened. It was just another defective MagiCan from Coca-Cola, part of a promotional campaign. Although the bomb squad did not find a bomb, it became evident that Coca-Cola had one. Just three short weeks after the introduction of MagiCans, Coke ceased the promotion.

This promotion created several problems for the company. Coke had intended to ship 750,000 MagiCans but only shipped 200,000. Thus the total number of prizes and the odds of winning those prizes were inaccurately advertised. The company had to look into the legal ramifications of this situation. In addition, water was placed in the cans to give them the weight of regular cans of Coke. Although the water was completely harmless, the company may also face some legal problems with consumers who drank it.

The most serious problem may be damage to the brand name. Anytime a promotional activity fails, the company risks damage to the brand. Coca-Cola received nothing but bad publicity from its MagiCan promotion and decided to withdraw the promotion before it received any more bad press. The negative publicity was a serious blow to Coca-Cola's image as a premier marketer.

Coca-Cola spent two years developing the MagiCan. The promotion was test marketed in Iowa and Illinois. Test-market data indicated potential problems. For instance, curious consumers actually pried open the can to look at the mechanism. Consumers also had trouble understanding the promotion and thought that cash popping out of cans was just a metaphor not to be taken literally.

Despite potential problems, Coca-Cola still launched the promotion. Caught up in the excitement, company executives lost sight of how truly unusual the promotion was. Unusual promotions require heavy advertising to provide additional explanations.

As Coca-Cola learned in this case, rushing to market without proper testing often leads to rushing out of the market. Furthermore, promotions that tinker with or place foreign objects in a consumable product, such as food or drink, require extreme caution. "When you are dealing with a food or beverage product, even one failure in a million is unacceptable," says John Lister, a brand and corporate identity consultant. Yet Coca-Cola, still enamored with the promotion, is considering relaunching MagiCans. This time the company will look at every structural, chemical, and marketing aspect of the MagiCan program.

### Questions

1. Do you think more extensive test marketing should be done with promotions like MagiCans? Give reasons to support your answer.
2. Should marketers put prizes in packages that contain food products? Would your answer depend on the types of packages? Give reasons to support your answer.
3. Do you think Coca-Cola should bring back MagiCans? Why or why not?

### References


Scott Hume, "Perrier Factor Doomed MagiCan," *Advertising Age,* 4 June 1990, p. 52.

Michael J. McCarthy, "Coca-Cola 'MagiCans' Go Poof after Just Three Weeks," *The Wall Street Journal,* 1 June 1990, pp. B1, B8.

Michael J. McCarthy, "MagiCan'ts: How Coca-Cola Stumbled," *The Wall Street Journal,* 5 June 1990, pp. B1, B8.

Don Schultz, "MagiCan Went Wrong, but Coca-Cola Remains Strong," *Marketing News,* 17 September 1990, p. 15.


## SIGNATURE SERIES VIDEO CASE

### The Louisiana Lottery

SIGNATURE SERIES VIDEO

*by Ken Brickman*
*Executive Director, Louisiana Lottery Corp.*

The Louisiana Lottery, video poker gaming, riverboat gambling, and a land-based casino in New Orleans were all in the headlines during 1995. But this was only the most recent debate over the "good" or "evil" of gambling. Since its founding in 1718, Louisiana has been in a strategic position at the mouth of the Mississippi River, and as an international port and popular tourist destination, the state, and particularly the city of New Orleans, has long followed its own morality, laws, and customs designed to accommodate international traders, pirates, opportunists, and other fun lovers and risk takers. By 1810, with a population estimated at only about 17,000, New Orleans had more gambling houses than Philadelphia, Baltimore, Boston, and New York combined.

The scandals and corruption of these early gambling

activities, not only in Louisiana but in most states, caused the U.S. Congress to pass a bill in 1890 that made the mailing of lottery materials illegal, including newspapers with lottery advertisements. The law also authorized the Postmaster General to intercept registry and money-order instruments to the benefit of any agent of a lottery company. The 1890 bill and subsequent legislation in 1894 ultimately created insurmountable obstacles to successful lottery operations.

The lessons of the Louisiana Lottery lasted until 1964, when New Hampshire became the first state in modern times to authorize a lottery. Three years later, New York followed, and then New Jersey. By the mid-1990s, there were only two states without some form of legalized gambling—Utah and Hawaii. The lure of instant wealth—by both state governments and lottery patrons—is simply too tempting to pass up.

The Louisiana Lottery enjoyed a phenomenal start, surpassing all prelaunch projections in sales. Sales of $288 million for the first seven months of operation were $38 million more than the initial sales projection of $250 million for the first full year of operations. Sales of instant, or "scratch" tickets, totaled over $354 million for the first twelve months, setting a new North American first-year per capita sales record of over $84 for instant tickets, surpassing the prior first-year record of $76 held by the California Lottery. Other forms of lottery games helped total first-year sales of the Louisiana Lottery to reach almost $476 million, representing per capita sales of over $112, which earned the Louisiana Lottery second place on the all-time per capita sales chart, second only to Florida at $131, which benefits from its winter "snowbird" tourists.

The advertising agency for the Louisiana Lottery, Bauerlein of New Orleans, used a somewhat different approach to introduce the lottery. As Robbie Vitrano, Bauerlein's president said, "The conventional wisdom for the industry was to use basic, generic themes such as sports and simple match games to teach new players about the game. We wanted to encourage participation by the simplicity of understanding the lottery, not discourage people by making the game appear too difficult. Research indicated that Louisianians wanted the Lottery to be a distinctly Louisiana game—one that reflected their lifestyle and interests. This dovetailed nicely with the fact that most people don't win and the population size of Louisiana is small, meaning relatively smaller jackpots compared to larger states. The creative approach was not to emphasize 'winning' the lottery, but to sell Louisiana and its pride and heritage along with the fun and entertainment of playing the lottery. Merely focusing on getting rich would eventually discourage potential lottery players."

The first direct competitive gambling alternative, in the form of video poker gaming, arrived in June 1992. Video poker machines are essentially slot machines displaying poker hands in place of traditional slot machine symbols, and they produce slips of paper representing winnings, which can be turned in to the retail operators for prizes up to $500. Rapid proliferation of video poker resulted in 13,500 machines within the first two years of operations. The next competitive gambling alternative—a riverboat casino—opened in October 1993, and by late 1995 a total of fifteen riverboat casinos, five Indian reservation land casinos, and a single land-based casino in New Orleans were in operation. The riverboats were drawing over 2 million patrons per month by the end of 1995, and these patrons were dropping almost $100 million each month at the gambling tables and in the slot machines.

The Lottery began feeling this competition almost immediately, and sales began slipping. Lottery sales peaked in 1993 at approximately $493 million but then dropped to about $354 in 1994. One of the reasons for the early success of the Lottery was the preference by much of the state's population for gambling-type entertainment. But the Lottery's extensive advertising and promotional campaigns also contributed to its success. Lottery advertising experts say well-planned and executed advertising campaigns also helped slow the flow of dollars to other types of gambling.

### Questions

1. Why is gambling so popular with so many people?
2. What factors attract people to play the lottery? Which are the most important in attracting new patrons? Which are most important in attracting regular patrons?
3. How can the Louisiana Lottery most effectively compete with other forms of gambling? What kinds of sales promotion techniques would be most effective?
4. Should the Louisiana Lottery emphasize awareness or persuasion in its promotional campaigns? How could personal selling help to promote products like the Lottery?

# PART FIVE INTEGRATIVE CASE

## KRAFT GENERAL FOODS

At the beginning of this century, James L. Kraft started delivering cheese in the Chicago area on a wagon drawn by a rented horse named Paddy. Almost eighty-five years later, Kraft, Inc. was acquired for a staggering $12.9 billion by Philip Morris Co. In 1989, Kraft was combined with Philip Morris's prior acquisition—General Foods—to form Kraft General Foods. This merger created the largest food company in the United States and Canada and the second largest in the world.

Philip Morris's diversification into the food business was a long-term strategy to reduce its dependence on tobacco products and to manage its cash flow by acquiring businesses in markets that would have a steady and stable demand for years to come. By 1992, Philip Morris was the proud owner of many well-known brands, such as Kraft, Kool-Aid, Maxwell House, Sanka, Cool Whip, Lender's Bagels, DiGiorno, Parkay, Breyers, Sealtest, Oscar Mayer, Entenmann's, Jell-O, and Tombstone Pizza, to name but a few. Operating revenues from food businesses in 1992 accounted for almost half of the operating revenues for Philip Morris. Cheese was the single largest food business for the company, yielding 20 percent of retail operating revenues from all food products in 1992 (see Exhibit 1).

With so many food brands, how can Kraft General Foods (KGF) market its products effectively? Increasing segmentation of the food market makes traditional mass marketing and "pull" strategies, such as national advertising and intensive distribution, tremendously costly and inefficient. Also, the increasing average size of supermarkets, the increasing mobility of the customers they serve, and the growing diversity in consumer preferences for packaged food make complete knowledge of customers a virtually impossible task.

However, KGF and other packaged-food manufacturers have discovered a new way of enhancing marketing effectiveness and achieving significant cost savings in reaching their customers: "micromarketing" strategies. They are geared toward tracking supermarket and discount store consumers, maintaining extensive databases on their preferences and purchases, segmenting grocery markets, and more efficiently targeting specific market segments through promotions. Micromarketing enables individual stores or store clusters to develop customized promotional programs for their specific customers. Aided by advanced technology and the techniques of direct marketing, micro-

*Exhibit 1*

Philip Morris's North American Food Businesses

Source: Philip Morris Annual Report, 1992.

| Food category | Contribution to company's 1992 retail operating revenues from food | Some prominent brands |
|---|---|---|
| Cheese | 20% | Kraft American, Kraft Velveeta, Kraft |
| Frozen/dairy foods | 15 | Breyer's, Sealtest, Cool Whip, Light n' Lively |
| Processed meats | 10 | Oscar Meyer, Louis Rich |
| Salad dressings, sauces, and spreads | 10 | Kraft (dressings), Good Seasons, Bull's Eye sauces |
| Coffee | 8 | Maxwell House, Sanka, Cappio, General Foods International |
| Baked goods | 8 | Boboli, Lender's, Entenmann's, Freihofer |
| Entree and side-dish preparations | 8 | Minute Rice, Log Cabin, Stove Top, Shake 'n Bake |
| Beverages | 6 | Kool-Aid, Capri Sun |
| Cereals | 6 | Shredded Wheat, Post |
| Others | 9 | |

marketing promises not only finer segmentation and more accurate targeting but also higher revenues for each promotion dollar spent.

Using micromarketing techniques, KGF identified six different consumer segments: full-margin shoppers (high-income, educated shoppers who buy often and buy what they want), planners and dine-outs (shoppers who plan their trips and also dine out often), commodity shoppers (lower-income shoppers with large families on tight budgets), frequent shoppers, "merchandise-ables," and "mini-baskets." These customer segments were developed through an extensive analysis of data from a number of sources, including scanner data on purchases by store, category, and product. Demographic and buying-habit information from over 30,000 food stores nationwide and geodemographic data of the sort used by direct marketers were used to identify shopper profiles and pinpoint their locale.

Compiling, maintaining, and constantly updating such voluminous databases are by no means simple tasks. But what is more important is making sense of the data and putting it to use. Here, KGF's organizational structure plays an important role. KGF Services, formed in 1992, provides marketing support to the brand managers of each KGF business unit. KGF Services coordinates with external agencies, such as A.C. Nielsen and Information Resources Inc., to obtain scanner and panel data. With fast, flexible computer systems, KGF Services can provide almost real-time feedback to managers. Today KGF has a multimillion-household database, probably the largest packaged-goods database in the country.

The database includes scanner data, coupon data, and information on advertising, merchandising, pricing, stockouts, and so on. One example of the type of information that can now be collected is the coupons from inserts in newspapers. Checkout scanners record the bar codes on the coupons, which indicate not only the amount of the coupon and the product involved but also the newspaper the coupon was in, which regional edition (if any), and the day the coupon appeared. Such data enable KGF Services to analyze differences in how micromarkets respond to changes in prices, media vehicles, and other aspects of promotion. In-store displays, coupon distribution, media advertising, inventory, and other aspects of merchandising can be tailored for each local market.

Highly detailed data on consumers and store sales have enabled KGF to target the volume-buying segments of the food market. KGF Services discovered that heavy users of KGF brands buy multiple brands across many food categories. KGF now focuses on these heavy users with promotions that simultaneously feature multiple brands. Using the same promotion tool for many brands saves money.

KGF's decision support systems also aid the retail stores that carry its products. Sales teams from KGF work with stores in a neighborhood to provide them with details on their shoppers. The stores can then change their own mix of products, adding profitable new ones and deleting unprofitable ones, deciding on appropriate displays and shelf space, and so on. KGF sales teams can also design micromerchandising programs for their customers. One retail chain installed drive-through windows for the benefit of a large customer segment that was already patronizing its stores, the "planners and dine-outs." KGF Services helped a five-store company based in Cashmere, Washington, called Martin and Scouten, pinpoint its customers and customize promotion programs. Each store was able to more precisely match inventory with demand—and also to sell more of the twelve KGF products it was promoting. Such micromarketing programs have enabled KGF to increase total product sales during promotional periods by as much as 23 percent.

The benefits of micromarketing are many. For companies like KGF, which sell in many product categories, micromarketing helps in devising the best possible promotional mixes and in economizing on promotions. Retailers involved in micromarketing programs benefit from knowledge of the types of customers shopping in their stores. Such information brings them more effective in-store promotions, better inventory management, higher sales, and increased operational efficiency.

Relationships between distribution channel members are increasingly characterized by the sort of "partnering" that KGF seeks with retailers. The information that flows between the partners creates a much stronger bond based on trust, cooperation, and mutual dependence. The marketing philosophy is unequivocally implemented when both the manufacturer and the retailer work in tandem for the benefit of the customer.

## Questions

1. How is micromarketing different from traditional methods of marketing in the food industry?
2. How are promotions used uniquely by firms using micromarketing?
3. What are KGF's methods of obtaining information on consumers? How does it use such information?
4. How does micromarketing change the relationship between manufacturers and retailers in the food industry? (Hint: Use your understanding of traditional channels and vertical marketing systems.)

## Suggested Readings

Michael Garry, "Knowledge Is Power," *Progressive Grocer,* May 1992, pp. 169–172.

Ken Partch, "Partnering," *Supermarket Business,* May 1992, pp. 29–34.

Lorraine Scarpa, "Fast, Flexible, Computerized, That's Today's Analytical World," *Brandweek,* 15 November 1993, pp. 25, 28, 32.

John Sinisi, "KGF's New Dressing," *Brandweek,* 28 September 1992, pp. 10, 12, 14, 15.

Michael Treacy and Fred Wiersema, "Customer Intimacy and Other Value Disciplines," *Harvard Business Review,* January–February 1993, pp. 84–93.

# PART FIVE ETHICS CASE

## THE SALE THAT NEVER WAS

Metropolitan Power & Light was a large combined gas and electric service utility with an industrial sales force of twenty-seven people. Its major competitor was Greater Edison Utilities, which also had an industrial sales force of some eighteen salespeople. Their service territories overlapped only in regard to types of energy. For example, Metropolitan had a natural gas franchise for part of the city of Applegate, and Greater Edison served that same area with electricity. In other areas, that pattern would be reversed. In some industrial parks, both companies could provide both types of service.

Ray Houser, a sales engineer for Metropolitan, had watched with great interest as his company revised his compensation to include a substantial commission for new business. Later Metropolitan adopted a commission formula that included additional compensation when a salesperson kept an existing customer from going to a competitor. For example, a large electric motor manufacturer had been buying energy for heating from Metropolitan's electricity division. A competing utility was urging the manufacturer to build its own cogeneration plant and produce its own electric power. Ray had worked with this manufacturer to solve some of its efficiency problems and had kept it from building a separate generating plant. Because this was a documented case of his holding a large industrial customer, his commission had been enhanced by $1,800.

The managers of Metropolitan had some qualms about paying salespeople for holding business because of the difficulty of documentation. They had a fear that some salespeople would spend too much time holding customers that really were not considering leaving. Ray had sympathy for their fear but felt very strongly that salespeople's time was better spent holding large existing accounts than chasing small new accounts.

The issue was debated but left unchanged until Greater Edison adopted a similar compensation structure for its salespeople. After several months of intense competition between the two sales forces, one of the Greater Edison salespeople approached Ray at a civic club meeting and joked about conspiring to try to steal each other's accounts and improve the size of both salesperson's commissions. Ray felt uncomfortable with the joke, even though he was convinced that the competing salesman was not serious.

- When is a joke not a joke?

Several weeks later, as a recession began to take hold, some industrial customers began cutting back energy use or, in some cases, shutting down plants. Because of the commission structure, Ray's total compensation fell by about 15 percent. The salesperson from Greater Edison, Bob Mackaby, called Ray and repeated his joke, but in a much more serious way. Bob suggested that they agree on which companies to approach with competitive proposals. Those proposals would be set up so the business would not actually be lost and counterproposals could be documented. Each salesperson's paycheck would be enhanced.

- Who would be hurt by this plan? Beyond the basic issue, are there other risks?

Ray was tempted. He knew he would be able to protect his present customers if such a deal was struck, and he would at least be fully prepared for frontal assaults from his major competitor. However, he was uneasy about "throwing" his proposals for new business to the competitor.

Over time, as Ray's paycheck began to diminish further, he began to seriously reconsider Bob's offer. Finally, he agreed to do two deals with his competitor.

First, Ray and Bob were going to make serious proposals to the two largest customers of each utility company. Ray had thought a lot about what it would take to win Greater Edison's largest customer, a regional plant for one of the major carmakers. He had also wondered about the vulnerability of his largest customer, which was a turbine-manufacturing plant of national note.

- What trust relationships are involved here? How are they affected by what has happened?

Ray was extremely surprised when he found that Bob had given him proposed figures different from those Bob had given to Ray's largest customer. Ray, in fact, had come in with a poor defending proposal and had lost some 60 percent of the customer's business. When Ray approached Bob, Bob laughed and said, "You weren't really taking all that seriously, were you? Besides, who would you complain to?"

- How would you feel if you were Ray? What would you do next?

# PART SIX
# PRICING DECISIONS



Squeri FoodService is one of the top 50 food distributors in the country. Dave Lind was fortunate to begin his career in Squeri's telemarketing department while in college. Not long after graduating from college, Dave worked his way up in the company to his current position as assistant director of purchasing.

With over seven thousand edible and non-food products, Dave Lind is in constant contact with hundreds of suppliers. Squeri spans the globe to bring their customers the finest products available. Dave is responsible for sourcing these products to meet their customers' needs. He works closely with Squeri's sales and marketing departments to make certain that they purchase what their customers want. This purchasing procedure needs to be efficient and timely, assuring that the customer gets the best and freshest goods on time. This process also helps Squeri minimize their cost by reducing waste which helps with profitability.

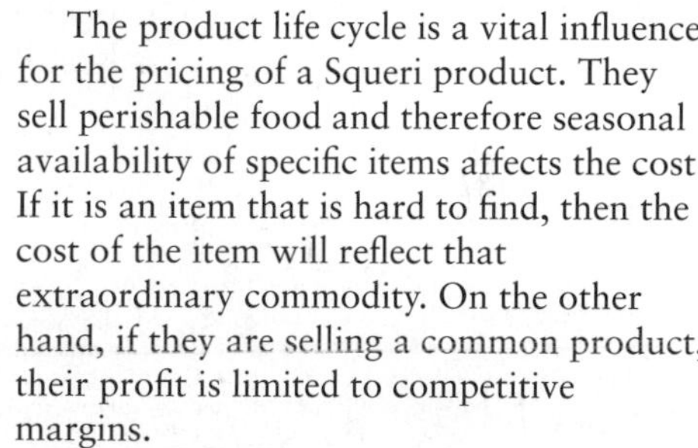

The product life cycle is a vital influence for the pricing of a Squeri product. They sell perishable food and therefore seasonal availability of specific items affects the cost. If it is an item that is hard to find, then the cost of the item will reflect that extraordinary commodity. On the other hand, if they are selling a common product, their profit is limited to competitive margins.

Dave says that he refers back to the information he learned while attaining his Bachelors of Business Administration degree. The knowledge he gained in his Business Marketing and Business Strategies courses has proven to be essential in his position.

Squeri FoodService is committed to enhancing their employees' knowledge and skills. By emphasizing their staff's education and ongoing professional improvement, Squeri provides their customers with the best service and support within the industry. Dave Lind has taken advantage of this. He attends management courses and buying seminars on a regular basis.

In the fast-paced food service industry, you have stay in touch with the constant change in product availability, client's needs, technology, and relationships. Armed with his Bachelors of Business Administration degree, work experience, and continuing education, Dave Lind is prepared to meet these challenges.

# CHAPTER 18

# PRICING CONCEPTS

## LEARNING OBJECTIVES

*After studying this chapter, you should be able to*

1 *Discuss the importance of pricing decisions to the economy and to the individual firm.*

2 *List and explain a variety of pricing objectives.*

3 *Explain the role of demand in price determination.*

4 *Describe cost-oriented pricing strategies.*

5 *Demonstrate how the product life cycle, competition, distribution and promotion strategies, and quality perceptions can affect price.*

The average 1994 baseball ticket price had risen to $10.45, and the total cost for a family of four to attend a major league baseball game was $95.80, according to a survey by *Team Marketing Report,* a sports-business newsletter. Its so-called Fan Cost Index, which also takes into account the price of food, souvenirs, and parking, had risen 26 percent since the newsletter began tracking the data in 1991.

The jump in ticket prices partly reflected the opening of a new park in Cleveland, where average ticket prices rose 39 percent, and Texas, where average ticket prices rose 35 percent. But it mainly resulted from the teams' need to make up for declining network TV revenue and to meet rising player payrolls.

Premium seats are getting more expensive at all the ballparks, according to *Team Marketing Report* editor Alan Friedman. "It's classic market segmentation," he says. "The high end keeps getting higher because of the number of ticket buyers who want the best seat with little regard for price." In 1994 the Milwaukee Brewers held the line on all tickets except their 3,000 best ones, creating a new category called Diamond Boxes. Featuring waiter service and other amenities, these seats went up $3 a ticket, to $17 and $18. The Cleveland Indians had no seats over $12 in their old Municipal Stadium, but they have about 15,000 such seats in their new Jacobs Field, or about a third of capacity. The Atlanta Braves, which in 1993 had about 5,000 seats priced over $12, increased the number to about 23,000 in 1994, driving their average ticket price up 23 percent. Overall, baseball teams priced 20 percent of tickets above $12 in 1993 and 30 percent of them over $12 in 1994.

At the same time, the number of low-end tickets is declining. The Texas Rangers had about 20,000 seats for less than $8 at their old stadium but have only about 6,000 in their new one. The Cleveland Indians reduced the number of seats selling for less than $8 from about 28,000 to about 5,000. (To be fair, few of the cheap seats in Cleveland's cavernous Municipal Stadium were ever occupied—although the top-priced ones weren't either.) *Team Marketing Report* found baseball's low-priced seats went from 33 percent of capacity in 1993 to 28 percent in 1994.

The trend is worrisome to some in baseball, who believe the sport's long schedule and need to compete with other summer entertainment requires popular prices. Of major league baseball's twenty-eight teams, eleven now have a Fan Cost Index of $100 or more. The highest is the New York Yankees, at $115.25.

Some baseball executives reject *Team Marketing Report*'s findings and the notion that their product is overpriced. The price of Yankee Stadium's soft drinks and hot dogs went up only because of bigger sizes, according to New York Yankee executive vice president David Susman. Although most ticket categories went up by $1, he says, in a city where a Broadway show costs a fortune and an average Knicks basketball ticket sells for $35, "$17 for the best seat in Yankee Stadium is a decent value."

Certainly an old baseball truth holds: Win, and the turnstiles will spin at any price. The Atlanta Braves, winner of 104 games in 1993, put through a 23 percent increase for 1994 and still got an advance sale of more than 3 million tickets. The Philadelphia Phillies, 1993 National League pennant winners, raised prices 19 percent and had an advance sale of 2 million tickets in 1994. "People ask, 'Are ticket prices too high?'" says *Team Marketing Report* editor Friedman. "The indication of that is when people stop consuming. There's no evidence of that yet."[1]

So what effect did the strike that prematurely ended the 1994 season have on ticket sales? Attendance at the home opener in Atlanta was 24,091, the smallest opening-day crowd since 1991.[2] The New York Yankees opened to about 6,500 fewer home fans than in 1994 and the Milwaukee Brewers drew only 31,426 out of a possible 53,192, their smallest opening day since 1993.[3] Kansas City opened to its smallest crowd since 1984.[4] But the Cincinnati Reds had sold 48,800 of a possible 52,952 season opener tickets two days prior to opening day.[5] Likewise, the Colorado Rockies had sold 47,000 of a possible 50,200 tickets the day before they opened. Boston's Fenway Park was sold out prior to the opener.[6] It appears that some fans are happy that baseball is back but others couldn't care less.

What type of pricing objective is major league baseball pursuing? How would you describe the demand for baseball's premium seats? What is the relationship between price and revenue? How does cost fit into the pricing equation? David Sussman of the New York Yankees mentions other forms of entertainment as competition. How does competition affect price?

*1 Discuss the importance of pricing decisions to the economy and to the individual firm.*

## THE IMPORTANCE OF PRICE

Price means one thing to the consumer and something else to the seller. To the consumer it is the cost of something. Price to the seller is revenue, the primary source of profits. In the broadest sense, price allocates resources in a free-market economy. With so many ways of looking at price, it's no wonder that marketing managers find the task of setting prices a challenge.

### WHAT IS PRICE?

**price**
Perceived value of a good or service.

**Price** is the perceived value of a good or service. Perceived value in today's society is most commonly expressed in dollars and cents. Thus price is typically the money exchanged for a good or service.

In a study of 2,000 consumers, 64 percent said that a "reasonable price" is the most important consideration in making a purchase.[7] "Reasonable price" really means "perceived reasonable value" at the time of the transaction. One of the authors of this textbook bought a fancy European-designed toaster for about $45. The toaster's wide mouth made it possible to toast a bagel, warm a muffin, and, with a special $15 attachment, make a grilled sandwich. The author felt that a toaster with all these features surely must be worth the total price of $60. But after three months of using the device, toast burned around the edges and raw in the middle lost its appeal. The disappointed buyer put the toaster in the attic. Why didn't he return it to the retailer? The boutique had gone out of business, and no other local retailer carried the brand. Also, there was no U.S. service center. Remember, the price paid is based on the satisfaction consumers expect to receive from a product and not necessarily the satisfaction they actually receive.

Price can be anything with perceived value, not just money. When goods and services are exchanged, the trade is called barter. For example, if you exchange this book for a chemistry book at the end of the term, you have engaged in barter. The price you paid for the chemistry book was this textbook.

### PRICE AS AN ALLOCATOR OF RESOURCES

Let's return to the monetary notion of price, which plays a crucial role in the U.S. economic system. We live in an economy that depends on a complex system of prices to allocate goods and services among consumers, governments, and businesses. It is a **mixed economy,** one in which both the government and the private sector exercise economic control. It is also an example of **capitalism,** an economic system characterized by private ownership of productive resources and an allocation of goods and services according to signals provided by a free market. We live in a mixed capitalistic society.

**Outward Bound courses are popular despite the hefty price tag of $2,000 to $3,000. People are willing to pay that price because the perceived value includes personal and spiritual growth.**

Courtesy Outward Bound and Cardinal Communications Group, Inc.

**mixed economy**
Economy in which both the government and the private sector exercise economic control.

**capitalism**
Economic system characterized by private ownership of productive resources and allocation of goods and services according to signals provided by a free market.

Consumers play an important part in the allocation process through the exercise of their dollar votes. If people believe that a merchant has set a fair price for a good or service, they vote for (buy) that product. For example, a consumer who uses Colgate toothpaste is in effect saying, "Keep producing Colgate; it meets my value expectations better than other products do." Businesses that do a good job of satisfying the needs of the consumer receive more dollar votes (sales). Those businesses may then use the earned revenue to buy more resources in order to produce more goods and services. Companies that do not satisfy the consumer (and thus lack dollar votes) cannot effectively compete for resources. They must eventually switch to another product or go bankrupt.

## THE IMPORTANCE OF PRICE TO MARKETING MANAGERS

**revenue**
Price charged to customers multiplied by the number of units sold.

**profit**
Revenue minus expenses.

Prices are the key to revenues, which are in turn the key to profits for an organization. **Revenue** is the price charged to customers multiplied by the number of units sold. Revenue is what pays for every activity of the company: production, finance, sales, distribution, and so on. What's left over (if anything) is **profit.** Managers usually strive to charge a price that will earn a fair profit.

To earn a profit, managers must choose a price that is not too high or too low, a price that equals the perceived value to target consumers. If a price is set too high in consumers' minds, the perceived value will be less than the cost, and sales opportunities will be lost. Lost sales mean lost revenue. Conversely, if a price is too low, it may be perceived as a great value for the consumer, but the firm loses revenue it could have earned. Setting prices too low may not even attract as many buyers as managers might think. One study surveyed over 2,000 shoppers at national chains around the country and found that over 60 percent intended to buy full-price items only.[8] Retailers that place too much emphasis on discounts may not be able to meet the expectations of full-price customers.

Trying to set the right price is one of the most stressful and pressure-filled tasks of the marketing manager, as trends in the consumer market attest:

- Confronting a flood of new products, potential buyers carefully evaluate the price of each one against the value of existing products.
- The increased availability of bargain-priced private and generic brands has put downward pressure on overall prices.
- A series of inflationary and recessionary periods has made many consumers more price-sensitive.
- Many firms are trying to maintain their market share by cutting prices. For example, when Compaq Computer lost market share and profits, it introduced a new line of low-priced computers and dropped the suggested retail price of most of its existing machines by 32 percent.[9] It now sells more personal computers than any firm in the United States.

In the organizational market, where customers include both governments and businesses, buyers are also becoming more price-sensitive and better informed. Computerized information systems enable the organizational buyer to compare price and performance with great ease and accuracy. Improved communication and the increased use of telemarketing and computer-aided selling have also opened up many markets to new competitors. Finally, competition in general is increasing, so some installations, accessories, and component parts are being marketed like indistinguishable commodities (such as natural gas and bauxite).

2 *List and explain a variety of pricing objectives.*

## PRICING OBJECTIVES

To survive in today's highly competitive marketplace, companies need pricing objectives that are specific, attainable, and measurable. Realistic pricing goals then require periodic monitoring to determine the effectiveness of the company's strategy.

For convenience, pricing objectives can be divided into three categories: profit-oriented, sales-oriented, and status quo.

## PROFIT-ORIENTED PRICING OBJECTIVES

Profit-oriented objectives include profit maximization, satisfactory profits, and target return on investment. A brief discussion of each of these objectives follows.

### Profit Maximization

*Profit maximization* means setting prices so total revenue is as large as possible relative to total costs. (A more theoretically precise definition and explanation of profit maximization appears later in the chapter.) Profit maximization does not always signify unreasonably high prices, however. Both price and profits depend on the type of competitive environment a firm faces, such as being in a monopoly position (being the only seller) or selling in a much more competitive situation. (See Chapter 2 for a description of the four types of competitive environments.) Also, remember that a firm cannot charge a price higher than the product's perceived value.

Many firms do not have the accounting data they need for maximizing profits. It sounds simple to say that a company should keep producing and selling goods or services as long as revenues exceed costs. Yet it is often hard to set up an accurate accounting system to determine the point of profit maximization.

Sometimes managers say that their company is trying to maximize profits—in other words, trying to make as much money as possible. Although this goal may sound impressive to stockholders, it is not good enough for planning. The statement "We want to make all the money we can" is vague and lacks focus. It gives management license to do just about anything it wants to do.

### Satisfactory Profits

Satisfactory profits are a reasonable level of profits. Rather than maximizing profits,

By cutting ticket prices, airlines can sometimes increase profits. Because of the high costs of fuel, aircraft maintenance, and flight personnel, it may make more sense to fly a plane full of reduced-fare passengers than to fly a plane with fewer full-price passengers.

American Airlines

many organizations strive for profits that are satisfactory to the stockholders and management—in other words, a level of profits consistent with the level of risk an organization faces. In a risky industry, a satisfactory profit may be 35 percent. In a low-risk industry, it might be 7 percent. To maximize profits, a small-business owner might have to keep his or her store open seven days a week. But the owner might not want to work that hard and might be satisfied with less profit.

### Target Return on Investment

**target return on investment (ROI)**
Profit objective calculated by dividing a firm's net profits after taxes by its total assets.

The most common profit objective is **target return on investment** (ROI), sometimes called the firm's return on total assets. ROI measures the overall effectiveness of management in generating profits with its available assets. The higher the firm's return on investment, the better. Many companies—including DuPont, General Motors, Navistar, Exxon, and Union Carbide—use target return on investment as their main pricing goal.

Return on investment is calculated as follows:

$$\text{Return on investment} = \frac{\text{Net profits after taxes}}{\text{Total assets}}$$

Assume that in 1996 Johnson Controls had assets of $4.5 million, net profits of $550,000, and a target ROI of 10 percent. This was the actual ROI:

$$\text{ROI} = \frac{550{,}000}{4{,}500{,}00}$$

$$= 12.2 \text{ percent}$$

As you can see, the ROI for Johnson Controls exceeded its target, which indicates that the company prospered in 1996.

Comparing the 12.2 percent ROI with the industry average provides a more meaningful picture, however. Any ROI needs to be evaluated in terms of the competitive environment, risks in the industry, and economic conditions. Generally speaking, firms seek ROIs in the 10 to 30 percent range. For example, General Electric seeks a 25 percent ROI, whereas Alcoa, Rubbermaid, and most major pharmaceutical companies strive for a 20 percent ROI. In some industries, however, such as the grocery industry, a return of under 5 percent is common and acceptable.

A company with a target ROI can predetermine its desired level of profitability. The marketing manager can use the standard, such as 10 percent ROI, to determine whether a particular price and marketing mix are feasible. In addition, however, the manager must weigh the risk of a given strategy even if the return is in the acceptable range.

## SALES-ORIENTED PRICING OBJECTIVES

Sales-oriented pricing objectives are based either on market share or on dollar or unit sales. The effective marketing manager should be familiar with these pricing objectives.

### Market Share

**market share**
Company's product sales as a percentage of total sales for that industry.

**Market share** is a company's product sales as a percentage of total sales for that industry. Sales can be reported in dollars or in units of product. It is very important to know whether market share is expressed in revenue or units, because the results may be

*Exhibit 18.1*

Two Ways to Measure Market Share (Units and Revenue)

| Company | Units sold | Unit price | Total revenue | Unit market share | Revenue market share |
|---|---|---|---|---|---|
| A | 1,000 | $1.00 | $1,000,000 | 50% | 25% |
| B | 200 | 4.00 | 800,000 | 10 | 20 |
| C | 500 | 2.00 | 1,000,000 | 25 | 25 |
| D | 300 | 4.00 | 1,200,000 | 15 | 30 |
| Total | 2,000 | | $4,000,000 | | |

different. Consider, for example, four companies competing in an industry with 2,000 total unit sales and total industry revenue of $4 million (see Exhibit 18.1). Company A has the largest unit market share at 50 percent, but it has only 25 percent of the revenue market share. In contrast, company D has only a 15 percent unit share but the largest revenue share—30 percent. Usually, market share is expressed in terms of revenue and not units.

Many companies believe that maintaining or increasing market share is an indicator of the effectiveness of their marketing mix. Larger market shares have indeed often meant higher profits, thanks to greater economies of scale, market power, and ability to compensate top-quality management. Conventional wisdom also says that market share and return on investment are strongly related. For the most part they are; however, many companies with low market share survive and even prosper. To succeed with a low market share, companies need to compete in industries with slow growth and few product changes—for instance, industrial component parts and supplies. Otherwise, they must vie in an industry that makes frequently bought items, such as consumer convenience goods.

The early 1990s proved that the conventional wisdom about market share and profitability isn't always reliable. Because of a general recession and extreme competition in some industries, many market share leaders either did not reach their target ROI or actually lost money. The airline, microcomputer, and food industries had this problem. Procter & Gamble switched from market share to ROI objectives after realizing that profits don't automatically follow from a large market share. PepsiCo says its new Pepsi challenge is to be No. 1 in share of industry profit, not in share of sales volume.[10]

Still, the struggle for market share can be all-consuming for some companies. For over a decade, Maxwell House and Folgers, the biggest U.S. coffee brands, have been locked in a struggle to dominate the market. Their weapons have been advertising, perpetual rounds of price cutting, and millions upon millions of cents-off coupons. At this point, Maxwell House, a unit of Kraft General Foods, has regained a few drops of market share that it had lost to Folgers, a unit of Procter & Gamble, earlier in the war. Maxwell House's strategy has been to advertise heavily (spending over $100 million a year) and to introduce new products that lure consumers with taste rather than price. Examples include ready-made coffee in refrigerator cartons and coffee syrup, both designed for consumers to pour and microwave as needed. Nevertheless, Folgers is still the nation's best-selling coffee, although the Kraft

General Foods brands, which include Yuban and Sanka, account for a 35 percent market share. P&G has 32 percent of the U.S. coffee market.

Research organizations like A.C. Nielsen and Ehrhart-Babic provide excellent market share reports for many different industries. These reports enable companies to track their performance in various product categories over time.

### Sales Maximization

Rather than striving for market share, sometimes companies try to maximize sales. The objective of maximizing sales ignores profits, competition, and the marketing environment as long as sales are rising.

If a company is strapped for funds or faces an uncertain future, it may try to generate a maximum amount of cash in the short run. Management's task when using this objective is to calculate which price/quantity relationship generates the greatest cash revenue. Sales maximization can also be effectively used on a temporary basis to sell off excess inventory. It is not uncommon, for example, to find Christmas cards, ornaments, and so on discounted at 50 to 70 percent off retail prices after the holiday season. Management can also use sales maximization for year-end sales to clear out old models before introducing the new ones.

Maximization of cash should never be a long-run objective, because cash maximization may mean little or no profitability. Without profits, a company cannot survive.

## STATUS QUO PRICING OBJECTIVES

**status quo pricing**
Pricing objective that seeks to maintain existing prices or simply meet the competition.

**Status quo pricing** seeks to maintain existing prices or to meet the competition's prices. This third category of pricing objectives has the major advantage of requiring little planning. It is essentially a passive policy.

Often firms competing in an industry with an established price leader simply meet the competition's prices. These industries typically have fewer price wars than those with direct price competition. In other cases managers regularly shop competitors' stores to ensure that their prices are comparable. Woolworth's middle managers must visit competing Kmart stores weekly to compare prices and then make adjustments. In response to MCI's and Sprint's claims that its long-distance service is overpriced, AT&T struck back with advertisements showing that its rates are essentially equal to competitors'. AT&T was attempting to convince target consumers that it follows a status quo pricing strategy.

3 *Explain the role of demand in price determination.*

# THE DEMAND DETERMINANT OF PRICE

After marketing managers set pricing goals, they must set specific prices to reach those goals. The price they set for each product depends mostly on two factors: the demand for the good or service and the cost to the seller for that good or service. When pricing goals are mainly sales-oriented, demand considerations usually dominate. Other factors—such as distribution and promotion strategies, perceived quality, and stage of the product life cycle—can also influence price.

## THE NATURE OF DEMAND

**demand**
Quantity of a product that will be sold in the market at various prices for a specified period.

**Demand** is the quantity of a product that will be sold in the market at various prices for a specified period. The quantity of a product that people will buy depends on its price. The higher the price, the fewer goods or services consumers will demand. Conversely, the lower the price, the more goods or services they will demand.

This trend is illustrated in Exhibit 18.2A, which graphs the demand per week for

*Exhibit 18.2*

Demand Curve and Demand Schedule for Gourmet Popcorn

**(A) Demand curve**

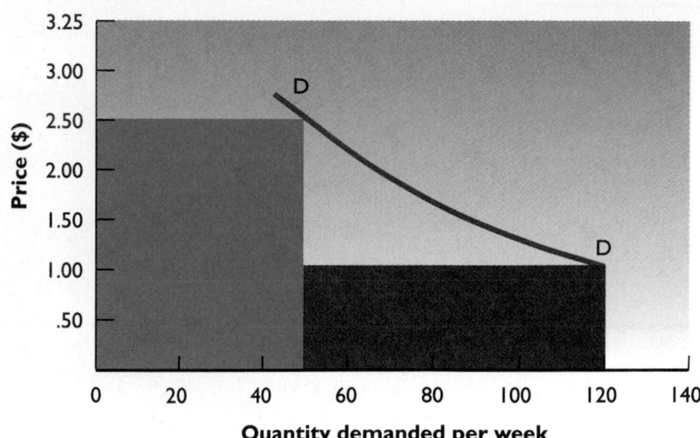


**(B) Demand schedule**

| Price per package of gourmet popcorn | Packages of gourmet popcorn demanded per week |
|---|---|
| $3.00 | 35 |
| 2.50 | 50 |
| 2.00 | 65 |
| 1.50 | 85 |
| 1.00 | 120 |

gourmet popcorn at a local retailer at various prices. This graph is called a *demand curve*. The vertical axis of the graph shows different prices of gourmet popcorn, measured in dollars per package. The horizontal axis measures the quantity of gourmet popcorn that will be demanded per week at each price. For example, at a price of $2.50, 50 packages will be sold per week; at $1.00, consumers will demand 120 packages—as the *demand schedule* in Exhibit 18.2B shows.

The demand curve in Exhibit 18.2 slopes downward and to the right, which indicates that more gourmet popcorn is demanded as the price is lowered. In other words, if popcorn manufacturers put a greater quantity on the market, then their hopes of selling all of it will be realized only by selling it at a lower price.

One reason why more is sold at lower prices than at higher prices is that lower prices bring in new buyers. This fact might not be so obvious with gourmet popcorn, but consider the example of steak. As the price of steak drops lower and lower, some people who have not been eating steak will probably start buying it rather than hamburger. And with each reduction in price, existing customers may buy extra amounts. Similarly, if the price of gourmet popcorn falls low enough, some people will buy more than they have bought in the past.

## The Concept of Supply

**supply**
Quantity of a product that will be offered to the market by a supplier, or suppliers, at various prices for a specified period.

**Supply** is the quantity of a product that will be offered to the market by a supplier, or suppliers, at various prices for a specified period. Exhibit 18.3A illustrates the resulting *supply curve* for gourmet popcorn. Unlike the falling demand curve, the supply curve for gourmet popcorn slopes upward and to the right. At higher prices, gourmet popcorn manufacturers will obtain more resources (popcorn, flavorings, salt) and produce more gourmet popcorn. If the price consumers are willing to pay for gourmet popcorn increases, producers can afford to buy more ingredients.

Output tends to increase at higher prices because manufacturers can sell more packages of gourmet popcorn and earn greater profits. The *supply schedule* in Exhibit

*Exhibit 18.3*

Supply Curve and Supply Schedule for Gourmet Popcorn

**(A) Supply curve**

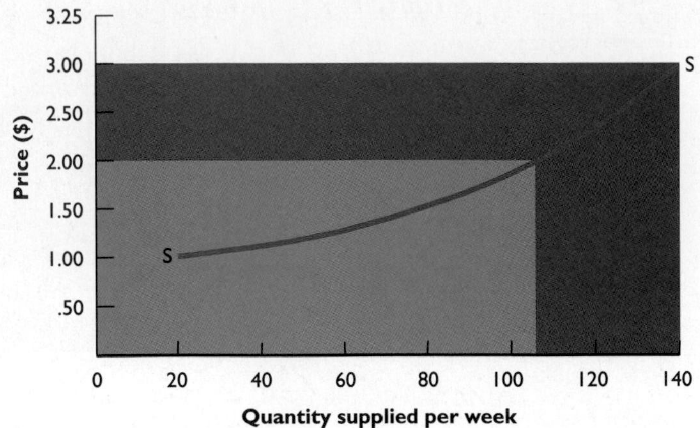


**(B) Supply schedule**

| Price per package of gourmet popcorn | Packages of gourmet popcorn supplied per week |
|---|---|
| $3.00 | 140 |
| 2.50 | 130 |
| 2.00 | 110 |
| 1.50 | 85 |
| 1.00 | 25 |

18.3B shows that at $2 suppliers are willing to place 110 packages of gourmet popcorn on the market but that they will offer 140 packages at a price of $3.

## How Demand and Supply Establish Prices

At this point, let's combine the concepts of demand and supply to see how competitive market prices are determined. So far, the premise is that if price is X, then consumers will purchase Y amount of gourmet popcorn. How high or low will prices actually go? How many packages of gourmet popcorn will be produced? How many packages will be consumed? The demand curve cannot predict consumption, nor can the supply curve alone forecast production. Instead, we need to look at what happens when supply and demand interact—as shown in Exhibit 18.4.

At a price of $3, the public would demand only 35 packages of gourmet popcorn. But suppliers stand ready to place 140 packages on the market at this price (data

*Exhibit 18.4*

Equilibrium Price for Gourmet Popcorn

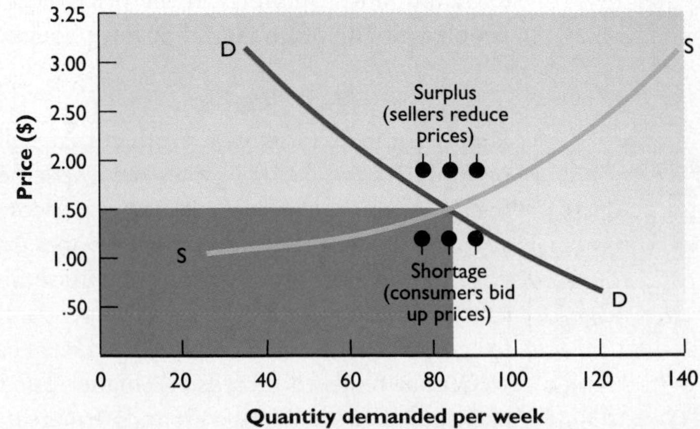

from the demand and supply schedules). If they do, they would create a surplus of 105 packages of gourmet popcorn. How does a merchant eliminate a surplus? It lowers the price.

At a price of $1, 120 packages would be demanded but only 25 would be placed on the market. A shortage of 95 units would be created. If a product is in short supply and consumers want it, how do they entice the dealer to part with one unit? They offer more money—that is, pay a higher price.

**price equilibrium**
Price at which demand and supply are equal.

Now let's examine a price of $1.50. At this price, 85 packages are demanded and 85 are supplied. When demand and supply are equal, a state called **price equilibrium** is achieved. A temporary price below equilibrium—say $1.00—results in a shortage, because at that price the demand for gourmet popcorn is greater than the available supply. Shortages put upward pressure on price. But as long as demand and supply remain the same, temporary price increases or decreases tend to return to equilibrium. At equilibrium there is no inclination for prices to rise or fall.

An equilibrium price may not be reached all at once. Prices may fluctuate during a trial-and-error period as the market for a good or service moves toward equilibrium. But sooner or later, demand and supply will settle into proper balance.

## ELASTICITY OF DEMAND

To appreciate demand analysis, you should understand the concept of elasticity.

**elasticity of demand**
Consumers' responsiveness or sensitivity to changes in price.

**elastic demand**
Situation in which consumer demand changes as price changes.

**inelastic demand**
Situation in which an increase or a decrease in price will not significantly affect demand for the product.

**Elasticity of demand** refers to consumers' responsiveness or sensitivity to changes in price. **Elastic demand** occurs when consumers buy more or less of a product when the price changes. Conversely, **inelastic demand** means that an increase or a decrease in price will not significantly affect demand for the product.

Elasticity over the range of a demand curve can be measured by using this formula:

$$\text{Elasticity (E)} = \frac{\text{Percentage change in quantity demanded of good A}}{\text{Percentage change in price of good A}}$$

If E is greater than 1, demand is elastic.

If E is less than 1, demand is inelastic.

If E is equal to 1, demand is unitary.

**unitary elasticity**
Situation in which an increase in sales exactly offsets a decrease in price so that total revenue remains the same.

**Unitary elasticity** (which is explained in more detail a bit later) means that an increase in sales exactly offsets a decrease in prices so that total revenue remains the same.

Easticity can be measured by observing these changes in total revenue:

If price goes down and revenue goes up, demand is elastic.

If price goes down and revenue goes down, demand is inelastic.

If price goes up and revenue goes up, demand is inelastic.

If price goes up and revenue goes down, demand is elastic.

If price goes up or down and revenue stays the same, elasticity is unitary.

Exhibit 18.5A shows a very elastic demand curve. Decreasing the price of a Sony VCR from $300 to $200 increases sales from 18,000 units to 59,000 units. Revenue increases from $5.4 million ($300 × 18,000) to $11.8 million ($200 × 59,000). The price decrease results in a large increase in sales and revenue.

Exhibit 18.5B shows a completely inelastic demand curve. The state of Nevada dropped its used-car vehicle inspection fee from $20 to $10. The state continued to inspect about 400,000 used cars annually. Decreasing the price (inspection fee) 50

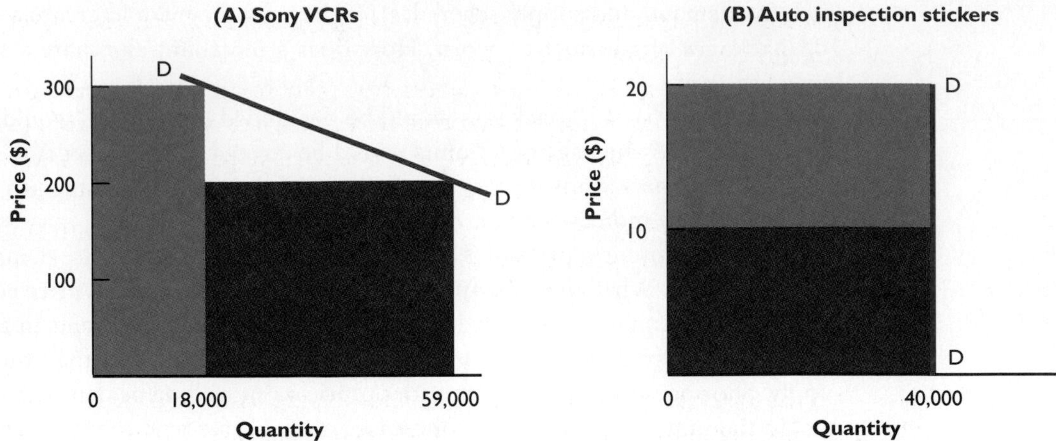


*Exhibit 18.5*

Elasticity of Demand for Sony VCRs and Auto Inspection Stickers

percent did not cause people to buy more used cars. Demand is completely inelastic for inspection fees, which are required by law. Thus it also follows that Nevada could double the original fee to $40 and double the state's inspection revenues. People won't quit buying used cars if the inspection fee increases—within a reasonable range.

Exhibit 18.6 presents the demand curve and demand schedule for three-ounce bottles of Spring Break suntan lotion. Let's follow the demand curve from the highest price to the lowest and examine what happens to elasticity as the price decreases.

## Inelastic Demand

The initial decrease in the price of Spring Break suntan lotion, from $5.00 to $2.25, results in a decrease in total revenue of $969 ($5,075 – $4,106). When price and total revenue fall, demand is inelastic. The decrease in price is much greater than the

*Exhibit 18.6*

Demand for Three-Ounce Bottles of Spring Break Suntan Lotion

**(A) Demand curve**

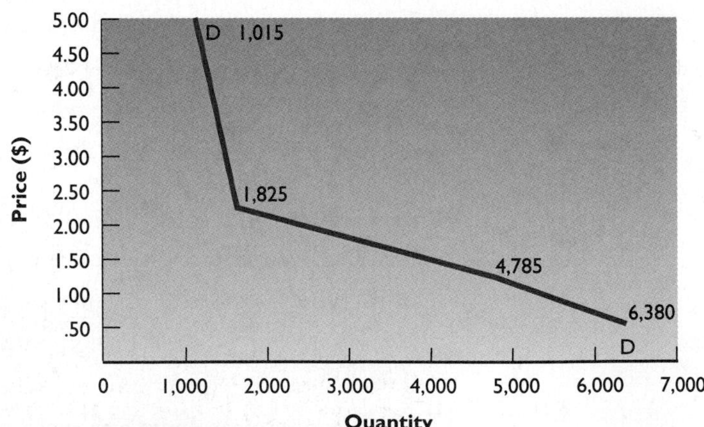


**(B) Demand schedule**

| Price | Quantity demanded | Total revenue (price x quantity) | Elasticity |
|---|---|---|---|
| $5.00 | 1,015 | $5,075 | Inelastic |
| 2.25 | 1,825 | 4,106 | |
| 1.00 | 4,785 | 4,785 | Elastic |
| 0.25 | 6,380 | 4,785 | Unitary |

increase in suntan lotion sales (810 bottles). Demand is therefore not very flexible in the price range $5.00 to $2.25.

When demand is inelastic, sellers can raise prices and increase total revenue. Inelastic demand for some goods considered essential in most American households, such as TVs and VCRs, has raised the typical retail price beyond the means of poor Americans. But the desire to have some of these products remains strong, and so poor consumers sometimes acquire these products by "renting to own." Some people claim, as the Ethics in Marketing box explains, that rent-to-own companies are taking advantage of poor people.

## Elastic Demand

In the example of Spring Break suntan lotion, shown in Exhibit 18.6, when the price is dropped from $2.25 to $1.00, total revenue increases by $679 ($4,785 – $4,106). An increase in total revenue when price falls indicates that demand is elastic. Let's measure elasticity of demand when the price drops from $2.25 to $1.00 by applying the formula:

$$E = \frac{\text{Change in quantity} \;/\; (\text{Sum of quantities} \;/\; 2)}{\text{Change in price} \;/\; (\text{Sum of prices} \;/\; 2)}$$

$$= \frac{(4{,}785 - 1{,}825) \;/\; [(1{,}825 + 4{,}785) \;/\; 2]}{(2.25) - 1 \;/\; [(2.25 + 1.00) \;/\; 2]}$$

$$= \frac{2{,}960 \;/\; 3{,}305}{1.25 \;/\; 1.63}$$

$$= \frac{.896}{.767}$$

$$= 1.17$$

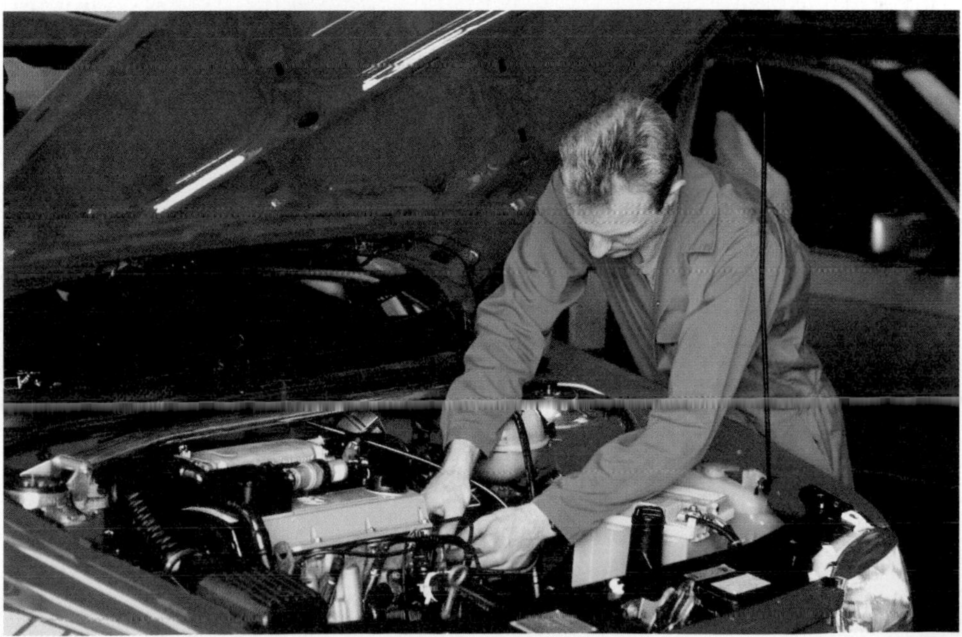

Because demand for new cars is elastic, people are more likely to get their cars repaired than to buy new ones when the prices rise too rapidly.

© Tony Stone Worldwide/Christopher Bissell

ETHICS IN MARKETING

**Is Renting to Own a Rip-Off?**

Since 1987, London-based Rent-A-Center has expanded briskly, using both acquisitions and aggressive marketing tactics introduced by its top executive, a former Pizza Hut marketing whiz. Rent-A-Center now thoroughly dominates the rent-to-own industry. Rent-A-Center USA controls 25 percent of the U.S. market; the chain has more outlets than its four biggest competitors combined.

The industry is known as rent-to-own because renters who make every weekly payment, usually for seventy-eight weeks, become owners. For low-income customers, Rent-A-Center has tremendous appeal. The chain gives them immediate use of brand-name merchandise, and the weekly payments are usually less than $20. Customers can eventually own the goods outright.

Unfortunately, customers who manage to make every installment may end up paying several times the item's retail value—at an effective annual interest rate, if the transaction is viewed as a credit sale, that can top 200 percent. In the Utah market, for example, Rent-A-Center customers pay a total of $1,033.56 over eighteen months for a new Sanyo VCR with a suggested retail price of $289.98—for an effective annual interest rate of a breathtaking 231 percent. Rent-A-Center denies that its transactions are credit sales, because most customers don't end up buying the product and they can cancel at any time. Thus, it argues, it doesn't charge interest at all.

Critics contend that Rent-A-Center employees also routinely encourage unsophisticated customers to rent more goods than they can afford. Then, when the customers fall behind in payments, Rent-A-Center repossesses the goods and re-rents them. The company says three out of every four are unable to meet all their payments. In fact, the company earns considerably more by renting, repossessing, and then re-renting the same goods than it does if the first customer makes all the payments. Derrick Myers, who was fired as manager of the Rent-A-Center store in Victorville, California, recalls one particular Philco VCR, for example. He says that it retailed for about $119 but that it brought in more than $5,000 in a five-year period.

According to a thick training manual, salespeople are supposed to quote the weekly and monthly rental rates. The manual doesn't instruct employees to quote the total cost, and former store managers say they made sure employees never did. Until recently, the total wasn't even on the price tag in forty states. Instead, the manual instructs employees to focus on "features and benefits," such as Rent-A-Center's free delivery and repair and, most of all, the low weekly price.

By design, the advertised weekly price yields each store about 3½ times the cost of purchasing the merchandise from Rent-A-Center headquarters. The total is jacked up further by a one-time processing fee (typically $7.50) and late fees (typically $5). The total price is usually revealed only in the rental agreement that customers sign at the end of the sales process, former store managers say.

To boost Rent-A-Center's profits, employees also push a "customer

Because E is greater than 1, demand is elastic.

But why is demand elastic when the price falls from $2.25 to $1.00? The demand schedule notwithstanding, in reality Spring Break cannot sell 1,825 units at $2.25 and an additional 4,785 units at $1.00. Instead, price is an either-or proposition. To sell 4,785 units at $1.00, Spring Break must sacrifice $1.25 on 1,825 units that could have been sold at $2.25. The total sacrifice when the price is dropped from $2.25 to $1.00 is $2,281 (1,825 units × $1.25). Demand must be sensitive enough to the price change to cover the sacrificed revenue, or else total revenue will fall (demand will be inelastic). Note that Spring Break does sell an additional 2,960 units (4,785 – 1,825) when it drops the price from $2.25 to $1.00. Thus the gross revenue gain from the price cut is $2,960 (2,960 units × $1.00). The gain of $2,960 is enough to offset the $1.25 per unit loss on the 1,825 units that could have been sold for $2.25. Therefore, by dropping the price from $2.25 to $1.00, total revenue increases by $679 ($2,960 – $2,281).

### Unitary Elasticity

The last price decrease for Spring Break suntan lotion is from $1.00 to 75¢. The increase in sales exactly offsets the decrease in price, so that total revenue remains the same. This situation, called unitary elasticity, is a fairly rare phenomenon. It could occur, for example, if all the people in the market for suntan lotion budget a certain amount of money for suntan lotion and will not deviate from that figure regardless of price. When price falls, they buy more suntan lotion, and when price goes up, they buy less.

### Factors That Affect Elasticity

Several factors affect elasticity of demand, including the following:

ETHICS IN MARKETING

protection" plan that offers minimal benefits but that 95 percent of customers end up subscribing to. "It's better than insurance," saleswoman Laura Daupino of the Bloomfield, New Jersey, store was overheard telling an unemployed welfare mother. Yet unlike insurance, the protection plan doesn't replace stolen or destroyed items or reimburse customers for their loss. It offers customers basically one benefit: It prevents Rent-A-Center from suing customers if goods are stolen or destroyed.

For Rent-A-Center, however, the protection plan is a $29 million annual revenue booster. The company racks up another $27 million from the other fees. On the other hand, Rent-A-Center has long justified its high prices by citing customer defaults and the costs associated with its free repairs.[11]

It can be argued that without rent-to-own operations, poor people would never be able to enjoy "the finer things in life." Do you agree? Do you feel that Rent-A-Center is exploiting the poor or providing a needed service? Is this simply a case of taking advantage of inelastic demand?



- *Availability of substitutes:* When many substitute products are available, the consumer can easily switch from one product to another, making demand elastic.
- *Price relative to purchasing power:* If a price is so low that it is an inconsequential part of an individual's budget, demand will be inelastic. For example, if the price of salt doubles, consumers will not stop putting salt and pepper on their eggs, because salt is cheap anyway.
- *Product durability:* Consumers often have the option of repairing durable products rather than replacing them, thus prolonging their useful life. For instance, if a person had planned to buy a new car and the prices suddenly began to rise, he or she might elect to fix the old car and drive it for another year. In other words, people are sensitive to the price increase, and demand is elastic.
- *Product's other uses:* The greater the number of different uses for a product, the more elastic demand tends to be. If a product has only one use, as may be true of a new medicine, the quantity purchased probably will not vary as price varies. A person will consume only the prescribed quantity, regardless of price. On the other hand, a product like steel has many possible applications. As its price falls, steel becomes more economically feasible in a wider variety of applications, thereby making demand relatively elastic.

4 *Describe cost-oriented pricing strategies.*

## THE COST DETERMINANT OF PRICE

Sometimes companies minimize or ignore the importance of demand and decide to price their products largely or solely on the basis of costs. Prices determined strictly on the basis of costs may be too high for the target market, thereby reducing or eliminating sales. Or cost-based prices may be too low, causing the firm to earn a lower return than it should. However, costs should generally be part of any price determination, if only as a floor below which a good or service must not be priced in the long run.

Cost may seem simple, but it is actually a multifaceted concept, especially for producers of goods and services. **Variable costs** are those that deviate with changes in the level of output; an example of a variable cost is the cost of materials. In contrast, a **fixed cost** does not change as output is increased or decreased. Examples include rent and executive salaries.

**variable cost**
Cost that deviates with changes in the level of output.

**fixed cost**
Cost that does not change as output is increased or decreased.

In order to compare the cost of production to the selling price of a product, it is

**average variable cost (AVC)**
Total variable costs divided by output.

**average total cost (ATC)**
Total costs divided by output.

**marginal cost (MC)**
Change in total costs associated with a one-unit change in output.

helpful to calculate costs per unit or average costs. **Average variable cost** (AVC) equals total variable costs divided by quantity of output. **Average total cost** (ATC) equals total costs divided by output. As plotted on the graph in Exhibit 18.7A, AVC and ATC are basically U-shaped curves. In contrast, average fixed costs (AFC) decline continually as output increases, because total fixed costs are constant.

**Marginal cost** (MC) is the change in total costs associated with a one-unit change in output. Exhibit 18.7B shows that, when output rises from seven to eight units, the change in total cost is from $640 to $750; therefore, marginal cost is $110.

All the curves illustrated in Exhibit 18.7A have definite relationships:

- AVC plus AFC equals ATC.

Exhibit 18.7

Hypothetical Set of Cost Curves and a Cost Schedule

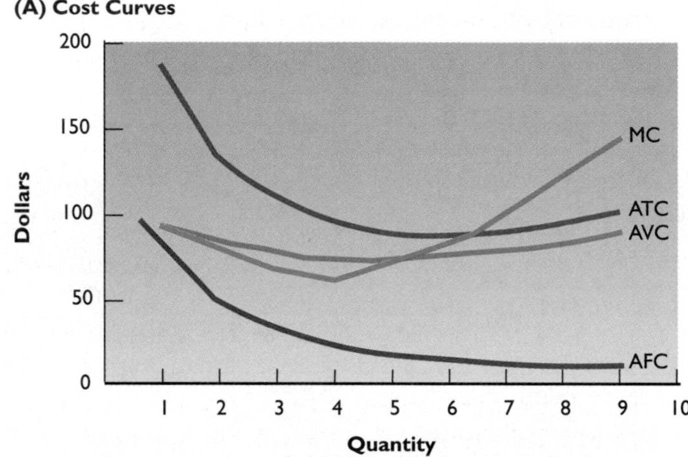


**(B) Cost schedule**

| **Total-cost data, per week** | | | | **Average-cost data, per week** | | | |
|---|---|---|---|---|---|---|---|
| **1 Total product (Q)** | **2 Total fixed cost (TFC)** | **3 Total variable cost (TVC)** | **4 Total cost (TC)** | **5 Average fixed cost (AFC)** | **6 Average variable cost (AVC)** | **7 Average total cost (ATC)** | **8 Marginal cost (MC)** |
| | | | TC = TFC+TVC | $AFC = \frac{TFC}{Q}$ | $AVC = \frac{TVC}{Q}$ | $ATC = \frac{TC}{Q}$ | $MC = \frac{\text{Change in TC}}{\text{Change in Q}}$ |
| 0 | $100 | $ 0 | $ 100 | — | — | — | — |
| 1 | 100 | 90 | 190 | $100.00 | $90.00 | $190.00 | $90 |
| 2 | 100 | 170 | 270 | 50.00 | 85.00 | 135.00 | 80 |
| 3 | 100 | 240 | 340 | 33.33 | 80.00 | 113.33 | 70 |
| 4 | 100 | 300 | 400 | 25.00 | 75.00 | 100.00 | 60 |
| 5 | 100 | 370 | 470 | 20.00 | 74.00 | 94.00 | 70 |
| 6 | 100 | 450 | 550 | 16.67 | 75.00 | 91.67 | 80 |
| 7 | 100 | 540 | 640 | 14.29 | 77.14 | 91.43 | 90 |
| 8 | 100 | 650 | 750 | 12.50 | 81.25 | 93.75 | 110 |
| 9 | 100 | 780 | 880 | 11.11 | 86.67 | 97.78 | 130 |
| 10 | 100 | 930 | 1,030 | 10.00 | 93.00 | 103.00 | 150 |

- MC falls for a while and then turns upward, in this case with the fourth unit. At that point diminishing returns set in, meaning that less output is produced for every additional dollar spent on variable input.
- MC intersects both AVC and ATC at their lowest possible points.
- When MC is less than AVC or ATC, the incremental cost will continue to pull the averages down. Conversely, when MC is greater than AVC or ATC, it pulls the averages up, and ATC and AVC begin to rise.
- The minimum point on the ATC curve is the least-cost point for a fixed-capacity firm, although it is not necessarily the most profitable point.

Costs can be used to set prices in a variety of ways. The first two methods discussed here, markup pricing and formula pricing, are relatively simple. The other three—profit maximization pricing, break-even pricing, and target return pricing—make use of the more complicated concepts of cost.

## MARKUP PRICING

Markup pricing, the most popular method used by wholesalers and retailers to establish a selling price, does not directly analyze the costs of production. Instead, **markup pricing** is the cost of buying the product from the producer plus amounts for profit and for expenses not otherwise accounted for. The total determines the selling price.

**markup pricing**
Pricing method that adds to the product cost amounts for profit and for expenses not previously accounted for.

A retailer, for example, adds a certain percentage to the cost of the merchandise received to arrive at the retail price. An item that costs the retailer $1.80 and is sold for $2.20 carries a markup of 40¢, which is a markup of 22 percent of the cost (40¢ ÷ $1.80). Retailers tend to discuss markup in terms of its percentage of the retail price—in this example, 18 percent (40¢ ÷ $2.20). The difference between the retailer's cost and the selling price (40¢) is the gross margin, as Chapter 13 explained. (See Appendix B for more information on markup pricing and the basic arithmetic of pricing.)

Markups are often based on experience. For example, many small retailers mark up merchandise 100 percent over cost (in other words, they double the cost). This tactic is called **keystoning.** Some other factors that influence markups are the merchandise's appeal to customers, past response to the markup (an implicit demand consideration), the item's promotional value, the seasonality of the goods, their fashion appeal, the product's traditional selling price, and competition. Most retailers avoid any set markup because of such considerations as promotional value and seasonality.

**keystoning**
Practice of marking up prices by 100 percent, or doubling the cost.

The biggest advantage of markup pricing is its simplicity. The primary disadvantage is that it ignores demand and may result in overpricing or underpricing the merchandise.

## FORMULA PRICING

A type of pricing similar to markup pricing is **formula pricing,** in which a predetermined formula is used to set price. One simple formula used by a marketing research firm (which should know better than to ignore demand) is to charge five times the cost of the fieldwork. Because fieldwork is normally the most expensive part of a research project, this approach normally covers all costs and produces a profit. More elaborate formulas are also used. For example, one manufacturer sets prices at 150 percent of direct labor costs plus 200 percent of material costs plus actual shipping costs.

**formula pricing**
Pricing method in which a predetermined formula is used to set price.

The main advantage of formula pricing is its simplicity. However, like markup pricing, it ignores demand.

**profit maximization**
Pricing method that sets price where marginal revenue equals marginal cost.

**marginal revenue (MR)**
Extra revenue associated with selling an extra unit of output.

**break-even analysis**
Method of determining what sales volume must be reached for a product before the company breaks even (total costs equal total revenue) and no profits are earned.

## PROFIT MAXIMIZATION PRICING

Producers tend to use more complicated methods of setting prices than distributors use. One is **profit maximization,** which occurs when marginal revenue equals marginal cost. You learned earlier that marginal cost is the change in total costs associated with a one-unit change in output. Similarly, **marginal revenue** (MR) is the extra revenue associated with selling an extra unit of output. As long as the revenue of the last unit produced and sold is greater than the cost of the last unit produced and sold, the firm should continue manufacturing and selling the product.

Exhibit 18.8 shows the marginal revenues and marginal costs for a hypothetical firm, using the cost data from Exhibit 18.7B. The profit-maximizing quantity, where MR = MC, is six units. You might say, "If profit is zero, why produce the sixth unit? Why not stop at five?" In fact, you would be right. The firm, however, would not know that the fifth unit would produce zero profits until it determined that profits were no longer increasing. Economists suggest producing up to the point where MR = MC. If marginal revenue is just one penny greater than marginal costs, it will still increase total profits.

## BREAK-EVEN PRICING

Now let's take a closer look at the relationship between sales and cost. **Break-even analysis** determines what sales volume must be reached before the company breaks even (its total costs equal total revenue) and no profits are earned.

The typical break-even model assumes a given fixed cost and a constant average variable cost. Suppose that Universal Sportswear, a hypothetical firm, has fixed costs of $2,000 and that the cost of labor and materials for each unit produced is 50¢. Assume that it can sell up to 6,000 units of its product at $1 without having to lower its price. Exhibit 18.9A illustrates Universal Sportswear's break-even point.

As Exhibit 18.9B indicates, Universal Sportswear's total variable costs increase by 50¢ every time a new unit is produced, and total fixed costs remain constant at

*Exhibit 18.8*

Point of Profit Maximization

| Quantity | Marginal revenue (MR) | Marginal cost (MC) | Total profit |
|---|---|---|---|
| 0 | — | — | — |
| 1 | 140 | 90 | 50 |
| 2 | 130 | 80 | 100 |
| 3 | 105 | 70 | 135 |
| 4 | 95 | 60 | 170 |
| 5 | 85 | 70 | 185 |
| *6 | 80 | 80 | 185 |
| 7 | 75 | 90 | 170 |
| 8 | 60 | 110 | 120 |
| 9 | 50 | 130 | 40 |
| 10 | 40 | 150 | (70) |

*Profit maximization

$2,000 regardless of the level of output. Therefore, 4,000 units of output give Universal Sportswear $2,000 in fixed costs and $2,000 in total variable costs (4,000 units × 50¢), or $4,000 in total costs. Revenue is also $4,000 (4,000 units × $1), giving a net profit of zero dollars at the break-even point of 4,000 units. Notice that once the firm gets past the break-even point, the gap between total revenue and total cost gets wider and wider, because both functions are assumed to be linear.

The formula for calculating break-even quantities is simple:

$$\text{Break-even quantity} = \frac{\text{Total fixed costs}}{\text{Fixed cost contribution}}$$

Fixed cost contribution is the price minus the average variable cost. Therefore, for Universal Sportswear,

*Exhibit 18.9*

Costs, Revenues, and Break-Even Point for Universal Sportswear

**(A) Break-even point**

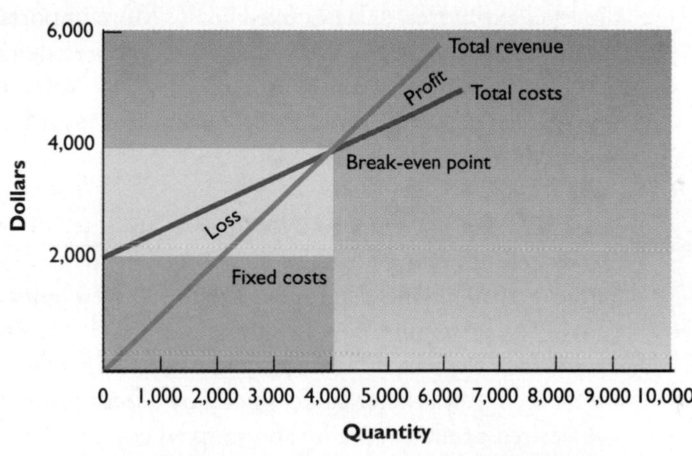


**(B) Costs and revenues**

| Output | Total fixed costs | Average variable costs | Total variable costs | Average total costs | Average revenue (price) | Total revenue | Total costs | Profit or loss |
|---|---|---|---|---|---|---|---|---|
| 500 | $2,000 | $0.50 | $ 250 | $4.50 | $1.00 | $ 500 | $2,250 | ($1,750) |
| 1,000 | 2,000 | 0.50 | 500 | 2.50 | 1.00 | 1,000 | 2,500 | (1,500) |
| 1,500 | 2,000 | 0.50 | 750 | 1.83 | 1.00 | 1,500 | 2,750 | (1,250) |
| 2,000 | 2,000 | 0.50 | 1,000 | 1.50 | 1.00 | 2,000 | 3,000 | (1,000) |
| 2,500 | 2,000 | 0.50 | 1,250 | 1.30 | 1.00 | 2,500 | 3,250 | (750) |
| 3,000 | 2,000 | 0.50 | 1,500 | 1.17 | 1.00 | 3,000 | 3,500 | (500) |
| 3,500 | 2,000 | 0.50 | 1,750 | 1.07 | 1.00 | 3,500 | 3,750 | (250) |
| *4,000 | 2,000 | 0.50 | 2,000 | 1.00 | 1.00 | 4,000 | 4,000 | (0) |
| 4,500 | 2,000 | 0.50 | 2,250 | .94 | 1.00 | 4,500 | 4,250 | 250 |
| 5,000 | 2,000 | 0.50 | 2,500 | .90 | 1.00 | 5,000 | 4,500 | 500 |
| 5,500 | 2,000 | 0.50 | 2,750 | .86 | 1.00 | 5,500 | 4,750 | 750 |
| 6,000 | 2,000 | 0.50 | 3,000 | .83 | 1.00 | 6,000 | 5,000 | 1,000 |

*Break-even point

$$\text{Break-even quantity} = \frac{\$2{,}000}{(\$1.00 - 50¢)} = \frac{\$2{,}000}{50¢}$$

$$= 4{,}000 \text{ units}$$

The advantage of break-even analysis is that it provides a quick estimate of how much the firm must sell to break even and how much profit can be earned if a higher sales volume is obtained. If a firm is operating close to the break-even point, it may want to see what can be done to reduce costs or increase sales. Moreover, in a simple break-even analysis, it is not necessary to compute marginal costs and marginal revenues, because price and average cost per unit are assumed to be constant. Because accounting data for marginal cost and revenue are frequently unavailable, it is convenient not to have to depend on that information.

Break-even analysis is not without several important limitations. Sometimes it is hard to know whether a cost is fixed or variable. For example, if labor wins a tough guaranteed-employment contract, are the resulting expenses a fixed cost? Are middle-level executives' salaries fixed costs? More important than cost determination is the fact that simple break-even analysis ignores demand. For example, how does Universal Sportswear know it can sell 4,000 units at $1? Could it sell the same 4,000 units at $2 or even $5? Obviously, this information would profoundly affect the firm's pricing decisions.

## TARGET RETURN PRICING

**target return pricing**
Pricing method that sets price where revenues from sales of a targeted quantity yield the target return on investment.

Target return pricing is one of the most popular methods of choosing a selling price. **Target return pricing** determines the break-even point (where costs equal revenues), plus a dollar amount equal to the desired ROI (return on investment) percentage. Thus when the targeted quantity has been sold, the company will have reached its target ROI. A marketer can easily figure a target-return break-even point by treating the desired profit as an addition to fixed cost. The desired level of profit (expressed in dollars) is typically a predetermined ROI.

Assume that Johnson Controls, an industrial controls manufacturer, has just spent $1 million developing a new heat-sensing unit. The firm has a 15 percent target ROI for the new product and therefore must earn a profit of $150,000. Fixed costs allocated to the new product by the accounting department are $65,000. Average variable costs are $14, and the tentative selling price is $60 each. The following calculation applies the basic formula:

$$\text{Fixed cost contribution} = \$60 - \$14 = \$46$$

$$\text{Break-even point ROI} = \frac{\text{Total fixed cost} + \text{Total desired profit}}{\text{Fixed cost contribution per unit}}$$

$$= \frac{\$65{,}000 + \$150{,}000}{\$46}$$

$$= 4{,}673.9 \text{ heat-sensing units}$$

If the marketing manager has forecast sales of about 4,700 units, then the target ROI will be slightly exceeded.

By plugging different prices into the formula, the marketing manager can determine how many units must be sold at each price to reach the target ROI. A comparison of the target ROI quantity and the sales forecast will tell the manager whether the ROI objective can be met at a given price.

5 *Demonstrate how the product life cycle, competition, distribution and promotion strategies, and quality perceptions can affect price.*

## OTHER DETERMINANTS OF PRICE

Other factors besides demand and costs can influence price. For example, the stage of the product's life cycle, the competition, product distribution strategy, promotion strategy, and perceived product quality can all affect pricing.

### STAGE IN THE PRODUCT LIFE CYCLE

As a product moves through its life cycle (see Chapter 9), the demand for the product and the competitive conditions tend to change:

- *Introductory stage:* Management usually sets prices high during the introductory stage. One reason is that management hopes to recover its development costs quickly. In addition, demand originates in the core of the market (the customers whose needs ideally match the product attribute), and thus demand is relatively inelastic. On the other hand, if the target market is highly price-sensitive, management often finds it better to price the product at the market level or lower. For example, when Kraft General Foods brought out Country Time lemonade, it was priced like similar products in the highly competitive beverage market because the market was price-sensitive.
- *Growth stage:* Prices generally begin to stabilize as the product enters the

Home computers were introduced to the market at relatively high prices, which allowed manufacturers to recover their development costs. As the product category enters the growth stage and new competitors are entering the market, prices are falling.

growth stage. There are several reasons. First, competitors have entered the market, increasing the available supply. Second, the product has begun to appeal to a broader market, often lower-income groups. Finally, economies of scale are lowering costs, and the savings can be passed on to the consumer in the form of lower prices.

- *Maturity stage:* Maturity usually brings further price decreases as competition increases and inefficient, high-cost firms are eliminated. Distribution channels become a significant cost factor, however, because of the need to offer wide product lines for highly segmented markets, extensive service requirements, and the sheer number of dealers necessary to absorb high-volume production. The manufacturers that remain in the market toward the end of the maturity stage typically offer similar prices. Usually only the most efficient remain, and they have comparable costs. At this stage, price increases are usually cost-initiated, not demand-initiated. Nor do price reductions in the late phase of maturity stimulate much demand. Because demand is limited and producers have similar cost structures, the remaining competitors will probably match price reductions.
- *Decline stage:* The final stage of the life cycle may see further price decreases as the few remaining competitors try to salvage the last vestiges of demand. When only one firm is left in the market, prices begin to stabilize. In fact, prices may eventually rise dramatically if the product survives and moves into the specialty good category, as horse-drawn carriages and vinyl records have.

## THE COMPETITION

Competition varies during the product life cycle, of course, and so at times it may strongly affect pricing decisions. For example, although a firm may not have any competition at first, the high prices it charges may eventually induce another firm to enter the market.

The salty snack business provides a good example of how high prices entice competition. In the 1980s, Borden noticed that the industry had only one big national competitor, Frito-Lay, which left room for a second. Also, yearly price increases by Frito-Lay kept profits rising about 20 percent annually. Borden made a full-scale commitment, and the strategy worked perfectly until 1982, when Anheuser-Busch decided to expand its Eagle Snacks division. Eagle won shelf space in supermarkets by reportedly paying retailers as much as $500 a linear foot and by dropping prices. Competitors fought back. By 1989 Eagle decided that it had to become more competitive to stay in the game, and it targeted Frito-Lay's Doritos tortilla chip business. Frito-Lay matched Eagle on every program. Eagle spent $15 million to $20 million in TV advertising and deep-cut price promotions. In 1992 Eagle had about a 4 percent market share but lost $20 million. It wasn't until the price war subsided in 1994 that Eagle Snacks finally turned a profit.[12]

When a firm enters a mature market without a "price umbrella" provided by a market leader, it has three options. It can price below the market, as Eagle Snacks did. Or, if the new competitor has a distinct competitive advantage, it can price above the market. Lifetime Automotive Products entered the windshield wiper market with wiper blades priced at $19.95, more than three times the average price. The firm's competitive advantage was a patented three-bladed wiper system that cleaned better than traditional wipers, plus a lifetime guarantee. Finally, companies can enter a market at the "going price," assuming that they can reach profit and market share objectives through nonprice competition. Entering at the existing price level helps avoid crippling price wars.

GLOBAL PERSPECTIVES

**Price Pressures in Europe**

In the past, even the slightest improvement in the economy of a European country would prompt price hikes of 5 percent or even 10 percent to boost corporate profits. But not anymore. As barriers to trade fall among member countries of the European Union, price competition is slowly increasing. Ultimately, the big winners will be Europe's consumers.

The signs of change are especially noticeable at the retail level. When Switzerland imposed a restaurant tax of 12.5 percent, both Burger King and McDonald's began big promotional campaigns, vowing to keep the price of fries and burgers from going up. In fact, both chains dropped the price of soft drinks. Walking through France's version of Wal-Mart, Continental Stores, shoppers are faced with a barrage of signs touting such bargains as "15 percent off Sanyo stereos" and "Today—take 200 francs off this Phillips vacuum cleaner."

Although prices are falling at the discounters and other retail shops, custom and traditional ways of doing business continue to prop up prices. For example, small appliance retailers had to fight off U.S. discounters in the 1950s and 1960s but still thrive in the central cities of Europe. Their appeal—and the reason for their continuing high prices—is the level of service they provide. European retailers, for the most part, have limited self-service.

A typical Shepra supermarket in France is only about one and a half times as big as a 7-Eleven store. But it is far more lavishly staffed. Usually, one or two employees are behind the meat counter, another is behind the cheese counter, and one is on hand to weigh customers' produce and help with their selections, along with the normal cadre of stockers and checkers. Obviously, labor costs limit retailers' ability to cut prices.

Other business customs also serve to limit price cutting. Downtown stores usually close for two hours at noon and in the evening at 6. Being open fewer and less convenient hours means that the facilities are being used less efficiently, which further drives up costs.

But customs may be changing. In 1995, Geneva, Switzerland, was filled with billboards making a radical announcement: Retailers would be allowed to stay open until 8 p.m. on Thursday nights. Migras, the local supermarket chain, fearing that shoppers might not come so late at night, offered a 10 percent discount on all groceries purchased between 6:30 and 8 p.m.

Why do you think prices are now coming down in Europe but have not in the past? If the downward pressure on prices leads to business failures and many people are laid off, will consumers really benefit? If hundreds of thousands of small retailers are put out of business by giant international discounters, what will happen to the economy? What will happen to Europe's traditional culture?

Price wars and intense competition are not limited to the United States. As the European Union moves toward greater economic unity, price cuts are becoming more common. Still, as the Global Perspectives box explains, the price cuts are limited by the old ways of doing business.

## DISTRIBUTION STRATEGY

An effective distribution network can often overcome other minor flaws in the marketing mix. For example, although consumers may perceive a price as being slightly higher than normal, they may buy the product anyway if it is being sold in a convenient retail outlet.

Adequate distribution for a new product can often be attained by offering a larger than usual profit margin to distributors. A variation on this strategy is to give dealers a large trade allowance to help offset the costs of promotion and further stimulate demand at the retail level.

Manufacturers have gradually been losing control within the distribution channel to wholesalers and retailers, which often adopt pricing strategies that serve their own purposes. For instance, some distributors are **selling against the brand.** They place well-known brands on the shelves at high prices while offering other brands—typically their private-label brands, such as Craftsman tools, Kroger pears, or Cost Cutter paper towels—at lower prices. Of course, sales of the higher-priced brands decline.

Wholesalers and retailers may also go outside traditional distribution channels to buy gray-market goods. As Chapter 12 explained, distributors obtain the goods through unauthorized channels for less than they would normally pay so they can sell the goods with a bigger than normal markup or

**selling against the brand** Stocking well-known branded items at high prices in order to sell store brands at discounted prices.

at a reduced price. Imports seem to be particularly susceptible to gray marketing. Porsches, JVC stereos, and Seiko watches are among the brand-name products that have experienced this problem. Although consumers may pay less for gray-market goods, they often find that the manufacturer won't honor the warranty.

Manufacturers can regain some control over price by using an exclusive distribution system, by franchising, or by avoiding doing business with price-cutting discounters. Manufacturers can also package merchandise with the selling price marked on it or place goods on consignment. The best way for manufacturers to control prices, however, is to develop brand loyalty in consumers by delivering quality and value.

## PROMOTION STRATEGY

Price is often used as a promotional tool to increase consumer interest. The weekly grocery section of the newspaper, for instance, advertises many products with special low prices. Crested Butte Ski Resort in Colorado, whose story introduced Chapter 15, tried a unique twist on price promotions. It made the unusual offer of free skiing between Thanksgiving and Christmas. Its only revenues were voluntary contributions from lodging and restaurant owners who benefited from the droves of skiers taking advantage of the promotion. Lodging during the slack period is now booked solid, and on the busiest days 9,000 skiers jam slopes designed for about 6,500. Crested Butte Resort no longer loses money during this time of the year.

Pricing can be a tool for trade promotions as well. For example, Levi's Dockers (casual men's slacks) are very popular with white-collar men ages 25 to 45, a growing and lucrative market. Sensing an opportunity, rival pantsmaker Bugle Boy began offering similar pants at cheaper wholesale prices, which gave retailers a bigger gross margin than they were getting with Dockers. Levi Strauss had to either lower prices or risk its $400 million annual Docker sales. Although Levi Strauss intended its cheapest Dockers to retail for $35, it started selling Dockers to retailers for $18 a pair. Retailers could then advertise Dockers at a very attractive retail price of $25.[13]

## THE RELATIONSHIP OF PRICE TO QUALITY

Consumers tend to rely on a high price as a predictor of good quality when there is great uncertainty involved in the purchase decision. Reliance on price as an indicator of quality seems to exist for all products, but it reveals itself more strongly for some items than for others.[14] Among the products that benefit from this phenomenon are coffee, stockings, aspirin, salt, floor wax, shampoo, clothing, furniture, perfume, whiskey, and many services. If the consumer obtains additional information —for instance, about the brand or the store—then reliance on price as an indicator of quality decreases.[15]

In the absence of other information, people typically assume that prices are higher because the products contain better materials, because they are made more carefully, or in the case of professional services, because the provider has more expertise. In other words, consumers assume that "You get what you pay for." One study has shown that some people believe "You get what you pay for" much more strongly than others. That is, some consumers tend to rely much more heavily on price as a quality indicator than others do.[16] In general, however, consumers tend to be more accurate in their price/quality assessments for nondurable goods (such as ice cream, frozen pizza, or oven cleaner) than for durable goods (such as coffeemakers, gas grills, or ten-speed bikes).[17]

When consumers lack the technical information needed for making purchase decisions, they may gauge the quality of products by price. That is, they may assume that the higher-priced products are also the highest quality.

© Tony Stone Worldwide/Jeff Zaruba

**prestige pricing**
Charging high prices to help promote a high-quality image.

Knowledgeable merchants take these consumer attitudes into account when devising their pricing strategies. **Prestige pricing** is charging a high price to help promote a high-quality image. A successful prestige pricing strategy requires a retail price that is reasonably consistent with consumers' expectations. For example, no one goes shopping at a Gucci's shop in New York and expects to pay $9.95 for a pair of loafers. In fact, demand would fall drastically at such a low price. Bayer aspirin would probably lose market share over the long run if it lowered its prices. A new mustard packaged in a crockery jar was not successful until its price was doubled.

Consumers also expect private or store brands to be cheaper than national brands. However, if the price difference between a private brand and a nationally distributed manufacturer's brand is too great, consumers tend to believe the private brand is inferior. On the other hand, if the savings aren't big enough, there is little incentive to buy the private brand. One study of scanner data found that if the price difference between the national brand and the private brand was less than 10 percent, people tended not to buy the private brand. If the price difference was greater than 20 percent, consumers perceived the private brand to be inferior.[18]

## LOOKING BACK

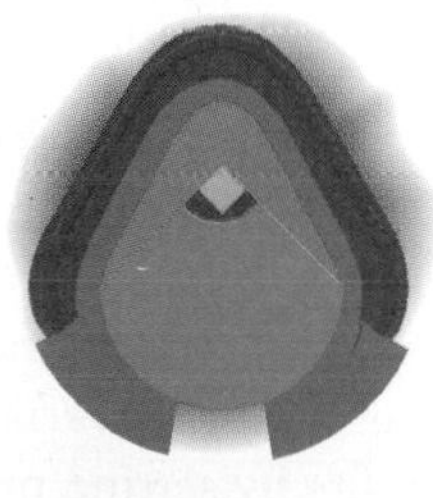

Look back at the story about pricing strategies in major league baseball that appears at the beginning of the chapter. One might argue that baseball owners are trying to maximize profits (or, at the very least, are striving for a satisfactory level of profits). Before the strike, by reducing cheap seats and installing more premium seating, they tried to squeeze more revenue from existing facilities. In other cases, they tried to maximize profits by building new stadiums with fewer bargain-priced seats. The logic behind this strategy is that the demand for premium seats is highly inelastic.

Cost plays several key roles in the pricing equation. First, it represents a floor below which a firm cannot price its products in the long run and remain in business. Second, controlling costs can add to a firm's profitability. For any given level of revenue that exceeds total costs, a lowering of costs will increase profits. Therefore, a firm can increase profit per unit in two ways: lowering costs or increasing price.

Competition can help hold down prices in the marketplace. A firm without competition that charges a high price will soon find competitors attracted to that market. As competitors enter the market, prices typically fall as firms compete for market share by lowering prices.

## SUMMARY

**1 Discuss the importance of pricing decisions to the economy and to the individual firm.** Pricing plays an integral role in the U.S. economy by allocating goods and services among consumers, governments, and businesses. Pricing is essential in business because it creates revenue, which is the basis of all business activity. In setting prices, marketing managers strive to find a level high enough to produce a satisfactory profit.

**2 List and explain a variety of pricing objectives.** Establishing realistic and measurable pricing objectives is a critical part of any firm's marketing strategy. Pricing objectives are commonly classified into three categories: profit-oriented, sales-oriented, and status quo. Profit-oriented pricing is based on profit maximization, a satisfactory level of profit, or a target return on investment. The goal of profit maximization is to generate as much revenue as possible in relation to cost. Often a more practical approach than profit maximization is setting prices to produce profits that will satisfy management and stockholders. The most common profit-oriented strategy is pricing for a specific return on investment relative to a firm's assets. The second type of pricing objective is sales-oriented, and it focuses on either maintaining a percentage share of the market or maximizing dollar or unit sales. The third type of pricing objective aims to maintain status quo by matching competitors' prices.

**3 Explain the role of demand in price determination.** Demand is a key determinant of price. When establishing prices, a firm must first determine demand for its product. A typical demand schedule shows an inverse relationship between quantity demanded and price. That is, when price is lowered, sales increase; and when price is increased, the quantity demanded falls. However, for prestige products, there may be a direct relationship between demand and price; the quantity demanded will increase as price increases.

Marketing managers must also consider demand elasticity when setting prices. Elasticity of demand is the degree to which quantity demanded fluctuates with changes in price. If consumers are sensitive to changes in price, demand is elastic. If they are insensitive to price changes, demand is inelastic. Thus an increase in price will result in lower sales for an elastic product and little or no change in sales for an inelastic product.

**4 Describe cost-oriented pricing strategies.** The other major determinant of price is cost. Marketers use several cost-oriented pricing strategies. To cover their own expenses and obtain a profit, wholesalers and retailers commonly use markup pricing; they tack an extra amount onto the manufacturer's original price. Like markup pricing, formula pricing sets prices using a predetermined formula based on variable and fixed costs. Another pricing technique is to maximize profits by setting price

### KEY TERMS

where marginal revenue equals marginal cost. Still another pricing strategy determines how much a firm must sell to break even and uses this amount as a reference point for adjusting price. Finally, a popular pricing method is target return pricing. Using this strategy, a firm calculates the break-even point and adds an additional amount so the total will equal its desired return on investment.

5 **Demonstrate how the product life cycle, competition, distribution and promotion strategies, and quality perceptions can affect price.** The price of a product normally changes as it moves through the life cycle and as demand for the product and competitive conditions change. Management often sets a high price at the introductory stage, and the high price tends to attract competition. The competition usually drives prices down, because individual competitors lower prices to gain market share.

Adequate distribution for a new product can sometimes be obtained by offering a larger-than-usual profit margin to wholesalers and retailers. Price is also used as a promotional tool to attract customers. Special low prices often attract new customers and entice existing customers to buy more.

Quality perceptions can also influence pricing strategies. A firm trying to project a prestigious image often charges a premium price for a product. Consumers tend to equate high prices with high quality.

## Discussion and Writing Questions

1. Why is pricing so important to the marketing manager?
2. In your opinion, has the role of price increased or decreased in importance relative to the other marketing mix variables? What developments have influenced your opinion?
3. How do consumers "vote" for products? What do consumer "votes" mean to manufacturers?
4. Comment on the following statement: "If demand for your product is inelastic, then your price is probably too low."
5. ✍ Your firm has based its pricing strictly on cost in the past. As the newly hired marketing manager, you believe this policy should change. Write the president a memo explaining your reasons.
6. Discuss several current consumer market trends influencing price.
7. How does the stage of a product's life cycle affect price? Give some examples.
8. Would you buy a private brand that was 50 percent cheaper than a nationally advertised brand? Why or why not?
9. List five products for which consumers often use price to gauge quality. Explain why you chose each product.

## Application for Small Business

Ann Boswell, an avid New Orleans gardener and horticulturalist, has always been intrigued with the smell of magnolia blossoms. After extensive tinkering with a number of ingredients, she has created a perfume that closely resembles the fragrance of the magnolia. She calls her perfume Southern Flower.

A New Orleans–based marketing research firm gave away free samples of Southern Flower in shopping malls throughout Louisiana and conducted a short interview with those who received the samples. The study estimated yearly demand in Louisiana would be as follows:

| *Price* | *Quantity* |
|---|---|
| $15.00 | 25,000 units |
| 20.00 | 20,000 |
| 22.50 | 19,000 |
| 25.00 | 11,000 |
| 27.50 | 10,000 |

Because the perfume uses real magnolia extract and is offered in a frosted, sculpted bottle with expensive foil packaging, the average variable costs are estimated at $13 per unit. Bottling machinery and factory rent are $40,000 annually.

Questions

1. Assuming that the market research studies are accurate, what price should be charged for the perfume?

2. Assume that fixed costs are $140,000 rather than $40,000. Should the company produce the perfume in the short run? In the long run?

3. Discuss the advantages and disadvantages of break-even analysis for a small business.

4. What is the break-even point for this perfume? Of what significance is that point?

## CRITICAL THINKING CASE

### Green Tortoise Bus Line

Take a trip back in time. In the 1960s, hippie buses flourished in the United States, traveling coast to coast. The ribald behavior of passengers and the cheap fares encouraged many riders to climb aboard.

Green Tortoise is a rolling remnant of the 1960s. The company owns nine antique buses whose average age is twenty years. They make regularly scheduled runs up and down the West Coast. In warmer months the company shuttles across the United States. Although most of the "gypsy" carriers have gone out of business, Green Tortoise still makes a profit. In 1981 the company bought out its last major competitor, the Grey Rabbit. It was a fitting end to the competition between the Tortoise and the Rabbit.

The buses have been modified to accommodate the passengers. The overhead racks have been converted into sleepers. When the seats flip down, they become sleeping platforms. The bus can sleep forty-five passengers. Roof racks for bicycles, kayaks, and canoes have been installed. The cost of renovating these buses runs $30,000. Despite their age, the company's buses are well maintained.

Creating a sense of adventure is the experience Green Tortoise provides. The driver, wearing red suspenders and sandals, greets the passengers. The back of the ticket stub says, "Know your limitations. Keep your wits about you." To this end, there is a sign on the visor warning, "If you downshift this transmission while going faster than 50 mph, it will blow up."

The bus makes some unusual stops. For example, on each trip between San Francisco and Seattle, the bus stops at the company's retreat off Interstate 5. The passengers are invited to participate in a communal cookout, sauna, and swim before continuing the journey. "It's adventure on the run," says Gardener Kent, owner and founder of Green Tortoise.

These bus trips are a niche business. The laid-back style of the bus line probably would appeal to only 5 percent of travelers, but 5 percent equals millions of people. Currently, Green Tortoise carries 10,000 passengers a year. Green Tortoise does not do any advertising except for handbills passed out by drivers and posted on college campuses. Demand for seats runs so strong that there is a waiting list to ride Green Tortoise.

Green Tortoise offers its passengers not only adventure but also a cheap fare. An average airline ticket between San Francisco and Seattle can cost over $400. Greyhound charges $101 for the one-way trip, but Green Tortoise offers "the adventure" for a mere $59. The bus line charges an additional $5 to strap a bike to the roof.

"This bus," says driver Steven Spahr, "gives people a chance to act like hippies for a night and then go back to the real world the next morning. That's something Greyhound just can't do." As passengers disembark at their final destination, they frequently hug the driver and often exchange names and phone numbers with other passengers.



Questions

1. Do you think Green Tortoise fares and Greyhound fares are elastic or inelastic? Give reasons to support your opinion.

2. Do you think Gardener Kent, founder and owner of Green Tortoise, is interested in maximum profits? Why or why not?

3. What costs should Green Tortoise consider when calculating its break-even point?

Suggested Reading

Bill Richards, "Trip on the Tortoise Can Be Hair-Raising If You Aren't Hip," *The Wall Street Journal*, 14 January 1991, pp. A1, A8.

**VIDEO CASE**

## The Electric Car

The electric car is a vehicle whose time has come—maybe. A lot depends on the pricing strategy.

Clean Car dealer Bell Ehuer sells the only electric car built in the United States for around $13,000. He expects to sell more than in the past because consumers can now claim a tax credit of 10 percent of the purchase price up to $4,000. Even so, his electric cars are still 50 to 100 percent more expensive than conventional cars.

For companies and government agencies that are expected to use clean cars in their fleets, the 10 percent tax break can add up to big savings. A Los Angeles company, Electric Cars of L.A., which converts gas vehicles to electric ones, is gearing up to meet the demand. The company president notes that the tax incentive reduces the cost of the conversion by $4,000. Virtually all Electric Cars of L.A. customers are fleet owners.

The key to penetrating the consumer market is not only economic but also psychological. When consumers think of electric vehicles, they think of golf carts.

### Questions

1. What can be done to increase consumer demand for electric cars? Is lowering the price enough?
2. Bell Ehuer advocates a government credit to make electric cars comparable in price to conventional ones. Is this a good idea?
3. The success of the electric car is a "chicken and egg" dilemma. To lower the cost of production, output (demand) must be increased. However, to increase demand, prices must be lowered. Prices can be decreased only when costs decrease, yet costs decrease only when production increases. Critique these statements.

# CHAPTER 19

# SETTING THE RIGHT PRICE

## Learning Objectives

*After studying this chapter, you should be able to*

1 *Describe the procedure for setting the right price.*

2 *Identify the legal and ethical constraints on pricing decisions.*

3 *Explain how discounts, geographic pricing, and other special pricing tactics can be used to fine-tune the base price.*

4 *Discuss product line pricing.*

5 *Explain how bidding differs from other forms of pricing.*

6 *Describe the role of pricing during periods of inflation and recession.*

7 *Discuss what the future might hold for pricing in the marketing mix.*

The drive, style, and feel of the small C-class Mercedes-Benz sedans, which made their debut in the U.S. market in late 1993, provided the first physical evidence of the manufacturer's rebirth as a maker of luxury automobiles. But the proof is in the pricing. Base-priced from $29,000 to $34,000, the four-cylinder C220 and the six-cylinder C280 represent the German company's boldest attempt at offering cars within reach of entry-level luxury-car buyers—potential customers it has been losing for years to lower-priced models from Lexus, BMW, and Infiniti.

The C-class sedans will actually sell for about the same price as the cars they replace, the smaller "Baby Benz" 190s, but the new models offer more room and better equipment. These are selling points the German auto maker has been touting aggressively to appeal to a luxury-car market that has become just as value-oriented as the market for low-priced Chevrolet Cavaliers.

"The customer is very much on the move, and we are trying very much to be ahead of him," acknowledges Helmut Werner, Mercedes-Benz's chairman. Werner "knows they have to offer something at a down-to-earth pricing level, which perhaps wasn't always the policy in the past," observes John Lawson, an industry analyst with DRI/McGraw-Hill in London.

The C-class cars mark a departure from the ultraluxurious, full-sized S-class sedans that Mercedes-Benz introduced in 1991 into the teeth of a recession. Priced from $69,000 to $119,900, the cars flopped. "Most wealthy people didn't get wealthy by being stupid," says Christopher Cedergren, senior vice president of AutoPacific Inc., an automotive-consulting group. "They don't mind spending the money. But they like to know they are getting their value for their dollar."

At $29,000, the entry-level C-class sedan sells for $700 less than the ES300, Lexus's entry-level sedan. Five years ago, the 190's base price was $11,450 more than the cheapest Lexus, a $21,050 ES250. "For Mercedes, the C-class cars really mark the first major product launch with an image and price that will stick through the '90s," says Susan G. Jacobs, an auto-industry consultant with Jacobs & Associates, in Rutherford, New Jersey. "They are recognizing that it's OK to be a luxury marque and to be a good value."

Analysts have been most impressed by Mercedes-Benz's decision to cut prices on some E-class sedans, the company's high-volume sedan line and most direct competitor to the popular Lexus LS400 and Infiniti Q45. Industry analysts, however, say it will be several years before they can say whether Mercedes-Benz has become a lean manufacturer—a must if the company hopes to sustain its value-pricing policies for any meaningful period.[1]

What are the advantages and disadvantages of setting a premium price on a product? What strategy is Mercedes-Benz following with its C-class cars? What is meant by "value pricing"?

1 *Describe the procedure for setting the right price.*

## HOW TO SET A PRICE ON A PRODUCT

Setting the right price on a product is a four-step process (see Exhibit 19.1):

1. Establish pricing goals.
2. Estimate demand, costs, and profits.
3. Choose a price strategy to help determine a base price.
4. Fine-tune the base price with pricing tactics.

The first three steps are discussed below; the fourth step is discussed later in the chapter.

### ESTABLISH PRICING GOALS

The first step in setting the right price is to establish pricing goals. Recall from Chapter 18 that pricing objectives fall into three categories: profit-oriented, sales-oriented, and status quo. These goals are derived from the firm's overall objectives.

A good understanding of the marketplace and of the consumer can sometimes tell a manager very quickly whether a goal is realistic. For example, if firm A has a 20 percent target return on investment (ROI) objective and its product development and implementation costs are $5 million, the market must be rather large or must support the price required to earn a 20 percent ROI. Assume that company B has a pricing objective that all new products must reach at least 15 percent market share within three years after product introduction. A thorough study of the environment may convince the marketing manager that the competition is too strong and the market share goal can't be met.

All pricing objectives have trade-offs that managers must weigh. A profit maximization objective may require a bigger initial investment than the firm can commit or wants to commit. Reaching the desired market share often means sacrificing short-term profit, because without careful management, long-term profit goals may not be met. Meeting the competition is the easiest pricing goal to implement. However, can managers really afford to ignore demand and costs, the life cycle stage, and other considerations? When creating pricing objectives, managers must consider these trade-offs in light of the target customer and the environment.

Exhibit 19.1

Steps in Setting the Right Price on a Product

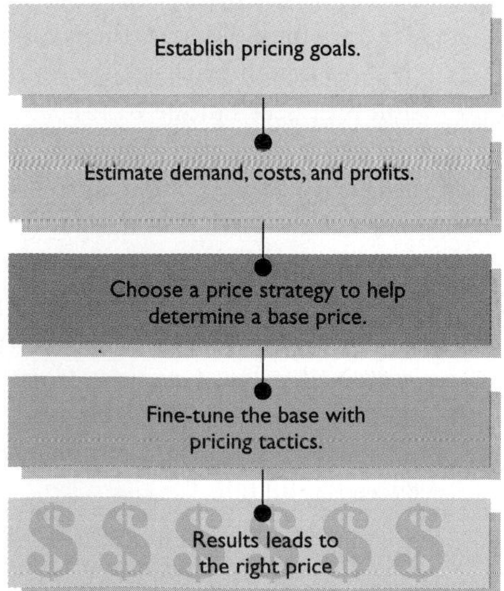

## ESTIMATE DEMAND, COSTS, AND PROFITS

Chapter 18 explained that total revenue is a function of price and quantity demanded and that quantity demanded depends on elasticity. After establishing pricing goals, managers should estimate total revenue at a variety of prices. Next they should determine corresponding costs for each price. They are then ready to estimate how much profit, if any, and how much market share can be earned at each possible price. These data become the heart of the developing price policy. Managers can study the options in light of revenues, costs, and profits. In turn, this information can help determine which price can best meet the firm's pricing goals.

## CHOOSE A PRICE STRATEGY

**price strategy**
Basic, long-term pricing framework, which establishes the initial price for a product and the intended direction for price movements over the product life cycle.

The basic, long-term pricing framework for the good or service should be a logical extension of the pricing objectives. The marketing manager's chosen **price strategy** defines the initial price and gives direction for price movements over the product life cycle.

The price strategy sets a competitive price in a specific market segment, based on a well-defined positioning strategy. For example, a carmaker like Mercedes-Benz would set a base price at one of the six price levels shown in Exhibit 19.2. The new E-class models are in the premium range. Changing a price level from premium to superpremium may require a change in the product itself, the target customers served, promotional strategy, or distribution channels. Thus changing a price strategy can require dramatic alterations in the marketing mix. A carmaker cannot successfully compete in the superpremium category if the car looks and drives like an economy car.

A company's freedom in pricing a new product and devising a price strategy depends on the market conditions and the other elements of the marketing mix. For example, if a firm launches a new item resembling several others already on the market, its pricing freedom will be restricted. To succeed, the company will probably have to charge a price close to the average market price. In contrast, a firm that introduces a totally new product with no close substitutes will have considerable pricing freedom.

The three basic strategies for setting a price on a good or service are price skimming, penetration pricing, and status quo pricing. A discussion of each type follows.

### Price Skimming

Price skimming is sometimes called a "market plus" approach to pricing, because it denotes a high price relative to the prices of competing products. Radius Corporation produces unique oval-headed toothbrushes made of black neoprene that look like a scuba diving accessory. Radius uses a skimming policy, pricing the toothbrushes at $9.95 compared to around $2.00 for a regular toothbrush.[2]

**price skimming**
Pricing policy whereby a firm charges a high introductory price, often coupled with heavy promotion.

The term **price skimming** is derived from the phrase "skimming the cream off the top." Companies often use this strategy for new products when the product is perceived by the target market as having unique advantages. For example, Caterpillar sets premium prices on its construction equipment to support and capture its high perceived value. Genzyme Corporation introduced Ceredase as the first effective treatment for Gaucher's disease. The pill allows patients to avoid years of painful physical deterioration and lead normal lives. A year's supply for one patient can exceed $300,000.[3]

As a product progresses through its life cycle, the firm may lower its price to successfully reach larger market segments. Economists have described this type of pricing as "sliding down the demand curve." Not all companies slide down the curve. Genentech's TPA, a drug that clears blood clots, was still priced at $2,200 a dose

*Exhibit 19.2*

Segmenting the Automobile Market by Price

| Price range | Model | | |
|---|---|---|---|
| **Ultra-premium** *(over $100,000)* | Lamborghini<br>Rolls Royce |  Lamborghini USA, Inc. |  By permission of Rolls-Royce Motor Cars Inc. |
| **Super-premium** *($60,000–$100,000)* | BMW 850Ci<br>Porsche 928 GTS |  BMW of North America, Inc. |  Porsche Cars North America |
| **Premium** *($40,000–$60,000)* | Mercedes E-Class<br>Lexus LS 400 |  Mercedes-Benz of North America, Inc. |  Lexus, A Division of Toyota Motor Sales, U.S.A., Inc. |
| **Moderate** *($15,000–$40,000)* | Buick Regal GS<br>Mazda Miata |  Buick Motor Division |  Mazda Motor of America |
| **Economy** *($10,000–$15,000)* | Saturn SL1<br>Honda Civic |  Saturn Corporation |  Honda Motor Company, Ltd. |
| **Basic** *(under $10,000)* | Geo Metro<br>Ford Aspire |  Chevrolet Motor Division |  Ford Motor Company |

four years after its introduction, despite competition from a much-lower-priced competitor.

Price skimming works best when the market is willing to buy the product even though it carries an above-average price. If, for example, some purchasing agents feel that Caterpillar equipment is far superior to competitors' products, then Caterpillar can charge premium prices successfully. Firms can also effectively use price skimming when a product is well protected legally, when it represents a technological breakthrough, or when it has in some other way blocked entry to competitors. Managers may also follow a skimming strategy when production cannot be expanded rapidly because of technological difficulties, shortages, or constraints imposed by the skill and time required to produce a product. As long as demand is greater than supply, skimming is an attainable strategy.

A successful skimming strategy enables management to recover its product development or "educational" costs quickly. (Often consumers must be "taught" the advantages of a radically new item, such as high-definition TV.) Even if the market perceives an introductory price as too high, managers can easily correct the problem by lowering the price. Firms often feel it is better to test the market at a high price and then lower the price if sales are too slow. They are tacitly saying, "If there are any premium-price buyers in the market, let's reach them first and maximize our revenue per unit."

Naturally, a skimming strategy will encourage competitors to enter the market. Intel introduced its powerful Pentium computer chips at $900 each for purchase in

Apple Computer, IBM, and Motorola jointly developed the Power PC chip as a direct challenge to Intel's Pentium chip. Because Intel was using a skimming strategy, the partners could seriously undercut Intel's price and still make money.

© Apple Computer, Inc.

large lots by computer manufacturers. Motorola saw an opportunity to penetrate Intel's market with a discount price. Motorola introduced its Power PC microprocessor, a chip comparable to the Pentium, at $280 each for purchase in large lots.[4]

Successful skimming strategies are not limited to products. Well-known athletes, entertainers, lawyers, and hair stylists are experts at price skimming. In the overnight delivery industry, World Courier has been a price skimmer for years. It charges three to four times as much as Emory and FedEx and still thrives. Why? It offers a unique service to a market niche that is willing to pay the price. The customer is most likely to be an international grain shipper, international lawyer, bank, or other financial institution that stands to lose hundreds or thousands of dollars with each day's delay in the delivery of its documents. The bigger shippers generally try to consolidate shipments, but World Courier uses the first available direct flight, even for one piece. Other couriers offer next-day service, but World Courier aims for 10 a.m. delivery everywhere in the world. The company will pick up as late as 8 p.m. in Europe and still guarantee delivery in New York by 9 a.m.

## Penetration Pricing

**penetration pricing**
Pricing policy whereby a firm charges a relatively low price for a product as a way to reach the mass market in the early stages of the product life cycle.

Penetration pricing is at the end of the spectrum opposite skimming. **Penetration pricing** means charging a relatively low price for a product as a way to reach the mass market. The low price is designed to capture a large share of a substantial market, resulting in lower production costs. If a marketing manager has made obtaining a large market share the firm's pricing objective, penetration pricing is a logical choice.

Penetration pricing does mean lower profit per unit, however. Therefore, to reach the break-even point, it requires higher-volume sales than would a skimming policy. If reaching a high volume of sales takes a long time, then the recovery of product development costs will also be slow. As you might expect, penetration pricing tends to discourage competition.

A penetration strategy tends to be effective in a price-sensitive market. Price should decline more rapidly when demand is elastic, because the market can be expanded through a lower price. Also, price sensitivity and greater competitive pressure should lead to a lower initial price and a relatively slow decline in the price later.

Schlitz, founded in 1849, enjoyed a long stint in the 1950s and 1960s as one of the premium, top-selling U.S. beers. But Schlitz ran into trouble when it started using a quicker, more cost-effective brewing method that earned bad press and perceptions of lower quality. That change, combined with poor marketing, led to seventeen straight years of sales declines. But between 1988 and 1994, Schlitz was gradually repositioned from the premium to the popular-price segment. For many older consumers, Schlitz is still a premium beer. Yet they can buy it for $3.99 a twelve-pack, as opposed to $5.99 or $6.99 for a premium beer. Sales of Schlitz have doubled since 1988 because of its penetration pricing strategy.

Southwest Airlines' success is also based on penetration pricing. By flying only the Boeing 737, it realizes efficiencies in stocking parts and training pilots and mechanics. It also saves by avoiding a costly computer reservation system, such as Apollo or SABRE, and not serving meals. Southwest has the lowest cost per seat mile in the industry. Costs per seat mile for the major carriers are USAir, 10.8¢; United, 9.6¢; Delta, 9.4¢; Northwest, 9.1¢; American, 8.9¢; and Southwest, 7.0¢. Around 800 people a week used to fly between Louisville, Kentucky, and Chicago; since Southwest entered the market, about 26,000 do. Similarly explosive growth took place after Southwest introduced a $49 fare on a St. Louis–Kansas City route that TWA had been flying for $250.[5]

Penetration pricing is the logical choice when demand is elastic and unit costs are low because of economies of mass production. A successful penetration strategy can effectively block the entry of competitors into the industry. For example, say that Invista Corporation's goal is a 12 percent return on investment, which is a normal profit in Invista's industry. Invista will reach this goal at a sales level of 80,000 units. Also assume that total market demand for the product is only 100,000 units and that any firm entering the industry would have a cost structure similar to Invista's. When Invista achieves its profit maximization goal by selling 80,000 units at $3.50 each, only 20,000 units of demand will remain for any potential competitor (see Exhibit 19.3). If a competitor entered the market and sold 20,000 units at $3.50 each, the competitor's average cost would be $16.00 (see the average total cost curve in Exhibit 19.3), for a total loss of $250,000 (average revenue $3.50 – average cost $16.00 = average loss per unit $12.50; $12.50 × 20,000 units = $250,000 total loss). If economies of mass production are lacking, profitable entry is impossible for almost any new competitor. Even a well-financed organization would have to be willing to sustain big short-run losses to penetrate the market.

The choice of pricing policies depends on competitive conditions throughout the world. For example, Levi Strauss has cut into the foreign market while sustaining its U.S. sales. The company's success lies in its skill at wielding a double-edged price strategy: penetration pricing in the United States and price skimming abroad. Sometimes companies reverse this approach, using penetration pricing in the international market and skimming in the domestic market.

## Status Quo Pricing

The third basic price strategy a firm may choose is status quo pricing, or meeting the competition (see also Chapter 18). It means charging a price identical to or very

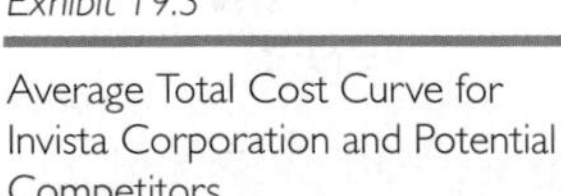

*Exhibit 19.3*

Average Total Cost Curve for Invista Corporation and Potential Competitors

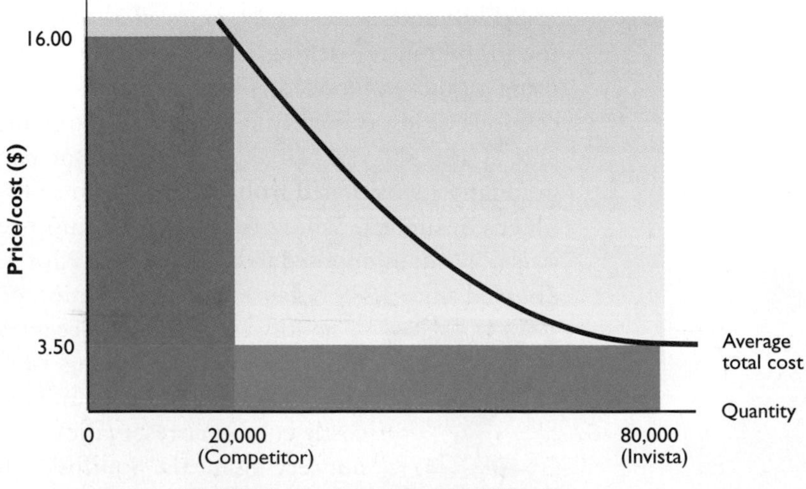

close to the competition's price. Montgomery Ward, for example, makes sure it is charging comparable prices by sending representatives to shop at Sears stores.

Although status quo pricing has the advantage of simplicity, its disadvantage is that the strategy may ignore demand or cost or both. But meeting the competition may be the safest route to long-term survival if the firm is comparatively small.

2 *Identify the legal and ethical constraints on pricing decisions.*

## THE LEGALITY AND ETHICS OF PRICE STRATEGY

As we mentioned in Chapter 2, some pricing decisions are subject to government regulation. Before marketing managers establish any price strategy, they should know the laws that limit their decision making. Among the issues that fall into this category are unfair trade practices, price fixing, price discrimination, and predatory pricing.

### UNFAIR TRADE PRACTICES

**unfair trade practice act**
Law that prohibits wholesalers and retailers from selling below cost.

In over half the states, **unfair trade practice acts** put a floor under wholesale and retail prices. Selling below cost in these states is illegal. Wholesalers and retailers must usually take a certain minimum percentage markup on their combined merchandise cost and transportation cost. The most common markup figures are 6 percent at the retail level and 2 percent at the wholesale level. If a specific wholesaler or retailer can provide "conclusive proof" that operating costs are lower than the minimum required figure, lower prices may be allowed.

The intent of unfair trade practice acts is to protect small local firms from giants like Kmart and Target, which operate very efficiently on razor-thin profit margins. However, state enforcement of unfair trade practice laws has generally been lax, partly because low prices benefit local consumers.

### PRICE FIXING

**price fixing**
Agreement between two or more firms on the price they will charge for a product.

**Price fixing** is an agreement between two or more firms on the price they will charge for a product. For example, suppose two or more executives from competing firms meet to decide how much to charge for a product or to decide which of them will submit the lowest bid on a certain contract. Such practices are illegal under the Sherman Act and the Federal Trade Commission Act.

The standing legal precedent related to price fixing is the Sacony-Vacuum case.[6] The courts ruled in this case that price fixing, or even the attempt to fix prices, is illegal *per se*. That is, the reasonableness or economic impact of the fixed prices is not a defense; the conspiracy itself is illegal.

This ruling has been applied to many forms of price setting by competitors. The following activities are all illegal *per se:*

- Maintaining prices by distributing price lists to competitors
- Agreeing on markups or discounts with competitors
- For members of professions, like surgeons, publishing and circulating minimum fee schedules within the profession

Offenders have received fines and sometimes prison terms. Price fixing is one area where the law is quite clear, and the Justice Department's enforcement is vigorous.

The Federal Trade Commission (FTC) sought to extend the definition of illegal circumstances to contexts in which no direct illegal secret agreements occur but where market signaling is used to communicate a company's intentions about prices. In a case involving DuPont and Ethyl Corporation, the FTC ruled that the following practices were illegal: giving customers more than thirty days' notice of price changes, to allow competitors to know of one's intentions; and granting "most favored customer status" to a company that guarantees a price at least as low as any other, thus discouraging spot discounts.

In 1994, the Justice Department filed a criminal indictment against General Electric and DeBeers Centenary AG for price fixing in the industrial diamond market. The diamonds aren't used in jewelry but rather in cutting tools for construction, oil drilling, and other work. The Justice Department could have brought a civil complaint but chose a criminal charge instead because the case was viewed as a "hardcore" price-fixing violation.[7] The case had not yet come to trial at the time this book was published.

The Justice Department filed a civil complaint against six major U.S. airlines for price fixing in 1992. They were charged with using their computer reservation systems to fix prices. The Justice Department claimed that the scheme cost U.S. flyers nearly $2 billion between 1988 and 1992. The case was settled in 1994 when the airlines agreed to quit sending coded messages about prices to each other through the reservation system. A class-action lawsuit filed on behalf of airline passengers was then settled by the airlines' offering discount coupons worth millions of dollars to passengers who flew during the late 1980s. The defendants were United, American, Delta, Northwest, and USAir airlines.[8]

Recently, the FTC has dusted off an old law to fight price fixing: Section 5 of the 1914 law that created the FTC, which prohibits "unfair methods of competition" (see Chapter 2). When a company publicly announces it will raise prices, it may illegally signal others to follow suit even though no agreement exists among the firms. The FTC used Section 5 to bring its first "invitation to collude" case when it charged that representatives of Quality Trailer Products, a Texas axle manufacturer, visited a competitor, American Marine Industries, and invited it to fix prices. Before the case was settled, American Marine went out of business. Quality Trailer signed a consent agreement barring it from any future price-fixing solicitations.[9]

Vigorous pursuit of price fixers has put a damper on their activities in the United States. But Russia's plunge into a market economy has left it unprepared to control price fixing by purported competitors, which is now quite common—as the Global Perspectives box explains.

GLOBAL PERSPECTIVES

**Price Fixing by Moscow's Capitalists**

When Russia adopted a market economy, Vladimir Grechanik, the top financial planner of Moscow's Bread Factory No. 14, went into a panic. After seventy years of government control of everything from the cost of raw materials to salaries, the factory suddenly would be able to set its own prices. He and his fellow producers anxiously tried to calculate how much flour would cost, how much transportation costs might rise, and what consumers would be willing to pay.

Just before prices were freed, Grechanik and executives from Moscow's other bread factories were called to a meeting at the Moscow Bread Consortium, the de facto ministry of bread. They eyed one another nervously, suspicious that, after years of mandated equality, the system might make rivals of former comrades. The bread consortium suggested raising the free-market bread price to three-and-a-half times the old price but not a kopeck more. The factory men were confused. In the old days, such a "suggestion" carried the full weight of a decree. But there were no certainties anymore. The new freedom was unbearable.

Left to his own devices, Grechanik returned to his office and got on the phone. For the next two days he and the other factory directors discussed their fears. Finally, they came to a decision: If the state was no longer to set prices, the factories themselves would jointly fix them—to ensure their mutual survival. "We all agreed on a single price," says Grechanik, as he walks past huge vats of flour on the factory floor. Lowering his voice, he confides, "I've heard that Bread Factory No. 26 is charging a little less, but I hope it's just a rumor."

## PRICE DISCRIMINATION

The Robinson-Patman Act of 1936 prohibits any firm from selling to two or more different buyers, within a reasonably short time, commodities (not services) of like grade and quality at different prices where the result would be to substantially lessen competition. The Robinson-Patman Act also makes it illegal for a seller to offer two buyers different supplementary services and for buyers to use their purchasing power to force sellers into granting discriminatory prices or services.

Six elements are therefore needed for a violation of the Robinson-Patman Act to occur:

**price discrimination**
Practice of charging different prices to different customers for the same product.

- There must be **price discrimination;** that is, the seller must charge different prices to different customers for the same product.
- The transaction must occur in interstate commerce.
- The seller must discriminate by price among two or more purchasers; that is, the seller must make two or more actual sales within a reasonably short time.
- The products sold must be commodities or other tangible goods.
- The products sold must be of like grade and quality, not necessarily identical. If the goods are truly interchangeable and substitutable, then they are of like grade and quality.
- There must be significant competitive injury.

The Robinson-Patman Act provides three defenses for the seller charged with price discrimination, described below. In each case the burden is on the defendant to prove the defense.

- *Cost:* A firm can charge different prices to different customers if the prices represent manufacturing or quantity discount savings. In terms of manufacturing, however, the courts have been willing to accept only price differentials resulting from transportation efficiencies, which can easily be verified from bills of lading. The courts generally have not viewed manufacturing efficiencies as a good reason for price differentials because of the difficulty in determining exactly the cost of specified units of a mass-produced product.
- *Market conditions:* Price variations are justified if designed to meet fluid product or market conditions. Examples include the deterioration of perishable goods, the obsolescence of seasonal products, a distress sale under

## GLOBAL PERSPECTIVES

To be sure, there are some emerging signs of free markets, as the monopolies that control prices for each segment of production start to crash against each other. The bread producers are protesting the prices set by the flour-mill conglomerate. The trade conglomerate of bakery stores is revolting against the prices set by bread producers. One store on Moscow's Kalanchovskaya Street has put up a sign over some stale bread at 3.50 rubles—well above the new fixed price—pointedly declaring its source was Factory No. 19. "We want everybody to know where it came from," says Nadeshda Verba, one of the store's employees.

There is one area where price competition seems to be emerging, ever so haltingly: the cake sector. Star Factory, notes Tamara Vlysko, deputy director of the bread consortium, sells its butter-cream *nochkas* for 54 rubles. But the following week, a rival, the Cheremushky Bread and Confectionery Plant, started offering *nochkas* for only 33 rubles. Star Factory's director flew into a rage. But rather than fight back in what might have been this city's first price war, he called Vlysko, the bureaucrat. "Why didn't you tell me what Cheremushky was charging for *nochkas*!" he sputtered. "No one's buying my cakes!" Vlysko suggested he might want to lower his price.[10]

Do you think that plunging into a free-market economy without first educating plant managers was a good idea? Should Russia set up an equivalent of our Federal Trade Commission? Do you think Russia can really convert to a market economy? Do you think it could convert in the next ten years?

court order, or a legitimate going-out-of-business sale. A produce warehouse may change its prices from one day to the next or even from one customer to the next, depending on the freshness of its fruits and vegetables. However, a shoe warehouse engaging in similar behavior might be viewed as practicing price discrimination. The courts have been rather liberal in accepting such a defense so as not to limit a firm's flexibility in responding to changing product or market conditions.

- *Competition:* A reduction in price may be necessary to stay even with the competition. Specifically, if a competitor undercuts the price quoted by a seller to a buyer, the law authorizes the seller to lower the price charged to the buyer for the product in question. Because the seller may elect not to reduce the price for all the other customers in that competitive area, price discrimination is being practiced. The courts have been willing to accept this defense, however, as long as the seller reduces the price to that charged by the competition, not less.

## PREDATORY PRICING

**predatory pricing**
Practice of charging a very low price for a product with the intent of driving competitors out of business or out of a market.

**Predatory pricing** is the practice of charging a very low price for a product with the intent of driving competitors out of business or out of a market. Once competitors have been driven out, the firm raises its prices. This practice is illegal under the Sherman Act and the Federal Trade Commission Act. Proving the use of this practice is difficult and expensive, however. A defendant must show that the predator, the destructive company, explicitly tried to ruin a competitor and that the predatory price was below the defendant's average cost.

Despite the difficulty of proving predatory pricing, a state court in Arkansas ruled that Wal-Mart had engaged in predatory pricing by selling pharmacy products below cost. Three pharmacies in Conway, Arkansas, claimed Wal-Mart was using predatory pricing to put them out of business. Wal-Mart admitted selling below cost but denied it was attempting to put anyone out of business. Wal-Mart noted that in 1987, when it started selling pharmaceuticals in Conway, there were twelve pharmacies and that the same twelve were still in business at the time of the court case. Also, the number of pharmacists had increased during that period from thirty-eight to fifty-eight, because several food stores had also opened pharmacies. Nevertheless, Wal-Mart lost the case.[11] It has been appealed to the Arkansas Supreme Court.

Federal courts have usually been much less hospitable to alleged victims of predatory pricing than to the alleged perpetrators. The U.S. Supreme Court threw out a $150 million judgment against B.A.T. Industries, which had been accused of trying to drive Brooke Group out of the generic cigarette market with predatory pricing. A federal jury threw out claims by Continental and Northwest Airlines that American Airlines was using predatory pricing in an attempt to drive them out of business.[12]

**base price**
General price level at which the company expects to sell the good or service.

*3 Explain how discounts, geographic pricing, and other special pricing tactics can be used to fine-tune the base price.*

## TACTICS FOR FINE-TUNING THE BASE PRICE

After managers understand both the legal and the marketing consequences of price strategies, they should set a **base price,** the general price level at which the company expects to sell the good or service (recall the car example in Exhibit 19.2). The general price level is correlated to the pricing policy: above the market (price skimming), at the market (status quo pricing), or below the market (penetration pricing). The final step, then, is to fine-tune the base price.

Fine-tuning techniques are short-run approaches that do not change the general price level. They do, however, result in changes within a general price level. These pricing tactics allow the firm to adjust for competition in certain markets, meet ever-changing government regulations, take advantage of unique demand situations, and meet promotional and positioning goals. Fine-tuning pricing tactics include various sorts of discounts, geographic pricing, and special pricing tactics.

## DISCOUNTS, ALLOWANCES, AND REBATES

A base price can be lowered through the use of discounts and the related tactics of allowances and rebates. Managers use the various forms of discount to encourage customers to do what they would not ordinarily do, such as paying cash rather than using credit, taking delivery out of season, or performing certain functions within a distribution channel.

### Cash Discounts

**cash discount**
Price reduction offered to a consumer, industrial user, or marketing intermediary in return for prompt payment of a bill.

A **cash discount** is a price reduction offered to a consumer, an industrial user, or a marketing intermediary in return for prompt payment of a bill. Prompt payment saves the seller carrying charges and billing expenses and allows the seller to avoid bad debt.

### Quantity Discounts

**quantity discount**
Price reduction offered to buyers buying in multiple units or above a specified dollar amount.

Probably the most common form of discount is the quantity discount. When buyers get a lower price for buying in multiple units or above a specified dollar amount, they are receiving a **quantity discount.** In theory, the quantity discount is based on the savings in transportation and other costs realized by the seller. Sellers offering quantity discounts also need to locate fewer buyers for the same number of units.

Sellers can offer quantity discounts on slow-moving items to increase their sales potential. Wholesalers can also use these discounts to discourage retailers from buying directly from the manufacturer. If the discount is close to what the retailers might receive by going directly to the manufacturer, they may continue to buy from the wholesaler.

By offering larger quantity discounts than competitors do, a firm can often gain profits and market share. For example, AT&T historically relied on systemwide averaging of long-distance telephone costs and prices. The resulting rates seldom considered differences in traffic density among long-distance routes. However, heavily used routes had much lower unit costs and were much more profitable. These were precisely the routes that MCI targeted with its Execunet long-distance service. Execunet was designed to appeal to large customers by offering deep discounts for high volume. This tactic enabled MCI to grow rapidly at the expense of AT&T.

**cumulative quantity discount**
Deduction from list price that applies to the buyer's total purchases made during a specific period, intended to encourage customer loyalty.

**noncumulative quantity discount**
Deduction from list price that applies to a single order rather than to the total volume of orders placed during a certain period.

MCI's discount on Execunet was a **cumulative quantity discount,** a deduction from list price that applies to the buyer's total purchases made during a specific period; it is intended to encourage customer loyalty. The buyer's purchases are totaled at the end of the period, and the discount received depends on the quantity (dollars or units) bought during that period. The discount percentage usually increases as the quantity purchased increases.

In contrast, a **noncumulative quantity discount** is a deduction from list price that applies to a single order rather than to the total volume of orders placed during a certain period. It is intended to encourage orders in large quantities. The size of this discount generally increases with the size of the order. The purpose is to reward buyers whose purchase patterns help the seller reduce costs. Specifically, as the size of the buyer's order increases, so do the transportation efficiencies that the seller can realize. For example, Coleman Products offers retailers quantity discounts on its outdoor products. The discount is substantial when a retailer orders enough merchandise to fill an entire trailer. By driving a single trailer from its Kansas plant to a retailer's warehouse, Coleman reaps big savings on transportation costs.

### Functional Discounts

A third common form of discount is the functional discount. When distribution channel intermediaries, such as wholesalers or retailers, perform a service or function for the manufacturer, they must be compensated. This compensation, typically a percentage discount from the base price, is called a **functional discount** (or **trade discount**).

**functional discount (trade discount)**
Discount to wholesalers and retailers for performing channel functions.

Functional discounts vary greatly from channel to channel, depending on the tasks performed by the intermediary. A typical discount schedule for a suggested retail list price of $500 would be discounts of 45 percent and 8 percent. The retailer's cost would be $275 ($500 minus 45 percent). The wholesaler would pay $253 ($275 minus 8 percent). Note that the total discount is not 53 percent (45 percent plus 8 percent) off the list price:

$$\$500 \times .53 = \$265$$
$$\$500 - \$265 = \$235$$

At 53 percent off the list price, the cost to the wholesaler would have been $235 instead of $253. Instead, discounts are figured on a chain basis from one level of the distribution channel to the next.

### Trade Loading and Everyday Low Prices

**trade loading**
Practice of temporarily lowering the price to induce wholesalers and retailers to buy more goods than can be sold in a reasonable time.

**Trade loading** occurs when a manufacturer temporarily lowers the price to induce wholesalers and retailers to buy more goods than can be sold in a reasonable time. Say that Procter & Gamble offers Super Valu an additional 30¢ off the normal price for a bottle of Prell. The Super Valu buyer jumps at the bargain and buys a three-month supply of Prell. Typically, Super Valu would pass along the discount to customers for about a month but then return to the original price for the last two months, thereby reaping some extra profit.

Trade discounts like these have more than tripled in the past decade, to around $36.5 billion in 1994.[13] The practice is most common in the consumer packaged-goods industry. An estimated $100 billion in grocery products, mostly nonperishables, sit at any one time on trucks and railcars or stacked inside distribution centers, caught in gridlock because of trade loading. This idle inventory is estimated to add about $20 billion a year to the nation's $400 billion grocery bill.[14]

However, it is estimated that such practices generate about 70 percent of wholesalers' profits and 40 percent of supermarkets' profits.[15] Wholesalers and retailers have understandably become addicted to trade-loading deals.

Unfortunately, trade loading ultimately costs consumers (and manufacturers) money, as shown in Exhibit 19.4. It "whipsaws" production and distribution and increases the manufacturer's costs. The largest U.S. packaged-goods manufacturer, Procter & Gamble, estimates it has created over $1 billion worth of unproductive inventory that has sat in P&G's distribution pipeline. Moreover, P&G's chairman Edward Anzt notes,

*Exhibit 19.4*

Costs of Trade Loading

Source: Patricia Sellars, "The Dumbest Marketing Ploy," *Fortune*, 3 October 1992, pp. 88–89. Original art by Jim McManus. Adapted by permission.

**With trade loading**

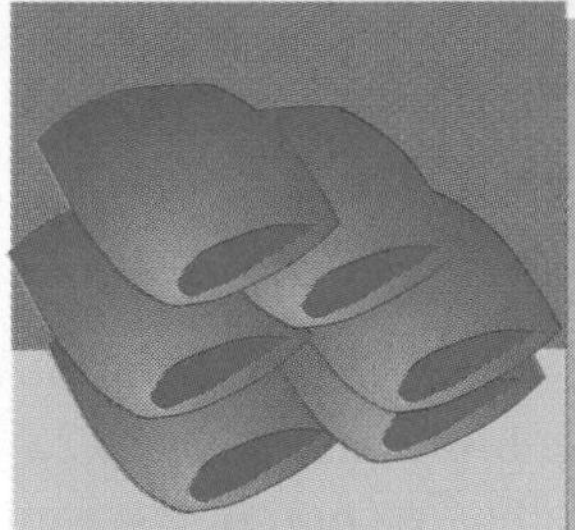

The manufacturer stockpiles ingredients and packaging supplies to meet peak production levels.

Plants prepare huge runs. Scheduling is chaotic, with more overtime and temporary workers.

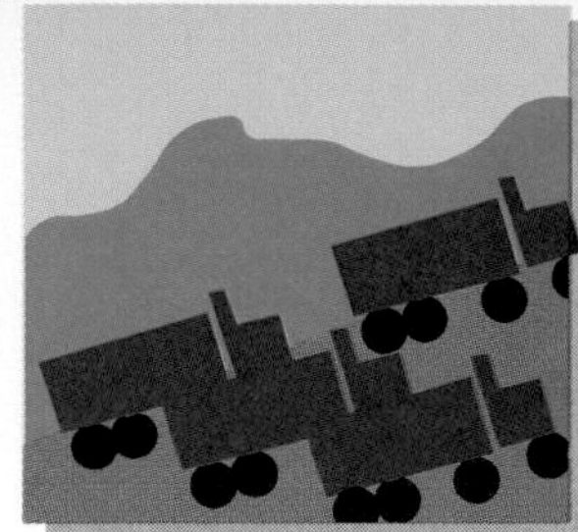

Freight companies charge premium rates for the manufacturer's periodic blow-out shipments.

Distributors overstock as they binge on short-term discounts. Cartons sit for weeks inside warehouses.

At distribution centers, the goods get overhandled. Damaged items go back to the manufacturer.

Twelve weeks after the items leave the production line, they may not be fresh for the consumer.

**Without trade loading**

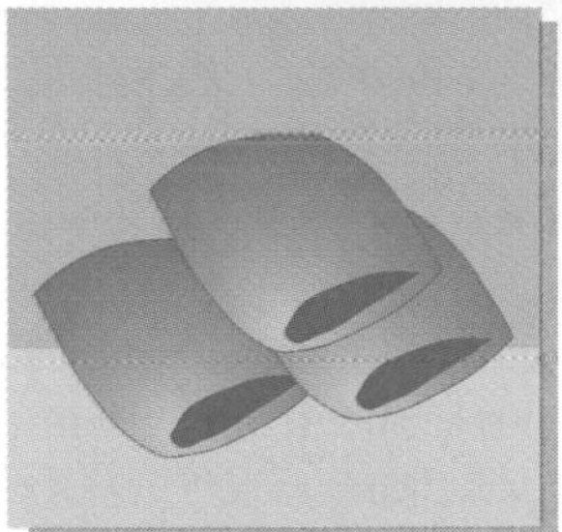

No more panic purchases are necessary. The company cuts down on inventories, freeing up cash.

Factories run on normal shifts. The company cuts down on overtime pay and supplemental workers.

The manufacturer eliminates peak-and-valley distribution. That helps it save 5 percent in shipping costs.

Wholesaler's inventories get cut in half. That means storage and handling costs decline 17 percent.

Retailers receive undamaged products. The perception of the manufacturer's quality improves.

The consumer gets the goods twenty-five days earlier, and—even better news—at a 6 percent lower price.

> Trade loading has caused the erosion of consumer loyalty. As retailers and wholesalers buy on deals and discounts, they pass wide price swings to consumers in an unpredictable pattern, and these shoppers, no dummies, increasingly "forward buy" themselves. People have reached the point where they won't buy unless a product is on sale. Shopping store to store for the best deal, they bulk up on whichever item—P&G's Crest or Colgate-Palmolive's Colgate, P&G's Tide or Lever Brothers' Wisk—is on promotion that week.[16]

**everyday low prices (EDLP)**
Price tactic of permanently reducing prices 10 to 15 percent below the traditional levels while eliminating trade discounts that create trade loading.

P&G has decided to attack the trade-loading problem with **everyday low prices** (EDLP), the tactic of offering lower prices (10 to 25 percent lower) and maintaining those prices while eliminating functional discounts that result in trade loading. Instead of selling, say, a case of cake mix for $10.00 most of the time and then for $7.00 to load the trade, P&G will sell the case for $8.50 all the time. By 1994 the company had introduced EDLP on about half its lines, including cake mixes, liquid laundry detergents, dishwashing liquids, fabric softener sheets, toilet tissue, and automatic dishwasher detergents. List prices have fallen 8 to 25 percent on items like Mr Clean, Jif peanut butter, and Pert shampoo. P&G plans to institute EDLP for all its products.

EDLP has sent the nation's wholesalers and retailers into shock, because it eliminates a major source of their profits. Some dealers have fought back. Chains with thousands of stores—such as Rite-Aid drugstores and A&P and Safeway supermarkets—are pruning the variety of P&G sizes they carry or eliminating marginal brands, such as Prell and Gleem. Super Valu, the nation's largest wholesaler, which also runs some stores, is adding surcharges to some P&G products and paring back orders to compensate for profits it says it's losing under the new pricing system. Certified Grocers, a Midwestern wholesaler, has dropped about 50 of the 300 P&G varieties it once stocked. Many other chains are considering moving P&G brands from prime eye-level space to less visible shelves. In P&G's place will be more profitable private-label brands and competitors' varieties.

In an attempt to quell the discontent, P&G has created a pay-for-performance fee for distributors that sell a target quantity of a specific brand over a six-month period. P&G claims that EDLP will ultimately help build brand loyalty, fend off private-label inroads into market share, and reduce manufacturing and inventory costs.[17] For now, the EDLP strategy is helping raise P&G's profits to their highest level since 1990.[18]

Will EDLP work for other packaged-goods manufacturers? One survey found that 75 percent were testing some form of EDLP.[19] Quaker Oats, Duracell, and (on a limited basis) Kraft General Foods are using it. Others, such as Ralston Purina and Colgate-Palmolive, have not changed their pricing tactics. A Colgate-Palmolive spokesperson says, "We will continue to deal with customers as they wish to be dealt with."[20]

## Seasonal Discounts

**seasonal discount**
Price reduction offered to buyers purchasing merchandise out of season.

A **seasonal discount** is a price reduction for buying merchandise out of season. It shifts the storage function to the purchaser. Seasonal discounts also enable manufacturers to maintain a steady production schedule year-round. For instance, to keep its sewing crew employed full-time, Jantzen swimwear offers seasonal discounts to retail stores in the fall and winter. One of the most familiar examples of a seasonal discount is the half-price sale on Christmas decorations that begins December 26.

It is true that sellers may not cover total costs when they offer deep seasonal discounts. However, as long as sellers cover variable costs and make a contribution to fixed costs, the total loss will be reduced.

## Promotional Allowances

**promotional allowance**
Payment to a dealer for promoting the manufacturer's products.

A **promotional allowance** (also known as a trade allowance) is a payment to a dealer for promoting the manufacturer's products. It is both a pricing tool and a promotional device. As a pricing tool, a promotional allowance is like a functional discount. If, for example, a retailer runs an ad for a manufacturer's product, the manufacturer may pay half the cost. If a retailer sets up a special display, the manufacturer may include a certain quantity of free goods in the retailer's next order. For example, Kraft General Foods regularly gives Kroger and other supermarket chains free cases of food products for performing specified services.

Like other forms of discounts, promotional allowances must be made available to all buyers on essentially the same terms. The Robinson-Patman Act bans differences in promotional allowances to similar purchasers of similar goods. For instance, suppose two retailers each buy twenty cases of soap. If one receives a $50 promotional allowance and the other receives $20, the transaction is illegal.

## Rebates

**rebate**
Cash refund given for the purchase of a product during a specific period.

A **rebate** is a cash refund given for the purchase of a product during a specific period. Rebates have become so common in the automobile industry that consumers find it unusual when a rebate is not offered.

The advantage of a rebate over a simple price reduction for stimulating demand is that a rebate is a temporary inducement that can be taken away without altering the basic price structure. A manufacturer that uses a simple price reduction for a short time may meet resistance when trying to restore the price to its original higher level. However, with rebates the price on the product remains constant, and the consumer may be less resistant to paying the regularly marked price once the rebate is discontinued.

Today manufacturers offer several different types of rebates:

Carmakers now offer a new kind of rebate: dollars off the price of a vehicle in exchange for using a credit card sponsored by the carmaker. These rebates not only encourage the purchase of a new vehicle; they also encourage the use of credit cards, which are a source of additional income for the sponsors.

- The *instant rebate* gives the consumer a refund at the time of purchase. For example, a jar of Jif peanut butter might have a peel-off rebate coupon that says, "25¢ off this jar of Jif now."
- A *product rebate* gives an extra product to the consumer, usually at the time of purchase. For instance, a can of Folger's coffee may have a free package of nondairy creamer attached to it.
- A *mail-in rebate* offers cash to consumers as a purchase incentive. To qualify for the mail-in rebate, consumers must often collect the proof of purchase required by the rebate offer, such as a label, bar code, or cash register receipt. They mail in proof to the company within a certain time limit and then wait up to eight weeks to receive the rebate.

products and consider transportation costs an important part of total costs. Instead of a single basing point, they use multiple basing points.

## SPECIAL PRICING TACTICS

Unlike geographic pricing, special pricing tactics are unique and defy neat categorization. Managers use these tactics for various reasons—for example, to stimulate demand for specific products, to increase store patronage, and to offer a wider variety of merchandise at a specific price point. Special pricing tactics include a single-price tactic, flexible pricing, professional services pricing, price lining, leader pricing, bait pricing, odd-even pricing, price bundling, and two-part pricing. A brief overview of each of these tactics follows, along with a manager's reasons for using that tactic or a combination of tactics to change the base price.

### Single-Price Tactic

**single-price tactic**
Policy of offering all goods and services at the same price.

A merchant using a **single-price tactic** offers all goods and services at the same price (or perhaps two or three prices). Retailers using this tactic include One Price Clothing Stores, Dre$$ to the Nine$, Your $10 Store, and Fashions $9.99. One Price Clothing Stores, for example, tend to be small, about 3,000 square feet. Their goal is to offer merchandise that would sell for at least $15 to $18 in other stores. The stores carry pants, shirts, blouses, sweaters, and shorts for juniors, misses, and large-sized women. The stores do not feature any seconds or irregular items, and everything is sold for $6.

Single-price selling removes price comparisons from the buyer's decision-making process. The consumer just looks for suitability and the highest perceived quality. The retailer enjoys the benefits of a simplified pricing system and minimal clerical errors. However, continually rising costs are a headache for retailers following this strategy. In times of inflation, they must frequently raise the selling price. The recession of the early 1990s resulted in the rapid growth of single-price chains.[21]

Stores like this one price every item the same, simplifying consumers' purchase decision. A single-price strategy has many benefits for retailers as well, although rapidly rising costs may create some headaches.

## Flexible Pricing

**flexible pricing (variable pricing)**
Price tactic in which different customers pay different prices for essentially the same merchandise bought in equal quantities.

**Flexible pricing** (or **variable pricing**) means that different customers pay different prices for essentially the same merchandise bought in equal quantities. This tactic is often found in the sale of shopping goods, specialty merchandise, and most industrial goods except supply items. Car dealers, many appliance retailers, and manufacturers of industrial installations, accessories, and component parts commonly follow this practice. It allows the seller to adjust for competition by meeting another seller's price. Thus a marketing manager with a status quo pricing objective might readily adopt this tactic. Flexible pricing also enables the seller to close a sale with price-conscious consumers. If buyers show promise of becoming large-volume shoppers, flexible pricing can be used to lure their business.

The obvious disadvantages of flexible pricing are the lack of consistent profit margins, the potential ill will of high-paying purchasers, the tendency for salespeople to automatically lower the price to make a sale, and the possibility of a price war among sellers. The disadvantages of flexible pricing have led the automobile industry to experiment with one price for all buyers. Ford started offering the Cougar at one price and has seen an 80 percent increase in sales. General Motors uses a one-price tactic for some of its models, including the Saturn and the Buick Regal.

## Professional Services Pricing

Professional services pricing is used by people with lengthy experience, training, and often certification by a licensing board—for example, lawyers, physicians, and family counselors. Professionals sometimes charge customers at an hourly rate, but sometimes fees are based on the solution of a problem or performance of an act (such as an eye examination) rather than on the actual time involved. A surgeon may perform a heart operation and charge a flat fee of $5,000. The operation itself may require only four hours, resulting in a hefty $1,250 hourly rate. The physician justifies the fee because of the lengthy education and internship required to learn the complex procedures of a heart operation. Lawyers also sometimes use flat-rate pricing, such as $500 for completing a divorce and $50 for handling a traffic ticket.

Those who use professional pricing have an ethical responsibility not to overcharge a customer. Because demand is sometimes highly inelastic, such as when a person requires heart surgery or a daily insulin shot to survive, there may be a temptation to charge "all the traffic will bear." Although drug companies are often criticized for their high prices, they claim that their charges are ethical. They say prices for new drugs need to be high to recover the research costs incurred in developing the drugs. The Ethics in Marketing story, which takes a more detailed look at Ceredase, mentioned earlier in the chapter, addresses this issue.

## Price Lining

**price lining**
Practice of offering a product line with several items at specific price points.

When a seller establishes a series of prices for a type of merchandise, it creates a price line. **Price lining** is the practice of offering a product line with several items at specific price points. For example, Hon, an office furniture manufacturer, may offer its four-drawer file cabinets at $125, $250, and $400. The Limited may offer women's dresses at $40, $70, and $100, with no merchandise marked at prices between those figures. Instead of a normal demand curve running from $40 to $100, The Limited has three demand points (prices). Theoretically, the "curve" exists only because people would buy goods at the in-between prices if it were possible to do so. For example, a number of dresses could be sold at $60, but no sales will occur at that price because $60 is not part of the price line.

Price lining reduces confusion for both the salesperson and the consumer. The buyer may be offered a wider variety of merchandise at each established price. Price lines may also enable a seller to reach several market segments. For buyers, the question of price may be quite simple: All they have to do is find a suitable product at the predetermined price. Moreover, price lining is a valuable tactic for the marketing manager, because the firm may be able to carry a smaller total inventory than it could without price lines. The results may include fewer markdowns, simplified purchasing, and lower inventory carrying charges.

**leader pricing (loss-leader pricing)**
Price tactic in which a product is sold near or even below cost in the hope that shoppers will buy other items once they are in the store.

Price lines also present drawbacks, especially if costs are continually rising. Sellers can offset rising costs in three ways. First, they can begin stocking lower-quality merchandise at each price point. Second, sellers can change the prices, although frequent price line changes confuse buyers. Third, sellers can accept lower profit margins and hold quality and prices constant. This third alternative has short-run benefits, but its long-run handicaps may drive sellers out of business.

Sellers face another major problem: trying to decide where to place the prices within a line. If the prices are too close together, buyers may wonder why the price of one article is higher than another. If the price lines are too far apart, the dealer may lose a customer who is looking for a price (and quality) somewhere between the existing prices. Also, salespeople will find it difficult to "trade up" customers (persuade them to buy higher-priced merchandise) if the price lines are too far apart.

ETHICS IN MARKETING

**Are Drug Prices Based on "All the Traffic Will Bear"?**

Although Ceredase is one of the most expensive drugs ever sold, it wins praise as a life-saving treatment. It has also become a lightning rod for criticism of high drug prices. "We were appalled" when the manufacturer, Genzyme, announced the pricing of Ceredase, says Abbey S. Meyers, president of the National Organization for Rare Disorders, a federation of 135 patient groups.

Genzyme is not the only drug manufacturer to be criticized for high prices. Patients have complained to Congress about the high prices of other advanced drugs, including Amgen's anemia drug erythropoietin, or EPO, which costs $4,000 to $6,000 a year, and Genentech's human growth hormones, which cost $12,000 to $18,000 a year. But Ceredase's pricing catapulted the issue to the top of the legislative agenda.

Ceredase substitutes for a missing enzyme that causes Gaucher's disease. Robin Berman, founder and medical director of the National Gaucher Foundation, says she knows her three sons with Gaucher's disease "would have been exceedingly ill, crippled and more than likely met an early demise" if Ceredase hadn't been available. But in her work with the foundation, Berman also talks with many people who are outraged by the drug's price.

There's no question that Ceredase, in its current form, is enormously expensive to make. For now, the company gets the enzyme from placentas, or afterbirths, collected from hospitals around the world. To produce a year's supply of Ceredase for an average patient takes 20,000 placentas, or about 27 tons of material. The drug is now used by about 1,100 patients, requiring almost 30,000 tons of placentas a year. Of Ceredase's $150,000 wholesale price for an average year's supply, more than one-third covers the costs of the placentas and processing. That's much higher than typical drug-manufacturing costs of 4 to 15 percent of the wholesale price. Genzyme plans to begin producing the drug through genetic engineering soon, which should eventually reduce its costs somewhat.

Genzyme executives expected to reach the break-even point on Ceredase in 1994, covering their development costs and other spending

## Leader Pricing

**Leader pricing** (or **loss-leader pricing**) is an attempt by the marketing manager to attract customers by selling a product near or even below cost, hoping that shoppers will buy other items once they are in the store. This type of pricing appears weekly in the newspaper advertising of supermarkets, specialty stores, and department stores. Leader pricing is normally used on well-known items that consumers can easily recognize as bargains at the special price. The goal is not necessarily to sell large quantities of leader items but to try to appeal to customers who might shop elsewhere.

**bait pricing**
Price tactic that tries to get consumers into a store through false or misleading price advertising and then uses high-pressure selling to persuade consumers to buy more expensive merchandise.

**odd-even pricing (psychological pricing)**
Price tactic that uses odd-numbered prices to connote bargains and even-numbered prices to imply quality.

## Bait Pricing

In contrast to leader pricing, which is a genuine attempt to give the consumer a reduced price, bait pricing is deceptive. **Bait pricing** tries to get the consumer into a store through false or misleading price advertising and then uses high-pressure selling to persuade the consumer to buy more expensive merchandise. You may have seen this ad or a similar one:

> REPOSSESSED . . . Singer slant-needle sewing machine . . . take over 8 payments of $5.10 per month . . . ABC Sewing Center.

This is bait. When a customer goes in to see the machine, it has just been sold, or else a salesperson shows the prospective buyer a piece of junk no one would buy. Then the salesperson says, "But I've got a really good deal on this fine new model." This is the switch that may cause a susceptible consumer to walk out with a $400 machine. The Federal Trade Commission considers bait pricing a deceptive act and has banned its use in interstate commerce. Most states also ban bait pricing, but sometimes enforcement is lax.

## Odd-Even Pricing

**Odd-even pricing** (or **psychological pricing**) means pricing at odd-numbered prices to connote a bargain and pricing at even-numbered prices to imply quality. For years many retailers have used this pricing tactic by pricing their products in odd numbers—for example, $99.95 or $49.95—to make consumers feel they are paying a lower price for the product.

Some retailers favor odd-numbered prices, believing that $9.99 sounds much less imposing to customers than $10.00. Other retailers believe that the use of an odd-numbered price signals to consumers that the price is at the lowest level possible, thereby encouraging them to buy more units. Neither theory has ever been conclusively proved, although one study found that consumers perceive odd-priced products as being on sale.[23]

Odd-even pricing curiously affects demand. Odd-numbered prices stimulate demand, and even-numbered prices curtail demand. Because people tend to buy more at odd-numbered

### ETHICS IN MARKETING

on the drug. Spending on Ceredase began in 1984, and it was introduced in 1991. Genzyme executives predict that from 1984 through 2002, when the patent on the genetically engineered version expires, the company will have an average annual return of about 25 percent on Ceredase.

Is that a reasonable return? Many critics say no. "There are a lot of businesses out there that are doing well with a lot less than a 25% after-tax return," says the father of a child who has Gaucher's disease. "Their profit margin is too high," says Senator Howard Metzenbaum, "particularly for an item costing as much as Ceredase." The Ohio Democrat co-sponsored a measure to change the orphan drug act—under which companies now receive seven-year monopolies on drugs they develop for rare diseases—to encourage more competition and lower prices.

Genzyme says it has taken steps to ensure that the drug's high price doesn't keep it out of the hands of those who need it. The company helps patients get insurance and provides the drug free to those who can't pay for it.

For some people, the drug's price is secondary. At the age of 26, Lenny Van Pelt, an attorney, suddenly developed a persistent bone pain in his right hip. After seeing fourteen doctors who diagnosed him with bursitis, arthritis, and leukemia, he was finally told he had Gaucher's disease. That was in 1986, when there was no effective treatment for Gaucher's. Over the next few years he underwent two hip-replacement surgeries costing about $80,000. He suffered four broken vertebrae and dangerously low blood counts. He lost forty pounds and two inches in height. "It was an incredible amount of devastation in a handful of years," he says. Ceredase, which his health insurance covered, halted the disease's progression. "It's worth the price because I got my life back," says Van Pelt, who gave up private law practice to assist Gaucher's disease patients with financial and legal advice.[22]

If you were the marketing manager for Genzyme, would you lower the price of Ceredase? Why or why not? If so, how would you determine the price? Do you think drug companies are charging too much? Do you think Genzyme's profit margin on Ceredase is too high?

*Exhibit 19.6*

Effects of Odd-Even Pricing

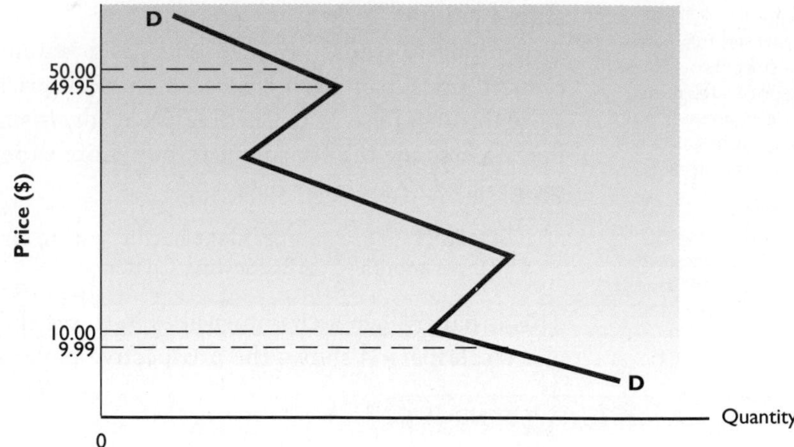


prices, demand is relatively elastic for odd-numbered prices and then inelastic for even-numbered prices, as shown in the downward slope of the demand curve in Exhibit 19.6. Such a situation creates a sawtoothed demand curve.

Even-numbered pricing is sometimes used to denote quality. Examples include a fine perfume at $100 a bottle, a good watch at $500, or a mink coat at $3,000. The demand curve for such items would also be sawtoothed, except that the outside edges would represent even-numbered prices and, therefore, elastic demand.

## Price Bundling

**price bundling**
Marketing two or more products in a single package for a special price.

**Price bundling** is marketing two or more products in a single package for a special price. Examples include the sale of maintenance contracts with computer hardware and other office equipment, packages of stereo equipment, packages of options on cars, weekend hotel packages that include a room and several meals, and airline vacation packages. Lotus now offers "suites" of software that bundle spreadsheets, word processing, graphics, electronic mail, and groupware for networks of microcomputers. Price bundling can stimulate demand for the bundled items if the target market perceives the price as a good value.

Services like hotels and airlines sell a perishable commodity (hotel rooms and airline seats) with relatively constant fixed costs. Bundling can be an important income stream for these businesses because the variable cost tends to be low—for instance, the cost of cleaning a hotel room or putting one more passenger on an airplane.[24] Therefore, most of the revenue can help cover fixed costs and generate profits.

The automobile industry has a different motive for bundling. People buy cars only every three to five years. Thus selling options is a somewhat rare opportunity for the car dealer. Price bundling can help the dealer sell a maximum number of options.

**unbundling**
Reducing the bundle of services that comes with the basic product.

A related price tactic is **unbundling,** or reducing the bundle of services that comes with the basic product. Rather than raise the price of hotel rooms, some hotel chains have started charging registered guests for parking. To help hold the line on costs, some department stores require customers to pay for gift wrapping.

## Two-Part Pricing

**two-part pricing**
Price tactic that charges two separate amounts to consume a single good or service.

**Two-part pricing** means establishing two separate charges to consume a single good or service. Tennis clubs and health clubs, for example, charge a membership fee and a flat fee each time a person uses certain equipment or facilities. In other cases they charge a base rate for a certain level of usage, such as ten racquetball games per month, and a surcharge for anything over that amount.

Health clubs often use two-part pricing, charging a fee for membership and additional fees for each use of the facilities.



Consumers sometimes prefer two-part pricing because they are uncertain about the number and the types of activities they might use at places like an amusement park. Also, the people who use a service most often pay a higher total price. Two-part pricing can also increase the seller's revenue by attracting consumers who would not pay a high fee even for unlimited use. For example, a health club might be able to sell only 100 memberships at $700 annually with unlimited use of facilities, for total revenue of $70,000. But perhaps it could sell 900 memberships at $200 with a guarantee of using the racquetball courts ten times a month. Every usage over ten would require the member to pay a $5 fee. Thus membership revenue would provide a base of $180,000, with some additional usage fees coming in throughout thc year.

4 *Discuss product line pricing.*

## PRODUCT LINE PRICING

**product line pricing**
Setting prices for an entire line of products.

**Product line pricing** is setting prices for the entire line of products. Compared to setting the right price on a single product, product line pricing encompasses broader concerns. In product line pricing, the marketing manager tries to achieve maximum profits or other goals for the entire line rather than for a single component of the line.

### RELATIONSHIPS AMONG PRODUCTS

The manager must first determine the type of relationship that exists among the various products in the line:

- If items are *complementary,* an increase in the sale of one good causes an increase in demand for the complementary product, and vice versa. For example, the sale of ski poles depends on the demand for skis, making these two items complementary.
- Two products in a line can also be *substitutes* for each other. If buyers buy one

This sort of *expected-profit criterion* is useful for a firm making many bids, with no single bid being crucial. According to an expected-profit criterion, the manager should choose the bid price that yields the highest expected profit. But the expected-profit criterion is not a good basis for decision making if the manager must also consider such factors as excess capacity, need to keep the assembly line running, or possible alternative uses of a new technology that will be developed under the bid. These objectives may motivate the manager to lower the bid price.

6 *Describe the role of pricing during periods of inflation and recession.*

## PRICING DURING DIFFICULT ECONOMIC TIMES

Pricing is always an important aspect of marketing, but it is especially crucial in times of inflation and recession. The firm that does not adjust to economic trends may lose ground that it can never make up.

### INFLATION

When the economy is characterized by high inflation, special pricing tactics are often necessary. They can be subdivided into cost-oriented and demand-oriented tactics.

#### Cost-Oriented Tactics

One popular cost-oriented tactic is *culling products with a low profit margin* from the product line. However, this tactic may backfire for three reasons:

- A high volume of sales on an item with a low profit margin may make it highly profitable.
- Eliminating a product from a product line may reduce economies of scale, thereby lowering the margins on other items.
- Eliminating the product may affect the price/quality image of the entire line.

**delayed-quotation pricing**
Price tactic used for industrial installations and many accessory items, in which a firm price is not set until the item is either finished or delivered.

**escalator pricing**
Price tactic in which the final selling price reflects cost increases incurred between the times when the order is placed and when delivery is made.

Another popular cost-oriented tactic is **delayed-quotation pricing,** which is used for industrial installations and many accessory items. Price is not set on the product until the item is either finished or delivered. Long production lead times have forced this policy on many firms during periods of inflation. Builders of nuclear power plants, ships, airports, and office towers sometimes use delayed-quotation tactics.

**Escalator pricing** is similar to delayed-quotation pricing in that the final selling price reflects cost increases incurred between the times when the order is placed and when delivery is made. An escalator clause allows for price increases (usually across the board) based on the cost-of-living index or some other formula. As with any price increase, management's ability to implement such a policy is based on inelastic demand for the product. About a third of all industrial products manufacturers now use escalator clauses. However, many companies do not apply the clause in every sale. Often it is used only for extremely complex products that take a long time to produce or with new customers.

Any cost-oriented pricing policy that tries to maintain a fixed gross margin under all conditions can lead to a vicious circle. For example, a price increase will result in decreased demand, which in turn increases production costs (because of lost economies of scale). Increased production costs require a further price increase, leading to further diminished demand, and so on.

#### Demand-Oriented Tactics

Demand-oriented pricing tactics use price to reflect changing patterns of demand caused by inflation or high interest rates. Cost changes are considered, of course, but mostly in the context of how increased prices will affect demand.

**price shading**
Use of discounts by salespeople to increase demand for one or more products in a line.

**Price shading** is the use of discounts by salespeople to increase demand for one or more products in a line. Often shading becomes habitual and is done routinely without much forethought. Ducommun, a metals producer, is among the major companies that have succeeded in eliminating the practice. Ducommun has told its salespeople, "We want no deviation from book price" unless authorized by management.

To make the demand for a good or service more inelastic and to create buyer dependency, a company can use several strategies:

- *Cultivate selected demand:* Marketing managers can target prosperous customers that will pay extra for convenience or service. Neiman-Marcus, for example, stresses quality. As a result, the luxury retailer is more lenient with suppliers and their price increases than is Alexander's Stores, a discounter. In cultivating close relationships with affluent organizational customers, marketing managers should avoid putting themselves at the mercy of a dominant firm. They can more easily raise prices when an account is readily replaceable. Finally, in companies where engineers exert more influence than purchasing departments, performance is favored over price. Often a preferred vendor's pricing range expands if other suppliers prove technically unsatisfactory.
- *Create unique offerings:* Marketing managers should study buyers' needs. If the seller can design distinctive goods or services uniquely fitting buyers' activities, equipment, and procedures, a mutually beneficial relationship will evolve. Buyers would incur high changeover costs in switching to another supplier. By satisfying targeted buyers in a superior way, marketing managers can make them dependent. Buyers will then tolerate higher prices—within reason.
- *Heighten buyer dependence:* Owens-Corning Fiberglas supplies an integrated insulation service (from feasibility studies to installation) that includes commercial and scientific training for distributors and seminars for end users. This practice freezes out competition and supports higher prices.

### RECESSION

A recession is a period of reduced economic activity. Reduced demand for goods and services, along with higher rates of unemployment, is a common trait of a recession. Yet astute marketers can often find opportunity during recessions. They are an excellent time to build market share, because competitors are struggling to make ends meet.

Two effective pricing tactics to hold or build market share during a recession are value pricing and bundling. *Value pricing,* discussed earlier in the chapter, stresses to customers that they are getting a good value for their money. Revlon's Charles of the Ritz, usually known for its pricey products, introduced the Express Bar during the recession of the early 1990s. The Express Bar, a collection of affordable cosmetics and skin treatment products, sold alongside regular Ritz products in department stores. Although lower-priced products offer lower profit margins, Ritz found that volume increases can offset slimmer margins. For example, the company found that consumers will buy two to three Express Bar lipsticks at a time. "The consumer is very conscious of how she spends her income and is looking for value and quality that she can find elsewhere in department stores," said Holly Mercer, vice president of marketing for Ritz.[25]

*Bundling* or *unbundling* can also stimulate demand during a recession. If features are added to a bundle, consumers may perceive the offering as having greater value. For example, assume that Hyatt offers a "great escape" weekend for $119. The pack-

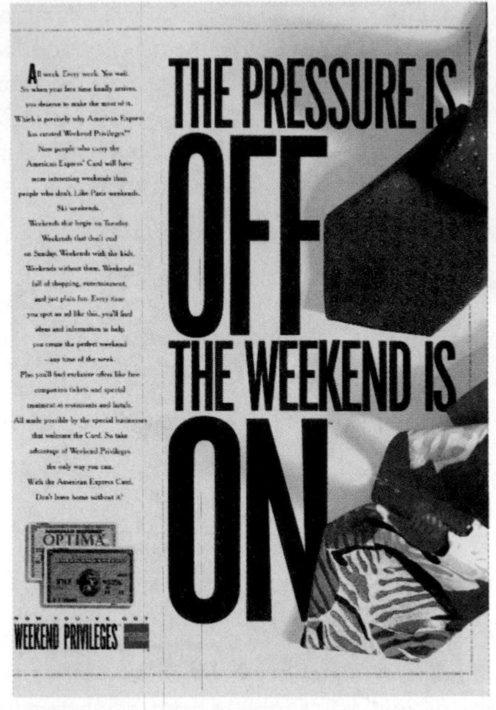


To stimulate demand for a product, a company might bundle the basic product with additional features. American Express, for example, provides "free companion tickets and special treatment at restaurants and hotels" to those who use its credit cards to charge weekend trips.

Courtesy American Express

age includes two nights' lodging and a continental breakfast. Hyatt could add a massage and a dinner for two to create more value for this price. Conversely, companies can unbundle offerings and lower base prices to stimulate demand. A furniture store, for example, could start charging separately for design consultation, delivery, credit, setup, and hauling away old furniture.

Recessions are a good time for marketing managers to study the demand for individual items in a product line and the revenue they produce. Pruning unprofitable items can save resources to be better used elsewhere. Borden's, for example, found that it made about 3,200 sizes, brands, types, and flavors of snacks—but got 95 percent of its revenues from just half of them.[26]

Prices often fall during a recession as competitors try desperately to maintain demand for their wares. Even if demand remains constant, falling prices mean lower profits or no profits. Falling prices, therefore, are a natural incentive to lower costs. During the last recession, companies implemented new technology to improve efficiency and then slashed payrolls. They also discovered that suppliers can be an excellent source of cost savings; the cost of purchased materials accounts for slightly more than half of most U.S. manufacturers' expenses.[27] General Electric's appliance division told 300 key suppliers that they must reduce prices 10 percent or risk losing GE's business. Allied Signal, Dow Chemical, United Airlines, General Motors, and DuPont have made similar demands of their suppliers. Specific strategies that companies are using with suppliers include

- *Renegotiating contracts:* sending suppliers letters demanding price cuts of 5 percent or more; putting out for rebid the contracts of those that refuse to cut costs
- *Offering help:* dispatching teams of experts to suppliers' plants to help reorganize and suggest other productivity-boosting changes; working with suppliers to make parts simpler and cheaper to produce
- *Keeping the pressure on:* to make sure the improvements continue, setting annual, across-the-board cost-reduction targets, often of 5 percent or more a year
- *Paring down suppliers:* to improve economies of scale, slashing the overall number of suppliers, sometimes by up to 80 percent, and boosting purchases from those that remain[28]

Tough tactics like these help keep companies afloat during economic downturns.

7 *Discuss what the future might hold for pricing in the marketing mix.*

## PRICING: A LOOK AT THE FUTURE

Predicting the future of anything is difficult. Nevertheless, a few changes in the area of pricing seem likely. One is related to the increase in direct-response marketing (mail order, catalog, telephone, and computer electronic catalogs). Their popularity means products will move more quickly from production lines to the consumer.

Faster distribution means that fewer funds will be tied up in finished goods inventory, a cost savings to the seller that may or may not be passed on to the consumer.

A closely related phenomenon is the United States' rapid transformation to an information-based society. Consumers and purchasing agents will be able to use their terminals to compare product alternatives and prices from several suppliers. The popular Prodigy information system, for example, gives detailed reports from sources like *Consumer Reports* and lists "best buys." Consumers will become more "price aware," and therefore elasticity of demand will increase, particularly for relatively homogeneous items.

An offshoot of the information society is the "cashless society," brought forth by electronic funds transfer. Buyers may come to think of price as an accounting entry, a more abstract concept. Moreover, when consumers no longer have to write a check or count out the dollars, money management may change. Record keeping will be more accurate, thanks to the electronic recording of transactions. On the other hand, the concept of price will be less concrete, which could lead to overspending.

The information revolution is already aiding managers in price decisions, and it will provide more benefits in the future. Electronic data-capture techniques, such as bar codes, make data available on a real-time, on-line basis. A district manager for a supermarket like Kroger can vary prices on Kraft's mayonnaise at different stores in the district and quickly determine elasticity of demand. Similarly, a manager can analyze the impact of a 5¢-off coupon (or any other value) almost immediately. New research technologies, such as single-source marketing research (discussed in Chapter 7), accurately measure elasticity of demand. As this technology spreads, managers will become far more accurate in setting the "right price."

## LOOKING BACK

Look back at the story about Mercedes-Benz that appeared at the beginning of the chapter. The advantages of premium pricing (skimming) are that development costs may be recovered more quickly if demand is inelastic, unit profits will be larger, and those who are willing to pay the premium price are, in fact, charged a premium price. On the other hand, premium pricing tends to attract competitors. Moreover, if a firm charges a premium price but doesn't have a distinct quality edge or other competitive advantage, sales will quickly evaporate.

Mercedes-Benz is following a penetration strategy with its C-class cars. It hopes to gain market share and profitability as well as stave off competition with its new price strategy. Mercedes-Benz is coupling a penetration price with value marketing—that is, offering a high-quality product at a fair price and with good service.

## SUMMARY

1 **Describe the procedure for setting the right price.** Setting the right price on a product is a process with four major steps: (1) establishing pricing goals; (2) estimating demand, costs, and profits; (3) choosing a price policy to help determine a base price; and (4) fine-tuning the base price with pricing tactics.

A price strategy establishes a long-term pricing framework for a good or service. The three main types of price policies are price skimming, penetration pricing, and status quo pricing. A price skimming policy charges a high introductory price, often followed by a gradual reduction. Penetration pricing offers a low introductory price to capture a large market share and attain economies of scale. Finally, status quo pricing strives to match competitors' prices.

**2 Identify the legal and ethical constraints on pricing decisions.** Government regulation helps monitor four major areas of pricing: unfair trade practices, price fixing, predatory pricing, and price discrimination. Enacted in many states, unfair trade practice acts protect small businesses from large firms that operate efficiently on extremely thin profit margins; these acts prohibit charging below-cost prices. The Sherman Act and the Federal Trade Commission Act prohibit both price fixing, an agreement between two or more firms on a particular price, and predatory pricing, undercutting competitors with extremely low prices to drive them out of business. Finally, the Robinson-Patman Act makes it illegal for firms to discriminate between two or more buyers in terms of price.

**3 Explain how discounts, geographic pricing, and other special pricing tactics can be used to fine-tune the base price.** Several pricing techniques enable marketing managers to adjust prices within a general price level in response to changes in competition, government regulation, consumer demand, and promotional and positioning goals. Techniques for fine-tuning a price can be divided into three main categories: discounts, allowances, and rebates; geographic pricing; and special pricing tactics.

The first type of tactic gives lower prices to those that pay promptly, order a large quantity, or perform some function for the manufacturer. Trade loading is a manufacturer's temporary functional discount to induce wholesalers and retailers to buy more goods than can be sold in a reasonable time. Trade loading increases inventory expenses and channel expenses and lowers the manufacturer's profits. A tactic meant to overcome these problems is "everyday low pricing," or maintaining low prices over time while eliminating the discounts that result in trade loading. Other tactics in this category include seasonal discounts, promotion allowances, and rebates (cash refunds).

Geographic pricing tactics—such as FOB origin pricing, uniform delivered pricing, zone pricing, freight absorption pricing, and basing-point pricing—are ways of moderating the impact of shipping costs on distant customers.

A variety of special pricing tactics stimulate demand for certain products, increase store patronage, and offer more merchandise at specific prices.

**4 Discuss product line pricing.** Product line pricing maximizes profits for an entire product line. When setting product line prices, marketing managers determine what type of relationship exists among the products in the line: complementary, substitute, or neutral. Managers also consider joint (shared) costs among products of the same product line.

**5 Explain how bidding differs from other forms of pricing.** Bid pricing is a process in which competing sellers state what they will charge to provide a good or service. Bid pricing is unique because the quantity demanded is indicated in the bidding specifications.

**6 Describe the role of pricing during periods of inflation and recession.** Marketing managers employ cost-oriented and demand-oriented tactics during periods of eco-

KEY TERMS

*bait pricing* 667
*base price* 656
*basing-point pricing* 663
*bid pricing* 670
*cash discount* 657
*cumulative quantity discount* 657
*delayed-quotation pricing* 672
*escalator pricing* 672
*everyday low prices (EDLP)* 660
*flexible pricing (variable pricing)* 665
*FOB origin pricing* 662
*freight absorption pricing* 663
*functional discount (trade discount)* 658
*joint cost* 670
*leader pricing (loss-leader pricing)* 666
*noncumulative quantity discount* 657
*odd-even pricing (psychological pricing)* 667
*penetration pricing* 651
*predatory pricing* 656
*price bundling* 668
*price discrimination* 655
*price fixing* 653
*price lining* 665
*price shading* 672
*price skimming* 648
*price strategy* 648
*product line pricing* 669
*promotional allowance* 661
*quantity discount* 657

nomic inflation. Cost-oriented tactics consist of dropping products with a low profit margin, delayed-quotation pricing, and escalator pricing. Demand-oriented pricing methods include price shading and increasing demand through cultivation of selected customers, unique offerings, and systems selling.

To stimulate demand during a recession, marketers use value pricing, bundling, and unbundling. Recessions are also a good time to prune unprofitable products from product lines. Managers strive to cut costs during recessions in order to maintain profits as revenues decline. Implementing new technology, cutting payrolls, and pressuring suppliers for reduced prices are common techniques used to cut costs.

7 **Discuss what the future might hold for pricing in the marketing mix.** Several trends in marketing are likely to affect pricing in the future. First, an increase in direct-response marketing is simplifying distribution and creating savings for sellers that may be passed on to consumers. Better and more accessible product information is likely to make consumers more price-sensitive. Electronic funds transfer may create a "cashless society," in which record keeping is more accurate but the concept of price more abstract. Finally, marketers' manipulation and analysis of pricing strategies are likely to become more effective with the use of new technology.

## Discussion and Writing Questions

1. Identify several new products on the market that have followed (a) skimming, (b) penetration, and (c) status quo pricing policies. Explain why you feel each company followed its particular policy.
2. Because of the multiple channels of distribution employed by many firms, the manufacturer has little authority over the final selling price of a product; therefore, the importance of price as a marketing variable is reduced. Evaluate this statement.
3. You are contemplating a price change for an established product sold by your firm. Write a memo analyzing the factors you need to consider in your decision.
4. Do you see everyday low prices as a solution to trade loading? Why are many manufacturers resisting EDLP?
5. What types of relationships exist among products in a product line? Discuss how they relate in terms of demand.
6. What factors influence whether or not firms bid?
7. Your firm submits a bid for an order of office furniture. List the ways you can ensure that the buyer will not overlook the high quality of your product, regardless of price.
8. How is the "information age" changing the nature of pricing?

## Application for Small Business

Traditionally, scuba diving operators have treated divers like rough and ready campers, people who don't mind close quarters with minimal amenities and dull food. Jim Munch founded Munch Diving Cruises in Fort Lauderdale, Florida, to reach a different market segment. He offers four-day cruises to a vicinity near Bimini in the Bahamas. The cruise features five dives per day, including night dives with towering reefs, deep walls of coral, and shipwrecks. The specially designed Munch Master boat can carry up to twenty customers. It contains staterooms with double bed and private bath, a sundeck with Jacuzzi, and delectable cuisine with an island flair. Best of all, the Munch Master's unique twin-hulled design minimizes wave action, so only the most delicate stomachs get upset.

Jim offers an excellent service, but he is worried about pricing. He knows that if he charges too much, he will attract competition. His boat is easily duplicable. Jim wants to offer a good value for the money to get repeat customers. On the other hand, his bank is pressing for a quick repayment on the note for his boat.

### Questions

1. Advise Jim on a price strategy.
2. What are some ways that he can fine-tune his base price?

## CRITICAL THINKING CASE

### Mahalo Air

Soon after Victor Weeks heard that a new local airline in Hawaii was offering tickets to other islands at almost half the regular cost, he called to reserve a $25 seat. By then Mahalo Air had cut its inaugural price to $10. Although one of Mahalo's competitors duplicated the $10 fare, Weeks walked away with a handful of Mahalo tickets. "I wanted to support them," he says.

Mahalo Air is flying into a market depressed by a steep drop in tourism. HAL Inc., owner of Hawaiian Airlines, has been driven into bankruptcy court, and Aloha and Hawaiian have been forced to trim seats. So desperate is the local industry's situation that the state of Hawaii has asked Congress to let it reregulate air travel.

Mahalo's founders "have spent too much time in the sun," says A. Maurice Myers, Aloha's president and CEO. "It's questionable whether two carriers can make it here. A third is ludicrous." But Mahalo says it can stretch the shrinking local market, long dominated by Hawaiian and Aloha, by emulating the mainland success of Southwest Airlines.

Mahalo's frills have been few indeed. Its first passengers faced delays, spotty air conditioning, and cramped turboprop planes. Nonetheless, its first month of flights sold out in four days. Mahalo takes forty minutes to fly from Honolulu to Maui, or about ten minutes longer than its jet rivals.

Mahalo's founders figure that Hawaiians, who lack ferries or other alternatives to air transportation, will go island-hopping more often to visit friends and relatives if air fares come down. Michael Nekoba, Mahalo's CEO, calculates that Mahalo can bite into 10 percent of the local market and turn a profit on a $30 one-way fare, a third off its rivals' discounted prices.

"It's kind of adventurous," says Weeks of Mahalo Air's scrappy-but-friendly ambience, compared with what he calls the corporate feel of Hawaiian and Aloha. The two long-established carriers are considerably less kind. "We are all subject to our dumbest competitor," says Bruce Nobles, president and CEO of HAL, who makes it a point to say that his company never matches Mahalo's fares but does sometimes match Aloha's fares when Aloha matches Mahalo's. "It was a question of us losing some money or more money. I chose to lose the least."

Mr. Iwamoto, who owns a 65 percent stake in Mahalo, says he understands his rivals' ire. The executive, whose business card features a winking, waving rabbit wearing a lei, says: "You can't blame them for complaining about us."[29]



#### Questions

1. What type of price strategy is Mahalo Air following? What dangers does this strategy present?
2. Is the airline using predatory pricing? Why or why not?
3. What price tactics could Mahalo use to alter its prices?

## VIDEO CASE

### Southwest Airlines

With over two decades of continued success, it is hard to believe that the plans for Southwest Airlines were first drawn on a cocktail napkin. At least this is the story that Herbert Kelleher, now Chairman of the Board, President, and Chief Executive Officer of the company, likes to share with people about the inception of the airline—an airline that is now one of the largest domestic carriers, as well as the most profitable in the United States.

Rollin King and Herb Kelleher conceived the idea

for a Texas intrastate airline in 1966. This idea was to provide low-cost air service to Houston and San Antonio from a Dallas base at Love Field. Implementing this plan was difficult in the regulated airline industry, and Southwest faced 34 judicial and administrative proceedings before its first flight took off in 1971.

While other airlines had agreed to leave Love Field and support the new Dallas-Fort Worth International Airport, Southwest never wanted to abandon Love Field and favored the less congested and closer-to-downtown location. However, other airlines believed that allowing a competing airline to fly from Love would jeopardize the financial future of the new DFW airport. Ultimately, Congress passed the "Wright Amendment" which limits regularly scheduled Love Field air service only to points within Texas and to its four contiguous states.

Early marketing campaigns centered around a "Luv" theme. The airline called itself, "The somebody else up there who loves you." Its headquarters has remained at Dallas Love Field despite the Amendment which has hindered its home-base growth.

Unlike most large air carriers who have suffered tremendous losses or even folded in bankruptcy, Southwest has been profitable every year since 1973. This can be attributed to its no-frills service which keeps its operating costs far below the competition.

- Only drinks and snacks (peanuts, pretzels, cookies) are served.
- Open seating and plastic reusable boarding passes are used.
- There is no baggage transfer to other airlines.
- Less congested airports, such as Love Field in Dallas and Midway in Chicago, are favored over larger, busier airports.
- Labor relations with its unions are characterized as "excellent."
- The time to "turn" an aircraft or the time spent at the gate between flights is usually 15 to 20 minutes, compared to the industry average of 55 minutes.

In addition, the company operates a point-to-point flight system. After the industry was deregulated in 1978, most carriers rushed to build complex hub and spoke systems. Southwest stuck to its original short-haul strategy with the average flight a mere 65 minutes. The airline has also maintained a fleet of only one type of aircraft, the 737, which leads to millions in savings because flight training and maintenance are greatly simplified.

The high frequency of flights and low fares attract business and leisure travelers alike, but the airline developed other marketing tools to lure customers. A pricing promotion, "Friends Fly Free," enables passengers to purchase one ticket and receive one free. Another marketing device, the airlines' frequent flyer program, is very simple because it is based on actual trips, not mileage. Each time they travel, passengers receive credit for each one-way trip. It is also very convenient to join by merely picking up a brochure at any Southwest counter.

As a short-haul niche carrier, the airline has differentiated itself with low fares and simple but fun service. The fun begins at the top with the wit and humor of Kelleher who has been known to dress up as Elvis and even arm wrestle another airline executive over an advertising slogan. Kelleher serves as an example for over 16,000 employees who display the same enthusiasm about Southwest and their jobs. Even Southwest's advertisements contain humor which has become symbolic of Southwest.

In 1993, the airline acquired Morris Air, a Salt Lake City-based regional carrier that mirrored Southwest's operation in many ways. Morris flew only 737s and concentrated on short-haul, low-cost service. While the purchase increased Southwest's fleet by 22 planes, the primary advantage of the acquisition was that Morris did not compete with Southwest in any market. This gave Southwest instant service in several cities in the far Northwest.

Southwest plans to continue expansion in the Midwest and western United States, but will not name which cities it is considering. Commenting on the carrier's future, Kelleher explains:

> I don't think anything will be different in the future. I'm talking about the philosophy of it, the foundation of it. I think that we will continue to emphasize that Southwest Airlines, in our opinion, is the best air transportation value in the industry. And that's a campaign that we launched several years ago. Basically, the core of it is "just plane smart," it's just plain smart to fly the carrier that has the best customer service record, one of the newest fleets in the industry, and the most hospitable people at the lowest price. It's really a value approach to marketing and I think that the decade of the '90s throughout its entirety is going to be very receptive to that approach.

Questions

1. Discuss the role of price in Southwest Airlines' marketing mix.

2. Describe Southwest's pricing strategy.

3. Compare Southwest's pricing strategy to the strategies of other major airlines such as American Airlines, United Airlines, and Delta Airlines.

4. Discuss Southwest's approach to fine-tuning the base price with pricing tactics.

5. Herbert Kelleher, Chairman of the Board, President, and Chief Executive Officer of Southwest Airlines says that the airline practices a "value approach to marketing." Explain this concept and cite evidence to support Mr. Kelleher's claim.

# PART SIX INTEGRATIVE CASE

## SOFTWARE PRICING

The decade of the 1980s witnessed a veritable revolution in microcomputers. The 1990s, however, promise to take software to new heights. Earlier, the hardware accounted for about 80 percent of the cost of a home or office computing system. Hardware today accounts for an average of only 20 percent of the system cost; software accounts for most of the cost of a computer system. Little wonder, then, that the worldwide packaged software market is growing at an unprecedented rate. Sales in 1994 were about $80.3 billion, almost double those of 1989.

Rapid growth in the software market could be attributed to many things. The two major reasons are the increasing use of microcomputers in most offices and many homes and the increasing diversity in consumer software needs. The market is expanding for both applications software (such as word-processing, graphics, and spreadsheet programs) and operating systems (such as DOS and Windows, which interact with hardware and provide the platform for applications software to work).

As the market grows, so does the competition for market share. In competitive markets, the importance of price as a strategic and competitive weapon cannot be understated. Competitive price strategies in the software market include traditional strategies such as penetration pricing and limited-time offers, as well as special "upgrade" pricing and "suite" pricing.

Many software firms seek to lure first-time users with special introductory prices. To popularize its OS/2 operating system, IBM marketed it at very low prices through mail-order retailers, software specialty stores, and general merchandise stores.

To retain current customers in a competitive market, almost all software developers offer new, improved upgrades at special prices. These "upgrade" prices are usually much lower than the price at which that version of the software is sold to new users. Many software developers also offer special "competitive upgrade" prices to users of competing software. For example, a spreadsheet developer may offer a low price to users of a different spreadsheet. Because learning the idiosyncracies of new software generally requires some time and effort, competitive upgrade pricing offers the extra incentive that may be necessary for users of a competitor's software to switch.

For computer users, the process of learning to use new software is a "sunk cost," and many are reluctant to switch once they have mastered a program. Thus many software developers, particularly the big firms, have decided that locking in new computer users is the best strategy for increasing market share. One key tactic, introduced in 1992, is the bundling of applications in a package called a "suite," which is offered at a discounted price. For example, Microsoft bundles its Microsoft Word word-processing program, PowerPoint graphics program, and Access relational database program into a bundle called Microsoft Office. Similar suites are offered by Lotus and Borland International. Buyers acquire compatible software programs at prices substantially lower than the cost of buying each individual program separately, but they are guided into using applications from only one manufacturer.

Price strategies that give computer users a break and increase software sales may seem to benefit both consumers and software development firms. However, the low prices have created complaints among current, loyal users. They resent having to pay the same as or even more than some new users pay. As for the software firms, the price wars are cutting into profit margins. Software prices and profits have both plummeted since 1990. Suite pricing may also be stifling innovation at a time when muscular new computer hardware is offering tremendous potential for new applications. When the market leaders are focused on compatibility and price, they may be less willing to innovate.

The price wars are also hurting software firms that have built their reputation on a single application program, even those that have been anointed the "best of the breed." For example, the Software Publishing Corporation, whose Harvard Graphics was the best-selling graphics program for many years, witnessed a rapid decline in sales, market share, and profits as competitors offered graphics programs in their suites.

Even though some of the graphics applications offered in suites were noticeably inferior to Harvard Graphics, consumers couldn't resist the low suite prices. The Software Publishing Corporation was forced to lay off 21 percent of its work force in 1993. Firms in this position have little choice but to expand into untried areas of software in order to compete.

Low introductory prices, discounted upgrade pricing, and cut-rate suite pricing will only prolong the price wars. Enticing users to switch software may seem to offer considerable potential for enhancing market share, but the risk is a full-fledged battle of the brands. At this point, the only limitation to all-out war remains the nonprice switching costs encountered by users.

## Questions

1. At what stage in the product life cycle is the computer software industry?
2. What are the similarities between the software market and markets for other products that are in the same stage of their product life cycle?
3. What are some of the price strategies used by software firms to attract new buyers?
4. What are the adverse effects of price wars?

## Suggested Readings

Phillip Anderson, "You, the Consumer, Can Save the Industry from Microsoft's Domination," *Infoworld,* 15 March 1993, p. 55.

Richard Brandt, "Software Will Play Hardball Again," *Business Week,* 10 January 1994, p. 82.

Garrett DeYoung, "Software Publishing Looks for a Rebound," *Electronic Business,* July 1993, pp. 77–80.

Ed Foster, "Borland's Upgrade Pricing Creates a Paradox of Its Own, *Infoworld,* 15 March 1993, p. 55.

Rosemary Hamilton, "User Skepticism Impels IBM to Remix Desktop Strategy," *Computer World,* 30 March 1992, pp. 1, 12.

Rick Whiting, "Full-Scale PC Software Price War Will Continue," *Electronic Business,* January 1993, pp. 80–81.

Shawn Willett, "Software Price Wars Don't Have a Big Effect on Buying Plans," *Infoworld,* 25 January 1993, p. 1.

# PART SIX
# GLOBAL MARKETING CASE

## PRICING EXPORTS THE HARD WAY

*Linda B. Catlin, Wayne State University, and Thomas F. White, Regis University*

Tim Ballard looked out his office window at the mountain in the distance and thought about the phone call he had just received from Finland. One of Tim's best international customers, Olë Kulla, is a small wholesaler who travels throughout much of Scandinavia. Olë handles several lines of high-priced gifts, including the solar-powered executive gifts that Tim's company, Solar World, manufactures. Olë had called Tim today to see if Solar World would be interested in setting up a distribution network in Russia, Latvia, and Lithuania.

Tim's initial response to Olë's question was no. "Thanks for thinking of us," he told Olë, "but I don't think we're interested in trying to do business in Russia. We're too small a company to take that kind of risk, and I don't have the manufacturing capacity to extend much beyond our present markets."

However, Tim listened carefully as Olë explained that Boris Ivanov, a Moscow entrepreneur whom Olë had met a year ago in Sweden, was looking for unusual gift items to sell in Russia, Latvia, and Lithuania. Boris, according to Olë, had established a sales network in the three former Soviet republics and was always looking for new products. Olë had shown Boris some of Solar World's executive gifts, and Boris had expressed a strong interest in the products. He asked Olë to call Tim and set up a meeting or at least a telephone conference to discuss the possibility of doing business.

"Boris has been extremely successful in setting up a business, now that individuals can own businesses in the former Soviet Union. He seems to understand the free-enterprise system very well," Olë told Tim. "I think it might be worth your time to talk with him about selling Solar World products in Russia."

Tim agreed to think over what Olë had said and to let him know if he wanted to contact Boris.

"The first thing I need to do," Tim thought after this telephone conversation, "is to get out the atlas and see where Lithuania and Latvia are located! I think I know where Russia is."

The next day Tim mentioned Olë's phone call to George Stephens, Solar World's sales manager. "I'm not convinced that this is something we want to pursue," Tim said, "but isn't it interesting that even a formerly communist country might be interested in buying our executive gifts?"

"I wouldn't dismiss the Russian's inquiry completely," George replied quickly. "I happened to be talking to Ben Rodriguez over at BR, Inc., yesterday, and he's just come back from a trip to Eastern Europe and Russia. He's planning to sell some of BR's specialty advertising items to Russia.

"Ben took a consultant with him when he went to Russia," George continued. "Maybe we ought to give her a call and see what's involved in doing business over there."

Later that week Tim did talk with Nina Churkin, the business consultant whom Ben Rodriguez recommended. Nina had been born and educated in the former Soviet Union. After she emigrated to the United States, she completed an MBA at a U.S. university. She advised Tim that if he had any interest in doing business in Russia, he would have to go there in person to meet Boris Ivanov.

"It's very difficult to do business long distance with anyone in Russia. Their communication system is not as reliable and advanced as in the United States, and personal relationships are much more important in doing business there than they are here," Nina told Tim. "Also, you need to be prepared to accept payment for your product in some form other than rubles or dollars."

"I don't understand," Tim said. "The firms I sell to in Finland and in Japan give me an international letter of credit, and I receive payment through the bank. I never even have to convert from another currency."

Nina laughed. "Unfortunately, Russia and the other former communist countries don't have many hard currency reserves. They are relying heavily on countertrade for obtaining products from the West."

"Countertrade? I don't know what that is," Tim said.

"There are several forms of countertrade. The simplest is barter. That's where you trade Boris a certain number of your products in exchange for an agreed-on number of one or more products produced in Russia.

An example of a Russian good he might be able to obtain for trade would be *matroyshka* dolls, those by colorfully painted nesting dolls that children love. Or some companies have access to *shapka,* the distinctive fur hats many Russians wear.

"Dolls? Fur hats? What would I do with dolls or fur hats?" Tim asked. "I don't sell children's toys or clothing. That sounds like a crazy way to do business."

"Countertrade sometimes takes a different form than straight barter. I think another way of doing it is called a buy-back agreement. In this situation, you would give Boris the technical information or specialized components he needs to make the executive gifts your company produces here. Then Boris produces those gifts in Russia and gives you a specified number on a regular basis as repayment for the technical information. You can sell those Russian-made gifts to your other customers, perhaps in Europe or back here in the United States."

"You mean I would sell our technical expertise to someone in Russia? How would I protect myself in that case? What would prevent him from using it and not paying me with finished goods?"

"Only a lawyer—and one familiar with Russian law as well as U.S. law—can answer those questions. You do need to be concerned about those issues."

Tim was intrigued, although somewhat perplexed, by what Nina told him. Using a countertrade arrangement in Russia might just give him the potential to increase his production without incurring more debt. And if the finished products were already in Europe, he could eliminate the transportation costs he now had to build in when shipping from the United States.

Tim called his banker to find out more about countertrade. His banker's response was negative. "Those payment arrangements are fraught with problems," the banker said. "My advice is don't have anything to do with companies or individuals who propose countertrade. An irrevocable letter of credit is the only way you should be doing business in the international market."

Although the banker had been helpful on many occasions when Tim had needed an increase in his line of credit, Tim also realized that bankers tend to be very conservative about business transactions that eliminate the bank as a financial middleman. And since he knew that Ben Rodriguez at BR, Inc., was considering exchanging his company's finished goods for Russian produced goods, Tim decided to regard his banker's advice as only one of many pieces to fit into what he was coming to regard as the countertrade puzzle.

Next, Tim contacted Lauren Kruph, a local attorney who was writing a comparative study of Russian and U.S. legal systems. Lauren confirmed Tim's concerns that there were a number of potential legal problems involved in doing business in Russia, especially if he decided to use countertrade.

"The problems almost certainly can be resolved," Lauren said, "but you will need to contact a Russian lawyer as well as a U.S. one. The process may be time-consuming and expensive. However, if this deal seems profitable enough in other respects, the legal expenses will be worth it.

Tim discussed the information obtained from Lauren, Nina, and the banker with his sales manager. They agreed that Tim should call Olë in Helsinki.

"I've decided to consider selling our products in Russia, Latvia, and Lithuania," Tim told Olë. "But first I want to suggest a possible deal between you and me. How about your buying the products from Solar World and then selling them to or countertrading them with Boris for some Russian products? That way, you can make a profit from this deal, too."

"I'm afraid my cash flow is not good enough for that kind of deal, Tim," replied Olë. "I already take some goods as countertrade for the Finnish and Swedish goods I sell to Boris. Possibly I could take some Russian products if Boris offers you the right ones in exchange for Solar World's products. But I can't directly buy your goods to sell or trade with Boris.

"I'm glad to know that you're anticipating the probability of a countertrade offer from Boris," Olë continued. "It's best if you're prepared to react to any of several different options he may suggest. Judging from what Boris projects he can do with the markets he wants to open up to Solar World's goods, I would guess you could eventually double your annual sales. Why don't I set up a meeting for the two of you here in Helsinki, and perhaps I can help with the negotiations?"

Olë had been Tim's first international customer and over the past six years had been a tremendous help in explaining the intricacies of doing business in Europe. Now Tim regarded Olë as a friend as well as a customer, and he appreciated Olë's offer to meet with Boris.

Tim agreed to a meeting with Boris in Helsinki and began to review Solar World's current position in preparation for his trip.

Solar World is a small firm, employing fourteen assemblers to make the company's products, including the solar-powered executive gifts that Olë sells, solar-powered flashlights and battery packs, high-tech micro-solar panels (on which the company has a monopoly), and educational solar kits. The company also employs three people in office and accounting jobs, plus George, the sales manager, and Tim, the company president. Solar World's annual sales are about $1.5 million; about a fifth of the sales, or $300,000, are made in Europe and Japan.

The firm's offices and plant are in a small, one-story office building in Colorado Springs, Colorado. The rest of the building is occupied currently, so any expansion in production facilities would necessitate moving to another site.

As Tim reviewed Solar World's position, he suddenly remembered an inquiry from a German wholesaler three months ago. The German firm wanted to represent the executive gift line in all parts of Europe south of Scandinavia, where Olë had exclusive distribution rights. The German representative estimated that eventually he would be buying 10,000 units per month, perhaps as soon as six months after his first purchase. Because of the large projected volume, which was several times the amount Olë sold now, the German wanted the products at a much lower price than Solar World sold them to the Finnish distributor. The German told Tim the end-user price he needed to move the projected volume, as well as the margin he would need to handle Solar World's products. Tim used these figures to work backward when setting a price for the German. Unfortunately, he discovered that the transportation and tariff costs would not allow Solar World enough profit to do this deal with its present cost structure. Moreover, the higher volume would require a second production shift with new employees and the many costs associated with those additional employees. Tim reluctantly had turned down this potential buyer. Now, however, with the possibility of getting finished products from a factory in Russia, Tim began to rethink his options regarding sales to the German firm.

Tim developed the following list of questions that he needs to answer before meeting with Boris:

1. Define a set of alternative proposals that Boris might suggest at the Helsinki meeting; use some aspect of countertrade as the basis for each proposal.
2. What are the pros and cons of countertrade for a firm the size and complexity of Solar World?
3. If Solar World accepts one of the countertrade proposals, what are the company's resources for selling or trading the goods it receives? How would the company price these countertraded goods? How should the company price its own goods under the countertrade conditions?
4. If Tim decides to sell the technology license to the Russian firm, how should he price it?
5. Which of the alternatives identified above is the best one for Solar World? Why?

### To the Student

How would you advise Tim in each area in preparation for the Helsinki meeting?

RAIN
C/F THERMOMETER

# Part Seven
# Contemporary Marketing Management



A position with a toy manufacturer during a work-study program in college gave Matthew Fenton a thorough understanding of how to market products to children. This experience, along with his double major in marketing and management, helped him land a job as an associate brand manager at Van Melle U.S.A.

Van Melle is an international company based in Breda, Holland. The century-old family business manufactures and markets candy. Van Melle U.S.A. is the U.S. branch of the operation. It oversees the marketing of two products: Mentos, the best-selling mint candy in the world, and AirHeads, the number-one fifteen cent, non-chocolate children's candy in the United States.

Brand recognition is important when selling candy to children. It is essential to stand out from the competition and catch kids' eyes. Packaging is a big part of Van Melle's sales strategy. The company recognizes that children are attracted to products that look outrageous. An interesting package design may convince a child to pick your product out of a display containing over a hundred other items.

Matthew's current tasks include package design, display design, coordinating research tests, analyzing promotional programs, and analyzing competitors. The continuing profitability of Mentos and AirHeads is one of the key measures of his job performance. Gradually, he will become more involved in long-term strategic planning for the company.

Matthew finds children's marketing very exciting. He enjoys the challenge of coming up with new ways to promote Van Melle's products to kids. He had to spend an additional year in college in order to participate in the work-study program that gave him his first real-world experience in business, but in the long run that investment has paid high dividends for his career.

# CHAPTER 20

# MULTICULTURAL MARKETING IN THE UNITED STATES

## LEARNING OBJECTIVES

*After studying this chapter, you should be able to*

1 *Analyze the cultural diversity of the United States.*

2 *Identify key characteristics of the African-American market and some elements of an effective marketing mix for this group.*

3 *Identify key characteristics of the U.S. Hispanic market and some elements of an effective marketing mix for this group.*

4 *Identify key characteristics of the Asian-American market and some elements of an effective marketing mix for this group.*

5 *Identify key characteristics of the Native American market.*

Cadillac is the number-one luxury auto among African-Americans, but more and more of them are driving off in imported cars. Cadillac is trying to woo some of them back with an aggressive promotional effort, aiming to thwart the importers that are making a play for the market segment—even though African-Americans represent only about 3.7 percent of the luxury car market.

Cadillac has been advertising in magazines oriented toward African-Americans for a number of years. But for the first time the company has targeted the market very specifically. Cadillac's own focus group research with African-American consumers revealed that the company suffers from a bit of an image problem. Baby boomers especially viewed the car as stodgy and were oblivious to Cadillac's newer cars.

In 1992 Cadillac introduced the Eldorado Touring Coupe and the Seville STS, both aimed squarely at the buyers who had been defecting to the imports. The redesigned models successfully pulled in other groups of buyers, but African-American baby boomers remained aloof. "It really came down to them not knowing about us," says Trina Barton, market strategy analyst for Cadillac. "When we told them about all of our achievements, they were surprised. We decided we needed to get our message out there."

Cadillac has done precisely that, sending out invitations for a test drive to 35,000 affluent African-American households nationwide. Consumers were told that, if they took a cruise in any new Cadillac before a certain date, Cadillac would make a $50 donation to the United Negro College Fund, the Sickle Cell Disease Association of America, or the Thurgood Marshall Scholarship Fund. The package sent out to younger consumers featured the 1994 Seville STS and Eldorado Touring Coupe and included a quote from *Car and Driver* magazine comparing the models to BMW and Mercedes-Benz.

In a study of 218 African-Americans who had bought luxury cars, J.D. Power & Associates found that Cadillac snared one out of three buyers. But the imports also pulled in their fair share, with Volvo nabbing 12.0 percent of the market, Mercedes-Benz 7.8 percent, Infiniti 5.0 percent, Acura 4.8 percent, and Lexus 3.3 percent. "That's the turf that Cadillac used to have," says Tom Healey, partner at J.D. Power & Associates. "Obviously, they still have a big part of it, but Lexus and Infiniti have picked up some of the market, and it's been at Cadillac's expense. I think what you're seeing now is Cadillac looking to grab back that share, especially now that they're more price competitive with the Japanese imports." [1]

The tactics used by Cadillac to recapture African-American buyers are an example of multicultural marketing. How do you think ethnic markets are changing in the United States? Are they homogeneous or diverse? How can ethnic markets be successfully reached?

1 *Analyze the cultural diversity of the United States.*

## THE UNITED STATES AS A MULTICULTURAL SOCIETY

The United States is undergoing a new demographic transition: It is becoming a multicultural society. The 1990 census found that eight in ten people in the United States are white, down from nine in ten in 1960. During the 1990s, the United States will shift further from a society dominated by whites and rooted in Western culture to a society characterized by three large racial and ethnic minorities: African-Americans, U.S. Hispanics, and Asian-Americans. All three minorities will grow in size and in share of the population while the white majority declines as a percentage of the total. Native Americans and people with roots in Australia, the Middle East, the former Soviet Union, and other parts of the world will further enrich the fabric of U.S. society.

The demographic transition has two basic causes. First, during the 1980s, 6 million legal immigrants came to the United States, 70 percent of whom were either Asian or Hispanic. Second, immigrants tend to have more children than the native-born population, as do Hispanic-Americans and African-Americans. Together, these factors are boosting the share of racial and ethnic minorities in the population.[2]

**multiculturalism**
Roughly equal representation of all major ethnic groups withiin a geographic area.

### ETHNIC AND CULTURAL DIVERSITY

**Multiculturalism** occurs when all major ethnic groups in an area—such as a city, county, or census tract—are roughly equally represented. Because of the demographic transition, the trend in the United States is toward greater multiculturalism.

Exhibit 20.1 depicts levels of multiculturalism by county. Four of New York City's five boroughs are among the ten most ethnically diverse counties in the country.[3] San Francisco County is the most diverse in the nation. The proportions of

*Exhibit 20.1*

Levels of Ethnic Diversity in the United States, by County

Source: James Allen and Eugene Turner, "Where Diversity Reigns," *American Demographics*, August 1990, p. 37. Copyright © American Demographics. For subscription information, please call (800) 828-1133.

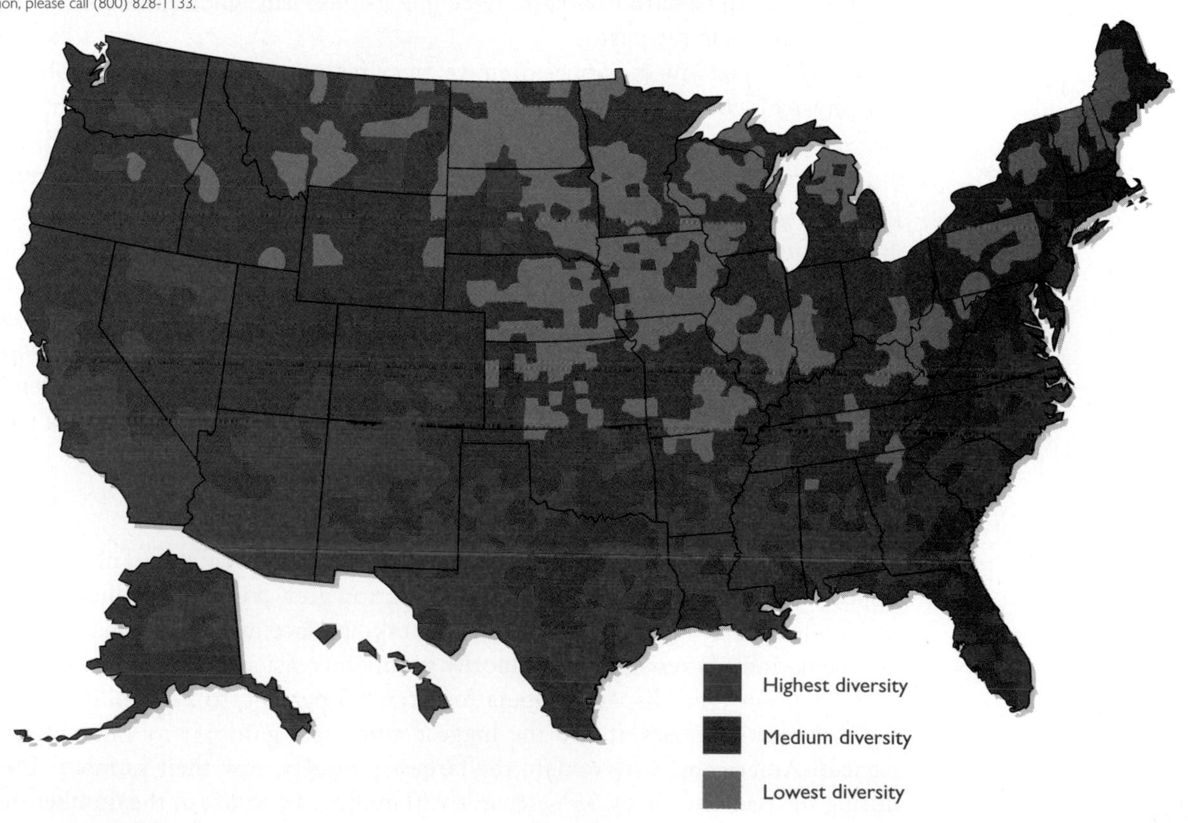

major ethnic groups are closer to being equal there than anywhere else. People of many ancestries have long been attracted to the area. The least multicultural region is a broad swath stretching from northern New England through the Midwest and into Montana. These counties have few people other than whites. The counties with the very lowest level of diversity are found in the agricultural heartland: Nebraska and Iowa.

## Social Implications of Multiculturalism

Multiculturalism will have a profound impact on society as a whole. If we count men and women as separate groups, all of us are now members of at least one minority group.[4] Without fully realizing it, we have left the time when the nonwhite, non-Western part of our population could be expected to assimilate to the dominant majority. In the future, everyone will have to do some assimilating.

Around 2010, the oldest non-Hispanic white baby boomers will start retiring. Therefore, the fastest growth between 1990 and 2010 within this slow-growing ethnic group will be in the older age groups, especially among those ages 55 to 64. Meanwhile, the maturing of the baby-bust generation will cause an absolute decline in the number of non-Hispanic whites ages 25 to 44.[5] Growth in the numbers of non-Hispanic white children will also lag behind growth in minority populations. These demographic shifts will have important consequences. As non-Hispanic whites age, they will be increasingly dependent on the productivity of black, Hispanic, and Asian workers. More than half the nation's new workers between 1990 and 2005 will be minorities, according to the Bureau of Labor Statistics. Increasingly, the fortunes of U.S. minorities will affect the well-being of the majority.

As multiculturalism takes hold, no single racial or ethnic group will have the political power to dictate solutions. Agreement on how to resolve almost any public issue is likely to be hard to obtain. Reaching a consensus will require more cooperation than it has in the past.

The U.S. economy continues to move away from manufacturing and jobs requiring physical skills toward services and jobs requiring knowledge and intellectual skills. More than ever, a college education will be the way to get ahead in U.S. society. But relative to rates for Asian-Americans and whites, African-Americans and Hispanics have lower overall education levels, and their college enrollment rates actually declined during the 1980s.[6] If these differences in educational attainment persist, they will produce sharply different socioeconomic profiles for the major racial and ethnic groups. Whites and Asian-Americans could increasingly dominate high-income, high-status occupations, leaving African-Americans and Hispanics with low-income, low-status occupations. Even if job discrimination suddenly disappeared, lower educational attainment would keep many minorities from entering newly opened doors.

## Marketing Implications of Multiculturalism

The demographic shift and growing multiculturalism create new challenges and opportunities for marketers. The U.S. population grew from 226 million in 1980 to 255 million in 1994, much of that growth taking place in minority markets. Asians are the nation's fastest-growing minority group, increasing 108 percent in the 1980s, to 7.3 million. The Hispanic population grew 53 percent, to 22.3 million; with 7.7 million new members, it had the biggest numerical gain of any minority group. African-Americans, who remain the largest minority, saw their numbers increase during the past decade by 13 percent, to 30 million. In contrast, the number of non-

*Exhibit 20.2*

Multicultural Makeup of the United States

Source: U.S. Department of Labor, Bureau of the Census projections.

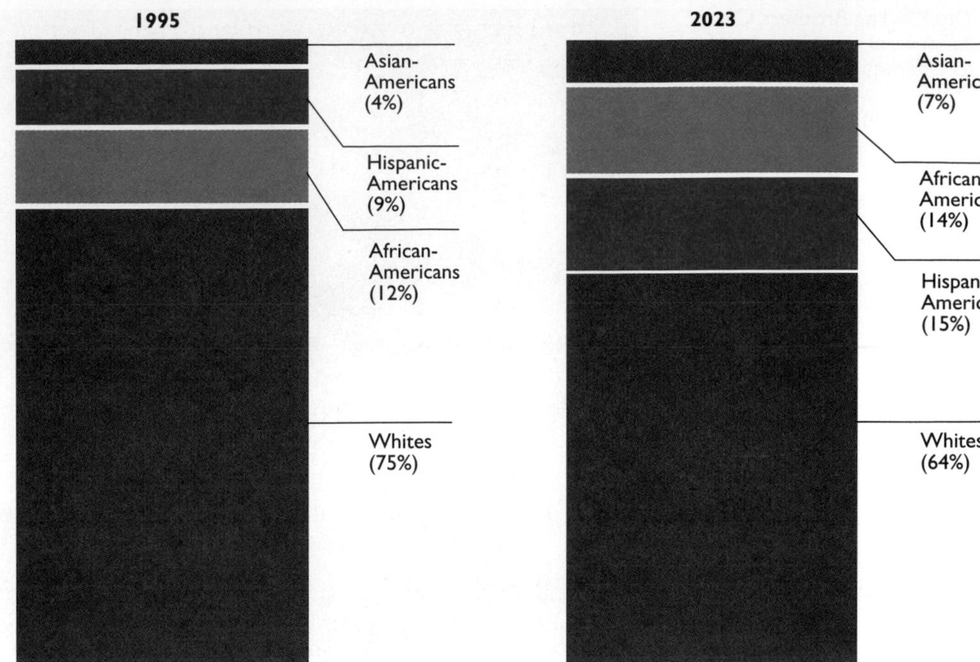


Hispanic whites grew by 4.4 percent. In 1994, about a quarter of the U.S. population were members of minority groups. The last census identified 110 different ethnic groups in the United States.[7]

Demographic shifts will be even more pronounced in the future. Exhibit 20.2 compares the 1994 population mix and the forecasted population mix for 2023. Note that Hispanics will be the fastest-growing segment of the population. The diversity of the U.S. population is projected to stabilize around 2023 as the birthrate among minorities levels off.

The marketer's task in a diverse society is more challenging because of differences in educational level and demand for goods and services. What's more, ethnic markets are not homogeneous. There is not an African-American market or a Hispanic market, any more than there is a white market. Instead, there are many niches within ethnic markets that require micromarketing strategies. For example, African Eye, which offers women's designer fashions from Africa, attracted a thousand women to a fashion show at Prince Georges Plaza near Washington, D.C. The show featured the latest creations by Alfadi, a high-fashion Nigerian designer, who also hosted the show. African Eye's dresses and outfits blend African and Western influences and are priced at $50 to $600. Says Mozella Perry Ademiluyi, the president and co-founder of African Eye: "Our customer is professional, 30 to 65, has an income level of $30,000-plus and often is well-traveled. They don't just want to wear something that is African. They want something that is well-tailored, unique, and creative as well."[8]

An alternative to the niche strategy is to maintain a brand's core identity while straddling different languages, cultures, ages, and incomes with different promotional campaigns. Levi Strauss, for example, publishes *501 Button-Fly Report* for 14- to 24-year-olds, with Spike Lee interviewing spelunkers, roadies, cemetery tour guides, and others on what they do in their jeans. For men ages 25 and up, Levi's runs separate ads on sports programs and in magazines, showing adults in pursuits like touch football and outings with the kids. A Hispanic campaign, in TV and outdoor

The Ringling Brothers Circus has several acts that appeal to different cultural groups. The Españas, for instance, perform on the Globe of Death.

Ringling Brothers Circus

advertising, follows two men through their day, from working to teaching a boy to play softball. *"Levi's siempre quedan bien"*—"Levi's always fit well"—is the theme.[9]

A third strategy for multicultural marketing is to seek common interests, motivations, or needs across ethnic groups. This strategy is sometimes called **stitching niches,** which means combining ethnic, age, income, and lifestyle markets, on some common basis, to form a large market. The result may be a cross-cultural product, such as a frozen pizza-flavored eggroll. Or it may be a product that serves several ethnic markets simultaneously. Ringling Brothers and Barnum and Bailey Circus showcases acts that appeal to many ethnic groups. It broadened its appeal to Asian-Americans by adding the "Mysterious Oriental Art of Hair Hanging." Marguerite Michelle, known as the "ravishing Rapunzel," is suspended in the air on a wire attached to her waist-length hair. When the circus comes to town, the Mexican-born Michelle also goes on Spanish-language radio shows to build recognition for Ringling in the Hispanic market. The circus is promoted as *"El Espectaculo Mas Grande del Mundo."*[10]

**stitching niches**
Combining ethnic, age, income, and lifestyle markets on some common basis to form a mass market.

## THE IMPACT OF IMMIGRATION

To a great extent, the U.S. demographic shift is due to immigration. During the past decade, 8.7 million people immigrated to the United States. Many who were already residing here resent these immigrants, especially when unemployment is high and social services are strained. A 1994 survey found that 61 percent of Americans want a decrease in immigration levels.[11] However, the economic benefits of being an open-door society far outweigh the costs.

Immigrants contribute to the economy as workers, consumers, business owners, and taxpayers. For instance, the 11 million immigrants who work earn at least $240 billion a year and pay more than $90 billion in taxes. One study estimated that immigrants receive only $5 billion in welfare, far less than they pay in taxes; however, another study claimed that immigrants, both legal and illegal, pay far less in taxes than they cost in government services.[12] There is no doubt, however, that immigrant entrepreneurs, from the corner grocer to the local builder, are creating jobs for other immigrants and for those born in the United States. Vibrant immigrant communities are revitalizing cities and older suburbs that would otherwise be suffering from a shrinking tax base. And the immigrants' links to their old countries are boosting U.S. exports to such fast-growing regions as Asia and Latin America.

The United States is also reaping a bonanza of highly educated foreigners. In the 1980s, 1.5 million college-educated immigrants joined the U.S. work force. High-tech industries, from semiconductors to biotechnology, are depending on immigrant scientists, engineers, and entrepreneurs to remain competitive. About 40 percent of the 200 researchers in the Communications Sciences Research wing at AT&T Bell Laboratories were born outside the United States. In Silicon Valley, California, much of the technical work force is foreign-born. At Du Pont Merck Pharmaceutical, a joint venture based in Delaware, a new antihypertensive drug was invented by a team that included two immigrants from Hong Kong and a scientist whose parents immigrated from Lithuania.

The next generation of scientists and engineers will be dominated by immigrants. The number of native-born citizens getting science PhDs has remained about the same, but the number of foreign-born students receiving science doctorates more than doubled between 1981 and 1991, to 37 percent of the total.[13]

The Immigration Act of 1990 has further increased the ranks of immigrants at the upper end of the socioeconomic scale. The law allows people who have no family in the United States to immigrate if they have highly prized work skills or are ready to make a significant business investment. The law nearly tripled the number of visas (to 140,000 a year) for engineers and scientists, multinational executives and managers, and other people with skills in demand. Investor immigrants, who will each put at least $1 million into the economy, account for 10,000 of those visas.

Regardless of their educational level, immigrants tend to join their peers, and their peers tend to live in large coastal cities. California, New York, Texas, Florida, Illinois, and New Jersey are expected to be home to three of every four new immigrants, who will be joining already-large minority populations in those states. In California, non-Hispanic whites will become a minority within the next two decades.

## ENTREPRENEURSHIP AND ETHNIC GROUPS

Today, minorities own about a tenth of the nation's 14 million firms.[14] During the past decade, every large minority group increased the number of businesses owned and rates of business ownership. But some minority groups have much higher rates of business ownership than others.

Nevertheless, business ownership is growing rapidly among all the major ethnic groups. The number of firms owned by Asians grew 89 percent during the past decade, not far behind the rate of Asian population growth. The number of firms owned by Hispanics grew 81 percent. Business ownership grew only 38 percent among African-Americans, but that growth rate was still faster than this group's population growth rate.[15]

The high rate of business ownership among Asians is due to several factors. First is their high level of educational attainment. In 1990, about 40 percent of adult Asian-Americans had completed college, compared with only 23 percent of whites.[16] Asian-Americans also have rather high incomes, so they have more capital to launch small businesses. Finally, a large share of Asian-Americans are recent immigrants, many of whom came to the United States specifically to go into business.

Examples of successful immigrants abound. Paul Yuan, for example, left Taiwan with his wife in 1975, seven days after their marriage. They eventually settled in Seattle with several thousand dollars in life savings and no work visas. Yuan was a college graduate, but for two years he worked in Chinese restaurants. In 1978 he became a legal resident and opened his own travel agency while working nights as a hotel dishwasher. By 1993, at 44 years of age, Yuan owned a thriving Seattle travel business, and he and his family lived in a $4 million house. Another example is Humberto Galvez, who left Mexico City for Los Angeles in 1965, at the age of 21. He started pumping gas and busing tables, working his way up the ladder, with a lot of bumps along the way. After starting and selling a chain of nineteen El Pollo Loco charbroiled chicken restaurants in the Los Angeles area, he now owns six Pescado Mojado ("wet fish") seafood diners, employing 100 workers. Examples like these not only prove the validity of the American Dream but also generate jobs and profits that fuel the U.S. economy.

*2 Identify key characteristics of the African-American market and some elements of an effective marketing mix for this group.*

## THE AFRICAN-AMERICAN MARKET

African-Americans, numbering 31 million in 1994, are the largest minority group in the United States. The proportion of the population that is African-American will continue to grow well into the next century, because the birthrate for African-Americans is 22.1 births per 1,000 persons, versus 14.8 for whites. Also, the death rate among African-Americans is lower than among the general population because their average age is younger.

The immigration of African-Americans from abroad is minimal compared with the large numbers of immigrants from Latin America and Asia. Immigration accounted for nearly 30 percent of total U.S. population growth during the 1980s, but it produced only 15 percent of the increase in the African-American population.

At the beginning of the twentieth century, over 90 percent of all African-Americans lived in the South. The growing industrial base in the North and lack of economic opportunity in the South started a massive movement of African-Americans out of the rural South, with the Northeast and the Midwest becoming the chief beneficiaries. In the 1970s, African-Americans began to migrate back to the South and West from declining northern industrial cities. Today, 53 percent of all African-Americans live in the South, 19 percent each in the Midwest and Northeast, and 9 percent in the West.[17] African-American population concentrations by county are shown in Exhibit 20.3.

The largest population of African-Americans in a metropolitan area occurs in New York City (see Exhibit 20.4). But the areas of greatest population growth among African-Americans are the outer suburbs surrounding central metropolitan areas. The African-American population of Gwinnett County, Georgia, north of Atlanta, increased 344 percent, for example, during the 1980s. In contrast, Gwinnett County's total population only doubled. Although the majority of both African-Americans and whites live in metropolitan areas, they tend to live in different communities. Half of whites, compared with just over a quarter of African-Americans, lived in suburban areas in 1990.

The African-American population is younger than the U.S. population as a whole. The median age of this group was 28.2 years in 1994, nearly five years younger than the median for all citizens. But, like the total population, the African-American population is aging. Between 1980 and 1994, the share of African-Americans 65 and older increased from 7.8 to 8.4 percent, and the median age rose by nearly three years.[18]

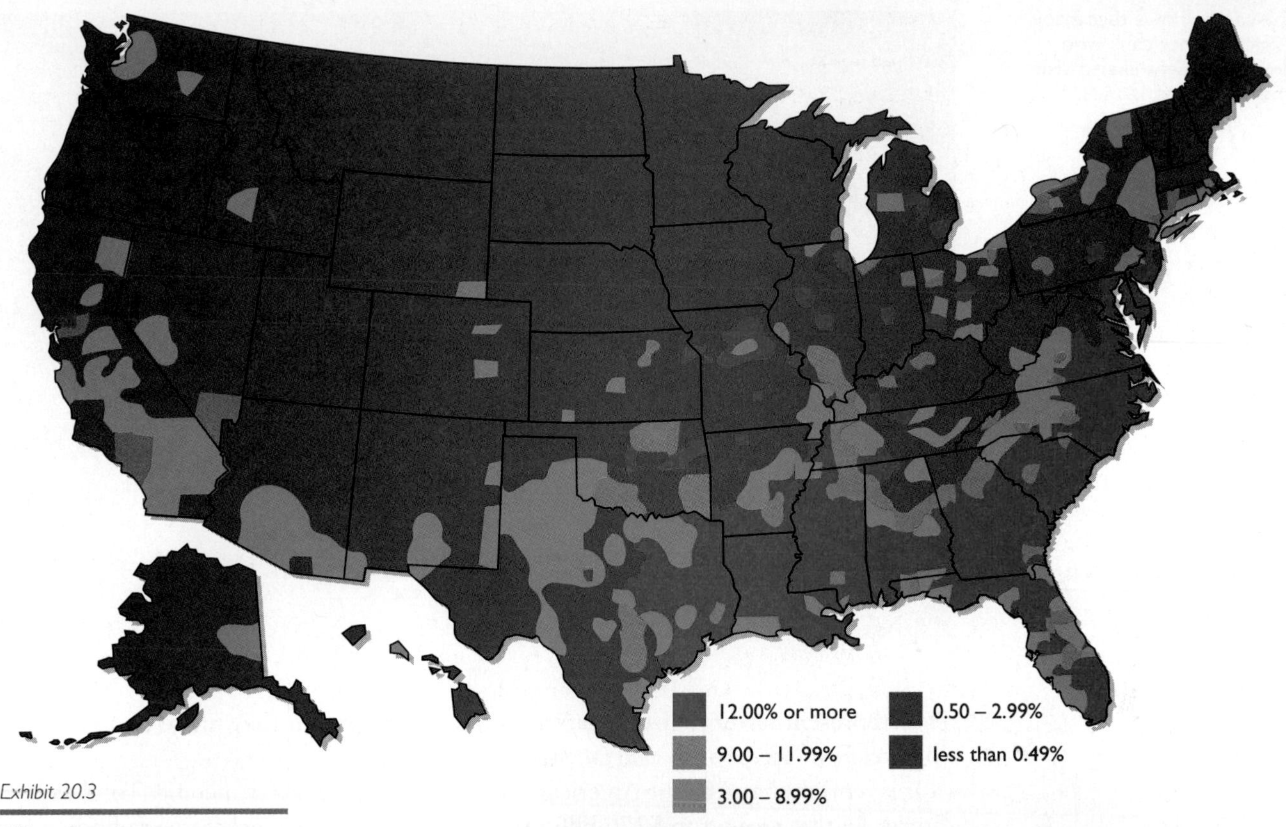


*Exhibit 20.3*

African-Americans as a Percentage of the Population in U.S. Counties, 1990

Source: Kathy Bodovitz, "Black America," *American Demographics* (American Diversity). Desk Reference Series no. 1, July 1991, p. 6. Copyright © *American Demographics*. For subscription information, please call (800) 828-1133.

*Exhibit 20.4*

Metropolitan Areas with the Largest African-American Population, 1990

Source: U.S. Department of Labor, Bureau of the Census, 1990.

| Rank | Metropolitan area | African-American population (in thousands) | Total population (in thousands) | Percentage of population that is African-American |
|---|---|---|---|---|
| 1 | New York, NY | 2,250 | 17,953 | 13% |
| 2 | Chicago, IL | 1,333 | 8,066 | 17 |
| 3 | Washington, D.C.–MD–VA | 1,042 | 3,924 | 27 |
| 4 | Los Angeles–Long Beach, CA | 993 | 14,532 | 7 |
| 5 | Detroit, MI | 943 | 4,665 | 20 |
| 6 | Philadelphia, PA–NJ | 930 | 5,899 | 16 |
| 7 | Atlanta, GA | 736 | 2,834 | 26 |
| 8 | Baltimore, MD | 616 | 2,382 | 26 |
| 9 | Houston, TX | 611 | 3,711 | 16 |
| 10 | New Orleans, LA | 430 | 1,239 | 35 |
| 11 | St. Louis, MO–IL | 423 | 2,444 | 17 |
| 12 | Newark, NJ | 423 | 723 | 58 |
| 13 | Dallas, TX | 411 | 3,885 | 11 |
| 14 | Memphis, TN–AR–MS | 399 | 982 | 41 |
| 15 | Norfolk–Virginia Beach–Newport News, VA | 398 | 1,396 | 29 |

## INCOME AND CONSUMPTION PATTERNS OF AFRICAN-AMERICANS

A substantial and growing African-American middle class has been overshadowed by the image of the low-income African-American. The concentration of poor African-Americans in densely populated urban areas makes them highly visible.

Research shows that many African-Americans who travel overseas like to visit the Caribbean islands.



They represent fewer than 30 percent of the U.S. poor, but they make up more than 40 percent of the poor in central cities.[19]

It is a myth that African-Americans have little discretionary income. Total expenditures by this group top $270 billion a year. Increasingly, marketers are finding the market segment very rewarding. The median income of dual-income African-American families is over $35,000, and about 13 percent of African-American families have incomes over $50,000.[20] Who are these affluent consumers? Like affluent whites, they tend to be well educated (32 percent college graduates), homeowners (77 percent), in the prime earning ages (66 percent between 35 and 55), married (79 percent), and suburbanites.[21]

Researchers have found some differences in consumption patterns between African-Americans and other groups. Consider the following:

> Several years ago, the Carnation Company discovered that per capita consumption of its Instant Breakfast Drink was unusually high among blacks. When mixed with milk, this sweet-flavored powder was intended to serve as a nutritionally complete, low-calorie breakfast. The high usage among blacks was puzzling, because blacks generally do not use diet products as heavily as whites. When Carnation investigated, it discovered that blacks were using the product as a supplement. Some customers were even drinking the product and eating a full breakfast simply because they liked the taste.
>
> Blacks and whites have different preferences in taste, too. Although blacks drink less coffee than average, they are much more likely than other Americans to lace their coffee with large amounts of sugar, cream, or nondairy creamer. Recognizing this trend, Coffee-Mate began marketing its product to blacks. It advertised in national magazines like *Ebony* and *Essence,* broadcast its message on local black radio stations, and used outdoor advertising in black neighborhoods. When it created a sweepstakes promotion that ran in local black newspapers, it generated double-digit increases in volume and share of sales among blacks.
>
> Candy, cookies, sweet snacks, and desserts are an important part of the black diet. Most blacks want something sweet with their meals. This is also reflected in their beverage choices and why Kool-Aid is a heavy favorite among blacks of all ages. The company's general marketing touts the fact that sugar-sweetened Kool-Aid has 25 percent less sugar than Coke or Pepsi. But blacks generally prefer to buy Kool-Aid in its unsweetened form and add lots of sugar themselves. The typical black household

spends 54 percent more than the average white household on sugar each year, according to the Consumer Expenditure Survey.

The difference between blacks and whites also shows up in packaging choices. Blacks have a strong preference for larger sizes of nonalcoholic beverages, for example. After the Coca-Cola Company discovered this phenomenon in the early 1970s, it began featuring and promoting 16-ounce bottles instead of the standard 12-ounce size when advertising to the black community.

Blacks are 50 percent less likely than whites to have taken a trip abroad in the last three years. When they do travel outside the U.S., blacks prefer destinations that are both "language comfortable" and "color comfortable," like the Caribbean, where blacks do not get hassled and feel unwanted because of their color. Language and skin color are strong bonds that outweigh cultural differences. As a result, blacks spend $60 to $70 million a year traveling to the Bahamas, according to *City Sun*.

Blacks heavily concentrate their vacations in the summer. They prefer to travel in groups, not as individuals, and they have a preference for tour packages. Blacks are far less likely than whites to go camping or hunting, however, and they are less likely to engage in adventurous or risky activities like bungee jumping. Instead, they prefer to relax and see the sights, shop, or party with friends.[22]

Source: *American Demographics* magazine © 1993. Reprinted with Permission.

## MARKETING MIXES FOR THE AFRICAN-AMERICAN MARKET

The size and purchasing power of the African-American market makes it an attractive target for the largest companies as well as for countless smaller ones. At least half of all Fortune 500 companies have launched some ethnic marketing activities.[23] Effectively penetrating the market, however, often requires a unique and distinctive marketing mix. Al Anderson, president of Anderson Communications Group, which specializes in marketing to African-Americans, notes, "Marketers must realize that black people are not dark-skinned white people."[24] African-Americans have unique desires, hopes, and preferences that require a specialized marketing mix.

### Product

Many firms are creating new and different products for the African-American market. Often entrepreneurial African-Americans are the first to realize unique product opportunities. For example, Olmec Corp. is a New York–based toy manufacturer created by Yla Eason when she couldn't find an African-American superhero doll to buy her son. Her $2 million company markets more than sixty kinds of African-American and Hispanic dolls. Eason has a distribution partnership with Hasbro. Today, both Mattel and Tyco Industries also market dolls that are more than Barbies in darker plastic. Tyco just introduced Kenya, who wears beads to adorn her cornrows. Like a Mattel doll called Shani, Kenya comes in a choice of three complexions: light, medium, and dark. Shani also has a new boyfriend named Jamal.

Kenya is not just a dark version of some other doll. Her hair, skin tones, and clothing were developed specifically for African-American girls.

© Tyco Corporation

In health and beauty aids, companies owned by African-Americans—such as Soft Sheen, M&M, Johnson, and ProLine—target the African-American

Many mainstream cosmetics companies, as well as cosmetics companies owned by African-Americans, have formulated new lines that feature a wide range of skin tones.



market. Huge corporations like Revlon, Gillette, and Alberto-Culver have either divisions or major product lines for the African-American market as well. Alberto-Culver, for example, has a hair-care line for this segment with seventy-five products. In fact, hair-care items are the largest single category within the African-American health and beauty aid industry. Maybelline has the largest share (28 percent) of the African-American health and beauty aid market with its Shades of You product line.[25]

Other entrepreneurs are capitalizing on African-Americans' growing market presence with "Afrocentric products" that stress African heritage and culture. Afrocentric products include art objects, books, jewelry, clothing, and services. "There's going to be a sustained demand for it," says Mohamed Diop, owner of Intercontinental Business Network, a New York importer of African cloth. "The interest now is much more of an intellectual interest, whereas in the '60s it was more of an emotional interest." More vendors also are marketing Afrocentric merchandise at two-day trade shows staged nationwide by Black Expo USA. The New York show drew about 75,000 people and 350 vendors, 90 of whom sold Afrocentric products at a specially designed African village.[26]

A variety of Afrocentric goods and services have taken hold in the wedding industry. The Always and Forever Wedding Chapel in Detroit offers a variety of products, including ancient rites performed by Yoruban priestesses and wedding-gown designs imported from Africa. The ceremony includes dancers to entertain the guests, drummers to announce the bride, and corn kernels to throw as a wish for fertility. Imperial Broom Company sells colonial-style brooms to people wanting to "jump the broom," in which a couple leaps into matrimony over a broom lying on the ground. The ritual, based on the broom as a symbol of the home in parts of Africa, was begun by slaves because they initially weren't allowed legally to marry. Danita Rountree Green has sold about 6,700 copies of her primer *Broom Jumping: A Celebration of Love* and started the newsletter *Broom Lady* to advertise Afrocentric bridal services.[27]

About a third of the nation's largest African-American–owned firms cater to the African-American market. Food processing, computer software, and construction are the three main industries in the twenty-five largest African-American–owned companies.

Not to be outdone by entrepreneurial firms, large companies are jumping on the bandwagon. JCPenney added two clothing sections to more than 100 stores, one called the African Collection (authentic African clothing) and the other called Africa Year (clothing styled in the United States but made of African fabrics). It also issued a specialty catalog that offers many of the same clothes by mail. Macy's flagship store in Manhattan is selling Cross Colours, a line of brightly colored clothing that its tags describe as ethnically inspired. Nike and Converse sell jogging suits and other exercisewear featuring African prints. Speedo, the California swimsuit company, had the same idea. Many small stores in big cities have started selling clothes, suspenders, and sunglasses with African prints. Todd Oldham, Mark McNairy, Antoinette Linn, and a few other major fashion designers have used African-print fabrics in their collections.[28]

African-American consumers tend to be heavy users of certain product categories that are not specifically produced for the African-American market. For example, they buy more than their share of VCRs, compact disc players, answering machines, home furnishings, major appliances, jewelry, watches, computers, candy bars, nondairy cream substitutes, corn, syrup, and tomato sauce. The African-American market also represents one of the fastest-growing segments of the tourism, financial planning, and health care industries.[29]

## Promotion

About 3 percent of all promotional dollars spent in the United States are specifically targeted toward African-Americans. But the dollar figure is growing rapidly, in part because African-Americans viewing advertisements in black media (media targeted toward African-Americans) as opposed to white media have been found to have higher personal identification with the brand. Further impetus for promotion targeting African-Americans comes from a study that found 58 percent of African-Americans feel advertisements are designed only for the white population.[30]

One company that reaches out to African-Americans is McDonald's, which bases its target spending on "share of stomach." African-Americans account for 15 percent of its business, or "share of stomach," so the group gets 15 percent of the marketing and advertising effort. Marketing professionals praise one McDonald's Breakfast Club campaign, which features "buppies" (black urban professionals) talking like African-Americans instead of whites.

Maybelline also targets African-Americans. Initial marketing efforts for its Shades of You cosmetics line focused on the frustration that many African-American women feel in tracking down the right colors for their complexions: "Five stores, fourteen lipsticks, and a half day later, I'm still a shade off." A later Maybelline campaign was a bit more mainstream. A print ad for nail polish, for example, said, "Some women can't be fooled. They know color has to do more than just look pretty.

A natural born wiz? Get real." The ad did include a more targeted tag, however: "Coordinated shades created expressly to flatter your looks." The ads ran in black-oriented magazines, including *Essence* and *Upscale*. Maybelline added a point-of-purchase display so women could put their hands up against the product shades to find a good match. "That's really important for this market because there are so many skin tones for women of color," notes Carolyn McHenry-Weiss, marketing manager for the Shades of You line. Maybelline also relies on a variety of grassroots events to help build a positive image for the brand, including donations to the National Coalition of 100 Black Women. And an annual Shades of You Salute to You promotion honors six "unsung heroes" among one city's African-American community. Each woman receives a $1,500 donation to the charity of her choice. The Shades of You brand has become so popular that Maybelline has licensed the name to No Nonsense pantyhose for a new line of hosiery.[31]

In general, the companies that are most effective in reaching the African-American market are soft-drink, fast-food, automobile, tobacco, and liquor companies and, to a lesser extent, packaged-goods companies. But even within these more progressive industries there are laggards. Jeff Burns, vice president of Johnson Publishing, publisher of *Ebony,* singles out BMW and Volvo. "Blacks buy 20 percent of the Volvos bought in this country and yet Volvo does no marketing to the black community," he charges.[32]

To win the praise of African-American consumers today, marketers must do more than just use African-American models or run ethnic ads. They must use sensitive, effective promotions, which often means working with African-American ad agencies. Some believe that, all things being equal, African-American ad professionals are more effective than whites at targeting African-Americans. "The truth is that general market agencies are not prepared by inclination or background to speak to the black community," says Byron Lewis, chairman and CEO of UniWorld Group/New York. "These general market agencies have an ivory tower approach to marketing to blacks."[33] African-American agencies also claim they can help companies avoid inadvertent stereotyping, as in a Westin Hotels & Resorts ad that featured an African-American woman as director of housekeeping or a car ad from Toyota (generally considered a progressive company) that said, "Car red. Knuckles white."[34]

One example of a company trying to create ethnically sensitive promotions is Pillsbury. Pillsbury marketing executives had never gauged African-Americans' response to the white lumberjack character who promoted their Hungry Jacks pancake and biscuit products. When they did, they discovered that "there were blacks using our products, but they weren't using them to the same level as the general population," says Amy Hilliard-Jones, Pillsbury's director of advertising.[35] So Pillsbury banished the lumberjack in test ads for African-American consumers by UniWorld agency. Instead, the ads ran a colorfully printed slogan, "You look Hungry Jack," and featured an African-American family eating together.

Advertising agencies are also creating public service announcements against racism. For example, the Smith/Greenland agency developed a campaign encouraging racial tolerance. The ads have no pictures, only copy (see Exhibit 20.5). The American Association of Advertising Agencies' Ad Council is creating an antidiscrimination campaign expected to last ten years. One of the ads opens with a shot of babies of various races in side-by-side cribs in a hospital nursery. The spot then whips through a montage of harsh scenes of violence and prejudice that take place from childhood to old age, closing on a graveyard. As the babies play, a voice-over says, "Here's one time it doesn't matter who your neighbor is," and when the cemetery is shown, "Here's the other." The final tag is "Life's too short. Stop the hate."[36]

Some promotion that targets African-Americans is controversial. R.J. Reynolds stopped marketing its Uptown cigarettes to African-Americans after complaints by black leaders. The malt liquor industry also receives its share of criticism, because its primary market seems to be the inner city. Malt liquor ads often feature rap heroes like Ice Cube and Geto Boys. The promotions have had themes of getting a cheap drunk and enhancing sexual prowess.[37] Liquor and cigarette promotions like these are decried because consumers potentially face serious health risks. The Ethics in Marketing story on page 704 presents a different type of ethical dilemma.

## Distribution

Many of the nation's largest retailers target African-Americans. Toys R Us hired minority ad agency The Mingo Group to create a comprehensive marketing and communications program targeting African-American consumers. For its Looking Good campaign, which emphasizes the store's clothing, Kmart appointed minority-owned agency Burrell Inc. to develop special advertising for African-American women between the ages of 18 and 49. The ads appeared in such national ethnic magazines as *Ebony, Essence,* and *Class,* in African-American local newspapers, and on radio stations in ten markets.[39]

Spiegel, the large catalog retailer, joined with the publisher of *Ebony* to develop a fashion line and catalog aimed at African-American women. Spiegel maintains that this group spends 6.5 percent of family income on apparel, compared with an average of 5 percent for all women. This catalog, to be called *E Style,* features clothes designed especially for African-American women. Its first issue was mailed to 1.5 million African-American women, including *Ebony* subscribers and current Spiegel customers.[40]

*Exhibit 20.5*

Public Service Announcement Stressing Racial Tolerance

Source: Smith/Greenland Incorporated Advertising.

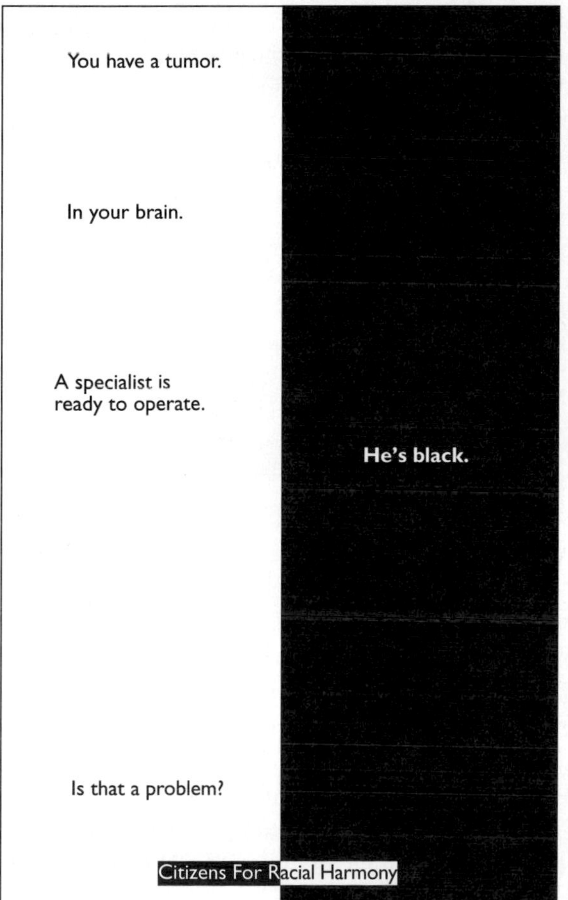


Pizza Hut is making minority franchises a priority. Pizza Hut is estimated to have about 300 minority-owned stores and now includes the nation's largest African-American–owned fast-food franchise company. Larry Lundy, who had been the chain's vice president of restaurant development, bought thirty-one stores in the New Orleans area for a price estimated at $15.5 million.[41]

Shopping malls are also being developed for the African-American market. Researchers have found that African-Americans, on an average trip to a mall, spend $51.21, or 5.1 percent more than whites.[42] On the eastern edge of Atlanta, bordered on one side by palatial homes and on the other by public housing, the South DeKalb Mall restyled itself as an "Afrocentric retail center."

ETHICS IN MARKETING

**Should Promotion Cost More Than the Contribution?**

*Harper's* magazine reported without comment that Miller Brewing gives $150,000 a year to its black scholarship program but spends double that amount to tell the public about the fund. Miller won't comment on the figures but notes that the Thurgood Marshall Scholarship Fund keeps eighty-seven deserving African-American students in college.

Noel Hankin, director of corporate relations for Miller Brewing, says part of the promotion budget goes to expensive television plugs linking Miller and the fund. Miller also bought advertising in African-American publications saluting black education. The ads carried modest logos for Miller and for the fund, as well as an 800 number for those who wish to contribute or get more information. The fund spends about $348,000 a year on the students, Hankin says, and Miller is by far the largest contributor. Miller spends more on promoting the fund to attract donations than it receives in contributions to the fund.

The tiny Thurgood Marshall Scholarship Fund wants to get out from behind the shadow of the well-known United Negro College Fund, a prodigious fundraiser. The UNCF aids African-American private colleges. The Thurgood Marshall fund serves a larger number of African-American public universities, which enroll more than 70 percent of all students at historically black schools. "Yes, we do mention Miller, but for good reason; we're the ones promoting the awareness of the fund," Hankin says.

It isn't unusual for firms to donate far less than they spend on promoting charities. "A ratio of 2-to-1 or 3-to-1 is common," says Craig Smith, president of Corporate Citizen, a Seattle think tank that studies corporate giving.[38]

Is something fundamentally wrong when the gift is less than the money spent promoting the company's largess? What about the argument that, if the firm couldn't promote its gift, there might not be a gift? Would you support a federal law that would disallow a tax deduction for a gift if the dollar value is less than the money spent on promotion?



Now 85 percent of the stores are owned by African-Americans. The mall increased the number of carts run by minorities and doubled the number of cultural shows. Almost all the mall's advertising is now aimed at African-Americans. Several mall retailers tailor their goods to African-Americans. Camelot Music more than doubled its selection of gospel, jazz, and rhythm-and-blues music. Foot Locker stocks styles that sell well in African-American markets, such as suede and black athletic shoes and baseball shirts from the Negro Leagues of the 1930s.

For many local residents, the mall has become a focal point for racial pride. People shop there out of loyalty to the neighborhood; they delight in seeing signs of African-American culture. Edward Price, an associate manager at Southern Bell, spent nearly $800 on Christmas gifts at South DeKalb. "We need something to rally around," he says. "I want to drop as much money into that mall as possible."[43]

But many upper-income African-Americans who live near the mall drive twenty minutes to shop elsewhere. They say the mall's selection is too limited, and they scoff at the notion of fashions aimed at them. Emerson Bryan, an official with the Atlanta Regional Commission, lives less than two miles from the mall, but other than buying toothpaste and filling prescriptions, he says, "I don't do my major shopping there." He says South DeKalb sells "ethnic variety" clothes that he couldn't wear to work. "When the stores see an area that's all black, they assume we're all the same," he says. "They assume we're all rappers. We're not."[44]

## Price

Product pricing is the one element of the marketing mix least affected by multicultural marketing. Unique specialty items are usually relatively expensive regardless of the ethnic market they are produced for. In contrast, consumer products in intensively competitive markets, such as hair-care items, are priced very competitively.

One controversial aspect of pricing is whether the poor pay more. U.S. Census Bureau data show that very often the poor are members of a minority group. In his 1964 book, *The Poor Pay More,* David Caplovitz reports the results of a study of consumer behavior among low-income families in four New York City public housing projects. Caplovitz was interested in what durable goods poor consumers own, where they shop, how much they pay, what method of payment they use, and how secure their finances are in general. He concluded that "society now virtually presents the very poor risks with twin options: of forgoing major purchases or of being exploited."[45]

A more recent study by the Department of Consumer Affairs in New York City showed that Caplovitz's findings are still relevant. An investigation of food prices and cleanliness of stores in poor, middle-income, and affluent New York City neighborhoods revealed that consumers in poor neighborhoods pay 8.8 percent more than consumers in middle-class neighborhoods do for the same groceries.[46]

The problem faced by the poor is illustrated by Jean Shelby, a Chicago inner-city resident:

> Jean Shelby receives Fingerhut catalogs, where the boldfaced price isn't the total cost but the amount per month. One recent offer: "TV/VCR combination, $59.64 per month." The deal appealed to Ms. Shelby, who supports herself and four children on $597 a month from her part-time receptionist's job, food stamps and $422 in Supplemental Security Income for one child. She bought the set, committing herself to 19 monthly payments. . . . The total she will pay, including finance charges at a 24.9 percent annual rate: $1,133.16. The same set can be found in the suburbs for as little as $499. Why not save up and buy the set outright? "I want things right away," Ms. Shelby says.
>
> Fingerhut's chairman, Theodore Deikel, acknowledges that much of the merchandise could be bought elsewhere for less, but he says Fingerhut provides a real value by extending credit to people most big companies wouldn't touch and by delivering name-brand merchandise to their homes. "We're trying to give them something they don't otherwise get," says Deikel.
>
> But to cover its higher credit risks, Fingerhut charges annual interest rates of up to 24.9 percent. That means people like Ms. Shelby may pay nearly seven percentage points more than the average rate banks charge the more-affluent on credit-card purchases. Officials of the Minnetonka, Minn., company note that finance fees can be avoided by paying the full cash price listed in its catalogs, but they say only 30 percent of orders are handled that way.
>
> The discount stores, outlet malls and warehouse clubs that have redefined suburbia's idea of a bargain have largely bypassed inner-city neighborhoods like Ms. Shelby's. These retailers see bigger opportunities in serving the more-affluent middle class. The inner city is "a much harder market to make money in" because of higher costs for insurance and security and larger losses to theft, says Carl Steidtmann, chief economist at the Management Horizons retail consulting unit of Price Waterhouse.[47]



In summary, firms that target the low-income market admit prices are higher than in higher-income areas. The higher prices are justified, they say, because the costs of doing business in low-income areas are greater. Moreover, they note, if the disadvantaged consumer did not pay more, the retailers simply wouldn't serve the market.

*3 Identify key characteristics of the U.S. Hispanic market and some elements of an effective marketing mix for this group.*

## THE U.S. HISPANIC MARKET

By the end of 1995, the Hispanic population will approach 26 million people, and the year 2010 should see a Hispanic population of nearly 39 million.[48] Hispanics are one of the fastest-growing minority groups in the United States.

Four states now have more than a million Hispanic residents: California, Texas, New York, and Florida. By 2000, two more states will join this club: Illinois and New Jersey (see Exhibit 20.6). Twenty states had at least 100,000 Hispanics in

*Exhibit 20.6*

States with the Largest Hispanic Population, in Thousands

| Rank | State | 1990 | 2000 |
|---|---|---|---|
| 1 | California | 7,737 | 10,144 |
| 2 | Texas | 4,358 | 5,979 |
| 3 | New York | 2,216 | 2,681 |
| 4 | Florida | 1,585 | 2,412 |
| 5 | Illinois | 905 | 1,193 |
| 6 | New Jersey | 740 | 952 |
| 7 | Arizona | 691 | 1,073 |
| 8 | New Mexico | 581 | 825 |
| 9 | Colorado | 425 | 594 |
| 10 | Massachusetts | 288 | 378 |
| | ***Total U.S.*** | 22,449 | 31,066 |

1990. The greatest metropolitan concentration is in Los Angeles County, where over 3 million Hispanics live. Dade County (Miami) is a distant second, with more than 950,000 Hispanics. Cook County (Chicago) ranks third, with almost 700,000 Hispanics. About two-thirds of all Hispanics live in just twenty-five metropolitan areas. A large percentage (43 percent) live in the suburbs.[49] Today, the number of Hispanics in California, Texas, New York, and Florida is greater than the entire U.S. Hispanic population of 1980. The 1990 census showed that 70 percent of the Hispanic population is still concentrated in those four states. However, future censuses will show a greater dispersion of the Hispanic population.

## HISPANIC SUBMARKETS

The concept of diversity is nowhere more evident than in the Hispanic culture. Mexican-Americans make up 60 percent of U.S. Hispanics and are highly concentrated in the Southwest. Puerto Rican–Americans are the second-largest Hispanic subgroup, at just 12 percent, but they dominate the Hispanic population of New York City. Cuban-Americans are the majority of Hispanics in South Florida, although they are just 5 percent of all U.S. Hispanics. The remaining 23 percent of Hispanics trace their lineage to Spain, South America, or Central America.[50]

Mexican-Americans are the youngest Hispanic subgroup, with a median age of just 24, according to the Current Population Survey. Cuban-Americans are the oldest, with a median age of 39. Cuban-Americans are also the best educated: 20 percent of them who are 25 or older have attended at least four years of college. This college-educated share slips to 15 percent for "other" Hispanics, 10 percent for Puerto Rican–Americans, and 5 percent for Mexican-Americans.[51]

Advertising to Hispanic-Americans often means choosing between the English and Spanish languages. It's a difficult decision, because researchers disagree on which language is appropriate for different kinds of advertising. One study of language use found that most Hispanics think and speak in Spanish in common situations. In other words, Mexican-Americans who are having fun at a party, singing in the shower, praying, thinking, or watching television are likely to choose Spanish, according to Market Development in San Diego. But 80 percent of Mexican-born permanent residents speak at least some English, and 90 percent of first-generation, U.S.-born Mexican-Americans speak English well. A growing number of upwardly mobile, assimilated Hispanics use English in their business and professional lives. But 70 percent of Hispanics speak Spanish at home.[52]

Marketers cannot assume that they can simply use Spanish instead of English to promote to Hispanics. They must take other steps to make sure their message will be understood and be relevant. First, the translation must be correct. Coors beer blundered in converting the slogan "Get loose with Coors" into Spanish; the slogan was mistakenly translated as "Get the runs with Coors."[53] Advertisers who are ignorant of subtle dialect differences among Hispanic groups may also run into trouble. In its early marketing efforts, Tang, the instant breakfast drink, billed itself as *jugo de china,* which is a Puerto Rican term for orange juice. But to all other Hispanics, the phrase is meaningless; *jugo de naranja*—juice of oranges—would be a better choice. Another Hispanic subsegment was puzzled by a phrase that translated as "low asphalt" and wondered why it would be an attractive feature for a cigarette.[54]

Today, marketing managers are carefully targeting major segments of the Hispanic market. One series of Campbell Soup ads, for instance, feature a woman cooking, but the individual ads differ in such details as the character's age, the setting, and the music. In the version for Cuban-Americans, a grandmother cooks in a plant-filled kitchen to the sounds of salsa and merengue music. In contrast, the Mexican-American ad shows a young wife preparing food in a brightly colored "Southwestern-style" kitchen, with pop music playing in the background.

## HISPANIC INCOME DISTRIBUTION

The total purchasing power of the Hispanic market in the United States is over $170 billion annually. Median family income for Hispanics in 1991 was $28,890, compared with $33,000 for the general population. Twenty-one percent of all Hispanic households have incomes over $35,000, and 8 percent have incomes over $50,000. Some Hispanic communities are quite affluent. In Miami, over 33 percent of the Hispanic households have incomes greater than $35,000, which is higher than the national average.[55]

Incomes are not equally distributed among Hispanic subcultures. According to the 1990 census, the median income of Cuban-Americans was $31,300, the highest of any Hispanic group. The comparative figure for Mexican-Americans was $22,200 and for Puerto Rican–Americans, $19,900, according to the U.S. Census Bureau. Puerto Rican–Americans living in New York City unfortunately have a poverty rate of 41 percent, compared with the national average of 14 percent.[56]

Miami has the second-highest total of Hispanic-owned businesses, according to Census Bureau figures, trailing only Los Angeles. But Miami's Hispanic businesses reported $500 million more in revenues than those in Los Angeles. Analysts attribute the higher revenue per business to Miami's established Cuban-American community.[57]

## MARKETING MIXES FOR THE HISPANIC MARKET

The diversity of the Hispanic population and the language differences create many challenges for those trying to target this market.

### Product

Hispanics, especially recent immigrants, often prefer products from their native country. Therefore, many retailers along the southern U.S. border import goods from

The tradition in many Hispanic cultures of shopping every day for fresh produce carries over to shopping patterns in the United States. Supermarkets serving U.S. Hispanics carry an abundance of fresh and sometimes exotic fruits and vegetables.



Mexico. In New York City, more than 6,000 *bodegas* (grocery stores) sell Puerto Rican–Americans such items as plantains, chorizo (pork sausage), and religious candles. The *bodegas* also serve as neighborhood social centers. Fresh produce is usually very important to Hispanic groups, because of their tradition of shopping every day at open-air produce markets in their native country.

Many Hispanics are loyal to the brands found in their homeland. If these are not available, Hispanics will choose brands that reflect their native values and culture. Research shows that Hispanics often are not aware of many mainstream U.S. brands. In general, Hispanics tend to be more brand loyal than African-Americans or Asian-Americans.[58]

Because many U.S. consumer product companies have cut back on product development, importing brands from Latin America means they can gain entry to new categories without spending much on research and expensive product launches. Instead, they can rely on the brand loyalty that Hispanic immigrants brought with them when they came to the United States.[59] Many U.S. companies have acquired Latin brands in international expansions. For example, PepsiCo, which bought a controlling interest in Gamesa, one of Mexico's biggest cookie makers, has begun selling Gamesa products to U.S. Hispanics.

Procter & Gamble noted that many retailers in Southern California were importing its Ariel detergent from Mexico. Ariel is offered in more than fifty countries and is one of the world's leading detergents. P&G is now trying to get Hispanics to switch to a new, U.S.-made version of Ariel called Ariel Ultra. Although the product has several key benefits over the imported Ariel, sales are slow. Ariel Ultra is selling well to white consumers, but Mexican-Americans prefer the original version. Tradition seems to be the main motivation.

Using a different tactic, Pepsi is importing Mirinda, its popular Mexican soft-drink line, into California. Mirinda—which comes in orange, apple, strawberry, and grapefruit flavors—could be expanded to other U.S. markets if it does well in California. Cadbury Beverages is evaluating options for its flavored mineral water called Peñafiel, which sells well in Mexico but has limited distribution in California. Goya Foods, whose sales rose from $300 million in 1990 to over $480 million in 1994, attributes its success to such products as *nopalitos* (sliced cactus), *tostones* (green fried plantains), and *harina pan* (a corn flour).[60]

A number of unique services have been created for the Hispanic market. For example, La Rosa del Monte moves households back and forth between the islands of Puerto Rico and Santo Domingo and to eight sites in the United States with large Hispanic populations. These include Miami, Orlando, and Chicago. La Rosa makes moving more affordable by doubling up customers' possessions in large containers. "If we don't have enough freight to fill a container, the customer may have to wait a month or two" for delivery, La Rosa says. But the wait cuts costs by two-thirds, to an average of $1,500 for the typical household.

## Promotion

Most promotional dollars targeting the Hispanic market are spent in an attempt to get them to buy mainstream goods and services. For example, Hispanics are 27 percent more likely than non-Hispanics to buy contact lenses (probably because of the relative youth of the Hispanic market). There is, of course, no such thing as a Hispanic contact lens. But Pearle Vision Centers advertise in Spanish.

Financial institutions are also targeting the Hispanic market. Valley National Bank, which is headquartered in Phoenix and claims a 40 percent share of the Hispanic market in Arizona, formed a Hispanic market committee to develop a program called Spanish Customer Assistance. One of the most popular elements of the program is *El Centro de Informacion en Español,* a twenty-four-hour telephone hot line that provides bank information and services in Spanish. To make Hispanic customers feel at home, bank employees are attending Spanish-language classes after working hours. Branch signs and promotional materials are being displayed in Spanish as well as English.[61] The bank airs commercials on Hispanic TV stations and runs print ads developed specifically for Spanish-language publications. It also is sponsoring events like the Tucson International Mariachi Conference and the Hispanic Women's Conference, making public service announcements, and providing financial advice on talk shows. Financial assistance is being provided to a summer library outreach program and a Hispanic Leadership Conference.

Media preferences among Hispanics vary widely from market to market. A survey of 5,000 households in ten markets in the continental United States, conducted by San Antonio–based Hispanic Marketing Research & Communications, found that

- 60 percent of the Hispanic market listens to Spanish-language radio at least once in a while. In McAllen, Texas, 70 percent listen exclusively to Spanish radio; in San Antonio, only 25 percent do.
- 40 percent of the nation's Hispanics watch Spanish-language television, and between 14 percent (San Antonio) and 50 percent (Los Angeles) watch only Spanish-language television. Hispanics tend to switch to English-language television as soon as they understand enough English, but they keep listening to the music of their heritage on Hispanic radio stations.
- Spanish-language newspapers are read by 20 percent of the nation's Hispanics. In Miami, which has two daily Spanish-language newspapers and dozens of weeklies, 35 percent of the Hispanic market reads them exclusively. But markets like San Antonio and Houston have no Spanish-language dailies at all.[62]

Spanish-language television is a growing presence, with at least 40 percent of U.S. Hispanics watching it at least some of the time. Three Spanish-language networks are in operation in the United States.

© Robert E. Daemmrich/Tony Stone Images, Inc.

The number of Spanish-language media outlets in the United States has increased steadily during the past decade. There are now 42 major Spanish-language magazines, 31 English or bilingual Hispanic-oriented magazines, and 103 Hispanic newspapers. Among the Spanish-language magazines, the leaders are *Mas* and *Una Nueva Vida*. Among the major English and bilingual Hispanic magazines are the *Vista* newspaper supplement, *Hispanic,* and *Hispanic Business.*[63]

TV and radio outlets have expanded as well. Four national Hispanic radio networks air Spanish-language programming over 600 stations. An estimated 80 percent of Hispanics listen to radio. The second most popular radio station in Los Angeles is KWKW, "*La Mexicana.*" As for television, there are three Spanish-language networks: Univision, Telemundo, and Galavision. Galavision, a basic-cable network covering 39 percent of Hispanic homes, targets the Mexican-American viewer, with all its programming produced in Mexico. Univision and Telemundo, broadcast networks, cover 90 percent and 85 percent of Hispanic households, respectively. Hispanics spend 26 percent more time watching TV than the general population.[64]

In 1993, advertisers spent over $800 million on promotions aimed specifically at Hispanics. That amount is large and growing, but it is still less than 1 percent of all U.S. advertising spending. Coca-Cola is one of the largest Hispanic promoters in the United States. Its *El Super Concurso de el Magnate* sweepstakes for Coca-Cola Classic generated more than half a million responses from its Hispanic viewers. The new "*Sabor para siempre*" ("Taste for always") tag line was also introduced during the sweepstakes. Commercials for Coke's promotion were aired exclusively on the twenty-three Telemundo network affiliates. They featured Andres Garcia, the popular star of Telemundo's *"El Magnate" novella* (Spanish soap opera). Retail displays offering sweepstakes coupons were available in nineteen markets. The grand prize winner received a new Ferrari and appeared on "*El Magnate,*" and eighteen other winners were given free trips to Miami and $1,000 each. The contest was one of the largest media merchandising promotions ever directed at Hispanic consumers. Coca-Cola has also sponsored other national promotions for Hispanics, including a tie-in with "*MTV Internacional.*" Diet Coke ran a Hispanic version of its Crack the Code promotion.[65]

## Distribution

The most visible distribution channel to Hispanics consists of retail grocery stores. In general, says Gloria Alvarez, director of operations for the Mexican-American Grocers Association, such retailers have become much more sophisticated in how they merchandise to Hispanics.[66] They now offer more full-service meat counters, better produce, and bilingual signs.

Developing a retailing mix for Hispanics is becoming more difficult. One reason is that immigration from Latin American countries is increasing. As a result, supermarkets have to cater to more people with different product preferences. In the Los Angeles area, although 80 percent of the Hispanics are from Mexico, many other countries are now represented. A second complicating factor for retailers is acculturation. Their customers may be immigrants, but they may also be second- and third-generation Hispanics whose buying habits have moved closer to those of whites.

Supermarkets are taking a variety of approaches to appeal to Hispanic customers. Some supermarket chains, such as Ralph's and Lucky, operate Hispanic-oriented stores using the same name as their other units. Other chains, such as Vons with its Tianguis stores and Quality Foods with Viva, both in the Los Angeles area, use different names. Vons, for instance, formed a separate eight-person management team to develop the Tianguis format. Its customer was pictured as an unacculturated Hispanic who had been in the United States for less than two years and couldn't speak English. When the first Tianguis store opened, it had a fiestalike atmosphere. Stands served Mexican foods, walls were splashed with bright colors, shoppers were serenaded with live mariachi bands, and shelves were stocked with empanadas, handmade tortillas, and other items usually found only in specialty shops. Making the extra effort to cater to prospective customers' needs paid off. In less than three years, Tianguis became one of the most profitable chains in the crowded and competitive Los Angeles grocery retail market.[67]

Targeting Hispanics can be profitable for supermarkets of all sizes. Sedano's Supermarkets, with twenty-one South Florida stores and annual sales of more than $200 million, dominates the Hispanic grocery business in Miami. Varadero Supermarkets, Sedano's chief Hispanic competitor, will do $100 million worth of business this year with only six Miami stores.

Specialty wholesalers are also being created to serve the Hispanic supermarkets. Midway Importing, for example, sells health and beauty aids produced in Mexico to Tianguis, Ralph's, Albertson's, Alpha Beta, and other grocery store chains. Chris Hartmen, president of Midway, notes:

> Many of these products have been up here for the last 20–25 years. But they've always come through black market groups' picking them up and distributing them—never with an organized approach—mainly in southern California, Chicago, and Texas. . . . The products have been way overpriced, because they've gone through several layers of distribution. No one has ever worked with these products in an organized fashion. It has always just been, "Let's get it over here, and it will sell." We're trying to make the marketplace more efficient and effective.[68]

More efficient distribution has brought down prices.

Mainstream retailers have also been actively targeting the Hispanic market. Kmart, Montgomery Ward, Wal-Mart, and Mervyn's have hired ethnic specialists and tested ethnic promotional campaigns. Those moves have spurred retailers like JCPenney and Sears to boost ethnic ad budgets. JCPenney spends about $6 million per year on Hispanic marketing, for Spanish-language TV commercials, brochures and credit applications in Spanish, and Hispanic fashion shows.

Shopping malls are also trying to attract Hispanic customers. The Tucson Mall in Arizona advertises on three Spanish-language radio stations and hires a mariachi music group to help it celebrate the Mexican holiday Cinco de Mayo. Half the mall's staff is bilingual.

4 *Identify key characteristics of the Asian-American market and some elements of an effective marketing mix for this group.*

## THE ASIAN-AMERICAN MARKET

By the end of 1994 there were almost 9 million Asian-Americans. During the past decade, the Asian-American population growth rate was twice that of Hispanics, six times that of African-Americans, and twenty times that of whites.[69] Like Hispanic-Americans, Asian-Americans are a diverse group, with thirteen submarkets. The five largest are Chinese (1.6 million), Filipino (1.4 million), Japanese (848,000), Asian Indians (815,000), and Koreans (799,000).

Immigration accounted for nearly three-fourths of the increase in the Asian-American population during the 1980s and early 1990s.[70] Of the two major streams of immigrants, one consists of people from Asian countries from which large numbers of people had already immigrated to the United States (for example, China, Korea, and the Philippines). This group tends to be well educated and ready to move quickly into the mainstream of U.S. society. The other group comprises immigrants and refugees from some of the war-torn countries of Southeast Asia: Vietnam, Laos, and Cambodia. Many in this group began their lives in the United States on welfare and lack the education and skills to move out of poverty.

Fully 56 percent of Asian-Americans live in the West, compared with 21 percent of all people in the United States. Eighteen percent of Asian-Americans live in the Northeast, 14 percent in the South, and 12 percent in the Midwest. Twelve states (California, Hawaii, New York, Illinois, New Jersey, Texas, Massachusetts, Pennsylvania, Virginia, Florida, Michigan, and Washington) each have over 100,000 Asian-Americans, five more states than in 1980. Nearly four out of ten Asian-Americans live in California, and about one out of ten lives in Hawaii.[71]

Asian-Americans are highly urbanized, with 93 percent living in a metropolitan area—half in central cities and half in suburbs.[72] In contrast, whites are twice as likely to live in suburbs as in central cities.

The high level of Asian immigration to the United States has created a youthful population. The average age of Asian-Americans is just 30, compared with 36 for whites. As Asian-Americans enter their peak earning years, their relatively high incomes will increase further.

### ASIAN-AMERICAN INCOME AND EDUCATION

Asian-American households are more affluent than those of any other racial or ethnic group, including whites. Their median household income was about $38,000 in 1993; 32 percent of Asian-American households have incomes of $50,000 or more, compared with only 29 percent of white households.[73] The high household incomes of Asian-Americans may be due in part to their concentration in Los Angeles, San Francisco, and Honolulu, where salaries are high to compensate for the cost of living.

Another reason for high household incomes is Asian-Americans' high level of education. Among adults 25 or older, 14 percent have been to college for five or more years, compared with only 9 percent of the total population. An additional 21 percent of Asian-Americans have completed four years of college, versus only 13 percent of the total population.

A third reason for the lofty household incomes of Asian-Americans is their lifestyle. Seventy-four percent live in married-couple households, versus 72 percent of whites and 43 percent of African-Americans.[74] Married-couple households typically have two or more earners, which boosts income.

A final reason for higher incomes is the high rate of business ownership among Asian-Americans. During the past decade, they have created new businesses faster than any other U.S. population group.[75] Different subgroups tend to gravitate toward different specialties. The Chinese, for instance, are often found in retail, wholesale, and financial enterprises but rarely in construction or transportation. The Japanese prefer construction and transportation to retail and service establishments. Retail-oriented Korean-Americans have become a major force in food marketing.

Why does the Asian-American community start so many new businesses? A key factor is the Asian immigrants' tradition of self-employment. They also turn to their fellow immigrants for help in raising money to start businesses. Asian-Americans pool their money in a **keh**, or cooperative, typically made up of about twenty members. Members contribute a fixed sum (usually $100 to $1,000) every month, and the total is awarded in full to a different member each month. Once the monthly payout cycle has been completed, the *keh* disbands. *Kehs* are a source of interest-free venture capital as well as a forum for exchanging business tips. There is little chance that a member would dare to stop contributing to the pot after getting his or her share. Reneging on a financial pledge to others violates Asian concepts of personal and family honor.

**keh**
Asian-Americna cooperative of about twenty people who combine their money and award it to one member each month and then disband after everyone has participated in the payout cycle.

Asian businesses are typically family owned and operated. During start-up, when money is scarce, they often draw on unpaid workers from the extended family. Extended kinship networks also enable immigrant households to share rents or mortgages, provide free child care, and ensure economic security against loss of employment by other household members.

Many Asian-American businesses serve internal markets—that is, others in the Asian-American community. Business owners tend to employ people from their own subgroup. These practices tend to strengthen the community's economy. In San

This herb shop in Chicago not only is owned by an Asian-American but also is in business expressly to serve the needs of other Asian-Americans.

Francisco's Chinese community, for instance, a dollar turns over five or six times before it leaves.[76]

## MARKETING MIXES FOR THE ASIAN-AMERICAN MARKET

Because Asian-Americans are younger and better educated and have higher incomes than average, they are sometimes called a "marketer's dream."

### Product

As a group, Asian-Americans are more comfortable with technology than the general population is. They are far more likely to use automated teller machines, and many more of them own VCRs, compact disc players, microwave ovens, home computers, and telephone answering machines.[77]

However, Asian-American subgroups often have dramatically different preferences, as one study found:

> Most Asian-Americans drink plenty of soda. Koreans are the exception, and only 52.1 percent of this group reported drinking soda in the previous three months. At the same time, Koreans drink more 7-Up than any other soda, a big difference from Asian-Americans in general, whose top soda preferences are Coke (55 percent) and Pepsi (18 percent).
>
> Bud's the king of beers for Asian-Americans, too, and it was the preferred brand of 44.2 percent of respondents. Coors (15.3 percent) was No. 2 and Miller (11.4 percent) No. 3. Light beer was preferred by 46.8 percent. Scotch is the preferred liquor, named by 28.7 percent of Asian-Americans. Johnnie Walker (18.8 percent) and Chivas Regal (14.6 percent) were the top two brands.
>
> Asian Indians were the biggest perfume users, and 68.1 percent had used some kind of fragrance in the previous three months. Filipinos were close behind, at 67.5 percent. The Japanese, at 35.7 percent, used perfume the least. Overall, Chanel (20.4 percent) was the preferred brand.
>
> Considering the state of the U.S. auto market, it would be natural to assume that Asian-Americans prefer Asian cars. The survey indicated otherwise. In fact, Ford was the auto of choice for 28.7 percent of respondents. The second choice was Toyota, at 21.9 percent. Only 9.1 percent owned Hondas.
>
> Asian-American consumers show no reluctance to purchase American products, even when Asian or other foreign alternatives are available.[78]



A number of products have been developed specifically for the Asian-American market. For example, Kayla Beverly Hills salon draws Asian-American consumers because the firm offers cosmetics formulated for them. Anheuser-Busch's agricultural products division sells rice to Asian-Americans, who are rice connoisseurs. The company developed eight varieties of California-grown rice, each with a different label, to cover a range of nationalities and tastes. Its Taste the Tradition ads, devised by multiethnic Los Angeles agency Muse Cordero Chen, played up similarities to Asian-grown rice, which is stickier than the kind most Westerners eat. The ads captured such nuances as the differences in Chinese, Japanese, and Korean rice bowls. Sales of Anheuser-Busch's Asian rice brands are now growing more than 10 percent a year.[79]

### Promotion

Cultural diversity within the Asian-American market complicates promotional efforts. Although Asian-Americans embrace the values of the larger U.S. population, they also hold on to the cultural values of their particular subgroup. Consider language. Many

Asian-Americans speak their native tongue at home, particularly Koreans and Chinese. Filipinos are far less likely to do so. Or consider big-ticket purchases. In Japanese-American homes, the husband alone makes the decision on such purchases nearly half the time, compared with the wife making the decision about 6 percent of the time. In Filipino families, however, wives make these decisions a little more often than their husbands do, although by far the most decisions are made by husbands and wives jointly or with the input of other family members.[80]

Misunderstanding the cultural differences among Asian-Americans can lead to some embarrassing gaffes. Metropolitan Life Insurance angered potential customers when it ran an ad in a Korean magazine showing a family in traditional dress—Chinese dress, that is. During Chinese New Year, Coors got complaints for reinforcing sexual stereotypes in an ad showing an exotic-looking woman wrapped in the folds of a silk dragon. A spokesperson says the brewer's advertising has since gotten away from "women and dragons." In another case, a company placed a Chinese-language ad to wish the community a happy new year but ran the Chinese characters upside down.[81]

Some very successful American advertising campaigns simply don't translate well among some Asian-Americans. The Pepsi Challenge, for example, would be seen as negative and rude. It's considered impolite to compare products and say one is better. Comparative advertising is shunned in China, Hong Kong, Taiwan, Japan, and the Philippines, among other places.[82] Ads stating that "We do everything better" are seen as bragging and lacking in consumer empathy. And it's usually not a good idea to try to translate humor. One long-distance phone company ran a tongue-in-cheek ad listing ten ways to save money on phone bills. One suggestion was to move before the phone bill arrives. Some Asian-Americans took this example seriously and were offended by its dishonorable suggestions. Advertising agencies like Lee Liu and Tong Inc. of New York City, which specializes in the Asian-American market, are attracting mainstream advertisers that want to avoid such problems.[83]

Unlike U.S. Hispanics, who are best reached via radio, Asian-Americans can best be reached through ethnic newspapers. Several Asian-language national newspapers are published in cities with large Asian populations. They include the *Korean Times* (Los Angeles, New York, Chicago, San Francisco, Seattle, Toronto, Houston, Las Vegas, and Washington, D.C.), *Chinese Daily News* (New York, Los Angeles, San Francisco, Chicago, Houston, Toronto, Vancouver, Boston, Atlanta, Honolulu, and Washington, D.C.), and *Philippine News* (Los Angeles, San Francisco, and New York). Asian-Americans can also be reached with television, but usually it is less cost-effective. However, the fall 1994 television schedule inaugurated the first prime-time Asian-American program, a sitcom called "All-American Girl" and featuring Korean-American comedian Margaret Cho.[84]

The most effective promotions stress the basic values that are important to Asian-Americans. In rank order, they are family security, self-respect, freedom, happiness, and true friendship.[85] An effective promotional campaign should show how a good or service will enhance the Asian-American's chances of living up to these important values.

## Distribution

Asian-Americans spend over $38 billion a year on retail purchases. Many of these dollars flow to other Asian-Americans who operate flower shops, grocery stores, appliance stores, and other small businesses.[86] After all, these are the businesses best equipped to offer the products that Asian-Americans want. For example, at first glance the Ha Nam supermarket in Los Angeles's Koreatown might be any other grocery store. But next to the Kraft American singles and the State Fair corn dogs are jars of whole cabbage kimchi. A snack bar in another part of the store cooks up aromatic mung cakes, and an entire aisle is devoted to dried seafood. In most U.S. supermarkets, bags near the checkout counter are filled with charcoal. Here, they are filled with rice.

Asian-Americans are also creating their own retail chains. One thriving chain is called 99:

> The number nine represents good fortune to the Chinese—the company operates eleven supermarkets in southern California. The chain operates two types of stores—99 Price for smaller stores in neighborhoods with close-up competition from other Oriental stores, and 99 Ranch for larger, more modern-style superstores.
>
> The 99 Ranch market in Anaheim carries 30,000 different packaged products with only about 15 percent comprised of American branded grocery, frozen food, and dairy products. The vast majority of 99's merchandise is provided by "literally hundreds" of import suppliers, many specializing in food from individual countries.
>
> A stroll up and down the seemingly endless aisles creates three distinct impressions. The first is the feeling of walking in and out of the United States, with shelves on one side housing familiar national brands, and those on the other packed with Oriental specialties. The second is the constant feeling of having "seen those items before" in other sections . . . and that's because you have. Innumerable teas and herb drinks, myriad fruit juice combinations and coffees, canned pigeon and quail eggs, bags of dried, seasoned and pickled vegetables, bottled beverages and sauces and endless grain products loom before the shopper in numerous locations of the store. The brands may be different, but the products are the same . . . or are they?
>
> "Not to the Chinese, Japanese, Korean or Vietnamese customer," says the store manager. "They all have distinct preferences based on their own cultures and customs, and they demand exactly the right items, and in the particular brands they have always known." This fierce brand loyalty extends to American products as well.
>
> The third dominant impression is service and selection in the perishables departments. Seafood and meat offerings are mind-boggling; a fully-staffed [counter] about 200 feet along the back of the store is devoted to an almost incredible selection, and this does not include several large cases of self-service and frozen seafood, meats and poultry in other locations of the store. Fish and shellfish are displayed live, already cleaned and trimmed or whole in the case, and in water-filled, serve-yourself bins, and varieties range up to 60 on a given day.[87]
>
> As seen in *Supermarket Business*, Richard DeSanta, "California's Oriental Stores: The Ultimate Niche Marketers," November 1991, 25–30.

Because Asian-Americans have a tendency to live in neighborhoods of people with the same ethnic background, specialized retail centers have naturally evolved. In suburban Orange County, California, Vietnamese immigrants have improved a once-barren area. The signs at the strip mall are almost exclusively in Vietnamese. An indoor mall, called Asia Garden, is packed on Sunday mornings. About 50,000 weekend shoppers patronize the 800 shops and restaurants, buying herbal medicines and dining on snail-tomato-rice-noodle soup. In the mornings, people may attend Buddhist ceremonies in makeshift temples; in the evenings they can applaud Elvis Phuong, complete with skintight pants and sneer.

Some entrepreneurs are building large enclosed malls that cater to Asian consumers. At the Aberdeen Centre near Vancouver, British Columbia, nearly 80 percent of the merchants are Chinese-Canadians, as are 80 percent of the customers. The mall offers fashions made in Hong Kong, a shop for traditional Chinese medicines, and a theater showing Chinese movies. Kung fu martial-arts demonstrations and Chinese folk dances are held in the mall on weekends.

5 *Identify key characteristics of the Native American market.*

## THE NATIVE-AMERICAN MARKET

Asian-, Hispanic-, and African-Americans have been discussed in some detail because they are the largest ethnic minority groups in the United States. A smaller group that must be singled out because of its role in U.S. history is the Native Americans. The census counted nearly 1.9 million Native Americans in 1990, up from fewer than 1.4 million in 1980. This 38 percent leap exceeds the growth rate for most other minority groups.[88]

The strong bonds that Native Americans still feel to their native culture are renewing their communities. Native Americans have not yet erased the poverty and other ills that affect many of them. But many living on and off the reservations have made educational and economic progress. A college-educated middle class has emerged, Native American business ownership has increased, and some tribes are creating good jobs for their members.

Native American businesses have some important competitive advantages because of the "sovereignty" afforded reservations. Many local, state, and federal laws do not apply on the reservations. They have no sales or property taxes, so cigarettes, gasoline, and other items can be sold for low prices. Reservations can also offer lucrative activities not permitted off the reservation, such as gambling. It is estimated that Native American tribes are now generating revenue of over $3.2 billion each year from gambling.[89]

## LOOKING BACK

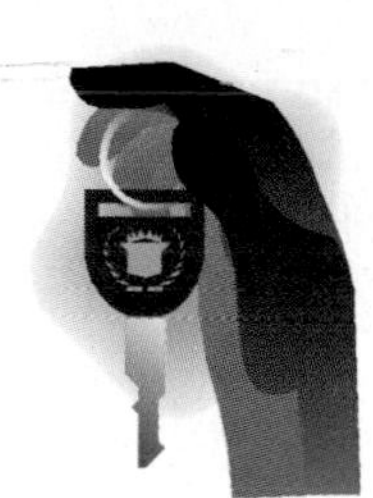

Like Cadillac, more and more consumer goods companies are creating specific marketing mixes for ethnic and cultural submarkets. The reason for this new targeting effort is the rapid growth of ethnic markets in terms of both population and income. Marketers have found that subcultures often respond best to products and promotion designed specifically for them.

The three major ethnic groups—African-Americans, Hispanic-Americans, and Asian-Americans—are quite distinct from one another. There is also significant diversity within the Hispanic and Asian-American markets. Diversity demands either crafting unique marketing mixes or "stitching niches" together to form a mass market. A company that doesn't consider the multicultural nature of U.S. society will find itself at a disadvantage in the marketplace.

## SUMMARY

1 **Analyze the cultural diversity of the United States.** The multicultural nature of the United States means that no longer can various ethnic groups be expected to assimilate into white, Western culture. In the future, no single ethnic group will be large enough to dictate political policy. As the United States continues to become a service-dominated economy, education will be the means for minorities to fully participate.

Much of the growth in the U.S. population since 1980 has occurred in minority markets. In 1994, about 25 percent of the U.S. population consisted of minorities. That figure should reach 36 percent by 2023, with the Hispanic-Americans growing most rapidly in number. Immigration has also served as a major source of growth in minority markets.

From a marketing perspective, multiculturalism increases the complexity of the marketing function. Demand for goods and services is often culture-driven. Within the large ethnic markets, the marketing mix is further complicated by the many submarkets. Marketers who want to reach these submarkets have to follow a niche strategy; try to maintain a brand's core identity while straddling different languages, cultures, ages, and incomes; or seek common interests, motivations, or needs across ethnic groups, which is called "stitching niches."

2 **Identify key characteristics of the African-American market and some elements of an effective marketing mix for this group.** In 1994, the 31 million African-Americans constituted the largest minority group. The proportion of the population that is African-American will continue to grow into the twenty-first century. Today, 53 percent of all African-Americans live in the South, 19 percent each in the Midwest and Northeast, and 9 percent in the West. The African-American population is younger than the U.S. population as a whole, with a median age of 27.9. Within this group is a substantial and growing middle class. Expenditures by African-Americans now top $270 billion annually.

In the marketing mix, the product element may vary to reflect African-Americans' unique desires, hopes, customs, and preferences. Health and beauty aids are one product category that has developed special lines for African-Americans. In addition, "Afrocentric products" stress the African heritage and culture of African-Americans. Specialized promotion for this market is growing rapidly. The most effective promotions avoid racial stereotypes. As for distribution, some special stores and shopping areas have developed to cater to this market. Although pricing is relatively uniform among all U.S. ethnic groups, some are concerned that the poor pay more because of their limited options.

KEY TERMS

*keh* 713

*multiculturalism* 691

*stitching niches* 694

3 **Identify key characteristics of the U.S. Hispanic market and some elements of an effective marketing mix for this group.** The Hispanic population is about 26 million, and it is growing much faster than the general population. The Hispanic market consists of three main submarkets: Mexican-American, Puerto Rican–American, and Cuban-American. The Cuban-Americans are concentrated in Florida, Puerto Rican–Americans in New York City, and Mexican-Americans in the Southwest. Mexican-Americans are the youngest, with a median age of 24; Cuban-Americans are the oldest at 39. Cuban-Americans are the most highly educated subgroup. The total purchasing power of the Hispanic market is over $170 billion per year. Median family income for U.S. Hispanics in 1991 was $28,890, compared with $33,000 for the general population.

Marketers have found that U.S. Hispanics often prefer products from their native country, especially if they are recent immigrants. They are very brand loyal. Marketers also need to be aware of the three main Hispanic submarkets when designing promotions. Subtle differences in culture and language often make it necessary to design different promotional programs for these different subgroups. Spanish-language broadcasting outlets and publications are the most effective means of reaching them. In terms of distribution, special retail chains and stores have developed. For instance, the Tianguis and Viva supermarket chains target the Mexican-American community; Sedanos serves Cuban-Americans.

4 **Identify key characteristics of the Asian-American market and some elements of an effective marketing mix for this group.** By the end of 1994 there were almost 9 million Asian-Americans. During the past decade, the Asian-American population growth

rate was 108 percent, twenty times that of whites. There are thirteen submarkets within the Asian-American community. Fifty-six percent of all Asian-Americans live in the West, compared with 21 percent of the general population. Most Asian-Americans live in a metropolitan area. The average age of Asian-Americans is 30. This group is the most affluent of any racial or ethnic group, including whites, with a median income of $38,000 in 1993. The main reason for their affluence is their high education level. Among adults, 14 percent of Asians have been to college for five or more years, compared with only 9 percent of the general population. Asian-Americans also have the highest rate of business ownership among minority groups.

Asian-Americans tend to be good customers for technologically advanced products. As with the U.S. Hispanic market, the Asian-American market is divided into subgroups based on country of origin, with definite product preferences among those subgroups. Language and cultural differences also complicate promotion, although Asian-Americans as a whole embrace traditional U.S. values. Various ethnic newspapers help marketers reach the Asian-American subgroups. Asian-Americans often establish stores and shopping areas serving their own ethnic group. For instance, in Southern California the 99 supermarket chain serves Asian-Americans, and the Asia Garden mall almost exclusively reaches Vietnamese customers.

5 **Identify key characteristics of the Native American market.** American Indians are simultaneously renewing some aspects of their native culture and developing a college-educated middle class (although many Native Americans still live in poverty). Competitive new businesses are developing on the reservations, which have no sales or property taxes.

## Discussion and Writing Questions

1. What does it mean to say that the United States is becoming a multicultural society?

✍2. Suppose you have seen the following statement in the newspaper: "People are basically the same everywhere, and we all want the same things. There is no need to create a special marketing mix for ethnic groups. Everyone, for example, likes Coca-Cola." Write a letter to the editor replying to the assumptions behind this statement.

3. Describe the ethnic mix of the U.S. population in 1993 and the projected mix for 2023. What are the implications of the changes?

4. Do you think the poor pay more? Do a simple market-basket survey in your own market. Pick ten items, and compare prices in a poor area and an affluent one. Describe your findings and develop reasons for them.

✍5. The marketing concept says to meet the needs of the consumer. Your boss says, "R.J. Reynolds was just responding to the needs of the marketplace with Uptown cigarettes. The same is true of selling malt liquor in poor neighborhoods." Write a memo explaining why you agree or disagree.

6. Retailers targeting the poor often admit that, with interest charges, the poor pay two or three times the price for which a television or other appliance could be purchased at a major discount chain. "The poor," they say, "can't get credit at national discounters. Either they buy from us and pay a lot more, or they do without." Discuss the ethics of this statement.

7. Do you agree that, because Asian-Americans can get interest-free loans from a *keh*, they have an unfair advantage over other ethnic groups in creating new businesses? Why or why not?

8. Why is it difficult to create a national promotional campaign for Asian-Americans?

9. Because Native Americans are exempt from many local, state, and federal laws, do they have an unfair advantage over other businesspeople? Why or why not?

## Application for Small Business

Robert Brown owns a Los Angeles travel agency that

caters primarily to the African-American market. Every August, the ocean liner *Majesty of the Seas* takes over 1,200 adventure seekers to the Caribbean.[90] Most of them are African-American. The so-called Festival at Sea sells out earlier and earlier every year. Robert's target market is African-Americans who have household incomes of $35,000 or more.

### Questions

1. Robert wants to book more customers for the Festival at Sea. How do you suggest that he reach his target market?
2. How should Robert promote the cruise?

## CRITICAL THINKING CASE

### Quaker Oats

In 1992 Quaker Oats broke up its ethnic marketing group, prompting speculation that other marketers would start reducing spending to target Asian-Americans, African-Americans, and U.S. Hispanics. Instead, such spending appears to be rising. The question is, Who controls the checkbook?

Ethnic marketing departments, usually run by minority executives, introduced many companies to racially targeted marketing in the 1980s. The new departments started as relatively weak advisers to brand managers but became more influential as companies gave more weight to ethnic markets. Minorities buy half of Quaker Oats' corn products, for instance, and Quaker's spending to reach minorities has tripled in recent years.

Quaker now says ethnic markets are too important to isolate in a single office. When the company disbanded its ethnic marketing department, it returned responsibility for ethnic markets to brand managers. "We don't want an ethnic marketing group out there as a dangling modifier to the rest of the business," says John Blair, Quaker's vice president of marketing. "We want ethnic marketing deeply embedded in every business manager in this company."

Minority suppliers fear they will lose customers without strong minority-run ethnic departments. "If brand managers could have done this job, they would have been given the responsibility in the first place," says Ken Smikle, publisher of *Target Market News,* which tracks ethnic marketing. "We're not talking about an ethnically diverse category of executive here."

Lafayette Jones, president of North Carolina's Segmented Marketing Services, says minority suppliers must learn how to deal with brand managers to survive. He notes that his firm still does work for Procter & Gamble, which took the same tack as Quaker Oats. Quaker's Blair concedes that the company's brand managers are still mostly white, but he says they must take ethnic marketing seriously—and turn to experts "to help them with the segments they don't understand. It opens up opportunities for minority vendors."



### Questions

1. Do you think Quaker Oats and Procter & Gamble made the right decision when they eliminated their ethnic marketing departments? Why or why not?
2. Do you agree with minority suppliers who worry about losing business without the ethnic marketing departments? Support your answer.
3. Why do you think large consumer goods companies created ethnic marketing departments originally?

### References

Patricia Braus, "What Does Hispanic Mean?," *American Demographics,* June 1993, pp. 46–58.

"Complexity of Asian American Market Causes Some to Stay Away," *Marketing News,* 17 January 1994, pp. 6, 9.

"Marketers Miss Out by Alienating Blacks," *The Wall Street Journal,* 9 April 1993, p. B8.

Eugene Morris, "The Difference in Black and White," *American Demographics,* January 1993, pp. 44–46.

Leon Wynter, "Business and Race," *The Wall Street Journal,* 16 November 1992, p. B1.

**VIDEO CASE**

## Ethnic Foods

The global village may be shrinking because of jet travel, but its kitchen is expanding. Ethnic cuisine is one of the fastest-growing segments in the U.S. food industry. In one poll, 26 percent of the people interviewed claimed that they now eat ethnic food more often than they did just three years earlier. Immigration from Latin America and Asia, as well as Americans' discovery of their own ethnic roots, has been responsible for this growth.

Here are some examples that show how popular ethnic cuisine has become:

- The Steiner Food Chain has gone from selling an inventory of 40 ethnic items to over 2,700 in a few years—resulting, of course, in increased revenue for the firm.
- Americans now eat more salsa than ketchup.
- Sylvia Woods, the Queen of Soul Food, expanded her 31-year-old restaurant in Harlem because of growing demand. She has also begun producing a line of soul food products to be sold in grocery stores. Sylvia sells bottled sauces in both New York and New Jersey.
- Glory Foods, in Columbus, Ohio, more than doubled its projected revenues in its first nine months of operation. It sells turnip greens, blackeyed peas, cornbread mix, and pepper-vinegar.

### Questions

1. More than 12,000 new food products are introduced in the United States every year. What can marketers of ethnic foods do to increase their chances of success?

2. The rise in demand for some types of ethnic foods can be attributed to immigration. What about the other ethnic foods?

3. For what other multicultural goods and services do you foresee rapidly increasing demand? Why?

# CHAPTER 21

# ETHICS AND SOCIAL RESPONSIBILITY

## Learning Objectives

*After studying this chapter, you should be able to*

1 *Explain the meaning of business ethics.*

2 *Describe the nature of ethical decision making.*

3 *Discuss several current ethical dilemmas.*

4 *Analyze ethical issues related to global marketing.*

5 *Discuss corporate social responsibility.*

6 *Explain the ways in which marketing meets its social responsibility.*

7 *Discuss consumerism.*

Every year, some 400,000 Davis, Jennings, and Raven guns are churned out by three offshoot companies of the Jennings family. Selling for as little as $35, versus $600 for higher-quality weapons, these are the starter guns for the fearful, the criminal, and increasingly the very young. To a startling degree, they also figure disproportionately in robberies and murders, piling up an alarming toll of casualties and an unending litany of violence. The small Davis .380 derringer is especially popular among criminals, according to the Bureau of Alcohol, Tobacco, and Firearms, because of its potent firepower and the ease with which it is concealed. Although high-powered weapons dominate the headlines in fleeting moments of mass murder, these three brands of small-caliber pistols are far more lethal because of their sheer numbers, rock-bottom prices, and easy availability.

A five-month investigation by *The Wall Street Journal* followed these handguns from the factory to the middleman and ultimately to the street. Low costs and high production are key. It takes a mere three minutes to completely assemble a Raven, compared to about half an hour for more expensive guns. Unlike standard guns, which use stainless steel, the Raven and its offshoots are made from cheaper materials. As a result the Jennings family wares typically won't withstand much use compared with better-quality guns.

Although Davis, Jennings, and Raven pistols all have minimal safety devices, they don't have other features that often appear on higher-quality guns to help prevent accidental discharge. Officials at the Bureau of Alcohol, Tobacco, and Firearms say the guns generally fail the "drop test" and can discharge if loaded and dropped to the floor. But that shortcoming isn't a violation of any law, because under the Gun Control Act of 1968, the test applies only to imported revolvers, not U.S.-made pistols. In fact, there are no safety requirements for U.S.-made guns, making them one of the least-regulated hazardous products in the United States.

In many ways, the Jennings family business is so typical that it's easy to lose sight of the product's main feature: It kills. The guns that leave the Jennings family's factories are first bought by wholesalers, who in turn sell the weapons to gun stores and pawnshops for legitimate trade. Often, though, the pistols are bought in bulk at retail by illegal dealers—particularly in states where gun laws are lax—and smuggled by bus or train to urban centers for resale. On the street, the buyer may pay more than triple the normal retail price to avoid required waiting periods, registration, and restrictions based on age and felony convictions.

Like any other business, the Jennings clan target their market. The Davis, Jennings, and Raven pistols sell in all sorts of neighborhoods throughout the United States, but too often the buyers are inner-city youths. Some neighborhoods have become virtual free-fire zones. For example, a Raven gun was used by a 15-year-old to rob and murder three cocaine dealers in Brooklyn. A 14-year-old in California was suspended from school after a Jennings .22 was found in his locker. And a 5-year-old in the Bronx was found carrying a loaded Raven to kindergarten in his pocket. The Jennings family denies that their guns figure predominantly in the inner city. Their customers, they say, "are just regular, everyday people who don't have the finances to buy higher-priced guns."

"We have a fire burning, and these companies are throwing gasoline on it," says Josh Sugarmann of the Violence Policy Center, which studies violence prevention. "These people know what the inner-city gun buyer wants."

The Jennings company is not under any legal obligation to control the markets it sells to, nor is it required to comply with any safety standards. But some companies have made changes out of a sense of social responsibility. For example, Wal-Mart stopped selling handguns altogether. Its decision was based on customers' indications that they prefer to shop at a retail store that does not sell handguns. Wal-Mart made this decision in a period of significant controversy over guns and violence, during which Congress passed the Brady Bill mandating a five-day waiting period for handgun purchases. But Wal-Mart management denies that this legislation had any bearing on its decision. Similarly, Toys R Us has stopped selling certain realistic toy guns as a result of an increase in shootings that involve children and teenagers. In several instances, teenagers have pointed toys guns at police and police have shot at the teens, causing death or injury.

Not everyone sees handguns as a problem. The National Rifle Association ran an ad campaign in women's magazines that played on concern about being the victim of armed criminals. The immediate purpose of the ads was not to promote gun ownership but to offer an 800 number that women could call with questions about self-defense. The NRA added callers' names to its mailing lists for direct-mail campaigns.[1]

Should the Jennings companies feel some responsibility to control the violence their guns are involved in? Should the guns' safety standards be raised to avoid accidental firing? Should Wal-Mart deny consumers the opportunity to buy handguns in their retail outlets? Should Toys R Us feel compelled to stop selling popular toy guns because of a few incidents involving police and children? Are these companies exercising social responsibility, or are they taking away consumers' buying-decision power? Is the NRA justified in using scare tactics to get more women on its mailing lists?

1 *Explain the meaning of business ethics.*

**ethics**
Moral principles or values that generally govern the conduct of an individual or a group.

## ETHICAL BEHAVIOR IN BUSINESS

**Ethics** refers to the moral principles or values that generally govern the conduct of an individual or a group. Ethics also can be viewed as the standard of behavior by which conduct is judged. Standards that are legal may not always be ethical, and vice versa. Laws are the values and standards enforceable by the courts. Ethics are personal rather than societal moral principles and values.

Defining the boundaries of ethicality and legality can be difficult. Often judgment is needed to determine whether an action that may be legal is indeed ethical. For example, advertising liquor, tobacco, and X-rated movies in college newspapers is not illegal in many states. But is it ethical? In the following situations, judgment plays a major role in defining ethical and legal boundaries. After you read each one, try to determine whether it can be placed neatly into one of the following categories: ethical and legal, ethical and illegal, unethical and legal, unethical and illegal.

- Saturday morning television is filled with commercials promoting fat-filled foods to children. For example, Pizza Hut, Little Caesar's, McDonald's, Burger King, and Wendy's promote only their high-fat foods to children on Saturday morning television, even though these restaurants have healthier items available. Researchers found in 1993 that 41 percent of the advertised foods got a third or more of their calories from fat, compared to 16 percent in 1990. Commercials for high-fat foods have increased despite federal recommendations that children follow a low-fat diet.[2]
- The U.S. Department of Health unveiled a series of radio and television advertisements urging sexually active young people to use latex condoms. These ads were meant to help slow the spread of HIV, the virus that causes AIDS. In one ad, a woman and a man are kissing and giggling and talking about whether he brought a condom. Because he did not, she flicks on the light and puts an end to their lovemaking. Then male and female announcers explain that the use of a latex condom can prevent HIV infection. Religious groups believe these ads result in sexual arousal and promote promiscuity instead of abstinence.[3]
- Members of morning walking clubs, which often walk in the local mall, have to pass food courts. Most members of the walking clubs are the elderly, seeking a healthier lifestyle in a climate-controlled environment. Some of the restaurants in the food courts have begun opening as early as 6 a.m. to serve mall walkers after their morning stroll. Many of them offer low-priced breakfast specials and two-for-one specials. However, most of the breakfast items they sell are fat-filled treats, such as biscuits, chocolate cookies, muffins, and doughnuts. Some senior-citizen advocates feel that purchasing these fat-filled foods defeats the whole purpose of exercising and that mall management is taking advantage of senior adults.[4]
- Big U.S. baby formula companies give free sample packs of formula to new mothers leaving hospitals with their infants. Formula companies have also given money to the American Academy of Pediatrics; in turn, members of the Academy recommend those formulas and give samples to mothers. A change in formula can make a baby sick; therefore, a mother is reluctant to change formula after her baby becomes accustomed to it. Abbott Laboratories, which holds 51 percent of the baby formula market, has used these tactics to promote its Similac formula. Critics note that the price of a thirteen-ounce can of Similac increased from 75¢ in 1980 to $2.25 in 1993.[5]
- Barney is a large purple dinosaur who appears in his own television show on

PBS, "Barney and Friends." Parents are upset because pledge drives interrupt "Barney and Friends." These pitches offer Barney tapes and toys to those who contribute to public television. The Federal Communications Commission is investigating whether these campaigns violate rules on advertising to children during children's shows. PBS representatives feel that soliciting during children's shows is acceptable because the local station and the children's shows are both supported by individuals' contributions.[6]

As you probably noticed, few of these situations fit neatly into one category. Some are clearly legal but could be viewed as ethical by some consumers and unethical by others. Although others were ruled illegal, a case could be made for their legality and ethicality.

How do people develop an understanding of which types of behavior are ethical? **Morals** are the rules or habits that people develop as a result of cultural values and norms. Culture is a socializing force that dictates what is right and wrong. Moral standards may also reflect the laws and regulations that affect social and economic behavior. Thus morals can be considered a foundation of ethical behavior.

**morals**
Rules or habits that people develop as a result of cultural values and norms.

Morals are usually characterized as good or bad. *Good* and *bad* have different connotations, including "effective" and "ineffective." A good salesperson makes or exceeds the assigned quota. If the salesperson sells a new stereo to a disadvantaged consumer knowing full well that the person can't keep up the monthly payments, is the salesperson still a good one? What if the sale enables the salesperson to exceed his or her quota?

Another set of connotations for *good* and *bad* are "conforming" and "deviant" behavior. A doctor who runs large ads for discounts on open-heart surgery would be considered bad or unprofessional, in the sense of not conforming to the norms of the medical profession. *Bad* and *good* are also used to express the distinction between criminal and law-abiding behavior. And finally, the terms are defined by religions, which differ markedly on what is good or bad. A Moslem who eats pork would be considered bad, as would a fundamentalist Christian who drinks whiskey.

## MORALITY AND BUSINESS ETHICS

Today's business ethics are actually a subset of the values held by society as a whole. The values businesspeople use to make decisions have been acquired through family and through educational and religious institutions. Moreover, social movements, such as those against nuclear power and for women's rights, also shape businesspeople's decision making.

Ethics are very situation-specific and time-oriented. Nevertheless, everyone must have an ethical base that applies to conduct in the business world and in personal life. One approach for developing a personal set of ethics is to examine the consequences of a particular act.[7] Who is helped or hurt? How long-lasting are the consequences? What actions produce the greatest good for the greatest number of people?

A second approach stresses the importance of rules. Rules come in the form of customs, laws, professional standards, and common sense. Consider these examples of rules:

Always treat others as you would like to be treated.

Copying copyrighted material is against the law.

It is wrong to lie, bribe, or exploit.

The last approach emphasizes the development of moral character within individuals. Ethical development can be thought of as having three levels:[8]

Business ethics grow out of the larger society's values. The public's interest in protecting the environment, as demonstrated by this protest against destruction of the Hawaiian rainforest, has given rise to "green marketing" techniques.

© G. Brad Lewis/Tony Stone Images, Inc.

**preconventional morality**
Basic level of moral development, which is childlike, calculating, self-centered, and even selfish, based on what will be immediately punished or rewarded.

**conventional morality**
Intermediate level of moral development, which is based on loyalty and obedience to the organization's or society's expectations.

**postconventional morality**
Most advanced level of moral development, in which people are less concerned about how others might see them and more concerned about how they see and judge themselves over the long run.

- **Preconventional morality,** the most basic level, is childlike. It is calculating, self-centered, and even selfish, based on what will be immediately punished or rewarded. Fortunately, most businesspeople have progressed beyond the self-centered and manipulative actions of preconventional morality.
- **Conventional morality** moves from an egocentric viewpoint toward the expectations of society. Loyalty and obedience to the organization (or society) become paramount. At the level of conventional morality, an ethical marketing decision would be concerned only with whether or not it is legal and how it will be viewed by others.
- **Postconventional morality** represents the morality of the mature adult. At this level, people are less concerned about how others might see them and more concerned about how they see and judge themselves over the long run. A marketing decision maker who has attained this level of morality might ask, "Even though it is legal and will increase company profits, is it right in the long run? Might it do more harm than good in the end?"

Unless managers and workers take positive action, business ethics is nothing more than empty moralizing. A businessperson with a mature set of ethical values accepts personal responsibility for decisions that affect the organization and the community. When making business decisions, he or she takes into account their effects on the needs and desires of employees and on the consumers who may be directly and indirectly affected. Will these decisions create goodwill and be in consumers' best interests, too? How will these decisions affect the social structure that enables the company to exist?

## ETHICS AND MARKETING MANAGEMENT

Many consumers perceive marketing activities as unethical and manipulative by nature. For instance, consumers often equate marketing with misleading advertisements, pushy salespeople, and high prices for poor-quality products. Indeed, some areas of marketing are particularly vulnerable to unethical behavior: product management, retailing, advertising, distribution, pricing, and personal selling. Consider the following statistics, which seem to show that people in the United States, in general, distrust businesspeople and marketers:

- A *Business Week*/Harris poll indicated that white-collar crime is thought to be very common (by 49 percent of respondents) or somewhat common (41 percent), and 46 percent of respondents believe that the ethical standards of business executives are only fair.
- A *Time* magazine study suggested that 76 percent of the populace see a lack of business ethics in business managers as contributing to the decline of U.S. moral standards.
- A Touche Ross survey reported the general feeling, even among businesspeople, that business ethics problems portrayed in the media have *not* been overblown or exaggerated.
- A Gallup study found that of all the various occupations, selling and advertising were judged to be at the bottom of the scale for honesty and ethical standards.[9]

Marketing managers must often weigh the needs of the organization against the needs of others (for instance, customers, suppliers, or society as a whole). Objective marketing considerations can conflict with ethical standards. For example, salespeople find themselves facing conflicting wants from the customer: high-quality products and low prices. They can feel tremendous pressure to compromise their own personal ethics for the apparent good of the business, the customer, or themselves.[10] Rigid sales or production quotas, risk of losing the sale, increased competition, lack of ethical guidelines, and greed often lead to unethical behavior in marketing.

Some of the major ethical problems confronting marketing managers are listed in Exhibit 21.1.

*Exhibit 21.1*

Possible Unethical Practices by Marketing Managers

- Bribery, gift giving, and entertainment
- False or misleading advertising
- Unfair manipulation of customers
- Misrepresentation of goods, services, and company capabilities
- Lies told to customers in order to make the sale
- Price deception
- Price discrimination
- Product deception
- Unfair remarks about the competitor
- Exploitation of children and underprivileged groups in marketing strategies
- Sex-oriented advertising appeals
- Invasions of customer privacy
- Manipulation of data (falsifying or misusing statistics or information)
- Misleading product warranties
- Unsafe products
- Smaller amounts of product in same-size packages
- Stereotyped portrayals of women, minority groups, and senior citizens

2 *Describe the nature of ethical decision making.*

## ETHICAL DECISION MAKING

How do businesspeople make ethical decisions? There is no cut-and-dried answer. One study of marketing executives and marketing researchers found that three factors influence their ethical judgments:[11]

- *Extent of ethical problems within the organization:* Marketing professionals who perceived fewer ethical problems in their organizations tended to disapprove more strongly of "unethical" or questionable practices than those who perceived more ethical problems. Apparently, the healthier the ethical environment, the greater the likelihood that marketers will take a strong stand against questionable practices.
- *Top-management actions on ethics:* The research also showed that top managers can influence the behavior of marketing professionals by encouraging ethical behavior and discouraging unethical behavior.
- *Organizational role (executives versus researchers):* Marketing executives expressed stronger disapproval of some questionable practices than did marketing researchers.

### ETHICAL GUIDELINES

**code of ethics**
Guidelines developed by a company to help its employees make ethical decisions.

Many organizations have become more interested in ethical issues. One sign of this interest is the increase in the number of large companies that appoint ethical officers—from virtually none in 1988 to 15 percent to 20 percent of large corporations by 1993.[12] In addition, many companies of various sizes have developed a **code of ethics** as a guideline to help marketing managers and other employees make better decisions. Some of the most highly praised codes of ethics are those of Boeing, GTE, Hewlett-Packard, Johnson & Johnson, and Norton Company.

Creating ethics guidelines has several advantages:

- It helps employees identify what their firm recognizes as acceptable business practices.
- A code of ethics can be an effective internal control on behavior, which is more desirable than external controls like government regulation.
- A written code helps employees avoid confusion when determining whether their decisions are ethical.
- The process of formulating the code of ethics facilitates discussion among employees about what is right and wrong and ultimately creates better decisions.[13]

Businesses, however, must be careful not to make their code of ethics too vague or too detailed. Codes that are too vague give little or no guidance to employees in their day-to-day activities. Codes that are too detailed encourage employees to substitute rules for judgment. For instance, if employees are involved in questionable behavior, they may use the absence of a written rule as a reason to continue, even though their conscience may be saying no.[14] The checklist in Exhibit 21.2 is an example of a simple but helpful set of ethical guidelines. Following the checklist will not guarantee the "rightness" of a decision, but it will improve the chances of the decision's being ethical.

Although many companies have issued policies on ethical behavior, marketing managers must still put the policies into effect. They must address the classic "matter of degree" issue. For example, marketing researchers must often resort to decep-

*Exhibit 21.2*

Ethics Checklist

Source: Adapted from Michael R. Hyman, Robert Skipper, and Richard Tansey, "Ethics Codes Are Not Enough," *Business Horizons*, March-April 1990, pp. 15–22.

- Does my decision presume that I or my company is an exception to a common practice or convention? In other words, do I think I have the authority to break a rule?
- Would I offend customers by telling them about my decision?
- Would I offend qualified job applicants by telling them about my decision?
- Have I made this decision without input from others, so that important issues might be overlooked?
- Does my decision benefit one person or group but hurt or not benefit other individuals or groups?
- Will my decision create conflict between people or groups in the company?
- Will I have to pull rank (use coercion) to enact my decision?
- Would I prefer to avoid the consequences of this decision?
- Did I avoid truthfully answering any of the other questions by telling myself that I could get away with it?

tion to obtain unbiased answers to their research questions. Asking for a few minutes of a respondent's time is dishonest if the researcher knows the interview will last forty-five minutes. Should researchers conducting focus groups inform the respondents that there are observers behind a one-way mirror? Often, when respondents know they're being watched, they stop talking and interacting freely. Does a client have an ethical right to obtain questionnaires with the names and addresses of respondents from a market research firm? Many of these concerns have been addressed by the Professional Standards Committee of the American Marketing Association. A copy of the American Marketing Association's code of ethics, adopted in 1987, is shown in Exhibit 21.3.

Even the best ethics programs don't always work. Dow Corning was among the first corporations to set up a formal ethics program. Through a committee made up of company executives, Dow Corning's program sought to create a corporate culture with high ethical standards. The company audited compliance with its standards, communicated with employees about ethics, included ethics in training programs, and surveyed employees about their ethics practices twice a year. Yet the system seemingly failed. Dow Corning was accused of covering up safety problems with the silicone breast implants the company produced. Internal documents suggest that Dow Corning was aware of the safety problems for years and tried to keep the public from learning of them.[15]

3 *Discuss several current ethical dilemmas.*

## CURRENT ETHICAL DILEMMAS

Today marketing managers face several ethical issues. Three of the major ones are tobacco and alcohol promotion, consumer privacy, and so-called "green marketing." Limited space prevents us from exploring many other ethical dilemmas, including marketing to young children, marketing that promotes sexual harassment, misleading advertising and product labels, and marketing to the disadvantaged.

### TOBACCO AND ALCOHOL PROMOTION

Never have the tobacco and alcohol industries experienced such strong attacks as they have in the 1990s. One example is the criticism of R.J. Reynolds Tobacco Company's promotion of its Camel brand with a cartoon mascot, Joe Camel. Some of the Camel ads have targeted women. For instance, full-color ads show female camels smoking cigarettes at a "watering hole" while male camels keep a close eye on them. Critics feel these ads may encourge young women to smoke.[16]

*Exhibit 21.3*

American Marketing Association Code of Ethics

Source: American Marketing Association

Members of the American Marketing Association (AMA) are committed to ethical professional conduct. They have joined together in subscribing to this Code of Ethics embracing the following topics:

**Responsibilities of the Marketer**

Marketers must accept responsibility for the consequences of their activities and make every effort to ensure that their decisions, recommendations, and actions function to identify, serve, and satisfy all relevant publics: customers, organizations, and society.

**Marketers' professional conduct must be guided by:**

1. The basic rule of professional ethics: not knowingly to do harm;
2. The adherence to all applicable laws and regulations;
3. The accurate representation of their education, training, and experience; and
4. The active support, practice, and promotion of this Code of Ethics.

**Honesty and Fairness**

Marketers shall uphold and advance the integrity, honor, and dignity of the marketing profession by:

1. Being honest in serving consumers, clients, employees, suppliers, distributors, and the public;
2. Not knowingly participating in conflict of interest without prior notice to all parties involved; and
3. Establishing equitable fee schedules including the payment or receipt of usual, customary, and/or legal compensation for marketing exchanges.

**Rights and Duties of Parties in the Marketing Exchange Process**

Participants in the marketing exchange process should be able to expect that:

1. Participants and services offered are safe and fit for their intended uses;
2. Communications about offered products and services are not deceptive;
3. All parties intend to discharge their obligations, financial and otherwise, in good faith; and
4. Appropriate internal methods exist for equitable adjustment and/or redress of grievances concerning purchases.

It is understood that the above would include, *but it is not limited to,* the following responsibilities of the marketers:

*In the area of product development and management,*

- Disclosure of all substantial risks associated with product or service usage;
- Identification of any product component substitution that might materially change the product or impact on the buyer's purchase decision;
- Identification of extra-cost added features.

*In the area of promotions,*

- Avoidance of false and misleading advertising;
- Rejection of high-pressure manipulations or misleading sales tactics;
- Avoidance of sales promotions that use deception or manipulation.

*In the area of distribution,*

- Not manipulating the availability of a product for purpose of exploitation;
- Not using coercion in the marketing channel;
- Not exerting undue influence over the reseller's choice to handle a product.

*In the area of pricing,*

- Not engaging in price fixing;
- Not practicing predatory pricing;
- Disclosing the full price associated with any purchase. In the area of marketing research,
- Prohibiting selling or fund-raising under the guise of conducting research;
- Maintaining research integrity by avoiding misrepresentation and omission of pertinent research data;
- Treating outside clients and suppliers fairly.

**Organizational Relationships**

Marketers should be aware of how their behavior may influence or impact on the behavior of others in organizational relationships. They should not demand, encourage, or apply coercion to obtain unethical behavior in their relationships with others, such as employees, suppliers, or customers. Marketers should:

1. Apply confidentiality and anonymity in professional relationships with regard to privileged information;
2. Meet their obligations and responsibilities in contracts and mutual agreements in a timely manner;
3. Avoid taking the work of others, in whole, or in part, and represent this work as their own or directly benefit from it without compensation or consent of the originator or owner;
4. Avoid manipulation to take advantage of situations to maximize personal welfare in a way that unfairly deprives or damages their organization or others.

Any AMA member found to be in violation of any provision of this Code of Ethics may have his or her Association membership suspended or revoked.

Critics also claim that the Joe Camel campaign targets children and teenagers in an attempt to turn them into smokers. Several studies show that this claim may have some basis. For instance, studies published in the *Journal of the American Medical Association* found that Camel ads are highly effective in reaching children. In one study, many members of a small group of 6-year-olds were nearly as familiar with Joe Camel as they were with the Disney Channel's Mickey Mouse logo. Another study found that, when consumers were asked to judge the age of models in cigarette ads, 17 percent of the models were perceived to be under the age of 25, an apparent violation of the tobacco industry's voluntary advertising code. Additionally, cigarette ads featuring young people were found to appear more often in magazines with younger audiences.[17]

Studies like these have prompted the U.S. Surgeon General to call for a ban of all tobacco advertising in magazines and in retail stores. (Tobacco advertising is already banned from the airwaves.) Other branches of the federal government are also seeking to control tobacco advertising. The U.S. Supreme Court has ruled that smokers may sue cigarette makers for hiding or distorting the health dangers of tobacco, which gives tobacco companies a substantial incentive for being truthful and including disclaimers on packages and in ads. Congress is also considering some antismoking laws, including ones that would allow individual states to regulate tobacco advertising, prohibit tobacco ads that can be seen by minors, limit outdoor advertising, and end tax deductibility for tobacco products. The Federal Trade Commission is under pressure to prohibit advertising of any kind for low-tar cigarettes, which are thought to lull smokers into a false sense of security. Efforts like these have spilled over to the states as well. One California bill would ban the use of cartoons in advertising for dangerous products, especially cigarettes.[18]

Although tobacco advertising is now banned from TV and radio, activists claim that the ads are sneaking onto the airwaves when television cameras focus on a stadium scoreboard or zoom in on an outfielder. In response to public sentiment, several big sports stadiums are eliminating tobacco ads.[19]

The state government of Minnesota erected this billboard to counteract tobacco companies' advertising. A number of government entities have undertaken similar marketing campaigns as the substantial health and social costs of smoking have become clearer.

© Mitch Kezar/Tony Stone Images, Inc.

Antismoking activists are not just trying to ban tobacco advertising; they are also using modern marketing techniques to "sell" their point of view. In California, for example, sophisticated ads funded by the state's cigarette tax attempted to persuade the state's 7 million smokers to kick the habit. The campaign targeted young women, teenagers, and immigrants. It was estimated to have cost the tobacco industry some $1.1 billion in lost sales in California.[20]

The alcoholic beverage industry has not fared much better. Beer commercials are limited to one minute per hour during college basketball championship games. The U.S. Surgeon General has also attacked alcohol advertising, assert-

To forestall criticism and further restrictive legislation, tobacco and alcohol marketers are spending many millions of dollars on advertising that preaches moderation and, for kids, postponement of adult habits.

© 1990 Anheuser-Busch, Inc., St. Louis, MO

ing that its reliance on sex and sports imagery encourages underage drinkers. Low-alcohol, brightly labeled alcoholic drinks have come under fire because critics feel this packaging will lure teenagers and increase alcohol abuse among them. Congress is thinking about requiring health warnings in all alcoholic beverage ads. One bill would require alcohol ads to warn that drinking can lead to birth defects and addiction.[21]

The Bureau of Alcohol, Tobacco, and Firearms has spoken out against many alcohol products that it feels are aimed at inner-city dwellers. Examples include PowerMaster, a potent malt liquor whose name had to be changed because of its connotation of strong alcoholic content, and St. Ides Premium Malt Liquor, whose commercials use rappers like Ice Cube and the Geto Boys to lure young drinkers. Colt 45, a high-octane malt liquor, targets young inner-city youth by its use in ads of a first-generation college graduate role model. Use of this role model is part of Colt 45's effort to have a hipper image, a change from its mid-1980s appeal to older black men.[22]

Many tobacco and alcohol companies are submitting to activists' pressures with new campaigns telling kids not to smoke and drink. The big tobacco companies and their trade group, the Tobacco Institute, have launched youth antismoking campaigns focusing on the peer pressure associated with smoking. Anheuser-Busch spends millions annually on its Know When to Say When campaign. Likewise, Miller Brewing has tripled spending on its responsible-drinking program, which it emphasizes during holidays and spring break.[23]

Critics question the sincerity of tobacco and alcohol companies' antismoking and antidrinking ads. Many feel the ads challenge children to smoke and drink. Others believe the industry's efforts to discourage teen drinking and smoking have been drowned out by the overabundance of upbeat ads. Still others feel the ads are the industry's last effort to fend off possible regulation.[24] In fact, beer companies are not just trying to discourage regulation but are earnestly trying to keep beer ads from being banned altogether.

Because the banning of alcohol and tobacco advertising could have a very big economic impact, others are also concerned. The Leadership Council on Advertising Issues estimates that if tobacco advertising were banned, 7,904 newspaper jobs would disappear and 165 magazines would go out of business. If beer and wine advertising on television were canceled, another 4,232 jobs would be lost, plus an enormous chunk of network sports programming. Without ads for hard liquor, another 84 magazines would fold, including many for African-Americans.[25]

Tobacco and alcoholic beverage companies can't necessarily escape the pressure by shifting into overseas markets. Tobacco companies, in particular, are facing tougher laws and regulations all over the world. The executive body of the European Union has recommended a ban on tobacco ads throughout the trade bloc. It would eliminate tobacco ads from magazines and other publications, billboards, and movie theaters and prohibit tobacco company logos on T-shirts and on the sides of racing cars. Ads would be allowed only inside tobacco shops. The European Union's ban on TV tobacco advertising took effect in 1991. Other countries—among them Taiwan, Australia, China, and Thailand—are also seeking to curb tobacco advertising or to stiffen regulations. Canada has some of the world's toughest antismoking regulations. Tobacco display advertising is banned from retail stores. Cigarette packages must be printed with large health warnings and must include inserts detailing the hazards of smoking. Canadian law also bans tobacco advertising in newspapers and magazines and on billboards.[26]

In contrast, Hungary may loosen its regulation of tobacco advertising. Cigarette ads were banned in 1978, but the country is considering a bill allowing cigarette ads if the state funds an antismoking movement.[27]

## CONSUMER PRIVACY

Today's computer technology can collect and analyze mountains of data. Thus it is easy for companies to compile alarmingly detailed profiles of millions of their customers, with everything from salaries and home values to ages and weights of family members.

Sometimes the companies that collect the information sell it to direct marketers. Many consumers resent this use of information provided in business transactions. In one study, almost eight in ten U.S. citizens agreed that if the Declaration of Independence were to be written today, they would probably add privacy to the list of fundamental rights—along with life, liberty, and the pursuit of happiness. The majority also believed that they have lost all control over the use of personal information.[28]

The number of marketers that have been entangled in consumer privacy issues is mounting. American Express has acknowledged that information about its cardholders' lifestyles and spending habits was offered for joint marketing efforts with merchants. After the news created controversy, Blockbuster Entertainment scrapped plans to sell to direct marketers information about its customers' video-renting habits. Equifax, the giant credit-reporting agency, with 120 million names in its files, also gave up the practice of providing mailing lists to direct marketers after the New York State Attorney General threatened a lawsuit.[29]

Even physicians and pharmacists routinely open their patient records to data collectors, who sell the records to pharmaceutical companies wanting to know exactly how well their products are selling. Critics of this practice say the custodians of medical records have no right to share such information with an unregulated business without patients' knowledge or consent. The practice especially alarms patients with AIDS, mental illness, and other conditions in which a breach of privacy can have far-reaching consequences.[30]

Many companies are using the privacy issue as a marketing weapon. AT&T aired television ads attacking MCI's Friends & Family program, which offers 20 percent off some calls in exchange for customer referrals. In one AT&T ad, a woman becomes outraged when a telemarketer asks for the phone numbers of people close to her.[31] In another ad, a man returns home to be bombarded by nasty messages on his answering machine from friends whose names and numbers he gave to MCI.

Technological advances enable computers to build models of customer behavior based on previous transactions. For instance, when people call 800 or 900 numbers, caller ID services can be used to record their phone number, and then the company can find their names and addresses and put them on a mailing list.[32] New legislation is being considered that would require callers' consent before their personal information is reused or sold.

But even by sending in a coupon, filling out a warranty card, or entering a sweepstakes, consumers are volunteering information to marketers. That information can be combined with information from public records to identify, as targets for marketing efforts, clusters of consumers who have similar interests and income. Retailers can compile similar lists with information from checkout scanners. Critics feel these practices are an invasion of consumers' privacy. Consumers are unknowingly arming marketers with information that will help the marketers sell them more goods and services.[33]

**green marketing**
Marketing of products and packages that are less toxic than normal, are more durable, contain reusable materials, or are made of recyclable materials.

## GREEN MARKETING

**Green marketing** refers to the marketing of products and packages that are less toxic than normal, are more durable, contain reusable materials, or are made of recyclable materials. In short, these are products considered environmentally friendly, and their marketers are "environmentally responsible."

The vast majority of U.S. citizens are worried about the environment. Most tend to blame businesses for the environmental problems they see. One study revealed these findings:

- More than eight in ten say industrial pollution is the main reason for our environmental problems.

Aveda is but one of many companies that have adopted an environmentally responsible marketing program. Aveda produces all-natural skin-care products, developed without animal testing and packaged in recycled materials.

- Nearly three-quarters of the public say the products that businesses use in manufacturing also harm the environment.
- Six in ten blame businesses for not developing environmentally sound consumer products.
- About two-thirds disapprove of the packaging used by fast-food businesses and consumer product manufacturers.[34]

Consumers blame themselves, too. Seventy percent say consumers are more interested in convenience than in environmentally sound products. Over half admit they are not willing to pay more for safer products. Companies like Bic, which specializes in disposable products, found that consumers are happy to pay for convenience. They don't seem to mind that the 4 million pens, 3 million razors, and 800,000 plastic lighters that Bic produces annually end up in landfills. In fact, the company's two refillable pens account for less than 5 percent of sales, a figure that has been steadily declining.[35]

Still, many companies are becoming environmentally sensitive. The Duracell and Eveready battery companies have reduced the levels of mercury in their batteries and will eventually market mercury-free products. Sanyo sells its rechargeable batteries in a plastic tube that can be mailed back. The company then recycles both the tubes and the cadmium batteries. Turtle Wax car-wash products and detergents are biodegradable and can be "digested" by waste-treatment plants. The company's plastic containers are made of recyclable plastic, and its spray products do not use propellants that damage the ozone layer in the earth's upper atmosphere. Similarly, L'eggs redesigned its trademark plastic egg package and replaced it with a more environmentally friendly cardboard package.[36]

Critics contend that green marketing campaigns are nothing more than an attempt to capitalize on people's concerns about the environment. One research group studied thirty-five U.S. corporations and found that many of them are using "green marketing" as a smokescreen while they continue to pollute the environment.[37]

Many companies have also been charged with making false or misleading environmental claims in their packaging or advertising. In response, many states and the Federal Trade Commission have issued guidelines for green marketers. For instance, California's truth-in-environmental-advertising law makes it harder for companies to use the words *recycled* and *recyclable* for packaging. The FTC's guidelines strongly encourage manufacturers and marketers to back up environmental claims with competent and reliable scientific evidence and to avoid overstating a product's environmental benefits.[38]

U.S. consumers are not the only ones becoming environmentally sensitive. Around the world, consumers and marketers alike are taking steps to preserve the earth and its atmosphere. Germany is one of the most environmentally advanced countries. One German law calls for 60 percent of packaging to be recycled within five years of the law's passage. German carmakers are now installing plants to recycle car parts. In Canada, a federal program called Environmental Choice sets environmental standards for products claiming to be environmentally friendly. Guidelines have been introduced for thirty-four product types, and more than 600 products have been certified through the program.[39]

4 *Analyze ethical issues related to global marketing.*

## ETHICS IN GLOBAL MARKETING

As the number of multinational firms increases, companies and nations inevitably become more interdependent. Hence, they must learn to cooperate for their mutual benefit. However, because of cultural differences, increased interdependence also heightens the potential for conflicts, many of which involve marketing ethics.[40] In addition, developing nations may have trouble imposing their marketing, environmental, and human rights regulations on large multinational firms.

These are some of the major ethical issues faced by international marketers:[41]

- *Traditional small-scale bribery:* payment of a small sum of money (for example, a "grease payment" or kickback), typically to a foreign official, in exchange for his or her violation of some official duty or responsibility in an effort to speed routine government actions
- *Large-scale bribery:* relatively large payment (for example, a political contribution) intended to allow a violation of the law or to influence policy directly or indirectly
- *Gifts, favors, and entertainment:* lavish gifts, opportunities for personal travel at the company's expense, gifts received after the completion of a transaction, expensive entertainment
- *Pricing:* unfair differential pricing, questionable invoicing (when the buyer requests a written invoice showing a price other than the actual price paid), pricing to force out local competition, dumping products at prices well below those in the home country, pricing practices that are illegal in the home country but legal in the host country (for example, price-fixing agreements)
- *Products and technology:* products and technology that are banned for use in the home country but permitted in the host country or that appear unsuitable or inappropriate for use by the people in the host country
- *Tax evasion:* practices used specifically to evade taxes, such as transfer pricing (adjusting prices paid between affiliates and the parent company so as to affect profit allocation), "tax havens" (shifting profits to a low-tax jurisdiction), adjusted interest payments on intrafirm loans, questionable management and service fees charged between affiliates and the parent company
- *Illegal or immoral activities in the host country:* practices such as polluting the environment; maintaining unsafe working conditions; copying products or technology where protection of patents, trade names, or trademarks has not been enforced; short-weighting overseas shipments so as to charge a phantom weight
- *Questionable commissions to channel members:* unreasonably large commissions or fees paid to channel members, such as sales agents, middlemen, consultants, dealers, and importers
- *Cultural differences:* differences between cultures involving potential misunderstandings related to the traditional requirements of the exchange process (for example, transactions regarded as bribes by one culture but acceptable in another)—including gifts, monetary payments, favors, entertainment, and political contributions that are not considered part of normal business practices in one's own culture
- *Involvement in political affairs:* marketing activities related to politics, including

the exertion of political influence by multinationals, marketing activities when either the home or the host country is at war, and illegal technology transfer

## CULTURAL DIFFERENCES IN ETHICS

Studies have suggested that ethical beliefs vary only little from culture to culture. However, certain practices, such as the use of illegal payments and bribes, are far more acceptable in some places than in others. Some countries have a dual standard concerning illegal payments. For example, German businesspeople typically treat bribes as tax-deductible business expenses. In Russia, bribes and connections in the government are essential for doing business. For bureaucratic tasks, such as registering a business, bribing a public official is the fastest method. It usually costs about 100,000 rubles ($500). What we call bribery is a natural way of doing business in some other cultures. For global marketers, it may be best to adopt a "When in Rome, do as the Romans do" mentality.[42]

Yet another example of cultural differences is the Japanese reluctance to enforce their antitrust laws. Everyday business practices, from retail pricing to business structuring, ignore antitrust regulations against restraint of trade, monopolies, and price discrimination. Not surprisingly, the Japanese are tolerant of scandals involving antitrust violations, favoritism, price fixing, bribery, and other activities considered unethical in the United States.[43]

**Foreign Corrupt Practices Act**
Legislation prohibiting U.S. corporations from making illegal payments to public officials of foreign governments in order to obtain business rights or enhance their business dealings in that country.

Concern about U.S. corporations' use of illegal payments and bribes in international business dealings led to passage of the **Foreign Corrupt Practices Act** in 1977. This act prohibits U.S. corporations from making illegal payments to public officials of foreign governments to obtain business rights or to enhance their business dealings in that country. The act has been criticized for putting U.S. businesses at a competitive disadvantage. Many contend that bribery is an unpleasant but necessary part of international business.[44]

## EXPLOITATION OF DEVELOPING COUNTRIES

For companies, the benefits of seeking international growth are several. A company that cannot grow further in its domestic market may reap increased sales and economies of scale not only by exporting its product but also by producing it abroad. A company may also wish to diversify its political and economic risk by spreading its operations across several nations.

Expanding into developing countries offers multinational companies the benefits of low-cost labor and natural resources. But many multinational firms have been criticized for exploiting developing countries. Although the firms' business practices may be legal, many business ethicists argue that they are unethical.[45] The problem is compounded by the intense competition among developing countries for industrial development. Ethical standards are often overlooked by governments hungry for jobs or tax revenues.

Take the tobacco industry, for instance. With tobacco sales decreasing and regulations stiffening in the United States and Western Europe, tobacco companies have come to believe that their future lies elsewhere: in Asia, Africa, Eastern Europe, and Russia. Despite the known health risks of their product, the large tobacco companies are pushing their way into markets that typically have few marketing or health-labeling controls. In Hungary, Marlboro cigarettes are sometimes handed out to young fans at pop concerts. Since 1987, cigarette advertising on Japanese television has soared from fortieth to second place in air time and value; it appears even during children's shows.[46]

Interestingly, at a time when smoking is being discouraged in the United States, U.S. trade representatives are talking to developing countries like China and Thailand about lowering their tariffs on foreign cigarettes. Japan, Taiwan, and South Korea have already given in to the threats.[47] Entering these developing countries, the tobacco companies and trade representatives insist, will help U.S. tobacco manufacturers make up for losses in their home market.

Environmental issues are another example. As U.S. environmental laws and regulations gain strength, many companies are moving their operations to developing countries, where it is often less expensive to operate. These countries generally enforce minimal or no clean-air and waste-disposal regulations. An increasing number of U.S. companies have located manufacturing plants called *maquiladoras* in Mexico, along the U.S.-Mexican border. Mexico has few pollution laws, and so *maquiladoras* have been allowed to pollute the air and water and dump hazardous wastes along the border. Many blame the *maquiladoras* for "not putting back into the border area what they have been taking out," referring to the region's inadequate sewers and water-treatment plants. Because Mexico has been eager to attract foreign employers, *maquiladoras* pay little in taxes, which would normally go toward improving the infrastructure. Ciudad Juarez, a populous and polluted *maquiladora* city bordering El Paso, Texas, generates 22 million gallons of sewage a day. It has had no sewage system at all.[48] Many fear that the North American Free Trade Agreement (NAFTA) will result in further environmental problems in Mexico, as well as in Canada and the United States, because of the environmental compromises required to ensure passage.

5 *Discuss corporate social responsibility.*

## CORPORATE SOCIAL RESPONSIBILITY

Ethics and social responsibility are closely intertwined. Besides questioning tobacco companies' ethics, one might ask whether they are acting in a socially responsible manner when they promote tobacco. Are companies that produce low-cost handguns socially responsible in light of the fact that these guns are used in the majority of inner-city crimes? **Corporate social responsibility** is business's concern for society's welfare. This concern is demonstrated by managers who consider both the long-range best interests of the company and the company's relationship to the society within which it operates.

**corporate social responsibility**
Business's concern for society's welfare, demonstrated by managers who consider both the long-range best interests of the company and the company's relationship to the society within which it operates.

### THE CASE FOR SOCIAL RESPONSIBILITY

Several arguments might lead a company to practice social responsibility.[49] The arguments for social responsibility include the following:

- *Changing public expectations:* Before the 1960s, the general understanding between business and society was that economic growth was the source of all progress. The mission of business, and the extent of its social responsibility, was to produce goods and services at a profit. We now recognize that economic growth sometimes has **social costs**, which are costs not directly paid for by individual consumers but borne by society as a whole. Examples include pollution, a massive underprivileged class, deteriorating cities, traffic congestion, unsafe work environments, and many other social problems. The new contract between society and business expects that business will reduce these social

**social cost**
Cost not directly paid for by individual consumers but borne by society as a whole.

costs. Society now feels that business organizations must work for social as well as economic progress.

- *Long-run self-interest:* By helping to make the environment a better place in which to live and work, business creates conditions that are favorable for its survival and profitability. Enlightened self-interest dictates a concern for social problems. Business cannot hope to remain viable in a deteriorating society.
- *Avoidance of government regulation:* If business doesn't respond properly to societal concerns, the political system is left to address these issues. The political response is often legislation. Regulations and laws tend to restrict a company's decision-making freedom and reduce strategic options. History has proved that business irresponsibility has led to new regulations and, in some cases, formation of new regulatory bodies. Examples include the truth-in-lending and truth-in-packaging laws, the Environmental Protection Agency, and the Consumer Product Safety Commission.
- *Business's useful resources:* Business has the economic tools to take effective action: managerial talent, technical knowledge, and financial and physical resources to help remedy society's ills. Business is also known for its innovative and efficient use of resources. Therefore, business should be encouraged or even forced to try solving social problems.

## THE CASE AGAINST SOCIAL RESPONSIBILITY

Despite the strong case for social responsibility on the part of business, some critics don't support the concept wholeheartedly or oppose it entirely. The arguments against social responsibility include the following:

- *Business's lack of understanding:* The free-enterprise system is designed to allocate resources for the production of private goods and services. Preferences and desires for public goods and services, such as children's welfare programs and training for the hard-core unemployed, are not revealed through the marketplace. Therefore, business has no mechanism for discovering needs for social programs. Also, business success is measured by achieving tangible goals, such as attaining a certain market share or level of profitability. How would business measure the success of a social program? A firm doesn't reach profit goals in pollution control or affirmative action programs.
- *Increase of business power:* Without overall controls, guidelines, and success measures, a corporation's social actions can be arbitrary. A corporation may decide to make a grant to a museum or hire the disadvantaged solely on the basis of what management thinks is important. When managers make such decisions about social investments, they have no guidelines and are not accountable for their actions. Managers, in effect, are imposing taxes on the public by using stockholders', consumers', and employees' money for public purposes. In addition, by taking over activities traditionally in the domain of government or community agencies, business may become more powerful than it should be.
- *Dilution of responsibility to shareholders:* Theodore Levitt, a marketing philosopher, and Milton Friedman, a noted economist, argue that the social responsibility of business is to earn an adequate return for the stockholders. Levitt says that business should take care of the material aspects of welfare and that government should handle the general welfare. The business of business is earning

profits. Friedman says that the sole responsibility of business is to employ its resources in activities that yield profits, so long as business stays within the framework of the laws established by society. If profits are diluted too much by spending for social causes, stockholder returns will be too low to attract capital to the firm, ultimately leading to the company's downfall.

- *Creation of a disjointed effort:* Because business has no overall guidelines to follow in setting up social programs, companies will pursue whatever they think is important. The result will be a disjointed, unfocused, random pattern of programs. Only government can determine social priorities and then focus resources to achieve social goals.

## SOCIAL RESPONSIBILITY TODAY

Despite the arguments against social responsibility, most large corporations feel they should do more than simply earn a profit. Public opinion favors the practice of social responsibility by business. For years, however, managers have been struggling with the issue.

In the beginning it was argued, in the manner of Levitt and Friedman, that businesses' first and only responsibility was to make a profit for stockholders. It became apparent, however, that this pursuit of financial gain had to take place within the laws of society. Social legislation of the 1970s made this fact clear. The result was the creation of several government bodies—including the Environmental Protection Agency, the Equal Employment Opportunity Commission, the Occupational Safety and Health Administration, and the Consumer Product Safety Commission—that recognized the environment, employees, and consumers as *stakeholders* in business, who claim both legal and ethical rights to the corporation.[50] These corporate stakeholders include

Customers, clients, consumers (direct and indirect)
Debtors (financial institutions, bondholders)
Employees
Government (local, state, federal)
Managers
Organized labor
Owners (stockholders)
Public-at-large
Suppliers[51]

Business managers have had to learn how to balance their commitments to the corporation's owners with their obligations to this growing group of stakeholders.

Earning an adequate return is still considered a firm's main social responsibility. If the company receives enough "dollar votes" for its goods and services to meet profit objectives, the firm's output is meeting society's material needs. Today, however, a firm must also develop environmental controls, provide equal employment opportunities, create a safe workplace, produce safe products, and do much more.

**pyramid of corporate social responsibility**
Model that suggests corporate social responsibility is composed of economic, legal, ethical, and philanthropic responsibilities and that the firm's economic performance supports the entire structure.

One theorist suggests that total corporate social responsibility (or CSR) has four components: economic, legal, ethical, and philanthropic.[52] The **pyramid of corporate social responsibility,** shown in Exhibit 21.4, portrays economic performance as the foundation for the other three responsibilities. At the same time that it pursues profits (economic responsibility), however, business is expected to obey the law

Exhibit 21.4

Pyramid of Corporate Social Responsibility

Source: Adapted from Archie B. Carroll, "The Pyramid of Corporate Responsibility: Toward the Moral Management of Organizational Stakeholders," *Business Horizons*, July-August 1991, pp. 39–48.

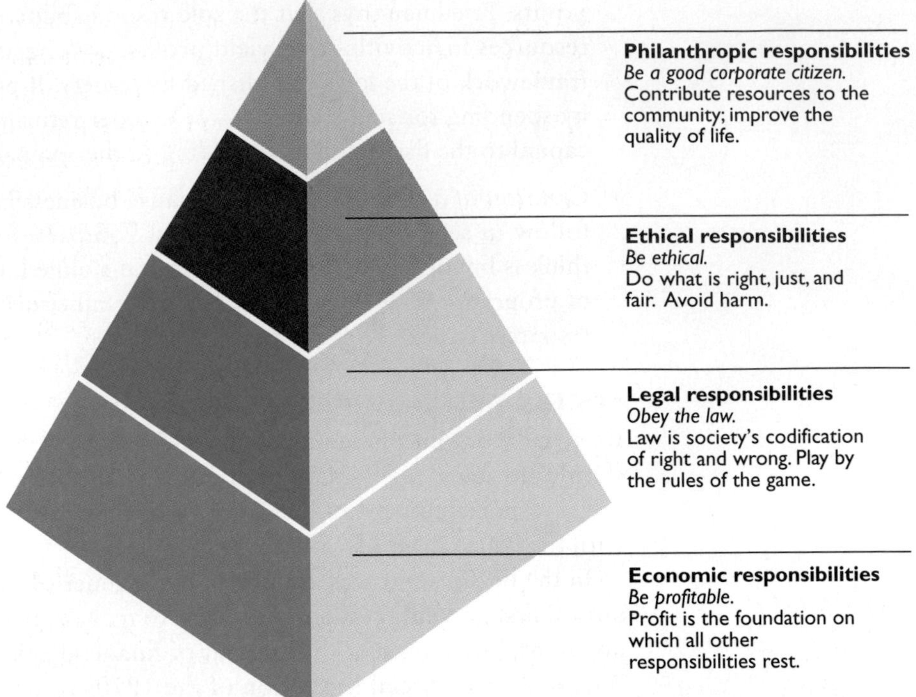


(legal responsibility); to do what is right, just, and fair (ethical responsibility); and to be a good corporate citizen (philanthropic responsibility). These four components are distinct but together constitute the whole. Still, if the company doesn't make a profit, then the other three responsibilities are moot.

A study by Mutual Benefit Life found that 91 percent of the CEOs interviewed believed their organizations are obligated to meet the community's needs rather than leave such support to government and the not-for-profit sector. Another survey asked MBA students and executives of the 1,000 largest U.S. companies whether business should undertake more social programs. An overwhelming majority of both today's and tomorrow's leaders believe that business must become more socially responsible.[53]

Many companies are already working to make the world a better place to live. Consider these examples:

- Metropolitan Life donates over $1 million a year and Levi Strauss over $500,000 to AIDS education and support services.[54]
- Ben & Jerry's, the premium ice cream maker, sent seven workers to live with Cree Indians in Canada to see how they've been displaced by a new hydroelectric power complex.[55]
- Jantzen, the world's leading swimsuit manufacturer, makes direct grants through its Clean Water campaign to organizations that preserve and clean up beaches and waterways.[56]
- Apple Computer donates about $8 million in computer equipment and advice to U.S. schools annually.
- G.D. Searle began a program in which its representatives regularly call hypertension (high blood pressure) patients, reminding them to take their medicine.[57]
- Ricoh, a Japanese office equipment maker, has developed a reverse copier that strips away the toner and allows the copy paper to be used again.[58]

Multinational companies also have important social responsibilities. In many cases a corporation can be a dynamic force for social change in host countries. For example, multinational corporations played a major role in breaking down apartheid (separation of the races) in South Africa, through their economic pressure on the South African government. Over 300 apartheid laws were compiled over the years, based purely on the pigmentation of people's skin. Among other things, these laws forced blacks to live in the most arid regions of South Africa, banned mixed marriages, and segregated the schools. To protest apartheid, many multinational corporations closed their South African operations altogether. Other companies refused to trade with South Africa. These actions seriously impeded South Africa's economy, and by the end of the 1980s the government began making major social reforms.[59] Once apartheid officially ended in the early 1990s, many of the companies that had participated in the boycott resumed their operations in South Africa.

6 *Explain the ways in which marketing meets its social responsibility.*

## THE MARKETING OF SOCIAL RESPONSIBILITY

Social responsibility programs require planning and organization. They also require the efforts of the entire corporation, not just of the marketing department. However, the discussion that follows pertains only to the marketing aspects of social responsibility.

The vehicle for marketing social responsibilities in most companies is the consumer affairs department. In the past this department only handled consumer complaints and distributed consumer education materials, mostly about company products. Examples include S Johnson and Sons' booklets on home decorating, gift making, and antique furniture and General Mills' Betty Crocker advisory service on cooking. Other consumer affairs departments take on broader social causes, as does Seagram's campaign against drunk driving. Modern consumer affairs departments monitor company advertisements, provide input for product design, research consumer satisfaction, develop warranties and guarantees, increase product safety, oversee product packaging and labeling, choose suppliers, and improve quality control.[60]

Almost all major U.S. corporations competing in consumer markets now have a formal unit that handles consumer affairs. The chief consumer affairs officer in many companies has a role in policy making and influences decisions about handling consumer inquiries, processing consumer complaints, developing consumer education programs, and researching consumer satisfaction.[61] During the remainder of the 1990s, consumer affairs departments will broaden their influence over marketing activities. Moreover, in more firms the top consumer affairs person will report directly to the CEO. Consumer affairs department budgets will grow to meet these new and expanding responsibilities.

7 *Discuss consumerism.*

## CONSUMERISM

**consumerism**
Political and economic struggle to increase the rights and powers of buyers in relation to sellers.

The concepts of social responsibility and consumerism go hand in hand. If every organization practiced a high level of social responsibility, the consumer movement might never have begun. **Consumerism** is a struggle for power between buyers and sellers. Specifically, it is a social movement seeking to increase the rights and powers of buyers in relation to sellers.

Sellers' rights and powers include the following:

- To introduce into the marketplace any product, in any size and style, that is not hazardous to personal health or safety, or if it is hazardous, to introduce it with the proper warnings and controls
- To price the product at any level they wish, provided they do not discriminate among similar classes of buyers
- To spend any amount of money they wish to promote the product, so long as the promotion is not defined as unfair competition
- To formulate any message they wish about the product, provided that it is not misleading or dishonest in content or execution
- To introduce any buying incentives they wish

In contrast, these are buyers' rights and powers:

- To refuse to buy any product that is offered to them
- To expect the product to be safe
- To expect the product to be essentially as the seller represents it
- To receive adequate information about the product

## THE HISTORY OF CONSUMERISM

Contrary to popular opinion, consumerism is not new. The roots of this social movement can be traced to the nineteenth century. The first consumer protection law, passed in 1872, made it a federal crime to defraud consumers through the mail.

Perhaps the first general consumer outcry was heard in 1906, with the publication of Upton Sinclair's *The Jungle*. The book was a devastating exposé of the U.S. meat-packing industry. The following excerpt from *The Jungle* describes some of the horrors:

> These rats were nuisances, and the packers would put poisoned bread out for them and they would die, and then rats, bread and meat would go into the hoppers together . . . . Men, who worked in the tank rooms full of steam . . . fell into the vats; and when they were fished out, there was never enough of them to be worth exhibiting—sometimes they would be overlooked for days, till all but the bones of them had gone out to the world as Durham's Pure Leaf Lard![62]

Sinclair's book helped ensure passage of the Pure Food and Drug Act of 1906 (see Chapter 2).

Throughout the late 1960s and mid-1970s, consumerism became quite influential. Inspired by the crusades of Ralph Nader and others, consumerism peaked during this period. It was less influential in the 1980s and early 1990s. Several factors account for the decline in consumer activism:

- Today's consumers seem more satisfied with the goods and services being placed on the market. A Gallup poll found that nearly half the respondents feel U.S. products are very high in quality, and two-thirds believe U.S. products better suit their needs than foreign-made goods.[63]
- The growing sense of social responsibility in U.S. business has heightened managers' awareness of consumer issues.[64] As a result, managers have been able to foresee and prevent problems that anger consumers.
- Demographics is also a factor. The social unrest of the 1960s was a response partly to the U.S. role in the Vietnam conflict and partly to big increases in the proportion of 18- to 20-year-olds in the U.S. population. Rapid increases in the numbers of this specific age segment were enough to cause social and economic

disharmony. Compared to previous generations, this group was more resistant to government, authority figures, and the accepted culture.[65] Today's far smaller group of 18- to 20-year-olds suggests to some demographers that interest in the consumer movement will remain unchanged for some time.

This plateau in consumerism does not suggest that consumer abuse no longer exists. For instance, some companies use sham marketing research studies for fund-raising and "sugging"—selling under the guise of research. High-pressure selling and outright fraud are still used in marketing condos, lake lots, and other things. Prospective buyers are promised wonderful gifts if they will visit the site in person. Unfortunately, a "personal computer" can turn out to be a hand-held calculator; a "car phone" may actually be a toy phone shaped like a car.

## BUSINESS RESPONSE TO CONSUMERISM

Only a few firms have been guilty of consumer abuse. Billions of satisfactory exchanges occur every day. Some companies enjoy an excellent reputation. Exhibit 21.5 shows the most-admired U.S. corporations. To come up with the list, *Fortune* magazine asked more than 10,000 senior executives, outside directors, and financial analysts to rate the ten largest companies in their own industry on quality of management; quality of goods or services; innovativeness; long-term investment value; financial soundness; ability to attract, develop, and keep talented people; responsibility to the community and environment; and wise use of corporate assets.

Many companies are taking innovative measures to respond to consumer needs. Whirlpool spends over $500,000 a year operating a nationwide, toll-free complaint line. Pennsylvania Power and Light Company (PP&L) pioneered the utility-consumer conference. It now conducts regular meetings between PP&L departments and consumer panels.

Many consumer organizations have written codes of conduct for companies to follow. One set of guidelines comes from a coalition of environmentalists and other groups in the wake of the 1989 Alaskan oil spill, one of the worst oil spills in history. Referred to as the "Valdez Principles," after the Exxon tanker involved in the spill, this voluntary code of conduct (see Exhibit 21.6) guides companies toward

*Exhibit 21.5*

Most-Admired U.S. Corporations

Source: Adapted from Tricia Welsh, "Best and Worst Corporate Reputations," *Fortune*, 7 February 1994, pp. 58–66. 

| Rank | Previous year's rank | Company (and industry) |
|---|---|---|
| 1 | 2 | Rubbermaid (rubber and plastic products) |
| 2 | * | Home Depot (specialist retailers) |
| 3 (tie) | 5 | Coca-Cola (beverages) |
| 3 (tie) | * | Microsoft (computer and data services) |
| 5 | 4 | 3M (scientific and photo equipment) |
| 6 (tie) | * | Walt Disney (entertainment) |
| 6 (tie) | 18 | Motorola (electronics/electrical equipment) |
| 8 (tie) | 9 | J.P. Morgan (commercial banking) |
| 8 (tie) | 6 | Procter & Gamble (soaps, cosmetics) |
| 10 | 17 | United Parcel Service (trucking) |

*Exhibit 21.6*

Valdez Principles

Source: Adapted from Rajib N. Sanyal and João S. Neves, "The Valdez Principles: Implications for Corporate Social Responsibility," *Journal of Business Ethics*, December 1991, pp. 883–890. Reprinted by permission of Kluwer Academic Publishers.

**1. Protection of the biosphere**
We will minimize and strive to eliminate the release of any pollutant that may cause environmental damage to the air, water, or earth or its inhabitants. We will safeguard habitats in rivers, lakes, wetlands, coastal zones, and oceans and will minimize our contribution to the greenhouse effect, depletion of the ozone layer, acid rain, or smog.

**2. Sustainable use of natural resources**
We will make sustainable use of renewable natural resources, such as water, soils, and forests. We will conserve nonrenewable natural resources through efficient use and careful planning. We will protect wildlife habitat, open spaces, and wilderness while preserving biodiversity.

**3. Reduction and disposal of waste**
We will minimize the creation of waste, especially hazardous waste, and whenever possible recycle material. We will dispose of all waste through safe and responsible methods.

**4. Wise use of energy**
We will make every effort to use environmentally safe and sustainable energy sources to meet our needs. We will invest in improved energy efficiency and conservation in our operations. We will maximize the energy efficiency of products we produce and sell.

**5. Risk reduction**
We will minimize the environmental, health, and safety risks to our employees and the communities in which we operate by employing safe technologies and operating procedures and by being constantly prepared for emergencies.

**6. Marketing of safe products**
We will sell goods or services that minimize adverse environmental impacts and that are safe as consumers commonly use them. We will inform consumers of the environmental impacts of our goods and services.

**7. Damage compensation**
We will take responsibility for any harm we cause to the environment by making every effort to fully restore the environment and to compensate those persons who are adversely affected.

**8. Disclosure**
We will disclose to our employees and to the public incidents relating to our operations that cause environmental harm or pose health or safety hazards. We will disclose potential environmental, health, or safety hazards posed by our operations and will not take any action against employees who report any condition that creates a danger to the environment or poses a threat to health and safety standards.

**9. Environmental directors and managers**
We will commit management resources to implement the Valdez Principles, to monitor and report upon our implementation efforts, and to sustain a process to ensure that the Board of Directors and Chief Executive Officer are kept informed of and are fully responsible for all environmental matters. We will establish a Committee of the Board of Directors with responsibility for environmental affairs. At least one member of the Board of Directors will be a person qualified to represent environmental interests before the company.

**10. Assessment and annual audit**
We will conduct and make public an annual self-evaluation of our progress in implementing these Principles and in complying with all applicable laws and regulations throughout our worldwide operations. We will work toward the timely creation of independent environmental audit procedures, which we will complete annually and make available to the public.

Whirlpool Corporation, headquartered in Benton Harbor, Michigan, is a prime example of a company that is responsive to consumer needs.

Courtesy of Whirlpool Corporation

higher environmental standards. Companies are encouraged to sign the code and adhere to its principles.[66]

Perhaps the business world's attitude toward consumerism is best expressed by business leaders themselves:[67]

> Every decision involves giving up something to get something . . . . The real intelligent course involves being sure that you deliver the quality the customer expects, not sacrificing quality to increase earnings. And if you make that call correctly, you may make a little less today but you're likely to make more in the future. So I think when an individual's goals or a corporation's goals are very much out of line with society's goals, they're in trouble . . . . The fact is you can't be a large, successful corporation and be working against the public will; not for long.
>
> —Richard Hecker, chairman and CEO, DuPont

> The only way for a corporation to exist and capitalism to survive is to be part of the whole society. We depend upon a healthy environment to sell our products, to hire people, to have customers to sell to . . . . I really do think, particularly the large corporations, if they are going to survive as entities, the only way to do that is feel a responsibility to the communities that [they] operate in. Companies have to be concerned with the owners—the shareholders, the employees, and the customers. And the fourth is the communities [they] operate in, whether that's the country [they] operate in or a local community.
>
> —David T. Kearns, chairman and CEO, Xerox

> Corporations can be short-sighted and worry only about our mission, products, and competitive standing. But we do it at our peril. The day will come when corporations will discover the price we pay for our indifference. We must realize that by ignoring the needs of others, we are actually ignoring our own needs in the long run. We may need the goodwill of a neighborhood to enlarge a corner store. We may need well-funded institutions of higher learning to turn out the skilled technical employees we require. We may need adequate community health care to curb absenteeism in our plants. Or we may need fair tax treatment for an industry to be able to compete in the world economy. However small or large our enterprise, we cannot isolate our business from the society around us. Nor can we function without its goodwill.
>
> —Robert D. Haas, president and CEO, Levi Strauss

If companies across the country adopted the philosophy of these three executives, then consumerism might die for lack of issues. Such philosophies, universally adopted, would also go a long way toward making U.S. firms competitive in world markets.

## LOOKING BACK

In light of what you have learned in this chapter, think back now to the opening story on the marketing of handguns. You will probably agree that gunmakers should be more socially responsible in marketing their products. You may also agree that gunmakers should be more concerned with product safety instead of producing as many guns as possible for the least cost.

Although quite a few companies in the United States lack a sense of social responsibility, many others try hard to be socially responsible. For example, both Wal-Mart and McDonald's have programs to employ the disabled. Wal-Mart is also a good corporate citizen: In the 1992 Presidential election, the company was responsible for registering 150,000 voters.

## SUMMARY

1 **Explain the meaning of business ethics.** *Ethics* refers to moral principles governing the conduct of an individual or group. Judgment is often needed to determine what is ethical versus what is legal. Morals are rules or habits that people develop as a result of cultural values and norms. Morals can be considered the foundation of ethical behavior.

2 **Describe the nature of ethical decision making.** Business ethics may be viewed as a subset of the values of society as a whole. The ethical conduct of businesspeople is shaped by societal elements, including family, education, religion, social movements, and so on. As members of society, businesspeople are morally obligated to consider the ethical implications of their decisions.

Ethical decision making is approached in three basic ways. The first approach examines the consequences of decisions. The second approach relies on rules and laws to guide decision making. The third approach is based on a theory of moral development that places individuals or groups in one of three developmental stages: preconventional morality, conventional morality, or postconventional morality.

Consumers often perceive marketing activities as unethical and manipulative. Marketers may find themselves in situations in which the needs of the business and the needs of customers, suppliers, or society as a whole are at odds. Three major factors have been found to influence the ethical behavior of marketing professionals: the extent of ethical problems within an organization, top management's actions regarding ethics, and the individual's role within an organization.

Many companies develop a code of ethics to help their employees make ethical decisions. A code of ethics can help employees identify acceptable business practices, can be an effective internal control on behavior, can help employees avoid confusion when determining the ethicality of decisions, and can facilitate discussion about what is right and wrong.

3 **Discuss several current ethical dilemmas.** The major ethical dilemmas for marketing managers explored in this chapter include tobacco and alcohol promotion,

consumer privacy, and green marketing. Other issues that were not discussed in this chapter are marketing to young children, marketing that promotes sexual harassment, misleading advertising and product labels, and marketing to the disadvantaged.

4 **Analyze ethical issues related to global marketing.** Marketing managers selling their goods or services globally should also be aware of what is considered ethical behavior in other countries. For example, bribery is often a standard business practice in other countries, although it is considered illegal and unethical in the United States. Multinational marketers must also be careful not to exploit developing countries that have unsophisticated marketing and environmental regulations.

5 **Discuss corporate social responsibility.** Responsibility in business refers to a firm's concern for the way its decisions affect society. There are several arguments in support of social responsibility. First, many consumers feel business should take responsibility for the social costs of economic growth. A second argument contends that firms act in their own best interest when they help improve the environment within which they operate. Third, firms can avoid restrictive government regulation by responding willingly to societal concerns. Finally, some people argue that because firms have the resources to solve social problems, they are morally obligated to do so.

In contrast, there are critics who argue against corporate social responsibility. According to one argument, the free-enterprise system has no way to decide which social programs should have priority. A second argument contends that firms involved in social programs do not generate the profits needed to support the business's activities and earn a fair return for stockholders.

In spite of the arguments against corporate social responsibility, most businesspeople believe they should do more than pursue only profits. Although a company must consider its economic needs first, it must also operate within the law, do what is ethical and fair, and be a good corporate citizen.

KEY TERMS

*code of ethics 729*

*consumerism 743*

*conventional morality 727*

*corporate social responsibility 739*

*ethics 725*

*Foreign Corrupt Practices Act 738*

*green marketing 735*

*morals 726*

*postconventional morality 727*

*preconventional morality 727*

*pyramid of corporate social responsibility 741*

*social cost 739*

6 **Explain the ways in which marketing meets its social responsibility.** Marketers have met their social responsibilities by setting up consumer affairs departments to monitor company advertising, product design, consumer satisfaction, product safety, product packaging and labeling, supplier selection, and quality control. Consumer affairs departments also handle consumer inquiries, process consumer complaints, develop consumer education programs, and create warranties and guarantees.

7 **Discuss consumerism.** Consumerism is a social movement in which buyers struggle to increase their rights and power in relation to sellers. Originating during the late nineteenth century, consumerism in the United States became an active and influential movement in the 1960s and 1970s. The decline of consumer activism in the 1980s and early 1990s is believed to be the result of several factors. First, consumers appear to be more satisfied with the goods and services provided in today's marketplace. Second, marketers have become more sensitive to consumer concerns. Finally, social unrest has declined in general because of changing demographics and the end of the Vietnam conflict.

## Discussion and Writing Questions

1. Cite examples of preconventional, conventional, and postconventional moral conduct in marketing.

✍2. Write a paragraph discussing the ethical dilemma in the following situation and identifying possible solutions: An insurance agent forgets to get the required signature from one of her clients who is buying an automobile insurance policy. The client acknowledges the purchase by giving the agent a signed personal check for the full amount. To avoid embarrassment and inconvenience, the agent forges the client's signature on the insurance application and sends it to the insurance company for processing.

✍3. Write a paragraph discussing the ethical dilemma in the following situation and identifying possible solutions: A local fire alarm manufacturer relies on the door-to-door selling efforts of its sales staff. The company provides its sales force with a selling kit that includes newspaper clippings about fire victims, including photographs of badly burned children. The salespeople use the clippings to make people aware of the need for early fire detection.

4. Describe an ethical dilemma in contemporary marketing not covered in this chapter. How do you feel about the firm's solution?

5. What is green marketing? Why is it controversial?

✍6. You have been invited to debate the question of how much responsibility businesses should assume for the welfare of society and the environment. Draft notes of your position, and anticipate the response of your debating partner.

7. Why did the consumer movement fade in the 1980s and early 1990s?

8. In today's marketplace, many businesses seem to have become more responsive to consumers. Suggest possible reasons for this trend.

## Application for Small Business

Enviro Care is a "green" store owned by a California couple. The birth of their son on Earth Day 1990 gave them the idea to start a retail business selling organic clothing and other environmentally friendly items. Enviro Care had its first profit two years after it began operation.

Enviro Care is no different from more than 200 other environment-minded small businesses in the United States. Kevin Connelly, publisher of *Natural Connection,* a trade journal for small retailers of environmental products, has seen the owners of these businesses learn late that success requires more than a concern for ecology: "A lot of these people got into this on principle but had no business or retail background."

Many environmentally conscious entrepreneurs thought consumers would be eager to buy their products. They underestimated the challenge of fundamental business tasks, like marketing new products. Kevin formed the National Green Retailing Association to help entrepreneurs who own environment-friendly stores. The group has biannual meetings, focusing on consumer education and the business of retailing. It also provides the trade journal for the owners of environment-related businesses. Kevin hopes these efforts will help Earth-friendly retailers succeed in a tough market.[68]

### Questions

1. Do you think consumers would purchase a product just on the basis that it is environmentally friendly?

2. Would you frequent a store or purchase goods and services on the basis that they are environmentally friendly?

3. What other programs could the National Green Retailing Association offer that would appeal to ecologically friendly entrepreneurs?

4. What different challenges face a small "green" retailer, who has a concern for the environment but not a business background, that might not face other companies?

## CRITICAL THINKING CASE

### Hooters, Inc.

Everyone seems to be taking sides when it comes to Hooters. The many fans of the fast-growing restaurant chain like its affordable food and drink, served up by friendly waitresses in a cheery atmosphere. Typical Hooters outlets feature rustic pine floors and tables, spicy chicken wings, and beer by the pitcher. TV monitors run nonstop sports videos, and the background music is golden oldies from the 1960s.

Critics claim the chain's appeal is blatantly sexist, from its name (slang for breasts) to the showcasing of its waitresses, called "Hooter Girls" and dressed in skimpy, revealing uniforms. Critics accuse the chain of fostering a climate in which sexual harassment can thrive. "The name should be changed because of the derogatory references to human anatomy," says the leader of a Fairfax, Virginia, group founded to protest the opening of a Hooters outlet.

Big profits can still be made from sexism, even in the 1990s. From its birth in 1983 in Clearwater, Florida, Hooters has grown into a nationwide network of 68 casual eateries in sixteen states. It expects to reach 200 restaurants by the end of 1994. Systemwide sales, in company-owned units and outlets owned by fifteen franchisees, totaled $100 million in 1991. Typical Hooters restaurants serve an average of 500 customers a day, with waiting lines at lunch and dinner.

Hooters uses every opportunity to flaunt its naughty name. The chain annually sells about $5 million worth of Hooters T-shirts, hats, calendars, and other items. The controversial Hooter Girl uniform consists of running shoes, bright orange running shorts, and a cut-off T-shirt with the company's logo—an owl with two very large, saucer-shaped eyes—and the motto "More than a mouthful." (A company executive insists that the motto refers to Hooters' hamburgers.)

Company officials say the chain's approach to sex is no different from that of *Sports Illustrated* magazine, which publishes an annual "swimsuit" issue. The magazine's readers "aren't checking out those girls' SAT scores," says the company's marketing vice president, adding that Hooters "doesn't cross the line of what the majority of people think is acceptable." Patrons claim the Hooter Girl uniform is no different from what you might see on someone in the mall or at the park.

All the same, at a time when national concern over men's sexual behavior has reached fever pitch, the chain's "Boys will be boys" attitude outrages feminists. The executive vice president of the National Organization for Women says Hooters "contributes to an atmosphere of sexual harassment." She further contends that Hooters resembles a nightclub or strip joint more than a neighborhood cafe.

Protests focusing on Hooters' image have picked up as the chain has begun aggressive expansion beyond its Sunbelt base. In Fairfax, Virginia, a group that included the mayor and city council members collected 200 signatures on an anti-Hooters petition. In addition to requesting that the restaurant change its name, the group said employees should be allowed to wear uniforms "reflective of a basic family atmosphere." As it turned out, the outcry and attendant publicity helped attract a standing-room-only crowd to the restaurant's opening.

Recent trends in advertising seem to reveal a backlash against sensitivity regarding sexism. Hooters advertisements have blatantly promoted their sexist image. This "politically incorrect" approach appears to be working quite well, but the question remains: Can the restaurant survive and continue to grow without a change in the hostile environment?

#### Questions

1. Hooters seems to be doing quite well despite charges that it promotes sexual harassment. Why do you think this is so?
2. Do you feel Hooters should be more socially responsible in its marketing techniques? Why or why not?
3. If you were the marketing vice president of Hooters, how would you address criticism of your marketing approach?

#### References

Eugene Carlson, "Restaurant Chain Tries to Cater to Two Types of Taste," *The Wall Street Journal,* 20 March 1992, p. B2.

John P. Cortez and Ira Teinowitz, "More Trouble Brews for Stroh Bikini Team," *Advertising Age,* 9 December 1991, p. 45.

# CHAPTER 22

# STRATEGIC PLANNING, FORECASTING, AND CONTROL

## LEARNING OBJECTIVES

*After studying this chapter, you should be able to*

1 *Describe the concept of strategic planning.*

2 *Identify the steps in the strategic planning process, and explain how businesses define their mission and set objectives.*

3 *Explain how businesses form strategic business units.*

4 *Explain how businesses conduct situation analyses.*

5 *Discuss the techniques for developing, evaluating, and selecting strategic alternatives.*

6 *Explain how firms implement strategies and alter strategies when necessary.*

7 *Identify several techniques that help make strategic planning effective.*

8 *Describe seven sales forecasting techniques.*

9 *Discuss global issues in strategic planning and forecasting.*

10 *Describe the concepts of marketing control and the marketing audit.*

What is now the nation's number-one bookseller was born in 1971, when Barnes & Noble founder and CEO Leonard Riggio bought a single stagnant Manhattan store. Today it's a 937-store chain. Why? Credit two profound insights into what consumers really want and a readiness to make big bets on that understanding.

Insight 1: "Shopping is a form of entertainment," as Riggio phrases it. Consumers aren't corporate purchasing managers, singlemindedly seeking specific commodities at the best possible price. To consumers, shopping is a social activity. They do it to mingle with others in a prosperous-feeling crowd, to see what's new, to enjoy the theatrical dazzle of the display, to treat themselves to something interesting or unexpected.

Riggio learned to craft stores that provide this sort of shopping experience: a high-visibility, upscale, usually suburban location to draw the crowds where they live; enough woody, traditional, soft-colored library atmosphere to please the book lovers; enough sophisticated modern architecture and graphics, sweeping vistas, and stylish displays to satisfy fans of the theater of consumption.

Customers at Barnes & Noble superstores settle at the many heavy chairs and tables to browse through piles of books; they fill the cafes that Riggio put into the superstores to increase the festivity; they hang out in their chosen sections to pick up like-minded lovers of sports and fitness, high-toned fiction, New Age emoting, or gay and lesbian studies. Consumers attend the readings and signings; they bring their kids to the puppet shows and story hours; they read the accolades for Barnes & Noble bookstores in newspapers and lifestyle magazines and are captivated.

Insight 2: Books are consumer products. "People have the mistaken notion that the thing you do with books is read them," Riggio says. "They think all a book is about is information." In truth, maybe 5 percent of what gets printed gets read, and those who read most are also the biggest accumulators of unread volumes. People buy books for what the purchase says about them—their taste, their cultivation, their trendiness. Their aim, says Riggio, is to connect themselves, or those to whom they give books as gifts, with all the other refined owners of Edgar Allan Poe collections or sensitive owners of Virginia Woolf collections.

The consequence is that, if you try, you can sell books as consumer products, with seductive displays, flashy posters, and an emphasis on the glamour of the book as an object and the fashionableness of the best-seller and the trendy author. Riggio has found he can even wrap his customers in the glamour, by sending them out with shopping bags sporting his trademark high-style sketches of famous authors. "It's amazing," says Riggio, "how people almost *wear* the bag that they take from the store."

Before developing the superstore formula, Barnes & Noble grew by spurts of innovative retailing. It was the first bookseller to discount and to stay open on Sundays, for example. But with the superstore formula, the company has hit on a model for future internal growth, with economics as investor-friendly as the stores are consumer-friendly. By 1994 Barnes & Noble had 280 superstores, up from 23 in 1989.[1]

The success of Barnes & Noble has been the result of good strategic planning. What is the role of strategic planning in an organization? What is the key factor in making strategic planning work? Where do forecasting and control fit into strategic planning?

From "Looking into the Customer's Soul" in Myron Magnet, "Let's Go for Growth," *Fortune*, 7 March 1994. 

1 *Describe the concept of strategic planning.*

## THE NATURE OF STRATEGIC PLANNING

Effective decision making is based on sound planning, which is one of marketing managers' three main functions (organizing and controlling marketing activities being the other two). Specifically, marketing managers must develop both long-range (strategic) and short-range (tactical) plans. Next, they and other managers must organize the firm's resources to carry out the plans effectively and efficiently. Finally, marketing managers create a monitoring system to correct deviations from the plans or change the plans if necessary.

**strategic planning**
Managerial process of creating and maintaining a fit between the organization's objectives and resources and evolving market opportunities.

**Strategic planning** is the managerial process of creating and maintaining a fit between the organization's objectives and resources and the evolving market opportunities. The goal of strategic planning is long-run profitability and growth. Thus strategic decisions require long-term commitments of resources.

A strategic error can threaten the firm's survival. On the other hand, a good strategic plan can help protect a firm's resources against competitive onslaughts.[2] For instance, if the March of Dimes had decided to focus on fighting polio, the organization would no longer exist. Most of us view polio as a conquered disease. The March of Dimes survived by making the strategic decision to switch to fighting birth defects.

Strategic marketing management addresses two questions: What is the organization's main activity at a particular time? And how will it reach its goals? Here are some examples of strategic decisions:

- Black & Decker's decision to buy General Electric's small consumer appliance division (a strategic success)
- Sears and IBM's joint effort to create the Prodigy on-line computer service (a billion-dollar investment; outcome unknown, but results are positive to date)
- McDonnell Douglas's decision to build the MD-11 passenger aircraft (moderate success)
- Procter & Gamble's decision to move to everyday low pricing (implemented in 1992; moderate success)
- Delta Airlines' decision to acquire most of PanAm's European routes (outcome unknown, but Delta suffered huge losses and was still struggling in late 1994)
- Sara Lee's decision to diversify out of food and to build powerful brand names in clothing (very successful acquisitions of the rights to market Hanes and Bali underwear, Coach leather goods, and Donna Karan hosiery)

All these decisions have affected or will affect each organization's long-run course, its allocation of resources, and ultimately its financial success. In contrast, an operating decision, such as changing the package design for Post's cornflakes or altering the sweetness of a Seven Seas salad dressing, probably won't have a big impact on the long-run profitability of the company.

2 *Identify the steps in the strategic planning process, and explain how businesses define their mission and set objectives.*

## THE STRATEGIC PLANNING PROCESS

The strategic planning process has eight phases: (1) defining the business mission, (2) setting the objectives, (3) establishing strategic business units (when necessary), (4) conducting a situation analysis, (5) developing strategic alternatives, (6) selecting an alternative, (7) implementing the selected strategy, and (8) altering the selected strategy when necessary (see Exhibit 22.1). Let's look at each of these phases.

*Exhibit 22.1*

Strategic Planning Process

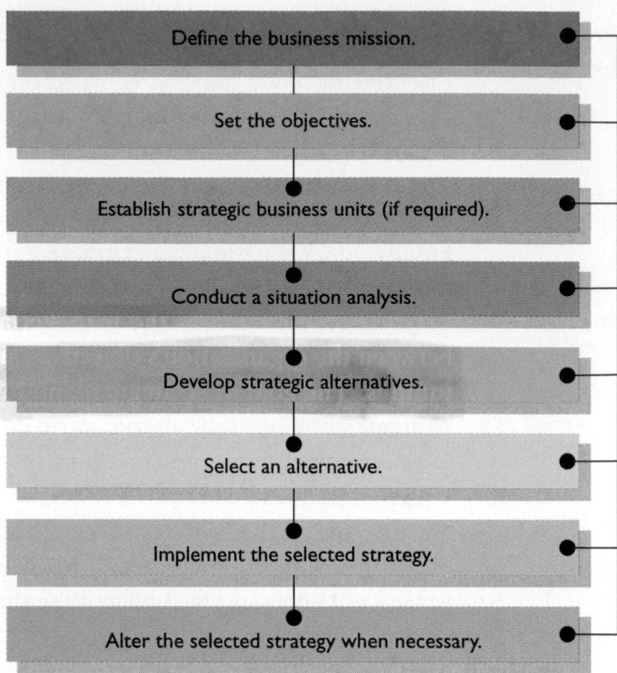


## DEFINE THE BUSINESS MISSION

Perhaps the single most important aspect of strategic planning is answering the question "What business are we in and where are we going?" The answer is the firm's mission statement. The way the firm defines its mission profoundly affects long-run resource allocation, profitability, and survival. A survey of 463 large organizations found that of twenty-five commonly used management tools, the three most popular and effective are mission statements (94 percent), customer surveys (90 percent), and total quality management, TQM (76 percent).[3] (TQM was discussed in Chapter 8.)

As mentioned briefly in Chapter 1, a mission statement should focus on the market or markets the organization is trying to serve rather than on the good or service offered. Otherwise, a new technology may quickly make the good or service obsolete and the mission statement irrelevant to the company's functions. For example:

- If Frito-Lay had decided that it was in the corn chip business, it would not be an industry leader today. Frito-Lay defines its mission as being in the snack food business.
- Anheuser-Busch says, "Beer is and always will be our core business. However, other business complementary to beer will be developed over the long term in order to maintain Anheuser-Busch as a growth company."[4]
- The mission of Saturn Corporation, a subsidiary of General Motors, is "to design, manufacture, and market vehicles to compete on a global scale, as well as re-establish American technology as the standard for automotive quality."[5] Saturn sees its market as small-car consumers who have been committed to the imports.

## SET THE OBJECTIVES

After management agrees on a mission statement, it must set objectives. Good objectives are realistic, measurable, time-specific, and consistent, and they indicate the priorities of the organization. Exhibit 22.2 shows some well-stated and poorly stated objectives. Notice how well they do or do not meet the following criteria:

*Exhibit 22.2*

Examples of Marketing Objectives

| Well-Stated Objectives | Poorly Stated Objectives |
|---|---|
| Our objective is to increase market share from 30 percent to 40 percent in 1997 by increasing promotional expenditures 11 percent. | Our objective is to be a leader in the industry in terms of new product development. |
| Our objective is to spend 12 percent of sales revenue between 1996 and 1997 on research and development in an effort to introduce at least five new products by 1998. | Our objective is to maximize profits. |
| Our objective is to achieve a 12 percent return on investment with a payback on new investments of no longer than four years. | Our objective is to be the best that we can be. |
| | Our objective is to better serve the customers. |

- Objectives must be *realistic*. Unrealistic objectives give no direction and are soon rejected by both management and labor. For example, an organization with limited resources and strong competitors that says its objective is achieving 90 percent market share in six months would simply be fantasizing.
- Objectives must be *measurable* in order to determine if progress is being made. To say "We want to be the best that we can be" or "We want to maximize profits" is little more than mouthing platitudes. Such statements give management a license to do whatever it wants. The reply to any difficult question about management's decisions and actions could simply be, "Oh, we're trying to maximize profits!"
- Objectives must be constrained by a specific *time* period, which tells managers how long they have to meet their goals.
- Company objectives need to be *consistent*. It is not possible to "maximize both sales and profits" or "achieve the greatest sales at the least cost" or "design the best product in the shortest possible time." These objectives are in a tradeoff relationship, meaning that pursuing one complicates, or even prevents, pursuit of the other. Here are some important tradeoffs: high profit margins versus high market share; deep penetration of existing markets versus development of new markets; profit goals versus nonprofit goals; high growth versus high stability.
- Objectives should be *prioritized* so managers and workers will know what needs to be done first.

Good objectives serve several functions:

- Provide direction for lower-echelon marketing managers
- Motivate employees and create something to strive for
- Form a basis for control, a way to measure the effectiveness of a plan
- Telegraph marketing philosophy, provide clues to the thinking of top management and to organizational philosophy, and help create a singleness of purpose

**strategic business unit (SBU)**
Subgroup in a larger organization, with a distinct mission and specific target market of its own, control over its resources, its own competitors, and plans independent of the other subgroups of the total organization.

*3 Explain how businesses form strategic business units.*

## ESTABLISH STRATEGIC BUSINESS UNITS

After defining its mission and setting objectives, the organization may need to set up a **strategic business unit** (SBU), which is a subgroup within the larger organization. When properly created, an SBU has the following characteristics:

A distinct mission and a specific target market

Kraft General Foods is a giant corporation with many strategic business units. One SBU markets desserts, including Jell-O.



- Control over its resources
- Its own competitors
- A single business or a collection of related businesses
- Plans independent of the other SBUs of the total organization

In theory, an SBU should have its own resources for handling basic business functions: accounting, engineering, manufacturing, and marketing. In practice, however, because of company tradition, management philosophy, and production and distribution economies, SBUs sometimes share manufacturing facilities, distribution channels, and even top managers.

SBUs often develop as the company grows. At first, many small firms have few products and serve only one or two target markets. As time goes on, however, they may diversify by offering different types of products. In addition, they may begin to serve different distribution channels and target markets or even enter the international market. For instance, PPG Industries, formerly Pittsburgh Plate Glass, evolved from a small plate-glass manufacturer to a $7.5 billion organization. PPG now has a number of SBUs offering products ranging from chemicals to precision instruments.

There is no "right" number of SBUs for a firm to have. The number depends on management's willingness to delegate authority, the resources available, and the ability to identify natural and logical business units. Kraft General Foods' SBUs already include breakfast foods, desserts, pet foods, and beverages. The firm's ground-breaking work in biotechnology may lead to a new generation of intravenous fluids for critically ill patients—and yet another SBU.

4 *Explain how businesses conduct situation analyses.*

## CONDUCT A SITUATION ANALYSIS

After defining a mission and establishing any required SBUs, the next step in the strategic planning process is conducting a situation analysis. Among the tools available for analyzing an organization's situation are SWOT, strategic windows, and differential advantage.

### SWOT

**SWOT analysis**
Analysis of a firm's strengths, weaknesses, opportunities, and threats.

A situation analysis is sometimes referred to by the acronym SWOT, meaning that the firm should identify its internal strengths (S) and weaknesses (W) and examine external opportunities (O) and threats (T). In essence, a **SWOT analysis** allows the company to determine its present status, its current capabilities, and its future expectations. A SWOT analysis prompted dog-food maker Alpo to get into the cat food business.

General Mills conducted a SWOT analysis and learned that large-volume cereal brands are more efficient to manufacture and promote—and thus more profitable. For cold cereals, a large volume is considered to be only 1 percent of the U.S. cold cereal market.[6] One of General Mills' strengths is its old, well-known cereal brands, such as Wheaties, Cheerios, and Kix. Management made a strategic decision to maintain the market share of its successful older cereal brands and to increase the market share of the remaining older brands. Top management set this goal for General Mills brand managers: Improve a third of the existing products every year with significant changes in taste, texture, nutrition, or packaging. By 1994, the company had twelve brands that each had at least a 1 percent share of the market, up from seven brands in 1986.

## STRATEGIC WINDOWS

**strategic window**
Limited time during which the fit between the key requirements of a market and the firm's competencies are at an optimum.

Another technique for examining opportunities is to seek strategic windows. A **strategic window** is a limited time during which the "fit" between the key requirements of a market and the firm's competencies are at an optimum. For instance, the air freight business was a slow-growth industry for many years. FedEx saw a strategic window for regularly planned shipments of high-value, low-weight merchandise. The rest is history.

During the past decade, General Mills management noted that the U.S. food industry was growing at only 1 percent a year. For the company to grow faster than 1 percent a year, it had to take market share from competitors. General Mills management also realized that a strategic window was open in the restaurant business. The popularity of both Mexican and Italian food was mushrooming. General Mills management realized that a strategic opportunity existed for popularly priced, sit-down Italian and seafood restaurants. After extensive marketing research, General Mills created the Red Lobster, Olive Garden, and China Coast restaurant chains. Red Lobster and Olive Garden have made a major contribution to General Mills' profits. China Coast is still too new to have made a significant impact.

## DIFFERENTIAL ADVANTAGE

An excellent way to examine opportunities is to seek a differential advantage over the competition. As Chapter 15 explained, a differential advantage is one or more unique aspects of an organization that give it an edge over competitors. Without a differential advantage, target customers don't perceive any reason to patronize one organization instead of another.

A differential advantage can exist solely in the firm's image; for example, frequent flyers perceive American Airlines as "the best" full-service airline. A differential advantage can also exist in any element of the marketing mix. Bang and Olufsen's differential advantage is its ability to produce ultrahigh-quality stereo systems. Kraft General Foods' differential advantage lies in its distribution system; it can reach virtually all U.S. supermarkets and fast-food stores and command adequate shelf space. Promotion and price can also provide a differential advantage.

There are two basic sources of differential advantage:

- *Superior skills:* Managers' and workers' unique capabilities may distinguish them from the personnel of competing firms. For example, in the production of titanium dioxide, DuPont has an exceptional competitive advantage based on superior skills. Its technicians created a production process using low-cost feedstock, giving DuPont a 20 percent cost advantage over competitors. The cheaper feedstock technology is complex and can only be accomplished by investing about $100 million and several years of testing time. Another example of superior skills is the Biltmore Resort in Phoenix, which has consistently won Mobil's coveted five-star rating. There are fewer than twenty five-star

Cost-saving manufacturing processes, as at this paper mill, are one source of differential advantage. Competitors with higher manufacturing costs have a disadvantage in the marketplace.



hotel/resorts in the United States. The Biltmore management has the skills needed to maintain a commendable level of service.

- *Superior resources:* Superior resources are a more tangible form of differential advantage. Examples include the scale of a manufacturing facility, a location,

Superior quality is undeniably a differential advantage. Some consumers are willing to pay more if they believe they are getting a better product.

a distribution system, the availability of computer-aided design and manufacturing, or a family brand name. Coke is a brand name of immeasurable value. Foremost-McKesson, the huge wholesaler to drugstores and hospitals, found that its competitive advantage stemmed from customer knowledge and a superior information system.

Differential advantage enables a firm to deliver superior customer value, attain lower relative costs, or both. Chapparal Steel, for example, is the leading low-cost U.S. steel producer because it uses only scrap iron and steel and uses a very efficient continuous-casting process to make new steel. In fact, Chapparal is so efficient that it is the only U.S. steel producer that ships to Japan. Similarly, Fort Howard Paper's differential advantage lies in its cost-saving manufacturing process. Fort Howard uses only recycled pulp, rather than the more expensive virgin pulp, to make toilet paper and other products. The quality, however, is acceptable only to the commercial market, such as office buildings, hotels, and restaurants. Therefore, the company does not try to sell to the home market through grocery stores.

Superior customer value is a function of superior quality. For instance, the French cruise line Pakquey has a reputation for offering impeccable service. The brand name BMW signifies quality to many car buyers. Salomon has gained a dominant position in the ski bindings market with a stream of innovations. Because superior quality sells products, many companies are adopting TQM programs as a source of differential advantage, as the Creating Customer Value box illustrates.

5 *Discuss the techniques for developing, evaluating, and selecting strategic alternatives.*

## DEVELOP STRATEGIC ALTERNATIVES

To discover a marketing opportunity, strategic window, or potential differential advantage, management must know how to identify the alternatives. One method for developing alternatives is the strategic opportunity matrix (see Exhibit 22.3), which matches products with markets. Firms can explore these four options:

**market penetration**
Marketing strategy that increases market share among existing customers.

**market development**
Marketing strategy that attracts new customers to existing products.

**diversification**
Marketing strategy that increases sales by introducing new products into new markets.

- *Market penetration:* A firm using the **market penetration** alternative would try to increase market share among existing customers. If Kraft General Foods started a major campaign for Maxwell House coffee, with aggressive advertising and cents-off coupons to existing customers, it would be following a penetration strategy. Customer databases, discussed in Chapter 7, help managers implement this strategy.
- *Market development:* **Market development** means attracting new customers to existing products. Ideally, new uses for old products stimulate additional sales

Exhibit 22.3

Strategic Opportunity Matrix

| | Present product | New product |
|---|---|---|
| **Present market** | **Market penetration:** Kraft General Foods creates a major promotion campaign with an increased budget for Maxwell House coffee. | **Product development:** ConAgra creates Healthy Choice frozen dinners. |
| **New market** | **Market development:** McDonald's opens restaurants in Moscow. | **Diversification:** LTV develops the monorail for the Dallas–Fort Worth airport. |

CREATING CUSTOMER VALUE

**Graniterock**

Graniterock is a Baldrige Award winner in the small business category. Based in Watsonville, California, just south of San Francisco, Graniterock produces rock, sand, and gravel aggregates, ready-mix concrete, asphalt, and road treatment. It also has a highway-paving operation. In addition, the company sells a wide range of building materials—such as brick, concrete block, wallboard, and decorative stone—that are manufactured by outside suppliers.

The industry in which Graniterock competes is fiercely competitive, and most competitors are now large, publicly traded firms. Traditionally, the industry has been a commodity business, with most customers buying from the lowest bidder.

In this difficult environment, Graniterock has significantly increased market share. Its productivity has steadily increased, and revenue per employee has risen to about 30 percent above the national industry average. Turnover and absenteeism have steadily decreased. Because of the company's extensive attention to safety, Graniterock's worker's compensation rates have declined to less than half the industry average. Costs of resolving customer complaints are 0.2 percent of sales, a tenth the industry average. And Graniterock has nearly a 10-point lead over the customer satisfaction level of its best competitor.

Graniterock's evolution to its current level of performance is typical of many firms. For the first few years after starting its total quality program in 1985, progress was slow and uneven. However, quality improvement gained momentum when Graniterock adopted the Baldrige Award criteria as a process template, which several other recent Baldrige Award winners also have done.

The comprehensive approach to quality is illustrated by Graniterock's nine corporate objectives, which drive the long-term planning process:

*Customer Satisfaction and Service.* To earn the respect of our customers by providing them in a timely manner with the products and services that meet their needs and solve their problems.

*People.* To provide an environment in which each person in the organization gains a sense of satisfaction and accomplishment from personal achievements, to recognize individual and team accomplishments, and to reward individuals based upon their contributions and job performance.

*Product Quality Assurance.* To provide products which provide lasting value to our customers and conform to state, federal, or local government specifications.

*Profit.* To provide a profit to fund growth and to provide resources needed to fund achievement of our other objectives.

*Management.* To foster initiative, creativity, and commitment by allowing the individual greater freedom of action (in deciding how to do a job in attaining well-defined objectives).

among existing customers while also bringing in new buyers. McDonald's, for example, has opened restaurants in Russia, China, and Italy and is eagerly expanding into Eastern European countries. In the nonprofit area, the growing emphasis on continuing education and executive development by colleges and universities is a market development strategy.

- *Product development:* A product development strategy entails the creation of new products for present markets. The "eating healthy" trend of the early 1990s led ConAgra—maker of Banquet, Morton, Patio, and Chun King frozen dinners—to develop Healthy Choice frozen dinners, which are low in fat, cholesterol, and sodium. Responding to the same trend, Kraft General Foods introduced no-cholesterol mayonnaise, and General Mills and Kellogg brought out high-fiber, low-fat, and low-sodium cereals. Managers following this strategy can rely on their extensive knowledge of the target audience. They usually have a good feel for what customers like and dislike about current products and what existing needs are not being met. In addition, managers can rely on the established distribution channels.
- *Diversification:* **Diversification** is a strategy of increasing sales by introducing new products into new markets. For example, LTV Corporation, a steel producer, diversified into the monorail business. Sony practiced a diversification strategy when it acquired Columbia Pictures; although motion pictures are not a new product in the marketplace, they were a new product for Sony. Coca-Cola manufactures and markets

CREATING CUSTOMER VALUE

*Community Commitment.* To be good citizens in each of the communities in which we operate.

*Financial Performance and Growth.* Our growth is limited only by our profits and the ability of Graniterock people to creatively develop and implement business growth strategies.

*Production Efficiency.* To produce and deliver our products at the lowest possible cost consistent with the other objectives.

*Safety.* To operate all Graniterock facilities with safety as the primary goal. Meeting schedules or production volume is secondary.

Since 1985, Graniterock has traced its improvement in achieving these nine objectives with a large chart called the Quality by Design Timeline. The chart also includes projections for several years into the future. The intent of the chart is to graphically link long-term planning, annual planning, and the contribution of each employee.

In keeping with the thrust of the Baldrige Award, Graniterock makes customer satisfaction a key element of its operations. It measures satisfaction levels of both its immediate customers (the contractors) and the end users of its products. To deliver high customer satisfaction levels, Graniterock has developed partnering relationships with contractors and supports the contractors with a variety of services. For example, a customer who is dissatisfied with any product is asked to short-pay the monthly invoice. The customer deducts from the bill an amount that compensates, at the customer's discretion, for whatever the problem may have been. This technique quickly identifies problems so they can be corrected. It also indicates to the customer that Graniterock is confident of delivering high-quality goods and services. As mentioned earlier, the annual cost of this short-pay system is only 0.2 percent of sales.

Graniterock also regularly compares its customer satisfaction levels to those of its direct competitors. Competitive assessments indicate that Graniterock maintains superior performance on virtually all of the thirteen attributes measured. The differences between Graniterock and its competitors are particularly evident for the most important attributes, to which Graniterock devoted its initial attention and efforts.

The construction industry has not generally adopted total quality management. Graniterock could find no other firms in its industry applying statistical process control to reduce defects and no other cement firms tracking on-time delivery. Graniterock has clearly demonstrated, however, that quality-improvement concepts can be very successfully applied in its highly variable, project-oriented business. It has also demonstrated that the early adoption and use of quality concepts provides a significant differential advantage.[7]

Selling granite is a simple business. Do you think Graniterock is overplanning? Why or why not? In commodity businesses—such as concrete, rock, and sand—sales usually go to the low-cost producer. Do you think Graniterock's emphasis on quality will price it out of the market? Defend your answer.

water-treatment and water-conditioning equipment, which has been a very challenging task for the traditional soft-drink company. A diversification strategy can be quite risky when a firm is entering unfamiliar markets. On the other hand, it can be very profitable when a firm is entering markets with little or no competition.

### SELECT AN ALTERNATIVE

The next step in developing a marketing strategy is to select one or more of the options. A corporation's philosophy and culture affect that selection. The choice also depends on the tool used to make the decision.

### Market Share versus Profit

Companies generally have one of two philosophies about when they expect profits. They either pursue profits right away or first seek to increase market share and then pursue profits. In the long run, market share and profitability are compatible goals.

A study of the relationship between market share and profitability reported these findings: A brand with the number-one market share had an average return on investment of 31 percent; the number-two brand, 21 percent; the number-three brand, 16 percent. Brands with the fourth-largest market share or less had a return on investment of 12 percent or less.[8] This far-reaching study found that the pattern was consistent in both the United States and Europe. It included service firms as well as manufacturers of industrial products, consumer durables, and consumer nondurable goods. Note, however, that these statistics are averages. In any specific situation, the relationship between market share and profits may not hold.

Moreover, another study suggests that the effect of market share on profitability depends on the dollar value of the market share.[9] That is, having the dominant market share in a $10 million market is not the same as being the number-one firm in a $1 billion market. Apparently, market share is more likely to determine profitability at certain levels.

Many companies have long followed this credo: Build market share, and profits will surely follow. Michelin, the tire producer, consistently sacrifices short-term profits to achieve market share. But attitudes may be changing. Lou Gerstner, CEO of IBM, has stressed profitability over market share, quality, and customer service since taking over in 1993.[10]

## The Role of Corporate Culture

Corporate culture also plays an important role in the choice of a strategic alternative. Corporate culture is the pattern of basic assumptions an organization has accepted to cope with the firm's internal environment and the changing external environment. If these assumptions have worked fairly well, management will tend to consider them valid. Therefore, new members of the organization should also consider them the correct way to perceive, think, and feel about the firm's internal and external environments.

Internally, corporate culture is concerned with such issues as worker loyalty, centralization or decentralization of decision making, promotion criteria, and problem-solving techniques. Corporate culture regarding the external environment is revealed by the way the firm reacts to problems and opportunities. Organizational response to the external environment can be categorized into four types:

- *Prospector:* focuses on identifying and capitalizing on emerging market opportunities, thus emphasizing research and communication with the market. Because of its strong external orientation, the prospector tends to build and maintain an excellent information system and product development program. A prospector prefers strategic alternatives that tap new markets or that devel-

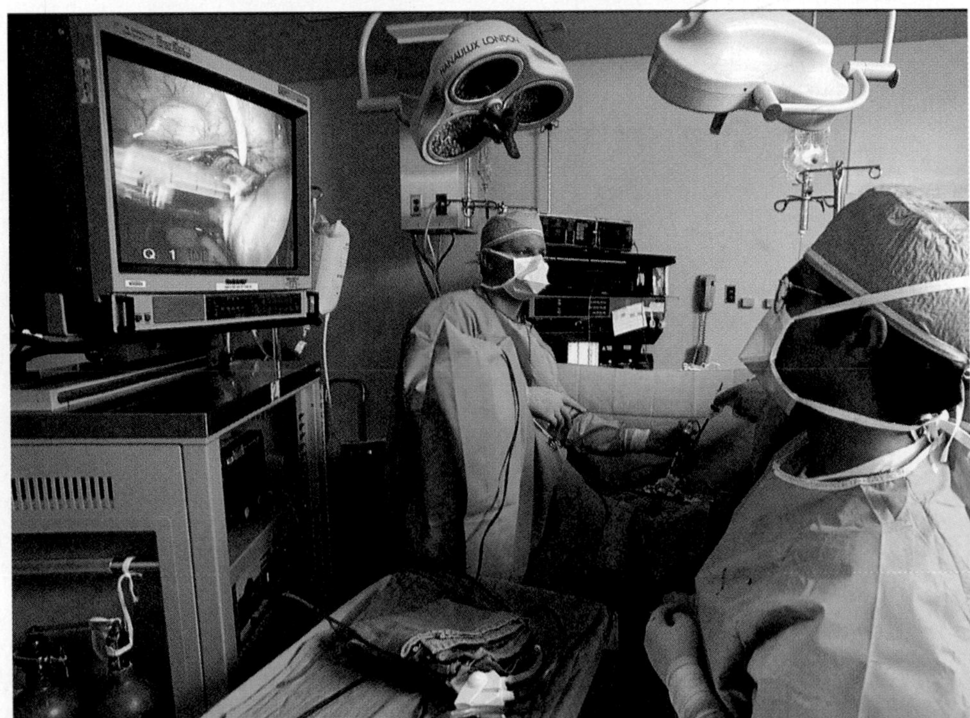

The corporate culture of a "prospector" emphasizes research and product development based on the market's needs. U.S. Surgical, a prospector, sells laparoscopes for precise, minimally invasive surgery, which allows patients to heal quickly and keeps costs under control.

op new goods and services. Both Ralston Purina and Philip Morris have a prospector culture. They are both leaders in bringing new consumer goods to market. U.S. Surgical is also a prospector. The fastest-selling surgical instruments today are those that use laparoscopes to do procedures through tiny incisions. U.S. Surgical has almost an 85 percent market share of the $3 billion laparoscopic instrument market.[11] About half of U.S. Surgical's sales come from instruments introduced within the past five years.

- *Reactor:* the opposite of the prospector. Instead of looking for opportunities, it responds to environmental pressures when forced to do so. The reactor is a follower, not a leader, and lacks a strategic focus. Emphasis is on maintaining the status quo despite environmental change. A reactor will avoid any strategic alternative that takes it out of its niche or that calls for bold, risk-taking action. Reactors include Woolworth's, Wrigley's, and Revco Drug. American Motors before its demise and AT&T before deregulation were also reactors.
- *Defender:* has a specific market domain and does not search outside that domain for new opportunities. Instead, it tries to "defend its turf." A defender looks favorably on any strategic alternative that helps reduce operating costs. The risk, however, is that market changes might go unnoticed. Even if the defender detects such changes, it typically is unable to adjust its business practices in response. American Home Products, a defender, has probably undermined its future. Its corporate culture has emphasized strict cost controls for years. Until recently, managers had to get central management's approval for any expenditure over $500. New product development suffered as a result.
- *Analyzer:* tends to be both conservative and aggressive. It usually operates in at least one stable market and tries to defend its position in that market. An analyzer also tries to identify emerging opportunities in other markets. Unlike the prospector, the analyzer is not an aggressive risk taker. Usually "second in" to new product markets, the analyzer does have the advantage of observing and learning from other firms' new-product problems. Delta Airlines, Bethlehem Steel, Aetna Insurance, and Alberto-Culver can be categorized as analyzers.

In summary, the same strategic alternative may be viewed entirely differently by firms with different corporate cultures. A highly desirable alternative for one organization may be completely unattractive to another firm.

## Tools for Selecting a Strategic Alternative

Four techniques help managers choose a strategic alternative: the portfolio matrix, the market attractiveness/company strength matrix, response functions, and the PIMS program. Let's look at each technique.

*Portfolio Matrix.* Recall that large organizations engaged in strategic planning may create strategic business units. Each SBU has its own rate of return on investment, growth potential, and associated risk. Management must find a balance among the SBUs that yields the overall organization's desired growth and profits with an acceptable level of risk. Some SBUs generate large amounts of cash over and above what is required for operating expenses or for more marketing, production, or inventory. Other SBUs need cash to foster growth. The challenge is to balance the organization's "portfolio" of SBUs for the best long-term performance.

To determine the future cash contributions and cash requirements that can be expected for each SBU, managers can use the Boston Consulting Group's portfolio matrix. A matrix is a self-contained framework within which something originates

*Exhibit 22.4*

Portfolio Matrix for a Large Computer Manufacturer

Note: The size of the circle represents the dollar sales relative to sales of other SBUs on the matrix—for example, 10x means sales are ten times greater than those of the next largest competitor.

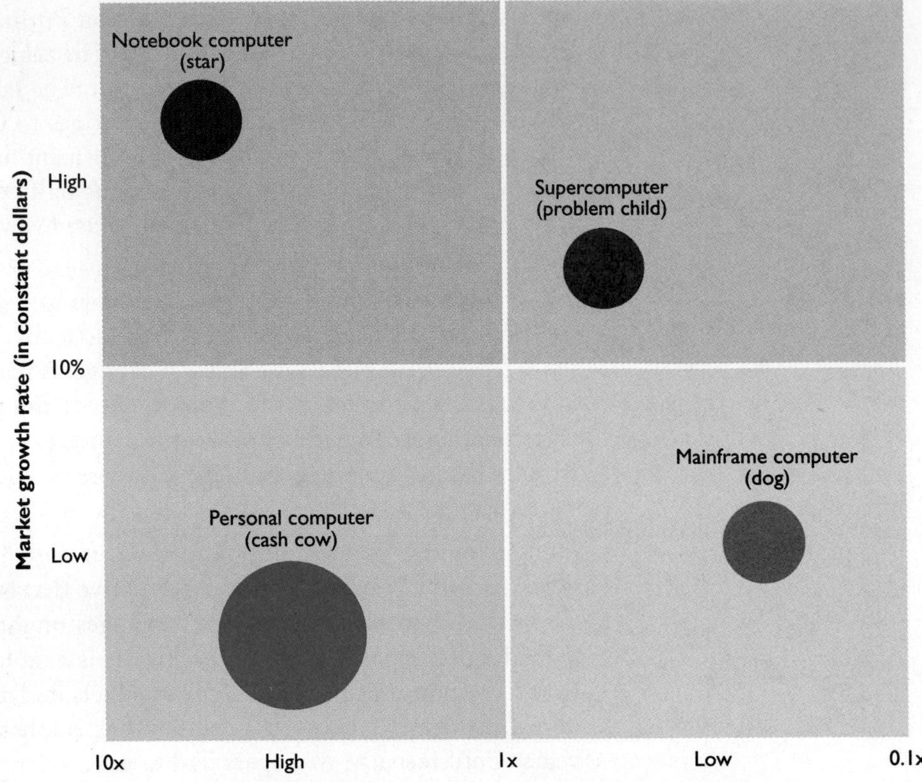


**portfolio matrix**
Tool for allocating resources among products or strategic business units on the basis of relative market share and market growth rate.

and develops. The **portfolio matrix** classifies each SBU by its present or forecasted growth and market share. The underlying assumption is that market share and profitability are strongly linked. The measure of market share used in the portfolio approach is *relative market share,* the ratio between the company's share and the share of the largest competitor. For example, if firm A has a 50 percent share and the competitor has 5 percent, the ratio is 10 to 1. If firm A has a 10 percent market share and the largest competitor has 20 percent, the ratio is 0.5 to 1.

Exhibit 22.4 is a hypothetical portfolio matrix for a large computer manufacturer. The size of the circle in each cell of the matrix represents dollar sales of the SBU relative to dollar sales of the company's other SBUs. These are the categories used in the matrix:

**star**
In the portfolio matrix, a business unit that is a market leader and growing fast.

- *Stars:* A **star** is a market leader and growing fast. For example, computer manufacturers have identified the notebook model as a star. Star SBUs usually have large profits but need a lot of cash to finance rapid growth. The best marketing tactic is to protect existing market share by reinvesting earnings in product improvement, better distribution, more promotion, and production efficiency. Management must strive to capture most of the new users as they enter the market.

**cash cow**
In the portfolio matrix, a business unit that generates more cash than it needs to maintain its market share.

- *Cash cows:* A **cash cow** is an SBU that usually generates more cash than it needs to maintain its market share. It is in a low-growth market, but the product has a dominant market share. Personal computers are categorized as cash cows in Exhibit 22.4. The basic strategy for a cash cow is to maintain market dominance by being the price leader and making technological improvements in the product. Managers should resist pressure to extend the basic line unless they can dramatically increase demand. Instead, they should allocate excess cash to the product categories where growth prospects are the greatest. For instance, Clorox Corporation owns Kingsford Charcoal, Match Charcoal Lighter, Prime Choice steak sauce, Cooking Ease spray lubricant for frying foods, and a restaurant chain. Its cash cow is Clorox bleach, with a 60 percent market share in a low-growth market. Clorox Corporation was highly successful in stretching the Clorox line to include a liquid formula in addition to the original dry bleach. Another example is Heinz, which has two cash cows: catsup and Weight Watchers frozen dinners.

**problem child (question mark)**
In the portfolio matrix, a business unit that shows rapid growth but poor profit margins.

- *Problem children:* A **problem child,** also called a **question mark,** shows rapid growth but poor profit margins. It has a low market share in a high-growth industry. Problem children need a great deal of cash. Without cash support, they eventually become dogs. The strategy options are to invest heavily to gain better market share, acquire competitors to get the necessary market share, or drop the SBU. Sometimes a firm can reposition the products of the SBU to move them into the star category.

**dog**
In the portfolio matrix, a business unit that has low growth potential and a small market share.

- *Dogs:* A **dog** has low growth potential and a small market share. Most dogs eventually leave the marketplace. In the computer manufacturer example, the mainframe computer has become a dog. Other examples include Jack-in-the-Box shrimp dinners, Warner-Lambert's Reef mouthwash, and Campbell's Red Kettle soups. Frito-Lay produced several dogs in the late 1980s, including Stuffers cheese-filled snacks, Rumbles granola nuggets, and Toppels cheese-topped crackers—a trio irreverently known as Stumbles, Tumbles, and Twofers. The strategy options for dogs are to harvest or divest.

After classifying the company's SBUs in the matrix, the next step is to allocate future resources for each. The four basic strategies are to

- *Build:* If an organization has an SBU that it believes has the potential to be a star (probably a problem child at present), building would be an appropriate goal. The organization may decide to give up short-term profits and use its financial resources to achieve this goal. Procter & Gamble built Pringles from a money loser to a record profit maker in 1994.
- *Hold:* If an SBU is a very successful cash cow, a key goal would surely be to hold or preserve market share so the organization can take advantage of the very positive cash flow. Bisquick has been a prosperous cash cow for General Mills for over two decades.
- *Harvest:* This strategy is appropriate for all SBUs except those classified as stars. The basic goal is to increase the short-term cash return without too much concern for the long-run impact. It is especially worthwhile when more cash is needed from a cash cow with long-run prospects that are unfavorable because of a low market growth rate. For instance, Lever Brothers has been harvesting Lifebuoy soap for a number of years with little promotional backing.
- *Divest:* Getting rid of SBUs with low shares of low-growth markets is often appropriate. Problem children and dogs are most suitable for this strategy. Procter & Gamble dropped Cincaprin, a coated aspirin, because of its low growth potential.

**market attractiveness/company strength matrix**
Tool for allocating resources among strategic business units on the basis of how attractive a market is and how well the firm is positioned to take advantage of opportunities in that market.

*Market Attractiveness/Company Strength Matrix.* A second model for selecting strategic alternatives, originally developed by General Electric, is known as the **market attractiveness/company strength matrix.** The dimensions used in this matrix—market attractiveness and company strength—are richer and more complete than those used in the portfolio matrix but are much harder to quantify.

*Exhibit 22.5*

Market Attractiveness/Company Strength Matrix

Note: Circle size represents dollar sales volume relative to sales of other SBUs on the matrix.

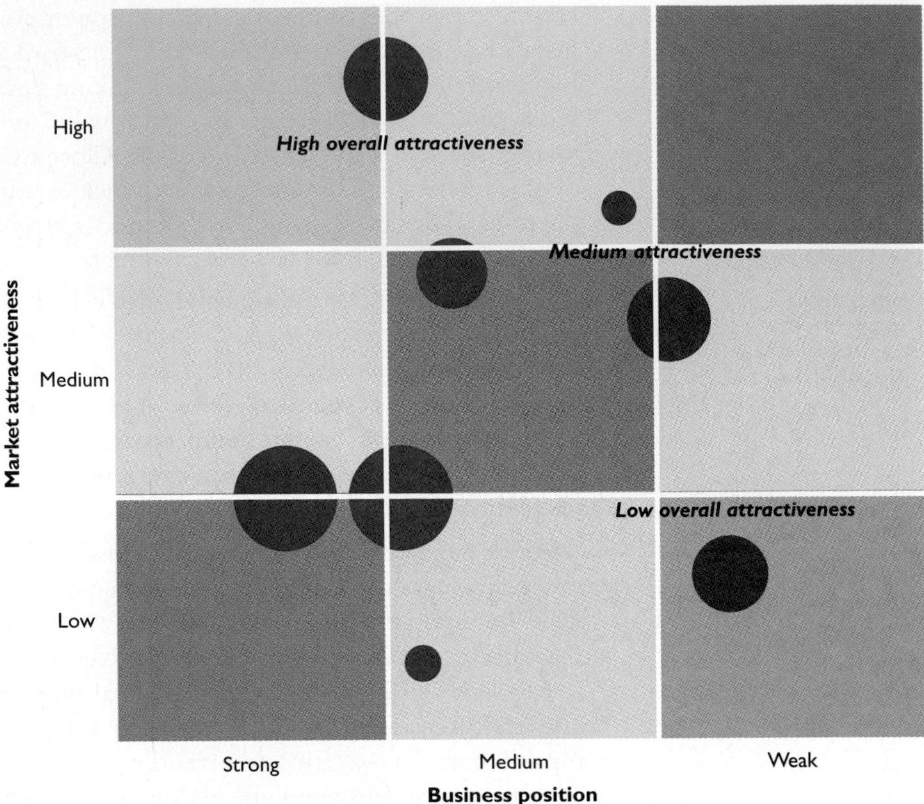


Exhibit 22.5 presents a market attractiveness/company strength matrix. The horizontal axis, business position, refers to how well positioned the organization is to take advantage of market opportunities. Does the firm have the technology it needs to effectively penetrate the market? Are its financial resources adequate? Can manufacturing costs be held below those of the competition? Will the firm have bargaining power over suppliers? Can the firm cope with change? The vertical axis measures the attractiveness of a market, which is expressed both quantitatively and qualitatively. Some attributes of an attractive market are high profitability, rapid growth, a lack of government regulation, consumer insensitivity to a price increase, a lack of competition, and availability of technology. The grid is divided into three overall attractiveness zones for each dimension: high, medium, and low.

Those SBUs (or markets) that have low overall attractiveness should be avoided if the organization is not already serving them. If the firm is in these markets, it should either harvest or divest the SBUs. The organization should selectively maintain markets with medium attractiveness. If attractiveness begins to slip, then the organization should withdraw from the market.

Conditions that are highly attractive—an attractive market plus a strong business position—are the best candidates for investment. For instance, Black & Decker used marketing research to uncover a market for the "serious do-it-yourselfer." These people were willing to pay a premium price for quality home tools. For example, research found that this group of consumers wanted a cordless drill that didn't run out of power before the job was complete. Black & Decker responded with a new line called Quantum. The line sold over $40 million in its first year.[12]

**response function**
Graphed relationship between a marketing mix (or component of the mix) and sales to a specific target market.

*Response Functions.* A third analysis technique is the use of response functions. **Response functions** are graphed relationships between a marketing mix (or component of the mix) and sales to a specific market target. Some planners substitute profits for sales when plotting response curves.

The graphs in Exhibit 22.6 show how two strategic business units in the same firm might view their response functions. The exhibit shows that sales are much more responsive to changes in price for the small-car SBU (graph A) than for the large-car SBU (graph D) if other response variables for each SBU are assumed not to change. Similarly, increasing the number of outlets has a greater impact on small-car sales (graph B) than on large-car sales (graph E).

On the other hand, personal sales effort is much more effective for large cars (graph F) than for small cars (graph C). Thus managers of the large-car SBU may find that the size and caliber of their sales force are critical to the SBU's success. Some sales would be generated without any personal selling, thanks to advertising and sales promotion—a phenomenon called the *market minimum.* As salespeople are added, sales begin rising at an increasing rate and then decrease. Finally, sales peak when $P_2$ salespersons have been hired. This upper limit of sales that can be generated by the sales force is called the *market potential.* The difference between the market minimum and the market potential is the *marketing sensitivity of demand.* By allocating more resources to the sales staff, management can increase total revenues to $S_2$. Beyond that point, additional salespeople do not generate additional sales.

Although response functions are helpful in choosing among alternatives, they have an important drawback. A response function is only as good as the assump-

*Exhibit 22.6*

Hypothetical Response Functions for General Motors SBUs

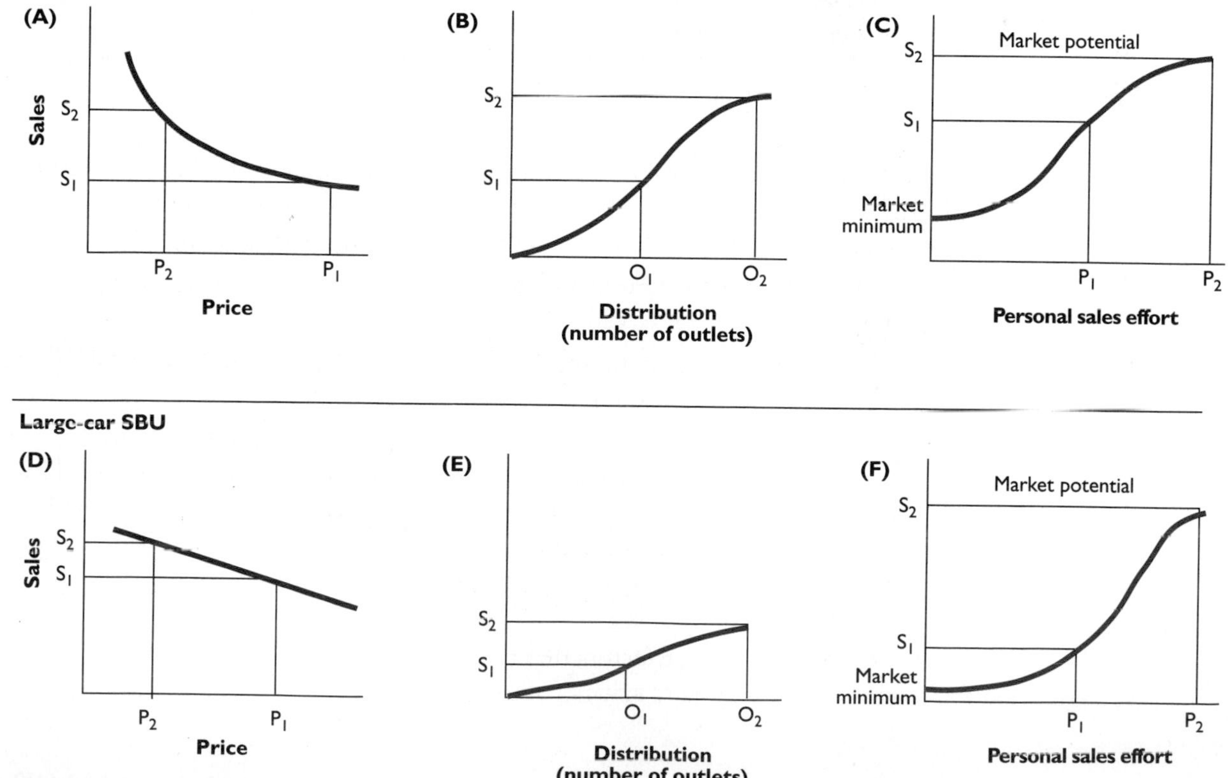

tions behind the curve. If the assumptions are wrong, then the curve is wrong. Moreover, even if the assumptions are correct at the time an alternative is chosen, the rapidly changing external environment may change relationships among variables. Thus marketing managers must continually reevaluate alternatives. They should also periodically use past experience, marketing research, and executive judgment to reassess the shapes of the response functions.

**profit impact of market strategy (PIMS)**
Method for analyzing strategic alternatives that involves consulting a database summarizing the financial and market performance of 3,000 strategic business units of more than 450 firms.

*PIMS Program.* The fourth tool for analyzing strategic alternatives is called the **profit impact of market strategy (PIMS)** program. The Strategic Planning Institute provides companies with a database summarizing the financial and market performance of 3,000 SBUs of more than 450 firms. PIMS focuses on the links among various factors and profitability (specifically, return on investment); its database includes successful firms and "real losers." The database includes large and small companies; markets in North America, Europe, and elsewhere; and a wide variety of products, ranging from candy to heavy capital goods to financial services.

For each SBU, three kinds of information are presented:

- *Market conditions:* distribution channels used by the SBU, the number and size of customers, and rates of market growth and inflation
- *Competitive position:* the SBU's market share, relative product quality, prices and costs relative to the competition, and degree of vertical integration relative to the competition
- *Financial and operating performance:* annual figures over periods ranging from two to twelve years

Detailed analysis of the PIMS database has produced some key findings:

- In the long run, the one factor that most affects an SBU's performance is the quality of its products relative to those of competitors. A quality edge boosts performance in two ways. In the short run, superior quality yields increased profits through premium prices. In the longer term, superior or improving quality is the most effective basis for growth. Quality leads to both market expansion and gains in market share.
- Market share (relative to the largest competitors) and profitability are strongly linked.
- The need to invest a lot in the SBU is a powerful drag on profitability. Investment-intensive businesses are those that use a great deal of capital per dollar of sales or per employee.
- Although market growth and relative market share are linked to cash flow, many other factors also influence performance.
- Vertical integration is a powerful strategy for some kinds of businesses but not for all. For businesses with a small market share, return on investment is highest when the degree of vertical integration is low. But for businesses with an average or above-average market share, return on investment is highest when vertical integration is either low or high and lowest when vertical integration is in the middle.
- Most of the strategic factors that boost return on investment also contribute to the long-term market value of an organization.[13]



For access to the PIMS database, companies pay about $20,000 to $40,000 per year and agree to make their data available on a confidential basis; data are pooled so individual businesses cannot be identified. The database contains successes, failures, and also-rans. The data provided by a business cover the market environment, competition, strategy pursued, and financial performance, plus projections of future sales, prices, and costs. A business may obtain insights on its own strategy from PIMS results tailored to its needs.

6 *Explain how firms implement strategies and alter strategies when necessary.*

## IMPLEMENT THE SELECTED STRATEGY AND ALTER IT WHEN NECESSARY

The seventh phase of the strategic planning process is implementation. Implementation requires the delegation of authority and responsibility, the determination of a time frame for completing tasks, and the allocation of resources. Sometimes a strategic plan also requires task force management. A *task force* is a tightly organized unit under the direction of a manager who, usually, has broad authority. A task force is established to accomplish a single goal or mission and thus works against a deadline. Toyota created a task force to build and market its luxury car, the Lexus. AT&T assigned a task force to develop marketing plans that would protect its long-distance market from MCI and Sprint.

Implementing a plan has yet another dimension: gaining acceptance. New plans mean change, and change creates resistance. One reason people resist change is that they fear they will lose something. When new-product research is taken away from marketing research and given to a new-product department, the director of marketing research will naturally resist this loss of part of his or her domain. Misunderstanding and lack of trust also create opposition to change.

After an organization implements its strategic plan, it must track results and monitor the external environment. As mentioned in Chapter 2, the one certainty about the external environment is that it will continually change. And as it changes, managers will be pressed to adjust the strategic plan. The key to organizational survival is their willingness to examine the changing environment and to adopt appropriate new goals and behaviors. Yet, they must not simply be willing to change; they must know how to change.

A key tool in evaluating the strategic plan is the marketing audit. The marketing audit uses financial and nonfinancial reports to evaluate the organization's goals, strategies, and performance. The marketing audit is discussed later in the chapter.

Organizations, especially large ones, have much inertia. They are set up as efficient machines, and it is hard to change one part without adjusting everything else. Yet organizations can be changed through leadership, preferably in advance of a crisis. An example of fresh leadership brought in to overcome inertia is Seisuke Ueshima, the new president of Yamaha, whose story is told in the Global Perspectives box.

7 *Identify several techniques that help make strategic planning effective.*

## HOW TO MAKE STRATEGIC PLANNING WORK

In the past decade, intense domestic and international competition has led many firms into strategic planning as a faddish prescription for survival. Many companies regarded strategic planning as a once-a-year, mechanistic process. Today, however, attitudes toward strategic planning have matured, and companies have become more effective in using it.

Effective strategic planning requires continual attention, creativity, and management commitment:

GLOBAL PERSPECTIVES

**Yamaha**

Yamaha makes audio equipment and is the world leader in pianos, horns, and other musical instruments. Consumers used to buy just about whatever the company made, particularly musical instruments, a business it dominates in Japan. But swelled by success, Yamaha meandered into sidelines that shared unique materials or manufacturing techniques with its core business—but little else. Its craftsmen were expert at bending and laminating woods for piano cabinets. After extending the technique logically to guitars and drums, the company applied it to the less familiar domains of skis, tennis rackets, and furniture. Similarly, from electronic organs it branched blithely into the cutthroat competition of TVs, VCRs, and audio equipment.

This obsession with production techniques put the company out of touch with its markets. Says Jeff Camp, an analyst for Jardine Fleming Securities in Tokyo: "Instead of just worrying whether they are building things right, they should be asking, Why are we building this product?"

That's what Seisuke Ueshima, Yamaha's new president, is asking. A marketing pro, he came from sister company Yamaha Motor, which makes motorcycles, boats, snowmobiles, and water scooters. But even if he finds inefficient operations, his options are limited. "We can't just downsize the organization through layoffs as American companies do," he says. Japan's tradition of lifetime employment requires Yammaha to create new jobs before chopping old ones.

Where will the jobs come from? Yamaha is now the leading maker of chips that enable microcomputers, video games, and keyboards to create sounds. The company expects sales to boom as computers evolve into multimedia players that manipulate video, still images, and sound. But Yamaha's future remains tied to musical instruments, which account for 56 percent of sales.

Yamaha's strategy is to go upscale, moving to expensive instruments that generate increased sales and profits in a stagnant market. The Disklavier, for example, is a high-tech answer to the player piano that costs from $8,000 to more than $30,000. The Disklavier combines a standard grand or upright piano with a built-in computer that can record and play back performances, including those of famous pianists. After a slow start the strategy is working, especially in the United States. Disklaviers account for 20 percent of Yamaha's total piano sales, or roughly $100 million, a proportion the company hopes to double by 1998.

In the past Yamaha might have applied this technology to some unfamiliar market. Now it is proceeding more methodically. "We are studying new markets very carefully now before introducing new products," Ueshima says. In the tough economy of the 1990s, versatility may yet be a blessing, but discretion has its rewards.[14]

How do you think Yamaha got into its current position? Do you think that the notion of lifetime employment is realistic in today's global economy? Do you think that "going upscale" is a good strategic move for Yamaha?

From Brenton Schlender, "The Perils of Losing Focus," *Fortune*, 17 May 1993. 

- Strategic planning is not an annual exercise, in which managers go through the motions and forget about strategic planning until the next year. It should be an ongoing process, because the environment is continually changing and the firm's resources and capabilities are continually evolving.
- Sound planning is based on creativity. Managers should challenge assumptions about the firm and the environment and establish new strategies. For example, major oil companies developed the concept of the gasoline service station in an age when cars needed frequent and rather elaborate servicing. They held on to the full-service approach, but independents were quick to respond to new realities and moved to lower-cost self-service and convenience-store operations. The majors took several decades to catch up.
- Perhaps the most critical element in successful strategic planning is top management's support and participation. For example, most department stores struggled during the late 1980s and early 1990s; many even faced bankruptcy. But from 1984 to 1994, the Dillard's chain opened or acquired over 240 department stores. Dillard's is either No. 1 or No. 2 in every market where it has a presence. The chain succeeded because top management defined its strategic mission and then made sure that mission was carried out.

Three additional examples of successful strategic planning follow: AT&T, Michelin, and McDonald's.

### AT&T

In 1984, the U.S. Justice Department forced AT&T to separate itself from

Strategic planning is most successful when the whole company, starting with the management team, understands the strategic mission and concentrates on carrying it out. At Dillard's, a fast-growing department store chain, management includes William and Alexa Dillard and their five children: Bill, Mike, and Alex and Denise and Drue.

Jackson Hill/Southern Lights

the Bell telephone companies. AT&T's first decade without the "baby Bells" was not easy nor without mistakes. At the outset, AT&T thought it knew what customers *needed.* It took most of the past decade to learn that customer satisfaction is giving customers what they *want.*

After losing major battles to MCI and Sprint, AT&T has finally learned how to compete. AT&T's computer business is a case in point. Because AT&T's long-distance network is so highly computerized, managers thought that people would jump at the chance to buy computers from AT&T. The company was wrong. Finally AT&T merged with an established computer company, NCR, which was recently renamed AT&T Global Information Solutions.

Cellular telephone technology was invented in the Bell Laboratories. But AT&T was required to leave the broad commercialization of that invention to others. Later it found that wireless communications technology is critical to providing "anytime, anywhere" telephone service. AT&T finally merged with the nation's largest cellular service company, McCaw Cellular Communications.

AT&T is now armed with a new strategy: to build on its position as the world's networking leader. The firm's main strength is its ability to build and manage networks. Networks are AT&T's core business. AT&T seeks continually to improve its own network and those of other telephone service providers around the world in order to make communications technology more useful to customers. Its efforts, in turn, increase network use. The more the network is used, the more money AT&T earns. But the network doesn't stand alone. It is enhanced by the company's differential advantage: the ability to combine communications, computing, and network products and systems.

AT&T's differential advantage is its ability to build and manage communications networks.

© 1994 AT&T

Each SBU at AT&T is responsible for its own markets, focusing on its own customers and competitors and developing the right products for its distinctive situation. Each is expected to be profitable in its own right and to support the corporate goal of at least 10 percent earnings growth each year. To do this, the SBUs focus on value-added goods and services that offer potential for high margins. The information industry worldwide currently generates about $900 billion in annual revenues and is expected to grow to $1.4 trillion by 1996.[15] AT&T fully expects to get its fair share.

## GROUPE MICHELIN

French tiremaker Michelin, which also makes maps and restaurant guides for car drivers, has long had a corporate culture that stresses secrecy, loyalty, hard work, and the quest for long-term market share.[16] The desire for secrecy is legendary. Michelin once refused to let French President Charles de Gaulle visit its plants. On another occasion it let a factory burn down rather than allow firefighters inside. Yet these days Michelin admits experts from General Motors, its largest customer, which insists on being involved with suppliers in product development.

To control the quality of its product, Michelin insists on producing all the materials for its tires, including steel belting and synthetic rubber. It also spends heavily on research, laying out 5 percent of sales in bad times as well as good.

In 1990 Michelin bought Uniroyal Goodrich Tire Company, which gave it a 20 percent global market share and sales of over $10 billion.[17] But by 1991, debt from the expansion had plunged the family-controlled company into deep financial trouble. Costs were out of control, and proud Michelin was getting complaints from valued customers and distributors. Sears, Roebuck, Michelin's biggest U.S. distributor, complained of too-slow delivery and warned that it was starting to buy more tires from Michelin's archrivals: Goodyear, Bridgestone of Japan, and Pirelli of Italy.

Belatedly, realizing that he had been too slow to modernize, family patriarch François Michelin started reinventing his own company. He began tearing down strict, inward-looking management systems that he had long considered a key to his success. He slowly, uncomfortably, started lifting the secrecy that had kept Michelin from communicating properly even internally. Its test tracks, for example, had been off-limits even to most senior executives. "Some information, even if you needed it you couldn't get it," says Bill Elks, a manager at a South Carolina plant.[18]

Many decisions had been centralized. "When I joined the company 15 years ago, one of the things that surprised me was that budgets didn't exist," says Bob Rawley, the plant manager at the South Carolina plant.[19] Executives applied to a central authority for investment authorizations. The system made it hard for executives to control costs or even to know how much things cost. Big customers had trouble getting Michelin's highly structured plants to respond to unexpected orders.

"We have seen the risks of a too-systematic approach," says Edouard Michelin, the heir apparent to the CEO position. A convert to such management innovations as "empowering" employees by removing supervisors, he has begun overruling some of the old guard, urging new ideas in Europe, Asia, and the United States. At Michelin's U.S. truck tire factory, for instance, managers let employees revamp work schedules, and the new schedule includes several twelve-hour shifts. Some senior officials tried to block the longer shifts, fearing reduced productivity and accidents. But Edouard Michelin shrugged off the complaints and let the new system be adopted.

Some managers worry privately that Michelin isn't decentralizing fast enough to keep up with competitors. But Sears says Michelin is jumping faster these days to fill orders on time.

## McDONALD'S

McDonald's accounts for nearly 40 percent of all fast-food hamburgers sold. It operates over 10,500 restaurants. Of these, more than 2,600 are located in forty-nine countries outside the United States. Its largest international markets are Japan, England, Germany, Australia, and Canada. Worldwide, McDonald's serves over 22 million customers per day.

McDonald's is a strong believer in planning. Its mission, derived from its strategic plan, is to be in the fast-food business with an emphasis on hamburgers. Company president Michael Quinlan says, "McDonald's hamburgers is what we are."[20] The strategic focus includes quality, service, cleanliness, and value—or QSCV, in company language. A director explains that McDonald's will try anything, as long as it improves Q, S, C, or V.

McDonald's strategic plan calls for increasing sales by adding restaurants, improving international profitability, and maximizing sales at existing restaurants. McDonald's accomplishes its first goal by adding over 600 restaurants each year. It plans to foster international growth by opening new restaurants (of the 600 opened per year, over 200 are international), introducing new products, and practicing more effective marketing. To better understand how McDonald's plans to increase sales of existing stores, let's examine its marketing mix.

## Product

Part of McDonald's product plan relates to service and image, and the rest focuses on new products. Field inspectors check on all the stores to make sure franchisees are minding their QSCVs. McDonald's tries to add one new product about every five years. However, the company has had more and more trouble coming up with a winner that guarantees mass appeal and profits. McRib, for example, was tested in 3,500 stores. Lots of people tried McRib once but didn't like the sloppiness or the taste.

In the 1990s McDonald's has been closely examining the pizza market, which is growing at about 11 percent annually. In the late 1980s it test marketed a pizza roll, called McPizza. McPizza failed miserably. To maintain QSCV, it was frozen and shipped to retail stores, but unfortunately it tasted like frozen pizza. McDonald's next effort, simply called McDonald's pizza, is freshly made using conveyer ovens that blast hot air over the top and bottom of the dish. The process leaves little room for error and produces a hot pizza in about five minutes. When it started testing this pizza, McDonald's took on such rivals as Pizza Hut, Little Caesar's Pizza, and Domino's. McDonald's must make sure that pizza doesn't cannibalize its evening sandwich sales.

Although pizza looks somewhat promising, the company is also testing breakfast burritos, a Quarter Pounder Ranchero burger, and a Western Omelet McMuffin. Its McLean burger, which appeals to health-conscious consumers, is only a very modest success.

## Distribution

McDonald's is always looking for new and more efficient ways to deliver supplies to its stores. It boasts one of the most sophisticated physical distribution systems in the world.

As for the location of its outlets, McDonald's started by building new stores in the suburbs of large cities and then spreading to smaller towns. Now the company is trying to build more restaurants in big cities. It is also cultivating semicaptive markets—toll roads, military bases, museums, and hospitals, for example, where there are a lot of people with limited dining choices.

## Promotion

McDonald's spends over $1 billion a year on promotion. The company's promotion plan stresses product quality because research has shown that consumers don't seem to think much of McDonald's hamburgers, despite the billions they've eaten.

The company's advertising agencies create more than 200 distinct advertisements a year. Many stress the slogan "McDonald's . . . food, folks, and fun" and feature shots of tasty-looking products. McDonald's also targets some promotions to subsegments of its market, such as minorities and the elderly. For example, it runs over thirty different promotions annually for the Hispanic market.

McDonald's has begun testing a point-of-sale computer system that tracks individual customer spending and automatically creates bonus coupons after certain spending levels have been reached. A test store in Paramus Park, New Jersey, had 9,500 customers signed up for the Frequent Customer Club in the first ninety days.[21]

### Pricing

McDonald's pricing plans for its domestic restaurants call for prices that will yield the company a 20 percent return on equity. Prices of its products are adjusted periodically to maintain the target return. Like other fast-food chains, McDonald's successfully introduced "value pricing" in the early 1990s (see Chapters 8 and 19).

A big chunk of McDonald's revenues comes from franchisees. Franchisees pay 11.5 percent of their revenue to the corporation for rent and services. The franchise system is just one part of the comprehensive strategy that keeps the McEngine running.

8 *Describe seven sales forecasting techniques.*

## SALES FORECASTING

A key to McDonald's successful strategic planning is effective sales forecasts. Poor forecasting can be very costly for a company. For example, in 1993 Fruit of the Loom forecasted a slowdown in underwear and apparel sales. It cut back production sharply. In 1994, almost overnight, demand soared because consumers had not been buying much underwear in the early 1990s. Fruit of the Loom hired back thousands of laid-off workers but still lost over $200 million in sales in 1994 because it didn't have enough product.[22]

The sales forecast for a strategic plan is what determines the plan's desirability. Generally, the greater the revenue potential and the lower the competitiveness of an alternative, the greater a plan's attractiveness.

### THE SALES FORECASTING PROCESS

**sales forecast**
Estimate of a firm's future sales or revenues for a specified period.

The **sales forecast** is an estimate of a firm's future sales or revenues for a specified period. One type of forecasting is a process that flows downward from estimates of overall economic activity, to industry sales trends, to company sales and revenues (see Exhibit 22.7). Forecasting company sales and revenues is itself a three-step process, beginning with estimating sales and revenues for individual products, then product lines, and finally a total for the entire company. This is the complete process:

1. *Evaluate national trends:* Marketing managers often forecast sales by starting with overall estimates of economic activity and narrowing them down to a specific product. For example, a forecast might begin with a national economic forecast of the gross domestic product (GDP). GDP is the total value of all final goods and services for a specified period. Unless the company is very large, it will usually obtain GDP forecasts through secondary sources—for example, a major bank, the federal government, a consulting firm, or a university. GDP forecasts are important for most marketers, because sales of most companies' goods and services tend to increase when GDP rises.
2. *Forecast industry sales:* The overall economic health of the country usually has a major impact on individual industry sales. The key to forecasting industry

*Exhibit 22.7*

Sales Forecasting Process

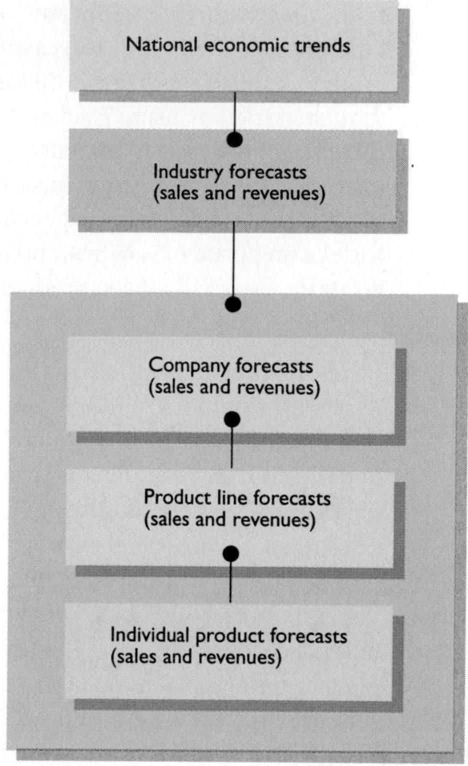


**market sales potential**
Maximum amount of product that can be sold in a given industry with maximum marketing expenditures under existing marketing mixes within a specific external environment.

sales is to determine **market sales potential,** which is the maximum amount of product that can be sold in a given industry with maximum marketing expenditures under existing marketing mixes within a specific external environment. Obviously, market sales potential changes as the environment changes. For example, the market sales potential for frozen yogurt and for low-fat and low-salt frozen dinners increased as U.S. consumers became more health-conscious.

3. *Measure individual product sales potential:* After estimating sales for every industry in which the firm competes, managers prepare sales forecasts for individual products. Industry sales forecasts place limits on potential product sales. That is, sales for a given product cannot exceed sales of the industry in which the good is sold, unless it is sold in several industries. Also, the competitiveness of each industry has an impact on sales potential for a single product. For example, competition in the fresh-pork industry became so intense that Swift's fresh-pork sales forecasts looked dismal. Swift actually sold the division. Arco Chemical also sold assets because of intense competition in its industry.
4. *Forecast company sales:* When forecasts have been completed for each individual product, they are totaled to form a product line forecast. In larger firms these are summed together to obtain an SBU (strategic business unit) forecast. Finally, the sales forecasts for each SBU are added together to provide the firm with a company sales forecast.

## CONTEMPORARY SALES FORECASTING TECHNIQUES

Marketing managers can use a number of methods to estimate sales for products, product lines, companies, and industries. These include the jury of executive opinion, sales force composite, Delphi technique, moving average, regression technique, multiple-factor index approach, and purchase intent scale.

## Jury of Executive Opinion

**jury of executive opinion**
Sales forecasting technique that surveys a group of executive experts.

One popular method of forecasting is the **jury of executive opinion,** which is based on the assumption that a group of executive experts can arrive at a better forecast than statisticians using a scientific approach. A jury of executive opinion relies on the executives' past experience and intuition regarding the future. Often the technique is applied in a group meeting until everyone reaches a consensus.

Unfortunately, this simple technique is usually not very reliable. It is used mainly for existing products. When applied to new goods and services, it is usually even less accurate, especially if the product requires an unfamiliar channel of distribution.

## Sales Force Composite

**sales force composite**
Sales forecasting technique that surveys the sales force.

A second popular technique is also subjective. The **sales force composite** uses the opinions of the sales force to create a forecast. It assumes that salespeople, who are in daily contact with the marketplace, are in the best position to project future sales. Participating in the establishment of sales estimates also is assumed to motivate salespeople to achieve their objectives.

The sales force composite, like executive judgment, is often unreliable. Some marketing managers use a historic inflator or deflator to improve the quality of the estimate. For example, if the sales force tends to underestimate actual sales by 10 percent (which makes it easier to achieve a quota), then the current estimate can be raised by the same percentage.

## Delphi Technique

**Delphi technique**
Sales forecasting technique that asks outside experts to express an anonymous opinion, review a summary of others' opinions, and express themselves again in order to reach consensus.

The **Delphi technique** is similar to both the jury of executive opinion and the sales force composite in that it solicits opinions about the future from groups of people. The Delphi technique, however, seeks opinions of experts outside the firm, such as government or university economists or other professional futurists. Sometimes the information is sought by mail or electronic mail so opinions can be gathered conveniently from experts all over the world.

Each member of the forecasting team submits a sales estimate and the rationale behind the figure. Next someone, usually an in-house person, summarizes all the information and resubmits the summary to the team. This process is repeated until a consensus emerges. Team members often remain anonymous so no one has to defend his or her views.

The Delphi technique is used regularly by over a hundred large companies, such as Lockheed. The major disadvantage of the technique is that it can be time-consuming and costly.

## Moving Average

**moving average**
Sales forecasting technique that combines sales data from several of the most recent years and uses an average to obtain the next year's forecast.

A **moving average** combines sales data from several of the most recent years and uses an average to obtain the next year's forecast. Every year, the oldest year in the previous calculation is dropped and the year just completed is added—hence the term *moving average.*

Assume that a solar irrigation pump company sold 950 units in year 1, 525 in year 2, and 1,100 in year 3. In year 4, the company sells 1,500 units. If management uses a four-year moving average, the sales estimate for the fifth year would be as follows:

$$\text{Moving average} = \frac{950 + 525 + 1{,}100 + 1{,}500}{4}$$

$$= \frac{4,075}{4}$$

$$= 1,019 \text{ units in year 5}$$

This technique is based on the assumption that relatively recent experience is the most valid basis for forecasting the next year's sales. However, giving equal weight to the years used in the evaluation may or may not be a good idea. One or more of the years may have been an aberration.

## Regression Technique

**regression**
Sales forecasting technique that uses statistics to define a relationship between past sales (a dependent variable) and one or more independent variables.

In statistics, a **regression** is an attempt to define a relationship between past sales (the dependent variable) and one or more independent variables, such as price, competitors' prices, per capita income, industry advertising expenditures, or new housing starts. Simple regression employs only one independent and one dependent variable. However, because many factors influence a product's sales, this technique has limited value to marketing managers. It would be unusual for one independent variable, such as price, to explain much more than half the total variation in a firm's sales from year to year. Therefore, marketing managers rely on multiple regression (more than one independent variable) to derive a formula that will accurately describe a relationship between sales and several independent variables.

## Multiple-Factor Index

Many consumer goods companies have found that sales potential can be estimated by using an index. Fisher-Price, for example, might assume that the demand for preschool toys is directly related to the number of preschool children in the United States. If New Mexico contains 1 percent of all preschool children in the country, then Fisher-Price might assume that 1 percent of all preschool toys will be sold in New Mexico. Rarely, however, is a single factor a highly reliable estimate of sales potential. Family income, location of toy store outlets, family size, education level of the head of the household, and other factors probably influence the sale of preschool toys. Therefore, it is usually best to use a multiple-factor index when trying to forecast sales.

One of the oldest and most popular multiple-factor indexes is the *Annual Survey of Buying Power*, published by *Sales & Marketing Management*. The index reflects relative consumer buying power in different regions, states, and metropolitan areas. *Sales & Marketing Management*'s index of the relative buying power of an area is given by this formula:

$$B_i = 0.5y_i + 0.3r_i + 0.2p_i$$

where

$B_i$ = percentage of total national buying power found in area $i$

$y_i$ = percentage of national disposable personal income originating in area $i$

$r_i$ = percentage of national retail sales in area $i$

$p_i$ = percentage of national population located in area $i$

For example, suppose that New Mexico has 1.11 percent of the U.S. disposable personal income, 0.96 percent of U.S. retail sales, and 0.93 percent of the U.S. population. The buying power index for New Mexico would be as follows:

$$0.5\ (1.11) + 0.3\ (0.96) + 0.2\ (0.93) = 1.02$$

Thus 1.02 percent of the nation's preschool toy sales would be presumed to occur in New Mexico.

The weights used in the buying power index are somewhat arbitrary. They were established for medium-priced consumer goods. Consequently, Fisher-Price would have to adjust the index to make it more meaningful for preschool toys.

## Purchase Intent Scale

**purchase intent scale**
Survey question that measures a person's propensity to buy a product.

The **purchase intent scale** is a type of survey question that quantifies the likelihood that a consumer will buy a particular product (see Exhibit 22.8). The scale is typically used to forecast demand for new products. In fact, it is applied throughout the new product development process.

Marketing managers ask the purchase intent question during concept testing to get a rough idea of demand. They want to quickly eliminate potential "dogs," carefully look at products for which purchase intent is moderate, and push forward the projects that seem to have star potential. At this stage, investment is minimal and product modification or repositioning is easy.

As the product moves through the development process, the product itself, the promotion strategy, price levels, and distribution channels become more concrete and focused. Managers evaluate purchase intent at each stage and refine demand estimates.

The crucial decision for new product introduction typically follows test marketing. Immediately before test marketing, commercial researchers often place the final, or near-final, version of the product in consumers' homes in test cities around the country. After a period of in-home use, usually two to six weeks, a follow-up survey is conducted among participants to find out their likes and dislikes. In addition, the survey asks participants how the product compares to those they already use and what price they would pay for it. The critical question, near the end of the questionnaire, is purchase intent.

The purchase intent scale is a good predictor of consumer choice for frequently purchased and durable consumer products. The scale is very easy to construct, and consumers are simply asked to judge their own likelihood of buying the new product. From past experience in the product category, a marketing manager can translate consumer responses on the scale to estimates of purchase probability. Obviously, some who claim they "definitely will buy" the product will not do so. In fact, a few who state that they "definitely will not buy" the product *will* buy it.

Assume that historical follow-up studies have told the manufacturer of a new coffeemaker the following about purchase intent for small electrical appliances:

*Exhibit 22.8*

Purchase Intent Question for a New Coffeemaker

If this new coffeemaker sold for approximately $35 and was available in the stores where you normally shop, would you

Definitely buy the coffeemaker .......... 1

Probably buy .......... 2

Probably not buy .......... 3

Definitely not buy the coffeemaker .......... 4

63 percent of the "definitely will buy" actually buy within twelve months.
28 percent of the "probably will buy" actually buy within twelve months.
12 percent of the "probably will not buy" actually buy within twelve months.
3 percent of the "definitely will not buy" actually buy within twelve months.

Now suppose that in-home market research for the coffeemaker resulted in these findings:

40 percent definitely will buy.
20 percent probably will buy.
30 percent probably will not buy.
10 percent definitely will not buy.

Assuming that the sample for the in-home marketing research study was representative of the target market, purchase intent can be calculated as follows:

$$(.4)(63 \text{ percent}) + (.2)(28 \text{ percent}) + (.3)(12 \text{ percent}) + (.1)(3 \text{ percent}) = 34.7 \text{ percent}$$

In other words, the formula shows that nearly 35 percent of the target households will purchase the coffeemaker. The manufacturer would be deliriously happy at a sales potential this high for the new coffeemaker. In the world of new product development, however, purchase intent is very rarely this high.

What should a company do if it doesn't have historical follow-up information? A reasonable but conservative estimate would be that 70 percent of the "definitely will buy" will actually buy, 35 percent of the "probably will buy," 10 percent of the "probably will not buy," and 0 percent of the "definitely will not buy."

9 *Discuss global issues in strategic planning and forecasting.*

## GLOBAL ISSUES IN STRATEGIC PLANNING AND FORECASTING

Chapter 3 noted that world markets are merging and that many traditional market boundaries are disappearing. Progressive companies all over the world are taking advantage of the changing marketplace by developing a global vision. With a global vision come new rules of international competition and dramatic changes in strategic planning. In industries ranging from automobiles to fast food and commodity chemicals, firms are finding that what worked in international marketing in the past may not work well today.

Strategic planners must recognize how globalization manifests itself in different industries. Many of the following patterns are usually present:

- Disappearing "national" market boundaries as competitors and customers cross traditional geographic borders to buy and to sell
- Declining numbers of competitors and increasing size of the remaining players as the smaller firms or firms with a narrow geographic focus are absorbed by the larger ones or are forced out of the market
- Competition among the same group of world-class players in every national market
- Increasing interdependence among national or regional markets as developments or marketing strategies in one location affect markets elsewhere

- Growing similarity among some segments of customers worldwide as gaps in their lifestyles, tastes, and behavior narrow[23]

Recall that the third step in the strategic planning process is to conduct a situation analysis. Here are several key questions marketing managers should ask in examining global SWOT:

- What is our current competitive profile compared with local and global rivals? What unique areas of competence do we enjoy? What other strengths do we have? In what areas are we weak?
- How are we perceived by our customers or members of the trade in local markets? Is the "global" nature of our company perceived as an advantage or a disadvantage?
- Is our current global strategy in line with our competitive posture in individual markets? Is the strategy building on our strengths and shoring up our weaknesses?
- How can we turn our global scope into a differential advantage? Are there areas in which we are not exploiting the economies of scale that come with our global size? How well and how fast do we transfer innovations globally? In what areas can we improve our efficiency internally or in the marketplace?
- How does the current profile of our management compare with those of our competitors? Do we have the skills needed locally and in headquarters to implement our strategy? Is our organizational structure in line with the strategy? How can it be improved to help with implementation?[24]

Del Monte marketing managers conducted research to help them understand how consumers perceive Del Monte fruits and juices in various countries. The research discovered that consumers around the world use canned fruits differently—for example, with cream topping in the United Kingdom but without topping elsewhere. They also found that, although Del Monte is a known brand and has a good reputation, consumer loyalty was low and consumers were increasingly opting for value-priced private brands.

To build on high international awareness of the Del Monte brand, and also to explain why Del Monte costs more than other brands, the company created a TV advertising campaign that communicated the freshness of Del Monte's canned products without showing how they were actually used. The commercial, called "The Man from Del Monte," emphasized same-day picking and packing under the uncompromising control of a Del Monte inspector. This highly successful commercial was shown in several countries in Europe and the Middle East, with the words translated into local languages.[25] The communication strategy proved effective because it was built on important insights from factual self-analysis.

The sales forecasting techniques discussed in this chapter can be applied in any country. The *Annual Survey of Buying Power* used in the multiple-factor index approach covers only the United States, but the U.S. Department of Commerce offers several publications that can help a global marketer in preparing a sales forecast. Updates of *Foreign Economic Trends and Their Implications for the United States* are issued semiannually for most countries in the world. The pamphlets describe economic trends in the country and analyze their implications for U.S. foreign trade. *Overseas Business Report,* published annually, deals with the basic economic structures, trade regulations, practices and policies, market potential, and investment laws in a group of countries. A similar publication is *International Marketing Handbook,* published by Gale Research Company, which provides an annual marketing profile for 142 nations.

**10** *Describe the concepts of marketing control and the marketing audit.*

## CONTROL OF MARKETING PROGRAMS

The desirability of one plan over another is often determined by the revenue that the alternative plans will generate. Forecasts are the basis for making revenue estimates. But once a plan is chosen and implemented, its effectiveness must be monitored. *Control* provides the mechanisms for evaluating marketing results in light of the plan's goals and for correcting actions that do not help the organization reach those goals within budget guidelines. Even if a firm is lucky enough to reach its goals without good controls, the chances are that some resources will have been wasted.

Although companies of all sizes have made great strides in instituting marketing controls, they often do not finish the process. For example, many companies have inadequate controls in the areas of product deletion, marketing cost allocations by functions or product lines, promotion effectiveness, and customer service.

### FORMAL VERSUS INFORMAL CONTROL

**formal control**
Written, management-initiated mechanism that influences the probability that employees and systems will function in ways that support the stated marketing objectives.

**informal control**
Unwritten, typically worker-initiated mechanism that influences individual or group behavior.

There are two broad classes of control within marketing organizations: formal and informal. A **formal control** is a written, management-initiated mechanism that influences the probability that employees and systems will function in ways that support the stated marketing objectives. An **informal control** is an unwritten, typically worker-initiated mechanism that influences individual or group behavior. Informal controls can back up formal controls to make the entire operation more efficient.

Informal control has three subsets:

- *Self-control:* occurs when a person sets personal objectives, monitors their attainment, and adjusts behavior if the objectives are off course. For example, say that Sandra Kerr, an account executive with a large New York advertising agency, has a chance to bid on a $50 million advertising budget for a division of Chrysler. The presentation must be ready within a month. Sandra exercises self-control by working nights and weekends to prepare the proposal.
- *Social control (also called small group control):* occurs when the marketing work unit sets standards (norms), monitors conformity with the standards, and takes action when a member deviates from them. Because the group has no formal authority, the action usually is limited to ostracizing the person. Salespeople, for example, might set norms for expenses, sales volume, or filing dates for paperwork.

- *Cultural control:* evolves over time. Culture, in this context, consists of the values and prescribed patterns that guide worker behavior within an entire organization. Cultural control stems from the slow accumulation of organizational stories, rituals, legends, and norms of social interaction. For instance, Procter & Gamble has tried to create what it calls a culture of "total quality" and the notion that workers should go the extra mile to ensure that quality. The company's Hatboro, Pennsylvania, plant was gearing up to launch a new children's NyQuil cough syrup in time for the winter cold season. Just days before the production line was to start rolling, the factory received from a supplier 3 million NyQuil boxes printed upside down. If the faulty boxes had been run through the machine that inserts the bottles, the tops of the bottles would have ended up at the bottom of the boxes. The packages would not have stood up on the store shelves. There was not enough time to bring in engineers to design new parts. Instead, two mechanics worked around the clock for three days, and even missed the plant's annual picnic, to develop a system of springs and brushes that turned the boxes around and kept them open so NyQuil bottles could be inserted properly.

## HOW CONTROL WORKS

Because informal controls, by definition, are not under management's direct influence, the focus here is the formal control systems used to ensure that events conform to plans. The flowchart in Exhibit 22.9 traces the steps of a basic control system. The process starts while planning is taking place. After the managers set goals, they must develop standards to measure performance. When standards have been set, the managers can then put the plan into action. Next, the managers measure performance to make sure standards have been met. If they have been, actions continue. Otherwise, the managers study deviations from standards to determine whether they fall within acceptable boundaries. If the deviations are not significant, actions continue with minor changes. When the deviations are major, the plan is halted. To revise the plan or perhaps scrap it, the managers analyze cause-and-effect relationships.

Assume that Jane French, the sales manager of Joy Manufacturing, a producer of heavy industrial equipment, decides that key accounts (customers with over $500,000 sales potential per year) are not getting the attention they deserve from the sales force. Her goal is to increase the calls made to key accounts. She decides that instead of demanding a key account quota from the sales force, she will use positive motivation. She develops a new commission scheme that provides a 2-percent-of-net-sales bonus on key account sales, or $1,500—whichever is greater. She then sends a letter to each salesperson with a list of key accounts in the territory. The standard she sets is a minimum average increase in calls on key accounts of 25 percent per month over the same period a year ago. By studying summary data from individual call-record sheets, she will measure performance.

During the first six months after the new system is installed, calls on key accounts increase on average by 31 percent, and key account sales rise 43 percent over the same period a year ago. The plan is conforming to French's standards. During the seventh month, however, the percentage increase slips to 26 percent and then falls to 22 percent. Although French is concerned about deviation from the standard, she doesn't consider it a major problem. Yet the general trend is disturbing, so she asks the eight regional managers to discuss it with the sales force and to report back within a week. All reports reflect the same situation. Key accounts are now being visited so often (an average of three times per month) that many sales calls are unproductive. The sales force then begins to call on other accounts and prospects where sales potential is better.

After studying the reports, French is satisfied that the key accounts are getting enough attention and that diverting time to other accounts might be more productive. She keeps the key account plan in force to provide incentives to call on key accounts but lowers the standard to an average increase of 15 percent over the previous year. In this example, the general goals were being met, but the control system required a refinement in the standards.

Three useful tools of marketing control are sales analysis, cost analysis, and the marketing audit. Sales analysis and cost analysis are explained in Appendix C; let's look now at the marketing audit.

*Exhibit 22.9*

Basic Formal Control System

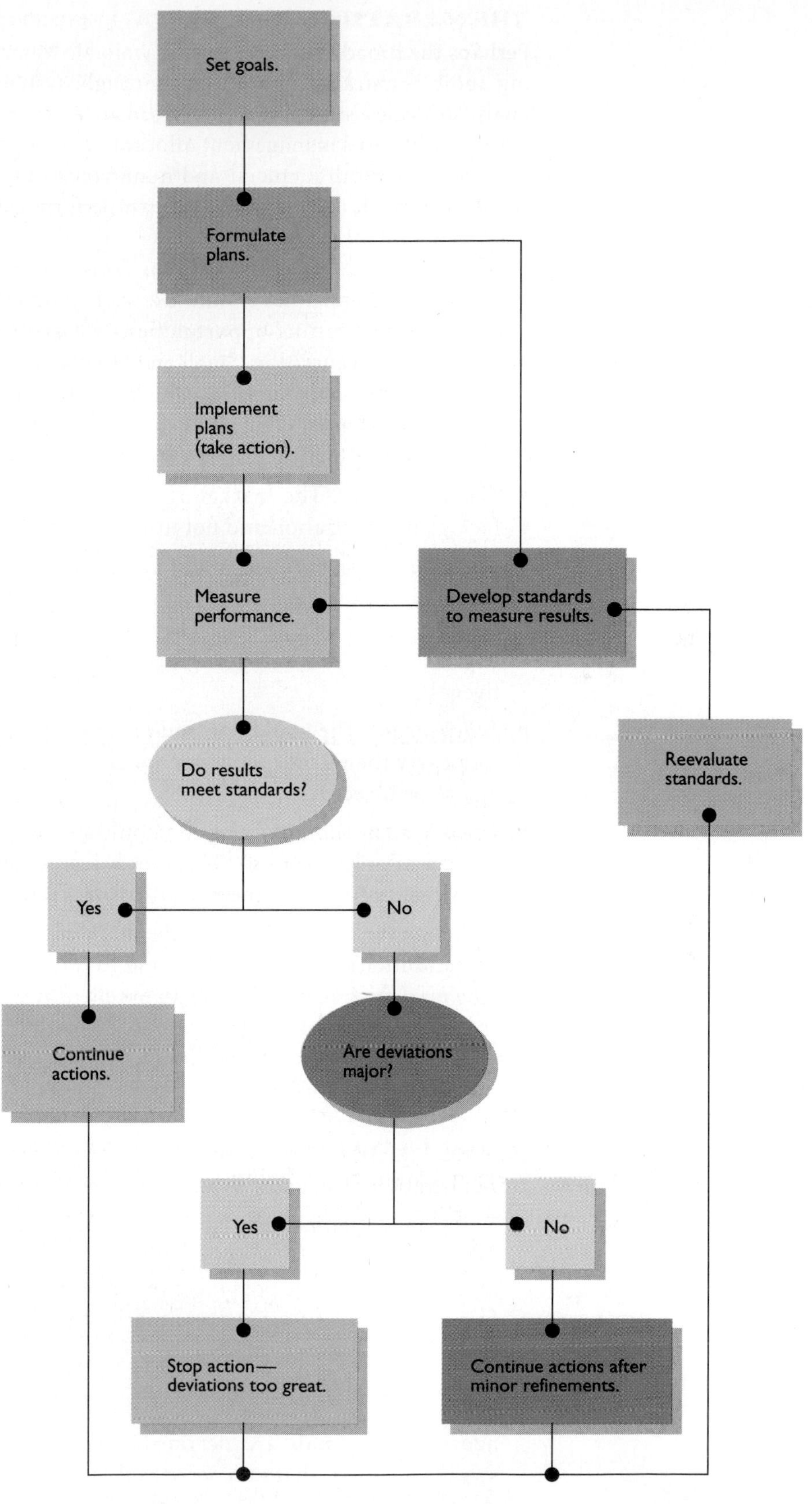

## THE MARKETING AUDIT

**marketing audit**
Thorough, systematic, periodic evaluation of the goals, strategies, structure, and performance of the marketing organization.

Perhaps the broadest control device available to marketing managers is the marketing audit. A **marketing audit** is a thorough, systematic, periodic evaluation of the goals, strategies, structure, and performance of the marketing organization. A marketing audit helps management allocate marketing resources efficiently. This tool, incorporating both financial and nonfinancial reporting, is mainly futuristic and strategic; it is not preoccupied with past performance but instead looks to the future allocation of marketing resources.

Marketing audits are not solely for firms having trouble meeting their marketing objectives. All companies should use such audits to uncover potential weaknesses and identify cost-cutting opportunities. Nor are marketing audits restricted to any single form of organization. Small and large organizations, service firms, and manufacturers all rely on the marketing audit. As strategic planning becomes more popular, the use of the marketing audit should increase.

The marketing audit has four characteristics:

- *Comprehensive:* The marketing audit covers all the major marketing issues facing an organization and not just trouble spots.
- *Systematic:* The marketing audit takes place in an orderly sequence and covers the organization's marketing environment, internal marketing system, and specific marketing activities. The diagnosis is followed by an action plan with both short-run and long-run proposals for improving overall marketing effectiveness.
- *Independent:* The marketing audit is normally conducted by an inside or outside party that is independent enough to have top management's confidence and to be objective.
- *Periodic:* The marketing audit should be carried out on a regular schedule instead of only in a crisis. Whether it seems successful or is in deep trouble, any organization can benefit greatly from such an audit.[26]

Although the main purpose of the marketing audit is to develop a full profile of the organization's marketing effort and to provide a basis for developing and revising the marketing plan, it is also an excellent way to improve communication and raise the level of marketing consciousness within the organization. That is, it is a useful vehicle for selling the philosophy and techniques of marketing to other members of the organization.

### Marketing Audit Procedure

Administration of an audit requires decisions on three important and related issues:

- *Scope of the audit:* The audit is an information-gathering process. If it is to fully evaluate a firm's overall marketing operation, the audit should collect as much information as possible given the firm's resources. For example, a small firm may find that a limited audit is most useful, because the firm may lack the resources to both collect detailed information and implement a large number of the suggestions that may emerge from a comprehensive audit. Although there is no "best" format for all organizations, the major areas usually addressed in an audit are identified in Appendix C. This outline includes many specific questions that may serve as a checklist.
- *Data collection:* Data are compiled from three main sources: internal interviews, external interviews, and secondary sources. Internal interviews, with key individuals in the organization, seek to get information on all aspects of

the organization's operations, competencies, and constraints. The internal interviews should be supplemented by interviews with key members of the organization's external publics, such as customers, suppliers, competitors, and stockholders. The audit should also tap all pertinent secondary sources of data available in files or in the literature. However, secondary sources do not provide reliable information unless they have been compiled with marketing audits in mind. Furthermore, these data must be carefully evaluated to make sure they are relevant. Together, these three sources of information offer a broad base for assessing an organization's marketing operations. The number of sources consulted and the amount of data collected depend on the scope of the audit.

- *Selection of an auditor:* Marketing audits may be conducted by someone from within or from outside the firm. In a firm with severely limited resources, a high-ranking staff member or companywide auditing committee may conduct the audit. However, self-audits lack the objectivity of independent audits by outsiders. Self-audits are less likely to challenge "sacred cows," because it is hard for people objectively to critique decisions made or influenced by them or their close colleagues. A third party, with whom people can talk openly without feeling any threat toward their position in the organization, can report insights that might not be offered as candidly to someone from within the organization.

### Postaudit Tasks

After the audit has been completed, three tasks remain. First, the audit should profile existing weaknesses and inhibiting factors, as well as the firm's strengths and the new opportunities available to it. Recommendations have to be judged and prioritized so that those with the potential to contribute most to improved marketing performance can be implemented first. The usefulness of the data also depends on the auditor's skill in interpreting and presenting the data so decision makers can quickly grasp the major points.

The second task is to ensure that the role of the audit has been clearly communicated. It is unlikely that the suggestions will require radical change in the way the firm operates. The audit's main role is to address the question "Where are we now?" and to suggest ways to improve what the firm already does.

The final postaudit task is to make someone accountable for implementing recommendations. All too often, reports are presented, applauded, and filed away to gather dust. The person made accountable should be someone who is committed to the project and who has the managerial power to make things happen.

## LOOKING BACK

Look back at the story about Barnes & Noble at the beginning of this chapter. The role of strategic planning at Barnes & Noble, or any other organization, is to provide a long-run vision for the firm. Strategic planning thus guides the long-term commitment of resources. Managers have found that defining the mission of their organization helps them direct and focus their activities. Organizations function better as a result and become more responsive to the changing environment. Therefore, strategic planning is very important for efficiently reaching long-run goals.

The key factor in making strategic planning work is top management's commitment to the process. Top management's participation is required as well.

Forecasting, an important part of strategic planning, helps marketing managers choose a course of action. Forecasted sales, profit, and market share are among the most important criteria in choosing a strategic alternative. Control makes certain that a plan reaches its goals by comparing outcomes of the plan with standards. When deviations are identified, corrective actions can be taken to get marketing back on the right path.

## SUMMARY

1 **Describe the concept of strategic planning.** Strategic planning requires long-term planning, organization of resources to carry out the plans, and adjustment of the plans when necessary. The strategic plan affects the long-run course of the organization, its use of resources, and its long-term financial success.

2 **Identify the steps in the strategic planning process, and explain how businesses define their mission and set objectives.** The eight steps in the strategic planning process are to define the business mission, set the objectives, establish strategic business units (if required), conduct a situation analysis, develop strategic alternatives, select an alternative, implement the selected strategy, and alter the selected strategy when necessary.

A firm defines its mission by answering the question "What business are we in?" It then sets objectives related to that mission. Good objectives are realistic, measurable, time-specific, and consistent, and they indicate the priorities of the organization.

3 **Explain how businesses form strategic business units.** As firms become larger and more complex, many decide to restructure into strategic business units (SBUs). Each SBU should have a distinct mission and target market, control over its own resources, its own competitors, and a single business or collection of related businesses.

4 **Explain how businesses conduct situation analyses.** A situation analysis, sometimes called a SWOT analysis, requires that management identify the firm's (or SBU's) internal strengths (S) and weaknesses (W) and also examine external opportunities (O) and threats (T). One technique for examining opportunities is to seek strategic windows, limited times during which the "fit" between the key requirements of a market and the firm's competencies are at an optimum. A differential advantage is a unique aspect of a firm or its product offering that causes target customers to patronize the firm rather than its competitors. A firm can achieve a differential advantage through superior skills or superior resources.

5 **Discuss the techniques for developing, evaluating, and selecting strategic alternatives.** The strategic opportunity matrix can be used to help management develop strategic alternatives. The four options are market penetration, product development, market development, and diversification.

Marketing managers then have four main tools for evaluating strategic alternatives. First, the portfolio matrix is a method of determining the profit potential and investment requirements of a firm's SBUs by classifying them as stars, cash cows, problem children, or dogs and then determining appropriate resource allocations for each. A more detailed alternative to the portfolio matrix is the market attractiveness/company strength matrix, which measures company and market viability. The third technique for evaluating strategic alternatives uses response functions, or graphed relationships, to analyze the impact of marketing mix variables on sales. The fourth tool, PIMS (profit impact of market strategy) analysis, uses a computer database to compare a firm's market conditions, competitive position, and financial performance to those of other firms in order to forecast profitability. Corporate culture often plays an important role in selecting a strategic alternative.

6 **Explain how firms implement strategies and alter strategies when necessary.** Implementation requires the delegation of authority and responsibility, the determination of a time frame for completing tasks, and the allocation of resources. Sometimes a strategic plan also requires task-force management. A task force is established to accomplish a single goal or mission and thus works against a deadline.

After an organization implements its strategic plan, it must track results and monitor the external environment. A key tool in evaluating the strategic plan is the marketing audit, which uses financial and nonfinancial reports to evaluate goals, strategies, and performance.

7 **Identify several techniques that help make strategic planning effective.** First, management must realize that strategic planning is an ongoing process and not a once-a-year exercise. Second, good strategic planning involves a high level of creativity. The last requirement is top management's support and cooperation.

8 **Describe seven sales forecasting techniques.** Sales forecasting is a process of estimating sales for products, product lines, companies, and industries. Contemporary forecasting employs seven techniques: jury of executive opinion, sales force composite, Delphi technique, moving average, regression technique, multiple-factor index, and purchase intent scale. The best tools for forecasting demand for new products are the Delphi technique, the multiple-factor index approach, and the purchase intent scale.

9 **Discuss global issues in strategic planning and forecasting.** Managers deciding to "go global" must make some dramatic changes in their strategic planning. Competitors are usually bigger, and target markets may have local quirks that complicate marketing decisions. However, global firms often have a differential advantage, in both their home market and international markets. No matter where firms sell their products, sales forecasting techniques remain the same. Publications are available that provide economic and market data for foreign markets.

10 **Describe the concepts of marketing control and the marketing audit.** A marketing control system ensures that marketing goals are achieved within guidelines. Controls are either formal (instituted by management) or informal (unwritten and typically initiated by workers). The control process begins during planning. Managers develop standards to measure performance. If measured performance does not meet standards, deviations are examined, and action may be halted if deviations from the standards are unacceptable.

The marketing audit is the process of evaluating the goals, strategies, structure, and performance of the marketing organization. The marketing audit should be comprehensive, systematic, independent, and periodic. Administration of an audit requires decisions about the scope of the audit, data collection methods, and selection of an auditor. Postaudit tasks include interpreting the data, communicating the results, and implementing the recommendations.

KEY TERMS

*cash cow* 768
*Delphi technique* 780
*diversification* 764
*dog* 769
*formal control* 785
*informal control* 785
*jury of executive opinion* 780
*market attractiveness/company strength matrix* 769
*market development* 763
*marketing audit* 788
*market penetration* 763
*market sales potential* 779
*moving average* 780
*portfolio matrix* 768
*problem child (question mark)* 769
*profit impact of market strategy (PIMS)* 772
*purchase intent scale* 782
*regression* 781
*response function* 771
*sales force composite* 780
*sales forecast* 778
*star* 768
*strategic business unit (SBU)* 759
*strategic planning* 757
*strategic window* 761
*SWOT analysis* 760

## Discussion and Writing Questions

✍1. Create a marketing plan to increase enrollment in your school. Write down each step, and describe the controls on the plan's implementation.

2. Why is a differential advantage critical to a firm's success?

3. Cite examples not mentioned in the chapter of specific strategies that firms use to achieve a differential advantage.

✍4. The CEO of IBM, Louis Gerstner, commented, "We're not going to play the market share game, just to hold some theoretical market share. Profitability is the most important thing." Write an analysis of the controversy over market share versus profit, referring to Gerstner's position and its pros and cons.

5. In your opinion, what type of organizational culture is best for the organization? Why?

6. Discuss four characteristics of the marketing audit.

✍7. Choose a company (real or hypothetical), and write some specific guidelines for that company to use in conducting a marketing audit.

8. Cite an example from your experience where a company would have benefited from a better control system.

## Application for Small Business

Jan Thomas is a 51-year-old grandmother, as well as chairman of a company based in New Orleans that does $1.2 million in sales each year. Her company, Jan Thomas Products, grew out of a product idea Jan had when bathing her grandson. Her idea was to create a "sponge car seat" to cradle a child in, thus freeing the mother's hands for washing the baby. The company now offers a variety of products for cleaning babies.

### Questions

1. What might be an appropriate mission statement for Jan Thomas Products?

2. What factors should Jan consider when forecasting sales for the next year?

3. Jan has only twelve employees. Does she really need any type of control system? Explain your answer.

**CRITICAL THINKING CASE**

## S.C. Johnson & Son

Commonly known as Johnson Wax, this outfit has long profited by sticking to niche marketing powered by strong R&D and heavy advertising. Johnson's brands—which include Pledge furniture polish, Glade air freshener, Raid bug spray, and Edge shaving gel—command huge market shares against a group of much smaller competitors. Consumers buy these products only a few times a year rather than a few times a week, so they aren't highly sensitive to price competition. Thus Johnson can command large profit margins while still repelling the private-label competition. Revenues at the privately held company have grown about 12 percent annually since 1988.

Johnson may be getting too big, however. In 1993 it paid nearly $1.2 billion, ten times more than it had ever spent on an acquisition, to buy Drackett Co. The deal brought Johnson a cabinetful of leading household brands, including Windex, Drano, and Vanish toilet-bowl cleaner. The company also got something it didn't bargain for: a phalanx of heavyweight competition, like Procter & Gamble and Clorox. Says Richard Posey, Johnson's executive vice president for North American consumer products: "Our competitive set has changed fundamentally. It's like moving from Triple A baseball to the majors."

But Johnson has been training for the big leagues for several years. Since 1991 the 108-year-old company has overhauled factories, consolidated international operations, and recast itself more clearly as a provider of products that clean, shine, and debug the home. Says CEO William George: "We're more focused. We're using our resources where they have a better chance of success." Johnson has sold most of its hair- and skin-care brands—with the notable exception of Edge for men and Skintimate for women, which continue to outsell Gillette in the shaving business.

To meet its new competitive threats, Johnson has increased its already substantial global advertising budget (now running about $500 million, a hefty 14 percent of sales), stepped up innovation, and quickened its expansion overseas. With Glade Plug-Ins, invented in Switzerland and launched in Australia, the company has breathed new life into its once stagnant air freshener business. Johnson turned these long-lasting fragrance dispensers, which fit into electrical outlets, into hot sellers in the United States and many of the forty-eight other countries where the company operates.

To better compete with firms that enjoy huge economies of scale, Johnson has mounted a concerted effort to cut costs. A paternalistic company with a tradition of lifetime employment and mind-numbing assembly lines, the company has now begun embracing self-directed work teams. Says chairman Samuel Johnson, a member of *Fortune*'s Business Hall of Fame, a great-grandson of the founder, and a noted environmentalist: "We have to guard against the diseases of complacency and arrogance."



Questions

1. How would you phrase the mission statement for S.C. Johnson & Sons?

2. What differential advantages, if any, does Johnson have?

3. If you had to make recommendations using the market attractiveness/company strength matrix, what would they be?

Reference

Ronald Henkoff, "When to Take On the Giants," *Fortune,* 30 May 1994, pp. 111, 114.

**VIDEO CASE**

## Polygram

Polygram, a recording company owned by the giant Dutch company Phillips, recently purchased Motown for about $300 million. The acquisition now gives Polygram the best collection of artists in American pop music. Motown needed Polygram's strategic management capabilities. Many music industry observers felt that Motown had lost its strategic vision and ability to spot market trends. For example, the company missed the popularity and growth of rap music, for the most part. Polygram, in turn, wanted the Motown name and its talent.

The catalog of Motown songs and artists is known worldwide. The music of Stevie Wonder, the Jacksons, Diana Ross, Smokey Robinson, and others are music standards in many cultures. These legends define Motown's value. The use of their songs in commercials and movie soundtracks continues to generate significant cash flow worldwide.

Polygram also feels that many opportunities exist in nonmusic ventures. One project being discussed is a movie based on the life of Stevie Wonder. A second concept under review is Motown restaurants. Polygram has made four major acquisitions in recent years and now feels that it is time to focus on internal growth.

Questions

1. Where would Motown be classified in the portfolio matrix? How might Polygram attempt to reposition it?

2. What strategic opportunities do you see for Polygram now that it has acquired Motown?

3. Discuss some of the potential threats facing Motown.

# PART SEVEN
# INTEGRATIVE CASE

## LEVI STRAUSS AND COMPANY

Levi Strauss began his business venture in the late 1800s in San Francisco, stitching surplus tent canvas into work pants for gold prospectors. Today the world's largest apparel maker has cornered a 22 percent share of the $6 billion jeans market. Trailing directly behind Levi Strauss are Wrangler (13 percent), Lee (11 percent), and Gitano (5 percent). These four jeans manufacturers control over 50 percent of the market. Another 20 to 25 percent of the market is composed of the private-label jeans of stores like JCPenney, The Gap, and Sears. Blue denims are the biggest-selling jeans (70 percent of market), followed by colored denims (20 percent). Acid-washed, stone-washed, oversized, and distressed-denim jeans are some of the most popular looks today.

### Target Market for Blue Jeans

In 1989 the industry sold 350 million pairs of jeans, more than enough for every person in the United States to have a new pair. Still, the market for jeans has declined quite a bit since its peak in 1981, when the industry sold 520 million pairs. The main problem is the shrinking population of 14-to-24-year-olds, the key market segment for jeans. Baby boomers have always been one of the major market segments. However, as these consumers enter midlife, they buy fewer pairs of jeans and begin looking for different products. They continue to wear blue jeans, but mostly on weekends. They simply do not wear out their jeans as fast as they once did.

Each of the four major jeans manufacturers has taken a different approach to segmenting the market. In the past, Gitano used sultry models to promote its jeans. This sort of image advertising appealed to young women. The company then realized that many of its loyal customers were older and had children of their own. In an effort to expand its market, the company broadened its appeal. Gitano's Spirit of Family campaign is aimed at mom and her teenage daughters.

Lee competes in all market segments but has directed its TV advertising to women. The company chose to focus on women for two reasons: Women constitute about 40 percent of the market, and they buy most of the children's clothes. The company emphasizes the product benefits—comfort and fit. Lee adopted the slogan "Nobody fits your body . . . or the way you live . . . better than Lee." The company targets the male market through the use of print advertising trying to maintain a "family brand" image.

Wrangler, manufacturer of the official jeans of the Pro Rodeo Association, concentrates on the blue-collar male market. Long associated with its hard-core cowboy positioning, the company is broadening its market to include consumers who might imitate the cowboy look. To reach this new market, Wrangler hired Texas Rangers' pitcher Nolan Ryan as a spokesperson for its products.

Levi Strauss has segmented the market not only by age but also by region and ethnic group. The company hired Spike Lee to direct a series of documentary-style ads for its 501 brand. Spike Lee has tremendous appeal with 14-to-24-year-olds. The company targets the market of 7-to-11-year-olds with the Wild Creatures campaign featured on Saturday morning television. In the West and Southwest, the company hits the Hispanic market with the appeal that jeans are appropriate for all occasions. This group wears jeans mostly for work only.

### Product Line Adaptation

Levi Strauss produces a wide range of products. In addition to its denim jeans, the company makes a complete line of clothing.

The company has never lost sight of the changing marketplace. Levi Strauss was one of the first companies to adapt its product line to the changing lifestyle of aging consumers. In 1978, market research indicated that older men preferred dress slacks to jeans. Levi Strauss introduced Action Slacks—comfortable, easy-to-clean slacks with an expandable waistband. Levi Strauss made middle-aged adults feel good about their older bodies; no matter how much exercise people get as they age, their bodies just don't maintain youthful contours. By 1985 Action Slacks brought the company over $100 million in sales.

The company has another product hit with the Dockers line of clothing. Levi Strauss identified a new consumer who wanted something between jeans and Dad's pressed slacks. The Dockers line is not new to Levi Strauss. The company had marketed a line of loose-fitting chino pants under the name Dockers in both Japan and Argentina with little success. The key to the product's success in the United States is that the slacks are available in a multitude of colors. With a line of coordinated shirts and a massive promotional campaign, Dockers has become a major product category that did not previously exist. Even stores like Sears and JCPenney have created special Dockers departments. Without merchandising support from Levi Strauss, many of these stores would have missed this Dockers market segment.

### LeviLink Computer Network

Making jeans is mostly a manual job. Workers hand-sew almost every seam and button on a pair of jeans.

In an industry with rapid changes in fashions and fads, retailers seldom stock large quantities of any specific size or style. Lower inventories reduce the risk to retailers when a specific style falls out of fashion but increase the risk of lost sales due to stock outages. This problem is even more severe for large retail chain stores. These stores often handwrite all orders and then send them to a central purchasing department for processing. Restocking an item can take as long as three weeks. LeviLink, Levi Strauss's new computer system, is streamlining these procedures.

Each store is connected directly to Levi Strauss by computer terminal. After the orders are entered into the terminal, the store receives the shipment within six days. The faster turnaround time offers two key advantages. First, it eliminates a lot of lost sales due to stock outages. Second, the system helps reduce the risk of stocking huge inventories in a constantly changing fashion business. The company estimates that for the retailers using LeviLink, sales have increased 20 to 30 percent.

Levi Strauss CEO Bob Haas decided to put $500 million into the restructuring of Levi Strauss's manufacturing and distribution systems by the end of 1995. The ultimate goal is to bring the equivalent of just-in-time manufacturing to the apparel business. When an order for a pair of jeans is entered into the system, the system can request that another pair of jeans be made. The company is also using the system to adjust the quantities of materials it orders from suppliers. By tying the production system closer to product sales, Levi Strauss has eliminated the need for large inventories of fabrics in warehouses next to manufacturing facilities.

### New Retail Outlets

In 1994, the Federal Trade Commission cleared the way for Levi Strauss to open its own retail stores, something the firm had been banned from doing since 1978. Although Levi Strauss does not intend to become a high-volume retailer, it does hope to open 200 stores nationwide by 1999, in downtown areas and upscale suburban malls. Each new store is expected to be one of three types: a joint venture with an existing retail chain, a Levi Strauss–owned Original Levi's Store, or a Levi Strauss–owned Dockers Shop.

### Questions

1. Propose a business mission statement for Levi Strauss for now and the future.
2. Compare Levi Strauss to its competitors in today's market. Predict which competitors may challenge Levi Strauss's leadership in the jeans market.
3. Examine Levi Strauss's differential advantage. Propose a plan for Levi Strauss to maintain this advantage.
4. Prepare a situation analysis for Levi Strauss. Predict possible threats and weaknesses that might hamper growth at Levi Strauss.
5. Evaluate the corporate culture of Levi Strauss. Is this the type of company you would like to work for?

### Suggested Readings

Bernie Knill, "Lesson from Levi's: Quick Response

Too Slow for the '90s," *Industry Week,* 2 May 1994, pp. A16–A21.

Russell Mitchell and Michael Oneal, "Managing by Values," *Business Week,* 1 August 1994, pp. 46–52.

Nina Munk, "Designing Ambitions," *Forbes,* 28 February 1994, p. 136.

Bill Richards, "Levi Strauss Plans to Open 200 Stores in 5 Years, with Ending of FTC Ban," *The Wall Street Journal,* 22 December 1994, p. A2.

# PART SEVEN
# ETHICS CASE

## THE INFLATABLE RÉSUMÉ

Each year, several million people are hired based on information obtained during an interview or listed on their résumé. Each year, some significant number of people get a job by falsifying their résumé. Bill Myer, a graduating senior at a major Midwestern university, had read articles about people fired years later for having lied on their résumés. He was determined to tell the truth on his until he was confronted with a statement by one of his fraternity brothers: "If you believe in yourself, you need to give the interviewer something to believe in as well." "What do you mean when you say 'Give them something to believe in'?" asked Bill. "I mean expand your job descriptions and experience so they fully understand that you are an experienced and capable worker," replied his friend. Bill gave some thought to his friend's specific suggestions:

1. Expand your description of each job and your work history so they show your managerial capability, even though you may not have served in a management position.
2. If you have not had the chance to hold office in student organizations, describe the jobs you have done for those organizations with significant titles that you have given yourself. For example, if you parked cars at the fraternity spring formal, you would give yourself the title of Director of Logistics Committee.
3. Round up your grade point average or simply pick out the courses that you have done well in and report only the grade point average for them.

- What are the risks involved in doing the things that Bill's friend suggested? Do you think interviewers have seen these things done before?

Bill's friend made some other suggestions:

4. Make summer jobs sound more important by giving yourself a job title whether you had one or not.
5. Cite references of very important people at the university whether they know you well or not, because no one ever checks résumé references.
6. Add courses to your résumé that will make you appear to be more outstanding, whether you took them or not, because no one ever checks transcripts.

- Are the temporary advantages gained by this level of résumé deception worth the risk? How might interviewers check your character by checking résumé items?

The final advice given by Bill's fraternity brother involved the following:

7. Drop some experience anecdotes into a job interview that do not appear on the résumé and then apologize for forgetting to add them. Leave the impression that there may be a number of other great experiences that you did not bother to put on your résumé.
8. In the interview, mention the names of others who could have been references that the interviewer will recognize. The names will leave a good impression, and again, no one ever checks.

- Do interviewers check references, transcripts, and other such background material? What is the risk of doing what Bill's friend suggests?

Bill asked himself whether his résumé would look competitive with other résumés if he was completely truthful. He felt that some interviewers would not be as willing to talk with him without an inflated résumé but that others would probably find it refreshing that he had not tried to inflate his background.

- Do you agree with Bill's perceptions? What advantages would there be to being completely honest on a résumé?

# APPENDIX A: CAREERS IN MARKETING

You can use many of the basic concepts of marketing introduced in this book to get the career you want by marketing yourself. The purpose of marketing is to create exchanges that satisfy individuals as well as organizational objectives, and a career is certainly an exchange situation for both you and an organization. The purpose of this appendix is to help you market yourself to prospective employers by providing some helpful tools and information.

## AVAILABLE CAREERS

Marketing careers have a bright outlook for the latter half of the 1990s. The U.S. Bureau of Labor Statistics estimates that employment in marketing fields will grow 30 percent by the year 2000. Many of these increases will be in the areas of sales, public relations, retailing, advertising, marketing research, and product management.

### SALES

There are more opportunities in sales than in any other area of marketing. Sales positions vary greatly among companies. Some selling positions focus more on providing information; others emphasize locating potential customers and closing the sale. Compensation, often salary plus commission, sets few limits on the amount of money a person can make and therefore offers great potential. Sales positions can be found in many organizations, including manufacturing, wholesaling, retailing, insurance, real estate, financial services, and many other service businesses.

### PUBLIC RELATIONS

Public relations firms help create an image or message for an individual or organization and communicate it effectively to the desired audience. All types of firms, profit and nonprofit organizations, individuals, and even countries employ public relations specialists. Communication skills, both written and oral, are critical for success in public relations.

### RETAILING

Retail careers require many skills. Retail personnel may manage the sales force and other personnel, select and order merchandise, and be responsible for promotional activities, inventory control, store security, and accounting. Large retail stores have a variety of positions, including store or department manager, buyer, display designer, and catalog manager.

### ADVERTISING

Many organizations employ advertising specialists. Advertising agencies are the largest employers; however, manufacturers, retailers, banks, radio and television stations, hospitals, and insurance agencies all have advertising departments. Creativity, artistic talent, and communication skills area few of the attributes needed for a successful career in advertising.

### MARKETING RESEARCH

The most rapid growth in marketing careers is in marketing research. Marketing research firms, advertising agencies, universities, private firms, nonprofit organizations, and governments provide growing opportunities in marketing research. Researchers conduct industry research, advertising research, pricing and packaging research, new product testing, and test marketing. Researchers are involved in one or more stages of the research process, depending on the size of the organization conducting the research. Marketing research requires knowledge of statistics, data processing and analysis, psychology, and communication.

### PRODUCT MANAGEMENT

Product managers coordinate all the activities required to market a product. Thus they need a general knowledge of all the aspects of marketing. Product managers are responsible for the successes and failures of a product and are compensated well for this responsibility. Most product managers have previous sales experience and skills in communication. The position of product manager is a major step in the career path of top-level marketing executives.

## WHERE TO LOOK

Not many people are fortunate enough to have a job fall into their lap when they graduate. It is your responsibility to find a career that satisfies both your needs and the needs of the employer.

So, where do you look? Several resources help narrow the search. Some of the obvious places to check are parents, friends, family members, career planning and placement centers, career counselors, and the companies themselves. A list of not-so-obvious resources is shown in Exhibit A.1.

*Exhibit A.1*

Selected Sources for Finding Out about Marketing Careers

Source: Adapted from *Occupational Outlook Handbook, 1994–1995 Edition* (Washington, DC: U.S. Department of Labor, Bureau of Labor Statistics, 1994), p. 44.

*Advertising Career Directory*
(Hawthorn, NJ: Career Press)

American Marketing Association, *Careers in Marketing*
(Chicago)

*Business Week Careers*

*Changing Times Annual Survey: Jobs for New College Grads*

Chemical Marketing Research Association, *Careers in Industrial Marketing Research*
(New York)

College Placement Council, *CPC Annual*

Dow Jones & Co., *Managing Your Career*
(published twice a year)

Lebhar-Friedman, Inc., *Careers in Retailing*
(published annually)

Magazine Publishers Association, *Guide to Business Careers in Magazine Publishing*
(New York)

*National Employment Business Weekly*

*Peterson's Business & Management Jobs*
(published annually)

U.S. Department of Labor, *Occupational Outlook Handbook*
(Washington, DC: published biennially)

*Exhibit A.2*

Compensation for Selected Marketing Positions

| Position | Compensation |
|---|---|
| *Advertising* | |
| Advertising media planner | $15,000–$35,000 |
| Assistant account executive | $18,000–$40,000 |
| Account executive | $25,000–$60,000 |
| Account supervisor | $40,000–$70,000 |
| *Marketing research* | |
| Analyst | $22,000–$35,000 |
| Project director | $40,000–$60,000 |
| Research director | $70,000–$100,000 |
| *Product management* | |
| Market analyst | $15,000–$30,000 |
| Assistant product manager | $17,000–$35,000 |
| Group manager | $37,000–$75,000 |
| Group product manager | $40,000–$100,000 |
| *Retailing* | |
| Trainee | $17,000–$25,000 |
| Chain store manager | $18,000–$90,000 |
| Buyer | $20,000–$60,000 |
| Department store manager | $30,000–$100,000 |
| *Sales* | |
| Trainee | $15,000–$30,000 |
| Real estate agent | $15,000–$100,000 |
| Insurance agent | $17,000–$100,000 |
| Manufacturer's representative | $20,000–$80,000 |
| Field salesperson | $23,000–$45,000 |
| Sales manager | $31,000–$75,000 |
| Securities salesperson | $35,000–$200,000 |

## COMPENSATION

Many college graduates want to know how much they will get paid in their new career. Although this is a topic that should be considered in your selection of a company, it should not be the only one. It is up to you to decide which criteria are most important in choosing a job.

Exhibit A.2 shows the average compensation range for various marketing positions. These ranges vary depending on your education and preference for geographic location. In addition to salary, marketing positions may include a company car, bonuses, or expense accounts, forms of compensation that are not common in other professions.

## GETTING THE JOB

Before you begin to look for a job, you need to make a self-assessment and develop your résumé and a cover letter.

### SELF-ASSESSMENT

When it is time to look for a job, it is important that you have a good idea of your personal needs, capabilities, characteristics, strengths, and weaknesses. The idea is to prepare so you will be able to market yourself the best you can.

The following questions will help you analyze what is important to you in choosing the kind of work you will do and the kind of employer for whom you will work:

1. What do I do best? Are these activities related to people, things, or data?
2. Do I communicate better orally or in writing?
3. Do I consider myself a leader of a team or a group?
   a. Do I see myself as active participant in a team or group?
   b. Do I prefer to work by myself?
   c. Do I prefer working under supervision?
4. Do I work well under pressure?
5. Do I like taking responsibility? Or would I rather follow directions?
6. Do I enjoy new products and activities? Or would I rather follow a regular routine?
7. When I am working, which of the following things are most important?
   a. Working for a regular salary?
   b. Working for a commission?
   c. Working for a combination of both?
8. Do I prefer to work a regular 9 a.m. to 5 p.m. schedule?
9. Will I be willing to travel more than half the time?
10. What kind of work environment do I prefer?
    a. Indoors or outdoors?
    b. Urban setting (population over a million)?
    c. Rural community?
11. Would I prefer to work for a large organization?
12. Am I willing to move?
13. Where do I want to be in three years? Five years? Ten years?

## THE FAB STUDENT MODEL

The FAB matrix is a device adapted from personal selling that can help you market yourself to potential employers. FAB, which stands for Features-Advantages-Benefits, relates your skills to an employer's needs by citing the specific benefits you can bring to that company.[1] People want benefits, whether they are buying a car or hiring a marketing graduate to fill a job vacancy. An employer needs information that indicates how hiring you will specifically benefit the firm.

Exhibit A.3 on page 802 is a model of FAB for students. The first step in FAB is as critical for you as it is for the salesperson: determining what the customer needs. In the case of the employer, needs are what the job requires or the problems to be solved. These needs should be listed in priority order, starting with the most important. Step 2 matches each need with a particular feature of the applicant (skill, ability, personality characteristic, educational attainment). In step 3, you arrange the needs and features in a FAB matrix where they become information points that you can use to construct a cover letter, résumé, or interview presentation.

You must approach a prospective employer with complete knowledge of that employer's features and job needs. Using the FAB matrix, you can match features with needs in a systematic, complete, and concise way.

*Exhibit A.3*

The FAB Matrix

| **Need of employer** *"This job requires . . ."* | **Feature of job applicant** *"I have . . ."* | **Advantage of feature** *"This feature means . . ."* | **Benefit to employer** *"You will . . ."* |
|---|---|---|---|
| Frequent sales presentations to individuals and groups | Taken 10 classes that required presentations | I require limited or no training in making presentations | Save on the cost of training and have employee with ability and confidence to be productive early |
| Knowledge of personal computers, software, and applications | Taken a personal computer course and used Lotus in most upper-level classes | I can already use Word 5.0, Lotus, dBase, and other software | Save time and money on training |
| Person with management potential | Been president of student marketing group and social fraternity president for 2 years | I have experience leading people | Save time because I am capable of stepping into leadership position as needed |

## RÉSUMÉ AND COVER LETTER

When developing a résumé, you need to capture on paper your abilities, education, background, training, work experience, and personal qualifications. Many of these points can be developed from the FAB matrix or other self-assessment techniques. Your résumé should also be brief, usually no more than one page. The goal is to communicate your qualifications in a way that will obtain a positive response—an interview—from potential employers.

The cover letter is, in some ways, more important than the résumé. It must be persuasive, professional, and interesting. Ideally, it should set you above and apart from the other candidates for the position. Each letter should look and sound original, tailored to the specific organization you are contacting. It should describe the position you are applying for and arouse interest, describe your qualifications, and indicate how you can be contacted. Whenever possible, cover letters should be addressed to the individual, not the title. Sample résumés and cover letters can be found in your local library or student placement center. Follow up the letter and résumé with a telephone call.

## THE INTERVIEW

The interview is the most important part of the job search process. An interview often decides whether or not you get the job. Here are some suggestions for before, during, and after an interview, as well as some questions interviewers frequently ask and some good questions you may want to ask them:

### Before the Interview

- Interviewers have varied styles: to name a few, the "Let's get to know each other" style, the quasi-interrogation style (question after question), and the tough, probing why, why, why style. Be ready for anything.
- Practice being interviewed with a friend, and ask for a critique.

- Prepare at least five good questions whose answers are not readily available in company literature. (Obtain and read this literature, such as brochures, advertisements, catalogs, and annual reports, beforehand.)
- Anticipate possible interview questions, and frame suitable answers.
- Avoid "back to back" interviews, as they can be exhausting.
- Dress for the interview in a conservative style rather than in the height of fashion.
- Plan to arrive about ten minutes early to collect your thoughts before being called.
- Review the main points you intend to cover.
- Try to relax.

## During the Interview

- Give a firm handshake in greeting the interviewer. Introduce yourself using the same form the interviewer has used (that is, use first names only if the interviewer does so first). Make a good initial impression.
- Maintain enthusiasm throughout the interview.
- Good eye contact, good posture, and distinct speech are musts. Don't clasp your hands or fiddle with jewelry, hair, or anything else. Sit comfortably in your chair. Do not smoke, even if given permission. Bring extra copies of your résumé with you.
- Know your "story" in detail. Present your selling points. Answer questions directly. Avoid one-word answers, but don't be wordy.
- Let the interviewer take the initiative often, but don't be passive. Find a way to direct the conversation to those things you want the interviewer to hear.
- The best time to make your most important points is toward the end of the interview, in order to leave on a high note.
- Don't be afraid to "close" the interview. You might say, "I'm very interested in the position, and I have enjoyed this interview."

## After the Interview

- Upon leaving, make a note of any key points. Be sure you know who is to follow up on the interview and when a decision is to be made.
- Objectively analyze your performance during the interview.
- Send a thank-you letter that mentions any additional points of information you may have left out.

## Questions Frequently Asked by Employers

- What are your long- and short-range goals and objectives, when and why did you establish them, and how are you preparing yourself to achieve them?
- What do you see yourself doing five years from now?
- What do you really want to do in life?
- How do you plan to achieve your career goals?
- What do you expect to be earning in five years?
- Why should I hire you?
- What do you think it takes to be successful in a company like ours?

- In what ways do you think you can make a contribution to our company?
- What qualities should a successful manager have?
- What do you know about our company?
- Do you think your grades are a good indicator of your academic achievement?
- What college subjects did you like most? Least? Why?
- What have you learned from your mistakes?
- How would you describe the ideal job for you following graduation?[2]

### Questions to Ask Employers

- What are the opportunities at this company for personal growth?
- Identify typical career paths based on past records. What is a realistic time frame for advancement?
- How is an employee evaluated and promoted?
- Describe a typical first-year assignment.
- Tell me about your initial and advanced training programs.
- How would you describe our company's personality and management style?
- What are your expectations for new hires?
- What are the characteristics of a successful person at your company?
- What are the company's plans for future growth, and how will they affect me?[3]

## FOLLOW-UP

The in-company interview can run from a few hours to a whole day. Your interest, maturity, enthusiasm, assertiveness, logic, and knowledge of the company and the position you seek will all be under scrutiny. But you also need to ask questions that are important to you. Find out about the environment, job role, responsibilities, opportunities, and any current issues that may be of interest. To avoid future embarrassment, try to remember the names of the people you have met. If all goes well, you may be working for this firm in the near future. Good luck!

# APPENDIX B: FINANCIAL ARITHMETIC FOR MARKETING

Marketing arithmetic plays an important role in managing a business and setting price strategies. Marketing managers must decide when to add or drop products and know how to evaluate the performance of products, product lines, and even divisions. These decisions require a basic understanding of accounting concepts. In this appendix you will learn about income statements; the relationships among costs, stock turnover, and profits; several techniques for evaluating an investment; and the way to calculate markups.

## THE INCOME STATEMENT

The income statement (also called the operating statement or profit-and-loss statement) summarizes the financial results of a firm's operations for a specific period, usually a month, quarter, or year. The ultimate objective of preparing the statement is to determine whether the organization earned a profit or suffered a loss.

The statement is divided into two sections: heading and body. The heading reveals the company name and the period covered by the statement. Note that the company in Exhibit B.1 on page 806 is Malibu Surfboards, a surfboard retailer, and the income statement is for the calendar year 1995. The statement's body contains an itemized listing of revenues and expenses. The left side of the body shows the three key elements: revenues, costs, and in this case a net profit. The profit results from revenues being greater than the costs. Let's examine each component in greater detail.

### REVENUES

*Gross sales* are the total amount billed to customers during the year. Sales returns occur because not all customers are satisfied with their purchases. Perhaps a surfboard was bought as a gift for a person who doesn't like the ocean. A board may have been defective.

Malibu offers a ninety-day payment plan without charging interest. A buyer can put a third of the purchase price down and pay the balance within ninety days. Malibu management, however, prefers that buyers pay cash and offers a 3 percent discount for immediate full payment. The *sales discounts* row reflects the dollar amount of cash discounts given to purchasers during 1995.

*Net sales* are gross sales minus sales returns and discounts. The income statement for Malibu shows net sales of $221,950.

### COSTS

Malibu incurs various expenses in the process of selling surfboards. A major cost is the cost of the surfboards sold to customers during 1995, called *cost of goods sold.* The cost of goods sold depends on three items: beginning inventory, net purchases, and ending inventory.

*Exhibit B.1*

Malibu Surfboards Income Statement for the Year Ended December 31, 1995

| | | | | |
|---|---|---|---|---|
| **Revenues** | | | | |
| Gross sales | | | | $227,880 |
| Less: Sales returns | | | $ 1,570 | |
| Sales discounts | | | 4,360 | 5,930 |
| Net sales | | | | $221,950 |
| **Costs** | | | | |
| Cost of goods sold | | | | |
| Beginning inventory, 1/1 at cost | | | $41,800 | |
| Add: Purchases at billed cost | | $91,720 | | |
| Freight-in | | 1,970 | | |
| Less: Purchase returns and allowances | $ 970 | | | |
| Purchase discounts | 1,750 | 2,720 | | |
| Net purchases at cost | | | 90,970 | |
| Cost of goods available for sale | | | 132,770 | |
| Less: Ending inventory at cost 12/31 | | | 31,500 | |
| Cost of goods sold | | | | 101,270 |
| Gross profit | | | | $120,680 |
| Operating expenses | | | | |
| Marketing expenses | | | | |
| Salaries of salespeople | | $39,590 | | |
| Promotion costs | | 5,200 | | |
| Delivery and shipment | | 4,500 | $49,290 | |
| General and administrative expenses | | | | |
| Salaries of office workers | | $12,500 | | |
| Rent | | 16,100 | | |
| Insurance | | | 4,280 | |
| Office supplies | | 1,818 | | |
| Utilities | | 3,627 | 38,326 | |
| Total operating expenses | | | | $ 87,615 |
| **Net profit before taxes** | | | | **$ 33,065** |

Malibu starts each year with a certain amount of merchandise on hand for sale to customers, called *beginning inventory.* During the year, the stock of inventory on hand is supplemented by purchases from surfboard manufacturers, which are called *purchases at billed cost.* Freight charges for new surfboards are called *freight-in.*

Sometimes the purchase of goods for inventory involves returns and allowances. These are caused by goods arriving in damaged condition, late delivery, and goods sent by the manufacturer in error. *Purchase returns and allowances* represent credit given by manufacturers to Malibu for one of these three reasons. *Purchase discounts* are discounts given by surfboard manufacturers when Malibu pays promptly.

By adding purchases during the year and freight-in expenses to the beginning inventory and then subtracting Malibu's purchase returns and allowances as well as purchase discounts, we arrive at the *net purchase at cost.* Then by adding the beginning inventory and the net purchases at cost, we have the *cost of goods available for sale* during 1995. If we now subtract Malibu's *ending inventory at cost* on December 31, we can determine the *cost of goods sold* during the year, as shown in Exhibit B.1. The cost of goods sold is $101,270.

*Gross profit* (gross margin) is the money left to cover the expenses of selling the surfboards and operating the business. It is determined by subtracting the cost of goods sold from net sales:

| | |
|---|---|
| Net sales | $221,950 |
| Less: Cost of goods sold | – 101,270 |
| Gross profit | $120,680 |

*Operating expenses* consist of marketing expenses and general and administrative expenses. These expenses arise from marketing activities and the running of the business. *Marketing expenses* include *salespeople's salaries, promotion costs* (such as brochures and advertising), and *delivery and shipment costs* of phone and mail orders for surfboards. *General and administrative expenses* are for such items as *salaries of office workers; rent* for the building; *insurance* of various types; *office supplies* such as paper, pencils, order forms, and computer ribbons; and *utilities,* including water, telephone, and electricity bills. Operating expenses for Malibu total $87,615.

*Net profit before taxes* represents the amount Malibu earned in 1995. It is what's left after subtracting the cost of goods sold and the operating expenses from sales revenues. Notice that net sales and net profits are not the same thing. A company may have large sales and little or no profits.

A condensed income statement for Malibu would be

| | |
|---|---|
| Revenue (net sales) | $221,950 |
| Costs (of goods sold) | – 101,270 |
| Gross profit | $120,680 |
| Expenses | – 87,615 |
| Net profit before taxes | $33,065 |

## COSTS, STOCK TURNOVER, AND PROFITS

A very important relationship exists among costs, sales, stock turnover, and profit. *Stock turnover* refers to the number of times during a period (usually a year) that the average amount of goods on hand is sold. Stock turnover rate is a measure of the number of times the average inventory is sold per year. The higher the turnover, the more quickly the inventory is moving.

Stock turnover can be calculated on the basis of retail price or of cost. Malibu's income statement reflects inventory valued on a cost basis, so we will use the following formula:

$$\text{Stock turnover rate} = \frac{\text{Cost of goods sold}}{\text{Average inventory at cost}}$$

The average dollar value of inventory at cost is calculated as follows:

$$\text{Average inventory at cost} = \frac{\text{Beginning inventory} + \text{Ending inventory}}{2}$$

$$= \frac{\$41,800 + \$31,500}{2}$$

$$= \$36,650$$

$$\text{Stock turnover rate at cost} = \frac{\$101{,}270}{\$36{,}650}$$

$$= 2.8$$

There is no exact measure of a "good" stock turnover rate. The rate varies by industry. Supermarkets, for example, often have a stock turnover rate of about 20, whereas an appliance retailer may have a rate of 3 or 4.

The benefits of rapid stock turnover are limited investment in inventory, less need for storage space, newer merchandise, and fewer markdowns. Generally speaking, high stock turnovers lead to higher profits. There are exceptions to this rule, however. Assume, for example, that a dealer reduces its stock and holds sales constant (resulting in an increase in turnover). Buying in small quantities may mean the loss of quantity discounts; higher expenditures for receiving, checking, and marketing merchandise; and greater correspondence and clerical costs. In this situation, profits fall.

## RETURN ON INVESTMENT

Return on investment (ROI) can be used as a yardstick to discover which investment opportunities offer the highest returns. It is the ratio of net profit after taxes to the investment used to make the net profit, multiplied by 100. Investment is not shown on the income statement, but it is on the balance sheet (statement of financial condition). The balance sheet, the other basic financial statement of a company, details assets, liabilities, and net worth.

Return on investment is often calculated by manufacturers for various new product opportunities to determine which, if any, the company should pursue. These are then compared with the cost of capital for the firm. *Cost of capital* is the weighted average of the cost of various types of funds the company uses, such as bonds and common stock. The ROI formula is as follows:

$$\text{ROI} = \frac{\text{Average earnings after taxes and depreciation}}{\text{Average investment}}$$

If product X has average earnings of $15,000 per year and an average investment of $105,000, then estimated ROI is $15,000 ÷ $105,000, or 14.3 percent.

ROI calculations can vary greatly depending on the depreciation and tax criteria used. Obviously, the same policies must be in force when comparing two new product alternatives, or the comparison will be "apples and oranges" instead of "two apples."

Return on investment requires that costs and revenues be projected for the estimated life of the product. To avoid too much long-range guessing, some marketing managers calculate ROI for fixed periods—for example, at the end of the first, third, and fifth years. The major problem with this simple formula is that it does not account for the time value of money. Two products may have identical rates of return but different investment and cash-flow periods. One product may have a high initial investment and become profitable eight years after introduction. A second product with the same ROI may have a moderate initial investment and reach profitability during the first year. The second product would certainly be more desirable because of the lower initial outlay and faster return. These profits can be reinvested or used in the business again.

### NET PRESENT VALUE

Let's carry the evaluation of new products one step further using the net present value approach. *Net present value* accounts for the time value of money. Assume one product

| | Product M | | | Product N | | |
|---|---|---|---|---|---|---|
| Year | Net cash flow | (If) (14%) | Present value of cash flow | Net cash flow | (If) (14%) | Present value of cash flow |
| 1 | $ 50,000 | .88 | $ 44,000 | $ 10,000 | .88 | $ 8,800 |
| 2 | 40,000 | .77 | 30,800 | 20,000 | .77 | 15,400 |
| 3 | 30,000 | .71 | 21,300 | 30,000 | .71 | 21,300 |
| 4 | 10,000 | .64 | 6,400 | 40,000 | .64 | 25,600 |
| 5 | 5,000 | .57 | 2,850 | 50,000 | .57 | 28,500 |
| | $135,000 | | | $150,000 | | |
| Present value | | | $105,350 | | | $99,600 |
| Less cost | | | – 10,000 | | | – 10,000 |
| Net present value | | | $ 95,350 | | | $ 89,600 |

*Exhibit B.2*

Net Present Value of Products M and N with $10,000 Cost

would return $1 million tomorrow and another product would return $1 million five years from now. If everything else is the same, the first product is more desirable. Would you rather have $1,000 today or twenty years from now? If you took that $1,000 today and invested it at 18 percent per year, the compounded value would be $27,393 at the end of twenty years! The longer it takes to receive money in the future, the less it is worth today. This is the notion of present value, usually called discounting.

Assume that a firm has two products, M and N, and each has a five-year life span. The cost of both projects is $10,000, and the cost of capital to the firm is 14 percent. The expected cash flows and present values are shown in Exhibit B.2. The actual dollar cash flows for products M and N are $135,000 and $150,000, respectively. Without considering the time value of money, the firm should go with product N. However, Exhibit B.2 shows that product M's largest cash flows occur soon after the product is launched and that product N's major cash flows occur later in the life cycle. The net present value of product M is $5,750 greater than that of product N. Why? Again, $1 received and reinvested today is worth more than $1 received and reinvested tomorrow.

## PAYBACK PERIOD

The payback period is the number of years it takes the firm to recover its original investment by net returns before depreciation but after taxes. Assume that a company is considering two new products and that each has a development cost of $300,000. Net returns forecasted for each product are as follows:

| *Year* | *Product A* | *Product B* |
|---|---|---|
| 1 | $150,000 | $40,000 |
| 2 | 105,000 | 60,000 |
| 3 | 55,000 | 80,000 |
| 4 | 25,000 | 120,000 |
| 5 | 5,000 | 200,000 |

As you can see, product A has the quickest payback: three years. It pays back half the original investment the first year, another $105,000 the second year, and the remainder in the third year. The shorter the payback period, the more quickly the firm recovers its original investment. Product B has a payback of four years, taking a year longer to recoup the original new product investment. If payback were the only criterion, the firm would choose product A.

As you might imagine, this decision could be a mistake. Payback analysis ignores the cash flows after the break-even point is reached. Product A, a faddish item, has a very short life cycle. Product B, on the other hand, reveals continued growth from the first year. Projects with longer payback periods traditionally are part of long-range planning, for many new products do not yield their highest returns for a number of years.

Payback analysis also ignores the magnitude of the original cost. Note, for example, that both products had development expenses of $300,000. But what if product A's development cost had been $25,000 and product B's had been $4 million? The firm may have selected product A simply because it lacked funds or was unwilling to risk $4 million.

Payback analysis does have some good points. It can be argued that paybacks of three or four years or longer are so uncertain that it is better not to consider them at all. In our simple example, we assumed that each year's cash flow was equally likely to materialize. Also, a company that has limited development funds must concentrate on products that offer a quick return.

## MARKUP PRICING

Assume that a retailer determines from past records that operating costs have been 32 percent of sales and profit has been 7 percent—a total *gross margin* of 39 percent. To establish a selling price for new merchandise, it can simply mark up the cost of the goods by 39 percent and still cover operating costs and earn a profit. However, if 7 percent is considered an unsatisfactory profit, the merchant will have to add more than 39 percent to the merchandise costs. An experienced retailer also expects a certain amount of *retail reduction:* markdowns, thefts, and employee discounts. If these three factors amount to 5 percent of sales, the retailer will have to use a markup of 41.9 percent to earn a 7 percent profit. The formula is

$$\text{Markup} = \frac{\text{Gross margin (39\%)} + \text{Retail reduction (5\%)}}{100\% + \text{Retail reduction (5\%)}}$$

$$= \frac{44\%}{105\%}$$

$$= 41.9\%$$

To achieve a *maintained margin* of 39 percent, the retailer must use an initial markup of 41.9 percent.

Sometimes retailers must establish a retail price based on a predetermined maintained margin and the unit cost. Suppose a merchant wants a gross margin of 41.9 percent (on retail) and has a merchandise cost of $3.46 per item. The formula for determining the retail price is

$$\text{Retail price} = \frac{\text{Cost (\$3.46)} \times 100}{100\% - \text{Markup (41.9\%)}}$$

$$= \frac{\$3.46 \times 100}{58.1}$$

$$= \$5.96$$

In the absence of any markdowns, theft, or other discounts, a selling price of $5.96 will provide the merchant with the desired gross margin on retail.

# APPENDIX C: TOOLS OF MARKETING CONTROL

Two important tools of marketing control in the financial area are sales analysis and marketing cost analysis. Moreover, as the importance of service and quality have increased, more companies have started using the marketing audit, a tool for strategic control. An examination of these techniques follows.

## SALES ANALYSIS

All marketing plans of profit-oriented firms and of many nonprofit organizations involve sales of a good or service. Therefore, most organizations have revenue-related goals. *Sales analysis* refers to the general effort to evaluate the firm's success in the marketplace. Sales volume analysis and market share analysis are two of the most commonly used tools for this purpose.

### SALES VOLUME ANALYSIS

*Sales volume analysis* is the detailed examination of sales volume data for the purpose of appraising a marketing plan. It is the simplest, most common type of sales analysis performed by marketing management. It reflects the target market's reactions to the firm's offerings and the organization's achievement of goals.

*Macrosales analysis* is the analysis of total or aggregate market performance. *Microsales analysis* subdivides total sales volume on some basis, such as territory or product, for a more in-depth examination of sales. By examining total sales performance, the marketing manager can determine trends in total sales activity. Usually company sales are compared to those of the industry to see how well the firm or strategic business unit is performing relative to the competition.

Exhibit C.1 shows that total sales for Jones Pump Company increased by $2.5 million from 1991 to 1992. Sales grew at an annual rate of 25 percent from 1992 through 1994, but the increase for 1995 was only 15 percent. Further insight can be

Exhibit C.1

Sales of Jones Pump Company

| Year | Company sales volume (in millions) | Increase | Company sales forecast (in millions) | Difference (in millions) |
|---|---|---|---|---|
| 1995 | $22.4 | 15% | $24.0 | – $1.6 |
| 1994 | 19.5 | 25 | 19.4 | + 0.1 |
| 1993 | 15.6 | 25 | 15.6 | — |
| 1992 | 12.5 | 25 | 12.0 | + 0.5 |
| 1991 | 10.0 | — | 9.5 | + 0.5 |

| Year | Industry sales volume (in millions) | Increase | Estimated market share | Actual market share | Difference |
|---|---|---|---|---|---|
| 1995 | $158.3 | 25.0% | 16.0% | 14.2% | –1.8% |
| 1994 | 126.6 | 15.5 | 15.0 | 15.4 | +0.4 |
| 1993 | 109.6 | 21.0 | 14.0 | 14.2 | +0.2 |
| 1992 | 90.0 | 30.0 | 14.0 | 13.9 | –0.1 |
| 1991 | 69.1 | — | 13.0 | 14.5 | –1.5 |

*Exhibit C.2*

Jones Pump Company Sales by Territory

| Territory | Estimated sales (in millions) | Actual sales (in millions) | Sales difference (in millions) |
|---|---|---|---|
| 1 | $ 8.0 | $10.0 | + $2.0 |
| 2 | 12.0 | 8.4 | – 3.6 |
| 3 | 4.0 | 4.0 | — |
| *Total* | $24.0 | $22.4 | |

*Exhibit C.3*

Jones Pump Company Sales by Product Line, Territory 2

| Product line | Estimated sales (in millions) | Actual sales (in millions) | Sales difference (in millions) |
|---|---|---|---|
| Municipal water system pumps | $ 3.5 | $3.6 | + $0.1 |
| Oil field pumps | 4.9 | 4.8 | – 0.1 |
| Sludge pumps | 3.6 | 0.0 | – 3.6 |
| *Total* | $12.0 | $8.4 | |

gained by looking at the industry volume section, which shows the rate of growth for the industry during the same periods. Jones Pump Company outperformed the industry in 1993 and 1994 but fell behind in 1995. In fact, 1995 seems to have been a problem year. Sales were $1.6 million, or 7 percent, below Jones's forecast. Similarly, the firm achieved only 89 percent of its forecasted market share—14.2 percent actual market share versus 16.0 percent estimated market share. This kind of macrosales analysis provides warning signals that further analysis is necessary. Something went wrong in 1995, and Jones needs to discover the cause.

The shortfall in Jones's sales can be more closely examined by allocating sales volume by territory and product. Exhibit C.2 shows that the sales staff met the forecast in territory 3 and went 25 percent over the estimate in territory 1. Territory 2 achieved only 70 percent of its estimate. Thus the problem seems to lie in territory 2.

The next step is to analyze sales in territory 2 by product line (see Exhibit C.3). The culprit is the sludge pump product line. Jones manufactures specialty pumps used by the construction and petroleum industries and by municipal water systems. Territory 2 encompasses the West Coast and the Southwest. Further inquiry by top management reveals that a San Francisco manufacturer is selling an imported pump designed for the same market that Jones serves. The imported pump has a better service record, develops more horsepower per unit of energy, and costs 30 percent less than the Jones model. Because the model is so specialized, the sales representative for the San Francisco manufacturer knows all the potential buyers west of the Mississippi River. Although Jones has many loyal customers, they cannot pass up a better pump at a much lower price.

## MARKET SHARE ANALYSIS

Sales volume analysis measures performance in absolute terms but does not measure the company's activities relative to the overall market. Nor does it take the competition into account. An increase in market share usually indicates that the firm's marketing mix is more effective than that of its competitors. A declining market share may indicate a need to investigate potential problem areas.

Like sales volume analysis, *market share analysis* is generally most meaningful when data are broken down by sales territory, customer type, and product category. A marketing manager may find, for example, that an overall increase in market share is due to increased sales to a particular type of customer.

## MARKETING COST ANALYSIS

A basic concept in accounting is matching revenues and the costs incurred in generating those revenues. As noted, sales revenue may indicate marketing success. But what role do costs play? Cost analysis is one of the most important techniques for maintaining marketing control.

*Marketing cost analysis* is based on the allocation of marketing costs by product, customer, distribution channel, or territory to measure the efficiency of the firm's marketing mix. The marketing mix is a basis for the allocation of direct costs of many types—for example, advertising costs, test-market expenses, and sales force expenses. In turn, marketing costs play an important role in determining the profitability of a product or product line.

Accounting information has become more readily available in recent years for two reasons: more sophisticated accounting systems and more common use of the computer. For accounting information to be useful for marketing cost analysis, it must be reallocated twice. The first reallocation is from natural to functional accounts, and the second is from functional accounts to market segments. These reallocations provide a basis for both marketing cost analysis and profit analysis.

### NATURAL ACCOUNTS TO FUNCTIONAL ACCOUNTS

*Natural accounts* are accounts that carry the name of the category for which the expenditure was made. Examples include rent, salaries, office supplies, insurance, and equipment. *Functional accounts,* on the other hand, are classified according to marketing activity. The number and names of the accounts vary from firm to firm. Functional accounts often include personal selling, advertising, storage, packaging, shipping, order filling, billing, market research, and delivery. Most marketing expenditures are made to accomplish a specific task—for instance, to develop a specific product, to promote a specific product, or to deliver a specific product. Marketing managers need to know whether such activities are increasing or decreasing the profitability of the firm.

To determine the profitability of specific marketing activities, funds must be reallocated from natural to functional accounts. Consider this example. Assume that J.J. Uniform Supply, a small uniform supply company, had a net profit of $8,500, as shown in Exhibit C.4. The first step is to allocate the expenditures from natural

*Exhibit C.4*

Income Statement for J.J. Uniform Supply

| | | |
|---|---|---|
| Sales | $75,000 | |
| Cost of goods sold | − 44,000 | |
| | | $31,000 |
| **Expenses** | | |
| Salaries | $ 13,000 | |
| Office supplies | 4,000 | |
| Rent | 3,500 | |
| Insurance | 2,000 | |
| Total expenses | | − 22,500 |
| Net profit | | $ 8,500 |

| Natural accounts | | Functional accounts: Personal selling | Advertising | Storage | Delivery and installation |
|---|---|---|---|---|---|
| Salaries | $13,000 | $ 8,000 | $ 2,000 | $ 1,500 | $1,500 |
| Office supplies | 4,000 | 2,000 | 1,000 | 500 | 500 |
| Rent | 3,500 | — | 1,000 | 2,000 | 500 |
| Insurance | 2,000 | — | 500 | 1,000 | 500 |
| *Total* | $22,500 | $ 10,000 | $4,500 | $ 5,000 | $3,000 |

*Exhibit C.5*

Reallocation of J.J. Uniform Supply Cost from Natural Accounts to Functional Accounts

accounts to functional accounts, as shown in Exhibit C.5. Note the breakdown of salary expenses: $8,000 (the majority) for a commissioned salesperson; $2,000 for a free-lance artist doing advertising layouts, $1,500 for a warehouse stocking clerk, and $1,500 for a delivery person who works after school. Half the office supplies were consumed in the sales effort, and the remainder were used for advertising, record keeping, and delivery. Because storage takes up more than half the building, it is charged with over half the rent ($2,000), and the rest is allocated using the same principle. The storage-facility insurance costs $1,000 annually; drafting equipment and tables used to prepare advertisements are insured for $500, and the delivery vehicle is insured for $500.

## FUNCTIONAL ACCOUNTS TO MARKET SEGMENTS

Assume that Joe and Jane, owners of J.J. Uniform Supply, are concerned that the three markets they serve may not all be profitable. Jane decides to continue the analysis by allocating the functional costs by customer type (see Exhibit C.6). Because 67 percent of the sales are made to industrial customers, this percentage of cost of goods sold is allocated to the industrial market ($29,333). The same process is followed for the retail and institutional markets. The sales representative spent 70 percent of his time calling on industrial accounts, 25 percent calling on retailers, and 5 percent calling on institutional customers. Advertising is strictly direct mail, and

*Exhibit C.6*

Reallocated Income Statement for J.J. Uniform Supply

| | | Marketing segment (customer type): Industrial | Retail | Institutional |
|---|---|---|---|---|
| Sales | $75,000 | $50,000 | $20,000 | $5,000 |
| Cost of goods sold | – 44,000 | – 29,333 | – 11,733 | – 2,934 |
| Gross margin | $31,000 | $20,667 | $ 8,267 | $2,066 |
| **Expenses (functional)** | | | | |
| Personal selling | $10,000 | $ 7,000 | $2,500 | $ 500 |
| Advertising | 4,500 | 2,157 | 768 | 1,575 |
| Storage | 5,000 | 3,333 | 1,333 | 334 |
| Delivery | 3,000 | 2,000 | 800 | 200 |
| *Total expenses* | $22,500 | $14,490 | $5,401 | $2,609 |
| Net profit | $ 8,500 | $ 6,177 | $2,866 | ($ 543) |

Jane's files reveal that 623 pieces were sent to industrial customers, 222 to retailers, and 455 to institutional customers—for a total of 1,300 advertising pieces. Thus \$2,157 of advertising expenses was allocated to the industrial customers (623 ÷ 1,300 = 0.4792 × \$4,500 = \$2,157). Storage and delivery costs were distributed using the percentage of sales accounted for by each market.

Using the allocation procedure, Joe and Jane find that their firm is earning a 12 percent profit in the industrial market, 14 percent in the retail market, and losing money in the institutional area. What action should Joe and Jane take at this point? They have several options:

- They could drop out of the institutional market. Because the market is currently unprofitable, the company could avoid serving institutional customers.
- The advertising expenditures–to-sales ratio is very high in the institutional market. Joe and Jane could examine their promotion program and try to raise institutional advertising effectiveness.
- Only 5 percent of the sales effort is being devoted to the institutional market. A stronger sales effort coupled with a more effective promotion program might make the institutional market profitable.

Although J.J. Uniform Supply is a profitable company as a whole, only the industrial and retail markets are generating profits. Servicing institutional accounts actually lowers overall profitability. Before Joe and Jane take any action, however, they should consider future trends in the institutional market. If, for example, the number of competitors is expected to decrease and the average size of an institutional account to increase, they may decide to stay in the market.

## A MARKETING AUDIT OUTLINE

A marketing audit is a comprehensive review of a profit-oriented or nonprofit organization's marketing activities. As the following outline shows, the audit embraces the organization's marketing orientation, planning, target market strategies, distribution decisions, product strategies, pricing strategies, and promotion strategies.

**I. Orientation**

1. Has the firm established a marketing orientation? That is, has the firm identified the benefits that particular customers seek and developed programs based on this input?
2. Are personnel efforts focused on satisfying the wants of actual or potential customers, rather than on programs, rules and regulations, or their own personal well-being?
3. Does the firm define its business in terms of benefits its customers want rather than in terms of goods and services?
4. Does the firm try to direct its products only to specific groups of people or to everybody?
5. Is the firm's main goal to maximize customer satisfaction or to get as many customers as possible?
6. Does the firm seek to achieve its goal chiefly through coordinated use of marketing activities (product, distribution, promotion, and pricing) or only through intensive promotion?
7. Does the firm have a mission statement, and is it translated into operational terms regarding the firm's objectives?

## II. Marketing Planning

A. *The External Environment*

1. Social: What major social and lifestyle trends will have an impact on the firm? What action has the firm been taking in response to these trends?
2. Demographics: What impact will forecasted trends in the size, age, profile, and distribution of population have on the firm? How will the changing nature of the family, the increase in the proportion of women in the work force, and changes in the ethnic composition of the population affect the firm? What action has the firm taken in response to these developments and trends? Has the firm reevaluated its traditional products and expanded the range of specialized offerings to respond to these changes?
3. Economic: What major trends in taxation and in income sources will have an impact on the firm? What action has the firm taken in response to these trends?
4. Political, Legal, and Financial: What laws are now being proposed at federal, state, and local levels that could affect marketing strategy and tactics? What recent changes in regulations and court decisions affect the firm? What political changes at each government level are taking place? What action has the firm taken in response to these legal and political changes?
5. Competition: Which organizations are competing with the firm directly by offering a similar product? Which organizations are competing with the firm indirectly by securing its prime prospects' time, money, energy, or commitment? What new competitive trends seem likely to emerge? How effective is the competition? What benefits do competitors offer that the firm does not? Is it appropriate for the firm to compete? Could the firm more usefully withdraw from some areas in which there are alternative suppliers and use its resources to serve new, unserved customer groups?
6. Technological: What major technological changes are occurring that affect the firm?
7. Ecological: What is the outlook for the cost and availability of natural resources and energy needed by the firm?

B. *Needs Assessments*

1. Are needs assessments undertaken?
2. Have secondary data been used in the needs assessments? If so, is the information current? Classified in a useful manner? Impartial? Reliable? Valid?
3. What does the firm want to learn from the needs assessments?
4. Are surveys used in the needs assessment process? If so, is each and every question necessary? Can the firm determine what will be done with the information from every question? Do the respondents have the ability to answer the questions accurately? Will respondents provide the information? Are the questions threatening or too personal? Are the questions worded simply enough to be understood by individuals with a low education level? Is the sample size appropriate?

5. How has the firm used the information it has generated about its markets and other publics for improving products?
6. What are the evolving needs and satisfactions being sought by the firm's customers?
7. Who buys the firm's products? How does a potential customer find out about the organization? When and how does a person become a customer?
8. What are the major objections given by consumers as to why they do not buy the firm's products?
9. How do customers find out about and decide to buy the organization's products? When and where?
10. Are evaluative reports written on the needs assessment studies? If so, are the needs assessment reports too long or too technical? Do they provide a summary of the high points that are of most interest to the reader?

C. *Objectives and Mission*

1. What is the mission of the firm? What business is it in? How well is its mission understood throughout the organization? Five years from now, what business does it wish to be in?
2. What are the stated objectives of the organization? Are they formally written down? Do they lead logically to clearly stated marketing objectives?
3. Are the organization's marketing objectives stated in hierarchical order? Are they specific so that progress toward achievement can be measured? Are the objectives reasonable in light of the organization's resources? Are the objectives ambiguous? Do the objectives specify a time frame? Are the objectives that are concerned with effectiveness benefit-oriented?
4. Does the firm have both long-term and short-term plans? Do the short-term plans contribute to achievement of the long-term plan?
5. Are the objectives and roles of each element of the marketing mix clearly specified?
6. What policies inhibit the achievement of the firm's objectives with respect to organization, allocation of resources, operations, hiring and training, products, pricing, and promotion?
7. Should the firm seek to expand, contract, or change the emphasis of its offerings or selected target markets? If so, in which product areas and target markets, and how vigorously?

D. *Marketing Planning and Evaluation*

1. Does the organization have a marketing planning and evaluation system?
2. Does the marketing planning and evaluation system include an annual program evaluation as well as a longer-term, firmwide evaluation (marketing audit)?
3. Is this firmwide evaluation conducted every five years or less to assess the overall status of all the firm's products and marketing activities? Does the audit describe the current marketing situation as well as speculate about the relevant future?

4. Is someone in the firm held accountable for ensuring that the recommendations of the marketing audit are implemented?
5. Are annual marketing plans developed, implemented, and used as the basis for evaluation?
6. Does the organization carry out periodic reviews of its programs and evaluations of its resource allocation decisions? How and with what results?
7. Is the long-term marketing audit a summation, synthesis, and integration of annual evaluations?
8. Are the short-term evaluation procedures (monthly, quarterly, and so on) adequate to ensure that the firm's long-term objectives are being achieved?
9. Should the firm enter, expand, contract, or withdraw from any existing segments?
10. What should be the short- and long-term cost and revenue consequences of these changes?
11. Does it seem that the firm is trying to do too much or not enough?
12. What are the core marketing strategies for achieving the agreed objectives? Are they sound?
13. Are the stated objectives being met, and are these objectives appropriate?
14. Are enough resources (or too many resources) budgeted to accomplish the marketing objectives?
15. Are the marketing resources allocated optimally to prime market segments and products of the organization?
16. Does the firm offer the intended benefits to customers? Are customers satisfied with these benefits?
17. In which particular areas should the firm make special efforts to improve its effectiveness?
18. Do any programs seem to have excessive costs? Are these costs valid? Can cost-reducing steps be taken?
19. Do forms and procedures make it hard or easy for someone to do business with us? Is more information asked for than is necessary? How are the data used?
20. What is done with negative feedback about staff from customers? How are complaints handled?
21. What is the firm's reputation among its various shareholders?
22. What are the organization's major strengths and weaknesses?

**III. Target Market Strategies**

A. *Target Markets*

1. Are the members of each product's target market homogeneous or heterogeneous with respect to geographic, sociodemographic, and behavioral characteristics?
2. What are the size, growth rate, and national and regional trends for each of the organization's market segments?

3. Is the size of each market segment sufficiently large or important to warrant a unique marketing mix?
4. Are the market segments measurable and accessible? That is, are the market segments accessible to distribution and communication efforts?
5. Which are the high-opportunity and low-opportunity segments?
6. What are the evolving needs and satisfactions being sought by target markets?
7. What benefits does the organization offer to each segment? How do these benefits compare with the benefits offered by competitors?
8. Is the firm offering products to people who are not adequately served by other organizations?
9. Is the firm positioning itself with a unique product? Is the product needed?
10. Is the firm targeting any unresponsive markets? If so, what contributes to their unresponsiveness?
11. How much of the firm's business is repeat versus new business? What percentage of the public can be classified as nonusers, light users, and heavy users?
12. How do current target markets rate the firm and its competitors, particularly with respect to reputation, quality, and price?
13. What is the firm's image with the specific market segments it seeks to serve?
14. Has the firm been efficient and effective in meeting customers' needs?

B. *Other Publics*

1. What publics other than target markets (financial, media, government, citizen, local, general, and internal) represent opportunities or problems for the firm?
2. What steps has the firm taken to deal effectively with key publics?
3. What does each public seek from the firm (that is, what's in it for them)?

## IV. Distribution Decisions

A. *Strategic Distribution Decisions*

1. Has there been a recent evaluation of the firm's existing distribution pattern?
2. Is there a written statement of distribution objectives?
3. Should the firm try to deliver its offerings directly to customers, or can it better deliver selected offerings by involving other organizations?
4. Are members of the target market willing and able to travel some distance to buy the product?
5. How good is access to facilities? Can access be improved? Which facilities need priority attention in these areas?
6. How are facility locations chosen? Is the site accessible to the target markets? Is it visible to the target markets?
7. When are products made available to users (season of year, day of week, time of day)? Are these times most appropriate?

8. Are timing decisions based on analysis of customers' preferences? To what extent do the choices reflect employee convenience? Inertia from the past?

**V. Product Strategies**

A. *Product Management*

1. What are the major products offered by the firm? Do they complement each other, or is there unnecessary duplication?
2. Where is the firm and each major product in its life cycle (calculated by using market share or sales)?
3. Are the development of new products, termination of old products, and allocation of resources given the correctly priority according to each product's life cycle?
4. Is the type of management used at each stage of the life cycle appropriate?
5. What are the pressures among various target markets to increase or decrease the range and quality of products?
6. What are the major weaknesses in each product area? What are the major complaints? What goes wrong most often?
7. Does the physical appearance of the facility create an environment that complements and enhances the product itself? Does it aid in the customer's satisfaction? Is the environment relaxing and comfortable?
8. Is the product name easy to pronounce? Spell? Recall? Is it descriptive, and does it communicate the benefits the product offers? Does the name distinguish the firm or product from all others?

B. *New Product Development*

1. Have new-product committees been established? Do they keep senior management involved and informed?
2. What major new products are in the planning stages?
3. Is the firm sufficiently organized to gather, generate, and screen new product ideas?
4. Has a feasibility analysis been conducted to examine the costs and benefits of the proposal? Has the firm set criteria regarding feasibility?
5. Does the firm carry out small-scale tests with major new products before launching them?
6. Are personnel resources sufficient for evaluating and launching new products? Do the firm's personnel have appropriate expertise?
7. Are promotional efforts for new products adequate?

C. *Diffusion of New Products*

1. Has the firm identified opinion leaders to help speed the rate of diffusion of products?
2. Are the opinion leaders contributing to diffusion?

D. *Product Retrenchment*

1. Are the firm's managerial resources spread too thin?

2. What can the firm do to manage effectively with reduced resources?
3. What products are being, or should be, phased out?
4. How does the organization determine which products are to be terminated?
5. Is there a regular review process to identify candidates for termination?
6. Could the resources allocated to particular products generate greater total benefits if they were reallocated?
7. Is the firm assigning the highest-caliber people to the highest-priority products?
8. What strategies are used for terminating products so customer dissatisfaction and internal opposition are minimized?
9. Is retrenchment being implemented as part of the firm's overall plan so all concerned know why it is taking place and are aware of its implications?

## VI. Pricing Strategies

### A. *Pricing Objectives and Policies*

1. What are the firm's objectives in pricing each product?
2. Is there a current written pricing policy statement?
3. Is the statement specific enough to give guidance to pricing decisions?
4. Does the pricing policy address all functions or objectives of price?
5. What mechanisms does the firm have to ensure that the prices charged are acceptable to customers?
6. If a proposed price increase or decrease is put into effect, how will the number of customers change? Will total revenue increase or decrease?

### B. *Price Setting*

1. What are the procedures for establishing and reviewing pricing policy?
2. Are prices reviewed at least annually?
3. Which method is used for establishing a price: going rate, demand-oriented, or cost-based?
4. What discounts are offered and with what rationale?
5. Can the firm identify, classify, and equitably allocate the costs associated with each product?
6. What is the typical price of similar products?
7. Has the firm considered psychological dimensions of price in its initial price decisions as well as in its price revision decisions?
8. Are price increases keeping pace with cost increases or general inflation levels?
9. Does the firm use price promotions effectively?
10. Do interested prospects have opportunities to sample products at an introductory price?
11. What methods of payment are accepted? Is it in the firm's best interest to use these various payment methods?

## VII. Promotion Strategies

### A. *Strategic Promotion Decisions*

1. Are there clear objectives for each element of the communication mix? How are promotion activities related to these objectives?
2. How does a typical customer find out about the firm's products? Word of mouth? Personal selling? Advertising? Publicity?
3. Does the message the firm delivers gain the attention of the intended target audience? Does it address the wants of the potential target market, and does it suggest a means for satisfying these wants? Is the message appropriately positioned?
4. Is the firm getting adequate feedback from its promotional efforts?
5. Is the firm's promotion effort effectively informing, persuading, educating, and reminding customers about its products?
6. On what basis does the organization measure the effectiveness of its various communication programs?
7. Does the firm have a tendency to overpromise?
8. How is the budget for each promotional element determined? Does it appear to be at the appropriate level? How does the organization decide on which products or markets to concentrate promotion?
9. Is promotion expenditure regarded as a cost or as an investment?

### B. *Advertising and Publicity*

1. Is there a well-conceived publicity program?
2. How is public relations normally handled by the firm? By whom?
3. Is the publicity effort directed at all the firm's key publics or restricted only to potential customers?
4. What does the advertising/publicity budget permit? If a greater amount were spent on this activity, would there be a proportionately greater benefit to the firm and its customers?
5. Have those responsible for the firm's publicity established and nurtured close working relationships with reporters and editors in each of the media outlets?
6. Is an effort made to understand each of the publicity outlets' needs and to provide each one with the types of stories that will appeal to its audience in forms it can readily use?
7. Which of the following media are currently being used: daily newspapers, articles and letters to the editor, weekly newspapers, weekly newsmagazines, monthly magazines, telephone directories, television, news and talk shows, radio spots, guest appearances, exhibitions, billboards, catalogs, posters, fliers, newsletters?
8. Has the firm chosen the type of media that will best reach its target markets?
9. Are the types of media used the most cost-effective, and do they contribute positively to the firm's image?
10. Are the dates and times the advertisements will appear the most appropriate?

11. Does the organization use an outside advertising agency? What functions does the ad agency perform for the organization?
12. Is the firm using all available public relations avenues?
13. Has the firm prepared several versions of its advertisements?
14. What system is used to handle consumer inquiries resulting from advertising and promotion? What follow-up is done?
15. Are news clippings or records kept for evaluating the firm's ability to get accurate and favorable media coverage?
16. How are the advertising and public relations programs evaluated? How often?
17. What does the annual report say about the firm and its products? Who is being effectively reached by this vehicle? Does the benefit of this publication justify the cost?

C. *Personal Selling*

1. How much of a typical salesperson's time is spent soliciting new customers as compared to serving existing customers?
2. How is it determined which prospect will be called on and by whom? How is the frequency of contacts determined?
3. What incentive does the sales staff have for encouraging more business?
4. How is the sales force organized and managed?
5. Has the firm prepared an approach tailored to each prospect? Does this approach emphasize benefits to potential customers rather than benefits to the firm? Does the firm address the question "What's in it for them?"
6. Has the firm matched its sales personnel with the type of buyer characteristic of the target market?
7. Do the firm's sales representatives generate enthusiasm for the firm's products?
8. Is there appropriate follow-up to the initial personal selling effort? Are customers kept informed on the status of their orders? Are they made to feel appreciated?

D. *Sales Promotion*

1. What is the specific purpose of each sales promotion activity? Why is it offered? What does it try to achieve?
2. What categories of sales promotion are being used? Promotional pricing? Free offers? Contests?
3. How is their effectiveness evaluated?

# GLOSSARY

## A

**accelerator principle (multiplier effect)** Phenomenon in which a small increase or decrease in consumer demand produces a much larger change in demand for the facilities and equipment needed to make the consumer product.

**accessory equipment** Goods, such as portable tools and office equipment, that are less expensive and shorter-lived than major equipment.

**adaptive selling** Sales technique using a pitch adapted for each prospect in response to the specific sales situation.

**administered system** Vertical marketing system in which a strong organization assumes a leadership position.

**adopter** Consumer who was happy enough with a trial experience with a product to use it again.

**advertising agency** Organization that handles the advertising and promotion functions for other organizations.

**advertising appeal** Reason for a person to buy a product.

**advertising campaign** Series of related advertisements focusing on a common theme, slogan, and set of advertising appeals.

**advertising objective** Specific communication task a campaign should accomplish for a specified target audience during a specified period.

**advertising response function** Phenomenon in which spending for advertising and sales promotion increases sales or market share up to a certain level but then produces diminishing returns.

**advertising** Impersonal, one-way mass communication about a product or organization that is paid for by a marketer.

**advocacy advertising** Form of advertising in which an organization expresses its views on controversial issues or responds to media attacks.

**AIDA concept** Model that outlines the process for achieving promotional goals in terms of stages of consumer involvement with the message; the acronym stands for Attention, Interest, Desire, and Action.

**all-you-can-afford approach** Method of setting a promotion budget that relies on determining how much the marketer can spend.

**annual purchasing contract** Type of purchasing contract that provides a discount schedule for purchases over the period of the contract.

**applied research** Attempt to find practical solutions to existing or potential real-world problems.

**arbitrary allocation** Method of setting a promotion budget that picks a dollar amount without reference to other factors.

**AS/RSAS/RS (AS/RS)** Technology that enables material handlers to automatically store and pick goods from a warehouse or distribution center, in order to decrease product handling, increase order fulfillment accuracy, and increase on-time shipments.

**aspirational group** Group that someone would like to join.

**assumptive close** Technique of ending a sales presentation by assuming the prospect is going to buy.

**assurance** Knowledge and courtesy of service employees and their ability to inspire trust.

**ATC (average total cost)** Total costs divided by output.

**atmosphere** Overall impression conveyed by a store's physical layout, decor, and surroundings.

**attitude** Learned tendency to respond consistently toward a given object.

**attitudinal objective** Promotional objective that seeks to improve or change a product's image by changing consumers' attitudes toward it.

**audience duplication** Situation in which the same audience is reached by two different media vehicles.

**audience selectivity** Ability of an advertising medium to reach a precisely defined market.

**audit** Examination and verification of the sale of a product.

**automatic identification (auto ID)** Use of identification technology to mark and read products as they enter and leave the supplier's warehouse or as they are received by a manufacturer or retailer.

**automatic storage and retrieval systems (AS/RS)** Technology that enables material handlers to automatically store and pick goods from a warehouse or distribution center, in order to decrease product handling, increase order fulfillment accuracy, and increase on-time shipments.

**automatic vending**
Form of nonstore retailing that uses vending machines to offer products for sale.

**AVC (average variable cost)** Total variable costs divided by output.

**average total cost (ATC)** Total costs divided by output.

**average variable cost (AVC)** Total variable costs divided by output.

**awareness objective** Promotional objective that seeks to increase consumers' knowledge of a product or brand.

## B

**baby boomer** Person born between 1946 and 1964.

**backward integration** Retailer's or wholesaler's acquisition of an intermediary closer to the manufacturing stage or performance of the functions formerly performed by an intermediary closer to the manufacturing stage.

**bait pricing** Price tactic that tries to get consumers into a store through false or misleading price advertising and then uses high-pressure selling to persuade consumers to buy more expensive merchandise.

**balance of payments** Difference between a country's total payments to other countries and its total receipts from other countries.

**balance of trade** Difference between the value of a country's exports and the value of its imports during a certain time.

**bar code (universal product code, UPC)** Series of thick and thin vertical lines, readable by computerized optical scanners, that represent numbers used to track products.

**base price** General price level at which the company expects to sell the good or service.

**basic research** Attempt to expand the frontiers of scientific knowledge without concern for commercial viability.

**basing-point pricing** Price tactic that incorporates the freight cost from a given (basing) point, regardless of the city from which the goods are shipped.

**behavioral objective** Promotional objective that aims to change a buyer's behavior or prompt the buyer to take some action.

**BehaviorScan** Single-source research program that tracks the purchases of 3,000 households through store scanners.

**belief** Organized pattern of knowledge that an individual holds as true about his or her world.

**benchmarking** Rating a product against the world's best products of all types.

**benefit segmentation** Method of dividing markets based on the benefits customers seek from the product.

**bid pricing** Process in which potential sellers are invited to state, either orally or in writing, what they will charge to provide a good or service.

**birdyback** Form of intermodal transportation combining the use of truck and air freight to move containerized goods.

**blanket purchasing contract** Type of purchasing contract that requires the supplier to provide a certain amount of product at the same price each month during the course of a year.

**boycott** Exclusion of all products coming from certain countries or companies.

**brainstorming** Technique for generating new product ideas in which group members propose, without criticism or limitation, ways to vary a product or solve a problem.

**brand equity** Value of successful company and brand names.

**brand loyalty** Consumer's consistent preference for one brand over all others in its product category.

**brand manager** Person who is responsible for a single brand.

**brand mark** Elements of a brand that cannot be spoken, such as symbols.

**brand name** Part of a brand that can be spoken, including letters, words, and numbers.

**brand** Name, term, symbol, design, or combination thereof that identifies a seller's products and differentiates them from competitors' products.

**break-even analysis** Method of determining what sales volume must be reached for a product before the company breaks even (total costs equal total revenue) and no profits are earned.

**broker** Wholesaling intermediary that brings buyers and sellers together.

**business analysis** Stage in the product development process in which demand, cost, sales, and profitability estimates are made.

**business product (industrial product)** Product used to manufacture other goods or services, to facilitate an organization's operations, or to resell to other customers.

**business product distributor** Wholesaler that buys business products and resells them to business customers.

**business service** Expense item obtained from an outside provider that does not become part of a final product, such as janitorial, advertising, legal, management consulting, marketing research, maintenance, and other services.

**business-to-business marketing** Marketing of goods and services to individuals and organizations for purposes other than personal consumption.

**buyer for export** Intermediary in the global market that assumes all ownership risks and sells globally for its own account.

**buyer**
Person who selects the merchandise for retail stores and may also be responsible for promotion and for personnel.

**buying center** Group consisting of all those who are involved in a purchase decision for an organization.

## C

**cannibalization** Phenomenon in which sales of a new product cut into sales of a firm's existing products.

**capitalism** Economic system characterized by private ownership of productive resources and allocation of goods and services according to signals provided by a free market.

**cash cow** In the portfolio matrix, a business unit that generates more cash than it needs to maintain its market share.

**cash discount** Price reduction offered to a consumer, industrial user, or marketing intermediary in return for prompt payment of a bill.

**cash-and-carry wholesaler** Limited-service merchant wholesaler that sells for cash and usually carries a limited line of fast-moving merchandise.

**category killer** Discount specialty store that carries a narrow merchandise selection and that dominates its segment.

**category manager** Person responsible for multiple product lines within a product category.

**central-location telephone (CLT) facility** Specially designed room used for conducting telephone interviews for survey research.

**chain store** Retail store that is one of a group owned and operated by a single corporation with central authority.

**channel captain (channel leader)** Member of a marketing channel that exercises authority and power over the activities of other channel members.

**channel conflict** Clash of goals and methods between distribution channel members.

**channel control** Situation that occurs when one marketing channel member intentionally affects another member's behavior.

**channel leader (channel captain)** Member of a marketing channel that exercises authority and power over the activities of other channel members.

**channel of distribution (marketing channel)** Set of interdependent organizations that ease the transfer of ownership as products move from producer to business user or consumer.

**channel power** Capacity of a particular marketing channel member to control or influence the behavior of other channel members.

**channel** Medium of communication—such as a voice, radio, or newspaper—for transmitting a message.

**closed-ended question** Question that asks the respondent to make a selection from a limited list of responses.

**CLT (central-location telephone) facility** Specially designed room used for conducting telephone interviews for survey research.

**co-branding** Placing two or more brand names on a product or its package.

**code of ethics** Guidelines developed by a company to help its employees make ethical decisions.

**COFC (container on flatcar)** Form of intermodal transportation involving containers that can be transferred from rail or truck onto ship or barge.

**cognitive dissonance** Inner tension that a consumer experiences after recognizing an inconsistency between behavior and values or opinions.

**cold calling** Form of lead generation in which the salesperson approaches potential buyers without any prior knowledge of the prospects' needs or financial status.

**commercialization** Final stage in the product development process, consisting of tasks necessary to begin marketing the product.

**communication** Process by which we exchange or share meanings through a common set of symbols.

**comparative advertising** Form of advertising that compares two or more specifically named or shown competing brands on one or more specific attributes.

**competitive advertising** Form of advertising designed to influence demand for a specific brand.

**competitive parity** Method of setting a promotion budget that matches a competitor's spending.

**component lifestyle** Practice of choosing goods and services that meet one's diverse needs and interests rather than conforming to a single, traditional lifestyle.

**component part** Finished item ready for assembly or product that needs very little processing before becoming part of some other product.

**computer-assisted interviewing** Interviewing method in which the interviewer reads the questions from a computer screen and enters the respondent's data directly into the computer.

**concentrated targeting strategy** Marketing approach based on appealing to a single segment of a market.

**concept of exchange** Idea that people give up something to receive something they would rather have.

**concept test** Evaluation of a new product idea, usually before a prototype has been created.

**concurrent (parallel/simultaneous) engineering** Product development process in which all relevant functional areas and outside suppliers participate at all stages, thereby streamlining the development process and reducing its cost.

**consideration set (evoked set)** Group of brands, resulting from an information search, from which a buyer can choose.

**consultative selling** Sales practice of developing long-term relationships with customers and providing them with information that will help them solve their problems and achieve their short-term and long-term goals.

**Consumer Product Safety Commission (CPSC)** Federal agency established to protect the health and safety of consumers in and around their homes.

**consumer behavior** Processes a consumer uses to make purchase decisions, as well as to use and dispose of purchased goods or services; also includes factors that influence purchase decisions and the use of products.

**consumer decision-making process** Step-by-step process used by consumers when buying goods or services.

**consumer product** Product bought to satisfy an individual's personal wants.

**consumer sales promotion** Sales promotion activities targeted to the ultimate consumer.

**consumerism** Political and economic struggle to increase the rights and powers of buyers in relation to sellers.

**container on flatcar (COFC)** Form of intermodal transportation involving containers that can be transferred from rail or truck onto ship or barge.

**containerization** Putting large quantities of goods in sturdy containers that can be moved from ship to truck to airplane to train without repacking.

**continuous improvement** Commitment to constantly seek ways to do things better.

**continuous media schedule** Media scheduling strategy, used for products in the latter stages of the product life cycle, in which advertising is run steadily throughout the advertising period.

**contract logistics** Manufacturer's or supplier's use of an independent third party to buy and manage an entire subsystem of physical distribution, such as transportation or warehousing.

**contract manufacturing** Private-label manufacturing by a foreign company.

**contract warehousing** Agreement between a manufacturer and a public warehouse facility to provide storage space for a specified period.

**contractual system** Vertical marketing system composed of independent firms at different channel levels (manufacturer, wholesaler, retailer) coordinating their distribution activities by contractual agreement.

**convenience product** Relatively inexpensive item that merits little shopping effort.

**convenience sample** Nonprobability sample that uses respondents who are convenient or readily accessible to the researcher.

**convenience store** Miniature supermarket, carrying only a limited line of high-turnover convenience goods.

**conventional channel** Network of loosely aligned manufacturers, wholesalers, and retailers that bargain with each other at arm's length, negotiate aggressively over the terms of sale, and otherwise behave independently.

**conventional morality** Intermediate level of moral development, which is based on loyalty and obedience to the organization's or society's expectations.

**cooperative advertising** Arrangement in which the manufacturer and the retailer split the costs of advertising the manufacturer's brand.

**core service** Most basic benefit a customer is buying.

**corporate social responsibility** Business's concern for society's welfare, demonstrated by managers who consider both the long-range best interests of the company and the company's relationship to the society within which it operates.

**corporate system** Vertical marketing system in which one firm owns successive stages in a channel of distribution.

**corrective advertising** Advertisement that is run to amend the false impressions left by previous promotion.

**cost per contact** Cost of reaching one member of the target market.

**cost per thousand (CPM)** Standard criterion for comparing media, computed by dividing the price of a single ad by the audience size in thousands.

**countertrade** Form of trade in which all or part of the payment for goods or services is in the form of other goods or services.

**coupon** Certificate that entitles consumers to an immediate price reduction when they buy the product.

**CPM (cost per thousand)** Standard criterion for comparing media, computed by dividing the price of a single ad by the audience size in thousands.

**CPSC (Consumer Product Safety Commission)** Federal agency established to protect the health and safety of consumers in and around their homes.

**credence quality** Characteristic of a product that consumers have difficulty assessing even after purchase because they do not have the necessary knowledge or experience.

**crisis management** Coordinated effort to handle the effects of unfavorable publicity or of another unexpected, unfavorable event.

**cross docking** Method used by many distribution centers to increase efficiency, in which goods are moved directly from the receiving dock to the shipping dock or are held in a temporary area before moving them to the outbound dock, without putting the goods into storage.

**cross-tabulation** Type of data analysis that relates the responses to one question to the responses to one or more other questions.

**culture** Set of values, norms, attitudes, and other meaningful symbols that shape human behavior and the artifacts, or products, of that behavior as they are transmitted from one generation to the next.

**cumulative quantity discount** Deduction from list price that applies to the buyer's total purchases made during a specific period, intended to encourage customer loyalty.

**customer satisfaction** Feeling that a product has met or exceeded the customer's expectations.

**customer value triad** Goods quality, service quality, and value-based prices—the components of customer value.

**customer value** The ratio of benefits to the sacrifice necessary to obtain those benefits.

**cycle time** Time from when production begins until the good is received by the customer.

## D

**database marketing** Creation of a large computerized file of customers' and potential customers' profiles and purchase patterns as a tool for identifying target markets.

**decision support system (DSS)** Interactive, flexible information system that enables managers to obtain and manipulate information as they are making decisions.

**decline stage** Fourth and final stage of the product life cycle, in which sales drop and falling demand forces many competitors out of the market.

**decoding** Interpretation of the language and symbols sent by the source through a channel.

**delayed-quotation pricing** Price tactic used for industrial installations and many accessory items, in which a firm price is not set until the item is either finished or delivered.

**Delphi technique** Sales forecasting technique that asks outside experts to express an anonymous opinion, review a summary of others' opinions, and express themselves again in order to reach consensus.

**demand** Quantity of a product that will be sold in the market at various prices for a specified period.

**demographic segmentation** Method of dividing markets based on demographic variables, such as age, gender, income, ethnic background, and family life cycle.

**demography** Study of people's vital statistics, such as their age, race, and location.

**department store** Retailer that carries a wide variety of shopping and specialty goods, including apparel, cosmetics, housewares, electronics, and sometimes furniture.

**derived demand** Demand that results from demand for another product.

**development** Stage in the product development process in which a prototype is developed and a marketing strategy is outlined.

**differential advantage** Set of unique features of a company and its products that are perceived by the target market as significant and superior to the competition.

**diffusion** Process by which the adoption of an innovation spreads.

**direct channel** Distribution channel in which producers sell directly to consumers.

**direct foreign investment** Active ownership of a foreign company or of overseas manufacturing or marketing facilities.

**direct marketing (direct-response marketing)** Techniques used to get consumers to buy from their homes, including direct mail, catalogs and mail order, telemarketing, and electronic retailing.

**direct retailing** Form of nonstore retailing that occurs in a home setting, such as door-to-door sales and party plan selling.

**direct-response advertising** Advertising that calls for consumers' immediate action, or a direct response.

**discount store** Retail store that is one of a group competing on the basis of low prices, high turnover, and high volume.

**discrepancy of assortment** Lack of all the items a customer needs to receive full satisfaction from a product or products.

**discrepancy of quantity** Difference between the amount of product produced and the amount a customer wants to buy.

**discretionary income** Income after taxes and necessities.

**distribution center** Type of warehouse that specializes in making bulk or breaking bulk and that strives for rapid inventory turnover.

**diversification** Marketing strategy that increases sales by introducing new products into new markets.

**dog** In the portfolio matrix, a business unit that has low growth potential and a small market share.

**drop shipper** Limited-service merchant wholesaler that places orders for its customers with the manufacturer but does not physically handle the products it sells.

**DSS (decision support system)** Interactive, flexible information system that enables managers to obtain and manipulate information as they are making decisions.

**dual distribution (multiple distribution)** Use of two or more channels to distribute the same product to target markets.

**dumping** Practice of selling products either below cost or below their selling price in their domestic market.

## E

**early adopter** Consumer among the second group to adopt a new idea or product, frequently an opinion leader.

**early majority** Third group of consumers to adopt a new idea or product, characterized by their deliberation.

**economic order quantity (EOQ)** Order volume that minimizes order processing costs and inventory carrying costs.

**EDI (electronic data interchange)** Computer technique that electronically transmits data about retail inventories to warehouses so orders can be filled more quickly and accurately.

**EDLP (everyday low prices)** Price tactic of permanently reducing prices 10 to 15 percent below the traditional levels while eliminating trade discounts that create trade loading.

**80/20 principle** Idea that 20 percent of all customers generate 80 percent of the demand.

**elastic demand** Situation in which consumer demand changes as price changes.

**elasticity of demand** Consumers' responsiveness or sensitivity to changes in price.

**electronic data interchange (EDI)** Computer technique that electronically transmits data about retail inventories to warehouses so orders can be filled more quickly and accurately.

**empathy** Caring, individualized attention to customers.

**empowerment** Practice of giving employees expanded authority to solve customer problems as they arise.

**encoding** Conversion of the sender's ideas and thoughts into a message, usually in the form of words or signs.

**environmental management** Implementation of strategies that attempt to shape the external environment within which a firm operates.

**environmental scanning** Collection and interpretation of information about forces, events, and relationships that may affect the future of an organization.

**EOQ (economic order quantity)** Order volume that minimizes order processing costs and inventory carrying costs.

**escalator pricing** Price tactic in which the final selling price reflects cost increases incurred between the times when the order is placed and when delivery is made.

**ethics** Moral principles or values that generally govern the conduct of an individual or a group.

**evaluation** Phase of the marketing process in which marketers gauge the extent to which objectives have been achieved during a specified time period.

**everyday low prices (EDLP)** Price tactic of permanently reducing prices 10 to 15 percent below the traditional levels while eliminating trade discounts that create trade loading.

**evoked set (consideration set)** Group of brands, resulting from an information search, from which a buyer can choose.

**exchange control** Law compelling a company earning foreign exchange from its exports to sell that foreign exchange to a control agency, usually a central bank.

**exclusive dealing** Channel control practice in which a manufacturer prohibits its dealers from carrying competing products.

**exclusive distribution** Form of distribution that establishes one or a few dealers within a given area.

**exclusive-territory policy** Channel control practice in which a manufacturer requires an intermediary to sell only to customers located within an assigned territory.

**experience quality** Characteristic of a product that can be assessed only after purchase or use.

**experiment** Method of gathering primary data in which one or more variables are altered to measure their relative influence on another variable.

**export agent** Intermediary who either lives in a foreign country and performs the same functions as a domestic manufacturer's agent or lives in the manufacturer's country but represents foreign buyers.

**export broker** Broker that operates primarily in exporting agricultural products and raw materials.

**exporting** Practice of selling domestically produced products in another country.

**express warranty** Written guarantee that a good or service is fit for the purpose for which it was sold.

**extensive decision making** Most complex type of consumer decision making, used when buying an unfamiliar, expensive product or an infrequently bought item; requires use of several criteria for evaluating options and much time for seeking information.

**external information search** Process of seeking information in the outside environment.

**extra inducement close (negotiation)** Technique of withholding a special concession until the end of the selling process and using it to close a sale.

## F

**factory outlet** Off-price retailer that is owned and operated by a manufacturer and that carries the manufacturer's own line of merchandise.

**family brand** Practice of using the same brand name to market several different products.

**family life cycle (FLC)** Series of life stages determined by a combination of age, marital status, and the presence or absence of children.

**FDA (Food and Drug Administration)** Federal agency charged with enforcing regulations against selling and distributing adulterated, misbranded, or hazardous food and drug products.

**Federal Trade Commission (FTC)** Federal agency empowered to prevent persons or corporations from using unfair methods of competition in commerce.

**feedback** Receiver's response to a message.

**field order taker** Someone who visits existing customers regularly, checks inventory, writes up new orders, and then delivers and stocks the product for the customers.

**field service firm** Firm that specializes in interviewing respondents on a subcontract basis.

**fishbone diagram** Graph resembling the skeleton of a fish that helps managers visualize cause-and-effect relationships for problems.

**fishyback** Form of intermodal transportation combining the use of truck, rail, and ship or barge to move containerized goods.

**fixed cost** Cost that does not change as output is increased or decreased.

**FLC (family life cycle)** Series of life stages determined by a combination of age, marital status, and the presence or absence of children.

**flexible pricing (variable pricing)** Price tactic in which different customers pay different prices for essentially the same merchandise bought in equal quantities.

**flighted media schedule** Media scheduling strategy in which ads are run heavily every other month or every two weeks, to achieve a greater impact with an increased frequency and reach at those times.

**FOB origin pricing** Price tactic that requires the buyer to absorb the freight costs from the shipping point ("free on board").

**focus group** Group of seven to ten people with desired characteristics who participate in a group discussion about a subject of interest to a marketing organization.

**follow-up** Final step of the selling process, in which the salesperson ensures that delivery schedules are met, that the goods or services perform as promised, and that the buyers' employees are properly trained to use the products.

**Food and Drug Administration (FDA)** Federal agency charged with enforcing regulations against selling and distributing adulterated, misbranded, or hazardous food and drug products.

**Foreign Corrupt Practices Act** Legislation prohibiting U.S. corporations from making illegal payments to public officials of foreign governments in order to obtain business rights or enhance their business dealings in that country.

**formal control** Written, management-initiated mechanism that influences the probability that employees and systems will function in ways that support the stated marketing objectives.

**formula pricing** Pricing method in which a predetermined formula is used to set price.

**forward buying** Practice of purchasing in advance of need to take advantage of promotional discounts offered by suppliers.

**forward integration** Manufacturer's or wholesaler's acquisition of an intermediary closer to the target market or performance of the functions of an intermediary closer to the target market.

**four P's** Product decisions, distribution (or place) decisions, promotion decisions, and pricing decisions, which together make up the marketing mix.

**frame error** Error that occurs when the sample drawn from a population differs from the target population.

**franchise outlet**
Retail store owned and operated by an individual who is a licensee of a larger supporting organization.

**franchise**
Right to operate a business or to sell a product.

**franchisee**
Individual or business that is granted the right to sell another party's product.

**franchisor**
Individual or business that grants operating rights to another party to sell its product.

**freight absorption pricing** Price tactic in which the seller pays all or part of the actual freight charges and does not pass them on to the buyer.

**freight forwarder** Carrier that collects less-than-carload shipments from a number of shippers and consolidates them into carload lots.

**frequency** Number of times an individual is exposed to a given message during a specific period.

**frequent-buyer program** Promotional program in which loyal consumers are rewarded for making multiple purchases of a particular good or service.

**FTC (Federal Trade Commission)** Federal agency empowered to prevent persons or corporations from using unfair methods of competition in commerce.

**full-line wholesaler (general merchandise wholesaler)**
Wholesaler that stocks a full assortment of products within a product line.

**full-service merchant wholesaler** Wholesaler that assembles an assortment of products, provides credit for clients, offers promotional help and technical advice, maintains a sales force to contact customers, and delivers merchandise and that may offer research, planning, installation, and repair.

**fully industrialized society** Society that is an exporter of manufactured products, many of which are based on advanced technology.

**functional discount (trade discount)** Discount to wholesalers and retailers for performing channel functions.

## G

**gap model** Model of service quality that identifies five key discrepancies that can cause problems in service delivery and influence evaluations of service quality.

**GATT (General Agreement on Tariffs and Trade)**
Multinational agreement that reduces tariffs and other barriers to trade, the eighth version of which was signed in 1994 by representatives of 117 countries.

**General Agreement on Tariffs and Trade (GATT)**
Multinational agreement that reduces tariffs and other barriers to trade, the eighth version of which was signed in 1994 by representatives of 117 countries.

**general merchandise wholesaler (full-line wholesaler)**
Wholesaler that stocks a full assortment of products within a product line.

**generation X** People who are currently between the ages of 18 and 29.

**generic product name** Name that identifies a product by class or type and cannot be trademarked.

**generic product** No-frills, no–brand name, low-cost product.

**geodemographic segmentation** Method of dividing markets based on neighborhood lifestyle categories.

**geographic segmentation** Method of dividing markets based on region of the country or world, market size, market density, or climate.

**geographic selectivity** Ability of an advertising medium to cover a specific area.

**global marketing standardization** Production of uniform products that can be sold the same way all over the world.

**global marketing** Use of a global vision to effectively market goods and services across national boundaries.

**global vision** Ability to recognize and react to global marketing opportunities, awareness of threats from foreign competitors in all markets, and effective use of global distribution networks.

**gray marketing** Selling trademarked products through unauthorized channels.

**green marketing** Marketing of products and packages that are less toxic than normal, are more durable, contain reusable materials, or are made of recyclable materials.

**gross margin** Amount of money the retailer makes, stated as a percentage of sales, after the cost of goods sold is subtracted.

**growth stage** Second stage of the product life cycle, characterized by increasing sales, heightened competition, and healthy profits.

## H

**heterogeneity** Characteristic of services that makes them less standardized and uniform than goods.

**hierarchy of effects model** Model that outlines the six-stage process by which consumers make purchase decisions: awareness, knowledge, liking, preference, conviction, and purchase.

**high-involvement decision making** Process of deliberately searching for information about products and brands in order to evaluate them thoroughly.

**horizontal conflict** Channel conflict that occurs among channel members on the same level that handle the same manufacturer's brands, such as between two different wholesalers or two different retailers.

**hygiene factor** Factor that contributes to customer dissatisfaction.

**hypermarket** Retail establishment that combines a supermarket and discount department store in one large building.

## I

**ideal self-image** The way an individual would like to be.

**implementation** Phase of the marketing process in which marketers turn their plans into action assignments and ensure that these assignments are executed in a way that will accomplish the marketing plans' objectives.

**implied warranty** Unwritten guarantee that the good or service is fit for the purpose for which it was sold.

**incremental productivity approach** Method of determining the optimal sales force size, in which salespeople are added as long as the total sales increase is greater than the increase in selling cost.

**independent retailer** Individual or partnership that owns one or several retail establishments that are not part of a larger retail organization.

**individual branding** Practice of using a different brand name for each product.

**industrial distributor** Full-service merchant wholesaler that sells to manufacturers rather than to retailers.

**industrial product (business product)** Product used to manufacture other goods or services, to facilitate an organization's operations, or to resell to other customers.

**industrializing society** Society characterized by the spread of technology to most sectors of the economy.

**inelastic demand** Situation in which an increase or a decrease in price will not significantly affect demand for the product.

**inflation** General rise in prices resulting in decreased purchasing power.

**infomercial** Thirty-minute or longer advertisement that looks more like a TV talk show than a sales pitch.

**informal control** Unwritten, typically worker-initiated mechanism that influences individual or group behavior.

**information processing** Type of service that involves the use of technology or brainpower.

**informational labeling** Labeling designed to help consumers make a proper product selection and lower their cognitive dissonance after the purchase.

**InfoScan** Scanner-based, national sales-tracking service for the consumer packaged-goods industry, using data from purchases at retail stores.

**innovation** Product perceived as new by a potential adopter.

**innovator** Consumer among the small group who first adopt a new idea or product and are eager to try.

**inseparability** Characteristic of services that allows them to be produced and consumed simultaneously.

**inside order taker** Someone who takes orders from customers over the counter, on the sales floor, over the telephone, or by mail.

**institutional advertising** Form of advertising designed to enhance a company's image rather than promote a particular product.

**intangibility** Characteristic of services that prevents them from being touched, seen, tasted, heard, or felt in the same manner in which goods can be sensed.

**intensive distribution** Form of distribution aimed at having a product available in every outlet where target customers might want to buy it.

**intermodal transportation** Combination of two or more modes of moving freight.

**internal information search** Process of recalling past information stored in the memory.

**internal marketing** Policy of treating employees as customers and developing systems and benefits that satisfy their needs.

**interpersonal communication** Direct, face-to-face communication between two or more people.

**introductory stage** First stage of the product life cycle, which represents the full-scale launch of a new product into the marketplace.

**inventory carrying cost** Total of all expenses involved in maintaining inventory, including the cost of capital tied up in idle merchandise, the cost of obsolescence, space charges, handling charges, insurance costs, property taxes, losses due to depreciation and deterioration, and opportunity costs.

**inventory control system** Method of developing and maintaining an adequate assortment of products to meet customers' demands.

**ISO 9000** European Union's standards for quality assurance procedures, controls, and documentation.

**JIT (just-in-time) inventory management** Redesigning and simplifying manufacturing by reducing inventory levels and delivering parts just when they are needed on the production line.

**joint cost** Cost that is shared in the manufacturing and marketing of more than one product in a product line.

**joint demand** Demand for two or more items that are used together in a final product.

**joint venture** Arrangement in which a domestic firm buys part of a foreign company or joins with a foreign company to create a new entity.

**jury of executive opinion** Sales forecasting technique that surveys a group of executive experts.

**just-in-time (JIT) inventory management** Redesigning and simplifying manufacturing by reducing inventory levels and delivering parts just when they are needed on the production line.

**keh** Asian-Americna cooperative of about twenty people who combine their money and award it to one member each month and then disband after everyone has participated in the payout cycle.

**keiretsu** Japanese society of business, which takes one of two main forms: a bank-centered keiretsu, or a massive industrial combine centered around a bank; and a supply keiretsu, or a group of companies dominated by the major manufacturer they provide with supplies.

**keystoning** Practice of marking up prices by 100 percent, or doubling the cost.

## L

**laboratory (simulated) market test** Presentation of advertising and other promotion materials for several products, including a test product, to members of the product's target market.

**laggard** Consumer among the final group to adopt a new idea or product, characterized by ties to tradition.

**late majority** Fourth group of consumers to adopt a new idea or product, characterized by their reliance on group norms.

**lead generation (prospecting)** Identification of those firms and people most likely to buy the seller's offerings.

**lead qualification** Determination of a sales prospect's authority to buy and ability to pay for the good or service.

**lead time** Time between when a customer places and receives an order.

**leader pricing (loss-leader pricing)** Price tactic in which a product is sold near or even below cost in the hope that shoppers will buy other items once they are in the store.

**learning** Process that creates changes in behavior, immediate or expected, through experience and practice.

**licensing** Legal process whereby a licensor agrees to let another firm use its manufacturing process, trademarks, patents, trade secrets, or other proprietary knowledge.

**life cycle cost** Expected additional outlay a customer incurs over the life of a product.

**lifestyle** Mode of living as identified by a person's activities, interests, and opinions.

**limited decision making** Type of decision making that requires a moderate amount of time for gathering information and deliberating about an unfamiliar brand in a familiar product category.

**limited-service merchant wholesaler** Wholesaler that performs only a few of the full-service merchant wholesaler's activities.

**line extension** Practice of adding products to a product line.

**logistics** Procurement and management of raw materials for production.

**loss-leader pricing (leader pricing)** Price tactic in which a product is sold near or even below cost in the hope that shoppers will buy other items once they are in the store.

**low-involvement decision making** Process of deciding to buy a product in which the consumer experiences little perceived risk, low identification with the product, or little personal relevance.

## M

**Maastricht Treaty** Agreement among the twelve members of the European Community to pursue economic, monetary, and political union.

**macrosegmentation** Method of dividing business markets based on such general characteristics as geographic location, type of organization, customer size, and product use.

**mail-order wholesaler** Limited-service merchant wholesaler that sells goods by catalog to businesses, institutions, government, and other organizations.

**major equipment (installation)** Capital good, such as a large or expensive machine, mainframe computer, blast furnace, generator, airplane, or building.

**mall intercept interview** Survey research method that involves interviewing people in the common areas of shopping malls.

**manufacturer's brand** Manufacturer's name used as a brand name.

**manufacturers' agent** Wholesaling intermediary that represents one manufacturer or several manufacturers of complementary lines and follows the terms set by the manufacturer.

**marginal cost (MC)** Change in total costs associated with a one-unit change in output.

**marginal revenue (MR)** Extra revenue associated with selling an extra unit of output.

**market attractiveness/company strength matrix** Tool for allocating resources among strategic business units on the basis of how attractive a market is and how well the firm is positioned to take advantage of opportunities in that market.

**market development** Marketing strategy that attracts new customers to existing products.

**market grouping** Trade alliance in which several countries agree to work together to form a common trade area that enhances trade opportunities.

**market manager** Person who is responsible for coordinating the marketing efforts designed to reach a particular group of customers.

**market opportunity analysis** Description and estimation of the size and sales potential of market segments of interest to a firm and assessment of key competitors in these market segments.

**market penetration** Marketing strategy that increases market share among existing customers.

**market sales potential** Maximum amount of product that can be sold in a given industry with maximum marketing expenditures under existing marketing mixes within a specific external environment.

**market segment** Subgroup of people or organizations sharing one or more characteristics that cause them to have similar product needs.

**market segmentation** Process of dividing a market into

meaningful, relatively similar, and identifiable segments or groups.

**market share approach** Method of setting a promotion budget that allocates the amount needed to maintain or win a certain market share.

**market share** Company's product sales as a percentage of total sales for that industry.

**market** People or organizations with needs or wants and with the ability, and the willingness, to buy.

**marketing audit** Thorough, systematic, periodic evaluation of the goals, strategies, structure, and performance of the marketing organization.

**marketing channel (channel of distribution)** Set of interdependent organizations that ease the transfer of ownership as products move from producer to business user or consumer.

**marketing concept** Idea that the social and economic justification for an organization's existence is the satisfaction of customer wants and needs while meeting organizational objectives.

**marketing intelligence** Everyday information about developments in the marketing environment that managers use to prepare and adjust marketing plans.

**marketing mix** Unique blend of product, distribution, promotion, and pricing strategies designed to produce mutually satisfying exchanges with a target market.

**marketing myopia** Practice of defining a business in terms of the goods and services it produces rather than in terms of the benefits customers seek.

**marketing objective** Statement of what is to be accomplished through marketing activities.

**marketing orientation** Philosophy that assumes responsiveness to customer wants should be the central focus of all marketing activities.

**marketing research** Process of planning, collecting, and analyzing data relevant to marketing decision making.

**marketing strategy** Plan that involves selecting one or more target markets, setting marketing objectives, and developing and maintaining a marketing mix that will produce mutually satisfying exchanges with target markets.

**marketing-controlled information source** Product information source that originates with marketers promoting the product.

**marketing** Process of planning and executing the conception, pricing, promotion, and distribution of ideas, goods, and services to create exchanges that satisfy individual and organizational objectives.

**markup pricing** Pricing method that adds to the product cost amounts for profit and for expenses not previously accounted for.

**Maslow's hierarchy of needs** Method of classifying human needs and motivations into five categories in ascending order of importance: physiological, safety, social, esteem, and self-actualization.

**mass communication** Communication to large audiences.

**mass merchandising** Retailing strategy of using moderate to low prices on most merchandise, coupled with big promotion budgets, to stimulate high turnover of products.

**master brand** Brand so dominant in consumers' minds that they think of it immediately when a product category, use situation, product attribute, or customer benefit is mentioned.

**materials-handling system** Method of moving inventory into, within, and out of the warehouse.

**maturity stage** Third stage of the product life cycle, in which sales begin to level off and the market approaches saturation.

**MC (marginal cost)** Change in total costs associated with a one-unit change in output.

**measurement error** Error that occurs when there is a difference between the information desired by the researcher and the information provided by the measurement process.

**media mix** Combination of media to be used for a promotional campaign.

**media schedule** Designation of the media, the specific publications or programs, and the insertion dates of advertising.

**medium** Channel used to convey a message to a target market.

**merchant wholesaler** Institution that buys goods from manufacturers and resells them to businesses, government agencies, and other wholesalers or retailers and that receives and takes title to goods, stores them in its own warehouses, and later reships them.

**micromarketing** Marketing program tailored to prospective buyers who live in small geographic regions, such as neighborhoods, or who have very specific lifestyle and demographic characteristics.

**microsegmentation** Method of dividing business markets based on the characteristics of decision-making units within a macrosegment.

**missionary sales representative** Someone who works for a manufacturer to stimulate goodwill within the channel of distribution and to support the company's sales efforts.

**mixed economy** Economy in which both the government and the private sector exercise economic control.

**MNC (multinational corporation)** Company that moves resources, goods, services, and skills across national boundaries without regard to the country in which the headquarters is located.

**modified rebuy** Buying situation in which the purchaser wants some change in the original good or service.

**monopolistic competition** Form of economic competition in which a relatively large number of suppliers offer similar but not identical products.

**monopoly** Form of economic competition in which one firm controls the output and price of a product for which there are no close substitutes.

**morals** Rules or habits that people develop as a result of cultural values and norms.

**motive** Driving force that causes a person to take action to satisfy specific needs.

**moving average** Sales forecasting technique that combines sales data from several of the most recent years and uses an average to obtain the next year's forecast.

**MR (marginal revenue)** Extra revenue associated with selling an extra unit of output.

**multiculturalism** Roughly equal representation of all major ethnic groups withiin a geographic area.

**multinational corporation (MNC)** Company that moves resources, goods, services, and skills across national boundaries without regard to the country in which the headquarters is located.

**multiple distribution (dual distribution)** Use of two or more channels to distribute the same product to target markets.

**multiplier effect (accelerator principle)** Phenomenon in which a small increase or decrease in consumer demand produces a much larger change in demand for the facilities and equipment needed to make the consumer product.

**multisegment targeting strategy** Marketing approach based on serving two or more well-defined market segments, with a distinct marketing mix for each.

## N

**NAD (National Advertising Division)** Complaint bureau for consumers and advertisers, part of the Council of Better Business Bureaus.

**NAFTA (North American Free Trade Agreement)** Treaty establishing the world's largest free-trade zone, which includes Canada, the United States, and Mexico.

**NARB (National Advertising Review Board)** Appeals board for cases in which the National Advertising Division rules in favor of the complaining party.

**National Advertising Division (NAD)** Complaint bureau for consumers and advertisers, part of the Council of Better Business Bureaus.

**National Advertising Review Board (NARB)** Appeals board for cases in which the National Advertising Division rules in favor of the complaining party.

**need-satisfaction approach** Sales pitch that focuses on satisfying a prospective buyer's particular needs.

**need** Anything an individual depends on to function efficiently; root of all human behavior.

**negotiation (extra inducement close)** Technique of withholding a special concession until the end of the selling process and using it to close a sale.

**networking** Process of finding out about potential clients from friends, business contacts, coworkers, acquaintances, and fellow members in professional and civic organizations.

**new buy** Buying situation requiring the purchase of a product for the first time.

**new product committee** Ad hoc group whose members represent various functional interests and who manage the new product development process.

**new product department** Separate department that manages the new product development process on a full-time basis.

**new product strategy** Plan that links the new product development process with the objectives of the marketing department, the business unit, and the corporation.

**new product** Product new to the world, the market, the producer, the seller, or some combination of these.

**niche** One segment of a market.

**noise** Anything that interferes with, distorts, or slows down the transmission of information.

**nonaspirational reference group** Group with which an individual does not want to associate.

**nonbusiness marketing** Marketing activities conducted by nonbusiness organizations.

**nonbusiness organization** Organization that exists to achieve some goal other than the usual business goals of profit, market share, and return on investment.

**noncumulative quantity discount** Deduction from list price that applies to a single order rather than to the total volume of orders placed during a certain period.

**nonmarketing-controlled information source** Product information source that is not associated with advertising or promotion.

**nonprobability sample** Any sample in which little or no attempt is made to get a representative cross section of the population.

**nonprofit organization marketing** Effort by public and private nonprofit organizations to bring about mutually satisfying exchanges with target markets.

**nonstore retailing** Practice of selling goods and services to the ultimate consumer without setting up a store.

**norm** Value or attitude deemed acceptable by a group.

**North American Free Trade Agreement (NAFTA)** Treaty establishing the world's largest free-trade zone, which includes Canada, the United States, and Mexico.

## O

**objective and task approach** Method of setting a promotion budget that begins with promotional objectives, defines the communication tools required to achieve those objectives, and then adds up the costs of the planned activities.

**observation research** Research method that relies on three types of observation: people watching people, people watching physical phenomena, and machines watching people.

**odd-even pricing (psychological pricing)** Price tactic that uses odd-numbered prices to connote bargains and even-numbered prices to imply quality.

**off-price retailer** Retailer that sells at prices 25 percent or more below traditional department store prices because it pays cash for its stock and usually doesn't ask for return privileges.

**oligopoly** Form of economic competition in which a small number of firms dominate the market for a good or service.

**on-line database vendor** Intermediary that acquires databases from database creators.

**on-line database** Database accessible by anyone with the proper computer facilities.

**open-ended question** Question worded to encourage unlimited answers phrased in the respondent's own words.

**operations-oriented pricing** Policy of varying prices to coordinate supply and demand and encourage maximum use of productive capacity.

**opinion leader** Individual who influences the opinions of others.

**optimizer** Type of business customer that considers numerous suppliers, both familiar and unfamiliar, solicits bids, and studies all proposals carefully before selecting one.

**order entry** First step in order processing, in which a customer order is taken.

**order getter** Someone who actively seeks buyers for a product.

**order handling** Second step in order processing, in which the order is transmitted to the office, usually on a standardized order form, and then to the warehouse floor.

**order processing cost** Total of operating expenses for the ordering or purchasing department, costs of required follow-up, operating expenses for the receiving department, expenses incurred in paying invoices, and the portion of data-processing costs related to purchasing and acquiring inventory.

**ordering cost** Average cost per order, calculated by dividing the order processing cost by the number of orders placed per year.

## P

**packaging** Container for protecting and promoting a product and making it safer and more convenient.

**parallel (simultaneous/concurrent) engineering** Product development process in which all relevant functional areas and outside suppliers participate at all stages, thereby streamlining the development process and reducing its cost.

**Pareto analysis** Method for identifying a company's biggest problems that uses a bar chart to rank causes of variation in production or service processes by the degree of their impact on quality.

**patronage-oriented pricing** Policy of setting prices at a level that will maximize the number of customers using a service.

**penetration pricing** Pricing policy whereby a firm charges a relatively low price for a product as a way to reach the mass market in the early stages of the product life cycle.

**people processing** Type of service directed at the customer.

**percent of sales approach** Method of setting a promotion budget that allocates an amount equal to a certain percentage of total sales.

**perception** Process by which people select, organize, and interpret stimuli into a meaningful and coherent picture.

**perceptual mapping** Means of displaying or graphing, in two or more dimensions, the location of products, brands, or groups of products in customers' minds.

**perishability** Characteristic of services that prevents them from being stored, warehoused, or inventoried.

**personal selling** Direct communication between a sales representative and one or more prospective buyers, for the purpose of making a sale.

**personal selling** Planned presentation to one or more prospective buyers for the purpose of making a sale.

**personality** Way of organizing and grouping the consistencies of an individual's reactions to situations.

**personalized economy** Economic structure in which goods and services are delivered at a good value on demand.

**persuasive labeling** Labeling that focuses on a promotional theme or logo rather than on consumer information.

**physical distribution service** Interrelated activities performed by a supplier to ensure that the right product is in the right place at the right time.

**physical distribution** Ingredient in the marketing mix that describes how products are moved and stored.

**piggyback (trailer on flatcar, TOFC)** Form of intermodal transportation combining the use of truck and rail to ship containerized goods.

**PIMS (profit impact of market strategy)** Method for analyzing strategic alternatives that involves consulting a database summarizing the financial and market performance of 3,000 strategic business units of more than 450 firms.

**pioneering advertising** Form of advertising designed to stimulate primary demand for a new product or product category.

**planned obsolescence** Practice of changing a product's style so that it becomes outdated before it actually needs replacement.

**point-of-purchase display** Promotional display set up at the retailer's location to build traffic, advertise the product, or induce impulse buying.

***poka-yoke*** Japanese concept that means finding ways to minimize human error by changing the design.

**portfolio matrix** Tool for allocating resources among products or strategic business units on the basis of relative market share and market growth rate.

**position** Place that a product, brand, or group of products occupies in consumers' minds relative to competing offerings.

**positioning** Developing a specific marketing mix to influence potential customers' overall perception of a brand, product line, or organization in general.

**possession processing** Type of service directed at something the customer owns.

**postconventional morality** Most advanced level of moral development, in which people are less concerned about how others might see them and more concerned about how they see and judge themselves over the long run.

**postsale service** Service that occurs after the transaction.

**poverty of time** Lack of time to do anything but work, commute to work, handle family situations, do housework, shop, sleep, and eat.

**preconventional morality** Basic level of moral development, which is childlike, calculating, self-centered, and even selfish, based on what will be immediately punished or rewarded.

**predatory pricing** Practice of charging a very low price for a product with the intent of driving competitors out of business or out of a market.

**preindustrial society** Society characterized by economic and social change and the emergence of a rising middle class with an entrepreneurial spirit.

**premium** Extra item offered to the consumer, usually in exchange for some proof of purchase of the promoted product.

**prepared sales presentation** Structured, or canned, sales pitch.

**presale service** Service that furnishes the customer with information and assistance in the decision-making process.

**prestige pricing** Charging high prices to help promote a high-quality image.

**price bundling** Marketing two or more products in a single package for a special price.

**price discrimination** Practice of charging different prices to different customers for the same product.

**price equilibrium** Price at which demand and supply are equal.

**price fixing** Agreement between two or more firms on the price they will charge for a product.

**price lining** Practice of offering a product line with several items at specific price points.

**price shading** Use of discounts by salespeople to increase demand for one or more products in a line.

**price skimming** Pricing policy whereby a firm charges a high introductory price, often coupled with heavy promotion.

**price strategy** Basic, long-term pricing framework, which establishes the initial price for a product and the intended direction for price movements over the product life cycle.

**price** Perceived value of a good or service.

**primary data** Information collected for the first time and used to solve a particular problem.

**primary membership group** Reference group with which people interact regularly in an informal, face-to-face manner, such as family, friends, or fellow employees.

**private brand** Brand name that a wholesaler or a retailer uses for products it sells.

**private warehouse** Storage facility either leased or owned by a company that needs to store a large amount of its own merchandise.

**proactive management** Practice of altering the marketing mix to fit newly emerging economic, social, and competitive trends.

**probability sample** Sample drawn from a population in which every element has a known nonzero probability of being selected.

**problem child (question mark)** In the portfolio matrix, a business unit that shows rapid growth but poor profit margins.

**problem recognition** Result of an imbalance between actual and desired states.

**processed material** Good used directly in manufacturing other products.

**producer segment** Portion of the business-to-business market consisting of individuals and organizations that buy goods and services for use in producing other products, for incorporation into other products, or for facilitation of the organization's daily operations.

**product advertising** Form of advertising that touts the benefits of a specific good or service.

**product assortment (product offering)** The mix of products offered to customers by the retailer.

**product category** All brands that satisfy a particular type of need.

**product development** Marketing strategy that entails the creation of new products for present markets; process of converting applications for new technologies into marketable products.

**product differentiation** Marketing tactic designed to distinguish one firm's products from those of competitors.

**product item** Specific version of a product that can be designated as a distinct offering among an organization's products.

**product life cycle** Concept describing a product's acceptance in the marketplace over four stages: introduction, growth, maturity, and decline.

**product line depth** Number of product items in a product line.

**product line pricing** Setting prices for an entire line of products.

**product line** Group of closely related products offered by the organization.

**product manager** Person who is responsible for several brands within a product line or product group.

**product mix consistency** Extent to which product lines are similar in terms of end use, distribution outlets used, target markets, and price range.

**product mix width** Number of product lines that an organization offers.

**product mix** All the products that an organization sells.

**product modification** Change in one or more of a product's characteristics—for example, its quality, functional characteristics, or style.

**product offering (product assortment)** The mix of products offered to customers by the retailer.

**product-review committee** Group of high-level executives—representing the marketing, production, and finance departments—appointed to review products for elimination from a company's product line.

**product** Everything, both favorable and unfavorable, that a person receives in an exchange—for example, a good, a service, or an idea.

**production orientation** Philosophy that focuses on the internal capabilities of the firm rather than on the desires and needs of the marketplace.

**profit impact of market strategy (PIMS)** Method for analyzing strategic alternatives that involves consulting a database summarizing the financial and market performance of 3,000 strategic business units of more than 450 firms.

**profit maximization** Pricing method that sets price where marginal revenue equals marginal cost.

**profit** Revenue minus expenses.

**promotion plan** Carefully arranged sequence of promotional efforts designed around a common theme and geared to specific objectives.

**promotion** Communication by marketers that informs, persuades, and reminds potential buyers of a product in order to influence an opinion or elicit a response.

**promotional allowance** Payment to a dealer for promoting the manufacturer's products.

**promotional mix** Combination of promotion tools—including advertising, public relations, personal selling, and sales promotion—used to reach the target market and fulfill the organization's overall goals.

**promotional strategy** Plan for the optimal use of the elements of promotion: advertising, public relations, personal selling, and sales promotion.

**prospecting (lead generation)** Identification of those firms and people most likely to buy the seller's offerings.

**PSA (public service advertisement)** Announcement that promotes the programs, activities, or services of a government entity or nonprofit organization.

**psychographic segmentation** Method of dividing markets based on personality, motives, lifestyle, and geodemographics.

**psychological pricing (odd-even pricing)** Price tactic that uses odd-numbered prices to connote bargains and even-numbered prices to imply quality.

**public relations** Marketing function that evaluates public attitudes, identifies areas within the organization that the public may be interested in, and executes a program of action to earn public understanding and acceptance.

**public service advertisement (PSA)** Announcement that promotes the programs, activities, or services of a government entity or nonprofit organization.

**public warehouse** Independently owned storage facility that stores merchandise for others and that may specialize in certain types of products, such as furniture, refrigerated foods, or household goods.

**publicity** Public information about a company, good, or service appearing in the mass media as a news item.

**pull strategy** Marketing strategy that stimulates consumer demand to obtain product distribution.

**pulsing media schedule** Media scheduling strategy that uses continuous scheduling during the best sales periods and a flighted schedule at other times.

**purchase intent scale** Survey question that measures a person's propensity to buy a product.

**purchasing contract** Agreement in which a business buyer promises to purchase a given amount of a product within a specified period.

**purely competitive market** Form of economic competition characterized by a large number of sellers marketing a standardized product to a group of buyers who are well informed about the marketplace.

**push money** Money offered to channel intermediaries to encourage them to "push" products—that is, to encourage other members of the channel to sell the products.

**push strategy** Marketing strategy that uses aggressive personal selling and trade advertising to convince a wholesaler or a retailer to carry and sell particular merchandise.

**pyramid of corporate social responsibility** Model that suggests corporate social responsibility is composed of economic, legal, ethical, and philanthropic responsibilities and that the firm's economic performance supports the entire structure.

## Q

**QFD (quality function deployment)** Technique that helps companies translate customer requirements into goods specifications by using a quality matrix to relate what customers want with how goods will be designed.

**quality function deployment (QFD)** Technique that helps companies translate customer requirements into goods specifications by using a quality matrix to relate what customers want with how goods will be designed.

**quantity discount** Price reduction offered to buyers buying in multiple units or above a specified dollar amount.

**question mark (problem child)** In the portfolio matrix, a business unit that shows rapid growth but poor profit margins.

**quota** Limit on the amount of a specific product that can enter a country.

**quota** Statement of the individual salesperson's sales objectives, usually based on sales volume alone but sometimes including key accounts (those with greatest potential), new accounts, and specific products.

## R

**rack jobber** Full-service wholesaler that performs the merchant wholesaler's functions and some usually carried out by the retailer, such as stocking shelves.

**random error** Error that occurs because the selected sample is an imperfect representation of the overall population.

**random sample** Type of probability sample in which every element of the population has an equal chance of being selected as part of the sample.

**raw material** Unprocessed extractive or agricultural product, such as mineral ore, lumber, wheat, corn, fruits, vegetables, or fish.

**reach** Number of target consumers exposed to a commercial at least once during a specific period, usually four weeks.

**reactive management** Practice of waiting for change to have a major impact on the firm before deciding to take action.

**real self-image** The way an individual actually perceives himself or herself.

**rebate** Cash refund given for the purchase of a product during a specific period.

**recall objective** Promotional objective aimed at increasing the percentage of the target market that can recall the campaign's message and the product.

**receiver** Person who decodes a message.

**recession** Period of economic activity when income, production, and employment tend to fall.

**reciprocity** Practice in which business purchasers choose to buy from their own customers.

**reference group** Group in society that influences an individual's purchasing behavior.

**referral** Recommendation to a salesperson from a customer or business associate.

**refusal to deal** Channel control practice in which a producer refuses to allow certain intermediaries to carry its products.

**regression** Sales forecasting technique that uses statistics to define a relationship between past sales (a dependent variable) and one or more independent variables.

**relationship marketing** Strategy of developing strong customer loyalty and forging long-term partnerships by creating satisfied customers who will buy additional products from the firm.

**reliability** Ability to perform a service dependably, accurately, and consistently.

**reminder objective** Promotional objective used to cue the consumer that the product is available.

**reorder point** Inventory level that signals when more inventory should be ordered.

**repositioning** Changing consumers' perceptions of a brand in relation to competing brands.

**resale restriction** Channel control practice in which the producer stipulates to whom distributors may resell its products and in what geographic territories they may be sold.

**research design** Outline of which research questions must be answered, where and when data will be gathered, and how the data will be analyzed.

**reseller market** Portion of the business-to-business market consisting of retail and wholesale businesses that buy finished goods and resell them for a profit.

**response function** Graphed relationship between a marketing mix (or component of the mix) and sales to a specific target market.

**responsiveness** Ability to provide prompt service.

**retail life cycle** Identifiable cycle of growth and decline that retailing institutions go through, which includes four distinct stages: (1) introduction, (2) growth, (3) maturity, and (4) decline.

**retailer** Firm that sells mainly to consumers.

**retailing** All activities directly related to the sale of goods and services to the ultimate consumer for personal, nonbusiness use or for consumption.

**retailing mix** Combination of the six P's—price, place, product, promotion, personnel, and presentation—to sell goods and services to the ultimate customer.

**revenue-oriented pricing** Policy of setting prices at a level that will maximize the surplus of income over expenditures.

**revenue** Price charged to customers multiplied by the number of units sold.

**reverse channel** Distribution channel in which products move from consumer back to producer.

**risk** Uncertainty about long-term, life cycle costs of buying a good or service.

**ROI (target return on investment)** Profit objective calculated by dividing a firm's net profits after taxes by its total assets.

**routine response behavior** Type of decision making exhibited by consumers buying frequently purchased, low-cost goods and services; requires little search and decision time.

## S

**safety stock** Extra merchandise kept on hand to protect against running out of stock.

**sales force composite** Sales forecasting technique that surveys the sales force.

**sales forecast** Estimate of a firm's future sales or revenues for a specified period.

**sales orientation** Philosophy that assumes buyers resist purchasing items that are not essential.

**sales presentation** Face-to-face explanation of a product's benefits to a prospective buyer.

**sales promotion** Marketing activities—other than personal selling, advertising, and public relations—that stimulate consumer buying and dealer effectiveness.

**sales promotion** Offer of a short-term incentive in order to induce the purchase of a particular good or service.

**sales territory** Particular geographic area assigned to a salesperson.

**sample** Subset for interviewing drawn from a larger population.

**sampling error** Error that occurs when a sample is not representative of the target population in some way.

**satisficer** Type of business customer that places an order with the first familiar supplier to satisfy product and delivery requirements.

**satisfier** Factor that contributes to customer satisfaction.

**SBU (strategic business unit)** Subgroup in a larger organization, with a distinct mission and specific target market of its own, control over its resources, its own competitors, and plans independent of the other subgroups of the total organization.

**scaled-response question** Closed-ended question designed to measure the intensity of a respondent's answer.

**scrambled merchandising** Practice of offering a wide variety of nontraditional goods and services in one store.

**screening** Stage in the product development process that eliminates ideas inconsistent with the organization's new product strategy or obviously inappropriate for some other reason.

**search quality** Characteristic of a product that can be easily assessed before purchase.

**seasonal discount** Price reduction offered to buyers purchasing merchandise out of season.

**seasonal media schedule** Media scheduling strategy that runs advertising only during times of the year when the product is most likely to be used.

**secondary data** Data previously collected for any purpose other than the one at hand.

**secondary membership group** Reference group with which people associate less consistently and more formally than a primary membership group, such as a club, professional group, or religious group.

**segmentation base (variable)** Characteristic of individuals, groups, or organizations used as a basis for dividing a market into segments.

**selective distortion** Process whereby a consumer changes or distorts information that conflicts with his or her feelings or beliefs.

**selective distribution** Form of distribution achieved by screening dealers to eliminate all but a few in any single area.

**selective exposure** Process whereby a consumer notices certain stimuli and ignores other stimuli.

**selective retention** Process whereby a consumer remembers only that information that supports his or her personal beliefs.

**self-concept** How a consumer perceives himself or herself in terms of attitudes, perceptions, beliefs, and self-evaluations.

**selling against the brand** Stocking well-known branded items at high prices in order to sell store brands at discounted prices.

**selling agent** Wholesaling intermediary used mostly by small firms on a commission basis and contracted to sell the manufacturer's entire output.

**selling team** Combination of sales and nonsales people, under the direction of a leader, whose primary objective is to establish and maintain a strong relationship with a particular customer or customers.

**sender** Originator of the message in the communication process.

**service mark** Trademark for a service.

**service** Product in the form of an activity or a benefit provided to consumers, with four unique characteristics that distinguish it from a good: intangibility, inseparability, heterogeneity, and perishability.

**shopping product** Product that requires comparison shopping, because it is usually more expensive than a convenience product and found in fewer stores.

**SIC (standard industrial classification system)** Detailed numbering system developed by the U.S. government in order to classify business and government organizations by their main economic activity.

**silent close** Technique of ending a sales presentation by saying nothing and waiting for the prospect to make a response.

**simulated (laboratory) market test** Presentation of advertising and other promotion materials for several products, including a test product, to members of the product's target market.

**simultaneous (concurrent/parallel) engineering** Product development process in which all relevant functional areas and outside suppliers participate at all stages, thereby streamlining the development process and reducing its cost.

**single-price tactic** Policy of offering all goods and services at the same price.

**single-source research** System for gathering information from a single group of respondents by continuously monitoring the advertising, promotion, and pricing they are exposed to and the things they buy.

**situation analysis** Extensive background investigation into a particular marketing problem.

**social class** Group of people in a society who are considered nearly equal in status or community esteem, who regularly socialize among themselves both formally and informally, and who share behavioral norms.

**social cost** Cost not directly paid for by individual consumers but borne by society as a whole.

**social marketing** Application of marketing methods to spread socially beneficial ideas or behaviors.

**socialization process** How cultural values and norms are passed down to children.

**societal marketing concept** Idea that an organization exists not only to satisfy customer wants and needs and to meet organizational objectives but also to preserve or enhance individuals' and society's long-term best interests.

**spatial discrepancy** Difference between the location of the producer and the location of widely scattered markets.

**specialty merchandise wholesaler** Wholesaler that offers part of a product line to target customers but in greater depth than general merchandise wholesalers offer.

**specialty product** Product for which consumers search extensively and are very reluctant to accept substitutes.

**specialty store** Retail store specializing in a given type of merchandise.

**SQC (statistical quality control)** Method of analyzing deviations in manufactured materials, parts, and goods.

**standard industrial classification system (SIC)** Detailed numbering system developed by the U.S. government in order to classify business and government organizations by their main economic activity.

**standing-room-only close** Technique of ending a sales presentation by urging customers to buy right away because the product is selling so well that it may not be available later.

**star** In the portfolio matrix, a business unit that is a market leader and growing fast.

**statistical quality control (SQC)** Method of analyzing deviations in manufactured materials, parts, and goods.

**status quo pricing** Pricing objective that seeks to maintain existing prices or simply meet the competition.

**stimulus discrimination** Learned ability to differentiate among stimuli.

**stimulus generalization** Form of learning that occurs when one response is extended to a second stimulus similar to the first.

**stimulus-response approach** Sales pitch applying the concept that a given stimulus will produce a given response.

**stimulus** Any unit of input affecting the five senses: sight, smell, taste, touch, hearing.

**stitching niches** Combining ethnic, age, income, and lifestyle markets on some common basis to form a mass market.

**stockout cost** Cost of being out of stock, which includes direct costs due to lost sales and indirect costs due to the loss of dissatisfied customers.

**straight commission** Method of compensation in which the salesperson is paid some percentage of sales.

**straight rebuy** Buying situation in which the purchaser reorders the same goods or services without looking for new information or investigating other suppliers.

**straight salary** Method of compensation in which the salesperson receives a salary regardless of sales productivity.

**strategic alliance (strategic partnership)** Cooperative agreement between business firms, taking the form of a licensing or distribution agreement, joint venture, research and development consortium, or partnership.

**strategic business unit (SBU)** Subgroup in a larger organization, with a distinct mission and specific target market of its own, control over its resources, its own competitors, and plans independent of the other subgroups of the total organization.

**strategic channel alliance** Producers' agreement to jointly use one producer's already-established channel.

**strategic partnership (strategic alliance)** Cooperative agreement between business firms, taking the form of a licensing or distribution agreement, joint venture, research and development consortium, or partnership.

**strategic planning** Managerial process of creating and maintaining a fit between the organization's objectives and resources and evolving market opportunities.

**strategic window** Limited time during which the fit between the key requirements of a market and the firm's competencies are at an optimum.

**subculture** Homogeneous group of people who share elements of the overall culture as well as unique elements of their own group.

**summative close** Technique of ending a sales presentation by summarizing the product's benefits and asking for the sale.

**supermarket** Large, departmentalized, self-service retailer that specializes in foodstuffs and a few nonfood items.

**supplementary service** Service that supports or enhances the core service offered by an organization.

**supply** Consumable item that does not become part of the final product.

**supply** Quantity of a product that will be offered to the market by a supplier, or suppliers, at various prices for a specified period.

**survey research** Technique for gathering primary data in which a researcher interacts with people to obtain facts, opinions, and attitudes.

**SWOT analysis** Analysis of a firm's strengths, weaknesses, opportunities, and threats.

## T

**takeoff economy** Period of transition from a developing to a developed nation, during which new industries arise.

**tangibles** Physical evidence of a service.

**target market** Group for which an organization designs, implements, and maintains a marketing mix intended to meet the needs of that group, resulting in mutually satisfying exchanges.

**target return on investment (ROI)** Profit objective calculated by dividing a firm's net profits after taxes by its total assets.

**target return pricing** Pricing method that sets price where revenues from sales of a targeted quantity yield the target return on investment.

**tariff** Tax levied on the goods entering a country.

**technical specialist** Sales support person with a technical background who works out the details of custom-made products and communicates directly with the potential buyer's technical staff.

**telemarketing** Type of personal selling conducted over the telephone.

**temporal discrepancy** Difference between when a product is produced and when a customer is ready to buy it.

**test marketing** Stage in the product development process during which a product is introduced in a limited way to determine the reactions of potential customers in a market situation.

**time management** Efficient allocation of time to tasks, based on their priority and urgency.

**TOFC (trailer on flatcar, piggyback)** Form of intermodal transportation combining the use of truck and rail to ship containerized goods.

**total quality management (TQM)** Coordination, throughout the entire organization, of efforts to provide high-quality goods, processes, and services in order to ensure customer satisfaction.

**TQM (total quality management)** Coordination, throughout the entire organization, of efforts to provide high-quality goods, processes, and services in order to ensure customer satisfaction.

**trade agreement** Agreement to stimulate global trade.

**trade allowance** Price reduction offered by manufacturers to intermediaries, such as wholesalers and retailers.

**trade deficit** Excess of imports over exports.

**trade discount (functional discount)** Discount to wholesalers and retailers for performing channel functions.

**trade loading** Practice of temporarily lowering the price to induce wholesalers and retailers to buy more goods than can be sold in a reasonable time.

**trade sales promotion** Sales promotion activities targeted to a channel member, such as a wholesaler or retailer.

**trademark** Legal, exclusive right to use a brand name or other identifying mark.

**traditional society** Largely agricultural society, with a social structure and value system that provide little opportunity for upward mobility.

**trailer on flatcar (TOFC, piggyback)** Form of intermodal transportation combining the use of truck and rail to ship containerized goods.

**transaction cost** Immediate financial outlay or commitment a customer makes.

**transaction service** Service that is directly associated with the exchange transaction between a firm and its customers.

**truck jobber** Limited-service merchant wholesaler that performs the functions of salesperson and delivery person.

**two-part pricing** Price tactic that charges two separate amounts to consume a single good or service.

**tying contract** Channel control practice in which a manufacturer sells a product to an intermediary only under the condition that it purchase another (possibly unwanted) product.

## U

**unbundling** Reducing the bundle of services that comes with the basic product.

**undifferentiated targeting strategy** Marketing approach based on the assumption that the market has no individual segments and thus requires a single marketing mix.

**unfair trade practice act** Law that prohibits wholesalers and retailers from selling below cost.

**uniform delivered pricing** Price tactic in which the seller pays the actual freight charges and bills every purchaser an identical, flat freight charge.

**unique selling proposition** Desirable, exclusive, and believable advertising appeal selected as the theme for a campaign.

**unitary elasticity** Situation in which an increase in sales exactly offsets a decrease in price so that total revenue remains the same.

**unitization** Increasing the efficiency of handling small packages by grouping boxes on a pallet or skid for movement from one place to another.

**universal product code (UPC) (bar code)** Series of thick and thin vertical lines, readable by computerized optical scanners, that represent numbers used to track products.

**universe** Population from which a sample is drawn.

**unsought product** Product unknown to the potential buyer or known product that the buyer does not actively seek.

**UPC (universal product code, bar code)** Series of thick and thin vertical lines, readable by computerized optical scanners, that represent numbers used to track products.

**urgency close** Technique of ending a sales presentation by suggesting a reason for ordering soon, such as an impending price increase.

**usage rate segmentation** Method of dividing markets based on the amount of product bought or consumed.

## V

**value analysis (value engineering)** Systematic search for less expensive substitute goods or services.

**value engineering (value analysis)** Systematic search for less expensive substitute goods or services.

**value-based pricing** Pricing strategy that starts with the customer, considers the competition, and then determines the appropriate price.

**value** Enduring belief that a specific mode of conduct is personally or socially preferable to another mode of conduct.

**variable cost** Cost that deviates with changes in the level of output.

**variable pricing (flexible pricing)** Price tactic in which different customers pay different prices for essentially the same merchandise bought in equal quantities.

**vendor analysis** Practice of comparing alternative suppliers in terms of attributes that the buying center views as important.

**venture team** Entrepreneurial, market-oriented group staffed by a small number of representatives from different disciplines.

**vertical conflict** Channel conflict that occurs between different levels in a marketing channel, most typically between the manufacturer and wholesaler or between the manufacturer and retailer.

**vertical marketing system (VMS)** Network of producers and intermediaries acting as a unified system.

**VMS (vertical marketing system)** Network of producers and intermediaries acting as a unified system.

**want** Recognition of an unfulfilled need and a product that will satisfy it.

**warehouse club** Limited-service merchant wholesaler that sells a limited selection of brand-name appliances, household items, and groceries on a cash-and-carry basis to members, usually small businesses and groups.

**warranty** Guarantee of the quality or performance of a good or service.

**wheel of retailing** Model describing the constant changes in retailing in which new retail institutions enter a market as low-cost, low-price operations and gradually increase services and prices.

**wholesaler** Firm that sells mainly to producers, resellers, governments, institutions, and retailers.

**workload approach** Method of determining the optimal sales force size, in which the total time required to cover the territory is divided by the selling time available to one salesperson.

**zone pricing** Modification of uniform delivered pricing that divides the United States (or the total market) into segments or zones and charges a flat freight rate to all customers in a given zone.

# ENDNOTES


## Chapter 1

1. Earl Naumann, *Creating Customer Value* (Cincinnati: Thomson Executive Press, 1994), pp. 87–88.
2. Peter D. Bennett, *Dictionary of Marketing Terms* (Chicago: American Marketing Association, 1988), p. 115.
3. Philip Kotler, *Marketing Management*, 8th ed. (Englewood Cliffs, NJ: Prentice-Hall, 1994), p. 9.
4. "Smart Selling: How Companies Are Winning Over Today's Tougher Customer," *Business Week*, 3 August 1992, pp. 46–48.
5. "Customers Must Be Pleased, Not Just Satisfied," *Business Week*, 3 August 1992, p. 52.
6. Loren Berger, "Who's Minding the Gun Counter?" *Business Week*, 25 October 1993, p. 120.
7. Berger, p. 122.
8. Berger, p. 122.
9. Susan Caminiti, "The New Champs of Retailing," *Fortune*, 24 September 1990, p. 98.
10. Leonard L. Berry, A. Parasuraman, and Valarie A. Zeithaml, "Improving Service Quality in America: Lessons Learned," *Academy of Management Executive*, 8, no. 2 (1994), p. 36.
11. "Smart Selling," p. 46.
12. Malcolm Fleschner with Gerhard Gschwandtner, "The Marriott Miracle," *Personal Selling Power*, September 1994, p. 25.
13. "Flexible Work Arrangements Continue to Find a Home at Companies," *Wall Street Journal*, 19 January 1993, p. A1.
14. Sharyn Hunt and Ernest F. Cooke, "It's Basic but Necessary: Listen to the Customer," *Marketing News*, 5 March 1990, p. 23.
15. "King Customer," *Business Week*, 12 March 1990, p. 9.
16. Gary Samuels, "CD-ROM's First Big Victim," *Forbes*, 28 February 1994, pp. 42–44.
17. Samuels, p. 42.
18. Cyndee Miller, "Theaters Give 'Em More Than Goobers to Win Back Viewers," *Marketing News*, 1 October 1990, pp. 1, 20.
19. "King Customer," p. 89.
20. Sharon E. Beatty, "Relationship Selling in Retailing," *Retailing Issues Letter* [Arthur Anderson & Co. and the Center For Retailing Studies at Texas A&M University], November 1993, p. 1.
21. Earl Naumann and Patrick Shannon, "What Is Customer-Driven Marketing?," *Business Horizons*, November-December 1992, pp. 44–52.
22. Susan Caminiti, "Finding New Ways to Sell More," *Fortune*, 27 July 1992, pp. 100–103.
23. Kotler, pp. 26–29.
24. Naumann and Shannon, p. 50.
25. "King Customer," p. 90.
26. Cyndee Miller, "Nordstrom Is Tops in Survey," *Marketing News*, 15 February 1993, p. 12.
27. "The Rebirthing of Xerox," *Marketing Insights*, Summer 1992, pp. 73–80.
28. "King Customer," p. 91.
29. Fleschner, p. 26.
30. From William Echikson, "The Trick to Selling in Europe," *Fortune*, 20 September 1993, p. 82.
31. Kotler, p. 738.
32. Naumann, pp. 21–23.

## Chapter 2

1. Elyse Tanouye, "Owning Medco, Merck Takes Drug Marketing the Next Logical Step," *Wall Street Journal*, 31 May 1994, pp. A1, A5. Reprinted by permission of the *Wall Street Journal*, © 1994 Dow Jones & Company, Inc. All Rights Reserved Worldwide.
2. Susan Hwang, "From Choices to Checkout, the Genders Behave Very Differently in Supermarkets," *Wall Street Journal*, 22 March 1994, pp. B1, B10.
3. Hwang, pp. B1, B10.
4. "No 'Me Too' for These Two," *Marketing News*, 14 May 1990, pp. 1, 10.
5. "Welcome to the Age of 'Unpositioning,'" *Marketing News*, 16 April 1990, p. 11.
6. Adrienne Ward Fawcett, "Fast Cars, Gas Grills, and Cable," *Advertising Age*, 18 April 1994, p. 13. Reprinted with permission. Copyright © Crain Communications, Inc., 1994.
7. "Myths in Progress," *American Demographics*, August 1992, pp. 40–41.
8. "Gimme a Double Shake and a Lard on White," *Business Week*, 1 March 1993, p. 59.
9. "How to Deal with Tough Customers," *Fortune*, 3 December 1990, pp. 38–48.
10. "Shades of Green," *Wall Street Journal*, 2 August 1991, pp. A1, A8.
11. "Will Consumers Ever Buy Again?" *Brand Week*, 27 July 1992, p. 36.
12. "Trading Fat Paychecks for Free Time," *Wall Street Journal*, 5 August 1991, p. B1.
13. Bradford Fay, "The Great Time Famine," *Marketing Research*, September 1992, pp. 50–51.
14. John Robinson, "As We Like It," *American Demographics*, February 1993, pp. 44–48.
15. "Work Force 2005," *American Demographics*, May 1992, p. 59.

16. "This Bud's for You. No, Not You—Her," *Business Week,* 4 November 1991, p. 86.

17. "Targeting the Professional Woman," *Brandweek,* 31 January 1994, pp. 18–24. Copyright © 1991 Adweek, L.P. Used with permission from *Brandweek.*

18. Patricia Braus, "Sex and the Single Spender," *American Demographics,* November 1993, pp. 28–34.

19. "Home Alone—with $660 Billion," *Business Week,* 29 July 1991, pp. 76–77.

20. "Home Alone," pp. 76–77.

21. "Forever Single," *Adweek's Marketing Week,* 15 October 1991, p. 20.

22. Braus, p. 30.

23. Braus, p. 30.

24. "New Projections Show Faster Growth, More Diversity," *American Demographics,* February 1993, p. 9.

25. "Snapshots of the Nation," *Wall Street Journal,* 9 March 1990, pp. R12–R13.

26. James McNeal and Chyon-Hwa Yeh, "Born to Shop," *American Demographics,* June 1992, pp. 34–39. Copyright © 1992 *American Demographics.* Reprinted with permission.

27. McNeal and Yeh, pp. 34–39.

28. "Photography Companies Try to Click with Children," *Wall Street Journal,* 31 January 1994, pp. B1, B8.

29. Susan Mitchell, "How to Talk to Young Adults," *American Demographics,* April 1993, pp. 50–54.

30. "Understanding Generation X," *Marketing Research,* Spring 1993, pp. 54–55.

31. "Xers Know They're a Target Market, and They Hate That," *Marketing News,* 6 December 1993), pp. 2, 15.

32. "Survey Sheds Light on Typical Boomer," *Marketing News,* 31 January 1994, p. 2.

33. Cheryl Russell, "The Master Trend," *American Demographics,* October 1993, pp. 28–37.

34. Russell, pp. 28–37.

35. Russell, pp. 28–37.

36. Ruth Hamel, "Raging against Aging," *American Demographics,* March 1990, pp. 42–45.

37. "American Maturity," *American Demographics,* March 1993, pp. 31–42.

38. Michael Major, "Promoting to the Mature Market," *Promo,* November 1990, p. 7.

39. "Bond Stronger with Age," *Advertising Age,* 28 March 1994, p. 5–6.

40. "Baby-Boomers May Seek Age-Friendly Stores," *Wall Street Journal,* 1 July 1992, p. B1.

41. "Changing Times," *Wall Street Journal,* 22 March 1991, p. B6.

42. "Americans on the Move," *American Demographics,* June 1990, pp. 46–48.

43. William Frey, "The New White Flight," *American Demographics,* April 1994, pp. 40–47.

44. Louis Richman, "Why the Middle Class Is Anxious," *Fortune,* 21 May 1990, pp. 106–109.

45. "The Incredible Shrinking Middle Class," *American Demographics,* May 1992, pp. 37–38.

46. "Mad Money," *American Demographics,* July 1993, pp. 26–32.

47. "Like Old Times," *Wall Street Journal,* 14 February 1994, pp. A1, A4.

48. "The Global Patent Race Picks Up Speed," *Business Week,* 9 August 1993, pp. 57–58.

49. "Closing the Innovation Gap," *Fortune,* 2 December 1991, pp. 56–62.

50. "Report on R&D Spending Hints at Loss of U.S. Competitive Strength," *Marketing News,* 22 June 1992, pp. 1, 8.

51. "Could America Afford the Transistor Today?" *Business Week,* 7 March 1994, pp. 80–84.

52. "Report on R&D Spending," pp. 1, 8.

53. "Could America Afford," pp. 80–84.

54. "Firefight over the Weapons Labs," *Business Week,* 7 June 1993, pp. 104–106.

55. "Closing the Innovation Gap," p. 57.

56. "Report on R&D Spending," p. 8.

57. "Closing the Innovation Gap," p. 58; "On a Clear Day You Can See Progress," *Business Week,* 29 June 1992, pp. 104–105.

58. "Closing the Innovation Gap," p. 58.

59. Daniel Burrus, "A Glimpse of the Future," *Managing Your Career,* Spring 1991, pp. 6, 10. Reprinted by permission of the *Wall Street Journal,* © 1991 Dow Jones & Company, Inc. All Rights Reserved Worldwide.

60. Fay Rice, "The New Rules of Superlative Service," *Fortune,* Autumn/Winter 1993, pp. 50–53.

61. Brent Bowers, "How a Device to Aid in Breast Self-Exams Is Kept off the Market," *Wall Street Journal,* 12 April 1994, pp. A1, A11. Reprinted by permission of the *Wall Street Journal,* © 1994 Dow Jones & Company, Inc. All Rights Reserved Worldwide.

62. "Cereal Giants Battle over Market Share," *Wall Street Journal,* 16 December 1991, p. B1.

63. "Sindy vs. Barbie in Court: Are They Twins?" *WE/MBI,* 13–26 July 1992, p. 1.

## Chapter 3

1. Bob Ortega, "Penney Pushes Abroad in Unusually Big Way as It Pursues Growth," *Wall Street Journal,* 1 February 1994, pp. A1, A8.

2. Michael Czinkota and Ilkka Ron Kainen, "Global Marketing 2000: A Marketing Survival Guide," *Marketing Management,* Winter 1992, pp. 37–43.

3. William J. Holstein, "The Stateless Corporation," *Business Week,* 14 May 1990, pp. 98–105. Reprinted by permission of the *Wall Street Journal,* © 1994 Dow Jones & Company, Inc. All Rights Reserved Worldwide.
4. Bruce Hager, "Can Colgate Import Its Success from Overseas?" *Business Week,* 7 May 1990, pp. 114–116.
5. "International Experience Will Be Essential for Business Leaders of Tomorrow: Commentary by Lester Pullen," *Marketing News,* 10 December 1988, p. 14; see also Christopher Bartlett, "What Is a Global Manager?" *Harvard Business Review,* September-October 1992, pp. 124–132.
6. Edmund Faltermayer, "Is 'Made in the U.S.A.' Fading Away?" *Fortune,* 24 September 1990, pp. 62–73.
7. "Competitiveness: How U.S. Companies Stack Up Now," *Fortune,* 18 April 1994, pp. 52–64.
8. Paul Krugman, "Competitiveness: Does It Matter," *Fortune,* 7 March 1994, pp. 109–116.
9. U.S. Central Intelligence Agency, *The World Fact Book* (Washington, DC: Government Printing Office, 1993), p. 334; U.S. Department of Commerce, Bureau of the Census, *Statistical Abstract of the United States* (Washington, DC: Government Printing Office, 1993), p. 722.
10. U.S. Central Intelligence Agency, p. 334; U.S. Department of Commerce, p. 722.
11. Jeremy Main, "Manufacturing the Right Way," *Fortune,* 21 May 1990, p. 54–64.
12. Edward O. Wells, "Being There," *Inc.,* September 1990, pp. 143–145.
13. Krugman, p. 110.
14. "Competitiveness," p. 54.
15. "Competitiveness," p. 64.
16. Neil Jacoby, "The Multinational Corporation," *Center Magazine,* May 1970, p. 37.
17. Robert Reich, "Who Is Them?" *Harvard Business Review,* March-April 1991, pp. 77–89.
18. "The Stateless Corporation," *Business Week,* 14 May 1990, pp. 98–105.
19. Cyndee Miller, "Levi to Sever Link with China; Critics Contend It's Just a PR Move," *Marketing News,* 7 June 1993, p. 10. Reprinted with permission of American Marketing Association.
20. Theodore Levitt, "The Globalization of Markets," *Harvard Business Review,* May-June 1983, pp. 92–102.
21. Saeed Samiee and Kendall Roth, "The Influence of Global Marketing Standardization on Performance," *Journal of Marketing,* April 1992, pp. 1–17; see also James Willis, Coskun Samli, and Laurence Jacobs, "Developing Global Products and Marketing Strategies: A Construct and a Research Agenda," *Journal of the Academy of Marketing Science,* Winter 1991, pp. 1–10.
22. Adam Snyder, "Global Marketing: We Are the World," *Superbrands 1990: A Special Supplement to Adweek,* August 1990, pp. 59–68.
23. M. Katherine Glover, "Do's and Taboos: Cultural Aspects of International Business," *Business America,* 13 August 1990, pp. 2–6.
24. "How Motorola Took Asia by the Tail," *Business Week,* 11 November 1991, p. 68.
25. "Trainers Help Expatriate Employees Build Bridges to Different Cultures," *Wall Street Journal,* 14 June 1993, pp. B1, B6.
26. "In the New Vietnam, Baby Boomers Strive for Fun and Money," *Wall Street Journal,* 7 January 1994, pp. A1, A5.
27. "Is Democracy Bad for Growth?" *Business Week,* 7 June 1993, pp. 84–85.
28. "China: The Emerging Economic Powerhouse of the 21st Century," *Business Week,* 17 May 1993), pp. 54–68.
29. "China," pp. 54–68.
30. John Keller, "Little Beijing Firm Aims to Be China's Dun & Bradstreet," *Wall Street Journal,* 6 April 1994, pp. B1, B6. Reprinted by permission of the *Wall Street Journal,* © 1994 Dow Jones & Company, Inc. All Rights Reserved Worldwide.
31. Igor Reichlin, "Crash Course in Capitalism for Ivan the Globetrotter," *Business Week,* 28 May 1990, pp. 42–44.
32. Vladimir Kvint, "Don't Give Up on Russia," *Harvard Business Review,* March-April 1994, pp. 4–12.
33. Kvint, pp. 4–12.
34. Kenneth Sheets, "Fields of Russian Dreams," *U.S. News & World Report,* 4 June 1990, p. 59.
35. Linda Robinson, "Daring to Be Different," *U.S. News & World Report,* 7 May 1990, pp. 38–43; see also "The Big Move to Free Markets in Latin America," *Business Week,* 15 June 1992, pp. 50–55.
36. Thomas Kamm, "Brazil Swiftly Becomes Major Auto Producer As Trade Policy Shifts," *Wall Street Journal,* 18 April 1994, pp. A1, A4.
37. "Why Detroit Doesn't Need the Protection It Wants," *Business Week,* 8 February 1993, p. 32.
38. "109 Countries Sign Ambitious Trade Pact," *Dallas Morning News,* 16 April 1994, pp. 1A, 11A.
39. "GATT's Payoff," *Fortune,* 7 February 1994, p. 28.
40. Bob Davis and Laurence Ingrassia, "Trade Pact Is Set by 117 Nations, Slashing Tariffs, Subsidies Globally," *Wall Street Journal,* 16 December 1993, pp. A3, A13; Bob Davis, "Unexpected Obstacles Are Threatening to Delay or Derail Congressional Approval of GATT Pact," *Wall Street Journal,* 8 April 1994, p. A14; Louis Richman, "What's Next after GATT's Victory?" *Fortune,* 10 January 1994), pp. 66–69.

41. Marie Anchordoguy, "A Brief History of Japan's Keiretsu," *Harvard Business Review,* July-August 1990, pp. 58–59.
42. Robert Cutts, "Capitalism in Japan: Cartels and Keiretsu," *Harvard Business Review,* July-August 1992, pp. 48–50.
43. "U.S. Sees Progress in Talks with Japan, but Seeks More Action on Trade Gap," *Wall Street Journal,* 31 July 1992, p. B2.
44. "Border Crossings," *Business Week,* 22 November 1993, pp. 40–42.
45. "How NAFTA Will Help America," *Fortune,* 19 April 1993, pp. 95–102.
46. "How NAFTA Will Help," pp. 95–102.
47. "How NAFTA Will Help," pp. 95–102.
48. "How NAFTA Will Help," pp. 95–102.
49. "How NAFTA Will Help," pp. 95–102.
50. "Road to Unification," *Sky,* June 1993, pp. 32–41.
51. Tony Horwitz, "Europe's Borders Fade, and People and Goods Can Move More Freely," *Wall Street Journal,* 18 May 1993, pp. A1, A10. Reprinted by permission of the *Wall Street Journal,* © 1993 Dow Jones & Company, Inc. All Rights Reserved Worldwide.
52. Rahul Jacob, "The Big Rise," *Fortune,* 30 May 1994, pp. 74–90.
53. Jacob, pp. 74–90.
54. "Greasing the Skids for Exports," *Business Week,* 31 January 1994, pp. 66–68.
55. S. Tamer Cavusgil and Shaoming Zou, "Marketing Strategy–Performance Relationship: An Investigation of the Empirical Link in Export Market Ventures," *Journal of Marketing,* January 1994, pp. 1–21.
56. "Shaping Up by Shipping Out," *Business Week,* 19 April 1993, p. 121.
57. "Making Global Alliances Work," *Fortune,* 17 December 1990, pp. 121–123.
58. "How Toshiba Makes Alliances Work," *Fortune,* 4 October 1993, pp. 116–120.
59. Joel Bleeke and David Ernst, "The Way to Win in Cross-Border Alliances," *Harvard Business Review,* November-December 1991, p. 130.
60. "FedEx: Europe Nearly Killed the Messenger," *Business Week,* 25 May 1992, p. 124.
61. "The New U.S. Push into Europe," *Fortune,* 10 January 1994, pp. 73–74.
62. David Szymanski, Sundar Bharadwaj, and P. Rajan Varadarajan, "Standardization versus Adaptation of International Marketing Strategy: An Empirical Investigation," *Journal of Marketing,* October 1993, pp. 1–17.
63. "Don't Leave Home without It, Wherever You Live," *Business Week,* 21 February 1994, p. 21.
64. "Global Ad Campaigns, after Many Missteps, Finally Pay Dividends," *Wall Street Journal,* 27 August 1992, pp. A1, A8.
65. "Machine Dreams," *Brandweek,* 26 April 1993, pp. 17–24.
66. "Pushing U.S. Style, Nike and Reebok Sell Sneakers to Europe," *Wall Street Journal,* 22 July 1993, pp. A1, A8.
67. "Ewing Shoots to Shoe Planet," *Brandweek,* 7 March 1994, p. 10.
68. "Hmm. Could Use a Little More Snake," *Business Week,* 15 March 1993, p. 53.
69. "The Rumble Heard round the World: Harleys," *Business Week,* 24 May 1993), pp. 58–59.
70. "When Slogans Go Wrong," *American Demographics,* February 1992, p. 14.
71. "Greeks Protest Coke's Use of Parthenon," *Dallas Morning News,* 17 August 1992, p. 4D.
72. "Pizza in Japan Is Adapted to Local Tastes," *Wall Street Journal,* 4 June 1993, p. B1.
73. "Now a Glamorous Barbie Heads to Japan," *Wall Street Journal,* 5 June 1991, pp. B1, B8.
74. Cyndee Miller, "U.S. Firms Lag in Meeting Global Quality Standards," *Marketing News,* 15 February 1993, pp. 1, 6, reprinted with permission of American Marketing Association; Ronald Henkoff, "The Hot New Seal of Quality," *Fortune,* 28 June 1993, pp. 116–120.
75. "Steel Rulings Dump on America," *Wall Street Journal,* 23 June 1993, p. A14.
76. "Why Countertrade Is Hot," *Fortune,* 29 June 1992, p. 25; Nathaniel Gilbert, "The Case for Countertrade," *Across the Board,* May 1992, pp. 43–45.
77. "Revolution in Japanese Retailing," *Fortune,* 7 February 1994, pp. 143–146.

## Chapter 4

1. Kathleen Deveny, "Cereal Firms Make a Pitch to Snackers," *Wall Street Journal,* 1 July 1993, pp. B1, B11. Reprinted by permission of the *Wall Street Journal,* © 1993 Dow Jones & Company, Inc. All Rights Reserved Worldwide.
2. Sally D. Goll, "From Soap to Luxury Cars, Consumer Tastes Develop," *Wall Street Journal,* 18 October 1993, p. A10.
3. Narasimhan Srinivasan and Brian T. Ratchford, "An Empirical Test of a Model of External Search for Automobiles," *Journal of Consumer Research,* September 1991, pp. 223–242.
4. John R. Hauser and Birger Wernerfelt, "An Empirical Test of a Model of Consideration Sets," *Journal of Consumer Research,* March 1990, pp. 393–408.

5. This section is based on Srinivasan and Ratchford, pp. 223–242; Peter D. Bennett and Gilbert Harrell, "The Role of Confidence in Understanding and Predicting Buyers' Attitudes and Purchase Intentions," *Journal of Consumer Research,* September 1975, pp. 110–117; Richard D. Johnson and Irwin Levin, "More Than Meets the Eye: The Effect of Missing Information on Purchase Evaluations," *Journal of Consumer Research,* September 1985, pp. 169–177.

6. Joel Huber and Noreen M. Klein, "Adapting Cutoffs to the Choice Environment: The Effects of Attribute Correlation and Reliability," *Journal of Consumer Research,* December 1991, pp. 346–357.

7. Yigang Pan and Donald R. Lehmann, "The Influence of New Brand Entry on Subjective Brand Judgments," *Journal of Consumer Research,* June 1993, pp 76–86.

8. Itamar Simonson, "The Influence of Anticipating Regret and Responsibility on Purchase Decisions," *Journal of Consumer Research,* June 1992, pp. 105–118.

9. Don Umphrey, "Consumer Costs: A Determinant of Upgrading or Downgrading of Cable Service," *Journalism Quarterly,* Winter 1991, pp. 698–708.

10. Wayne D. Hoyer and Steven P. Brown, "Effects of Brand Awareness on Choice for a Common, Repeat-Purchase Product," *Journal of Consumer Research,* September 1990, pp. 141–149.

11. Gail Tom, "Cueing the Consumer: The Role of Salient Cues in Consumer Perception," *Journal of Consumer Marketing,* Spring 1987, pp. 23–27.

12. Craig A. Kelley, William C. Gaidis, and Peter H. Reingen, "The Use of Vivid Stimuli to Enhance Comprehension of the Content of Product Warning Messages," *Journal of Consumer Affairs,* Winter 1989, pp. 243–266.

13. Richard Gibson, "Anheuser-Busch Makes Price Moves in Bid to Boost Sales of Flagship Brand," *Wall Street Journal,* 28 February 1994, p. A7A.

14. William Boulding and Amna Kirmani, "A Consumer-Side Experimental Examination of Signaling Theory: Do Consumers Perceive Warranties as Signs of Quality?" *Journal of Consumer Research,* June 1993, pp. 111–123.

15. Teresa M. Pavia and Janeen Arnold Costa, "The Winning Number: Consumer Perceptions of Alpha-Numeric Brand Names," *Journal of Marketing,* July 1993, pp. 85–98.

16. Diane Crispell and Kathleen Brandenburg, "What's in a Brand?" *American Demographics,* May 1993, pp. 26–32.

17. Ruth Hamel, "States of Mind," *American Demographics,* April 1992, pp. 40–43.

18. Kathleen Deveny, "What's in a Name? A Lot If It's 'Texas,'" *Wall Street Journal,* 24 November 1993, pp. T1, T4.

19. Elizabeth J. Wilson, "Using the Dollarmetric Scale to Establish the Just Meaningful Difference in Price," in *1987 AMA Educators' Proceedings,* ed. Susan Douglas et al. (Chicago: American Marketing Association, 1987), p. 107.

20. Sunil Gupta and Lee G. Cooper, "The Discounting of Discounts and Promotion Thresholds," *Journal of Consumer Research,* December 1992, pp. 401–411.

21. Dana Milbank, "Made in America Becomes a Boast in Europe," *Wall Street Journal,* 19 January 1994, p. B1.

22. Kevin Goldman, "Volvo Features Accident Survivors in Ads," *Wall Street Journal,* 8 October 1993, p. B3.

23. Kathleen Deveny, "Marketers Exploit People's Fears of Everything," *Wall Street Journal,* 15 November 1993, pp. B1, B3.

24. David A. Aaker and Kevin Lane Keller, "Consumer Evaluations of Brand Extensions," *Journal of Marketing,* January 1990, pp. 27–41.

25. Ellen R. Foxman, Darrel D. Muehling, and Phil W. Berger, "An Investigation of Factors Contributing to Consumer Brand Confusion," *Journal of Consumer Affairs,* Summer 1990, pp. 170–189; Damon Darlin, "Where Trademarks Are Up for Grabs," *Wall Street Journal,* 5 December 1989, pp. B1, B5.

26. Carrie Dolan, "Levi Tries to Round Up Counterfeiters," *Wall Street Journal,* 19 February 1992, pp. B1, B6.

27. Yumiko Ono, "Land of Rising Fun: With Careful Planning, Japan Sets Out to Be 'Life Style Superpower,'" *Wall Street Journal,* 2 October 1992, pp. A1, A11.

28. Susan Mitchell, "How to Talk to Young Adults," *American Demographics,* April 1993, pp. 50–54; "In the Wake of the Baby Boom," *Sales & Marketing Management,* May 1993, p. 48.

29. Steven Lipin, Brian Coleman, and Jeremy Mark, "Pick a Card: Visa, American Express, and MasterCard Vie in Overseas Strategies," *Wall Street Journal,* 15 February 1994, pp. A1, A5.

30. Kevin Goldman, "BMW Banks on Affordability and Safety," *Wall Street Journal,* 17 January 1994, p. B3; Kevin Goldman, "BMW Shifts Gears in New Ads by Mullen," *Wall Street Journal,* 21 May 1993, p. B10.

31. Kathleen Deveny, "Putting It Mildly, More Consumers Prefer Only Products That Are 'Pure, Natural,'" *Wall Street Journal,* 11 May 11 1993, pp. B1, B8.

32. William Echikson, "Inventing Eurocleaning," *Fortune,* Autumn/Winter 1993, pp. 30–31.

33. Yumiko Ono, "Broadening War against Smoking Proves a Blessing to Gum Makers," *Wall Street Journal,* 29 March 1994, p. B9.

34. Kevin Goldman, "Volvo Seeks to Soft-Pedal Safety Image," *Wall Street Journal,* 16 March 1993, p. B6.

35. Gabriella Stern, "Heinz Aims to Export Taste for Ketchup," *Wall Street Journal,* 20 November 1992, p. B1.

36. Beth A. Walker and Jerry C. Olsen, "Means–End Chains: Connecting Products with Self," *Journal of Business Research,* March 1991, pp. 111–118.

37. John W. Schouten, "Selves in Transition: Symbolic Consumption in Personal Rites of Passage and Identity Reconstruction," *Journal of Consumer Research,* March 1991, pp. 412–425.

38. Yumiko Ono, "Home Hair-Color Sales Get Boost as Baby Boomers Battle Aging," *Wall Street Journal,* 3 February 1994, p. B6; Suein L. Hwang, "To Brush Away Middle-Age Malaise, Male Baby Boomers Color Graying Hair," *Wall Street Journal,* 2 March 1993, pp. B1, B10.

39. Marc B. Rubner, "The Hearts of New-Car Buyers," *American Demographics,* August 1991, pp. 14–15.

40. Grant McCracken, "Who Is the Celebrity Endorser? Cultural Foundations of the Endorsement Process," *Journal of Consumer Research,* December 1989, pp. 310–321.

41. Mary Walker, Lynn Langmeyer, and Daniel Langmeyer, "Celebrity Endorsers: Do You Get What You Pay For?" *Journal of Consumer Marketing,* Spring 1992, pp. 69–76.

42. Kevin Goldman, "Candice Bergen Leads the List of Top Celebrity Endorsers," *Wall Street Journal,* 17 September 1993, pp. B1, B6.

43. Marilyn Lavin, "Husband-Dominant, Wife-Dominant, Joint: A Shopping Typology for Baby Boom Couples?" *Journal of Consumer Marketing,* 10, no. 3 (1993), pp. 33–42.

44. Michael B. Menasco and David J. Curry, "Utility and Choice: An Empirical Study of Wife/Husband Decision Making," *Journal of Consumer Research,* June 1989, pp. 87–97.

45. Robert Boutilier, "Pulling the Family's Strings," *American Demographics,* August 1993, pp. 44–48.

46. Ellen R. Foxman, Patyria S. Tansuhaj, and Karin M. Ekstrom, "Family Members' Perception of Adolescents' Influence in Family Decision Making," *Journal of Consumer Research,* March 1989, pp. 482–491.

47. James U. McNeal and Chyon-Hwa Yeh, "Born to Shop," *American Demographics,* June 1993, pp. 34–39.

48. James U. McNeal, "The Littlest Consumers," *American Demographics,* February 1992, pp. 48–53; "The Littlest Advisors," *American Demographics,* April 1990, pp. 14–15.

49. "The Future of Households," *American Demographics,* December 1993, pp. 27–40; Margaret Ambry, "Receipts from a Marriage," *American Demographics,* February 1993, pp. 30–37; see also Robin A. Douthitt and Joanne M. Fedyk, "Family Composition, Parental Time, and Market Goods: Life-Cycle Trade-Offs," *Journal of Consumer Affairs,* Summer 1990, pp. 110–133; Robin A. Douthitt and Joanne M. Fedyk, "The Influence of Children on Family Life Cycle Spending Behavior: Theory and Applications," *Journal of Consumer Affairs,* Winter 1988, pp. 220–248.

50. Kenneth Labich, "Class in America," *Fortune,* 7 February 1994, pp. 114–126.

51. David W. Helin, "When Slogans Go Wrong," *American Demographics,* February 1992, p. 14.

52. Yumiko Ono, "Pizza in Japan Is Adapted to Local Tastes," *Wall Street Journal,* 4 June 1993, p. B1.

## Chapter 5

1. David Stipp, "GM and Utility Mount Charge on Electric Autos," *Wall Street Journal,* 19 May 1993, p. B1. Reprinted by permission of the *Wall Street Journal,* © 1993 Dow Jones & Company, Inc. All Rights Reserved Worldwide.

2. Michael D. Hutt and Thomas W. Speh, *Business Marketing,* 4th ed. (Fort Worth, TX: Dryden Press, 1992), p. 3.

3. U.S. Department of Commerce, Bureau of the Census, *Statistical Abstract of the United States* (Washington, DC: Government Printing Office, 1990), pp. 771, 772, 780.

4. *Selling to Government Markets: Local, State, and Federal* (Cleveland, OH: Government Product News, 1991), p. 1.

5. Larry C. Giunipers, William Crittenden, and Vicky Crittenden, "Industrial Marketing in Non-Profit Organizations," *Industrial Marketing Management,* 19 (1990), p. 279.

6. "Johnson & Johnson, Voluntary Hospitals Reach Supplies Agreement," *Wall Street Journal,* 10 November 1992, p. B5.

7. Robert W. Haas, *Business Marketing Management* (Boston: PWS-Kent, 1992), p. 16.

8. Robert W. Haas, p. 16.

9. Tom Stundza, "Metal Cans Lusting for Market Share," *Purchasing,* 22 February 1990, pp. 61–64.

10. Jim Mele, "Leasing: Preparing for the 1990s," *Business Week,* 19 March 1990, pp. 23–32.

11. Frank G. Bingham, Jr., and Barney T. Raffield III, *Business Marketing Management* (Cincinnati, OH: South-Western, 1995), p. 12.

12. Bridget O'Brian, "Airlines' Ailments Give Most of Their Suppliers Big Headaches as Well," *Wall Street Journal,* 31 December 1991, p. A1.

13. "Pushing Drugs to Doctors," *Consumer Reports,* February 1992, pp. 89–94. Copyright 1992 by Consumers Union of U.S., Inc., Yonkers, NY 10703–1057.

14. Bradley Johnson, "The Preferred Chip," *Advertising Age,* 7 October 1991, p. 22.

15. Allyson L. Stewart, "The Challenges of Business-to-Business Marketing in Europe," *Marketing News,* 6 December 1993, p. 11.
16. Philip Kotler, *Marketing Management,* 8th ed. (Englewood Cliffs, NJ: Prentice-Hall, 1994), p. 210.
17. George Anders, "Managed Health Care Jeopardizes Outlook for Drug Detailers," *Wall Street Journal,* 9 October 1993, p. A1.
18. Earl Naumann, *Creating Customer Value* (Cincinnati, OH: Thomson Executive Press, 1994), pp. 62–66.
19. Robert W. Haas, pp. 196–197.
20. Steven Volder Haas, "Contract Bold Step for EDS," *Fort Worth (Texas) Star-Telegram,* 18 December 1991, p. 1.
21. Tom Hayes, "Using Customer Satisfaction Research to Get Closer to the Customers," *Marketing News,* 4 January 1993, p. 22.
22. James Brien Quinn, Thomas L. Doorley, and Penny C. Paquette, "Beyond Products: Services-Based Strategy," *Harvard Business Review,* March-April 1990, pp. 58–60, 64–67.
23. Kevin T. Higgins, "Business Marketers Make Customer Service Job for All," *Marketing News,* 30 January 1989, pp. 1–2.
24. Bingham and Raffield, pp. 47–48.
25. "Ford, Citibank Launch Card," *Marketing News,* 15 March 1993, p. 1; Terry Lefton, "Ford Forays into Citi Card Charge," *Brandweek,* 15 February 1993, p. 2.
26. Bingham and Raffield, p. 48.
27. Hutt and Speh, p. 265.
28. James B. Treece, Karen Lowry Miller, and Richard A. Melcher, "The Partners," *Business Week,* 10 February 1992, pp. 103–104.
29. Stipp, p. B12.
30. Stipp, p. B12.


## Chapter 6


1. Laura Bird, "Limited Inc. Structures a 'Casual' Plan for Expansion," *Wall Street Journal,* 26 September 1994, p. B4.
2. "Coke Targets Young Men with OK Soda," *Marketing News,* 23 May 1994, p. 8.
3. *Wall Street Journal,* 2 August 1990, p. A1.
4. Gregory A. Patterson, "Waterbed Makers Target Younger, Groovier Snoozers," *Wall Street Journal,* 28 April 1994, pp. B1, B14.
5. Dwight J. Shelton, "Regional Marketing Works and Is Here to Stay," *Marketing News,* 6 November 1987, pp. 1, 25.
6. Cara Appelbaum, "Forget about Global, Coke's Gone Texas," *Adweek's Marketing Week,* 9 March 1991, p. 10; Kathy Thacker, "Coke Woos Texas with Major Push," *Adweek's Marketing Week,* 15 April 1991, pp. 1, 4.
7. Excerpted from Allyson L. Stewart, "Rules of the Toy Game Different for Europe's Kids," *Marketing News,* 25 October 1993, p. 9, by permission of the American Marketing Association.
8. Yumiko Ono, "Food Firms Concoct Dino Nuggets, Gaudy Yogurt to Attract Kids," *Wall Street Journal,* 12 April 1994, pp. B1, B7; "Those Little Kids Have Big Pockets," *Wall Street Journal,* 26 August 1992, p. B1; Laura Zinn et al., "Teens: Here Comes the Biggest Wave Yet," *Business Week,* 11 April 1994, pp. 76–86.
9. Scott Donaton, "The Media Wakes Up to Generation X," *Advertising Age,* 1 February 1993, pp. 16–17; Cyndee Miller, "Xers Know They're a Target Market, and They Hate It," *Marketing News,* 6 December 1993, p. 2.
10. "How Spending Changes during Middle Age," *Wall Street Journal,* 14 January 1992, p. B1.
11. "New Ford Mustang Designed to Attract More Female Buyers," *Marketing News,* 3 January 1994, p. 27; Fara Warner, "New Cadillac Reconnaissance: Women and African Americans," *Brandweek,* 28 February 1994, pp. 1, 6; Fara Warner, "Midas Increases Bid to Attract Women," *Brandweek,* 14 March 1994, p. 5; Pam Weisz, "There's a Whole New Target Market Out There: It's Men," *Brandweek,* 21 February 1994, p. 21; Adrienne Ward Fawcett, "Ads Awaken to Fathers' New Role in Family Life," *Advertising Age,* 10 January 1994, pp. 5–8.
12. Cyndee Miller, "Give Them a Cheeseburger," *Marketing News,* 6 June 1994, pp. 1, 6.
13. Fara Warner, "I'd Gladly Pay You $5,000 Now for a Cask of Single Malt, Much Later," *Brandweek,* 7 March 1994, p. 24; Fara Warner, "Trading In, Trading Up, Buyers Drive Status Cars," *Brandweek,* 7 March 1994, p. 25.
14. Kevin Helliker, "U.S. Discount Retailers Are Targeting Europe and Its Fat Margins," *Wall Street Journal,* 20 September 1993, pp. A1, A4.
15. Betsy Spethmann, "Pipeline to Youth: Coke Surf Deal Set," *Brandweek,* 1 November 1993, p. 8.
16. Christian DelValle and Jon Berry, "They Know Where You Live—and How You Buy," *Business Week,* 7 February 1994, p. 89.
17. *VALS 2: Your Marketing Edge for the 1990s* (Menlo Park, CA: SRI International).
18. Martha Farnsworth Riche, "Psychographics for the 1990s," *American Demographics,* July 1989, p. 30.
19. Kate Fitzgerald, "Happy Birthday (Name Here)," *Advertising Age,* 21 February 1994, p. 17.
20. " x $ = ?" *Brandweek,* 31 January 1994, pp. 18–24.
21. Thomas Exter, "Boozing Boomers," *American Demographics,* December 1991, p. 6.
22. Fara Warner, "Subaru Pitches 600,000 of Its Rivals' Customers," *Brandweek,* 1 March 1993, p. 4.

23. "Hot Spots," *Business Week,* 19 October 1992, pp. 80–88.
24. "IBM Realizes Marketing," *Marketing News,* 6 June 1994, p. 1.
25. "American Express Pulls Trigger with New Ads," *Marketing News,* 4 March 1991, p. 4.
26. Much of the material in this section is based on Michael D. Hutt and Thomas W. Speh, *Business Marketing Management,* 4th ed. (Hinsdale, IL: Dryden Press, 1992), pp. 170–180.
27. John H. Taylor, "Niche Player," *Forbes,* 1 April 1991, p. 70.
28. Tim Triplett, "Game Stores Find a Niche among the Competitive," *Marketing News,* 23 May 1994, p. 14.
29. "New Hershey Bar," *Wall Street Journal,* 27 February 1990, p. B1; "Mr. Maybelline Gives Cover Girl the Edge," *Adweek's Marketing Week,* 22 October 1990, pp. 6–8; James S. Hirsch, "Vacationing Families Head Downtown to Welcoming Arms of Business Hotels," *Wall Street Journal,* 13 June 1994, p. B1; Bradley Johnson, "Carnival Cruise Line Beckons Hispanics," *Advertising Age,* 25 January 1993, p. 46.
30. David L. Rados, *Marketing for Nonprofit Organizations* (Boston: Auburn House, 1981), p. 93.
31. Richard Brunelli, "Data Prompts Coors to Cap Dry Beer Plans for Now," *Adweek,* 14 May 1990, p. 6.
32. Tim Triplett, "Consumers Show Little Taste for Clear Beverages," *Marketing News,* 23 May 1994, pp. 1, 11.
33. Al Ries and Jack Trout, *Positioning: The Battle for Your Mind* (New York: McGraw-Hill, 1981), pp. 66–67.
34. Tim Triplett, "Marketers Eager to Fill Demand for Gambling," *Marketing News,* 6 June 1994, pp. 1, 2.
35. Laura Bird, "Major Brands Look for the Kosher Label," *Adweek's Marketing Week,* 1 April 1991, pp. 18–19.
36. "Shirley Young: Pushing GM's Humble-Pie Strategy," *Business Week,* 11 June 1990, p. 52.
37. These examples were provided by David W. Cravens, Texas Christian University.
38. Gerry Khermonch, "Kirin Presses into Mainstream," *Brandweek,* 16 May 1994, p. 12.
39. Cyndee Miller, "Firm Toots Milk Product as Hip Alternative to Soda," *Marketing News,* 23 May 1994, p. 6.

## Chapter 7

1. Joseph Rydholm, "Here's Looking at You, Kid," *Quirk's Marketing Research Review,* March 1993, pp. 27–29.
2. "More Marketers Are Going On Line for Decision Support," *Marketing News,* 12 November 1990, p. 14; Terrence O'Brien, "Decision Support Systems," *Marketing Research,* December 1990, pp. 51–55; "Database Is Nerve Center of Integrated Marketing Plan," *Marketing News,* 3 February 1992, p. 5.
3. "Hand-Held Computers Help Field Staff Cut Paper Work and Harvest More Data," *Wall Street Journal,* 30 January 1990, p. B1; "How Software Is Making Food Sales a Piece of Cake," *Business Week,* 2 July 1990, pp. 54–56.
4. "KGF Taps Database to Target Consumers," *Advertising Age,* 8 October 1990, pp. 3, 88.
5. PRIZM brochure (Alexandria, VA: Claritas, Incorporated).
6. "They Know Where You Live—and How You Buy," *Business Week,* 7 February 1994, p. 89.
7. Peter Pae, "American Express Company Discloses It Gives Merchants Data on Cardholders' Habits," *Wall Street Journal,* 14 May 1992, p. A3.
8. "How to Find Online Information," *American Demographics,* September 1993, pp. 52–55.
9. Ed Campbell, "CD-ROMs Bring Census Data In-House," *Marketing News,* 6 January 1992, pp. 12, 16.
10. Tibbett Speer, "Nickelodeon Puts Kids Online," *American Demographics: 1994 Directory of Marketing Information Companies,* pp. 16–17.
11. "Questionnaire Design Affects Response Rate," *Marketing News,* 3 January 1994, p. 14.
12. Carl McDaniel and Roger Gates, *Contemporary Marketing Research,* 2nd ed. (Cincinnati, OH: South-Western, 1993), pp. 223–226.
13. Diane Pyle, "How to Interview Your Customers," *American Demographics,* December 1990, pp. 44–45.
14. "King Customer," *Business Week,* 12 March 1990, p. 90.
15. "Network to Broadcast Live Focus Groups," *Marketing News,* 3 September 1990, pp. 10, 47.
16. William Wilson and Xiaoyan Zhao, "Perestroika and Research: Ivan's Opinion Counts," *CASRO Journal 1992,* pp. 27–31.
17. "There's No Mystery in How to Retain Customers," *Marketing News,* 4 February 1991, p. 10.
18. Michael McCarthy, "James Bond Hits the Supermarket: Stores Snoop on Shoppers' Habits to Boost Sales," *Wall Street Journal,* 25 August 1993, pp. B1, B8.
19. McCarthy, pp. B1, B8.
20. "K Mart Testing Radar to Track Shopper Traffic," *Wall Street Journal,* 24 September 1991, pp. B1, B5.
21. "Do Not Adjust Your Set," *American Demographics,* March 1993, p. 6; "Nielsen Rival to Unveil New Peoplemeter," *Wall Street Journal,* 4 December 1992, p. B8.
22. "Gadgets That Track Viewers," *Adweek,* 22 April 1991, p. 10.
23. "New Nielsen CEO Takes Steps to Revitalize Company," *Marketing News,* 22 November 1993, p. 7.
24. "Amid Share Slump, Market Researcher Plays Patch Up," *Wall Street Journal,* 25 April 1994, p. B4.

25. "Nielsen in Turmoil," *Advertising Age,* 15 November 1993, pp. 1, 21, 24; "Rivals Duel Bitterly for Job of Supplying Market Information," *Wall Street Journal,* 15 November 1993, pp. A1, A9.
26. "Researchers Rev Up," *Advertising Age,* 13 January 1992, p. 34.
27. "Nielsen Weighs Assets," *Advertising Age,* 12 August 1991, p. 29.
28. "Information Resources Wires the Drugstores," *Adweek's Marketing Week,* 27 May 1991, p. 34.
29. Laurence Gold, "The Coming Age of Scanner Data," *Marketing Research,* Winter 1993, pp. 20–24.
30. Laurence Gold, "New Technology Contributions to New Product and Advertising Strategy Testing: The ERIM Testsight System," speech by vice president of marketing, A.C. Nielsen Company.

## Chapter 8

1. Krystal Miller, "Chevy's Latest Revival Effort Is Customer-Driven," *Wall Street Journal,* 9 November 1993, p. B1.
2. Kenneth Labich, "Is Herb Kelleher America's Best CEO?" *Fortune,* 2 May 1994, pp. 45–52.
3. "Value Pricing Is Hot as Shrewd Consumers Seek Low-Cost Quality," *Wall Street Journal,* 12 March 1991, pp. A1, A5; "Value Marketing: Quality, Service, Fair Pricing Are the Keys to Selling in the '90s," *Business Week,* 11 November 1991, pp. 132–140; "GM, Pitching Value, Scores Cavalier Upset," *Wall Street Journal,* 11 May 1993, pp. B1, B2.
4. David Greising, "Quality: How to Make It Pay," *Business Week,* 8 August 1994, pp. 54–59.
5. Much of the material in this chapter regarding the customer value triad is based on Earl Naumann, *Creating Customer Value* (Cincinnati, OH: Thomson Executive Press, 1995).
6. Allan J. Magrath, "Marching to a Different Drummer," *Marketing Executive Report* [American Marketing Association], August 1992, p. 15.
7. Otis Port and John Carey, "Questing for the Best," *Business Week,* 25 October 1991, p. 10.
8. Keith H. Hammonds and Gail DeGeorge, "Where Did They Go Wrong?" *Business Week,* 25 October 1991, p. 35.
9. Jonathan B. Levine, "It's an Old World in More Ways Than One," *Business Week,* 25 October 1991, p. 28.
10. Jeffrey A. Tannebaum, "Small Companies Are Finding It Pays to Think Global," *Wall Street Journal,* 19 November 1992, p. B2.
11. Robert Neff, "No. 1—And Trying Harder," *Business Week,* 25 October 1991, p. 23.
12. Port and Carey, p. 10.
13. Port and Carey, p. 14.
14. Port and Carey, p. 14.
15. Kevin Kelly, "Motorola Wants to Light Up Another Market," *Business Week,* 14 October 1991, p. 50.
16. Richard Colby, "Oldest Rule, Newest U.S. Trend: Customer Comes First," *Sunday Oregonian,* 22 March 1992, p. R1.
17. Arthur R. Tenner and Irving J. DeToro, *Total Quality Management* (Reading, MA: Addison-Wesley, 1992), p. 9.
18. Levine, p. 27.
19. George Anders, "More Managed Health-Care Systems Use Incentive Pay to Reward 'Best' Doctors," *Wall Street Journal,* 25 January 1993, p. B1.
20. Port and Carey, p. 16.
21. Thane Peterson et al., "Top Products for Less Than Top Dollar," *Business Week,* 25 October 1991, p. 68.
22. David Woodruff and Jonathan B. Levine, "Miles Traveled, More to Go," *Business Week,* 25 October 1991, p. 71.
23. Michael Barrier, "Small Firms Put Quality First," *Nation's Business,* May 1992, p. 30.
24. Barrier, p. 22.
25. Levine, p. 27.
26. David Woodruff et al., "A New Era for Auto Quality," *Business Week,* 22 October 1990, p. 87.
27. Mike Vasilakes, "Wilson Oxygen Teams Up with Employees and Suppliers to Improve Quality," *Welding Distributor,* March-April 1993, pp. 65–70.
28. Much of the material in this section is adapted from Elayne Cree, "Baldrige Award Proves That Customer Defines Quality," *Marketing News,* 6 January 1992, p. 30.
29. Naumann, pp. 5–7.
30. Valarie A. Zeithaml, A. Parasuraman, and Leonard L. Berry, *Delivering Quality Service* (New York: Free Press, 1990).
31. Larry Armstrong and William C. Symonds, "Beyond 'May I Help You?'" *Business Week,* 25 October 1991, pp. 100–103.
32. Dori Jones Yang, "Northern Hospitality," *Business Week,* 25 October 1991, p. 118.
33. "Quality Service Commitment," *Services Marketing Today* [American Marketing Association newsletter], January-February 1992, p. 3.
34. "Piety, Profits, and Productivity," *Fortune,* 29 June 1992, p. 84.
35. Naumann, pp. 81–84.
36. Much of the material in this section based on Zeithaml, Parasuraman, and Berry and on Naumann.
37. John E. Martin, "Unleashing the Power in Your People," *Arthur Andersen Retailing Issues Letter* [Texas A&M University, Center for Retailing Studies], September 1994, p. 1.
38. Much of the material in this section is based on Naumann, pp. 101–121.

39. Bill Saporito, "Behind the Tumult at P&G," *Fortune,* 7 March 1994, p. 75.

40. Brian S. Moskal, "Consumer Age Begets Value Pricing," *Industry Week,* 21 February 1994, p. 36.

41. Gail Gilbert, "Customer Satisfaction Measurement Is Core of Firm's Quality Improvement," *Marketing News,* 4 January 1993, p. 18.

42. Much of the material in this section is based on Naumann, pp. 137–161. See also Frederick Herzberg, *Work and the Nature of Man* (New York: World Publishing, 1966).

43. Greising, p. 56.


## Chapter 9


1. Adapted from Gerry Khermouch, "Kodak Breaks with Past for Value Film Line," *Brandweek,* 17 January 1994, pp. 1, 6.

2. Chris Roush, "At Times, They're Positively Glowing," *Business Week,* 12 July 1993, p. 141.

3. Mark Robichaux, "Tabasco Sauce Market Remains Hot after 125 Years," *Wall Street Journal,* 11 May 1990, p. B2.

4. Mark Robichaux, "Avis Hit by Almost Every Obstacle in Franchise Book," *Wall Street Journal,* 3 May 1990, p. B2.

5. Terry Lefton, "Still Battling the Ozone Stigma," *Adweek's Marketing Week,* 16 March 1992, pp. 18–19.

6. Matthew Grimm, "Kentucky Fried (Not) Chicken Set to Turn Rotisseries on Full Blast," *Brandweek,* 12 July 1993, pp. 1, 6.

7. Barbara Holsomback, "F-L Takes Risk in Repositioning of Fritos Brand," *Adweek,* 25 February 1991, pp. 1, 4.

8. Seema Nayyar, "Gillette's New Dry Look," *Brandweek,* 1 February 1993, p. 3.

9. Pam Weisz, "Procter to Scope Out More Profit in Baking Soda Mine," *Brandweek,* 7 February 1994, pp. 1, 6; Pam Weisz, "Smithkline Finally Pops Soda Aquafresh—'without Grit,'" *Brandweek,* 18 April 1994, p. 3.

10. Marcy Magiera, "Levi's Dockers Look for Younger, Upscale Men with Authentics," *Advertising Age,* 18 January 1993, p. 4.

11. Eben Shapiro, "Low-Alcohol, Brightly Labeled Cocktails Stir Fears They Will Tempt Teenagers," *Wall Street Journal,* 8 April 1993, pp. B1, B5. Reprinted by permission of the *Wall Street Journal,* © 1993 Dow Jones & Company, Inc. All Rights Reserved Worldwide.

12. Laura Zinn, "Does Pepsi Have Too Many Products?" *Business Week,* 14 February 1994, pp. 64–66.

13. Fara Warner, "RJR Opts for Select Makeover," *Brandweek,* 14 June 1993, pp. 1, 6.

14. Joanne Lipman, "Maxwell House, Folgers Clash over Coffee," *Wall Street Journal,* 20 February 1990, p. B6.

15. Carrie Goerne, "Coffee Consumption Down, but Sales of Exotic Blends Perk Up," *Marketing News,* 20 July 1992, pp. 1, 22.

16. Terry Lefton, "Black & Decker's 'Demos' Lines," *Brandweek,* 28 June 1993, p. 4.

17. Gerald Schoenfeld, "Treat Old Products Like New," *Marketing News,* 31 July 1990, p. 15.

18. Schoenfeld, p. 15.

19. "Measuring Quality Perceptions of America's Top Brands," *Brandweek,* 4 April 1994, pp. 24–26.

20. Mark Zandler, Zachary Schiller, and Lois Therrien, "What's in a Name? Less and Less," *Brandweek,* 8 July 1991, pp. 66–67.

21. Cited in Alexandra Ourusoff, "Who Said Brands Are Dead?" *Brandweek,* 9 August 1993, pp. 20–33.

22. Peter H. Farquhar et al., "Strategies for Leveraging Master Brands," *Marketing Research,* September 1992, pp. 32–43.

23. Ruhul Jacob, "Asia, Where the Big Brands Are Blooming," *Fortune,* 23 August 1993, p. 55.

24. Holly Heline, "Brand Loyalty Isn't Dead—but You're Not off the Hook," *Brandweek,* 7 June 1993, pp. 14–15.

25. Diane Crispell and Kathleen Brandenburg, "What's in a Brand?" *American Demographics,* May 1993, pp. 26–32.

26. "Copying the Copycats," *Economist,* 12 September 1992, p. 78.

27. Kathleen Deveny, "Private-Label Unit Sales Drop but Can Big Marketers Relax Yet?" *Wall Street Journal,* 10 February 1994, p. B5; Eleena De Lisser and Kevin Helliker, "Private Labels Reign in British Groceries," *Wall Street Journal,* 3 March 1994, pp. B1, B9; Julie Liesse, "Big Name Marketers Are Being Stalked by Strong, High-Quality Store Brands," *Advertising Age,* 12 April 1993, pp. 1, 4.

28. Teri Agins, "Big Stores Put Own Labels on Best Clothes," *Wall Street Journal,* 26 September 1994, p. B1.

29. "Retailers Hungry for Store Brands," *Advertising Age,* 11 January 1993, p. 20.

30. Kathleen Deveny, "Sales of Private-Label Goods Keep Rising," *Wall Street Journal,* 5 October 1993, p. B8.

31. "The Dial Corp.: The New Name behind Some of the Best Names You Know," *Wall Street Journal,* 6 May 1991, p. R1.

32. Nancy Arnott, "Inside Intel's Marketing Coup," *Sales & Marketing Management,* February 1994, pp. 78–81.

33. Karen Benezra, "Kellogg, ConAgra to Walk up Cereal Aisle," *Brandweek,* 14 March 1994, p. 8.

34. Betsy McKay, "Xerox Fights Trademark Battle," *Advertising Age,* 27 April 1992, p. 139.

35. Carrie Dolan, "Levi Tries to Round Up Counterfeiters," *Wall Street Journal,* 19 February 1992, pp. B1, B8; Damon Dorlin, "Coca-Cola's Sprite Enters South Korea; Local Sprint Follows," *Wall Street Journal,* 21 February 1992, p. B5.

36. Adapted from Marcus Brauchli, "Chinese Fragrantly Copy Trademarks of Foreigners," *Wall Street Journal,* 20 June 1994, pp. B1, B5. Reprinted by permission of the *Wall Street Journal,* © 1994 Dow Jones & Company, Inc. All Rights Reserved Worldwide.
37. David Kiley, "For Schick's Tracer, Packaging Is Pivotal," *Adweek's Marketing Week,* 15 October 1990, p. 12.
38. Karen Benezra, "Coke Always & Everywhere," *Brandweek,* 14 February 1994, p. 4; Betsy Spethmann, "Patented Packages Become Equity Guard," *Brandweek,* 9 August 1993, pp. 1, 6.
39. Judith Springer Riddle, "The Old Salt Is Out at Old Spice," *Brandweek,* 13 September 1993, p. 10.
40. Howard Schlossberg, "Effective Packaging 'Talks' to Consumers," *Marketing News,* 6 August 1990, p. 6.
41. Dan Koeppel, "Spreckels Bags the Sack," *Adweek's Marketing Week,* 22 October 1990, p. 10.
42. Judith J. Riddle, "J&J Ready to Flip Lid on Tylenol," *Brandweek,* 3 May 1993, p. 3.
43. Riddle, p. 3.
44. Joe Schwaetz, "Americans Annoyed by Wasteful Packaging," *American Demographics,* April 1992, p. 13; Scott Hume, "Green Labels Good, but Confusing," *Advertising Age,* 9 December 1991, p. 43.
45. "A Biodegradable Plastic Gains Notice," *Wall Street Journal,* 4 February 1993, p. A1; Robert McMath, "It's All in the Trigger," *Adweek's Marketing Week,* 6 January 1992, pp. 25–28; Robert McMath, "Green Packaging That Works," *Adweek's Marketing Week,* 2 December 1991, pp. 28–29.
46. Pam Weisz, "Price Tools for Pfixer-Uppers," *Brandweek,* 18 April 1994, p. 8.
47. Beverly Bundy, "What's in It for You?" *Fort Worth Star-Telegram,* 4 May 1994, p. D1.
48. Jacqueline Simmins, "Using Labeling Rules to Pitch a Product," *Wall Street Journal,* 25 March 1994, p. B1.
49. Hugh Filman, "A Brand New World: Packaged Goods Companies Go Global with Their Wares," *Marketing Executive Report,* June 1992, pp. 22–23.

## Chapter 10

1. Adapted from "Failure of Its Oven Lovin' Cookie Dough Shows Pillsbury Pitfalls of New Products," *Wall Street Journal,* 17 June 1993, pp. B1, B8.
2. *New Product Management in the 1980s* (New York: Booz, Allen and Hamilton, 1982), p. 8.
3. Elaine Underwood, "Blue Collar Couture," *Adweek's Marketing Week,* 5 August 1991, p. 12.
4. Judith Springer Riddle, "Ban Extends to Hypoallergenic Line," *Brandweek,* 2 August 1993, p. 9.
5. "Pumping No-Iron Slacks," *Business Week,* 7 February 1994, pp. 30–31; Dan Koeppel, "Kingsford Achieves the Impossible," *Adweek's Marketing Week,* 2 September 1991, p. 6.
6. Seema Nayya, "Gillette's New Dry Look," *Brandweek,* 1 February 1993, p. 3.
7. Fara Warner, "Kleenex Goes National with High-Tech Bathroom Roll," *Adweek's Marketing Week,* 25 November 1991, p. 7.
8. Brenton R. Schlender, "How Sony Keeps the Magic Going," *Fortune,* 24 February 1992, pp. 75–84; Valerie Reitman, "Rubbermaid Turns Up Plenty of Profit in the Mundane," *Wall Street Journal,* 27 March 1992, p. B3.
9. Elyse Janouye, "Johnson & Johnson Stays Fit by Shuffling Its Mix of Business," *Wall Street Journal,* 22 December 1992, p. A1, A4.
10. Adapted from Yumiko Ono, "Adding Vitamins, Snack Makers Call Products More Healthful," *Wall Street Journal,* 26 May 1994, pp. B1, B7. Reprinted by permission of the *Wall Street Journal,* © 1994 Dow Jones & Company, Inc. All Rights Reserved Worldwide.
11. Robin T. Peterson, "Speed Is Critical in New Product Introductions," *Marketing News,* 1 March 1993, p. 4.
12. John Bussey and Douglas R. Sease, "Manufacturers Strive to Slice Time Needed to Develop Products," *Wall Street Journal,* 23 February 1988, pp. 1, 13.
13. Joseph B. White, Gregory A. Patterson, and Paul Ingrassia, "American Auto Makers Need Major Overhaul to Match the Japanese," *Wall Street Journal,* 10 January 1992, pp. A1, A10.
14. Earl Nauman, *Creating Customer Value* (Cincinnati, OH: Thomson Executive Press, 1994), pp. 66–70.
15. *New Product Management,* p. 3.
16. *New Product Management,* pp. 10–11.
17. Naumann, pp. 58–62.
18. Brian Dumaine, "Payoff from the New Management," *Fortune,* 13 December 1993, pp. 103–110.
19. Zachary Schiller, "At Rubbermaid, Little Things Mean a Lot," *Business Week,* 11 November 1991, p. 126.
20. Adapted from Gabriella Stein, "Heinz Aims to Export Taste for Ketchup," *Wall Street Journal,* 20 November 1992, pp. B1, B9. Reprinted by permission of the *Wall Street Journal,* © 1992 Dow Jones & Company, Inc. All Rights Reserved Worldwide.
21. David W. Cravens, *Strategic Marketing,* 4th ed. (Homewood, IL: Richard D. Irwin, 1994), p. 370.
22. Gerry Khermouch, "Seagram's Quest Aims Clearly at Canadian," *Brandweek,* 8 February 1993, p. 2.
23. Christopher Power, "Will It Sell in Podunk? Hard to Say," *Business Week,* 10 August 1992, pp. 46–47.
24. Power, p. 46.
25. Power, p. 46.
26. John Bissell, "What's in a Brand Name? Nothing Inherent to Start," *Brandweek,* 7 February 1994, p. 16.
27. Lawrence Ingrassia, "A Recovering Gillette Hopes for Vindication in a High-Tech Razor," *Wall Street Journal,* 29 September 1990, pp. A1, A4.
28. Bissell, p. 16.

29. Michael R. Czinkota and Ilkka A. Ronkainen, *International Marketing,* 3rd ed. (Homewood, IL: Richard D. Irwin, 1993), pp. 301–307.

30. "Category Management: Marketing for the '90s," *Marketing News,* 14 September 1992, pp. 12–13.

31. Richard Gibson, "Pinning Down Costs of Product Introductions," *Wall Street Journal,* 26 November 1990, p. B1.


## Chapter 11


1. Ronald Henkoff, "Service Is Everybody's Business," *Fortune,* 27 June 1994, pp. 48–49. © 1994 Time, Inc. All rights reserved.
2. Henkoff, pp. 48–49.
3. Henkoff, pp. 48–49.
4. "The Manufacturing Myth," *Economist,* 19 March 1994.
5. Paul N. Bloom and Torger Reve, "Transmitting Signals to Consumers for Competitive Advantage," *Business Horizons,* July-August 1990, pp. 58–66.
6. "Health Card for All in Clinton Plan 3 Officials Say," *Fort Worth Star-Telegram,* 10 April 1993, p. 1.
7. "That's Entertainment," *Services Marketing Today* [Services Marketing Division newsletter, American Marketing Association], May-June 1994, p. 4.
8. "Saturn, Luxury Car Brands Score Big," *Fort Worth Star-Telegram,* 17 June 1994, p. B4; Stephanie Anderson Forest, "Radio Shack Goes Back to the Gizmos," *Business Week,* 28 February 1994, p. 102.
9. Much of the material in this section based on Christopher H. Lovelock, *Services Marketing* (Englewood Cliffs, NJ: Prentice-Hall, 1991), pp. 13, 18–19.
10. "Baby Pictures Just a Phone Call Today," *Services Marketing Today* [Services Marketing Division newsletter, American Marketing Association], March-April 1994, p. 4.
11. Elaine Underwood, "Disney Charts Course to Sail into Cruises," *Business Week,* 7 February 1994, pp. 1, 6.
12. Kathy Brown, "A Burger and a Campaign to Go," *Adweek,* 14 January 1991, p. 6.
13. Henkoff, pp. 52, 56.
14. "Profiting from the Nonprofits," *Business Week,* 26 March 1990, pp. 66–74.
15. Patricia Seelers, "Yes, Brands Can Still Work Magic," *Fortune,* 7 February 1994, pp. 133–134.
16. "Bar Restricts Lawyer Ads," *Marketing News,* 11 May 1993, p. 11.
17. Much of the material in this section based on Lovelock, pp. 238–240.
18. Leonard L. Berry and A. Parasuraman, *Marketing Services: Competing through Quality* (New York: Free Press, 1991), pp. 151, 152.
19. Leonard L. Berry, A. Parasuraman, and Valarie A. Zeithaml, "Improving Service Quality in America: Lessons Learned," *Academy of Management Executive,* 8, no. 2 (1994), pp. 32–52; Henkoff, p. 60; "Flexible Work Arrangements Continue to Find a Home at Companies," *Wall Street Journal,* 19 January 1993, p. A1.
20. Larry Armstrong and William C. Symonds, "Beyond 'May I Help You?'" *Business Week,* 25 October 1991, p. 102.
21. Much of the material in this section based on Berry and Parasuraman, pp. 132–150.
22. Joshua Levine, "Relationship Marketing," *Forbes,* 20 December 1993, pp. 232–234.
23. "Car Rental: Hertz—#1," *Services Marketing* [Services Marketing Division newsletter, American Marketing Association], July-August 1993, p. 4.
24. Charles Fleming and Jathon Sapsford, "Visa, American Express, and MasterCard Vie in Overseas Strategies," *Wall Street Journal,* 15 February 1994, pp. A1, A5.
25. "Profiting from the Nonprofits," p. 67.
26. William L. Bulkeley, "Nonprofits Dig into Databases for Big Donors," *Wall Street Journal,* 8 September 1992, p. B1. Reprinted by permission of the *Wall Street Journal,* © 1992 Dow Jones & Company, Inc. All Rights Reserved Worldwide.
27. Dori Jones Yang, "When City Hall Learns to Think Like a Business," *Business Week,* 25 October 1991, p. 136.
28. "Profiting from the Nonprofits," p. 69.
29. Christian Basi, "Delivering A-Peeling Promotion," *Fort Worth Star-Telegram,* 18 June 1994, pp. B1, B12.
30. J. M. Prottas, "The Cost of Free Services: Organizational Impediments to Access to Public Services," *Public Administration Review,* September-October 1981, p. 526.


## Chapter 12


1. Marj Charlier, "Existing Distributors Are Being Squeezed by Brewers, Retailers," *Wall Street Journal,* 22 November 1993, pp. A1, A6.
2. Russell W. McCalley, *Marketing Channel Development and Management* (Westport, CT: Quorum Books, 1992), p. 3.
3. Richard A. Melcher, "Cut Out the Middleman? Never," *Business Week,* 10 January 1994, p. 96.
4. For an excellent discussion of channel evolution and structure, see Arun Sharma and Luis V. Dominguez, "Channel Evolution: A Framework for Analysis," *Journal of the Academy of Marketing Science,* 20, no. 1 (1992), pp. 1–15.
5. Julie Candler, "How to Choose a Distributor," *Nation's Business,* August 1993, pp. 45–46.
6. Elaine Underwood, "Timex on Upscale Watch," *Brandweek,* 26 April 1993, p. 4.
7. Eleena De Lisser, "PepsiCo's Taco Bell Unit Maps Further Diversification," *Wall Street Journal,* 14 May 1993, p. B4; Richard Gibson, "What'll It Be, Pal? Fill It

with Regular or an Order of Fries?" *Wall Street Journal,* 24 November 1993, p. B7; Betsy Spethmann, "Kellogg, Big G Test Vending," *Brandweek,* 15 November 1993, p. 8.

8. Jon Berry, "Ocean Spray Joins the Pepsi Generation," *Adweek's Marketing Week,* 9 March 1992, pp. 18–21; Gabriella Stern, "Phar-Mor Forges Stronger Ties with Manufacturers," *Wall Street Journal,* 8 March 1993, p. B4.
9. Yumiko Ono, "'King of Beers' Wants to Rule More of Japan," *Wall Street Journal,* 28 October 1993, pp. B1, B8.
10. E. J. Muller, "The Quest for a Quality Environment," *Distribution,* January 1992, pp. 32–36.
11. Robert F. Lusch, Deborah Zizzo, and James M. Kenderdine, "Strategic Renewal in Distribution," *Marketing Management,* 2, no. 2 (1993), pp. 20–29.
12. James E. Ricks, "Benefits of Domestic Vertical and Horizontal Strategic Alliances," *Journal of Business & Industrial Marketing,* 8, no. 4 (1993), pp. 52–57.
13. Eleena De Lisser, "PepsiCo Plans to Form 'Superbottler' in Latin America to Bolster Sales There," *Wall Street Journal,* 12 September 1993, p. A6.
14. Laurie P. Cohen, "The Man with the Midas Touch Meets His Match in the Nation's Steakhouse," *Wall Street Journal,* 3 January 1994, pp. B9, B12.
15. Ricks, p. 53.
16. For an excellent summary article on channel power, see John F. Gaski, "The Theory of Power and Conflict in Channels of Distribution," *Journal of Marketing Research,* Summer 1984, pp. 9–29; see also Jehoshua Eliashberg, "Multiple Business Goals Set as Determinants of Marketing Channel Conflict: An Empirical Study," *Journal of Marketing Research,* February 1984, pp. 75–88; Jean Johnson, Harold Koenig, and James R. Brown, "The Bases of Marketing Channel Power: An Exploration and Confirmation of Their Underlying Dimensions," in *1985 AMA Educator's Proceedings,* ed Robert Lusch et al. (Chicago: American Marketing Association, 1985), pp. 160–165; Robert Lusch and Robert Ross, "The Nature of Power in a Marketing Channel," *Journal of the Academy of Marketing Science,* Summer 1985, pp. 39–56.
17. For an excellent discussion of how to measure power, see Gary L. Frazier, "On the Measurement of Interfirm Power in Channels of Distribution," *Journal of Marketing Research,* May 1983, pp. 158–166.
18. Arieh Goldman, "Evaluating the Performance of the Japanese Distribution System," *Journal of Retailing,* Spring 1992, pp. 11–39.
19. Eric Michael Kennedy, "The Japanese Distribution System," *Business America,* 17 May 1993, pp. 20–21.
20. Valerie Reitman, "Manufacturers Start to Spurn Big Discounters," *Wall Street Journal,* 30 November 1993, pp. B1, B2.
21. Robert F. Lusch and Patrick M. Dunne, *Retail Management* (Cincinnati, OH: South-Western, 1990), p. 94.
22. Christina Duff, "Nation's Retailers Ask Vendors to Help Share Expenses," *Wall Street Journal,* 4 August 1993, p. B4.
23. Jennifer Lawrence, "Wal-Mart Draws Fire," *Advertising Age,* 13 January 1992, pp. 3, 43.
24. Dana Milbank, "Independent Goodyear Dealers Rebel," *Wall Street Journal,* 8 July 1992, p. B2.
25. Valerie Reitman, "Retail Resistance: Eliminated Discounts on P&G Goods Annoy Many Who Sell Them," *Wall Street Journal,* 11 August 1992, pp. A1, A6.
26. Jeffrey A. Tannenbaum, "Mail Boxes Etc. Delivers Profits but Not to Everyone," *Wall Street Journal,* 13 October 1993, p. B2.
27. Brent Bowers and Jeffrey A. Tannenbaum, "Small Businesses Laud High Court Ruling on Kodak," *Wall Street Journal,* 10 June 1992, p. B2.
28. N. Craig Smith and John A. Quelch, *Ethics in Marketing* (Homewood, Illinois: Richard D. Irwin, Inc.: 1993):480.
29. Smith and Quelch, p. 481.
30. Smith and Quelch, p. 481.
31. Larry S. Lowe and Kevin F. McCrohan, "Minimize the Impact of the Gray Market," *Journal of Business Strategy,* November/December 1989, pp. 47–50.
32. Donald A. Davis, "Seemingly No Relief," *Drug & Cosmetic Industry,* November 1993, p. 22; "Parfums Givenchy, Inc.," *Drug & Cosmetic Industry,* January 1993, p. 95.
33. Shira R. Yoshor, "Competing in the Shadowy Gray: Protecting Domestic Trademark Holders from Gray Marketeers under the Lanham Act," *University of Chicago Law Review,* 59 (Summer 1992), pp. 1363–1390.
34. Sam J. Alberts, "Trademarks and Gray Market Goods: Why U.S. Trademark Holders Should Be Held Strictly Liable for Defective Gray Market Imports," *George Washington Journal of International Law & Economics,* 25 (1992), pp. 841–873.
35. Daniel Lyons, "Gray Market 'Deals' Aren't Always a Deal," *Computerworld,* 1 February 1993, p. 98.
36. "It's a Catalog, B'Gosh," *Catalog Age,* June 1993, p. 28.
37. Allan J. Magrath, *How to Achieve Zero-Defect Marketing* (New York: American Management Association, 1993), p. 102.
38. Allan J. Magrath and Kenneth G. Hardy, "Six Steps to Distribution Network Design," *Business Horizons,* January-February 1991, pp. 48–52.
39. Tara Parker-Pope, "Texas Wineries: Red, White—and Blue," *Wall Street Journal,* 13 October 1993, pp. T1, T4.

40. Saul Klein, "Selection of International Marketing Channels," *Journal of Global Marketing,* 4 (1991), pp. 21–37; Erin Anderson and Anne T. Coughlan, "International Market Entry and Expansion via Independent or Integrated Channels of Distribution," *Journal of Marketing,* January 1987, pp. 71–82.
41. Anderson and Coughlan, p. 74.
42. Anderson and Coughlan, p. 72.
43. Arieh Goldman, "Japan's Distribution System: Institutional Structure, Internal Political Economy, and Modernization," *Journal of Retailing,* Summer 1991, pp. 154–183.
44. Kenneth G. Hardy and Allan J. Magrath, *Marketing Channel Management: Strategic Planning and Tactics* (Glenview, IL: Scott Foresman, 1988), p. 667.
45. Bryan Batson, "Chinese Fortunes," *Sales & Marketing Management,* March 1994, pp. 93–98.
46. U.S. Department of Commerce, Bureau of the Census, *Statistical Abstract of the United States* (Washington, D.C.: Government Printing Office, 1993), p. 784.
47. Joseph V. Barks, "Squeezing Out the Middleman," *Distribution,* January 1994, pp. 30–34.
48. Yumiko Ono, "As Discounting Rises in Japan, People Learn to Hunt for Bargains," *Wall Street Journal,* 31 December 1993, pp. B1, B4.
49. Barks, pp. 31–32.


## Chapter 13


1. Patrick M. Reilly, "Music Stores Grow Larger and Livelier, Adding Preview Posts, Apparel, Pizza," *Wall Street Journal,* 18 June 1993, pp. B1–B2.
2. U.S. Department of Commerce, Bureau of the Census, *Statistical Abstract of the United States* (Washington, DC: Government Printing Office, 1993).
3. Kevin Helliker, "Wal-Mart's Big Blitz into the Grocery Field Meets Stiff Resistance," *Wall Street Journal,* 9 October 1992, pp. A1, A7.
4. "Fortune's Service 500: The 50 Largest Retailers," *Fortune,* 30 May 1994, p. 214.
5. Gregory A. Patterson, "'Face Lift' Gives Sears a Fresh Look and Better Results," *Wall Street Journal,* 20 July 1993, p. B4; Kate Fitzgerald, "Sears to Retool Its Image," *Advertising Age,* 1 February 1993, pp. 1, 36.
6. Matt Moffett, "Chic Star of Mexican Retailing: Sears Roebuck," *Wall Street Journal,* 8 March 1993, pp. B1, B5.
7. Bob Ortega, "Penney Pushes Abroad in Unusually Big Way as It Pursues Growth," *Wall Street Journal,* 1 February 1994, pp. A1, A7.
8. Joseph Pereira, "Toys 'R' Them: Mom-and-Pop Stores Put Playthings Like Thomas on Fast Track," *Wall Street Journal,* 14 January 1993, pp. B1, B5.
9. Karen J. Sack, "Supermarkets: Sales and Earning Begin to Rebound, But . . . ," *Standard & Poor's Industry Surveys,* 5 May 1994, p. R87.
10. Judith Waldrop, "Eating Out, Going Up?" *American Demographics,* January 1992, p. 55.
11. Sack, "Supermarkets," p. R87.
12. Bill Saporito, "And the Winner Is Still . . . Wal-Mart," *Fortune,* 2 May 1994, pp. 62–70.
13. Bob Ortega, "Tough Sale: Wal-Mart Is Slowed by Problems of Price and Culture in Mexico," *Wall Street Journal,* 29 July 1994, pp. A1, A5.
14. "Fortune's Service 500," p. 214; "Top 50 General Merchandise Chains," *Standard & Poor's Industry Surveys,* 5 May 1994, p. R80; Christina Duff, "Blue-Light Blues: Kmart's Dowdy Stores Get a Snazzy Face Lift, but Problems Linger," *Wall Street Journal,* 5 November 1993, pp. A1, A6.
15. Emily DeNitto, "Hypermarkets Seem to Be Big Flop in U.S.," *Advertising Age,* 4 October 1993, p. 20.
16. "Supercenters: A Growing Threat," *Standard & Poor's Industry Surveys,* 27 January 1994, p. R75.
17. Laura Liebeck, "Supercenters to Have Upscale, Trendier Look," *Discount Store News,* 18 April 1994, p. 33.
18. Cacilie Rohwedder, "Europe's Smaller Food Shops Face Finis," *Wall Street Journal,* 12 May 1993, pp. B1, B10.
19. Gale Eisenstodt, "Bull in the Japan Shop," *Forbes,* 31 January 1994, pp. 41–42; Susan Caminiti, "After You Win the Fun Begins: Toys 'R' Us," *Fortune,* 2 May 1994, p. 76.
20. Neela Banerjee, "Pet Superstores Collar Rivals' Customers," *Wall Street Journal,* 18 November 1993, p. B14.
21. Julie Liesse, "Welcome to the Club," *Advertising Age,* 1 February 1993, pp. 3, S6.
22. Bob Ortega, "Retail Combat: Warehouse-Club War Leaves Few Standing, and They Are Bruised," *Wall Street Journal,* 18 November 1993, pp. A1, A6; "Competition from Warehouse Clubs Hits Peak," *Standard & Poor's Industry Surveys,* 5 May 1994, p. R88.
23. Elizabeth Malkin, "Warehouse Stores Move into Mexico," *Advertising Age,* 18 January 1993, pp. I3, I30.
24. Faye Rice, "Haute Discount," *Fortune,* 20 September 1993, p. 16.
25. Larry Jabbonsky, "Snapple Tends to Vending with 54-Selection Glass Bottle Unit," *Beverage World,* 28 February 1994, p. 4.
26. Betsy Spethmann, "Toys: A Venerable Retail Technique Opens New Doors of Opportunity," *Brandweek,* 14 February 1994, p. 38; Leah Singer, "Push-Button Profits," Success, October 1993, p. 18.
27. Laurie M. Grossman, "Families Have Changed but Tupperware Keeps Holding Its Parties," *Wall Street Journal,* 21 July 1992, pp. A1, A13; Suein L. Hwang, "Ding-Dong: Updating Avon Means Respecting History without Repeating It," *Wall Street Journal,* 4 April 1994, pp. A1, A4.

28. Robert F. McCracken, "Establishing a Market Presence in China: The Avon Experience," *East Asian Executive Reports,* 15 August 1993, pp. 10–11; James McGregor, "U.S. Companies in China Find Patience, Persistence, and Salesmanship Pay Off," *Wall Street Journal,* 3 April 1992, p. B1.

29. Denison Hatch, "Privacy: How Much Data Do We Really Need?" *Target Marketing,* February 1994, pp. 35–40.

30. George E. Bardenheier Jr., "More to Database Brand Building Than Filling Up a Lot of Mail Boxes," *Brandweek,* 2 May 1994, pp. 20–21; Timothy O'Brien, "Direct-Mail Scams Surge as Tele-Schemes Grow Stale," *Wall Street Journal,* 17 December 1992, p. B5.

31. Karen J. Sack, "The Outlook: Courting a More Reticent Consumer," *Standard & Poor's Industry Surveys,* 5 May 1994, p. R75.

32. Kyle Pope, "Forecasts Aside, Dealers of PCs Thrive Again," *Wall Street Journal,* 1 February 1994, pp. B1, B3.

33. Stephen Barr, "Option Play," *Adweek,* 7 December 1992, p. 21.

34. Gregory A. Patterson, "U.S. Catalogers Test International Waters," *Wall Street Journal,* 19 April 1994, pp. B1, B2.

35. William C. Moncrief et al., "Examining the Roles of Telemarketing in Selling Strategy," *Journal of Personal Selling & Sales Management,* Fall 1989, pp. 1–12.

36. Junu Bryan Kim, "800/900: King of the Road in Marketing Value, Usage," *Advertising Age,* 17 February 1992, pp. S1, S6.

37. Patrick M. Reilly, "Home Shoppers to Be Given Yet Another Service," *Wall Street Journal,* 14 January 1994, pp. B1, B10.

38. Patrick M. Reilly, "Home Shopping: The Next Generation," *Wall Street Journal,* 21 March 1994, p. R11.

39. William M. Bulkeley, "Online Shopping Fails to Fulfill Promise," *Wall Street Journal,* 21 June 1993, p. B5.

40. "15th Annual Franchise 500," *Entrepreneur,* January 1994, pp. 150–151.

41. Robert T. Justis and Richard Judd, *Franchising* (Cincinnati, OH: South-Western, 1989), pp. 35–55.

42. International Franchise Association, *Franchise Fact Sheet,* 9 November 1993.

43. Justis and Judd, pp. 7–10.

44. Jeffrey Tannenbaum, "Plan to Aid Franchises in Emerging Nations Starts Slowly," *Wall Street Journal,* 13 February 1992, pp. B2.

45. Roger Cohen, "Pizza and Persistence Win in Hungary," *New York Times,* 5 May 1992, pp. D1, D9.

46. Yumiko Ono, "Japan's Fast-Food Companies Cook Up Local Platters to Tempt Local Palates," *Wall Street Journal,* 29 May 1992, p. B1; John Labate, "Snapshot of the Pacific Rim," *Fortune,* 7 October 1991, pp. 128–129.

47. Karen J. Sack, "Retailing: Current Analysis," *Standard & Poor's Industry Surveys,* 27 January 1994, pp. R70–R71.

48. "Sporting Goods Dept. Localizes Mix," *Discount Store News,* 18 April 1994, p. 59.

49. Patricia Strand, "Work at Home, Shop at Home," *Advertising Age,* 10 January 1994, p. S7.

50. Laura Richardson, "Buying: Different Strokes for Different Folks," *Chain Store Age Executive,* January 1994, pp. 10MH–12MH.

51. "Supermarkets: Distribution Targeted under New Efficiency Plan," *Standard & Poor's Industry Surveys,* 5 May 1994, p. R90.

52. Kate Fitzgerald, "The Latest Side of Sears," *Advertising Age,* 2 May 1994, pp. 1, 48.

53. Elaine Underwood, "Big Retailers Focus on Frequent Buyers," *Brandweek,* 11 April 1994, p. 5; Cyndee Miller, "Catalogs Alive, Thriving," *Marketing News,* 28 February 1994, pp. 1, 6.

54. Dawn Wilensky, "Target Builds on Good Deeds with Habitat Program," *Discount Store News,* 18 April 1994, p. 38.

55. Richard Gibson, "Location, Luck, Service Can Make a Store Top Star," *Wall Street Journal,* 1 February 1993, p. B1.

56. Kate Fitzgerald, "All Roads Lead to . . . ," *Advertising Age,* 1 February 1993, p. S1.

57. Gerry Khermouch, "We Take You to Main Street, Which Stands against the Wal," *Brandweek,* 21 February 1994, pp. 26–28.

58. Suzanne Alexander, "Feisty Yankees Resist Wal-Mart's Drive to Set Up Shop in New England Towns," *Wall Street Journal,* 16 September 1993, pp. B1, B6; "Town Residents Oppose Proposed Wal-Mart Center," *Wall Street Journal,* 22 August 1994, p. B5.

59. Gibson, p. B1.

60. William M. Stern, "Bumpbacks in Minneapolis," *Forbes,* 11 April 1994, pp. 48–49.

61. Chip Walker, "Strip Malls: Plain but Powerful," *American Demographics,* October 1991, pp. 48–51.

62. Gregory A. Patterson, "More Stores Switch from Sales to 'Everyday Low Prices,'" *Wall Street Journal,* 12 November 1992, p. B1.

63. Cyndee Miller, "Glitzy Interiors Transform Stores into 'Destinations,' Boost Sales," *Marketing News,* 30 August 1993, pp. 1, 6; Christina Duff, "Megastores That Entertain and Educate May Signal the Future of Merchandising," *Wall Street Journal,* 11 March 1993, pp. B1, B3.

64. This list taken from Patrick Dunne et al., *Retailing* (Cincinnati, OH: South-Western, 1992), pp. 316–321.

65. Gordon C. Bruner, "Music, Mood, and Marketing," *Journal of Marketing,* October 1990, pp. 94–103; Kevin Helliker, "Harrods: Grandeur Comes at Grand Cost," *Wall Street Journal,* 1 December 1993, pp. B1, B6.

66. Cyndee Miller, "Research Reveals How Marketers Can Win by a Nose," *Marketing News,* 4 February 1991, pp. 1–2.
67. Patricia Sellers, "Companies That Serve You Best," *Fortune,* 31 May 1993, pp. 74–88.
68. These four factors taken from William Davidson, Albert Bates, and Stephen Bass, "The Retail Life Cycle," *Harvard Business Review,* 54 (November-December 1976), pp. 89–96.
69. Stephen Brown, "The Wheel of Retailing: Past and Future," *Journal of Retailing,* 66 (Summer 1990), pp. 143–149.
70. Eleanor G. May, "A Retail Odyssey," *Journal of Retailing,* 65 (Fall 1989), pp. 356–367.
71. Dunne et al., p. 98. This theory based on William R. Davidson, Albert D. Bates, and Stephen J. Bass, "The Retail Life Cycle," *Harvard Business Review,* November-December 1976, p. 89.
72. Sack, "The Outlook," p. R75.
73. This section based on Karen J. Sack, "U.S. Retailers Expand Abroad," *Standard & Poor's Industry Surveys,* 5 May 1994, pp. R78–R79.
74. Kevin Helliker, "U.S. Discount Retailers Are Targeting Europe and Its Fat Margins," *Wall Street Journal,* 20 September 1993, pp. A1, A4.
75. This section adapted from Laurie Petersen, "21st Century Supermarket Shopping," *Adweek's Marketing Week,* 9 March 1992, p. 9; Howard Schlossberg, "Tomorrow's Retailing Technologies on Display Today at Smart Store," *Marketing News,* 20 January 1992, p. 2.
76. U.S. Department of Commerce.
77. U.S. Department of Commerce.
78. Sack, "The Outlook," p. R76.


## Chapter 14


1. Thomas A. Foster, "Global Logistics Benetton Style," *Distribution,* October 1993, pp. 62–66.
2. John T. Mentzer, Roger Gomes, and Robert E. Krapfel Jr., "Physical Distribution Service: A Fundamental Marketing Concept," *Journal of the Academy of Marketing Science,* Winter 1989, pp. 53–62.
3. Mentzer, Gomes, and Krapfel, pp. 53–62.
4. Robert Selwitz, "How Swede It Is," *Distribution,* October 1993, pp. 58–61.
5. Peter Bradley, "Transportation Joins the Strategic Arsenal," *Purchasing,* 19 August 1993, pp. 65–68.
6. E. J. Muller, "Key Links in the Supply Chain," *Distribution,* October 1993, pp. 52–56.
7. Lisa H. Harrington, "Public Warehousing: The Original Third Party," *Distribution,* February 1993, pp. 47–52.
8. Lisa Harrington, "Cross Docking Takes Costs Out of the Pipeline," *Distribution,* September 1993, pp. 64–66.
9. Allan J. Magrath, *How to Achieve Zero-Defect Marketing* (New York: American Management Association, 1993), p. 128.
10. Jim Thomas, "A Prescription to Cut Health-Care Costs," *Distribution,* September 1993, pp. 68–71.
11. Tony Seideman, "BC Labels Turn High-Tech," *Distribution,* January 1993, pp. 83–84.
12. William M. Bassin, "A Technique for Applying EOQ Models to Retail Cycle Stock Inventories," *Journal of Small Business Management,* January 1990, pp. 48–55.
13. E. J. Muller, "The Best Game Nintendo Built . . . ," *Distribution,* December 1993, pp. 31–35.
14. Thomas A. Foster, "Logistics Costs Drop to Record Low Levels," *Distribution,* July 1993, pp. 6–10.
15. Karen A. Auguston, "Determined Distributor Meets JIT Demands," *Modern Materials Management,* August 1993, pp. 48–50.
16. Ernest Raia, "Saturn: Rising Star," *Purchasing,* 9 September 1993, pp. 44–47.
17. Risks of JIT inventory management from Paul H. Zipkin, "Does Manufacturing Need a JIT Revolution?" *Harvard Business Review* (January-February 1991), pp. 40–50.
18. Raia, p. 45.
19. Ven Sriram and Snehamay Banerjee, "Electronic Data Interchange: Does Its Adoption Change Purchasing Policies and Procedures?" *International Journal of Purchasing and Materials Management,* Winter 1994, pp. 31–40; see also B. Dearing, "The Strategic Benefits of EDI," *Journal of Business Strategy,* 11 (January-February 1990), pp. 4–6; Robert Monczka and J. Carter, "Implementing Electronic Data Interchange," *Journal of Purchasing and Materials Management,* 25, no. 1 (1989), pp. 26–33; J. V. Hansen and N. C. Hill, "Control and Audit of Electronic Data Interchange," *MIS Quarterly,* December 1989, pp. 403–413.
20. Kate Evans-Correia, "Purchasing Now Biggest EDI User," *Purchasing,* 21 October 1993, pp. 47, 59.
21. E. J. Muller, "Faster, Faster, I Need It Now!" *Distribution,* February 1994, pp. 30–36.
22. U.S. Department of Commerce, Bureau of the Census, *Statistical Abstracts of the United States* (Washington, DC: Government Printing Office, 1993), p. 631.
23. Stephen R. Klein, "Rail Industry Structure: Railroads' Second Golden Era May Be Dawning," *Standard & Poor's Industry Surveys,* 4 November 1993, p. R15.
24. Klein, "Rail Industry," p. R15.
25. Stephen R. Klein, "Rail Traffic: Rail Traffic Chugs to New Highs," *Standard & Poor's Industry Surveys,* 4 November 1993, p. R23.
26. U.S. Department of Commerce, p. 629.
27. Stephen R. Klein, "Trucking Markets in a State of Flux," *Standard & Poor's Industry Surveys,* 4 November 1993, p. R34.

28. U.S. Department of Commerce, p. 610.
29. U.S. Department of Commerce, p. 610.
30. George Adcock, "Ports Take Different Paths to Latin America, but All Want In on the Growing Trade," *Traffic World,* 14 March 1994, pp. 30–33.
31. Kurt Hoffman, "Overnight Air Logistics: Tune In to How Cable Giant HBO Gets Its Products in and on the Air," *Distribution,* January 1993, pp. 57–59.
32. "Air Cargo: Firm Growth Ahead," *Standard & Poor's Industry Surveys,* 1 July 1993, p. A41.
33. Klein, "Rail Traffic," p. R21.
34. Daniel Machalaba, "Rail Companies Track Benefits of Intermodal," *Wall Street Journal,* 29 November 1993, p. A9B.
35. Rose A. Horowitz, "Nabisco Biscuit Opts for Single-Source Contract for Intermodal Shipments, Taps the Hub Group," *Traffic World,* 4 October 1993, pp. 41–42.
36. Aysegul Ozsomer, Michel Mitri, and S. Tamer Cavusgil, "Selecting International Freight Forwarders: An Expert Systems Application," *International Journal of Physical Distribution and Logistics Management,* 23 (1993), pp. 11–21.
37. Richard Malkin, "AEI Enters a New Phase," *Distribution,* February 1993, pp. 60–63.
38. This section based on Jay Gordon, "Service Industry Logistics," *Distribution,* February 1992, pp. 27–31.
39. Krystal Miller and Richard Gibson, "Domino's Stops Promising Pizza in 30 Minutes," *Wall Street Journal,* 22 December 1993, pp. B1, B5.
40. Stanley Hoffman, "Hazmat: The New Facts of Life," *Distribution,* January 1993, pp. 40–44.
41. Karen Auguston, "Protective Packaging Gets Green and Lean," *Modern Materials Handling,* November 1993, pp. 44–45.
42. James Aaron Cooke, "Turning Trash into Cash," *Traffic Management,* October 1993, pp. 46–48.
43. Patrick Byrne, "A New Road Map for Contract Logistics," *Transportation & Distribution,* April 1993, pp. 58–62.
44. E. J. Muller, "Reduce, Reuse, Recycle," *Distribution,* November 1993, pp. 42–49.
45. E. J. Muller, "Third Party Catches On," *Distribution,* July 1992, p. 60.
46. E. J. Muller, "The Top Guns of Third-Party Logistics," *Distribution,* March 1993, pp. 30–38.
47. Thomas A. Foster, "Brewing Up a Logistics Partnership," *Distribution,* September 1993, pp. 49–52.
48. Joseph B. Barks, "Lost in 'The Quest'?" *Distribution,* August 1993, pp. 72–79.
49. John D. Schulz, "Sears, Schneider National Team Up to Cut Retail Giant's Logistics Costs," *Traffic World,* 11 October 1993, pp. 29–31.
50. "Shipping to the C.I.S. Deserves an 'E' for Export Effort," *Distribution,* September 1993, p. 24.
51. Karen E. Thuermer, "To Maintain a Stronghold, Improve Service, Carriers Invest in China's Decayed Infrastructure," *Traffic World,* 4 April 1994, pp. 18–19; Jesse Wong, "Freighted with Difficulties," *Wall Street Journal,* 10 December 1993, p. R4.


## Chapter 15


1. Marj Charlier, "How an Obscure Ski Hill Carved a Niche among Resorts," *Wall Street Journal,* 20 January 1994, pp. B1, B2.
2. Joseph Pereira, "Gillette to Launch Excel Razor in U.S., Backed by $80 Million Marketing Blitz," *Wall Street Journal,* 5 October 1994, p. B8; Bob Garfield, "What Taste? Diet Coke Ads Gulp Down Attitude," *Advertising Age,* 17 January 1994, p. 46; Melanie Wells and Marcy Magiera, "Diet Coke Bubbles Back with the Basics," *Advertising Age,* 17 January 1994, p. 4.
3. Kevin Goldman, "Winemakers Look for More Free Publicity," *Wall Street Journal,* 29 September 1994, p. B4.
4. Goldman, p. B4.
5. Riccardo A. Davis, "Kodak, Fuji Focus on Summertime Promos for Kids," *Advertising Age,* 15 March 1993, p. 36.
6. Philip J. Kitchen, "Marketing Communications Renaissance," *International Journal of Advertising,* 12 (1993), pp. 367–386.
7. Information on Compaq's Presario product line from Bradley Johnson, "Compaq's New PC Looks Homeward," *Advertising Age,* 13 September 1993, p. 12.
8. Kitchen, p. 372.
9. Ian G. Evans and Sumandeep Riyait, "Is the Message Being Received? Benetton Analysed," *International Journal of Advertising,* 12 (1993), pp. 291–301.
10. Major Gary Lee Keck and Barbara Meuller, "Observations: Intended vs. Unintended Messages: Viewer Perceptions of United States Army Television Commercials," *Journal of Advertising Research,* March-April 1994, pp. 70–77.
11. Jacob Jacoby and Wayne D. Hoyer, "The Miscomprehension of Mass-Media Advertising Claims: A Re-Analysis of Benchmark Data," *Journal of Advertising Research,* June-July 1990, pp. 9–16; Jacob Jacoby and Wayne D. Hoyer, "The Comprehension/Miscomprehension of Print Communication: Selected Findings," *Journal of Consumer Research,* March 1989, pp. 434–443.
12. AIDA concept based on the classic research of E. K. Strong Jr., as theorized in *The Psychology of Selling and Advertising* (New York:McGraw-Hill, 1925) and "Theories of Selling," *Journal of Applied Psychology,* 9 (1925), pp. 75–86.

13. Hierarchy of effects model based on the classic research of R. C. Lavidge and G. A. Steiner, "A Model for Predictive Measurements of Advertising Effectiveness," *Journal of Marketing,* 25 (1961), pp. 59–62. For an excellent review of the AIDA and hierarchy of effects models, see Thomas E. Barry and Daniel J. Howard, "A Review and Critique of the Hierarchy of Effects in Advertising," *International Journal of Advertising,* 9 (1990), pp. 121–135.
14. Barry and Howard, p. 131.
15. Lindsay Chappell, "PR Makes Impressions, Sales," *Advertising Age,* 22 March 1993, pp. S18, S32.
16. Laura Bird, "Critics Shoot at New Colt 45 Campaign," *Wall Street Journal,* 17 February 1993, pp. B1, B8.
17. David B. Jones, "Setting Promotional Goals: A Communications' Relationship Model," *Journal of Consumer Marketing,* 11 (1994), pp. 38–49.
18. Peter J. Danaher and Roland T. Rust, "Determining the Optimal Level of Media Spending," *Journal of Advertising Research,* January-February 1994, pp. 28–34; see also Barbara Jizba and Mary M. K. Fleming, "Promotion Budgeting and Control in the Fast Food Industry," *International Journal of Advertising,* 12 (1993), pp. 13–23.
19. Jizba and Fleming, p. 16.
20. James E. Lynch and Graham J. Hooley, "Increasing Sophistication in Advertising Budget Setting," *Journal of Advertising Research,* February-March 1990, pp. 67–75.
21. Jizba and Fleming, p. 16.
22. Lynch and Hooley, p. 74.
23. Lynch and Hooley, p. 68.
24. Ali Kanso, "International Advertising Strategies: Global Commitment to Local Vision," *Journal of Advertising Research,* January-February 1992, pp. 10–14.
25. Kevin Goldman, "Prof. Levitt Stands by Global-Ad Theory," *Wall Street Journal,* 13 October 1992, p. B7.
26. Kanso, p. 10.
27. Carolyn A. Lin, "Cultural Differences in Message Strategies: A Comparison between American and Japanese TV Commercials," *Journal of Advertising Research,* July-August 1993, pp. 40–47.
28. Goldman, p. B7.
29. Penelope Rowlands, "Global Approach Doesn't Always Make Scents," *Advertising Age,* 17 January 1994, pp. I1, I38.
30. "Procter & Gamble Co. Disposable Diaper Ads to Be Altered by Firm," *Wall Street Journal,* 30 December 1992, p. A2; "Miller Cancels Beer Ads as Agency Takes Icy View," *Wall Street Journal,* 3 March 1994, p. B8.
31. Jeanne Saddler, "General Nutrition to Pay FTC Penalty of $2.4 Million over False Advertising," *Wall Street Journal,* 29 April 1994, p. B4.
32. Jeanne Saddler, "Ads for Diets Spark Inquiry by Regulators," *Wall Street Journal,* 26 March 1993, pp. B1, B5.
33. William Wilkie, Dennis McNeill, and Michael Mazis, "Marketing's 'Scarlet Letter': The Theory and Practice of Corrective Advertising," *Journal of Marketing,* Spring 1984, pp. 11–31.


## Chapter 16


1. Raymond Serafin, "Mustang Love: Ford Revs Up Romantic Heritage to Sell New Model of Sports Car," *Advertising Age,* 4 October 1993, p. 4; Raymond Serafin, "New Mustang Ads Hope to Leap Generation Gap," *Advertising Age,* 22 November 1993, p. 40; Kathleen Kerwin, "Remembrance of Ponies Past," *Business Week,* 6 December 1993, p. 178; Cleveland Horton, "New Mustang Rides Crest of Airwaves," *Advertising Age,* 14 March 1994, p. 12.
2. "National Ad Spending by Media," *Advertising Age,* 29 September 1993, p. 64.
3. U.S. Department of Commerce, Bureau of the Census, *Statistical Abstract of the United States* (Washington, DC: Government Printing Office, 1993), p. 405.
4. Derived from Schonfeld & Associates, "Advertising-to-Sales Ratios, 1992," *Advertising Age,* 13 July 1992, p. 16.
5. "Radio & TV Broadcasting: Viewers Deluged with Ads," *Standard & Poor's Industry Surveys,* 13 February 1992, p. M26.
6. "Radio & TV Broadcasting: Commercials Clog the Airwaves," *Standard & Poor's Industry Surveys,* 12 May 1994, p. M35.
7. Amitava Chattopadhyay and Kunal Basu, "Humor in Advertising: The Moderating Role of Prior Brand Evaluation," *Journal of Marketing Research,* November 1990, pp. 466–476.
8. Marvin E. Goldberg and Jon Hartwick, "The Effects of Advertiser Reputation and Extremity of Advertising Claims on Advertising Effectiveness," *Journal of Consumer Research,* September 1990, pp. 172–179.
9. Rajiv Grover and V. Srinivasan, "Evaluating the Multiple Effects of Retail Promotions on Brand Loyalty and Brand Switching Segments," *Journal of Marketing Research,* February 1992, pp. 76–89; see also S. P. Raj, "The Effects of Advertising on High and Low Loyalty Consumer Segments," *Journal of Consumer Research,* June 1982, pp. 77–89.
10. David W. Schumann, Jan M. Hathcote and Susan West, "Corporate Advertising in America: A Review of Published Studies on Use, Measurement, and Effectiveness," *Journal of Advertising,* September 1991, pp. 35–56.
11. Eben Shapiro, "R.J. Reynolds Ads Spotlight Nonsmokers," *Wall Street Journal,* 25 July 1994, pp. B4.

12. Neela Baberjee, "Russia Snickers after Mars Invades," *Wall Street Journal,* 13 July 1993, pp. B1, B10.

13. Kevin Goldman, "Six Flags Puts a 'Suit' in Its Ads to Take Swipe at Disney's Parks," *Wall Street Journal,* 9 June 1994, p. B6.

14. Tahi J. Gnepa, "Observations: Comparative Advertising in Magazines: Nature, Frequency, and a Test of the 'Underdog' Hypothesis," *Journal of Advertising Research,* September-October 1993, pp. 70–75.

15. For a comprehensive review of academic research on the effectiveness of comparative advertising, see Thomas E. Barry, "Comparative Advertising: What Have We Learned in Two Decades?" *Journal of Advertising Research,* March-April 1993, pp. 19–29. See also Cornelia Pechmann and David W. Stewart, "The Effects of Comparative Advertising on Attention, Memory, and Purchase Intentions," *Journal of Consumer Research,* September 1990, pp. 180–191; Darrel D. Muehling, Jeffrey J. Stoltman, and Sanford Grossbart, "The Impact of Comparative Advertising on Levels of Message Involvement," *Journal of Advertising,* 4 (1990), pp. 41–50; Jerry B. Gotleib and Dan Sarel, "Comparative Advertising Effectiveness: The Role of Involvement and Source Credibility," *Journal of Advertising,* 1 (1991), pp. 38–45.

16. Dave Barrager, "Japan Tiptoes toward Comparative Ads," *Adweek,* 22 February 1993, pp. 10–11.

17. Joanne Lipman, "It's It and That's a Shame: Why Are Some Slogans Losers?" *Wall Street Journal,* 16 July 1993, pp. A1, A4.

18. Debra Goldman, "The French Style of Advertising," *Adweek,* 16 December 1991, p. 21; Lisa Bannon and Margaret Studer, "For 2 Revealing European Ads, Overexposure Can Have Benefits," *Wall Street Journal,* 17 June 1994, p. B8.

19. Johnny K. Johansson, "The Sense of 'Nonsense': Japanese TV Advertising," *Journal of Advertising,* March 1994, pp. 17–26.

20. Thomas R. King, "Disney's Mock Newscast Ads Draw Criticism That They Dupe Viewers," *Wall Street Journal,* 14 July 1994, p. B6.

21. Kevin Goldman, "Barrage of Ads in Super Bowl Blurs Messages," *Wall Street Journal,* 3 February 1993, p. B6.

22. Thomas R. King, "Studios Battle Clutter of TV Movie Spots," *Wall Street Journal,* 25 June 1993, p. B1.

23. Scott Donaton, "Increase in Ad Pages Seen as Temporary," *Advertising Age,* 15 November 1993, p. 33.

24. Derived from Radio Advertising Bureau, as reported in "Radio & TV Broadcasting," *Standard & Poor's Industry Surveys,* 12 May 1994, p. M35.

25. Shailagh Murray, "Commercial Radio Finds Eager Ears, but Few Ads, in the Former East Bloc," *Wall Street Journal,* 24 August 1993, p. A9.

26. "Network's Dominance Still Slipping," *Standard & Poor's Industry Surveys,* 12 March 1992, p. L28.

27. Kevin Goldman, "TV Promotional Clutter Irks Ad Industry," *Wall Street Journal,* 11 February 1994, p. B4; Kevin Goldman, "CBS Virtually Sells Out Ad Spots for Olympics at Healthy Prices," *Wall Street Journal,* 25 January 1994, p. B5; Kevin Goldman, "Roster for Super Bowl Ads Fills Up Early," *Wall Street Journal,* 13 December 1993, p. B6; Joe Mandese, "Cost to Make TV Ad Nears Quarter-Million," *Advertising Age,* 4 July 1994, p. 3.

28. Arch G. Woodside, "Outdoor Advertising as Experiments," *Journal of the Academy of Marketing Science,* 18, no. 3 (1990), pp. 229–237; Riccardo A. Davis, "Competition Ignites Outdoor Spending," *Advertising Age,* 11 April 1994, p. 32.

29. Hanna Liebman, "McDonald's Poised for New Billboard Buys," *Adweek,* 1 March 1993, p. 10; Scot Hume and Alison Fahey, "McDonald's Readies Major Blast via Outdoor Boards," *Advertising Age,* 30 March 1992, p. 58.

30. Kevin Goldman, "Philips Infomercial Does Its Thing in Popular TV-Watching Hours," *Wall Street Journal,* 22 September 1993, p. B8.

31. Kevin Goldman, "Three Place-Based TV Suppliers Tune In," *Wall Street Journal,* 28 April 1994, p. B6.

32. Timothy K. Smith and Thomas R. King, "Hard Sell: Madison Avenue, Slow to Grasp Interactivity, Could Be Left Behind," *Wall Street Journal,* 7 December 1993, pp. A1, A8.

33. Debra Aho, "France Says 'Oui' to Interactive Kiosk," *Advertising Age,* 8 November 1993, p. 25.

34. Joseph M. Winski, "In Interactive, Consumer Taking Control," *Advertising Age,* 5 April 1993, p. S2.

35. Laura Bird, "Loved the Ad. May (or May Not) Buy the Product," *Wall Street Journal,* 7 April 1994, p. B1.

36. Leah Rickard, "Ford Explorer Rides High with 'Jurassic,'" *Advertising Age,* 13 September 1993, p. 4; Laura Bird, "A Star Is Brewed as Beer Scores in Hit Film," *Wall Street Journal,* 8 July 1993, p. B8.

37. Adapted from Scott M. Cutlip, Allen H. Center, and Glen M. Brown, *Effective Public Relations,* 6th ed. (Englewood Cliffs, NJ: Prentice-Hall, 1985), pp. 7–17.

38. Richard Gibson, "Pillsbury's Telephones Ring with Peeves, Praise," *Wall Street Journal,* 20 April 1994, pp. B1, B4; Carl Quintanilla and Richard Gibson, "'Do Call Us': More Companies Install 1-800 Phone Lines," *Wall Street Journal,* 20 April 1994, pp. B1, B4.

39. Patricia Sellers, "The Best Way to Reach Your Buyers," *Fortune: Special Supplement,* Autumn-Winter 1993, pp. 14–17.

40. Judith Waldrop, "Educating the Consumer," *American Demographics,* September 1991, pp. 44–47.

41. Paula Nichols, "Reaching the Compassionate Consumer," *American Demographics,* November 1993, pp. 26–27.

42. John P. Cortez, "Put People behind the Wheel," *Advertising Age,* 22 March 1993, p. S28.
43. Joanne Lipman, "Product Plugs Dot Olympic Landscape," *Wall Street Journal,* 11 February 1992, p. B8.
44. Eric Wieffering, "Wal-Mart Turns Green in Kansas," *American Demographics,* December 1993, p. 23; Bob Ortega, "Wal-Mart Store Comes in Colors, but Is All Green," *Wall Street Journal,* 11 June 1993, pp. B1, B10.
45. James E. Lukaszweski, "How Vulnerable Are You? The Lessons from Valdez," *Public Relations Quarterly,* Fall 1989, p. 5; E. Bruce Harrison and Tom Prugh, "Assessing the Damage: Practitioners's Perspectives on the Valdez," *Public Relations Journal,* October 1989, p. 40.
46. Marcy Magiera, "Pepsi Weathers Tampering Hoaxes," *Advertising Age,* 21 June 1993, pp. 1, 46; Marcy Magiera, "The Pepsi Crisis: What Went Right," *Advertising Age,* 19 July 1993, pp. 14–15.


## Chapter 17


1. James S. Hirsch, "More Hotels to Offer Plan for Air Miles," *Wall Street Journal,* 24 August 1993, pp. B1, B4.
2. Scott Hume, "Trade Promotion $ Share Dips in '92," *Advertising Age,* 5 April 1993, pp. 3, 43.
3. Scott Hume, "Coupons Set Record, but Pace Slows," *Advertising Age,* 1 February 1993, p. 25; Scott Hume, "Coupons: Are They Too Popular?" *Advertising Age,* 15 February 1993, p. 32.
4. Kathleen Deveny and Richard Gibson, "Awash in Coupons? Some Firms Try to Stem the Tide," *Wall Street Journal,* 10 May 1994, pp. B1, B6.
5. "International Coupon Trends," *Direct Marketing,* August 1993, pp. 47–49; "Global Coupon Use Up; U.K., Belgium Tops in Europe," *Marketing News,* 5 August 1991, p. 5; Kamran Kashani and John A. Quelch, "Can Sales Promotion Go Global?" *Business Horizons,* May-June 1990, pp. 37–43.
6. Christy Fisher, "Candy Bars Pack On the Promotions," *Advertising Age,* 19 September 1994, p. 29; Jeanne Whalen, "A Sizzling Season of Fast-food Promos," *Advertising Age,* 30 May 1994, pp. 1–2.
7. Eben Shapiro, "Cigarette Makers Outfit Smokers in Icons, Eluding Warning and Enraging Activists," *Wall Street Journal,* 27 September 1993, pp. B1, B4; Kevin Goldman, "Philip Morris Dresses Up Virginia Slims," *Wall Street Journal,* 26 February 1993, p. B8.
8. Don E. Schultz, William A. Robinson, and Lisa A. Petrison, *Sales Promotion Essentials,* 2nd ed. (Lincolnwood, IL: NTC Business Books, 1993), p. 75; Gary McWilliams and Marc Maremont, "Forget the Green Stamps—Give Me a Ticket to Miami," *Business Week,* 24 February 1992, pp. 70–71.
9. Kate Fitzgerald, "Ale-ing Essayists Vie for Guinness Pub," *Advertising Age,* 16 May 1994, p. 38.
10. Daniel M. Gold, "Reggie's Year in the Trenches," *Adweek's Marketing Week,* 9 March 1992, pp. 28–29.
11. E. S. Browning, "Eastern Europe Poses Obstacles for Ads," *Wall Street Journal,* 30 July 1992, p. B6.
12. Kathleen Deveny, "Displays Pay Off for Grocery Marketers," *Wall Street Journal,* 15 October 1992, pp. B1, B5.
13. Kmart/Procter & Gamble Study, Point-of-Purchase Advertising Institute, as reported in Lisa Z. Eccles, "P-O-P Scores with Marketers," *Advertising Age,* 26 September 1994, pp. P1–P4; Deveny, p. B1.
14. "Technology Gives P-O-P a New Look," *Advertising Age,* 26 September 1994, p. P6; Bristol Voss, "Selling with Sentiment," *Sales & Marketing Management,* March 1993, pp. 60–65.
15. Joseph M. Winski, "Auto Shows Lure People Who Buy," *Advertising Age,* 22 March 1993, p. S24.
16. Hume, "Trade Promotion $ Share," p. 3.
17. Edward Mayo and Lance P. Jarvis, "The Power of Persuasion: Lessons in Personal Selling from the White House," *Journal of Personal Selling and Sales Management,* Fall 1992, pp. 1–8.
18. U.S. Department of Commerce, Bureau of the Census, *Statistical Abstract of the United States* (Washington, DC: Government Printing Office, 1993), p. 446.
19. Henry Canaday, "Where Will Sales Jobs Be in 1994?" *Personal Selling Power,* February 1994, pp. 28–29.
20. "1993 Sales Manager's Budget Planner," *Sales & Marketing Management,* 28 June 1993, p. 62.
21. Percentages based on 935,753 leads tracked by Inquiry Handling Service, Inc., San Fernando, CA, 1993.
22. Andy Cohen, "Face-to-Face Sales," *Sales & Marketing Management,* August 1994, p. 13.
23. Sue Kapp, "Prospects Stay Interested Six Months," *Business Marketing,* March 1990, p. 42.
24. Marvin A. Jolson and Thomas R. Wotruba, "Selling and Sales Management in Action: Prospecting: A New Look at This Old Challenge," *Journal of Personal Selling and Sales Management,* Fall 1992, pp. 59–66.
25. Betsy Wiesendanger, "Bigger Sales, Same Budget," *Sales & Marketing Management,* July 1993, pp. 46–53.
26. Nancy Arnott, "Break Out of the Grid!" *Sales & Marketing Management,* July 1994, pp. 68–75.
27. "1993 Sales Manager's Budget Planner," p. 65.
28. Andy Cohen, "Delivering the Right Pitch," *Sales & Marketing Management,* September 1994, p. 44; Sondra Brewer, "How to Present So Prospects Listen," *Personal Selling Power,* April 1994, p. 75.
29. Paul B. Thornton, "Eight Practices from the Best Presenters," *Personal Selling Power,* October 1993, pp. 50–51.
30. Rosann L. Spiro and Barton A. Weitz, "Adaptive Selling: Conceptualization, Measurement, and Nomological Validity," *Journal of Marketing Research,* February 1990, pp. 61–69.

31. Charles Surasky, "Customers Buy Benefits," *Personal Selling Power,* September 1994, pp. 66–67.

32. Charles Futrell, *Fundamentals of Selling,* 4th ed. (Chicago: Irwin, 1993), p. 24; Stephen X. Doyle and George Thomas Roth, "Selling and Sales Management in Action: The Use of Insight Coaching to Improve Relationship Selling," *Journal of Personal Selling & Sales Management,* Winter 1992, pp. 59–64. See also Bob Kimball, *Successful Selling* (Chicago: American Marketing Association, 1994).

33. Valerie Reitman, "Toyota Calling: In Japan's Car Market, Big Three Face Rivals Who Go Door-to-Door," *Wall Street Journal,* 28 September 1994, pp. A1, A6.

34. Perri Capell, "Are Good Salespeople Born or Made?" *American Demographics,* July 1993, pp. 12–13.

35. Sergey Frank, "Global Negotiating: Vive Les Differences!" *Sales & Marketing Management,* May 1992, pp. 64–69.

36. This section adapted from Rolph E. Anderson, Joseph F. Hair Jr., and Alan J. Bush, *Professional Sales Management,* 2nd ed. (New York: McGraw-Hill, 1992), pp. 172–177.

37. Melissa Campanelli, "Big Blue Retools," *Sales & Marketing Management,* June 1994, p. 88.

38. Mark A. Moon and Gary M. Armstrong, "Selling Teams: A Conceptual Framework and Research Agenda," *Journal of Personal Selling & Sales Management,* Winter 1994, pp. 17–30; Henry Canaday, "Team Selling Works," *Personal Selling Power,* September 1994, pp. 52–58.

39. Anderson, Hair, and Bush, pp. 183–184.

40. Robert G. Head, "Restoring Balance to Sales Compensation," *Sales & Marketing Management,* August 1992, pp. 48–53.

41. Head, "Restoring Balance," pp. 48–53.

42. Henry Canaday, "Creative Compensation," *Personal Selling Power,* April 1994, pp. 24–28.

43. Robert G. Head, "Select Salespeople Systematically," *Personal Selling Power,* May-June 1993, pp. 68–69.

44. Weld F. Royal, "From Socialist to Sales Rep," *Sales & Marketing Management,* August 1994, p. 63.

45. Ginger Trumfio, "Picking the Cream of the Crop," *Sales & Marketing Management,* March 1994, p. 34; "For Northwestern, Once Is Not Enough," *Sales & Marketing Management,* September 1992, p. 58.

46. Head, "Select Salespeople Systematically," pp. 68–69.

47. Robert J. Kelly, "Toward a More Diverse Sales Force," *Sales & Marketing Management,* March 1994, pp. 33–34.

48. "What's Selling? Sales Jobs," *Sales & Marketing Management,* September 1993, p. 11.

49. Patrick L. Schul and Brent M. Wren, "The Emerging Role of Women in Industrial Selling: A Decade of Change," *Journal of Marketing,* July 1992, pp. 38–54.

50. Bob Alexander, "Picture Perfect: How Kodak Trains for Sales Success," *Personal Selling Power* (March 1994):19–23.

51. Michael J. Major, "Sales Training Emphasizes Service and Quality," *Marketing News,* 5 March 1990, p. 5.

52. Bill Kelley, "Training: 'Just Plain Lousy' or 'Too Important to Ignore'?" *Sales & Marketing Management,* March 1993, pp. 66–70.

53. Malcolm Fleschner, "100% Success at Federal Express," *Personal Selling Power,* March 1994, pp. 44–52.

54. Lawrence B. Chonko, John F. Tanner Jr., and William A. Weeks, "Selling and Sales Management in Action: Reward Preferences of Salespeople," *Journal of Personal Selling & Sales Management,* Summer 1992, pp. 67–74; "Facts Survey," *Incentive: Special Supplement* (1994).

55. "1993 Sales Manager's Budget Planner," p. 74.

## Chapter 18

1. John Helyar, "Going Out to the Ballpark Costs More This Season, Especially for Best Seats," *Wall Street Journal,* 5 April 1994, p. B1.

2. Karen Allen, "Empty Seats for Some Openers," *USA Today,* 27 April, 1995, p. C1.

3. *Ibid.*

4. *Ibid.*

5. Don Collins, "Check of Ticket Sales Shows Parks Filling Up," *USA Today,* 26 April 1995, p. C1.

6. *Ibid.*

7. "Price Rises as Factor for Consumers," *Advertising Age,* 8 November 1993, p. 37.

8. "Retailers Are Giving Profits Away," *American Demographics,* June 1994, p. 14.

9. "A PC Price War Has Computer Buyers on a Shopping Spree," *Wall Street Journal,* 29 June 1992, pp. A1, A6.

10. "The Big Squeeze," *Adweek's Marketing Week,* 12 November 1990, p. 22.

11. Alix Freedman, "A Marketing Giant Uses Its Sales Prowess to Profit on Poverty," *Wall Street Journal,* 22 September 1993, pp. A1, A14.

12. Bill Saporito, "Why the Price Wars Never End," *Fortune,* 23 March 1992, pp. 68–78.

13. "Levi's Dockers Weigh into Casuals," *Adweek's Marketing Week,* 24 September 1990, pp. 26–27.

14. Akshay Rao and Kent Monroe, "The Effect of Price, Brand Name, and Store Name on Buyers' Perceptions of Product Quality: An Integrative Review," *Journal of Marketing Research,* August 1989, pp. 351–357; Gerard Tellis and Gary Gaeth, "Best Value, Price-Seeking, and Price Aversion: The Impact of Information and Learning on Consumer Choices," *Journal of Marketing,* April 1990, pp. 34–35.

15. William Dodds, Kent Monroe, and Dhruv Grewal, "Effects of Price, Brand, and Store Information on Buyers' Product Evaluations," *Journal of Marketing Research,* August 1991, pp. 307–319; see also Akshay Rao and Wanda Sieben, "The Effect of Prior Knowledge on Price Acceptability and the Type of Information Examined," *Journal of Consumer Research,* September 1992, pp. 256–270.
16. Michael Etgar and Naresh Malhotra, "Determinants of Price Dependency: Personal and Perceptual Factors," *Journal of Consumer Research,* September 1981, pp. 217–222; Jeen-Su Lim and Richard Olshavsky, "Impacts of Consumers' Familiarity and Product Class on Price-Quality Inference and Product Evaluations," *Quarterly Journal of Business and Economics,* Summer 1988, pp. 130–141.
17. Donald Lichtenstein and Scott Burton, "The Relationship between Perceived and Objective Price-Quality," *Journal of Marketing Research,* November 1989, pp. 429–443.
18. "Store-Brand Pricing Has to Be Just Right," *Wall Street Journal,* 14 February 1992, p. B1.


## Chapter 19


1. Oscar Suris, "Mercedes-Benz Tries to Compete on Value," *Wall Street Journal,* 20 October 1993, p. B1.
2. "What's Fair," *Wall Street Journal,* 20 May 1994, p. R11.
3. "What's Fair," p. R11.
4. Ken Yamada, "Motorola Challenges Intel in Pricing Its New Microchip," *Wall Street Journal,* 26 April 1993, pp. B1, B8.
5. "Is Herb Kelleher America's Best Manager?" *Fortune,* 2 May 1994, pp. 43–52.
6. *United States v. Sacony-Vacuum Oil Co.,* 310 U.S. 150 (1940).
7. "Price-Fixing Charges Put GE and DeBeers under Tough Scrutiny," *Wall Street Journal,* 22 February 1994, pp. A1, A8.
8. "Six Big Airlines Settle U.S. Suit on Price Fixing," *Wall Street Journal,* 18 March 1994, p. A2; "U.S. Steps Up Probe on Fixing of Air Fares," *Wall Street Journal,* 18 March 1992, p. A3.
9. "FTC Broadens Trust Powers with Old Law," *Wall Street Journal,* 30 September 1992, pp. B1, B2.
10. Adapted from Laurie Hays and Adi Ignatius, "Moscow's Capitalists Decide the Best Price Is a Firmly Fixed One," *Wall Street Journal,* 21 January 1992, pp. A1, A17. Reprinted by permission of the *Wall Street Journal.* © 1992 Dow Jones & Company. All rights reserved worldwide.
11. "Wal-Mart Admits Selling below Cost, but Denies Predatory Pricing Charge," *Wall Street Journal,* 24 August 1993, p. A9; "Wal-Mart Loses a Case on Pricing," *Wall Street Journal,* 13 October 1993, p. A3.
12. Patricia Sellers, "The Dumbest Marketing Ploy," *Fortune,* 3 October 1992, pp. 88–94.
13. "Do Low Prices Bore Shoppers?" *American Demographics,* January 1994, pp. 11–13.
14. Sellers, pp. 88–94.
15. "Eliminated Discounts on P&G Goods Annoy Many Who Sell Them," *Wall Street Journal,* 11 August 1992, pp. A1, A6.
16. Sellers, pp. 88–89. © 1992 Time Inc. All rights reserved.
17. "Broad Grocery Price Cuts May Not Pay," *Wall Street Journal,* 7 May 1993, pp. B1, B8.
18. "Value Pricing Pays Off," *Business Week,* 1 November 1993, p. 32.
19. "Value Pricing Pays Off," p. 32.
20. "Eliminated Discounts," pp. A1, A6.
21. "Single-Price Stores' Formula for Success: Cheap Merchandise and a Lot of Clutter," *Wall Street Journal,* 30 June 1992, pp. B1, B6.
22. "What's Fair?" p. R11.
23. Charles Quigley and Elaine Notarantonio, "An Exploratory Investigation of Perceptions of Odd and Even Pricing," in *Developments in Marketing Science,* ed. Victoria Crittenden (Miami: Academy of Marketing Science, 1992), pp. 306–309.
24. Francis Mulhern and Robert Leone, "Implicit Price Bundling of Retail Products: A Multiproduct Approach to Maximizing Store Profitability," *Journal of Marketing,* October 1991, pp. 63–76; Dorothy Paun, "Product Bundling: A Normative Model Based on an Orientation Perspective," in *Developments in Marketing Science,* ed. Victoria Crittenden (Miami: Academy of Marketing Science, 1992), pp. 301–305; Manjit Yadav and Kent Monroe, "How Buyers Perceive Savings in a Bundle Price: An Examination of a Bundle's Transaction Value," *Journal of Marketing Research,* August 1993, pp. 350–358.
25. "Value Strategy to Battle Recession," *Advertising Age,* 7 January 1991, pp. 1, 44.
26. "How to Prosper in the Value Decade," *Fortune,* 30 November 1992, pp. 89–103.
27. "Cut Costs or Else," *Business Week,* 22 March 1993, pp. 28–29.
28. "Cut Costs," pp. 28–29.
29. Michael Ybarra, "Price Cutting Airline Does No-Frills Hula," *Wall Street Journal,* 29 December 1993, pp. B1, B6.


## Chapter 20


1. Raymond Serafin and Riccardo Davis, "Detroit Moves to Woo Blacks," *Advertising Age,* 11 April 1994, p. 10; Fara Warner, "New Cadillac Reconnaissance: Women and African Americans," *Brandweek,* 28 February 1994, pp. 1, 6; Cyndee Miller, "Cadillac Promo Targets African-Americans," *Marketing News,* 23 May 1994, p. 12.

2. Martha Farnsworth Riche, "We're All Minorities Now," *American Demographics,* October 1991, pp. 26–33.
3. James Allen and Eugene Turner, "Where Diversity Reigns," *American Demographics,* August 1990, pp. 24–38.
4. Martha Farnsworth Riche, "We're All Minorities Now," *American Demographics,* October 1991, pp. 26–33.
5. "The Declining Majority," *American Demographics,* January 1993, p. 59.
6. Riche, p. 28; "Beyond the Melting Pot," *Time,* 9 April 1990, pp. 28–32.
7. William Dunn, "The Move toward Ethnic Marketing," *Nation's Business,* July 1992, pp. 39–44; "The Numbers Bear Out Our Diversity," *Wall Street Journal,* 24 April 1994, p. B1.
8. Dunn, p. 40; "How to Sell across Cultures," *American Demographics,* March 1994, pp. 56–58.
9. Jon Berry, "An Empire of Niches," *Superbrands: A Special Supplement to Adweek's Marketing Week,* Fall 1991, pp. 17–22.
10. Berry, pp. 17–22.
11. "Feelings about Foreigners," *Wall Street Journal,* 23 May 1994, p. B1.
12. "The Immigrants," *Business Week,* 13 July 1992, pp. 114–122; "Immigrant Tide Surges in '80s," *USA Today,* 29 May 1992, p. 1A; "It's Really Two Immigrant Economies," *Business Week,* 20 June 1994, pp. 74–78.
13. "The Immigrants," p. 117.
14. William O'Hare, "Reaching for the Dream," *American Demographics,* January 1992, pp. 32–36.
15. O'Hare, "Reaching," pp. 32–36.
16. O'Hare, "Reaching," pp. 32–36.
17. William O'Hare et al., "African Americans in the 1990s," *Population Bulletin,* July 1991, pp. 2–22.
18. O'Hare et al., pp. 2–22; 1994 projection by authors.
19. Judith Waldrop, "Shades of Black," *American Demographics,* September 1990, pp. 30–34.
20. "Blacks' Family Incomes Grew during 1980s, Census Says," *Fort Worth Star-Telegram,* 25 July 1992, p. A3.
21. William O'Hare, "In the Black," *American Demographics,* November 1989, pp. 24–25, 27–29.
22. Eugene Morris, "The Difference in Black and White," *American Demographics,* January 1993, pp. 44–46.
23. "Marketers Pay Attention! Ethnics Comprise 25 Percent of the U.S. Market," *Brandweek,* 18 July 1994, p. 26.
24. "Many Marketers Still Consider Blacks Dark-Skinned Whites," *Marketing News,* 18 January 1993, pp. 1, 13.
25. "Cosmetics Firms Finally Discover the Ethnic Market," *Marketing News,* 30 August 1993, p. 2.
26. "Black-Owned Firms Are Catching an Afrocentric Wave," *Wall Street Journal,* 8 January 1992, p. B2.
27. "Firms Cater to African-Style Weddings," *Wall Street Journal,* 24 August 1993, pp. B1, B2.
28. "Fabrics Industry Makes a Fashion Statement Out of Africa," *Dallas Morning News,* 26 July 1992, p. 24.
29. Ronald Miller and Pepper Miller, "Trends Are Opportunities for Targeting African Americans," *Marketing News,* 20 January 1992, p. 9; "Six Myths about Black Consumers," *Adweek's Marketing Week,* 6 May 1991, pp. 16–19.
30. "African Americans," *Adweek's Marketing Week,* 21 January 1991, pp. 18–20; Thelma Snuggs, "Minority Markets: Define the Consumer of the 21st Century," *Credit,* January-February 1992, pp. 8–11; "Minorities Show Brand Loyalty," *Advertising Age,* 9 May 1994, p. 29; "Surveys Point to Group Differences," *Brandweek,* 18 July 1994, pp. 32–35.
31. "Cosmetics Firms," p. 2; "Business and Race," *Wall Street Journal,* 7 September 1994, p. B1.
32. "African Americans," p. 19.
33. "African Americans," p. 19.
34. For articles on promotion stereotyping, see Robert Wilkes and Humberto Valencia, "Hispanics and Blacks in Television Commercials," *Journal of Advertising,* 18 (1989), pp. 19–25; Robert Pitts et al., "Black and White Response to Culturally Targeted Television Commercials: A Values-Based Approach," *Psychology and Marketing,* Winter 1989, pp. 311–328; Tommy Whittler and Joan DiMeo, "Viewers' Reactions to Racial Cues in Advertising Stimuli," *Journal of Advertising Research,* December 1991, pp. 37–46; William Qualls and David J. Moore, "Stereotyping Effects on Consumers' Evaluation of Advertising: Impact of Racial Differences between Actors and Viewers," *Psychology and Marketing,* Summer 1990, pp. 135–151; Richard Pollay, Jung Lee, and David Carter-Whitney, "Separate, but Not Equal: Racial Segmentation in Cigarette Advertising," *Journal of Advertising,* March 1992, pp. 45–57; David Strutton and Keith Tudor, "A Conceptually Based Discussion of Possible Antecedents and Societal Implications Associated with Marketing's Stereotypical Portrayal of Blacks," *Developments in Marketing Science: Proceedings of the 1991 Academy of Marketing Science Annual Conference,* ed. Robert King (Academy of Marketing Science, 1991), pp. 243–246; "What Role Do Ads Play in Racial Tension," *Advertising Age,* 10 August 1992, pp. 1, 35; and "Marketers Miss Out by Alienating Blacks," *Wall Street Journal,* 9 April 1993, p. B8.
35. "Waking Up to a Major Market," *Business Week,* 23 March 1992, pp. 70–73.
36. "Advertisers Promote Racial Harmony; Nike Criticized," *Marketing News,* 6 July 1992, pp. 1, 10.

37. "Fighting the Power," *Advertising Age,* 3 March 1991, p. 4; Thaddeus Spratlin, "The Controversy over Targeting Black Consumers in Cigarette Advertising," in *Developments in Marketing Science: Proceedings of the 1991 Academy of Marketing Science Annual Conference,* ed. Robert King (Academy of Marketing Science, 1991), pp. 249–252; Kathleen Deveny, "Malt Liquor Makers Find Lucrative Market in the Urban Young," *Wall Street Journal,* 9 March 1992, pp. A1, A4.
38. "Promotion Cost More Than a Contribution," *Wall Street Journal,* 29 April 1994, p. B1.
39. "Retailers Boost Efforts to Target African American Consumers," *Marketing News,* 22 June 1992, p. 2.
40. "Spiegel, Ebony Aim to Dress Black Women," *Wall Street Journal,* 18 September 1991, pp. B1, B7.
41. "Former Pizza Hut Official Takes Big Franchise Slice," *Wall Street Journal,* 24 March 1992, p. B1.
42. "After Demographic Shift, Atlanta Mall Restyles Itself as Black Shopping Center," *Wall Street Journal,* 26 February 1992, pp. B1, B5.
43. "After Demographic Shift," pp. B1, B5.
44. "After Demographic Shift," pp. B1, B5.
45. "Students Attempt to Find: Do the Poor Really Pay More?" *Advancing the Consumer Interest,* Spring 1992, pp. 30–33.
46. "The Poor Pay More for Food in New York, Survey Finds," *Wall Street Journal,* 15 April 1991, pp. B1, B4.
47. Francine Schwadel, "Urban Consumers Pay More and Get Less, and Gap May Widen," *Wall Street Journal,* 2 July 1992, pp. A1, A4. Reprinted by permission of the *Wall Street Journal,* © 1992 Dow Jones & Company, Inc. All rights reserved worldwide.
48. "The Largest Minority," *American Demographics,* February 1993, p. 59.
49. "One Million Hispanic Club," *American Demographics,* February 1991, p. 59; "Vivan Los Suburbios," *American Demographics,* April 1993, pp. 31–37.
50. "Specific Hispanics," *American Demographics,* February 1994, pp. 44–53.
51. "The Mexican Way," *American Demographics,* May 1992, p. 4.
52. "How to Speak to Hispanics," *American Demographics,* February 1990, pp. 40–41; Patricia Braus, "What Does Hispanic Mean?" *American Demographics,* June 1993, pp. 46–58.
53. Snuggs, pp. 8–10; see also Gonzalo Soruco and Timothy Meyer, "The Mobile Hispanic Market," *Marketing Research,* Winter 1993, pp. 6–14.
54. Stuart Livingston, "Marketing to the Hispanic Community," *Journal of Business Strategy,* March-April 1992, pp. 54–57.
55. "Habla Español?" *Target Marketing,* October 1991, pp. 10–14.
56. "The United States of Miami," *Adweek's Marketing Week,* 15 July 1991, pp. 19–22; "Hispanics' Tale of Two Cities," *U.S. News & World Report,* 25 May 1992, pp. 40–41.
57. "United States of Miami," p. 20.
58. "To Reach Minorities, Try Busting Myths," *American Demographics,* April 1992, pp. 14–15; "Poll: Hispanics Stick to Brands," *Advertising Age,* 15 February 1993, p. 6.
59. "Run to the Supermarket and Pick Me Up Some Cactus," *Business Week,* 20 June 1994, pp. 70–71.
60. "Run to the Supermarket," pp. 70–71.
61. "Deposit-Hungry Consumer Banks Courting the Nation's Hispanics," *American Banker,* 2 May 1990, pp. 1, 6.
62. Elizabeth Roberts, "Different Strokes," *Adweek's Marketing Week,* 9 July 1990, p. 41; see also "What Does Hispanic Mean?" *American Demographics,* June 1993, pp. 46–56.
63. "Advertising in Hispanic Media Rises Sharply," *Marketing News,* 18 January 1993, p. 9.
64. "Advertising in Hispanic Media," p. 9.
65. "Targeting Hispanics: NutraSweet Educates while Coke Titillates," *Marketing News,* 11 November 1991, pp. 1, 2.
66. "The Challenge of the '90s: Pinning Down the Hispanic Market," *Progressive Grocer,* June 1990, pp. 69–74.
67. Livingston, p. 56.
68. Greg Muirhead, "Mexican-American Influx Offers Chance for Growth," *Progressive Grocer,* April 1992, p. 4.
69. "Asian Americans," *CQ Researcher,* 13 December 1991, pp. 947–964.
70. "Asian Americans Increase Rapidly," *Futurist,* September-October 1991, pp. 51–53.
71. Adapted from William O'Hare, "A New Look at Asian Americans," *American Demographics,* October 1990, pp. 26–31. Reprinted with permission © *American Demographics,* October 1990. For subscription information, please call (800) 828-1131.
72. "Asians in the Suburbs," *American Demographics,* May 1994, pp. 32–38.
73. O'Hare, "New Look," pp. 26–31.
74. O'Hare, "New Look," pp. 26–31.
75. "Asian Americans," p. 953.
76. "Why Asians Can Prosper Where Blacks Fail," *Wall Street Journal,* 28 May 1992, p. A10.
77. "The California Asian Market," *American Demographics,* October 1990, pp. 34–37.
78. Jerry Goodbody, "Taking the Pulse of Asian Americans," *Adweek's Marketing Week,* 12 August 1991, p. 32. Used by permission of A/S/M Communications, Inc.

79. "Suddenly, Asian-Americans Are a Marketer's Dream," *Business Week,* 17 June 1991, pp. 54–55.
80. Goodbody, p. 32.
81. "Suddenly," p. 55.
82. "Complexity of Asian-American Market Causes Some to Stay Away," *Marketing News,* 17 January 1994, pp. 6, 9.
83. "Marketers Say Budgets Hinder Targeting of Asian Americans," *Marketing News,* 30 March 1992, p. 2.
84. Nejdet Delener and James Neelankavil, "Informational Sources and Media Uses: A Comparison between Asian and Hispanic Subcultures," *Journal of Advertising Research,* June-July 1990, pp. 45–52; "'All-American Girl' Puts Asians on the Dial," *Wall Street Journal,* 15 June 1994, p. B1.
85. Keun Lee and Nejdet Delener, "Values of Minority Orientals: Subcultural Comparisons Using a Three Dimensional Approach to Values Measurement," in *Developments in Marketing Science: Proceedings of the 1991 Academy of Marketing Science Annual Conference,* ed. Robert King (Academy of Marketing Science, 1991), pp. 255–259.
86. "Suddenly," p. 54; "American Dreams," *Wall Street Journal,* 16 June 1992, pp. A1, A5.
87. Richard DeSanta, "California's Oriental Stores: The Ultimate Niche Marketers," *Supermarket Business,* November 1991, pp. 25–30. Used by permission of the publisher.
88. "American Indians in the 1990s," *American Demographics,* December 1991, pp. 26–34.
89. "Struggling to Be Themselves," *Time,* 9 November 1992, pp. 52–54.
90. "Black Adventures," *American Demographics,* August 1994, p. 4.


## Chapter 21


1. Adapted from Alix M. Freedman, "A Single Family Makes Many of the Cheap Pistols That Saturate Cities," *Wall Street Journal,* 28 February 1992, pp. A1, A6–A7; Andrea Gerlin, "Wal-Mart Stops Handgun Sales inside Its Stores," *Wall Street Journal,* 23 December 1993, pp. B1, B8; Kevin Goldman, "NRA Calls Ads for Women Educational," *Wall Street Journal,* 28 September 1993, p. B6; Joseph Pereira and Barbara Carton, "Toys 'R' Us to Banish Some 'Realistic' Toy Guns," *Wall Street Journal,* 14 October 1994, pp. B1, B12.
2. Jerry E. Bishop, "TV Advertising Aimed at Kids Is Filled with Fat," *Wall Street Journal,* 9 November 1993, p. B1.
3. Helene Cooper, "CPC Advocates Use of Condoms in Blunt AIDS-Prevention Spots," *Wall Street Journal,* 5 January 1994, p. B1.
4. Wendy Bounds, "Active Seniors Do Laps of the Mall—Then Cool Down by Eating Fast Food," *Wall Street Journal,* 9 January 1993, p. B1.
5. Thomas M. Burton, "Methods of Marketing Infant Formula Land Abbott in Hot Water," *Wall Street Journal,* 25 May 1993, pp. A1, A5.
6. Mary L. Carnevalle, "Parents Say PBS Station Exploit Barney in Fund Drives," *Wall Street Journal,* 19 March 1993, pp. B1, B8.
7. This concept taken from Frank Bingham, Jr., and Barney Raffield, "An Overview of Ethical Considerations in Industrial Marketing," in *Developments in Marketing Science,* vol. 12, ed. Jon Hawes and John Thanopoulous (Akron, OH; Academy of Marketing Science, 1989), pp. 244–248; see also Michael Mayo and Lawrence Marks, "An Empirical Investigation of a General Theory of Marketing Ethics," in *1989 AMA Educators' Proceedings: Enhancing Knowledge Development in Marketing,* ed. Paul Bloom and others (Chicago: American Marketing Association), p. 95.
8. Based on Edward Stevens, *Business Ethics* (New York: Paulist Press, 1979).
9. These points taken from Gene R. Laczniak and Patrick E. Murphy, "Fostering Ethical and Marketing Decisions," *Journal of Business Ethics,* April 1991, pp. 259–271.
10. L. B. Chonko, B. M. Enis, and J. F. Tanner Jr., *Managing Salespeople* (Boston: Allyn and Bacon, 1992), p. 43.
11. Ishmael Akaah and Edward Riordan, "Judgments of Marketing Professionals about Ethical Issues in Marketing Research: A Replication and Extension," *Journal of Marketing Research,* February 1989, pp. 112–120; see also Shelby Junt, Lawrence Chonko, and James Wilcox, "Ethical Problems of Marketing Researchers," *Journal of Marketing Research,* August 1984, pp. 309–324; Kenneth Andrews, "Ethics in Practice," *Harvard Business Review,* September-October 1989, pp. 99–104.
12. Julie Amparano Lopez, "More Big Businesses Set Up Ethics Offices," *Wall Street Journal,* 10 May 1993, sec. B.
13. Adapted from Chonko, Enis, and Tanner, p. 43.
14. Michael R. Hyman, Robert Skipper, and Richard Tansey, "Ethical Codes Are Not Enough," *Business Horizons,* March-April 1990, p. 16.
15. John A. Byrne, "Best-Laid Ethics Programs . . . ," *Business Week,* 9 March 1992, p. 67.
16. Paul Nowell, "Critics Fuming over Joe Camel's Female Friends," *Houston Chronicle,* 19 February 1994, p. 1D.
17. Joanne Lipman, "Surgeon General Says It's Time Joe Camel Quit," *Wall Street Journal,* 10 March 1992, pp. B1, B7; see also John P. Pierce et al., "Does Tobacco Advertising Target Young People to Start Smoking? Evidence from California," *Journal of the American Medical Association,* 11 December 1993, p. 3154; Michael B. Mazis et al., "Perceived Age and Attractiveness of Models in Cigarette Advertisement," *Journal of Marketing,* January 1992, pp. 22–37.

18. Lipman, "Surgeon General Says," p. B1; Paul M. Barrett, "Surprise Court Ruling Could Have Big Impact Far beyond Cigarettes," *Wall Street Journal,* 25 June 1992, pp. A1, A10; Eben Shapiro, "FTC Confronts 'Healthier' Cigarette Ads," *Wall Street Journal,* 21 March 1994, p. B7; Larry Dietz, "Who Enjoys the Right of Free Speech? Jane Fonda, Joe Camel, You, and Me," *Adweek Western Advertising News,* 20 April 1992, p. 44.
19. Suein L. Hwang, "Some Stadiums Snuff Out Cigarette Ads," *Wall Street Journal,* 17 July 1992, p. B3.
20. Janice Castro, "Volunteer Vice Squad," *Time,* 23 April 1990, pp. 60–61; Eben Shapiro, "California Plans More Antismoking Ads," *Wall Street Journal,* 26 January 1993, p. B7.
21. Matthew Grimm, "Bud, Coors Mull 'Media' Strategy to Blunt Critics," *Adweek's Marketing Week,* 11 November 1991, p. 5; Eben Shapiro, "Low-Alcohol, Brightly Labeled Cocktails Stir Fears They Will Tempt Teenagers," *Wall Street Journal,* 4 August 1993, p. B1; Frank Rose, "If It Feels Good, It Must Be Bad," *Fortune,* 21 October 1991, pp. 91–100.
22. "Selling Sin to Blacks," *Fortune,* 21 October 1991, p. 100; Alix M. Freedman, "Heileman Tries a New Name for Strong Malt," *Wall Street Journal,* 11 May 1992, pp. B1, B5; Kathleen Deveny, "Strong Brew: Malt Liquor Makers Find Lucrative Market in the Urban Young," *Wall Street Journal,* 9 March 1992, pp. A1, A4; Laura Bird, "Critics Shoot at New Colt 45 Campaign," *Wall Street Journal,* 17 February 1993, p. B1.
23. Joanne Lipman, "Why Activists Fume at Anti-Smoking Ads," *Wall Street Journal,* 20 February 1992, p. B3; Julia Flynn Siler, "It Isn't Miller Time Yet, and This Bud's Not for You," *Business Week,* 24 June 1991, p. 52.
24. Lipman, "Why Activists Fume," p. B3; Siler, p. 52.
25. Joanne Lipman, "Foes Claim Ad Bans Are Bad Business," *Wall Street Journal,* 27 February 1990, p. B1.
26. Terry Adams, "Tobacco Ad Ban in EC Nearer," *Advertising Age,* 17 February 1992, p. 59; "EC Panel Proposes Ban on Nearly All Tobacco Ads," *Marketing News,* 24 June 1991, p. 21; Rosanna Tamburri and Christopher J. Chipello, "Court Upholds Canadian Ban on Tobacco Ads," *Wall Street Journal,* 18 January 1993, p. B5.
27. Barry Newman, "The Marlboro Man Gets Bushwhacked by an Old Red Foe," *Wall Street Journal,* 24 February 1993, p. A1.
28. Deborah Schroeder, "Life, Liberty, and the Pursuit of Privacy," *American Demographics,* June 1992, p. 20.
29. Peter Pae, "American Express Co. Discloses It Gives Merchants Data on Cardholders' Habits," *Wall Street Journal,* 14 May 1992, p. A3; "Blockbuster Video Says It Has No Plan to Sell Its Customer Lists," *Marketing News,* 4 February 1991, p. 2; see also the article that prompted the controversy, Michael W. Miller, "Coming Soon to Your Local Video Store: Big Brother," *Wall Street Journal,* 26 December 1990, p. 9; "Equifax Says It Will Stop Giving Mailing Lists to Direct Marketers," *Marketing News,* 16 September 1991, p. 21.
30. Michael W. Miller, "How Drug Companies Get Medical Records of Individual Patients," *Wall Street Journal,* 27 February 1992, pp. A1, A4.
31. Evan I. Schwartz, "The Rush to Keep Mum," *Business Week,* 8 June 1992, pp. 36–38.
32. Mary Lu Karnevale, "Caller ID Services Accused of Invading Individuals' Privacy," *Wall Street Journal,* 25 June 1993, p. B8.
33. Jonathan Berry, "A Potent New Tool for Selling," *Business Week,* 5 September 1994, pp. 56–62.
34. Joe Schwartz and Thomas Miller, "The Earth's Best Friends," *American Demographics,* February 1991, pp. 26–35; Joe Schwartz, "Americans Annoyed by Wasteful Packaging," *American Demographics,* April 1992, p. 13.
35. Schwartz and Miller, p. 28; Terry Lefton, "Disposing of the Green Myth," *Adweek's Marketing Week,* 13 April 1992, pp. 20–21.
36. Terry Lefton, "Beating the Green Rap," *Adweek's Marketing Week,* 27 January 1992, p. 6; Joe Schwartz, "Turtle Wax Shines Water, Too," *American Demographics,* April 1992, p. 14; "L'eggs to Scrap Plastic 'Egg' Package," *Marketing News,* 19 August 1991, p. 20.
37. "Research Group Says Some Green Marketers Are Only Pretending," *Marketing News,* 20 January 1992, p. 3.
38. Arthur S. Hayes and Junda Woo, "'Green Marketing' Labeling Law Piques Food Industry Coalition," *Wall Street Journal,* 24 February 1992, p. B6; Jeanne Saddler, "FTC Issues a 'Green-Marketing' Guide to Help Prevent Deceptive-Ad Charges," *Wall Street Journal,* 29 July 1992, p. B5.
39. "Free Trade's Green Hurdle," *Economist,* 15 June 1991, pp. 61–62; "In the Market for a Better World," *Maclean's,* 11 May 1992, p. E1.
40. Paul F. Buller, John J. Kohls, and Kenneth S. Anderson, "The Challenge of Global Ethics," *Journal of Business Ethics,* October 1991, pp. 767–775.
41. Adapted from Robert W. Armstrong, "An Empirical Investigation of International Marketing Ethics: Problems Encountered by Australian Firms," *Journal of Business Ethics,* March 1992, pp. 161–171.
42. See Russell Abratt, Deon Nel, and Nicola Susan Higgs, "An Examination of the Ethical Beliefs of Managers Using Selected Scenarios in a Cross-Cultural Environment," *Journal of Business Ethics,* January 1992, pp. 29–35; John Tsalikis and Osita Nwachukwu, "A Comparison of Nigerian to American Views of Bribery and Extortion in International Commerce," *Journal of Business Ethics,* February 1991, pp. 85–98; Daniel Treisman, "Korruptsia," *New Republic,* 11 May 1992, pp. 14–17.

43. Carla Rapoport, "Why Japan Keeps on Winning," *Fortune,* 15 July 1991, pp. 76–85; for more insight into Japanese attitudes toward business ethics, see Edwin Whenmouth, "A Matter of Ethics," *Industry Week,* 16 March 1992, pp. 57–62.

44. Tsalikis and Nwachukwu, p. 85.

45. John Dobson, "Ethics in the Transnational Corporation: The 'Moral Buck' Stops Where?" *Journal of Business Ethics,* January 1992, pp. 21–27.

46. "The Tobacco Trade," pp. 21–23.

47. "The Tobacco Trade," pp. 21–23.

48. Diana Solis and Sonia L. Nazario, "U.S., Mexico Take On Border Pollution," *Wall Street Journal,* 25 February 1992, pp. B1, B8; for more information on *maquiladoras* and the growth in the U.S.-Mexico border population, see also Blayne Cutler, "Welcome to the Borderlands," *American Demographics,* February 1991, pp. 44–49, 57; see also Dan Koeppel, "The New Borderland," *Adweek's Marketing Week,* 17 February 1992, pp. 19–24.

49. Pros and cons of social responsibility adapted from Rogene Buchholz, *Business Environment and Public Policy,* 3rd ed. (Englewood Cliffs, NJ: Prentice-Hall, 1989).

50. Archie B. Carroll, "The Pyramid of Corporate Social Responsibility: Toward the Moral Management of Organizational Stakeholders," *Business Horizons,* July-August 1991, pp. 39–48.

51. Dan R. Dalton and Catherine M. Daily, "The Constituents of Corporate Responsibility: Separate, but Separable, Interests?" *Business Horizons,* July-August 1991, pp. 74–78.

52. This section based entirely on Carroll, pp. 39–48.

53. Leo Northart, "At Issue: Corporate Social Responsibility," *Public Relations Journal,* August 1983, p. 3; "A Kinder, Gentler Generation of Executives?" *Business Week,* 23 April 1990, p. 86.

54. Barbara Clark O'Hare, "Good Deeds Are Good Business," *American Demographics,* September 1991, pp. 38–42.

55. Suzanne Alexander, "Life's Just a Bowl of Cherry Garcia for Ben & Jerry's," *Wall Street Journal,* 15 July 1992, p. B3.

56. Cara Appelbaum, "Jantzen to Pitch In for Clean Waters," *Adweek's Marketing Week,* 6 April 1992, p. 6.

57. Elyse Tanouye, "Drug Firms Start 'Compliance' Programs Reminding Patients to Take Their Pills," *Wall Street Journal,* 25 March 1992, pp. B1, B5.

58. Andrew Pollack, "Un-Writing a New Page in the Annals of Recycling," *New York Times,* 21 August 1993, p. 17.

59. Mzamo P. Mangaliso, "The Corporate Social Challenge for the Multinational Corporation," *Journal of Business Ethics,* July 1992, pp. 491–500.

60. Richard T. Hise, Peter L. Gillett, and J. Patrick Kelly, "The Corporate Consumer Affairs Effort," *MSU Business Topics,* Summer 1978, pp. 17–26.

61. Claes Fornell, "Increasing the Organizational Influence of Corporate Consumer Affairs Departments," *Journal of Consumer Affairs,* Winter 1981, pp. 191; Hise, Gillett, and Kelly, pp. 17–26.

62. Upton Sinclair, *The Jungle* (Garden City, NY: Doubleday, 1906), p. 41; see also Robert Hermann, "The Consumer Movement in Historical perspective," in *Consumer: Search for the Consumer Interest,* 2nd ed., ed. David Aaker and George Day (New York: Free Press, 1974), pp. 10–18.

63. "American Products: What Consumers Think," *Management Review,* May 1989, p. 14.

64. Barney Raffield, "Consumerism and Marketing Management Revisited: Enduring Implications for Marketing Managers," in *Developments in Marketing Science: Proceedings of the Academy of Marketing Science,* ed. Kenneth Bahn (Blacksburg, VA: Virginia Tech, 1988), pp. 242–246.

65. Les Carlson and Norman Kangun, "Demographic Discontinuity: Another Explanation for Consumerism?" *Journal of Consumer Affairs,* Summer 1988, pp. 55–73; see also Robert L. Egbert et al., "Demographic Discontinuity: Social-Psychological Implications of Rapid Changes in the Size of Youth Populations," report prepared for the George A. Miller Lecture Series, University of Illinois at Champaign, 1982; see also Richard A. Esterlin, *Birth and Fortune: The Impact of Numbers on Personal Welfare* (New York: Basic Books, 1980).

66. Rajib N. Sanyal, "The Valdez Principles: Implications for Corporate Social Responsibility," *Journal of Business Ethics,* December 1991, pp. 883–890.

67. Quotes taken from Charles E. Watson, "Managing with Integrity: Social Responsibilities of Business as Seen by America's CEO's," *Business Horizons,* July-August 1991, pp. 99–109.

68. "It Ain't Easy Being a Green Retailer," *Wall Street Journal,* 20 December 1993, p. B1.

## Chapter 22

1. "Looking into the Customer's Soul," *Fortune,* 7 March 1994, pp. 68–70.

2. Michael E. Porter, *Competitive Strategy: Techniques for Analyzing Industries and Competitors* (New York: Free Press, 1980).

3. "Management Tools That Work," *Fortune,* 30 May 1994, p. 15.

4. Anheuser-Busch, *1993 Annual Report* (St. Louis: Anheuser-Busch, 1993).

5. Saturn Corporation, *Face to Face with the Future* (Detroit: Saturn Corporation, 1994).

6. "A Boring Brand Can Be Beautiful," *Fortune,* 18 November 1991, pp. 169–178.

7. Earl Naumann, *Creating Customer Value* (Cincinnati: Thomson Executive Press, 1995), pp. 70–75.
8. "Dominant Brands Are Most Profitable Assets," *Conference Board's Management Briefing: Marketing,* October-November 1989, p. 6.
9. Michael Minor, "The Market Share Effect: A Review and Reconsideration," in *1989 AMA Educators' Proceedings: Enhancing Knowledge Development in Marketing,* ed. Paul Bloom and others (Chicago: American Marketing Association), pp. 121–125.
10. "Long-Term Thinking and Paternalistic Ways Carry Michelin to Top," *Wall Street Journal,* 5 January 1990, p. A1; "Gerstner Is Struggling As He Tries to Change Ingrained IBM Culture," *Wall Street Journal,* 13 May 1994, pp. A1, A6.
11. "Getting Hot Ideas from Customers," *Fortune,* 18 May 1992, pp. 86–87.
12. "A Star Is Born," *Fortune: Special Edition,* Spring 1994, pp. 45–47.
13. Robert Buzzell and Bradley Gale, *The PIMS Principles* (New York: Free Press, 1987).
14. Adapted from Brenton Schlender, "The Perils of Losing Focus," *Fortune,* 17 May 1993, p. 100.
15. AT&T, *1993 Annual Report;* "Could AT&T Rule the World?" *Fortune,* 17 May 1993, pp. 55–66.
16. "Long-Term Thinking," pp. A1, A4.
17. "TYRE Makers on the Rack," *International Management,* March 1993, pp. 40–43.
18. "Michelin Is Setting Out on the Road to Transformation," *Wall Street Journal,* 2 September 1994, p. B4.
19. "Michelin Is Setting Out," p. B4.
20. McDonald's, *1993 Annual Report,* p. 4.
21. "McD Rewards, Researches Frequent Customers," *Nations' Restaurant News,* 1 June 1992, pp. 7, 89.
22. "Too Much Pruning Stunts Fruit of the Loom," *Business Week,* 6 June 1994, p. 38.
23. Kamron Kashani, *Managing Global Marketing* (Boston: PWS-Kent, 1992), pp. 5–6.
24. Kashani, p. 90.
25. Kashani, p. 90.
26. Philip Kotler, *Marketing Management,* 8th ed. (Englewood Cliffs, NJ: Prentice-Hall, 1994).

## Appendix A

1. C. F. Siegel and R. Powers, "FAB: A Useful Tool for the Job-Seeking Marketing Student," *Marketing Education Review,* Winter 1991, pp. 6065.
2. Louisiana State University Placement Center, Baton Rouge, LA, 1993.
3. Louisiana State University Placement Center, Baton Rouge, LA, 1993.

# COMPANY AND ORGANIZATION INDEX

## A



## B



## C

# SUBJECT INDEX

## D

M

## T